Societies Around the World: Shorter Edition

Prepared by Howard Becker, University of Wisconsin, on the basis of the two-volume work by Irwin T. Sanders, Richard B. Woodbury, Frank J. Essene, Thomas P. Field, Joseph R. Schwendeman, and Charles E. Snow

Societies

Prepared at the University of Kentucky by:

IRWIN T. SANDERS, Editor
Professor of Sociology

RICHARD B. WOODBURY, Asst. Editor
Associate Professor of Anthropology

FRANK J. ESSENE
Associate Professor of Anthropology

THOMAS P. FIELD
Associate Professor of Geography

JOSEPH R. SCHWENDEMAN
Professor of Geography

CHARLES E. SNOW
Professor of Anthropology

Around the World

A NEW SHORTER EDITION: ESKIMO · NAVAJO · BAGANDA

CHINESE PEASANT · COTTON SOUTH · ENGLISH MIDLANDS

Edited in One Volume by Howard Becker · University of Wisconsin

THE DRYDEN PRESS · PUBLISHERS · NEW YORK

PHOTOGRAPH CREDITS: British Information Services, pp. xxiv; 252a, b, and c; 398d; 666a, b, and c; and cover. The Chemstrand Corporation, p. 532c (top). George A. Dale, U.S. Indian Service, p. 28b (bottom). Paul Guillumette, Inc., pp. 398b; 406a, b, and c; and cover. Dorothea Lange, Berkeley, Calif., p. 532c (bottom). National Film Board, p. 38a and cover. Milton Snow, Navajo Service, p. 142c (bottom). Milton Snow, U.S. Indian Service, p. 142c (top) and cover. U.S. Department of Agriculture, p. 398c and cover. U.S. Indian Service, pp. xxii, xxiii; 28b (top); 142a and b; and cover.

PREFACE TO THE SHORTER EDITION

IN THE LATE SPRING OF 1953 I was much gratified at receiving from my good friend Stanley Burnshaw of The Dryden Press two handsome volumes totaling nearly twelve hundred pages of fascinating reading. My gratification was heightened when I discovered that those whose names appeared on the title pages had done much more than set out juicy tidbits; they had closely organized over one hundred and sixty selections by about one hundred and twenty authors into an expository and social-scientific masterpiece that was also eminently teachable. Colleagues who shared with me the teaching of introductory courses at once agreed to the purchase of twenty sets to be used as assigned reading, and we soon added more, for our students were enthusiastic. Then, in the summer of 1954, Stanley Burnshaw wrote me a letter about like this:

> Dear Howard Becker:
>
> The group identified with *Societies Around the World* has decided that a one-volume edition would be a good idea. Although there is obviously plenty of editorial talent in the group, the task of shortening what is on every hand acclaimed as a first-class book is likely to be a little melancholy for those who have lived with it during the seven years of its development. Some of us think that you may possess the kindly ruthlessness of the surgeon; would you consider the operation? It's a queer one, for you'd simply be trimming a thoroughly healthy six-footer down to about four and at the same time keeping him as vigorous as he ever was and sufficiently recognizable so that his well-wishers won't say, "Have we ever been introduced?" If you're even mildly interested, let's talk things over at the Urbana meetings.

Well, I was interested, we did talk things over, we reached agreement, and we went to work. The result is now before you. It is, I think, a usable short version of the original, brought up to date here and there, and hence I now quote at length from the preface to the latter, where the purpose and character of, participation in, and acknowledgments for the book are admirably stated:

"For the past seven years, a group of social scientists—sociologists, anthropologists, and geographers—at the University of Kentucky has been developing a new approach to the study of society—one that presents, from an interdisciplinary point of view, the essential characteristics of a society, in terms of both its everyday workings and its organization.

"We have sought to build in the minds of beginning students a clear, meaningful concept of the social universe as an area of scientific study. Convinced that such a conception best prepares students for further work in history, government, social anthropology, and other fields, we have stressed society as the chief subject matter of the social sciences. The work does not try to teach the social sciences *per se*; the intention is rather to prepare the student for later study. . . . Even those students who do not go on to specialize in the social sciences, however, will gain, from the study of this material, in their understanding of the society in which they live and of the other societies of the world.

"*Societies Around the World,* the outcome of our undertaking, treats societies comprehensively. . . . Through selections from many authoritative sources representing a wide variety of approaches, methods, and points of view, each of the societies can be seen as a 'going concern.' Because each selection . . . is related to the basic study plan, the student can read purposively and intensively—and can develop in intellectual maturity.

"The selections are supplemented by a few original articles and are knit together by brief transitional comments and explanations. As the student compares one society with another, he will discern not merely the differences among six societies that are widely diverse geographically and encompass virtually the entire range of complexity known in human social groupings; more important, he will identify and understand the main characteristics of society in general.

"The Introduction . . . makes clear to the beginning student some of the elementary concepts useful in studying man, whether biologically or socially; in visualizing and understanding the habitat and economy of a group; and in analyzing social organization and sociocultural change. An outline, 'How to Study a Society,' orients the student and provides a basis for his use of the comparative method.

"[The first society presented is that of] the Eskimo, whose adaptation to a rigorous Arctic habitat has been ingenious and complex but whose social patterns are relatively simple. Next, the Navajo are shown to have made another kind of environmental adjustment, to a semi-arid climate; their social organization illustrates the operation of a matrilineal clan system. The Baganda of equatorial Africa, the third society studied, had a well-defined system of kingship long before their culture contact with Europeans; in recent generations they have undergone profound economic, political, and social change.

"Social change, one of the underlying themes of *Societies Around the World,* is illustrated with especial clarity in the [next] three societies . . . [Reluctance to change that until recently held readiness to change in check is revealed in] a study of the Chinese Peasant, who exemplifies the chief traits of a peasant society—the form of social grouping in which most of the world's population now lives. The Cotton South is then presented as an area undergoing swift economic and social change because of the industrialization of what was, only a century ago, an almost wholly agrarian society. The English Midlands, the last society studied, affords insight into the organization and problems of a contemporary industrial society.

"[The descriptions, comparisons, and analytic comments are then brought to a close] with a brief overview of the methods and content of the various fields of social science, in the expectation that the student will have new interests to satisfy and new questions for which to seek answers.

❋   ❋   ❋

"[Many] people, chiefly at the University of Kentucky, have contributed to the courses from which these two volumes have resulted. The co-authors listed on the title page are the major contributors to the project, which included several planographed editions. In addition, valuable contributions have been made by twelve other instructors who have taught the course. These valued colleagues are: C. Arnold Anderson, Percy Black, James W. Gladden, David L. Hatch, Catharine K. Haynes, James W. Hughes, Harry K. Hutter, Gordon Lewis, Willard E. Ruggles, Bernard H. Schockel, Willis A. Sutton, Jr., and Richard L. Tuthill.

"We have had the benefit of seminar and other discussions with a number of people who possess a first-hand knowledge of the six habitats and societies chosen. These include, for the Eskimo, George A. Dale, the late W. Elmer Ekblaw, Margaret Lantis, and E. S. Lusby; for the Navajo, Father Berard Haile and Clyde Kluckhohn; for the Baganda, Thomas Cullen, William S. Kajubi, and C. Amory Ross; for the Chinese Peasant, George B. Cressey, Francis L. K. Hsu, and Lewis S. C. Smythe; for the Cotton South we have drawn heavily upon the University of Kentucky staff members specializing in this area; and for the English Midlands, Jacqueline Tyrwhitt, W. Warren Haynes, and, especially, Catharine K. Haynes, who, during a year recently spent in England, devoted a great deal of time to gathering source material through interviews and library research . . . [Other detailed acknowledgments have been omitted as less relevant for the present edition.]

❋   ❋   ❋

"We have had the benefit of extensive collaboration by our colleagues Professor C. Arnold Anderson and Dr. Mary Jean Bowman through the intermediate stages of this project; they withdrew before the final versions were published. Nathalie F. S. Woodbury collaborated professionally and assisted in the technical details of preparing the manuscript.

"An expression of gratitude is also due to the publishers and authors who permitted us to make extensive use of their materials, as well as to the students at the University of Kentucky who volunteered many worth-while comments and often taught the instructors who, in turn, were teaching them.

I.T.S., R.B.W., F.J.E., T.P.F., J.R.S., C.E.S."

Resuming, now, my own prefatory remarks, let me say that in the abridgment, and in proofreading as well, I was greatly aided by my wife, Frances Bennett Becker, herself a qualified social scientist. We succeeded, as we hope, in compressing the selections without squeezing them dry of interesting and instructive detail. A few selections had to be omitted entirely, but these were very few.

Where the general introduction, beginnings of sections, interspersed comments, social-science generalizations, and conclusions are concerned, there was some abridging, but some augmenting, too. The book already showed emphasis on values and value-systems and made reference to a theme with which I have dealt from time to time; namely, secularization. Consequently, I increased the emphasis somewhat and developed the discussion of secularization further, particularly in conjunction with Percy Black's splendid section entitled "Some Social-Science Generalizations." In that section some twenty pages of my own were inserted, bearing the subtitle "Looking at Values and Value-Systems."

The insertion is the most compact statement on the general topic indicated that I have thus far succeeded in making, but it is probably too compact and schematic. At various points I have included references to more fully qualified and sustained theoretical treatment and to more adequate illustrations and empirical evidence; if these can be followed up by the reader, he may find that the added twenty pages were worth wading through. If not, some points will remain a bit obscure, at least to the beginning student, although the main ideas, I think, will be understood without much difficulty. The problem of the secularization of values and value-systems, especially in its relation to social change, does seem to me to be of central importance for several social sciences, and I hope that others share my opinion sufficiently to exercise a little patience when I am not lucid. In any event, I have tried to be as clear as possible within space limits, for I remarked many years ago that "obscurity is not profundity, and in spite of etymology the ponderous is not the weighty."

Some changes have been made in the maps for the sake of including all the important place names and names of natural features mentioned in the text. Several of these changes were based on the original compilation and cartography by Thomas P. Field. By providing two maps for each society treated—one a halftone relief map and the other the map included in the two-volume edition— we hope to have substantially helped the student in the important task of getting good geographic orientation.

Here and there some stylistic and terminological alterations in the editorial sections and passages were made, but these are of no great significance. In the Conclusions, I took the liberty of expanding the first two pages to about four, but without, I trust, changing Dr. Sanders' basic meaning in any fundamental way.

May the well-wishers of the two-volume edition find cause to extend their benevolence to the shorter version, and may new friends join them!

Madison, Wisconsin HOWARD BECKER
March 1956

NOTE

With a few exceptions, footnotes and references contained in the original selections that make up this volume have been omitted; those retained appear in parentheses in the text. Many subheads have been deleted or revised to fit the material actually quoted. In the present edition, nearly all indications of deletions have been omitted for the sake of greater reading continuity. *For scholarly purposes of citation or quotation, the two-volume edition, which remains in print, should be used* if for any reason reference to the original books and journals from which the selections are drawn is inconvenient or impossible.

Contents

PART ONE

THE BAGANDA

SOME SOCIAL-SCIENCE GENERALIZATIONS

PART TWO

SOCIAL CHANGE ON A WORLDWIDE SCALE 400

THE CHINESE PEASANT

THE COTTON SOUTH

THE AUTHORS OF THE SELECTIONS

PART I

THE ESKIMO

THE NAVAJO

THE BAGANDA

Introduction

Introduction

≪≪≪

Man must be understood within the context of the society of which he is a part. This holds true whether we consider man as a biological species or specific groups of men to which such labels as Chinese, Americans, or Poles have been applied. Man is a social animal; he *learns* most of his behavior from other people and acts primarily with reference to other people. In fact, he has recently been termed *Homo reciprocus,* Man the Reciprocal, because he becomes fully human only in and through give-and-take with others; he is "man in reciprocity."

Moreover, every person is a member of some society. Even those who claim to be "men without a country," or who join as nameless people the French Foreign Legion, carry into their daily activity much that they learned when they were growing up in the society on which they later turned their backs. Personality develops in social situations and tends to reflect the chief traits that one's society emphasizes.

All of this will become much clearer as we become familiar with the six societies treated in this book. These six have been selected from the many hundreds available because they represent most of the chief types of societies as well as the major habitat areas. They have been arranged in order of social complexity from the simple social organization of the Eskimo to the highly indus-trialized organization of the English Midlands, where the Industrial Revolution very early showed some of its most distinctive features. Intermediate societies are the Navajo Indian, with a simple clan system, the Baganda of East Africa, who had a well-defined political kingship as well as a clan system long before the white man came, the familistic Chinese peasant, and the rapidly changing plantation society of the Cotton South. In the section entitled "Some Social-Science Generalizations and Tools" these societies are viewed as examples of

2

types that, abstractly considered, are found among many peoples in many parts of the world.

But the purpose of this book is not merely to take you on a conducted tour of the world, fascinating as each of these peoples may prove to be. The real purpose is to set before you in bold outline the nature of this human universe we call society. Its common denominators should emerge as you note them systematically in one society after another. And while you are doing this you will find yourself comparing each of these societies with your own so that, by the time you have finished the book, you will see your own society in fresh perspective and be able to participate in it more intelligently.

Throughout this book emphasis will be laid upon understanding each society as an ongoing system. At times, the richness of detail will be absorbing, and we may fail to see what the connections with the system in its entirety are, although it may be granted that such connections often are not easy to see and sometimes may be so vague as to be of no ascertainable importance. Nevertheless, we should continually remind ourselves that each society is demonstrably a going concern. To change the figure of speech: Whether or not all the details can be fitted into the jigsaw puzzle, a sufficient number of them can be so fitted as to produce a fairly accurate general picture of the society. Of interest to us, then, will be the interrelations of this piece with that: the economic system and family life; government and education; religion and social class; technology and recreation, to mention but a few examples.

The attempt made in the pages that follow is not to convert you to any specific social-science discipline but rather to convince you of the importance of knowing more about society so that you will eagerly continue the study of human behavior. One important task of the social scientist is to describe accurately and dispassionately the influence of man on man, or groups of men on other groups. The resulting social arrangements take many forms. Some social scientists, particularly the economists, study the associations formed and the economic mechanisms set up to satisfy man's major material needs and even consider at times the way in which man satisfies certain intangible wants, such as a craving for beauty or the attainment of prestige. Political scientists examine the political behavior of man and study the governmental institutions that arise out of and in turn tend to control such behavior. Students of human geography see society against the habitat, or physical environment, and note the relations between the natural and the social worlds.

Physical anthropologists study man as a biological type, describing his development through the centuries and classifying him into racial divisions. Cultural anthropologists concern themselves with tools and techniques, language, beliefs, and values, social institutions, and every other man-made characteristic. Sociologists investigate especially the associative and dissociative life of man—how he joins up with and splits off from other human beings—but in this book the sociological emphasis is chiefly on association and particularly on those group patterns and types of associative interaction that recur over periods of time. In addition, the sociologist shares the interest of the social psychologist in learning more about the interaction between society and personality.

There is inevitably much overlapping of one social science with another, since they all focus on some phase of human relations. That is why none of the foregoing statements about any of the social-science disciplines can be considered adequate. They are merely a rough phrasing of the approach each uses in its efforts to derive basic principles from the scientific study of human behavior.

This book, therefore, concentrating as it does on the analysis of several societies, should give you sufficient background material to make your study of any social science much more effective. It will familiarize you with a number of key terms and concepts that should help you in reading social-science literature. At the same time, not only should it give you convenient technical terms for expressing ideas for which your former vocabulary was insufficient, but it should also show you that with a little care in expressing yourself clearly and unemotionally, you can go a long way with "layman's language"—good, plain English, although not necessarily everyday English.

How to Use This Book

First, start to form the habit, if you have not already done so, of using a suitable dictionary. It need not be a twenty-pounder, but neither should it be of the sort that comes as a premium with a trial subscription to the *Crossroads Courier*. (For terms that do not appear in your dictionary, you might consult E. B. Reuter, *Handbook of Sociology*, New York, The Dryden Press, 1941.)

Second, leaf through the book casually and read the selections that strike your fancy. If you are interested in marriage customs, notice how these compare in the societies described here. If you are concerned with the effect of Western culture on people who have not yet reached the Machine Age, read the concluding sections for each of the societies.

This kind of reading will raise questions in your mind. You may wonder why the Eskimo are willing in hard times to see their aged parents starved or even put to death, whereas the Chinese peasants supposedly do all in their power to respect and care for their parents. You then will ask yourself whether the difference lies in the fact that one is a hunting people and the other an agricultural people, that movement from place to place is common among the Eskimo and permanence of residence is characteristic of the Chinese. But you will remind yourself that the Baganda have long been agriculturalists and never seemed to develop any great affection for their parents, although they do take care to avoid the visitation of the spirits of departed ancestors by being kind to relatives before they die. As you pursue several such topics through three or four societies, you will become convinced that only by painstaking study of these societies as on-going systems will you be able to gain a thorough understanding.

Such a conviction, therefore, should make you willing to familiarize yourself with the following outline of how to study a society and to seek detailed answers to each of the questions found in it. This will prove meaningful only to the extent that you dig out the answers for yourself. The textual material is simply an aid to that end and in no way seeks to be predigested pabulum soothing you into an illusion of knowledge that cannot very well stand searching scrutiny.

To summarize concerning the use of this book: Make reasonably sure that you know what unfamiliar words mean; read casually and for enjoyment; speculate on what you have read, and try to reach some tentative generalizations of your own; dig more deeply into the material, and organize what you read around the questions asked in the how-to-study-a-society outline. Then go back to your earlier generalizations and see how they stand up. Critically evaluate the principles contained in "Some Social-Science Generalizations" (pp. 360-398) and look up supporting evidence to disprove any that do not ring true to you.

How to Study a Society

Before beginning the study of any specific society, it may be desirable to see a preview of the kind of topics about which you will be reading. The following outline not only will give you these but also will serve as a review guide when you try to put together in some logical order the many interesting facts you will learn.

A Topical Outline

A. Who are the people?
  1. What is their racial origin?
  2. How many are they? Are they increasing or decreasing?
B. What is their physical environment?
  1. In what part of the world do they live?
     a. Latitude and longitude.   c. Size of the area.
     b. In relation to neighbors.   d. Shape of the area.
  2. What is the topography of their living space?
  3. What kind of climate do they have?
  4. Is the soil productive?

5. Are there minerals, and do they use them?

6. How available is water: surface? underground?

7. What are the wild and domesticated (1) plants and (2) animals living in the area with them?

C. How do they make their living? (The maintenance institution.)

1. Of which of the resources available in their habitat do they make use?

2. What do they exchange with other people? To what extent?

3. What are their tools and techniques for:

   a. obtaining and preparing food? *d.* transporting things and people?

   b. obtaining shelter?   *e.* waging war?

   c. making clothing?   *f.* playing games?

4. What are their rules determining the control, distribution, and use of things?

   a. Does each family or some group produce all of its own needs or is there exchange with other members of the society? Barter? Sale? Capture?

   b. What is the division of labor? Does everyone work at every task, or do some people work at one thing and others at something else?

   c. What are their ideas about property? How permanent is ownership of goods?

   d. What are the rules determining who may have access to what areas or items in the habitat?

D. What are their social organizations and their social interactions?

1. What are the chief groupings or patterns of association among the people?

   a. Area or locality groups: community and settlement patterns.

   b. Political units:

      (1) on geographic basis: tribe or nation.

      (2) on institutional basis: government.

   c. Family and kinship groups.

   d. Sex groups.

   e. Age groups.

   f. Work and economic groups.

   g. Religious groups.

   h. Educational groups.

   i. Class and caste groupings.

2. What are the major social values of these people? What do they think is most important in life? What are their reasons for carrying on their lives, as they see them? How are these related to the physical environment? to the social organization? In what respects can these values be viewed as sacred, or secular, or both, in the most

general senses of those terms? in more specific senses? (Here you
may wish to consult the section entitled "Looking at Values and
Value-Systems.")
3. How are children and young people taught to become useful members
   of the society? (Socialization.)
4. How are members of the society controlled or guided to follow the
   prescribed ways of living? What are the norms, or "rules of the
   social game"?
5. How are the norms tied together to make up a social system? What
   social interactions (cooperation, competition, etc.) are most
   stressed?
E. What sociocultural changes have taken place?
   1. What has been learned about their history?
   2. What have been the main outside influences upon them? How have
      these been exerted?
   3. What have been the main changes in their lives?
   4. How and by whom have these changes been introduced?
   5. Have these changes been welcomed or resisted? How, and by whom?
      Have the norms and the value-system of the society become more
      sacred? more secular?

On Understanding a Society

Having gained from the outline above an over-all view of the subject matter of a
society, we now turn to a more detailed explanation of some of the topics on the
outline. First, we shall look at what might be called the background factors of a
society, concentrating chiefly upon Sections A, B, and part of C of the outline
above. Second. we shall inquire into the nature of a society, focusing on outline
Section D and part of C. Finally, we shall consider sociocultural change, mentioned in Section E.

BACKGROUND FACTORS

A SOCIETY CONSISTS OF PEOPLE. Before we can begin to understand how
people behave toward one another in a society, we must know something about
the people themselves. We must examine man's capacity for adjustment, upon
which the survival of any society depends; then we can consider a people's
physical appearance, and this will involve a brief discussion of racial traits.
Finally, we need to inquire into a people's numbers, to ask whether its total
population is increasing or declining, and to get information about the propor-

tion of males and females at various ages, of natives and foreign born, and so on for all important demographic° data.

Man's Capacity for Adjustment. Man is in one sense an animal. Like other animals, he seeks food, he reproduces his kind, he protects himself from his enemies, and he seeks to shelter himself from physical discomforts. His main biological purpose, then, is survival, both as an individual and as a species. Many social patterns, we shall notice later on, are attached to these survival needs, whereas others seem to have at most only a slight connection.

In some ways man as an organism is rather poorly equipped for the struggle for survival. He has no natural coat of fur to keep him warm; he also lacks the brute strength or speed of many animals, as well as the natural protective features that aid other species effectively. But man does possess some decided advantages. From the anatomical point of view, his ability to stand erect on two legs gives him considerable mobility and also leaves his arms free for tasks other than locomotion. The inherited ability to rotate the forearm without twisting the upper arm and to grasp with the hand makes man a "natural" maker and user of tools. The fact that man is omnivorous, or can eat both plants and animals, opens up wider sources of food than those available to those animals eating only plants (herbivora) or only animals (carnivora). As we shall see in our study of the Eskimo, man can eat and digest, if he has been brought up under the appropriate conditions, many foods that we with our acquired fastidiousness may consider entirely unsuited to human consumption.

Another advantage enjoyed by man is the prolongation of human infancy. Whereas the young of other animal species mature in a relatively short time, the human infant requires many years to become an adult biologically and socially. Thus parental care, with all that it means for the social development of the parents as well as the child, is required over a span of fifteen years or more—a period of plasticity during which the young can be taught a tremendously wide range of human knowledge and behavior patterns. This formative period makes possible the accumulation and transmission of the cultural heritage, which we shall discuss shortly.

But man's most significant biological feature is his large brain with its complex nervous system, which, along with the prolongation of infancy, makes human learning possible. Psychologists have learned the chief characteristics of this nervous system, how the organism responds to various stimuli, how learning occurs, the part played by the subconscious in daily life, and a number of other topics that give us a great appreciation for man as a biological species. We still have much to discover about the mental life of man, about how individuals

° *Demography.* The quantitative study of the vital processes and movement of human population, based upon census and registration data. (E. B. Reuter, *Handbook of Sociology,* New York, Dryden Press, 1941.) Where such data are lacking, there can be, at best, only rough estimates; but for many populations—that of China, for example —the demographer must still do the best he can even in the absence of reliable information.

acquire what is called their personality, and also about the delicate relations between the nervous system and bodily processes. We nevertheless know enough to assert that man's accomplishments are possible only because of the special powers that he possesses, however he has come to possess them.

Society depends on man's capacity for abstract thinking, and on his interest in and enthusiasm for solving problems. That is, man has the ability to adjust and to create, in relation to his natural environment, to his fellow human beings, and even to such ideals as political liberty. And it is this adjustment to such ideals, and man's attempt to realize them in everyday life, that make it possible to speak of a spiritual side of man and think of him as more than a biological organism. More thorough explanations of man's spiritual nature are provided by the great religions of the world, although these explanations differ from one another considerably. Social science must take these beliefs into account in understanding how a given society works, but it cannot pass on the correctness of any such explanation since the *final* arguments for or against it lie outside the social-science field.

Thus, a society is made up of people who are not mere automata but who are possessed of great adjustive and creative potentialities, who rise above the mere eking out of an existence to the consideration of beauty, love, freedom, and a number of other ideals incorporated in the great esthetic, political, and religious systems of the world.

The Species and Racial Stocks. Should a doctor traveling through Africa come upon a Pygmy suffering from excruciating abdominal pain, he could, if the diagnosis justified it, operate on the patient for appendicitis with the same assurance with which he would perform an appendectomy on you or anyone of your acquaintance. This is because the primary characteristics of the human organism are essentially the same for human beings everywhere. The location of the stomach, heart, appendix, backbone, and other organs does not change with skin coloring or social position. "The brotherhood of man" is a biological fact. All living men are classified as the same genus and species, *Homo sapiens.*

But secondary characteristics do differ, and it is these secondary physical traits, less important biologically but outwardly visible, that many people use as the basis for certain kinds of social distinctions. Nevertheless, in considering the secondary differences, let us not lose sight of the fundamentally unitary nature of man.

Man is an animal exceedingly difficult to classify physically into various subdivisions. If we take any given set of biological characteristics, such as skin and eye color, hair texture, height and weight, or facial features, we find that some people with the same skin color differ as to head shapes and facial features, that those with similar body builds may differ greatly as to type of hair and shape of head, or that those having heads much the same vary in heel form and calf muscles.

In spite of the difficulties, however, physical anthropologists have set up useful racial classifications, some much more detailed than others. For the purpose of this book we shall use the customary threefold classification of racial stocks—Mongoloid, Negroid, and Caucasoid—but we shall include as separate stocks the American Indian, the Australoid, and the Polynesian. All but the last two of these will be described in connection with the six societies taken up in this volume. The Navajo are American Indians, a stock that includes the Eskimo, who are more recent arrivals on this continent. The Chinese peasants are Mongoloid; the Baganda are Negroid; the Southern whites and the people in the English Midlands are Caucasoid.

But racial classifications lead us into interesting problems. For example, the Hindus of India and the Arabs of the Near East, even though their skin color is frequently very dark, are Caucasoid, like the Anglo-Saxons, because their other physical traits, such as hair texture and facial features, closely resemble those of Western Europeans. Such facts as these lead naturally into the question of the meaning of race. What is it after all?

Race is purely a matter of biology and nothing else. Every individual has two parents, each of whom genetically contributes equally to the heredity (nature) of their child. Thus each generation changes physically with new combinations of heredity. Racial populations, ever changing in themselves, absorb foreign strains along the contact borders of their countries. In modern times, the easy modes of travel have accelerated the amount and kind of interbreeding of human beings.

If race is physical—that is, biological—why introduce it into the study of society, or the social? For one thing, race differences, as is quite apparent, almost invariably create social distinctions between the groups possessing these differences. Just as some white people are inclined to look down on those differing in physical appearance, so the Mongoloids and Negroids time and again have looked with derision upon the white groups with whom they have had contacts.

An open-minded study of race and society will show that as far as modern science now knows there is no direct causal connection between skin color and morals, between head size and cultural achievement, or between racial stock and political institutions. People of all stocks, perhaps even the little-known Pygmy, have the ability to become "modern" if they want to and are allowed to. To account, therefore, for the great social differences in the world today, we turn to an examination of the cultural heritage rather than to racial ancestry alone, while realizing that this cultural heritage is also influenced by the physical environment in which a people lives.

Available Demographic Data. For most of the world's two billion people, accurate census records and vital statistics are not available. Nevertheless, before turning to the study of any society, we should discover as accurately as we can how many members it contains. If figures are available, we can subtract the death rate from the birth rate and derive the natural increase; or, if there has been any migration, we can find the net amount by comparing the number of those who have emigrated with the number of those who have immigrated. Certain sickness, or morbidity, rates, such as those for leprosy or smallpox, tell us much about the health of the people. So does a knowledge of the various age groupings, the ratio of women to men, racial divisions, occupational distribution, as well as other characteristics described by population experts.

In the case of some of the societies taken up in this volume, the demographic facts, unfortunately, are sketchy, but they nevertheless help round out the background necessary for understanding each of the people being studied.

A SOCIETY EXISTS IN SPACE. Societies, consisting as they do of people, must have a locale, or a physical setting. This we call the *habitat* and define it as *the physical features of their homeland that have been blended into something distinctive and identifiable as a place where men dwell.* These features, when considered from the standpoint of nature, are called *elements* and when viewed in terms of the way in which man lives are called *factors.* In other words, physical geographers could study the four elements of space, surface features, climate, and natural resources as part of the physical universe without relating them specifically to human life. That would give us knowledge of the duration of daylight as it is related to season and latitude, reasons for climatic conditions, spatial relations of mountains, plains, and plateaus, and presence of timber, petroleum, fish, and numerous other potential resources awaiting man's exploitation.

Another way of viewing the habitat, however, is to consider it as one of the conditioning influences of man's life and to notice how man adjusts to the elements mentioned above. This introduces us to the factors emphasized in human geography. Just as you can probably visualize a society better if you know what the people look like, so you can more quickly and effectively get some preliminary notions of the range of possibilities of family life or political organization if you know something about the habitat in which these social relations occur. Do members of the family spend winter under conditions of such intense cold that a sizable proportion of their time and effort is spent in keeping warm, or is the climate so mild that they can give their attention to a number of other things? Is their political unit so extensive and the terrain so difficult that communication between the capital city and outlying provinces is infrequent and unsatisfactory, or is their territory compact and easily administered? Is their creative skill great enough to enable them to overcome, or even turn to advantage, the handicaps that their habitat would otherwise impose?

In our treatment of the various habitats we use four general headings under which most of the information about the physical environment can be classified. These are space relations, including factors of location, size, and shape; surface features, with the factor of terrain; climate; and natural resources, comprising the factors of soils, minerals and rocks, water, natural vegetation (flora), and native animals (fauna).

Space Relations. The "where" factor of the habitat is based first on identification, or giving the place a name, as Gallup, New Mexico, or Scotland. Ordinarily when we explain location of a place to someone else, we use *relative location,* which states the political or physical boundaries of an area. A more precise way is *geomatical location;* it involves a global grid or lattice work of intersecting lines. The intersection of any two lines (coordinates) may be given one and only one mathematical expression in terms of latitude and longitude.

The importance of the factor of size is well known and is quite evident if we compare the physical potentialities of the British Isles with those of the Soviet Union.

Surface Features. Terrain involves principally the degree of slope to any given area of land. Where level land predominates, we speak of plains; if plains are elevated, plateaus. If the land is sloping, with low elevations, we talk of hill country; if altitudes are high and the gradients steep, mountain-and-valley country. The drainage pattern, with its lakes and streams, is also a part of terrain. Almost innumerable aspects of the terrain factor are interwoven with other factors as man works for his livelihood.

Climate. People tend to adapt their activities to the given climatic pattern of temperature and precipitation. If, for example, the climate is hot and wet (rainy tropical) throughout the year, certain plants and animals will exist and others will not. People will collect or produce certain foods, will construct shelters and clothing of available materials and in certain designs to meet problems of heat and wetness. Similar variations are to be found in cold climates of the world. If precipitation results in heavy accumulations of snow, men will conduct their activities to meet this condition as well as cold. Man must make some adjustment to extreme climates, although he often manages with surprisingly little, as the Indians of southern South America do. At the other extreme are the Eskimo, who, as we shall see, make a highly elaborate adjustment to their environment.

Natural Resources. Another factor is soil. Like climate and all the other factors, soil is not some one thing but rather a great many things. There are thousands of kinds of soil, which differ from one another in their physical structure, chemical composition, depth, and fertility.

These factors do not stand alone. It is the interaction and combinations of factors that make up the environment within which man's activities take place. The best physical and chemical properties in soil are useless for growing plants unless the climate is also favorable or unless man can devise some method of overcoming the climatic deficiencies. The fertile soils of the wet Yazoo Basin had to be drained before maximum utilization was achieved. So we see again the interrelations of terrain, climate, soil, vegetation, and human activity.

Men knew of and used many of the various rock and mineral formations in their natural environment long before the science of geology evolved. Obviously, the so-called industrial peoples make far greater use of this factor than do the nonindustrial. To know how and to what extent any human group uses minerals gives us an important key to understanding its cultural development. Naturally, it is only in human groups that have undergone certain kinds of cultural development that certain minerals can be used; uranium, necessary for atomic energy, provides a good example. This only underscores the fact that in a certain sense man makes his habitat.

The hydrographic factor denotes surface waters, underground waters, and the littoral, or coastal, zone. The nature and availability of water may deeply affect the life of any group. To the Eskimo, the ocean not only is a major source of food but also makes possible travel—in boats in summer or in sleds over the ice in winter. Agriculture depends on underground water in addition to rain; in dry regions, such as the greater part of the Navajo Reservation, farming can be practiced only in restricted areas and is at best a risky affair. Man's activities, especially his stripping large regions of vegetation, can greatly affect the water supply, because the water will not be retained but will run off, with disastrous effects in the form of floods and erosion.

Man makes a great many adjustments to the littoral, or coastal, conditions. The great fishing banks of the world are to be found in regions of wide continental shelf with shallow water and numerous shoals or islands. Shorelines indented with deep bays and harbors encourage sea commerce, whereas unbroken shorelines force man to construct breakwaters for harbor protection and limit his commercial activity. Thus, hydrographic factors are interwoven in the fabric of human activities.

Up to this point the discussion has concerned the nonliving factors of the natural environment, any or all of which may perhaps be found in worlds other than our own. The living, or biotic, factor takes on two forms: plant life, or flora, and animal life, or fauna. Plants and animals vary with the climate patterns, soil, terrain, and water factors that make up their natural environment. Nor do all classes of plants and animals lend themselves equally well to domestication. But irrespective of level of cultural attainment or economic status, all human society is dependent upon animal and plant life, which in turn is dependent upon the inorganic factors of the natural environment.

These, then, are the factors that combine in a variety of ways to make up a specific habitat. Although most of the emphasis in the descriptions to follow is upon society, the influence that many of these habitat factors have upon social life should not be overlooked. Such influences are perhaps most clearly shown in the major livelihood resource adjustments, to be described in detail for each society. As we proceed, we shall find societies in which manufacturing and commerce are the major types of livelihood. Careful consideration of these questions brings us back to the obvious fact that every society has a habitat, to which its members are constantly making adjustments. Out of these adjustments, in part at least, a *culture* has developed. A discussion of this is now in order.

A SOCIETY IS A PART OF CULTURE. *Culture Includes All That Is Man-made.* Up to this point we have been discussing natural conditions, biological and physical, which have a bearing upon man's participation as a member of society. Man is a part of nature, and so, in one sense, is his society. But social scientists have found it useful to distinguish between that which is *natural* and that which is *cultural*—that is, acted upon or created by man. Once this distinction was drawn, giant strides were made toward the understanding of society, because it was found that much of what was thought to be natural—and therefore apparently subject to unalterable natural laws—was really cultural and subject to the control of man. Since organized warfare, for example, is cultural, it can be modified, and in the years ahead disputes may be settled by much less devastating means.

This use of the word *culture* in so broad a sense differs from its everyday meaning of refinement or pursuit of the arts. In the social-science sense everyone has culture—not just those who speak French or appreciate classical music. When used in this book, therefore, culture describes all of man's hard-won accumulation, his social heritage. It has been called "the mode of life of a people. All that belongs to man which is socially rather than biologically transmitted." As the student moves into more advanced courses, he will probably pay less attention specifically to artifacts, or the material side of culture, and will make use of a definition such as the following: "The mass of learned and transmitted motor reactions, habits, techniques, ideas, and values—and the behavior they induce." In still other courses, where culture as an activity rather than as a museum collection is strongly stressed, still another definition may be used: "Culture is what remains of men's past, working on their present, to shape their future."

Usually, however, in any investigation we are concerned not with the total achievements of man through the ages (culture in the general sense) but rather with a single culture, or the lifeway of a specific people.

The Three Aspects of Culture. Man's social heritage is so tremendous and the man-made accompaniments of the life of any people so numerous that classification is essential for convenience. Any human group makes use of physical objects, such as religious paraphernalia, clothes, weapons, and an assortment of tools. These can be handled, felt, and photographed. We call them *artifacts,* because they have been made by man and are not natural objects, such as meteorites.

But there are parts of a social heritage other than the concrete or easily seen artifacts. People live in families, in neighborhoods, in communities; they have governments, economies, religions, and even elaborate educational systems —all of which consist primarily of patterns of social relations among the people who comprise the society. These social arrangements likewise are man-made and can be termed *sociofacts*. A city police department is an example of a sociofact.

Behind the sociofacts, however, are traditional ways of looking at things, belief systems, rules of behavior, and values. They are worked out and passed on by members of a society and are therefore cultural. These we term *mentifacts*, since they relate chiefly to the mental life of the people. The Golden Rule, for example, is a mentifact in some segments of American culture today.

The division of culture into these three aspects of *artifacts, sociofacts,* and *mentifacts* is for convenience of discussion only, since none of us customarily divides his daily life into three such compartments (see diagram, p. 148). Further, as is the case with most technical language—indeed, language of any kind—our terminology has defects. For example, artifact could be used to designate sociofact and mentifact too, for *all* culture is made by "art" and is "artificial" in that sense. What we here call artifacts might well be called "manufacts," for etymologically "manufacture" means to make by the hand (*manus*) of man. We could therefore say that culture is artifactual and that all artifacts are classifiable as: (1) made by hand, or manufacts; (2) made by society, or sociofacts, or (3) made by mind, or mentifacts. However, "artifact" has long been used by archeologists and others to mean "manufact," and there seems no good reason to disturb such established usage. We shall therefore continue to refer to tools, clothing, houses and similar shelters, etc., as artifacts; customary social arrangements such as marriage, kinship, nationhood, etc., as sociofacts; and ideas, theories, philosophies, religious beliefs, etc., as mentifacts. In brief,

artifact   = tool,
sociofact = custom,
mentifact = idea.

Obviously, it is usually impossible to transmit any one aspect of culture without bringing in both the others. A pencil, for example, must carry with it the custom of writing in certain social situations, and the language in which the writing is done cannot be dispensed with, either. Tool involves custom, and custom involves idea; or, in our terminology, artifact requires sociofact, and sociofact requires mentifact.

Many other interesting problems connected with the study of culture are not discussed here. The distinction between the natural and the man-made, between habitat and culture, is important in understanding any cultural problem. Just as we broke down the habitat into a number of factors, so we have divided the culture into aspects. As we turn to the study of society, our chief focus will be upon the sociofacts, but we must be ever mindful of the close tie-up between such matters as a people's material development and their social development, between a people's beliefs and their important social institutions.

THE NATURE OF SOCIETY

EVERY SOCIETY IS A UNIQUE PRODUCT. A society has been defined as "any permanent or continuing grouping of men, women, and children, able to carry on independently the processes of racial perpetuation and maintenance, on their cultural level." Its members have their own ways of getting things done—of rearing children, of procuring food, of propitiating the spirits, of enjoying leisure time—and they usually do these things in groups. These groups and their acts are directly connected with the cultural milieu of artifacts and mentifacts, as well as with the total social structure. And the natural environment has had its part particularly in conditioning the economic adjustments. The physical vigor of the people may give the group advantages over neighbors who are less strong. Leading personalities probably held the center of the stage long enough to do heroic deeds, give wise counsel, or perfect useful inventions. Everywhere we look we find the past lingering on in the present, and it is as we read about that past that we get helpful leads about the road that a society has traveled.

One thing is certain: To attempt to explain the nature of any society exclusively in terms of a single, narrow point of view is misleading and usually a betrayal of the facts. Most "vulgar Marxists," for example, would maintain that economic forces are the only clue to understanding a society's development; others seek an explanation in the Darwinian "struggle for existence," or in the density and qualities of population. Such theories fail through the "single-factor fallacy," i.e., they do not recognize the obvious fact that society is the product of many forces. Therefore, anyone continuing the study of social science today must be familiar with a number of fields so that he can apply from each field that which is pertinent to the problem he is investigating. Sometimes the available historical evidence gives the key, sometimes the cultural analyses of the social anthropologist; at others the sociological nuances of class differences or the subtle influence of climatic or population factors needs consideration. What is really demanded is theoretical flexibility that still permits consistent rather than opportunistic theory, respect for evidence, and knowledge of where to turn for possible insights.

ALL SOCIETIES HAVE COMMON DENOMINATORS. The elements common to all societies we shall stress more than their uniqueness. These are based on the fundamental proposition that *a society consists of social relations*—what can be called "the interaction of personalities through communication." That is, American society is made up not merely of more than 150 million isolated individuals but rather of innumerable social bonds that join various Americans together. With this in mind, we turn to a listing of the common denominators, or social ingredients, of any society. The first of these concerns the nature of a social relation.

A SOCIAL RELATION IS MADE UP OF STATUSES AND ROLES. Since people in contact with one another occupy social positions recognized by others, they are expected to carry out the roles, or behavior patterns, considered appropriate to their own social position, or status. In this sense, a society like ours is a vast collection of innumerable statuses—such as president, garbage collector, son, champion athlete, woman, child, banker, general, cook—that take on meaning in specific situations. Status has been quite well defined as "the position that the person occupies in relation to his fellows; also the position of a group in relation to other groups. A person's status in a group has a double aspect. On the one hand, it rests in the minds of his associates, since it is the way they treat him and consider him. On the other hand, status is registered in the mind of the individual himself, as a sort of reflection of how he stands in the eyes of others." If we knew, therefore, how those occupying these statuses were supposed to behave (their roles) in particular kinds of social situations, we would know a great deal about American society. What is a president supposed to do or not to do at the ceremony of taking the oath of office? How is a son supposed to behave toward his parents when they suggest that he not marry the girl to whom he is engaged? How is the champion athlete supposed to act toward his defeated opponent?

By the same token, we can learn to understand the societies that we hereafter study if we recognize the most common statuses and know how people in those positions are supposed to act in frequently recurring circumstances. A person's social role can be defined as "the part played by the person in the group or social situation; the function of a person in the group." The role is the active manifestation of the status.

(Some social scientists feel that it is unnecessary always to distinguish between role and status; hence they use role as inclusive of both. Moreover, they feel that when distinction is necessary, they can use the terms "enacted role" and "assigned role." Beyond this, they feel that status as a term is not sufficiently colorless for scientific use; it begs too many questions about prestige, for instance. Hence they often refer to status as "position"; instead of saying that a man has the status of pitcher, for example, they follow common usage and say that he has or plays the position of pitcher. Other writers, to be sure, use position in another sense, and in a succeeding paragraph we follow their practice. We need not worry further about these finespun distinctions. The authors of our selections do not always observe these distinctions, and certainly they seldom discuss role and status in the technical sense; but they nevertheless make themselves clearly understood. After all, that is the main thing.)

THROUGH SOCIAL VALUES AND SOCIAL NORMS THE CULTURAL HERITAGE BEARS UPON SOCIAL RELATIONS. Most people soon learn whether their position in a group, a community, or a society is considered high or low by the others associated with them. A person's position in a community, for instance, is a combination of his various statuses which have meaning for those within that community. Whether these are viewed as high or low depends on the social values which the members of the community accept and by which they rank the importance of various statuses against one another.

Social values have been briefly defined as "objects of human desire or appreciation: any objects, conditions, or principles around which meanings have grown up in the course of experience of social interaction." A *value-system* describes those values that are most often stressed or emphasized and that show what the people consider to be most important in everyday life. In America, for example, we stress individual rights, success, progress, the brotherhood of man, wealth, and efficiency—to name but a few—as being fundamental to our way of life. In other societies people may build their lives around a different arrangement of values, some of which, as in our own case, may be inconsistent with one another but all of which seem important. Knowing the value-system, then, helps one understand the significance of different statuses in society. Among the Eskimo we will find that the status of the hunter is highest, whereas among the Navajo it is of much less importance. This difference is not only related to the occupational differences but has been incorporated in the value-system as well. In the section entitled "Some Social-Science Generalizations and Tools" more detail about values and value-systems is provided.

Norms are the rules of the game by which members of society must abide in playing the various roles assigned to them. In many roles, such as those of husband and wife in our society, there is rather wide latitude of interpretation: our family can be patriarchal, with the father in charge, or matriarchal, with the mother in charge, or a companionship, in which the dominant status shifts from one to the other in keeping with the social situation being encountered. However, even in our society there are certain rules (norms) that cannot conveniently be violated: the husband must be the principal provider, or at least contribute to the support of his family, and parents may not punish their children in ways that are considered cruel or harmful.

Thus it is that culture, chiefly through the mentifacts of values and norms, pervades the social relations of a society and guides the people, at times without their awareness of what is happening, into socially approved conduct. For the purposes of this book, therefore, we shall assume that the value-system prevailing in a given society will be our guide to ranking the various statuses as to those considered more desirable and less desirable. We shall also view norms as the rules setting limits to the expression of the roles which the holder of a status might exercise.

SOCIAL RELATIONS VIEWED AT REST CAN BE CLASSIFIED INTO PATTERNS OF ASSOCIATION AND DISSOCIATION. The analysis of any society would be difficult indeed if we had to proceed from a listing of all possible statuses, a description of all possible roles, and a spelling out of the values and the norms. Somehow or other we must find a short cut to social description, since we cannot deal with thousands of possibilities simultaneously. As individuals we have hundreds of relations with other people, some fairly permanent and others quite temporary; all of our acquaintances, our neighbors, and others in our community whom we have never seen are likewise involved in an intricate web of relations.

The only way we can make sense out of such a seemingly confused maze is to follow the scientific procedure of classification. Fundamentally, people act either for and with one another, or against and apart from one another, or both for and against at the same time. That is, they either associate or dissociate or both. Technically, this is called *sociation—association*, dis*sociation*—but we need not worry about such special terms here. Moreover, we are concerned in this book chiefly with social systems that are not marked by much direct dissociation in the form of cutthroat competition, feuding, warfare, and so on—or at least these aspects are not much emphasized. Hence from this point on we shall refer primarily to patterns of association, always remembering, however, that in books designed for other purposes we might emphasize dissociation.

Again, our classification is further simplified by dealing with social relations in the broadest sense—that is, by making little of the distinction between social processes and social relation*ships*. Technically, social relations seen in motion are social processes, whereas social relations seen at rest are social relationships. By using social relations to mean either or both as occasion requires, we avoid making distinctions that, in this context, would amount only to hairsplitting.

At this point we want to classify in terms of social relations seen at rest; in the next section we shall deal with social relations seen in motion.

As we look at social relations in terms of the statuses connected (husband-wife, teacher-pupil, doctor-patient) we can begin to see that they readily fall into convenient groupings which we can term *patterns of association*. The totality of all of these patterns is called the *social structure*, or *social organization*.

The patterns of association that we have selected for emphasis in the societies to follow are six in number:

(1) Locality patterns—those with a spatial focus, such as the community.

(2) Family and kinship patterns—referring chiefly to biological relations.

(3) Economy patterns—the way in which people organize to meet most of their material needs.

(4) Governmental patterns—arrangements for the use and control of political power in the administration of justice, protection from foes, and promotion of the public welfare.

(5) Religious patterns—those groupings concerned with the unknown and the supernatural and usually involved in the promotion of moral and spiritual values.

(6) Patterns of class and caste—the relations within and between the layers of society.

A study of this list will show a number of omissions, such as age and sex, ethnic or racial groupings, educational patterns, and those focusing on mutual aid or recreation. But once we understand these six kinds, we shall find it easy to use the same kind of analysis for other patterns in which we may be interested.

Since the major purpose of the many pages that follow is to illustrate and document the rich varieties of these patterns of association, no attempt will be made to describe them here. It is important to remember that we begin to get the social-science approach to the study of society only as we see how each pattern stands out distinctly in its own right and at the same time is closely related to the others. When we do this, the term *society* ceases to be a blur and assumes definite characteristics that can be described and discussed intelligently with other people.

SOCIAL RELATIONS SEEN IN MOTION BECOME VARIETIES OF INTERACTION. The relations among those who form a group are not merely connections among people who recognize their common membership; these relations are also the channels through which flow the various kinds of interaction. Whereas the *patterns* of association relate chiefly to the collection of statuses of their members, the ongoing interactions are tied in with the carrying out of the roles.

There are several ways of viewing what happens when people get together to play, to study, to work, or to engage in any other activity. One way is to think only in terms of the specific activities and to try to classify these. By doing this we tend to duplicate the classification of the patterns of association, since there is a close correspondence, as we have seen, between status and role.

Another way of looking at the behavior of people in a group is to try to understand the kind of interaction that is occurring. Are these people *cooperating* and together trying to reach a common goal? Are they *competing* and trying to race one another to a common goal? Are they in *conflict* because they think they have antagonistic goals? Are they *accommodating*, trying to reconcile their differences by a "live and let live" policy toward one another? These interactions, and others, such as *assimilation* and *amalgamation*, will occasionally be called, for some purposes of this book, the *social processes*—although, much of the time, as stated earlier, we shall merely refer to social relations or to interactions. We need to know which of these receives the greatest emphasis in a given society if we are to assess properly the kind of behavior we observe. In America, for example, where competition runs through not only our business and our athletics but even our academic grading system, we are not surprised that "social climbing" —another form of competition—is an accepted preoccupation of many in the middle class.

A third way of viewing social relations is in terms of what have been called the *motivational* interactions of socialization and of social control. *Socialization* is the development of an individual into a person who knows his status and its appropriate role in one situation after another. It has been defined as "the process of learning to conform to group standards, mores, and traditions, and becoming imbued with a sense of oneness, intercommunication, and cooperation." (Note, however, that the group standards, the sense of oneness, and so on, may be of *any* kind—those of a criminal gang or of a charitable organization.) Socialization begins at birth and continues throughout life. Motivation enters in because through socialization the individual is influenced to *want* to do as an individual what "society" expects him to do as expressed in the norms. In other words, the family, the school, and the church in our society try to teach the maturing individuals how to behave and also to inculcate the social values and the accepted norms associated with "right" behavior.

Social control is viewed by some writers as the way in which society keeps in check deviant behavior, or the departure from the roles that society expects at a given time. Consequently, a group situation could be studied from the standpoint of how those with influence in the group keep the extremists from going too far in any direction—the hints they drop, the threats they make, and, in the final analysis, the carrying out of those threats in the form of punishment. Social control, like socialization, deals with motivation, since its operation seeks through fear of punishment or promise of reward to change unapproved behavior into that which is approved and expected.

SOCIETY CAN BE VIEWED AS A GOING CONCERN. As we summarize the brief consideration of society as a set of social relations, it is necessary to point out that such relations are tied in with the cultural heritage through the social values and the norms—that social relations consist of both statuses and roles. Through the classification of the status side of the relation, we arrive at patterns of association, which here receive primary emphasis, which can be studied satisfactorily, and about which numerous valid generalizations can be made. Through the classification of roles, we see the social relations from the kinetic point of view and trace the kinds of interaction that occur.

Somehow or other, if any society is to endure, it must maintain sufficient harmony within the patterns of association and the varieties of interaction to satisfy the needs of most of the people, to train a new generation, and to keep deviant behavior at a controllable level. For some of the societies that we are to study, this becomes very difficult as they are forced into a white man's world much more precipitately than in the past. Such a consideration leads us into the general topic of social change, to which we now turn.

Sociocultural Change

People today are acutely and at times painfully aware of living in a changing world. The older people try to cling to ideas and patterns of social organization that afforded them security in the past; younger people wonder just what to take hold of in order to gain the personal serenity that the times, troubled or otherwise, always require. To the social scientist, however, change is the normal condition of affairs, although he realizes that the types and the tempo of change do vary with time and place. Certain kinds of change can be guided once they are understood in a perspective that makes possible intelligent individual and group action.

In this concluding section we shall try to answer four questions briefly: What are the changes? What are the main classifications of change? Who and what are the agencies of change? And, finally, what implications do these facts have for social policies? In a sense, this is a review of all that has gone before, although some of the material will be set in a slightly different light.

WHAT ARE THE CHANGES IN CULTURE AND SOCIETY?

The word *sociocultural* conveniently ties together the ideas of *society* (without which there could be no culture, since people in association work out the culture traits) and *culture*, which, because of its cumulative character, generation after generation, may be viewed as embracing all that is man-made (artifacts, sociofacts, and mentifacts). This means that a society at any given time is a cultural product, although its members are constantly modifying their cultural world.

Therefore, sociocultural change covers all modifications in man's way of life. Illustrations would include the substitution of the automobile for the horse-drawn carriage; the development of an economy from an agricultural to an industrial type; alterations in religious organization and beliefs; or the replacement of an absolute by a constitutional monarchy with the introduction of the ballot and a representative assembly. Accompanying such changes there are always innovations in the status system and the working out of new roles for each status. Those who are unable to learn the new roles or fail to face the fact of changed social position are considered by the younger people as out-of-date; those who try to usher in change, whether prophets, inventors, or rebels, are willing and eager to take up new roles.

In summary, then, sociocultural change involves any reworking of any aspect of culture, whether it has to do with things or ideas. It also describes the changes in sociofacts, or patterns of association, and the changes in the expected behavior of the socialized individual. In order to think concretely on this topic, we must concentrate upon some one aspect—such as technology or the system of social values—and trace the change in it, after which we can relate it to the changes occurring in other aspects. Only then can we arrive at general conclusions about the sociocultural change of any given population at a specific point in time. In the societies we study in this book, we shall have ample opportunity to trace the changes that occur and, by the time we have studied the last society, we should have clearly in mind how sociocultural change affects practically every people and most details of their lives.

WHAT ARE THE KEY ASPECTS OF SOCIOCULTURAL CHANGE?

In the preceding section we briefly listed the major kinds of interaction: conflict, competition, cooperation, accommodation, and assimilation. Other classifications are also in use (for example, advance, accordance, contravention, differentiation, exploitation, institutionalization, etc.), but the terms we list are widely accepted and quite suitable for our present purposes. Essentially, they describe what happens when individuals or groups interact. Such interactions lead to change and, in one sense of the word, are the embodiment of change, since they represent society in action. (Here the interested student may refer to J. O. Hertzler, *Society in Action*, New York, The Dryden Press, 1954.) But their operation is really more related to the sociofacts, which we discussed earlier, along with the two "motivational" categories of socialization and social control.

Another set of categories we call *cultural*, for they describe how any culture trait, be it material, social, or mental, is introduced or altered in a sociocultural system. The cultural activity that accounts for most change is *borrowing*, when we view it from the standpoint of those taking over new traits. We call the same activity *diffusion* when we observe the spread of traits from one place to another.

A receiving culture seldom, if ever, accepts new things entirely and passively. Some parts are accepted and others rejected. What is taken in is subjected to changes in detail, meaning, or context. *Integration* is a term that helps to describe and analyze this refashioning of a new trait to fit into a sociocultural system so that it will be accepted by enough people to become a recognized way of behaving.

Some cultures today are being so bombarded with new traits that there is insufficient time for integration to occur. This leads to serious disturbance in social relations, sometimes resulting in widespread social disorganization. Change in a total culture is called *acculturation*. This may often be sudden and overwhelming, as when a primitive people is conquered by a technologically more advanced group. It may also be used to describe the changes that immigrants who move into a foreign culture adopt as they give up their old ways. In a sense, this second use of the word approaches the meaning of *socialization* already described.

Another major cultural activity is *invention*. Many important inventions (*e.g.*, the alphabet) were made only once and spread widely over the earth from one source, but someone or some group does have to originate them. Some inventions, such as farming, metallurgy, and pottery production, were probably made at least twice but certainly not a large number of times.

Loss of traits leads to some culture change. Usually loss comes from an "either-or" situation. We can have either horses or cars on our busiest streets, but we cannot have both without serious trouble. Often, it is obvious that more efficient traits replace less efficient ones. Inefficiency alone, however, does not automatically mean extinction. If the trait has high emotional values, it may be long retained. There is also cultural loss through lapse. No society ever succeeds in transmitting *all* of its culture to succeeding generations. Folksongs, for example, may slowly drop out of use, not because they are placed in an "either-or" situation or because they are inefficient, but because they are too hard to learn in all their details, or because other folksongs have more emotional appeal.

Invention, diffusion, integration, acculturation, and loss are thus major factors in culture change. Each may happen accidentally or incidentally. It is only as cultures become more complex that individuals often become self-conscious specialists in culture change. This leads us immediately into the question of who and what are the agencies speeding up and making possible the ease of culture transmission to all other parts of the world.

WHO AND WHAT ARE THE AGENTS OF CHANGE?

Borrowing, obviously enough, can occur only when there is social contact among peoples. This does not mean that the majority of members from the differing societies must be in communication with one another, for often one individual carries with him traits that change a whole lifeway of another people. Missionaries, for example, are among the most important culture carriers from the West. They may not always understand the role they play in this respect, but their whole life is dedicated to the initiation of change. Although a missionary's primary interest lies in bringing about a new religious orientation, he usually finds that to make his message effective he must undertake to heal the sick, teach people to read, promote agricultural efficiency, and carry on a number of other activities which seem to assist his work. Changes in religious beliefs lead in many cases to changes in family life, acceptance or rejection of governmental practices, modification of recreational patterns—a whole train of innovations that the missionary may never have intended in the first place. In terms discussed in the section "Some Social-Science Generalizations and Tools," he changes the holy values of a people, and thus may introduce other changes that eventually lead to extreme and even disastrous secularization, for in certain circumstances the accompanying disorganization may hinder not only his program but the actual welfare of the people themselves. That is why careful consideration must be given to the study of change.

For centuries, too, military leaders have gone forth in conquest. For every new territory subdued, a new government must be established. Some of these governments immediately try to make over the new areas into the image of the conqueror, much as we have tried to do in Germany or Japan; others are content with nothing more than taxation and a modicum of loyalty, leaving the people to follow their own customs without much disturbance. Businessmen, bringing in their cotton cloth, chewing gum, tobacco, firearms, printing presses, and innumerable other material traits, usher in much sociocultural change. Diplomats, sportsmen, tourists, explorers—all of these have their effect upon the peoples among whom they travel, and thus they become indirectly agents of sociocultural change.

But there are also impersonal agencies of change which are assuming increasing importance. American motion pictures have had much to do with changing some of the thought patterns and even the habits of certain groups in many foreign countries. International radio transmission is also influential. The best jazz orchestra in Zagreb, Yugoslavia, at the time of Tito's coming into power was made up of young men who had learned all they knew about jazz by listening regularly to the short-wave broadcasts of an American band. Through imitation and some improvisation they reached the point where they could easily have passed as an American musical organization.

Social policies and sociocultural change

Because of his ability and interest in tracing the social effects of many kinds of change, the social scientist is being increasingly employed by governments, business concerns, and religious groups to discover possible ways of blending new traits into the existing culture patterns of a given society. The social scientist is also being called upon to advise local communities as to the kinds of change which can best be initiated to bring about certain results desired by the members of the community. Even policy makers on a national scale are sensitive to the need for watching trends, whether through public-opinion analysis or other techniques of measuring popular reaction.

Anyone working in the field of intergroup or human relations is actually committing himself to some kind of attempted change. Hence he should be aware of how changes come about—via the social and cultural interactions—and of the ways which social scientists have worked out of looking at these activities in considerable detail. Advanced courses deal with some of the complex methodological problems involved in such research, but even so introductory a treatment as this book presents can help develop a systematic approach to the study of change, particularly with the use of the six living case studies in this book and the treatment of value-systems and social change that is offered in the section "Some Social-Science Generalizations and Tools."

Ourselves as a Society

Studying the societies described in this book should also help us understand American society better. As we learn to see life through the eyes of the Eskimo, the Navajo, the Baganda, the Chinese peasant, the people of the Cotton South, and the English "Midlanders," we shall become aware of the many ways in which our behavior must appear strange to them. And as we begin to place American society alongside other societies, we shall notice its significant characteristics.

Our first reaction to some of the societies described in this book may be one of wonder or even at times distaste; their foods are different from ours; religious ideas take on other forms; and health practices are far from scientific. Yet we shall also develop an appreciation for these people if we judge them not against our own background but against the circumstances under which their way of life has come into being and is even now being carried on.

Compare the Eskimo habitat with that of our own country. The United States has been favored with rich mineral deposits, and, until fairly recent times, an ever-beckoning frontier. Our location has made us feel militarily secure and at the same time has placed us astride many of the major commercial routes of the world. Thus, the understanding of our own society and our comparison of it with other societies should be based upon the realization that our forefathers had rich resources with which to build, and that the combination of these resources with ingenuity and hard work contributed much to our present position. Moreover, it is not very likely that the builders of America would have greatly surpassed the Indian in conquering the wilderness if they had not brought with them the accumulation of a civilization created out of inventions, products, and ideas from Asia, Africa, and Europe and rapidly adopted many traits from the Indians themselves.

The relatively abundant natural resources have played a part—though only a part, to be sure—in the growth of some of the mental characteristics that we Americans possess. One of these is our seeming indifference to waste. At first we think it strange that an Eskimo tries to eat almost every part of the animal he has killed and to use in other ways what he cannot eat. But people from other countries think it just as strange that in the opening of the West we allowed buffalo hunters to exterminate tremendous herds merely to get the buffalo hides. It is sobering to reflect that earlier generations, in their haste to "get ahead," mined the soil of its richness and let it wash or blow away and also stripped the hills of virgin forest with no thought of reforestation. We are now realizing that the abundance we once had on all sides has disappeared, and, instead of blithely using things up or throwing them away, we must stress conservation. Like many other societies, we may come to act upon the principle that "to waste is to do wrong," especially in view of the great needs existing in many parts of the world.

The family is another area in which we shall probably make frequent comparisons between our society and those described in this book. How strange, we may think, that the Navajo people trace descent through their mothers only and not through both their fathers and their mothers! Our study of these people will show us that, in the situations which they have faced, that system probably had some merits. Or, reading of the courtship and marriage practices of the Baganda may make us glad that in America women are not valued in terms of cows, or wives in terms of the cotton patch to be cultivated. But let us look more closely at our own family system. Foreigners think some of our ways most unusual. One of these is the practice we have developed of permitting young people to choose their own marriage partners—one of life's most important decisions—without any guidance from their elders. This is in direct contrast to the practice in most of the world, where parents arrange for the marriage of their sons or daughters. In this respect, our society represents an extreme position.

Coupled with this unusual freedom is the complicating error of the romantic fallacy, which assumes that one falls in love with the "one and only" and is forever blissfully happy when the knot is tied. Of course, if some dark morning there is an unhappy awakening and burnt toast becomes an issue, the only conclusion to draw is that one did not really find the "one and only" or else one would not be unhappy. Hence, the only way out is the divorce court and a search for a new mate. This, of course, is an overstatement of what life in America is like; most young people learn soon enough that successful marriages are made rather than fallen into, and that each partner has to work hard toward its success. Nevertheless, the "moonlight and roses" cult of our society, some of which was already well developed in the Old South, seems just as bizarre to many foreigners as do their family systems to us. That is to be expected even though we try to explain that our courtship patterns are based on the opportunity for boys and girls to meet under many conditions as they grow up; that it is also based on the growing insistence of parents that children, as they become able, select their own clothes, manage their own budgets, pick their own friends, take on summer jobs, and decide for themselves where they want to go to college. Thus the American youth, though inexperienced in many ways, is not necessarily as sheltered as is his counterpart in some societies. But even he has not had the rigorous training for adulthood that the children of the less industrialized societies acquire early in life.

We, too, have our taboos. Like almost all people, we forbid close relatives to marry; some religious denominations do not allow women to hold official positions on an equality with men; we do not desecrate or behave disrespectfully toward our flag; and we place strict limits on the use of certain kinds of language in polite society. The list could be greatly expanded. Most of these items seem perfectly normal; they should be accepted without question, we might say. But they do illustrate the fact that we, like all societies, have our set of taboos that have grown out of our historical past. In the section "Some Social-Science Generalizations and Tools," we shall analyze some of these taboos as aspects of sacred value-systems and see how secularization may limit their scope or even wipe them out.

We are apt to think the dress of other people quaint or picturesque without realizing that clothing represents their adjustment to their own climate and that it also shows social distinctions just as clearly as do overalls and the dinner jacket in the United States. The American woman paints her fingernails, and she wears sheer stockings in the coldest weather; American men wear useless buttons on the sleeves of their coats; and children repeat nursery rhymes whose original meaning was lost long ago. Again, we might ask, "Why not?" But it is well to remember when reading of unusual habits of other people that some of our national habits may be just as difficult for them to understand. We stand up, for example, in the seventh inning of a baseball game before our favorite team comes to bat. If a visitor to America asks us why we stand, we reply, "Oh, so our team will win." He then says, "I see, it is a prayer for victory." We point out that it is no prayer but just a custom and end up by being quite as confused as he in our search for a logical, scientific reason for this behavior pattern.

These observations all emphasize the point, which will be treated more fully later on, that American society, like any society, grows through adaptation to its resources and its historical experience, but that it does have common denominators with all societies in the form of taboos, customs, social values, and systems of social relations, such as the family. The content of any of these will differ in each society, but each will have them in some form. Thus, in looking at the values of the six peoples described in this book, we shall remember that we, too, have values around which our social life revolves. Our value-system, including as it does individualism, success, altruism, private owner-ship, democracy, wealth, respect for human personality, as well as a number of other values, must be understood by outsiders who hope to interpret our life correctly. Admittedly, we do not completely live up to the ideals these values express, nor are they all entirely consistent with one another, but we want to be judged in terms of these values and not by some other standard. In just the same way, we must try to understand others with reference to what they con-sider most important in life.

These few remarks about our rich and varied physical surroundings, our courtship patterns, our taboos and customs, and our value-system should be sufficient to suggest two things: first, in keeping with the outline "How to Study a Society," we should try to organize what we know about our own society; having done this, we can, secondly, try to compare traits of other societies with corresponding kinds of traits in our own society. In doing so, we shall learn to recognize many American behavior patterns that undoubtedly seem strange to other people. This does not mean that we shall think any the less of our own society; rather, we shall have a broader perspective in which to view the peoples of the world, and we shall be able to gauge more tolerantly the differences between their way of life and our own.

THE ESKIMO

Above: Part of an Alaskan reindeer herd being surrounded and "cut out" and corralled by Eskimo in Alaska. The entire community works together, with a long strip of burlap forming a temporary fence; the permanent corral can be seen in the background. Herding reindeer on a systematic basis is a new idea to the Eskimo, contrasting with their traditional hunting of migratory herds (which, in the wild state, are usually called caribou). *Left:* Old women fish for cod through holes chopped in the ice, leaving more active work to others. By means of a barbless hook and a line wound on two sticks, great numbers of fish can be taken, to be eaten fresh in the winter as a supplement to the reserves of dried fish and meat.

Right: Eskimo fishing boats meeting a Canadian government patrol ship on its annual cruise. Vessels of the Canadian and U. S. governments bring to the Eskimo many essential supplies and services: medical and dental care, assistance in the export and sale of ivory carvings and furs, and supplies of gasoline for boat motors, cooking, and lighting. *Below:* Tents and frame buildings are both popular in the arctic. The snow-block igloo was never common and was unknown in many areas. The "clothes line" is hung with fish, drying for winter storage, high out of reach of the dogs.

The Eskimo Habitat

Scale of Miles
0   200   400   600

ATLANTIC OCEAN

NORTH POLE

ARCTIC OCEAN

PACK ICE

SOUTHERN LIMIT OF

ICE CAP

BAFFIN BAY

Upernavik Island

Angmagssalik Island

ELLESMERE ISLAND

BAFFIN ISLAND

MELVILLE PEN.

VICTORIA ISLAND

BARREN GROUNDS

ARCTIC CIRCLE

HUDSON BAY

UNGAVA PENINSULA

TREE

NORTHERN LIMIT OF TREES

ARCTIC CIRCLE

Mackenzie River

Yukon River

BERING SEA

Point Hope

Kotzebue Sd.

Diomede Is.

St. Lawrence Island

Nunivak Island

Kodiak Island

Prince William Sound

Pavlov Bay

ALEUTIAN IS.

PACIFIC OCEAN

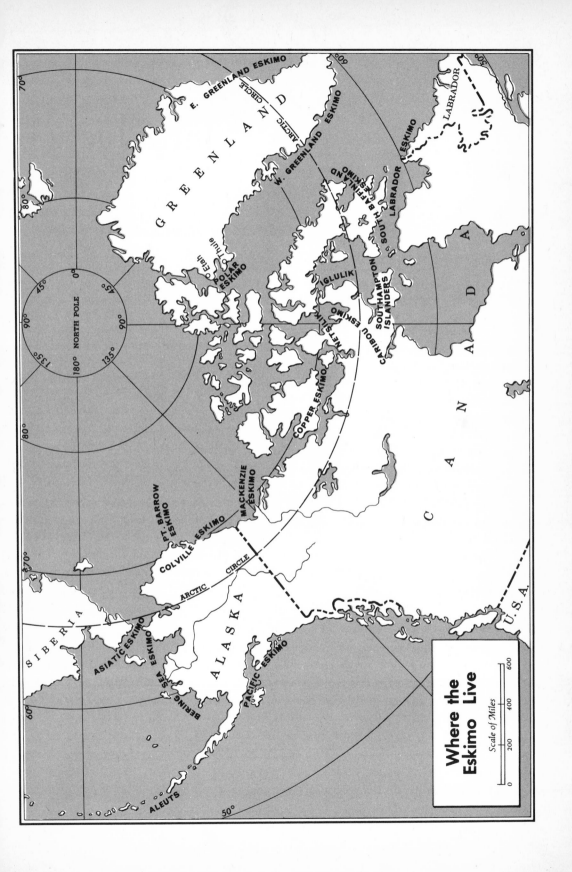

Where the Eskimo Live

Scale of Miles

0   200   400   600

Introduction

‹‹

The Eskimo are a fascinating people. The student who reads about them for the first time will be struck by the strange or different ways in which they carry on their daily round of activities. Their diet is amazing and has earned for them a derogatory Indian term meaning *raw meat eaters,* from which the word *Eskimo* is said to be derived. Their family pattern startles many, as does their matter-of-fact attitude toward mercy killings. However, as familiarity with the Eskimo increases, this fascination is based less on the bizarre and more on the remarkable ingenuity shown in the Eskimo adaptation to an almost impossible physical environment. The student will constantly ask, "Why do they stay there?" The answer lies partly in that hunting the Arctic animals is the only life they know; that they are habituated to the rhythm of their annual cycle, although they do not hesitate to assimilate many of the ways of the white man (tea, coffee, tobacco, firearms, kerosene lamps, needles, etc.).

The Eskimo call themselves *Inuit,* or The People. They consider themselves the center of the universe and in so doing display what is called *ethnocentrism,* or an exaggerated pride in one's own people and a tendency to consider one's own way the only right way.

The first selection is a brief summary of the physical traits of the Eskimo. Using these traits as criteria, we may note that the Eskimo are somewhat specialized members of the Mongoloid race.

TIME PERSPECTIVE

Centuries were required for the development and spread of Eskimo culture, with its remarkable adaptation and specialization. Today, the traditional culture has been modified by contact with Europeans and white Americans, especially since whaling flourished, and no Eskimo group can be found that has not undergone some changes. The main outlines of the earlier development of Eskimo culture will be treated in Selection 6, and in 19 and 20 more recent and rapid changes will be discussed.

PLACE PERSPECTIVE

The Eskimo live in the most northerly and most extended habitat of any primitive people. They are found from Eastern Greenland to the Asiatic mainland; from well above the Arctic Circle to areas below, which do not experience the periods of 24-hour darkness or 24-hour light. The Eskimo live under the flags of Denmark, Canada, the United States, and the Soviet Union. Despite this wide dispersion there is a remarkable uniformity to their culture, although there are some important differences based on habitat variations.

A careful reading of Selection 3, with frequent consultation of maps, will fix the location of the Eskimo groups. Their physical environment will be detailed vividly in Selections 4 and 5, which describe the features of the Arctic which the Eskimo have learned to use to advantage, as well as the extraordinary difficulties they face in the cold, the extreme seasonal changes, and the scarcity of plant life. In Selections 6 through 9, further information on the environment will be found in connection with the Eskimo techniques for making a living.

ECONOMIC AND SOCIAL ORGANIZATION

One of the purposes behind the first section of this book is to make available, in the language of various authors, accurate accounts of Eskimo life. The selections differ both in style and in the location of the Eskimo group being described. An illustration of this range of content will be found by comparing Selection 11, which deals with the Eskimo of Greenland, with 12, devoted to the Nunivak Islanders off the coast of Alaska. In these selections, as well as in those numbered 7 through 10, one will find not only a description of hunting techniques but an insight into the economic system which is definitely governed by fixed rules and practices, although these are not enforced by policemen or government officials.

Eskimo social organization is relatively simple. There are settlements, described in Selection 5, but these do not take on the permanent features of most modern communities. The family, as Selections 13 and 14 will show, is the basic unit of Eskimo life. Child rearing seems haphazard to the outsider, but the individual grows up to be self-reliant, skilled in what he needs to know, and happy. There is little that could be called government among them, although Selection 15, on the law-ways of the Eskimo, does show that there is rather severe group control when any individual menaces the welfare of others.

Eskimo religion is an integral part of the social organization. The Eskimo are polytheistic and rely upon the *shamans,* or religious leaders (often referred to by the native term, *angakok* or *angakut*), as well as upon amulets and other magical devices to protect them from the dangers of the spirit world. These religious ceremonies, taboos, and deities, are found in Selections 16 and 17. The songs in Selection 18 illustrate the creative ability of the Eskimo.

The concluding selections, numbered 19 and 20, tell about the most recent changes in the way of living of the Alaskan Eskimo. Primitive people everywhere in the world today are forced to learn many new ways in order to survive. Change itself is not new, but the rate of change is constantly increasing. And along with change goes the secularization of value-systems.

The People: Their Physical Features and Language

>>>

Although all mankind is alike in ultimate potentialities of mind and body, any group that remains isolated and inbred for a long enough time comes to share a unique combination of physical traits. Familiarity with these special traits makes it possible to identify a person as Eskimo by his outward appearance even though he gives up his fur clothing and other *cultural* traits.

• 1 • *Physical Traits of the Eskimo*
CHARLES E. SNOW

Today there are about 40,000 Eskimo, about half of whom are part white in their ancestry. Natives of mixed parentage are particularly common in Greenland, where they make up about three-fourths of the Eskimo population. Basically, the Eskimo are Mongoloid, like their relatives the American Indians, who preceded them across Bering Strait from Asia. The Eskimo have a yellow-brown skin, lighter than most Indians, but of course the hands and face are considerably darkened by exposure to sun, wind, and cold.

The Eskimo face, with its great size, looks "Oriental." It is large, square, and flat, with prominent cheek bones and often with heavy jowls. The nose is rather low and pinched between the eyes, and the nostrils are flaring. The eye slit is slanted upward and has a fatty fold of skin over the inner corner. This is called an epicanthic fold, and is particularly noticeable among women and children. Eye color is dark brown, except where mixture with whites has produced other colors.

The teeth are of excellent quality, evenly set in a broad dental arch. The back surfaces of the incisors are often curiously concave, with rims and hollows suggesting the shape of a scoop shovel. Most adults show extreme wear of the teeth from nearly constant use.

Hair is dark brown to black, generally straight and coarse. Grayness and baldness are rare. Eskimo have very little body hair, and the scanty beard of the men is plucked as a safeguard against ice forming there from the condensation of the breath.

In the central and eastern areas the Eskimo have long, narrow heads, relatively high and of large size. In the west the Eskimo have smaller, lower, and rounder heads.

In body build they are short and heavy-set, with relatively short legs and broad shoulders. They often have remarkably fine, small hands and feet. In stature, men average five feet three inches to five feet six inches, and women about five inches less.

Language has a particular value in tracing the history of a group of people, because it is one part of culture of which people are little conscious and which they rarely make any effort to modify. Therefore, the language of a group will be only slightly changed in the course of centuries, and groups whose languages were once identical will speak only slightly differing dialects even after being separated for many generations. It is also true, of course, that language will quickly absorb new words and thus will reflect with astonishing accuracy the contacts and influences which its speakers have undergone. But the linguistic expert can analyze the basic forms and structure of a language and discover much about its earlier, perhaps very remote, affiliations. The Eskimo have had relatively few outside contacts and influences, for they avoided the Indians, their only neighbors, and the Europeans came only recently, except in Greenland. Thus the situation described by Voegelin is significant in our attempt to understand the historical background of the Eskimo.

• 2 • *The Two Eskimo Languages*

C. F. VOEGELIN

That most Eskimo dialects are mutually intelligible is attested by Rasmussen who travelled across arctic America from Greenland to Alaska expecting to but failing to find numerous different Eskimo languages. "Yet the remarkable thing I found was that my Greenlandic dialect served to get me into complete understanding with all the tribes." Our authority cites characteristic experiences on his journey. When he arrived at the Lyon Inlet Eskimo, west of Baffinland, he says, "I was delighted to find that the difference in language was so slight that we had not the least difficulty in understanding one another. Indeed, they took us at first for tribesmen of kindred race from somewhere up in Baffin Island."

At Point Barrow Rasmussen says, "My Greenland accent and idiom occasioned no difficulty among the natives here; a fact which promised well for future work. All in all, we may conclude that essentially one Eskimo language is spoken all the way from Greenland to Alaska."

Birket-Smith [affirms] Rasmussen's ability to use Greenlandic among the Central dialects, and adds, "neither had the rest of us any difficulty in our daily intercourse

[Adapted from "North American Indian Languages Still Spoken and their Genetic Relationships," in Leslie Spier, *et al.*, eds., *Language, Culture, and Personality: Essays in Memory of Edward Sapir,* Sapir Memorial Publication Fund, Menasha, Wis., 1941. Pp. 16-17. Used by permission.]

with the Canadian Eskimos." As to diversity, "The difference between the individual groups may, perhaps, be compared with the difference between standard English and Scotch, and between standard Danish and Jutlandic. . . . Neither Jacob Olsen, a native of West Greenland, nor our Polar Eskimos had spent many days among the Canadian Eskimos, before they were able to talk freely with them upon all everyday subjects."

The first real break in languages is found in Alaska where Rasmussen says, "The Eskimo from the south and west of the Yukon spoke a dialect differing so considerably from the others that I found it, contrary to all previous experience, impossible . . . without the aid of an interpreter."

[We] find Dall reporting significant change of dialect at the Yukon delta group of Ekogmut. This was about where Rasmussen's Greenlandic Eskimo failed him. Until further work is done, particularly in Alaska, we may conclude that there are two Eskimo languages, Central-Greenlandic and Alaskan.

Not only in physical traits and language but also in many other aspects of their life— in the ways in which they gain their livelihood, in their social customs, and in their beliefs and ideals—there is a remarkable degree of uniformity among the widely dispersed Eskimo groups. Two things account for much of this homogeneity. First, as will be discussed in Selection 6, much of modern Eskimo culture developed in the central Arctic and has spread in a few centuries west to Bering Sea and east to Greenland. Second, the Arctic environment everywhere poses much the same problems, so that diversity has tended to be limited to such minor matters as the styles of decoration on clothing or the arrangement of the barbs on a harpoon tip. At this point we shall consider just what this environment is and what it means to those who live in it.

The Habitat

<<<<<<<<<<<<<<<<<<<<<<<<<<<<<<<<<<<<<<<<<<<<<<<<<<<<<<<<<<<<<<<<<<<<<<<<<<<<<<<<<<<<<<<<<<<<<<<<<<<<<<<<<<<<<<<<<<<<<<<<<<

The habitat factors to be presented for the Eskimo are those which answer questions for the first part of the outline on how to study a society (pp. 5-6). First are the three space relationships of (1) location, (2) size, and (3) shape of the habitat. A fourth factor, surface features, covers the questions of terrain and drainage. The remaining factors are (5) climate, (6) soil, (7) minerals and rocks, and (8) water, both surface and underground, (9) natural vegetation—flora, and (10) native animals—fauna.

The Eskimo occupy a vast, attenuated, collar-shaped region extending nearly 4000 miles across the Arctic fringe of North America and the adjacent corner of Siberia. It is a region of innumerable islands, bays, and narrow channels, with much of the coast steep and rocky and much of the inland either mountain or tundra. There are thus relatively few places that are ideal for settlement and many large areas are almost uninhabited. The majority of settlements are on the coasts. For purposes of study and comparison, the Eskimo have been divided by Birket-Smith into seventeen groups, each made up of several smaller, entirely independent bands composed of several families who live and work together. Such bands or communities number about 160, and each may include from a mere handful of families to over a hundred.

Nearly every group of families, whether large or small, moves from place to place with the seasons, going where the best hunting is to be found. But although they may scatter for part of the year and sometimes change the location of the winter village, they never stray from a particular region which they think of as their own. Each group can therefore be identified by the name of the geographical region in which it stays, or by some important feature, such as an island or river.

35

• 3 • The Regions where the Eskimo Live

THOMAS P. FIELD

The Eskimo are widely dispersed across the Arctic of North America. Eskimo settlements are generally confined to the littoral of the tundra. Major exceptions to this general pattern are found in northwestern Alaska with the Colville Eskimo and in the Barren Grounds of Canada with the Caribou Eskimo. Though the littoral of the tundra extends for many thousands of miles, the settlements are found only where a combination of natural features make for good hunting. Eskimo settlements are small and isolated from neighbors. Each of these communities tends to develop a character of its own and the people identify themselves by the community name such as Kuskokwigmiut (people of Kuskokwim) and Nuniwagamiut (people of Nunivak).

Because of the elongated habitat it is convenient to speak of the Alaskan, the Central and Greenland Eskimo. One of the best groupings is that made by Kaj Birket-Smith (in *The Eskimos,* 1936) which is the basis of the system that follows.

ALASKAN ESKIMO

Aleut: From the Near Islands in the western Aleutians eastward to the northeast point of Kodiak Island and the opposite mainland. Their settlements are found on the Rat, Andreanof, Fox, and Shumagin Islands as well as both sides of the Alaskan Peninsula as far eastward as Pavlov Bay.

Asiatic: The extreme eastward points of Siberia—Cape Dezhnev and Cape Chaplina, St. Lawrence Island and the twin Diomede Islands.

Bering Sea: From Point Hope southward to Bristol Bay including the Kuskokwim delta, Nunivak Island and the opposite mainland, the Yukon delta, and Point Hope.

Colville: Across the northwestern interior east of Point Hope, following the Kobuk, Noatak, and Colville Rivers.

Point Barrow: From Wainwright northeastward to Point Barrow.

Pacific: Kodiak Island and Cook Inlet eastward to Prince William Sound.

CENTRAL ESKIMO

Mackenzie: Herschel Island eastward to Liverpool Bay including the delta of the Mackenzie.

Copper: Victoria Island and the opposite mainland including Minto Inlet, Prince Albert Sound, Union Strait, Coronation Gulf, and Queen Maud Gulf.

Netsilik: Adelaide and Boothia Peninsulas including lower Back River and Pelly Bay.

Caribou: Baker Lake, Chesterfield Inlet, Rankin Inlet, Kazan River, and south to the timber line.

Iglulik: East coast of the Melville Peninsula southward to Repulse Bay, Roe's Welcome Sound, and Southampton Island.

Southampton: Southampton Island.

South Baffinland: Home Bay, Cumberland Sound, Frobisher Bay, and westward along the south coast facing Hudson Strait.

Labrador: Atlantic Coast of Labrador westward to include the north and west coast of the Ungava Peninsula.

GREENLAND ESKIMO

Polar: Northwestern coast from Humboldt Glacier south to Melville Bay including the settlements of Etah and Thule. Hunting camps on Ellesmere Land.

West Greenland: Greenland's west coast, Melville Bay south to Cape Farewell and including Upernavik, Disko Island and Godthaab.

East Greenland: East Coast of Greenland from Scoresby Sound south to Angmagssalik Island.

In studying the Eskimo, it is important to know the *latitude* at which a particular group lives, because of its relation to the climate, the seasons, and the periods of light and darkness. The most southerly Eskimo settlements (those of Labrador) are at about 55° North latitude. The greatest number of the Eskimo live between 60° and 70°, and the northernmost, those of the Cape York region of northwest Greenland, at about 75° North latitude.

The latitude of an Eskimo settlement directly affects the lives of the people in it, because the great differences between summer and winter become more extreme to the northward. Many, but not all, Eskimo experience the "midnight sun" of the summer, since they live above the Arctic Circle, which lies at 66½° North latitude, and they experience the corresponding winter period when the sun is not seen for days or weeks and twilight takes the place of a true day with sunrise and sunset. Notice, however, in this section that there *is* a summer in the Arctic, even though it comes late, lasts only a short time, and is rarely very warm. This annual change in light and temperature affects almost every aspect of life in the Arctic. For example, travel is easiest in the winter over the ice of the sea or the snow-covered land. Also, it is only at certain times that important animals like the walrus or the caribou come together in large numbers to migrate and are thus relatively good hunting. Such prized delicacies as bird eggs are likewise available only for a few weeks of the year and the gathering of them takes precedence over all other activities at this time. So it will be seen that there are great *seasonal* changes in the occupations of an Eskimo, and indeed in the whole pace and orientation of his life. On the other hand, he pays little attention to the kind of unvarying daily routines which most of us follow, with the hands of the clock always determining whether we are to work or play, eat or sleep.

Seasonality, therefore, for the Eskimo is mainly a matter of alternations in the duration of light and darkness; with the Navajo (whom we study next) it is based on temperature changes; and with the Baganda it is tied in with rainfall.

• 4 • The Annual Cycle of the Seasons
EDWARD M. WEYER, JR.

In temperate and tropical latitudes daylight and darkness alternate diurnally with relatively slight seasonal variation. In the Far North, however, daylight and darkness are largely seasonal, and at the Pole they are entirely seasonal. There the sun remains above the horizon for approximately six months (actually the center of the sun is visible for almost a week longer, because of atmospheric refraction), and then disappears for the remainder of the year. No Eskimos, of course, live under this extreme condition. The northernmost tribe experiences four months of continual sunlight during the summer, followed by two months of alternating sunlight and twilight ushering in the darkness of winter. For three and a half months they do not see the sun at all, though during this time the darkness is partly relieved by twilight, when the sun is not far below the horizon. The darkness of winter is superseded by a lingering dusk, with

[Adapted from *The Eskimos: Their Environment and Folkways,* Yale University Press, New Haven, 1932. Pp. 16-20, 27-31. Used by permission.]

growing periods of sunlight until the sun once more circles the sky during all of the twenty-four hours. [This] represents the extreme case throughout the inhabited world. Other groups of Eskimos to the south experience the seasonal variation of sunlight to less degree.

SUN AND CLIMATE

The climate of the Arctic is influenced strongly by the seasonal distribution of sunlight and by the enfeebled effect of the sun in high latitudes. The *yearly total* number of hours of sunlight does not differ radically from the Equator toward the poles—what small change there is in high latitudes being a slight increase.

The height of the sun above the horizon influences the amount of its heat received at any point on the earth. When the sun's rays strike the earth at a low angle their effect is diminished. Striking the earth's outer atmosphere at an acute angle, the rays of the sun must, in the first place, pass through a greater thickness of air before reaching the surface of the globe. In other words, virtually a thicker blanket of air insulates the earth from the sun in high latitudes than in low. In the second place, each unit of heat from the sun, figuratively speaking, must distribute itself over a broader area. These two facts explain why the sun does not seem so warm when it is near the horizon.

The temperature at any point on the earth at a particular time of the year is basically determined, therefore, by the daily duration of sunlight in conjunction with the angle at which the rays of the sun fall. In summer in high latitudes these two factors work toward opposite effects: the days are unusually long —even twenty-four hours when the midnight sun is visible—but at the same time the sun never rises high in the sky. The length of day makes for warm weather, while the low position of the sun has a counteracting effect.

Almost as much heat is received at the surface of the globe in the polar regions in summer as at the Equator. The ratio, as given by Angot, is 494 for the North Pole, to 517 for the Equator at the summer solstice.

The dissipation of heat from the sun expended in melting the winter's accumulation of snow does not delay the advance of warmer weather as much as might be supposed, because the quantity of snow is slight over large areas. The cooling influence of the frozen ground, furthermore, is obstructed by the surface vegetation and the blanket of thawed earth, which even in the height of summer prevent thawing of the ground below a depth of about two feet. At Fort Yukon within seven feet of where a thermometer registered 100° F. in the shade there lay eternally frozen soil.

In winter, on the other hand, the shortness or total absence of sunlight combines with the narrowness of the angle at which the sun's rays strike the earth, to cause the polar regions to receive very much less heat than the equatorial.

ARCTIC SUMMER

Summer in the Arctic is [quite] short, and cool, especially near the sea. Inland, surprisingly hot temperatures are recorded. From Fort Yukon, on the Arctic Circle, for instance, the United States Weather Bureau has reported 100° F. in the shade. On the other hand, at Smith Sound the highest temperature recorded by MacMillan in four years was 63° F. There, the summer is very brief and for the most part cool; yet even so there is a complete disappearance of snow at sea level, a thawing of the surface soil, and a blossoming of plants.

Only a small proportion of the Eskimos live in what can be considered the high arctic belt, which includes northern Greenland and the Arctic Archipelago with the exception of the southern fringe of Victoria Island and the greater part of Baffin Island. In this belt the average temperature, even of the warmest month of summer, is within ten degrees (F.) above freezing, which is about the same as that during the coldest month of winter in Delaware. Thus, even on the extreme fringe of the inhabited world, the climate in midsummer is comparable with midwinter climate in a densely settled section of the temperate zone. Farther south in the Eskimo region the summer temperatures become increasingly milder; until at Dillingham, Alaska, near the southern limit of the Eskimos in the west, the average temperature of the warmest month (July) is 56° F., which is practically the same as the average of the coldest month at San Diego, California. Farther north within the province of Point Barrow on the northernmost point of Alaska; at Adelaide Peninsula, on the Arctic coast of Canada; and at Upernivik, in latitude 73° N. on the west coast of Greenland, the average temperature of the warmest month is approximately the same as the average temperature during the coldest month at Victoria, Canada; Portland, Oregon; Nantes, France; and Hankow, China.

[Temperature maps of the Arctic will indicate] . . . that the isotherm of 32° F. moves northward over the Eskimo region during April, May, and June, signifying that during these months the average temperature rises from below freezing to above freezing. This rise roughly marks the transition to the arctic summer. In any particular place the change is, as a rule, quite sudden. Everywhere within the Eskimo region it is complete, in that all the land at sea level is stripped of snow. Only north of the Eskimo lands does snow lie on the ground through the summer, specifically near the northern extreme of Greenland in latitude about 82° 30'. If it is true that the snow reported in this locality lay on open ground, not in ravines or other protected places, this is the only place of its kind known in the northern hemisphere.

Elsewhere permanent snow and land ice exist only on mountains and plateaus. The outstanding glaciated area within the regions we are studying is Greenland. About 86 per cent of the island, the entire interior of it, is covered by a shield of ice. In the Arctic Archipelago local areas are glaciated, such as in Grinnell Land and other parts of Ellesmere Island, in Devon Island, and Baffin Island.

With the approach of the warm period snow and ice at sea level melt. In general the ground becomes free of snow in June or July. There are extensive areas where the snow is gone by about the tenth of May, and does not return till the first of October. On the other hand, there are areas where the ground is free of snow for only a month or six weeks. River ice and lake ice usually break up about the same time that the snow disappears, or a little sooner.

Snow flurries may occur, to be sure, in some sections during any month of the year. Thus, at Ungava, Labrador, snow falls every month. And among the Iglulik Eskimos of the Melville Peninsula and northern Baffin Island none of the months is entirely free from snowstorms. In southern Greenland, snow falls occasionally even in July and August. The arctic summer[, however,] is virtually a snow-free period. [The sea ice breaks up as] early as May in parts of Bering Sea and in the waters of southern Greenland, and even in April in some places. [However, scattered] sea ice remains through the summer in some waters within the Eskimo regions.

On land the release from winter is remarkably sudden. The earth is scarcely bare before the hardy flora burst into life. Most plants of the Arctic are perennials; the brevity of the growing season excludes annuals. Plant forms must hurry their life cycles to fit the short summer from June to August. Roots, liberated from their long frosty imprisonment, quickly absorb moisture from the spongy tundra. Flower buds are not infrequently open before the snow is off the ground. At the first suggestion of spring they are ready to bloom. Development is almost explosive.

With the same suddenness come the migratory birds. The Danish Expedition in northeastern Greenland remarked that the snow melted away in one day; the birds arrived almost the same day, most of them at the same hour. It should be realized that a hundred species or more of birds nest largely or almost entirely north of the Arctic Circle. Mosquitoes also appear, which make living on the tundra miserable. Caribou become much more numerous in the so-called Barren Grounds, along the coast of Labrador, and in the Arctic Archipelago, whither they migrate in herds.

At the height of the arctic summer only one or two feet of the surface soil is thawed. Beneath is a solid platform of frozen earth. Because of this rock-like subsoil, drainage of the abundant ground water from the flat tundra is slow. The earth is soggy. Small clumpy protuberances of mossy earth, "niggerheads," offer the only secure footing to the traveler. Elsewhere he sinks sometimes knee-deep into the sodden soil.

The warm season is brief in duration. In contrast with the sudden awakening of spring, autumn is a quiet dying away of nature. Winter arrives stealthily, almost imperceptibly. In September some snow falls in most parts and small lakes and rivers freeze in the northern sections.

ARCTIC WINTER

The Eskimo lands do not become buried deep in snow. Whatever falls is not likely to melt, but the annual snowfall is only moderate or light, particularly in the central and northern regions. Around Coronation Gulf the yearly snowfall does not aggregate more than two or three feet. The total yearly precipitation in the Arctic Archipelago is less than eight inches, in many places probably only four inches. In addition to the lightness of the snowfall, winds sweep much of the surface bare.

Sea ice forms throughout most of the region during November, but this is a very variable phenomenon. The Polar Sea, it should be remembered, never freezes very deep. Some waters are kept free of solid ice throughout the winter by ocean currents.

During November the average tempera-

ture in the warmest Eskimo regions is but slightly below freezing; while in the central and northern sections it is as much as forty degrees (F.) below freezing. In January the divergence in temperature from south to north becomes even wider. Clearly, there is far less uniformity throughout the region with respect to winter temperatures than with respect to summer temperatures.

The southerly parts of the Eskimo region have a winter comparatively mild in the arctic sense. The average temperature in southernmost Greenland in January, the coldest month, is the same as that in Albany during the same month. And the average temperature during the coldest month at Dillingham, at the southeastern corner of Bering Sea, is the same as that in the coldest month at Montreal.

The Arctic Archipelago and the extreme northern border of North America, on the other hand, are subject to average temperatures of $-10°$, $-20°$, and even $-30°$ F. during the coldest period of winter. No averages comparable with these occur in the northern United States.

In the high arctic belt the winters are exceedingly cold; they are not, however, the coldest winters in the inhabited world. The coldest place where people dwell, or nearly the coldest place, is Verkhoyansk, in northeastern Siberia just north of the Arctic Circle. There the average temperature for the whole of January often is below $-58°$ F. and occasionally the temperature drops as low as $-94°$. Such a winter climate is far colder than that among any Eskimos.

At the approach of winter most of the birds of the Arctic and the greater part of the caribou, at least of Victoria and King William Islands, migrate southward. The scarcity of living forms and the gloom of the protracted twilight give the wintry tundra an extremely dismal cast. The Eskimos who inhabit this region see the sun during the height of winter for only a few hours each day.

In the face of conditions such as Weyer describes, it is important that people live in well-selected spots, protected if possible and near to game. The Eskimo, like most people, prefer to dwell in groups larger than solitary family units. In fact, in the areas where abundant food resources permitted, Eskimo settlements could reach a size of several hundred people. This was true in the past especially in the Aleutians and the Bering Sea. Ipiutak (see p. 46) was such a town in prehistoric times, and more recently both St. Lawrence Island (Selection 9) and Nunivak Island (Selection 12) had larger populations than today. In the central Arctic and in Greenland, Eskimo villages were small, since few people could be supported by the local food resources.

In Selection 3 the reader will have noticed that no Eskimo "tribes" are mentioned. Instead, they are merely listed as groups, each of which occupies a specific locality or region. The problem of what to call these groups has puzzled investigators of the Eskimo, but it now seems that "settlement" is the most satisfactory term to use.

The question of just why a particular place happens to be the site of an Eskimo settlement can be answered only by means of a fairly elaborate discussion of how the Eskimo make a living, which leads into a consideration of resources (see p. 12). This topic will be given more attention in Selections 6 through 10, but in the next selection the author explains some of the special circumstances that make certain places greatly preferred for settlements. It should be kept in mind that the author is writing specifically of the Polar Eskimo, on the northwest coast of Greenland, but much of what he says applies to all of the regions occupied by the Eskimo.

Dr. Ekblaw wrote from personal experience with the Eskimo, gained during a long stay in northwest Greenland. An expedition he made just before World War I was planned for a single year, but it was three years before he finally returned to the United States. After his regular supplies and his emergency supplies were exhausted, he had to live off the country, with the help of his Eskimo hosts. Thus he learned to appreciate the many important circumstances which make existence possible only in certain localities of the Arctic.

• 5 • Settlements of the Polar Eskimo

W. ELMER EKBLAW

The Polar Eskimo are solely a hunting people. Their fishing activities are so insignificant in their economy, so negligible in the contribution to their dietary, that they may be neglected. These Eskimo are essentially a coastal people, living on the shore, but hunting chiefly on the sea and deriving the major part of their living from it. Their food is almost exclusively meat and blubber, eaten boiled or raw. The vital organs are eaten raw. They have no vegetables, fruits or cereals, not even roots or berries. The fuel to heat their homes, and to light them, and to cook their food is blubber, of whale, por-

[Adapted from "Distribution of Settlement among the Polar Eskimo," *Bulletin of the Massachusetts Archaeological Society*, Vol. 8, No. 3, Andover, 1947. Pp. 40-43. Used by permission.]

poise (beluga or narwhal), walrus and seal, and sometimes of bear. The material of which they fashion their every item of clothing is of furs and hides, tanned and made pliant by scraping and chewing. Their whips, their dog harnesses and traces, their harpoon lines, their kayaks, are of leather from animal skins. Many of their tools and implements like harpoon points, are of ivory, their bows of caribou antler. Bone and horn are used for a few items of their home life. Except for soapstone pots and lamps and primitive ulus and other scrapers, practically all artifacts in their economy and culture are from animal sources, obtained by hunting and trapping.

The sites of their settlements must then represent primarily an adjustment to their hunting activities. Easy access to adequate and varied supplies of available game constitutes the major factor in choice of both summer and winter sites of settlement.

Settlements of the Polar Eskimo are widely scattered and separated along the whole coast of Thule. Many sites once occupied have been abandoned for years; some sites have been more or less continuously in occupance from time immemorial.

Eskimo sites consist of from a single igloo [permanent winter house, here built of stone] to five or six igloos at the most. No site affords enough game for a large number of hunters for continual residence throughout the year. Supply of game, too closely hunted, becomes depleted either through continued slaughter or through being frightened away after persistent or prolonged pursuit. Under such conditions even the most assiduous hunting within reasonable range of the settlement yields insufficient reward and dooms the people in that settlement to dearth and relative poverty. There is a very nice balance among area of hunting territory, sustained supply of game, intensity of hunting, and assured comfortable standard of living. Whenever the booty of the chase decreases, supply of meat and blubber for use in the igloo or tupik [the tent-like summer residence, of skins] diminishes, but more important than that is the consequence of limited

food for the dogs. With a well-fed powerful dog team of eight or ten dogs the hunter can sledge far to hunting-grounds wherever game is most abundant and having made his kill can haul a heavy load of flesh, blubber, and skins home to the settlement, or cache it along shore at some place where he can get it when he or his fellows need it. His wife's igloo will be well lighted and heated, his children well fed, healthy and happy, and his dogs kept numerous for replacements when needed and fit for the trail upon any occasion. The Eskimo of a settlement will then be prosperous and effective.

Consequently settlements are not only limited in number, but widely enough spaced and scattered along the coast to afford maximum territory for sustained and successful hunting. Since most of the game is in the sea, and conditions favorable for abundance and variety vary from one area to another, there can be no regularity or average in spacing of settlement or in number of families occupying any particular site. In an area of paucity and monotony of game, settlements must be widely spaced, with distances of as much as eighty to a hundred miles intervening, and the number of hunters in the settlement relatively few, in some places but two or three. Where game is abundant and varied, both on land and sea, there settlements are closer, in the most advantageous localities perhaps but twenty or thirty miles apart, and the number of hunters in a settlement rises at times to eight or ten.

Any one territory yields only a few species of game, limited variety of food, of furs, and of other raw materials. Some settlements yield greater variety but a smaller aggregate of supply; a very few supply both quantity and desirable diversity. For occasional change in dietary and in scenery, and required assortment of furs and skins for the several items of clothing for man and woman, Eskimo families change residence from one village to another almost every year, rarely living two years in succession at the same site.

Composition of the group of any settlement varies with every year. A group at a settlement one year disperses to several other settlements the next, and is replaced by families that the year before may have resided at as many sites as there are families. There is no continuity of settlement, or of composition of population at a settlement, from one year to the next. A site may be occupied one year and abandoned the next, particularly if it affords but limited choice or quantity of game.

Besides four desirable and rather permanently inhabited settlements, a dozen or fifteen other sites of more or less desirable residence afford varying quantities and variety of game, and remain in more or less constant occupance, sometimes with several hunters, sometimes with few.

Proximity, or easy accessibility of a site to hunting grounds not immediately surrounding it, constitutes a secondary advantage of considerable moment for its selection for settlement—and[, moreover,] the Polar Eskimo are sociable as we are and like to visit each other when travel conditions permit. Ease of movement from one village to another, by sea-ice, by land, or by icecap has been an important factor in choice of residence.

Whatever the attributes of site that determine its selection for summer settlement, they must include a sloping beach or delta to provide an easy gradient up which to drag the heavy carcasses of sea-animals killed and a wide strip between high tide and low tide for bringing in the kayaks and the game. Other essentials for the summer camp are a running stream to supply plenty of fresh water for cooking and drinking; an accessible gap in the coastal cliffs by which to reach the ice-cap for sledging to neighboring villages when need arises; and a wide and uninterrupted view of the sea toward which the tupiks are fronted, that folk may observe weather and ice conditions, approaching visitors, returning hunters, or perchance some valuable vagrant game. In addition, longest exposure to the sun, freedom from gales, and most favorable temperatures, are conditions which make a site desirable for summer occupancy.

Winter settlements are more firmly established at sites long since selected for definite advantages that they possess. Igloos, being of stone, must be built where suitable stone is available, and can not be removed from one site to another. Consequently winter settlements are more permanently fixed and regularly inhabited, generally in the very same places where the igloos were first built. Like summer villages, winter villages must insure as easy and trustworthy facilities for hunting as possible; consequently they are established where the shore slopes gently to make the ice readily accessible for sledge or kayak as the season permits; where issuing glaciers make gaps in the barrier cliffs and afford routes for sledge travel over the ice cap to other villages should necessity arise; and where any stores laid up in caches along the coast in successful summer hunting remain easily available.

In winter, when all land sources of fresh water are frozen, and all streams are dry, the only supply is from offshore icebergs, except the few places where small fresh-water lakes or ponds are near. Sites otherwise favorable become increasingly desirable if shoal water prevails near shore, upon which drifting bergs may ground and furnish potable and other domestic water. Should perverse currents or winds keep the bergs from grounding, then the Eskimo must sledge their supply of ice for their homes from remoter sources, a hazardous chance should inclement weather long prevail; or they must remove to a more favorable site.

Whereas summer villages may be located well into the depths of fjords and bays where seal bask in the sunshine and dovekies nest in the talus slopes and eiders on the islets, winter villages must be established near the mouth of the fjord or gulf, toward some shoal upon which icebergs ground conveniently, or some pool where tide or winds keep the ice open nearly or quite all winter, and sea animals haunt shallower coastal waters.

As [the] culture of the Eskimo has changed through the centuries, their choice of settlement has been decided upon different factors. Similarly, changes in ice and weather conditions; in character, habits, and haunts of game; in tides, currents and salinity of the sea; all of which must come again and again, have indisputably modified the location of both winter and summer settlement. Improved hunting equipment, larger sledges, better home equipment and a multitude of wares for better living, all provided by contact with the white man, and pur-chased with ivory and furs, have expanded appreciably the Eskimo's hunting range to grounds where game is abundant and trustworthily regular, and given them greater assurance of ample supplies of the necessities of life.

Hunting has ever been, and remains, the one significant activity of the Polar Eskimo. Their hunting economy forces upon them a definite place, as well as a way of living.

Making a Living

>>>

Eskimo are among the greatest hunters in the world, but to them hunting is not a sport or a form of recreation. It is the most serious occupation there is—a matter of life or death to the hunter and his family. A man plans his hunting with the same concentration, care, and energy that a businessman in the United States applies to planning a sales campaign or calculating his margin of profit.

The following selections deal primarily with the tools and techniques used for obtaining food and shelter, for making clothing, and for travel and transportation. In all these activities the Eskimo are famous for the ingenuity with which they make use of the available resources and for the elaborateness and effectiveness of some of their equipment and devices. But we must consider, as part of how they make a living, the question of which member of a family or community does what things, the problem of property and ownership, and the extent to which certain goods are exchanged for others. It is in the answers to these questions, rather than in the striking (but less far-reaching) differences in clothing, diet, housing, and so forth, that we shall find the most profound differences from our own life. Consider what it means to say that every Eskimo family or group of neighboring families is almost entirely self-sufficient. How many American families could provide everything they use, year in and year out? And think how strange to an Eskimo would be our ideas of land ownership, by which a person may own land whether he uses it or not; for Eskimo own no land and consider anyone entitled to whatever land he customarily uses.

But if Eskimo life seems almost wholly unlike our own, it must nevertheless be remembered that the things the Eskimo do still achieve the same basic purpose of providing food and shelter, thus ensuring the survival of the individual and the group. A better understanding of the continuity of this survival comes from a brief glimpse of Eskimo prehistory, particularly in the light of the material possessions which they used two thousand years ago.

· 6 ·   *Eskimo Prehistory*

RICHARD B. WOODBURY

INTRODUCTION

The first people that we can call Eskimo lived in the Arctic many centuries ago. All that we know about them is derived from archeology, that is, the study of those few imperishable things they left behind them, their ruined houses, a few tools, dishes, weapons and ornaments, and the accumulated rubbish of centuries. It is because many of these things are like those used by the Eskimo today that we can call the earlier people of the Arctic "Eskimo," but of their language, their religion, and their customs we know next to nothing. To judge from the objects found in archeological excavations, Eskimo life has gradually changed, going through a process of increasing specialization.

ESKIMO BEGINNINGS

To make clear the picture of early times in the Arctic, experts (such as Louis Giddings and Froelich Rainey) have suggested dividing archeological remains into the Palae-Eskimo (old Eskimo) and the Neo-Eskimo (new Eskimo). The Palae-Eskimo were nomadic or seasonal migrants, hunting caribou inland in the fall and winter, and moving to the coast in the spring to hunt sea-mammals and to fish. Their settlements have been found from Cook Inlet in Alaska to the western coast of Greenland, with no remains reported in Siberia. Besides their migratory life, which persists today for some Eskimo who shift periodically between coast and inland, the Palae-Eskimo are distinguished by the fact that their tools and weapons were mostly of chipped flint, and rarely of slate or ivory, both of which the Neo-Eskimo used in great abundance. One of the earliest Palae-Eskimo settlements for which a date has been established is that at Cape Denbigh, Alaska (about 200 miles

southeast of Bering Strait), which was occupied about 2000 years ago. How much older the beginnings of this culture may have been is not yet known.

For the Neo-Eskimo, the oldest stage so far identified is called the Old Bering Sea culture, and is at least 1300 years old. These Eskimo lived permanently on the coast and depended mostly on the hunting of sea mammals. It is probably they who developed what Birket-Smith calls the "Arctic coast culture proper" [see page 55] and which is often thought of as more typically Eskimo than the partly inland and partly coastal life of the Palae-Eskimo and their successors. A distinctive feature of Neo-Eskimo culture is the making of tools and weapons by grinding and rubbing instead of by chipping, and the very extensive use of ivory and slate. The pottery made by the Neo-Eskimo peoples was markedly inferior in workmanship and decoration to that of earlier times, and eventually some Eskimo gave up almost completely the practice of pottery making. In its place, simple containers were carved out of soapstone, not a difficult task even without metal tools. Because they tended to live in one place for the greater part of the year and to occupy the same village for many generations, their settlements are usually easier for archeologists to find, and they contain great quantities of broken, lost or discarded objects in the rubbish that piled up through the years.

THE IPIUTAK CULTURE OF POINT HOPE

Of all the Palae-Eskimo settlements so far discovered, that of Ipiutak, which was inhabited almost exactly 1000 years ago, is the one about which we know the most. It represents a late stage of Palae-Eskimo culture, so late, indeed, that the Neo-Eskimo pattern had already developed elsewhere in the Arctic and may have influenced the people of Ipiutak in some degree.

Their village lay at the tip of Point Hope, some 125 miles north of the Arctic Circle. As judged by the bones found in the refuse heaps, and by their tools, weapons and equipment, they lived chiefly by the hunting of land and sea mammals, with both birds and fish of minor importance. They probably spent the winter inland, where caribou were the chief game. Following the herds to the coast in the spring, they were then ready for the annual walrus migration to pass, and also hunted seals on the pack ice of spring and early summer. There is no evidence of whale hunting, which is, therefore, probably a Neo-Eskimo development and of lesser antiquity.

The village of Ipiutak was the spring and summer home of a large community, a larger group than could be supported at a place of less abundant resources. Just how many lived in the settlement is unknown, but it is certain that all of the 600 to 700 houses were not occupied at any one time. Instead, they represent annual additions and replacements by a group perhaps numbering as many as 1000 people. A typical house is square, about 12 to 15 feet across, with sod-covered walls sloping in toward a roof resting on four corner posts. Low benches on three sides of the house were covered with mats (and probably caribou skins, too), for sleeping, leaving room for a small floor area with a shallow depression in its center which served as a fireplace. The entrance was at the west, a short passage with no cold-trap on a lower level, such as many recent Eskimo houses have to prevent cold air flowing in the door. Wood must have been burned for cooking and heating, since no lamps have been found in which seal and walrus oil could have been used for fuel. Besides lacking lamps, they used no pottery, had no bow-drill, and made little use of ivory or slate for tools, preferring caribou antler and flint. A single small engraving tool of iron was found when the village of Ipiutak was excavated. It is not meteoric iron, but instead comes from Asia, proving that these Eskimo

were in touch, at least indirectly, with the people of the Old World.

The most impressive accomplishment of the Ipiutak Eskimo is their skillful and imaginative carving, which they used for decorating both everyday implements, like harpoon sockets, and ornaments whose use we do not know. Fantastic animal designs are somewhat like some known from western Siberia, again indicating an Old World derivation for part of Ipiutak culture. In graves they sometimes placed intricately carved ivory chains and swivels, perhaps copies of similar objects in metal, known or remembered from Siberia. The handsomest pieces of all are sets of flat ivory slabs which can be assembled to make masks or facial ornaments; they are decorated with carved and engraved designs, and with inlays of darker material.

The Ipiutak village at Point Hope is important for two reasons. First, it gives us a glimpse of Palae-Eskimo life a thousand years ago. Secondly, it shows that Eskimo life has developed since that time toward greater dependence on the resources of the coastal zone, while the inland phase of their life has decreased in importance. All Eskimo groups have not changed to an equal degree in this respect, but the shift in emphasis has nearly everywhere been strongly toward the coast.

THE OLD BERING SEA CULTURE

At the same time that people were occupying the Ipiutak village for part of each year, there was elsewhere a considerable number of more permanent villages, which we know something of from archeological excavations. Some of the oldest of these are in the Bering Sea area, on Cape Prince of Wales, on the Diomede Islands, and on St. Lawrence Island; hence, the name Old Bering Sea has been given to the culture which they reveal. These settlements are the first that can be identified as Neo-Eskimo, on the basis of some of the distinctive features that were noted a few paragraphs above. The material culture of the Old Bering Sea Eskimo resembles that of the coastal Eskimo of recent times so closely as to leave little doubt that a continuous development from one to the other has taken place.

[The Old Bering Sea Eskimo had many items of equipment that] have continued in use to the present. They travelled by kayak (the one-seater boat for hunters) and umiak (the larger boat), both common today. Sleds were small, probably pulled only by hand. The dogs they kept were smaller than Eskimo dogs of today, and they may have been used mainly for food. Their houses were rather small, semi-subterranean, and without the sleeping platform such as used at Ipiutak and common today. House entrances were long, and built lower than the floor of the house to keep cold air out. Thus, we see many features of present day Eskimo life already in existence in the Bering Sea area ten centuries ago. It is not claimed that they originated there, since some are much older and many can be traced back ultimately to the Old World. But it seems to be here that they became crystallized into the special economic and technological pattern that is characteristically Eskimo, a pattern so successful that it has persisted without many major changes until recent years.

An explanation of why this area should have been so important in the development of the Eskimo has been offered by Collins:

"The Bering Strait region was especially favored in the abundance of walrus. Indeed, it was probably the abundance of walrus, more than any other single factor, that made possible the initial concentration of population at numerous places around Bering Strait. With an assured food supply and with other basic needs of life thus provided, attention could be turned to other than subsistence activities, with the result that on the material side, at least, there was opportunity for the development of a technical and artistic virtuosity unequalled elsewhere in the Arctic."

THE SOUTHWESTERN ESKIMO AREA

Eskimo-like remains have been dated at about 1000 B.C. in the Aleutian Islands, and it was in this same area that the greatest density of population was achieved by the Eskimo in recent years, about 20 people to each square mile of land (in contrast to 0.5 to 3 in some parts of the Arctic). In general, the earlier cultures of this region seem similar to the Old Bering Sea culture in some respects, but less specialized toward the hunting of sea mammals. In the Aleutian Islands, especially, birds and fish have probably always been particularly important resources. Furthermore, development in the southwestern area has continued to be relatively independent of the more northerly Eskimo regions. One reason for some of this area's distinctive features is its closeness to Asia, towards which the Aleutians form a series of stepping stones. There has been a constant flow of new ideas and techniques from the west to the east, so that many things we think of as "typically" Eskimo can be found widely occurring in the Old World. The Kamchatka-Aleutian route was of some importance in this spread of ideas, particularly since it resulted in contact with a more southerly and more highly developed part of Siberia than did the Bering Strait route.

For the southwestern region, archeologists have disclosed a succession of cultural changes, covering the last eight to ten centuries. They are best known in certain sub-areas, namely, Cook Inlet, the Aleutian chain, and Kodiak Island. Although distinctive traits could be tabulated for the various periods and sub-areas, the area as a whole has remained somewhat apart from the rest of the Eskimo world. Its long separate history is reflected today in language, with the Yukon River forming an approximate boundary between the two Eskimo languages.

THE THULE CULTURE OF THE CENTRAL ARCTIC

Sometime after 1000 A.D. settlements appear in the vast region north and west of Hudson Bay which look very much like those of the modern Eskimo in Greenland, Labrador, Baffin Land, Point Barrow and northwestern Alaska. They belong to the Thule Culture, which is identified as the immediate source of the culture of the modern coastal Eskimo groups. As to its origins, the evidence points to a relationship with the Old Bering Sea culture, and suggests a gradual spread of Neo-Eskimo culture (of which both Thule and Old Bering Sea are examples) along the Arctic coast from west to east. This spread finally brought the Thule culture to the eastern coast of Greenland.

Some of the important elements of the Thule culture are the following: permanent houses of stone, whale bone and turf for winter occupation; conical tents for summer; the snow house (igloo) for temporary winter shelter; the dog sled, with the Asiatic style of tandem harness; both soapstone and pottery dishes. These people utilized more fully than many of their predecessors all the natural resources of the Arctic, hunting the whale, walrus, seal, bear, and caribou, trapping foxes and other smaller animals, and catching birds and fish in abundance. The importance of the whale and walrus is indicated by the later abandonment of many Thule settlements, in locations where a slight rise of the land (a process still going on) reduced the depth of channels and inlets so that these large sea mammals moved elsewhere.

An interesting development took place, starting in the 11th century, when Scandinavian settlers in Iceland began exploring and colonizing the coasts of Greenland. They first reported only occasional glimpses of the Eskimo, and found them so strange and different that they hardly considered them human beings. [Nevertheless, as] Norsemen settled in Greenland, the Eskimo began to obtain certain valued goods in trade, such as metal and cloth, but relations were rarely friendly. By the year 1400 the Eskimo had succeeded in driving out or exterminating the last of the white settlers, aided by a shift in the climate of Greenland that made the Norse farming and herding activities increasingly unsuccessful. The modifications in Eskimo culture resulting from these European influences were rather minor, but permit the Greenland settlements of this period to be identified by archeologists, who have given the name Inugsuk culture to this blend.

SUMMARY

A pattern of life that we can identify as Eskimo is very ancient in the Arctic, but as yet a single point of origin cannot be selected. From the time of the earliest Eskimo-like cultures to the present day, the influence of the Old World has been important. The importance of Asiatic influences is reflected in the fact that it is western Alaska, the Bering Sea, and the Aleutians where much of modern Eskimo culture seems to have developed. The Thule culture of central Canada stems from Alaska originally and in recent centuries has spread not only eastward to Greenland, but west again into Alaska, accounting for the considerable uniformity of all Eskimo groups except those of the extreme southwest.

• 7 • How the Eskimo Uses His Environment

EDWARD M. WEYER, JR.

CULTURAL ADJUSTMENTS

... Physically, the Eskimo is in all essential characteristics like other men. Strip him of his clothing, deprive him of his tools and implements, his dwellings, and his ability to create these things essential to life, and

[Adapted from *The Eskimos: Their Environment and Folkways,* Yale University Press, New Haven, 1932. Pp. 65-74. Used by permission.]

he would be scarcely more fit to survive in his northern environment than a savage from the tropical jungle. Clearly, with no more than his natural physical attributes he would soon perish.

The Eskimo cannot compete with the animals as an animal. He is not compelled to. What he lacks as a physical organism he acquires through ingenuity and invention. He survives, not chiefly through physical strength and endurance, as the animals do, but through mental capability. An ingenious hunting device can take the place of fleetness of foot or sharpness of tooth or talon; the use of fire and clothing can compensate for weak resistance against cold. In this manner, man's culture takes the place of physical adaptations among the lower animals. This is particularly true of his self-maintenance mores, his implements for securing food, and his clothes and dwellings.

The Eskimo culture is the growth of centuries. As with every culture, its evolution has been analogous to organic evolution among animals. Survival has been the criterion. The succession of variations, followed by the elimination of the inexpedient, and the selection and retention of the expedient, has perfected a harpoon head that will remain imbedded beneath the skin of the seal, walrus, or whale, and thereby prevent its sinking, a boot that is waterproof, and a method of glazing sledge runners that lessens friction on granular snow. Expediency or inexpediency in most culture traits is not a matter of immediate life or death. Yet selection continually goes on. Men can modify their culture, whereas animals cannot modify their bodily organisms appreciably. By repeated trial and error, unconscious for the most part yet rational in the final outcome, culture traits evolve.

This interpretation of cultural evolution applies in substance to all groups of people. Its application to the Eskimos, however, is uncommonly striking, partly because their adaptations are highly specialized and partly because they must struggle against an exceptionally severe natural environment.

The Eskimo is a cultural success. He survives farther north than any other people on earth, in exceedingly wretched and difficult conditions—an exemplification of man's cultural adaptability to nature in the raw.

The habitat of the Eskimos is at once one of the coldest parts of the world and one of the poorest in available fuel. With wood scarce, the Eskimo burns animal oil in stone or pottery lamps. Thus the blubber that keeps the seal warm in the polar sea heats the igloo. All the Caribou Eskimos, however, inland dwellers of the Barren Grounds of Canada, with the exception of the Hauneqtôrmiut and a very few Qaernermiut, pass even the coldest winters without any artificial heat whatever. Here the temperature falls sometimes as low as −50°, and the only way they can dry wet clothing is by their own bodily heat. Their only light during the long gloom of winter is a sort of tallow dip.

Human eyes cannot endure protracted exposure to the glare of sunlight on the snow. The glare is especially difficult to withstand in the Eskimo region during springtime, the result being snow blindness, which is sometimes permanent. To avoid this, the Eskimo peers through snow goggles, made of wood, ivory, or bone, with a narrow slit for each eye.

The throwing board which he uses to add impetus when hurling a weapon has the effect of lengthening his arm by a foot or so. Lacking the physical strength to handle the unwieldy carcass of the walrus, he has made use of the principle of the block and tackle.

Often obliged to hunt seals and other creatures in the open sea, the Eskimo has fitted himself for that element. His kayak, about the size of a small canoe, is perhaps the most seaworthy small craft in the world. Inasmuch as its frame of driftwood or saplings is covered over entirely with watertight skin save where the small circular manhole is left open, the paddler is able to propel his craft actually *through* waves that would swamp an undecked boat.

When a kayaker secures his waterproof

gut jacket about the hatch of the kayak at his waist and fastens the garment tightly around his wrists and face or neck, he makes the boat virtually part of his person. Nowhere can water enter the boat or even penetrate inside his clothing. Consequently, a skilful kayaker can capsize his boat and come up none the worse.

Even for the native unversed in the art of capsizing, the kayak is a remarkably effective craft. Few Eskimos can swim. Their failure to learn is due chiefly, of course, to the coldness of the water, but the author can testify that Eskimo children sometimes bathe in the Arctic Sea in summer.

The Eskimo utilizes the strength and hardiness of the dog by harnessing him to a sledge; and to protect his valuable animals' feet from sharp ice he makes little shoes for them. He also uses the dog in hunting. A keen sense of smell directs the animal to the breathing hole of the seal, and the Eskimo, following, benefits from his dog's faculty just as though his own nostrils possessed it.

INGENIOUS UTILIZATION OF SCANTY RESOURCES

The Eskimo shows remarkable ingenuity in making use of what simple resources his homeland offers, and, unlike the man with but one talent, makes the utmost of his scanty materials. His house of snow needs only to be mentioned in this connection. Knowing nothing of glass he fashions his window out of ice, or from the translucent intestinal membrane of a sea mammal, the gullet of the white whale or of birds, or the pericardium of the caribou. For thread he uses sinew, generally procured chiefly from the back and hind legs of the caribou but also from the white whale, and from the gullet, tail, back, and flippers of the seal. Whalebone serves as cord for lashing implements; and the thin fiber stripped from the surface of bird quills is used for finer lashing.

Only a small proportion of the Eskimos used metal before the coming of the white man. In the absence of metal the Eskimos used stone, of course, for blades and weapon points. They also used stone, commonly soapstone, for lamps and cooking pots. Iron pyrites, in addition, was of value in generating fire among practically all Eskimos. Everywhere, however, the Eskimos were familiar with the process of generating fire with a drill.

Stone for implements and iron pyrites were in general available to all Eskimos, though in some cases they would have to travel to procure them.

In natural resources, particularly in wood, the Eskimos of the central and northernmost regions are most poorly supplied. Their own resourcefulness is correspondingly conspicuous as under these circumstances they make their sledges of bone or ivory. In Baffin Island if wood is scarce the natives make a strange shovel-shaped sledge by stitching together sheets of whalebone. The height of ingenuity is displayed in the building of a sledge of frozen hide. Pieces of walrus skin or musk-ox skin are soaked in water, folded into the desired forms, and allowed to freeze solid. Thus the Eskimo fights the inexorable North with its own weapons; the extreme cold that makes his homeland a woodless country he utilizes in improvising his frozen sledge. This method is most common in the region of the Magnetic Pole, but is also practiced among the Iglulik and Copper Eskimos. The frozen hide is used chiefly for runners, the crosspieces being commonly of bone. The Arvilingjuarmiut (Pelly Bay) would roll up raw meat or fish in the hide that was to be frozen for sledge runners. After thawing, the skins were fed to the dogs that had drawn the sledge, while the contents were eaten by their masters. Boas mentions sledges of frozen salmon. Klutschak depicts a sledge of ice from Simpson Strait, and Boas refers to the making of a sledge by freezing together slabs of ice. Eskimos of the central regions are even known to make harpoon shafts by freezing walrus hide.

FOOD ECONOMY

General scarcity of food and seasonal variations in the quantity force the Eskimos to conserve and preserve their stores. They must hoard the products of the plentiful season as provision against want. Naturally this necessary economy in food influences the variety of the Eskimos' diet. Sometimes they are obliged to draw food from strange sources, and the Alaskan Eskimos, for instance, rob the nests of field mice and appropriate for their own consumption the titbits stored by these rodents.

The very thought of some of the Eskimos' delicacies turns the civilized stomach. Every afternoon the hunters of Diomede Island would squat around their meal of long-cached walrus meat, which lay on bare ground strewn with the excreta of dogs and people. The raw, rotten meat was reminiscent of highly ripe cheese. Strangely, these same Eskimos showed some reluctance about drinking water with a speck of dirt in it. Eggs they would eat in any stage of deterioration or incubation, discarding only the eyes of the embryo. The Eskimos of Bering Strait bury fish heads and allow them to decay until the bones become of the same consistency as the flesh. Then they knead the reeking mass into a paste and eat it. A few other examples of Eskimo food will indicate his lack of squeamishness: raw intestines of birds and fish, swallowed like oysters; live fish, gulped down whole, head first; slime scraped from a walrus hide together with some of the human urine used in the tanning process; fatty soup thickened with the blood of seal or caribou (common among most Eskimos); fat, maggoty larvae of the caribou fly, served raw; the contents of the caribou's paunch, left in the body so long that the whole mass has become tainted; deer droppings, munched like berries, or the feces taken from the rectum of this animal; and marrow more than a year old swarming with maggots.

These examples are rather convincing evidence that hunger is the best sauce. It should be added, however, that even the Eskimo exercises some discrimination against what would be injurious to health; also that he sometimes suffers from the folly of eating meat too long cached. The wonder is that a diet containing such foods does not cause more widespread disaster.

INGENIOUS HUNTING METHODS

The foregoing examples taken from the industries and diet of the Eskimos show how they circumvent the privations of their ungenerous habitat. It is significant that in an environment affording a minimum of natural resources they catch and kill the largest animals in the world—whales.

It is largely from the animals the Eskimo kills that he manufactures his hunting weapons. From the skin of the seal the Bering Strait native fashions a net with which to catch more seals. To attract fish to his hook the Diomede Islander attaches the bright orange flap from the corner of the beak of the crested auklet. From whalebone the Eskimo fashions "spring bait," one of the most ingenious of his hunting accessories. To make this he sharpens the end of a strip of the baleen, doubles the springy material up under tension, and ties it in that position with sinew. He buries the mass in fat and allows it to freeze. When the wolf is enticed and swallows it, the warmth of his stomach and his digestive juices release the barbed baleen, which pierces the creature internally and kills it.

To catch birds an Eskimo sometimes builds a small snow hut with a hole in the roof around which he scatters bits of meat and blubber as bait. From inside he deftly snatches the feet of the attracted birds. East Greenlanders, having poured train oil on the water so that swans alighting cannot easily take off, approach in a kayak and harpoon them.

The Eskimo acknowledges no superior throughout the animal kingdom. Though sometimes dangerously challenged, he remains the master of his stern world. The largest animals, as has been pointed out, are his prey. Indeed, he outwits all forms from the whale down to the tiniest creature. He even tricks the lice which infest his body, by drawing a piece of bear fur on a string under his clothes and pulling it out filled with the vermin.

Occasionally the Eskimos show an equally astonishing lack of resourcefulness, as, for instance, when Jenness observed that the Copper Eskimos obtained all their water throughout the winter from snow, being ignorant apparently of the fact that ordinary sea ice loses its salinity with age, and that an old cake of the previous winter will yield perfectly fresh water.

But, in general, the Eskimo has achieved harmony with his habitat. Generations of cultural evolution have developed a mode of living that fits his life-conditions. By mode of living we refer chiefly to his self-maintenance mores; and by life-conditions we mean the actual, physical, concrete, perceptible circumstances of his life. But here ends, in a large measure, the perfection of his judgment. Aside from his physical environment, the Eskimo faces another set of life-conditions, his spirit world. As with all peoples, though perhaps to a greater degree than among most groups, his imagination fills the world with ghosts, demons, and deities, to him just as exacting in their requirements as the forces of the natural world. And in his responses to this supernatural environment, in contrast with his responses to the physical environment, he often displays what, on the surface at least, might seem to be inefficiency and lack of economy. The [many] objects relinquished by all Eskimos for the use of the dead as grave deposits are a considerable economic sacrifice. And the stern taboo that Rasmussen observed among the Netsilingmiut "which forbade them even to make themselves new clothes or warmer sleeping rugs until they had shivered their way through the first of the snow right on into November," does not seem conducive to their immediate well-being. The question raised by cases such as these, however, can be fairly discussed only in connection with the broad subject of the Eskimos' religion, which is dealt with in later [sections].

The foregoing selection has discussed a few of the Eskimo's skillful ways of making up for the shortcomings of his environment. It is not an easy existence, and the Eskimo's life is one of constant risk, frequent hardship, and periodic threat of death by starvation. But through the centuries a great many ingenious ideas have been put to work to make it possible to live successfully without some of the resources that we tend to take for granted or think of as indispensable. The list on page 54 indicates just a few of the problems and challenges of the Arctic and the solutions made by the Eskimo.

The reader will find many more such problems in the ensuing pages (particularly in the selection on the Nunivak Eskimo), and he can continue and greatly expand this list of the specific solutions made by the Eskimo. Such a list serves to emphasize the severe limitations which the Arctic places on man's attempts to live there. Each of the Eskimo's "solutions" increased the extent to which he could profit from the particular resources of the Arctic—especially its abundant sea life, which in turn depends ultimately on the myriad small plants and animals that thrive in these less salty waters. But each new "solution" and more specialized technical adaptation also increased the Eskimo's dependence on the continuation of the special conditions to which their culture was suited. Such changes as the disappearance of whales in the bays and channels of the central Arctic had a disastrous and profound effect on the Eskimo of that region. Today the Eskimo everywhere find themselves in a changing world with the sort of handicaps that a few generations ago in the United States faced the craftsmen whose only skill was the making of fine carriages. Later, we shall consider in more detail the attempts the Eskimo is making to adapt to new conditions.

PROBLEM	SOLUTION
No agriculture and very few wild food plants.	Diet mostly meat and fish; all the organs are eaten and thus vitamins are obtained.
No trees for building houses.	Use of driftwood from forests of Canada, Alaska, and Siberia. Use of whale ribs for house frames, in some regions. Building of snow house, in some regions.
Not enough wood for fuel.	Use of seal and whale oil for heating and lighting.
Scarcity of wood in any form.	Elaborate techniques of piecing, lashing, and gluing in order to build up small bits of wood, bone, and ivory into sled runners, harpoon shafts, etc.
No wool or other woven cloth for clothes during long cold winter.	Very carefully tailored clothes of fur; both men and women wear fur trousers and boots. Baby carried inside mother's parka.
Glare of sun on ice and snow may cause blindness.	Slit goggles.
Many of the large and important animals (whale, polar bear, walrus) found mostly out at sea or on offshore ice.	Kayak provides fast, easy, and relatively safe travel even in rough water. Harpoon with detachable head and attached line reduces chance of losing animal, and bladder floats help to keep it from sinking.

We now turn to a description of some of the Eskimo hunting methods and the ways in which they differ from one part of the Arctic to another. These differences are worth noting, because there are such striking uniformities throughout the Eskimo region that variations tend to be overlooked. As Birket-Smith points out, they are differences in *emphasis*, most of them made necessary by the local conditions of shoreline, animal life, topography, seasonal cycle, and so on. On the basis of these regional variations, he has defined three subdivisions of the coastal type of life and also an inland type of Eskimo culture, as follows:

COASTAL ECONOMY

1. "High Arctic Culture," an extreme specialization based on the hunting of sea mammals. This type is exemplified by the Polar Eskimo of the northwest tip of Greenland, who live almost the year around under "winter" conditions.

2. "Arctic Coast Culture Proper," typical of the greater number of Eskimo groups. There is little dependence on the inland, and there are well-marked seasonal changes in hunting activities.

3. "Subarctic Culture," a specialization away from hunting on the ice, and with greater dependence throughout the year on hunting and fishing from boats in open water. This occurs in the southern parts of the Eskimo region, particularly in southern Greenland and the Aleutians.

"INLAND CULTURE"

The "inland culture" is limited to a few groups whose dependence on caribou hunting has increased at the expense of their coastal activities. These are found "in the flat delta of the Yukon and Kuskokwim, where fish abound, on the great coastal plains about the Noatak and Colville Rivers in northern Alaska, and lastly, on the Barren Grounds west of Hudson Bay."

A more detailed description of caribou hunting is given in the next selection. The people described are not the "Caribou Eskimo" of the Barren Grounds but dwellers on the coast of Labrador who make a yearly hunting trip of a few weeks and then return to the coast. Thus they do not quite fit into any of Birket-Smith's four types of Eskimo culture but, instead, combine characteristics of the "Arctic Coast Culture" and of the "Inland Culture."

The caribou they hunt are wild, native to North America, and somewhat larger and more vigorous than the domestic caribou of Lapland and Siberia, which are usually called reindeer. The two names are sometimes used interchangeably, since the New and Old World species are not greatly different from each other. Starting in 1891, Siberian reindeer began to be imported into Alaska to replace the seriously depleted wild herds. It has been difficult to persuade the Eskimo to herd them like cattle and to maintain their numbers, since the Eskimo have preferred to follow their traditional practice of hunting the reindeer periodically and letting them fend for themselves the rest of the time. The degree of success that is being achieved in Alaska, under a governmental program to place reindeer-herding on a permanent basis, is briefly discussed in the final selection on the Eskimo (see p. 127).

• 8 • Caribou-Hunting Activities of the Labrador Eskimo

FRANK G. SPECK

The indispensability of the caribou to the Eskimo here, if not to the same extent elsewhere, is shown in the following notes relevant to the present hunting life of the Eskimo from Hopedale to Nain.

In recent years the coast Eskimo ascended the rivers leading to the interior about the end of July or early in August and remained until September, when caribou skins cease to be fit to be made into clothing. It took as many as thirty sealskins to supply the family with materials each winter for boots, dog-sled traces and sealskin-hooded coats. Some of the hunters working on shares in the last few years have taken 300 to 500 annually in nets.

The time of the inland hunt has been changed somewhat in the last few years through the influence of the traders. They go inland just after Christmas and remain there until about the first of May.

The account of Dr. S. K. Hutton, an eyewitness to the event among the natives of the village of Okkak (between 1908-1912), is too vivid and intimate to overlook:

"On Easter Tuesday morning the sledges make their start, and track westward up the frozen rivers and through the winding valleys to the moss-covered wilderness where the reindeer find their food. The hunters have no luggage on their sledges; no tent, no sleeping gear, only a scrap of dried seal meat or fish for themselves and the dogs, and a gun, an axe, a knife, a packet of sticking plaster for the inevitable cuts, and a tin of grease for their sunburnt lips and cheeks —that is their whole equipment, with the occasional addition of a kettle for the making of a cup of Eskimo tea, weak as water, and flavoured with a mouthful of molasses out of a bottle.

"They start together, but after a while they get separated and travel in ones and twos, or alone. This man's dogs are slow and lag behind; the other man wants to try such and such a valley instead of the beaten trail; and so they separate.

"When night comes they build snow huts for shelter, and sleep on a bed of dogs' harness spread on the hard snow floor—not for any great comfort there is in it, but because if they left it outside the dogs would devour it in the night. In the morning each man boils his own tea and munches his own solitary feed or dried meat or ship's biscuit, harnesses his team, and drives on alone. Alone he travels where his fancy leads him; he will find the deer.

"How graphically they tell of the keen moment when they first see the deer. Cunning fellows, away they circle so as to come upon them from the lee side, and if they cannot see the herd, but only find tracks, they know how far away they are by the freshness of the spoor. They turn their sledges upside down before they get within range, and make the team lie down; then the dogs are safe, for they cannot drag an upturned sledge. Woe betide the luckless hunter who lets his dogs get too close; away they go—no power can stop them—they are as keen as wolves to do a little hunting for themselves, and for the nonce they have become wolves again.

"My neighbors liked to talk about the reindeer hunt. 'Ah,' they said, 'It is fine to see the herd upon the hillsides, all grey and white like the snow upon the rocks. Yes, there are many tuktu; you may watch them all day, marching along the hills, more and more and always more, a great, great number. Ah, it is fine to watch them—but only Eskimo eyes can see them, because our eyes are made for hunting.'

"However much the seals may mean to the Eskimos, it always seemed to me that

[Adapted from "Inland Eskimo Bands of Labrador," in Robert H. Lowie, ed., *Essays in Anthropology Presented to A. L. Kroeber*, University of California Press, Berkeley, 1936. Pp. 317-320. Used by permission.]

the reindeer hunt was the big event of the hunter's year. There never was such excitement as when the sledges were sighted—such roars of welcome, such a stampede over the ice, such a willing crowd to help with the groaning sledge."

We have a few facts in regard to the equipment of the Eskimo when inland to show the carrying over of their usual cultural traits in this environment. They entrain for this journey provided with sealskin tents of the conical form as made by the Indians, about fifteen feet in diameter at the base. The poles for these skin tents are made, kept, and carried with them during their moves. It has been mentioned that they journey to the hunting, trapping, and inland fishing grounds by means of their usual kayaks. Of especial importance, furthermore, is the observation that they carried with them, until about fifteen years ago, their stone lamps and the necessities for lamp cooking instead of resorting to wood for fuel. Now, however, they often burn wood, the material being gathered in favorable spots and conveyed with them in the kayaks. It is in the winter hunt in the interior that the coast Eskimo employ snowshoes, following the necessity of travel in deep snow which the Indians of the interior undergo.

In 1877, Edward W. Nelson was sent to Alaska by the United States Government, primarily for the purpose of making meteorological observations. For four years he made his headquarters at the trading post of St. Michael on Norton Sound, and whenever he could entrust his observations to others he made trips to various parts of Alaska, mostly by dog sled, in order to collect examples of Eskimo handiwork for the U.S. National Museum. He acquired a magnificent series of specimens, about 10,000 in all, many of which are illustrated and described in the report from which the following extract is taken.

Among the places Nelson visited was St. Lawrence Island. His account of what had just taken place there is a vivid example of what can happen when a new and strange cultural trait (in this instance, whisky) is introduced to a people without a knowledge of its appropriate use. The St. Lawrence Islanders went on "a prolonged debauch" just at the time when they should have obtained their great supply of winter meat from the annual walrus migration. Among peoples to whom whisky is a familiar part of their total cultural inventory, such indulgence would be tolerated only when it was least likely to interfere with indispensable economic pursuits.

It is worth noting that during this catastrophe the St. Lawrence Islanders' abhorrence of cannibalism was overcome by necessity, and yet a brutally practical approach was maintained; they evidently ate their children, since it would be the children who would be least able to carry on successfully if left to themselves. Even a single surviving man and woman could have preserved the greater part of the intricate skills and knowledge that are essential to life in the Arctic.

• 9 • Famine on St. Lawrence Island

EDWARD W. NELSON

The terrible famine and accompanying disease which caused the death of over a thousand people on St. Lawrence island during the winter of 1879 and 1880 was said to have been caused by the use of whisky. The people of that island usually obtained their

[Adapted from "The Eskimo about Bering Strait," *18th Annual Report, Bureau of American Ethnology*, Part 1, Washington, 1899. Pp. 268-270.]

supply of food for the winter by killing walrus from the great herds of these animals
that go through Bering Strait on the first ice
in the fall.

Just before the time for the walrus to
reach the island that season, the Eskimo obtained a supply of whisky from some vessels
and began a prolonged debauch, which ended
only when the supply was exhausted. When
this occurred the annual migration of the
walrus had passed, and the people were shut
in for the winter by the ice. The result was
that over two-thirds of the population died
before spring. The following spring, when
the *Corwin* visited the islands, some of the
survivors came on board bringing a few articles for trade. They wished only to purchase
rifle cartridges and more whisky.

During July, 1881, the *Corwin* made a
visit to this famine stricken district, where
the miserable survivors were seen. Only a
single dog was left among them, the others
having been eaten by the starving people.
Two of the largest villages were entirely
depopulated.

In July I landed at a place on the northern shore where two houses were standing,
in which, wrapped in their fur blankets on
the sleeping platforms, lay about 25 dead
bodies of adults, and upon the ground and
outside were a few others. Some miles to the
eastward, along the coast, was another village, where there were 200 dead people. In
a large house were found about 15 bodies
placed one upon another like cordwood at
one end of the room, while as many others
lay dead in their blankets on the platforms.

The first to die had been taken farthest
away, and usually placed at full length beside
the sled that had carried the bodies. Scattered
about such bodies lay the tools and implements belonging to the dead. In one instance
a body lay outstretched upon a sled, while
behind it, prone upon his face, with arms
outstretched and almost touching the sled
runners, lay the body of a man who had
died while pushing the sled bearing the body
of his friend or relative.

Others were found lying in the underground passageways to the houses, and one
body was found halfway out of the entrance.
Most of the bodies lying about the villages
had evidently been dragged there and left
wherever it was most convenient by the living during the later period of the famine.
The total absence of the bodies of children
in these villages gave rise to the suspicion
that they had been eaten by the adults; but
possibly this may not have been the case.
The strongest evidence in this regard, however, was in one village where there were
over two hundred dead adults, and although
I looked carefully for the bodies of children,
none could be found; yet there was no positive evidence that cannibalism had been
practiced by the natives. That this custom
sometimes prevailed, however, in ancient
times, during famines, I learned from the
Unalit; nevertheless they openly expressed
their abhorrence of the practice.

On the bluff at the northwest point of
this island we found a couple of surviving
families living in round-top, walrus-hide
summer houses. At the foot of the hill not
far from their present camping place was
a winter village, where about 100 people
lay dead; the bodies were scattered about
outside or were lying in their blankets
in the houses, as we had seen them in
other places.

The two families living there consisted
of about a dozen people; the adults seemed
very much depressed and had little anima-
tion. Among them were two bright little
girls, who had the usual childish carelessness, and kept near us while we were on
shore. When I shot a snow bunting near the
village they called to me and ran to show
me its nest on the hillside.

When I asked one of the inhabitants
what had become of the people who formerly lived on that part of the island, he
waved his hand toward the winter village,
saying, "All *mucky mucky*," being the jar-
gon term for "dead." [He seemed oblivious
to his gruesome surroundings.]

It is only on rare occasions that a community suffers such disaster from starvation as occurred on St. Lawrence Island. But Eskimo families are frequently hungry and are accustomed to constantly recurring periods of hardship and privation. Even the most expert hunter can have a run of bad luck, but if all the families in a settlement share their food and other resources, a family can survive such periods. This sharing is not at all a haphazard affair but is a well worked out tradition, deeply ingrained in every individual. Possibly nothing in our own society would appear more shocking or unbelievable to an Eskimo than the enormous differences in well-being among our population, unless it was a realization that there is often no satisfactory mechanism in our society by which the least fortunate are made the responsibility of those more favored by circumstances or ability. (On the other hand, the Eskimo would understand and appreciate the American ideal that individuals advance by their own efforts, and that new leaders arise from varied backgrounds in each generation.)

• 10 • The Owning and Sharing of Food

EDWARD M. WEYER, JR.

Summarizing . . . [a number of individual cases] seem to indicate that:

(1) Hunting grounds, or rather the privilege of hunting on them, is a communal right, except in rather rare instances.

(2) The hunter or hunters almost always have the preferential share in the game secured, but part of each catch is generally divided among the community or among those present at the apportioning.

(3) Stored provisions are normally the property of the family or household; but in time of scarcity there is a tendency toward communalism. Hospitality is stressed under all circumstances.

These generalizations signify that . . . there is a definite communalistic tendency, accentuated through privation. This tendency has evolved as an expedient adjustment to irregularities in food supply. Food constitutes the most important capital of the Eskimo. In quantity it fluctuates within wide limits, according to seasonal phases and vicissitudes of fortune. The seasonal fluctuations are smoothed out, as already mentioned in another chapter, by the storing of provisions. But even aside from broad seasonal variations, from time to time the individual or the family suffers through misfortunes that do not affect the community as a whole and is hard pressed by privation. Under such circumstances the larger unit, wherein fluctuations are less extreme, serves as a stabilizing factor. Membership in the community confers, in a sense, insurance for the individual and for the family. Through cooperation within the group, the ups and downs which would endanger the members if they were isolated are smoothed out. Frequent minor sacrifices on the part of the individual are substituted for less frequent, but more severe, misfortunes.

It must not be assumed, however, that this aspect of the property mores of the

[Adapted from *The Eskimos: Their Environment and Folkways,* Yale University Press, New Haven, 1932. Pp. 188-189. Used by permission.]

Eskimo manifests a deliberate group policy. The system grew by custom, without much reflection and without much foresight. Even in its present state, there is little implication that it is "just"; scarcely to any degree, if at all, has religion entered this phase of social life to sanction expedient mores.

Furthermore, individual interests rather than group interests are dominant. The group serves as an insurance organization, toward which there is little feeling of righteous responsibility, save in that kinship among its members makes the prosperity of one member the concern of another.

Communalistic practices are expedient among the Eskimos; but they are not without their handicaps. Individual effort is stifled to some degree. Accumulation of property by the individual is thwarted; even the most industrious and skillful person cannot attain economic prestige through his superior qualities. The social organization enforces upon the individual a sort of slavery.

Social Organization
and Interaction

‹‹

Among the most easterly of all Eskimo groups are the Ammassalik, or, as the name is sometimes spelled, Angmagssalik. They are the largest group on the east coast of Greenland, and their number has gradually increased to about 800, partly because the remnants of other Greenland communities have been attracted there since the establishment of a trading post in 1894. This group is a typical representative of what was described earlier as the "Arctic Coast Culture."

In the account of the Ammassalik Eskimo, and in the account of the Nunivakers which follows it, there will be considerable additional information on some of the topics already discussed under the heading "Making a Living." Notice particularly the description of what work is done by men and what is done by women, and the way in which they complement and depend on each other. Also, there is an interesting discussion of the structural details and furnishings of the winter house, in which several families live together. It is rather like a Pullman car (or French *wagon-lit*), as the author says, since each family has a small compartment curtained off from the main room. But besides these elements of "material culture"—the equipment for living—the way in which people get along with one another is described. In some ways this is an even more significant aspect of life than their houses, their hunting, and their clothing. There are certain ways in which people are expected to behave (roles), certain ways in which individuals are grouped into families and communities (patterns of association), and certain supreme values, to which everyone is expected to adhere. Key interactions such as conflict, cooperation, and competition, as well as socialization and social control, are also described.

• II • The Ammassalík Eskimo of Greenland

JEANETTE MIRSKY

In 1884 there were 371 Ammassalik Eskimos. They are an Eskimo group who inhabit and recognize as their home territory that long stretch of the east Greenland coast extending from the 65th to the 68th degree of latitude. The name is used by the Eskimo further south to indicate all those people within that district who go to a certain spot from the middle of May to the middle of June to hunt ammassat (capelins). The spot where the capelin run occurs is within the Ammassalik fiord, but there are no permanent dwelling places there.

ECONOMIC BACKGROUND

The Ammassalik look to the sea, for from the sea come their food, their clothes, their shelter, and their main means of intercommunication. The western drift of the Arctic Ocean brings Siberian driftwood to their treeless land. The sea washes up pumice stone used in preparing the hides. Though the land provides them with a certain amount of food—foxes, birds, berries, herbs (the hare, the reindeer, and the musk ox have long disappeared from their district)— they depend practically entirely on the skin, flesh, and blubber of the seal, the walrus, the bear, the narwhal, etc. The different kinds of seal are their great staple.

The Ammassalik have a vast territory at their disposal and they are well aware of it, knowing in detail the uninhabited coast line to the north of them as well as the various settlements to the south. But they are concentrated around the three large fiords of Sermilik, Ammassalik, and Sermiligak. In winter they live in settlements, each of which consists of one long house, and these are scattered along the shores of these three fiords, some only a few miles apart, some completely isolated. Neither the place nor the

composition of these settlements remains the same winter after winter. People live together because of preference, and thus settlements may be made up of families who are related to each other—brothers and their families, or an elderly couple and several of their married sons and daughters and their families—or just friends and their families. The people live in the winter houses from the end of September to the end of April. Then the settlements break up into individual small family units who spend the other months living in tents, moving about from place to place.

Property among the Ammassalik consists of food, dogs, blubber, house parts and tents, sledges, kayaks and umiaks and their accessories, hunting weapons—harpoons, lances, darts, throwing sticks, floats, fishing scoops, dredges, snares, slings, etc.—men's knives, saws, hammers, bow drills, and other tools, women's knives, scraping boards, needles and awls, twisting and plaiting implements, household utensils—skin bags used for storage, fire-making implements, lamps, drying frames, cooking pots and accessories, water and urine tubs, dishes and plates and spoons and ladles, trinket boxes and chests —clothing, headdress, bracelets, combs, backscratchers, buckles, beads, snow goggles, amulets, masks, drums, dolls, and toys. All these things are owned individually by the man or woman or child who makes or uses them and most of them are of a perishable nature.

Men and women have their own field of work. The man takes the initiative in the struggle for existence, not only in getting a wife—which generally takes on the aspects of a kind of robbery—but also in providing the food for the family by hunting the marine animals, and in deciding where the

[Adapted from "The Eskimo of Greenland," by Jeanette Mirsky, in Margaret Mead, ed., *Cooperation and Competition among Primitive Peoples,* copyright, 1937, McGraw-Hill Book Company, Inc., New York. Pp. 51-78. Used by permission.]

family shall live in summer and winter. He makes his hunting and working implements himself, and this is the basis for ownership. Every youth and man owns a kayak. The man also makes the tools and utensils and adornments used and owned by the women in their work and in the common household tasks. The women's work consists of skinning the animals brought in by the man and cutting up the meat. Upon them rests the complicated and difficult routine needed to convert the densely furred and fatty skins into leather suitable for use in clothes, boot soles, boat and tent coverings, dog harness, whips, harpoon lines, bags, sheaths, and needlecases. She also nurses the children, looks after the lamps, the cooking, the drying of wet clothes, the rubbing and drying and mending of all the boots; she sews the prepared sealskins into coverings for the kayak and umiak and assists the man in stretching the skins securely over the wood frame; she cooperates in the housebuilding in the autumn and in the tent raising in the spring; she rows the umiak and takes part in the capelin fishing, drying and preparing the scooped-up fish for winter storage. In addition during the autumn the women harvest wild berries and edible herbs and gather the mussels and small seafood to be found along the shore.

The division of labor is thus clearly marked between the sexes, yet there is no prohibition against a woman being a hunter. Each couple is at once the producer of the means of subsistence and of the necessary raw materials, the manufacturer of the finished product, and the direct consumer. Each couple is thus a completely self-sufficing unit and the struggle for existence is continuous, precarious, and dependent on factors outside the individual's control. Property consists of the basic needs of food, clothing, and shelter and the means of procuring those, and is for the most part perishable and barely above the subsistence level. In consequence wealth is fairly evenly distributed among the people. But within this equality there is a variation depending on individual ability. An angakok (shaman) is likely to have more possessions, obtained as fees for his services. But in general inequalities are not of quantity but of quality, so a man will not have two kayaks, but a skillful workman may have a better kayak than a less skillful one; a more skillful and enterprising hunter will have more to eat; everyone has clothes, but some will be made of skins that are worked and sewed and decorated by a more skilled woman; etc. Another factor in addition to the limitations set by the environment and the technology that tends to equalize the domestic economy and keep all property at the same level of distribution is the mobile life of the Ammassalik. Were it possible to accumulate large surpluses they would only prove a serious problem in their mobile summer life, and mobility is dictated by their pursuit of game.

It is important to remember that the Ammassalik depend largely upon seals and other blubbery sea mammals for their food, clothing, light, and heat and that, though the coastal waters are rich in these animals, it is impossible for them to accumulate great stores of food. And even were they able to, they have no way of preserving the meat and blubber from year to year. At the best they can keep food for a few weeks or months without spoiling. Therefore, if conditions are unfavorable for any protracted period then starvation faces them.

The technology of the Ammassalik reflects individualism in the procuring of animals and the manufacturing of articles. Whatever is possible for one person to handle is done alone, though two or more persons may cooperate in a task because it is pleasanter and easier. Thus cooperation is found principally in the whale hunts and shark roundups (formerly in reindeer and musk-ox drives), and to a lesser degree in the building and organizing of their winter houses. Yet within this cooperative framework an extraordinary amount of individualistic play is found. There are no rewards for certain individuals within the group enterprise, and this rules out any competitive element. In a whale hunt several men paddle out together in an umiak, one or all may harpoon, and when the whale is dead they tow it back to land, where the entire community shares in the kill. In a shark round-up, men, women, and children unite to secure as much of the school as possible: they all dig the hole in the ice, the women and children run up and down along the edge of the hole and shriek to attract the sharks to the surface, where they are harpooned by the men. In the reindeer drives the women and children set up the stone walls and drive the herd between these to a narrow spot where the hunters lie concealed. All these are cooperative enterprises in which the work and the rewards are shared by the whole community. These contrast strongly with the salmon fishing, the capelin hunting, and the berrying, in which several persons carry on the same work at the same time and at the same place without any cooperation or help. Each man works alone for his own end and the fact that other men are similarly engaged around him does not make the work cooperative. It is an individualistic note in the face of an environmental setting which indicates cooperation. And yet whether a man hunts by and for himself or with and for a group he uses the same tools, weapons, and implements. There is no specialization of roles in the cooperative ventures: any man can handle any phase of the work since each is master of all the needed techniques.

This is one of the factors that make it possible to understand the amount of individualism allowed within the winter long house. The winter settlements may be thought of as a federation of free and sovereign states, composed of members who can join or not at will, who are free to leave at any time, and who, while they are within the federation, retain a maximum of their individual rights. During the summer hunting season arrangements are made, purely on preference, as to who shall constitute the personnel of each house, and where they shall live. There is no competition for such house sites, for the territory is vast and there are a great number of vacant house sites whose old walls of turf and stone may be

used to advantage. The house itself consists of one room, varying in size from twenty-four to fifty feet in length, depending on the number of families to be accommodated. Along the back part of the house runs a wooden platform six feet wide that is the living quarters for the families. The props that support the roof also divide this platform into stalls, each of which is occupied by a family and which are partitioned off from the adjacent stalls by skin hangings. (In a stall six feet wide by four feet long a man, his two wives, and six children live.) Skin hangings are also used to line the inside of the entire house, and to pad the living platform. The platforms are used as beds by night and as the workroom for the women during the day. The unmarried men, big boys, and casual guests sleep on narrow benches which run under the windows on the opposite side of the house. Alongside the stall every family has its own lamp over which the cooking is done and the clothes and boots are dried out. Each woman cooks food in her own pot. Under the platform are kept the skin bags and wooden boxes which contain the family's tools and utensils. Outside the house each hunter has a stand on which his kayak rests. The picture given by such settlements is similar to that presented by a *wagon-lit*. The housemates cooperate to build the common outside covering and the food brought in is for the communal stores. But except for the containing walls of turf and stone the different parts are individually owned and contributed: the ridgepole, the props, the planks for the platform, the skin wall and platform coverings. The food, which is mainly acquired by individual efforts, is put into a common storeroom, though the skins are individually owned and used. In handling the food each woman cooks her own share in her own pot over her own lamp and then hands the prepared meat and soup around for all to share. Each house has several communal urine tubs but each family within the house has its private one. The latter are used for individual washing purposes—the women are constantly washing their hair in urine—but the stale urine is collected in the large group urine tubs for all the women to use in tanning the animal skins. Each compartment is a separate unit. Its occupants can, for the most part, do as they please while they are on the *wagon-lit* and they can get off at any place they choose. Only when hunting is bad and the supply of food and blubber is short—when the environment forces it—do the members cooperate more fully. Then only one lamp is lit, only one pot used. At such times, though, no person or family is obliged to remain within the group. In times of scarcity a man is free to leave whenever he pleases. This freedom makes intelligible the chief role of the "headman," whose authority is limited to acting as host when strangers arrive and to determining the division and arrangement of the stalls within the house.

In the entire arrangement of the winter settlement, which for the Ammassalik is the peak of cooperative activity, there is present no factor of competition since there is no limitation on either the territory or the house sites available or in preferable stall locations, and there is no obligation to become part of any group or to remain a part of a group so entered. There is a minimum of cooperation demanded or required. There is a maximal amount of individuality expressed in the living arrangements, the securing and cooking of food, and the ownership of everything except the walls which were originally made use of.

Outside these cooperative activities, the Ammassalik have only one hunting technique that requires the work of more than a single hunter. In the *ittuarteq* method of hunting seals two hunters must work in close harmony. [Two] holes are cut [in the ice], one large enough for a man to lie in, the other just big enough to accommodate a harpoon. Inside the larger hole a hunter peers into the water, watching for seals, while the other man manipulates the harpoon, which is tipped with pieces of white bone to lure the animals. When [one man] sees a seal opposite the point of the harpoon he gives an emphatic but cautious cry, at which the other man [quickly] strikes [at the animal].

All the other hunting methods require a single hunter. Whenever there is open water seals, walrus, narwhals, etc., are hunted from a kayak. Though two or more men might go out together, each in his own kayak, it is more common for a man to go out alone. To them kayaking implies a solitary venture, and so well is this understood that a good kayaker must be able to right himself by his own efforts when his kayak capsizes. When ice covers the fiord the commonest method is for a hunter to locate a seal hole and wait until the animal comes there to breathe. Since a seal has several holes it may be hours before the hunter's patience is rewarded. In the spring seals come up on the ice to sleep and sun themselves and then the hunter crawls slowly and carefully until he is within striking distance of his prey.

In the tasks performed by the women there is the same individualistic note. Cooperation exists between the adult women of a family; between co-wives, a wife and a mother-in-law, a wife and an unmarried sister-in-law, but such cooperation is not implicit in the tasks. Two women carrying out their share of the domestic economy can be considered as the equivalent of one extraordinary woman, a supercapable wife. It is better to have two women to take care of the game brought in by a capable hunter, but it is not compulsory to have more than one. Even the umiak is better rowed if there are two women rowers, but it can be rowed by one.

Possessing the necessary skill and owning her tools, a woman is not only a capable craftsman but she is fully equipped and ready to set up "shop" anywhere she pleases and to cooperate with any man. This fact must be constantly borne in mind to understand the freedom with which the individual woman can move about in the social setting. Every man must have a wife as an economic partner and it is desirable for him to have two such partners. A hunter is seriously handicapped if he has no wife, and if he has two he need be only inconvenienced if one of his wives leaves him.

There is no organized trade, but bartering is carried on. Bartering can include everything from a wife to a bone dart; it can be a permanent transaction or a temporary exchange. It is carried on in much the same informal way that small boys "swap" picture cards, marbles, and knives. The transactions vary with the individual and the article to be exchanged. In one instance two men had exchanged their wives and other possessions at the same time, the wives being just one on a list of items exchanged. When the time came to return what had been traded one of the men refused to return the wife because he did not want to have to return the other objects which he had acquired at the same time.

SOCIAL STRUCTURE

The same strong sense of individualism that characterizes the technology and economics of the Ammassalik is markedly present in their social structure. They have no political unity, no organized leadership, no social stratification. They have no complicated relationship system nor any set of kinship attitudes that defines by its terms the rights and obligations obtaining among its members. There is no set residence. The biological family constitutes the only recognized bond.

A few bonds unite the Ammassalik among themselves and set them off as a group from their neighbors. They use the same dialect, they are natives of the same territory, and they have a way of life that is slightly different from other Eskimo. The Ammassalik have *not* certain widespread Eskimo traits. Here we do not find hospitality wrestling matches, we do not find group ritual, they do not practice female infanticide, they do not substitute the murderer for the man he murdered, there are no *angakut* (shamans) contests. The absence of the first of these traits may be due to the fact that the Ammassalik are a small group who meet once a year during the capelin season. Each person is well known and there is no necessity of having contests in order to place a newcomer in the hierarchy of strength. This

fact may also explain the lack of angakut contests.

The attitude of suspicion and slander that exists between the Ammassalik and their nearest neighbors, the southeastern Greenlanders, is the same within the Ammassalik group. The attitude contrasts strikingly with their behavior. To all persons, whether in the group or outside the group, they behave hospitably, extending this hospitality to include food as well as shelter, enemies as well as friends. The widespread Eskimo pattern of including sex in the hospitality pattern, of a man offering his wife to a guest, is here carried on under the guise of the game of "Putting Out the Lamps," which may be played whether a guest is present or not. But a good host is one who always has the lamps extinguished in the evening when there are guests in the house. In this game both the married and the unmarried take part and complete liberty prevails. (The incest tabus which do not permit intercourse between parent and child or between siblings still hold.) Under cover of darkness a man may take any woman as his sex partner. In the summer when the family unit is small and light lasts far into the night the game is not played. Then two men will formally exchange wives, or an unmarried man will try and steal another's wife.

Under this pattern of extended hospitality runs the ever present note of suspicion and slander. It is present between the group as a whole and the outsiders, between members of one settlement and all other settlements, and between an individual and the rest of the group. The lack of political unity is carried to such extremes, the marked individualistic nature of the people is so opposed to the slightest suggestion of cohesion, that the same attitudes and feelings are found intratribally as well as intertribally.

There is no organized leadership, but there are recognized leaders. An outstanding hunter, a powerful angakok, a skillful drum singer—individual differences within the same field of endeavor are known and casually rated. But there is no "best" hunter, or "most powerful" angakok, or "most skillful" singer; there is no set point, no limit to what a role demands, and each man rolls up his own score for his own satisfaction and to his own interest. Leadership, such as it is, is ephemeral. A man's standing as a successful hunter may vary from season to season, depending on his luck as well as his skill.

Their kinship system is similar to ours; bilateral, counting sex, generation, and direct and collateral descent. A man, his wife or wives, and their children constitute the family. The man and woman unite their efforts to take care of themselves and of the immature children (the man may be the real or foster father, the woman the real or foster mother) and together they form a social and economic unit, a household, within which the young are cared for. But even within this small, closely related group there is a complete allowance for individuality. There is no set attitude that prevails between such fundamentally close relationships as parent and child, siblings, and the conjugal pair. There is a complete tolerance for the role the individual chooses to take in any of these relationships. A father may provide for his son, and this is the usual picture, but he may also abandon him; a mother may aid her daughter in getting a husband or may compete for her daughter's husband; a son may look out for his mother or he may not see her from one year to the next and be indifferent to her fate; siblings may live together and work together or they may be members of different settlements and strangers to one another. Marriage, which is extraordinarily brittle, cannot be said to have any norm of conduct as regards the conjugal pair; it is only when there are children born to a couple that there is a tendency toward stability; but even then the picture presented by the married couple is as varied as the number of marriages. This minimal kinship structure gives free play to the individuality of the persons within that structure. The high incidence of foster parents may be an important factor in giving this wide variation within the kinship structure, but it cannot be the cause of it since both real and

foster relatives behave in the same way.

With such a loose social structure the economic activities which stress the all-round ability of each man to get a living and the self-sufficiency of the conjugal pair harmonize completely.

It is absolutely necessary that a man marry. As soon as a youth is able to support a wife he is in a position to marry. Since supporting a wife depends directly on a boy's hunting ability, and since boys are trained to hunt seriously from the age of ten on, it often happens that boys marry at a very tender age. Marriage implies getting a woman to complete the unit of a domestic economy. The chief incentive to marriage is to have a wife to look after a man's things and dress his game, and so a mother will urge her son to marry because "she can scarcely see to sew any longer." This sometimes leads to very strange unions with a young man married to a woman old enough to be his mother. No man no matter how old he is can be without a wife, and in looking at the census we find that while there are widows there [seem to be] no unmarried widowers. Complete sex freedom exists before and after marriage. Marriage is deeply rooted in economic necessity and can be divided into two component factors; on the one hand a woman is a sex partner, and on the other an economic partner. In securing a sex partner a man does not have to marry. Any man who wants to may participate in the game of "Putting Out the Lamps," and a man has access to the unmarried girls and the temporarily unattached women. Both during the winter and during the summer a man's sexual wants can be easily gratified. If a man is married he can take advantage of the opportunities stated above and, in addition, he is free to exchange his wife with another man for as long as both want to. This whole pattern is congruent with the individualism that is characteristic of other activities; and in addition there is a slight note of helpfulness that pervades this sex field. A man whose wife fails to conceive and who is desirous of having children may call upon an angakok to cure her of her "sickness." The treatment consists of the angakok's journeying to the moon, whence a child is thrown down to the wife, who thus becomes pregnant, and as a reward for having made such an arduous trip the angakok has the right to have intercourse with the wife. That the treatment consists of both the angakok's journey and his copulating with the wife can be seen in the alternate method, which is to urge the wife to have intercourse with other men in order that she may conceive. Exclusive sexual prerogatives do not seem to be the cause for competitive claims.

There is competition, however, in securing a wife as an economic partner. In this competition there does not appear to be rivalry for a particular woman. Rather, there is a constant scrambling around for any woman if she is desirable. If she is attractive that is pleasant but not necessary[, hence choice is wide.] Competition enters into this acquiring of female economic partners because there is a limited number of women available—though there are 114 women to every 100 men—because of the economic drive to get a wife, because polygamy exists (all the good hunters try to get two wives to handle the game they bring in), and because marriages are brittle. The actual securing of a wife is simple and direct. There are no preliminaries, no prerequisites, either social or financial. A young man may give the father a payment in the shape of a harpoon, or knife, etc., for the privilege of marrying his pretty daughter; but often a father will give a present to a skillful hunter in order that the latter will marry his daughter; but by far the greater number of marriages are concluded by the simple act of a man's taking a woman, whether it be from her father or her husband. Women are taken by force, with the rewards going to the most powerful man. The economic character of the marriage is stressed in the reasons for which a woman is divorced. Unfaithfulness plays a small part. It is rather because she is a bad housekeeper, because she is a bad or negligent seamstress, because she eats too much. A man will divorce and leave his wife even though at the time she is pregnant or has children. While it is true that women are taken by force and kept or left at will, women are not cowed. There is as much freedom of choice for the women as for the men. A woman may take the initiative in the game of "Putting Out the Lamps," or in getting a desirable husband, or she may leave her husband because she wants to go to another settlement, or because he has abused her. The securing of wives is the focal point around which competition centers.

Since marriage is easily entered and as easily left, and since it is almost obligatory for adults to be married, it is regarded lightly and it is nothing for a young man or woman in the early twenties to have been party to five, six, or seven marriages. Marriages assume a more stable aspect when there are children born to a couple, but the children are no guarantee of stability. The whole field of marriage—outside the competitive securing of wives—reflects the individualistic note. A man is at liberty to treat his wife as he wants and the range of attitude goes from caressing to beating and stabbing, from devotion to desertion; and reciprocally a wife can "take it or leave it." Marriages are as varied as the people themselves.

Another factor that tends to keep the competition for wives in a constant state of flux is the high death rate among the hunters. Of the thirteen deaths reported during ten months among the Ammassalik all but three were men; of these ten, seven were twenty years and older.

Women are the primary source of quarrels, and such quarrels are carried on between individuals in a variety of ways. They may lead to murder, to revenge by theft, or to a drum match. Quarrels may occur between a man and his wife, between two men, or between two women. In any case there is no attempt on the part of outsiders to interfere in any way. It is quite ordinary to read such an account of a conjugal quarrel. "When Piutek saw the new wife she became angry and began to scold her husband. He flew into a passion, seized hold of her hair, and thumped her back and face with his clenched fists. Finally he stabbed her in the knee so that the blood spurted out. As is usual in such cases the other inmates of the house looked on with perfect composure at this connubial quarrel." There are no cases reported, however, of death resulting from such quarrels.

Drum matches are held both summer and winter. While this is a juridical procedure and a method of settling disputes, yet it conforms to the wider social pattern of singing songs for pleasure. (In fact old drum-match songs constitute part of the repertory of songs sung during the long winter nights.) Both men and women may sing, but they must do so in the traditional style which governs every expression, tone, sound, and movement, and those who cannot master the style are ashamed to sing or touch the drum. A match of this kind is not settled in one encounter, but is carried on for years, the parties taking turns visiting one another. For each new meeting the parties prepare and practice new songs, in which the crimes are vastly exaggerated, or, if they can find no new material that is suitable, they may father new crimes on their opponents or reproach them for deeds which may have been merely intended but never committed. They can enumerate the faults of the opponent's family living and dead. The opponents stand facing one another. They sing one at a time while the other party stands quietly and listens. The singer mocks the other in a number of ways, by snorting and breathing right in his face, by butting him with his forehead so that he tumbles over. The listener accepts this with the greatest composure and even laughs mockingly to show the audience his indifference. When the singer is about to butt him he shuts his eyes and advances his head to receive the blow. The match can thus go on all night, each man taking turns in beating the drum and singing but otherwise not budging from the spot. In the intervals between songs and before and after the match, the opponents do not show the slightest sign of their hostility but appear to be friendly. This is carried on before a large audience which follows every word and movement with keen enjoyment. A man has often several drum matches going on at the same time and, if during the years in which a match is going on one of the parties dies, the survivor prides himself on it and boasts of this fact to others. The same pattern that is found in these juridical drum matches is found in matches similarly carried on just for pleasure. In fact drum matches are the chief pastime of the Ammassalik.

Murder is of frequent occurrence. The lack of social forms makes it possible for a man to murder within the group without having any punishment visited on him. There is no blood feud, no retaliatory act, either physical or magical, no substitutive procedure, no purification rite, nothing. The man remains within the group and people are careful not to provoke so powerful a person. At the most his act can furnish material for a drum song. He is accepted realistically. In 1884 there were three murderers within the Ammassalik group. All were young men and angakut and they moved freely about. Not even murder alters the hospitality pattern. One young man who had killed his stepfather because the latter abused his mother "wanders all about the fiord, and even comes on visits by sledge and boat to the near relations of the murdered man. He is spoken of with dread, but not on account of the murder, but because as an angakok he has robbed so many souls from people who afterwards died." The two other murders were done because in one case a brother resented the harsh way his sister was treated by her husband when she broke a tabu; and in the other case a man killed his father-in-law, after he had been divorced from the man's daughter, because the older man had frightened him badly years before.

Religion among the Ammassalik is a highly individual affair carried on by angakut, each of whom has one or more spirit helpers who act as messengers and help him to get in touch with the spirit world. The religion centers about obtaining the means of subsistence and curing the sick. Any person of either sex may become an angakok, and the only differentiation among the various practitioners is based on personality traits, the acclaim going to the most fearless, the most adroit and cunning. There is a slight amount of cooperation needed to become an angakok. One must be taught by an established angakok how to go out to a lonely spot and there to rub a small stone on the top of a large stone for three days until this brings out the spirit of the rock. This procedure is repeated at different times during the next three or four years, during which time the disciple enters into communion with different spirits who become his *tartoks,* servants. Once a person has been instructed, the whole matter again becomes a personal affair. The angakut perform according to the shamanistic pattern of being securely bound, going into a trance in which their spirits speak and make their presence felt through them and making journeys to the moon, to the depths of the ocean, etc. They are all good ventriloquists and sleight-of-hand artists. Most of these seances are performed for the pleasure of it. In cases of illness the angakok goes into a trance to find out what has happened to the soul of the sick person—for all sickness can be traced to some harm which has happened to the soul, its having been abducted by an evil spirit, its having gotten lost, etc.—and if possible bring it back to the body. Such services are paid for in sledges, dogs, harpoon points, etc., ostensibly to the tartok who served the angakok in effecting a cure, but through the angakok who controls it.

The one time when there is a maximum of cooperation within the society is in times of famine, which occur only in winter. Then we find the individualistic stress that characterizes the winter settlements giving way to a certain cooperation motivated by the desire to live. Forced to extremes by the environment, the Ammassalik will cooperate. To conserve the blubber needed for heat and light, only one or two lamps will burn for all the housemates, and cooking will be communally done and shared. But even in

the face of this anyone is free to step outside the settlement and go to another, or to try to fend for himself. It is only as long as they choose to remain together, and the choice is open and free for each person to make, that they cooperate. Famine must be distinguished from "times of fast." The latter occur when there is a scarcity of seal meat though there may be plenty of other food. But when the pack ice is a solid mass for many weeks and hunting is impossible and the food is used up, that is famine. First the dogs are eaten. [If] the famine continues, the living are forced to eat the dead. They face this possibility quite realistically. They dread it, and those who have been forced to it shrink from speaking of it, but it does not drive them insane, they are not reproached for having been cannibals. As [though] to fortify this realistic acceptance of the inevitable there are tales told of people who grew so fond of human meat that they longed to taste it again.

In accordance with the theory that persons are adult as soon as they can maintain their part in the domestic economy, they remain an integral part of the group as long as they are able to carry on their tasks. Because of the high death rate among the men and the strenuous life they lead, old men are few. The Ammassalik do not, as the Central Eskimo do, consider a man dead when he is too old to hunt and ceremonially wall him up to die, but a very sick person who seems moribund will be thrown into the sea to avoid the necessity of handling his dead body. Of the six old men, between fifty and sixty, all but one were still good hunters, the remaining one had two capable sons who chose to look after their father. An elderly woman can still carry on her work, but this feeling against an individual remaining alive past the days of his usefulness is explicit in the case of a man who told his mother-in-law that she was so old she was of no use in the world and that she might as well be dead. After hearing this she threw herself into the sea. It is this attitude of being unable to provide for oneself or being past the useful age that is directly reflected in the position of the orphan. The orphan in tales and in fact is hungry, ragged, and abused. He may be killed, or abandoned; he is without strength in a society that values it above all else, without power where a powerful personality is a distinguishing mark, without any skill where skill is necessary to maintain life itself.

THE IDEAL PERSONALITY

The Ammassalik ideal man is one who is outstanding in skill, in strength, in power, a man who expresses his personality fully and without being deterred by economic, social, or supernatural sanctions. Such a man can take what he wants without fear, he can do as he pleases without being checked or ostracized, he is at once a terror and a pride. Such outstanding men are not classified, rated and compared one with another; there is no set number of such individuals allowed; each stands out clearly and when they compete they afford pleasure to the whole group. Prestige is a direct reflection of a powerful personality. And having set this as an ideal the Ammassalik accept all behavior by which such an individual manifests his greatness: violence, arrogance, aggressiveness.

The Ammassalik give all the rewards to those who are skillful in hunting, angakokism, or drum singing. With that as a basis a man is free to act as he pleases. The successful hunter or angakok can get two wives and he is welcomed as a son-in-law, a husband, and a housemate. The skillful drum singer who is inventive, a capable artist, and a clever composer may steal, murder, slander, etc., and yet win the community's approval by his superior ability in a drum match. These are the three avenues in which a man may become outstanding. [Nevertheless,] there is no competition among the big men for such high positions. Any number of men, all those who qualify by virtue of their skill and personality traits, can be termed important. The community is elastic and individual enough to allow each man to

think of himself as important and the only check on this is in those cases when one man has cut across the path of another; then the one who does not yield is the more important. And yet there is no open phrasing of competition. A man can show his bigness by going far away from everyone else and there maintaining himself and his family. The one time when competition does explicitly enter the social picture, the drum match, it quickly loses its character and becomes a game in which neither side wants to win, in which both are united in continuing the game and enjoying it.

The injection of strong personality, as an ideal, in a highly individualistic group is here carried out so that one proof of a man's power is seen in his disregard of customs and tabus. One way that people knew Avgo was a very powerful angakok was the way in which he married his mother-in-law while still married to her daughter.

Success and the attainment of prestige depend directly on a person's skill and personality alone. Conversely a person who has neither skill nor a marked personality to exploit with the sanction of his skill is the despised one, the butt of his fellows. Such a role is traditionally and factually taken by the orphan.

EDUCATION

Among the Ammassalik, children are greatly desired. Both male and female children are welcome since the one means future hunters and the other means hunters' partners. No sickly child, or one without a mother, is allowed to live, and in times of stress it is understood that children must be sacrificed before their parents, because even if they were kept alive by any such gesture they would be unable to cope with the environment and would quickly succumb. They are an investment that is not allowed to become a liability. It is essential to the infant's very life that cooperation exist between the parents in raising it. (There are exceptional cases in which a father or mother will desert, and then unless a foster parent

replaces the runaway in the household economy, the child will be abandoned to die.)
There is no conflict between the welfare of
the child and the practice of exchanging
wives.

A great number of "Petting Songs" sung
by the mother to her infant or young child
indicate a cherishing, tender attitude. If
the mother goes out of the house or tent
she carries her child with her strapped securely on her back and kept warm between
her fur blouse and her own body. A child
suckles until it is past two, but when it is
only a few months old it gets additional
food, meat that the mother has first masti-
cated thoroughly. Love and attention are
given the child the first time it wears a little
shirt, the mother kissing the child's breast,
shoulder, hips and navel in order that the
child may be healthy. This is continued each
time its shirt is put on until it is able to
walk.

Again, when the child cuts its first tooth,
it is the center of attention. This pattern
of giving the child some mark of attention
when it first performs some act that marks
a stage on the road to adulthood is observed
when a boy gets his first kayak, when he is
about twelve years old, and when he brings
home his first large game. There are, however, no rites to mark a girl's first menses
or a boy's puberty. Children are never punished, no matter how refractory they may
be.

The child is brought up in the midst of
the household. It goes from the small summer tent to a larger winter house, but wherever it goes it is an intimate part of the
family; it sees its mother at work, it awaits
its father's return with food, it watches as
the father makes his tools and implements,
it listens to the adult conversation, it hears
the songs that are sung and the tales that
are told on long winter nights, it goes with
the mother when she goes berrying or visiting or to a drum match, it sleeps under the
same cover as its parents. [Small] boys make
hunting implements and show an extraordinary skill in making the models, with which
they practice shooting and harpooning. A

boy usually gets his own kayak, made for
him by his father, when he is about twelve.
One boy who had received a kayak when
he was ten had within three years caught
thirty seals. Little girls are given dolls to
play with and to dress. The dolls are so
realistically made that if a child is born to
the couple for whom the dolls are named, a
baby doll is inserted in the mother doll's fur
blouse. The children themselves own all their
toys.

By the time a boy is thirteen to fifteen
he has become quite adept at making tools
and implements and has learned the technique of hunting. From that time on it is a
matter of constant practice. The transition
from play to adult occupations is made early
and follows a consistent training. The same
is true of girls, and by the time they are
this age they are able to do excellent sewing.

Within a tent or house the adults wear
only a *natit,* a G-string. Children go about
quite naked in the houses and tents until
they are almost grown up and do not put
on the natit until they are fifteen or sixteen.
As soon as a youth puts on a natit, the
women begin to smile at him and he is
ready for marriage. When the girls put on
their natit, they also put up their hair in a
topknot as a sign that they are ready for
marriage. Neither boy nor girl needs any
further preparation for marriage. Each can
carry on the work that is required of him;
they have liberal sex knowledge, for there
is no privacy achieved or desired in sex;
they have no social structure to learn, no
formalized ritual. They are as they are and
that is the way the society takes them.

SUMMARY

The Ammassalik have achieved a society
that is highly individualistic. Each couple is
a self-sufficing economic unit in a community with a minimum of social forms, and
there are no effective social sanctions to
regulate murder, competition for women, or
economic activities. There are occasions for
cooperation which are implicit in their relations with the environment, but when they
occur actual cooperation is minimized. There

are occasions for competition, and competition occurs realistically as conflict for the only fixed goods which are limited in their otherwise limitless environment—women to serve as economic partners. It is competition that is without rivalry. The one place where rivalry occurs is in the juridical drum songs, and these quickly lose that aspect and tend to become pleasant, sociable affairs which all enjoy. The society sets up no one goal, and a man can attain importance as a skillful hunter, or angakok, or drum singer if he also has the proper arrogant personality traits. Social cohesion is at a minimum.

All the way across the Arctic from the Ammassalik Eskimo live the Eskimo of the Bering Sea, one of whose settlements, on Nunivak Island, has been studied with unusual care. Dr. Margaret Lantis spent an entire year, from the summer of 1939 through the summer of 1940, living with the Nunivakers (or Nuniwagamiut, as they call themselves), and she returned for a shorter visit in 1946. Thus she was able to observe many aspects of their life very closely, coming to know them as individuals, and being accepted by them as a friend and neighbor. Such close acquaintance is important in studying "social organization," because outward appearances can be deceptive, and even the simplest sort of direct questioning can be misunderstood or resented when it comes from a stranger and a foreigner. After considerable time spent in studying such easily observed aspects of culture as hunting techniques and household furnishings, Dr. Lantis was able to investigate, on a friendly, intimate basis, some of the things we call "social organization." By this time she was able to begin seeing things from the point of view of the Nunivakers themselves, something absolutely essential for any attempt to understand a group of people other than one's own.

The report from which the following extract is taken contains the first half of Dr. Lantis' study of Nunivak, dealing with nonmaterial culture and including a long series of mythological tales. The information is presented under these main headings: (1) natural environment and economic factors, (2) ceremonialism, (3) religion, (4) recreation, (5) life crises—that is, birth, puberty, marriage, and death—(6) social organization, and (7) mythology.

It will be apparent to the reader that even the headings under which Dr. Lantis has arranged her data would hardly be the ones we might select for describing our own society. We might investigate the topic of "religion" as she has done, but would include such things as "churches," "clergymen," "morals," and "marriage," and would certainly not include "doctoring," which is an integral part of Eskimo religion. Likewise, for the Eskimo a discussion of "government" could hardly be carried on in the same terms as for ourselves, since the necessary controls exercised by society over its members are accomplished without elections, courts, police, taxes, or any of the other aspects of "government" in our society.

In order to appreciate the reasons for including certain details in this description of Nunivak Eskimo life, the reader will do well to have the following questions in mind, and notice what information would be useful in answering them:

What groupings exist among the people, on the basis of geography, kinship, sex, age, and economic activities?

What social control is accomplished by means of the family or household group, by
beliefs in the supernatural, by the system of leadership, by public opinion operating through such events as song contests or festivals, and by other means?

What organized institutions are there (such as the Kazigi, the men's house), and
what does each one accomplish?

By what means do individuals achieve recognition, approval, and social position?

What are the things in life that seem most important to the Eskimo people—their
dominant "values," the reasons for which they carry on their lives?

Some of these questions can be answered for the Nunivakers only partly on the
basis of information in the next selection, and should be kept in mind until Selections
13 to 17 are read. Moreover, since the Nunivakers' way of life differs in many small
details from that of every other Eskimo group, some statements made about them would
not be completely true for Point Barrow, for example, or for Greenland. On the whole,
however, the Nunivak outlook on life is quite typical of most Eskimo groups. In fact, there
are so many more Eskimo in the Bering Sea and Aleutian Islands regions than in the rest
of the Arctic, and so much of Eskimo culture developed here, that the term "representative" could perhaps be better applied to it than to the Central or Eastern Eskimo. It is
an accident of history that until recently such groups as the Nunivakers have received
much less attention than the Greenland Eskimo and others nearly as far from the true
center of the Eskimo world.

• 12 • *The Nunivak Eskimo of Bering Sea*

MARGARET LANTIS

THE ANNUAL CYCLE

Nunivak Eskimos had difficulty objecti-
fying and organizing their ideas on social
matters, but in regard to the material side
of their life they could name off their activities as if they had been drilled to do so.
Their interest in the annual cycle of food-
getting and in the movements from winter
village to seal camp to fish camp was [neces-
sary for several reasons]. For one thing the
seasons were well defined; not only the
great contrast between summer and winter,
but spring and autumn could be distinguished also. Their modes of travel were
completely different in summer and winter,
they lived in different villages, and for the
most part the birds and animals that they
caught were different in the two seasons.

Then spring was synonymous with the big
seal hunt, the break-up of the ice, and coming
of the birds; autumn brought big fish runs,
berries, and the large southward migrations
of birds. Finally—and this was especially important—the Bladder Feast provided a climax
and definitive end to the year. At this feast
the bladders of seals caught during the year
were inflated and returned to the sea. This
was thought to keep the supply of seals from
decreasing since an animal's soul was supposed to reside in his bladder. Like many
great festivals of Europe, it occurred in late
December.

It may be surprising to us but it is true
that these people paid relatively little attention to the coming and going of the sun.

[Adapted from "The Social Culture of the Nunivak Eskimos," *Transactions of the
American Philosophical Society*, N.S., Vol. 35, Pt. 3, Philadelphia, 1946. Pp. 171-173,
195-204, 217, 222-223, 229-239, 244-263. Used by permission.]

Since here on latitude 60° N. every day in the year has some sunlight, weather permitting, there is not the contrast between summer and winter solstices that occurs on latitude 70° N. On the other hand, the phases of the moon were watched carefully. So many activities were dependent upon or at least affected by the tides, even in winter when the sea was covered with ice; for example, tomcods could be speared through the ice profitably only when the water was nearing high tide. The people knew well the connection between the tides and the phases of the moon, of which they distinguished seven.

CEREMONIALISM

A surprising amount of Nunivak ritual was personal and individual. Although most of the Bladder Feast was communal, the most important part of the ceremony was given by lineages. This was the dispatching of the seals back to the sea and the singing of sacred hunting songs. The myths show that the people thought it quite possible for just one family to give a whole Bladder Feast. The Messenger Feast, it is true, was highly communal, the entire village cooperating to entertain another village. The Exchange Feast and other lesser dances were given by and for the whole community. These, however, were not essential to the spiritual and economic maintenance of the group. The ritual opening the spring hunting season *was* fundamental in Nunivak life, and every bit of this was carried out by families. There was no feeling that the whole village should work together. If one family got ready before the others and wanted to be in the hunt, that was all right. There was no feeling that the family was injuring the hunting prospects of the group; rather, there was secret admiration for the man who had made all preparations so speedily. The same was true for the beginning of cod fishing, salmon fishing, and egg gathering. All activities were begun by individuals or small groups.

There were three minor rituals for protection of the group, which usually were performed with the direction and assistance of the shaman. One was the purification of the kazigi. In winter and in summer the men cleaned out the kazigi, emptied the urine kantags and turned them upside down over the evil spirits to imprison and kill them. They swept the floor and drove out the evil that had accumulated, making a big noise and commotion, the shaman beating on the drum, the men dancing. In a tiny settlement without a medicine man, this could be done by laymen. The other bits of ceremonial business were the driving away of a storm and an eclipse. The shaman would sing and drum, the men usually accompanying him with the little rattle drums. If men were out traveling or hunting when a storm came up, they would beat on their kayak covers. The exact nature of the songs is unknown, but there seemed to be no essential priestly functions connected with them.

The life-crises observances, as stated elsewhere, were principally a family matter.

What rituals present among other Alaskan Eskimo groups did the Nuniwagamiut lack entirely? There was no ceremony addressed to the moon or the sun. The morning song may have had some connection with the sun originally, either on Nunivak Island or at the place from which the Nunivak people got this custom. It has not recently, however.

There was no first-salmon or any other salmon ceremony. There was no umiak-launching ritual. The umiak was not used for hunting. No memorial feast of any kind was given. Only rarely was a special feast or dance given in fulfillment of a vow for hunting catch. If a man did promise to give a feast in return for getting mukluk [Bearded Seal; in other contexts, mukluk is the word for waterproof fur boots] in the spring season, he would fulfill his vow at the next Bladder Feast. Somewhat more often, a person would promise a feast if a member of his family recovered from illness. This vow might be fulfilled at any time.

There was no purification of people except by washing in urine and rinsing in water, and by sweat bathing at beginning and end of the Bladder Feast and end of the spring hunt. The burning of grass, mentioned in the opening of the spring hunt, probably was purificatory, too; although this point was not brought out by the Eskimos themselves. Regarding sweat bathing in this area, one should remember that the sweat bath was a pleasure and was usually taken as such, rather than for ritual purification or the termination of taboos. It was a form of celebration comparable to feasting.

The most important item in ritual paraphernalia was the tambourine drum, with carved wooden handle. The drum of a grown man might be three feet in diameter, of a boy only one foot. The drumstick was a long flexible wand. Although there were no finger-masks, there were sticks with feathers dangling from one end, with which some of the men beat time to the music in the Messenger Feast. There was a kind of rattle-drum used by special performers in the Bladder Feast, two sticks might be struck together, and bangles on clothing might rattle, but there were no rattles consisting of small objects in a container. There were ceremonial headdresses and a great variety of masks varying from a simple piece of fur from an animal head to beautifully carved and painted wooden affairs with many attached parts. In ceremonies people wore their finest and fanciest garments, yet there was little clothing that had specific ritual significance, possibly the fur headdresses and armbands, certainly the dry-grass wrappings. [There] was a special lamp frame that was reserved for big festivals. All other paraphernalia seem to have been the personal property of the shamans, kept more or less secret from the laity.

In a description of the Nunivak ceremonial pattern, certain negatives are as essential as positives. The ceremonial pattern did *not* include formal prayers, offerings of wealth except a meager offering of food and a wish for good luck. It did not contain any harsh self-punishment (except fasting at puberty), ritual cannibalism, or other abnormal behavior. The shaman might go into a trance, as an exciting display of power more than anything else. Nunivak ceremony was notably healthy, consisting of dancing that was vigorous but not hysterical; feasting; singing of traditional songs; display of handcraft, wealth, and prized ancestral objects; games; wearing of masks and dramatic portrayals of spiritual or mystic beings.

RELIGION

The Supernatural. The Nunivak universe was peopled by several interesting races of supernatural beings, most of whom were conceived by the Eskimo clearly and in detail. Concerning the world levels other than our own, they were not so certain. Underneath this earthly level was a dark disagreeable world called da'laxpax, very dark (place), to which went the souls of all who died a natural death, including women who died in childbirth (the shamans thought). When a woman in one of the myths traveled in the underworld, she noticed her clothing was old and black. There was no one entrance to the underworld in the west or anywhere else. When the shaman went there for some reason, he made his own path by magic. Human souls just sank down through any crevice apparently.

Above the ordinary human level there were several smaller sky levels, . . . one shaman said two, another said four. In the lowest one of the sky worlds there were very large fruits. Sometimes the shaman would journey up there and bring back one of these fine big fruits. All those who were drowned, killed while hunting, frozen or murdered went to the sky, which was very pleasant. There seems to have been a belief in reincarnation which was not entirely clear and consistent. Little information on this was obtained. The souls of seals definitely were reincarnated year in and year out.

The greatest being, the ultimate control and protector of the whole universe, perhaps the Nuniwagamiut "Urgott" was tlam-choak, "universe (world) being" or "spirit of the world." No one had ever seen him, so no one knew what he looked like, but sometimes during a storm he was heard talking like a man. . . . Then Nunivakers added an element to the universe which other groups, so far as is known now, did not have: tlam-choak's "eye of the world." This was a great human eye somewhere up in the sky which saw everything man did, especially when one broke a taboo. The World-eye was not tlam-choak's eye, yet in effect and in practice it seemed to be. The eye was more than an eye, it was a power that sent punishment for taboo-breaking.

[Shamans] had no special ornaments on their parkas or caps, no special insignia. Aside from their "powers," which were really sleight-of-hand tricks, they did not differ essentially from laymen. Apparently the latter could occasionally see spirits in the same way as medicine men. This also is not entirely clear. It may have been that there were a number of men who were "sort of shamans," who had a few beneficial powers.

Shamans had few essential priestly functions. As stated elsewhere, they might drum and sing to drive away a storm for the benefit of the whole community. Yet individual hunters caught out in a storm could drum on their kayaks and sing their own power songs to the same end. The shaman directed many activities during the Bladder Feast and other ceremonies; yet a small settlement could and did hold a Bladder Feast with only the old hunters to initiate and direct it.

Shamans had no formal means of divination except possibly scrying [crystal gazing] . . . but in the past two generations they have got a name for themselves as prophets.

Even while (and because) people admired the medicine men for these and other powers, they feared and distrusted them. Nunivak shamans did not seem to acquire much wealth. If one, besides being a shaman, were a strong, industrious, and effective worker and hunter, he certainly would be able to dominate the community. But some shamans were cripples or sickly people or others who for some reason could not be outstanding hunters. Since they were not wealthy and were the targets for all suspicions of witchcraft, the shaman's position was not enviable. He was thought to kill people by sending his spirit helpers to cause some misfortune to them, or to enter the body of the victim, causing sickness.

The medicine man could not be entirely dispensed with, though. Nunivakers were singularly deficient in practical means of curing, so they had to turn to the shaman as their doctor.

Doctoring was the weakest sector of the culture. Nuniwagamiut were adequately fed, clothed, housed, had plenty of recreation, interesting and varied craft work (particularly for the men), no oppressive caste system of graded societies; they had free competition allowing any man to rise socially and economically by his own industry and skill. In the case of illness and accidents, however, the people could not care for themselves; they had to turn to the shaman. Yet they did not regard him as their benefactor. They feared him and resented his superior power over the supernatural.

RECREATION

There is one big and important generalization to be made concerning Nunivak games and sports: There were no games of chance. All were based on strength, speed, dexterity, skill of some kind or another. Even in the very few guessing games, such as guessing where the snare was buried in the sand, there was some measure of skill involved. And there was no betting on their guesses. Although in a few of the adults' games there was betting, it was certainly small-scale gambling and always gambling on one's own skill and that of one's partner. Probably in the old days nothing was bet except driftwood for the sweat-bath fire. No Nunivak man ever lost his parka or his wife by playing mumble-ty-peg.

Nunivak culture was particularly rich in forms of recreation. Best of all, it offered something to every element in the population and for every season. Although the adult males had the most highly organized games and contests and the only ones involving betting, there were distinctive forms of recreation for women, too. Both juggling and string games were limited to the female sex. In the telling of folk tales, old women were the usual performers and the best ones, although of course men sometimes were the raconteurs. As far as listeners were concerned, all ages and both sexes were permitted to listen.

The games and sports limited to adult males were tug of war, finger pulling, arm pulling, and similar contests, the formal dart game, . . . (on the principle of horseshoes), jumping over a swinging log, all performed in the kazigi, principally in winter. Outdoors in winter they had foot races and contests in throwing spears with spear thrower. In summer they had boat races, and young fellows went swimming by themselves.

In some games and sports both sexes participated at the same time: handball (in summer), skin tossing (principally in spring), racing games (summer), jumping rope. Although both sexes could dance and sing, the men had far greater opportunity in this respect.

As for the children, naturally the very young children amused themselves with unorganized play more than in formal games. But the culture did provide them with toys: dolls, model boats, whistles, tops, buzzes, balls, slings, darts, small bows and arrows, and jumping ropes. Small boys around six years old were expert with the slingshot, for example. With the exception of such model implements as darts, children had to keep their toys indoors in winter. However, outdoors in summer, indoors in winter, they always had something to keep their hands busy.

Although mumble-ty-peg was a game principally for young men and boys, girls did play it occasionally. More often the girls played balancing sticks, usually with the boys. Both of these games were important in keeping the children amused in the winter. In summer boys and girls together played racing games, hide-and-seek, the beach games, and handball, the latter the only game that brought all ages and both sexes together. The boys independently played darts, had contests in strength, and went

swimming. For the girls, the most important group amusement was "house," which not only entertained the little girls but also provided them an opportunity for naturalistic art. A girl, using the very nice ivory knife made for her by her father or grandfather, would cut and trace in snow or sand (usually the former) the scenes, people, or objects of her everyday surroundings. Boys similarly practiced carving, etching, and painting, not as a formal game but as a kind of imitative play. Also, at a surprisingly early age, both boys and girls took their place in the ceremonial and the social dances in the kazigi.

LIFE CRISES

In the Nunivak scheme of things there were three kinds of crises in an individual's life, a "crisis" being any pronounced, significant change. These three types were not consciously categorized by the Nunivak people themselves, but their behavior at different life crises was so consistently different that it is not difficult for a student of the culture to make the distinctions. Given their concept of the universe, the three patterns of life-crisis behavior are logical, not merely a hodge-podge of peculiar superstitions and outworn cultural survivals.

We must realize that they saw the universe as one great natural unit. We would call it a natural-supernatural unit. They thought often about this natural-supernatural world, thought about it enough to be able to organize their beliefs concerning it and their behavior toward it. Probably this explains why beliefs and behavior were inwardly consistent. The people had schematized the natural world around them. In contrast, they were not at all contemplative about their social environment. It was exceedingly difficult for them to explain any aspect of their social system, so far as they had a system. They had not objectified it. Their social behavior was not entirely inconsistent, of course; but the behavior of individuals toward each other in situations that did not directly involve the natural-supernatural, that is, in purely social situations, was relatively variable and inconsistent, and different from behavior in the system. Observances at life crises show these differences. Some personal crises involved the natural-supernatural world. The behavior at such times was different from that at crises with a primarily social significance.

One type of crisis behavior-pattern was connected with *physiological* change: childbirth, girl's puberty (prolonged but attenuated in menstrual periods), and death. To Nunivakers, these changes were not primarily of group concern. They mattered greatly in the life of the individual and they mattered in the natural world. The individual was in an unnatural, "unclean" condition and offensive to the natural-supernatural powers or he would be if he did not take certain precautions. He might also contaminate other people. It is astonishing how consistent was behavior following these crises: taboos on fresh foods, sexual satisfaction, wearing ornaments, joking and playing, on certain kinds of economic activity which involved the more important and sacred items of food supply, taboos to prevent contamination of important food-getting instruments such as kayak and harpoons, and finally taboos on looking up and around and on going bareheaded and barehanded, evidently to prevent contamination of the great universe powers. All of this was directed to securing the pity and respect of the beings of the natural-supernatural world and to prevent arousing their antagonism. Behavior at such physiological crises was not directed toward the community. The individual did not have to work or dance for the community; he did not have to give many presents to the community. So long as the person carried out the demands of that other world, the social world paid very little attention openly. Actually the people always showed a gregarious interest in such an important event in the life of a member of the group. But there was no big communal ceremony; the ritual was small and personal. The orientation of behavior toward the natural world rather than the social world is shown by the duration of most

of the taboos: "until the end of the next Bladder Feast." Until the Feast was successfully concluded, at which time everything was set right with the seals and the birds and other important beings, people had to be very careful about not giving offense to them. Other evidence of the nature of these taboos is given by the nature of punishment for breaking the taboos. The individual or his family was punished primarily, the community secondarily. When an individual broke a personal taboo, he ran the risk of becoming ill or having some other misfortune. The community would be affected only if the broken taboo involved the important food animals.

This brings us [now] to the second kind of life crisis, a change in one's status with regard to food getting. First berry picking and gathering of grass by a girl, first killing of a bird and a seal by a boy required recognition by the whole community. Since obviously these activities involved the food supply of the group, the parents of the child called these activities to the attention of the community by distributing gifts. *Certain ritual "firsts,"* which also involved the group, were handled in the same way. These were first appearance of a child at a ritual, first drum, first dancing in the kazigi.

The crises in this second large category, like the first, had to do with the great nonsocial universe. They represented first contacts with that universe by young individuals, and so far as those contacts might be offensive to the animals and involve danger to the food supply, taboos were in force. For example, when a boy caught his first hair seal, he could not eat any part of that kind of seal. But since the events at these changes of status involved more than the individual and the nonsocial world, there was this combination of taboo and distribution of wealth, that is, a combination of nonsocial and social. Thus the individual and the group participated in the crisis observances just as they participated in the effects of the crisis, which were continuation of food getting and continuation of ritual. There was another aspect of this sharing. Undoubtedly the spirits liked the traits of generosity, of attention to taboos and ritual details, and would repay both the group and the individual for them.

The third kind of crisis was a *change in social status*. To a Nunivaker, this was no crisis at all. Under this heading there came marriage, divorce, and adoption. These did not involve the food supply or the perpetuation of ritual; hence there were no taboos, and the community did not have any official part in these changes of status. Members of the community individually would show great interest in what were important events in the life of the principals; as a group, they were indifferent. This seems rather strange to us. We are undoubtedly right in assuming that these events were bigger to the individuals than outward social forms would indicate. (From actual observation, it would seem that becoming an orphan or being adopted into a strange family were the two most serious changes from the standpoint of personal development.) Yet the indifference of the supernatural, the absence of opportunity for social advancement by giving presents and feasts, and lack of other emotion-reinforcing acts and situations would keep these personal events from seeming overwhelmingly important even to the principals. We must not project into their lives our emotions.

Two other changes of social status were recognized by the village, for different reasons. When a novice shaman was ready, he demonstrated his powers in the kazigi before the assembled community. If he passed this test, he was recognized as a practicing shaman who could be called upon by the group. Whether he or his family gave presents for a feast is not known definitely. However, it seems unlikely. The second type of change involves the elevation of a man to the status of "chief," which came later in life.

Marriage. Before marriage, boys and girls were supposed to show a certain sedateness toward each other. Girls in particular were expected to walk, not run, to keep their eyes cast down, to refrain from taking the initiative in teasing and playing when they were in the presence of men and youths. The two sexes did spend very little time together, and even when they were in each other's presence, they talked at rather than to each other, giggled, and teased self-consciously. In the evening, particularly the very long summer evenings, the taboos were evaded somewhat. Boys and girls from ten to twenty years old played games together and adolescent flirtations flourished. The youngsters would develop shy, blushing "cases" which often included sexual intercourse and occasionally ended in marriage. But there was no frank, serious pairing off, and no working together. For example, a girl or young woman could not get into the kayak of any boy or man except her husband, a little brother, or an old grandfather. For a young couple to go off together for fishing before they were married was not proper.

Boys of fourteen or fifteen and tomboy girls of ten or eleven would go swimming together, nude. These same youngsters would sneak off on a summer evening for some rough, kidlike erotic behavior, which consisted of a boy catching a girl and hugging or caressing her. After this age, however, the boy began to associate with older boys, to think about seal hunting, to strut around and act lofty towards the girls because he was learning to take his place in the community as a hunter. He could not seriously think of marriage until after he had caught at least one of each kind of seal, including the adult bearded seal. He would be twenty or more when finally eligible to marry. Meanwhile, when he was between sixteen and twenty, most of the girls he had formerly played with were being married to older men. It was unusual if a girl were still unmarried at sixteen. Most girls were married when about thirteen, a few at eleven or twelve. The result was that not all young men could have wives younger than themselves. However, the "normal" marriage can be considered one between a youth of twenty and a girl of thirteen.

So far as kinship was concerned, the only marriages absolutely forbidden, aside from the usual parent-child and brother-sister ones, were marriages between *any people in uncle-niece or aunt-nephew relationship*. For example, a man could not espouse his brother's or his sister's daughter. He could, however, marry a parallel cousin's daughter even though, according to Nunivak terminology, he did call that cousin his brother or sister. A person could marry his serious partner or joking partner or a cross-cousin or a parallel cousin, although people were quite dubious about this last one.

Since all the villages intermarried, everyone on the island was related to everyone else. One could scarcely avoid marrying a distant relative. There was some intermarriage with people on Nelson Island and at Hooper Bay although this was necessarily infrequent. Nunivakers in the old days did not marry beyond those two localities. The Nunivak population therefore should be regarded as very inbred.

There were no formal rules of courtship, no plans for married life were made by the young couple, and they did not have intercourse before marriage (supposedly). The young man did not have to give service to the girl's family prior to marriage. When he was thinking about getting married, his mother made a nice wedding parka from furs that he himself had caught or obtained by trade, and she might also make boots. If he were quite anxious to win a particular girl, he would carve a belt buckle or some other trinket. Then most men would get a relative to make the proposal to the girl's family, an older brother, a grandmother, anybody. There was no rule about this. If the suitor was older and felt sure of himself or if he was away from all his relatives, he would ask for a girl himself. Occasionally, her parents would quietly take the initiative. This was not the proper procedure, though. If the young man was acceptable, he brought forth the fine new clothing for the bride. While he was staying in the kazigi with the other men, she took food to him in a new

dish, the best food that she could prepare. This was the public notification of the marriage, as if a tiny village needed any in a literal sense.

There was no other exchange of gifts, nothing that might be called the binding of a contract, unless the foregoing is considered such. The bride's family did not give a feast, her father did not give a sweat bath. As stated before, the community did not take part in this change of individuals' status. Neither man nor woman changed hairdress, type of ornaments, or cut of the clothing pursuant to marriage.

Following the marriage, the young man just stayed on in the girl's village if he was from another settlement, as was true frequently. If his family lived in the same village, he brought his own dishes and clothing to the house of his bride's parents but probably would leave his hunting gear in his father's storehouse. The rule of matrilocal residence was adjusted to fit circumstances as agreeably as possible. If a family had four sons and one young daughter, one of the sons would bring his wife home instead of going to her village. If the bridegroom did the customary thing and moved to the other village, he probably would use the kazigi to which his wife's father and brothers belonged, but he might use another kazigi because it was less crowded or nearer his wife's house or because some of his own kin stayed in it.

Marriages seem to have been contracted much more often in summer than in winter. There was a good reason for this. During the winter families crowded together in the winter houses, so that a young couple could have no privacy for the shy courtship or for the honeymoon. In the summer they could travel and camp out as much as they pleased. And they took full advantage of the opportunity. One principle of Nunivak marriage was that the husband and wife be in love. Of course a couple of middle-aged people, each of whom had been married three times before, would marry for material considerations. A young couple really would be in love and would not hesitate to show it. Not long after the marriage the bridegroom would take his wife to his home, for the chance to travel alone with her, to get the remainder of his personal possessions, or for various reasons. On this visit, the girl was given a new nickname by her husband's relatives . . . and the in-law taboos came into force.

A man never looked directly at or talked directly to his wife's mother or father, another of the many traits setting Eskimos of this region apart from those in the Arctic. Normally a man talked through his wife. If no intermediary was present, he would talk at his parents-in-law without looking at them. Naturally, he would always show the greatest respect and formality. If he met his mother-in-law on the trail, neither one need detour, but they would not look at each other as they passed. Although he talked freely enough with his wife's brothers and sisters, he rarely joked with them (if he did, it was without the sharpness of the joking partner); and the same was true of a woman and her husband's brothers and sisters. Between a woman and her parents-in-law there were the same taboos as between a man and his parents-in-law, except that they were not so rigorously observed. For example the woman could talk to her mother-in-law if necessary, while refraining from looking at her directly.

After the honeymoon, for the first few years of married life the young couple remained in the wife's home. We must remember, though, that the man spent almost all of his time in the kazigi, and for other reasons (discussed elsewhere) he scarcely belonged in his father-in-law's household. During his early married life he was emotionally tied to two groups: his parental family, and his wife and children. Yet, as pointed out in the introduction, there were other forces in the culture which prevented friction and held the couple together.

As the children grew up, certain taboos were enforced on brothers and sisters. Any child, both before and after adolescence, could address his parents directly and familiarly.

There were always the closest bonds between parents and children and between grandparents and grandchildren. But brothers and sisters gradually drew away from each other. After puberty, they never looked directly at each other and never talked freely. One might make a request of the other, formally. That was about the extent of their conversations. Even before puberty, from the time that the boy went to the kazigi, they did not play together unless they were taking part in a group game. Although in general among the children the age principle was in force, whereby any older child would ask any younger child to do things for him, among brothers and sisters the boy tended to domineer over the girl regardless of age. A lad of eighteen might take a big-brother protective attitude toward his little sister of five, but a boy of ten was usually quite indifferent to the wails of his eight-year-old sister or his eleven-year-old sister. Both he disregarded, unless he wanted them to do something for him. However, among the brothers of a family there were free demonstrations of affection. As the taboos on heterosexual behavior increased, inside and outside the family, the companionship among all boys increased. There was a similar situation among girls, although it was not quite so obvious. All these relationships among various members of the family had formal expression in the system of names and nicknames.

SOCIAL ORGANIZATION

Names, Nicknames. People must completely disregard the naming system and significance of names among the Eskimos of the Norton Sound region and northwest Alaska when studying the naming system of Nunivak, because it is entirely different in its *raison* and in practice. On the Lower Yukon, for example, a person was named for the most recently deceased individual in the community, regardless of sex and relationship to the child. The baby then became a reincarnation of the dead person.

Here is the Nunivak system. There was no ceremony, and no presents were given in the kazigi. The child was named for a relative, either a living relative or one who had died several years previously, not the most recently deceased. The baby was given a masculine or feminine name according to its own sex. There was no indiscriminate use of names.

Children were most often named for their grandparents. The genealogies show that twice as many boys were named for maternal grandfather as for father's father. With matrilocal residence, this is to be expected, since the baby belonged to the household of his mother's father. [The great-aunts] and great-uncles, uncles and aunts were honored in this way. Although this name (what will be called henceforth the "real name") was something very special, there was no legend connected with it and it was not owned by the lineage. In other words, people of different families bore the same name.

The name may not contain the soul of the individual, but it contains some other vital essence, something very special connected with the individual and possibly also with the family. The Nunivak people have gone to astonishing lengths to avoid use of the real name. First, there was teknonymy. A man was referred to as Father-of-John or Father-of-Mary, whichever was the eldest. A woman was Mother-of-John (or-Mary). When the oldest child died, the parents then were spoken of in connection with the oldest living child. However, age priority was not rigidly adhered to.

Second, there were descriptive nicknames, which derived from the traits of the individual himself or of the person for whom he was named, that is, he might receive both the real name and nickname of a relative. Most of these nicknames suggested no real opprobrium, were just amusing, and were used freely by everyone; for example, "Little-rail" applied to the tallest man on the island. Some were used more surreptiously. One fat dark-skinned woman, who probably had Negro blood, was called by the name of a male seal that has a brown face and strong odor and taste, by those who disliked her. Aside from the inherited ones, nicknames developed naturally in various ways. Joking partners seem to have been the originators of many of them.

There was still another way of getting a nickname. Names provided one more means of commemorating achievements. If a man did something of which he was proud, he would make up a name and apply it to a favorite son or grandson when the child was young. An interesting point is that such names tended to become reciprocal.

Third, the Nuniwagamiut have built up a thorough and rather complex system of nicknames, the basis of which has remained carefully hidden until the present. Probably it can best be explained by analogy to nick-naming in European cultures: James may be called Jimmie, Jim, or Jamey; Dimitri becomes Dima; Patricia becomes Patsy, Pat, or Patty. The Nunivakers have a directly comparable system, except that *kinship terms of reference are the bases of these pet names.* . . . The chief difference between these people and ourselves is that they have worked out their system much more logically and completely than we have.

The Lineage. Surrounding the individual, surrounding the biological family, there was the lineage, a social as well as biological continuum from generation to generation. The heritage which the lineage conferred on all its members was and is important to both Nunivak Islanders and ethnologists. In this heritage the central concept was the inogo. . . . The basic meaning is specific power, amulet, charm, magic helper. Inogos were innumerable. If we include all their forms, each person probably had two dozen inogos. He wore on a string around his neck or in the pocket of a suspender arrangement over the shoulders little carved figures for personal protection. He tied a tern's bill or a mink's nose or what-you-will to his fish trap. He tied small figures to his seal net. He secreted a mysterious bundle in his kayak when he went seal hunting in the spring. He carved the ivory toggles on his harpoon lines to resemble different creatures. And he called them all inogos.

The concept went even farther than

things, objects that a man could hold in his hand. A Nunivak male painted an inogo on his kayak cover, umiak cover, and double-bladed paddle, all the same inogo. These painted designs did not look exactly alike, but they all represented one and the same creature, usually a bird. In short, there were inogo animals. The design represented that animal and carried its power. The design was a talisman, the animal itself was a super-talisman. A man's animal helper was utilized in other ways. He made two flat stylized carvings in ivory of the head of the bird or body of the animal and placed one on each side of his sacred hunting hat. On the fore-shafts of his big harpoons for sea mammals, he carved and etched the same inogo crea-ture. He took the claws or the beak or the ears of a real animal of this species and used them when he needed their special powers. Furthermore, he did not have just one ani-mal helper; he had several. He had songs and stories about them, and the songs had power just as the designs had power.

How and where did a person get these dozens of inogos? Most of the amulets to prevent or cure illness were given to him by the shaman, for which in return he gave some gift. Some of the amulets with very specific powers for use in hunting, he also acquired from the shaman, for example, an inogo to make a walrus bleed much and die quickly. However, most of his inogos were inherited; not necessarily the actual bit of ivory carving or the sperm-whale tooth, but the *right* to use a whale's tooth or a carving of a flounder.

SOCIAL CONTROL

It is always artificial to divide culture into sections and treat each section as a separate unit. Usually it is possible, even advanta-geous, to do this even though it is admittedly artificial. In the case of Nunivak commu-nity organization, law-ways, social relation-ships aside from kinship, and economic status, a segmentation of the ethnographic material into these four categories would necessitate much repetition in presentation of the data and would violently tear apart

behavior which is meshed in functioning and which cannot function unless it is meshed.

ECONOMIC SEGMENTATION

Division of Craftsmanship and Labor. Nunivak had no guilds, no essential division in craftsmanship except a sexual division. All men of middle age made boat frames and house frames, made all tools, hunting and fishing implements, including women's things, did all the carving, etching, painting of wood, bone, antler, and ivory, even made their own masks and other ceremonial para-phernalia. Women made all baskets, mats, and pottery, did all the sewing, even the stitching of boat covers, made all sinew or grass threads, ropes and braids, including those used on hunting implements. The one exception to this was the stitching of the quiver, used in caribou hunting and war. A man made his own quiver completely, since it was thought that if a woman touched it, a man would not catch much game or shoot his enemy. In the preparation of skins, there was not such a clear-cut division. Men made raw hide lines for seal nets, harpoon lines, and the like. Women made lashings for boots and other skin ties on clothing. Women did all the work in preparing bird, animal, and fish skins for clothing, in pre-paring intestines, esophaguses, stomachs, bladders, and whole skins for pokes and floats. Men did most of the work of prepar-ing boat covers. Women could not wear or use the scarce, almost sacred blue paint (vivianite) but could apply paint made of ocher or soot to clothing, fancy bags, and ornaments.

Thus we see how dependent each group was upon the other for its comfort and con-venience in daily life. Men provided the family with its eating and storage dishes, cups, spoons, and buckets (that is, wooden buckets; women made leather buckets), gave the women their knives, scrapers, picks and pounders, sinew shredders, needles and needlecases, boot-sole crimpers, ornaments, combs and backscratchers, and their amulets. Women gave the men all their clothing and provided for the family all the cooking vessels and pottery lamps (there were no stone lamps), burden baskets, wall and bench coverings, besides many small objects such as cases for tools, bags for storing clothes, etc.

No adult could be lazy. Regardless of status, lineage, age, or physical condition, one had to work to the limit of one's capacity. Everyone was judged on this basis.

In division of labor aside from craftsmanship, there was again the primary sexual division, plus some separation of tasks on the basis of age. All men were hunters[, and] by a combination of hunting, collecting wood, and craftsmanship provided—besides food and clothing materials—shelter, transportation, and the production goods: kayaks; harpoons, nets, fishtraps, etc.; and tools. One might even add to the list of production goods and amulets which according to Nunivak notions were essential in hunting success. Finally, the men made some consumer goods, principally dishes and ornaments.

Women were expected to provide the remainder of the food: fish, shellfish, greens, and berries. On Nunivak Island much more than in the Arctic, these were important, constituting nearly half the diet. Although both sexes and all ages might gather mussels, this was usually a job for older children. For many tasks, there was no hard and fast rule. Men secured codfish and halibut with large composite hook and line, fishing on the open sea. Women and children fished for tomcods and other small fish from rocks along river or bay, using small hooks. Boys fished from kayaks in these protected waters. Women and girls speared tomcods through the ice on river or bay. Although the men preferred other methods, they would occasionally also resort to these unpretentious techniques.

Women secured some raw materials besides food, principally grass which was also more important here than in the far north, although these materials were not so numerous or so essential as the ones provided by men. Women's most vital work was the conversion of raw materials into consumer goods. Besides the boots, pottery, etc. already mentioned, the storage and preparation of all food was their most essential contribution to the economy, and seasonally a big task, as we have seen.

The above are types of cooperation in which each person performs by himself his own tasks which are parts of a larger process. House construction is a good example. Men made the excavation and did all the carpentry, a big task in building a log house with primitive tools. Women provided the grass, the pounded earth and sods to cover the roof. The man made the stone hearth; the woman made the skylight of walrus intestine and fishskin and the mats to cover walls and benches. There was also a slightly different form of cooperation. For example, the hunter himself skinned and butchered large bearded seals and walrus, his wife all the smaller seals. This was like the gathering of driftwood. Men brought in the big logs, women and children the smaller pieces. In addition, there were forms of cooperation in which two or more people worked together at the same task. In the family the principal one was fishing with seine or trap. Although two males might handle the large seines, the usual combination was husband and wife. The question of cooperation will be dealt with again later. The point made here is that males and females did occasionally do the same work and do it together.

Division of labor on the basis of age was as follows. Children of both sexes gathered the smaller pieces of driftwood and the boys broke it up for firewood. Although both sexes and various ages carried water, the task of cutting ice usually was given to the boys of early teen age. Girls began at an earlier age than boys to contribute labor to the family, by gathering grass, greens, and berries and by tending the babies. Although the boys ran errands and assisted the men here and there, the boys' work consisted largely in helping themselves rather than the family. That is, they were helping only themselves at the moment, by making their own crude toys, tools, and hunting implements, but in time by exactly these same activities they would be helping the household. At the other end of the age scale, the old people also did their share of the work. Old women, who could no longer walk far and carry great bundles of grass and whose hands were no longer good enough to skin a seal neatly, nevertheless kept busy twisting thread, making baskets, and repairing clothing. Old men similarly could handle fish nets and traps after their hands were too stiff and slow to handle the spears, and they could adz a piece of wood for the boatbuilder or housebuilder. Cripples specialized in craftwork in order to provide something of value to the wealthy family which in turn would give food to the poor person. Shamans, if physically able, were expected to hunt and do all the other work of a layman. Their special powers were an addition to, not a substitute for other labor and abilities.

Absence of Formal Economic Stratification. The conclusion to the above is that there was no stratification of society based on an essential difference of economic function. Ivory carvers were no higher in the scale than housebuilders, teachers no higher than fishermen. Every man was a housebuilder and an ivory carver, a teacher and a fisherman of sorts. Although men's and women's labor and crafts were different, neither sex was thereby made independent of the other. It was just the reverse. The mere fact that each sex performed specialized tasks meant that each was dependent on the other, producing an economic unit, the family, characterized by full cooperation within itself. It is true that man's position was higher than woman's. Baskets were not wealth, sealskins were. This sums up the difference. The only other possibility for stratification pertained to shamans. Their position in the community will be discussed separately.

POLITICAL SEGMENTATION

In political functions, there was some division. Of course the principal division of the total adult population of a community was again sexual. A woman did not openly and alone perform any function toward the community as a whole, that is, she had no role *directly* in relation to community affairs.

Hers were relationships with individuals. Primarily she was identified with her husband, the identification becoming more complete as they grew older. She assisted him in the performance of ritual, in his duties toward such individuals as his serious partners and toward the community. Actually a woman might be influential in the community through her gossip, her industry and maintenance of high standards of workmanship or of generosity, or her domination over some important man; but all this was unofficial, indirect, and variable. Hence only the men's roles are formally stated.

Types of Officials Not Present. As there were no caribou drives or other forms of communal hunting, there were no hunt chiefs. Hunting was carried on by families or by other small cooperative units either within the community or cutting across the communities. Brothers from different villages would move to the same spring camp and assist each other in seal hunting. Partners would operate a seal net together and divide the catch. The most interesting and significant point is that each family was free to open any seasonal food-getting activity without regard for the remainder of the community, and it could go wherever it pleased to do it. Yet there was a kind of control, unformalized. We shall encounter the same situation again and again. The older men who had the reputation of good hunters *influenced* the younger hunters in their decisions. They made suggestions, they set the example. They did not direct or coerce.

The same was true in warfare. There was no war chief. But some men's words were listened to more carefully than others'. The war stories show clearly the lack of formal authority, regarding preparation and conduct of battle, to argue out a point and finally to dominate. But he did not necessarily dominate the whole expedition or defense. He would win one point, only to lose another.

In communal ritual, the shaman naturally took a prominent part but he did *not* direct all aspects of the ceremonial; indeed he was not essential for anything except his own performance as a shaman. In small settlements the Bladder Feast could and would be held by laymen alone, the older and wealthier men directing the others.

Factors in Leadership. The bases for prestige, influence, dominance are difficult to ascertain and separate. All of the following must be recognized: (1) age of the individual and his knowledge of the experience and lore of past generations; (2) specific abilities, special experience and achievement; (3) personality traits apart from the foregoing; (4) wealth and handling of wealth, especially generosity; (5) family. One might also add (6) closeness to group opinion and group standards. However, this would function in at least three of the other five. The Nuniwagamiut themselves recognized all of these, although they appreciated the importance of personality probably least of all. They even recognized the contribution of the family—rather the lineage—toward the securing and maintenance of position by the individual.

Age.—Let us consider some of the age factors. On Nunivak *relative* age was important in various connections. To summarize data given elsewhere, in games and sports individuals entered and dropped out of the contest according to their relative age from the youngest to the oldest. In everyday life, tasks were passed along from older to younger. Younger people could not use the names of their elders and always must show them deference, with the exception of joking partners and certain close relatives. In the distribution of goods following feasts, first choice was given to the eldest and then down the line according to age. This same attention to old people and their ideas was shown in less formal ways in community life, until a person was obviously senile and his judgments unreliable.

Achievement.—In making one's place in the community, certain abilities, certain achievements were far more important than others. A man's success in hunting, assisted by an industrious wife, was the *only source of wealth* according to Nunivak ideology. They could not imagine wealth coming from

trade, shamanism, or craftsmanship alone. These could add to one's prestige and influence but were not a substitute. Let us look at an example. The head of one household was a fine carver. The household possessed by actual count more dishes, a greater variety of dishes, and all of them better made than those of other families. It also had a well-built house. Yet this family was very poor. It did not have enough seal oil to last through the year; its skin clothing was old and worn; it did not possess a seal net (which was made of rawhide); it did not have a surplus of the best food to give away at feasts. The family was not starving, it is true. It could live on fish, shellfish, reindeer, and greens. But it did not "rate."

Besides products of the hunt, there were other items which were reckoned as wealth: boats, tools and hunting implements, houses and storehouses. Even though all of these might be made by the very industrious and otherwise competent man who did not happen to be a good hunter, it was far easier for the hunter to secure them. If a man did not have large enough logs for a new storehouse or an umiak, he could barter for them giving sealskins in payment. If he needed a walrus tusk for his new harpoon, he could barter for one. Also one could secure the more valuable skins or additional skins to add to one's own catch. One woman pointed out that wealthy men wore eider parkas, wealthy women wore cormorant, both of them birds taken singly by spear. Poor people wore parkas made of murre or puffin skins, both of which could be secured in large numbers on the cliff rookeries. Although the value of the former skins was partly determined by social standards, there was also in eider an intrinsic value of warmth and durability, in cormorant a greater beauty in the iridescent black plumage which almost any people would recognize. The Nuniwagamiut were right in their estimation of the importance of hunting.

Success in hunting was the principal source of personal prestige. Whereas, momentarily, or in respect to a particular activity, a man might be esteemed for his dancing, mimicry, or composition of pleasing songs, for his umiak construction or ivory carving, his bravery in war, or for his cheerful friendly disposition, such rating was not formalized as it was in hunting. People would say, "He always makes good kayaks"; or "He composes the best songs." Of the great hunter, however, they said, "He caught ten mukluks in one season!" Since even good hunters got only three or four a season, one can understand the significance of ten. As we have seen, this rating according to the number of adult bearded seals killed did not depend solely upon the ease of reckoning the number of animals killed in comparison with the difficulty of judging quantitatively the good points of a dance or a wood carving. The hunting of these particular seals had been given a cultural significance beyond its intrinsic value. Naturally, if a man could combine other good qualities (according to Nunivak standards) with those of the good hunter, he had that much more prestige. But, as in the case of wealth, these were an addition, not a substitute. Being modest in regard to one's achievements, controlling one's anger, and similar traits made people like a man, but not admire him. Even the admiration for a fine mask did not equal the admiration for a dead bearded seal.

Success in hunting also gave a man and his family recognized *status* in the community and this status carried influence with it. In contrast to most cultures, it did not give recognized rights—only duties. There was really no political organization; but so far as there were political, economic, and social functions toward the community as a whole, all were aspects of this status. Specifically the situation was this: In a large village many men would be called "good hunter," but normally only one could be "best hunter" since only one kind of hunting catch was counted, viz., big bearded seals, and it seldom happened that two men caught the same high number of mukluk. If a man for several successive years remained at or near the top of the rating and was good in other kinds of hunting, people would begin to call him noga'tlpeax, high man, which meant also

"rich man." Note that this word has two meanings in free translation, "best hunter" and "wealthy man," even "chief." There was a word meaning "wealthy," literally "having goods," . . . but this did not denote the same thing as noga'tlpeax. Next, if a man combined with his prestige as a hunter, the trait of generosity in dealing with the members of the village and in maintaining or bettering the economic status of the village in relation to other communities, then he was given the title of oki'skax, which seems to mean literally "helper" . . . but is always translated "chief."

There was no such thing as an office of village chief which could be held by only one man at a time. In a prosperous village with one hundred inhabitants or more, there would be two or three chiefs. "Chief" was a title rather than an office. As stated before, none of these men had official rights or authority except the right to dominate others as a person, on the basis of prestige. The only role that might be called an office was "boss of the kazigi." Each kazigi had its recognized leader and authority, some old man who was a noga'tlpeax. It is difficult to see just what his duties were, yet everyone said that there was such a person. He probably took the initiative in suggesting that the kazigi be cleaned or repaired and assigned young men to do the work, superintended preparations for festivals, entertained guests from other villages.

Exactly where and when did people begin to call a man "chief"? Apparently at the Messenger Feast. Although the whole village cooperated in giving the Feast, there was always one wealthy man who acted as principal host. If he could give away goods so lavishly that he put the guests to shame and made his own village feel proud, the people would recognize him as their leader. Other incidental statements by informants indicated that a man who entertained generously at feasts within the village would gain either of the two titles, noga tlpeax or oki'skax, which actually were used interchangeably in reference to any one outstanding man. We see from this that the "high man" had many duties, more duties than rights. He had to show knowledge and caution in guiding the younger people; he must never cease to work hard and hunt vigorously; he had to know all the old rituals and taboos and must uphold them; he must help the poor people. But it was easier for him if he belonged to the right family.

The Family.—Nunivakers themselves recognized the importance of heredity and family status, although they expressed it differently from the way we would, and actually they saw the situation somewhat differently. When one old man was asked how a man became a chief, he said, "He knew all the songs." We must recall that a lineage possessed a mass of secret power songs and other amulets. If a man knew *all* of them and used them properly, he was bound to be a successful hunter. If a successful hunter, then he would have surplus goods. Here enters one necessary factor not controlled by lineage and songs: personality, particularly helpfulness and generosity. If a man distributed his surplus, then he was an acceptable chief. From specific cases, we see that actually a man did not need to be always open-handed in order to be called chief. If a man was a good hunter and especially if his father and grandfather had been good hunters, people would grudgingly and with disparaging comments give him his rightful title even if he was stingy. Sometimes a man even would claim the title when others thought he did not deserve it. As one would expect, there was a certain amount of rivalry, backbiting, and jealousy between chiefs. Although the eldest son of a chief certainly would have the title (unless completely incompetent), the grandson could not claim it without earning it in his own right. He had to reaffirm the superiority of his family.

Besides knowing all the songs of his paternal family, a chief had to know all the ritual of the group. He acted as director of ceremonial, the Eskimo master of ceremonies; the shaman assisted him as prompter for songs and other details. Sometimes the shaman himself had high enough economic status to be boss of the kazigi and take full charge of the ritual, with plenty of comment and assistance from the other older men of the community.

The important function of the paternal family in the personal success of its members was sensed by the people in other ways. Orphans or other poor boys were anxious to attach themselves to a stepfather or some other man who was a good hunter. Men complained bitterly that they had been orphans and had never been sponsored properly when they began their hunting career. A chief's son was called just that and was given advantages even in his early days as a hunter.

Lack of Formal Community or Tribal Organization. The statement was made earlier that Nunivak had no political organization. Any political organization seems to include four things, rather it is constructed of four things: (1) a territorial unit, in which there are (2) standardized relationships between leaders or officials and their following or constituency, (3) an ideology of group action and of individual action affecting the group, and (4) means (agencies) of control or coercion, to enforce that ideology and those relationships.

Aside from the relationships between boss of the kazigi and men of that kazigi or between the wealthy chief and the poor people of the community, there were no standardized relationships and even the former were poorly defined. The relations were man to man, not leader to group. The ideology pertained almost exclusively to individual behavior, not group behavior. Regarding both interpersonal relations and personal relations with the Supernatural, there was a clear code of behavior which anyone could state. A man should be kind and affectionate toward wife and children; he should provide well for them. A man should give to his serious partner any kind of help that that person needed. And so on. As one would expect, there were no organized agencies of control or coercion. How did the community function in the absence of authoritative chief, council, or police? Public opinion, guided by tradition or the personal opinion of a strong-minded sharp-tongued individual, the power of [the world spirit] to punish or the compulsive force of material necessity—these regulated conduct.

EXCEPTIONS: RELIGIOUS CONTROL.—The most obvious control of the individual was religious control by the Supernatural. In other words, Nunivakers were subject to internal sanctions rather than external sanctions; most of their transgressions were sins rather than crimes. They had a word meaning "taboo." . . . Here are examples of tabooed acts and their punishment. If a person ate his inogo [magic helper], he would get sick and die. If a person went away from a village feeling angry at any individual in that community, he would turn into a wandering spirit and never return. If he threw seal bones around, there would be a scarcity of seals. In this case, not only he but also the community would suffer; hence taboos were more or less a group concern. This seems to be the basis of public confession, which did not show the usual clear demarcation between social and supernatural but had aspects of both. When some calamity befell the individual or the group, the shaman would call the person or a person to confess in the kazigi his transgressions against the Supernatural. Aside from this, there were no ordeals, trials, or other public consideration of the matter. Divination by scrying was the only kind that the people knew about and no one could remember an instance of its having been used. Note that people were called upon to confess their sins, not their crimes. There was no formal punishment for illegitimacy or adultery. A woman need not confess and was not tried for beating her child or a man for deserting his wife and baby. We should remember here the group's indifference to change of the individual's social status such as marriage, divorce, and adoption. All are parts of their basic attitude toward the social. What we call social and political and conceptualize as superpersonal, they thought about very little and conceptualized only as "the people of the big kazigi" or "the people of Whetstone Village," a collective agglomeration of families, evidently not conceived as an organized unit.

CONTROL BY THE LINEAGE.—The one social unit that passed judgment and meted punishment was the family. Just as the family was the economic unit, so it was the juridical unit. The community did not punish the murderer; the family of the victim did. Members of the victim's generation, for example his brothers, were not normally the ones to avenge the death. The eldest son of the murdered person was taught from childhood that it was his duty to kill the murderer or possibly another man in the murderer's family. Hence the offender felt reasonably safe until the boys of his victim's family were grown. As for others in the community, they feared the murderer and avoided him as much as possible, yet lived and worked with him when necessary. Apparently the suppression of anger and resentment, the continuation of a frustration on the part of the victim's kin were not strong and did no great damage to their personalities because they shifted the burden onto the next generation. They looked forward confidently to the time when the score would be evened. And it was not possible to avoid revenge by any kind of payment to the offended group.

CONTROL BY FORMALIZED PERSONAL RELATIONSHIP.—In no situation not involving the family could one collect damages, for example, for an insult. If a person intentionally or accidentally killed another's dog or seriously damaged his boat, there might be some harsh words exchanged. Or both would complain to a chief or would try to get sympathizers among the old people. Many factors would influence public opinion.

It was stated above that adultery was not punished. A clear statement of the attitudes regarding sexual offenses was not obtained. For an unmarried girl to have intercourse and bear a child was no delict or sin unless it was a case of incest. The incestuous relations were father-daughter, mother-son, uncle-niece, aunt-nephew, brother-sister, probably parallel cousins although this was not so strict. For a man to father a child by any woman other than his wife was a scandal but was not punished in any way. For a woman to run away with a lover was a personal affront to her husband. He might or might not try to get her back. The code of morals did not require that he punish her or the other man in any specific way. This was a personal matter to be settled individually. A woman who had committed adultery might kill the child of such a love affair (this happened within recent years) or claim that it belonged to her husband, or admit its identity and give it away for adoption to anyone, relative or nonrelative, who wanted a child. An illegitimate child suffered very little disfavor. On the whole, the code was elastic.

Other offenses that are common in other groups and must be dealt with by law scarcely existed among these people, for example, theft. The culture made it almost impossible for one to steal. (1) There was no ownership of territory, hence no infringement was possible. A piece of land or a particular spot in a river created no wealth. All the animals and fish that were of most value ranged over considerable territory, whether land or sea, and the people ranged with them. What did produce wealth was the dipnet, the bow and arrow, the harpoon, the amulet, and all of these could be transported. Moreover, they could be protected easily. (2) All personal property was well known to others, besides being marked. A person might find a lost or discarded implement and repair it for his own use, but this would scarcely be called theft. (3) The most important property of the individual and the family was secret and protected by the Supernatural, viz., power songs and other powers. The people, seeing these supernatural powers as the ultimate source of their wealth and prestige, guarded them like early Venetian glassmakers guarding their formulae. (4) Food was constantly redistributed and furthermore attainable for any physically normal person. A man might not always have the choicest food, but he had some kind of food. Since raw materials besides food were given away by the wealthier people, basic economic necessity did not drive the individual to thievery. (5) Finally, there was very strong feeling against theft. A person who would steal was low indeed.

In spite of all these natural safeguards and this attitude, thefts were committed occasionally. Children sometimes raided food caches; children and adults stole driftwood from each other's piles of wood stacked around the coast; one might take the foxes or fish from another's trap. But that was all.

One misdemeanor of which people were always accusing each other, more or less openly and more or less seriously, was lying. They had good reason to do this. Most people's gossip contained a sting of unpleasant truth which one would like to label as false. Moreover, there were genuinely malicious lies. However, in such small communities, each person could be appraised accurately and no one could go too far. Note that there was little need to lie in order to protect oneself. The lies were accusatory, aggressive rather than protective. The only lies that a man was moved to make regarding himself —and these were infrequent—were claims that his grandfather was such and such a wealthy man when actually the relationship was distant, or that he himself had given away many kayaks when he was a young man. These point to the locale of stresses and frustrations in Nunivak life.

Since conduct was regulated so much by formalized interpersonal relationships, let us review them. The serious partnerships, like the lineage and biological family, gave security to the individual. Supposedly, man or woman could always turn to his partner for help, whether that partner was of the same sex or opposite sex. However, the relations between man and man, between woman and woman were strongest. Supposedly, too, in the intimacy of such a relationship, one could express oneself freely without fear that every statement would be ridiculed as so often happened in other situations. The joking partnerships provided release for other suppressed emotions, possibly not for the person who was doing the joking but for some friend or relative whose attitudes he expressed. Also it gave each person an opportunity to show his own wit and cleverness in playing a ticklish game. Finally, since the joking partners presumably belonged to different lineages . . . the relationship provided an occasion when one could make fun openly of a member of another lineage even though he was one's blood relative. Perhaps making fun of a relative provided some satisfaction. People naturally did not state their motivation. It should be remembered that the joking sometimes was given formally as a short song presented in the kazigi. The recipient had to show another set of qualities which Nunivakers esteemed in personal relations: patience, forbearance, good humor.

The social taboos between affinal relatives, between brothers and sisters, and the less stringent taboos between other blood relatives regulated conduct within the household. These taboos required distance and deference between individuals who otherwise might have quarreled very easily and disrupted the household or might have gone to the other extreme and committed incest. The principal taboo in force for all people inside or outside of the household was the name taboo. The various substitutes for real names in themselves established and at the same time gave notice of the degrees of intimacy and formality between people of differing age, kinship, and status.

CONTROL BY UNFORMALIZED RELATIONSHIPS. The unformalized personal relations are of course more difficult to state, yet just as important. There were a few strong, approved motivations which when properly expressed in action became personal qualities that the people esteemed. First, there was a sense, possibly one should call it a sensation, of compatibility and harmony; there was a desire to get along together, to avoid conflict. These required that the individual suppress anger and resentment, that he either suppress desires or else openly recognize them, leave the inhibiting situation and enter into a satisfying situation. This happened in marital separation.

In a positive way, these motivations required that a person be helpful. The man

loaned his tools, the woman helped another woman who was sewing her husband's kayak cover, whether the women were related or not. Also, a person subjugated his individual opinion to the opinion of the group when the latter became manifest. How could all this harmony develop? Responsiveness to others was developed in early childhood and fostered throughout life by the small size of the group and the intimate living arrangements. The face-to-face relationships throughout the year (one person rarely went off alone to hunt or to live) made possible a kind of communication that obviated stated laws and arguments. By bodily attitudes, tone of voice, and other bits of overt behavior, one person communicated to others more than he could say in a speech made in council; and his communication probably would be more honest. The speech might be an affectation, a selfconscious effort to meet cultural standards. On the other hand, the close attention to his work and lack of interest in another person's story on the part of a man merely sitting at work in the kazigi would express not so much an opinion as an attitude. By just such attitudes, the Nunivak community functioned.

SOCIAL INSTITUTIONS AND THEIR CONTROL

The Household. Within the community there were two institutions, i.e., localized associations of people. One was the household which, as we have seen, functioned by means of an interplay of personalities. There was no stated division of labor between the adult women who formed the nucleus of the household. One assumed some authority over the others on the basis of age, wealth, personality, or industry and technical ability. In some cases, two strong personalities had to make a series of adjustments which might bring momentary unhappiness. If they simply could not get along together, one family unit pulled out of the household; or if it had greater claim, from having built the house or from longer residence, it shoved the other out. Rarely did families remain together if they were openly quarreling.

The Kazigi. The other institution, the kazigi, was more formal. This is expectable since it contained more people and many who were not closely related by kinship. The fact that kazigis anciently were named shows that they were more stable, more institutionalized than the households even though their location and membership did change frequently.

The kazigi had many functions. Besides being an eating and sleeping place for the male population, it was the workshop for men and industrial training school for boys. It was the scene for competition in games and craftsmanship, for cooperation in work, in providing sweat baths and holding ceremonials. It was the stage for the shaman showing his powers, for the child making his or her debut, for the old men showing the things handed down from their fathers, for the women displaying their handiwork. Finally, it was the town hall. For its communal functions it had a leader, as we have seen.

A boy went into the kazigi to live when about five years old. What the kazigi may have represented long ago, it is impossible to say. In recent generations it has not in any sense functioned as a society or club. In other words, a person did not belong as to a club. In general, men lived in the kazigi nearest their individual homes. Yet it was observed that when one middle-aged man moved to the opposite end of the village from his kazigi, he continued to use his old one, not the one nearest his new house. According to their statements, people did this from habit, because they felt at home in a certain ceremonial house, were congenial with its inmates. In the same way there was supposedly no rule except proximity that determined which kazigi a new son-in-law should use when he moved into the village.

Within the "clubhouse" the "members" were arranged as follows: Men sat on the floor to work and eat, and they slept on the floor on their individual mats and furs; boys occupied the benches above them. They were grouped according to kinship. An uncle and his adopted nephew were in one part of the

kazigi, two middle-aged brothers in another part, and so on. When the habitual places of members of specific kazigis were ascertained, it was found that the wealthy man was on the right side (as one faced in from the entrance), usually at the center of the right side. (The number of kazigis examined was very small, however.) The rear directly opposite the entrance was the place of honor for guests and recognized chiefs, according to the men's statements. The two front corners near the entrance were occupied by poor people. Under the old system when men actually lived in the kazigi—today most men sleep in their own houses—probably there were never more than twenty adults in any one kazigi, although one old man said there would be as many as thirty in a very large one. In a structure reckoned as large in modern villages there would be twelve to fifteen married men; in a small structure five or six. If a village increased considerably in size, naturally an additional kazigi would be built.

The kazigi was not dichotomized except occasionally for social dances. Then it was divided on the basis of opposite sides of the room, not kinship. The two sides were not named. On such occasion, one group tried to outdo the other in dancing and in distributing gifts. It is noticeable that the kazigi was not divided for religious functions or games. In the same way as one side of the men's house entertained the other, so one kazigi entertained another kazigi in the same village. Then, when the whole village was host to another village, all ceremonial houses cooperated, holding their feasts and public performances in the largest one.

The Shaman-doctor Profession. There was another group in the community which, although unorganized, functioned as a closed group, namely the shamans. Shamans had powers, knew secrets that no layman knew. Besides their powers of flight, miraculous healing of wounds, and communication with the Supernatural, they had the ability to cure everyday ailments by methods that the layman never used. Although an ordinary person might occasionally see the same kind of spirits that the shaman saw, the latter had many more spirit helpers than the layman. He knew more songs and how to carve a greater variety of masks. In this situation it is not surprising that the people often feared the angakok. They often accused him of witchcraft whereas they rarely accused a layman. They hated him and would finally attempt to kill him. It is interesting that here is the only situation in which the community as a whole or even a large part of it would decide that an individual should be eliminated, would plot and carry out his murder. On the other hand, if a shaman did not lose many patients and became famous for his magical powers, the village would be proud of him. Even so, the shaman was a lonely person, apart from the remainder of the community, associating with his immediate family and with his helper, who was apparently a novice. To what extent did shamans work together? This is a difficult question to answer. It seems certain that there was collaboration, at least tacitly so far as they suspected but did not reveal each other's secrets. This, too, justifies the statement that shamans formed a closed group.

ECONOMIC RELATIONSHIPS AND CONTROL

Some aspects of Nunivak economics have little to do with community organization. Although they have been partially described in this section, more must be said. The first is ownership.

Concept of Ownership. Each person— man, woman, or child—owned his clothing, tools, dishes, ornaments, amulets. People borrowed each other's things freely, particularly within the household, but rights of ownership were recognized. In theory a woman could dispose of her handiwork as she pleased. Actually, in the old days there was no opportunity for this. In a well-adjusted family, husband and wife would discuss the disposition of their wealth, contributing ideas just as they had contributed labor in accumulating and preserving that

wealth. Today women have developed an industry that is entirely their own: coiled basketry. Although some women take the baskets directly to the traders and dicker for the goods that they want in exchange, many women still allow their husbands to do the trading.

Complete ownership by a child was recognized if the child had found or made the object himself. He could dispose of it entirely as he pleased, at least in most families. In some families a domineering parent gave the children very little freedom.

Family ownership or joint ownership— it is impossible to distinguish between them —appeared especially in regard to umiaks (or today, launches). Father and sons or several brothers, each a householder, would build a large boat and operate it together. There was no known instance of unrelated men owning a boat jointly.

Aside from boats, houses, and tools, the bulk of wealth and also the most necessary wealth, viz., food and raw materials, was owned by the biological family. An indication of attitudes toward family communal ownership is given by the rules of inheritance. After a death, neither the deceased's nor his family's goods were burnt or otherwise destroyed. All the personal possessions of the young son or daughter of a wealthy couple might be deposited on the grave, plus half the goods of the family. But, in the case of a mature person leaving small children to be cared for, Nunivak Eskimos never deposited all of the deceased's personal possessions, let alone those of the family. The attitude was that the surviving spouse or the eldest son would keep the things for the use of the children. If the sons and daughters were grown, possessions were divided among them. The sons received their father's tools, some of his hunting and fishing implements, his umiak. His kayak might or might not be left on the grave. This was at the discretion of the survivors. There was little that the daughters could receive for themselves. However, if a son-in-law had become a full member of the household, he might even have prior claim over the sons, provided he remained in the household and cared for his mother-in-law, as often happened. A man's brothers might receive some things. There seem to have been no rules, though, to determine just what or how much they would be given. After the death of a mature woman, the daughters continued to use her baskets, buckets and other things that might be called household goods, and even some of her ornaments, according to one informant. Since people stressed the great amount of goods which *some* families put in the grave of a beloved person, one can surmise that most people were not so lavish. A poor family, knowing how difficult it is to acquire good kayaks, could not afford to leave its only decent kayak on a grave. In such matters the Nunivakers were realistic.

Mobility of Wealth. The absence of private ownership of territory was conducive to mobility of population, to relatively little attachment to locality. The culture by a variety of means provided also a mobility of wealth. The constant redistribution of wealth had a leveling effect upon economic status . . . for any family. It also prevented the destitution of many people or permanent destitution. The means of distributing wealth have been cited in various connections. Here they will be merely summarized. (1) The most obvious was the distribution of goods in connection with ceremonial. (2) Day by day well-to-do families fed orphans and old people who had outlived their own children, in return for which the poor people did what work they could. Also, when a person was cutting and hanging up his fish to dry or putting it in pits, if anyone came saying that he needed fish, he would be given two or three for immediate use. One must never refuse a request for food. On the other hand one must not ask for it too often. (3) Every person was expected to work. Thus every able-bodied person was a primary and largely independent producer of wealth. As long as each man could go out and create his own wealth, it could not be concentrated in the possession of a few. (4) Women and children could own goods as well as men. (5)

Borrowing without payment of interest and barter without any medium of exchange provided the family with materials or tools which it might need in conjunction with those it already had, in order to create wealth. (6) Helping one's partners and other forms of cooperation served the same ends. (7) Lack of ostentatious destruction of wealth following a death kept the goods in use and in circulation.

Cooperation and Competition. All of this indicates a great deal of cooperation. The cooperation within the family, the household, the kazigi, and the village (diminishing in that order) have been discussed. Another kind of cooperation appeared in sea-mammal hunting. If one man sighted a seal or walrus and threw his harpoon, it was quite all right (with one or two exceptions) for any other men to throw their harpoons in an effort to hit the animal first or to assist in the final kill.

When a person saw one or more live walrus on the rocks in summer, he would run to his boat or to the village to get proper hunting implements and secure help. The first person he encountered, whether man, woman, or child, would be given a large part of any animal killed; some informants said half of the whole carcass. Certainly if this first person were a man capable of helping, he would receive a full one-half. In case the discoverer reached the kazigi without meeting anyone, he would give the half share to the oldest man in the clubhouse at the moment. There were no rules for division of a whale found dead or caught in a net. Nunivak Eskimos seemed to think a whale provided so much meat, blubber, and bone that everyone could have what he wanted.

When a small seal was seen on the ice in spring, the younger men were supposed to let an older hunter go after it first. The seal would then belong to him entirely, although he probably would give away parts of it. In open water in summer (when it was harder to hit seals), there was a free-for-all dash. However, again the older man of two who hit a small seal would be given title to it. A mukluk, on the other hand, would be divided in two, no matter how or where caught. The man who scored the first hit on a mukluk got the full credit for that animal, an important point. He also received all of the hide, intestines, forequarters, and bladder. The second man got the hindquarters. Beyond this, there were no strict rules. Probably a third man would receive the stomach and some of the meat. Usually only two or three cooperated in taking a seal. Actually, cooperation is not the word to describe these activities. Each man was out for himself, anxious to get as much as possible away from the other person. If the first man seemed stingy in allotting parts to the second and third, or if the latter asked for too much, there was resentment and grumbling.

Although there was considerable cooperation in Nunivak society, there were also competition and rivalry. When a wealthy man fed a poor man, this was really neither cooperation nor competition. In the first place, the giver expected labor in return for the gift of food and clothing or for the loan of tools, kayak, or dog team. Perhaps in the latter case he would receive some gift. In order to meet the Nunivak standards of personal behavior, one had to discharge these interpersonal social obligations. Among ourselves, a well-to-do householder feeding a poor man who is out of a job and in return having his garden weeded is analogous to the Nunivak behavior. Possibly one might call the above an instance of cooperation, but it is not ordinarily so labeled. One man is dependent upon the other. He works and he eats at the option of the other.

[All things considered], there seems to have been more competition in these larger, economically more secure villages than in the Arctic villages. People were rated not only as hunters but also as kayak-makers or seamstresses and basketmakers. That they did not keep these ratings indefinitely did not mean that individuals were not competing. Above all, they competed in distribution of goods. So often they used such expressions as these: "He tried to outdo the other chief." "My face got red because I could not give

as much as the others." "They recognized him as their chief because he always caught the most animals and he always had the most to give away at feasts."

If there was any one central point to which all Nunivak society was related, it was the position of the great hunter. [In sociological terminology, he was clearly a charismatic leader.]

CONCLUSIONS

Nunivak Culture as [a Balanced System.] One can see clearly, when surveying the total social culture, why Nunivak society has never become a large cohesive unit. Several tendencies prevented it: (1) the strong individualism in economic matters, including art and craftsmanship, a certain amount of individualism in religion and social relations; (2) the network of interpersonal relationships, especially in the partnerships, which cared for various needs that must be satisfied by some group in other cultures; (3) emotional strength of the biological family once it was well established, the children partly grown (remember, also, that life-crisis observances were conducted by the biological family); (4) religious strength of the lineage, which also had social and legal functions, notably in obtaining revenge for a murder; (5) absence of constant intercourse with other tribes (although there were warfare and trade, the whole island population did not need to be constantly and thoroughly organized to conduct or resist aggression; the natural environment assured the island of comfortable isolation for six months in each year); (6) absence of craft guilds, secret societies with limited membership, or a priesthood, any one of which might have sought to dominate society and in so doing could have organized it; (7) lack of any concept of land ownership, anywhere from individual to tribal ownership. It was not even necessary to have village organization, let alone tribal organization, since the kazigis could function jointly in lieu of duly constituted village authority. The lineages could have taken unto themselves political functions and did show some tendency to do that, but their power—hence their interest?—centered in religious and ceremonial functions.

There are subtle innuendoes of behavior in constant face-to-face relations which in the small community function very well in making known the attitudes, the wishes of members of that community. Of course there were leaders, the "wealthy men," who in most cases could assert and maintain their personal influence over other individuals by those very qualities which had made them wealthy men in the first place. The title was not conferred generation after generation regardless of personal worth. The shaman also had to have the qualifications expected of a shaman, else he could not maintain for many years his place of respect. None of these leaders exercised his rights, he only exerted his influence.

Since in this culture the position of the individual (any individual) was prominent and strong relative to the strength of the community, let us consider, in conclusion, why this has been so. In other words, what did Nunivak culture do for the individual?

There is a related question which we shall consider as part of the same problem because, if we get the answer to the one question, probably we have the answer to the other: How did the Nuniwagamiut obtain their morale? Even though there were some unhappy individuals on Nunivak Island, the emotional tone of the group was enviable. Morale is not easy to achieve, yet these people seem to have had it.

We give below some suggested explanations, not by any means exhaustive. Two known suicides (one of a very old man), one murder, and one attempted murder—not counting infanticide—within the past fifteen years show that Nunivak culture is of course not the perfect culture. At the same time, we must not forget that there are constitutional differences in the Eskimo as in any other race. Although we certainly recognize the individual differences, here we can only generalize what were strong impressions regarding the group, giving some evidence.

(1) Although any hunting-and-fishing people have more basis for fear of physical injury and violent death than agricultural peoples have, these Eskimos were not carrying on the extremely dangerous activities of the whale hunters and bear hunters both north and south of them. Furthermore, their culture provided some reassurance through the belief that people dying a violent death went to a pleasant sky world after death. Other sources of fear were warfare, vengeance for murder, quite rarely a fear of specific spirits, and witchcraft. Some of these might become irrational anxieties, admittedly. They are considered here only as occasions for fear in the presence of "real" danger. These four aspects of the old Nunivak life have now disappeared completely or partially, in descending order as given. Thus life has become more secure in the past fifty years. Not a single case that might be called Arctic hysteria was found in 1939-1940 or was reported from recent years. It may have existed in the far past, but it is this author's guess that it was not common. . . . In the future, as the Nunivak people are called upon to make more drastic adjustments to civilization and the present security drifts away, it is likely that there will be an increase in mild neuroses but not hysteria or serious psychosis.

(2) There was satisfaction of basic physical needs, this being due to a combination of natural and cultural factors. The people had not always abundant but at least adequate food, clothing, shelter, warmth, and illumination, affection in early life, sexual satisfaction in adulthood, care in old age. Recreation is partly physical, partly social. Whichever aspect is considered, recreation here was more than adequate. One inadequacy was the poor development of realistic medical care. Whether there was satisfaction of such psychogenic needs as the need for aggression is not considered here, as sufficient evidence is not at hand.

(3) The age factor needs further consideration by itself. No age group was in such a situation—relative to the whole community—that it suffered fear or anxiety, even though there was thorough recognition of authority of older over younger. There was not the situation found in some Arctic

Eskimo groups in which every aged person comes to be a burden and either commits suicide or is abandoned. On Nunivak a few old people without any vigorous young adults to support them have committed suicide. Other old people (who were already great-grandparents, living on into senility) have been well cared for by their offspring. Informants stress the distribution of fine new goods to the old people in every festival and dance in the old days, and they lamented the lack of care of the aged today.

An anxiety that does occasionally develop today (and may have existed anciently) may be attributed partly to an age factor, but other factors undoubtedly are more important. The youth who at nineteen years of age still does not have a kayak and hunting equipment of his own or who is not even loaned such equipment by an older man may suffer acutely for a while. Here, as in the case of the old person without support, the prime factor is the family with all that it possesses—or lacks—of economic security and personal adjustment. Age disabilities are secondary.

(4) In spite of the strong masculine-feminine segmentation of culture—stronger than in many cultures—shown for example in the difference in the forms of all utensils owned by males and by females, there was not great discrepancy in the status of men and women. Over the contents of the storehouse and the activities of the biological family, the woman had considerable authority besides her personal influence. Even though the various forms of artistic expression permitted her were more limited than in the men's art, she did have means of esthetic satisfaction. [And furthermore, the] woman even had forms of recreation that were all her own. Finally, by identification with the males of her family, she could obtain vicarious satisfaction of social and economic needs. This placed her in a dependent position, of course, and caused some insecurity. However, the social organization was such that some male—partner, brother, or uncle—would take responsibility for a woman and her children if her husband or father would not or could not.

(5) There was enough seasonal variation (but not such severe contrasts as one finds in the Arctic) so that the individual need not suffer monotony.

(6) In addition to the variety provided by the natural environment, the culture offered a variety of satisfactions for individual needs. This was made possible by the free competition in all fields of endeavor. Although a normal Nunivak male wanted to be a good hunter more than anything else, if he were not he still could obtain some satisfaction from his superiority as a carver, or as a shaman, or as a mimic and dancer. Very important is the fact that every individual had access to all occupations of his or her sex and to all forms of social participation. If frustrated in one direction, a personality was not thereby frustrated in all directions but could seek and obtain some compensation. The case material at hand bears this out. Moreover, there was free competition in sexual matters, outside the incest relationships. Spouses were chosen principally on the basis of compatibility, sometimes on the basis of immediate expediency (a hunter had to have a female helper and a woman needed a male provider). They were *not* chosen solely or primarily because of social status or other formal attainment.

Yet for the individual who needed greater than usual self-maximation, the culture did provide opportunities which we shall lump together under the term "social advancement." The young man from a capable, well-to-do family did have a much easier time in the socio-economic competition, but the intelligent industrious son of a poor family could raise himself socially.

(7) There were cultural mechanisms of emotional escape, provided by the Bladder Festival, Messenger Feast, and Exchange Feast. Ready-made means of emotional escape and release often are found in ceremonial.

The serious partnerships too were a means of satisfying not only food and sex needs, through the loaning of wives and through assistance in hunting, trading, and other activities, but also provided a kind of escape from the individual's personality weaknesses and his misfortunes. The serious partnerships strengthened the confidence of the individual by the assumption that a partner would stand by a person no matter what happened.

(8) There was satisfaction of one psychogenic need, particularly in childhood, which is so important that we shall consider it here in spite of our reluctance to discuss individually the psychogenic need. *There was little occasion for a person to feel rejected.* It is true that there was lack of security for a few children from broken families. However, ease of child adoption, the kazigi, and the communal household theoretically provided a place for every individual; and these cultural attempts to handle the situation were actually effective in most cases.

That there was local realization of the importance of "belonging" is shown in some of the folk tales; for example, the poor boy sitting alone by the kazigi entrance (that is, without relatives) and the young brothers in a deserted village are objects of pity by the narrator. In the stories, relief from the intolerable situation is obtained by magical means, leading finally to the profession of shamanism. There is some evidence that in real life this was a way out for the neglected child.

(9) Although individualism was strong, it did not lead to conflict and to an ultimate aloneness of the individual. There were counterbalances of individualism, for example, the necessity for cooperation in a number of situations and the satisfactions derived from cooperation.

(10) The standards, the rules, almost everything that might be called a "system" was in the hands of the people affected; or, if not actually in their control, the various parts of the culture were at least known to them so that there was a feeling of possession and identification in regard to their culture on the part of all the people. The only important part of Nunivak culture which was withheld was shamanism. Even here, however, the ultimate control over the practice of the medicine man rested in the community. There was no situation comparable to the conditions in our culture in which the lives of very many of the people are controlled by forms of social, economic, and political organization which may be completely unknown to those people. They see at most only the effects of such organization and of course do not understand what they see. Not having any control over the bulk of their culture, they cannot possibly manipulate or adjust to satisfy their individual and primary-group needs. But they are sure that someone else is so manipulating it. The results are suspicion, conflict, and either a helpless negativism or else revolt.

Freedom to change and adjust the culture—if not in the large and basic organization of it, then at least in its details—characterizes Eskimo life. Especially around the shores of Bering Sea where life was more secure, where people were not hounded by fears, there was a predominantly pragmatic attitude: the individual was free to try variation in all aspects of living. If his variant worked, if he "got away with it," he certainly had added something to his personal satisfaction and he probably had added something to the culture.

The two preceding descriptions of Eskimo settlements have supplied numerous details of the ways in which those particular groups are organized into effective social units and of how those units function to meet the many nonmaterial needs of human life. In the next four selections certain aspects of social organization will receive some additional attention.

Family life and the manner in which children grow up to become members of society are especially important matters to study in attempting to understand any society, because nearly everything which a person knows or does or thinks is greatly affected by his earliest years. It is then, at first mostly with the mother, then within the intimate circle of the family, that patterns of behavior, and the standards and values which govern later life, are acquired and become firmly fixed in each individual. Certain things are taught to children quite carefully, but far more are "picked up" from observation and habit, so that long before adulthood is reached a child is a thoroughgoing Eskimo in all his attitudes and emotions. Each of us thus becomes—through the socialization process—in our early years forever stamped with the distinctiveness that separates each society from every other.

There has been no one better qualified to write about the Eskimo than Knud Rasmussen. He was born in Greenland in 1879 of a Danish-Eskimo mother and a Danish father, and he grew up speaking Eskimo before he learned to read and write Danish. Proud of his Eskimo ancestry, he turned in his twenties to exploration of the Arctic and the collection of information about Eskimo life—particularly the stories, tales, and myths. With Peter Freuchen he founded a combination trading post and scientific camp in 1910 at Thule, on Cape York. His numerous books and reports, both in Danish and English, form a vast and valuable body of information on the Eskimo. One of his colleagues, William Thalbitzer, sums up his unique qualifications in these words: "The clear mirror of his soul reflects his Eskimo spirit blended with his European mentality."

One of the groups which Rasmussen studied intensively was the Netsilik Eskimo, who live in the Central Arctic, north and west of Hudson Bay. Their location has been given more precisely in Selection 3. Rasmussen in a section not quoted here describes the sexual patterns among the Netsilik. These patterns follow rather closely those discussed by Dr. Lantis for the Nunivak Islanders. Indeed, the discussion which follows is little more than a summary of facts given previously about Eskimo family life, though for a different Eskimo group.

• 13 • The Family Among the Netsilik Eskimo
KNUD RASMUSSEN

Man and wife live together like good comrades. Although the wife has been bought, acquired for a sledge, a kayak, or perhaps a piece of rusty iron, she is by no means treated as a chattel that has no right to any consideration. In theory, no doubt the husband is lord and master over her and never need ask, as among all primitive peoples. He can do as he likes with his woman. But despite the fact that this is the general and time-honoured view there is no sign of subjec-

tion. On the contrary, woman's behavior in the home is very self-assertive, and she is not only lively and loud-spoken but has considerable authority in both her early and her late years.

The only place where woman's lack of her rights seemed to me to be more manifest among Eskimos is in the Thule District in North Greenland. There in earlier times, that is to say before the arrival of Christianity, it was never considered to be good form

[Adapted from "The Netsilik Eskimos: Social Life and Spiritual Culture," *Report of the Fifth Thule Expedition, 1921-24*, Vol. 8, No. 1-2, Copenhagen, 1931. Pp. 190-195. Used by permission.]

for a woman to speak to a man without being spoken to; if visitors arrived she never addressed them, took no part in the general conversation, and on the whole did nothing except what her husband bade her do. This was the [prevailing] custom among the Polar Eskimos; but as soon as one had crossed Melville Bay and moved down toward the Upernivik District there was quite another tone; there the women were noisy and very unembarrassed, freely took part in the conversation around about and often in fact led the talk, always with a very keen sense of humor. There was similar freedom among the Netsilingmiut. The women were quite unconstrained and with their uncontrolled humor often appeared to dominate the company.

During months of intercourse with various families in snow huts and tents I made the observation that really there was not much difference in the tone between these so-called primitive housemates and man and wife in modern wedlock. It was positiveness, and an aptitude for a somewhat childish cavilling, that gave rise to squabbling; as a rule the causes were quite casual ones and, to the outsider not only trifling but ridiculous too. While the quarrelling went on the woman's brain always seemed to work more quickly than the man's, and her sallies would fall with such ready wit that they either left the husband entirely speechless or compelled him to seek refuge in the law of the strongest. I have seen some husbands in excitement or uncontrollable anger give their wives such a "clout" that for days she has had to go about with a florid black eye.

Children are treated well and affectionately, and in the event of food being scarce the parents willingly sacrifice themselves for their benefit; for to them it is quite natural that they themselves should starve if only the little ones have something to eat. Adoptive children, bought for a mere trifle, receive the same treatment and upbringing as their own children. The neglected, cowed and ragged orphans that once were a common type among the old Eskimos in Greenland are an unknown feature here.

All work has a natural distribution, roughly characterized by the fact that it is the man who procures food while the woman does all the house work. Her contribution to the upkeep of the home is set at a high value, and a clever seamstress enjoys genuine esteem. The woman has not only her special duties but also her rights; in her marriage she has her own property, her particular possessions being recognized as the lamps, pots . . . ulo, sewing needles, meat trays of wood . . . water containers . . . and the large horn ladles for boiled meat and soup, almost always of musk-ox horn. She brings all these things into the marriage as her trousseau and retains them in the event of a separation. To us these possessions may seem trivial; but as showing how highly they are valued by themselves, and that the most necessary household utensils cannot always be so easily procured, I might mention that Itqilik's wife Unalerssuaq, who had no soapstone cooking pot in her marriage outfit, bought one and paid for it—of course with her husband's approval—with a newly-born child. Naturally, a soapstone pot is not so high-priced if the family is in the vicinity of one of the places where soapstone is to be had, so that this particular bargain may be explained by the fact that the Itquilik family was right up at Arvertoq (Bellot Strait), and there it was impossible to get any of this material.

The Netsilik woman receives such a sober upbringing and spends her life under such hard conditions that as a rule she has no eye for ornament, not even beads; her sole luxury is a kind of sheath of wood or walrus ivory in which she can protect her hair. It . . . consists of two hollowed-out pieces which can take the braids and are tied on with strips of caribou skin. In the case of a young childless woman the strips must be put on so that white ones alternate with dark ones, but if a woman has nothing but dark strips round her "hair sticks" it means that she has a son.

Divorce is common as long as there are no children, and there are women who go through seven or eight trial marriages before they finally settle down.

Their pleasure in their offspring is great, and children always unite parents closely. If they cannot beget children a little adoptive child usually has the same effect and influence. Adoptive children are always bought, and the price paid for them varies greatly, although it is always high. Eqatlijoq for instance had bought her adoptive son for a soapstone cooking pot and a kayak, both very precious objects. They are usually bought when newly born, the reason being, of course, that a mother who does not intend to rear her child does not want the trouble of nursing it, especially as this also would mean that her next child would be so much the later in coming.

Most young men and women are "engaged" before they are born, which means that the parents agree that their children are to have each other. If the parents of an engaged couple live so far apart that they rarely or never see each other, the natural thing is that when they grow up they enter into a temporary marriage with another. As far as the woman is concerned this happens at a very tender age, thirteen to fifteen. One young man, Angutisugssuk, who lived in King William's Land, called a man right up at Repulse Bay his father-in-law. Angutisugssuk was then twenty years old and unmarried, because his mother-in-law had not yet given birth to his "intended". And so for the time being he was "second husband" in the house of Tarajorqaoq.

Actually the notion of illegitimate children seems unknown. At any rate I came across no case among the Netsilingmiut. The system seems to be that the woman, as soon as she is pregnant, stays with the man who is the father of the child. On the other hand there must be cases of children being born out of wedlock, for they know the term for this. . . . There seems to be no feeling of shame of having children out of wedlock, or at any rate I was unable to ascertain any. Among other Eskimos it is no unusual custom that such children are killed—it was once common in Greenland.

The procuring of abortion for the purpose of avoiding childbirth does not take place.

Polygamy is known, but of course it cannot be general owing to the great inferiority of women as to number. If a man has more than one wife it is consequently always a sign of good standing and especial skill as a hunter. Though jealousy is no unknown feeling, concubines usually get on well together. Polyandry is also practiced, it being no rare occurrence for a woman to have two husbands. A grown man is a helpless being if he has no woman to make his clothes, and so it will happen that a husband will call a good comrade who is alone to share his wife with him. It is seldom, however, that these marriages run smoothly, especially if the men are young, for it very often ends in one of them being killed. Naturally, a wife can never ask a good friend to come in as a partner in her marriage; that is a right that exclusively belongs to the husband.

The Caribou Eskimo are one of the few remaining inland groups. They live on the Barren Grounds west of Hudson Bay. At the present time they are in danger of dying out, because the herds of caribou, on which they have depended for food and clothing, are seriously depleted. This is largely due to the introduction of firearms and the resulting overhunting. A vivid picture of their life today is given in Farley Mowatt's *People of the Deer*. In the thirty years since Birket-Smith's researches, many changes have taken place.

To most of the Caribou Eskimo, the salt water is and always will be something strange. They are thus unlike all other Eskimo groups, spending all or nearly all of the year away from the sea and its resources for food and clothing. Here we have a few details of the way in which their children pass their time between the more serious tasks of learning adult occupations.

• 14 • Childhood Among the Caribou Eskimo

KAJ BIRKET-SMITH

One cannot say that there is a lack of *purposeful* education among the Caribou Eskimos, as the parents little by little teach their children what they think is right. It might rather be said that there is a want of *systematic* education, but I am not sure even of that, for the necessary manual accomplishments and moral principles, however primitive they may be, are gradually impressed upon the children. It is true that one does not notice Eskimo upbringing much. No parent will ever beat his child.

The children are allowed to do practically as they like; but on the whole they are astonishingly obedient and well brought up. The hare is the "bogey man" of the Eskimo children. "Look out, the hare is coming!" is the standing cry for frightening children into being good. If this does not work, the parents give it up. Even when there is really something at stake they do not take more forcible measures. I remember the days when we starved together with the Eskimos on lower Kazan River. The only game to be had were ptarmigan and owing to lack of ammunition, they had to be knocked over by stones or shot with the bow and arrow. Our already slender chances on these occasions were constantly spoiled by a four-year-old boy who insisted upon joining in the hunt and who always scared the birds away; but no one forbade him to go with us.

Children are looked upon as being particularly exposed to the influence of evil powers. For this reason our collection only includes one child's dress, and even then it is new; nothing would persuade any parent

to sell clothing which their children had worn. They were even reluctant to part with urine scrapers. Among the Padlimiut on Sentry Island it was only with great difficulty that I was allowed to photograph the children. In other places this gave no trouble; but in some of these cases it was because no one suspected what a camera was. Many children, boys at any rate, are richly decorated with amulets. If a child dies while an infant, it is necessary that the next one to be born in the family be made unrecognisable to the evil spirits; it must, at any rate among the Qaernermiut, have a special dress.

Many children's games are a mimicry of the life and doings of the grown-ups. On Sentry Island, high up, there was a number of stone settings which represented kayaks. They belong to an earlier period, whereas close to the Harvaqtormiut camp Nahiktartorvik, at lower Kazan River, there are two stone settings from recent times; they represent houses, or rather platforms, on which the little girls play "housekeeping".

A number of toys are copies of the possessions of the adults.

Proper toys are not lacking either. The girls have dolls. . . . Two dolls from the Padlimiut, south of Hikoligjuaq, are of caribou skin and represent a man and a woman in their under dress . . . the faces are not indicated on either of them.

A common toy is the *buzz*. . . . A specimen from the Padlimiut, Hikoligjuaq, consists of a circular disc of unhaired caribou skin with a diameter of 6 cm and two small holes in the middle. . . . A sinew-cord runs

[Adapted from "The Caribou Eskimos: Material and Social Life and Their Cultural Position," *Report of the Fifth Thule Expedition, 1921-24,* Vol. 5, Copenhagen, 1929. Pp. 288-292. Used by permission.]

through both holes and forms a small loop, whilst the two free ends are furnished with two small strips of hairy sealskin. The total length of the cord is 60 cm. By holding the cord at both ends and first swinging the disc a few times round so that the cord becomes twisted, the disc can be made to rotate rapidly with a buzzing sound by alternately bringing the hands closer together and further away from each other. From the regions west of Hudson Bay Boas figures a buzz of bone or gristle.

The wind-wheel . . . consists of a flat piece of wood pointed at both ends, the edges bevelled off at opposite sides like a very crude propeller. In the centre is a hole for the handle. When this toy is moved against the wind the wings revolve.

The bull-roarer . . . is also known. . . . A pop-gun . . . consists of a small tube, for instance a bird bone, through which the boys send a ball of chewed lichen by means of a rod. [Children also play with whistles.] The bones in the head of the trout are also used as a kind of toy; according to their shape they are given various names such as "bear paw", "owl", etc.

Many games require no particular toy or plaything. "Catch" is commonly played, and in the light summer evenings the camp resounds with, "you are on". Similar games are . . . [one] in which some are "caribou" and others "wolves" who pursue them.

Hide-and-seek is often played. It is called . . . by the same name as is also a game which is very like "hunt the slipper". In winter they play . . . gliding down a slope on a caribou skin. . . . [Another] game . . . consists in several—always little girls, I believe—swinging round until they become dizzy.

[In another game] two girls stand face to face, let their knees go quite slack and then bob quickly up and down by the ankles without lifting the toes from the ground; at the same time they jabber a rigmarole at incredible speed.

Another game for girls is . . . hopping with bent knees alternately on the right and the left leg, almost like Russians do. Young girls amuse themselves sometimes by "playing," i.e., flipping the finger-nails against the upper teeth, commencing with the little finger; they are astonishingly adept at producing various tones in this manner.

At the close of childhood there are no puberty ceremonies in the proper sense. The most marked is the change for the young girl who, at her first menstruation, assumes the long frock-hood. She must then eat with a man who is under taboo . . . for instance owing to a death, whereby his taboo is removed. . . . Otherwise only shamans may eat with menstruating women, and therefore at each period a woman must cook her food in a separate pot. She must not eat raw or rotten meat, and, the first time she menstruates after a birth, she must not eat the head of any animal.

Boys are regarded as grown up when they begin to really take an active part in the hunt. The first time a boy kills a caribou, it must be cut up in the house, which is otherwise taboo; the skin must be presented to a man and the meat must be eaten by everyone in the settlement except women and small children. When he has caught his first seal, all the men and women in the settlement must make a cut in the skin of its head. No woman may touch the blood, but the meat must be cooked and eaten by each sex separately, but with the usual exclusion of women with infant children. The heart must be eaten in the boy's own tent.

The fact that the next selection comes from a scholarly journal devoted to criminology reflects the widespread interest that exists in the ways in which nonliterate peoples achieve the controls for which we have elaborate systems of laws, police, courts, and prisons. Although at first glance the system used by the Eskimo appears totally unlike ours, it is in reality similar. Our legal system is a formal expression of ancient traditional ways by which society protects its members against the excesses of individuals or minorities. Eskimo society, unlike our own, is composed of such small groups that face-to-face discussion and settlement of difficulties can usually take the place of more formalized techniques of control. Even though Eskimo "law" is unwritten, and is based on very different attitudes and values from our laws, it is nonetheless binding in the circumstances to which it applies. Many of the things of which Dr. Hoebel writes have been mentioned in previous selections, but are here brought together in terms of the Eskimo in general rather than of certain groups.

• 15 • Social Controls

E. ADAMSON HOEBEL

LEGAL HOMICIDE

Homicide is not a legal absolute. The Eskimos, for example, recognized several forms of homicide as legally acceptable which our law defines as criminal murder.

Infanticide, invalidicide, senilicide and suicide are all forms of homicide accepted by Eskimo society. They are all, in whole or in part, responses to the basic principle of Eskimo society that only those may survive who are able (or potentially able) to contribute actively to the subsistence economy of the community.

An infant is only potentially productive. It is up to each family to decide for itself whether its present resources are sufficient to nourish the infant through its non-productive years. There will be no social blame if a negative decision is reached.

Children subsist at their mothers' breasts for two to four years at least, and frequently much longer. The need for mobility and the unceasing effort required by woman's work make it difficult, if not impossible, for the mother to nurse more than one child at a time. Surplus children are subject to disposal. This is effected by offering the child for adoption, and if there are no takers, by infanticide. Childless couples are eager to adopt in order to have a back-log against old age. In western Alaska survivors to make

memorial offerings are desirable. An abandoned child may be adopted without further ado. Children offered for adoption are exchanged for a gift.

Female children are the most frequent victims of infanticide because of two discriminating factors. (1) The male is the primary food-getter. (2) The tendency towards patrilocal residence means that the adult female will on marriage more often be lost to her parents than will be a male child. Hence, the baby girl is a poorer risk as an investment in old age security. The selective effect on the population is to be seen in the data brought together by Weyer. In fourteen Eskimo groups outside of East and South Greenland (where infanticide is rare) the ratio of girls to boys among children under ten years of age ranges from forty-two to ninety-two girls to each hundred boys. Among adults the proportions are reversed. So high is occupational mortality among men, that in twenty Eskimo groups only three had fewer women than men, while in half the groups there were more than one hundred and ten women to a hundred men. Were it not for infanticide there would be one and a half times as many adult females as there are males in the average Eskimo community.

Senilicide and invalidicide are rooted in the same conditions as infanticide. Though

[Adapted from "Law-ways of the Primitive Eskimos," *Journal of the American Institute of Criminal Law and Criminology*, Vol. 31, Chicago, 1940-41. Pp. 670-682. Used by permission.]

others may decide that the day of an aged one is done, the request for death comes usually from the old person. The act must be performed by a relative, else it is apt to be considered murder.

Stabbing, hanging, strangulation, blocking up in a snow house to freeze and starve, and abandonment in the open are all used by various Eskimos.

Though infanticide is casually accepted, according to reports on the Eskimos, senilicide gives rise to greater emotional conflict. Not infrequently the aged one has to insist on his "right" to be killed.

Suicide by the senile, the invalided, and hunters faced by drowning in a storm, is also wide-spread.

All these forms of homicide are legal in the Eskimo's point of view—*acceptable homicide*—because the strain upon the community well-being is eased through the act. No external tension results since there is no status struggle involved. Neither the individual nor the kinship group is challenged by outgroup forces. The loss of the person can be gracefully accepted without need for retaliation or legal satisfaction. To the individual the transition from death to after-life is made easy in the belief that all who die violently, as well as the mother lost in child-birth, are transported directly to the best of the Eskimo heavens.

Cannibalism induced by starvation is legally acceptable. Eskimo anthropophagy is non-epicurean and non-religious. To the Eskimo, it is a necessary evil, regrettable, but valuable.

"Many people have eaten human flesh," admitted a native of King William Island, "but never from any desire for it, only to save their lives, and that after so much suffering that in many cases they were not sensible of what they did."

Cannibalism, therefore, is an emergency measure, socially recognized, acceptable and regrettable.

HOMICIDE AND SEXUAL COMPETITION

. . . The arena of sex is the primary breeding ground for trouble and law. Rasmussen found that all of the adult males in the fifteen Musk Ox Eskimo families had been involved in murder, either as principals or as accessories; furthermore, "the motive was invariably some quarrel about a woman."

Murder springs from other motives as well. Among the Alaskan Eskimos on the West coast, Nelson reported that murder for economic gain was so regular that among the Malemute "only relatives or formal friends dared to hunt together" for fear one hunting partner might slay the other. Jenness reports trivial insults as the cause of several Copper Eskimo murders, as one woman stabbing another in the stomach because of a taunt of sterility (this is the sole reported instance of murder done by a female among the twenty-seven specific cases found in the literature), or a man disemboweling another to demonstrate the falsehood in the victim's assertion that the slayer did not know how to make a sharp knife.

Murder results quite regularly in the murderer taking over the widow and children of the victim. In many instances the desire to acquire the woman is the cause of the murder, but where this is not the motive, a social principle requiring provision for the bereaved family places the responsibility upon the murderer.

Blood revenge executed by kinsmen of a murdered party is expected among all Eskimos (so far as the data go), save the Copper, Iglulik, and East Greenlanders, among whom it is optional according to the "strength" of the surviving kinsmen. This, coupled with the protectorate principle means, as Birket-Smith notes, that a man will raise as his own son, the son of his victim, a boy who, when he grows to manhood, may be the one to exact blood vengeance upon his foster-father.

The execution of blood revenge may be immediate or long postponed. In the latter case, a Central Eskimo murderer may live on amicable terms with the people who must take vengeance on him, until one day, perhaps after years, he is suddenly stabbed or shot in the back; or if the revenge-takers wish to be more sporting, he is challenged to a wrestling match, to suffer death if he loses, and reputedly, to have the privilege of killing another of the victim's family if he wins.

Among all Eskimos except West Greenland, where the avenger announced the offense for which the victim was about to die, revenge is exacted by stealth while the murderer is busily engaged. H. König calls attention to the fact that the old Scandinavian law demanded the verbal pronouncement of the death warrant before the slaying of an outlaw and suggests that the practice was transmitted by them to the Greenland Eskimos of this locale.

CRIMINAL HOMICIDE

A killer who kills several persons at once may enhance, not injure, his prestige in the community. Not so, the homicidal recidivist. He becomes a social menace, liable at any time to strike down another victim. As a general menace, he becomes a public enemy. As a public enemy, he becomes the object of public action. The action is legal execution.

The single murder is a private wrong redressed by the kinsmen of the victim. Repeated murder becomes a public crime punishable by death at the hands of an agent of the community.

[Such punishment exists] among all the Eskimos reported on, save the East Greenlanders. The important element is that the executioner, who undertakes the slaying, seeks and obtains the community approval for his act of riddance. When such approval is obtained no blood revenge may be taken on the executioner, for his act is not murder. It is the commission of a public sentence, for and in the name of the people, and the responsibility is theirs. Furthermore, revenge is precluded for the simple reason that unanimous consent involves the consent of the murderer's relatives, if any be in the community.

As a double safe-guard against blood revenge on the executioner, close kinsmen may be called upon to carry out the community will. In 1921, for instance, the headman of the Arviligjuarmiut was deputed by his fifty-four co-villagers to execute his own brother, who occasionally went berserk, having killed one man and wounded others in his fits. The headman went reluctantly to his brother and explaining his position, asked how he chose to die, by steel, thong, or shot. The brother chose the latter, and was killed on the spot.

At Point Barrow, on the north Alaskan coast, a brother and an uncle shot and killed their kinsman who had murdered ten to twelve victims whom he had ambushed on his march from Herschel Island to the Point. The man had been publicly whipped by the whaling captains at Herschel on injunction of the local missionary, for the reason that he had exposed a baby to die. All the Eskimos had reacted with disgust to such unheard-of punishment, for to their mind, "to whip a man does not cure him." But even so, the man had become a homicidal lunatic to be removed.

It is generally reported that *de facto* murder is not essential in establishing one as a public enemy. Threats and abuse of others may lead to the same end. The obnoxious person is first ostracized, then liquidated if he continues his bothersome behavior.

CRIMINAL SORCERY AND PERFIDY

Sorcery and chronic lying are placed in the same category as homicidal recidivism. Because the sorcerer is a killer, and because the perfidious man is thought to be a public danger, both are liable to execution at the public command. Outside of West Greenland, a sorcerer may be killed by the relatives of a victim of sorcery, when a shaman names the sorcerer as guilty.

In West Greenland the natives treat all sorcery as an offense against the group punishable by death at the hands of the group.

The execution of liars is reported from Greenland to Alaska, but no actual cases are given. Nor is the reason for such drastic action given.

EVIDENCE

In the small Eskimo community the question of evidence in disputes does not raise a great problem; sufficient direct information seems usually to be at hand. When fact is not known, however, resort may be had to divination, but apparently only when an element of sin enters into the offense, or as among the Copper Eskimos, at least, when a death through sorcery has occurred. Divination is by weighing. A thong is looped around the head of a reclining person, or a bundled coat, or even the diviner's own foot. When the proper spirit has entered the object, the questions may be put. As it is hard or easy to lift, the answer is "yes" and "no". In Nunivak, according to Dr. Lantis, divination is had by peering into still water which has been poured into the abdominal cavity of a dressed animal. The image of the guilty person may be seen.

REGULATED COMBAT

Homicidal dispute, though prevalent, is made less frequent in many Eskimo groups by recourse to regulated combat-wrestling, buffeting, and butting. Buffeting is found among the central tribes along the Arctic Circle from Hudson Bay to Bering Straits. Wrestling occurs in Siberia, Alaska, Baffin Land and Northwest Greenland. Head-butting as a feature of the song duel occurs in West and East Greenland. All three forms are a type of wager by battle.

In buffeting, the opponents face each other, alternately delivering straight-armed blows on the side of the head, until one is felled and thereby vanquished. Butting accompanies the singing in the song duel in Greenland. The singer, if so inclined, butts his opponent with his forehead while delivering his exculpation. The opponent moves his head forward to meet the blow. He who is upset is derided by the onlookers and comes out badly in the singing. As juridical forms, boxing and butting are more regulated than feudistic homicide, since the contests are announced and occur on festive occasions when they are looked upon as a

sort of sport performance before the assembled community. Stealth, cunning and ambush are not part of such contests; the strongest wins by pitted strength. The object to the boxing and butting contests is not annihilation, but subjection. Nor is there any concern with basic justice.

Boxing and butting are apparently available as means of settling all disputes except homicide.

Wrestling serves much the same function, though it may have a more deadly outcome in Baffin Land and Labrador, where the loser may be slain by the victor. The wrestling duel is occasionally used as the means through which blood revenge may be carried out. It is more sporting, however, for Boas tells us that if the murderer wins, he may slay yet another of his victim's kinsmen.

JURIDICAL SONG CONTESTS

Deserving of fame are the *nith* songs of the eastern and western Eskimos. Elevating the duel to a higher plane, the weapons used are words—"little, sharp words, like the wooden splinters which I hack off with my ax."

Song duels are used to work off grudges and disputes of all orders, save murder. An East Greenlander, however, may seek his satisfaction for the murder of a relative if he is too physically weak to gain his end, or if he is so skilled in singing as to feel certain of victory. Since East Greenlanders get so engrossed in the mere artistry of the singing as to forget the cause of the grudge, this is understandable. There, singing prowess equals or outranks the gross physical.

Among the East Greenlanders song duels may be carried on for years, just for the fun of it. But elsewhere, grudge contests are usually finished in a single season. Traditional songs are used, but special compositions are created for each occasion to ridicule the opponent and capitalize his vulnerable foibles and frailties.

In West Greenland, the singer has the vocal backing of his household. In preparing for the contest he sings his songs until all his household knows them perfectly. When the actual contest is in full swing, his householders reinforce' his words in chorus. In spite of the nastiness of the insults hurled, it is good form for neither party to show anger or passion. And it is expected that the participants will remain the best of friends thereafter. The West Greenlanders, in contrast to the men of the East Coast, use self-deprecation, "the self-irony which is so significant in the Eskimo character," though at the same time the opponent is lashed with weighty accusations and sneering references.

Among the Polar Eskimo the song duel is also used, but without the head butting and buffeting.

Among the Iglulik Eskimos, north of Hudson Bay, contest singing is also an important art. Among these people, anyone who would be considered an effective singer must have a "song cousin." This is an institution built upon the basis of "formal friendship," a comradeship bond which was widespread among the aborigines of the western hemisphere. Song cousins try to out-do each other in all things, exchanging costly gifts and their wives whenever they meet. Each delights to compete with the other in the beauty of his songs as such, or in the skillful composition and delivery of metrical abuse. When song cousins expose each other, it is for fun, and is done in a light-hearted humorous manner. When a man takes up a grudge song-duel, however, the tenor of the songs is different. Though the cast of the songs is humorous, for effect, insolence, derision, and the pictured ludicrousness of the opponents are the stuff they are made of. As in Greenland, the one who can win the audience, or silence his opponent, is victor, but in any event, winner and loser are expected to be reconciled, and they exchange presents as a token of settlement.

Further inland, among the Caribou Eskimos, who are located at the very center of the whole Eskimo territory, the song duel is also found. . . . The occurrence of the song duel complex all down the west coast of Alaska and even out into the Aleutian Islands shows how basic (and possibly, ancient) a form it is among the Eskimo.

The song duels are juridical instruments insofar as they do serve to settle disputes and restore normal relations between estranged members of the community, and insofar as one of the contestants receives a "judgment" in his favor. But like the medieval wager of battle the judgment bears no relation to the rightness or wrongness of the original actions which give rise to the dispute. There is no attempt to mete justice according to rights and privileges defined by a substantive law. It is sufficient that the litigants (contestants) feel relieved—the complaint laid to rest—a psychological satisfaction attained; this is justice sufficient unto the needs of Eskimo society as the Eskimos conceive it.

Unlike wager of battle, however, there is no ordeal element in the song duel. Supernatural forces do not operate to enhance the prowess of the singer who has "right" on his side. Let it be remembered that "right" is immaterial to the singing or its outcome (though the singer who can pile up scurrilous accusations of more or less truth against his opponent has an advantage in fact). As the court-room joust may become a sporting game between sparring attorneys-at-law, so the juridical song contest is above all things a contest in which pleasurable delight is richly served, so richly that the dispute-settlement function is nearly forgotten. And in the forgetting the original end is the better served.

In these ways, Eskimo society, without government, courts, constables, or written law, maintains its social equilibrium, channelling human behavior according to its own accepted standards, buttressing the control dikes along the channels with primitive legal mechanisms, or their equivalents.

The Supernatural World

>>

Every human being has felt, at least occasionally, that the world in which he finds himself is tremendously large, powerful, and uncontrollable, and a natural result of such feelings is the conclusion that the world is dominated by forces vastly greater than those of mankind. Ideas about the nature of the world vary from group to group but almost always include many beliefs concerning the mysterious and inexplicable aspects of life, the things that are "beyond nature" in the sense that they lie entirely outside the everyday cause-and-effect world in which man can control and predict. The term "religion" is often applied to these beliefs and to the practices that go with them, but it is misleading if it is taken to mean what "religion" happens to consist of in our society. For the Eskimo, religion includes a body of beliefs (or myths) concerning the origin of certain features of the natural world, and a large number of practices and techniques by which man maintains a proper relationship with the supernatural forces governing the world. It is not something that is of interest only on Sunday, and it does not include the idea of "worship." Just what Eskimo religion does consist of will be made clear in the next selection, which explains how drastically the Eskimo's view of religion differs from ours. Moreover, this selection will help to make clear the fact that the realm of the sacred, as we shall discuss it later, includes much more than religion in any defensible sense of the latter term.

This selection should be read with the realization that many aspects of the religious life of the Eskimo have already been dealt with in the earlier selections. In the account of the Ammassalik, the higher status of the shaman (angakok) is shown on pages 63 and 71; his answer to a woman's sterility on page 68, and his initiation, conduct of the seance, and the pay received on page 70. The shaman receives much attention in the article on the Nunivakers.

Burial customs and beliefs about the dead have been discussed in Selections 9, 11, 12, and 15. Information on curing the sick has been presented also in Selections 11 and 12. Views on the supernatural world are described by Mirsky and Lantis; information about evil spirits has been presented in Selections 12 and 14; communal confessions are described in Selections 11 and 12; amulets will be discussed in detail in Selection 17. Such information, piecemeal though it may be, will give the passage which follows greater significance.

· 16 · The Religion of the Eskimo
MARGARET LANTIS

SHAMANISM

Becoming a Shaman. At Pt. Hope on the northwest coast of Alaska, Umigluk when a young man and a fast runner was sent on a long errand. On the way he heard paddles dipping slowly in water, a boat came circling down as from the moon and stopped by him. A shaman who had died some time before stood up in the boat and asked about his family. Umigluk replied that they were fine. The man sank down and another rose, wearing fine clothes, and mittens with pieces of metal on them. He seemed to have one big eye instead of two. He danced, his mittens rattling. A white ermine, then a brown ermine appeared, and one chased the other around the gunwale, which entertained Umigluk. The shaman spirit reappeared and spoke of the broken tabus that had caused his death. Then the boat disappeared and Umigluk continued on his way.

Although by the time he reached home he had forgotten the vision, during the next four days Umigluk did strange things that he could not account for. He was "crazy" (delirious?) but gradually recovered. Thereafter, the spirit in the fancy clothing took possession of Umigluk when he drummed and went into a trance in the men's ceremonial house. In this state, he learned eight songs and the spirit's name, and with this assistance became a great shaman.

There was always the belief that the novice shaman dies or nearly dies and recovers and always the idea of spiritual appointment even though the appointment was secured differently. Eastern and Western Eskimo shamans differed in that the former deliberately sought power through solitude, concentration, and physical self-mortification, while the latter were un-selfconscious—although equally suggestible—in undergoing the same conditions. The spiritual beings of their locality just came to them out of their normal solitude. At the same time, both were trained in certain earthly techniques, better demonstrated in performances by skilled mature shamans. And in both regions there was a tendency for shamanism to be carried on in certain families. This does not contradict the idea of spiritual election.

The Shamanistic [Seance.] In East Greenland, the shaman is placed on the floor with his drum and drumstick on a flat stone beside him. His feet rest on the lower edge of the dry skin hanging in front of the entrance. With his hands behind him and his head forced down between his knees, he is bound tightly. A thong is bound around his head, which helps him to see clearly when all the lamps have been extinguished. He

[Adapted from "The Religion of the Eskimos," in Vergilius Ferm, ed., *Forgotten Religions: a Symposium,* Philosophical Library, New York, 1950. Pp. 312-320, 322-328, 330-331, 334-336. Used by permission.]

becomes stiff and unconscious though his feet move convulsively, rattling the dry skins at the door, which sound as if caught in a rushing wind. His spirit-helper appears and sets the drum dancing around the shaman's head.

Holm described such a seance in which he participated in 1884.

The drum now started into motion, dancing first slowly, then with ever increasing speed, and mounted slowly up to the ceiling. Now ensued a veritable pandemonium of noises, a rattling, a blustering, and a clattering, sounding now like a machine factory, now like great winged creatures. At one moment it was the angakok one heard, succumbing to a power mightier than himself, groaning, wailing, shrieking, whining, whispering; now came the sound of spirit-voices, some deep, some feeble, others lisping or piping. At frequent intervals a harsh, demoniacal, mocking laughter made itself heard.

The drum was manipulated with extraordinary dexterity, frequently making the round of the house, and particularly often floating above my head. The beating of the drum was often accompanied by singing, which ever and anon was subdued, as if it proceeded from the nether world. Lovely women's voices were sometimes heard from the background. Then once more that deafening chorus of clattering, rattling and blustering noises—the drum fell to the ground with a crash and all was still. This was the signal for the entrance of the dreaded monster, *Amortortok* . . . it has black arms and anyone whom it may happen to touch turns black and is bound to die. It walked with a heavy tread round the house and on the platform and roared out crying "a-mo! a-mo!" All cowered into the furthest recesses of the platform for fear that the monster might touch them. It dinned in my ears and tried to tear away from me the skin on which I sat, in order to get me up in a corner with the other people, but only succeeded in tearing the skin.

After this and other supernatural creatures had gone, a man asked Sanimuinak, the shaman, whether the lamp could be relighted. Sanimuinak replied in his natural voice that his spirit helper was present and the lamps could not be lighted just yet. But finally it retreated.

On such an occasion, the shaman perhaps is journeying to the moon to get a child for a barren woman, a service for which he is paid later, as for all other services. When, after such a journey, he finally returns to himself and the lamps are lighted, his hands are free of lashings, and he is perspiring and limp from exhaustion.

Nature of the Shamanistic Experience. There is no doubt of the shaman's sincerity even though he used ventriloquism, sleight-of-hand tricks, and the elation, exhaustion or other abnormal states of his spectators to assist him. In most Alaskan seances there used to be also prolonged dancing, drumming and chanting to the point of frenzy, at which the shaman would be contorted and would make the cries of all kinds of animals and birds or speak in some strange language. In Alaska, the shaman might be killed, after elaborate preparations, and return to life. This was pure trickery. Yet the initiative, strength, and reassurance to others that these unusual people—men and women—could demonstrate is impressive.

The condition of the shaman in his novitiate and to some extent in his mature performance resembles the progress of schizophrenia: a panic state at first when he or she has auditory or other hallucinations and realizes that there is something strange about him. He has a period of profound perplexity, withdrawal, unsureness of himself. He may be catatonic or hebephrenic, or each successively. Then his beliefs regarding the beings that he has seen, his relationship to them, his powers to do remarkable things, as well as his fears, autistic speech and other abnormal behavior become organized into a system. This is so real and coherent to him that songs, masks and other carvings, and specific tabus are accepted as logical products of experience. If this really is a kind of schizophrenia, we can assume that the self-induced ecstasy or hypnotism, disturbing and exhausting as it is, nevertheless is far more satisfying than the original anxieties from which these experiences grew. In many of the cases for which there is biographical information, there does seem to have been some unusual difficulty in early life, although not enough is known so that this can be asserted for every case.

Once the nature of the experience becomes unquestionable, no matter how bizarre, then the portrayals of it are acceptable. He henceforth lives two kinds of lives, in two different systems of relationship, and convinces others that he does.

This leads to two conclusions: (1) If indeed the shaman's experience is schizophrenic, it is nevertheless controlled, and the sufferer recovers. He does not become irretrievably disorganized or so paranoid that he cannot be tolerated by his fellowmen. (2) The remainder of the community accepts the possibility of such dual functioning, that is, in relationship to the social environment and to the natural-supernatural enviroment.

On the first point, it has been suggested regarding Yurok Indian women of northern California that those who could organize and control their abnormal behavior became medicine women while others who showed similar early behavior but who could not direct it in a way that the community understood became merely neurotic or "crazy." The same appears to be true of the Eskimos.

In regard to the second point, not only shamans can see ghosts, little people who live in crevices, or animals that can take human form. Probably every Eskimo at some time will see, hear, or feel awesome things, even outside the angakok's seance. But he escapes from the encounter unharmed, may even acquire some special gift of his own, if he is unafraid and does what

is proper for that kind of Being. Here shows up the suggestion (emotional preparation) from myths, organized religious belief, and stories of others' personal experiences. He who has seen the vision himself cannot deny that it is possible for another man.

Also, it is noticeable to those who know Eskimos intimately that they all, to some extent, are living a dual life. The Eskimo's "good humor is a conspicuous characteristic." People have referred to his highly buoyant nature, optimism, volatile laughter, his "effort to get the maximum joy possible out of the passing moment."

> But sound the depths of his mind, and this joviality and good nature appear as but a defensive veneer. At bottom his thoughts revolve about the misfortunes that are unpredictable and inescapable. (E. M. Weyer, *The Eskimos,* 1932.)

Functions of the Shaman. His greatest services to the community, in the Eskimo view, were given by providing food (animals and fish) and by curing illness. He also helped to change the weather, prevent or repair injuries, bring personal success of various kinds, divine the cause of present difficulties or prophesy the future, and combat sorcerers. Any one with so much greater knowledge and power than ordinary people might do great evil as well as great good. Not infrequently, especially in Alaska, there was an uneasy suspicion and antagonism between shamans and the remainder of the community.

Among the Western Eskimos where there were elaborate ceremonials, highly developed art, and a larger population than in the Central Region at least, the shaman had greater opportunity for leadership, and used it, sometimes overbearingly.

COSMOLOGY

General Attitudes. Eskimos are not much interested in origins or ends of existence, rather, concentrating their attention on the present. An occasional individual does spec-

ulate and try to find philosophical explanation of life, but most people try to account
only for today's illness or shortage of food,
and account for it as due to specific acts of
people, living or dead, or of evil beings. As
Essene says, the lack of cosmological cycles
of myths (though they do have separate
myths) shows that Eskimos have not tried
to systematize their world, either natural or
social.

Though the Eskimo view of the world
is remarkably concrete in its visual and auditory imagery, there is no fixed canon. As
Birket-Smith says, they lay no claim to a
revealed religion, stated once and for all
time. To them, their view of life is a series
of rational conclusions based on observation
and experience. It can be modified, added to
by new experience, hence is relative. The
only difference from modern scientific views
of the world is that the Eskimos and many
people like them have not been able to observe and test enough. So they fill in the
gaps with imagination and careful reasoning
from wrong primary assumptions. These
processes tend to make the religion highly
personal.

Belief: Spirits. Eskimo cosmology is an
almost complete animism. Everything seems
to have a soul-spirit. Geographical features,
all the animals (except the dog, in some
areas), lamp, entranceway and other items
of structures and furnishings, tools, clothing,
all have souls. A mussel or a little pond may
seem weak and insignificant items of the
natural world, yet the mussel's spirit may
guard a child against drowning, hence be
worn as a protective amulet, and the pond
may be inhabited by a dragon-like creature,
hence be avoided.

Belief: Deities. In Labrador and Greenland, the idea of a ruler of the spirits was
developed, to the point that the Labrador
people assigned supreme control of all
tornrait [spirits] to Torngarsoak. He, as husband of the Sea Goddess, became one of two
principal deities and was thought to preside
over the sea animals. In most places, however, Sèdna the Sea Goddess herself or the
Moon-man controlled the sea animals, hence

held power of life or death for the Eskimos.

When a group feared starvation, it im-
plored the shaman to visit Sedna and prevail upon her to release some animals for
the penitent people. He undertook the hazardous journey, overcoming several obstacles,
and finally by cajoling Sedna and by comb-
ing her hair reduced her antagonism to man
and got her to send out some of her offspring, the sea animals. Upon the angakok's
return home, he would call upon individuals
to confess their sins, or he would make specific accusations, and people at the seance
hurriedly confessed their infractions of tabus,
as we have seen. If the animals still did not
appear, further explanation was necessary,
for example that Sedna still was not sufficiently placated. Her relationship to men
and animals was not questioned any more
than the relations of great deities in other
religions.

The Moon-man came into his own in the
Norton Sound and Kotzebue Sound areas
of Alaska (at least as far north as Pt. Hope)
where he was thought to provide the [needed]
animals. [Eclipses] of the moon naturally were
much feared, but the shaman usually could
set things right. While the Eastern Eskimos
did not think that the Moon-spirit controlled
the sea-animals, they did believe that it was
a man, that he would befriend orphans or
others, and that he could make women
pregnant.

Sila is the most remote, most pervasive,
most impersonal, abstract of all *inuat. Silap
inua* is the Spirit of the Air, almost the
Spirit of Heaven or the Universe. Sila also
seems to mean, in Greenland and Alaska,
spiritual power or understanding. Unlike
Sea Goddess, Sun, and Moon, no earthly
origin is presupposed for Sila. Nearly all
groups speak of this deity as masculine, yet
he never is seen—only heard occasionally in
the wind. He is a great and stern supporter
of the system of tabus, seeing transgressions
and punishing them with bad weather,
dearth of game, and sickness. Although Sila
can be kind—just as we say that the weather
is kind—Sila can be terrifying also, especially
if an Eskimo has not treated the food-

animals properly. Among the Iglulirmiut and neighboring peoples who have developed most highly the cult of the Sea Goddess, *Silap inua's* powers evidently are not so inclusive in this regard. Sila is not a Supreme Being, able to control Sun, Moon, monsters, and all other independent spirits, but he is the most intellectualized of the deities, with a consistent awesomeness and none of the human-like vagaries that other Eskimo deities are subject to.

Belief: Human Souls. It is doubtful whether most Eskimos believe in multiple souls as has been claimed. . . . This much can be said of Eskimos generally; they believe in:

1. A soul-being that can become a soul-spirit like other supernatural beings. Occasionally the shadow is identified with it. In different places it takes other forms: a ball of fire or a light, steam, a skeleton.
2. The name, which has personal qualities but has no form, no lasting existence as a separate entity. It does not go to the afterworld.
3. The life essence, warmth, breath.

Because of the special importance of his name to a person, several devices to avoid saying the name are used (nicknames, teknonymy, etc.), and quite widely a child is named for the most recently deceased in the community, regardless of sex. . . . Perhaps all Eskimos formerly believed in reincarnation although it usually was not the name-soul that was reborn.

Morality in Relation to Cosmology. Let us see first what is regarded as good behavior and what is bad. Eskimos esteem hard work, alertness and awareness, consideration for the feelings of others (tactfulness), generosity, skill (hunting, for a man; sewing, for a woman), and physical courage, demonstrated in suffering violence. They disapprove quarrelsomeness, stinginess, theft, tabu-breaking, and murder. Aside from incest prohibition (which does not extend to cousins) and observance of sex tabus in certain ritual periods, sex has not been part of the tabu system. It can be seen that the traits listed combine in support of strong community life.

Sin here, as elsewhere, is any offense to the Supernatural, a transgression of divine law. In the Eskimo system, what is thus offensive and deserving of punishment appears somewhat more materialistic and non-social than in many systems.

Fear of the dead seems to increase as we go north. Possibly the anxiety regarding subsistence spreads until it covers all relations with the natural-supernatural world. For example, an illness usually is assumed to indicate that the Spirits have been offended; if they are offended, they may send even greater danger such as storm or epidemic. Illness and death then may induce greater anxiety than that to be expected for the sickness of one person. Morality thus is maintained by the most basic fears.

Illness in Relation to Cosmology. If spirits or sorcerers cause sickness, just how can they accomplish this? How can the illness be cured? The Polar Eskimos and apparently most others of Greenland and Canada believe that sickness is due only to loss of the soul, which either has been stolen or has been frightened or tormented out of the patient. The shaman then goes on a spirit-flight to recover the soul, having "diagnosed" the case by deciding the probable means of losing the soul. In Labrador, the Coronation Gulf area (Copper Eskimos), and Alaska—probably elsewhere—there is an alternative explanation, especially in cases of pain rather than general debility: a sickness has been implanted in the patient. The shaman, male or female, then may sing, dance, exhort, and contort, to drive out the sickness, finally sucking or pulling it out triumphantly.

Conclusion. (1) There was no basic male-female dichotomy of Supernatural Beings or even of the greatest Powers. A large proportion of the myths deal with interpersonal relations, especially male-female relations, but this probably is attributable more to the very personal, here-and-now character of the religion. (2) There was no clear human-animal dichotomy. Any person's soul could travel away even while he was still living and could encounter animals' soul-spirits. Animals could take human form and live among people—at least, this had occurred in the past. (3) There was no preoccupation with the dead, indicated by the very meager funeral, little concern regarding after-life, no ancestor-worship or other cult of the dead, no personification of death, and the willing-ness to use an infant's body or parts of an adult corpse as an amulet or magic agent. On the Pacific coast of Alaska this went to an extreme of making a human "poison" used in whaling, a practice undertaken by only the powerful whalers, however. (4) Religion had a physical orientation, indicated by the following: (a) most tabus related to the food supply; (b) in the myths, the savior characters saved people from physical dangers rather than from sin (this was visualized as a personal contest, with the protagonist pictured as a strong, clever person, not a pure, meek one); (c) a human origin or physical identity was attributed to most supernatural powers, Sila being the only completely disembodied one.

SUMMARY

Despite the great distances covered, there is remarkable uniformity in Eskimo religion. It evidently was strong and satisfying, to last through long migrations and subsequent isolation. Regional differences were prin-cipally differences of emphasis and elabo-ration. For example, the tabus to enforce rigid separation of land and sea animals were more numerous and inclusive among Central Eskimos, while in Alaska such tabus might differ from family to family. The following generalizations are given, there-fore, with the reservation that there are such local differences.

First, symbolism of fluidity, changeabil-ity of life, even of unreliability, and a lack of symbolism indicating attachment to the land are noticeable. There is a Sky Deity but no Earth Deity except dwarfs and other local trolls. The prominence of bird guar-dian-spirits in Alaska and of bird characters in the myths of all regions seems especially typical. This fluidity probably reflects the ancient as well as modern mobility of the Eskimos, who must be continually moving about in search of food and who most often seek that food from the sea.

Second, there is much individualism in the religion: (1) The shaman gains his power in solitude and in highly personal experience rather than by elaborate initia-tion given by community or priesthood. (2) There is little chanting in unison and ap-parently no dancing in unison east of the Copper Eskimos, and even in the Western Region the individual usually sings and dances his own composition. (3) Man's re-lation to the supernatural most often is sym-bolized as a personal struggle, both in myth and in the shaman dramas. There is notice-able lack of myths concerning migration, war, daily life and the origin of daily cus-toms, or other examples of community effort.

Third, some aggression is shown in the religious experience, but evidently there is not so much as might be expected from the amount of individualism. Although shamans formerly had to enter contests, it was not essential for the layman to wrestle with evils in order to have religious experience and obtain supernatural aid. The person who starved, nearly drowned, or died (became unconscious), the child who was sickly or mistreated saw the spirits whether he sought to or not. The aggressor, the one who showed violence toward his people, was a wrong-doer, while the sufferer of violence was thought to be rewarded in after-life. As for aggression characterizing the religion as a whole, religion to the Eskimos was not a militant cause and not enforced on others. The Eskimo in religion, as in many of his social relations, was passive—he did as the Spirits directed him to do and assumed that others must do the same.

Fourth, a here-and-now orientation char-acterizes the religion and even the mythol-ogy more than most other bodies of belief. Although etiological and teleological beliefs and tales are not lacking, they are not elaborated or organized into a cosmogony. Because in the past their expectations of punishment for tabu-breaking were so immediate and vivid, and not relegated to the after-world, Eskimos' attention to details of behavior, especially toward the game animals, and their anxiety regarding broken tabus were great. We must not be condescending or condemnatory of those tabus, ludicrous as they may seem to us. In terms of daily life, Eskimo tabus had meaning, and the religion was vital.

Fifth, the factor of abnormality in Eskimo religion undoubtedly has been overemphasized in several accounts of it. The religious leaders did go through periods characterized by behavior that could be called abnormal in almost any culture's standard of normal behavior. The important point regarding Eskimo shamans is that they did pass through their difficulties, gain self-assurance, and learn to control and organize their peculiarities so that they could assure others also.

Thus, in considering the functions of Eskimo religion, we see that for many individuals, regarded as individual personalities (notably the shamans), religion redirected, channeled, and formalized their aberrant behavior, which probably had arisen from social causes. It substituted supernatural guardians for human guardians who too often were lacking, and it gave opportunity for emotional release that some people could not get adequately in everyday life. For the community, religion mitigated the physical threats to existence, which most people normally feared much more than their social threats, and it consolidated the community by making each person's relations with the Supernatural important for the welfare of all.

Amulets are important to the Eskimo, as previous comments have indicated. An understanding of just what they are will be easier if some specific examples are considered. In the next selection, Knud Rasmussen has collected a number of these "magical" beliefs of the Copper Eskimo. Many of them depend on the simple principle of "like produces like," so that the bones of a seal caught by a good hunter will bring luck in hunting, and the claws of a falcon will give courage to their wearer.

• 17 • *Amulets*
KNUD RASMUSSEN

Amulets are called . . . "attachments," and people say of them: . . . "no matter what it is, one must simply be pleased with it". Among the more important amulets, however, there are: ermines, because they make one light of foot; the skin of the great northern diver, which gives strong life, for this bird hangs on to life very tenaciously; skins of gulls make clever fishermen, especially if at birth one has been wiped clean with one of these skins; wolf bones make men clever hunters; bones of a dog have the effect that, if one is murdered by men, revenge will be taken by the soul of the dog; the skin of a red-throated diver, especially if one has been wiped clean with one of these at birth, gives health and long life; a piece of skin from the head of a black bear, sewn on to the back of the inner coat, gives strength; bees, sewn into a piece of skin and placed in the

[Adapted from "Intellectual Culture of the Copper Eskimos," *Report of the Fifth Thule Expedition, 1921-24*, Vol. 9, Copenhagen, 19-32. Pp. 47-49. Used by permission.]

armhole of the inner coat, give hard blows when boxing and great ability to stand hard blows; the head, claws or skin of a falcon give courage, for a falcon is not afraid of attacking birds bigger than itself; parts of an eagle's beak or claws give luck in all kinds of hunting.

If it is desired that a little girl should become a clever seamstress, her first little piece of sewing must be fastened to the sleeve of the person who first took her when she was born.

When a young woman, pregnant for the first time, notices life in the child, one of her kamiks must be pulled off and she must walk about a whole day with one foot in her stocking only. This gives easy delivery.

Otherwise a special kayak amulet is the skin of a red-throated diver. It must be pushed right into the kayak in front of the skin one sits on. A bee may also be put there; it must not have been sewn up in skin, but must have a thin line of skin around it. Finally, one may also place a blown-up seal or caribou bladder in . . . the kayak.

For a boy a toy is made out of the metacarpal bones of a seal, a thong being run through them; these the boy throws about outside. If the bones have been taken from a seal caught by a good hunter they will give the boy luck when sealing in later life.

Some boys must always wear their hair long; if it is cut, their life spirit is also cut over. Sometimes there is a special reason for this custom. Netsit was once nearly killed by an accidental shot, and his foster father decreed that his hair should never be cut.

If a ptarmigan is placed on an infant boy's back and quickly taken away again, it will become the boy's pugjut: that by which the child can bob down and become invisible; his enemies will then go right past him without seeing him. The beak alone, or the head and foot of the ptarmigan, will be worn by him as an amulet.

The small snails one finds in the country are hung round the necks of dogs as amulets. A dog with an amulet of this kind will notice at once when bad weather is approaching; it will become restless and warn its master.

A boy must have the head of an ermine fastened to his cap; this will make him clever at catching ermines.

Near the part of the chest that moves when breathing small boys must have a lock of hair of an old man or woman sewn on. This gives vigour.

Young men and women must now and then swallow the spittle of an old man or woman. This will give them vigour.

We are inclined, in the western world, to think of the composing of songs and poems as accomplishments of only a gifted few, and as something remote from the daily life of ordinary people. But in simpler societies everyone takes part in singing and the recitation of stories and poems, creating anew as well as recalling old traditions. The subjects of songs are drawn from the daily life of the singer and are entirely familiar to his audience, necessitating no preliminary explanations and permitting great brevity of form. The two songs which follow are from the great collections made by Knud Rasmussen. To be appreciated fully, they must be imagined as sung in a vigorous manner, accompanied by drumming on a sealskin tambourine, with the wealth of pantomime and gesture of which the Eskimo are such masters.

• 18 • Some Eskimo Songs

SONG OF A DEAD ONE

*(Dreamt by a North-American
Eskimo)*

Joy fills me,
When the first daylight breaks in,
And the great sun
Glides silently forward in the sky.

But I, however, lie anxiously and full of fear.
How the busy swarming of maggots fright-
ens me!
They gnaw themselves into the cavity of the
collarbone,
And tear away my eyes.

Anxiously I lie here and meditate.
Say to me, was it then so beautiful on earth?
Remember the winters,
When worries corroded us,
Worries for soles to shoes,
Worries for leather to boots,
Was it so beautiful then?

Anxiously and fearfully I lie here.
But was I not always in troubles?
Even in the splendid summer,
When the hunting failed,
And there was not a fragment of fur
Left in the house for clothes,
Was it so beautiful then?

Anxiously and fearfully I lie here,
But was I not always in troubles,
When I stood on the ice of the sea,
And became quite out of my mind,
Because no salmon wanted to bite?

Or was it so beautiful then,
When I stood sweating and red and em-
barrassed
In the whirl of the feasthouse,
And the choir ridiculed me,
Because I got stuck with my song?
Was it so beautiful then?

Say to me, was it so beautiful on earth?
Here joy fills me,
When the first daylight breaks in,
And the great sun
Glides silently forward in the sky.
But I, however, lie anxiously and full of fear.
How the busy swarming of the maggots
frightens me!
They gnaw themselves into the cavity of the
collarbone,
And tear away my eyes.

AN OLD NARWHAL-HUNTER
YEARNING FOR HIS YOUTH

(Eskimo of Greenland)

Ijaja-a———ijaja———aje
I want to try
To push away my thoughts,

My great thoughts,
Ijaja-a———ijaja———aje.

* * *

May my song
Free me from them,
May my song healingly
Breathe through my throat,
May my little song
Dispel from my soul
My great worries,
Ijaja-a———ijaja———aje.

But no, no, no,
It is impossible
To drive away the grief from my throat,
It is impossible to loosen the thronging tears,
Ijaja-a———ijaja———aje.

[Translated into English by Kyllikki Lassi, from Knud Rasmussen's *Thulefahrt*, 1926,
and *Grönlandsagen*, 1922.]

My eyes are tired,
My extinguished eyes!
No more will they follow the narwhal,
When it rushes up from the depths
To break the wave of the sea.
No more will my muscles tremble,
When I seize the harpoon,
Ijaja-a——ijaja——aje.

Or, if only all the souls
Of the sea-animals, which once I killed,
Gave me their help,
To banish my heavy thoughts!
If the memory of the earlier hunts
Could only free me

From the weakness of old age,
Ijaja-a——ijaja——aje.

* * *

The throat songs of many narwhals
Sounded through heavy breathing,
When wildly it stormed:
Deep tunes and shrilling flutes!
Others rested sleepily
On the mirror-like waters.
I sing of the memories of my youth.
And together with the breath of life
My song breaks down from my throat!

Sociocultural Change
and Social Policy

»»»

Except for a brief excursion into Eskimo prehistory, we have so far been concerned chiefly with the Eskimo as they were in the eighteenth and nineteenth centuries, before the changes brought about by extensive contacts with the white man's world during the last 100 years. There have always been changes taking place in the Eskimo way of life, but until recently they were very slow and were rarely more than gradual modifications of long-established traditions. But when the whaling ships of many nations came into the Arctic area, and the Russians began their immense fur trade in the Arctic, and the Hudson's Bay Company established trading posts all the way to the Arctic Ocean, and Americans poured into Alaska during the gold rush, the isolation of the Eskimo was over. Today it is impossible to find any Eskimo settlements that have not felt the impact of civilization to some degree, and in many places the Eskimo are hardly distinguishable, at first glance, from the mixed American and European population among whom they live.

What have we done for (or to) the Eskimo? Those who lament for the romantic past may feel that the invasion of the Eskimo's lands by outsiders has been an unmitigated evil. But events cannot be halted or changed in order to keep the Eskimo as a sort of living museum exhibit of the "noble primitive." The Eskimo are changing, for better or for worse, and only a careful scrutiny of their past and present situation can help us determine what their fate will be. One effect of white contact has been to improve the Eskimo's chances for benefits from modern medical science, but this is at least partly offset by the great decline in health resulting from a poorer diet (caused by the introduction of bread, coffee, and sugar) and the introduction of tuberculosis, measles, and chicken pox, which have often proved deadly diseases to people with no previous exposure to them. The Eskimo has been quick to accept certain mechanical devices and items of equipment, adapting

121

them for his own use with skill and ingenuity. In the realm of social organization he has
been more conservative, and changes often are the unforeseen result of new circumstances,
such as the effect on courtship and marriage of wage-earning in place of hunting. To a
high degree such changes could be anticipated and modified to the mutual advantage of
both Eskimo and newcomer, but only if sufficient information is available and if there is
a willingness to recognize that the most obvious and the easiest solution to a problem is
not always the best one.

The next two selections deal with the effect of our civilization on Eskimo life in
Alaska. Effects have been equally profound in the Canadian Arctic and in Greenland, but
it happens to be Alaska that is the responsibility of the United States, and we as citizens
will ultimately determine what policies our government follows in dealing with the Alaskan
Eskimo. Both the authors of these accounts are familiar with the Arctic, but since their
experiences have not been identical, their observations and opinions differ somewhat.
Mrs. MacCarthy writes from her experience as a Navy employee at Barrow, where she and
her husband were engaged in research. Mr. Dale's acquaintance with the Arctic covered a
period of 15 years. Owing to lack of space, many details have been deleted from his original report, but by this time the reader will already be familiar with much of the culture
of the Eskimo and will be able to evaluate for himself the innovations that are described.

• 19 • Point Barrow Today

ELIZABETH MacCARTHY

Barrow Village is, undoubtedly, the largest
community of Eskimos in Alaska, and perhaps in the world. The population has increased from about 300 in 1945 to about 1000
today. They have moved in from other
places on the arctic slope, attracted by jobs
open to them working for the Navy at nearby
Point Barrow.

The Barrow Eskimo has been in fairly
constant contact with white men for a number of years now. Whalers have been landing there to trade since the 1850's and there
has been an established trading company
there since approximately 1880. Other "civilizing" influences have been the mission
established by the Presbyterian church, the
government school and the hospital. The
government has maintained a weather station there for some years, as well as a post-
office. Then during the past four years the
government project at Point Barrow has
brought hundreds of white men to work,

just a few miles from their village, as well
as a few white women. Many of the teachers
and other government workers in the village
have had their families with them there.

One of the first evidences of the Eskimo's adoption of white culture is the new
type of house he is building. I might mention, first of all, that we have seen only one
snow house since our arrival here last April,
and that one was out on the tundra, about
twelve miles from the Base. It probably was
built for a temporary hunting shelter. We
have seen a number of the remains of old
Eskimo houses, those built with driftwood
for corner posts, usually, and the jaws and
ribs of whales giving additional support.
There are, also, some Eskimo families now
living over at the village in shacks, built in
the white man's tradition, but made from
scrap material, old packing boxes, driftwood
and tar paper for walls or roofing, as well
as blocks of sod for insulation. However,

with the increased prosperity of the past few years, a great many of the men have been building new houses for their families. The material has been brought in by the Navy, on its annual ship expedition, and by the Alaska Native Service freighter, which makes one trip up during the summer, if ice conditions make it possible.

The Eskimo does not have to buy a lot to put the house on. He selects his site, evidently any suitable unoccupied space, gets permission from the "Town Council," and begins construction.

The new houses are of varying sizes. The smaller are one-room boxes, with a single window, perhaps. Others have several rooms, and frequently among these is a lean-to shed kitchen, often seen in the more primitive type of house. They have been taught to use modern insulation, although it is doubtful if they can afford to buy adequate amounts of insulation material. Usually the house is built by the owner, although he sometimes employs assistance. Very few of the houses are painted. The high cost of paint is probably the controlling factor there, as well as the fact that wood deteriorates very little in this climate, because, as can be seen from their clothes, the Eskimo does enjoy color.

One thing is very plain when looking over the village, and that is the fact that there is no town planning board. The houses face at all possible angles to each other, and are clustered over the surface of the slope in a crazy-quilt pattern. During the months of the year when the ground is covered with snow the village has a certain charm, although it is obvious even then that a great deal of trash is lying about. However when the snow melts away, during June, usually, and the ground begins to thaw, then the place loses all of its former charm, and both the accumulated filth and its odors become very evident.

Many of the Eskimo families move out of their "town houses" when summer comes and live in tents during the warmer months. One large group of them moved out toward the Point where hunting and fishing are both good at that time. Those who have boats take them along, naturally. This change of residence is in the best Eskimo tradition, of course. A modern variation is that the actual moving is usually accomplished by means of a rented tractor that tows the large sled, on which is piled all the equipment necessary for the summer living.

When it comes to furnishing his house, the Eskimo has been fairly sensible in selecting first only those things that might lighten his labors—such as improved stoves, sewing machines, dishes, pots and pans, and occasional tables. He has been much less interested in beds and chairs, probably partly because of the fact that his house was already overcrowded.

When it comes to clothes we can see for ourselves that there is more and more a tendency for the natives to imitate the dress of the white men, while meanwhile the whites are adopting some parts of the Eskimo costume—the fur boots, mukluks, and the jacket with the fur ruff around the face that we call a parka, although the proper Eskimo name is the Artiga, I believe. In recent years the younger Eskimo men and women have been ordering from the mail order places the same kind of clothes they see the white people wearing. I have seen several of the young girls with the "stateside" variety of winter coats, and the custom of wearing a scarf tied around the head has been taken up by most of the women. They still have their warm furs, usually worn with the snow shirt cover to keep the fur clean and dry, although a few of the more "advanced" wear the furs uncovered, as practically all the white people do. At the Base the men seem to be adopting more and more of the white man's clothing, beginning with the caps and shoe pacs, and then taking up the shirts and trousers, belts, jackets, heavy wool socks and underwear.

They seem to rely on caribou and reindeer meat as their staple food, rather than the flesh of sea animals. Some of their meat they still secure by hunting, but a large part of it is bought from one of the owners of herds of reindeer maintained out on the tundra, a number of miles from the village.

Muktuk and the rest of the flesh of the whale is still considered a great delicacy, and they eat walrus and seal and polar bear, when these are obtainable. In the summer they do some fishing and they kill ducks and geese in large numbers. They like most of the beverages we use—tea, coffee, and Coca-Cola. (This they buy in sirup form and mix their own.) There seems to be very little drinking of alcoholic drinks at Barrow, according to what information I have. They like eggs and some of them make very good bread. The wives are more likely to make biscuit, from flour, water, and some form of fat. They are very fond of oranges and apples and most varieties of canned fruits. They use very little salt and do not care for pepper and other spices. They are inordinately fond of chewing gum, and on the occasions when we have gone over to some celebration, almost every Eskimo present was chewing gum. They like nearly all sweets, but particularly chocolates.

The Eskimos at Barrow are still as fun-loving as most writers have pictured their ancestors. They enjoy jokes and take everything possible as a joke, including accidents to themselves and others, if not too serious. One white man who rides over to the Base every day on the "Eskimo Taxi" (two tracked trailers, joined together and pulled by a "Cat") told us that during the half hour ride there are always several card games going on, and many of those not playing cards are engaging in the sort of horse-play you would expect in a bunch of young high school boys. During their noon hour, after they have finished eating, they occupy time until the whistle blows in pitching horseshoes. They also have baseball and basketball teams, in season, and their teams play against the teams organized among the men who are living at the Base. Sometimes they beat the white men, and sometimes they lose.

They are fond of music also, it seems, and a large number of them have radios and record players. Incidentally they get the electricity to run their radios and record players, also an occasional washing machine, by rigging up their own private power plants, and getting two or three neighbors to share the expense of running it for the privilege of having some of the electricity. The Eskimo foreman here at the Laboratory has such an arrangement with a neighbor. He pays about $20 a month for two 60 watt bulbs that can be turned on at night in his home.

This past year there has been an Eskimo movie place at Barrow, also, with the same shows given there as are being shown in other Alaska towns. The admission is 75 cents, I believe. The movies are no doubt having a large influence on the Eskimo population. We hope that some of it will be good. And speaking of moving pictures, many of the Eskimos have cameras and use them well.

In addition to their own traditional celebrations, they have taken over several of the white man's holidays—notably the Fourth of July is celebrated, Thanksgiving and Christmas. The Fourth of July is celebrated with games of an athletic nature, to begin with—competitive games, archery and target-shooting, with a lively baseball game as the grand finale of this part of the day's entertainment. That night there is usually some dancing. We notice that they are somewhat shy of dancing before the white people, and that the older men and women are more likely to dance than the younger group. (Meanwhile out on the outskirts of the scene the younger children can often be seen having their own dance-play.) One of the young men told a friend of ours that many of the younger Barrow Eskimos would like to learn to do American style dancing, but that the Barrow minister would not allow it. He added that many of them hope to build some sort of community house of their own, and that when they have that building "We won't have to ask anyone."

Thanksgiving is usually celebrated with a dance.

Christmas is an occasion for the giving of gifts, as it is with us. Most of these will be ordered long in advance from any of the mail order houses, unless they have friends outside who will buy for them. Some of them have trees and put up Christmas decorations, although, of course, there are no trees growing within many miles of their homes.

The church has had a wonderful opportunity to be of service to the Eskimo. In the early days, we are told, most of the Eskimos accepted the Christian religion whole-heartedly. Many of them are still very religious, but the younger generation seem to be slipping away.

Last Saturday night I went over to an organ concert at the Barrow church. They have a new Hammond organ, and an organist from Fairbanks came up to give a concert and some instruction to the minister's assistant, a native, who acts as an interpreter at services as well as playing the organ for the services. There was a charge of $1.00 for adults, to pay the expenses of the woman who came up to give the concert—about $150 round trip for the plane fare. The church was crowded, and whole families came, all the children as well as the adults, and many babies in parkas on their mothers' backs. The audience was very well behaved and listened attentively.

Just this fall the government awarded Wien Airlines a mail contract, by which Barrow is to get weekly letter mail, weather permitting, and parcel post mail every other week. The village postmaster reported that 5000 pounds of mail were expected in on the plane last week. This will mean a great deal to the natives in ability to buy many articles at a more reasonable price than they have had to pay before this. It also means that they have a means of getting to the outside world, if they wish to do so, and have the plane fare. This is quite a change from mail once a year on the boat and about twice a year by dog team and sled.

There are two stores in Barrow. One is privately owned, and the other is the "Native Store," that is the one owned and operated by the Alaska Native Service. Prices here are cheaper than at the privately owned store, but still high.

Some of the wise and more provident Eskimos have bank accounts, usually in the Bank of Fairbanks, since a representative of that firm comes up about once a month to receive deposits and cash checks. The Eskimo saves his money to buy lumber for a new house, or a boat or a tractor, just as people outside do.

The coming of the Alaska Native Service freighter is the big event of the year, since it brings new supplies for the native store, the new teachers for the school, frequently, and the supplies ordered by separate Eskimo families. We went over when the ship was being unloaded, and it was extremely interesting to see the variety of goods strewn over the beach.

At present there is a small general hospital at Barrow, and additional quarters for taking care of T.B. patients are under construction. There has been no physician there for several months—only two white nurses and some native assistants.

One favorite topic here is what will happen to the Eskimo at Barrow if the Navy should close up shop at the Base. Many think that the Eskimo has lost the ability as well as the desire to maintain an existence by hunting. Others say that even if the Eskimo wished to earn a living by hunting there are not enough wild animals left on the slope to feed the number of Eskimos resident here. Some of the more vigorous could be depended on to go south to seek work, but undoubtedly many of the older and less able would have a hard time. One man told us that he thought that the only solution would be for the government to feed them.

• 20 • Northwest Alaska and the Bering Sea Coast

GEORGE A. DALE

TECHNOLOGICAL CHANGES

Diet. Present-day diet represents an extensive intermingling of early and modern habits and customs, as to food selection, and ways of procuring, preparing, and storing various foods. Eskimo who live in areas where fish, game and other natural foods are available depend upon these foods to a great extent. This is both a matter of choice (we like the foods mother used to give us) as well as a matter of necessity. Natural foods are often available at little or no cash outlay, and form an important subsistence diet. Only in rare and isolated cases, however, do individuals or small groups "live off the country" for more than a few days at a time. Usually subsistence foods are combined with foods from the trading post. If limited in the store food they can buy the first choices are usually sugar, tea, flour, and canned milk. More affluent families eat dried or canned fruits, pilot bread, crackers, and coffee. The list grows with the ability to buy until most staple nonperishable grocery items are included. Essentials such as matches, soap, and baking powder are purchased. Not a food, but considered an essential, is tobacco in a variety of forms, including snuff and leaf chewing tobacco. Candy bars, bubble gum, and pop are consumed in large quantities if income permits. Unfortunately, these non-essentials are frequently consumed in quantities all out of proportion to income, and replace essential items.

It should be noted that the nutritional status of many modern Eskimos is bad. This is largely due to a poor choice of foods bought from the traders. Surveys indicate that the nutritional status is better among those Eskimo using larger amounts of Native foods.

Fishing. Salmon are caught throughout the Bering Sea Coast area and in the streams emptying into the Bering Sea, by a variety of methods, including gill netting, fish wheels (in the streams), in set nets placed on the beaches, and by gaffing salmon in shallow streams. Fish wheels are an innovation reported to have been brought in from the Columbia River. They are made of saplings, scrap lumber, and chicken wire and require the use of nails, staples and other manufactured items.

Chee fish, [ling cod, and whitefish are] caught in large basketwork traps [which] are of primitive design but are constructed of an interesting combination of driftwood frames and poultry netting.

Tomcod are taken near shore through holes in the sea ice. The primitive gear consists of a baleen line weighted with stone lashed to a piece of ivory, which is especially fashioned as a sinker. This is equipped with a barbless bone hook suspended in combination with a bone or ivory lure. Present day equipment often includes hooks made by drilling canine teeth of dogs, the baleen lashing being inserted at one end of the tooth and nails bent and sharpened to form a barbless hook at the opposite end. Washers, bolts or other heavy bits of metal are frequently attached as sinkers. Baleen lines are preferred to cotton or linen lines, as ice will less readily form on the baleen line. Large quantities of tomcod are eaten by the people, often raw and frozen. The manner of eating them resembles eating corn on the cob.

Needle fish and black fish, found in brackish streams throughout the tundra area, are still caught in considerable quantities in primitive traps made of long splints of driftwood bound with willow withes to form a conical basket trap. Many times these traps are made with the use of modern materials, such as woven wire netting.

Herring are widely available throughout the Eskimo area. They are usually caught in commercially made nets, or in nets made at home from commercial twine. For storing, herring are woven together in long strips by means of wisps of beach grass passed through their gills, and are hung over crude racks to dry. They are an important item of dog food during the winter.

Whaling. The bow head whale is taken for the most part between Bering Strait and Point Barrow. The methods of taking whales represent a wide range of cultural adaptation. Whale crews may go out in either wooden whale boats such as were used by early commercial whalers, or in an umiak. The umiak is commonly driven by an outboard motor, although in stalking the whale the motor may be shipped inboard and the boat propelled by homemade paddles. Whales are shot with a heavy shoulder gun, shooting a specially designed whale bomb which explodes in the body of the whale and at the same time attaches a line to the carcass. Additional lines are often attached by means of harpoons after the animal has been shot. Whale bombs cost about $15 apiece and are a common item in the annual requisitions for Native stores at Barrow, Pt. Hope, Pt. Lay and Wainwright. Many combinations of primitive and modern gear are used in towing the whale and in cutting and processing the blubber and meat.

Whale hunting is such an important event that it is celebrated by a mixture of primitive and modern social and religious expressions. One of the writer's associates reports being invited to the ceremony preceding a whale hunt at Pt. Hope. All present were invited, as a part of the ceremony, to eat a piece of the flipper from a whale caught the preceding season. Prayers were offered in Native, and other traditional ceremonials were observed. Not to leave anything undone which might assure success in the hunt, they also asked the local missionary to offer prayers "white man style" in behalf of the successful hunt.

The whaling crews are very carefully selected, the captain of each boat being chosen on the basis of demonstrated prowess in earlier hunts. Special dances and rites are held celebrating a successful whale hunt. A special feature of these celebrations is "blanket tossing."

Hunting [beluga or small white] whales involves an extensive mixture of primitive and modern methods. "Drives" are organized in which gasoline powered boats are used to surround schools of the beluga and drive them into shallow water where they can be shot with rifles. They are then retrieved with primitive harpoons. The harpoon lines may carry floats to serve as markers, either an inflated seal skin or an empty 5-gallon gasoline can. Social custom is rigidly observed in regard to giving the choicest meat to the most expert hunters and in making sure that everyone in the village receives a share. Beluga fat and meat are stored in ice caves. The meat, freed of blubber, is also dried. The stomach of the beluga is filled with chunks of blubber and hung in a cool place, where the blubber slowly renders.

Hunting. The many species of hair seal, including the spotted harbor seal, and ribbon seal, as well as the larger bearded seal (oogruk), are extremely important even in the modern Eskimo economy. They are frequently shot on the ice or in the water and occasionally speared direct. They are retrieved with a harpoon, with a long-handled gaff hook, or with a grapple. The last consists of a block of wood roughly pear shaped and bearing four nails bent and sharpened to form a crude grapple hook. A length of raw-hide line is attached. The grapple is used by throwing it beyond the floating body of the seal and pulling it across the carcass to engage the hooks, and then pulling the animal within reach of the shore or ice. During the war, when ammunition was scarce, several communities revived the use of whale-sinew nets as a means of beating the ammunition shortage. Many old techniques are retained in the seal hunt, but modern equipment is utilized wherever it is convenient or feasible. For example, the seal hunter covers himself with a parka of white cotton drill. One Eskimo showed the writer a seal lure made from broken phonograph records. The primitive material for such a lure was baleen but this ingenious hunter had found that phonograph records could be heated in hot water and fashioned into a lure more easily than making a lure of baleen.

Walrus are likewise hunted by a combination of traditional and modern techniques. An old-style skin boat driven by a modern outboard motor is used to approach the ice floes where the walrus congregate. As the boat nears the floes the motor is stopped to avoid any disturbing noise, and the hunters approach silently with paddles, until within gunshot. Walrus dead in the water are retrieved with harpoons or grapples. As walrus are too large to pull into the umiak they are butchered with steel knives in the water alongside and lifted aboard piecemeal. A head or flipper too heavy to bring aboard by hand is hoisted with a crude boom rigged with small steel blocks and manila line.

Walrus meat and blubber are stored in ice caves and become an important part of the winter food supply. Ivory is allowed to cure for a year or two and is then carved into curios for the tourist trade.

Considerable conflict between traditional and modern customs is centered around walrus hunting. The Fish and Wildlife Service wisely makes drastic efforts to conserve walrus, as they are supposedly decreasing in numbers. Reports are frequently made of extensive kills of walrus on the Siberian side of the straits and this slaughter further reduces the size of the herds. There are laws prohibiting the shooting of walrus for ivory only, and hunters are encouraged not to shoot the animals under conditions which make the recovery of carcasses unlikely. There are laws prohibiting the shipment of raw ivory from the Territory in order to discourage ivory hunting, and to protect the supply of ivory upon which the Eskimo is dependent for his sale of carved articles.

The Pt. Hope Eskimos have [a rather] interesting technique of polar bear hunting during the occasional bright days of early spring. The dirty yellowish-white color of the bears is an almost perfect camouflage against the sea ice. However, when the sun shines the bears cannot help casting black shadows on the surface of the ice. An Eskimo, on top of a snow-covered igloo in the village, scans the ice floats with a telescope, watching for these shadows. The location of the bears is reported to hunters, who then stalk the animals and kill them with rifles. The meat is a common article of food, but the skins are generally sold to traders and taxidermists.

Old Eskimos have reported to the writer that caribou were caught in early times by driving small bands through the streams and lakes and killing them with spears from kayaks. The modern procedure is to stalk these animals in the open hills and shoot them with rifles. Hunters pack meat to camp on packboards or in small saddle bags on the backs of dogs. When caribou runs are heavy many animals may be killed and left scattered, to be picked up later for dog food. Occasionally carcasses are dragged into heaps to serve as fox bait throughout the winter. Present day remnants of these wasteful practices result in many violations of game laws. Legally the Eskimos are limited to two caribou per person, as are white hunters. Violations result in arrest and fining or jailing of violators, with the result that families suffer from the absence of the hunter.

The management of domestic reindeer herds, based on modifications of methods used in handling cattle in the States, has been difficult for the Eskimo to understand and master. They tend to regard the reindeer as they do the caribou, as a game animal, and to hunt them as such. The reindeer industry which was started about 1900 has nearly disappeared, due to losses of deer to wolves and to the deer joining migrating wild herds. Present efforts are being made to aid individual herd owners to develop herds from which animals can be sold to both Eskimos and whites, to provide meat to the buyers and cash income to the owners. This is in sharp contrast to the old Eskimo pattern of communal ownership of resources.

The individual herd ownership plan now developing appears promising. Eight or ten Eskimo herd owners have developed their herds to the point where they are realizing a cash income from them.

Beaver, rabbits, and other small land animals are important in the Eskimo economy, and muskrat and fox are valuable as a source of cash. Wolves, too, are a source of cash income from the sale of pelts and the payment of bounty. Techniques involved in taking these animals illustrate a free intermingling of modern and traditional methods.

Geese, brant, loons, cranes, murres, puffins, sea parrots, ptarmigan and many other kinds of birds are extensively used for food, and the skins and feathers have many uses. Nets, bolas, bows and arrows, and spears are all used to some extent in taking birds. A modern shotgun and a .22 caliber rifle are preferred to other methods, however, when cash income permits hunters to buy guns and ammunition, and many hunters are expert marksmen.

In certain instances (e.g., netting puffin), it is apparently more sure and certainly less expensive to use the older methods instead of guns, as the large numbers of birds taken makes the cost of guns prohibitive.

Vegetable Food. The tin pail has largely replaced the skin bag or grass basket for gathering berries. The pressure cooker, the glass preserving jar, and the tin can with the home can-sealing machine have, in places, been added to the refrigeration of food in ice cellars, freezing food out of doors, or preserving in seal oil. Wherever soil and climate permit, simple gardening is practiced to a limited extent. Techniques of gardening are relatively modern, as gardening was not a part of the early cultural pattern. Preparation of garden soil ranges from hand spading of small plots to plowing of several acres with a community-owned tractor. In larger projects commercial fertilizer and insecticides are used. Fish offal, seaweed, and shells are used to a limited extent to enrich tundra soil and to improve fields of potatoes, carrots, turnips, rutabagas, and cabbage, the most common vegetables produced.

The Old and the New. It is startling evidence of the range of cultural adaptation to see an ivory-tipped harpoon, a thermos bottle, and an alarm clock clustered together on the wall of a hunter's home. The cultural range represented in this assortment of instruments is small, however, compared to those situations in which a hunter helplessly adrift on an ice floe becomes the object of a highly organized search by airplanes and helicopters directed by radio.

In general, it may be safely said that the modern Eskimo increasingly adopts the white man's tools, instruments, and procedures as his income increases. However, certain items from the older culture cannot be satisfacto-

rily replaced in the modern culture and have, on the contrary, been adopted in modified form by the newcomers to the Arctic. For example, Eskimo women find no other form of knife as versatile and useful as their semi-lunar ulus. The parka as a cold weather garment has no satisfactory substitute and has influenced the design of military clothing for Arctic wear.

Shelter. Since the Eskimo has no highly effective means of transportation his shelter must be made of materials close at hand. Semi-underground structures (igloos) are usually built of sod and driftwood. Where wood is scarce whale bones are used in lieu of wood for house framing. Scrap lumber, which is usually dunnage thrown overboard from freighters, scrap corrugated iron, window sashes, nails, hasps and staples, and padlocks are typical manufactured articles incorporated with the primitive materials in house construction. The houses retain their floor plan of a single circular room reached by a low tunnel. In a few instances the tunnels go under the floor with access holes in the floor. Crude doors of skins and canvas at the entrance to the living room proper and at the outer entrance to the tunnel protect the living room from drafts. A common modification is the addition of a stovepipe projected through the roof by means of a safety thimble improvised from a 5-gallon oil can. In addition to the stovepipe many igloos are fitted with a square wooden ventilator extending far enough above the roof to be clear of the maximum snow level. The lower end of the ventilator is closed with a crude slide. There are still a considerable number of igloos, particularly on Diomede and King Islands, which lack the stovepipe and are heated by seal oil lamps. Others depend on the heat from gasoline or kerosene pressure lamps. Those who can afford to, substitute primus stoves for seal oil lamps for cooking.

Igloos on Diomede Island and King Island are built largely of stones combined with driftwood and whalebone and with the usual addition of scrap lumber, corrugated iron, window sash, etc. Crevices between stones are packed with soil and moss. Use of stones is dictated not only by their availability, but by the fact that there are no easily accessible growths of tundra to provide suitable sod blocks. Lacking sod roofs, Diomede Islanders use discarded walrus skin umiak coverings for roof material in somewhat the same manner as composition rolled roofing is used. Diomede Island homes are built step-fashion into the side of the hill so that one man's roof may be another's terrace. The King Island homes cling to a steep cliff; the outer edges of the floors are supported by crude scaffolding of driftwood, the inner or hill edge of the floors being supported directly on the rocks.

Where timber is available (e.g., Kobuk and Kostak River valleys) the Eskimo home is usually a one-room log cabin with a sod roof. It usually has a floor of rough lumber, or if of dirt it is frequently covered with spruce boughs which are changed at intervals. Such cabins usually have two windows built into the walls, rather than used as skylights as is common in the coast igloos. Modern building materials are used in these cabins much as in igloos. In general the cabins are drier and in many ways more satisfactory than the igloos, but being above ground they are not as warm and require more fuel.

At Deering, Kotzebue, Elephant Point and other locations where dunnage from freighters is available, nondescript shacks are built of all sorts of scrap material. Combined with driftwood and sod may be boards, corrugated iron, 5-gallon gas cans (hammered flat), paper cartons flattened and used for insulating, canvas, skins, 50-gallon gas and oil drums, and other miscellaneous items. The resulting buildings are in many ways the least satisfactory of any Eskimo dwellings.

The extent to which Eskimos will adopt modern housing when their economic status permits is well illustrated at Pt. Barrow. For several years these people have had an abnormally large cash income from their employment at a nearby contractor's camp. Under the guidance of a government agent they have purchased materials in the States with which many have built four and five room homes to replace their igloos or shacks. These houses are two-story insulated frame structures, usually with sleeping quarters on the second floor and louvres in the floor to permit heating of the upstairs with waste heat from the first floor rooms. Such homes are feasible largely because a local coal deposit makes fuel relatively abundant and inexpensive.

The common canvas tent serves as a home for Eskimo families so frequently that it is entitled to consideration under the general topic of shelter. The 7 by 9 or 8 by 10, or in some cases a large tent, is a "must" for almost every family. As a matter of choice the tents are frequently erected in the immediate vicinity of the more permanent homes and the people move into them in mild weather. They serve as shelters when hunting, travelling, attending reindeer round-ups, or on other occasions. A small tent, well banked with snow and with the floor covered with reindeer skins, can be made surprisingly warm with a minimum of fuel in temperatures as low as 40° below zero.

In many villages there may be one or several bath houses. A hut 6 feet in diameter and 5 feet high will be heated to an almost unbearable temperature by an open fire. Five or six men will then crowd in, strip, close the smoke hole, and throw water on hot stones, creating a very effective sweat bath.

Eskimos have adopted primus stoves and sheet iron wood-burning camp stoves almost universally because of their convenience and economy of fuel. Those who cannot afford to buy such stoves improvise them from 5-gallon oil cans, 50-gallon oil drums, or similar containers.

Candles, kerosene lamps, and lanterns are widely used as a source of light. Those able to afford them frequently use the gasoline or kerosene pressure lamps. Wind chargers are popular and practical in many areas where there are almost continuous winds. Although first cost is high they are economical in the long run since there is no need of paying freight on petroleum. Buckets and galvanized wash tubs are in great demand. Many Eskimo women spend a great deal of their time melting snow or carrying water and washing clothes in metal tubs with washboards.

Eskimos have made a very wide adaptation of modern materials in the building and furnishing of their homes. This varies in proportion to the ability of the individuals to buy and the availability of materials. There is a wide use of modern hand tools in the construction of even the most primitive dwelling.

Clothing. As is true of food, clothing is usually a mixture of commercial clothing bought from the trader or mail order company and the old type of skin clothing. Mixtures may also occur within the same item of clothing. For example, a fur cap or mittens of unplucked beaver may be lined with cotton flannel or sateen. Seal skin mukluks [boots] may be decorated with bright woolen ties and pompons. Within an individual costume the mixture may range from an extreme of one or two articles of store clothing (e.g., canvas work gloves or long part-woolen underwear) combined with all Native clothing to an almost complete outfit of manufactured clothing with perhaps only a Native-made fur cap. Many items of manufactured clothing are not effective substitutes for Native fur clothing in extreme cold weather. On the other hand, rubber shoe pacs for use in mild wet weather are usually superior to and more durable than Native seal skin water boots. As in the choice of hunting equipment and tools the Eskimo skillfully chooses combinations of old-style and modern clothing which contribute the most to his comfort, safety and convenience. One interesting example is the almost universal substitution of cheap colored sun glasses for the wooden carved slit goggles as a protection against glare.

As a means of increasing his cash income the Eskimo have widely accepted the suggestions of traders, teachers, and others for modifying their Native garment patterns to make the garments more salable. White women will not wear the traditional shirt type parka which must be put on or taken off over the head, as it musses the hair almost beyond repair. To make parkas more salable they are shortened to jacket length, and zippers are inserted, making an easily removable coat style parka. The demand for these and for ski garments now exceeds the supply. Another concession to market demands is to have skins commercially tanned, as the odor of urine-tanned skins is offensive to many.

While perfectly willing to make these zippered garments for sale, Eskimos for practical reasons prefer the old type for their own use. Some exhibit a general contempt for the innovation. An old Eskimo woman watching the writer struggle with a cold parka zipper, frozen solid by a single drop of water, said, "White man too damned much nice—maybe freeze to death."

Women's outside garments for ordinary wear are similar to men's, but often more elaborately decorated. Decoration often consists of insets of white reindeer skin forming patterns at the sides of the parka hood and over the shoulders. Certain patterns are characteristic of certain villages, so that a woman's parka may automatically announce her home town. Clothing decoration is an important part of the primitive costume. Women spend many hours in making elaborate patterns for the cuffs and hems of parkas. These are made of small squares or other geometric figures of different colored skins to form designs. Certain missionary groups have discouraged such decoration as "works of the devil," but the unadorned garments which result are a drab affair indeed as compared with the beautiful garments which these people are able to make. Seamstresses have a great deal of pride in their workmanship and there is keen competition among them. Within a village each woman's produce is carefully evaluated by her neighbors. Even the teeth marks on the mukluk soles serve to identify the seamstress.

Transportation. The Eskimo is moving from his primitive era of foot and dogsled transportation to the air age without intervening stages. Large numbers of Eskimo now are able to travel by plane from their home villages in remote parts of the Territory. This travel is usually at their own expense and for the reasons of seeking employment, medical and dental aid, and for many other reasons. Air travel has a great appeal to them and they occasionally sacrifice necessities to buy plane tickets. The arrival of a plane is always a matter of excitement and interest in a small village.

Many Eskimo, both men and women, are carried in planes at the expense of various salmon packing companies. Canneries located in Bristol Bay recruit labor from as far north as the Norton Sound area. Company chartered planes call for and return workers to their homes at the beginning and end of the packing season. Students en route to Government boarding schools or to the States to attend college almost invariably travel by air. The writer was recently aboard a PAA clipper en route from Fairbanks to Juneau in company with 30 Eskimo students going to Mt. Edgecumbe School, an Alaska Native Service boarding school near Sitka. The stewardess confided that Eskimo are excellent plane passengers, although predisposed to air sickness. A limited number of indigent students, dependent children, and others are transported by air as beneficiaries of the Alaska Native Service or of welfare agencies. Air transport has been a life saver to many Eskimos in isolated areas who were ill or injured.

Although the Eskimo, like his white contemporary, depends largely on planes for long distance travel throughout the year, he still uses dogteams for local winter travel and [for] hauling. Tending the long trap lines, particularly those far from the villages, requires dogteams, as do also hunting and trips to and from hunting and trapping camps. Personal travel between neighboring villages is largely by dogteam. A few dogteam mail contracts still remain for short hauls which cannot be serviced by local planes. Expenditures of public funds, however, are being diverted from dogteam trails and shelter cabins to the development of airfields in the small villages, thus facilitating

the use of small planes for local transportation. All of this will eventually result in displacement of the dogteam for all except local hauling and trapline use.

In the coastal waters the umiak still remains an important means of transportation, especially when equipped with an outboard motor. In many places the umiaks have been replaced by wooden whaleboats or by nondescript locally-built wooden boats decked over and equipped with inboard motors. Many of these violate almost all known safety precautions, particularly in the handling of gasoline, and it is only Eskimo skill as boatmen which keeps the number of casualties relatively low. Boats of minimum draft are used as tugs in moving shallow draft barges to transport freight from coastal points to inland river villages. However, the umiak remains the most important means of water travel to the more remote villages, such as Diomede and King Islands, where rocky beaches make the use of heavier boats impracticable. The kayak has been modified less than the umiak, as it is too small to permit attachment of an outboard motor. It functions largely as a piece of hunting equipment, and airplanes and power boats have infringed very little upon its highly specialized use.

Communications. To secure a working knowledge of English is the most critical communication problem of many Alaska Eskimos. A large part of the population older than 30 suffers an employment handicap because of their meager use of English. They can converse in broken English, but their comprehension is too limited to assure ready understanding of spoken or written instructions. Much interest in learning English was shown during the war, when oldsters wanted to correspond with absentee sons. Village teachers and literate neighbors were frequently asked to read and write letters. Many older Natives are impressed by the importance of signatures and can write theirs, although unable to write even simple letters.

Although most of the men within the selective service age bracket had attended village schools, many were excluded from the Armed Forces because they were unable to meet the minimum literary tests. Living in isolated villages, attending church services conducted in Eskimo by lay readers or with such Eskimo as the missionary could acquire, and with little other use for English, skills gained in school were soon lost. Since the war there has been a marked increase in the use of English. Returning servicemen had learned to rely on English as their common language and many others had worked in English-speaking labor groups. Continuing emphasis on English in village schools, increasing use of English in homes of younger families, and increasing contacts with English-speaking immigrants to the Territory, plus more interest in radio broadcasts and in periodicals are producing a steady growth in ability to use English.

In spite of these changes it is still necessary to use an interpreter in speaking to many community groups to be sure that they all understand. It is amusing to address a group through a formal interpreter only to have the discussion following the talk proceed in broken English in which all but a few will participate.

Only the smallest and most remote villages and isolated groups are [altogether] without radio communication. In almost every village there are radio receivers, individually owned by the trader, teacher, or some Eskimo family. These sets supply news broadcasts, fur market quotations, and news of plane movements to the entire village.

Summary. Activities associated with securing food, shelter, and clothing, and with transportation and communication have expanded to include numerous kinds of unskilled and semi-skilled wage work. The wages are spent for a wide variety of products of white technology, for example, canned food, airplane fares, commercial telegrams, and radio sets. At the same time, the Eskimo has increased his cruising range. He has added to his general effectiveness in adapting many of the white man's products to his traditional activities in hunting, fishing, travelling, and mode of life in general. Examples

of these adaptations are the rifle, outboard motor, primus stove, shoepac, etc. The result is an extensive intermingling of modern and primitive technology. Casual observation might indicate that the white technology is rapidly dominating this mixture, both in number of items and in effectiveness, and that this mixture is beneficial to the Eskimo. More critical evaluation raises serious doubts as to the overall advantages to the Eskimo of these technological adaptations. First, the improved hunting equipment has been made available primarily because whites entered the Eskimo area seeking game and fur, as well as other resources. They brought with them other techniques beyond the Eskimo's control, for example, capital resources, shipping, credit, and engineering services. As a result he now "gets the little end of the deal" in spite of adopting freely from the white technology. Secondly, the white attitude of exploitation through trade, credit, etc., worked to the Eskimo's disadvantage. Third, the Eskimo loses identification and status in the resulting mixed communities through disuse of his own social organization and only partial acceptance into the white organization. As a result his system of values suffers and with it his own self-esteem.

SOCIAL ORGANIZATION

Courtship. In small villages courtship retains many of its early social implications and techniques. These may be modified or in some cases driven underground by disapproval of missionaries or teachers. Older patterns may be disturbed by such events as young men becoming independent of parental and group ties when leaving the community to work for wages. Instead of gaining prestige and eligibility as a suitor because of skill as a hunter he becomes a wage earner. At the same time he is absent more or less permanently from his home village and from eligible girls. Opportunities for wage work are frequently localized, as at Barrow. This reduces the ratio of men to women in certain villages and gives an excess of men in others. Both conditions disturb the opportunity for marriage, tending to destroy established courtship patterns.

Missionaries have probably had less effect on patterns of courtship than on actual marriage practices. Some Missions provide group recreational activities for mixed groups of young people as part of their church programs. These have only minimum effect on established courtship patterns. The physical, social, and economic structure does not readily permit courtship practices common in white communities.

Village schools have little effect on courtship patterns. Since they ordinarily extend only through the sixth grade most boys and girls have left school prior to developing courtship interests. Older girls occasionally remain in school but boys of equal age have usually quit school to assist their fathers in the trapline, in hunting, and in other activities. Thus courtship interests develop for the most part after leaving school.

Boarding high schools located at Mt. Edgecumbe (near Sitka) and White Mountain (near Nome) together enroll over 600 students, including about 200 Eskimos. In these schools elaborate precautions are taken to prevent promiscuity. Many recreational activities are provided, such as athletics, dances, movies, parties, hikes, picnics, swimming, and summer camps. There are numerous opportunities for church going. Advisors assist the young people in acquiring the approved dating techniques. Under these conditions many "cases" develop. Courtships flourish but few marriages develop. Although many of the boarding school students are of marriageable age and courtship and marriages are not discouraged, it is only rarely that couples marry while still in school. Only infrequently couples who have courted at school marry even after leaving school. Occasionally unmarried boarding school girls become pregnant, some of them marrying the father of their child, and others offering their child for adoption. Still others keep their children and are supported in part by the aid-to-dependent-children program of the Federal Security Agency.

Marriage. In remote villages many couples are married according to old custom. Such marriages may simply consist of the young man and woman establishing a household. They may be in an independent household or live with the parents of either spouse or with another family. Convenience, choice, and available space seem largely to dictate the place. Such marriages may or may not be recognized by the community council or by observance of some formality.

The more astute missionaries and teachers recognize without question families established through such marriages. Teachers, missionaries, occasionally U.S. Commissioners, nurses, and other interested persons frequently try to acquaint the couples who have been married according to local customs or common law procedures with the legal advantages and improved inheritance rights of children of being married by a religious or civil ceremony. Occasionally couples who have been married for many years without benefit of law or clergy arrange to be married by a Commissioner or clergyman. Probably a majority of the present-day Eskimo couples arrange for religious or civil marriages before establishing their homes.

A "marriage commissioner" is an official appointed by a District Court who has authority to perform civil marriages. This legal provision is in answer to the demand from remote communities for a readily available means of being legally married. U.S. Commissioners have duties similar to those of a Justice of the Peace in the States, including the authority to perform civil marriages. The marriage commissioner's authority is limited to that of performing marriages, however, and his jurisdiction does not extend to other matters of law.

Broken Homes. The high incidence of tuberculosis is a common cause of broken homes. Where the fathers are hospitalized children are usually kept with the mother, who is given assistance from the Alaska Native Service or from the Territorial Department of Public Welfare. Where the mother is hospitalized the breakup of the home is usually more complete, as the father seldom has facilities or ability to take care of the children. Such children are placed with relatives or in institutions.

Liquor is probably directly or indirectly the cause of more broken homes than any other single factor. Impoverishment of a home due to excessive use of liquor invites T.B. Also, many homes are broken for varying lengths of time, sometimes permanently, by the imprisonment of one of the parents for drunkenness.

Many Eskimo young people leave their homes prematurely to attend Government operated boarding schools or mission schools. Low income is often a factor in requesting admission to boarding schools. Many others seek admission because they live in villages too small to provide upper grade and high school facilities. Many of the children from homes broken by liquor and other causes are enrolled in boarding schools. Separation of the child from his home to attend boarding school occasionally results in a permanent separation. The distances and travel costs are too great to permit summer and other vacation visits to their homes.

The causes of broken homes and the number of broken homes have increased beyond the capacity of simple community measures for caring for children by redistributing them among families of next of kin or in childless families. Welfare programs, including foster home placement, boarding home care, and mission homes have largely supplanted the procedures formerly possible in the relatively simple community.

Infanticide. There may be extremely rare cases which are undetected. Infrequent cases are reported which may be deliberate attempts at infanticide. They can probably be equally well accounted for as sheer neglect, usually associated with excessive drunkenness of the parents. The writer has first-hand knowledge of a few cases occurring since 1940 in which infants have been "accidentally" smothered; one in which an infant was left in an unheated cabin; one in which the infant was left at the side of the road in a suitcase. There is only a remote possibility that these cases are remnant expressions of the early custom of deliberately exposing children to die. One of the writer's co-workers, who was a teacher on St. Lawrence Island from 1924 to 1937, reports two cases of known infanticide. One was the choking of a newborn infant that was obviously deformed and the family concluded it could never live and be self-supporting. The second was the drowning of a newborn infant at a hunting camp. This child was the offspring of a father and his stepdaughter, and the motive for killing the child appeared to be to remove it as evidence of incest.

Killing of the Aged Infirm. This practice, to relieve the group from supporting them, is not now known. A middle-aged Eskimo confided to the writer that this was the practice many years ago. He had never known of a case first-hand but his father had told him about it. He added, "We take good care of our old people now because pension money helps everybody." The Eskimos have been quick to recognize the value to the household of having an old age pensioner in their midst. They are industrious about establishing claims for Old Age Assistance benefits. Establishing proof of age for people over 65 is very difficult and sometimes impossible, due to lack of birth records or other acceptable documentary evidence. This difficulty has proven a readily understood argument in favor of birth registrations. As a result Eskimos cooperate readily in filing birth certificates and supplying other data for vital statistics. Responsibility for birth and death records falls upon teachers, missionaries, commissioners, physicians and others. Traders cooperate readily in establishing proof of age, since Old Age Assistance beneficiaries represent cash income at the trading post.

Polygamy. Two instances are reported on St. Lawrence Island by the teacher mentioned above. One was a Siberian Eskimo who had brought his two wives to St. Lawrence for a visit, liked the country, and remained. He was threatened by the local missionary because of his polygamous family but it never became "convenient" for him to return to Siberia. The second case was where a young widow was taken into the home of a man and wife because she had no hunter to support her after her husband's death. She became in effect an additional wife but the motive was apparently her economic need.

Unmarried Mothers. Exploitation, particularly by white men, of Eskimo girls results in so many unmarried mothers that this type of family requires separate recognition. These cases reached a peak during World War II. Men of the Armed Forces were responsible to a lesser degree than were the men of the civilian labor gangs. In many cases unmarried mothers elect to take the responsibility for their children. They support them in boarding homes or institutions or maintain them in homes which they establish with the aid-to-dependent-children grants. A few unmarried mothers return to the parental homes and the children become members of the parental group. Occasionally unmarried mothers later marry, the husband assuming responsibility for her child. Frequently, however, the mother does not marry the putative father of her child, as he more often disappears as soon as the girl's pregnancy is detected. Lack of basis for prosecution, unwillingness of the girl to press legal action, and an all too common attitude of indifference for the welfare of both the unmarried mother and her child make it extremely easy for the fathers of these children to escape all responsibility.

COMMUNITY ORGANIZATION

There are no predominantly Eskimo villages in Alaska which are incorporated under Territorial laws. Nome, an incorporated town, has a larger population of Eskimos than whites. The business and social life of the town is dominated by the white minority. Lacking incorporation, a village has no local authority to enact ordinances and regulations. There are no formally elected Council or Mayor and no law enforcement officers. These unorganized groups of people constituting a village are without means of formal corporate action, except where organized under a Department of the Interior charter.

Furthermore, the substitution of wage work for hunting, and many other aspects of white culture are tending to modify the older forms of community organization to the point where its effect on individuals and groups within the community is considerably weakened.

At present the head man, called the chief, mayor, or chief councilman, is chosen by an informal election, often by a voice vote. Since there are no ordinances specifying terms of office, date of elections, eligibility of voters, qualifications of candidates, etc., these particulars may vary from time to time. Elections are often held at Christmas time, as this holiday is the time of year when the greatest number of people are usually in the villages.

Qualifications for becoming a chief or mayor vary widely. Usually he is chosen from among the older men. In some villages being able to speak, read and write English is also regarded as a qualification. However, the best interpreter in the village is not necessarily the chief. Abilities as a hunter or trader, and general qualities of leadership, affect selection. Men who are very poor by village standards and who have not demonstrated success in some endeavor are not commonly elected chief.

The writer knows of no case in which a woman has been made chief or elected to the council. They do participate freely in the community discussions which are often an adjunct to council meetings. In a few cases, women's organizations (e.g., mothers' clubs organized by teacher or nurse) bring considerable pressure on village affairs. Such women's groups have exerted a strong influence in some villages to prevent the admission of liquor licenses, to prohibit the showing of movies in competition with church activities, etc.

Some of the chiefs and their councils, usually with consent of the majority of the community, prepare simple statements prohibiting certain activities, such as importation of liquor, unchained dogs, and illegal cohabitation. These informal statements are of little effect, inasmuch as they are not based on a legal code and there is no provision for enforcing them. Without a legal basis of operation, the power of taxation, and means of law enforcement, the position of the chief and council is frequently weak and ineffective. A few of them exert a considerable amount of influence and control by virtue of their natural leadership and prestige.

In general, however, the chief and the council are not in a position to deal effectively with individuals or groups who choose to violate acceptable local standards of conduct. The chief and council are often reluctant to evoke Territorial or Federal laws to punish violators. They may be unaware of applicable laws or of ways of securing enforcement. In reference to game laws, they may not be in sympathy with the law or they may be afraid of reprisal if they inadvertently or knowingly violate the game laws whose applicability to their means of making a living may be debatable.

Lacking incorporation under Territorial law, 35 villages have been incorporated under the provisions of the Indian Reorganization Act (the Wheeler-Howard Act) of the Department of the Interior. In 1936 its provisions were made applicable to Alaska. This act provides that Native communities having a common bond of residence or occupation and meeting certain other requirements could be incorporated under a charter from the Department of the Interior and function as a corporate unit in the transaction of business, borrowing money, loaning money to individuals, organizing of cooperative stores, and other enterprises, and in preparation and enforcement of local law codes. Prerequisite to the granting of a charter is the submission of a constitution and by-laws prepared by the people and approved by the Secretary of the Interior. The final act in securing a charter is the ratification of the constitution and by-laws by a majority vote of the village. The chief advantage in incorporation is eligibility to borrow money for community business enterprises from a revolving credit fund established for this purpose by the Government. Three villages have organized stock company trading posts in their villages; 24

have incorporated to form a purchasing agency (Alaska Native Industries Cooperative Association, ANICA) with headquarters in Seattle. This agency buys supplies for the village stores in large quantities to give the stores the price advantage of mass purchasing. For 1948 the total purchases of the stores from ANICA totaled $750,000, computed as landed cost value at the stores. Local retail value of this is approximately $1,000,000.

The provisions of the Indian Reorganization Act have brought to these villages the whole modern organizational complex of incorporation, chartering, ratification, credit, mass-purchasing, and distribution. Success of these village enterprises is evidence that Eskimos have the ability to act in accordance with this complex pattern. To a great extent the board of directors of the village store replaces the village council. The chairman of this board may in many respects function as a chief. The entire life of the village is greatly influenced by the cooperative trading post. With an increase in cash economy, plus the cooperative plan whereby accumulated store profits become available for general community improvement, the village store replaces the subsistence economy to a considerable extent and becomes the center of gravity of the economic system.

In many cases the informal, poorly organized village structure co-exists with the more formal organization stipulated by the Indian Reorganization Act. In communities where hunting is still predominantly an economic activity, a distinguished hunter may be the chief, and by virtue of his leadership exert a great deal of positive direction over his constituents in hunting activities. At the same time another man in the village may be chairman of the board of directors of the village store and exert extensive direction and leadership. Conflicts, jealousy, and complications are common, but, on the whole, democratic processes prevail and the community benefits by what each leader is able to contribute from his skill and experience.

The schools have relatively little effect upon community organizations other than as a general aid to the acculturation process. Alaska Native Service teachers are also trained to serve as community leaders and consultant-advisors to the community. They are usually ex-officio members of the village council or board of directors of the village store, and advise in all matters pertaining to Government relationships. They assist with clerical work, provide fur market information from radio broadcasts, and assist in many other ways.

Missions have only slight effects on community organization in most places. Certain missions in the Kotzebue area, however, combine trading and evangelism and maintain a system of exploitative tithing. Here the missionary is often the trader, or else the mission arranges with the trader to collect tithes on all furs and other produce brought in by the Natives. The Eskimos are instructed in the mission church services not to accept any trade goods in exchange for their furs until the trader has given a tithe to the mission. Fortunately, exploitation by fostering hysterical fear of the afterlife is not characteristic of the missions in general. Where it has been practiced, the mission has an economic interest and vigorously opposes the village organization.

The trader is an extremely important factor in village organization, often completely dominating village life. As a source of supply of manufactured necessities, he can control the action of individual trappers by granting favors or withholding credit. The plan of operation was usually to keep the Eskimo in debt, demand all his furs and other produce, and control him by threat of refusing credit for future needs. Trappers who sold their furs to itinerant fur buyers were punished by withholding credit. The trader was usually the postmaster and scribe for the village and capitalized fully on the advantages of this strategic position. Mail order catalogues were "accidentally" lost instead of distributed. One woman ordered a layette from a mail order house, but the order did not clear the local post office until too late—she was forced to buy the necessary outing flannel and other baby supplies from the local trader. Relief checks and old age assistance checks, coming to illiterate Natives, were endorsed by marks—witnessed by the trader—and the recipient had no way of knowing what portion of the check was credited to his account on the trader's books. In many cases the traders kept no books.

In addition to these sharp practices, many traders used whiskey shamelessly and openly in controlling trappers. The net result was a virtual state of peonage for the Eskimos, whose existence from season to season was dependent largely upon credit from the traders. Isolation, illiteracy, absence of schools and teachers, and poor transportation and communication were all assets to such a pattern of operation. One old-time trader recently mistook a school teacher for a tourist and remarked, "These damned Government teachers are making these Natives so smart we can't make any money off them any more."

A more refined type of monopoly is practiced by large trading firms having control of lighterage facilities at Nome, Kotzebue, Bethel, and a few other strategic coastal points. These companies own and operate most of the tug and barge equipment necessary for lightering freight between steamers and the beach. The bulk of supplies, including fuel oil, foodstuffs, and heavy freight, used in the Arctic enters the country through these few ports or satellite ports under the control of companies operating at Nome or Kotzebue. Prices are exorbitant. Competition is effectually stifled. The entire economy of the country suffers. These companies are large enough to send lobbyists to Congress where the usual pressure techniques are applied to protect these vested interests in their exploitation.

To summarize, an examination of present day Eskimo community organization reveals a practical ingenuity in adapting and combining organizational methods equal to that displayed in adapting technological processes.

SOCIAL CONTROL

The normal family continues to be an important element in social control, but its effectiveness is weakened by the numerous cases of family break-downs resulting from various causes, such as tuberculosis, liquor, etc. Eskimo parents are skillful in controlling children by suggestion and persuasion. Serious child-parent conflicts are rare. Family affection runs high, and feelings of close kinship and mutual emotional dependence are obvious. Children are present and a part of all community activities. If they go to sleep at a meeting, they may be held in their mother's arms or laid in some convenient place. Sleeping babies and older children lie across their mothers' laps during dances in the kazigi. When three-year-olds venture from the audience to attempt a few dance steps with the adult performers, their efforts are invariably greeted with friendly laughter and encouragement. The child has abundant opportunity to recognize himself as a member of the family and of the village group.

Partly due to this close feeling of group kinship and partly due to the pressure of opinion in a small group, public opinion is a strong influence controlling the individual. Control is informal and casual, but relatively ineffective only with strong-minded recalcitrants who are determined to have their way.

Religion is relatively weak as a means of social control, since the old control by the supernatural has largely disappeared. Such beliefs in the supernatural as do remain are limited largely to the old people. The shaman has found the doctor, the Public Health nurse, school teachers trained in first-aid, and the attractions of a modern hospital to be tough competition in the healing art. His prestige in all departments has suffered accordingly. Shrewd nurses sometimes enlist the shaman to sing his song in combination with her treatment when the attitude of the patient may be helped.

Present-day churches and missions exert social control in many ways. They are centers of public opinion; they express approval of desirable conduct; they counsel against and frown upon many undesirable forms of conduct. They provide acceptable social activities in competition with the undesirable activities associated for the most part with liquor. Likewise, the schools provide village library facilities, recreation, and sponsor and encourage many activities which exert an indirect social control over the entire community.

Law-ways in an Eskimo community are difficult to detect without making an intimate and detailed study, such as that of the Nunivak group by Lantis. In isolated villages the white man's laws have little effect on the Eskimos because they do few things to violate them. Convictions for violent crimes, such as murder and rape, do not occur more frequently than among the white population. In the more primitive communities, being jailed may add to a man's prestige rather than serve as a warning example to his fellows. The odium of being punished by temporary loss of freedom seems small compared to the distinction of a free airplane ride from the village to jail and return. In addition, the returned culprit can report a warm place to stay, no work to do, and good meals furnished free during the period of his imprisonment.

Tax laws and voting laws control Eskimos as they do their white neighbors. Laws controlling titles in real estate affect Eskimos only slightly since they live for the most part on the public domain. They are eligible to acquire land under the same homestead laws as the whites.

It should be noted that within the last four years, Eskimos have been elected to the Territorial Legislature and now have at least a minority voice in the making of Territorial laws. The Eskimos elected are widely recognized as leaders, both by their own people and by their white contemporaries. They are respected by their white colleagues as effective and competent members of the Territorial Legislature.

Liquor as a technique of social control is widely used by the whites in the exploitation and control of the Eskimos. An able liquor lobby prevents more than a minimum legal control over the sale and distribution of liquor in the Territory. Public opinion is largely indifferent to the violation of such laws as exist. None of the restrictions on the sale of liquor to Indians which exist in the States apply in Alaska. With this lack of regulation, unscrupulous, greedy traders supply them with liquor and cheat them shamelessly. Men are "rolled" in "dives" and their wages stolen. Eskimo girls in Nome and Fairbanks are debauched and prostituted openly in the bars. Recognizing the dangers associated with the use of liquor, the majority of Eskimo villages have operated an informal local option and kept liquor licenses out of their villages.

ATTITUDES AND BELIEFS

Generalizations concerning attitudes and beliefs must be tentative because of the variations between individuals and between groups. In general Eskimos have a great admiration for white technology and a desire to acquire its products. They also seek the advantage of the white man's institutions. Some of them retain a genuine skepticism about the white man's religion, possibly growing from the very evident lack of agreement among whites concerning their own churches. Representatives of various churches try to win Eskimos to their faith, often raising questions and doubts about other denominations in so doing. The predicament of an old Eskimo illustrates this. Approaching a school supervisor who had just arrived in the village, he said, "Are you another Jesus man?" The supervisor assured him that he was not a missionary, to which the Eskimo replied, "Maybe you can help me think about something. Teacher says we all go to hell if we work on Saturday." (The teacher was a Seventh Day Adventist.) "Missionary (a Lutheran) says we go to hell sure if we work on Sunday. Now what is poor Eskimo to do when two white people say different things? I guess we'll just have to go to hell Eskimo way." In view of such confusion, their attitude of skepticism is a compliment to their good judgment.

Their attitude toward education is universally favorable. They accept without reservation or wishful thinking the fact that the white man has come to stay and the necessity of mastering his language. They regard the school as a source of many useful services as well as an opportunity for their children to receive an education. Villages where schools have not been established are persistent in their efforts to secure them.

The Eskimo's attitude toward himself is an important aspect of his over-all adjustment. He is a chronic extravert, except in larger centers where he is constantly the target of the white man's discrimination. He is frequently rebuked and exploited. In spite of this he maintains a loyalty to those of his white associates whom he has genuine reason to regard as his friends.

Suggestions for Additional Reading

Some of the most useful sources of information on the Eskimo have been quoted at length in the preceding pages. *The Eskimos,* by Edward M. Weyer, Jr., is one of these, a careful compilation of details about every aspect of Eskimo life and of the area in which they live. We have also quoted from several volumes of the *Report of the Fifth Thule Expedition,* and there is a wealth of additional material in this series. Some of the best and most accessible accounts of the Eskimo of a generation or two ago are in the Annual Reports of the Bureau of American Ethnology, Smithsonian Institution, Washington, D.C.

In addition to scientific reports, there are a considerable number of books written by travelers and visitors to the Arctic, as well as some fine fictional accounts, which describe admirably the land, the life, and the feelings of the Eskimo. Only a few can be mentioned here. *Salamina,* by Rockwell Kent (Harcourt, Brace and Co., 1935), is a vivid account of

Kent's long visit to the west coast of Greenland, generously illustrated with drawings which successfully combine attractiveness and accuracy. A lively fictional account of Eskimo life in northern Greenland has been written by Hans Ruesch, with the appropriate title, *Top of the World* (Harper and Bros., 1950, and Pocket Books, Inc., 1951). *Kanguk, a Boy of Bering Strait, as Told to William Albee* (Little, Brown and Co., Boston, 1939), is an autobiography, the recollections of an old man, told with simplicity and vigor and illustrated by himself; it presents an Eskimo view of Eskimo life in the days when the white man had as yet caused very little change from long-established and traditional ways. Another volume with illustrations by an Eskimo, which again catch the bleak but intense mood of Arctic life, is *Igloo Tales,* by Edward L. Keithahn, illustrated by George Aden Ahgrupuk (Education Division, U. S. Indian Service).

Out of the experiences of his years in Greenland, Peter Freuchen has written two imaginative but accurate stories of Eskimo life, *Eskimo* (Horace Liveright, 1931) and *Ivalu, the Eskimo Wife* (Lee Furman, Inc., N. Y., 1935). A more recent but equally enthusiastic admirer of the Arctic is Gontran de Poncins. He has produced a book of remarkably fine photographs of the Canadian Eskimo, with considerable personal and rather impressionistic comment in addition. The book is titled simply *Eskimos* (Hastings House, N. Y., 1949). Another nonprofessional but informative account of the Eskimo of this area is Farley Mowat's *People of the Deer* (Little, Brown and Co., Boston, 1952). In recent years such popular and semipopular periodicals as *Natural History, The Saturday Evening Post,* and *The National Geographic Magazine* have contained numerous excellent articles on the Eskimo, often liberally illustrated.

Finally, there should be mentioned the names of a few of the outstanding experts whose writings we were unable to include in the present volume because of lack of space: Franz Boas, Diamond Jenness, Therkel Mathiassen, Vilhjalmur Stefansson, and William Thalbitzer.

THE NAVAJO

When a Navajo becomes ill or engages in some critical undertaking, such as a long journey, he asks the "singer" to perform one of the many complex ritual chants which will bring about a good relationship between the individual Navajo and the forces of the supernatural world all about him. For this ritual a "dry painting" (*top*) is made of many colors of sand, pollen, and dry pigments, to symbolize certain deities and natural forces, such as the winds, the rain, or the rainbow. The singer (*bottom*) then performs his series of chants, while the "patient" is seated on the painting.

The last three decades have seen in the United States a new feeling of responsibility for the welfare of the Indians, whose continent we now occupy. No tribe in the country is as large today as the Navajo tribe, and few are in greater need of medical care, schools, roads, and other forms of assistance. The Navajo Service, an agency of the Department of the Interior, brings medical attention to the people (*top*) in their homes and also has established hospitals. *Bottom:* A Navajo house is built of heavy poles and sticks, covered with a thick layer of earth to serve as insulation as well as to keep out the rain. The metal stovepipe and the steel axe, at right, are recent innovations.

GREAT PLAINS

SANGRE DE CRISTO MOUNTAINS

Pecos River

Rio Chama

Rio Grande

Rio

Mt. Baldy

Mt. Taylor

SAN JUAN MOUNTAINS

Ute Peak

Chaco Wash

LUKACHUKI MTS.

TUNICHA MTS.

CHUSKA MTS.

Canyon de Chelly

Wash

DEFIANCE PLATEAU

River

CARRIZO MTS.

Chinle

CHINLE VALLEY

PLATEAUS

San Juan

Navajo Mt.

Black Mesa

River

COLORADO

River

Little Colorado

San Francisco Peaks

Colorado

Grand Canyon

BASIN AND RANGE

The Navajo Habitat

Scale of Miles

0   20   40   60

35°

35°

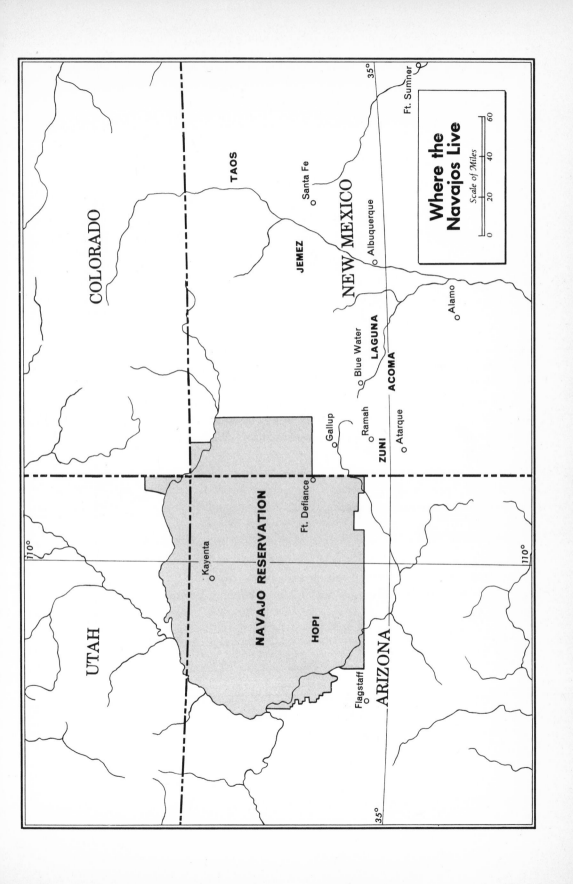

Where the
Navajos Live

Scale of Miles

0   20   40   60

COLORADO

NEW MEXICO

TAOS

Santa Fe

JEMEZ

Alamo

Blue Water

LAGUNA

ACOMA

Ft. Sumner

35°

Gallup

Ramah

ZUNI

Atarque

Ft. Defiance

NAVAJO RESERVATION

Kayenta

HOPI

Flagstaff

ARIZONA

UTAH

110°

110°

35°

Albuquerque

Introduction

<<<<<<<<<<<<<<<<<<<<<<<<<<<<<<<<<<<<<<<<<<<<<<<<<<<<<<<<<<<<<<<<<<<<<<<<<<<<<<<<<<<<<<<<<<<<<<<<<<<<<<<<<<<<<<<<

Just as the Eskimo amaze foreigners with their ingenuity, so the Navajo impress out-siders with their dignity. They have learned to adapt to their dry habitat, which lies chiefly in Arizona and New Mexico, and have developed a philosophy of life based on submission, on realistically accepting what each day brings instead of striving for goals beyond their attainment. Much of their religious ceremonialism, which is a key to understanding their culture, was borrowed from the Pueblos several hundred years ago when the Navajo first came into the area; many traits such as the use of horses and sheep are reminders of the days of Spanish Conquistadores; the current tensions, relatively new in Navajo life, stem from overcrowding due to population increase and unwise use of natural resources.

PLACE PERSPECTIVE

To understand the Navajo, one has to understand his habitat: the precarious exist-ence based on a short growing season and the ever-present threat of drought; the over-grazed hillsides; the scenic gorges, which hinder communication; the snow-covered moun-tain peaks, where winter's violence matches summer's heat; the sparse growth of piñon, juniper, cactus, and sage, with sufficient supplies of timber located here and there on the 25,000 square mile reservation.

TIME PERSPECTIVE

There is a curious connection between the Eskimo and the Navajo that one hardly expects to find. The Athabaskan Indians, who in Northern Canada came into contact with the Eskimo, are of the same linguistic stock as the Navajo now located thousands of miles away in the American Southwest. This is proved conclusively by the fact that the Navajo speak an Athabaskan language which is quite unlike the non-Athabaskan lan-guages of the Pueblo tribes around them. The story of their migration and the result-ing development of their culture is set forth in Selection 22.

ECONOMY AND SOCIAL ORGANIZATION

It was only after contact with the Americans at the time of our Civil War that the Navajo took up the pastoral way of life with much enthusiasm. Prior to that they had been partly agricultural and had lived from raiding their less mobile neighbors, both Indians and Mexicans. They proved so troublesome to the American authorities trying to administer this area, acquired by the Mexican War from Mexico, that Kit Carson was given the job of rounding them up and putting them in a military camp at Fort Sumner, New Mexico. When they went back to their canyons and desert stretches, they were given sheep, among other things, and they took up herding. They kept on farming small patches of moist soil, and some began to work as day laborers for the Indian Service, the railroads, and the mining concessions on the Reservation. Thus we cannot think of the Navajo as a true pastoral type in the way that the Eskimo represent the hunting type of economy. The Navajo are rather semipastoral, this emphasis being of comparatively recent origin. They had had sheep and goats since the Spaniards visited the Southwest, but had never looked upon flocks as a major source of livelihood.

Many readers will be confronted here for the first time with a clan system, in which descent is traced through one side of the family only (in the case of the Navajos, the mother's side); the clan regulates the ownership and inheritance of property, as well as the choice of mates. Further insight into this socioeconomic arrangement is provided by Selection 32, which is a verbatim autobiographical account of a rather unusual Navajo man. All authorities agree that this account rings true.

The clan and family organization, together with a detailed description of Navajo infancy and childhood, is portrayed in several selections. In the discussion of Navajo political structure, one learns, for example, that the Navajo tribe was seldom closely knit as a political unit but that the real authority lay in the hands of a series of local leaders, each with power only in his immediate area. This explains why the white military leaders found it difficult to make treaties which the Navajo would observe, since one leader did not feel obligated to keep what some other local leader had signed.

A major focus of Navajo life is in their religion: in the ritualization which surrounds almost every daily activity, in the majestic chants which provide occasions for a social gathering, for religious expression, and for healing.

SOCIAL AND CULTURAL CHANGE

The Navajo call themselves *Dineh,* "the people." Ask the Navajo where he lives and he will answer, "Dineh Twah," meaning "among the Navajo people." His way of life is a proud way and, although scornful at times of other ways, he is able to take numerous foreign traits and fit them into his culture. This is how he has survived. But today the "American way" constitutes a major threat, in the opinion of many of the older Navajo. Certain of these would prefer to be left alone to follow ancient patterns of life. Others are demanding their rights as citizens of the United States and are asking for sums of money which older treaties promised would be set aside for the education of Navajo children.

Today the question is "Will the Navajo find a way out of his present dilemma?" Has the Navajo finally come to the end of his success in resisting or adapting to change? Is his proud way doomed? What, if anything, should our national government and the several state governments be doing to meet the Navajo demands?

The two spellings of the name of these people need not be confusing. Those of us preparing this book prefer to use *Navajo*, the older, Spanish spelling, and we have done so throughout; other writers prefer *Navaho*, a form we retain when quoting from their original works.

The People

>>

The Navajo are interesting people. Their physical traits are described in the next selection. But of importance too is their fertility. They are now the largest group of Indians in the United States and also one of the fastest-growing groups. In 1868 their number was estimated at 8000–15,000; now they number about 65,000. Looking at population growth from another point of view, we find that the Navajo had a birth rate in 1940 of 36 as compared with 24 for other Indians and about 20 for the United States as a whole. (The birth rate is the number of infants born annually for each 1000 people in the total population; the death rate is the number of persons who die annually for each 1000 people.) The death rate for the Navajo was 16, for all Indians 13, and for the United States about 10. If we subtract the death rates from the birth rates we get the natural increase, which in the case of the Navajo is 20, all Indians 11, and the United States 10. In other words, the Navajo, far from dying out, are growing through natural increase twice as fast as the rest of the country.

• 21 • Physical Traits of the Navajo
CHARLES E. SNOW

The Navajo population is now about 65,000 and they are increasing by more than 1000 a year. Racially the Navajo belong to the group of American Indian tribes termed *Pacifid,* probably one of the last series of migrant groups to enter North America from the great Mongoloid reservoir of Asia. The type today is found among the Indians of Alaska and the Canadian Pacific coast areas.

The interbreeding of the Navajo with the Pueblo and other Indian tribes and recently with Spanish and American whites has produced great variation in body build, facial features, skin and eye color, and other physical features.

In stature, Navajos are fairly tall compared with other Indian groups. Men average five feet six inches, and women five feet one inch. They tend to be light in weight, men averaging 140 pounds, but there is great variation among individuals. In general, Navajos are of medium body build, although they can be roughly divided into two groups, one being short and stocky, like the Pueblo Indians, and the other taller, leaner, and larger boned.

Skin color is variable, from light to dark shades of yellow-brown. Similarly, hair varies somewhat, usually being black and straight but sometimes dark brown with a slight waviness. Body hair is scanty, and beards are sparse, although some men develop straggly moustaches.

Eyes are dark brown, but again there is some variation with mixed dark and light eyes among people of mixed ancestry. The "oriental" eye, consisting of a fold of skin slanting across the inner corner of the eye, occurs fairly commonly among children and women.

Navajos' heads are frequently flattened at the back as a result of the cradle board used in infancy, but too great flattening is not admired. Even without the effects of cradling, heads are relatively round, with low crowns. Faces are both long and broad, with prominent cheekbones accentuating the large features. The nose is frequently aquiline. As with the Eskimo, shovel-shaped front teeth are common. The teeth are generally excellent, with little decay and little crowding.

The racial traits described above are inherited biologically. But the social heritage is important, too. This we term culture, signifying that it is man-made and handed down from parent to child—not through genetic processes but through training and education to the point that it seems as much a part of the individual as do his hands and feet.

Before turning to a description of the growth of Navajo culture, which is the next selection, let us review the nature of culture as it was set forth on pages 14-15. The following diagram illustrates the interrelations among the three aspects of culture, which are discussed in the next selection.

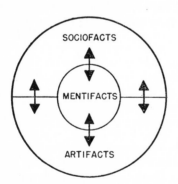

The whole circle represents culture, which is actually indivisible. But from its whole can be sorted out for examination the artifacts, sociofacts, and mentifacts, all in close touch with each other as the arrows show. Beliefs and values (mentifacts) are centrally placed for they actually pervade the utilization of the material possessions as well as the preference for varying kinds of social arrangements.

You will notice that Dr. Farmer's account deals with the artifacts (for example, bows and arrows), sociofacts (bands of people, under the leadership of a headman), and mentifacts (legends and clan stories). This selection is not an attempt to describe all of Navajo culture in terms of these three aspects—these "tools, customs, and ideas"—but it does show how major historical events brought about changes in the Navajo way of life.

• 22 • The Growth of Navajo Culture

MALCOLM F. FARMER

. . . The western garb of blue jeans, colored shirts, high-heeled boots, and wide-brimmed hats of the men, the wide flowing skirts and bright velveteen blouses of the women, the distinctive woolen rugs and blankets, silver and turquoise jewelry, flocks of sheep and goats, colorful ceremonials, sand paintings, all make up a familiar sight in the present-day Navaho culture. However, these and many other traits found among the people today are not original with Navaho. They have been taken over from many sources and under various conditions. The Navaho have been great culture-borrowers, taking over traits from every group with whom they came in contact during their migrations. It is very difficult to determine the basic culture pattern of the group because of this [characteristic].

The Navaho are not indigenous to the southwest. Their ancestors began to arrive about 1300 A.D. This time is believed to mark the real invasion of any numbers, because it was then that the Pueblo people who had held that part of the southwest for so many hundreds of years were withdrawing to the present Pueblo centers; the pressure of invading people, among other causes, was becoming an important force. These movements opened areas for settlement, and the ancestors of the Navaho and other Apachean groups began to establish their territories.

The origin of the ancestors of the Navaho is not entirely clear, but anthropological investigations over a period of years have given much information. The language has been one of the best keys. . . . Language then indicates that the Navaho and other Athapaskans of the American southwest are northern in origin, and divided from the southeastern fork of the Athapaskan people as they moved south from Canada. The purity of the language and the close relationship to the northern nucleus also indicates that this break did not take place until a fairly recent time.

The Navaho-Apache when they entered the southwest were quite different in many cultural aspects from the present-day Navaho or their ancestors of two hundred years ago. Informants say that the people then wore clothing of yucca and grass fibers twisted and braided. Men wore breech cloths, sandals, and sometimes leggings. Women wore skirts and sandals. Both used blankets which often had rabbit fur twisted on the fiber wefts. They also used some buckskin for clothing. Later this material was more commonly used. This was when the influence of the Plains tribes became stronger, and was probably some years after the Navaho-Apache arrived in the southwest. Many of the Pueblo groups show the effects of this same influence. The Navaho-Apache gained their livelihood by hunting game and gathering wild plants that were edible. The men hunted with sinew-backed bows and arrows of solid wood. Groups very often stalked the game, hid near game trails, and imitated game calls. Sometimes they drove deer and antelope into corrals. The Navaho-Apache were also acquainted with the bison. Its range may have been crossed in their travels, and there is evidence also that the bison ranged into the eastern side of the Great Basin in pre-historic times. Many parts of the bison are still used ceremonially. Before, during, and after hunts, the men used many rituals. Everything had to be done just right in order to assure success not only in the hunt of the moment but for future hunting as well. Their only domestic animal was the dog.

Houses were made by arranging three forked poles in a conical framework and

[Adapted from "The Growth of Navaho Culture," *The San Diego Museum Bulletin,* Vol. 6, No. 1, San Diego, 1941. Pp. 8-16. Used by permission.]

covering it with other timber, brush, and earth. Sometimes, the informants say, juniper bark was used for a covering. Crude circular wind-breaks were made by setting tree branches in a circle and leaving an opening at one side. Dwellings usually had the doorway to the east. Arts and crafts were probably not elaborate. The Navaho made a few baskets, usually bowl-shaped of coiled weave. Pitched water bottles were also made, but this trait was no doubt taken over from an alien group, perhaps the Ute. It is not definitely known if pottery was made at this time.

From about 1400 to 1600 A.D. the Navaho-Apache lived in the northwestern part of New Mexico centering somewhere on the upper San Juan and east towards the Chama River. Some of the first amalgamations with other southwestern groups took place during this time. The Navaho genesis legend and the clan stories tell of this period. Many clans joined the Navaho-Apache, and the group became more powerful. It is no wonder that the Navaho culture of today is such a conglomerate with mixing occurring at this early date. At least eight clans trace their beginnings to this period. The culture of the whole group was changing, notably on the religious side. Much of the ritualism, as mask dances, the use of corn meal and pollen, perhaps sandpainting, ceremonial wands, and much other ceremonial paraphernalia that can be traced to Pueblo influences was coming into use. A very important thing was the change in food habits. The Navaho-Apache, formerly hunters and wild food gatherers, now began to plant corn and pumpkins and soon became excellent farmers.

In 1539 an influence came into the southwest that was destined to change the whole life of the Navaho-Apache. It was in that year that Fray Marcos de Niza, a Franciscan monk, made his famous exploration trip into the region as far north as the Zuni towns. He was soon followed by another Spaniard, Francisco Vasquez Coronado, who with a party of about two hundred and fifty Span-

iards on horseback, and three hundred Indians, made conquests in the Zuni towns. So started the Spanish invasion of the southwest. Of great importance was the introduction of horses, sheep and goats. The Navaho-Apache soon made use of these domestic animals, mostly for food. Changes also took place in the Navaho-Apache clothing habits. The Spaniards' tight-fitting leather knee-length breeches, leggings, and shoes with hard soles and soft uppers, were taken over by the men, and soon became very popular. At this same time, and until 1700, the Navaho-Apache became raiders. With the introduction of the horse as a riding animal, swift movements over long distances became possible and the Rio Grande Valley and the Acoma-Zuni area began to feel the force of the Navaho-Apache warriors. Various attempts to Christianize the Navaho-Apache took place during this period.

In 1680 an event took place that had an important effect on Navaho-Apache culture. This was the Pueblo Revolt against the Spaniards. The Spaniards retreated down the Rio Grande and returned in 1692 causing many of the Pueblo people to flee to the wilder sections of the province. So it came about that many Pueblo people went into the country of the Navaho-Apache and lived there for a number of years. This contact resulted in many more Pueblo traits being incorporated in the local culture pattern. Perhaps one of the most important of these elements was weaving. It may be that the Navaho-Apache had done some weaving before, but all the historical evidence so far found indicates that it was at this time that the craft gained its dominant place. Of the elements of the craft, the sheep and goats were obtained from the Spaniards, and the mechanics of weaving from the Pueblo Indians. The blending and the unique results of these were Navaho. Clothing for both men and women was made. Other elements of the craft, such as the belt loom and knitting, were also in common use after this time. Another culture trait that seems to date from this same period is the building of stone towers. Because of the raiding in which the people were constantly engaged, they had to be on the look-out at all times for retaliating war parties entering their own country.

During the time after 1600 A.D. the Navaho began to spread out over northwestern New Mexico. They divided into bands, usually under the leadership of a headman. These bands had a certain amount of contact with each other, but they operated independently to a great extent. This system caused a lot of difficulty for the Spaniards, because if they caught up with one group and perhaps made a treaty with them, soon a second band would become active elsewhere and begin raiding. In later times the American military forces had the same difficulty. They would make a treaty with what they thought to be all the Navaho, and it would turn out to be with only one band. By the year 1750, the Navaho had spread west to the region of Canyon de Chelly, Arizona, and south to Mount Taylor, New Mexico. . . . The pattern of their culture was now fairly well established. As the Navaho extended their territory, the contact between the groups became less. The general pattern remained fairly stable but many local differences were developing.

The men, in 1750, wore short buckskin breeches, buckskin shirts, and hard-soled moccasins of Spanish style. They also, on occasion, wore cotton pants of a Spanish type. These were loose with a slit on the outside of the leg almost to the knee. The Navaho also had some woven woolen shirts. Under these clothes they wore the traditional breech cloth. Women wore Pueblo style moccasins with wrap tops, and a black dress trimmed with red and blue designs. The dresses were made by sewing two woolen blankets together along the top edge and sides leaving a hole for the head and one at each side for the arms. The dress was never worn draped over one shoulder in the Pueblo manner. A woven sash was also worn. The dress may have been an adaptation of the Pueblo women's dress, or, as has

been suggested, it was a copy in woven material of the dress of buckskin worn by Plains Indian women. This costume was used by Navaho women until well into the American period.

A very characteristic Navaho craft, silver working, had its beginnings in the middle 1800's.

The next event that had great importance to the Navaho was in 1864. It was at this time that the "Great Walk" to Fort Sumner took place. Due to continued raiding by the Navaho, United States military forces, under Col. Kit Carson, rounded up the Navaho in 1863 and 1864 and took them to Fort Sumner on the Pecos River in New Mexico. Over 8,000 men, women and children were there at one time. This reservation was a failure, and in 1868 the Navaho were returned to their old country under a treaty with the government. Some of the changes that took place during the captivity are still established in Navaho culture. Women's clothing was changed from the old woolen dress to the wide skirt still seen today. The blouses also date from this time. The Navaho came in contact with many other Indian groups during this time and many traits were taken from them. The domination of the United States government was established during this period and the effect is still in evidence.

In this rather brief account, some of the major influences that have shaped the culture of the Navaho Indians have been noted. As they have taken over traits, they have cleverly shaped them to their own needs and ideals. They have the faculty of taking over, reshaping, and improving crafts in such a manner that they seem typically Navaho. Flood farming, sheep raising, weaving, silver working, are only a few of the major items. The Navaho is passing through many trials due to land problems, over-grazing, over-population for the available land area, commercialization, and many other factors. The culture of the Navaho is still dynamic, and is today absorbing American culture traits and adapting them to fit Navaho needs.

The Habitat

»»

The Navajo live on the Colorado Plateau in the "four corners" area, where the states of Arizona, New Mexico, Utah, and Colorado come together. Although a few Navajo do live in Colorado, the reservation and most off-reservation settlements lie in the three other states. Traditionally the Navajo country extended eastward to the Rio Grande valley, and the prehistoric as well as the historic record indicates that the range of these people has been greater than it is today.

To the north, northeast, and northwest of the Navajo's plateau habitat is mountainous, broken country; to the east, the Great Plains grasslands; and to the west and south, the Basin and Range country, primarily a desert region which climatically is a northern extension of the Sonoran Desert. Traditionally the Navajo have recognized territorial boundary markers. These are their holy mountains, only four of which are used as boundaries by any one Navajo group. They include the San Francisco peaks to the west, Navajo Mountain to the northwest, the San Juan mountains to the northeast, Mount Baldy to the east, and Mount Taylor to the south.

The area dealt with in the following selections comprises the reservation and the land immediately adjoining to the east and south. An introductory sketch of this region is given in a report of J. A. Krug, former Secretary of the Interior.*

The Navajo Indian Reservation is an area approximately the size of the State of West Virginia, located in northeastern Arizona, northwestern New Mexico, and the southeast corner of Utah. When the tribe returned from military captivity at Fort Sumner in 1868, the land reserved for its use amounted to about 3,500,000 acres. Subsequently the reservation was increased at various times to a present total of 15,444,952 acres. Not all of the Navajos live on the reservation, however.

* From *The Navajo: A Long-Range Program for Navajo Rehabilitation*, U. S. Department of the Interior,Washington, 1948. Pp. 1-3.

A considerable number live on individual Indian allotments and areas of public domain immediately east of the reservation in New Mexico, and there are small nonreservation colonies at Ramah, south of Gallup; at Canoncito, 40 miles west of Albuquerque; and at Alamo (Puertocito), 80 miles southwest of Albuquerque, all in New Mexico. In aggregate, there are approximately 16,000,000 acres, or 25,000 square miles, of land used by the Navajos.

The population density of about 2.1 persons per square mile appears low in comparison with that of Eastern States, but the Navajo lands are actually much more densely populated than similar areas in the surrounding country. While in the surrounding areas substantial communities have been established by non-Indians, centers with integrated systems of improved roads, irrigation facilities, water and sewage systems, schools, medical services, post offices, libraries, public parks, and other common improvements, there is nothing comparable on the Navajo Reservation.

The Navajo lands are of striking beauty but low productive value. As Lee Muck states: "It is a land of high plateaus, flat-top mesas, inaccessible buttes, deep canyons, and sand and gravel washes. . . . The rocks are chiefly sedimentary in formation. The climate is arid, the vegetation sparse, and a very substantial part of the area may be classified as unsuitable for any productive use." More than 1½ million acres are too rough, inaccessible, or barren to be used even for grazing. Precipitation varies from about 5 inches annually in the lower elevations to a little over 20 inches in the mountains, but much of it falls in torrential summer showers. Winters are cold but comparatively open. In the spring there are violent winds with attendant dust storms. Summers are hot and dry. Vegetation is typical of the upland desert and varies from shrub types to potentially luxurious mountain meadows. By far the greater proportion is of the grassland, sage, and woodland types. There are 260,000 acres of merchantable ponderosa pine.

Soil erosion has irreparably damaged many thousands of acres of Navajo land and, with self-generating momentum, threatens the entire range-land economy of the tribe. Some 2,000,000 acres of productive . . . land have been denuded and exposed to erosion. Navajo livestock in their desperate search for sustenance have climbed the steep, eroding slopes, destroyed the sparse clumps of grass, and trimmed the browse as high as they could reach. The vegetation which once checked the run-off is now gone. Torrential floods rush down the unprotected slopes with destructive fury, carving deep gullies all the way from the mountains to the major streams. . . .

As has been noted, the Navajo lands have been enlarged fivefold since the tribe was released from captivity. There have been other attempts to obtain additional land, although none has been successful in recent years. There is now a statutory restriction against the use of either Federal or tribal funds for the purchase of land for Indians in Arizona and New Mexico. Existing law prohibits the addition of public lands to reservations in Arizona and New Mexico without the consent of Congress.

In our effort to understand more about the physical environment to which the Navajo must adjust we will consider first the surface features, then the climate, and, finally, the natural resources. Selection 23 is from Cosmos Mindeleff, who traveled through Navajo country and wrote a report on Navajo Houses for the *Annual Report of the Bureau of American Ethnology* in 1895–96. Mindeleff describes the heart of Navajo country.

• 23 • The Surface Features
COSMOS MINDELEFF

It would be difficult to find a region of equal size and with an equal population where so large a proportion of the land is so nearly worthless. This condition has had an important effect on the people and their arts, and especially on their houses.

The region may be roughly characterized as a vast sandy plain, arid in the extreme; or rather as two such plains, separated by a chain of mountains running northwest and southeast. In the southern part of the reservation this mountain range is known as the Choiskai [Chuska] mountains, and here the top is flat and mesa-like in character, dotted with little lakes and covered with giant pines, which in the summer give it a park-like aspect. The general elevation of this plateau is a little less than 9,000 feet above the sea and about 3,000 feet above the valleys or plains east and west of it.

The continuation of the range to the northwest, separated from the Choiskai only by a high pass, closed in winter by deep snow, is known as the Tunicha mountains. The summit here is a sharp ridge with pronounced slopes and is from 9,000 to 9,400 feet high.

Still farther to the northwest, and not separated from the Tunicha except by a drawing in or narrowing of the mountain mass, with no depression of the summit, is

another part of the same range, which bears a separate name. It is known as the Lukachukai mountains. Here something of the range character is lost, and the uplift becomes a confused mass, a single great pile, with a maximum altitude of over 9,400 feet.

The western and northwestern parts of the reservation might also be classed as mountainous. Here there is a great mesa or elevated tableland, cut and gashed by innumerable canyons and gorges, and with a general elevation of 7,500 to 8,000 feet. Throughout nearly its whole extent it is impassable to wagons.

The base of the mountain range has an average breadth of only 12 or 15 miles, and is a pronounced impediment to east-and-west communication. It is probably on this account that the Navaho are divided into two principal bands, under different leaders. Those of one band seldom travel into the territory of the other. The Navaho of the west, formerly commanded by old Ganamucho (now deceased), have all the advantages in regard to location, and on the whole are a finer body of men than those of the east.

On the west the mountains break down into Chinlee valley by a gradual slope—near the summit quite steep, then running out into table-lands and long foothills. This

[Adapted from "Navaho Houses," *17th Annual Report, Bureau of American Ethnology*, Part 2, Washington, 1898. Pp. 477–480.]

region is perhaps the most desirable on the reservation, and is thickly inhabited. On the east the mountains descend by almost a single slope to the edge of the approximately flat Chaco valley. In a few rods the traveler passes from the comparatively fertile mountain region into the flat, extremely arid valley country, and in 50 or 60 miles' travel after leaving the mountains he will not find wood enough to make his camp fire, nor, unless he moves rapidly, water enough to carry his horses over the intervening distance.

Throughout the whole region great scarcity of water prevails; in the large valleys during most of the year there is none, and it is only in the mountain districts that there is a permanent supply; but there life is almost impossible during the winter. This condition has had much to do with the migratory habits of the people, or rather with their frequent moving from place to place; for they are not a nomadic people as the term is usually employed.

[The] San Juan river forms a short section of the northeastern boundary of the Navaho country, and this is practically the only perennial stream to which they have access. It is of little use to them, however, as there are no tributaries from the southern or reservation side, other than the Chaco and Chelly "rivers," which are really merely drainage channels and are dry during most of the year. The eastern slope of the mountain range gives rise to no streams, and the foot of the range on that side is as dry and waterless as the valley itself. One may travel for 20 miles over this valley and not find a drop of water. Except at Sulphur Springs, warm volcanic springs about 30 miles south of the San Juan, the ordinary traveler will not find sufficient water between the foot of the mountains and the river, a distance of over 50 miles. Such is the character of Chaco valley. But the Indians know of a few holes and pockets in this region which yield a scanty supply of water during parts of the year, and somewhere in the vicinity of these pockets will be found a hogán or two.

Chaco wash or river, like most of the large drainage channels of this country, has a permanent underflow, and by digging wells in the dry, sandy bed it is often possible to obtain a limited supply of water. This is well known to the Navaho, and 90 percent of the houses of this region are located within reach of the wash, whence the supply of water which the Navaho deems essential is procured.

On the western slope of the mountains and in the canyons and cliffs of the high table-lands which form the western part of the reservation, the water supply, while still scanty, is abundant as compared with the eastern part. In the mountains themselves there are numerous small streams, some of which carry water nearly all the year; while here and there throughout the region are many diminutive springs almost or quite permanent in character. Most of the little streams rise near the crest of the mountains and, flowing westward, are collected in a deep canyon cut in the western slope, whence the water is discharged into Chinlee valley, and traversing its length in the so-called Rio de Chelly, finally reaches San Juan river. But while these little streams are fairly permanent up in the mountains, their combined flow is seldom sufficient, except in times of flood, to reach the mouth of Canyon Chelly and Chinlee valley. However, here, as in the Chaco, there is an underflow, which the Indians know how to utilize and from which they can always obtain a sufficient supply of potable water.

The whole Navaho country lies within what the geologists term the Plateau region, and its topography is dictated by the peculiar characteristics of that area. The soft sandstone measures, which are its most pronounced feature, appear to lie perfectly horizontal, but in fact the strata have a slight, although persistent dip. From this peculiarity it comes about that each stratum extends for miles with an unbroken sameness which is extremely monotonous to the traveler; but finally its dip carries it under the next succeeding stratum, whose edge appears as an escarpment or cliff, and this in turn stretches out flat and uninteresting to the horizon. To the eye it appears an ideal country for traveling, but only a very slight experience is necessary to reveal its deceptiveness. Everywhere the flat mesas are cut and seamed by gorges and narrow canyons, sometimes impassable even to a horse. Except along a few routes which have been established here and there, wagon travel is extremely difficult and often impossible. It is not unusual for a wagon to travel 50 or 60 miles between two points not 20 miles distant from each other.

· 24 · Climate
THOMAS P. FIELD

The climate of the Navajo country is that of a middle-latitude steppe—dry, with 12 to 18 inches of annual precipitation, steppe vegetation, and at least one month below 32° F. Though the latitude is considerably less than that usually associated with this climatic type, the generally high elevation of the Colorado Plateaus brings it in accord with this classification. To reach a desert, the Navajo need only go downhill, down to the floor of a major canyon or down to the Painted Desert.

The influences of the climate on cultural activities are many and varied. For instance: (1) winter hogans are located at lower elevations than the summer ramadas (shades); (2) winter hogans, to be comfortable, must be located near a good wood supply because Navajo winters are severe; (3) the high mountain pastures are too cold and too snowbound for winter grazing, necessitating seasonal shifts; (4) in summer the family moves out of the winter hogan and lives under the scanty shelter of the ramada; (5) when a person is diagnosed as having been made ill by lightning from one of the many thunderstorms, the Shooting Chant is used; (6) several of the gods are direct expressions of weather forces; (7) the violence of the conflict between gods is believed to create rain; (8) weather varieties are given sex distinction, gentle rains are female and storms are male; (9) the deep planting of corn; (10) the "ten-gallon" Stetson hats of the men, all reflect the conditioning influence of climate upon the Navajo way of life.

The climate of the Navajo country is a part of a great world pattern of climates. On all continents with land lying between 30° and 40° of latitude the western interior portions are dominated by arid or semi-arid climates. The climatic map of Africa is one of the best illustrations of this phenomenon, a core of desert which faces westward, and a surrounding crescent of less arid climates. This is true of the Sahara in the Northern Hemisphere and of the Kalahari in the Southern Hemisphere. The core of desert for the Navajo country is found in the Sonoran Desert of northwest Mexico. This desert is as much as five hundred miles from the Navajo thus making them on the fringe of an arid climate rather than in its center. Poleward, equatorward and eastward from the desert cores the climate becomes more humid. Five hundred miles east of the Navajo country one finds the first signs of agriculture becoming dominant over pastoralism. The poleward reduction of aridity is less pronounced over the same distance but the same tendency is noted. It can be said with fair certainty that, regardless of the many factors that influence the climate, the latitude of the Navajo country combined with its central western position will result in some form of an arid climate.

It is useful to note at this point that the forces acting to make weather and the resulting climate are dynamic forces, forces with movements of clock-like regularity, forces that can combine to produce gentleness or violence by chance or by predetermined mixtures. The grandest of these forces is the "march of the four seasons." This patterned, constant change of earth-sun relationships results in the seasonal sequence of winter, spring, summer and autumn. The winter solstice is the period of lowest sun, the summer solstice is the period of highest sun. Earth-sun relationships are the making of climate and since the relationship is constantly changing, constantly shifting the position of high sun, is it not only reasonable to expect that climatic areas would shift as well? Such climatic shifts are well-recognized. They are most important in understanding the climate of the Navajo. During the spring and early summer the climate of the Sonoran Desert infringes farther and farther poleward. This results in a Sonoran climate for the Navajo during this period. Imagine the situation of the Navajo farmer at this time. He calls corn "that which you eat," yet the spring and early summer, the planting season, are the period of greatest drought. The Navajo country then is not far enough south to be constantly under the desert influence, but during the early summer it is strongly under its influence.

The winter months find the Navajo country in a very different climatic environment. The southerly shift of the sun has moved the Sonoran climate equatorward placing the Navajo farther from its center. Following the established pattern the Navajo country comes under the influence of more northerly climates. The keynote of these climates is cyclonic storms, atmospheric disturbances resulting from the interplay of warm, moist and cold, dry masses of air. Cyclonic storms are rain-makers. Cyclonic storms migrate from west to east with the prevailing westerlies. Being on the southern fringe of these storm tracks results in only infrequent invasions into the land of the Navajo. The resulting small amount of precipitation would not be worthy of mention in humid lands but to the land of the Navajo it is a vital matter. Poor winter rains mean reduced pasture and low water supply.

Elevation plays a role in shaping the character of the Navajo's climate. The reservation is considerably more than a mile above sea level. Increasing elevation results in marked reductions in temperature. Because of the elevation the climate is colder than would be expected at this latitude. This lowered temperature acts both to the benefit and hindrance of the Navajo. Summer days often record high temperatures but the rarified atmosphere reduces evident heat discomfort. (This lack of discomfort often leads to sunstroke for those who are inexperienced.) The Navajo seldom has any complaint against the heat but cold is a different matter. Frost comes early and a lack of fuel resources drives him to the lower elevations. Abrupt changes in elevation in the Navajo country are largely confined to the backbone of mountains which run from the Zuni reservation north toward the San Juan River and in the depressions made by the San Juan and Colorado Rivers. The mountains may be thought of as wringers which, by mechanical action force the air to rise, to cool and to precipitate. The precipitation record of the various weather stations on the reservation clearly shows that increasing elevation results in increased precipitation. As much as 24 inches annually is recorded at the higher stations and it would be presumed that the mountain tops would exceed this amount. In the instance of the canyons a reverse situation applies. There is a lack of exposure, nothing to cause the air to rise, cool and precipitate. Thus we find the driest areas at the lowest elevations. Most Navajo are forced to live in the midground between these two extremes. Living in the midground between 3 and 24 inches of annual precipitation certainly has obvious disadvantages from an agricultural point of view.

Air masses are born in centers of action that give them their distinguishing characteristics and send them outward to make weather in those areas that lie in their path. For the Navajo one center of action and source region is the Canadian north and the Arctic. From this source region originate masses of cold, dry, heavy air. A second source region lies over the Aleutian Islands. From this region comes cold, moist, moderately heavy air. Both of these source regions send air masses curving southeastward across the United States in increasing numbers as autumn blends into winter. To the south of the Navajo country lie three source regions. The first of the southern source regions lies over the Gulf of Mexico and the Caribbean Sea. From this region originate warm, moist, light air masses which circulate northward. The second region lies over the Mexican Plateau and is the source of warm, dry air masses. The third region lies over the Pacific and produces warm, moist air masses similar to those from the Gulf of Mexico. Air masses from these southern sources are of more common occurrence over the land of the Navajo in summer than in winter.

It is only in the broadest sense, however, that air masses can be referred to as the weather-makers of an area. The particular character of an air mass, the immediate state of the pattern of circulation and the atmospheric results of interaction between two air masses makes the expected weather fit into only the most general sort of category—such seasonal generalities as winter cold, spring drought, late summer rains and the early frosts of autumn. If the generalities of air mass invasions and conflict were unalterably fixed the weather phenomena for a given season would be the same year after year. Also there would be no variation between years as to temperature, precipitation and related features. The weather of the Navajo country instead of being characterized by constancy is in fact characterized by change and violation of the generalities. Variations from normal or average are the rule rather than the exception. Extreme shifts in temperature and precipitation from year to year are common. The Navajo country is noted as the area of greatest absolute range of temperature in the United States, 134°F. (Absolute range means the difference between the coldest it has ever been and the hottest it has ever been.) In this case, Keams Canyon, Arizona, has recorded a high of 104°F. and a low of −30°F. In winter, sudden changes in temperature are most frequent. They occur when cold polar air masses invade the area.

The occurrence of precipitation is of vital importance to the Navajo. Not only is he concerned with how much precipitation occurs but also with the factor of how much for how long. This concern of the Navajo is not unwarranted. He lives in a land that experiences long gentle rains in the winter —rains that produce little volume. His summer rains are often short and violent—rains that run off in floods rather than soaking into the ground.

Winter precipitation is largely the result of air mass interaction. The land is being constantly overrun by cold air masses from the north. On occasions however, warm, moist air from the Pacific flows northward. This warm, moist, light air is forced up by the heavy surface air. The lifting process combined with the cooling by contact causes condensation in the warm air. The resultant precipitation is usually that of light, steady rain or snow. Such precipitation makes living difficult and miserable for the Navajo. Stock losses from cold and starvation occur and the problem of getting about becomes almost impossible. Still, this winter precipitation is vital, it soaks into the ground, feeds the springs and is available as ground moisture for crops. The winter (Jan., Feb., March) precipitation averages only about 2.5 inches but it reduces the aridity in an effective manner.

Precipitation varies widely from month to month, and even at the rainiest of stations as many as 10 of the 12 months have in one year or another experienced a complete absence of rain.

Mid-summer is the time of the "Mexican Monsoon". July and August are the wet months for the Navajo. The intense heating of the land during the late spring and early summer results in a lowering of air pressure. This extensive and lasting area of low pressure becomes the attracting force for both tropical and polar air masses. Warm, moist tropical Gulf air masses and similar tropical Pacific air masses migrate toward this center of low pressure.

Because the distance inland is great these air masses lose much of their moisture enroute but on occasion they have the carrying power to penetrate the land of the Navajo. When they do arrive, the Navajo experiences thunderstorms. These thunderstorms may be the result of the rising land causing the air to cool and precipitate. On the other hand the conflict between a tropical air mass and one from polar sources can also produce widespread thunderstorms.

Summer thunderstorms, regardless of their cause, may vary greatly in their intensity and the amount of resultant precipitation. It is not uncommon to see the rain from a large thundershower evaporate before it can reach the surface. On the other hand a real deluge may result. Gladys A. Reichard describes this second type in her book, *Spider Woman*.*

. . . "It's raining again." And that look of satisfaction typical of the Navajo when they are pleased, settles on her face.

We continue our weaving placidly although the storm is gaining in velocity. This is a male [violent, as contrasted to a gentle, "female"] rain with wind, thunder, and lightning, sharp lightning. I have learned to lay my door over the supports of the entry when it rains. Quite satisfactory to keep the house dry, but it cuts off most of our light. So we cover the weaving and just sit, as small as we can make ourselves, and look at each other. Suddenly there comes a cry from Maria Antonia's house, a startled cry of fear. The settlement is galvanized into action. Marie darts up, I thrust the army blanket at her. She rushes out while I put on my rain things.

I try to go out but the rain sends me back. There is no going between drops, no walking between puddles. The settlement has become a single puddle in which shoes slip and slide. I see my relatives running about barefoot. The women have hastily thrown on their blankets, but their ruffled skirts drip water. Tom and Curley's son have been shovelling to divert the water from the houses, and they are soaked.

* From *Spider Woman*, The Macmillan Company, New York, 1934. Pp. 85-86, 90-93. Used by permission.

Next day we learn the results of the tornado [really a thunderstorm] and take a trip to survey the havoc. It has raised the water level of the large reservoir near Ganado, empty all summer, five feet. But it has ripped out entirely the diversion dam which controlled the ditches. The place where it stood used to look like a smooth lake. It has now become a wide forty-foot cañon. Concrete piers are torn completely away, their mass dumped in the side of the wash at intervals half a mile down. The traders tell me the waves rose as high as the telephone poles in front of their place. In the sixty years of their experience they remember nothing like this. Poor old blind Tonto, the twelve-year-old son who led him through life, and his little grandson were drowned just outside their hogan. No one knows how many sheep were lost.

A few days later in the course of our conversation Red-Point remarks casually: "It's awful dry. We need rain."

From what has been reconstructed of the early history of the Navajo there emerges the story of his constant effort to adjust to the climate of the plateau country. Considerable admiration is due the Navajo for his success in meeting the problems presented by a vagrant climate that does little to make the job of adjustment easy.

In the period between the arrival of the Navajo in the Southwest and the arrival of the Spanish in the 16th Century the Navajo changed from full-time nomadic hunters and gatherers to nomadic part-time farmers. This partial adaptation to the well-established Pueblo way of life was successful. The early Spanish historians recorded the Navajo as a farmer and trader. From the climatic point of view this would indicate that the good years, for the Navajo type of economy, outnumbered the bad. These good years allowed the Navajo to prosper and in doing so led him further away from his traditional way of life. All progress and success were dependent upon the good years in a land where the bad years can be frequent.

The Navajo situation might be summarized as follows: (1) the primitive nomad arrives in a land which provides a good life to a more advanced and highly skilled people; (2) by acculturation the nomad achieves the means to obtain a subsistence-plus economy; (3) the good years seem very good and yet the cultural advance has not been so great as to make the bad years seem too abnormal; (4) he rises to a cultural level which is incompatible with the climate and other resource features of the habitat. Then even those years that formerly seemed good are only mediocre; (5) a considerable measure of release is found through the introduction of pastoralism; (6) there is continued self-destroying movement toward the present need for a drastic course of action, action in the form of enforced migration, change in occupation or the acceptance of charity to support a lost cause.

The mid-latitude steppes of the Southwest have been and still are areas of hazard for agricultural and pastoral people. When the Navajo first entered the territory of the present reservation he could easily see that he was not the first to farm the canyon floors. Many have speculated as to why these ancient people abandoned their well-made homes, their canyon floors and their defensible position. It seems improbable that a single answer to this question would suffice for all cases of abandonment. War, plague, overpopulation and climatic change have all been advanced as answers, but no one is considered as all inclusive. However, if we look closely at the inherent character of the local climate and relate these facts to the mode of life much of the abandonment seems explained.

When precipitation, its incidence and amount, and seasonal distribution are average at near-critical levels it is to be expected that an exact level will not be held from one year to the next. Arid climates are noted for being erratic. For the Navajo or the Anasazi who preceded him a combination of slight variations could upset the balance of forces which gave him a favorable climatic situation. The simple fact is that they run out of water.

The modern Navajo is vitally concerned with the natural resources of his reservation, the full utilization of which is of the greatest importance if the Navajo economy is to achieve a better balance. The known resources divide themselves into two types: (1) those that can be utilized by the Navajo directly—*i.e.*, the pasture, the farm land, irrigation and domestic water, fuel wood, saw timber, and building materials; (2) those that can be exploited by the employment of outside capital—*i.e.*, petroleum, rare minerals, including uranium, and the locale and desirable climate for motion-picture sets.

In the following selection the blend of the two types is evident. Since the Navajo were originally hunters, it seems appropriate first to note what wildlife still exists and the connection between its decrease and the coming of domesticated animals. Then further mention will be made of water, although preceding selections have made frequent reference to its scarcity. The value of water, a vital natural resource which many of us in well-watered areas take for granted, is an ever-recurring theme in this section. The overuse of range lands, with the resulting erosion and more rapid run-off, means that now less water remains in the ground to supply vegetation.

The next selection will also describe briefly the timber and mineral resources. When this has been done, it will be possible to turn to a study of Navajo economy in Part III, where the soil as a resource will be discussed in connection with farming and more details about livestock will be presented.

The chief enemy of wildlife has not been the hunter. It has been the rapid increase of sheep and other livestock competing for food, devastating the cover, and destroying the factors that held back moisture for a steady flow of water into the streams. In other words, just as destruction of grass, of soil, of water, and of woodland has been brought about by excessive grazing, so has destruction of wildlife been largely brought about by overgrazing. It is hoped that the reverse may take place, namely, that restoring the range through controlled grazing will also restore the chances of the surviving wild species increasing their numbers.

Within the past few years, the District has been thoroughly surveyed with regard to water. The location of all known springs, dug wells, and charcos or reservoirs has been determined and mapped with pertinent information as to their condition. Where the map showed blank spots, in which there was no water, the country was searched for possible spots where reservoirs might be built to collect natural run-off.

The location of a reservoir and its effectiveness is conditioned by a number of physical factors, however, as well as the human desire for water. A reservoir at the foot of a small rock would not collect very much water, for the mouth of the funnel would not be sufficiently large, so to speak. On the other hand, if the area drained is mostly sand, the waters are likely to disappear into the ground before they get to the reservoir. The condition of the soil in District 1 (northwestern corner of Reservation) is such that many reservoirs built with the hope of collecting water have never done so, or the reservoir basin itself proved to be too porous to hold what water did run into it.

In the light of this experience, it appears unfeasible to build many more earth reservoirs in this area. Best hope now seems to be to build cement-walled reservoirs wherever a rock-bottomed gorge may be found in an area devoid of springs or deep ground water. This greatly limits the prospect of collecting natural run-off for stock waters.

Careful geologic surveys have also been made to determine where deep, drilled wells would provide assured water. In many parts of the District, it has been discovered that the tilt and structure of the rock formations is such that no wells can be developed, however great the expenditure. This applies to much of the northern part of the District.

Where this is so, the only future prospect for making maximum use of the vegetation in such areas, is to adjust stock movements and land use claims with the aim of getting more persons to move their flocks onto this range during the few weeks or months when reservoirs may contain water or when snow is on the ground. Such a plan, following reduction of stock to carrying capacity of the District, is being studied. This would place more owners on the waterless, winter range than now, but should allow more sheep from the District to secure winter forage while relieving the overgrazed sections.

Since 1935, ten drilled wells have been completed in District 1, ranging in depth from 430 feet to 1,420 feet. Seven of these produce water, but three proved to be dry holes. These wells often cost as much as $5,000 or more to drill because of the inaccessibility of the country and their great depth. The Navajos must be educated, therefore, to keep small children from dropping stones down the pipe to "hear the splash," to assume responsibility for reporting damage or neglect of any sort, and to take the initiative in cleaning out springs and repairing reservoirs.

[Adapted from unpublished materials, U. S. Department of the Interior, Washington, D. C.]

Making a Living

»»»

We now turn from the consideration of the habitat itself—which is a part of nature, although it is in many ways influenced by the presence of man—to the Navajo's adjustment to this living space. This reintroduces the concept of culture which was described just prior to Selection 22. As man sets about the task of making his houses, providing food, and placating the spirits, he reacts to the physical environment about him. He makes artifacts: tools such as a digging stick to use in planting corn, blankets to keep him warm, jewelry to delight the eye, or medicine bundles to be used in curing the sick. He also develops ways of getting along with his fellows through special kinds of family groups, property systems, or a tribal council, to mention but some of the sociofacts. Although these seem less directly connected with the habitat, they, too, in societies such as the Navajo, show its influence. And if we turn to the legends, myths, beliefs, and values (mentifacts), we again can see symbolic use made of natural landmarks or certain plants or animals.

But it is through culture that man transcends some of his environmental handicaps, since he can gain by trade what his own habitat could never provide, and he can take over (borrow) traits—ideas, fashions, domestic animals, seeds, machines—from other cultures and add them to his own. With such points in mind it will be interesting to note the Navajo adjustments which in the next six selections deal chiefly with making a living and thus stress the material side of the culture.

Although Selection 26 treats briefly a number of the points discussed in detail later on, it provides an effective introduction to many facets of Navajo life.

• 26 • Navajo Farmer
MARY AND JOHN COLLIER, JR.

Now Johnny Chee has been home from the Army more than two years. The joy of homecoming has been replaced by the wonder of what is going to happen to him, for

162

unlike most Americans he is a ward of the Government.

Day breaks late this first Friday in February. In the first cold light the three Navajo hogans of Johnny Chee's family stand out like black rocks on the sage covered plain of Burnt Corn Valley. In the pole corral near the hogans a lamb is bleating, an early lamb, born out of season.

Wisps of smoke begin to rise from the smoke holes of the three hogans, silvery threads of smoke that rise unbroken in the icy morning air. Everyone is getting up. You are asleep on a sheepskin, and then you wake and sit up, rub your eyes and you are up. No clothes to change, no clothes to put on, because the Navajos rarely remove their clothes at night. So Johnny Chee sits up and rubs his eyes. So do his two little brothers and his younger sister. Old Grandfather Fast Horses coughs hard and spits into the dead fire. Johnny's father, Isaac Chee, rolls a cigarette. Johnny's mother kindles the fire from the dying coals in the oil drum that serves as a stove, while his grandmother rummages about in some flour sacks to make fried bread for the early meal.

Nobody is talking much yet, just grunting and mumbling as each thinks over the tasks for the day. Grandmother sees the nearly empty flour sacks. Will someone go to the post today to get more? Old Grandfather, feeling all his aches, thinks of times when he was a boy and would run out to greet the dawn. Yes, he would run five miles into the dawn and five miles back. That was the way it was when he was a boy. Johnny's mother thinks of the younger boys. They should be in school, but she is keeping them home to look after the sheep.

Isaac Chee, a strong, quiet, capable man in his late fifties, is thinking as all fathers must about the family finances. Should he pawn his silver belt again? The two younger boys are laughing. Teasing each other with their private jokes, they splash water from the little basin as they wash their faces. Mother starts to check them, then remembers that with the snow on the ground, water

is not so precious, but in a month or so they'll be hauling it four miles from the windmill. Sister gathers up the sheepskin beds and shakes them out over the racks outside the hogan. She gives a kick to shake the dust from her skirt and smooths down her frayed velour blouse.

But Johnny is thinking hardest. All winter he has been idle, just puttering around. Fried bread and coffee are good, but not when it's all you have to eat. Where is there a job in the lonely plains of Burnt Corn Valley? Jobs are far away in Winslow, Flagstaff, or even California. His heart is heavy with the thought of leaving home.

Coffee is boiling on the oil drum stove. Mother pats a ball of dough into a tortilla and drops it into the sizzling fat. Sister spreads a cloth on the floor and passes out cups and spoons, and the family settles down for breakfast.

Old Grandfather Fast Horses spits again and begins one of his long speeches. "I suppose you've been everywhere now," he begins, nodding at Johnny. "I suppose you've traveled everywhere and seen everything. I suppose you've traveled so far that you came right to where the land went into the sky."

"No, Grandfather," Johnny explains again. "The land is always under the sky. The land is like a big melon, and I was like an ant going around and round."

Old Grandfather spits skeptically. "Ants and melons! We had much finer stories to tell when I was a boy

"Well, Grandfather, he's back," laughs Johnny's mother, "and that's a wonderful thing. To travel as far as Johnny traveled and still get home!"

"He's home," observed grandmother tartly, "but how long will he stay home? What's the matter with all the young people today? Always running around and round like they had no home."

Johnny finishes his coffee, throws the dregs toward the fire, and gets up. "I'll go for the horses, Father; then we can go to the post. Maybe there'll be some news."

Johnny and his father hitch up the bat-

[Adapted from "Navajo Farmer," *The Farm Quarterly,* Vol. 3, No. 3, Cincinnati, 1948. Pp. 17-20, 22-24, 103-106. Used by permission.]

tered wagon and start off for the trading post.

THE INDIAN TRADER

The trail to the post is two parallel ruts that runs through the sage and skirts the red mesas that wall one side of the valley. Now it dips precipitously into a wash and back up again, the horses struggling though the wagon is empty. In the ten miles to the post they pass perhaps eight or a dozen hogans, huts of wood and earth, so much a part of the land you might not see them. Most of the way there is only the spacious vista of plains, mesas, and sky that make up the Navajo world.

The trading post is the hub of the scattered trails leading to it from all directions. Beside the red sandstone post there is a missionary church and a government day school. There is a scattering of hogans of Indians who work in the school, in the post, or who have some obscure business of their own, an excellent medicine man, a young man who owns a truck, a blacksmith with a little forge who puts on horseshoes and fixes loose wagon wheels.

At the post wagons and saddle horses are hitched everywhere. Everyone has come to trade and hear a little news. Everyone is busy and self-contained. Some are watering their horses at the pump, others are loading bales of alfalfa for their horses, for spring grass is still a long way off. Others just stand along the wall in the sun looking wise and thoughtful. The women in their bright velveteen blouses and long full skirts push their way in or out through the heavy door of the post.

Inside, the trader stands patiently behind the counter. Navajos crowd the counter, squat against the wall, recline against the grain bags. There is a gentle hum of voices. News is going around. Fifty intent eyes sweep the shelves of the trader's store. Men look earnestly at a rack of new saddles, at coils of white lariat rope, at a new plow with a crimson painted plowshare. They look at the great, wide brimmed, tall crowned Stetson hats that swing from the rafters

overhead. Their women look longingly at the bolts of velvet, royal purple, peacock blue, and burgundy red and the many-striped Pendleton blankets that every well dressed Navajo woman must wear. Children stand in a silent circle around the candy counter, admiring each piece like a jewel from a foreign world. Then one by one the Navajos do their buying, flour, coffee, lard, and a little sugar. They buy it all very slowly, thinking about all the fine things that they would like to buy, but it is the flour that they finally ask for.

Isaac Chee unbuckles his great silver concha belt with smiling sky blue turquoises on each concha. He offers it to the trader for pawn. The trader makes out a pawn ticket.

"All I can offer is forty dollars. You know how things are," the trader says in Navajo, sweeping his arm toward the gleaming racks of pawn that stand just behind him. Thirty, fifty silver belts, strings and strings of turquois bracelets, rings, thousands of dollars worth of credit in pawn. "Look at all that! Everyone wants to borrow money. In six months the pawn is supposed to be dead, and where is the money? If I were to sell the pawn, everyone would feel bad and say I was not their friend. This concha belt was your uncle's. It has been here. before. It is a fine old belt. I'll put you down for forty dollars. . . ." He enters the figures in the credit book by Isaac Chee's name where thirty dollars is still outstanding. "Can't you make some money, Isaac? Look, last week I heard the railroad needs section hands in San Diego, and next month the orange growers will want many men...."

"All this work is so far away," replies Isaac. "You know lambing time is soon and I have fine lambs coming. There will be wool in May."

"Yes, but only a handful. Your father used to have three hundred head."

"Yes," Isaac nods slowly. "I have only thirty head now. My permit allows thirty-five. Yes, it is very hard."

Johnny puffs silently at a cigarette. His father is buying his groceries now. Two sacks of flour, lard, coffee, one can of peaches for a treat. Johnny suddenly smiles. Not a smile of humor or pleasure, but a particular Navajo smile that says, "This is life. This has happened before."

"I think that I will go again, Father." Johnny is saying. "San Diego." Again the smile. "What day it is?" he is asking the trader. "Will the mail bus go by here tomorrow?"

THE NAVAJO PROBLEM

Last winter [1947] the public "discovered" the Navajos and their privations. Clothing and food were sent from dozens of organizations. A Wisconsin housewife sent a pretty white dress "for a Navajo baby." A home economics class in Oklahoma sent ten dollars. Congress appropriated $2,000,000 for emergency relief.

Navajos have multiplied beyond the point where the arid and eroded land can support them.

The day of reckoning was put off by WPA and CCC. Then came the war, and 3,600 Navajo service men were sending home their allotment checks and some 15,000 were working in defense industries and agriculture. The war's end brought . . . a showdown. The defense workers returned to unemployment on the reservation. Then the veterans returned. By the middle of last winter the "52-20" checks were gone. Starvation stalked the reservation.

Why should a vigorous expanding people want to live in such a land? This area has always been their home. In its severity it spells trust and peace. Each canyon, each rolling hill, is part of the Navajo personality; each rock is a friend and each trail an old song that fills the heart with strength. The land was not always desert. In the old days there was plentiful game, enough grass, and above all there was space for a free spirit, for flocks of fine sheep, for rich living. The Navajos' love of their land permeates their whole approach to life. This land between the four sacred mountains is the center of the Navajo universe, and who would want to live elsewhere?

"IT IS ALL FOOD"

Traditional Navajo foods are the direct product of the land. In the old days mutton and goat meat from the family herd was the base of the diet, and there was corn, squash, beans and melons that the family raised by dry farming or got through trading with the Hopi farmers. Navajos learned to use every part of the animal and plant, and as a result the old diet was remarkably well balanced.

The Navajos eat all the internal organs and entrails. They empty and wash the stomach, stuff it with a dressing made of the blood and rough flour and a little fat, tie it up and boil it. They wash the small intestines well, wind them about with a string of fat and roast them over the coals. The heart, lungs, liver, second stomach, windpipe and stomach bag they cut up in small pieces and fry. The head and feet they singe, cook in hot ashes, then take off the hide and eat the inside. The ribs they roast over coals. The rest of the meat they may roast or pound with fat and fry in a pan or slice and hang over a wire to dry. They boil all the bones for soup.

They have ingenious ways of using plants in all stages of maturity. They boil young corn sprouts for greens, roast young stalks in ashes, make a soup from the undeveloped ears when the corn first comes into silk, and from the first milk ears till the corn is dry they have innumerable ways of baking breads, cakes and mushes. Squash blossoms they boil with fat and meat for flavor. They eat melons immature as well as ripe, "as soon as they have flavor," and dry them in the sun to store for winter.

CHURRO RUSTLER

The Navajos got their sheep in the first place by stealing them from the Spaniards who wrote in their archives, "We are the shepherds of the Navajos." But they couldn't steal the knowledge of animal husbandry and have always thought of the sheep, like the wild animals they know, as independent beings capable of taking care of themselves. Children were sent out with the flocks, not to supervise their grazing, but simply to see that they all returned to the hogans at night. Breeding followed its natural course and lambs were born from February to May.

These sheep, descendants by natural selection from the Spanish Churro, are light in weight, but quick and hardy. They will scramble over steep rocks where a Rambouillet wouldn't dare go. Since the 1880's Government officials and traders have been trying to "improve" the Navajo stock.

Recognizing, at last, the many valuable characteristics of the old type sheep the Indian Bureau and the Bureau of Animal Industry opened the Sheep Laboratory at Fort Wingate, New Mexico, in 1937 as a joint project to improve the Navajo sheep. In a series of experiments they are crossing the old breed with such long staple sheep as the Romney and Corriedale and, at the same time, trying to improve the Navajo sheep by selective breeding. They count on twenty years' work to establish a definite breed, but already considerable progress has been made.

When the railroads reached the southwest the Navajos were urged to increase their flocks for the eastern markets. From 15,000 sheep and goats in 1870 they increased to a million in the early 1930's. This, of course, led to overgrazing.

In the old days a family felt free to move anywhere on the reservation. Now there is no unclaimed grazing land and they settle down to a limited radius, knowing that if they roam some other family will claim their grazing rights. So the range around the family hogans and water holes was cropped even closer. The lamb and wool crop fell off, a fact which the Navajos failed to appreciate since they thought in number of sheep rather than weight per sheep.

The eroded state of the Navajo range was common knowledge when the dust bowl dramatized the importance of conservation. The technical brains of the Department of Agriculture focused all their energies on saving the soil; and a virtual army of technologists, agronomists and engineers moved in. The Navajo reservation was used as a vast field laboratory and, as much of the work was primary experimental research, many mistakes were made. Some positive things were accomplished. Hundreds of wells were dug and drilled for stock water, springs were developed and storage dams built, water spreading structures were designed to block arroyos in eroding valleys. The continuous drought of the past ten years has kept the Navajos from seeing any improvement in their range. They share the common belief that if it would only rain the problem would take care of itself.

The most drastic program of the conservationist was stock reduction. The goats, they said, cropped the range too short. The horses ate more than they were worth and the sheep would have to be reduced almost in half. To the Navajo this logic was incomprehensible and shocking. They resisted the program one hundred per cent. The Indian Service went ahead with its orders and reduced the herds by force, shooting sheep and goats and dumping the carcasses in trenches. The Indian Service had every intention of balancing the loss in economy. But politics being what they are, most of the planners went on to other jobs. All that remains is the sheep reduction.

"THAT WHICH YOU EAT"

Navajos believe the first man and woman were created from two ears of corn. In Navajo the word for corn means "That which you eat," so that it stands symbolically for all food products. Navajo corn is the same corn that the early inhabitants of the southwest, the cliff dwellers, cultivated near their canyon homes. Corn of myriad colors, red, blue, yellow, black, white, variegated, pink, dark red, blue spotted grey, and black tipped. This corn, unlike other varieties, can be planted as deep as twelve inches because of its elongated mesocotyl. This extra depth, bringing it closer to the moisture, means survival on the desert. Indian corn also develops a single large radicle which descends to the sub-soil and finds water at critical times when ordinary corn with its shallow roots would surely dry up. And even when the stalk is poorly developed, Indian corn can produce ears, sometimes longer than half its own length. These characteristics come undoubtedly from centuries of careful selection of seed corn from the best ears of the crop. Navajos did not originate this tradition, but they carried it on faithfully in the choice of seed for corn and all other crops.

"For desert farming you can't beat the Indian methods," Indian Service men say.

The Navajo farmer squats on one knee and with a stick digs a hole eight or ten inches deep. His wife or daughter follows, putting in not two or three kernels, but a small handful; "four for the cutworm, four for the crow, four for the beetle, and four to grow." Sixteen shoots to push their way through the earth's surface, sixteen sprouts to brace themselves together against the spring sandstorms, sixteen stalks to withstand the devastation of desert mice. Then the farmer's wife sprinkles the richer top soil back into the hole, pats it down gently with her foot, leaving a little depression to hold any chance rain, and moves on to the next hole eight or ten feet away. The clusters are planted far apart because there just isn't enough moisture to support them any closer together.

Beans are often planted between the rows of corn, getting the benefit of shade and wind break of the corn stalks. Melon and squash are usually planted in another plot. Where modern machinery is not available wheat is planted in the same way as corn, with many seeds dropped into one hole. "If you let the wind plant the wheat, the wind will take it away later." And this is literally true, for shallow planted seed in loose soil surely belong to the wind.

Navajos are reluctant to disturb the soil, for they know that breaking the earth's surface can be disastrous. The priceless moisture can be lost, the wind can blow the field away in a whirlwind of dust, and delicate plant shoots can be buried in wind drifted sand. So Navajos plow with caution. Under extreme conditions they do not plow at all, nor do they disturb the surrounding weeds that hold the earth and give protection to the young corn. All they do is dig a hole and drop in the seeds. Where the soil is firmer

and moisture more plentiful, they plow and cultivate with an ingenious tool of their own design.

The farmer chooses a plot for dry farming very carefully, usually making use of some underground water table. He plants in the path of water seepage, a declivity in the desert, a basin of rock, or to the leeward of a sand hill which stores water from the winter snows and summer rains, depending on his deep rooted crops to find their way down to water.

Navajos living in valleys use the spring run-off for one good irrigation. In late April they plow their fields and build dikes around them. Then comes an agonizing wait. If he plants too soon the spring winds will cut the young plants to ribbons; if too late, the wind and sun have dried the streams and his ditch will be filled with dust. When he dares wait no longer he turns the water into his field to soak. Next day he breaks the dike and the water flows on to his next field and so on as long as the water lasts. A few days later he digs his holes and plants. This is his only irrigation, for the summer torrents carry fifty per cent silt and are useless for agriculture.

In a few places on the reservation there are year round springs and streams and on the bigger washes and rivers large storage dams have been built. Here plowing with horse and tractor are possible and conventional irrigation techniques are practiced.

NAVAJO ECONOMICS

The Navajos' only dependable income comes twice a year, in the spring when they sell wool, and in the fall when they sell lambs. Silver and rug weaving are the only other traditional sources of income. As these no longer bring in enough to support the growing population, the Navajos are turning increasingly to wage work. The reservation offers at present only limited opportunities, and most Navajos must leave home to find work to balance the dwindling economy. It is the problem of the off-reservation Navajos that has given us the picture of their inadequate education. Even the returned veterans with three years' service find themselves unequipped to meet the standards of the white world.

Many people are impatient with the slow transition of the Navajo from their ancient life. Every effort is being used to awaken their self-determination. Some enthusiasts are ever urging the Navajos to take over trading posts by imposing restrictive regulations on the traders. But others feel that planners who are encouraging business and industrial ambitions among the Navajo people must not forget the importance of helping them get a realistic picture of how our business and industry functions. Many students of this problem say, "Continued subsidy or economic protection will not really help them. Unless they learn to meet the legitimate competition of the white world they will never be able to 'stand on their own feet,' but will remain dependent on the government."

EDUCATION

During most of the half century that we have been trying to educate the Navajo both the Indian Service and missionaries have started with the assumption that to educate an Indian you had first to strip him of every vestige of Indian culture. The Navajo language was forbidden, the home life was considered an evil influence, and Indian ceremonies of any kind tools of the devil. The result has been that after four or five years the child is sent back to his family, hopelessly split between the white man's world and his Indian culture. He is not "Americanized," for a new culture is not assumed so easily. He has been told that everything his beloved parents did was wrong, but he has not been given any better tools to take the place of Navajo ways. He has neither learned to make a better way of life on the reservation or to find a new home for himself elsewhere.

During the past fifteen years tremendous efforts have been made to establish a program that would preserve the Indian's personality, and at the same time give him the benefits of modern education. The plan is now to cause as little change as possible in the child's home pattern and to base the educational program on the pattern he knows. To the surprise of many people, the old people show no great prejudice toward education as long as it does not attack their culture or disrupt their homes.

One of the newest programs is the development of written Navajo. Many teachers believe the children will learn to read and write faster in their native tongues than in English. In a few schools today both children and adults are being taught to read and write the Navajo language on an experimental basis. These classes may develop into a reservation-wide program if they are successful.

Selection 26 should have established a feeling for the "Navajo way," and the critical reader is likely to desire more facts. From what sources and in what manner does the Navajo gain his livelihood? The original Navajo hunted the native animals and gathered wild plants and their products. As we have already seen, Pueblo influences resulted in the addition of farming, and the Spanish influence in the addition of livestock, which were pastured on natural grasses. The climate, however, forced the Navajo to engage in seasonal pastoral migrations in search of pastures. Until the land became too crowded, the Navajo moved about enough to be called a nomad. Nowadays, the modern Navajo is making several other economic adjustments: mining, logging, arts and crafts, and miscellaneous wage work. This complex of economic adjustments is the subject of Selection 27.

• 27 • *The Navajo Economy*

CLYDE KLUCKHOHN AND DOROTHEA C. LEIGHTON

LIVESTOCK

For the year 1940, 44 per cent, or nearly half, the total income of The People came from livestock. Three-fourths of this income resulted from sales of livestock.

The importance of livestock in the total Navaho economy can, however, be easily misunderstood from these data. In 1940, Navahos on and off the Reservation owned about 432,000 sheep, 71,000 goats, 16,000 cattle, and 38,000 horses. But they were far from evenly divided among The People: 2,500 out of the 9,500 Navaho families owned no livestock at all; about 4,000 families owned less than 60 head of sheep; at the other end of the scale, 110 families owned more than 500 head each. Hence it is obvious that a high proportion of the tribe's total livestock income—and indeed of the total income—was concentrated in a small number of well-off families.

AGRICULTURE

Agriculture is estimated to be the source of only about one-seventh of all Navaho income. Not more than 50,000 acres (one-fourth of 1 per cent of the Reservation) are now devoted to agriculture, and of these less than half (23,500 acres) are in irrigated tracts with an assured supply of water. . . . However, this distribution of total income cannot be taken without serious qualification, for estimating the value of foods consumed is difficult and unsatisfactory.

Agriculture today is the basis of the subsistence economy, as it has been for at least three hundred years. Almost every family raises some of its food, and many families live for weeks at a time chiefly from the produce of its gardens and fields. There is considerable variation between parts of the Reservation in the amount of "income" from agriculture—in one district it is esti-

mated at 40 per cent—but throughout the Reservation it is the mainstay of life for all save the most prosperous families.

Maize and squash are the staple crops, but melons are a valued addition, and in some areas beans, wheat, and oats are important. On the ditch-irrigated farms along the San Juan River, as many as 42 different crops are now raised. Demand for fruit trees is great, and it is clear that Navahos would go in for fruit production on a large scale if suitable opportunities could be provided.

In 1944 the total number of acres planted by Navahos under the jurisdiction of the Navajo Service totaled about 32,000. Acres harvested were as follows:

Maize	18,320	Alfalfa	3,818
Other Cereals	1,085	Other Forage	1,335
Potatoes	713	Wild Hay	418
Beans	1,501	Grapes	535
Squash	942	Tree Fruits	9,118
Melons	615	Garden	417

Trustworthy figures on average yield per acre were unavailable, but there was general agreement among competent judges that the average Navaho farmer obtains less from his farm land than the average white farmer in the Southwest would obtain. This is partly because adequate machinery is lacking, but even more because crop rotation, use of fertilizer, planting at the right time, and proper techniques of irrigation have been neglected. One experienced observer says that most Navahos earn only about $20 per acre from irrigated land as against the $100 per acre of their white neighbors.

WILD PLANTS AND ANIMALS

Livestock now eat most of the wild plants which furnished food for The People in the old days. Even so, almost every family will have a few dishes of wild greens during the

[Adapted from and reprinted by permission of the publishers from Clyde Kluckhohn and Dorothea Cross Leighton, *The Navaho*, Cambridge, Mass.: Harvard University Press, Copyright, 1946, by The President and Fellows of Harvard College. Pp. 19-24, 29-33.]

summer, and the poorer families still occasionally utilize certain wild seeds as cereals. The fruits of several species of cactus are gathered to make confections.

There are, however, a number of plants which furnish cash income as well as food. Herbs are gathered and sold for ceremonial purposes and for use as household medicines; some of the rarer species can be sold within the tribe for high prices.

The important wild plant resource is the pinyon nut, of which a sizable harvest is gathered every three or four years. Four-fifths of these nuts are sold to traders and go eventually to New York market, where they are salted and packaged for sale like peanuts. In 1936 a single trader paid $18,000 for the nuts. In such a good year they furnish a poor man with a cash crop that is comparable to the fall sales (surplus animals) of well-to-do livestock owners.

Game counts for little in the Navaho economy nowadays. It furnishes a few meals for the family during the year, and in some seasons rabbits and prairie dogs may tide a family over until it can produce or purchase other meat. Furs—coyote and wildcat skins and, in some areas, beaver—account for only a minute proportion of commercial income ($3,770 in 1940).

WAGE WORK

In 1940 about a third of all Navaho income was in the form of wages. On the Reservation the government is the chief employer of Navahos, supplying 84 per cent of wages in 1940, 33 per cent to regular employees and 51 per cent for temporary or irregular work. Almost half of the government payments in that year went to Civilian Conservation Corps employees. By 1942, when the CCC was liquidated, about 400 Navahos were employed in regular established positions of the Navajo Service, and about 780 were employed on a temporary or irregular basis, about 260 of these in tribal enterprises. . . . Navahos are on the government payroll as interpreters, teachers, day-school assistants, matrons, advisers, maintenance workers at agency plants, road and irrigation employees.

Other Reservation wage employment comes from traders, who use Navahos as interpreters and handy men; from missionaries, whom they serve as interpreters and guides; and from some of the more prosperous Navahos, who employ their tribesmen during the lambing, shearing, and harvesting seasons.

Fees for performing ceremonial rites should also be mentioned as a source of individual income. The sum total probably does not bulk large in cash terms, but to many families the income in livestock, goods, and cash earned by one or more of their members is of considerable importance, and the prosperity of certain families is based primarily upon the substantial fees charged by famous Singers.

Navahos have for years worked for white ranchers around the Reservation on a seasonal basis or during the seasons of heavy work. Some work for the Santa Fe Railroad. In ever increasing numbers they are going as seasonal laborers to the beet fields of Colorado; to Arizona mines, and to ranches as far away as Texas. Since 1940 the large ordnance depots near Gallup and Flagstaff have employed many Navahos. In 1944, Navahos earned $785,000 in planting, weeding, and harvesting irrigated crops at Bluewater, New Mexico.

AGRICULTURE

Floodwater farming is the common type, but ditch irrigation is practiced in a few regions. For the most part, The People have tried to take over the white agricultural techniques with which they are familiar, in so far as they have been able to purchase factory-made equipment. Close to the railroad and to centers of white influence, metal ploughs, barbed-wire fences, and the like are the rule today, although in more remote regions like that of Navaho Mountain digging sticks and brush fences are still common. Even where white techniques have been followed, however, The People still have much to learn about their application.

The old sunwise and other ceremonial ways of planting have almost disappeared, but most Navahos still use the Indian method of planting corn in hills rather than in rows. Planting dates are determined by various means—at Navaho Mountain, for instance, by the position of the Pleiades—and simple folk rites continue to be a basic part of agriculture.

ANIMAL HUSBANDRY

The techniques of animal husbandry have been derived first from the Spanish-speaking peoples of the Southwest (for whom many Navahos have worked as herders) and more recently from government stockmen, although there are a few minor variations which are distinctly Navaho. White influences have come to predominate more and more in recent years. Now one seldom sees undocked sheep, or flocks in which ewes and rams are herded together throughout the year. Most herding is done by children, however, and adult Navahos often herd on horseback—a practice disapproved by most white experts. Furthermore, the flocks are usually corralled for too many hours during the heat of the summer days.

Navaho sheep average about 6 pounds of wool when sheared, and only 57 lambs survive for each 100 ewes, while sheep owned by whites in nearby regions average 8 pounds of wool and produce 70 lambs per 100 ewes. Part of the trouble comes from the practice of using children for sheepherders, which means that, instead of utilizing distant ranges and moving the flock frequently, the flock is kept near home and brought back to the same corral every night.

On the whole, Navaho livestock enterprise is uneconomic. Because of terrain and available forage, because of herding practices, and because sheep provide wool as well as meat and can be slaughtered and consumed more easily and quickly than cattle, sheep are usually more suitable to Navaho economy. But other animals are not used to the best advantage. Goats are valued for their milk and their intelligence in the flock, but too many of them are kept. Cattle are owned by only an occasional family except in a few parts of the Navaho country, and their number and distribution are not at the optimum. Indeed, probably half of the total carrying capacity of the range has been used by nonproductive stock: excess horses, old cows and steers, and goats.

REGIONAL VARIATIONS IN ECONOMY AND TECHNOLOGY

In view of the numbers of The People and the size of their country, it is hardly surprising that the words "always" and "never" may seldom be used with any exactness. Regional and local variations in many features of the way of life are numerous and multiform. In large part, these reflect differences in the intensity of contacts with whites in accord with the location of the area, type of terrain making for greater or lesser isolation, etc. Moreover, sustained contact with the Ute and Piute Indians on the north has produced modifications of a different sort from those of the southern and eastern regions, where various Pueblo tribes or Jicarilla Apaches have been the neighbors of most influence.

Other differences are due to climates, soils, and topography. Along the northern, western, and a portion of the southern boundary of the Reservation stretches a broad C-shaped belt where the environment favors a livestock economy and where, except for a few localities, farming is of decidedly secondary importance. This type of economy also is characteristic of the eastern Navaho country, though in the "checkerboard" sections factors of land ownership and competition with non-Indian operators pose rather different problems. In most of the great central and eastern portion of the Reservation, conditions permit the development of considerable cropland, most of which is in small tracts conveniently located for receiving flood waters or sufficiently high to enable utilization of the increased rainfall in dry farming. These more favorable conditions have fostered an economy in which livestock and crops are about equally important. In a few restricted areas (Shiprock, Chinle, Ganado, and Tuba City) soil conditions and assured water supply permit intensified farming, and livestock plays a secondary or insignificant role.

Since the Navajo dwelling excites so much curiosity on the part of the tourist and is such an interesting adjustment to available materials and to the climate, a special description seems in order.

• 28 • Navajo House Types
GORDON B. PAGE

The "Pile Stick" type is still found all over the Reservation . . ., but is by no means the predominating type. [In this there is a foundation of three poles locked together. Over this foundation more logs are leaned, and then the whole structure is liberally plastered with earth which is packed hard by hand pressure.] There appears to be no outstanding type of structure, but rather a general plan, which is followed in construction, using whatever materials happen to be most accessible to the builder. Variations of the "Pile Stick" hogan are dependent on the materials used in building. At Naschiti an orthodox "Pile Stick" frame was used, but instead of the usual sides built up of logs chinked with mud, a long strip of canvas was wound about the frame, creating a "tipi" effect.

Occasionally a square, rectangular, or poly-sided hogan is desired. For this a trench two feet deep is dug along a line scraped in the earth, and upright posts, seven feet in length and roughly squared, are set up vertically in the trench, to form the walls. Beams are laid across a ridge pole set on the walls, to form a slightly pitched roof.

A site having been chosen, cleared, and leveled if necessary, the construction of a hogan will follow in this order. If there is plenty of timber available, and if the builder is able to obtain help from his neighbors or kinsmen, he may build the eight-sided type. . . . Posts are sunk in the earth at the corners . . . with two feet of their length below the surface; then poles, logs, or in some cases, railroad ties, are laid parallel to the ground, with their ends meeting at the posts. The interlocking sides are built up a few feet, and then a cribbed roof . . . roughly dome-shaped, is built over the whole. When the structure has been thoroughly chinked with mud, and the roof tamped with earth, the hogan is finished. . . .

In areas where timber is scarce, two types of dwellings are found; the stone house and the dug-out. The stone house is sometimes built on the conventional circular plan, but sometimes it is rectangular. The walls of stone houses are built up higher than those of timber houses, the former usually rising to a height of seven or eight feet. The stone blocks are dressed enough to give a finished appearance to the exterior, and are built up with mud mortar. The rectangular stone house has a pitched roof; the circular house has a cribbed roof.

The ownership of a stone hogan implies the possession of a certain degree of wealth. The stone must be hauled in wagons, and the laborers, even though they be men of the owner's clan, must be fed and housed. Thus the expenses incurred in building a stone house are considerably greater than in a timber house.

Contrasting with the stone house is the dug-out, at the other end of the architectural scale. Although warm in winter and cool in summer, it is far from pretentious in appearance. To construct this dwelling a deep excavation is made into a hill or bank which faces east. The structure is a single room approximately twelve feet square, with walls seven to eight feet high. The east wall, with

[Adapted from "Navajo House Types," *Museum Notes*, Vol. 9, No. 9, Museum of Northern Arizona, Flagstaff, 1937. Pp. 47-49. Used by permission.]

the exception of a two foot opening for the door, is sometimes formed of poles banked with earth. Usually the roof is cribbed and tamped with earth. This type of dwelling may be seen on the low mesas to the east of Tolani Lakes and in the Kayenta district.

The hogans described so far have been the permanent or winter quarters of the Navajo. In the summer the people move to the valleys where they cultivate crops. Here they live in temporary camps until after the harvests. If the family is well-to-do, the summer house usually is a tent but most of the summer camps are those structures commonly known in the Southwest by the Spanish name *ramada*. These consist of four upright poles, forked at the top, into which other poles are laid, forming the rectangular framework. . . . Slender roof poles are laid horizontally across the framework to provide support for the brush roof. Sometimes poles and brush are laid against the windward side to form a protective wall. The ramada provides a cool, shady shelter, admirably adapted to the summer climate of the region.

Still another type of summer dwelling is the forked-stick tripod overlaid with brush, being a variation of the "Pile Stick" hogan. No earth is placed over the brush, as is the case in winter hogans. In regions where timber is scarce, the poles of the summer house are taken out of the ground after harvest season and hauled away in wagons to the winter camp. In well forested areas, however, the timber frames are left in place.

AUXILIARY ARCHITECTURAL FEATURES

Doors for all types of hogans are similar. They consist either of an old blanket, suspended from the lintel, or a plank framework fastened with battens and hinged with leather or tin. Most hogans do not have windows. However, a few stone hogans, usually of the square or rectangular shape, have small glass windows in frames.

As an open fire is a necessity in heating the hogan, provision must be made for the escape of the smoke. Therefore, most hogans have an opening about three or four feet square in the roof. In imitation of the white man's chimney, a good many hogans boast ingenious, home-made chimneys contrived from bottomless kettles, buckets, and tin cans strung together with wire, the top suspended from the beams of the smoke hole, the flaring bottom covering the oil drum or open fire.

Cupboards to hold personal possessions are simply boxes from the trading post, or more often, the interspaces between the logs of the hogan.

The trading post is a central feature of the Navajo economy today, as Selection 26 has already shown. The account which follows not only gives the historical background but shows the functions that these trading posts perform. In one sense, they may be viewed as a community center for many otherwise isolated family groups.

• 29 • *Trading on the Reservation*

Presumably the Navajos had worked out some peaceful scheme of trading goods among themselves and with other tribes long before the Spaniards contacted them in the 16th and 17th centuries. At any rate, within the next hundred years, earliest-known writ-

[Adapted from unpublished materials, U. S. Department of the Interior, Washington, D. C.]

ten records referring to the Navajos indicate that, in the late 1700's and the early 1800's, the Navajos had become master weavers, owners of innumerable sheep, and possessors of many horses. They were well-clothed, and their leaders were wearing fine silver jewelry. Not all of this was the result of plunder. Early trade was rapidly making its impress upon Navajo destiny.

Exchanges within the tribe, such as corn for sheep, undoubtedly took place peacefully and continuously in the distant past. Upon special occasions such as dances and "sings" very likely a practice prevailed similar to that of today where gifts are given to medicine men and honored friends, articles and coins are given to the girls of the squaw dance and the male singers, and friendly swapping takes place among the festival makers. The importance of this type of internal exchange is not to be underestimated in promoting satisfactions among the people. It is said, for example, that much of the product of silver-smiths on the Reservation even today is traded internally and does not make its appearance among the commercial trade channels, until deposited as pawn for credit at the trading posts.

Unfortunately, not much is known as to the nature and the economic consequences of this internal exchange. We do not know very well the precise nature of the financial obligations between Navajos, or the social expectations concerning goods between relatives, clan members, rich and poor, or medicine men and Navajo society. We do not know clearly as to whether these relationships tend to even out, so that all of the participants tend to stay on the same economic level as a consequence of the exchanges, or whether the net result is to put certain persons in the strategic position of automatically accumulating a concentration of wealth. We do know that among many other peoples a key to what happens within an economy may be obtained from a knowledge of how the excess is distributed. This is a relatively unexplored area.

But it is the Navajo blanket that early assumed the major role in bringing influences from outside through trading. Before the appearance in Navajoland of the American system of trading with its stores of set prices to everybody and with the traders devoting all of their time to trade behind the counter, the woolen goods manufactured by the Navajos were the most important medium for the external exchange with the Pueblos, Havasupais, Apaches, and Utes, as well as the New Mexicans. By the process of primitive trade, Navajo blankets occasionally filtered eastward to the tribes of the Great Plains, while to the Navajos came such things as sea shells from the far distant Pacific.

American traders first came to the Navajos early in the 1800's. These were Mormons —traveling traders and missionaries—bringing horses for blankets.

Today the most important avenue of trade is through the fixed trading post of which there are approximately a hundred, not to mention the posts outside of but near to the boundaries of the Reservation. Supplementing these to a slight degree are the occasional fairs on or in the vicinity of the Reservation. In 1938 was inaugurated the first Navajo Tribal Fair as a further means of giving the tribal members experience in this phase of their life. The store or trading post and the fair both mark a definite advance over the primitive barter system in bringing buyer and seller together whenever one is ready to engage in such exchange.

Development of fixed trading posts, however, did not take place until after 1868 upon the return from Bosque Redondo. As late as 1876, only one post was reported to be operating actually within the Reservation.

Later, trading posts began to multiply, so that the bulk of present day trading posts was established after 1890, and the most active period of trading post establishment took place from 1900 to recent times. At present there is little likelihood of many new posts appearing on the Reservation.

Most of the trading posts in this section, (northwestern part of reservation), are stone buildings with trader's living quarters adjoining. Nearby each post is a camp hogan so that a Navajo family coming to the post from a distance may stay overnight. The trading post itself is likely to be situated at some strategic point such as a watering place or road intersection but otherwise isolated, and it is not unusual for Navajo families to be situated 25 or 30 miles away from a post.

During the year, Indian families will come to the trader to secure such things as flour, coffee, sugar, baking powder, velveteen, overalls, tobacco, or other odds and ends for food, clothing, or general living. They may bring in an occasional rug on which to make the trade, they may pawn a piece of silver and turquoise with the trader for credit, or the purchase may be on unsecured credit. In the spring at shearing time, wool will be brought to the trader; and in the fall lambs will be brought in, so that spring and fall are the occasions for cleaning up one's indebtedness with the trader and re-establishing credit for the following year.

Historically, then the trader was the one functional link between the Navajo and the White culture. Outside of the short list of rations issued by the Government, it was the trader who first made available to the Navajo the growing list of goods on which he has become increasingly dependent. It was the trader who offered an outlet for the rugs, wool, and lambs so that an exchange could be effected for White man's goods. It was the trader who exercised influence upon the Navajo in stimulating his desires for different kinds of goods, and who also exercised an influence upon the types of things produced by the people.

More influential than this in many respects, were the personal, man-to-man relationships which the trader established with Hosteen (Mr. Navajo). The trader was the one White man, outside of the soldiers and the distant governmental officials, to whom to come for all sorts of advice—business, personal, and medical. Having no place to keep occasional important papers and having little comprehension of their significance, it would be with the trader that they were deposited, if kept at all. In times of drought or other distress, it was the old-time trader who dug into his own pockets and financed the emergency relief measures. It was the old-time trader who assumed a host of responsibilities which the Government had not undertaken —all the way from ministering to the sick and feeding the poor, through making coffins and helping to bury the dead.

Among the Navajos, the trader is still the primary non-governmental contactor with the outside world. He still maintains that unique man-to-man relationship which was formerly widespread throughout most of America in the form of the rural storekeeper, but which has become merely a memory or bit of ancient history for so many city people.

With the rapid multiplication of trading posts since 1900, the new traders have come to the Reservation during a period in which many changes have taken place in the outside world as well as within the Reservation. For example, it was not until the late 1800's that John Wanamaker at his store in Philadelphia introduced America to the one-price store in which all customers paid the same price for an article, rather than each customer haggling for hours over the price of each item.

Prime characteristic under the surface, however, of this dynamically changing scene is that forces have been gathering beyond the power of any individual trader or Navajo to adjust. The national and world depressions, the changing role of the wholesaler, changes in the markets for wool and sheep, the on-coming of wages, the advent of the automobile, and the many complicated economic inter-relationships are greater · than the individual as forces. Control of trade has rapidly become a matter of studying and controlling institutions rather than single persons.

Any account of Navajo life would be incomplete without some mention of the crafts of weaving and silver work. These are assuming increasing economic importance because of the tourist and off-reservation demand. The following selections provide an interesting account of the origin, production, and symbolism of Navajo rugs and of silversmithing among the Navajo.

• 30 • Navajo Weaving

DANE AND MARY ROBERTS COOLIDGE

ORIGIN

It was the Spider Woman who taught the Navajos how to weave and for many hundred years they left a spider-hole in the center of every blanket as an acknowledgment of her aid. When the great ruins of Pueblo Bonito were inhabited, a Kisani woman wandered away from that village and took refuge among the nomadic Navajos. One day as she was walking across the plains she saw smoke rising from a small hole and, looking down into it, she beheld the Spider Woman—weaving her web.

By magic she enlarged the hole and invited the girl to come down; and there, one by one, she taught her to make four different blankets. The fourth was the Pretty Design, embroidered in black on white cotton cloth, which survives to this day in the ceremonial skirts and sashes of the Hopi and other Pueblo tribes. After the blankets the girl learned to weave baskets, and in the bottom of nearly every Navajo Wedding basket can still be seen the spider-hole, plugged with buckskin.

But when the early Indian traders began to buy Navajo blankets for bed covers they refused all that had this hole. So the Indians gradually ceased paying their tribute to the Spider Woman, and only when some weaver was afflicted with Blanket Sickness did she leave a half-concealed slit. But, now that the purpose of this aperture is known, a blanket containing a spider-hole is worth more than one without.

When the Kisani woman returned to the Navajos she called for native cotton,

which then grew like grass on the flats, and for yellow and black dyes. Then she made the blankets, just as the Spider Woman had shown her, and the Navajo women imitated her. While the girl was weaving, some Kisani men who had heard of her discovery came and watched her a long time. Then they went back home and began to make Pretty Design sashes, and these are still woven only by men. But the Navajo women developed many beautiful patterns and weaves; and when European sheep were stolen from the Spaniards, they perfected the Navajo Rug.

DYES AND WOOL

The wool was cut from these first sheep with knives. It was cleaned by washing in suds made from the crushed roots of Soap Weed, a slender-leaved Yucca, and dyed with native vegetable dyes. The first blankets, however, were made in natural colors of the wool—white, black, yellowish brown, and gray made of black and white, mixed. To these colors were added a greenish-yellow made from rabbit-bush flowers, a dull red from mountain mahogany roots and a blue from sumac boiled with blue clay. But as soon as they came in contact with Mexican traders they began to use indigo blue; and a scarlet red, made from the cochineal insects found on cactus leaves.

The coming of Spanish soldiers to New Mexico gave the Navajos another source of colors—their uniforms. The bright red of the infantry and the yellow of the cavalry were either bought or taken from the bodies

[Adapted from "Navajo Rugs," *Enjoy Your Museum*, No. 4a, Esto Publishing Company, Pasadena, 1933. Unpaged. Used by permission.]

of those killed—and *bayeta,* that rarest and most precious of blanket materials, was obtained by unravelling the fabric. This colored yarn was generally split and retwisted and, spun fine and hard, was used to make Squaw Dresses or other show garments for men or women. After a short time the traders began to introduce English broadcloth—the familiar "red cloth" of Indian barter—and, until Germantown yarns were brought in, this material was unravelled and respun.

No *bayeta* has been made for over fifty years now and it is very difficult to identify the cloth. But the fact that it has been respun gives the best clue, as the roughness and the tiny knots made by the first weaving can be felt by running the fingers lightly over the surface. It is hard and close-woven and the reds in particular have a brilliant sheen, although toned down by half a century of use.

About 1880 the first aniline dyes were introduced and the result was an orgy of glaring colors and color combinations which nearly ruined the rug market. As these blankets became more and more violent the traders finally refused to buy them and within a period of ten years they had almost disappeared. But in their place there came the stable-dyed Germantown yarns in many beautiful colors, and by re-spinning these soft zephyrs the women made finer blankets than ever.

Back to their natural colors—with indigo and fast red aniline dyes supplied for contrast—the patient weavers at last settled down to produce the standard, commercial rug. But nothing could keep down their creative instinct, and the restrictions of the traders only resulted in more attention to weave and design. It is the mothers of the tribe—the old, skilled weavers—who are the leaders; and from their memories of early days they have reproduced many ancient patterns.

The latest trend is shown in the effort of certain traders to bring back the early blanket, with its natural colors and vegetable dyes in beautiful shades of tan, brown and walnut. The golden-tan backgrounds of the new Sand-painting Rugs are exact reproductions of native sand. But the trade still demands its gorgeous reds and the bright colors commonly called "Indian."

SPINNING AND WEAVING

The Navajo loom is crude and primitive but no effort to modify it has ever succeeded, for it is perfectly suited to its purpose. Being a nomadic people, it is often necessary for these Indians to move in order to get grass for their sheep. To attempt this with a Colonial spinning wheel on the pack would never do at all so the old-fashioned hand-spindle is used. And to lash anything on a horse more cumbersome than a half-made blanket on its warp-poles is absolutely impossible.

Outdoors under the cedar trees, where the weaver can watch her children herding the sheep, she sets up two uprights and two cross-poles, between which the smaller warp-frame is stretched. When grass gets short she can roll up her rug and move on. Half in sun and half in shadow she sits on a sheep-skin with her moccasined feet tucked under her and makes up the design as she weaves.

The warp is stretched tight by the weight of rocks and, with the polished batten-stick turned edgewise to separate the cords, she lays out her balls of yarn and begins. In and out she threads the hardspun wool stopping at intervals to hammer it down with the back of the broad-bladed batten. Little hanks of bright-colored yarn hang from the blanket as the pattern begins to take shape. There are borders, symbols, ancient designs and, recently, figures of gods and men; while at her side, looking on, some little girl cards the wool and spins it into the first coarse yarn.

At last the rug is done and, tying it behind her saddle, she rides to the trader's post to exchange it for flour, coffee, sugar.

DESIGNS AND SYMBOLISM

The patterns of Navajo rugs are innumerable—and no two alike. A thousand pillow-tops can be examined until the eyes ache from the strong colors, but no two will be alike. Not for any price will the weavers duplicate a pattern, although they can copy any design that is shown them. It is just that it is bad luck to make two of a kind. And the more beautiful, the more perfect the rug is, the more careful they are to break the pattern somewhere to avoid the curse of perfection—the appearance of rivalling the handiwork of the gods.

This is characteristic of rug-makers all through the Orient, but so subtly are the variations made that only a careful check will reveal them. The Navajos are especially adept at concealment. A different shade of red in the background near the end, as if the weaver had run out of yarn; a deft break in the pattern, a different number of stripes and diamonds, or a reversed arrangement of design. And, when a solid border surrounds the blanket—somewhere, generally near a corner, a thin devil-line or spirit-line will be made "to let out the evil spirits."

The designs for rugs come from many sources, including the ancient symbols found on the pottery of the cliff-dwellers, whose ruined houses are found all over the Reservation. From them comes the swastika . . . but for some reason it is seldom used by the Indians except at the insistence of the traders. With the Navajos it is the sign of the Whirling Logs, deeply reverenced in the Night Chant Ceremony, and for that reason probably used with reluctance.

Nearly all the patterns used on rugs are associated with rain, storms and clouds. In a country with such scanty rainfall, all ceremonies, prayers and symbolic designs have been concentrated upon the idea of obtaining water to support their animals and crops. The principal figures found in good weaves are square mountains used for borders, triangular clouds, parallel lines for falling rain, jagged lightning and little, zigzag flashes.

Since curves are very difficult to weave, triangles are used to represent the cloud-forms and cloud terraces of Pueblo pottery —often called cloud-ladders—upon which the gods, who come to earth at night, are sup-posed to ascend to heaven at dawn. A straight line, with little lines on the lower side like the teeth of a rake, means falling rain; a triangle with curved sides coming to a point like a water-spout is called far-off falling rain. A diamond, composed of two triangles, signifies rain clouds. A vertical straight line with a triangular hump on its left-hand side is the Humpback Yeibitchai —the god who carries a black bag of rain on his back.

So much the Indians will tell us, but not their traditional significance. Behind every color, every sun-dog, every animal and bird form, there is a deeper and more hidden symbolism. White is more than white—it is the color of Early Dawn, the symbol of the East where the Yeibitchai dwell, to whom prayers are offered up at dawn. Blue is more than blue—it is the symbol of the South.

Yellow is the color of the West, where the Turquoise Woman lives, who keeps watch over women and their children. Pollen shaken from the feathers of a pair of yellow warblers will bring happiness to the home. Good things come from the West, where at evening Yellow Twilight is seen. He is a god, like Early Dawn, and is mentioned in their prayers. Black is for the North, whence comes evil and witchcraft. It is cold and violent and malevolent. Strong winds and storms come from there. But it is also the color of night—and of black clouds, which are good. It is the color for the male element in life, just as blue is female.

Red is the symbol of the Sun and of halos. In sand-paintings the gods always stand on sun-dogs, short bars of blue and red. It is a holy color, little used except in connection with the gods and with the rainbows, which are their pathway through the sky.

MODERN RUGS

Most blankets have no such story to tell; and, when they do, few are told. The Navajo Rug, it might as well be admitted, is made by the Indians to sell. When they want a blanket to wear they go to the trader and buy one—a fine, soft Pendleton made of Oregon wool, much better to sleep in and to wear. Every Navajo has a robe—the first ones were buggy-robes—and it is a beautiful sight to see a crowd of them at some night Chant, each wrapped in a blanket which is Indian in design, though manufactured by a white man.

The first Navajo blankets were made to be robes. They were warm, watertight and would turn the winter wind; but now they no longer serve that purpose. They are rugs —sold as rugs and used as rugs—and only in saddle-blankets and gaily tasselled sitting-blankets does the woman weave for herself. At the big dances and "sings" some gorgeous specimens can be seen, but her greatest art is applied to the making of Modern Rugs.

At the great autumn fairs held at Gallup and Shiprock their finest handiwork is exhibited and the judges award a prize for the best. Some of the points by which they are chosen are the smoothness of the weave, the dying and blending of the colors, and the beauty and originality of the design. To make these prize rugs thin and hard the yarn is often respun five times and hammered tight with the batten. Every line of the pattern is clean and straight and the colors are perfectly dyed. The grays and other backgrounds are evenly mixed and many daring effects are achieved, but it is mostly among the Native Dyed and Sand-painting Rugs that the prize-winning exhibits are now found.

The first Sand-painting Rug was made in 1910—and by a man, Hosteen Tla.

When the sand-paintings were first handed down to mortals they were expressly forbidden to reproduce them except in colored sands. Only the gods could paint them on buckskin and fabric—and even the sand-paintings must be wiped out before the end of the day. So the Navajo had always been taught; but when, in 1883, Washington Matthews published his first great book on the Navajos, he reproduced copies of four sand-paintings.

This defiance of the Yeibitchai alarmed the Indians and when, shortly afterwards, both Matthews and his Medicine Man became deaf and finally died, it was looked upon as the vengeance of the gods. Especially as they died of apoplexy, the dreaded Yei-bitchai Sickness. For thirty years—until Hosteen Tla—no one dared to make sand-painting pictures; but he was a *hatali* himself and he prayed long to Pretends-to-see-People, the mystic who had originated the rites, before he made his first blanket.

It was a reproduction of Whirling Logs, one of the four which Matthews had used, and for three years the Navajos waited to see him struck blind or paralyzed. But Tla prayed and offered sacrifices to the gods and at last he sold his blanket—for a thousand dollars. Others rushed in then—Sand-painting Rugs were all the rage—until a woman weaver became blind. After that even the boldest hesitated and now the Ceremonial Blanket, representing dancers in the ceremonies, has largely taken the place of real Sand-painting Rugs.

This is a reproduction of some dancer —or of a Yeibitchai sand-painting of dancers from which one figure has been left out, or the number of eagle-plumes changed. Anything to avoid the wrath of the Yeibitchai, whose victims are stricken by some disease of the head. Deafness, blindness, facial paralysis, apoplexy—these awaited the imitators of Tla, and they turned to less jealous gods. But after twenty years the old man is still well and prosperous and the ancient fear of the gods is passing.

By making this first blanket he set a new style, both in weaving and in color. The heads of the male gods are round and he succeeded in weaving a curve, one of the first. For the background of this great ceremonial picture he used the natural wool of an old breed of sheep which is the exact color of sand—a golden tan. This same effect is achieved by dyes, native and aniline; and so, developing side by side but in different ways, the Sand-painting and Native Dyed Blankets have created a new vogue in Modern Rugs.

• 31 • Navajo Silver Work

RUTH F. KIRK

. . . Silver came into possession of the Indians from raids on the Spanish, who were notable artists in metal, but coins and silver were scarce, and the hostility between the Spaniards and the Indians precluded cultural exchanges. So it remained for the Americans to bring knowledge of the handicraft to the Indians. After the campaign of 1851-2, Capt. H. L. Dodge wrote a letter to the editor of the Santa Fe *Weekly Gazette* in which he reported that he had with him at Fort Defiance, Arizona . . . a Mexican silversmith and an assistant. So the seed of the art was planted in Navaho-land. A man named Herrero Delgadito was the first Navaho Indian to learn the craft, apparently sometime between 1853 and 1858.

Since silver was so scarce, the output must have been very small, because the Navaho in captivity at Bosque Redondo in 1863 had little jewelry and the craft did not prosper during those four years.

After the return from captivity, silversmithing was started anew and by 1880, when Indian traders ventured into the formerly hostile land of the Navaho, Mexican smiths are known to have been wandering through the territory making silver ornaments and taking horses in exchange for their labor.

The Indians had learned that coins could be hammered into ornaments, and from soldiers they had obtained American coins to use for that purpose. . . . The silversmiths preferred the Mexican coins . . . as their higher silver content rendered them more malleable and hence easier to pound. In making jewelry from coins, the Indians first melted a sufficient number in a pottery crucible, then poured the molten silver out and hammered it until it was the required thickness for the piece to be made.

In the craft's earliest days, the work was unbelievably crude, but in 1883 Matthews reported that the introduction of fine files and emery paper had brought a great improvement in the fifteen years of his observation.

In casting, which apparently was introduced about 1875, the silver had first to be melted and then poured into a mold which had previously been carved from sandstone. Then, when cooled and set, the piece required a great deal of filing and smoothing.

About 1880 the first turquoise was set in silver. Excepting for the turquoise wampum from earlier times, turquoise was very scarce and it was to be another thirty years or more before turquoise became readily available, so early Navaho jewelry had very few stones.

The Indians made jewelry solely for their own use, and bartered it one to the other, but none had been made up for commercial sale. In 1899, it is reported that Mr. Herman Schweizer of the Fred Harvey Company attempted to get jewelry made for his company, from a trader in Thoreau. Apparently, little success attached to this first endeavor.

Between the years of 1880 and 1900, a Navaho man made a fine appearance, dressed in the typical short trousered costume of the times, and adorned with jewelry of his own contriving. He wore large silver loop earrings, usually with a bead at the bottom of each loop, a heavy plain silver necklace with a crescent . . . pendant, and usually a wampum necklace or two as well. On his left arm appeared a . . . bowguard to protect his wrist when he used his bow and arrows. He wore rings, also one or more bracelets, usually of one or two ounce weight. The center of attraction was his huge concho belt, with slots cut in the center of each concho to permit stringing on leather. The first buckles were small and functional, but soon attained more importance until large, handsome buckles became the style. Silver

[Adapted from "Southwestern Indian Jewelry," *Papers of the School of American Research*, Archaeological Institute of America, Santa Fe, 1945. Pp. 8-14, 16-20, 23. Used by permission.]

buttons on his moccasins, and perhaps on his trouser seams, completed his adornment, unless he wore over one shoulder a medicine bag, which almost invariably was ornamented with a solid row of silver buttons.

The necklace might have been a Pueblo type, especially in the first days of the silversmithing craft, with crosses and a large cross pendant instead of a crescent. The Indians were willing to borrow their lucky charms from any source and a cross had no religious significance either to the Pueblo or to the Navaho.

These styles were still in vogue when John J. Kirk, my husband, started his career as an Indian trader, in 1910. It was a common practice at that period to use the one and two ounce bracelets in lieu of money for buying supplies at the trading post. Cash was always scarce and a one ounce bracelet worth one dollar was easier for an Indian to carry on his wrist than a coin in his pocket, not to mention his liking for the decorative effect. The Mexican peso from which such bracelets were fashioned cost fifty cents, and fifty cents was the average value of the work involved in making a bracelet. The two ounce size, of course, was worth two dollars, and buttons of various denominations were used as small change. Very little turquoise was available, even most of the wampum was of shell or coral, and turquoise stones for setting in silver jewelry could be obtained only after about 1912.

As tourists discovered New Mexico [and Arizona], the demand for Indian jewelry outgrew the realm of curios, and transcended the scope of costume jewelry. Gradually it took its place as classic adornment with sports wear and various other types of clothing. Even on inexpensive jewelry, the art of the Indian maker left an indelible influence, giving each piece a unique quality of integrity and charm which made it permanently a source of pleasure to the owner.

During these good years of development of Indian jewelry not all went well. This comparatively new product, with its ready market among tourists, proved too great a temptation to men with machines. A belt that required a week or more to pound by hand, and thus provided a bare livelihood for the craftsman and a small profit to the trader who financed him and marketed the belt, could be made in a few minutes with a machine. And then the [inferior] machine-made product was advertised as "Indian made" because Indians had been hired to operate the machines! While such imitators rolled up wealth, and threatened the hand-made craft with extermination, Secretary Ickes helped the Indians by ordering that only hand-made Indian jewelry could be offered for sale by stores in National Parks. This was a boon to the Indians and contributed considerably toward keeping the craft going during trying depression years following 1929.

The Arts and Crafts Board was organized in 1938 by the federal government with the twin objectives of improving the status of the silversmith and the development of new markets for Indian jewelry. It started with a set of standards and the idea of hallmarking eligible pieces of jewelry. For silversmith improvement guilds were established to train apprentices, and for those who finished their training a minimum wage scale was established.

The overall results of the Arts and Crafts Board effort have been good. They revived and improved the old plain designs in both cast and hammered jewelry, and they brought about considerable improvement in soldering and finishing. They encouraged the use of sterling silver (925 fine) instead of coin silver (900 fine) which had always been preferred, and sterling takes a nicer finish.

If the Indians can be protected from machine competition and if they achieve a happy blending of old and new forms—with better equipment and improvements in technique; if they enjoy demand not only from tourists but also from a discerning public at large; and if they receive aid and encouragement from all their friends and well wishers, the Indians of the Southwest may be standing at the threshold of a silvercraft development that might well be the artistic and economic salvation of these tribes.

Social Organization
and Interaction

〈〈

Most of us are primarily interested in getting along as best we can in a relatively complex modern industrialized society. At first the Navajo may seem remote, to say nothing of
being quaint. But an understanding of how their society is put together, of how their economy and family are intertwined, of how their religion and education are connected, and
of how their sense of being Navajo is based primarily on a linguistic, cultural unity will
do much to show us what threads need to be followed in an analysis of a more highly
differentiated society such as ours.

Societies are the central theme of this book. These are made up of people who share
a common culture and who have definitely prescribed ways of behaving toward one another in keeping with the statuses which they—the social actors—occupy. We shall understand the Navajo way of life when we can eventually state what a Navajo farmer would
do under certain circumstances, how a Navajo mother would discipline her three-year-old,
what behavior is expected of the Navajo at the trading post, what role the representative
on the tribal council is supposed to play, how the singer is greeted and assisted in his performance of a chant.

Although the selections which follow deal with specific aspects of the social organization (that is, with certain sociofacts) each description shows how the specific topic being
discussed is related to other social groupings and institutionalized forms of behavior. In
other words, our purpose is not merely to master the details of any one grouping or institutionalized pattern, such as the clan system, in and of itself but also to see how such a
pattern fits into the total society, what functions it performs, and how its modification
would be apt to change other formalized ways of behavior.

Some of the parts of the social-organization puzzle which are included in this section
and which have to be fitted together are the kinship and clan system, property and in-

heritance relationships, courtship patterns and husband-wife relationships, parent-child relationships, the headman's connection with his followers, the kinds of social control that the Navajo people exercise upon one another, and the simple but strongly-defended forms of religious organization.

Laura Thompson has given a good picture of the fundamental organizational relationships—matrilocal family, matrilineal clans, and the "outfit," or local land-use community.*

> The smallest Navaho socio-economic group is the matrilocal family consisting of husband, wife (or wives, about 7 per cent of the families being polygamous), and unmarried children. The family occupies a single hogan. Although the husband is the family's formal head, husband and wife share family responsibilities, the wife's position in this matrilineal society, wherein a large share of the property and its control is in the woman's hands, being perhaps somewhat more advantageous than that of her husband.
>
> Farming and herding are usually cooperative tasks shared by a larger kinship unit; namely, the extended family consisting of the biological families of a woman and her married daughters as well as unattached collateral relatives. The hogans occupied by such a group are usually within "shouting" distance. In the extended family the position of the maternal uncle is important, for he exercises many functions which usually fall to the father in general American society.
>
> Navaho families are also grouped into large matrilineal clans, of which there are sixty or more cutting across the local divisions. Navaho clans regulate marriage, for a Navaho may not marry within his own clan (i.e., his mother's clan) or that of his father. Hence clans are important in establishing the individual's large circle of relations and kinship obligations.
>
> Of far more importance to the government administrator than the clan grouping, however, is that of the "outfit" or local land-use community.

Each *land use community* can be identified with a specific area of country which includes range, farm land and habitations. The occupants lay claim to the country as their own on the basis of ancestral settlement and present use. It is because of the territorial land use characteristics that this social grouping has been called the land use community. Cooperative community labor and leadership exhibits itself most often in general problems relating to range use, water, subjugation and development of farm land, the construction of dams, tanks, irrigation systems, and the presentation of a united front toward those who attempt to encroach upon the community rights. (Solon T. Kimball and John H. Provinse, "Navaho Social Organization in Land Use Planning," *Applied Anthropology*, vol. I, Boston, 1942. Pp. 22–23.)

* Adapted from "Personality and Government: Findings and Recommendations of the Indian Administration Research," *America Indigena*, Vol. 10, No. 2, Mexico, 1950. Pp. 143-145.

Such groups are called "outfits," the head of a prominent nuclear family being the leader. There are great variations in size, composition, and area of Navaho "outfits" and the facts concerning them have been systematically assembled for only a few parts of the Navaho reservation. The hogans of an "outfit" may extend over a large land-use area, in some cases from 12,000 to 80,000 acres. On the other hand, constituent families of an "outfit" do not necessarily occupy contiguous lands.

The next selection, entitled "Son of Old Man Hat," requires a brief explanation. It consists of excerpts from the life history of an old Navajo, whose reminiscences about his life were translated by an English-speaking Navajo and recorded by Walter Dyk. A selection of the most interesting material was made; it was put into chronological order, and the interpreter's faulty English smoothed. Dyk retained, however, much of the Navajo flavor of the account, as well as such devices as constant repetition.

The narrator, Left Handed, was born in 1868 during the repatriation from Fort Sumner, New Mexico. Owing to the illness of his mother he was adopted by his mother's sister, Abaa, who was of the Bitahni clan. Left Handed's adopted father was Old Man Hat, who was of the Many Goats clan. Many of the persons introduced in the story are in some manner related to Left Handed and his family. It should be noted, however, that the title "mother" or "father" is often used by him as an honorary title to denote an older person rather than as a kinship term.

The Navajo portrayed in this story are clearly preoccupied with the job of making a living from their sheep and goats. The white world was only beginning to reach into the reservation at this time.

• 32 • Son of Old Man Hat
WALTER DYK

LEARNING TO GRIND CORN

In the winter, when they both went out, my mother used to tell me to grind up corn. So while I stayed at home, watching the place, I used to grind corn for our food, but I never ground enough. Once she told me to grind some, but it was a little too hard for me; I wasn't strong enough to break up all the kernels. All at once, as I was grinding, a man came in. His name was Red Wife Beater. He said, "Are you grinding corn?" I said, "Yes, I'm grinding some corn." "Do you have to grind corn?" he asked. I said, "Yes." "Why do you have to grind up corn?" "Because we want to eat it," and I said, "My mother told me to grind it." "Why doesn't she grind it? You can't grind all that corn. You're not strong enough." I had a dishful of corn sitting beside me. He said, "Get up." I got up, and he began to grind the corn. While he was grinding he said, "Look, and watch how I'm

[Adapted from Son of Old Man Hat: A Navaho Autobiography recorded by Walter Dyk, Copyright, 1938, by Harcourt, Brace and Company, Inc., New York. Pp. 9, 16-18, 27, 34-35, 68-71, 78-81, 104-118. Used by permission.]

holding this rock. Watch how I'm working it." I did, and I learned how to hold the grinding-stone and how to work it. My mother never did show me how to hold the rock, and how to use it. She'd just say, "Go ahead and grind up the corn," that was all, and then she'd go out with the herd. After he'd ground it all up he said, "Now I've made it easier for you. Go ahead now, and grind it a little finer." Then he went away.

LEARNING TO CONFORM

There are many things like that, and many a thing I learned that way. I said all kinds of things that I shouldn't have said and did a lot that I shouldn't have done, but I always learned a lesson from them. Every time I said something that I shouldn't have said they'd tell me I shouldn't say it. From there on I wouldn't say it any more. And when I did something I shouldn't have done it was the same, they'd tell me I shouldn't do it. Many things are like that, and I got to know them all. That's the way to be when you are young, and that's the way I was.

SON OF OLD MAN HAT LEARNS ABOUT THE YEIBICHAI AND WHAT SINGERS WILL DO TO DISOBEDIENT CHILDREN

After some days we moved again across a little valley towards the south, to Sand Lake. When we got there they said, "Now we're close to the chant. We can go there from here, for it's close at hand." My father and mother and three others got on their horses and rode over. The next day they all came back bringing corn, watermelons, cantaloupes and peaches. They said, "Everything is good and ripe now. Over at the chant they have all kinds of things to eat. And today the Yeibichai will be going around to different hogans, and they'll begin dancing tonight."

That's what they said when they came back, to make me scared of the Yeibichai, I guess. My father said, "These Yeibichai are going around to different hogans today,

looking for children. They have a sack into which they put the children who have disobeyed their fathers and mothers. They may come here today. So you must do what you're told. When they come you must get water and wood, so that they won't bother you. They'll know, then, that you are a good boy. Those children who are bad they whip first, after that they put them in their sacks and take them home. There they dig a hole and build a fire. That's where they bury the children and cook them, in order to eat them. So you must do what you're told to do."

I asked my mother, "Where do these Yeibichai live?" "They live in the rocks, in walls of rock. That's where they're from, and that's where they take the children. "Will you do what you're told to do?" I said, "Yes." "And will you herd the sheep all the time?" I said, "I will. I'll herd the sheep all the time." "Well, then," she said, "I won't tell the Yeibichai about you."

LEARNING ENDURANCE

About this time I used to race by myself early in the morning while it was still dark, and in the middle of the day and in the evening. In the middle of the day when it got real hot, when the sun was right in the middle of the sky, I used to run a race under the sun, while the sun was looking down on me. That's the time the sun is having dinner. When he sees me running a race under him he'll try to get me a horse. The sun that we see in the sky, is our father, and I'm his son; that's why when I race under him, when he sees me running, he knows I'm after something, he knows I'm after a horse. And soon enough I'll get a horse from my father, the sun, and from there on I won't be on foot any more. It's as when you're working for something, trying your best to get it. Even though it's hard to get you must try and try to get the thing you want. That's the way I used to be: I worked hard for everything.

In the summertime I used to put a lot of sand in my moccasins. I'd squeeze my feet into them even though it hurt. At first I had a hard time running, but after a while I began to get used to it. From there on I hardly knew I had dirt in my moccasins; I could carry it all as far as I wanted to go. I put the sand in my moccasins to toughen my feet, so as to be able to run anywhere, through sand and through snow and not mind it, so that when I wanted to go through the sand and the desert I could stand it, even though the sand was deep, without getting tired, even though the snow was twelve inches deep or more I could run through it as though there were nothing on the ground. That's how I raced for six miles in order to make my feet and legs strong and my muscles hard. And I used to take a mouthful of water and holding it in my mouth, run up a great big hill. I did this so as to develop strong wind. I breathed only through my nose while running.

In the winter, when the snow was on the ground, not the first snow that comes but the second,—the second, you know, is colder than the first,—I used to race early in the morning while it was still dark. Even though it was a real cold morning I had to get up without anything on, except my moccasins and my G-string, and run for a long distance. While I'd be running on my way I'd go under a young tree and shake the snow on myself. This was a hard thing to do. If you're not strong, every time you shake the snow onto yourself, you'll say, Ah! Before I'd start back for home I'd throw myself in the snow and roll around in it for quite a while. When I'd get home I wouldn't go inside, I'd stop by the doorway, turn around again and run for the water. If there was thick ice on top of the water I'd get a stick or a piece of rock, break the ice, take off my moccasins and jump in. I'd stay in the icy water as long as I could stand it, turning over and over, hollering and screaming so as to develop a good voice. Then I'd get out and put on my moccasins and start for home. While I'd be running on my way my body would be covered with a thin coat of ice, cracking all over me. . . . That was the hardest thing; I sometimes

couldn't stand it. Before going in the hogan I'd roll in the snow once more. Then I'd go in, but I shouldn't go near the fire. I had to stay away from the fire, until all the ice had melted off my body.

There are only two months in the winter during which one should race and do all these things, from the first of December until the last of January.

That's what the old people taught their children. "Every child should race and go into the icy water and the snow, so as to be tough and brave and quick and strong, so that even if something very serious should happen to you you'll be able to stand it, and if anything should try to scare you, you won't scare easily, you'll be strong all over. You'll be as brave as a mad dog, able to jump on anything that gets after you, even though it's tough and strong, even though it's big. That's what all the racing and bathing is for." So, even when I was small, I started doing this in order to make myself tough and get all the things I wanted.

FAMILY JEALOUSIES AND QUARRELS

At that time my father was also married to Bitahni's Sister. She was a clan mother of mine and my mother's clan sister. We were all living together in one hogan. I don't know how he came to be married to her. Maybe my mother told him to marry her, or it may be my father asked my mother, saying he wanted to marry her. Anyway my father had two wives, but it wasn't long before my mother and her sister quarreled.

One afternoon my father and mother began fighting. I was sitting outside watching them. Finally my father threw my mother down and sat on her. Then my uncle's sister dragged Old Man Hat off my mother, and my mother got up and went after my father again. My uncle's sister let them go; she was standing there, watching them too. My mother was just like a man; she was a strong woman. They were fighting for a long time, and then the old man was thrown, and my mother was on top of him. He got up with her, and they wrestled around, fighting and cussing. They fought and fought for a long time. At last they stopped, they must have tired, and just cussed each other. My mother sure did swear and cuss my father and her sister. It was all due to jealousy.

It was evening by the time they quit. My father went inside the hogan and packed his stuff and started to go away. He was going to leave my mother. As he tried to go she cried out and grabbed him and began begging him not to leave her. Then he put down his pack, and for a long time after that they talked. At last they all apologized to one another, and my uncle's sister built a fire.

Sometime after this my mother and father got into a quarrel again over her sister. They quarreled and swore and cussed each other for a long time, and my mother was crying. Then she went out and separated her sheep and goats from my father's herd and saddled her horse and put all her stuff on it. She had only one horse. She got on it and told me to come. I went up to her, and she reached down and lifted me up and sat me behind her. Then we started off and left my father. We went on, driving the herd, and soon we got to Flowing From Rocks. We passed there and went on and got to Anything Falls In that evening where we camped that night.

The next morning she packed all the stuff on the horse again and said, "We'll go back, my son, to your father. We left your poor father yesterday, and he's all alone now. We'd better go back to him." So we turned around and drove back the sheep. When we got home my father was sitting in the hogan smoking. As soon as we got inside she walked up to him and put her arms around his neck and held him against her breast. She was crying and talking, saying, "I'll be with you all the time. I'm not going to treat you like this any more. Forgive me, my husband. I'm sorry for what I've said and done to you. I'm very sorry. Forgive me, right now." And she said again, "I'm not going to treat you

like this any more in my life. I'll be with you always."

WHO HAS MULES SPENDS THE WINTER LEARNING SONGS AND PRAYERS

That was all he said to his nephew, and then he started singing. He started a song from here, from the earth, and went along up to the sun and around and back and came to earth again. There were four long songs. My father said, "You need learn only these four songs. If you learn these four, fix them well in your mind, the rest will be easy." Towards midnight, or a little after, while they were working on the songs I fell over and went to sleep. From there on I don't know what they said, or how long they sang. Early in the morning my mother woke me and told me to go out and get some wood and build up the fire. She had the fire started. They were still sitting up. They said, "It's morning now," and Who Has Mules said, "I'd better be going back." My father said, "All right," and he went home.

That day I went out with the herd and was herding all day, but he didn't come. The next day my father and I were herding. When we came back in the evening there was a big pile of wood, but he wasn't there, he'd gone back home. After we had supper he came, and as soon as he arrived they started in. My father said, "Now, I guess, you remember all you learned the night before last."

Then he said, "Now you can go ahead and repeat all the songs. Start from where we started and repeat every one. I'll just listen to see if you get it all." So he repeated all the songs; he started from here and went up to the sun and around until he came to earth again, to the middle of his hogan. My father said, "That's right. I know you've got them all now. Every song you repeated is right. You didn't miss anything. I think you got everything the first time. Once you learn it, it won't go away from you. You'll remember them always. I know you won't forget them."

While they were working on the songs again that night I fell asleep. In the morning when my mother woke me they were still up, they'd been up all night again. From there on he came every two or three days. That winter we didn't do anything, nor go any place. Those two were working on the songs, prayers and stories all that winter. All that I did was herd, sometimes by myself, sometimes I'd go out with my father or mother, sometimes my mother went out with the herd by herself.

Late in the spring, after he'd been gone again for two days, when I came back with the herd in the evening, there was a big pile of wood. That night he came, and they started on the songs. After Who Has Mules was through repeating all the songs and all the prayers that go with them and all the stories about them, the stories about the sheep, horses, properties and other things, my father said, "Now you've learned everything. You remember everything from where we started to where we stopped. Now I know you remember things, and I think you're a smart man. There are lots of people who can't learn these songs, and now you've learned a few of them. When you start using them on your stocks and properties, if you do it right, you'll soon have everything. Now you can go ahead. You wanted to learn, and I told you you could. I promised you, and I've given it to you." He cupped his hands and spread them out before him and said, "You see, you think there is nothing in my hands, but my hands are full. Everything is overflowing, things are falling out of my hands. That's the way you'll be later on. So just stick to it and learn some more if you want to.

"You must remember everything I've said to you. I told you that I had a handful of things, and that you'd be that way sometime, but you'll have to have a hard time first. You won't get this way just as soon as you learn all the songs about them. You have to work for all these things, you have to go through many dangerous places, down in the arroyos, in the canyons, and climb up and down mountains. You have to kick sticks and rocks and get splinters in your feet and hands and be cut. You may think you'll get them all as soon as you learn the songs, but you must suffer a great deal before you get them. After you've suffered, then, for all your knowing you'll have a handful of things, and you'll look at them and won't know what to do with them. But you'll use them all the time. After you get all this stuff your children will have everything. They won't starve, they won't be ragged, they won't hunger for meat and other things. They'll have everything, if you have it on hand for them. And you can help the poor and others with it all the time. That's after you get all these things, but before that you must be stingy."

They were up all night. Early in the morning my father said, "Now you've learned all that I know, all the songs, prayers and stories. I wanted you to learn, for you are my only nephew. I know you wish to have lots of stock and property, and I know you need them, I know you have children. I don't want your children to go starving. So, now, you can go ahead, tend to your stocks and properties, and do it right. And don't talk roughly, because you've learned many songs and prayers. If you know the songs and prayers you don't want to talk roughly. If you do you won't get these things, because all the stocks and properties will know that you'll be rough with them. They'll be afraid and won't want to come to you. If you think kindly and talk in the kindest manner then they'll know you're a kind man, and then everything will go to you. So, now, just go ahead, this is all I want to say to you. This will be the end." That's what my father said, and Who Has Mules went home.

THE COYOTES KILL THE LAMBS AND THE SHEEP FREEZE TO DEATH

In the fall when it got real cold we moved up on Black Mountain to Aspens Coming Down. There we lived all winter, and in the spring they took the sheep to Keams Canyon. A few days after they returned from that place they wanted to move, because there wasn't any grass on the mountain. The sheep had plenty of feed, but the horses were getting poor. So we moved, past Water In Bitter Weeds and on to Sweet Water. There wasn't any feed at all around there, so after two days we moved again. That night we camped at Two Red Rocks Pointing Together, and the next morning we moved to Dry Around The Water. But there wasn't much water there, so we passed that place and went on to Flowing Through Rocks and stopped and camped on top of that wash. There was plenty of water; the horses had water, and the sheep had water too.

We thought there'd be some feed, but there was nothing. The stock had nothing to eat, and so we moved again. When we arrived at the San Juan, where all these washes end, we stopped and camped close to the river by a big rocky hill, called Coiled Mountain. All around upon that little mountain was lots of feed.

After we'd camped there some people came and visited us. They thought we hadn't sheared yet, but over half the herd was done; only a few, the ewes, still needed shearing. When they started in they killed a billy-goat and sold the skin at the store. They got a dollar for it and bought some grub. Skins were worth a whole lot, and after they'd sheared all the sheep they killed ten billy-goats, all at once, and the fellows who helped us got a skin apiece. We kept five and the wool. We sold the wool and the hides and bought more stuff, flour, baking powder, coffee, sugar and other food, and a lot of drygoods, calico and things like that, and different kinds of dishes.

The day after they returned from the store they said, "We have our wool all sold now. I guess we'd better start moving back." We'd come by way of the canyon, but we didn't go back that way; we took a short cut over the rocks. We camped overnight among the rocks, and the next morning when the sun was pretty well up we moved to White With Reeds. It was hot then, early in the summer.

There wasn't any rain at all, or any cloud. It was hot and getting worse every day. . . . Nobody did anything or went any place, and I did nothing but herd. Then we heard that my father, Choclays Kinsman, had moved down to the flat and was living at Hawohi Water. They wanted to move to where he was living, and so we started for that place. It wasn't very far, but when we got to Hawohi Water no one was there. They'd lived there all right, but they'd moved back toward Black Mountain. There were fresh tracks around, so we followed them all the way to Lines Of Thin Rocks.

The next morning we followed that little canyon to Solid Rocks Upward. They said, "There used to be water there." My father rode over, and when he came back he said, "I think there's enough for the horses." So he drove them over, and only the horses had water. We stayed until it got cool and then started again and got to Flowing Through Rocks in the evening. There'd been water in that wash, but there wasn't any now. The wash was dry. We camped there, and the sheep were thirsty. They were making a great noise, crying for water. So that evening my father and I took them to Black Rock Standing. The moon was shining, and there we watered the herd. There was plenty of water in that wash. When they'd had enough they all quieted down, and then we got some for ourselves and started back. It was close onto midnight.

There was no cloud anywhere and no rain. Everything was dried up, no grass, no weeds, no feed for the stocks, nothing green all over the flat and the valley. The sheep had enough, because they can eat anything, but the horses were poor. They were starving. My father, Choclays Kinsman, came to our place and said, "I'm living a little above Black Rock Standing. That's where we moved to. We couldn't find any feed at all any place. The sheep are all right, but the horses are starving. I don't know what to do about it. Do you know of any place where we can find feed for them? We've got to do something. We've got to go around and see where there's some feed." My father said,

"I've been moving and riding around, looking for feed for the stocks, and asking the people I get to see about grazing, but it's the same all over, no rain and no green spot, no place at all."

We stayed at this place many days. Then all at once they said, "We'll move again." We moved, passing Many Streams, and on past The Lake, past Anything Falls In to Flowing From Tassel Rock. From the mouth of that little canyon out into the valley where the water spreads was a nice level place all sandy. There my father, Slim Man, lived. He had a farm in the valley, and the corn was ripe. My mother went over to the hogan where he lived and brought back some corn. She used to call his wife, my daughter. She said, "My daughter said to me, 'You can come and get corn and make yourself some corn-bread whenever you want to. When you come just go into the field and help yourself. Take all the corn you want.' That's what my daughter said, so I must go and make us some corn-bread. Slim Man wasn't at home. I asked for him. I said to my daughter, 'Where has my son gone to?' She said, 'He's staying with another woman.'" He'd married another woman, who was a Red Clay, and from there on he had two wives.

There we located all during the fall and had corn right along. When fall came we helped them take it in off the field and lay it out to dry. About then my father, His Horse Is Slow, came to our place. Old Man Hat said, "I can't think any more. I've been thinking and worrying about the stocks all summer, but now I've given up, because I can't find a place where there's any feed for them." His Horse Is Slow said, "That's the way it's been with me too, but I've found a good place to go. I heard there's lots of feed for the stock down at Navaho Mountain, and that's where I'm going. Some fellows from there had nice fat horses. They said there's lots of feed over there. So that's where I'm going soon. I was figuring on going to Blue Wash, but they say there isn't any feed around there, that place is still worse, all the stocks are starving to death. That's why I think I'll go to Navaho Mountain." Before he left he said to my father, "We'll start moving for that place together."

The next day we moved to Mouth Of The Canyon, close to his place. They had their corn all in too, and put away, buried in a hole. He came to our place, and they started to talk about the grazing. That was all they were talking about. Finally they said, "We'll all start moving together for that place where they say there's good grazing." Early next morning he came again and said, "You folks can go ahead. You can move today, or you can stay two or three days more. It's up to you." Right away my father said, "I guess we'd better start this morning, because we'd like to get to that place as soon as we can. The stock is getting poorer all the time." His Horse Is Slow said, "All right, you can go ahead and we'll go just as soon as we get ready. Once we start we'll go right along. So you people had better go now."

We moved that morning. In the evening we got to Two Streams Run Together. A little way below there we camped. The next morning we got the horses and started moving again, and that night we camped at Trail Through The Woods. In the morning, after we'd eaten, we packed our horses, and when we had everything ready we started on. We passed Trail Going Over Rocks and Solid Rock Places and got to Many Streams Coming Out At One Place where we camped that night. In the morning my father brought back the horses, we had everything ready, and after we ate we packed them and started when the sun was pretty well up. We got to the foot of the cliff and started climbing. It was a bad place, but it was the only place where there was a trail. We had a hard time getting the sheep and horses on top. They were slipping and falling on the rocks. We were climbing all forenoon. From there we went on through a wood and beyond the wood was sagebrush. We went quite a way through that to a lake, called Lake Between The Rocks, and that's where we camped.

Giving Out Anger was living there, quite a distance from the lake. His son and his son's uncle were young men, and they used to run a race to the lake early every morning. By that time it had frozen a little on top like crust. We used to hear them go. They said to me, "Don't lie in bed too long. As soon as morning comes get up and put on your moccasins and run a race to the lake. Get in as your brother and uncle are doing." So I'd get up in the morning and put on my moccasins and when I'd hear them coming I'd start for the lake too, and I'd be hollering. When they'd get to the lake they'd take off their moccasins and jump in, and I'd do the same. But I never stayed in the water long. It was too cold for me. I'd get in and roll a while and then put on my moccasins and start for home. Those two would still be swimming in the lake.

We stayed at this place a few days, and then moved again. We'd waited long enough for the other people. We went down the valley towards Tall Mountain and on to Lower Valley where we camped that night. The next morning we started down the trail of a canyon on the east side of Navaho Mountain. Fresh tracks were coming up. That was Giving Out Anger's herder who'd been down there with the sheep. We went down the trail to the foot of the canyon and camped.

In the canyon was lots of salt-weed, and that's where Giving Out Anger's herder had taken their sheep. They'd been down for salt-weed, perhaps the day before; the tracks looked that way. As I was walking around, not far from where we'd camped, I got to a hole where they used to bury corn. It was about four feet deep, and down at the bottom stood a great, big, black wether. I called my mother, and the two of us began taking it out. We had a hard time. When we got it out she undid her red belt and tied it to one of the horns, and then we chased it towards our herd and turned it loose.

While I'd been walking around out in the salt-weed a man had come to our place. He was a Bitahni. My mother said, "A man came to our camp, your grandfather, Old Man Won't Do As He's Told. He took his horse to where he wants to hobble it."

That evening when it got dark my mother said, "Let's kill that wether. It's good and fat." My grandfather got some cedar bark and softened it, that's what we used for a light, and all of us went out and rounded up the herd. We could tell that wether easily, because it was black, and it was running around in the herd. While Won't Do As He's Told held up the light my mother caught the wether, and we took it back to camp and killed it. It was sure fat. Old Man Won't Do As He's Told butchered it, and that's what we had that night, nice, fat meat for lunch.

The next day my mother said to my grandfather, "Put the meat up on a tree. When you go back you can take it all with you, my uncle." He took the meat and put it on a tree and gave my mother and father thanks. "Thank you very much for the meat. I'll have nice, fat meat with me when I get home. That's what I want and like to have, and now you've given it to me, and I've got some meat now." He stayed with us all that day and night again. The next morning he went home, and we started moving again that morning also, following the canyon down towards the north.

As we were moving along close by the trail called Trail Going Towards Navaho Mountain a Paiute came driving some horses towards me. I was riding at the head of the sheep, holding them back, because we wanted them to go slowly, and my father and mother were way behind me. The Paiute let his horses go and rode right past me and started chasing back the sheep. He was waving at them, saying, Shah! Shah! Shah! The sheep were scared and stopped, and some of them turned back. About that time my father and mother caught up with me. Then the Paiute let the herd go and rode up to them and said, "What do you want to drive your sheep down in this canyon for? This isn't your place. This is all mine. So take your sheep back on the canyon, and stay upon the canyon with your sheep. I don't want any Navaho to come down in this canyon. I don't want any of them to live around here." I was going along slowly at the head of the sheep and could hear them talking to each other. They were both talking as loud as they could.

My father said, "Maybe you think that way. What do you think you are? You're just a Paiute, that's all. I'm not a bit scared of you. You think you scare me, but you can't scare me at all. All around here, all over around Navaho Mountain, belongs to me. It doesn't really belong to me, it belongs to all the Navaho; so you've got no business riding up to me like this."

As I went over a little hill with the sheep I could still hear him talking. I went quite a way with the herd before they caught up with me again. My mother said, "We had a quarrel with Nabahadzin. He didn't want us to stay in this canyon, so we quarreled and cussed each other." My father said, "This canyon has water quite a way below here. We'll camp by that water."

We stayed at that place three days, and those people caught up with us. The day after they arrived we all started moving again. They said, "Quite a way below here's another spring, and there's a little bigger space than this. We'll move down and live there for the winter." It was a long way, way down close to the San Juan.

While we were living there we had a little snow. A few days later my father, His Horse Is Slow, said, "I want to go up on the canyon to look around and see if there's any feed." He rode his horse on top of the canyon and was gone all day until the sun was almost down. When he came back he said, "Up on the canyon the snow is about a foot deep, but there's plenty of feed, lots of grass for the horses and lots of different weeds for the stock. It's a big space, so we'd better move on the top, because it's a better place." Right away my father and mother said, "We'll do that." The next day we all started to move. We took our sheep and horses up first, and afterwards the other people took up theirs.

There we stopped and camped and lived, right in this space. Ten days after we got on top we took the herd down in the canyon for salt-weed. We took the horses down

also. After we brought our sheep back they began lambing. It was cold, about the middle of the winter, but the lambs were getting along fine. Giving Out Anger and his sister and another outfit of his had moved above us.

After many of the lambs had been born we took the herd in the canyon again for salt-weed. The mothers of the lambs went down all right, but the lambs wouldn't go, because the trail was too narrow there at the edge of the canyon where it started down. My mother said, "Stay there with the lambs, and I'll take down the sheep." She went on, and I stayed with the lambs, and they all lay down.

When the sun was low my mother called me, and I went down, and we started driving up the sheep. My father was in the canyon with the horses. When we were close to the top I went ahead to where the lambs had been, but they were gone. When all the sheep came up I said to my mother, "The lambs have gone." The sun was almost down. We'd figured on camping at the edge of the canyon. She said, "They may have gone back home. I'd better go after them." She left, and I was herding around waiting for my father. When he came up with the horses I said, "The lambs went back home, and my mother's gone after them." He began to track them. He hadn't gone very far from where I was, and there two of them were lying. The coyotes had been after them. It was like that all the way to our home. The coyotes had killed nearly all of them. Only about twenty got back. In places two, three and four of them were lying, some still alive and walking around, pretty well chewed up. "It's that way all the way to our home," my father said when he returned.

We started back, but it was a long way to where we lived, and we didn't get very far before it was dark. We took the sheep down in a little hollow, and there we stayed, walking around them all night. They were making so much noise, crying for their little ones. It seemed like a long night. By midnight I was so tired from walking around them and weak and hungry. It was sure a long night. Early in the morning we went on. As soon as we started they wanted to run. My father got on his horse and tried to stop them; he got out his robe and waved it, but still they wanted to go. I couldn't do anything; I just walked behind them. When we got close to our camp he let them go, and they were running around there, looking for their little ones, making an awful noise.

I was walking way behind the herd. I tried to run, but I couldn't, I was too weak and so hungry and tired. I hadn't slept all night. Close to our home I was about to cry. My mother met me, and I said, "I'm weak, and I'm starving." She said, "You better hurry back. The food is cooked and ready to be eaten." I said, "I can't go any faster, I'm so weak." She grabbed me and shed a little tear and took hold of my arm and started back with me. Everything was ready, some meat was cooked and other food. My father was just beginning to eat. My mother said, "Only about twenty lambs came back. I got home when it was real dark and found only a few of them running around. I've been taking care of them all night. I didn't sleep either, for I thought if I let them go they'd run away, or the coyotes would get after them again."

We lived there for many days. Then we heard Giving Out Anger's outfit had been shaking their hands. They said they found out by hand-shaking that we'd have a bad winter. This winter it would start snowing early. The snow would be deep, over above the sagebrush. But we didn't believe them. They worked a few days making a trail and then moved down into the canyon on the east. We stayed on top with His Horse Is Slow.

The first snow that fell was only about six inches deep. Then we moved about four miles north, close to the point, where there was lots of wood, but His Horse Is Slow lived on at that same place. After we moved my father herded the sheep while my mother and I put up a small hogan. In a few days the clouds gathered from all over, and soon they were right close above us. It was that way all day, and that night it started snowing. In the morning when we got up it had snowed about a foot. It snowed all that day and all night, all the next day and all night again. In the morning it stopped. It had snowed from two and a half to three feet. It was over the sagebrush. The herd couldn't go very far, so it stayed around the hogan. Those people were right, but, I guess, it snowed that deep all over, even down in the canyon.

It stopped snowing early in the morning. As soon as it stopped the clouds broke up and moved away. By daylight it had all cleared off, and the sun was shining, and a warm breeze came up and the snow began to melt. By afternoon the snow had almost turned to water, but when the sun was pretty well down it began to get cold. We thought the snow would be gone the next day, but that night it was cold, and the snow turned to ice. For two nights it was bitter cold, and the sheep were getting on top of one another and killing themselves that way. We tried to stop them but we couldn't, it was too cold for them. When we took one pile apart there'd be another. Soon we just gave up, we couldn't do anything with them, so we let them go. In those two nights a lot of them were killed, smothered, crushed and squeezed to death.

My mother was crying, but my father was quiet; he didn't say anything about it, only my mother was crying. Then he said, "Well, you mustn't cry. You mustn't cry for the sheep. You shouldn't cry for them. They belong to someone who made them. He gave them to us, and we've been using them for many years. Now who made the sheep wants his sheep back, so he's taken them. He took them away from us because we've had them and used them for many years. Perhaps he thought we were satisfied. So you stop crying and don't think about it, don't worry about it and don't be sorry. Even if we lost every one we'd soon get them all back again."

We hadn't put up a corral, and that day we took all the dead sheep and made a corral of them. They'd quit squeezing one another, but they were starving to death, because there wasn't any feed, only the sagebrush, that was all they ate, nothing besides. So they died of starvation. They kept on dying, we couldn't do anything. The ice was as hard as a rock and a foot thick. I tried to chop through it, but I couldn't. We couldn't do anything. We couldn't move to any other place, and so we just stayed there.

This happened the middle of December. Toward the end of January, all at once, it began to blow. It blew a breeze all day and night. By next afternoon the ice had melted away. Only in places where there was shade, as under the trees, under the rocks or sagebrush, there was still a little left. And so the ice melted away after we'd lost nearly all our sheep and goats.

About that time His Horse Is Slow came to our place. He was so surprised. He said, "I'm sorry for you folks, that you've lost all your sheep. We lost some, but not many. We lost only a few head, because where we're living there's a thick wood, and in that wood it didn't snow deep. It only snowed on the trees, not on the ground. That's why we didn't lose very many. You should have stayed with us," he said. "I'm so sorry for you folks."

Then we moved to where we'd lived before, close to His Horse Is Slow. We stayed there at that place several days, and then they said, "We'll move down in the canyon again for salt-weed." We went down, and His Horse Is Slow came after us. We stopped and camped a little while and then started back up the canyon. We'd stay at one place for a few days and then start moving again. We kept doing that the whole month of February, all the way up the canyon, moving a little way and camping for two or three days.

We got to where the Paiute had met us, and where my grandfather, Old Man Won't Do As He's Told, visited us, and finally we got back to where we'd lived for a while, where the lake was. The lake didn't have much water in it, even though it had snowed deep that winter. It had just soaked into the ground, and so the lake was pretty well down. The grass was getting green. It was early in the spring, and I was happy about it. I was so eager to see the green grass.

There we lived for a little while. It was nice and warm. In a few days the grass was about three inches high, and there was enough feed for the horses and sheep. His Horse Is Slow came to our place and said, "I went to Water Under The Rocks where we buried our corn. At that place it's pretty dry. It looks as though it didn't snow over there. But in Another Canyon and at The Middle Wash it's nice and green, everything is getting green. I think there's enough feed for all the stock. It looks better than around here, so we'd better be all moving to that place." Right away they wanted to go.

TALK TO THE SNAKES, THE LIGHTNING AND THE BEARS

Several days after we killed the beef it snowed. After the snow my father started telling me about the snakes. He said, "You should talk to the snake. When you talk to a snake he'll know just what you're saying to him. He can hear you. If you talk to the snake the snake won't bother you. Maybe you'll step on a snake sometime when you're walking along, but the snake will know who you are, and even though you stepped on him he won't move, he won't try to do anything to you. So in the summertime, when all the snakes come out, the first one you see you want to talk to. In that way the snake will know you all the time. The same with the lightning. You must talk to the lightning too. When you first see the lightning and hear the thunder you should talk to them, and they will know who you are all during the summer. The same with the bear. When you go up on the mountain the first bear that you see, or even the track of one, you must talk to it, and they'll know you all the time, all during the summer. In that way they won't harm you; they won't bother you at all."

My mother had many prayers. When she made corn-mush—she made it every other day—she had sticks to stir it with, and when she thought the mush was done she'd take the sticks out and raise them. While she was holding them up she'd say a prayer. She used to say, "We'll have something all the time. . . ."

THE END OF OLD MAN HAT

He was lying still, just breathing a little all that night, and just as morning came, just as you saw a little white and blue sky coming over the mountain, he passed away. He died that morning and all his relatives and friends began to cry. As soon as he died they told me to go and round up the horses, and while his relatives and friends were holding him and crying I started out, and while I was running I was crying too. I caught my father's racehorse and rounded up the others and drove them back. Everybody had left him and come outside.

We used to have a blue horse. It was the best horse in the bunch. I put a rope around that horse's neck and led him over to the hogan where my father was and put the saddle and bridle on him. Some of his relatives were still inside, fixing him up. They put new moccasins on his feet and cut a great big buckskin of his in half and put it around him for leggings. They dressed him in all his clothes and put on two bunches of beads that he had.

When he was dressed one of his nephews and I went in and got him. Our hair was untied, and we were covered with ashes. We put him on the horse and all his things beside him. There were two big bundles of stuff, and then we started off. The other fellow was leading the horse, and I was by my father, holding him, so he wouldn't fall off. We went to a little cliff and put him in a hole under the rocks and built a wall around him and covered him with rocks and all the poles we could find, and over that we put some dirt. We fixed him so nothing would bother him. After that we destroyed all his things and faced the horse to the north and killed it.

Then we started back, running and jumping over the bushes, so no evil spirit would catch up with us. When we got home we set fire to the hogan in which he died, and after that his brother, Choclays Kinsman, came up with a rifle and shot the racehorse. We were standing by him, and he said to us, "Face the horse to the north." We went over and faced it north, and then he shot another. We went over and faced that one to the north again, and he turned around and shot another one, and we faced that one to the north. As he was turning to shoot again a fellow came up and grabbed his rifle and begged him not to kill any more.

A little way from home they had a pail of water ready for us to wash in. It was mixed with the leaves of a tree struck by lightning. We washed the ashes off ourselves over there and then went back in the other hogan. There was a place for us two, right beside each other, on the north side. Everybody else was on the south side. When we got inside we put our clothes back on, and while we were dressing the others started cooking. It was almost noon. All this time we hadn't eaten anything. They'd said, "Nobody should eat until everything has been fixed up."

When the food was cooked we started eating. We had ours apart from the other people. They said to us, "You two have to eat separately, not with the others, and you shouldn't leave anything in the dish. You must eat up everything. If you want more they'll put some in your dish, just enough for you to eat. And you mustn't touch anything, nor bother anything. You mustn't bother the fire. And nobody should walk in front of you, or go near you. You two mustn't separate. Whenever one wants to go out to take a leak, you should both go. Even though the other doesn't need to, you both should go. You have to stay right by each other, so nothing will go between you. None of you should go between them," they said. "When any of you go out you shouldn't go towards the north, nor look towards the north. As soon as you go out turn around towards the south. You should only be on the south side of the hogan, and none of you should look around. You might see something. If you look around you might see evil spirits, and that'll be bad for you. You'll get sick from it and die. You mustn't say, 'evil spirits,' and you mustn't say, 'grave,' and you shouldn't face toward where the hogan was burned. You have to do these things and not say things like that for four days. During the four days you must all be quiet. Don't do anything, or say anything out loud. You must all go easy on everything."

Three days after he was buried they got some soap-weed and hauled some water. That was for us and the others too, but ours was separate. Early the next morning we all got up and washed ourselves all over. When we were through the two of us washed our clothes and hung them up to dry. It was before the sun was up. Then the other fellow and I took our corn pollen and went out towards where we'd buried the body. Quite a way from the hogan we stopped and put some pollen in our mouths and some on top of our heads, and some we sprinkled about, naming the body and saying, "You've gone away from us now by yourself." Those were the only words we said, and then we turned around and started home.

Inside the hogan we gave the corn pollen to the fellow sitting by the doorway, and then all the people began taking some and saying their prayers, saying, "We'll live long, and we'll live good lives. We'll be on the good path, on the happy path all the rest of our lives." After that they talked to us, telling us how to take care of ourselves, and how to take care of the others. "In that way," they said, "you'll live a long and good life. And some day the same thing will happen to you. When you die you'll be fixed just the same way."

THEY DIVIDE THE OLD MAN'S GOODS AND MOVE AWAY

After we were through with all these doings we rounded up the horses and saddled them and put on all our stuff and moved away to a place called Salt Water. When we got to that place all the sheep and horses were there, and there was a crowd, all my father's relatives and a lot of people from different places, talking about how they'd divide the things up. My father's brother, Choclays Kinsman, got on his horse and rode over where the sheep were, and everybody moved there after him. He said, "I'll give sheep to every one of you. Some will get twenty head, some fifty, and some of you will get a hundred. In that way everyone of you will get some sheep. I'll do the same with the horses. I'll give each of you a horse or two. I don't want any sheep or horses for myself, because I've got enough. But it's up to you, my relatives and friends, if you want to give me a sheep or a horse it'll be all right. I'll be thankful for it. But before I start giving them out to you I want my boy to have his first. We'll all help separate my boy's sheep and horses, and then I'll start giving you some."

They separated the sheep for us, and my mother and I had a little over five hundred head. And they separated fourteen horses of mine. My father came up to me and said, "Get two more out of that bunch. Any two you like." So I went over and got me a young mare and a three-year-old stallion. I didn't get any of his sheep. He'd had close to nine hundred head, but his clan relatives got them all. They got all his cattle too. But the cattle were up on Black Mountain, so all the people who were related to him went up there and rounded them up and gave one or two heads to each other. There was only one steer in the bunch, and my father's brother kept that for himself.

How do you reckon your kin? The answer to this simple question is a variable one which depends upon the system of kinship reckoning used by the people questioned. In our society we count as kin blood relatives through both the mother's and the father's side of the family. Without becoming involved in relatives-by-marriage, we have four grand-

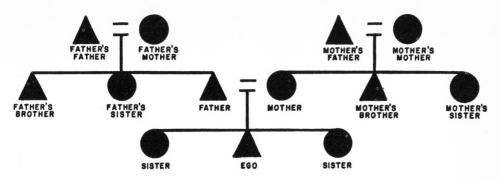

A bilateral kinship system.

parents, two parents, brothers and sisters, aunts and uncles on both sides, all of whom are close blood kin. In the figure on the preceding page this blood relationship is shown. It is from this base that we build our whole family line.

Suppose, now, that your method of reckoning kin was altered so that your blood line was reckoned through the male side only. You would then have only one blood grandparent, your father's father, and your only aunts and uncles would be your father's brothers and sisters.

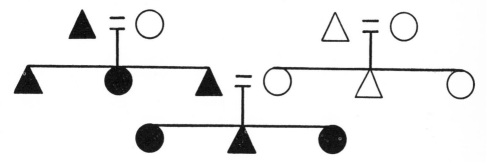

A patrilineal kinship system.

How people reckon their kin is a vital element of their society. It gives an initial bias to the way they live. The Navajo would never expect to inherit property from his paternal uncle, and if he were down on his luck he would first turn to his blood relatives, his mother's people. The Navajo would accept this pattern of action because he traces his blood line through his mother.

When people belong to a kinship group through a single blood line, they are members of a clan. The word clan, however, can be deceptive, because it does not specify the reckoning system. Male-line-derived clans are variously termed patriclans, gentes, or patrilineal clans. Female-line clans are termed matriclans, clans, or matrilineal clans. The Navajo reckon their kin through the female line, and these lineages may rightfully be called clans.

The Navajo recognizes his father's clan as a secondary but important feature of his lineage. Every Navajo individual is, however, a member of his mother's clan and, of course, of his maternal grandmother's clan. Conversely, since a man and wife should never be of the same clan, an individual is always of a clan different from that of his father.

Every Navajo is a member of a family, an extended family (several families who are related), an "outfit" (several extended families forming an economic group), and a clan. These are the patterns of associations that are easily recognized by them. Our use of the word "Navajo" refers to the society or "tribe." This larger category is not fully understood by the ordinary people. They think only in terms of the radius of their outfit, which is their world.

The first article on the Navajo clan, and Selections 35 and 36, are by Gladys A. Reichard, Professor of Anthropology, Barnard College, Columbia University. Dr. Reichard, who has been a student of the Navajo for more than twenty-five years, has published extensively on these people.

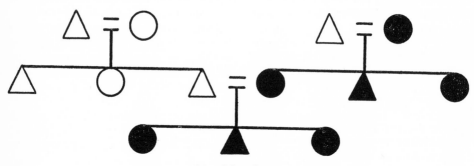

A matrilineal kinship system.

• 33 • Clan Functions

GLADYS A. REICHARD

Compared with western pueblo clan functions those of the Navajo are relatively simple. The main function is to regulate marriage and in doing so indirectly to affiliate clans. By bringing the clans into close relationship through encouraging marriages between them the clan performs an economic function. For naturally, if clan members are exchanged, as when a brother and sister marry a sister and a brother the gifts passing between the clans tend to neutralize one another. Or, if three brothers of one clan marry three sisters of another the second gains in wealth while the first becomes more closely related through good-will. Thus there is a constant interchange.

The Navajo clan has no political functions. Those who are at present called clan heads fill a position which is artificial in the old Navajo organization. Most of the informants say there was no such thing as a clan head. Political functions, such as they

[Adapted from "Social Life of the Navajo Indians with Some Attention to Minor Ceremonies," *Columbia University Contributions to Anthropology*, Vol. 7, New York, 1928. Pp. 30, 32, 34-35. Used by permission.]

were, were vested in the Peace and War chiefs whose functions and clan affiliations cannot at present be ascertained.

At first glance it would appear that in religious matters the clan played no role at all. One thing is clear, namely, that the chants are not clan property. They are individual possessions which can be secured primarily only by those having and proving sufficient intelligence, not only to learn them, but to learn them well. The custodian of a chant teaches it preferably to his son who is, of course, not a member of his clan. But if all the sons fail to be interested in learning the chant, or if they lack the ability (the standard of which is high) the chanter might teach his ritual to anyone who fulfills the requirements.

Consequently although Navajo clans have powerful social and economic functions, such as regulating marriage and consequent friendly affiliation and serving to keep individual property within the clan, other functions such as political and religious ones are very weakly developed. This feature is in marked contrast to some of their pueblo neighbors whose clans function most importantly in the two latter respects.

The preceding discussion of clan functions has to do only with an individual's own clan. In brief we may say that the chief functions of the Navajo clan are social with very slight evidence of religious restriction as in the *anadji* ceremony. The father's clan has the same function namely, a social one, which works out in a different way. Two individuals whose fathers belong to the same clan no matter if they are absolute strangers will by that fact establish a relationship which manifests itself chiefly in the giving of gifts and in hospitality which is more marked than usual.

Membership in a father's clan or clan-group exerts a very powerful influence upon kinship terms also. Two men who belong to the same clan are reckoned as clan brothers after the first generation regardless of blood relationship. That is, a man will call his mother's brother *ci-dai* (man speaking, male relative one generation removed ascending or descending older than I, related through a first intermediate female relative in direct or collateral line). But all members of succeeding generations will reckon their relationship on the basis that these men belong to the same clan and are therefore brothers. Without bearing this principle in mind one could not define the kinship system of the Navajo.

Thus we find that although the Navajo clan is strikingly maternal, the father's clan functions as strongly in a different direction. This phenomenon again illustrates the danger of dependence upon catchwords ("maternal sib," "social functions").

• 34 • Clan Origins

KATHERINE LUOMALA

Some of the clans become so closely associated through the intermarriage of their members, or other local ties, that they regard themselves as constituting a group of related clans, but not related closely enough to develop marriage taboos. There are about a dozen of these groups scattered about the reservation. They are unnamed.

The number of clans among the Navaho has been variously estimated as fifty-one by Matthews, fifty-eight by the Ethnologic Dictionary, and forty-nine by Reichard. The counting of clans is rendered difficult because many clans have duplicate names which may be translated differently by different people. Then, too, names of extinct clans have been forgotten or are known to only a few.

The names of the clans are based, for the most part, on localities figuring in their early history. Also a clan may be named

[Adapted from *Navaho Life of Yesterday and Today,* United States Department of the Interior, National Park Service, Berkeley, 1938. Pp. 88-90.]

after the alien tribe from which the clan ancestors came.

The female members of a family are not the only ones to live in the same locality generation after generation. Their clan relatives are also territorially restricted to the pastures and sites of an area, in which the individual families of the clan hold adjoining lands, basing their claims on generations of occupation.

A local band was the basis of almost every clan. Though the origin legends are a mixture of fact and fancy, they indicate, in a general way, how the tribe grew. Bands of wandering Navaho met other hunting tribes using the same lands, and if their language was similar, relationships were soon established. Pueblo people, who had abandoned their communities because of famine or the attack of enemies, fled to the wilderness, and after a time intermarried with the Navaho.

In the version of the origin legend given by Matthews . . ., we have a charming mythological account of clan origins, which is summarized here as a matter of literary interest and not for any historical value it may have. The goddess Esdzanadle, or Changing Woman, was lonely as she lived on the western ocean in her splendid house, so she made people from her epidermis.

These people formed the original clans of the Navaho. At last the clans decided to leave her. She said, "It is a long and dangerous journey to where you are going. It is well that you should be cared for and protected on the way. I shall give you five of my pets—a bear, a great snake, a deer, a porcupine, and a puma—to watch over you."

She also gave them five magic wands of turquoise, white shell, haliotis [generic term for abalone, a Pacific Ocean shell fish], black stone, and red stone. The people, as they wandered, grew thirsty, so a man of the clan with the turquoise wand struck it into the ground and made a water hole. A woman of another clan said the water was bitter, and she gave the clan the name of Bitter Water. Later, they met a band living near a spring, called Coyote Spring, and these people were named Coyote People after the water hole. They met some of the Apache, who begged to marry the Navaho girls. Later some Zuni, driven by famine, came to the San Juan, and joined a Navaho clan. . . . The Navaho tribe became powerful enough to raid the Pueblos: one man raided Red House, a pueblo, from which he brought back a girl who founded the Red House Clan. In this fashion, so the Navaho relate in their legends, the fifty or so clans of the Navaho tribe of today were created.

Ordinarily one would expect a discussion of property and inheritance to be included in the description of the economy, but in the case of the Navajo the clan is the key to understanding these matters. Therefore, the clan system has been explained first, followed by Dr. Reichard's account of property and its inheritance.

Among the Navajo, as among the Eskimo, the ideas about property are quite different from ours and we shall again be reminded of the problems created when we try to introduce our system of land ownership among a people who through the years assigned property rights to those who used, rather than had legal title to, a piece of land.

• 35 • Property and Inheritance
GLADYS A. REICHARD

Ownership of personal property is purely individual among the Navajo. There is no sex discrimination. Property consists of: livestock, goods, and intangible property. . . . Each individual has his own stock. In the Crown Point district where the land is favorable for cattle-raising the Indians count their wealth in cattle and horses. In most other places sheep and goats do better, but everyone has horses.

Each woman or child who may be seen with a flock has charge of the sheep of a number of people. She has her own and those of her sisters, brothers or husband, or perhaps her mother's and father's. Or she may be caring for the animals belonging to her maternal uncle or to some of her cousins. There is no absolute rule as to whose flocks shall be tended by any individual. The matter depends upon convenience and circumstances. There is also no strict clan definition as to care. A woman may include the sheep of her father or his brother with hers. But the individual animals are always known and no mistake is made in ownership. Family-groups always keep their flocks separate even though the flocks of several are pastured in a given area.

Suppose a rich boy, Chiki, goes to school when he is very young. This circumstance will by no means deprive him of his income. His kinsmen—brother, cousin, maternal uncle or whoever can do so—will care for his cattle, sheep and horses. Even though he be away as long as ten years he may return to find his flocks and herds greatly increased and improved. His kinfolk will treat his animals as well as their own. When he returns he will not think of paying them for their attention, nor would they expect it. There is ideal trusteeship which is rewarded only by reciprocity, if the need arises.

"Intangible property" consists of chants and all that goes with them—song, dance, medicine bundles, prayersticks, etc.—formulas for increasing flocks and horses, power and knowledge. . . .

Knowledge too whether acquired by formal instruction or by experience is valuable. It is transferable and heritable. It is usually very closely related to chant wisdom or medicine-lore. A man may teach it to another and receive payment for the instruction without in any way lessening his own wisdom or power. The young man would expect to give his teacher a large gift during the long period of instruction and the Chanter would expect it. But the Chanter must not, in any contingency, specify the amount to be paid. If he did he would lose his own power, the Chant would lose its power and the man who paid would gain nothing by his effort. On the other hand, if the learner did not voluntarily pay a generous sum to his teacher he would lessen his chances of gaining power. He would be considered niggardly and people would not hire him to sing for them as often as they would a more liberal man. The total amount paid is large but indefinite since gifts are presented at intervals for many years. I should not be surprised if the entire payment for learning a major chant totaled one thousand dollars or more. A singer renders to his teacher the entire fee received for the first four performances of his chant. Besides, the instructor receives a part of the fee of every subsequent chant given by his students as long as he lives. This is a kind of royalty.

Another kind of power possessed by some Navajo is the ability to divine. This power is innate and can therefore be taught to certain individuals only if they have the intangible "something" within them. The capacity for divination is a source of income. A man is paid a small sheep or a dollar and a half to prescribe a particular chant as a cure.

I shall not be able to give nearly all the classes of intangible property which exist. I cite the few I have heard of which show that the Navajo is rich not only in material property but also in imaginative and supernatural wealth. There are sacred names for sheep, horses, and hard goods, the knowledge of which will cause the particular animal or commodity to increase for the owner of the name.

Ceremonial paraphernalia cannot be eas-

[Adapted from "Social Life of the Navajo Indians with Some Attention to Minor Ceremonies," *Columbia University Contributions to Anthropology*, Vol. 7, New York, 1928. Pp. 89-94. Used by permission.]

ily classified. A ceremonial basket, for example, may belong to a family until a ceremony has been performed. Then it becomes the property of the man who conducted the ceremony. He may give it away or sell it. But if the family has been obliged to borrow the basket, they pay the Singer two or three dollars and return it to its owner.

The foregoing description refers to personal property and under this title we may properly place everything which is owned by the Navajo. The materials and powers owned may be disposed of as well as used by the individual possessing them. When we consider real estate it cannot be placed in the same category. Land is "owned" only in the sense that it is "used." Pasture land and water supply really go together in the minds of the Navajo. Anyone may pasture his stock where he will and he may use the available water. But no one would deliberately drive his sheep on to land which is being grazed to its full capacity by another. If a newcomer came to a certain territory the matter of grass and water would be talked over with those already there and an agreement made. To the whites who map out rights, privileges and ownership so thoroughly it is incredible that people can live like this. They set up no boundaries, each goes where he will, each uses all the water he needs. If the supply becomes exhausted he moves to another place where it is better. And all this without dissension or bad feeling. Once in a very long time a Navajo might be found who is stingy with land or water. Public opinion is sufficient to demand more altruistic behavior. Public opinion would put him down as a miser, he would be despised and life for him would be very unpleasant. Stephen says that grazing land is family property. I have not been able to corroborate his statement.

Land for purposes of cultivation is also needed. The garden is close to the summer abode of the family and it, like pasture-land, is owned only when used. A family usually has a winter hogan and one or more summer homes where pasturage is good. They

move about within the environs of these places and in this respect only are they nomadic. Gardens are planted each year and cared for. But should a place be deserted for several years anyone may use the house and garden and establish his family there. He would know, of course, whether or not the original family had left temporarily or permanently.

There are conflicting opinions as to the ownership of gardens:

"The farm is, as a rule, the property of the husband who disposes of it before death," according to the Franciscans.

Stephen claims that the woman owns the house and all domestic gear. The man must plant the garden for the woman even though he may have his own garden elsewhere.

Chee Dodge (Crystal) says the farm belongs to the one who starts it and descends in his or her clan.

George Bancroft (Tuba City) says a woman owns the farm and her relatives inherit in the following order: mother, sisters or brothers.

I could get no response except astonishment about the ownership of house and farm adjoining. A man has a hut built when it is necessary but *he* does not *own* it. Neither does his wife nor his children nor any of his relatives. Everyone owns it who uses it. The idea that a house could be individual property amazed Navajo who had had very little contact with whites. But if a woman, the head of a household, should die her daughter who lives at home would automatically become the head of the house. If there were no daughter a son might bring his wife home or the hogan would be abandoned. The matter depends entirely on the number, relationship and residence of the survivors and on other circumstances.

I quote the following remark on garden produce, "The man cares for the corn, but the women and children may help and when the corn is ripe it belongs to everyone."

An excellent illustration of the ownership of real estate is furnished by Tuli of Shiprock. Much land is being irrigated in the Shiprock area because of the elaborate system supplied by the San Juan River. Tuli is a very enterprising young man who has been educated at the Government schools. He is ambitious and energetic. He took up an irrigated claim which had already been fenced. It consisted of twenty acres. The improvement which was noticeable from the summer of 1924 when he first began to work it until the summer of 1925 when I visited him again was astounding. But Tuli is not sure—basing his opinion on old Navajo custom—that he will retain the twenty acres. For a woman owned the ten acres which he took up but had fenced twenty and she moved to Crown Point. If no white man interferes Tuli can be reasonably sure that he can keep the twenty acres, for it is very unlikely that the original owner would even attempt to establish a claim. However, if she did, Tuli would yield the ten acres if she came to live there and continued to keep them up. On the other hand if she, influenced by whites, should claim the land with Crown Point as a point of vantage, Tuli who is very good-natured, might yield, but I am sure could not fail to harbor resentment.

The illustration brings up one of the most difficult questions in the assimilation of two civilizations. Our property ideas are so utterly different from those of the Navajo that there seems to be hardly any principle intelligible to the natives which an official might follow no matter how fair-minded he might be. In all probability Tuli's problem if left alone will solve itself. But on other parts of the reservation complex situations arise again and again. For instance, at Crown Point land has been homesteaded. At the same place and elsewhere allotments have been made. These two methods of assigning land have been used by the U.S. Government with the aim of benefiting the Navajo. But they have of necessity been worked out according to our own views of economy. The requirements of homesteading are difficult for the Navajo to understand, but in most cases they can be lived up to. It is when questions of inheritance come up that

the white man is nonplussed in dealing with the Navajo. The viewpoint is simple enough but difficult to comprehend by one born and raised in our tradition. Land is used not owned, therefore it cannot be disposed of. If a man dies, his survivors may continue to use the land as he has been doing; if there are no survivors or if they do not care to stay, the land is there and anyone else may use it.

But with land ownership which enters into homestead rules and allotments, the matter changes in all its aspects. The Navajo are being taught to "own" real estate. Let us go on the hypothesis that he may learn the lesson of real estate ownership within the next few years. Will the problems of the Government be settled as simply as that? By no means, for though property ideas be reconstructed the hydra of Navajo inheritance raises its seven heads.

A man owns much personal property; he learns to realize also that he owns land and water rights and can dispose of them. He dies. Who inherits his property? How is a re-allotment to be fairly made? We all know how the matter would be settled by us. We have a patrilineal type of social organization and although it has broken down considerably in favor of the bilateral type, nevertheless our laws of inheritance are based on it. The Navajo, on the other hand, have a strictly matrilineal organization. The only tendency toward two-sided inheritance is the very weak one of courtesy gifts. All the laws are based on inheritance in the maternal line.

For this reason a man's children inherit very little, almost none, of his property. If he has made an oral will the family will do all in its power to carry it out. If not, his brothers and his mother's brother will determine how the property shall be disposed of. The most important thing is to keep it all, or nearly all, in the clan. The little which the children inherit is calculated on the basis of age, not of sex: older children get a little, younger children none. The widow also gets almost nothing.

Under ordinary circumstances a man's

sister and brother, or his mother, if she is living, will inherit the bulk of his property. If they are not living his sisters' children or their daughters' children are the next in succession.

A married woman's property goes to her children if they are married or mature; if they are small, her brother takes precedence. His sisters' children are, however, his legal heirs.

An unmarried woman's possessions go to her sisters and brothers.

As was pointed out earlier, social organization actually consists of people in relation to one another; people behave toward each other in keeping with the status which each respectively occupies. In the selection which follows, a number of statuses will be described, together with the roles associated with them. For example, you will read, among other things, about the husband-wife and the mother-child relationships; about father-child and maternal-uncle-nephew relationships, as well as those between mother-in-law and son-in-law. This selection, too, provides helpful information regarding the relative statuses of men and women.

• 36 • The Family and Marriage

GLADYS A. REICHARD

The Navajo family is unilateral counting descent in the mother's line. The normal members of the family are children, parents, maternal grandparents and maternal great-grandparents, for it is not at all unusual to find four generations living. The feeling about the dwelling is that wherever the mother is, is home. In a single household may be found the mother, her daughters and their unmarried children and so on.

When a girl marries, the mother has a hogan or shade—according to the time of year—built somewhere near her own for the daughter and her family. My observations lead me to believe that the chief reason for a separate domicile is the mother-in-law taboo. For although the husband is not permitted to speak to his mother-in-law and avoids coming into her presence, nevertheless, the daughter and her children spend most of their time at grandma's.

The mother of the family plays a large role in the social and economic life. She possesses a number of sheep and goats—oftentimes more than her husband—and has charge of them. The flocks are frequently large consisting of the sheep and goats belonging to the mother, to some of her sisters or brothers or to her husband. Sometimes the mother tends them herself. It is more customary, however, for her to see that they are cared for by the children of from seven to twelve years of age, for the mother of a household has plenty of work which keeps her occupied at home. Old women who no longer have children or large households to attend to may also guard the sheep.

But at times of crisis, as for example, when the sheep must be rounded up for dipping or shearing, or during lambing time, the whole family aids. The mother, father and older children riding horseback assist at the work.

The woman has to do all the cooking

[Adapted from "Social Life of the Navajo Indians with Some Attention to Minor Ceremonies," *Columbia University Contributions to Anthropology*, Vol. 7, New York, 1928. Pp. 51-61, 68-73, 87-88. Used by permission.]

and must care for the house and children. When domesticated animals are killed she has charge of skinning the animals and of drying or cooking the meat; she makes all the clothing except the moccasins for the female members of the family and occupies herself with weaving rugs in her spare moments. The cash or produce received by a woman from products of her own manufacture are hers to use or to dispose of at will.

Socially, the position of the Navajo woman is high. She has a voice in all family affairs and many times her decision on a matter is final since she may have control of the family purse-strings according to the relative wealth of herself and her husband. It should not be inferred however that wealth is the main cause of the woman's high prestige. For she is held in general regard and the feeling of the family for her opinion is something which one finds difficult to describe.

[Numerous] examples might be cited to show the woman's influence in the decision of family questions but of course the amount of prestige which a woman enjoys must vary greatly in different families. The Navajo woman works hard and in general enjoys great respect and has unusual authority. The general tendency, even in spite of the theoretical power of the avunculate is for sons, brothers and husband to consult the maternal head of the house and to respect her opinion.

In religious matters the woman has privileges similar to the men. There is no ceremony or part of one which she may not learn if she has the ability. She may learn the songs and ritual, she may superintend the making of sand-paintings, she may say the prayers and, as proof of her complete knowledge of a given rite she may learn the long mnemonic myth. Finally she may be provided with the . . . [prayer stick] which is given to each singer by his or her teacher.

The position of the Navajo woman in political life is interesting. Although the political organization . . . of the tribe is not well known there is sufficient evidence to show that women were on a level with men

even here. War set the criterion of political prestige. Names indicate the fact that women went to war as, for example, Mother-went-to-War-when-carrying-her . . . Mother-was-at-War-with-the-Hopi . . . and Woman Chief . . . . At the tribal assembly . . . women who had achieved much in war had a voice in the council and might even become chiefs. Chee Dodge heard of one who was chief because she had seen the war party kill an enemy. The greatest honor which could be given a Navajo individual was to be acclaimed chief. The institution of the tribal assembly fell into disuse so long ago that the functions of the chiefs are vague but the office carried prestige perhaps rather than executive power. Whatever the privileges may have been they were as readily bestowed upon women as upon men.

In general discussions of the position of woman there is, I believe, too great a tendency to be content with the conclusion that position is "high" or "low." There goes with the catchword an implication that if the position of one sex is high that of the other must be low. The Navajo data do not bear out the implication. The Navajo man of intelligence is a most important factor in the community. He is the repository of sacred lore which is precious to every individual. By virtue of his ability to learn chants and perform cures he is considered a man of good judgment, a kindly spirit and one who may be appealed to as an authority not only in religious but also in political or other worldly matters.

The notion that in a society having mother-descent and the avunculate the father is a nonentity in the household is also an erroneous one. The Navajo father, although he is not constantly busy as is the mother, has important duties. He attends to the horses and cattle, regulates irrigation and cultivates the crops. The children have about the same attitude toward the father as our children have—except that they do not consider him the family bank! When he sits about the home he plays with the children and pets the little ones. He takes delight in making simple toys for them. Many children weaı heavy silver ornaments made for them by their fathers. Older children and women will sometimes show large collections of bracelets and rings of different sizes which they have worn from babyhood up.

The fact that relationship in the father's clan is carefully checked up and that kinship is determined on that as a basis is another evidence that relationship with the father and his family is not considered as inferior to that reckoned through the mother —it is merely different.

We may summarize thus: the Navajo woman enjoys great economic and social prestige as the head of the house and clan and as the manager of economic affairs, and she is not excluded from religious ritual or from attaining political honors. The man enjoys the privileges and prestige of the political and religious life and is by no means unknown to, or unloved by, his children.

The practice of polygyny increases the number of the actual members of a household and it is often difficult to get clear in one's mind the relationship of the many individuals comprising a household. There is no distinction made between the children of the father and mother of the household and other children who may be living there. Adoption is not formal but children unfortunate enough to lose a mother are taken and raised with the rest.

Theoretically the children of a deceased mother are brought up by their maternal grandmother, and the husband goes back to his mother's home to live. In actual practice there is as much variety as we find in our own society since the custom is subservient to convenience and circumstances.

We may conclude then that although the tendency is for women to care for their deceased daughter's children, the actual adoption depends upon other factors such as economic condition of the family concerned, closeness of affiliation with the father's family, desire of grandparents or of the second wife for the children, or other practical considerations.

Except for [one] example ... I have found no examples of the mother's brother taking

care of the children although the avunculate is highly developed among the Navajo. The maternal uncle has many privileges and along with them certain obligations but adopting his sister's children seems not to be one of them. He must look after his sisters' children but that would imply finding a home for them rather than actually caring for them himself. The personal relation between him and his nephews is a very close one, the younger man having in reality two fathers, one who pets him and plays with him, who teaches him the things men learn and do, that is, his biological father; and the other, his maternal uncle, one who does the same things but who in addition has social obligations and privileges which cannot be shouldered by the real father.

The analogy between personal attitude and kinship terminology cannot be applied to the relationship between a man and his sister's daughter. In this connection his privilege or power seem to determine his attitude. He has power to regulate her life in many respects. Especially he is allowed to decide whom she shall marry. This is perhaps the most strongly recognized of his privileges although he must be consulted in all family matters.

As provision is always made for the care of young children, so old people are usually made comfortable. The duty devolves upon the members of the family according to convenience. The daughter or grand-daughter customarily assumes the responsibility but if the old man or woman has no daughter or grand-daughter the sister's daughter would be looked to next. I have seen old blind and crippled men who were kindly, often tenderly, led about by the young men or women of the family. They usually have a large pile of sheepskins and blankets upon which to recline—the other members of the family have one or two— they occupy the warmest place in the hogan and they are patiently waited on.

The care of the unfit is a family matter which is taken over by individuals who feel themselves responsible usually because of relationship to the persons concerned.

If pueblo marriage may be defined as

"brittle monogamy" Navajo marriage may be called "brittle polygyny." It is not unusual to find a man who has more than one wife. Polygyny has of course been forbidden by the U.S. Government and now one wife is all that is officially recognized. In the past family instability seems to have been common. Instability would account for the large amount of polygyny which prevailed if we accept the hypothesis that the sexes were equal in number. This is the opinion of a number of Navajo informants. The marriage ceremony was held for only the first of a man's wives. If the couple did not get along well together the man could leave. Since the woman is economically independent his leaving did not affect her economical status in any way. The man would return to his mother's house or "go to live with" another woman. The causes for separation vary: jealousy is sometimes given as a cause, laziness on the part of either man or woman or general incompatibility may be other reasons. A woman who does not attend to the household duties and a man who does not look after his wife's property are considered lazy. A husband may leave a disobedient wife. "She does not *always* have to obey her husband but she ought to sometimes to get along."

Sometimes a man may settle a disagreement with his wife by paying her a given sum. The request to leave would then be withdrawn and the two might live together in perfect harmony for an indefinite period, perhaps for life. An example was given of a "mean" type of woman who would quarrel with her husband periodically, each time requiring him to make a settlement in order to stay with her. After she had acquired the bulk of his wealth she might make him leave her anyway. Actions like this were not condoned nor did they happen frequently but they were possible.

From a number of examples in the genealogies as well as from remarks made about duplicate marriages it seems justifiable to conclude that sterility or even temporary inability to function sexually is sufficient reason for a man to leave a woman. Usually the men who have the greatest number of wives one after the other have no children with the ones they have left.

The matter of family instability is one which is comparable with conditions in our own society. Families may be unstable for the first few, perhaps as many as five, years but if two individuals live together that long and have a child or two the group becomes stable and there may be no change except the addition of children for many years. The custom of polygyny may make for stability or instability according to the view one takes. If a man takes his wife's sister, daughter or niece and at the same time continues to live with his wife and to have children with her as well as with the other woman I should say the family becomes more stable rather than less so. On the other hand, a man might take a new wife from another family and thus upset the whole pattern of residence. This might or might not make for instability depending upon the individuals concerned. Men may be found who have lived with one and the same woman for thirty, forty or fifty years. It is not unusual to find that they have never lived with anyone else. Other instances show that men after a period of philandering settle down and remain faithful to one woman. Another type of man goes through a long period of change, he lives with a woman two or three months—or years—then leaves her and goes to live with another. He will have many children in various parts of the reservation. But when he becomes middle-aged he will settle down, perhaps with a woman past the age of child-bearing, and live with her the rest of his life.

Tradition has it that one rich man had twelve wives at one time. In the genealogies the record is nine and the man did not live with all at the same time. I have no case where a man lived with more than three at once.

Whereas the custom of marrying more than one woman of the same clan is by far the most common, it sometimes happens that a man marries women of two or more different clans. But when he takes a second wife from a clan other than the first wife's he is obliged to pay a certain sum to his first wife's family. It is said that a man sometimes secures a second wife from the family of his first wife by threatening to take one from another clan.

Marriage is by gift rather than by purchase.

MARRIAGE PREFERENCES

The most outstanding feature of the Navajo marriage is not the relationship of the man and woman who marry but rather the relationship existing between the numerous wives chosen by one man or the relationship between the individuals of intermarrying pairs. Of the 1,025 marriages recorded there is only one example of marriage between cross-cousins. In the old days cross-cousins married without social sanction. They married in secret, no gift was given and no ceremony was held; hence the union was not legitimate. The types of marriage we find among the Navajo are, I am convinced, directly related to two factors: 1st, the tendency to affiliate clans and to bring them into close social and economic harmony; and 2nd, the practice of polygyny. The first of these factors is the more important for the fact that polygyny is customary is not determining in any way, but it certainly lends itself admirably to the process of clan affiliation.

Before discussing clan preferences it may be well to review the limitations in choosing mates. First of all there is strict clan exogamy: "A person who would marry a woman of his own clan or clan-group would go crazy and jump into the fire." . . . Parallel cousins may not marry since they are sisters and brothers.

Different attitudes prevail regarding marriage outside the tribe. Some say that those who marry outside are not the best Navajo. "Maybe it is all right at Zuñi where they do not live so well as over this way (Ganado) but not here and it is not done very often." But the same people treat marriages between school boys and girls in a different light. These are sanctioned, allowance being made for changing customs. Even school boys and girls of the same clan or clan-group

may marry although the old folk do not thoroughly approve.

The custom of the levirate was quite common years ago but has been more or less abandoned lately. Hastin Jake knew a man who married his brother's widow but soon left her. Others say that a man's brother had the first rights to the widow and she could not marry another without his consent unless she paid his family. Or, other members of the deceased husband's clan have a prerogative and the widow is not free until they give her up.

Many more examples might be given but the tendency for clan members to seek mates for their relatives in a few neighboring clans is brought out by any typical family which has married children enough to pick and choose. But although preferences are very strong they do not take precedence over family standing. The first thing a man considers in choosing a wife for his son is the position of the woman's family in the community. Industry, cleanliness, hospitality and prosperity are the criteria upon which a family is rated. Wealth of course counts for a good deal but the character of the members of the family is far more important. The clan to which the woman belongs is also important but family position necessarily establishes clan position. A process somewhat like the following prevails in choosing a mate: Suppose a man and woman have a large number of children who live to a marriageable age. When they think it time for one of their sons to marry they will look around for a mate in some family which they consider a good one to affiliate with. The girl's family never takes the lead in making a match. "People would laugh" if they did, or "it would look as if they wanted to get rid of their girl." The father of the boy takes the initiative rather than his mother's brother. But if the father is "not so bright as the mother" she might get her brother to make the negotiations with the girl's family. The matter is talked over in family council and in choosing a wife for a son the father's voice is final and may override that of the maternal uncle whereas the opinion of the *girl's* maternal uncle may take precedence over her father's or even over her own. Now let us suppose a girl is agreed upon, the proposal is made and accepted and the marriage takes place. Then it may be that the girl's family has also a son whom they will later marry to the sister of their son-in-law. Now in the first family there are a number of unmarried children and the second family may know of mates for them although not in the immediate family, nevertheless they will be clan members and mutual influence will be exerted to have them seek mates from the first family. And so it goes until we have an intricate network of clan and family alliances which is so complex that it defies any attempt to discover whether the affiliations are due primarily to desire for clan or family union or whether they are due merely to proximity of habitat. The fact, however, that some unions are made with the Father's relatives who are not clan members leads us to suppose that family wishes are very little, if at all, subservient to clan influences.

While theoretically matrilocal residence is the rule there are exceptions due to circumstances or to preference; just as in placing orphans, convenience is more potent than custom. If there is no daughter to care for a home upon the death of a mother a son may take his wife to his mother's home and the two keep it up.

AVOIDANCE

The observance of the mother-in-law taboo is more rigid among the Navajo than some other old customs. Adoption of orphans, residence and even clan endogamy may upon occasion be subordinated to convenience, but not so avoidance. I worked with Sydney and his father-in-law, Sandoval, sporadically for two months in the summers of 1923 and 1924. I spent much time at Sydney's home near Shiprock and made several excursions to Salt Canyon where Sandoval lived. Sydney's mother-in-law was never in sight. But in the summer of 1925 as I passed through Shiprock I stopped to see Sydney and his wife, Mary, only to find Mary dangerously ill. Her mother was taking care of her. She had been isolated in a hut near her house. At the time Sydney was not at home but when he was, both he and the old lady located the other before they moved from house to hogan in order that they might avoid each other.

One of my most sophisticated interpreters told the story of his marriage. He said, "When I married I told my wife and her family I was going to treat her mother just like my own mother." Her mother was so chagrined at his lack of respect for her that in deference to her wishes the boy avoided her.

I cite these examples to show that the avoidance custom is one which dies hard. From the point of view of conservatism the custom belongs in the same class with belief in ghosts and witches, which beliefs never *quite* free a Navajo individual.

The taboo begins as soon as the proposal of marriage is accepted and lasts until the death of the individuals who observe it. Even if the wife dies the husband continues to avoid her mother. Thus if a man has been married a number of times in different families he must avoid a number of women. Since avoidance begins with the engagement a woman may not attend her daughter's wedding. She may sit within hearing distance but may not enter the hogan or shade. If she does not know her son-in-law she may peek into the hogan through a crack so that she will thereafter know how he looks so she can avoid him. "A woman believes she will go blind if she looks at her son-in-law."

Among the Mescalero Apache the group of women a man must avoid is rather extended. Not so among the Navajo. Avoidance here applies only to son- and mother-in-law. Very, very long ago a sister would not pass an object to her brother directly but would put it down and let him pick it up or would pass it to someone else to hand to him. But the Navajo "got over that." I could find no evidence of anyone who observes the custom. It is true that although Tuli never heard of the restriction he felt that a "man would rather get the object himself than have his sister pass it."

JOKING

The joking relationship which is the antithesis of avoidance is one with which the Navajo are thoroughly familiar. As is not uncommon in North America two kinds of joking are recognized. The most extreme permits obscene teasing and obtains between cross-cousins (*bi-zedi*) who, it will be remembered, are not potential mates. The term *bi-zedi* is used by two female cousins or by two cousins of opposite sex, but two male cousins are also accustomed to tease each other. Tuli says he teases his cross-cousins but if they "get mad" he stops. If they tease back he continues and if four or five of them co-operate they succeed in "teasing him down." This type of teasing includes twitting about sex matters.

Tuli says that maternal uncle and nephew (*bi-dai-bi-da*) also tease but do not become obscene. Tuli teases *bi-da* about girls of his uncle's father's clan and the uncle teases Tuli about girls of his (Tuli's) father's clan. Teasing about sex ("not bad") may be indulged in also by a maternal uncle and niece, paternal uncle or aunt and nephews and nieces. But if sisters and brothers teased each other about such things they would "jump into the fire."

From a very reliable informant I found that the following individuals also may joke:

"Maternal grandmother and maternal grandson may tease but not bad."

"Father-in-law and son-in-law may joke bad."

But since the Navajo are great teasers and always enjoy a personal joke it is not quite easy to determine where they draw the line between "bad" and "not bad," that is, when it is allowable to joke in an obscene way and when not. Evidently teasing about sex is not always considered obscene and certain persons may be privileged to joke about members of the opposite sex of the father's clan who would not be permitted to carry the custom as far as actual obscenity.

"A Navaho woman's most treasured possession is her child, and to all children she is almost invariably kind. She may be capable of butchering a sheep or whipping a horse like a man, but she will not punish a child beyond a little slapping and a sharp word. Children screaming or crying and the scolding voice of an angry mother are seldom heard among the Navahos." (Statement in *The Padres' Trail,* January 1948, published by the Franciscan Fathers of Saint Michael's Mission in Arizona.)

When we compare this approach with that commonly found in our own society, we can readily see that every people has worked out ways of helping the child develop the kind of personality which is most desired by the majority. Socialization is the term frequently used to describe the process by which a child is taught the many roles he is supposed to play as he matures toward full participation in adult society.

• 37 • *Navajo Infancy and Childhood*
CLYDE KLUCKHOHN

. . . Almost all of the data utilized in this chapter were obtained among the group of about five hundred Navaho Indians living near Ramah, New Mexico. Although these Indians live in close proximity to ranchers and not far from a Mormon and a Spanish-American village, intimate contacts have been minimal because of the linguistic barrier. The first school for this group opened only in 1943 and until this time they had been almost completely let alone by the Indian Service and by missionaries. Hence acculturation, other than in the realm of material objects, has been relatively slight.

THE FIRST MONTH

Abundant corn pollen is sprinkled on the baby's head as soon as delivery is complete. . . . The midwife then ties the cord with a piece of homespun wool or a string picked up from the floor and cuts it (formerly, and still sometimes, with a flint knife, but more often with a pair of scissors or a kitchen knife). . . . Unless the baby is already crying or breathing well, it is shaken, massaged on the chest, or patted on the back or held by the feet with the head downwards. It is then wrapped tightly in a woolen blanket or in cotton cloths and a sheepskin and placed near the fire. The head is propped with blankets so that it will not get out of shape.

The bath is given with soap and warm water in an old piece of crockery or a dishpan. There is a great fear of the blood connected with birth so that in many families the receptacle is afterwards thrown away. In any case the bath water is carefully disposed of in a hole outside the hut which has been prepared for this purpose. . . .

The baby is dried with a towel. A cloth band (sometimes with a little cotton directly over the navel) is wrapped tightly around the abdomen. The whole body to the neck is then swathed firmly in cloths (usually old flour or sugar sacks) which are tied both at the shoulder and hip levels. Thus bundled, the baby is wrapped in a sheepskin (fur side toward the body) and laid at the left of the mother, towards the north, with its head pointing to the fire.

The exhausted mother is lying down near the fire on the south side of the hut. She is usually given a tea brewed from juniper branches or from plant leaves. Her first food should be cornmeal mush unseasoned, and indeed in strict theory she should eat nothing but this for four days. . . . Nowadays the mother gets a hearty meal as soon as she wants it. In most cases she does not drink anything but coffee or tepid to warm water until her milk has begun to come freely.

Except when the mother is seriously ill, a relationship of almost constant physical proximity between child and mother begins after the child's first bath and is unbroken until the child can walk. Night and day, wherever the mother goes, whatever she is doing, the baby is either being held by her or is within sight of her eye and almost always within reach of her hand. As soon as she is physically able, the mother herself responds to every manifestation of want or discomfort on the part of her child. Her usual first response whenever the child cries is to place it to her breast. If this fails to produce quiet the baby will be cleaned and dried, cuddled, talked to or sung to. The baby is totally helpless; it can only cry. Wriggling is hardly an outlet for the Navaho baby since it is wrapped so tightly.

The baby's routines are simple and infinitely repeated. He is bathed in warm water every day, or sometimes every other day, depending in part on weather conditions. The cloths that serve as diapers are changed when the baby is bathed and usually one or more other times during the day. Frequency of changing varies greatly depending upon the relative restlessness of the baby and upon family habits. . . . Under such conditions it is not surprising that skin irritations are frequent. A reason frequently given for denying the baby freedom of hands and arms is to prevent it from scratching itself. (Another reason given is warmth.) Sometimes mittens are put on the baby's hands to control scratching during the periods the baby is unwrapped. The baby's face may also be largely covered to prevent scratching.

The length of daily periods of being unwrapped during the first month average about two hours, but the range of variation is considerable. In no case did the infant have less than an hour (usually before and/or after the bath) to kick and squirm freely, but where members of the family had a good deal of free time or where the baby was ill or uneasy, this figure mounted to four or even five hours a day, usually in stretches of an hour to an hour and a half at a time.

In every case the baby gets a good deal of affectionate attention. He is, of course, fed and held by the mother. He is also held, touched, and talked to by the grandmother, aunts, father, older brothers and sisters, and indeed by all relatives who come and go in the hogan.

According to the Navaho ideal, a child is nursed immediately it begins to cry. During the first month of life ideal and practice nearly coincide. Only occasionally is there any delay, as when the mother rouses slowly from sleep during the night or is outside the hogan for a few minutes or is busy with some task which cannot be put aside the instant the baby cries. . . . The willingness of a mother to feed her infant on his terms is doubtless increased by the fact that she is never more than a few feet from her child in and around her one-room shelter. She sits on the floor (there being no chairs), and the infant is easily pulled near her. Since the mother wears only a loose blouse and no underwear the derangement of her clothes is negligible.

MONTHS TWO AND THREE

After about four weeks the child is put onto a cradle board. Sometimes this occurs earlier—as soon as the cord has fallen off and the navel completely healed. The permanent cradle represents a considerable expenditure of labor and, since the cradle will be thrown away if the child dies in it, the family does not wish to risk putting the child into the cradle until the chances for its survival are good. Another factor is the mother's desire for movement. So long as the baby is shifted merely from one hut or windbreak to another nearby, the wrappings of cloth and sheepskin serve very well. But if the mother wishes to go to the trading store or to visit relatives she must take the baby with her on horseback or wagon and for this the protection of the permanent cradle is thought necessary. The same cradle may be used for a succession of brothers and sisters if all have lived, but the cradle is painted afresh with red ochre for each new occupant.

The permanent cradle is not made casually, although these days one sees a few for which boxes or store boards are used. The cradle is ordinarily made by the father from a pine tree which has not been struck by lightning nor badly broken by wind nor rubbed against by a bear.

The board proper contains one or more small holes in the lower part to allow for the drainage of urine. Sometimes this bottom is made of two boards tied together so as to form a trough-like cradle instead of a perfectly flat one. At the top is placed a narrow padded strip as a pillow. Over this is arched a wooden hood one-and-a-half to three inches wide which clears the child's forehead by some inches. To the bottom is lashed a foot-rest. There are varying sets of holes toward the bottom of the board so that the cradle can be lengthened as the baby grows taller.

Tassels of fringed buckskin in the upper corners of the cradle are seen less and less frequently today, but a turquoise setting or bead for a boy and a white shell for a girl are still prevalent forms of decoration. A squirrel tail is often fastened to the cradle because young squirrels fall without injury. Buckskin pouches with amulets and herbal medicines are also attached for magical protection.

Within the cradle the baby is wrapped

tightly in a number of cloths as he has been during the pre-cradle period. Sometimes the two legs are separated and each tightly encased. The child is strapped to the cradle by means of a lacing cord which is passed in zig-zag fashion between cloth or buckskin loops attached to the sides of the board and is finally fastened through a loop on the footboard. A cloth is attached to the top and, resting on the hood, can be lowered to cover the whole cradle and keep out light, flies, and cold (and probably oxygen as well). Except in the case (sometimes) of babies under six weeks or two months, the head is not strapped and the baby can freely move this part of its body.

The cradle is a strong focus of Navaho sentiments. A young man or woman will point proudly to one still hanging in their parents' hogan and say "That is the cradle in which I grew up."

A soft and ample pad of cloths, cliff-rose bark, or folded blanket is placed back of the child's head to prevent undue flattening. This raised pad is in the form of a hollow triangle (open at the top side). It is supposed to keep the baby's neck straight and to make the neck grow long, but the main point is that the hollow within the pad allows the back of the head to get round. A very flat head is not admired, and a grown child will sometimes openly blame his mother for not taking precautions to prevent this.

The proportion of each day that the baby spends tightly laced in his cradle varies with his age and with the temperament and situation of the mother. If she has older children to assist her in household tasks, she is likely to keep the child out of the cradle for longer intervals than a mother who must do all the work of the household as well as care for the baby. However, since healthy babies sleep most of the time in the early months and do not need to be removed from the cradle for nursing, they can be and often are left there most of the time except when they are bathed or when the cloths which serve as diapers are changed.

A daily bath is not given quite as scrupu-lously as during the first month. The children are talked to in a somewhat more personal way as they come to recognize individuals and to respond.

All the elders make a great fuss over each succeeding event in motor development. This seems to follow the same general pattern as with white children. At least the ranges are about the same. The averages (especially for certain later developments such as walking) appear to be a bit later.

MONTHS FOUR TO TWELVE

From an objective point of view the features of this period are: more or less the ordinary course of human motor development, a greater proportion of time out of the cradle, gradually increasing ingestion of foods other than milk, accelerating frequency of nursing, and the growth of the symbolic significance of nursing.

Although tied to the cradle during part of their waking hours each day, Navaho children nevertheless get some chance to explore their bodies and other individuals with their hands, to move their limbs, to try out their muscular equipment in a variety of ways. Apparently this limited practice is sufficient because there seems to be comparatively little difference between Navaho and white children in the ages at which motor skills are developed though the relevant figures have not yet been fully analyzed. With both there is, of course, considerable individual variation.

The Navaho say that a child sits up when it has two teeth. The average of fifty-one cases for sitting with slight support is 4.2 months, of forty-eight cases it is 5.3 months for sitting alone. By five months or a little later children will also reach for and grasp things and put their feet in their mouths. As they acquire teeth they have the same need for things to chew on as do our children. Bones, beads, and other hard objects are freely given them. Thumb-sucking is very rare, and we have never observed 'obsessive" thumb-sucking or a child asleep with its thumb in its mouth. When excited or disturbed, a child will not infrequently put the index or some other finger in its mouth. Occasionally the mother will put a baby's whole fist in its mouth to quiet it. Sometimes a mother will also pacify a small baby by putting her own finger in its mouth.

At eight to nine months most babies will stand when supported under the arms (two cases were observed at a little less than seven months), and some will raise themselves to a standing position. At about ten to twelve months they will walk when led, and the first independent steps usually come from two to six months later. These signs of development are aided and encouraged, but the Navaho mother counts it no disgrace that the child takes his time to grow up.

Of one feature of development the Navaho make a little ceremony. The first laugh is eagerly watched for. The person who sees it first must give a present to each other member of the family. When visitors come to the hogan it is polite for them to enquire "Has the baby laughed yet?" The ceremony consists in the mother's holding the baby's hands out straight while some member of the family (usually a brother or sister) puts a pinch of salt and bread and meat on each hand. Today store candy is sometimes used. The food is then immediately taken away— "so that the baby will learn not to be selfish." The father or mother then kills a sheep and distributes this to relatives along with a bit of salt for each piece.

The hours spent in the cradle steadily diminish as the child grows older. Some families put the baby in the cradle relatively little after he is able to sit up—mainly for traveling and for protection at night. Other families take the onset of crawling or scooting as a signal for freeing the child from the cradle almost all of the day. But conservative Navaho opinion insists that the cradle is the normal place for the infant until he can walk independently.

Children of six months average 4.2 hours daily out of the cradle, those of nine months 5.8, those of eleven months 9.3 (a good many children of this age are out of the cradle entirely). Younger children out of the cradle are held in the arms or lap of the mother or some other relative or are allowed to lie on a pile of skins or blankets to kick freely. Those who can scoot or crawl are permitted to move about on the floor of the hut for brief periods so long as someone is able to keep an eye on them so that they do not get too near the fire.

Especially from the time a baby is able to sit up, it is offered any and all foods available that can be eaten with its equipment of teeth. Bread dipped in broth or coffee, canned tomatoes, fruit, rice, cooked cereal, soft store cookies, and squash are usually among the first solid foods in a baby's experience. Bones, bits of pork rind, and pieces of meat to suck on are also commonly given the child from the time its teeth begin to appear. Gradually the child is taught to use a cup or bowl instead of a bottle—with weak, heavily sweetened coffee as the inducement. Squash, bits of potato, pieces of softened meat are fed with a spoon, and the child is encouraged to hold the spoon himself.

The Navaho formula continues to be: "Feed a child whenever it cries, day or night. Give it anything that the people it sees are eating if it will eat." Permitting a four-months old child to have as much coffee as it likes shocks most whites. Indeed the practice of letting a child eat whenever it cries seems to most whites bad for the child as well as inconvenient for the mother. But the psychological consequences are probably highly beneficial. Previous to a child's ability to state its wants verbally, others can respond only to its crying or fidgeting. The important thing among the Navaho is that something is always done when the child manifests discomfort or demands attention in this way. It is now generally agreed that among all human beings many of the most deeply rooted aspects of a personality take their form in the first year of life. They are the more tenacious because they are unverbalized. These basic "unvoiced" attitudes grow in large part out of the interaction between the baby's manifestations of his wants and needs and the responses which surrounding individuals (and especially the mother) make to them.

TODDLERS

The child who can walk alone has completely abandoned the cradle, although usually this has been quit (at least for the daytime when not traveling) a little earlier. Certain routines change. The bath, for example, is seldom given more than once a week with a yucca suds shampoo of the hair perhaps once in two weeks. The toddler now runs about exploring his world. He grabs cats and dogs who are so unwary as to permit themselves to be caught. Parents or other elders seldom discourage a child's cruelties to animals. They will often join in the laughter of the other children at a dog's yelp when it is kicked or has its tail pulled by a baby. Even special tortures such as running a needle and thread through a kitten's ear are tolerated.

The child runs from person to person and is petted by each in turn or consoled if it has met with some small accident. The father will take a toddler who wakes fretful from a nap in the heat and soothe him in his arms. Any older person rushes to the child when he screams after a fall or a slight burn or an ant bite. At the same time the Navaho method is generally to let learning occur through such minor injuries but not to rub the lesson in by further punishment. After the safety of the cradle is gone, the child's principal protection is the presence of elders. But their backs must sometimes be turned, and children learn the realities of fires, knives, and sharp claws through experience. Navahos spend comparatively little time in verbal warnings, in imaginatively enlarging upon such dangers and their consequences and making generalizations. White practice perhaps tends to make some children unduly fearful and dependent. Navaho practice tends to make children better able to look after themselves, as far as the external world is concerned.

Almost all training in the first two or three years of life is delayed, gradual, and gentle. The positive side of child training in this period is mainly a matter of constant encouragement in the acquisition of language and of other skills. Someone is always talking to the baby, giving him words to imitate, telling him especially the proper kinship terms with which to address his various relatives, praising him whenever his random babblings happen to hit a meaningful sound combination or when his imitations are understandable.

No fuss is made about food or sleep. The child sleeps when and where he chooses. He eats (of what is available) what he pleases and when. "The baby knows what is best for him," Navahos say. Some of all the dishes prepared for the rest of the family are offered the baby, but none are forced upon him. When the family buy sweets or soda pop at the trading store, the youngest gets as much as he will take—or at least his fair share and usually more.

The youngest child is definitely the kingpin of the household. After he can walk he tends to get progressively less of his mother's undivided attention, it is true. His mother will tell an older child to amuse him, and toddlers are bounced, carried around on the hip, and entertained in every conceivable way by elder siblings, especially sisters.

According to psychoanalytic conceptions, the Navaho infant has exceptionally favorable opportunities for developing a secure and confident adult personality. Apart from sickness (which is of course responded to), there appear to be only two slight liabilities in the pre-weaning period. Teasing of children of nine months or a year and over is not infrequent—even by the mother. Sometimes it takes mildly sadistic forms, as when a child reaches for the cigarette the mother is smoking and she holds the burning end toward him. There are also delays in the response to crying, even of pre-verbal children. A child of seven or eight months may cry fifteen or twenty minutes during the day before a busy mother picks him up. During the night sometimes soundly sleeping parents are very slow to rouse.

But there is no sudden and harsh attempt to compel the child to control his eliminative activities. Older persons are almost always quite tolerant of displays of aggression (even blows with sticks and other objects) and temper tantrums. When a toddler has something taken from him or fails to get what he wants, he will scream, arch his back, brace himself, hold his breath, and be quite inconsolable until his elders give in (which they do more often than not) or somehow distract him. If a child holds his breath so long that it begins to get stiff, cold water will be thrown in its face.

White observers often comment that Navahos "spoil" their younger children. They do *indulge* them, but they seldom "spoil" them in the original sense of the word, i.e. to deform or ruin the character. The "spoiled" child is the one who is petted one moment and neglected or beaten the next—regardless of his behavior. The Navaho toddler is given self-confidence by being made to feel that he is constantly loved and valued. Navahos sometimes comment that they spoil the last baby in a family, but here again this must be translated to mean "indulge even more than earlier children."

Nor is it true that Navaho children experience no restrictions. Whites who go into a Navaho hut and see a crawler put into its mouth a lump of dirt from the floor or a cup which the dog has just licked, or see a four-year old sticking a nail through a cat's ear, are likely to get the impression that the words "No" and "Don't" are never used to Navaho children. This is far from being the case. *T'adoo* (equivalent to "stop that") is one of the most frequently heard words where small children are present. Probably there are *fewer* "don'ts" than among whites. This is partly because there are fewer prohibitions put upon biological impulses, partly because Navaho life is simpler and there are fewer objects that a child can destroy or be harmed by, and partly because there are no taboos on "dirt" or "germs". On the other hand, the number of "superstitious" taboos which are enforced upon the child are much more numerous. In other words, the number of interferences and prohibitions to the child's activity in the form "I don't want you to do that" is relatively small, but the number in the form "Such and such will happen to you if you do that" is fairly high. If parents are not ultimately responsible for denials and restrictions, then it is of no use for a child to try to coax or cajole them. One hears many straightforward requests and even demands from children to their elders but little wheedling; plenty of crying but comparatively little whining.

Let us now turn from a chronological review to a topical treatment which will include data on children of two years and more of age (all unweaned and recently weaned children).

THE BABY AND THE CRADLE

During many hours of the day and all of the night, the cradled baby's bodily movements are sharply restricted by the cradle. Its position is varied from the horizontal to the upright, but the baby cannot move much of its own volition. There is, however, a certain uniformity of environment when the baby is moved from one place to another—regardless of who does the moving. It is also to be noted that the entire body as an extended unit receives the impact when the child is rocked or moved.

The infant's sensory contacts are also limited by the cradle. It can see well—more than most white babies when its cradle is upright—and of course its hearing and sense of smell are not interfered with. Perhaps the greatest limitation is on the sense of touch.

Certain aspects of cradling have obvious survival advantages. The cradle board and the thick swaddling provide a measure of protection against harmful insects and snakes. The heavy canopy, which may be raised or lowered slightly, guards the child's eyes against the direct rays of the bright sun out of doors, and if when the mother is traveling on horseback with her baby, the horse should buck or shy or fall and the baby be dropped, the hood provides excellent insurance against head injury. After the child has begun to creep, it can be put in the cradle to protect it from getting too close to the fire during occasional moments when all other persons may be out of the hut. In a crowded dwelling where toddlers and older children may be scuffling about, the baby is probably safer in his cradle than on a sheepskin on the floor as the other children sleep.

The cradle is often placed in an upright position after the child has been nursed. White pediatricians have suggested that this habit may help the baby in digesting his food much as being held upright helps the white baby to "bubble". Margaret Fries also suggests that the custom of propping the cradled child in an upright position before he can *crawl* or even sit may facilitate walking.

In addition, there appear to be important psychological advantages to cradling. The cradle, like the womb, is a place where movement is restricted, where support is always present, and where changes resulting from movement or from temperature fluctuations are minimized in their effect.

Likewise, the cradle permits babies, who could not otherwise sit up unaided, to assume for long periods a position other than that of lying down, out of touch with what is going on around them. When the weather is warm or mild, and the family is lounging or eating under the trees outside, for instance, the cradle is ordinarily propped against a tree. This means that the child's face and eyes are on about the same level as those of the adults who are sitting near him. In this, as in several other ways, the Navaho child from the very beginning is part of the total society rather than being isolated or segregated from it, "just a baby", as in white families.

One judge of the merits of cradling is the baby itself. We have frequently observed babies crying both to be released from the cradle and to be put back into it. The former predominates with children of six months and more. There is evidence that with younger children the protection (or habit?) of the cradle has a strong appeal especially when the child is sleepy. Many children have difficulty in becoming accustomed to sleeping outside the cradle. During wakeful hours, however, children of six months and older apparently begin to feel the confinement as frustration and will wail to be released or at being put back into the cradle. The average age at which the cradle is hung up and no longer used *at all* is 11.6 months (range 8 to 15½ months).

NURSING AND WEANING

In general, however, at the weaning period the Navaho child comes to learn effectively that the world around him makes demands, imposes restrictions, and gives punishments, as well as supplying reassurances and rewards. Although the Navaho continue to allow great latitude with respect to activities that are severely regulated by white parents (such as eating and sleeping), the weaned child must face keenly-felt deprivations. Latterly he has been accustomed to nurse as much for comfort or libidinal pleasure as for nourishment. Now this solace is denied him even when he is tired, cross, or frightened. No longer is everything done for him with hardly any effort on his part; instead he must learn to feed, wash, and dress himself. To be sure, these activities do not have the same significance for Navaho children as for whites. The etiquette of eating is simple, to say the least. Washing is a matter of hands and face and an occasional yucca suds shampoo of the hair. Except for removing and putting on shoes, dressing takes place more nearly weekly than daily. Nevertheless, life must have a very different quality for the nursing than for the weaned child. Upon the nursing child the only restrictions imposed are those which the cradle places upon movement, and even this restriction usually is terminated while the child still nurses. No longer are almost all his responses rewarded, no longer does his mother devote herself mainly to his comfort and pleasure. The mother averages only about an hour a day out of sight of the nine months old child but nearly three away from the eighteen-months old baby. After the child really begins to talk, he finds that all responses and rewards are made much more selectively by his elders—he has to do the right thing for attention and praise. Sometimes crying is responded to only by placing the child on a water barrel or elsewhere in isolation until it stops.

On the other hand, it must not be forgotten that the number of older persons who are available to respond to the child is unusually large. One of the most common sights in an extended Navaho family is that of a toddler (especially one who has been recently weaned and feels himself rejected by his mother) running from one woman in the group to another and receiving some sign of affection from each.

If the initial experiences with the mother have been good (which is usually the case), it seems to be one or more of the older brothers and sisters who bears the brunt of the hostility generated at the period of weaning.

Little hostility appears to be generated against the father during this early period. He is usually out of the child's sight a great part of the time, and when he is present his role is very positive: he seldom disciplines and he pets and comforts (especially the child recently displaced by weaning). He cannot give the reward of nursing, but he does supply candy and other food tidbits. He also will often hold the baby while the mother is cooking or engaged in some other urgent task, particularly when an older sister of the baby is not available.

TOILET TRAINING

Not until he can talk and understand is pressure put on a child to learn Navaho conventions of excretion. If a child who can walk and talk (or at least respond to speech) starts to urinate inside the hut, he is told to go outside to do this, and an older child will gently lead him out. At first elimination is permitted just outside the door; later the child is expected to go away into the bushes or behind a ledge of rock. For a long time he is not punished for lapses or accidents but encouraged to act like his elders. Before going to sleep at night, he is taken out and is also advised not to eat or drink much for some time before going to bed. No special "baby words" are used with children in referring to urine or feces.

After a time, the youngster who continues to wet or soil himself is teased or scolded by his relatives. In some families the buttocks of older children are slapped though ordinarily Navaho children are switched on the legs, not on the buttocks.

In short, the two evacuation activities of the child are uniquely free from parental interference for a long time. Whatever may be the sensations associated with evacuation or retention of urine or feces, the processes are subject for some time to the impulses of the child, unmixed with parental punishment. The conflict between the child and its parents because of the discipline of cleanliness which is so critical in child development among us is postponed for at least a year and usually, for all practical purposes, for two years.

DISCUSSION

The most striking theoretical question which emerges from this consideration of some of the main aspects of Navaho infancy is this: how can this picture be reconciled with the facts on Navaho witchcraft, on the states of morbid melancholia and endemic uneasiness which have been well documented for adult Navaho? How can the anxiety level be so high among a people where infants are nursed whenever they want to be, where childhood disciplines are so permissive, where there is so much genuine affection for children? If the writings of certain psychoanalysts were literally true (and the whole truth), adult Navahos ought to have calm and beautifully adjusted personalities. However, this is most certainly not the case. In spite of the fact that Navaho infants receive a maximum of protection and gratification, they tend to be moody and to worry a great deal when they become adults.

The explanation may rest in part upon the frequent ill health of Navaho children, upon teasing, upon refusals of the breast to toddlers, and upon delays in response to crying or upon other factors (such as genetic ones) that have been overlooked. But the main point is probably not that the theorists are utterly wrong but that they claim too much for the earliest years and do not pay enough attention to later events and to the total situation in which the mature person finds himself. [It may well be that the] high degree of tension observed among adult Navaho may be traced partly to the exceedingly grave pressure to which Navaho society is at present subject, and also to the conflicts caused by weaning, other experiences of later childhood, and beliefs about supernatural forces.

In the two selections that follow are discussed some of the more important characteristics of Navajo political structure. The first selection describes the tribal assembly (Nah-Sit) at which major problems were discussed, and decisions reached about the emergencies facing the Navajo people. But in addition to such formal assemblies Navajo culture provided certain traditional punishments for witchcraft, homicide, sex irregularities, theft, and intoxication. The coming of the white man with his concepts of European law wrought some changes in the old Navajo common law, and these are also briefly mentioned.

The second article indicates how loosely knit was the Navajo tribal organization and how "the political unit was really the natural community, environmentally defined." The role of the chief or headman, as described in these two selections, will emerge as something quite different from what is usually depicted in Western movie scenarios.

• 38 • Navajo Common Law
RICHARD VAN VALKENBURGH

EARLY POLITICAL ORGANIZATION

There is scant information available dealing with the early political organization of the Navajo. Aged informants state that there were twelve chiefs: six War Chiefs and six Peace Chiefs. There was no caste as there was and still is among the Hopis; a Navajo leader's rank being determined by his ability. A prevailing tone of democracy ran through the entire organization. Choice of leaders was by popular selection from the rank and file based upon an individual's particular abilities. War Chiefs were chosen for their ability as warriors and Peace Chiefs for their eloquence and discrimination.

THE EARLY TRIBAL ASSEMBLY

There was a close association between the ceremonial and political life of the early Navajo, as indicated by fragmentary scraps of the archaic tribal assembly known as the *Nah-sit*.

The last *Nah-sit* was held for a woman called *Etsan Chon* at a place called *Tsin-si-cod-ni*, or "Cottonwood Trees," at a location some twelve miles east of Chinlee towards Lukachuki. This occurred over one hundred years ago, and another was to have been held just prior to the exile to Bosque Redondo in 1863. It was during this exile that the one hundred and thirty-two chants of

[Adapted from "Navajo Common Law," *Museum Notes*, Vol. 9, Nos. 4 and 10, 1936-37, pp. 17-19, 51-53; Vol. 10, No. 12, 1938, pp. 39-42, Museum of Northern Arizona, Flagstaff. Used by permission.]

the ceremonial were lost, upon the deaths of the men who knew them.

During the days when the *Nah-sit* was held, the tribe was not so widely diffused as it is today, the concentration being along the Carrizo Mountains, Lukachuki Mountains, Chuski Mountains, and Defiance Plateau. It was then possible for all the people to assemble at the appointed place when the ceremony was called.

The meetings came in two and four year intervals, and could be called in an off year should a tribal emergency arise.

A date was set for the *Nah-sit* early in the winter, soon after the harvest. On the appointed date a four day dance was held. After a twelve day period, another four day dance would be held, and this would continue throughout the entire winter. The twelve day intervals would allow for other duties and ceremonies such as the Mountain Chants and the Night Chants, Needle Chants and Hail Chants. The *Nah-sit* closed with a four day dance in the spring, and on the fifth day, or the day after the dance, spring planting would begin.

The *Nah-sit* was held as a prayer for abundant water and fertility of the soil, as well as for political purposes. When the assembly was called, the leaders would select a group of young men, some of which would go to the tops of the four sacred peaks for prayer and to return with water from the peaks. Another group would be sent to the Salt Lake south of Zuni. This group carried corn pollen as offering to the Goddess of the lake. As soon as the offering was made, clay was taken, and returned to the place where the assembly was being held. This clay was placed upon the lips of the dancers, for the purpose of drawing rain.

The dancers were composed of selected young people, dancing in couples—a man and woman together. Sometimes the partners would dance throughout the whole winter, and in the spring, with the closing of the dance, would return home to arrange for marriage. No face paint was used, other than the clay upon the lips; the dancers wore their best clothing, and only young

people highly respected by the tribe were allowed to dance.

Between the dances, the tribe met and discussed any emergency that may have arisen. When alien difficulties were concerned, the War Chiefs were in charge of the discussion. When domestic problems arose, the Peace Chiefs took charge. Women were permitted to act as War Chiefs if they had taken part in raids or fights with the enemies.

LATER POLITICAL ORGANIZATION

During the period of exile at Bosque Redondo, the entire governmental structure of the Navajo was destroyed. After the tribes returned to their homes, few of the old chiefs remained, and they retained their power by the general consent of the people, but with the recognizance of the Agent.

[Such traditional leaders] represented the Navajo to the Agents, and counciled for their people in the matters of annuities, law enforcement and governmental programs as formulated by the Indian office.

During the period of the years between 1869 and 1895 all the important tribal councils took place at Fort Defiance, those of lesser importance taking place at dances. The political discussions of today that the Navajos hold at their dances are reminiscent of the above period and that preceding it.

WITCHCRAFT

Witchcraft is the most heinous of all Navajo crimes, for it affects the health and wealth of not only the individual, or individuals, but it terrorizes the whole countryside as well. The practice, although now rare, is not as uncommon as most people believe. In recent years employees of the Indian Service have been forced to publicly burn medicine bags of suspected witches in order to quell the wrath of the Navajos. Within the past five years a witch was killed by a semi-educated boy, who, probably because of his education, had lost some of the superstition and terror that most Navajos have of these "poisoners".

Usually the suspected witch is a medicine

man who is attempting to gain wealth by blackmail; in other cases individuals with warped minds have been known to be accused of the practice. Sometimes individuals will charge other persons of witchcraft if they have a grievance against them.

The offence of witchcraft is against the individual or individuals (who have been half-frightened to death) and who are really sick, and also against the family group which it affects economically; and further, against the community which it has thrown into terror. Should a witch publicly admit his crimes (they sometimes did), or even be strongly suspected on circumstantial evidence, the punishment sanctioned by the countryside is death. The kinsmen of the witch will not demand blood money. It is further believed that undetected witches eventually will be struck by lightning.

HOMICIDE

Homicide is a not too common crime among the Navajo. There is a much lower percentage per capita than among the White and Spanish-American populations of the Southwest. There have not been over five murders on the Navajo Reservation during the past year (1936). Examination of old government records shows the ratio to be very low.

Since 1810, the major cause of Navajo homicide has been the introduction of intoxicants. Previous to that and to date, the other predominant causes are inter-clan or family feuds, personal insults, and domestic difficulties.

A murder having been committed there must be some settlement. Retribution for murder is asked by the family group of a murdered person, first in the form of a payment of goods. In the old days, a wealth of shells, turquoise, coral, buffalo hides, and other skins were demanded. Later, "live stock" was exacted as a penalty, or the minimum of four horses for a man and five horses for a woman. Today in remote regions, this penalty, with additions, is exacted and if not paid the murderer is turned over to the Federal authorities for punishment.

But if a man should murder an immediate clansman, nothing would be done by the family of the murdered man; "It is between ourselves," they would say. But should a distant clansman murder a member of a family, they would say, "We are not related and will attempt to exact the penalty."

Death by accident, such as wrestling, riding on a borrowed horse, etc., is, in a way, considered murder so the relatives of the dead person would ask for payment. Should this be refused, "blood revenge" might be sought.

We find, then, that the basis of Navajo thought in regard to homicide is first that of payment. The human being, having an economic value to the family, has been taken away, and thus, for this loss, the family should receive recompense in tangible goods. Further, we find that, should this recompense be refused, revenge enters the picture and an attempt is made to equalize by killing. While this is general, we do find cases where no payment has been demanded, but blood revenge has been arbitrarily exacted.

NAVAJO CONCEPTS OF JUSTICE

Primitive Navajo justice as we have seen was fundamentally governed by concepts developed from traditions. Each breach in the rules of Navajo behavior had a specific justice whether enforced by mortals or by supernatural beings. Even though justice might be meted by mortals, Navajos feel that a further reckoning had to be made with the gods. Today, much of the primitive concept remains. However, at present the Indian Bureau has established a series of Indian courts which are presided over by Navajo judges. These judges are generally guided by the Code of the Indian Service, a set of laws based on those of the United States and independent of Indian traditions. Nevertheless the Navajos cling to their primitive philosophy, and their psychological behavior is determined more by this than by the white man's laws. It is no wonder that they are sometimes bewildered by the injunctions of the Indian court which has sentenced them.

ETIQUETTE AND HOSPITALITY

The most favored visitors are members of the immediate family group. Others welcome are men of standing, medicine-men, headmen, old friends, etc. Clansmen are welcome for a short stay, and travelers are welcome for an overnight stay.

One cannot state that any visitors are welcome to stay as long as they wish. The duration of a visit, unless for a specific purpose, such as assisting in lambing, shearing, harvest, etc., is usually three or four days for members of the immediate family. Should the visitors mention that they are in need of something, the hosts make every reasonable effort to supply that need. Should the hosts feel that the guests are staying too long, they hint thus: "I have to be off. I won't be here for some time."

When the guests prepare to depart, the hosts make no direct statement of an intended visit. They will hint: "Well! We will be at your camp to help with the harvest, shearing, . . ." etc.

Mutton feasts are always given the honored visitor. One of the best methods to incur displeasure is for a man to stay in a camp while the men are absent. For a guest to leave camp without announcing his plan of departure is cause for suspicion and on the next visit, no hospitality is offered.

The worst offenders are those who "crawl around the hogan at night and attempt to be familiar with the women." Another offender is he who "comes to the camp with an intention of gaining power over some one there."

A man traveling is not welcomed by lone women unless they are willing to allow him full privileges. Long ago, honored guests were accommodated by slave women.

Asking an individual his name is highly discourteous. By necessity, should the name be mentioned, there is danger of the owner having the ear drums dry up. Forfeits are demanded for the over use of clan names by non-clan affiliates. No woman ever dances with a relative or clansman at a Squaw Dance. A guest should never cut a portion from the middle of a melon or a piece of meat, but should cut his piece from the end. A man or boy should never touch sisters or female cousins, and should address them with the decorum taught him by his parents. Maternal uncles may address their nieces as they wish. Sometimes the jocularity becomes rather *risque,* if not lewd.

EXTRA-MARITAL BEHAVIOR

There are religious injunctions governing extra-marital behavior. In the past the punishment [for violations] seems to have been similar to the reputedly practiced mutilation of the Western Apaches. We have encountered no informant who remembers seeing a mutilated woman, but some oldsters tell that their grandparents spoke of such cases. The first offense caused the removal of the nose, the second, the removal of the ears, and the third, the punching out of the eyes. In the recorded tradition of the Navajo chief Goatso, the famed organizer of the clans into the tribe, it is related that he subjected some of his women to mutilation.

Today the offense is treated in a milder manner. One sees and hears of bruised bodies and blackened eyes, but generally no great violence takes place. Sometimes women become incensed at the antics of unfaithful spouses. We have on record the event of a Navajo wife belaboring her wayward man with a singletree. Normally such cases are settled by a cash or goods payment.

Sex in the philosophy of the Navajo is not based upon white man's concepts. It is purely biological and socio-economic in function. Fundamentally, it is stripped of any sentiment as we know the word.

THEFT—ROBBERY

Old time Navajo punishment required the thief to return the property or its equivalent plus a fine equal to the value of the property. No dishonor was attached to a thief as long as he was not actually caught. The dishonor consisted in getting caught red-handed. Long ago the Navajo made the bulk of their income from their depredations on the Rio Grande villages. Thievery and plunder was the profession of every able bodied man. Even after the terrific ordeal that the tribe endured between 1864-1868 at Fort Sumner, before they were home six months they were stealing Ute and Zuñi stock. Some of that old spirit remains today. Aliens are legitimate prey.

The Indian court gives a labor sentence of not over six months.

Robbery with weapons is rare, and if such should occur it is usually accompanied by intoxicants and violence. Cases of this description are generally turned over to the Federal courts.

INTOXICATION

Intoxicants were introduced to the Navajo by the New Mexican pueblos or villages located on the eastern boundary of the Navajo habitat. There was no stigma attached to selling spirits to Indians sixty years ago, and the traffic was considered legitimate. We find in the letters of Gov. James Calhoun of New Mexico, written 1849 to 1853, that spirits were an important item in the government issues to Indians.

Before the introduction of white or Indian courts, the Navajo method of handling a violent and intoxicated tribesman was to lasso him, tie him up, and turn him loose when he sobered up.

Today, if arrest is made in a town or city, the case is handled in the regular channels. If on Federal lands, trial is held before the Indian courts. The usual sentence for drunkenness alone is $30 fine or 30 days in jail.

• 39 • Navajo Political Structure
W. W. HILL

Speaking in a strictly political sense, a Navaho tribe does not exist. Such cohesiveness as occurs in a national sense is due to a common linguistic and cultural heritage, to the occupation of a defined territory, and to a common designation for themselves, *dine* "people," as against all others. The Navaho have never functioned as a unit in a concerted action. Never have all of them been brought, even temporarily, under the leadership of a single or individual group for a common purpose.

The fundamental political entity of the Navaho is the natural community. This unit is an economic one, geographically determined and distinct. The Navaho territory is one in which the location of natural resources necessary for subsistence occur at scattered locations and usually sharply defined by natural barriers. As their basis, such units had land fit for agriculture, which was located with reference to surface or sub-soil irrigation, readily available timber for building and household use, water for domestic purposes, and, after 1870, pasturage for sheep. The population of these units varied in relation to the natural resources. No reliable figures are available but estimates range from ten to forty families.

These natural communities were economically self-sufficient. Their problems were locally their own. They acted without reference to other such units, and often to the detriment of the others.

In recent years, 1874-75 and later, this separatist situation has been further reinforced by the establishment of trading posts, missions, schools, etc., in and near these key areas. Likewise, whatever incentive might have once existed for cooperation on a tribal basis against territorial aggression has been removed by government protection.

Community leadership was vested in one or more individuals whose duties involved the direction of domestic affairs and warfare. The Navaho recognized a distinct dichotomy of interest in these two cultural phases and seldom did one man fill both

[Adapted from "Some Aspects of Navajo Political Structure," *Plateau*, Vol. 13, No. 2, Museum of Northern Arizona, Flagstaff, 1940. Pp. 23-28. Used by permission.]

offices. The choice of the war leader (war *natani*) or leaders was entirely dependent upon ritual attainment. Anyone who had acquired the knowledge of one or more of the War Ways, upon which the success of any punitive venture was thought to depend, was eligible as a leader. Because of practical field experience these individuals were also in charge of defense operations, if the occasion arose.

Unlike the war leader, the local headman or peace *natani* was chosen. Factors governing the choice included exemplary character, oratorical ability, personal magnetism, and proven ability to serve in both the practical and religious aspects of the culture. It was a foregone conclusion that the chosen individual would be a practitioner and it was necessary that he control at least the Blessing Way Ceremony.

The people of a district met or were canvassed to determine the eligible candidate. In this the women had as much voice as the men. Usually the choice was nearly unanimous. If two men appeared to have nearly equal capabilities they might be asked to make speeches in order to determine the selection. Once a decision had been reached the man was notified and the induction ritual performed.

Not only was a personal investigation involved in the choice but the characters of the man's relatives were examined as well. The position was not hereditary, though a tendency for an individual to be succeeded by a son or sister's son was recognized. The *natani* was a local community head, and kinship figured in an election only in the normally expectable prejudice for a relative. These last features present a real anomaly for a people who otherwise possess such a strong matrilineal bias.

Tenure of office was assumed to be for life. Normally, however, headmen resigned when advanced age prevented them from adequately coping with the amount of work and responsibility which the office entailed. In this case they customarily recommended a successor. If an incumbent proved unworthy or lacking in ability he would either be ignored by the group or informed that his term of office was over. In either case a successor would be chosen.

Occasionally a woman might be chosen for the position of *natani*. Whether such a person acted in the full capacity of her male counterpart is difficult to determine. Certainly they acted as arbitrators in domestic affairs and may have directed economic procedure. In at least one case a woman was an important figure in war.

The induction of a headman into office was usually accompanied by a ceremony. The man was first anointed on the mouth and lips with pollen. This was [said] to give him strength and wisdom and "to enable a man to make 'powerful speeches and talks'." The pollen used was purported to have been grown on the four sacred mountains. This was mixed with pollen from the yellowbird, bluebird, oriole, and mockingbird. Next a piece of spruce and dirt from the four sacred mountains was placed in the man's moccasins. Occasionally tobacco from these four localities was given to the candidate who smoked it in a "mirage" stone pipe or, if this was lacking, a corn husk cigarette was substituted. All proceedings were accompanied by song. According to the Franciscan Fathers headmen underwent this ceremony four times. They also state that the headmen were distinguished by a costlier robe, and an arrowpoint, feather, or stone of the "mirage" type tied to the hair.

After the installation, the headman addressed the gathering, asking them for help and for obedience, the group answering in the affirmative. Sometimes the group removed their moccasins during the ceremony to signify their willingness to obey the *natani*.

According to Slim Gambler, it was customary for the newly elected man to journey to the four sacred mountains and plant corn at each one.

The obligations and duties of the headman were manifold, and, as he had no coercive power, his success and efficiency depended entirely upon his personal qualities and abilities. He was expected to address his own and other communities at public and ceremonial gatherings. While these talks might refer to specific problems, they were usually ethical and moral in their scope, admonishing the people to live in peace, righteousness, and to be diligent and hard working. As most headmen were accomplished raconteurs, various traditional and mythological tales were used to emphasize the points.

The *natani* acted as general economic director and encouraged productive activities. He planned in advance the work for the community, set the time for planting, and superintended planting, cultivation, and harvesting. He instructed in the proper techniques of agriculture and pastoralism. Any communal work was under his supervision.

In the legal sphere he arbitrated disputes over damages, acted as mediator in quarrels between individuals, remonstrated with wrong-doers, and adjusted family difficulties. Family difficulties most frequently involved marital disputes and desertion. Indigent individuals without relatives were considered his responsibility and a headman's menage usually included a number of such dependents. He was the diplomatic representative between his own and other communities,

tribes, and governments. He was expected to dispense hospitality to visitors.

Generally two or three men acted as assistants and advisors to the headman and were appointed by him. They were detailed to various duties in his absence. No recognized tribal or community council existed, though individual expression was encouraged at any public gathering.

Neither the headman nor his helpers were paid for their services. In rare cases, if the *natani* were absent, his farm would be cared for by the community, but this was the only form of compensation which was made.

In summary: no centralized authority existed among the Navaho. The political unit was the natural community, environmentally defined. Over this was a non-hereditary elective headman, whose influence permeated every sphere of the culture except warfare, which was usually in the hands of a separate religious leader. This headman had no coercive power and his efficacy and tenure depended entirely upon personal qualities and practical abilities.

The character of religious beliefs and practices of the Navajo differs greatly from that of the Eskimo. To be successful the Eskimo shaman must become "possessed." Navajo religious expression is more formalized and less individual. The word "singer" probably best describes the Navajo religious leader. The "singer" is concerned with the *form* as well as the *spirit* of religious practices. Both the shaman and singer work toward a common objective—the attainment or retention of the good will of the supernatural world. In the following selections it should become clear that the religion of the Navajo is radically different from our own; he is concerned only with the "here and now"; religion is never separate from everyday living, and much religious effort is directed toward the physical well-being of the individual. A useful distinction between religion and other aspects of the sacred is to be found in the section entitled "Looking at Values and Value-Systems." The same section contains a distinction between ritual and ceremonial that is also important for some purposes.

• 40 • The Ritualization of Everyday Behavior
W. W. HILL

One of the characteristics of Navaho culture is the unusual amount of ritual that has been

integrated in the affairs of everyday life. So thorough have been the adjustments of the

[Adapted from "The Agricultural and Hunting Methods of the Navaho Indians," *Yale University Publications in Anthropology*, No. 18, New Haven, 1938. Pp. 177-182. Used by permission.]

ritual and material sides of the culture that to the Navaho mind they appear indistinguishable.

[There are] two types of ritual . . .: a personal, simple, folk knowledge, exoteric in character, which forms a part of the agricultural process, and a more complex esoteric type which, while personal in character, is confined to a small part of the population. The latter type is associated with hunting and with ceremonies of the Rain Way chant variety.

Both exoteric and esoteric rituals are basically the same in pattern. They consist of a minor rite, or various minor rites, placed and used in different combinations. The variation in complexity is enormous. The ritual may be a simple act taking only a moment to transact, or it may be a sequence of such acts which take days to perform. However, in every case it is fundamentally a shamanistic performance varying mainly in degree of elaborateness.

While there is a general feeling that certain ceremonies should occur during certain seasons of the year and while particular ones, such as those connected with agriculture, are of necessity performed during the summer, there is actually no fixed order followed. The performance of rituals is dependent on the necessity of the moment and their occurrence is irregular.

It is apparent that, once established, these ritual patterns have spread or included many activities. . . . The simple exoteric type which appears in connection with agriculture is also applied to other everyday pursuits. The following random examples will serve to illustrate the extent to which such ritual observances (prescriptions, tabus, and the like) are integrated in other phases of Navaho culture.

No wood from a grave, from a house in which a person has died, or from a woodpile of a dead person can be used for building fires. Similarly, the wood used in building chutes and pounds, brush shelters for hunters, eagle catching pits, and sweat houses, or wood from trees struck by lightning, touched by a bear, or on which a deer has rubbed its horns is not used for fires because it is thought to cause illness. Once the fire is built no one is allowed to step over it, except during ceremonies.

The implements used to stir food have to be made of more than one element, because only food for ceremonial purposes can be stirred with a single stick. Food must always be stirred in a clockwise direction.

All animals and their products (e.g., milk, cheese) must be cooked before being eaten. This is not necessary in the case of some vegetable foods "because the sun has already cooked them." When bread, pots, or cooking stones are removed from the fire the depressions left by them in the ashes are smoothed over and a prayer is said asking for good fortune. If mush is set out to cool prayers are said for good weather and for riches. At the conclusion of meals the legs are rubbed while asking for good health.

Many individual food tabus exist. Anyone who has had the Shooting Way chant performed over him may not eat heads, feet, lungs, hearts, intestines, or tails, else the ceremony will be nullified. Those over whom the Flint Way chant has been performed must not eat from a metate or with a knife.

Blessing Way songs are sung before retiring and on arising in the morning. If young people are allowed to sleep late it is believed that they will become ill. The ashes from the fireplace are removed as soon as the family arises. If they are taken out before dawn they are thought to act as pollen offerings to the gods. Ashes may not be removed during the day because this is conceived as a gesture of disrespect toward the sun. In removing the ashes, they must not be spilled as this is thought to make a path by which "poverty" may enter the house. The house is swept clean each morning in the belief that a clean home is an invitation to the gods to come and visit.

This type of ritual is employed at the time wild plants and piñon nuts are gathered. On the way to gather seeds the women sing songs which are thought to insure a good harvest. Before leaving to collect the harvest of piñon nuts, a piñon nut is crushed and rubbed on the face while saying, "May

I have good luck in getting seeds." No one is allowed to shake the nuts from the trees because the bears employ that method in getting nuts and would be angered if a human used it.

Simple ritual of this type has also been incorporated into the technological processes. When dressing skins, a turquoise or a white shell bead is placed in the pole on which the hide is scraped. This is believed to protect the joints of the worker from becoming stiff. If the tanner leaves his work he must lay the pole on the ground or he will be visited with this affliction. When rubbing the hide the tanner allows no one in the hogan else, it is believed, the hide will dry out.

If visitors arrive when pottery is being made, the potter rubs clay on their faces and arms to prevent the pots from cracking during the process of firing. Designs on pots must never form a completed circle. The potter would become ill if this happened. This also applies to designs occurring on basketry. When weaving, a woman sings songs which are thought to facilitate the work. Songs of the same type are sung to lighten loads that are being carried,

When a hogan is built, the doorway must face to the east and the poles must be placed one after another in a clockwise direction. The same tabus that apply to the wood used for fires apply to the timbers used in building. No one may enter or leave a hogan other than by the doorway and no one may pass anything out of the hogan except through the door "because only the dead are taken out through the walls." If a crow or an owl alights on a hogan it must be killed or bad luck will result. Before a hogan can be occupied it must have the foundation poles blessed and a Blessing Way ceremony held in it.

When arrows are made they must have on the shafts one straight line and two zigzag lines. These represent the lightning which the Monster Slayer used in hunting. The Navaho make no flint points "because they belong to the Holy People." They believe that the Holy People leave them scattered around in exchange for the prayer sticks which are offered.

Ritual observances are even connected with the more personal activities. As previously mentioned, it is tabu to step over a fire. Nor is one person allowed to step over another. This is believed to bewitch the person, especially if the person who steps over you wears the talisman of some chant that has been performed over him. Women are required to sit with their legs under them and to one side, men with their legs crossed in front of them, because it is said that in the beginning Changing Woman and the Monster Slayer sat in those positions. An individual should not whistle after dark because only "devils" whistled at that time.

It is not permissible to cut the hair, because this is believed to cut off the rainfall. A person over whom a chant has been performed must wear the talisman of that chant in his hair; for example, men who have had the Chiricahua Wind Way chant performed over them wear a turquoise, women a white shell bead. Those who have been treated by the Shooting Way chant wear a turquoise or an olivella shell.

When smoking in a group, the man who lights the pipe takes one puff and passes the pipe clockwise to his neighbor, who follows the same procedure. When the pipe returns to the first man he takes two puffs and passes it around again; the third time three puffs; the fourth time four puffs. The smoking is then at an end.

Particular songs are reserved for use during sweat baths. Before a bath the bather throws fresh dirt on the sweat house. This is believed to prevent poverty. Before entering the sweat house a man must tie the foreskin over the end of the penis to prevent blindness, and must shout an invitation to the Holy People and men to come join him in the bath. No one is allowed to sleep in a sweat house without first poking a hole in the roof.

Rites and observances of this type have also found foothold in the social structure. Many are connected with childbirth. The newborn child is placed with its head toward the fire to make the head round. Songs are often sung over newborn children to make them healthy and strong. A squirrel skin is tied to a cradle to prevent the child from being hurt should the cradle fall.

Death is also surrounded by many simple exoteric rites. An attempt is always made to remove a person from the hogan before death sets in, else the hogan must be abandoned. Mourners must not talk or spit on the way to the grave and must return by a different route than the one they took to it. All participants at a funeral must take sweat baths to cleanse themselves after the proceedings.

When a new local leader is installed, various members of the community secure earth from the tops of four mountains located in the cardinal directions. This earth is dusted into the moccasins of the chosen man to confirm his appointment.

Ritual also plays an important part in sports. Innumerable songs for success in gambling are known and sung at appropriate times. These are believed to bring the gambler good luck, but their use is looked upon as being not quite sportsmanlike. Men and race horses are treated with herbs and pollen to make them fleet footed.

These random examples, taken from varied activities, give an approximation of how often the simple exoteric type of ritual appears in the activities of everyday life. It is impossible to guess as to the activity with which this type of ritual originated. It probably represents a heritage of folk tradition and shamanistic procedure, primarily Great Basin in character, to which have been added embellishments, which I conceive as borrowed from the Pueblos, but given a more generalized form.

The esoteric type of ritual characteristic of hunting has also encompassed other activities. These ceremonies are generally complex and the ritual well stylized. The proceedings are always directed by a shaman leader. This man controls the esoteric knowledge of the ritual, the correct execution of which is believed to insure success to the activity involved. He has entire control of the action of all participants.

Other recurring traits in this ritual pattern include continence, purification, offerings, prayers and songs, restrictions on sleeping and urinating, insistence on a serious demeanor of the participants, and the construction of shelters believed in themselves to possess magical power.

Continence is one of the prerequisites of success in all ritual activities of the Navaho. It is always required during the course of the ceremony and usually goes into effect four days before the ceremony, not to terminate until four days following. This tabu is generally removed by ritual purification.

Ritual purification is accomplished by bathing or burning incense. The bathing consists either of taking sweat baths or washing the hair in yucca suds. The extent to which the cleansing is indulged depends on how intimate a part the individual plays in the ritual. Purification before the ceremony is thought to remove impurities and condition the person for the ritual ordeal; purification after the ceremony lifts all the religious restrictions.

Offerings are made in the form of "jewels," pollen, or prayer sticks. The kind of "jewels" and pollen, and the constituent parts and decoration of the prayer sticks vary with the ceremony. These offerings are given in the spirit of supplication and are not believed to have compulsive effect.

Songs and prayers are sung and said at specified intervals throughout all rituals. The correct rendition of these is believed to be paramount to the success of the ceremony and the slightest mistake will nullify all the results. Each activity has particular sets of songs and prayers which belong to it alone.

A serious demeanor during all activities involving ritual is thought essential. It is believed that any levity on the part of any of the participants not only endangers the success of the activity, but is also apt to bring misfortune on the transgressor.

Another constant factor of ritual activity is the construction of shelters according to ritual procedure. They are usually built with reference to the cardinal points, have the entrance in a specified direction, and with the construction following a clockwise or front to back progression. The purpose of these structures varies with the different activities; for example, the brush shelters used in hunting symbolize for the Navaho a corral and are believed to have power to draw the game to the hunters. In the Rain Ceremony the boughs covering the ceremonial hogan point downward and are thought to have the compulsive effect of imitative magic which will bring down the rain.

The ritual pattern characterized by these traits, besides its use in hunting and in the Rain Ceremony, is fundamental to the healing chants, girls' puberty rites, marriage ceremonies, warfare, trading expeditions, and trips to the lakes south of Zuñi in quest of salt. The pattern may have originated with the elaborated shamanistic healing procedures and been transferred to other activities.

It is dangerous to attempt an analysis of the function of ritual among a primitive people. However, among the Navaho, a few possible explanations are suggested by the phases of culture which are ritualized. First, rituals are found integrated into any given complex of practical procedures at points where uncertainties due to environmental factors are neither explained nor controlled, and at points where technical proficiency or scientific knowledge are unequal to the task at hand. It would therefore seem plausible to infer that they offer a mechanism whereby an individual is able to compensate for his inadequacies.

A second rôle of ritual in Navaho culture, and one of which the Navaho is fully aware, is its social aspect. The larger rituals usually occur in periods of comparative economic inactivity and offer, apart from their religious connotations, an opportunity for the coming together of large bodies of people to seek release from economic hardships through the less serious forms of social expression accompanying all ceremonies.

Another possible function of Navaho ritual rests entirely on the psychological principle that man must have release from the specific exactments of his culture. If this be accepted it might be possible to explain on these grounds the complete reversal of common behavior and social usage during the hunt. However, this would seem only to explain the form the ritual takes, rather than the function of the ritual itself.

Irrespective of its functional significance there is no doubt but that a harmonious adjustment has been achieved between the religious and material sides of Navaho life. What is more notable is that, while contacts with modern white culture have altered to some extent the material side of Navaho life, the religious side has remained intact or, at most, absorbed innovations into the old patterns.

• 41 • *The Great Chants of the Navajo*
CLYDE KLUCKHOHN

The great chants are religious liturgies. The two rituals most often given—the Night Chant and the Mountain Chant—may only be held in the months of late autumn and early winter, when the snakes are hibernating and "when the thunder sleeps." A devout Navajo will not even sing their songs in spring or summer, for if he did he would surely be bitten by a snake or struck down by the lightning.

The Night Chant and the Mountain Chant are complex five or nine day dramas, founded upon elaborate myths, events of which are represented by that most consummate of Navajo arts—the sand-painting (better called the dry-painting), replete with rite of penitence and purification, with song and prayer and masque. The ritual is so rich that seldom is a *hatali* (a singer of the sacred songs) completely familiar with more than

[Adapted from "The Great Chants of the Navajo," *Theatre Arts Monthly*, Vol. 17, No. 8, New York, 1933. Pp. 639-645. Used by permission.]

one of the nine day ceremonies. In the Night Chant alone there are more than four hundred songs, to say nothing of dry-paintings, dances, and all the minutiae of ritualistic preparation of masks, prayer sticks and other ceremonial paraphernalia. No iota of this is committed to permanent record. Every rubric is carried in the *hatali's* head and transmitted by him to his students and assistants.

Of these liturgies there were probably more than fifty, but today the song-priests lack their accustomed acolytes, and one wonders if even the Mountain Chant and the Night Chant will survive another generation.

These ceremonies are ostensibly given to cure one individual from some disease, or simply from persistent bad dreams and a troubled spirit. Just as certain chants are appropriate to certain seasons, so also some chants are believed to be especially efficacious for certain illnesses. The patient and his relatives pay the fees of the chanter (who will be a specialist in the rite selected) and his assistants. They share also in the not inconsiderable expenses of providing ceremonial equipment and hospitality to visitors.

Nevertheless, the chants are of importance for group and tribal life. They are a tremendous social occasion, a time for the coming together of a tribe which lives apart. (50,000 Navajos are scattered over 30,000,000 acres.) But no spirit of levity, like that of the *anaji,* pervades the precincts of the ceremonial *hogan.* An atmosphere of serene friendliness reigns. Indeed, as at the Athenian Lennea and the Great Dionysia, it is expressly enjoined that wrongs both public and private must be temporarily forgotten. Matters of the common weal are discussed at open meetings held in intervals between the ceremonies. Young Navajos are initiated into the tribe and into tribal secrets. They are shown the masks of Talking God, of House God, of Changing Woman, of the Bearer of the Sun, of the Black Elder of the Gods, of White Shell Woman, of Fringed Mouth and Humpback, of that "divine knight errant of the Navajo Pantheon," the Slayer of the Alien Gods or Descended with the Lightning, and his brother, the Child of the

Water. All the Navajos present try to right their relation to the supernatural world and to obtain relief for ailments physical or mental. Prayers are said for the whole people (and even for Mexicans and Anglos), for rain and crops and health and general prosperity.

The nine-day ceremonies usually fall naturally into three divisions. The first four days are given over principally to the purification of the patient by emetic, medicine, and sweat-bath; to sacrifice to the gods; to the preparation and consecration of the extensive ceremonial equipment: prayer sticks, cigarettes, herbal medicines, shell and turquoise, rock crystal, wild tobacco, specular iron ore, corn meal, baskets, drum and drum sticks, pollen from corn and also from grasshoppers, yellow warbler, and bluebird. The succeeding four days are focused upon the making of the dry-paintings and attendant visits of the personators of the gods and treatment of the patient. The ninth night is devoted to a splendid public ritual which is the culmination of all the prayerful activity of the preceding period.

The most attractive episode in the first division of the Night Chant is "No Sleep on the Trail of the Gods," which Washington Matthews has called "The Vigil of the Gods." The masks of eighteen to twenty-four of the gods are lined in rows in the ceremonial lodge, appropriate sacrifices are made, prayers are said all through the night. Finally the song-priest chants before the mask of each god in turn the Song of Waking:

He stirs, he stirs, he stirs,
Among the lands of dawning, he stirs, he stirs;
Now in old age wandering, he stirs, he stirs;
Now on the trail of beauty, he stirs, he stirs.

The sandpaintings are begun not long after sunrise and they must be destroyed and carried out of the ceremonial *hogan* before sunset. When the picture is completed, an elaborate exemplification of the laws of sympathetic and holophrastic magic begins. The divine figures are sprinkled with meal.

Plumed wands are erected. If there be a rainbow in the painting, a seashell filled with water is placed at one end; pollen is applied to the divine figures. The patient enters to the accompaniment of a song and the rattling of a gourd and sprinkles the picture with pollen and meal. Personators of the gods enter, perform various rites, and depart. The patient sits on the dry-painting and is anointed with pollen and finally with the sand and mineral of the painting itself. He leaves. Others touch ailing parts with material from the picture. The material is carried out in deerskins to be deposited at the foot of trees at the four cardinal points.

The final night there is continuous singing and dancing from sunset, when, as the Navajos say, "the basket is turned down" (a basket is inverted to serve as a drum), until the rising sun is greeted with the melodious Bluebird Song. The first event is the painting of the First Dancers who daub themselves simultaneously with white clay. They face the east, and the right hand is painted first, they whiten the body from above downward, singing:

Now the holy one paints his form,
The Wind Boy, the Holy One, paints
his form.
With the dark cloud he paints his form,
With the misty rain he paints his form,
With the rainy bubbles he paints his
form,
To the ends of his toes he paints his
form,
To the plume on his head he paints his
form.

The masque itself is what H. B. Alexander calls "the most poetic description of the genius of the thundercloud and rain in Indian literature." A brilliant setting is formed by myriad fires which glow, sputter, blaze to reveal clinging clusters of Navajos, ghostly trees, and murky mesas. Teams of dancers from different districts who have been practising for weeks, composing new songs and rehearsing old ones succeed each other endlessly. There is the same spirit of competition which prevailed in the Greek theatre. Nor is the counterpart of the satyr play lacking . . . The clownish Water-Sprinkler God dances in and out of time and gets in the way of the line of dancers.

Some songs are made up of meaningless syllables. Others have a vivid literary quality. For example:

I am the Slayer of the Alien Gods,
Where'er I roam,
Before me
Forests white are strewn around,
The lightning scatters;
But 'tis I who cause it.

This passage from the myth of one rite of the Mountain Chant is a final answer to those who assert that the Amerind has no feeling for the landscape about him and for the land itself:

But instead of looking south in the direction in which he was going he looked to the north, the country in which dwelt his people. Before him were the beautiful peaks with their forested slopes. The clouds hung over the mountain, the showers of rain fell down its sides, and all the country looked beautiful and he said to the land "Ahalani!" (Greeting!) and a feeling of loneliness and homesickness came over him and he wept and sang this song:

That flowing water! That flowing
water!
My mind wanders across it.
That broad water! That flowing water!
My mind wanders across it.
That old age water! That flowing
water!
My mind wanders across it.

The Mountain Chant is more seldom given than the Night Chant and is, if anything, more spectacular. By the ninth day a huge crowd has gathered and horses and covered wagons and (today) automobiles encircle the communal cooking shelter, and the ceremonial *hogan,* the area in front of which has been leveled for the public exhibition. All afternoon at isolated spots in the timber little groups gather to rehearse the *ah leel,* the vaudeville acts of the evening.

The performers are watched and encouraged by neighbors and relatives. Meanwhile men and boys are cutting, hauling, and piling cedar and juniper for the great fires and to form the enormous corral within which the evening's rituals will take place.

Just as the last lights flicker on the mesas, the song-priest marches around the corral, sprinkling meal and pollen and chanting prayers of consecration. The waiting crowd throngs into the enclosure, carrying blankets and babies, coffee pots and food. Complete darkness falls, and the tension grows momentarily more expectant. At last the great piles are lighted. Flames soar. The heat scorches and the retreating spectators pack themselves close against the tree limbs which form the enclosure. While the heat is still intense, the twelve Turn-to-White dancers rush in, shouting, twirling their staves tipped with white eagle down. They are stripped to the g-string, but their bodies are plastered with white clay. Nearer and nearer they circle to the blaze. At last one dancer gets the tip of his stave in the fire. "Turn to white!" shouts the crowd and he, quickly sliding the ring concealed in his hands down his stave, triumphantly exhibits the feathers that have just sprouted to replace those which were burned off.

There follows a series of *ah leel*. A man rubs his hands, producing a sparkling, crackling flame; a turtle climbs a tree; there is the arrow-swallow dance; feathers rise out of a basket and dance in the air before a young girl; green corn grows and yucca blossom, though it is December. The plumed arrow dance is given by different teams to the whizzing of the bullroarer (which the Navajos call the "groaning stick"). Here too, as in the Night Chant, there are elements of comic relief. A dirty old man enters, stumbles about in the manner of the "low comedy", disappears, reappears with a strapping man dressed as an hideous old crone.

Throughout the whole performance, one notes how much more scope the Navajos give individual expression in religious drama than do their Pueblo neighbors. Pueblo dances are team dances, there are no "stars." Pueblo ceremonies are of and for and by the whole community. Navajo ceremonies are primarily to cure a single tribesman. The Pueblo Indian is the representative of the almost perfectly developed community life. The Navajo is the free individualistic child of the desert.

The dancers and the acts come and go. It gets very cold and many spectators crawl beneath their blankets to sleep a little. But just as the horizon begins to change from blue-black to grey, the Fire Dance begins. The twelve dancers storm in, chasing each other with brightly flaming juniper torches and shouting the Fire Song. Now they are bathing each other's bodies in flame, now they are trampling in the coals that surround the still flaring central fire. Suddenly with whoops of laughter they vanish into the grey morning, still beating their torches on each other's backs.

The song-priest faces the east and chants:

The curtain of daybreak is hanging,
The Daylight Boy,
From the land of day it is hanging,
Before him, as it dawns, it is hanging,
Behind him, as it dawns, it is hanging,
Before him in beauty it is hanging,
From his voice in beauty it is hanging.

• 42 • *Navajo Folktales*

RAYMOND WILKIE

Folktales are an important part of Navajo culture, reflecting almost every aspect of and giving a rationale to many traditional but non-rational patterns of behavior. Included in the concept of folktales are all traditional prose tales handed down by word of mouth from one generation to another.

The sacred stories or myths are considered to be absolutely true, not to be questioned, and must be re-told in letter-perfect fashion. Navajo myths are organized into a continuous, integrated pattern, and many motifs which are found as isolated fragments among North American Indians are here related to the total pattern.

The non-sacred stories or folktales may often contain supernatural elements, but they are not believed to be absolutely true and have less emotion attached to them than have the myths. The most popular and numerous of the Navajo non-sacred folktales are those about gambling and about Coyote the Trickster.

The principal distinguishing characteristics of Navajo mythology are to be found in the style and in the manner of organization of the motifs. None of the particular incidents in the mythology are unique to the Navajo; most of them are widespread in the Southwest and many are found over most of North America. The organization of many motifs into a single integrated pattern is an outstanding characteristic, but not a unique one, being also found among the Pueblo Indians from whom the Navajo undoubtedly derived much of their mythology. Throughout the mythology there are recurrent stylistic patterns which emphasize color, direction, and number symbolism. The acquisition of ceremonies from the gods appears at the end of almost every myth and there is a strong tendency toward the pairing of characters in a male-female or dominant-submissive pattern.

Like the sacred stories of every people, Navajo myths sanction existing customs, especially those concerned with the family and related social structures. There are myths for every important social event and condition—birth, marriage, death, housebuilding, travel, fertility, harvest, healing—which explain what people do at these times and why they do it. The reason most often given for these acts is that the gods acted this way in the myths.

CREATION MYTH

From the beginning, according to the Navajo, there existed a series of six worlds, one above another. Beneath the present world were four lower worlds and above it was the sky world. Each of the lower worlds was inhabited by a different kind of animal or divine people, the first world containing ants, the second swallows, the third grasshoppers, and the fourth the Yei or gods, and other minor supernaturals.

Water Monsters, who controlled the waters in each of the worlds, were angered by the witchcraft, adultery, and quarreling of the inhabitants, and floods were produced which forced successive flights to the next higher world. In the fourth world the Yei created First Man and First Woman from ears of corn and they, being partly divine, gave birth to First Boy and First Girl, the parents of the first Navajo. Also among the children of First Man and First Woman were two hermaphrodites who invented pottery, weaving, hoes, and axes.

After a large number of Navajo had been created and had intermarried with the Pueblo and Mirage Peoples, a quarrel arose between First Man and First Woman. They separated and First Man took all the other men with him across the River of Separation where they lived without the women for four years.

After the separation was ended, two girls who had been left behind attempted to swim the River and were dragged under by Tieholtsodi the Water Monster. Some of the Yei went to the home of Tieholtsodi to rescue the girls and while there, Coyote the Trickster stole two of Water Monster's children. When the angry parent sent a flood in retaliation, the people escaped to the present world through hollow reeds which magically grew to the sky. The hole through which entrance into the present world was effected is called the Emergence Hole and is the place where the spirits of the dead, called Tchindi, go down to their dwelling place in the lower world.

Soon after the Emergence, First Man and First Woman created various objects and natural phenomena including the mountains, the stars, the sun, and the moon. The sun and the moon were fashioned of turquoise and white shell, respectively, and were given to two supernaturals to carry across the sky. The Bearer of the Sun, known also as Sun Father, is the parent of the twin culture heroes of the Navajo.

Coyote the Trickster created evil or senseless things and hindered First Man in his attempts to create the world. When First Man created the stars, Coyote threw them into the sky without patterning them as had been intended. When First Man threw a light object into the water and said, "If this floats, men will live forever," Coyote threw a stone in and said, "If this sinks, men will die."

TWIN HEROES

The second part of the Navajo mythology deals with the twin culture heroes and their adventures. The mother of the twins was Turquoise Woman who was created by the union of Earth Mother and Sky Father. The fathers of the culture heroes were the Sun and the Water who magically impregnated Turquoise Woman. After their birth the boys magically grew to maturity in four days and started on a journey to their father, the Sun. Their purpose was to obtain magical weapons with which to slay the monsters who had destroyed most of the Navajo. These monsters had been born during the Separation of the Sexes as a result of the sexual misconduct of some of the women. This is an implicit warning to Navajo women that aberrations from the path of virtue will not go unpunished.

The youths succeeded in reaching their father's home in the East on a rainbow bridge after evading various obstacles—cutting reeds, boiling sands, cane cactus, bears, snakes, lightning, and the Symplegades, rocks that rush together to crush people who go between them—with the aid of magical incantations given them by Spider Woman, a beneficent supernatural. At the house of Sun Father, they were subjected to various paternity tests including being thrown against flint spikes, being put in a super-heated sweat-house, smoking poisoned tobacco, and being pushed off a cliff. With the aid of various deities, including Niltsi the Wind, who whispered advice, the hero youths survived the tests, and the Sun, forced to acknowledge his paternity, gave them lightning bolts, flint armor, and rainbow rafts with which to combat the monsters.

The twins returned home and killed many of the monsters, including the Giant Elk, the Giant Eagle, the People-Who-Killed-By-Staring, the Bear-Who-Tracks, the Traveling Stone. The monsters Hunger, Poverty, Death, Syphilis, and Cold were spared because each promised to do something useful for the Navajo. Hunger encourages the pleasures and virtues of hunting; Poverty gives incentive for work and the creation of new things; Death prevents over-population of the earth; Syphilis punishes promiscuity; and Cold prevents drought.

The various tests, obstacles, and monsters encountered by the twin heroes are motifs which are widespread over North America, and some, such as the Symplegades, have a world-wide distribution. Usually however, they appear as individual, isolated episodes. The paternity tests in Navajo mythology are usually presented as son-in-law tests among other North American Indian tribes. In borrowing motifs, the Navajo have reworked them to fit their own stylistic pattern and have organized them into one integrated system.

ORIGIN OF THE CLANS

[The third section of the Navajo mythology relates how the Navajo clans originated. For an account of this see Selection 34.]

MISCELLANEOUS MYTHS

In addition to the three main parts of Navajo mythology there are numerous myths only incidentally related to the central theme. Stories about Coyote the Trickster fall into this category. Trickster stories are favorites among American Indians, although the Trickster is often represented by some other animal, i.e., Raven, Mink, or Blue Jay on the North Pacific Coast. Coyote stories are characterized by sadism, sexual aggression, perversion, trickery, and stupidity. Some episodes display only one of these themes; others use two or more. Usually, Coyote is the trickster, but sometimes the dupe. He appears in both sacred and non-sacred stories, but is only a minor character in the former. In many of the tales Coyote is killed, but he always returns to life. In addition to the creation of death and the scattering of the stars, previously mentioned, the following tales are characteristic of his secular adventures.

When Coyote stories appear in the mythology, they are sometimes strung together in a series of tests or adventures. More often, they are short episodes which relate how he created some phenomenon inconvenient to the Navajo. The majority of Coyote tales are non-sacred and told simply for vicarious enjoyment of forbidden adventures or for the humor inherent in viewing misfortune produced by someone else's stupidity.

Gambling stories are popular among the Navajo, as among the other Indians of western North America for whom gambling is not merely a game but a serious preoccupation. Coyote is often the gambler, but all animals and people are assumed to be born gamblers. One such myth tells of a gambler who won all the possessions of the Pueblo people and even the people themselves as his slaves.

Probably the most recurrent theme in Navajo mythology is that of the hero (and sometimes, but rarely, the heroine), who has various adventures, finally receiving ceremonies from the gods for the benefit of the Navajo. Such a hero was Scavenger Boy, a typical "poor boy who made good." As a youth Scavenger Boy was captured by the Pueblo people and made a slave. As one of his tasks, he was lowered over the edge of a cliff to capture some baby eagles, but on the advice of Niltsi the Wind, the youth refused, and instead threw itching dust down on his masters. When the parent eagles returned, they were thankful to the youth for saving their children and carried him to their home in the sky world. There, Scavenger Boy de-

feated the enemies of the eagles, the hornets and bees, with magic given him by Spider Woman. As a reward, he was given the daughter of the Eagle Chief and many healing ceremonies which he took back to his people. He also returned to his former masters, the Pueblo people, and unrecognized by them, agreed to perform a healing ceremony for their itching. He required for the ceremony that their most valuable white shells and turquoise be draped around his body, but when this had been done he rose to the sky clothed in their most precious possessions, thus taking revenge for his years of slavery.

All the miscellaneous myths are related, though often by a tenuous connection, to the central body of the mythology. They derive much of their strength from the fact that each is connected with some ceremony which is important socially and psychologically to the Navajo people.

FUNCTION

One of the primary functions of mythology in Navajo culture is to sanction existing patterns of behavior and to furnish models of virtue. Explanations of marriage customs, puberty rites, birth and death ceremonies, and of every type of social activity are given by the divine precedent. Any question of "why" in regard to non-rational cultural behavior is always answered by the myths. The gods acted in this way and instructed the Navajo to do the same.

In the education of the children, the myths provide ideal types for both boys and girls. Boys are encouraged to simulate the Warrior Twins and other culture heroes; girls model themselves after Turquoise Woman. Also, as an aid in maintaining discipline, Navajo parents threaten disobedient children with being cooked and eaten by evil Yei.

As part of the ceremonials, mythology aids in maintaining social solidarity and serves as a focus for the great seasonal gatherings described previously in "The Great Chants of the Navajo." Revival of mythology and ceremonialism serves as an indirect means of expressing resentment against the engulfing civilization of the United States and against the Christian religion.

Mythology functions psychologically to provide a sense of security in a universe which viewed without it appears neutral if not hostile to man. If all natural phenomena are manifestations of supernatural forces which can be controlled by proper actions and magic rites, then there is nothing in the universe to fear. This sense of security in the present world is augmented by the mythological continuity with the past which makes the Navajo feel secure in the knowledge that he is the center of the universe and the principal purpose of its creation.

The mythology also helps maintain psychological integrity by providing approved targets for aggressive tendencies which cannot be expressed against the real objects of frustration. It is the witches and Tchindi, primarily, who serve as scape-goats and prevent the expression of intra-family hostility which might have disastrous consequences.

In the telling of thinly-veiled stories about witches who are uncles, fathers, brothers, sisters, etc., individuals have an opportunity to direct hostilities against approved targets. Also, rites to counteract the influence of the evil spirits give the individual the feeling of doing something, and the participation of his family in the ceremony gives him a sense of being wanted.

Most of the secular folktales are about Coyote and about gamblers. These stories told purely for entertainment furnish vicarious enjoyment of tabooed sadistic and sexual acts. They also provide vicarious destruction of authority and the glory of identification with courageous and all-conquering heroes.

The mythology of the Navajo has been studied as intensively as that of any primitive group in the world. The characteristics which have most impressed ethnographers, including Washington Mathews, Clyde Kluckhohn, Gladys Reichard, and Father Berard Haile, are the extreme use of symbolism and the theme of obtaining ceremonies from the gods. Every character and incident in the myths has related color, direction, and number symbols; almost every myth ends with the description of ceremonies which the hero has been given by the deities.

The mythology reflects a large part of Navajo culture, but being essentially traditionalistic it often reflects the culture as it was in past centuries. Integration of the mythology with other aspects of the culture, especially through the religious ceremonies, is so complete that abstraction of the myths from the daily economic and social activities often does violence to the situation as viewed by the Navajo. In order to properly appreciate the meaning of Navajo mythology, the reader should constantly bear in mind the socio-economic context in which the folktales, both sacred and non-sacred, are told.

A Note on Social Values and Social Status

One of the best ways of finding out about a status system is to sort out the social values, or chief points of emphasis around which the major social relationships are centered. As we think back over the selections just read, what are the things or ideas that the Navajo people consider most important? For what are they willing to make great sacrifices? What gives an individual among them much prestige? As we saw in the case of the Eskimo, those who conformed to the social values to the greatest degree had the highest social status. The same holds true for the Navajo, but the value-system differs and one becomes prominent for reasons different from those stressed by the Eskimo. The following listing is merely suggestive as a summary of some of the main points covered thus far. As a summary, it does not include distinctions between prestige, esteem, rank, etc.

I. TRADITIONAL NAVAJO SOCIAL VALUES, A KIND OF MENTIFACT

Men	*Women*
Wealth (personal property and livestock)	Weaving skill
Personal qualities, especially generosity and hospitality	Wealth (personal property and livestock)
Clan connection	Personal qualities, especially industry and responsibility
Possession of ceremonial knowledge	Clan connection
Skill in handling livestock	Possession of ceremonial knowledge

II. STATUS SYSTEM

A. Within the biological family, Navajo woman's status is high, owing in large measure to the clan's being matrilineal and to her economic independence.

B. Within extended families, those who possess the traditional values in greatest degree are looked up to for advice and leadership.

C. At times, two or more extended families living in proximity are informally joined in an "outfit." The individuals with most possessions or prestige often held themselves responsible to the trading post for the debts incurred by others in the outfit.

D. The Navajo people, even before the coming of the Americans, were led by a series of local leaders, each acquiring status in a fairly well-defined area but having authority only over those in that area. When such a leader visited elsewhere, people considered him an individual of some importance but one who was out of his "bailiwick." The power of these leaders was never fixed; each might have 2000 to 5000 followers. Approximately 70 percent of these leaders were succeeded by their sisters' sons or someone else in their lineage. Only about 20 percent were succeeded by their own sons.

E. Navajo follow the "strain toward consistency" in that they are distrustful of extremes. If a man becomes too wealthy or too powerful, he is accused of witchcraft and viewed with suspicion and even fear by others.

F. Navajo look down upon (assign low status to) those who are congenitally lazy or who show anger.

G. There is much effective mobility by families up and down the social scale. A family's fortunes rise if the family includes a successful singer. Promising boys are urged into this training.

Sociocultural Change
and Social Policy

‹‹

W hat should be the governmental policies with regard to the Navajo, both in terms of helping them meet the difficulties of their environment and adjusting to the white man's way which surrounds them? There is no easy answer to this question, since a change introduced to give greater economic security sets in motion changes in family life and makes it hard to see in advance just what the consequences of any particular policy may ultimately be.

Some of the most ambitious planning for the Navajo was carried on while Julius A. Krug was Secretary of the Interior, and these proposals carry the title of "The Krug Plan." Here are the chief points of that plan as described by the Colliers in their article "Navajo Farmer," mentioned earlier.

With 60,000 Navajos living on a reservation that can only maintain 20,000 on a minimum standard it is evident that either the land must be made to produce more or some of the people must leave their homes. Secretary of the Interior Julius A. Krug proposed a plan designed to do both of these things. Soil conservation, irrigation projects and range improvement would be used to increase the productivity of the land and a large group of Navajos aided in finding a place in the white world. The Secretary has asked Congress to appropriate $90,000,000 to be spent over a ten year period for the rehabilitation of the Navajo and Hopi, whose reservation lies within that of the Navajo.

Under the Krug plan additional schools would be built and educational facilities expanded. Along with this would go a health program and additional hospitals.

The isolation in which these people live would be broken by construction of new roads and improvement of old roads and trails. To improve communications in the territory telephone and radio facilities would be increased and air transport within the reservation would be promoted.

Soil and water conservation programs would aid the dry farmers and the herdsmen would benefit by the range improvement program, which is part of the plan. Irrigation projects now underway would be completed and extended to add 58,500 acres of irrigated land to the 23,000 acres already under water.

A small amount of the total fund would go toward the development of community enterprises and industries and a revolving loan fund would be made available to individual Navajos to establish themselves in business or to acquire capital equipment. It is estimated that with all of these improvements the number of Navajos that the reservation can support could be raised from 20,000 to 35,000.

This leaves 25,000 Navajos who cannot expect to make a living on the reservation. What of them? Under the plan 1,000 Navajo families, or about 5,000 people, would be resettled on a new irrigation project below Parker Dam on the lower Colorado River. This is Indian land and is open to any Indian groups in the Colorado watershed. The remaining Navajos would be helped in finding employment and adjusted to industry and agriculture off the reservation.

The United States Congress has dealt none too kindly with the Krug Plan and, as a consequence, we are still in the midst of what might be called a makeshift policy. Facing up to the problems of the Navajo gives us some idea of what colonial powers such as Britain, France, and the Netherlands face when they try to determine policies for many different peoples in large areas of the world. This should be borne in mind while we read the next selection, on the Indian Service. The concluding selection, on the Navajo in the machine age, reminds us of the genius these people show in adapting foreign ways to their purposes and their ability to give innovations a peculiarly Navajo touch.

• 43 • The Indian Service

ALEXANDER H. LEIGHTON AND DOROTHEA C. LEIGHTON

The problem of the Navaho is essentially the problem of all of us—adjustment to life. With our biological needs, our dependence on other people, our temperaments, our beliefs, and our prejudices, we must constantly adjust ourselves as best we can to a changing world. The matter is not a simple one for us nor is it for the Navahos, and no single or magic recipe has yet been found.

Medicine alone is not the answer, nor is

education, religion, economics, agriculture, industry, nor radical change in patterns of behavior and belief. All these and other phases of life must be taken into consideration together.

The Navahos have serious difficulty gaining a bare subsistence; poor health drags them down; ignorance interferes with efficient use of what resources they possess; their historical experiences give them little reason to trust anybody; and the beliefs and traditions which bear them up make them distant and ultraconservative. And yet, they must adjust themselves, in a few short years, to a white civilization that was thousands of years in the making, which is infinitely complex and full of contradictions, and which, while promising wealth, surplus possessions, and numerous mechanical conveniences also brings economic depressions and wars to the home of the bewildered Indians.

The purpose of the Office of Indian Affairs is to help the Indians make this adjustment and the present day policies have a history that goes back beyond the eighteenth century. A few years ago in his Annual Report, the Commissioner of Indian Affairs said:

European colonizers and their descendants brought to America ideas of land ownership, morality, government, and religion which were meaningless to the native American. In time these ideas became dominant to the exclusion of Indian habits of thought. Since we were a humane Nation and were not bent on de-destroying the Indians we assumed the responsibility of showing them how our ideas operated. We wanted them to learn our ways so that they could exist side by side with us. In other words, we instituted a system of Indian education which is with us today.

We took away from the Indian all but a tiny fraction of his wealth in land, water, and other resources, and even his food supply, insofar as that consisted of game and wild products; and by doing so we charged ourselves with the responsibility of keeping the Indian from starvation. Furthermore, since the Indian's understanding of property differed from ours, it was obvious that he would not long retain the little property left him if he was not protected. That made it necessary to erect trust-barriers around him which would prevent predatory men from making off with the means by which the Indian was to be taught a new way of existing.

By placing trust-barriers around Indian property, we exempted his land from State and local taxation. In taking this action we were subjecting the Indian to possible discrimination on the part of the States which would have resulted in leaving him without health care, education, roads, or any of the services which a State renders its people. States and local communities cannot furnish services without revenue. Once again, then, it became necessary for the Federal Government to assume an obligation toward the Indian tribes whose property it was seeking to protect.

The Indians became, and in many cases remain, wards of the Government. During World War I so many of them volunteered to fight in the Army that in 1924 citizenship was conferred on all Indians.

The headquarters for Government regulation of Navahos is located at Window Rock, Arizona. Formerly, the reservation was divided into six different districts, each with a complete and independent administrative organization. This led to much confusion of policy and duplication of effort, and was abandoned in 1933 in favor of a coordinated over-all management. One of the compelling needs for the change was the serious soil erosion all over the reservation which could be better handled if the whole area was treated as a unit than if each of the six subdivisions had its independent and often incompatible ideas. Soil conservation and the control of the causes of erosion has been a major preoccupation ever since.

As the range became overgrazed the water which fell on the surface and which should have been caught and held by surface growth, swept down the steep slopes and cut deep arroyos. Some of these stretched for more than a hundred miles, cutting the bottoms out of fertile valleys.

In order to preserve some animals alive, it has been necessary to bring about drastic reductions in the number of sheep and other stock. While this has caused widespread hardship and suffering, it is evident that in the long run it will benefit the Indians. A careful study of the facts indicates that over-population was one important reason why in recent years the sheep's wool has been poor and the lambs light. By reducing the number of animals on the range, the same amount of fodder can produce better sheep and thus raise the income.

Therefore, concomitant with the reduction in numbers, there has been an effort to improve breed and breeding practices. The tribe has spent considerable money buying good rams which are rented out to individual owners, and the Government has established a laboratory at Fort Wingate to experiment with developing the best type of sheep for the range, for the uses of the Navahos, and for the commercial market.

Moreover, a livestock disposition project was established to make it possible for the Navahos to sell their poor quality sheep, which commercial buyers would not take and which pulled down the quality of the flock if kept and used for breeding. These sheep are bought for a reasonable price and sold as fresh meat locally or canned for use in reservation schools and hospitals. While not profitable commercially, the meat is nevertheless perfectly good nutritionally, and has been of great help in improving the diet in government institutions where meat was otherwise too costly to be frequently served.

Actual results of the various efforts can be seen in these figures assembled in 1943:

Since 1931, Navaho sheep reduced from 575,000 to 346,000.

Since 1931, Navaho lambs *increased* from 317,000 to 346,000.

Since 1931, weight of lambs increased from 53 to over 60 lbs.

Since 1931, weight of fleece increased from less than 4 to 6 lbs.

Since 1931, if wool is worth 30¢ and lambs worth 10¢ a pound, the value of these products increased from $2,126,747 to $2,861,236.

In spite of these figures, the Navahos do not yet recognize very thoroughly the need and benefits in stock reduction and the program has encountered severe opposition. Some Navahos[, however,] are cooperative and in the course of time it is probable that all will see the benefits. Unfortunately, the ill feeling attached to stock reduction has spread to other Government activities, so that school, medical care, and all other contacts have suffered at times.

In order to carry out the reduction program, the reservation, which had just been consolidated from the six independent divisions, was re-divided into 18 districts. All are now under the head office at Window Rock but a District Supervisor is in charge of each district and represents the General Superintendent locally. The District Supervisor is responsible for the carrying out of Government programs in his district with the exception of education, health, and construction, but even here there is, or should be, close collaboration. His duties, therefore, include administrative relations with Indians, law and order, work programs on farm, range, and livestock, distribution of relief, selective service, and rationing. His principal aids are the Range Riders who have most of the direct contact with Indians. [Two] of the eighteen Supervisors, and eleven of the twenty Range Riders are themselves Navahos.

The Farm Program is mostly restricted to the irrigated areas, where Indians are supervised in their use of water, and encouraged to improve their farming practices. No control is exercised over other farms, beyond requiring a permit for breaking uncultivated ground.

The over-all soil conservation program is linked with the school system. Much emphasis is placed, especially in the high schools, on the need for and methods of saving the soil from further destruction.

Education for Navaho children started in a day school which soon became a boarding school at Fort Defiance after the return from Fort Sumner. Eventually other boarding schools were built in different parts of the reservation, but many of the children were taken as far away as Pennsylvania and California. In these schools there were children from many tribes, from parts of the country with different climatic conditions and ways of making a living. Consequently, not much could be done in teaching the children of each tribe how to get along best with its particular conditions. Instead they were taught as if they were white children and would always live in white communities. Ninety-five per cent of the children went home and entered a life for which their education had given them little preparation and many handicaps. Moreover, the schools in which they had spent their early years had been much like orphan asylums, and had deprived them of the many advantages of character formation afforded by family life in even the poorest Indian home.

In recent times, there has been an attempt to adapt the boarding schools on the reservation to present-day needs by making two of them Vocational High Schools, and a third an Agricultural High School where students can get practical instruction that will help them in life under reservation conditions if they are unable to leave. Instruction is also afforded in the usual academic courses, and in types of work that will enable them to support themselves in white society if they wish to do so and it becomes possible. The other five boarding schools limit instruction to six or eight grades.

In addition there are almost fifty day schools scattered over the reservation. These have become important community centers where the children learn, the parents use the laundry, bathing, and shop facilities, and where various specialists such as doctors, nurses, and home economics teachers give demonstrations, and meet otherwise inaccessible people. A number of children also attend Mission boarding schools, both on and off the reservation, and a much smaller number go to Government schools away from the reservation.

Many children attend school for only two or three years, but an increasing number are continuing to the higher grades or high school, and a few go to college. Although, legally, it is a punishable offense to keep children from school, the law is not enforced. The following table shows the proportion in and out of school:

SCHOOL ATTENDANCE OF NAVAHO CHILDREN
AGED 6 - 18

	Number in Navaho Service schools '42-'43	Estimated number, all schools	Estimated number of children	Percentage in school
6-12 yrs. of age				
Day-school	1789	1995		
Boarding School	1320	2008		
Total	3109	4003	8285	49%
13-18 yrs. of age				
Day-school	262	353		
Boarding School	1102	1406		
Total	1364	1759	6215	28%
Total, all ages	4473	5762	14,500	40%

The education given in the day schools is not so intense as in the boarding schools, but it is probably more extensive since many more persons, both old and young, attend or have contact with the day schools than with the boarding schools.

AVERAGE DAILY ADULT ATTENDANCE FOR
EDUCATIONAL ACTIVITIES 1942 - 43

	At boarding schools	At day schools	Total
Men	48.2	310.9	359.1
Women	59.5	426.1	485.6
Total	107.7	737.0	844.7

It would seem that the best hope of raising the general level of literacy in the tribe is the day school.

A large and important branch of the Navaho Service is that which deals with health, and in it lies one of the best means of establishing better collaboration between the Indians and our white society. Illness is a matter of much concern to the Navaho, and he is perhaps more willing to try new methods of healing than new methods of raising sheep.

Hospital facilities are excellent, and are being used increasingly. The largest hospital is at Fort Defiance, where there are 250 beds, 100 of which are for tuberculous patients.

The limited field work done at present amounts to examination and immunization of day school pupils by the doctor from the nearest hospital; examination and treatment of other patients who meet him at the schools on these trips; and occasional visits by specialists to the boarding schools. The field program is the one most in need of expansion and the day schools offer an excellent starting point for demonstrations and education in health matters.

The Government has also taken a hand in organizing the tribe politically. It will be remembered that in the first chapter we said that originally there was no one leader of the whole Navaho tribe but there were a number of men who stood out from the rest for their force of character and who served as leaders for smaller or larger numbers of their people, usually their clansmen. This sort of leadership depended entirely on group support, and if the individual fell into disfavor for any reason his leadership vanished. The Government was slow to recognize this state of affairs in its early contact with the Navahos, and dealt with men who were only self-appointed leaders but who were amenable to the Government's ideas. There were even attempts to create tribal leaders by executive order when the existing chiefs refused to cooperate.

In 1923 an attempt was made to remedy the situation by creating a Navaho Council. Largely because its members were simply carefully selected "yes-men" who did not represent the tribe, nothing came of the effort. In 1925 small units were decreed within the tribe known as "chapters," each about the size of a township, and they were instructed to elect certain officers and to handle their local business through them. It

was a technique quite unfamiliar to the Indians, and not very satisfactory, but it gave them some experience in handling elections and finding out how various men among them behaved in public office. In 1937 a set of rules of election and procedure for the Council was drawn up, and after its approval in 1938 by the Secretary of the Interior, it became the basis for the present tribal government.

According to these Rules, the Council has 74 members, the number of representatives from each district depending on the population. These men are elected for a four-year term, and meet two or three times a year. As it operates at present, the Council passes on expenditure of tribal funds; defines conditions of tribal membership; regulates the domestic relations of Navahos, including marriage, divorce, and inheritance; and administers justice. The Council also expresses opinions regarding Government acts and advises the Government.

While this type of self-rule has not yet entirely proved itself, it has come nearer the mark than any previous effort, and gives evidence of possessing spontaneity, the will to survive and to speak for the tribe. The idea of reservation-wide tribal government is finding acceptance and it will probably grow in flexibility and responsiveness as time goes on. The indications are that the individual members are more and more reporting to their communities and obtaining validation or refutation of their decisions in Council.

One important phase of government in which the Navahos have a large share is the administration of justice. Except for major crimes, all offenses committed on the reservation and which cannot be settled privately are tried before a court composed of three Navaho judges, or in some cases associate judges. They observe a code of laws which was adopted in 1937, and take tribal custom into account in making decisions. Under some circumstances there are provisions for calling a jury. A group of Navaho policemen who travel about the reservation maintain order and enforce the law; one of their chief duties is to control traffic in liquor; therefore they nearly always appear at the public ceremonials, where drinking frequently takes place. The most frequent causes of arrest are drunkenness and domestic difficulties. Sentences for misconduct consist of fines, or alternately a number of days in jail corresponding to each dollar of the fine. Four jails are maintained on the reservation and the prisoners do much useful work [during the time they are] serving their sentences.

The Navaho tribe and the Government have set up a number of projects known collectively as "tribal enterprises." Two of these have already been mentioned in the discussion of stock improvement, namely the Livestock Disposition project and the Livestock Improvement project. The largest and most important of the undertakings from the commercial point of view is the sawmill located on the plateau above Fort Defiance. Large ponderosa pines that are ripe or overripe are harvested scientifically so that the forest is not depleted.

Another enterprise of potential importance is the Arts and Crafts Guild. This organization is devoted to improving the standards of workmanship for weaving and silverwork, seeing that craftsmen get a better return for their products, and finding and developing a dependable, high-class market for the goods. The war has caused a decline in the amount of handicrafts produced, but probably it will revive later.

Finally there is the flour mill at Round Rock which was established in the center of the wheat-growing area of the reservation to give the Indians an opportunity to have their wheat processed near home and to provide a market.

All of these projects have aided the Navaho economy. It remains now to find trained and capable Navahos to take over their operation for the future. Perhaps the best source of such managers will be the men returning from the armed forces at the close of the war.

In addition to these industries, certain natural resources on the reservation are leased by the tribe to commercial operators who employ many Navahos. Such resources include coal, oil, helium, vanadium, and copper. [Recently uranium has also become important. There are a] few individual Indians [who] own and operate small coal mines.

The plans and the goals of the Navaho Service are excellent, and one cannot help being moved with admiration, but it must be remembered that although much has been accomplished a great deal is still in the form of intention rather than realization. Every step forward is achieved with great difficulty. There is the conservative resistance of the Indians and there is the indifference or active (if covert) hostility to the Government program on the part of some of its employees although numerous others work effectively toward accomplishment of the aims. Frequent misunderstandings occur because of cultural and language differences between Indians and whites. There is political pressure, or the threat of pressure, from individuals who want to get the Indian land, who are opposed to Indian cooperatives, who want to keep the Indian standard of living low so that labor will be cheap and profit greater on articles of trade, and who want to cut down the Federal money spent on Indians. There are also people who mean well for the Indians, but who attack the Government's program because they wish the Indian christianized and forget that freedom of religion is not limited to Christians. They would have Indian education carried out in mission schools with only financial aid from the Government, thereby depriving the Indian of the rights embodied in the non-sectarian public schools which other Americans can attend. These attacks and **interferences are not well balanced by other forces, because the Navahos are unable to vote and because the general public pays little attention to the Indian problem and leaves the field clear for those who are in** it for the special reasons [which have] already [been] mentioned.

• 44 •   The Navajo in the Machine Age

CLYDE KLUCKHOHN

A fifth columnist who, by mistake, dropped by parachute into the interior of the Navaho Reservation would feel himself very far from civilization. The first human beings he met would almost certainly speak no word of any European language. They probably would have seen airplanes in the sky previously, but they might well never have seen a locomotive. If he were so lucky as to find an English-speaking Navaho, our fifth columnist would doubtless discover that he was within thirty miles of a trading store operated by whites and perhaps even that near to a post office. But the post office might be (as is that at Kayenta, Ariz.) 165 miles from the nearest railroad station.

The determinants of Navaho population growth are probably manifold, but of one factor there can be no doubt: the Navaho capacity for adapting to a capitalistic, competitive, individualistic economy. The old saw, "Let's give the country back to the Indians," is no longer a pleasantry among many stockmen of New Mexico, Arizona, Colorado, and Utah. The Navahos are *taking* the country back. Each year, as their numbers grow, they spread over more range beyond legal limits.

The Navahos, then, are distinguished among American Indians by the ease and alacrity with which they have adjusted to the impact of our culture while still retaining many aboriginal traits and very definitely preserving the coherent framework of their own cultural organization. It is almost true to say that in some areas the culture of the Navahos has altered more in the past generation than has the culture of their neighbors, the Pueblo Indians, in the whole four hundred years during which these town-dwelling Indians have been in sustained contact with European civilization.

The intensity of these [contacts] must not be overestimated. The Navaho country is enormous (about sixteen million acres) and, except on its southern border, isolated from railroads and main highways. Within this vast area, schools and other agencies of governmental influence were few and far between until very recently. It is, of course, this insulation from our society (plus their own numbers) which helps to explain the fact that in 1942 the culture of the Navahos still retains its integrity and coherent form in spite of the many borrowings from Western technology.

Seen against the perspective of other early New World cultures, Navaho material culture was basically very simple.

The simplicity of Navaho material culture is not to be traced entirely to the accidents of historical experience. As a people, the Navahos appear to be rather poorly gifted mechanically. Some nonliterate groups, like the Eskimos, have a deserved fame for the ingenuity of the devices they have developed to face a severe environment. The Navahos seem, by contrast, singularly uninventive.

With these generalizations as a background, let us see what proportion of Western traits these adaptive people have taken over, what is the nature of the adaptations they have made, and which sectors of their material culture remain at the aboriginal level.

The basis of the food economy continues to be agriculture. Although floodwater farming remains basic, irrigation is practiced in some places. Simple exoteric magical rites persist—but so do they in European peasant and American folk cultures. The Navahos, encountering no ritualistic resistance, have taken over our agricultural technology in so

[Adapted from "The Navahos in the Machine Age," *The Technology Review*, Vol. 44, No. 4, Massachusetts Institute of Technology, Cambridge, 1942. Pp. 178-180, 194-197. Used by permission.]

far as they have become familiar with it and to the extent that they have been able to purchase factory-made equipment. In sharp contrast, many of the Pueblo Indians today continue to thresh in the fashion described in the Bible in spite of full familiarity with the combine and plenty of money to buy such devices.

The importance of domestic animals in present-day Navaho economy has often been exaggerated. An appreciable number of families have no food animals at all, and many families can eat meat only infrequently. But Navaho herders, especially the women, will lavish time and effort to preserve an individual animal. I have often seen a woman sitting for hours at a time with several newborn lambs under her capacious skirts when an unseasonal snowstorm has occurred at lambing time.

Most Navahos are good botanists. Some of their medicine men can distinguish as many as four hundred species and know one or more uses for each; and almost any adult can find and use a hundred different plants. Today the herbs are employed mainly in folk remedies and in curing-ceremonials.

Similarly, hunting contributes but a small fraction of the daily fare. Deer, antelope, and the larger game animals must be hunted ritually, and since such ritual hunting is seldom carried out today, game counts for virtually nothing in the Navaho budget. In most regions the weapons are now guns, but in certain isolated corners of the Navaho country bows and metal arrows are still in use. Steel traps are employed by the poorer families in obtaining prairie dogs and other animals. Aboriginal traps are now limited to the catching of birds for ceremonial purposes.

Food preparation is much closer to the aboriginal tradition than is food production. Except for coffee, tea, wheat flour, occasional canned goods, and the use of flesh of domestic animals, the cuisine of the Navahos shows comparatively little white influence. In all likelihood mutton, goat, and beef are prepared in the fashion formerly used for venison. The taste for coffee and tea was acquired during the Fort Sumner period, and coffee is today an indispensable part of every meal. The use of mealed wheat flour also dates from that time and has gradually supplanted hand-ground corn flour. Despite the fact that salt can be bought at every trading store, many Navahos still make long journeys to various "sacred" salt deposits. Although this procedure is often more expensive than buying salt at the store, the aboriginal habit persists, partly because of established preference for the taste of the salt from the natural deposits, partly because salt-gathering is a highly ritualized activity.

Pottery and basketry are today made exclusively for ceremonial purposes, and the Navahos are relying more and more on the pottery and basketry produced by other Indian tribes.

Most containers are at present derived from our culture. Every Navaho house contains pots and pans, cloth sacks, and trunks or suitcases in which ornaments and family treasures are stored. Likewise, store axes and a few other metal tools are normally found. Indeed, apart from lariats and hobbles of rawhide, infrequent bows and arrows, rocks for grinding corn and medicines, and a few crude handmade objects such as troughs hollowed out of logs, almost all implements are now of white manufacture. The principal exceptions are ceremonial articles. The houses of ceremonial practitioners (about one adult man in every four or five practices some sort of ritual for pay) contain buckskin pouches for keeping ritual equipment, wooden composite fire drills for kindling ceremonial fires, and other archaic objects.

Log cabins based on white prototypes are now common in the regions closest to railroads. In the main, however, the native type of house and lean-to still prevails, for a variety of reasons: In the first place, greater imitation of European examples would be expensive in materials, and the natives lack carpentry skills. In the second place, the hogan is an excellent simple adaptation to the climate. I have found hogans generally more comfortable than the cabins of white homesteaders. In the third place, religious rites cannot be carried on except in a native type of house. Few Navahos have abandoned their religion, so that practically everyone who lives in a white-style cabin must also have a hogan.

Horseback travel by trail and wagon road is still the staple form of transportation. The Navaho country is perhaps the only part of the United States where one may see great numbers of farm wagons, including covered wagons. Buggies are seen now and then. The oldest type of Navaho saddle was made of two hide cylinders stuffed with hair and attached by wide strips. It was placed on the horse's back and secured by a girth. Now, however, the land of the Navaho is one of the best places to see cowpuncher saddles in their old luxuriance and variety.

Fifteen years ago, Navaho-owned automobiles were rarities. Today, perhaps one family out of every twenty-five or thirty owns a car. Very few are bought new.

Most persons, if they know nothing else about the Navahos, realize that they make rugs. At first, their textiles were made as wearing apparel, but by 1890 they were producing mainly a coarse rug for commerce. Although several revivals of old designs and of vegetable dyes have occurred since then, the product remains commercial.

Experimentation in weaving has been limited almost exclusively to design. Pueblo Indians never departed from their original simple, banded patterns. The Navahos' lack of conservatism, their lively imagination, and their splendid sense of humor are shown in the riotous colors and elaborate patterns which they have produced.

A Navaho family, however, makes all the tools the weaver needs, save for her tow cards. This fact is to be traced in part, I think, to the relative conservatism of the women. At any rate, the same thing is far from true of the other great Navaho craft, silversmithing. The smiths, who are mostly men, obtain both tools and materials entirely from white traders. It is true that silver mining could hardly be expected, but the forging of their own tools would be quite possible. Here again the creativeness of Navahos is as artists—in making new designs for stamp dies or for casting, in evolving new forms and arrangements.

For all practical purposes the applications of electricity, probably the most conspicuous feature of our machine culture, have not impinged on the Navahos at all. But it must be remembered that throughout New Mexico and Arizona only the few towns of any size have power plants, and extensive areas have no telephone or telegraph communication. One application of electricity—the radio—may well have a fairly wide distribution among the Navahos before too long. Within the last few years the Office of Indian Affairs has installed broadcasting units at twenty or more localities to insure communication when roads are impassable and snow and ice make the telephones uncertain. The stations are used primarily to enable the Navaho Central Agency to transmit instructions and receive reports. Already some broadcasts are in the native language, and Indian Service representatives are encouraging the purchase of receiving units by families who can afford them.

What generalizations can we draw from this hasty survey? First, we note that the bulk of Navaho material culture now shows European derivation or influence, and that their nonmaterial culture as yet does not. This finding is in full accord with the general anthropological induction that the nonmaterial culture of a people is much the more resistant to change. A second anthropological theorem which receives further confirmation is that those aspects of material culture which have persisted at about the aboriginal level tend strongly to be associated with ritual activity. A final generalization which also seems to be widely true, at least in nonliterate societies, is that women are more conservative than men: Food preparation, women's costume, women's commercial craft—in all of these we notice more preservation of ancient patterns. The really astonishing thing, as one experiences the totality of Navaho life today, is the degree to which these Indians have taken over aspects of our technology without sensible alteration to the distinctive flavor of their own way of life.

Suggestions for Additional Reading

Many readers, after this introduction to the Navajo, will want to acquire more information about them. This interest may be amply satisfied because of the volume of technical information available, the accessibility of the Navajo to the tourist, and the recurrence of Navajo subjects in the press and popular literature. The record of the Navajo is also available on film through educational, advertising, and commercial motion pictures. The beautiful photography of the magazine *Arizona Highways* (Arizona State Highway Department, Phoenix) often includes the Navajo and their land. Recently, Navajo life has been splendidly documented in *Navaho Means People,* by Leonard McCombe, Evon Z. Vogt, and Clyde Kluckhohn (Harvard University Press, 1951).

Probably the best fictional account of Navajo life is Oliver La Farge's Pulitzer Prize novel *Laughing Boy* (Houghton Mifflin, Boston, 1929, and Penguin Books, 1944). A popularly written but authentic account of a Navajo girl's life, *Dezba,* by Gladys A. Reichard (Augustin, New York, 1939) forms a companion volume. The development of a popular Navajo artist, Beatien Yazz, through the encouragement of his talents by his white friends, is delightfully told by Alberta Hannum in *Spin a Silver Dollar* (The Viking Press, N. Y., 1946).

The arts and crafts of the Navajo are the subject of many nontechnical volumes, often lavishly illustrated, and well worth a careful reading before a visit to the Southwest. Among these are Gladys A. Reichard's *Navajo Shepherd and Weaver* (Augustin, N. Y., 1936) and Charles A. Amsden's *Navaho Weaving, Its Technic and History* (Southwest Museum, Los Angeles, 1934). *The Navajo and Pueblo Silversmiths,* by John Adair (University of Oklahoma Press, Norman, 1944) is an excellent introduction to that subject, which is also treated more briefly in several pamphlets issued by the Laboratory of Anthropology, Sante Fe, New Mexico.

Among the best and most inexpensive publications on the Navajo are those of the United States Indian Service, Department of the Interior, Washington, D. C. Through the Haskell Institute, Lawrence, Kansas, they have issued a series of attractively illustrated bilingual readers for use in Navajo schools. Although they are extremely simple in content and style, both the text and the many pictures by Navajo artists are well worth the attention of the interested student. The Indian Service also distributes several pamphlets giving up-to-date information on Indian tribes, including the Navajo.

Those who wish to consult technical reports will find much additional information in some of the volumes quoted in this book, as well as references to other sources. In 1940, Clyde Kluckhohn and Katherine Spencer published *A Bibliography of the Navaho Indians* (Augustin, New York), an invaluable guide. More recent publications are listed in the bibliography of Gladys A. Reichard's *Navaho Indian Religion* (Bollingen Series XVIII, Pantheon Books, New York, 1950), which also serves as an excellent survey of what many consider the most appealing and interesting aspect of Navajo life.

For a description of a European people living a life in some respects almost as "primitive" as that of the Navajo, see Howard Becker's *Man in Reciprocity* (Frederick A. Praeger, New York, 1956), Chapter 4. The society described is that of the Scottish Outer Hebrides.

A Review of the Chief Aspects of Societies

Before we move on to the study of the Baganda, the third society in this series, we shall do well to take stock of what we have learned about society thus far. These findings can then be tested against what we learn about the Baganda. By now, the pattern followed in the study of each society should be evident; the few comments below follow the chief headings of that outline. We cannot begin to review in any detail all of the main themes, but we can select just a few as a reminder.

THE PEOPLE

The Eskimo and the Navajo belong to the Mongoloid racial stock; the Baganda, whom we are about to study, to the Negroid stock. Much research points to the fact that, so far as we now know, no racial stock is hereditarily intellectually superior to any other, but that representative groups of every race have all made different adjustments to different habitats and historical experiences. Nor is it fair for their inherent intellectual ability to be judged in terms of their present-day cultural achievement as viewed solely through American or European eyes. The question to ask is: "What would members of the white race have done if faced with similar habitats and with the same historical past?"

THE HABITAT

Although all factors of the habitat are interrelated we have chosen for convenience of discussion to classify ten of these factors under four divisions: location, size, and shape; surface features; climate; and natural resources (soil, minerals, water, flora and fauna). It is obvious that the Eskimo and the Navajo face great obstacles in the physical environment, and part of understanding their society involves finding out how they adjust to such conditions.

MAINTENANCE INSTITUTIONS

As has been indicated early in this book, the social scientists make a useful distinction between nature and culture. Race and habitat are a part of nature; the former is biologically transmitted and the latter is subject to the laws of the physical universe. But when man is introduced into the picture, he begins to develop and transmit to succeeding generations customary patterns of behavior, and also to alter features of his environment. It is at these points that culture, which is man-made, comes into play and provides the starting point for the social scientist.

Therefore, we have gone into considerable detail about ways in which the Eskimo and Navajo obtain their food through the use of weapons and tools that they have made; we have noted also their types of shelter, clothing, and transportation as important cultural traits. They both use domesticated animals; they both have a system of exchange and, along with it, some ideas of private property, different though they are from ours in certain respects.

In a rough sort of way, what we have been describing here is the economy of a people, which really consists of more than the materials produced or the technology used in producing them; it consists also of the relationships between producer and consumer, the division of labor, and the complex relationships of ownership and inheritance. As we study the Baganda we shall find that the kingship, or political institution, plays an important role in the working of the economy, particularly with respect to the distribution of goods produced. Here again, reference to Becker's *Man in Reciprocity*, Chapters 19, 20, and 21, should prove helpful.

SOCIAL ORGANIZATION

In one sense the economy, seen as a set of social relations, is a part of social organization but is often conveniently treated separately. The Eskimo, with a relatively simple organization, differ from the Navajo, with their clan system, which regulated several aspects of their life. Sociofacts, such as a family system, an "outfit," a tribal council, are, like artifacts, a part of culture. To understand social organization, however, we must know more than merely the human relations that exist among the people. We must also understand what holds them together and keeps them in force from generation to generation. This leads into a description of such mentifacts as social values, norms, mythology, or sets of beliefs. These mentifacts need not be concerned with merely answering questions about the unknown or with elaborating standards of right and wrong; they can deal with economic matters too, such as folk beliefs about the right time to plant corn, proper food for a child to eat, or the way in which clothing should be worn to keep one warm or cool.

To understand the Baganda, just as has been true of the Eskimo and Navajo, we must locate each major type of social grouping, find out the relations among its members along with their rights and duties, and then see what function the social grouping performs for the society as a system. As we do this we shall begin to get an insight into the leadership structure of the society and to see the part played by the mentifacts in the everyday behavior of the people in various group situations.

SOCIAL CHANGE

Today, in a world of rapid movement, people can no longer remain relatively isolated as in the past. They are in position to overcome many of the difficulties of their environment by borrowing cultural traits from other people. The Eskimo are attaching outboard motors to their umiaks, are using the rifle in place of stone age weapons, and are taking many ideas from the white man about religion, social security, and community life. The Navajo are getting most of their supplies from the trading post and are coming face-to-face with the American idea of private ownership of land. The Baganda, to be studied next, present an even more striking example of social change. A full analysis of *cultural* change would involve detailed descriptions of changing technology as well as the new developments in social organization. Since the emphasis here is upon societies, the stress is placed primarily upon *social* change, which, of course, cannot be altogether separated from other aspects of culture. It is obvious to anyone that not all changes are necessarily beneficial; whether they are or not depends upon the value-judgments of the person making the appraisal.

Familiarity in a systematic way, then, with the people, their habitat, economy, social organization, and changes under way should give us an appreciation for any society we study, even our own.

THE BAGANDA

Right: Cotton has become a major crop of the Baganda, partly because of the encouragement of the British Government. It has been realized that by the production of such crops as cotton and coffee, for which there is demand in world markets, the Baganda and the other tribes of the Uganda Protectorate will be able to pay for internal improvements they desire. Among these are educational and health services. The income from cash crops also pays for such things as automobiles and radios, which people the world over seek in their struggle to raise their living standards. Besides aiding in the change to a cash economy, the British have tried to encourage the preservation of traditional patterns of communal life. *Below:* A drainage ditch is dug, as part of a program of soil conservation and reduction of erosion.

In many parts of Africa, native kingdoms had developed several centuries before the white man's "discovery" of the continent. In Uganda, the kings ruled through a highly elaborate system of chiefs and courtiers and were attended with great pomp and pageantry when they made royal appearances. In particular, the Kabaka, as the Baganda King was called, had a series of royal drums (*top*) which were played by the royal drummers on such occasions. *Below:* The trappings of royalty represent a blend of the traditional, such as the royal leopard skins, with the new, in the form of European innovations.

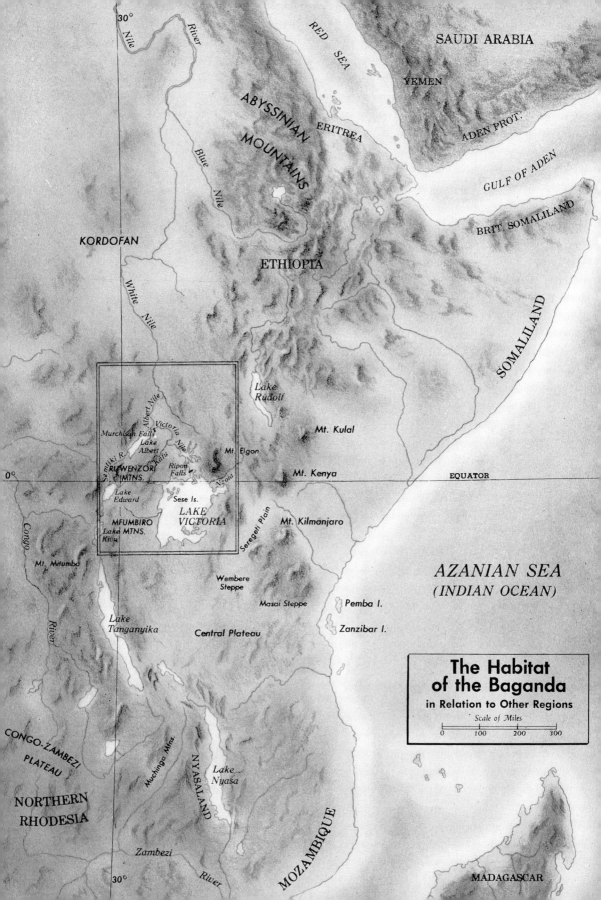

The Habitat
of the Baganda
in Relation to Other Regions

Scale of Miles

0   100   200   300

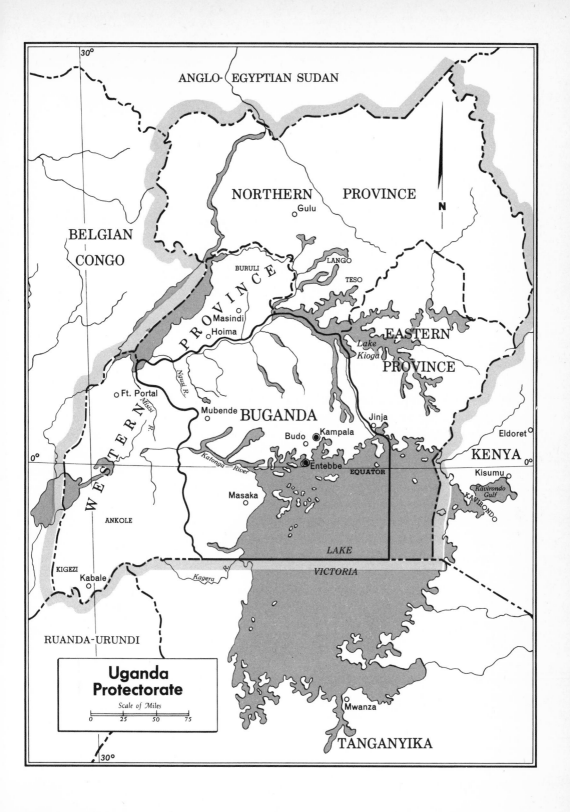

ANGLO- EGYPTIAN SUDAN

BELGIAN
CONGO

NORTHERN   PROVINCE

Gulu

BURULI

LANGO

TESO

Masindi

Hoima

Lake
Kioga

EASTERN

PROVINCE

Ngusi R.

Musi R.

Ft. Portal

WESTERN   PROVINCE

Mubende

BUGANDA

Jinja

Eldoret

Budo   Kampala

Katonga River

Entebbe

EQUATOR

KENYA

Kisumu

Kavirondo
Gulf

KAVIRONDO

Masaka

ANKOLE

LAKE

KIGEZI

Kabale

Kagera R.

VICTORIA

RUANDA-URUNDI

Mwanza

**Uganda
Protectorate**

Scale of Miles

0   25   50   75

TANGANYIKA

Introduction

<<<<<<<<<<<<<<<<<<<<<<<<<<<<<<<<<<<<<<<<<<<<<<<<<<<<<<<<<<<<<<<<<<<<<<<<<<<<<<<<<<<<<<<<<<<<<<<<<<<<<<<<<<<<<<<<<<<<<<

W e now shift our attention from North America to Africa, where we are to study the Baganda people, who live in a modified equatorial habitat. Their physical environment offers striking contrasts, both in climate and resources, to the Eskimo and Navajo habitats. The Baganda are by tradition an agricultural people; their total of more than a million greatly surpasses the numbers of either the Eskimo or the Navajo. Their social structure, with a highly developed political system superimposed upon an older clan system, is much more complex than the societies studied heretofore in this book.

PLACE PERSPECTIVE

Africa is assuming an increasing geographic and strategic importance because of the large-scale economic developments being carried on by the British and other Western powers in their African dependencies. Since India has become independent, Britain has turned to Africa as the source of much of her needed raw materials. Furthermore, Africa is closer to Britain than was India, and the lines of communication are less vulnerable to attack in time of war.

The Uganda Protectorate is a part of British East Africa, which also includes Kenya, Tanganyika, and Zanzibar-Pemba. Uganda is politically oriented to the east, whereas its flora and fauna are more typical of those found in Central Africa. A number of tribes, each with its own customs and its own special relationship to British authorities, live in Uganda. Of these, the Baganda are often considered the "most advanced."

The Baganda live in the province of Buganda, one of the four major political subdivisions of the Uganda Protectorate. Their habitat is north and northwest of Lake Victoria, the second largest fresh-water lake in the world. The Equator passes through Buganda, but what would be an oppressive equatorial climate is modified by the fact that

254

most of the province is about 4000 feet above sea level. Thus the elevation here plays the same role as it does among the Navajo.

TIME PERSPECTIVE

In order to understand the various accounts of Baganda life, it is necessary first of all to read them against the historical background of these people. Mention will frequently be made of the invading conquerors from the north, supposedly with much Caucasian, or white, blood in their veins. They are variously called Hamites or Galla, with the term Bahima being used specifically for those who settled in what is now southeast Uganda, or Ankole. The Bahima were a herding people who brought their flocks with them, as well as a culture more highly developed materially and socially, which they proceeded to force upon the loosely-organized Bantu agriculturists of the area. The effectiveness with which the Bahima asserted their authority in Ankole and in Buganda was quite different. In Ankole, they set up a kingdom in which the royal family remained aloof from the Bantu peasants, whom they governed almost as serfs; in Buganda, there was much more fusion and certainly an advancement both in standard of living and in political institutions.

In understanding the Baganda, therefore, one should bear in mind the constant culture changes which were produced by contact between the African groups themselves. But there was another important influence at work before and during the initial impact of Western culture—namely, the coming of the Arab traders in quest of slaves and ivory.

Eventually, with the increased activity of the missionaries and British commercial interests, Arab influence lost out and natives turned more and more to Western nations. By 1900 British control had reached the point where the Baganda king was willing to sign the well-known Uganda Agreement, in which he was recognized as sovereign of the Baganda people but subject in many respects to the control of high British officials resident in Uganda.

The study of the Baganda is therefore interesting not only because it shows us the achievement of a people once far removed from the rest of the world but because it affords us a case study of what happens to a nonliterate people when it is brought into close contact with our dynamic contemporary culture pattern.

LUGANDA, THE BAGANDA LANGUAGE

The student will avoid some confusion if he remembers that the Baganda people change the first part of a word (prefixes to a common stem) in order to denote a change in meaning. The stem -ganda, for instance, with various prefixes takes on new meanings: Baganda, which denotes the tribe or the people; Luganda, which is the language they speak; Muganda, the name for an individual member of Baganda society; and Buganda, the territory or country inhabited by the Baganda people. In earlier accounts (such as those of Roscoe) this area was usually referred to as Uganda, but in more recent times Uganda has denoted the enlarged protectorate under the British, with Buganda being the preferred term for the province where the Baganda people live.

A PREVIEW OF SELECTIONS ABOUT THE BAGANDA

Some of the selections contained here are based on the writings of John Roscoe, an Anglican missionary, who, as a result of his early acquaintance and long contact with the Baganda, gives us a microscopic account of their pre-European way of life. His facts, vividly describing the past, are brought up to date by selections such as those by Lucy P. Mair. These show the rapid changes which have occurred since the Baganda began to grow cotton around 1906, to turn from a subsistence to a cash economy, and in other ways to feel the influence of western civilization. Before reading any selection be sure that you note the period of time it is describing. We have not attempted to deal with recent events, such as the deposing of the Kabaka (king) in 1953 and his reinstatement in 1955, for one crisis so rapidly succeeds another that any effort to keep up-to-date would be nonsensical.

The People

>>>

The Baganda are members of the Negroid race, one of the three great races of living mankind. Most physical anthropologists divide the Negroids into two groups, African Negroes and Oceanic Negroes. The African Negroes, numbering more than one hundred million, live in central and southern Africa. Their northern boundary is approximately 12° North Latitude. African Negroes are subdivided into a number of smaller groups, which are classified differently by various anthropologists. The classification most commonly used is the following:

Subgroup	Location	Description, Remarks
Bushman-Hottentot	Southwest Africa	Very short, wrinkled, yellow-skinned, inner-eye fold, steatopygous (large, protruding buttocks).
Forest	West Africa	Brown to black skin, ancestors of Negroes taken as slaves to America; considered "true" type.
Pygmy	Scattered through Congo basin	Shortest of all people, infantile body proportions, reddish brown skin.
Sudanese	French Sudan	Darkest of all people, tall, muscular.
Nilotes	Upper Nile	Tallest of all people, dark skins.
Hamitic	N.E. Africa	Tall, slender, narrow nose, brown skin.
Bantu	East and S.E. Africa	See detailed description below of Baganda, which applies to all Bantu.

Of the seven racial subgroups of African Negroes, four, or possibly even five, appear in Uganda.

• 45 • Racial History and Population Distribution of Uganda

S. J. K. BAKER

Four racial strains have contributed in varying degree to the composition of the population now residing within Uganda. A pygmy, or perhaps a primitive negro strain, appears among certain fragmentary groups which have been driven into the remoter and less accessible parts of the Protectorate. Examples of such groups are to be found mainly on the extreme western outskirts, where their members gain a precarious living from hunting and the gathering of wild fruits, to which may be added a little primitive cultivation. It is said, though, that certain pygmy elements survive inside the Mabira Forest within forty miles of Kampala. In view of their numerical weakness one may pass without delay from these primitive peoples to a consideration of the Bantu negro. The representatives of this strain, fundamental in the present population of Uganda, are now found mainly in the south and west of the country, where they form the bulk of the population on the plateau and the cultivating element in the highlands. The Hamitic or Bahima strain was probably the next one to intrude into the area. Tradition links the Bahima with the Galla, bringing them from the north-east, and an analysis of their present-day distribution shows that they have penetrated south-westwards into Western Uganda and beyond what are now the Protectorate boundaries into Ruanda and Urundi. The Bahima element is strongest in Ankole, where the incoming herdsmen were able to take advantage of the natural abundant pasture in the highlands and on the adjacent plateaux. Here the invaders have remained quite distinct from the Bantu cultivators whom they brought into subjection. Further north, Toro and Bunyoro have a physical character less favourable to large-scale pastoralism, and the Bahima have been unable so completely to preserve their identity. The greatest degree of fusion between the two elements has taken place in Buganda—in the fertile region of the "Victorian" Plateau—where the Bahima, though remaining as a feudal aristocracy, have lost their pastoral mode of life and have tended to become absorbed in the mass of Bantu cultivators. There is much truth in the idea that the social progress of the Baganda and the historical development of their kingdom have arisen out of the fusion of these two different strains. The fourth racial element in the population of Uganda is Nilotic. The representatives of this type entered from the north-west at a comparatively recent date and they have penetrated south-eastwards at least as far as Kavirondoland. The Madi, the Acholi, and the Lango are held to be Nilotic tribes. Their line of movement cut across the earlier one which brought the Bahima into Uganda and much inter-mixture between the two types must have taken place. They are to be compared with the Bahima in that they have a considerable amount of Hamitic blood . . . and in that their traditional occupation seems to have been the keeping of cattle. The Nilotic tribes of Uganda, however, are known in addition to be careful cultivators of grain.

In the Province of Buganda there is a strong concentration of population in the vicinity of Lake Victoria, a fact which has its counterpart in the centralisation of the administrative, commercial and educational services around Kampala and Entebbe. . . . Buganda is *par excellence* the region of plantain culture, though cotton has achieved importance as a commercial crop in modern times.

A second area of concentration occurs in the south central area of the Eastern Province, after a break which may at one time have constituted a kind of marcher zone between Buganda and Busoga. In the southern part of this area the plantain, if not the predominant food crop, is at least an important means of subsistence, while in the north

[Adapted from "The Population Map of Uganda: a Geographical Interpretation," *The Uganda Journal*, Vol. 1, No. 2, Kampala, 1934. Pp. 138-144. Used by permission.]

the millet complex is definitely dominant. The abundant labour supply is one of the factors favourable to the success of large-scale cotton cultivation in the Eastern Province, and the both relative and absolute acreage under this crop, has increased rapidly in recent years. This development inevitably involves a challenge to the historical supremacy of the Kampala-Entebbe focus. As late· as 1925, the Phelps-Stokes Commissioners were able to make the following statement in their report: "The Kingdom of Buganda is at present the centre of everything in the Protectorate and all the roads lead to Kampala its capital, so that it is impossible to get anywhere in Uganda with ease, except from Kampala or by roads radiating from that city. It should be pointed out that Kampala is not merely the centre of communications; it is also the intellectual centre of the whole Protectorate." They went on to predict that with the arrival of the railway a second centre would arise in Eastern Uganda. The railway has arrived, numerous roads have been constructed in the Eastern Province, new schools have been built and the predicted tendencies are certainly in operation. Kampala still retains much of its nodality, but a disturbance in the regional balance has undoubtedly taken place, providing the geographer with an illustration of the dynamic character of the facts which he is studying.

The presence of unpopulated districts in close proximity to these populous areas is to be explained in terms of health conditions. The sleeping sickness epidemic of the early twentieth century played havoc in the area east of Jinja. The tragic scale of this devastation is illustrated by a statement taken from the 1920 edition of the Handbook of Uganda: "Before the advent of sleeping sickness Saza Chief Nanyumba had 17,000 fighting men at his command. He has now 105 tax payers." The disease is now under control, though here as elsewhere along the lake shore the tsetse fly *Glossina palpalis* is still to be found.

A zone by nature thinly occupied covers the greater part of the Interior Plateau and in it pastoral activities together with the cultivation of drought-resisting cereals assume an important rôle. Its continuity from south-west to north-east is interrupted by the north-westward extension of the populous zone around the shores of Lake Kioga. The presence of another tsetse fly, *Glossina morsitans,* which brings disease to cattle, explains the total depopulation of certain areas in Southern Ankole. . . . The sparse distribution of people in Buruli, especially on the south side of the Kafue River, would seem to be partly due to historical causes, for here lay the marcher zone between the rival kingdoms of Buganda and Bunyoro. Finally, beyond the populous districts of Lango and Teso, the whole of north-eastern Uganda is sparsely peopled by semi-nomadic tribes.

Population increases upon approach to the Western Highlands. Kigezi and Western Ankole have a dense distribution comparable with that across the boundary in Ruanda and Urundi. Toro and Bunyoro are less thickly populated. In the West Nile Highlands, beyond the valley of the Nile, there dwells a considerable population of Nilotic stock in whose rural economy the keeping of cattle and the cultivation of millet play a prominent part.

Since our interest in this section of the book is the people of Buganda—that is, the Baganda—we turn now to a brief description of their physical appearance.

· 46 · *Baganda Physical Traits*

CHARLES E. SNOW

Over a million people live in Buganda, nearly all belonging to the Bantu subgroup of the Negroid division of mankind. However, as indicated in the last selection, the

Baganda have mixed with several other Negroid groups. This mixture is probably the reason that two distinct types of body build can be distinguished. A shorter, sturdier type with darker skin is common among the lower social classes, and a taller, lighter, more slender form, with long, thinly muscled arms and legs, narrow hips, and smaller facial features occurs among the upper classes.

The skin color of both groups is a dark chocolate brown, but with some variation among individuals of mixed ancestry and a somewhat lighter shade among members of the royal families. Bodies of both men and women are practically hairless, and the abundance of sweat glands causes a glistening appearance. Hair is black, generally woolly and wiry. Beards are usually scanty.

Eyes are dark brown and are set wide apart; they appear large and wide-open because they lack the skin folds overlapping the eyelids at either corner, such as may be seen in many Whites and Mongoloids.

Head shape is long and oval, with narrow, flat sides and with the back of the head projecting prominently, forming a characteristic profile. Foreheads are usually upright or even bulging. The brows are smooth. Ears are small and set close to the head. The face is oval, moderately short, with pronounced protrusion especially around the mouth (known technically as prognathism). The nose is concave in profile, flat with wide-flaring nostrils. The teeth are generally of excellent quality, erupting completely and evenly without crowding.

The Habitat

》》》

In the nineteenth century, Africa came to be known as the Dark Continent. Probably the skin color of some of its inhabitants, the unexplored interior areas, and its shadowed jungles all contributed to the name. Even today Africa remains relatively unknown to the outside world despite a century of systematic exploration and description. The following selection provides a general perspective of Africa as it is today. Such an article was not felt to be necessary for the Eskimo or Navajo, since they both live in better known North America.

• 47 • Africa
ROBERT G. AND M. S. WOOLBERT

FROM PAST TO PRESENT

Civilization first developed in Africa, along the lower Nile, some six thousand years or more ago. Despite this long head start Africa, taken as a whole, is today the least developed of the great continents. Her history, except for that of her Mediterranean shore, is almost unknown, although future investigations will undoubtedly disclose much new information about Africa's past. At Zimbabwe in Rhodesia, for instance, there are ruins which may reveal a whole new chapter in Africa's history when their origin is learned. One of the first things we must fix in our minds is that Africa has not always been inhabited by the peoples we now find there. Great migrations have, even within historic time, resulted in the mass movements of tribes, peoples and whole races.

Another all-important fact is that Africa, viewed as a habitation for human beings, consists of two distinct parts.

What divides Africa into two unequal

[Adapted from "Look at Africa," *Headline Series*, No. 43, Foreign Policy Association, New York, 1943. Pp. 7-8, 10-11, 27-29, 50, 58, 62-64, 72. Used by permission.]

parts is the Sahara and its eastern extensions in Egypt and the Sudan. Long experience has proved this wide belt of sand, steppe and rock to be one of the world's most effective barriers to human intercourse. Indeed, Sahara is the Arabic word for "wilderness." This desert zone, 1,000 miles or more in width, extends over 3,000 miles from the shores of the Atlantic to the Red Sea. The only break is the valley of the Nile, nowhere more than a few miles across. The ancient Egyptians and Greeks had relations with Nubia and Ethiopia. But the connection was tenuous, and had to be maintained via the Red Sea as well as the Nile. For, between Aswan in Upper Egypt and the place where the Blue and White Niles join at Khartoum, navigation is impeded by no less than six cataracts.

For many purposes, then, we may say that there are two Africas. The larger of these is that lying south of the Sahara. Here dwell the hundred million real Africans, the Negroes. This is the Africa to which we are going to give our attention.

THE REAL AFRICA

Where the Negroes came from and when they entered Africa is a matter of conjecture. According to one theory, they arrived on the east coast as early as 30,000 B.C. From here they spread west and south, dispossessing the smaller and more primitive races. Today, the principal remnants of these older peoples are the Pygmies, who have taken refuge in the dense forests of the Congo, and the Bushmen and Hottentots of South Africa, whom both Negroes and whites have pushed out into the arid regions around the Kalahari Desert.

Much later we find the Arabs moving down the east coast as far as the Tropic of Capricorn, carrying on trade and setting up towns. From Morocco Islam was carried south across the desert to West Africa. Here, during the period of the Middle Ages in Europe, flourished a succession of Negro empires with a surprising degree of culture,

carrying on a lively trade across the Sahara with the Mediterranean countries.

THE LAND AND ITS PRODUCE

The tropical zone claims a greater proportion of Africa than of any other continent. Except for a few areas where the high elevation provides a more temperate climate, tropical Africa is not a white man's country. Until further advances are made in the techniques of acclimatization, this vast equatorial area will remain the almost exclusive preserve of the black race.

Africa is the second largest of the continents. Its area of some 12,000,000 square miles is over three times that of Europe. Its coastline affords few good harbors. This fact has naturally influenced the commercial development of Africa. Even today most of its modern harbors have had to be created by extensive dredging and other costly works.

On no other continent is the proportion of land below 600 feet so small as in Africa. From one point of view this is fortunate, for in the tropics upland areas are likely to be better drained and healthier than lowlands. It so happens in Africa that by far the larger part of the lowlands are desert or steppe rather than the marshy, wet rain forest so typical of tropical lowlands in South America and southeastern Asia.

Tropical Africa possesses the largest potential supply of water power in the world. Of the 500,000,000 estimated horsepower in all countries, Africa accounts for nearly 200,000,000—or 40 per cent. All except a minute fraction of this is located in the vast undeveloped area between the Limpopo River and the Sahara. These facts have led some enthusiasts to predict a bright industrial future for Africa, especially for the Congo basin where about two-thirds of this potential power is to be found.

[Air travel is developing rapidly in Africa] but the heavy loads will still have to be borne by ground transportation—water, railroad and highway. Rivers were the main avenues by which Central Africa was explored. Today they serve as arteries of traffic. Unhappily, cataracts and other hindrances to navigation detract from their value. The cataracts of the Nile . . . obliged the British to lay rails parallel to that river.

Africa has fewer miles of railroad than any other continent. In only two places do rails span the continent—both in its narrow southern part. It was only a few years before World War II that the standard-gauge line across French North Africa from Casablanca to Tunis was completed. The ambitious Cape-to-Cairo scheme of Cecil Rhodes has never materialized, and perhaps it never will.

THE PEOPLE

The Bantu Negroes number around forty millions and occupy a third of the continent. Like the Sudanese Negroes, they show Hamitic strains in varying degree, particularly in East Africa, where the two groups intermingle. The Bantu languages all belong to a common family—a fact of considerable importance in the cultural unity of central and southern Africa. The Bantu have in turn been subdivided for purposes of classification into three groups according to their location: Eastern, Southern, and Central.

Among the Eastern Bantu the more advanced peoples are found north and west of Lake Victoria. The Baganda, for example, have a highly developed social and political organization under a limited monarchy where the king still reigns under British rule. In Kenya there are the Kikuyu and Akamba who, unlike their hostile neighbors, the pastoral and nomadic Masai, cultivate the soil. Along the coast and in the islands live the Swahili Bantu, on whose language is based the commercial tongue of East Africa. It is spoken widely by travelers and traders as far as Arabia and Madagascar.

Among the Southern Bantu are many noted peoples and "nations," such as the Zulu, Basuto, Bechuana, Matabele and Mashona.

Much less is known of the history of the Bantu in Central and West Central Africa and of their "empires" mentioned by the Portuguese explorers. They live in the part of Africa where conditions are least hospitable to the white man. Whether their own institutions or those of any Negro people survive the impact of European civilization is problematical. If not, these as well as other African peoples are in for a long period of readjustment, the outcome of which cannot be predicted. Few of the Bantu have been converted to Islam, and those chiefly along the east coast where Arab culture has influenced them directly.

In Uganda the story is quite different. Here there are only some 2,000 whites, mostly in government service or trade, out of a total of nearly 4,000,000 inhabitants. [The official 1948 population figures for Uganda are:

African Negroes	4,953,000
Indians (mostly from Western India)	33,900
Europeans (mostly English)	7,600
Goans (Portuguese colony in Western India)	1,500
Arabs (includes Arab-Negro crosses)	1,400
Total	4,997,400

The total population exceeded previous estimates by almost one million. Better medical care and improved sanitation are responsible for the sharp increase in the number of people.]

Very little land is owned by non-Africans. Yet production is extensive and expanding. Education is largely in the hands of thousands of native teachers, and goes up through the college level, including instruction in medicine, engineering and other practical professions. In Uganda the Negroes are demonstrating what they can really do to improve their own status—with help rather than repression from the whites.

A rediscovery of Africa is in process. The vast potentialities of the second largest continent are only beginning to be realized. Newspapers and magazine articles have usually been extremely optimistic about the new Africa. A few have gone as far in the other direction, pointing out the racial tensions, disease, harsh climate, and other difficulties that will stop economic progress. Even since the next article was written violence in Africa has attracted worldwide attention. What might in the past have seemed a local problem is now seen as one of international importance. Some of the basic reasons for Africa's significance appear in the following selection.

• 48 • The Growth of Africa's World Role

HAROLD R. ISAACS

POSTWAR ECONOMIC DEVELOPMENT

Because of the shrinkage of empire elsewhere, of the acute pressure on Europe's own economies, and of the steadily rising strategic and economic importance of Africa, the African colonies have become more precious than ever in the eyes of the colonial powers. They are driven to try to maintain and increase the African contribution to their own economic existence, even if this requires large new investments they cannot easily make.

All the major colonial powers have announced plans for economic development in Africa on a large scale during the next ten years. Their estimated projected investment totals $7 billion for this period.

The development schemes of the Western powers all lay heavy stress on projects designed to improve the economic status of the Africans. There are a number of projects for agricultural, educational, health and industrial development aimed at expanding the internal African market. Some of these are actually under way now. But according to the UN's *Review of Economic Conditions in Africa for 1950,* the greater part of current European economic effort in Africa is still concentrated on increasing production of raw materials and food for export, improving transport and communications, and

This emphasis on primary exports rather than on internal development is characteristic of all colonial economy and is especially marked in Africa. In 17 African countries, more than 70 per cent of the total export production is confined to one, two or three commodities. These have generally been agricultural products (sugar, cacao, cotton, palm oil, sisal), while key minerals are steadily assuming a greater weight in the export picture. By 1949 African exports had increased by 23 per cent in quantity over 1937. Africa was shipping raw materials to Europe at the rate of $2.5 billion a year and to the United States at the rate of more than $500 million a year.

Many of these raw materials are vital to Western economy and to the Western military machine. Africa produces one-fifth of the world's copper and tin (Congo, Northern Rhodesia, Nigeria); nearly one-fourth of its manganese (Gold Coast, Union of South Africa); more than one-half of its gold (Union of South Africa, Congo, British West Africa); palm oil, 70 per cent (Nigeria, Congo); sisal, 75 per cent (British East and Portuguese Africa); cobalt, 80 per cent (Congo, Northern Rhodesia, Morocco); industrial diamonds, 98 per cent (Union of South Africa, Congo); columbium, 99 per

[Adapted from "Africa, New Crises in the Making," *Headline Series,* No. 91, Foreign Policy Association, New York, 1952. Pp. 11-15, 19-25. Used by permission.]

cent (Nigeria); pyrethrum, 100 per cent (British East Africa). Uranium is supplied in major quantities by the Congo and will also be provided by South Africa, where it is to be processed as a by-product of the gold mines.

The effort to step up this production and speed its movement has been greatly spurred by the rearmament needs of the Western world. As a result, the accent on African welfare has been substantially reduced. . . .

. . . Although some efforts are being made to raise the economic status of Africans, the main trend in European economic activity in Africa is toward further improvement of the economic status of Europeans. This means a widening, instead of a narrowing, of the wide economic gap between European and African—a gap which represents the essence of the explosive situation in Africa. A recent world survey by the UN placed the annual per capita income of Africans at $75, compared to $50 in Asia, $380 in Europe, and $1,100 in North America. But even the figure of $75 is deceptively high, for it represents the income of both Europeans and Africans.

STATES OF MIND

In Africa, as anywhere else, there is not a state of mind; there are states of mind. These are always elusive, more so in Africa than elsewhere because the white man has dug so deep a gulf between himself and the African and because so little effort is being made to find out what Africans, in their various groups or segments, are thinking and feeling.

Certain facts are plainly visible. Since the end of the Second World War more and more Africans have been aroused to a new sense of their problems, their needs, and the effort to better their lot. The war itself directly affected the lives of tens of thousands of Africans who fought in European armies on African, European and Asian battlefields. These men, like a similar group of Asians a generation earlier, returned to their homelands with widened horizons and fresh notions about their own future.

A whole new set of ideas, aspirations and expectations was set in motion among the small but important segment of educated Africans by the eloquent promises of wartime Allied propaganda, especially the Atlantic Charter. These ideas were directly or indirectly absorbed to an unmeasurable extent by the "uneducated"—or traditionally educated—African as well. Postwar disillusionment has sharpened their awareness of the world they live in; it has started them on a more realistic process of self-education about their place in the world and their chances of improving it. "We know now," said one African in what may be a typical comment, "that we shall advance not on the basis of the Europeans' readiness to concede to us, but on the basis of our own capacity to grow strong enough to know what we want and to take it."

MISTRUST OF WHITES

Basic in this whole picture is the African's attitude toward the Europeans. His feeling is rooted in his whole experience, going back generations to the brutalities of the slave-trading era, the later wars of colonial conquest and penetrations, the succeeding years of European consolidation at African expense. This pattern has varied widely in different places, but it has included the frequent pre-empting of the African's lands; the crowding of masses of Africans in some areas into hopelessly inadequate "reserves"; the weakening or breakup of his tribal life and its replacement, in many instances, by the most degraded kind of industrial exploitation and urban existence, as in the Union of South Africa.

The African's need to become part of the modern world places an inescapable burden of change on the African. Some anthropologists tend to idealize the tribal life from which the African is being wrenched. Yet the fact seems to be that the traditional tribal life can no longer adequately serve the African's needs. He must find his way to some new and broader coherence if he is to thrive in the future. Until he does, he must carry with him not only the burdens imposed by the white man's rule, but those imposed by his own past.

One common result of the African's experience is that he often does not trust the white man, even the one who comes with benevolent purpose, and generally does not believe the white man even when the white man tells the truth.

The changing concepts of Africans have led to an increasingly critical view of Christianity. There are said to be as many as 20 million African Christians—many more, at any rate, than in all areas of Asia combined. By far the greatest portion of existing educational facilities for Africans in Africa is maintained by mission effort. Not a few notable missionaries have tried to live and function in Africa in a manner consistent with their beliefs. But the African Christian, to a growing degree, has become aware of the wide gulf between Christian profession and Christian behavior as generally exemplified by the European both in Africa and in his own homeland. Younger Africans, especially, have begun to reject European rationalizations for this gulf. A standing joke among them is to offer to go as missionaries to convert Europe's savages to Christianity.

The rising mood of self-assertion among Africans is reflected in the frequent rejection of European control of African churches, or in abandonment of Christianity altogether. In Nigeria a new religious movement has spread widely, borrowing some features of Christianity but combining them with much older African beliefs. Some young Africans rebound all the way back to ancestral religions; others move toward their own varieties of agnosticism. A sign of the times among young men in Kenya is the dropping of baptismal Christian given names.

In the rural hinterlands similar moods are often more obscurely expressed. In Uganda in British East Africa a returning East African was recently struck by the widespread revival among his people of the ancient ceremony of the blood oath. "It is a strong thing, the blood oath," he explained. "It imposes on a man ties of brotherhood with another man that are far stronger even than family ties. Men in my country are reaching out to each other in this way. They had no specific purpose in mind, and I came to realize it was a way of beginning to come together to take some kind of a stand. I found among my people even in the remote villages a feeling that was an old feeling, yet a new feeling. It was that they were being treated like animals and that the white man would never treat them in any other way. Even old folks were repeating the phrase which some said had come up from South Africa: 'Don't kill the white man; just hate him, for he will never change his ways.'"

RACE FEELING

In colonial Africa the superiority of the white man and the inferiority of the black man is automatically assumed at virtually every point of contact between the two. This fact, with all its variants and complexities, dominates all European-African relationships. In a setting of rising tension and conflict the primary emotion it induces in the black man is hostility, and in the white man it is fear.

The intensity and consciousness of these emotions vary on a wide scale. The color bar stands at different heights in different parts of Africa, ranging from implicit attitudes in some regions to highly explicit legal barriers in others. It is made to appear less obtrusive in French and Portuguese Africa. In British Africa the intensity varies in relation to the size and character of the white population. In some areas, such as the Gold Coast and Nigeria, where there are only small groups of white officials and residents, although segregation is practiced, the relationship between the races is much less emotionally charged. In other areas, which have large white settled minorities—in Kenya and Southern Rhodesia but most of all in the Union of South Africa—the fear of the African majority has assumed almost psychotic proportions. There the maintenance of white supremacy is the paramount aim, and in Rhodesia and the Union it is aggressively enforced by the white man's laws.

In these areas it is the white man who puts his relationship with the African on a straight racist footing, and the African must inevitably react on the same terms, for he has small chance to do otherwise. The extent and depth of African feeling can scarcely be measured by examining the few organized outlets for self-expression which he is allowed. It must be appraised in terms of the whole complex of attitudes and circumstances which lie behind the increasingly frequent eruptions of criminal violence, particularly in the Union of South Africa.

We now turn from the survey of Africa as a continent in crisis to a consideration of a specific section of Africa astride the equator. Tropical Africa has not attracted white settlers to any great extent.

The following selection narrows the geographic survey to Uganda alone. Noteworthy is the small percentage of land covered by forest. Probably the most widespread misconception of Negro Africa is that it is covered with tropical jungles. There is some dense forest or jungle, but it is concentrated near the coast, in the river valleys, and along the shores of lakes. The characteristic plant zone of Uganda, as well as of most African countries, is savanna—that is, tropical grassland.

• 49 • Uganda, the Protectorate
HOMER L. SHANTZ

Uganda . . . with an area of 81,000 square miles lies on the equator and on the northwest shore of Lake Victoria . . . from which the Nile flows over a low escarpment to form Ripon Falls. . . . The Nile flows through Lake Kioga, a papyrus swamp covering thousands of square miles. Mount Elgon on the southeast border and the Ruwenzori range in the southwest are the principal mountains.

The vegetation varies from the tropical rain forests of about a thousand square miles such as the Bugoma and Budonga forests east of Lake Albert, the temperate rain forests of about a thousand square miles such as are found on Mount Elgon and the Ruwenzori range, through the grassland types. The high-grass low-tree savanna covers about 37,000 square miles of the central part of the colony and includes the large papyrus swamp which surrounds Lake Kioga. The acacia-tall grass savanna of 15,000 square miles lies farther north. Along the Kenya border in the northeast a more open type of about 8,000 square miles is of acacia-desert grass savanna. In the north and east there are also many thickly wooded areas of dry forest of about 3,000 square miles, valuable for timber and gums. The mountain grassland of the southwest of about 16,000 square miles is excellent grazing land and suitable for cool-weather crops.

LAND USE

The forests occupy about 2,000 square miles, about 2.5 per cent of the area, and furnish timber of unusual value. The woodlands cover about 3,000 square miles, less than 4 per cent, valuable for timber, wood . . . and gums. There are in addition re-

[Adapted from "Agricultural Regions of Africa, Part 2: Vegetation and Potential Productivity of the Land," *Economic Geography*, Vol. 17, No. 3, Worcester, Mass., 1941. Pp. 228-230. Used by permission.]

sources from the savanna area which furnish valuable timber trees such as iroko (m'vule) . . . and such economic products as shea butter.

About 71,000 square miles, 87 per cent, is grazing land of high carrying capacity, some as good as any in Africa. Grazing land of low carrying capacity covers not over 8,000 square miles, 10 per cent of the area. Almost the total area of 79,000 square miles is suitable for sheep and goats. Cattle find about 31,000 square miles, 38 per cent, unusually favorable. Here are produced cattle, goats, sheep, and donkeys. The total animal units amount to about 2,471,000, 31 per square mile of grazing land. Wild animals are abundant over much of the area and ivory is an important export product.

LAND CLASSIFICATION

Not much of the cool-weather crop land has been developed, since under natural conditions most of it is excellent grazing land and is occupied by a cattle raising people. This area of about 17,000 square miles, 21 per cent of the total area, produces under European supervision coffee and tea, and by natives bananas, beans, peas, coffee, potatoes, and wheat. Warm-weather crop land is far more extensive and amounts to about 56,000 square miles, 69 per cent of the total area.

A great variety of crops can be grown but two crops stand out: first, bananas as a food crop; and second, cotton as a money crop.

The chief crops grown by Europeans are rubber, tobacco, cotton, and maize. But this production is very small as compared with the native production of bananas, cotton, millet, sweet potatoes, sorghum, manioc, sesame, beans, maize, peas, groundnuts, rice, sugar cane, tobacco, chillies, and rubber. The northern portion of the colony has a drier climate and is especially adapted to such crops as sorghum, millet, manioc, and cotton. Here sorghum and manioc become food crops instead of the banana which is the food crop of the south and central portion. The fields of banana are as characteristic of Uganda as fields of corn are characteristic of Illinois. In the north, grains are stored by order of the government against periods of drought and famine. The natives with plenty of food crops have been induced to produce cotton as a money crop.

Very little of the land of Uganda is suitable for grazing only, but a part of the drier northeast portion of about 8,000 square miles, 10 per cent of the area, can be so designated.

The exports from Uganda are cotton, cottonseed, coffee, hides, skins, rubber, chillies, sesame, and ivory, and amount to about $281.00 per square mile of agricultural land.

• 50 • *Buganda, Home of the Baganda*

FRANK J. ESSENE

Buganda is one of the four provinces of the Uganda Protectorate, the other three being Western Province, Eastern Province, and Northern Province. These last three provinces are the result of political manipulations. Each of them contains separate kingdoms and smaller political units that the British have united in various combinations for administrative purposes. Buganda, on the other hand, is a single native kingdom as well as a province. The Baganda people make up the bulk of the population. Buganda's outer boundaries have been un-

changed since 1900. Buganda is the stable core of Uganda Protectorate.

One reason for the stability of Buganda's borders is that almost all are set at natural barriers. The Victoria Nile and Lake Kioga form the eastern border. The marshy river Kafu, the Ngusi River, and the southern corner of Lake Albert make up the northern edge of Buganda. The Misisi River and various swamps mark the western limits. The extreme southern part follows the artificial boundary of 1° South Latitude for a short distance on land and continues out to the middle of Lake Victoria. The actual land boundary for most of southern Buganda is the shoreline of Lake Victoria.

Politically, Lake Victoria is divided between the provinces of East Africa that front upon it. Buganda owns nearly one third of Lake Victoria, some 7970 square miles. The Sese Islands lie within Buganda's share of the Lake. Natives of the Sese Islands, the Basese, were once bitter enemies of the Baganda. Early in this century these natives, who numbered about 20,000, were all taken inland to save them from sleeping sickness which was ravaging their islands. The tsetse fly which carries the disease was later eradicated and the Basese were taken back to their island homes.

The total area of Buganda is 25,390 square miles, almost exactly the size of the Navajo reservation. Included in the total area is 8,095 square miles of water, mostly of Lake Victoria. Over a million Baganda live on 17,295 square miles of land. Thus the population density of about 60 persons per square mile of land is 25 times that of the Navajo. Yet, in relationship to the natural resources and technology available, Navajo land is much more overcrowded.

Three factors of location have influenced the history of Buganda: being well inland, at the source of the Nile River, and straddling the equator. The inland location was the main barrier to early European exploration. However, speculation about the source of the Nile was one of the reasons that European exploration centered about this area in the latter half of the nineteenth century. The equatorial location, even though somewhat modified by an elevation of 4,000 feet, results in too hot a climate to attract European settlement.

Uganda Protectorate is a political unit that resulted from expediency and compromise. However, most of its boundaries have geographical validity. Uganda is essentially a basin nearly surrounded by mountains or highlands. In the northwest corner a break in the highlands lets the Nile River through but does not provide an easy route for man to travel. The only part of Uganda's boundary that does not present topographic barriers to man is in the south. However, Lake Victoria nearly fills this open area as the mountains of Kenya and Ruanda dip down close to its shores.

Some aspects of Buganda's geologic history have obvious effects today. When dinosaurs were living, all Uganda's streams flowed west into the equivalent of the Congo River. Remnants of the channels showing this drainage pattern still exist. In comparatively recent times, the Ruwenzori range (and other mountains along the Belgian Congo boundary) pushed up faster than the streams could cut channels. Much water was trapped so that large swamps and lakes resulted. Some water managed to break through to the north and eventually almost all Uganda came to be drained by the Nile. Drainage is so imperfect that large shallow lakes, such as Victoria and Kioga, many smaller lakes, swamps, and sluggish rivers still dominate the landscape.

Of Buganda and Lake Victoria Roscoe says:

> . . . It is hilly and well watered, and almost every valley is swampy ground, while some valleys contain deep water held up by papyrus growth extending from hill to hill often a mile across. The country is almost always green with numberless evergreen trees. . . . The sloping sides of the hills are favorite sites for building of huts. . . .
> The lake [Victoria] on the western and north-eastern side is surrounded by hills and high land, though there are spots with gently rising plains, which give the impression of being almost level with the surface of the water. . . . In some places the hills run down to the shore, and end abruptly in sheer precipices with rocky faces rising over a hundred feet from the water.
> . . . The water is beautifully fresh, and appears most pleasing to the eye of the traveler. . . . It is also sweet to the taste. . . . The lake is an attractive sight, as it flashes and ripples in the warm sun-

shine, with its fringe of never fading trees with their shades of green lighted up with bright colours of tropical flowers, or the beautiful water plants and lilies floating gracefully in shallow water.*

In several respects the climate of Buganda is more temperate than tropical. The mean monthly temperature is within two or three degrees of 70° Fahrenheit the year around. However, on any single day the temperature may be fifteen or twenty degrees higher in the afternoon than at sunrise. The absolute range of temperature recorded at Kampala is 35° Fahrenheit, with the highest temperature ever recorded, 91° and the lowest 56°. In the northern part of Buganda temperatures average a few degrees higher and the absolute range is slightly greater.

Rainfall varies from about 55 inches a year along the shores of Lake Victoria to some 35 inches annually in the northwestern part of Buganda. Kampala, only a few miles from Lake Victoria, has an average of 46.2 inches of rain yearly. The usual rainfall pattern is a fair amount of rain each month with the heaviest rain concentrated near the

* From *Twenty-five Years in East Africa*, Cambridge University Press, Cambridge, 1921. Pp. 57-59, 78. Used by permission.

spring and fall equinoxes. (Actually, every day is almost an equinox in Buganda. March 21 and September 21 are better marked here as the days when the sun passes directly overhead.) Nearly all rain is due to thermal convection in association with warm, moist air masses. Afternoon thunderstorms are most common. Occasionally, hail falls in local areas.

The factors entering into the production of rainfall in tropical Africa are variable and complex. [Compare these with those described in Selection 24.] Two permanent high pressure areas that center over the Sahara and Kalahari deserts and the low pressure cyclonic region in the western Indian Ocean are of major importance. Most rain that falls in Buganda comes from evaporation of the Indian Ocean. The heaviest rains in Buganda occur along with southeast winds. These ocean-moist air masses pick up further moisture from Lake Victoria which leads to quick production of rain. (The water of Lake Victoria itself is also derived from Indian Ocean evaporation.) The winds that cross Lake Victoria exert a cooling influence in addition to bringing rain. Entebbe averages 2 degrees Fahrenheit cooler and about 20 inches more rain annually than Mwanza, a Tanganyika town on the opposite side of the lake.

Making a Living

>>

Whether man in the tropics is a hunter, gatherer, herder, or farmer, he literally sweats out a living. There is no danger of frosts killing man's crops, but neither do frosts kill the ubiquitous insect pests. Cattle do not die of exposure, but they are killed by many insect-carried forms of disease. Tropical hunters and gatherers have an even more precarious hold on life than herders or farmers. Wild animals are usually scattered and wary. Meat spoils so quickly that holding a surplus for emergency use is impossible. Wild plant foods that man can eat are few, hard to obtain, and usually difficult to prepare. Tropical areas may be thinly settled but none is uninhabited. Man is most adaptive, for in one way or another he manages to survive in all parts of the world.

The most obvious problem of the tropics is the hot climate. Man must adjust his activities to the extreme climatic conditions. The usual working day is from early morning to 10:00 or 11:00 A.M. and from mid- or late-afternoon to dark. This split shift is more efficient than it appears. Physical labor during the hottest part of the day would be relatively unproductive.

People in the tropics usually wear little or no clothing. The Baganda are exceptional in that they were wearing long bark-cloth robes when the first European explorers reached them. Baganda clothing, however, was draped loosely on the body. It did not keep the wearer too warm, as the tailored clothing of Europeans often does.

Since housing in hot areas usually has as its primary function the shedding of rain, the roof is the most carefully constructed part of the building. Roofs are almost always thatched except where Europeans have introduced corrugated iron. Thatched roofs are built up in several layers, with the result that rain penetrates only part way through it. When the sun's rays strike the wet thatch, the water evaporates and the house interior is cooled in the process. The greatest drawback of thatched roofs is the ease with which they catch fire. Thus cooking is often done away from the house to reduce the fire hazard. Building materials are plentiful in the tropics. Small tree trunks and branches are used for house frameworks. Palm leaves and wide-bladed grass provide material for thatching.

The Baganda formerly supplemented their food supply with wild game. Antelopes, buffaloes, and small mammals helped vary their predominantly starchy diet. But the intro-

271

duction of firearms brought about the virtual extinction of larger game animals in Buganda. A Muganda now eats large game about as often as an American eats venison. Lions and leopards used to prey upon Baganda cattle. Only an occasional leopard is seen today. The Baganda killed both these members of the cat family to protect their prized herds, and presented the skins to their chiefs and king.

Unlike ourselves, the Baganda have no revulsion against eating insects. Termites (often erroneously called white ants) and the kungu fly are favorite tidbits. Locusts are also eaten. Wild plants make up a small part of a Muganda's diet since few wild plants in Buganda are edible. Mushrooms, greens, seeds, and tubers are eaten. All the domestic plants are exotics—they came originally from wild plants in other parts of the world. Native plant life has many uses to the Baganda other than dietary. The dense-grained tropical woods, such as mahogany, are excellent for woodworking. Grass and palm leaves are useful for thatching and weaving. The inner bark of the wild fig trees is pounded into a paperlike textile called bark cloth. Selections 55, 56, and 57 include detailed descriptions of woodworking, basketry, and bark-cloth manufacture. Local clays are available for the making of pottery. Both iron for tools and salt for table use had to be imported, as neither occurs in significant amounts in Buganda.

The indirect use of Buganda resources through agriculture and the keeping of domestic animals is described in several of the following selections. Perhaps the reader will be confused in the references to the Baganda as basically banana growers as compared to statements that plantains are their staple food. The words "banana" and "plantain" are sometimes used interchangeably and sometimes not. In the latter case bananas usually indicate a type of plantain that is edible raw, whereas plantains are those that require cooking before being eaten. The cassava plant, mentioned several times, is known to most of us as tapioca. However, the tapioca we use is a highly refined product quite different in appearance from the large tuber from which it originally comes. Groundnuts are more commonly known as peanuts in the United States. Other plants described in the next two selections are familiar in name and should be no problem to identify.

In the first of the following two selections the two general types of agriculture in Uganda and their associated crops are dealt with. Only the first of these types is characteristic of Buganda, and it is described in greater detail in Selection 52.

• 51 • Agriculture in Uganda
HAROLD B. THOMAS AND ROBERT SCOTT

In a country such as Uganda, with its wide range of soil and climate, and with its multiplicity of tribes with varying social conditions, native agriculture is much diversified in accordance, primarily, with the dietetic requirements of the people, and these requirements are largely determined by the soil and climatic conditions under which the people live. In general, apart from the arid north-eastern portion of the Protectorate,

[Adapted from *Uganda*, Oxford University Press, London, 1935. Pp. 112-124. Used by permission.]

these conditions have created two broad types of vegetation belts, of which the first may be termed the rain forest, elephant-grass, plantain type, and the other the short-grass, grain type. The former type is usually associated with a fairly heavy loam soil which through its formation resists erosion to some extent, although normally subjected to heavy rainfall, whereas the latter is usually associated with a lighter, more sandy soil, which is very liable to serious erosion. These two main types of vegetation affect the distribution of domestic animals; it will be found that cattle are much more abundant in the short grass, grain country, and this factor, of course, has a bearing on the agricultural practice of the neighbourhood.

With these conditions in mind, it can be said that native agriculture falls naturally into two categories. One comprises a plantain-eating, settled agricultural people, practising a comparatively intensive system of agriculture, which has as its foundation the plantain garden, or *lusuku,* in and around which are grown the other food crops and, since the introduction of Western ideas, the 'cash' crops. Under this system the family is the unit, the village being conspicuously absent, and the control of a number of families and of some share of their productivity is evidence of wealth. Characteristic of the other category is a grain-eating, cattle-owning people, practising a shifting cultivation, and an extensive system of agriculture, congregating often in villages and regarding the ownership of cattle as the index of prosperity.

The main plantain areas of the Protectorate are the Buganda Province, the districts of Busoga, Bugishu, and part of Budama in the Eastern Province, part of Bunyoro in the Northern Province, and Toro, Kigezi, and part of Ankole in the Western Province. Throughout these areas the principal source of food supply is plantains, which are supplemented by sweet potatoes and cassava. This starchy diet is augmented by simsim, ground-nuts, beans, and miscellaneous vegetables which provide an ingredient of protein and fat and add a relish to what is generally considered to be tasteless food. A few plants of sugar cane, chillies,

and ginger can usually be found on any holding, often in the plantain garden itself, but these are merely subsidiary and only grown in small quantities.

A typical native holding consists of a plantain garden within or near which is the house, made of wattle and daub with a thatched roof—although corrugated iron roofs are coming into use. Near at hand are an area under economic crops and a number of small plots of various food crops, several of which are often mixed together in the same plot. The whole area under cultivation in an average holding may extend to about eight acres, of which the plantain garden occupies three acres, and the cotton plots three acres. The balance of the area contains small plots of the miscellaneous crops mentioned above and often a plot of coffee. No definite rotation is practised; the land is usually cropped until yields indicate that soil fertility has become exhausted, when the land is allowed to revert to bush and new land is cleared for future plantings.

Most of the cultivated land in Buganda Province is in private ownership. The larger estates are breaking up into peasant holdings, but a majority of Baganda are still rent-paying tenants of some landowner. The standard annual rent is shs. 10/- for each holding, and in addition the tenant is liable to pay to the landowner a regulated money tribute in respect of his plots of cotton and coffee. The fact that plantains are grown tends to anchor the people to their gardens and causes them to grow their other crops within a short distance of their homes.

In [much of] the Eastern Province there is a pronounced dry season which prevents the successful cultivation of the plantain. In general the soils are less fertile than in the plantain-growing areas, and more rapidly become exhausted. The staple diet is grain, and the most important crop is the small millet, *Eleusine coracana.* Over the greater part of these areas coffee will not produce, so that all economic and food crops are annuals. Holdings are therefore rarely compact. Plots may be near to the house or a mile away where the cultivator may have chosen a piece of land which is especially fertile, or one that he considers to be suitable for a particular crop.

Throughout the non-plantain areas, and particularly in the Eastern and Northern Provinces, food shortages are by no means infrequent.

The most widely occurring type of soil in the Protectorate is red loam overlying a very compact clay subsoil. The soil colour varies from a bright red, when there is little organic matter, to a dark chocolate colour under an old stand of elephant grass. The depth of soil may be as much as 15 inches. The subsoil is red, and very hard when dry, and usually contains a layer of murram of varying depth. During the first year of cultivation there is little or no erosion, but afterwards, through loss of organic matter, erosion becomes more general.

Erosion is not so serious in Buganda and Busoga where the red soils are found and where cotton blocks on the scale general in the Eastern Province are not common. It is, however, a problem which is likely to become of first importance in certain areas, particularly those carrying an increasing animal population.

When cultivation ceases over a particular area, it is native practice to leave the land rough, dead grass and sticks and the remains of previous crops not being removed. Soon, weeds occupy the ground and give some protection to the soil.

There are very few instances of large-scale farming among natives. The limit of size of a unit of cultivation in Buganda and in other areas where agriculture is fairly stable is almost invariably that required to support a peasant family; and in the non-plantain districts also plots are only large enough to fulfil a family's requirements.

The implement most commonly used is the short hoe with a handle which is straight for the greater part of its length but ends in an acute angle. The heart-shaped blade is tied to this lower arm of the handle in such a way that it inclines back towards the user. The handle, except among certain of the Nilotic tribes, is so short that a stooping position has to be adopted, but this hoe is used for all digging and weeding work. Imported hoes, square bladed and with a ring through which the shaft is passed, are also in general use. The blade is at right angles to the shaft, which is 3 feet long so that the hoe is effective for digging work. . . . Other implements in general use are knives, axes, a small type of adze, and in plantain districts a broad-bladed, heavy knife which is used for cutting down the bananas.

It has been the policy of the Government, acting through the Agricultural Department and the Provincial Administration, to introduce ploughing wherever conditions are suitable. There are a few ploughs in use in most districts, but the greatest development has taken place among the Teso and their relations in Bukedea county. In Teso alone there are now about 10,000 ploughs, the ratio being about one plough to eight men. Progress in other districts where vegetation is of the short grass type is slow but steady. The adoption of ploughing is being followed by the introduction of cultivators and harrows.

Where ploughing is practised cattle are used in the plough teams, there being commonly four, though sometimes six, oxen to a team. Apart from this use, for the most part in breaking up land for cotton, stock play a very minor part in agriculture.

Native agriculture has not yet reached the stage at which specialization on the production of a particular crop is practised. There are a few groups such as the salt-workers of Katwe and the Bakenyi of Lake Kyoga who exchange salt and fish for food and beer. The Batuku of the Semliki valley are provisioned by the Baamba tribe in exchange for meat, and the Bakonjo hill-men of Ruwenzori exchange wheat, potatoes and tannias for other foods grown by the plain-dwellers. With these exceptions there is very little exchange of foodstuffs.

Labour, where used in harvesting food crops, is not generally paid except by a feast after the work is finished. An ox may be killed and beer made for all those who assisted. The hill people of Bugishu will, however, pay with food for labour from the plains, and the Baganda may pay immigrant labour from the Western Province and Nilotic districts sometimes in the same manner, sometimes in cash.

There is little system in the marketing of native produce . . . Markets have been established in townships and in many native centres purely to supply local demands for foodstuffs, and the amounts there sold are very small. The marketing of cash crops such as ground-nuts, simsim, and coffee in any considerable quantity has hitherto been effected through the many Indian bazaars throughout the country. Indian shopkeepers in these bazaars bought small lots of produce for low prices, or exchanged them for cheap cloth, salt, cigarettes, and other petty luxuries. There were also, and are still, many itinerant buyers purchasing produce in the villages by similar methods. The grade of produce bought in this matter is naturally often low and the consideration received by the producer offers no inducement to increase production. but these deterrents to economic expansion are now capable of control through the Native Produce Marketing Ordinance, 1932. This legislation allows the number of buyers of a specified produce to be limited, and the marketing of produce to be confined to recognized centres.

At the present time native agriculture in Uganda is almost entirely in the hands of peasant producers, and apart from the use of ploughs in certain areas, the whole of the cultivation is done by hand . . . It is true that in Buganda, where much land is in private ownership, there are numerous large estates owned by wealthy landowners, but these have not been developed on estate lines, the land being farmed by tenant farmers who pay rent to the owner.

Most of the land is farmed on an eight to ten years' cycle, and for at least half of this period the land is fallow and out of cultivation. During the fallow period the land is allowed to revert to bush in order to restore the fertility which has been lost during the time when the area was under crops.

No system of manuring is practised, and it may be said that the necessity for such manuring is not as yet appreciated.

Since the cultivation of economic crops is of recent introduction, and the advancement of the country is dependent on the increase of the production of these crops together with foodstuffs, and therefore on the maintenance of soil fertility, the education of the people, both young and old, in agricultural matters plays an important part. This very necessary agricultural education is given in a number of ways. So far as the younger generation is concerned, all schoolmasters, before taking up their duties as teachers in the elementary schools, have to take a course of instruction at one of the Government farm schools at Bukalasa and Serere. In the elementary schools nature study forms an essential part of the training of the pupils who, in addition to theoretical training, maintain a school garden. Vocational training in agriculture for small-holders is given in the schools mentioned above. Two farm schools for sons of landowners have been established and are maintained by missions.

Apart from the above, a number of African Agricultural assistants and instructors are employed by Government. These are of two grades, one consisting of men who have received an advanced training in agriculture, and the other of lower-grade instructors conversant with the primary rules of crop husbandry. Their efforts are directed towards the improvement of agricultural practice among the people themselves, and they work under the guidance of officers of the Agricultural Department. It will of course be obvious that the whole organization of provincial administration is intimately concerned with agricultural education in the broadest sense of the term, in that every effort is made to inculcate in the minds of native farmers the necessity for, and the benefits to be derived from, a higher standard of agriculture.

At this stage of development, as is to be expected, there is as yet little move towards co-operation, though signs of interest in its possibilities are already apparent among thinking native producers. In districts where ploughs are used several persons will combine to purchase a plough, which is then shared by the group. In Buganda, associations have been formed by the growers themselves, with the object of selling cotton and other crops collectively, the reduction of the cost of transport to markets and the bulk sold permitting of a higher price being obtained. In one association in Bulemezi county, Buganda, a cess is collected from members which is used to create a fund to be devoted to the erection of produce stores and to assist financially those members who, through loss of crops, are unable to meet demands made on them for taxes. In Bugishu district the first step has been taken toward what will, it is hoped, lead to the eventual formation of a co-operative society among the coffee-growers in that area.

It will be seen that the bulk of the native agriculture at the present time has developed along the lines of peasant small-holders producing their own food supply plus a considerable amount of economic crops, and it is safe to assume that future development will, in the main, continue on these lines.

Cotton is the crop of incomparably the greatest economic importance, and the type grown has proved itself to be well suited to the country, and commands a ready sale. But the cultivation of coffee is becoming of increasing importance, and its cultivation is being extended to new districts when experiments have proved such new areas to be adapted to its cultivation. The possibilities of other sources of agricultural wealth, as for instance, tobacco in Bunyoro, are not being neglected, but it is upon these two crops, cotton and coffee, that the prosperity of the natives of Uganda will rest, so far as can be seen, for many years to come.

• 52 • Baganda Farming

N. S. HAIG

On a typical hillside . . . viewed from a neighboring one, cultivation starts on the lower slopes just beyond the fringe of forest or swamp. Each homestead is surrounded by a large banana garden with bark cloth trees dotted here and there through it; the other crops, such as cotton, coffee and food crops, are cultivated farther away from the house compound. During recent years, cotton cultivation has increased to such an extent that clearings have crept farther and farther up the hillsides, and in many places the whole of the top half of a hill has been cleared and planted with cotton. It is frequently maintained that soil erosion in Buganda Province has not yet commenced to any dangerous extent, and such an assertion is presumably based on the amazing recovery under rest of which the soil in most parts of the Province is capable, unless deterioration has already gone too far. A careful inspection of some of the most thickly populated areas, however, will show that this is a mistaken idea. Although there is no immediate danger of large contiguous areas of land becoming completely worked out, the sum total of the small patches of land which have been ruined by careless cultivation must amount in the aggregate to a very considerable figure.

The cotton acreage alone in Buganda Province now approaches half a million acres, and this and sweet potatoes, one of the main food crops of the Baganda, are the two most dangerous crops from the point of view of soil erosion. A good cotton crop results in comparative wealth to the grower, and a large proportion of his money is devoted to the cultivation of a still larger acreage of cotton during the coming year, without due regard being paid to the maintenance of soil fertility. The supply of im-

[Adapted from "An Agricultural Survey in Buganda," *The East African Agricultural Journal*, Vol. 3, No. 6, 1938. Pp. 451-455. Used by permission.]

migrant labour during recent years, with the possible exception of 1937, has been more than sufficient to fulfill the requirements of Baganda growers.

Land in Buganda Province is mainly privately owned by the Baganda. Under the Uganda Agreement in 1900, approximately half of the total area of the present province was assured in private possession to the King, his relatives and certain Chiefs. Since that time very numerous changes have taken place through inheritance and sale, the larger estates being split up and sold. At the present time [1938], there is a growing desire on the part of tenants to possess their own land, and big estates are being more and more cut up and purchased in lots of from five to thirty acres, the price varying from Sh. 5 to Sh. 100 per acre and upwards according to its proximity to large townships. This general trend is very desirable, and it is found that the owners of these "small holdings" are much more open to advice on better farming methods than the ordinary tenant on someone else's land. It is difficult for a landlord to evict a tenant unless the latter grossly misuses the land. Some mention should be made here of the liabilities of a tenant. His obligations to the landlord are:—

(a) the payment of *Busulu* or rent.

(b) the payment of *Envujo* (crop tax).

(c) certain minor obligations in respect of beer making, also a tribute on bark cloth trees.

Busulu, formerly paid in kind or by labour performed, was changed later to an annual tax. *Envujo* dates back to a considerably earlier period than *Busulu,* and was always paid in kind. Nowadays it is assessed on the acreage under economic crops (e.g. cotton and coffee), grown by each tenant, and is a money tax. Payments of the above taxes gives a tenant the right to cultivate what crops he pleases on his holding and assures him reasonable security.

Cultivation throughout Buganda Province is entirely by hand. Only three agricultural implements are employed—the hoe, a short knife with a curved blade, and the cutlass. The hoe used by the Baganda, has a short handle and usually an imported blade, though the locally-made blade may sometimes be seen. . . . The curved knife is used by the women for cutting off and peeling plantains, and to some extent for miscellaneous agricultural purposes. The cutlass is used for general purposes such as the cutting down and splitting of plantain stems for use as a mulch.

The usual time-table of the working day is as follows. Both men and women start work in the fields almost as soon as it is light, and the women work until about ten o'clock, when they go home to prepare the mid-day meal. The men go on working until about half-past eleven, when they come home and dinner is eaten about twelve o'clock. Both men and women resume work about three o'clock when it begins to get cool; the men work in the fields up to about five o'clock, and the women are occupied with fetching water and preparing the evening meal. There are, however, many individual exceptions to this rule.

While in most cases the plots owned by each cultivator are centred round his homestead, in areas such as this where land is scarce many cultivators have also been forced to take up plots on the fringes of cultivation, which may be at some distance from the main part of their holding. Some of these plots may be so distant that a considerable amount of time is wasted in walking to them for field work. Statistics were collected of the proportion of such plots, as they give in some sense a measure of the pressure upon the land by the farming community. In this *mutala* [hill slopes, separated by swamps, on which villages and gardens stand], out of a total of 778 plots measured at the two surveys, 119 plots or 15 per cent were separated from the main holding of the owner.

Of the crops grown by the average farmer in Buganda the banana garden is permanent, as also is the coffee plot. Apart from these, all crops grown are annual ones. A properly cared-for banana garden should last up to fifty years if kept enriched and mulched with dead leaves from banana plants, and other household rubbish such as banana and sweet potato peelings. Unfortunately, the standard of cultivation of banana gardens has declined very much of late.

The coffee plot can only be called semi-permanent. Interplanting with cotton, or beans, or groundnuts is usual for the first few years at least. Much propaganda has been done to encourage the use of Elephant grass or other grasses as a mulch for coffee, but results to date are disappointing.

The common practice after clearing a piece of new land is to plant early sown cotton, e.g. in May or June. This will be harvested in January and February, and the plants uprooted and burnt in March, after which food crops will be planted, either beans or groundnuts singly or mixed, and often interplanted with a few maize plants. As soon as these are harvested, a late-sown crop of cotton is planted. Beans and ground-nuts are very commonly sown between the rows of cotton, and help largely to check soil wash on hilly land, as well as providing an additional source of food. This succession of food crops followed by cotton may continue for several years, sometimes for as many as seven or eight years when land is scarce, by which time the soil has become powdery on the surface and has lost its texture and fertility. It is all too common to find that a farmer will now plant coffee in this worn-out soil, thus giving a permanent crop the worst possible start. Cotton may even be taken as a catch crop in the young coffee for another two years.

In areas where land is still fairly abundant, the above rotation will occupy three to four years, and the land will then be rested for a similar period. When land is scarce, and cultivation has to be extended to cover six or eight years on the same plot, weed growth is encouraged to a certain point, the weeds being dug into the soil in an attempt to enrich it.

Sweet potatoes are not included in the above rotation. They are planted in a separate plot, and may follow each other year after year, or may be rotated with maize or simsim, to be followed later by bananas. Sweet potatoes may be planted continuously on the same plot until it has to be abandoned. Groundnuts are usually given preference as regards soil; they are frequently planted in "virgin" soil, or taken after the first crop of cotton on freshly cleared land.

A proper picture of Buganda agriculture is incomplete without the realization of the extent to which the people move about from one village to another. Probably the chief method by which soil fertility is maintained and restored is not by any system of management or rotation, but by the fact that when the cultivators find their crop yields are diminishing, they leave the village and move to another.

Throughout the Elephant grass areas cattle are only kept very sparingly. On this *mutala,* three cattle only are owned by residents, but are not kept on the actual *mutala.* Poultry, sheep and goats are kept by all families and the average number per taxpayer was found to be: poultry, 4.59; goats, 1.12; sheep, 0.20. A number of rabbits are also kept for sale by some of the residents. The keeping of live stock therefore hardly enters into the agriculture of the area, and no bad effects are caused through overgrazing by stock. It is the duty of the children to herd the sheep and goats which find plenty of rough grazing; beyond this, no special feeding is supplied, except that banana peelings mixed with a little salt are sometimes given in the evenings. Both sheep and goats are used for consumption by the owner's family rather than for sale, but a salable goat may fetch from Sh. 6 to Sh. 30 and a sheep from Sh. 6 to Sh. 15. The dried skins may fetch up to Sh. 1 apiece.

John Roscoe, in describing Baganda life of half a century ago, furnishes many details about the king's herds, which were tended by the Bahima herdsmen. Among other things he pointed out the following:

Peasants were afraid to own more than one or two cows lest they excite the cupidity of the chiefs. Should they have a large herd the chief would have robbed them of their cattle. Peasants who owned cows sent their boys out to herd them, since girls and women were forbidden by custom to do this work and no woman was allowed to milk cows. Poor people took their cows into their houses by night, and made special places of beaten earth for them to lie upon, with a gutter to carry any water off.

A great number of other taboos surrounded the care of cattle and the use of milk products. These taboos were largely borrowed from the Bahima. For example, no one was ever allowed to boil milk except in the making of a milk cake shortly after a calf was born. The people believed that boiling milk would cause the cow to go dry. After milk utensils had been washed with water they were held over a fire made of cow-dung and sweet-smelling grass. The milk would absorb a smoky flavor from the vessels and would not be considered fit to drink without it. Milk was drunk curdled or clotted, except by children, who drank it fresh. Butter was made in a large bottle-gourd, holding from three to four quarts. The gourd was plugged with grass and rocked back and forth. After the butter had formed it was shaken onto a plaintain leaf or a wooden bowl, was slightly washed, and was then used in cooking or for smearing on the baby.

Only the chiefs would have cattle killed for food, but would choose for this purpose a male animal or an aged or barren cow. Peasants in parting with a cow would sell it or kill it in the market, where they sold the meat immediately. Should an animal die from sickness, the herdsmen unhesitatingly ate the meat, devouring everything except the skin and bones.

Goats played a significant part in Baganda life. For one thing, they were frequently used to pay any fines the peasant might be charged with. Every household would thus keep one or two of these animals around, sheltering them in the house at night tethered by a foot to pegs in the ground under the slope of the roof. No taboos were attached to goats, and they were preferred as food to sheep, although the people never used goat milk. Sheep found less favor with the people since there was a strong taboo against women eating mutton. Also, men were afraid that a sheep's ghost would haunt them if the animal saw them in the act of slaughtering.

Although Roscoe and Johnston were writing about the Baganda of forty or fifty years ago, many of their observations still hold true today. Few natives use oxen as draft animals; they still are most reluctant to kill off scrub stock in the interest of better breeding practices; and while cattle may be killed for their meat by the wealthy, a poor man seldom eats beef except when a cow dies or is accidentally killed.

• 53 • *Modern Animal Husbandry*
HAROLD B. THOMAS AND ROBERT SCOTT

It is a matter for conjecture when cattle were first introduced into Uganda, but it is probable that the Zebu was established before the arrival of the Longhorn, which

[Adapted from Uganda, Oxford University Press, London, 1935. Pp. 195, 197-198, 206-211. Used by permission.]

apparently accompanied the ancestors of the Bahima when they first arrived in the Protectorate, possibly some four to five hundred years ago. Crossbred strains between these two groups occur alongside the comparatively pure parent breeds, and occupy the greater part of the Buganda Province.

In Buganda a greater degree of interest in stock is evinced than in most parts of the Eastern and Northern Provinces. This attitude can, however, be regarded as of comparatively recent growth, since it seems probable that the Baganda, prior to the nineteenth century, while always anxious to obtain cattle in their raids, valued them only as a source of meat. When they began to expand from the rain-forest, elephant-grass zone in which their kingdom was first established, and entered the savanna country which had previously been the outer fringe of Bunyoro, the king's herds were established in those savanna areas, notably in Bugerere. On the Sese Islands, and probably also in south Kyagwe, however, cattle-keeping would appear to have been an earlier practice, and a recognized sacrifice to Mukasa, the principal deity of the Baganda, took the form of white cattle in units of nine. The management of the herds, also, seems to have reached a considerably higher standard throughout Buganda than in the Eastern Province. The animals were housed and ticks were carefully removed from them; they were supplied with fodder and salt at frequent intervals, and the owner commonly kept them in his own hut and tended them carefully. The rinderpest epizootic of 1914, however, caused heavy loss and many owners then combined their surviving stock into one composite herd, for which paid herdsmen were responsible. This change was bad, inasmuch as it tended to divorce the cattle from village life.

In the more recent past the ownership of cattle in Buganda was in the hands of chiefs and richer peasants who, while keenly interested in their stock as a tangible mark of wealth, were content to have their cattle herded by half-bred Bahima or others who almost invariably had the bad points of the Muhima without his knowledge and ability

to look after cattle. There has been a welcome recent extension of ownership following on the opening up of areas in which cattle can be purchased cheaply, and the Baganda peasants are acquiring them to an increasing extent. Unfortunately, the tradition that if a herd is to be properly cared for it is essential to employ herdsmen from the Western Province persists, and these men assume almost complete control of the stock. Any statement made by them as to the health of the animals or any explanation as to a decrease in milk or numbers is usually accepted without question by the owners. Influenced by a dawning suspicion that all is not well, the Baganda are, however, beginning to show a desire for the knowledge which will enable them to make a greater economic use of their animals, but much careful work will have to be undertaken before the tribe as a whole will be able satisfactorily to control and develop its resources of cattle.

Goats are widely distributed throughout the Protectorate, and are of great importance in the economic scheme of the natives: if, in the scale of native wealth, cattle represent pounds, then goats may be taken as representing shillings. The majority of the goats are short-haired and of a great variety of colour—the Baganda have over twelve different names distinguishing the colours of goats. In certain hilly areas a type which has a distinctly longer coat than is usual in the lowlands can be observed. Goats are valued by their native owners principally as slaughter stock: the meat is consumed by the family and near neighbours and the skins sold. The milk of goats is not acceptable to most natives.

Sheep are kept for their flesh (which, however, is seldom eaten by Baganda women, being tabu to them), and their skins are also sold. . . . Sheep are less hardy than goats.

The castration of surplus males is becoming increasingly popular, so that the scrub bull will in time be eliminated, and in addition this policy brings about an increased and better meat supply from bullocks [steers]. This meat, being cheaper and more palatable than that obtained from . . . [un-castrated] animals, is being bought to an increasing extent, thus improving the dietary of natives. Considerable progress has been made in encouraging the consumption of better meat, and it is hoped that native owners will become accustomed to sell stock readily.

The Government conducts experimental stock farms, and similar institutions are maintained by the native administrations, with the close cooperation of the Veterinary Department in all branches of work. At all the farms, [moreover,] a close study is being made of various indigenous breeds. The animals are maintained in conditions slightly better than those prevailing throughout the country, but generally not dissimilar, with a view to breeding out particular weaknesses.

There are as yet few foundations on which an extensive native dairy industry could be built. The native cow does not give a heavy yield—three-quarters of a gallon a day over eight months is exceptional—but the average fat content is high. Butter is commonly made and, although sometimes converted into indifferent ghee, is seldom eaten, but is mainly used as an unguent. There is evidence that when improved methods of management are more generally understood and followed, the yield of milk can be increased; and a number of posts have been established to demonstrate improved methods of preparing butter and ghee. It is essential, however, that more milk should be available for infants and calves before any considerable quantity is used for other purposes, and great caution is therefore being observed in the development of the live stock industry.

It is, indeed, improbable that animal products in general will represent a substantial proportion of the exports from Uganda for some years. The once prosperous trade in hides and skins, the average value of which was £178,133 for the years 1927-9, has greatly deteriorated, to some extent as a result of the world economic depression. The value of the exports in 1934 was only £29,232, and the average value over the three preceding years only £32,846. Extensive propaganda work in connexion with the preparation of hides and skins is, however, continuously undertaken.

The native veterinary assistants are a valuable link between the more backward people and the European staff. Any native assistant who shows special aptitude is sent to the veterinary laboratory for a month or two annually, to undertake a 'refresher' course.

A highly popular step in Buganda has been the inauguration of meat inspection classes for native market masters. Only the simplest aspects of meat inspection, mainly methods of dealing with *cysticercus* or "measly" meat (an intermediate stage of a tapeworm commonly encountered in man), tuberculous carcasses, and anthrax, receive serious attention.

The primary aim of educational work is, however, to reach the mass of stock-owners and, after obtaining their trust, to persuade them to help freely in the control of disease and its eradication, and to secure greater benefits, both in improved health and increased prosperity, from the management of their live stock. There seems to be no doubt but that the more intelligent methods of stock-keeping which are being slowly inculcated will result not only in an increase of the wealth of the community, as measured by material possessions, but, by bringing an adequate diet within reach of all, in a widespread amelioration of the physical condition of the natives.

The following description, though written fifty years ago, still holds true for the great majority of Baganda. A few of the wealthier and better educated Baganda live in houses partially European in style and follow European rules of etiquette in eating. However, rich and poor Baganda eat approximately the same types of food. The significance is that the Baganda had fairly well solved the problem of diet and housing before the British came and have seen no reason to change.

• 54 • *Food and Shelter*

HARRY H. JOHNSTON

FOOD

As regards the *food* of these people, they are fond of meat when they can get it, either by killing goats, sheep, cattle, or wild animals. Meat is sometimes cooked in water with red pepper and the spicy grains of the amomum, or it is grilled over the fire on a rough gridiron. A common practice is to run lumps of flesh on to wooden spits and stick them up in a slanting position over the fire. Fish, of course, enters largely into the diet of the people, and locusts, white ants, and the kungu fly are also eaten. A kind of thick soup or curry is made of meat or fish, which is eaten with banana "stodge" as a relish.

The staple food is *bananas*. Sweet potatoes are also eaten, boiled or roasted, and ground-nuts and grains, such as Indian corn, but to a very limited extent. You frequently meet children herding goats in the fields or along the roads, and these invariably have a roasted potato in one hand and a small store of raw ones in the other. They are very quick at answering questions as to the correct road to any village, and munch away at the roasted potato in the intervals between question and answer. These random snacks of bananas or potatoes seldom answer the purpose of a regular meal. The fixed repast consists of bananas, or rather plantains, prepared in the following way: A large earthenware pot is filled with plantains, then covered over with banana leaves, and a little water added. The plantains are first of all peeled, and as they grow limp in the boiling, they fuse into a solid mass. The pot is supported over the fire by three stones of sufficient size, placed in position to serve as a tripod. Instead of stones for this purpose one occasionally sees three old pots, inverted, placed round the fire, and the cooking-pot set on top of them. When the mass is

cooked, the pot is taken off the fire, some fresh banana leaves are put on the ground, and the content is turned out on to the leaves by inverting the cooking-pot. The cooked bananas have a mashed appearance, but you can still detect the shape of the original fruit in the heap.

If they can afford it, they have a soup, curry, or gravy to eat with the bananas. Some meat is boiled down, or some fish is cooked in a small earthenware pot, not much bigger than an ordinary sugar-bowl. When the family has gathered together for the meal, each member of it washes his or her hands by pouring water out of a jar on the fingers, one person pouring the water whilst another twirls and rubs his fingers. Then the person who poured the water hands the jar to the other, so that he in turn may rub and wash his hands. There is no towel for drying; it is sufficient to give the hands a few violent shakes. Then they sit round the mass of banana pulp, men, women, and children altogether. The soup or gravy is sub-divided between one or two other small earthenware bowls, so that a person has not to lean across the food to reach it. The heap of food is then parcelled out into a number of little mounds, and each person has one in front of him. He takes up a piece of the mashed plantain, forms it more or less into a ball in his hand, then dips it into the gravy. If he considers that there is little chance of the gravy dripping from the ball while it is on its way to his mouth, he raises the ball quietly and disposes of it. If he suspects that there is to be a drip, he casts a hurried glance at the ball of food as it is raised out of the gravy, and regulates the pace to the mouth so that it arrives just before any drop has fallen. If a drop has fallen on the ground, he disposes of the ball first, and then casts a rueful glance at the

[Adapted from *The Uganda Protectorate*, Vol. 2, Hutchinson, London, 1904. Pp. 649-657, 671-674. Used by permission.]

spot where it fell. Every drop of the soup is precious, and very little of it is wasted. The youngsters of the family, having had less experience and less tact in regulating the quantity of soup each time, and the rate at which the piece of food should be conveyed to the mouth, frequently waste some; but this is soon noticed, and the elder members of the family charge the younger ones with the waste, especially if there are several dipping in the same bowl. The youngster admits at once the heinousness of the offence, and in order to guard against a repetition of it he first of all dips the ball in the bowl, then touches it on his mound of banana pulp in order to catch any loose drops of gravy, and then conveys it to his mouth. He takes care next time to pick up the part of the mound on which he touched the loose drop on the last occasion, immerses it in the bowl, touches it again on the mound, and so on; so that by this method none at all of the gravy is lost. The pieces of meat or fish used in making the soup are allowed to remain for the end, and are then distributed so that each person gets at least one morsel. When the meal is over, the hands are again washed.

Plantain pulp is nourishing food. Thousands never eat anything else. It does not follow that the people are not hardy because they are fed on this soft, bulky food. "I have seen," writes Mr. Cunningham, "boys and men whom I have overtaken on the road start off to race my bicycle, and keeping up the race for a distance of five miles without effort, even at the rate of eight or nine miles an hour."

The favourite *drink* of the Baganda is "mwenge," a kind of sweet beer which is made from the juice of the banana. For this purpose a small kind of banana is usually employed which grows very sweet, as it ripens after the bunch has been cut from the tree. This liquid, when first brewed, is perfectly delicious. After twenty-four hours it begins to ferment, and may become a very heady, intoxicating beer. I am not aware that the Baganda make that porridge-like beer from various kinds of native grain which is so common elsewhere in Africa; nor do they, as is done both to the east and to the west, make a fermented drink out of honey. As soon as the Sudanese from the Upper Nile settled in the country as soldiers or soldiers' followers, they introduced the bad practice of distilling a heady spirit from bananas, and this when drunk by the Baganda renders them quite mad. They get tipsy over their banana drink when it becomes fermented, but not stupefied or frantic.

It is said that there are no fewer than thirty-one distinct kinds of bananas cultivated in the Kingdom of Uganda. Some of these are short, squat bananas prized for their sweetness and beer-making qualities. Others, again, are of the kind known to us as plantains—of considerable length, not excessively sweet when ripe, and used by the Baganda in an unripe state, and consequently without any sweetness at all. The banana is too much the main staple of food. When on rare occasions a drought visits the country, and the bananas fail to bear fruit, the people are on the verge of starvation, since they grow a very insufficient supply of any other vegetable food. Sweet potatoes are cultivated, and the English potato has been adopted with approval, but it is cultivated in large quantities more for sale to Europeans than to be eaten by the people themselves. A little maize and still less sorghum is grown for food. Eleusine [small millet] is rare. There are practically two harvests of everything (except bananas, which produce all the year round), and these are coincident with the two short dry seasons which follow the heavy rains of the winter and summer.

There is a considerable growth of *mushrooms* throughout the whole country, and *five species* are wholesome. They are much liked by the Baganda, and are equally appreciated by Europeans. The flavour of one kind is quite sufficient to provoke the raptures of a gourmet. The Baganda grow sesamum, which produces a seed full of oil.

No less than twenty kinds of peas and beans, certain herbs the leaves of which greatly resemble spinach, and various seeds, fruits, roots, and leaves of the forest are in use as articles of food. The sugar-cane grows most luxuriantly in the regions near the lake shore or near rivers, and produces an excellent cane sugar. Before the arrival of Indians and Europeans, however, the Baganda never made sugar. They only chewed the stalk of the cane for its delicious sweet juice. Tomatoes grow abundantly in Buganda now, and are no doubt eaten by the natives, who also sell them to Europeans. The coffee-tree is possibly indigenous to the forests of Uganda and the neighbouring islands. The Baganda chew the sweet pulp around the beans but make no use of coffee as a beverage. . . . [They also eat] the Cape gooseberry, the fruits of which have an agreeable sub-acid flavour, and a taste very much like cherries.

SHELTER

The *house* in Uganda, or in countries subject to Uganda influence, differs from any other in Negro Africa. The huts of the peasants, of course, come back somewhat closely to the common beehive shape, though they exhibit a larger porch. The typical Uganda house, however, is constructed as follows: The ground plan is an almost perfect circle with, generally, two doorways, one opposite the other. Outside the front doorway the roof is prolonged into a kind of porch which opens out in a great horse-shoe shape, something like the old "coal-scuttle" bonnet. The doorway is fairly lofty —much more so than in any other type of Negro house—but the door-posts, which are generally small tree-trunks encased in a reed covering, converge somewhat in their upper extremities, so that the shape of the door is a very long oval. The interior of a chief's house has a general level of the floor raised at least a foot above the ground by a hard structure of clay smeared over with mud and cow-dung, so that it is absolutely smooth, and in some places is shiny and black with the polish of feet going to and

fro. Other daises often rise in steps above the level of the floor. The roof is relatively very high in the centre. It is composed of a vast framework of palm-frond stems or flexible sticks lined inside with closely tied canework. This frame work of the roof really extends uninterruptedly to the ground, and round the edge of the hut and its narrow verandah, if it has one. It is strengthened from the ground upwards by a circle of poles which are placed perpendicularly in the ground all round the periphery of the house, and which fit into the roof just where it begins to slope upwards towards the apex. The roof is supported in the interior by tall, straight poles made of the stems of the wild date palm. In the fore part of the hut, near the main door, at about an equal distance between the projection over the porch and the apex of the roof, there is a screen or partition wall with supports in the centre made of these date-palm columns going right up to the roof.

In all Uganda buildings of the old type (I am obliged to put in this proviso, because the Baganda are changing their customs so rapidly, and many of them are now building houses after the European style in bricks) the palm-trunk column is an ever-present and picturesque feature. The dwellings of kings and chiefs, churches, mosques, and schools are all distinguished by this forest of smooth, straight, slender palm-trunks. Their use enables the Muganda of the better class to give his roof a high pitch and his dwelling a stateliness which makes it something far superior to the ordinary African hut, however extensive may be the ramifications of these low-pitched dwellings. Of course the houses of the peasantry are greatly inferior in appearance to those of the gentle-folk, and many of them at a distance look like untidy haycocks. The better class of dwellings is in itself a special feature of Uganda and such countries to the west as follow Uganda fashions. The thatch is extremely thick, perhaps as much as a foot in density. It is of fine long grass, and all over the front of the house, over the porch and a portion of the verandah, the grass is shaved off with sharp knives to a smooth edge. This gives the house a very neat aspect, and is a great improvement on the untidy, weeping straws which usually terminate an African's thatch. The interior of the house and the outer walls of the porch and front verandah are most neatly covered with canework. This is made of the long stalks of the elephant grass packed closely together in an upright position, and bound by transverse bands of bast. This canework is almost a specialty of the Baganda, and with it they clothe unsightly poles, which then become glistening columns of pale gold. Doors are even made of this canework. The apex of the roof is usually finished off by a cap composed of several flounces of thatch, one on top of the other.

A large house may contain, besides the central fireplace (generally a raised dais of hard clay on which stand the three big round stones which compose the African's grate), from one to five sleeping berths, usually beds of raised clay partially surrounded by screens. It has been already explained that a partition of palm-trunks rising to the ceiling cuts off the front part of the hut into a sort of semi-circular hall, and helps to ensure a certain amount of privacy for the interior. Behind the broad opening in this palm-trunk partition is placed a screen of matting, which enables people to pass to the right or left of the interior of the hut, but prevents any one gazing direct from the doorway on the inmates. Curiously enough, in many of the houses, even of the better class, there is a partition on the left of the interior from the principal entrance which serves as an enclosure for cattle, one or more milch cows being kept there with their calves. Some of these cows are extremely tame, and walk in and out of the houses with great care and deftness, never upsetting or injuring the frail screens through which they have to pass. It may be supposed that these tame cows introduce a certain amount of dirt and smell into the house; but as regards cleanly habits they seem to be as well trained as a domestic dog or cat.

At the back of the principal dwelling-house there are smaller and less neatly built huts which serve as cooking places, and sometimes as separate dwellings for supernumerary women or children, and attached to every establishment is a privy. In the courtyard which contains the principal dwelling there may still be seen a small fetish hut near the house and close to the gateway leading into the courtyard. Every Uganda house of importance has attached to it a series of neatly kept courtyards surrounded by tall fences of plaited reeds. In visiting a chief one may pass through four or five of these empty courtyards, in which followers of the chief stand or squat under shady trees. Any really big chief or the king of Uganda would have in one of these courtyards a band of music, a number of men with drums, fifes, and horn trumpets, who would greet the arrival of distinguished strangers by striking up some melody. Or a couple of these may be seated on the ground playing tunes on the "amadinda," a xylophone. These courtyards are called "kisikati" (in the plural "bisikati"). The reed fencing that surrounds them is usually of the [same type which] follow[s] roadways in towns or settlements for miles, enclosing the plantations and settlements of well-to-do individuals. These fences, behind which rise handsome shade-trees or bright green bananas, give a singularly civilised aspect to the broad roads which traverse townships.

The Uganda *town* is a series of villa residences surrounded by luxuriant gardens. Occasionally there is an open square formed by the meeting of two broad roadways, and this may be the site of a market or a place of reunion for the people. Narrow paths may circulate between the huts of peasants or as by-ways, but as a rule the Muganda prefers to make roads as broad as those in vogue in civilised countries at the present day. The public ways are kept fairly free from the growth of vegetation, but no attempt is made, of course, to metal their surface, and consequently the heavy rains cut deeply into their clay soil, so that the roads in their present condition are quite unsuited to wheeled traffic.

Among the Eskimo and Navajo the arts and crafts were at most the products of part-time specialists. The full-time artisans described in the following selection indicate the much greater complexity of Baganda society. Baganda technology is considerably more advanced than that of the peoples previously studied. This is in part due to the advantage of specialization. However, it does not follow that the Baganda are superior artistically. Navajo silver work or Eskimo ivory carvings are as good or better artistically than anything produced in Buganda. Generally speaking, among all people one technique, or at most only a few, receive the greatest emphasis. Products of this technique are usually very finely made. Other artifacts that could benefit from care in manufacture are made in a slipshod fashion. It is fair enough to state then that one group makes, say, better pottery than another, but it is most difficult to judge the over-all artistic ability of the people.

• 55 • The Royal Craftsmen

MARGARET TROWELL

Most of the highly skilled craftsmen are old men—the last of their kind. Their tale is always the same, the young men will not be bothered to learn the crafts for they see no future in them. In the old days the crafts-man had . . . prestige, however poor and humble he might be; any modern office boy with a smattering of booklearning now considers himself to be superior. The economic factor too is one which deserves further study. The African peasant has not yet learnt to think clearly in terms of shillings and cents with regard to his indigenous products. The blacksmith commands a higher price than his work warrants in a good many cases because superstition still gives it a value beyond the merely utilitarian; on the other hand the potter, whose work demands more time and skill, is underpaid because with his poor technique he cannot compete with imported enamelware and old petrol tins.

THE SMITH

There is more historical or legendary material available concerning the origins of the blacksmith's craft than of any other. This is to be expected, because everywhere in Africa the smith, his forge and his work seem to hold an especially important, often almost sacred, position in the eyes of the people. It is still today one of the largest of the peasant industries in Buganda and in the past must have ranked as second to none. It is more highly organized than any other craft.

In every other craft the leader of the royal craftsmen and often his second in command holds a hereditary position and comes from one particular clan although the workmen under them may be of any clan. But among the smiths many of the clans seem to have their own closed groups, where all the workmen will be of the one clan and where only a certain type of work is done. Thus the *Nvubu* (Hippopotamus) clan have always been the makers of the royal shields, and the bracelets, anklets and other ornaments for the King's wives; while the *Ente* (Cow) clan make the weapons and agricultural implements needed for the Lubiri [Royal Enclosure].

[Adapted from "Some Royal Craftsmen of Buganda," *Uganda Journal,* Vol. 8, No. 2, Kampala, 1941. Pp. 47-55, 58-61. Used by permission.]

Driving out of Kampala on the Entebbe Road one passes the market place of Katwe just outside the township borders; from a dilapidated oblong mud hut open to the road comes the clink of hammer on iron. This is the smithy of the *Ente* or Cow clan, and here you can watch them making spears, adzes, axes, hoes, large digging spears, knives for peeling bananas, others for cutting meat, awls, needles and bells of various kinds, for cattle, hunting dogs and decorating babies' legs "to make them walk."

It is a large and busy smithy with two separate sets of fire and bellows. A young lad will be working the bellows, pumping the bamboo rods up and down at an incredible speed with seemingly tireless energy, in fact this working of the bellows in a smithy seems to be the one job in all Africa where rapid hard work is expected and given. The bellows . . . consist of two clay bowls each with a long stem looking like enormous shallow pipes set close at a slight angle to each other. These are covered with a goat skin tied tightly round the neck of each bowl; up from the centre of the skin above each bowl comes a bamboo rod and it is these that the boy pumps up and down forcing the air out through the stem of each bowl in turn. The air is sent into a large clay nozzle . . . and out into the charcoal fire. A hole in the ground nearby holds water which is sprinkled with a mop of banana leaves over the fire to damp it down.

The smiths squat on the floor nearby, each with his stone anvil. . . . Each will have a heavy piece of iron like a flattened stick for his hammer, . . . and a chisel . . . held in a cleft stick.

Katongole, the head of the *Ente* clan, is by right of his position the hereditary chief smith. The original Katongole came from Bunyoro and settled in Budu where members of the clan have always been known for their work as smiths, working the iron themselves right up from the ironstone. All the work which is done for the Kabaka [the native king] in this smithy is still made from iron smelted in Koki, although work made for sale is made from scrap iron bought in the towns.

In all about twenty men of the Cow clan are members of this smithy. They will be called in by Katongole in rotation to do their three months work a year as royal smiths of the Kabaka. During this time each man must produce a certain tribute, this was given to me as 7 spears . . . 20 "digging spears," . . . 25 polished knives . . . 80 peeling knives . . . 15 adzes . . . 7 awls . . . 40 small needles and 30 large needles. . . . What work they do over and above this may be sold for their own profit, although they must buy their own scrap iron to melt down for their own work. The privileges which they enjoy are the same as those of other royal craftsmen—free land, no taxation and no other form of compulsory labour. In the old days the smith, like the potter could not be killed for human sacrifice; and during the times of such sacrifices it was customary for him to carry his smith's hammer as a badge of office in order that no mistake might be made!

Of all the crafts the smith's was the most hedged round with taboos. If women could not be present at the digging of clay and the firing of pots, they were kept even more strictly from contaminating the smith or any of his work. While working he could have no intercourse with his wife, he could not even feed or talk with other people, his food would be brought to him and left at the smithy door. Today these customs are not strictly observed and passers-by will stop to chat at the smithy door, yet one feels the craft still has its pride and dignity of position which sets it apart from any other. The smith is not pessimistic that his trade will die out, on the contrary Katongole assured me that even an educated schoolboy would be glad to become a smith. They do not seek fresh openings for their skill; on my enquiry as to whether they undertook such jobs as the repair of bicycles I was told proudly that the royal smiths of the Cow clan had no need of such work and would not touch it, unless of course they were personally ordered to do so by the Kabaka. Meanwhile they had all the work they needed in the making of agricultural implements "for, as every woman knows a garden would not prosper if cultivated with foreign implements." This apparently refers only to knives for cultivating, for practically all Baganda that I have asked use an imported "jembe" [long-handled hoe] rather than the old Buganda hoe.

The only grumble on the part of the smith was concerning the price he was paid for his labour, although as far as I could tell he was considerably better paid than the potter considering the amount of skill and labour involved. . . . The word *Mukemba* is used for the pay of a blacksmith and also for the fee for divination; it does not seem to be used for payment to a potter or other craftsman.

DRUMS

Every event in life has had its significance marked with its own particular drum beat—birth, marriage, death, the accession to power or wealth, the return of the warrior—for each the call of the drum has gone forth, the message has rung out across the valley. Drums have a magic of their own, a power to fill the world with a throbbing mystery of sound. When the King walks clad in barkcloth through his courts preceded by drums and horns one feels the old dignity and power of a great native chief. When at night in the flickering light of torch and fire half-seen figures dance and move to the throb of the drum and the monotonous chant of harp and pipes, then into the light strides a minstrel to tell again some tale of warrior's prowess or of past glories of the tribe, one is caught up by the strange glamour of movement and sound.

At the workshop [described here] some ten or a dozen men are constantly at work making and repairing drums. Apart from the hereditary Kawula and Kasimba the workmen are of any clan and hold their position by sheer merit. As royal craftsmen they are entitled to wear the skin apron and are exempt from any kind of tax or compulsory labour, and hold free land.

The drums made here are chiefly. *Ngoma*, short stocky drums made of a hollow block of wood narrowing at the base with cowhide stretched top and bottom lashed together with thongs; they range in size from little ones under a foot high used at ceremonies for the birth of twins to huge fellows some five feet or more in height. They are the drums which beat on ceremonial occasions and which today call folk to school or church; the tall *Engalabi* for dance and song are of a different type.

In front of the open shelter which forms the workshop stand a row of . . . logs hollowed and shaped ready to be covered with the skins. Cut from unseasoned wood from trees in the Kabaka's forest land they have been smeared with cowdung to prevent them from splitting and have stood for months in the shelter to dry out.

The choice of the skins for covering the drums was a matter of more importance than the choosing of the wood. . . . Today every good *Engoma* has its fetish rattling inside; these are popped in at the last moment by Kasimba himself, who sends away his men on some errand while he does it, thus preserving an air of mystery about the proceedings.

Today an ox is always slaughtered especially for its hide, although most of the old ceremonies are done away with. The fresh skin is dried in the sun for two days and then buried in the swamp for several days until it is soft and pliable and afterwards cleaned and scraped.

Inside the shelter a man is preparing the long thongs of twisted cowhide which will be used later to lash together the skins which cover both ends of the drum. When he has finished the long twisted cord will be hung outside from tree to tree to dry and then stored until it is needed.

Another man is cutting the covering skins. He cuts a circular piece of hide considerably larger than the top of the drum and another large star-shaped piece with four points for the bottom. The skin is still wet from its soaking in the swamp so that as it dries on the drum it will shrink and become taut.

He roughly fastens the two skins together over the drums, then fetches his awl and a length of twisted thong that he may begin the final lacing. This is slow work and will take him several days if the drum is a large one. When it is finished he will leave it for a week and then if necessary tighten up the thonging; then, if it is to give out one particular note in a battery of drums he will tune it by driving little wedges of wood under the thongs.

A long band of hide is fixed to the drum by which it may be carried or hung in the drum-house, and two loops through which to thrust the drumsticks. Today these are all of wood but in the old days certain of the royal drums were beaten with human bones from victims slain for the purpose.

As well as the *Engoma* type of drum there is also the *Engalabi* or dancing drum. This is a long cylindrical drum some three or four feet high. The head is larger than the rest and is about eight inches deep. This is covered with the skin of the . . . water lizard pegged round about an inch below the top. The whole length of the drum is hollowed out and as it is not covered with skin or thonging is smoothed and polished on the outside to a much higher degree than the *Omulugwa* or the *Engoma*. The bottom end of the *Engalabi* widens out again into a flange, and this is left uncovered. These drums used also to be played by the Baganda to cheer them on the march.

THE POTTER

Possibly it was because of the rarity of these craftsmen in the early days that they were held in such high honour, so much so that in the times of human sacrifice when numbers of people were killed to the glory of the King the lives of the potters were always spared.

Cooking pots too, had an almost sacred value—were they not as a man's mother? . . .

The Baganda themselves all agree that the Banyoro are better potters than they are themselves, and a large number of the potters in Buganda are Banyoro, or their fore-fathers came from Bunyoro originally. According to their legends most of the crafts are not of local origin but their first workers came in from surrounding tribes. It is interesting that this should be so for it bears out the opinion which can but be formed from a study of their work today. Skilled workers though the Baganda can be, they show very little creative imagination or adaptability but are content to follow out old techniques and old forms without any real desire to put new life into them.

The pottery of Buganda can be divided into two main groups; coarse unglazed red earthenware and fine black pottery.

There are two types of earthenware pot in common use . . . the waterpots [and cooking pots. The waterpots] consist of an almost spherical bowl over a foot in diameter with a short neck some six inches across with or without a turned-out lip. . . . Cooking pots are bowls varying from one to three feet in diameter.

Near the towns the use of . . . [pottery cooking pots] is giving way to that of aluminum sauce-pans, for although these may cost four times as much they will last far longer. Some African women who can afford to buy sauce-pans, however, still say that food is better when cooked in . . . [clay pots]; while the peasants away from the towns would almost always use them.

Even in the towns . . . [pottery pots] are still more popular for water than the old tins and kettles which are the modern substitute. The water keeps cooler in them and, according to most African women, tastes better.

The fine black pottery is not commonly used by the Bakopi, the peasants; but can only be found in the households of the rich. Nowadays it is being made for sale to Europeans. It is very fine and delicate, and, considering that it is all coiled pottery, for the wheel is not yet used in the country, its shape is almost perfect. Unfortunately it is very porous and brittle owing to bad firing.

There are many more variations of shape than in the common red earthenware. Bowls of various sizes and slightly different shapes are made to hold vegetables and sauces... such are small waterpots with long narrow necks copied from gourd shapes ... milkpots of the same shapes as the wooden ones made by the Banyankole.

It can safely be stated that during the last thirty years no new shapes or types of pottery have come into being in this country with the exception of a few freak copies of European flower vases, candle sticks and ash trays; this in spite of such a sudden influx of tableware and ornaments from Europe and Japan as can seldom have happened before in history. The average Muganda potter has as yet realised no connection between his own work and imported china, and refuses to believe that it is also made of clay and by similar processes to his own.

If no new types of pottery have been evolved technical methods are also at a standstill.

Although communities of potters are to be found in certain districts, small individual potteries are to be found in all parts of the country. Where there are good clay deposits a number of potters will tend to congregate, and as the craft is to a large extent hereditary sons will set up on their own in the district in which they have grown up. Any youth may apprentice himself to a potter without payment of any kind, but as a general rule the craft will run in families.

• 56 • *Some Commonplace Crafts*

HARRY H. JOHNSTON

CANOE-BUILDING

The Uganda *canoe,* like the Uganda house and road, is a thing peculiar to Uganda. The germ of the idea possibly may be seen in the tube-like vessels which ply on all parts of the Albert Edward, and which, like the canoes of the Baganda, are made of boards sewn together with thongs. The foundations of the boat consist of a keel made from the long, slender stem of a tree, which may be as much as fifty feet long. The keel is straightened and slightly warped, so that it presents a convex aspect to the water. This long tree-trunk is a semicircular hollow, the interior having been burnt out with fire, aided by the chipping of axes, and it is of sufficient girth to form by its breadth the bottom of the canoe. The prow end of the keel projects for a considerable distance out of the water sloping upwards, as the Baganda generally load more heavily the after part of the canoe. Along the rim of the hollow keel the first long plank of the canoe side is fixed at an angle of perhaps twenty degrees. Its bottom edge is firmly *sewn* to the upper rim of the keel by fine wattles, made generally of the flexible rind of the midribs of the raphia palm. Innumerable holes are pierced in the lower edge of the board and the upper rim of the keel with a red-hot spike of iron. A small pair of iron pincers draws the thin wattle through these holes, and in this way the board which is to form the first plank of the canoe sides is firmly fixed to the edge of the keel. A second and broader board is again sewn to the upper edge of the first one. When this has been repeated on both sides, the canoe is made, but it is rendered firmer and more stable by the insertion of the transverse poles which serve as seats and stays. The prow and the stern are finished off by another hollowed half-cylinder of wood stitched to the ends of the planks. The prow end of the keel is also strengthened by a long bent pole with a backward twist

[Adapted from *The Uganda Protectorate*, Vol. 2, Hutchinson, London, 1904. Pp. 659-664, 657-658. Used by permission.]

being securely fastened to the keel. The top of this prow is generally ornamented by a pair of horns, and it is steadied by a stout rope being carried tightly from the uppermost point of the prow to the nose or beak of the canoe. Along this string hangs a fringe of banana filaments or bunches of grass. The joins in the planks and between the lower planks and the keel are generally covered by narrow rods on both sides, over which the bast which makes the stitches is tightly tied. Finally, the outside of the canoe is given a coat of grease to stop up chinks and holes, and is further smeared with red clay both inside and out, so that the canoe is sometimes almost the colour of vermilion.

It is curious that with all these ingenious notions about boat-building, the Baganda have never conceived the idea of using sails, and even now, when they are familiar with Arab daus on the lake and European sailing vessels, they still prefer to propel their canoes entirely by paddles. The paddle, unlike so many Uganda implements, is not particularly artistic in shape or design, nor has it that charming ornament characteristic of the canoe paddles of Benin. The paddles are stout and strong, with a heart- or spade-shaped blade, about three to four feet in length, and cut out of a solid piece of wood. Like the canoe, they are generally smeared with fat and red clay. All these canoes and planks are *hewn*. No such thing as a saw exists anywhere in Negro Africa, unless where introduced by Europeans. Planks are often obtained by splitting tree-trunks by means of wedges, and adzing down the thick layers of wood to the required thinness.

WOODWORK

The Baganda carpenters now make chairs after the European model—in fact, a curious relic of the Speke and Grant expedition remained in the perpetuated camp stools. These useful articles were much admired by the Baganda, and after the departure of Speke and Grant two or three which were left behind in the possession of Mutesa were imitated over and over again by the carpenters, and now no person of importance is without one of these portable seats. . . . Gourds are cut into many different shapes for drinking vessels, or are left in their natural form to serve as bottles and beer calabashes. The exterior of these gourds is also covered with ornament drawn by means of red-hot needles.

Another article in which they display exquisite taste is the long tube made simply of a hollowed cane with which they suck up banana beer (the object being to draw up only the liquid into the mouth, and not fragments of pulp or rind). This cane is enclosed in a covering of tightly plaited straw, many different colours being used in the plaiting, the result being a really exquisite piece of workmanship. Wooden spoons of quaint shape are cut out of solid blocks of the same hard wood which is used for canoe planks, and ladles are made of the same material.

BASKETRY

Basketwork is also much developed amongst these people. . . . Many of the plaited baskets of black and white straw are charming in design. . . . Some of their workmanship makes one imagine that a fine chainwork of bast or the stiff rind of palm midribs may have preceded goldsmiths' work in early days, and have been imitated by the goldsmiths subsequently. The Baganda will make necklaces composed of links of palm rind fitting one into the other, and resulting in a chainwork of extraordinary suppleness and finish.

The Baganda make mats of three kinds ordinarily. In the Sese Islands bundles of papyrus stalks are roughly fastened with bast string. The result is a soft mat of great springiness and by no means of ugly appearance, as the dry papyrus fades to a pleasing grey-green. Elsewhere in Uganda very finely-plaited mats are made, the finest form of all being something like the Swahili "mikeka," which is varied by charming patterns of different coloured dyes. The material out of which most of the finer mats are made is the fibre derived from the fronds of the *Phoenix* or raphia palms. The Baganda make excellent ropes, almost good enough for exportation; also string of various degrees of fineness. The rope is generally made from the fibre of a species of *Hibiscus,* of *Sanseviera,* and of the bast of raphia and date palms. The string is made of various kinds of bast or hemp.

LEATHERWORK

Leather is dealt with successfully in the making of sandals, and occasionally of caps, boxes, or the tops of drums. Skins of wild beasts are beautifully dressed, being rendered perfectly soft and supple on the undersurface. The hide is continually scraped with a knife till all the fibres are loosened, and it is then rubbed with sand and fat.

ROAD CONSTRUCTION

The Uganda road is like the old Roman road. It aims, or attempts to aim, straight at its destination, perfectly regardless of ups and downs. The natives never dream of negotiating a hill by taking the road around it by a gentle gradient. [The] roads are carried with tolerable correctness from point to point along the shortest route. It is when the Baganda come to one of their many thousand marshes that they show both perseverance and skill. . . . Uganda is a sort of "switchback-railway country," with lofty hills and broad valleys which are marshes choked with vegetation and often filled with magnificent forest. Across these marshes the Baganda build causeways, which, though perhaps not sufficiently strong for heavy wheeled traffic, are generally quite solid enough for foot passengers and people on horseback. [Their] weakness seems to lie in the perishable nature of the foundations. The immense quantity of papyrus leaves and branches which are thrown down at the bottom of the causeway rot by degrees and shrink in volume. This causes holes to form in between the poles. At the same time, one has only to travel in countries like Uganda outside the limits of Uganda civilisation to realise what a boon these dry roads are across the interminable marshes.

• 57 • Bark-Cloth Making

A. D. F. T.

It is probable that the Baganda brought with them to Uganda the art of making bark-cloth, and it has been fostered by them ever since; but it was not till the reign of Semakokiro, probably towards the end of the 18th Century, that they covered their nakedness, inadequately concealed by skins, with bark-cloth, which they adopted as a national dress. In the reign of Mutesa (1857-1884), that remarkable person allowed certain favoured people to substitute cotton clothing for bark-cloth, but it was abandoned by the general public in favour of European materials only in comparatively recent times. Yet even to-day it is very commonly used as clothing by women of the upper classes in their homes, and generally by the poorer people.

As blanket, mattress, shroud, bundle-wrapping and so on, it is invaluable. And Europeans, attracted by its rich shades of red-brown and its texture, employ it for panelling, cushions, chair seats, blotters, calendars, and such other things as an imaginative mind may suggest. They even employ those on which patterns are described . . . as wall decorations.

It was Zakaliya who first showed me the

[Adapted from "Bark-Cloth Making in Buganda," *The Uganda Journal,* Vol. 1, No. 1, Kampala, 1934. Pp. 17-19. Used by permission.]

method of making bark-cloth. Awakened early one morning on *safari* by the woodpecker tap of his mallet as it came across the quiet valley, mingling with the lowing of cattle and the sound of women's voices as they hoed their fields, I got up to investigate. Picking my way along a narrow path between walls of dew-drenched elephant grass, cheered by the jolly song of a black chat [a common bird], I presently emerged into a clearing. There he was, squatting in a low thatched shed open on three sides, hammering a bark-cloth . . . on a log which stretched the 18 feet of the shed's length. The disreputable remains of a brown felt hat sat on his head, his face was spattered with latex from the beaten bark and his hands moved only quicker than his tongue. Two merry eyes twinkled when he saw me. "Good morning, Sir, you are up early this morning," he said, laying down his mallet, his old face creasing into a thousand wrinkles of a toothless but altogether charming smile. "My luck's in to-day that you should come and visit me." "But mine will be in too, Zakaliya, if you will tell me how you do your work," I replied. Now, Zakaliya was not only an artist in his trade but a born showman, and it was a lucky fate that led me to him. Not only did he like describing the process of bark-cloth making, but he enjoyed the superiority which the telling gave him in the eyes of the curious, who by this time had gathered round. "That I will!" he exclaimed. And, prompted by occasional questions, he shewed me in the next day or so the mysteries of an art centuries old. "Of course," he began, "I am making only a small barkcloth and working on it myself. I began at 7 o'clock and should finish by 12. This came off a small tree; but if I had taken the bark of that tree," pointing to one 12 inches in diameter and uniform in thickness to a height of ten feet, where it branched, "I could get two bark-cloths, and others yield three or even four. And sometimes two or three of us work together on a big barkcloth. Well, suppose we begin with the bark removed from the tree and ready for con-

verting into cloth. . . . I first begin beating it on the underside with this mallet . . . whose face, as you see, has big grooves," holding up a mallet with a 9-inch handle and a head shaped like a mill-stone, 6 inches across and 3 inches deep. "When the underside has been beaten twice, the upper surface is then beaten twice. That is, the bark is laid on this log . . . and then hit with a mallet backwards and forwards from one side to the other, the mallet changing hands in the middle of the cloth and every square inch receiving attention." He started with it rolled up at his feet and gradually unrolled it as he beat, pushing it over the log away from him rather as a sewing machine moves on material as it is sewn. When he had beaten it on both sides, he folded it in half and beat it again using more force; and before he had finished with the . . . [coarser mallet] the bark was folded into four thicknesses. The next mallet with finer grooves came into use and the bark—which had begun to assume the appearance of cloth—was folded yet again into eight thicknesses. Zakaliya then hit with greater force and the cloth rapidly increased in width. The process was then reversed as the bark-cloth was gradually unfolded and the beating progressed. Small sections of cloth were folded into pads and beaten with great energy, and the unfolding went on steadily.

When the cloth has been beaten as much as is good for it, and all moisture is expressed, it is spread in the sun for 5 to 15 minutes, according to the strength of the sun. It then has its final beating . . . with the third and last mallet . . . whose grooves are the finest of all, the bark-cloth being opened out entirely for this beating. All mallets are made of . . . a very hard, tough, white wood. Incidentally, these last for years and when not in use are kept carefully tied up in old bark-cloth. One beating on each side completes the third stage, and the cloth is then spread in the sun for some hours to dry out thoroughly.

Next day it is left in the sun all day to be coloured, since the colouring is done purely by the sun, except in Buddu where the process is helped by steaming . . . mainly the varying shades of red are obtained by leaving the cloth in the sun for varying periods—several days in the case of the very dark red cloths.

When the colouring process is completed, the cloth is left out in the night air for a couple of hours, from about 6 o'clock to 8 o'clock, to get damp. Next morning it is folded into a strip about 8 or 9 inches wide and kneaded with the hands and fingers for a couple of hours, by which time it should be soft and ready for sale, after tears have been mended with bark fibre and any necessary patching has been done.

Social Organization

and Interaction

»»»

In our study of the important patterns of association, such as the family, the clan, the political complex, religion, and social class, mention will be made of the relationships connected with them (husband-wife, clan chief-member, king-subject, and priest-worshipper). The accounts frequently describe in considerable detail just what roles, or behavior patterns, people who hold a particular status are supposed to follow under certain circumstances. The norms, sometimes in the nature of taboos, set rigid limits on the performance of these roles. Furthermore, with the Baganda, as with the Eskimo and the Navajo, the social values are the bases for the determination of social position.

Previous selections have necessarily touched upon some phases of Baganda society. Economic life in particular cannot be considered apart from the social system in which it is found. However, the identification of the different patterns of association, their interrelations, and the ideology behind them have yet to be presented. In this introduction a schematic picture of Baganda society will be given. Subsequent selections will provide more detailed material about Baganda social institutions.

The kind of social interaction most often dealt with is accommodation, or the adjustment of social statuses and roles to the new practices from Western Europe. An interesting case study in social control is found in Selection 68, in which sanctions against traditional native marriage arrangements are taken up.

The Baganda family is the foundation of Baganda society as well as the basic economic unit. The family may be either monogamous or polygynous, the latter being a strongly entrenched institution that has survived despite missionary efforts to outlaw it. A man pays a bride-price for a wife. This does not mean that women are classed as simple purchases; rather, the bride-price is a means of making marriage more stable. The missionaries recognize this value of the bride-price and encourage the custom. Residence after marriage is patrilocal. The husband is traditionally the head of his family. His position has weakened somewhat in recent years, but he still usually dominates his household.

The biological family is the basic social unit for the Eskimo and Navajo also. However, a polyandrous Eskimo family, an extended Navajo family, and a Muganda with perhaps ten wives appear to have little in common. The difference seems greater when the rules of residence are considered. The Eskimo family may move away to another village, the Navajo family almost always stays near the wife's kin, whereas a Muganda brings his wife to his own house. The details vary greatly, but the family core, husband-wife-children living together fairly permanently, always remains.

The Baganda are organized into clans as well as family units. The simplest definition of a clan is that it is a unilineal descent group; that is, it traces relationship through one parent only and forbids marriage within this line of descent. The Navajo clan, described in some detail previously, is matrilineal. The Muganda, on the other hand, takes his clan membership from his father unless he is the descendant of a king (Kabaka). The Kabaka must marry a commoner and his children take the clan of their commoner-mother. Kingship passes from clan to clan, so that no one clan becomes dominant.

Each Muganda, except the descendants of kings, is a member of a patrilineal clan. Some twenty-nine clans still exist of the thirty-six that were functioning eighty years ago. Clans are strongly exogamous—marriage within the clan is still unthinkable. The economic and religious functions of the clan, once important, are now much weakened. Their former economic significance was in the control of land by the clan and the sharing of goods and services by clan members. Clan temples and priests have been replaced by Christian churches and missionaries. A clan member still has his totem, but most of its religious significance has been lost. Clan chiefs still hold office, but the position, stripped of most of its economic and religious powers, is not important.

Kingship, hereditary through the male line, was well established in Buganda when the first white explorers arrived. The king's power was absolute. In addition to his temporal power, the king was also semi-holy. When he died, he became a national god. The British policy was to take away the absolute power of the Baganda king while backing him as a limited ruler. Their king is still the symbol of Baganda unity.

In the old days, the prime determinant of high social status was royal favor. All high officers had to curry the king's favor with extravagant praise and frequent presents. Lesser officers in turn promoted their interests with presents to the higher officials, and this system extended down to the lowest social level. Wealth, then, could be used to increase one's status but did not directly measure social standing. British control has greatly decreased bribe-taking by officials. Ownership of property is now one of the more important determinants of status.

Certain craftsmen had fairly high status in pre-British times, as was indicated in the preceding selections. In modern times, those with the most formal schooling are likely to have fairly high prestige. However, it is the occupation for which schooling qualifies one that determines status, not knowledge in itself.

Before the missionaries came, much of Baganda religion was closely tied to family, clan, and king. Each family had its shrine and household god; each clan had its temple, priest, and clan gods; and the dead kings and other high gods were national figures. Ancestor worship was basic to all this. All gods except the highest were once Baganda people. They protected their living descendants if the living performed the correct religious rites. Missionaries from the Church of England, the Roman Catholic Church, and the Mohammedan religion have nearly destroyed this part of Baganda beliefs. However, the less formalized magical and religious practices still survive. These include fertility rites, amulets, fortune telling, and black magic.

Mythology helped hold the social structure together. Legendary history told of the past glories of the Baganda. Each king was given his share of noble exploits. The kingly line itself was traced back to a mythical tribal founder. There were also moral fables that showed the advantage of following the approved rules of life. Proverbs, as the distilled wisdom of the past, justified particular actions in the present. In addition there were many folk tales that were purely for entertainment.

In brief, an average Muganda in pre-Christian times had loyalties to his family, clan, and king. Ties to each of these were forged by custom, precept, religion, and royal authority. English dominance over the Baganda led to modifications in the social structure. Although some of the following selections will criticize various British policies, Buganda is often cited as the model native African kingdom.

Harold B. Thomas and Robert Scott, authors of Selections 53, 58, and 70, were administrative officers in the Uganda Protectorate Government. Their comprehensive reference book *Uganda* is the modern counterpart of Sir Harry Johnston's two-volume work *The Uganda Protectorate*. Four of the selections on social organization and one on cultural change are by Lucy P. Mair. Dr. Mair, a social anthropologist at the London School of Economics, is an authority on colonial administration, and her field work in Africa has included intensive investigation of Buganda.

· 58 · The Family

HAROLD B. THOMAS AND ROBERT SCOTT

THE FAMILY THE BASIS OF THE SOCIETY

The economic unit in native society is for the most part still the family and not the individual. The maintenance of the customary standard of living, and, in particular, the production of both foodstuffs and marketable crops, normally represents the well-balanced efforts of the members of a household from the time when they have the strength to uproot a weed. In most areas of the Protectorate other than Buganda the continued occupation of a plot of land is entirely due to the family's energy in keeping their preserves under cultivation, and individual ownership (as we understand the term) of

[Adapted from *Uganda*, Oxford University Press, London, 1935. Pp. 277-283. Used by permission.]

the sources of wealth, land and cattle, is never absolute. In Buganda the titles of estates secured to natives by the Uganda Agreement of 1900 . . . have unquestionably been granted to individuals, with the result that a foreign conception of individual ownership of land has been introduced. Similarly, the advancement of the country both intellectually and materially has stimulated individual enterprise and produced a wage-earning class. These changes, however, have had little effect on the basic economic fabric: the estates are being split into family holdings and the wage-earners still maintain their links with the soil through their families. It may, perhaps, be well to emphasize the fact that the native family economy has no relation to 'communism'. Each family's interests are carefully defined and jealously guarded, and communal action which limits proprietorship, such as the accumulation of common grain reserves against a famine, is neither spontaneous nor welcome.

It may be explained that the term 'family' used above should be understood in its restricted sense, as describing a number of persons living together, and forming one household. In the majority of tribes a larger family consisting of all persons having a common grandfather, or sometimes greatgrandfather, is recognized, and its head, usually the senior male representative but sometimes a member elected by the rest, has certain responsibilities, rights, or claims on his descendants. . . . Commonly, however, the family in its economic aspect consists of a household, but here it should be made clear that this term does not necessarily imply a group of persons consisting only of a husband, a wife, and children. The old custom of polygamy still survives, chiefly among the pagans and Muhammadans, but also among Christians. . . . Where a household contains more than one wife, the women's work is sometimes undertaken as a common task and apportioned fairly between both or all, as in Bunyoro; sometimes the husband hoes a food plot of sufficient size for each wife, which she afterwards plants and tends, as among the Lugbara. Usually, however, the household consists of a married man, his wife, children, female dependents, who may include his deceased brothers' widows, and their children. There are now no slaves, although some Nilotic households still include an unexplained male member, who prefers to retain his subordinate status rather than renounce the privileges enjoyed by even the servile members of a family. Paid servants are rarely found in native households anywhere in Uganda.

DIVISION OF LABOUR WITHIN THE FAMILY

The division of labour within the family is still based to a large extent on custom, although the traditional apportionment of tasks has been modified by the large increase in the production of marketable crops. . . . The common belief that the male Bantu recline at ease with their pipes and gourds of beer while their women folk work for them is a half truth, based on imperfect observation. The men's work is usually performed between dawn (6 a.m.) and 8 a.m. and between 4:30 and 6 p.m., and is not necessarily continuous throughout the year. These hours are very generally maintained, and natives have on occasion given up profitable small-holdings which they were required to cultivate on scientific lines rather than perform the few hours' additional labour necessary daily. The lighter work of the women is spread more evenly over the day, although some of their tasks also are seasonal. Although the men have therefore greater opportunity for enjoying themselves as they please than their women folk, it need not be assumed that their share of the work is less exigent of their energies than the women's.

It is of interest to note the apportionment of the family work among the Baamba, who form perhaps the most primitive Bantu tribe in the Protectorate. The husband builds and maintains in good repair a hut for each of his wives and for any children who sleep away from their mother. He clears the ground for new plots and cuts down or destroys trees where necessary. From the wood he fashions spoons and porridge-sticks. He manufactures the family's supply of bark-cloth, beer, and drums. Finally, he hunts and traps animals for food. The wife cultivates the food plots and keeps them weeded, and collects edible grubs and ants. Her regular daily tasks consist of attending to the younger children, gathering the firewood, drawing water, and cooking. She also makes bowls and pots of clay, and baskets. If her husband leaves home on a visit she accompanies him in order to carry his loads. The elder unmarried children assist their father or mother, according to sex, while the younger boys herd the goats and sheep.

A division of household labour on this basis was probably general among the Bantu tribes before the introduction of economic crops. To-day the woman's share of the work remains [much] the same, while the man's is almost completely altered. The limitation of hunting has made one of his chief occupations into an occasional sport, and the importation of cheap cloth and implements has made it more profitable for him to earn money and provide for the family's needs in the market than to engage in home manufacture. The men, therefore, either adopt some trade, such as carpentry, or grow economic crops. The women have no part in the technical work of their men folk, but they frequently take some share in the cultivation of marketable crops. In most tribes labour on the economic crops is shared in much the same manner as the work of food production: the husband does the initial clearing and the wife the planting and weeding. It is, however, not uncommon to employ hired labour for the hard work of the clearing operations.

There is no evidence that has come to notice to show that any class of work is regarded as 'tabu' to either sex among the tribes of the Protectorate. Among many of the tribes there is now little sign that a rigid distinction between 'manly' spheres of labour and 'womanly' spheres of labour ever existed. The more important Bantu peoples, the Baganda, Basoga, and Banyoro, for example, do not consider it proper that a woman should engage in the building of a house, cattle herding, butchery, beer brewing, or bark-cloth making, but have no strong antipathy to the undertaking by men of tasks normally regarded as women's, except perhaps the cultivation of food crops after the spade-work has been done. Where cattle are considered a mark of social superiority, there is a distinct tendency to exclude women from any work associated with them. . . .

POSITION OF WOMEN AND MARRIAGE

The woman's position in a native household is to a great extent secured by the fact that most marriages between natives are incapable of being easily dissolved. There are four recognized forms of marriage, into any one of which a native may enter, according to his spiritual beliefs. Under the Marriage Ordinance, he may either be married in a church duly licensed for the celebration of marriages, or, civilly, before a District Registrar of Marriage. If he chooses either of these alternative forms he may be punished as a bigamist if by native custom he has already married another woman, or if he should subsequently take a second wife. If he is a Muhammadan he will be married before a registrar who is usually the local *mwalimu* (teacher), appointed under the provisions of the Muhammadan Marriage and Divorce Ordinance, and his matrimonial affairs are throughout governed by Kuranic tradition. The majority of natives, however, adheres to the forms of marriage sanctioned by tribal usage.

DOWRY

Native custom almost always demands that the stability of the marriage shall be guaranteed by the transfer of certain property by the bridegroom to the bride's family. . . . The payment of the recognized 'dowry' by the husband to the bride's family is an essential part of the marriage, and may be said to 'legalize' the union.

The payment of 'dowry' has frequently been misrepresented as the payment of a given price for the girl. As has been indicated above, however, the 'dowry' is in fact a form of insurance against the frivolous dissolution of the marriage by either party.

Even among the Baganda, who have been

most influenced among all the tribes of the Protectorate by European ideas and, in particular, by missionary teaching, the 'dowry' is still an essential element in marriage. The former principles governing its payment, and return in certain circumstances, have, however, undergone considerable modification, and it is now often regarded as being in the nature of a *douceur* to be retained by the father-in-law. The change is perhaps due to the fact that in Buganda the bridegroom as often as not pays in cash. Elsewhere the 'dowry' is usually assessed in cattle or goats, and is accompanied by several prescribed presents which probably had a ritualistic significance in the past but have none now. . . . The value of the 'dowry' ordinarily paid varies in different tribes, and in many instances a maximum has been established by the responsible Native Council. The actual amount required is subject to agreement, sometimes between the suitor and the girl's father, sometimes between the elders of the two clans concerned.

Once contracted in due form, most marriages are permanent. Their stability is not endangered to any great extent by the very frequent infidelities of both parties. Formerly, one of the most fruitful causes of bloodshed within a tribe was adultery, which was not, however, regarded as endangering the stability of the home, but as affecting the rights of the husband. The offence is now treated as a tort in the majority of native courts, and the guilty male is forced to pay handsome compensation to the injured husband. In default, he may be committed to prison, and if he repeats his offence more often and more

promiscuously than public opinion will tolerate, he may have to pay the compensation and go to prison as well. Exceptionally, Banyankole women are considered as being entitled, after marriage, to have sexual intercourse with whomsoever they please. Elsewhere the guilty wife is usually beaten by her husband, with the full approval of her family. Sexual promiscuity not affecting the marriage bond is deprecated by most tribes but very widely practised. It does not usually involve the parties concerned in any court proceedings, although if pregnancy results the male is usually fined, or forced to marry the girl, or to pay compensation to her family. There is, however, no moral stigma attached either to adultery or to fornication. The ease with which legal proceedings in the tribal courts can be brought prevents contentions between the various parties concerned from becoming a disruptive element in society.

The solidarity of the family in economic matters is complete, in that there is a place in the domestic organization for every member whatever his relationship to the head of the household may be. As each family is self-supporting, there are no unwanted children and no poor. Aged relatives are always sure of some means of support; and, except where missionary teaching has been most intensive, there is no material distinction between 'lawfully' born and 'illegitimate' children. The young man can be reasonably sure that his family will assist him in providing a 'dowry' against the time of his marriage; and the young woman has the protection of her family at all times.

• 59 • *Marriage in Buganda*

LUCY P. MAIR

MARRIAGE AS A PROBLEM OF CULTURE CONTACT

Adherence to the Christian code in matters of sex is often taken as the acid test of a genuine conversion; but the conflict between this code and the values implicit in the native social structure has led in Africa to the open rejection of this aspect of

[Adapted from "Native Marriage in Buganda," *International Institute of African Languages and Cultures, Memorandum 19,* London, 1940. Pp. 1-17, 22-29, 31-33. Used by permission.]

Christianity as inacceptable, expressed in the foundation of numerous independent churches permitting polygamy) . . . In popular terminology the word 'polygamy' is usually taken to mean any departure from the Christian standard of an exclusive sexual partnership between one man and one woman, deriving ethical as well as legal recognition in the eyes of the community from the ceremony which signalizes its inception. As one hears it used by Europeans in Africa, it may cover the faithful observance of a contract made in due legal form, but involving obligations other than those imposed by the Christian ceremony, acts of adultery which do not lead to the dissolution of marriage, re-marriage after a divorce in recognized form, mere sexual promiscuity, or the transient non-legalized unions for a period of cohabitation and economic co-operation that have been observed to be on the increase in modern conditions in many areas. In the same way the adjective is used indiscriminately of an African who marries two wives and a European who had a wife and a mistress, and it is assumed that the common element in the two cases is an indulgence of sexual passions beyond the bounds set by the Christian code.

At the present day the people as a whole can be said to be nominally Christian. That is to say, the public practice of the pagan religion and the open profession of its dogmas are entirely abandoned, the king is a member of the Native Anglican Church, and the position of Christianity as the official religion is manifested in the various understandings whereby quotas of posts under the native government are reserved for Protestants and Roman Catholics respectively. I have been told by missionaries and native clergy that in the outlying regions there are still many pagans. . . . There is a Moslem minority, but Christianity is necessarily the religion of all who have had more than a rudimentary education, since the whole educational system is based on the activity of Christian missions.

Thus every individual Muganda is logically committed, on the basis of a vow made in childhood, or possibly by others on his behalf in infancy, to Christian standards of conduct.

Boys and girls who are baptized while at school are asked before the ceremony to promise, the former that they will keep to one wife, the latter that they will refuse to live with a husband who brings in additional women to his household; and those who are baptized in infancy are later asked to make the same promises. As a preliminary to confirmation, the conduct of the candidates must be declared satisfactory by a committee.

Departures of all kinds from Christian standards are a frequent topic of sermons, particularly by the native clergy, who usually class together as the typical manifestations of pagan behaviour . . . breaches of the sexual code, . . . drunkenness, and recourse to divination by the mediums of the pagan deities. Backsliders are not refused admission to church services, the argument being that church attendance may lead them to repent. Whether they are refused communion I am doubtful. The attempt to apply this sanction impartially might lead to highly embarrassing situations with important personages; I saw one such personage at the Christmas Communion service at N——, who to my knowledge and to that of the entire native community, has nine wives in addition to the lady who sat at his side.

The conclusion of a marriage according to native custom, even though the marriage may be monogamous, is condemned by the Church partly on the ground that the religious ceremony and the Christian vows are essential elements in the marriage of Christians, and partly because the native celebrations involve the consumption of beer.

In the case of its own employees the mission can take disciplinary action against breaches of the Christian code. . . . In the little communities of teachers and clergy, with a group of Europeans as nucleus, formed by the principal mission stations, one sees a much closer adherence to Christian norms than elsewhere. Here the sanctions are operative which are probably the strongest incentives to conformity at home—an effective public opinion (based on the genuine conviction and example of the European group) and the fact that deviation from the accepted norms leads to loss of status and possibly of income.

In the training of native clergy, who for the past ten years or so have been expected to attain a fairly high educational level, ideals of the matrimonial relationship are stressed which go beyond the mere observance of the marriage vows—such as equal companionship, respect for the wife, sharing of property, and joint administration of income.

In Uganda, as in England, the norms inculcated by the Church are not identical with those enforced by the State. The High Court has ruled that an African who has accepted Christianity has thereby abandoned the right to contract a marriage in accordance with native custom, and it would seem to follow that the only marriage which a Muganda can legally contract is one in accordance with Protectorate law. This, of course, permits civil as well as religious marriage, but in practice those Baganda who bind themselves to a monogamous marriage invariably go through the religious ceremony. The State, however, will divorce parties who have been married by the Church, on grounds determined by Protectorate law; but the Church will not bless a second marriage of a divorced person. The grounds on which divorce can be obtained are more limited than was the case in England even before the recent amendment of the law. A husband can divorce his wife for adultery; but a wife is only entitled to a divorce if the husband's adultery is aggravated by incest, bigamy, cruelty, or desertion. She may also, as in England, divorce him if he is guilty of rape, sodomy, or bestiality; and if he abandons the Christian religion and contracts a polygamous marriage. . . . Thus a Muganda seeking divorce must go to the High Court. Only three or four such cases have occurred.

Sanctions of political nature for Christian marriage also operate through the organs of the native administration. The law which the native courts administer nowhere explicitly provides for this. They have instructions, issued in 1923, to hear no claims arising out of a second marriage by a man who already has contracted a Christian union; but neither Protectorate law nor the law of Buganda lays down that only a Christian marriage is valid, even in the case of baptized natives. However, in practice this is the only form of marriage which the native courts will recognize. Only one type of matrimonial case comes before them—that involving the abduction of a wife. The Native Adultery and Fornication Law . . . of 1917 established maximum penalties of 480s. for adultery and 600s. for the abduction of a married woman, the criminal penalty being imposed to prevent collusion by husbands in their wives' adultery in order to obtain damages, a practice that has developed in parts of East Africa where adultery is treated as a civil offence. The wording of this law makes it applicable both to Christian and native customary marriages, but it is the definite policy of the native government to apply it only to the former. The fine normally imposed is 200s., but even this would represent more than a year's cash income for many Baganda; and the liability of the adulterer to this heavy penalty is in native opinion one of the most significant characteristics of the Christian contract. Another way in which official disapproval of polygamy is shown is in connexion with the annual count of heads which the native authorities are required by the Protectorate Government to make. They are asked to report, among other data, the number of married and unmarried adults. In the case of a polygamous household, whether or not the wives have been formally married in accordance with native custom, all but one are returned as unmarried.

The institution of marriage in Ganda culture has the same three aspects as have been described in connexion with Christian marriage and with the form of marriage imposed by Protectorate law—a code of behaviour, involving on the one hand restrictions on the free play of sexual impulse and on the other positive rules of conduct between husband and wife, the conclusion of a contract in accordance with recognized forms, from which legal consequences flow, and sanctions for both code and contract. Though some points of the code may now be generally disregarded, it continues to command the theoretical approval of all Baganda; those who violate it do not defend their action by elaborating an alternative morality of their own. . . .

According to the Ganda sexual code, which still commands general respect in theory, however much it is disregarded in practice, girls should remain chaste up till marriage, and the responsibility for this is held to rest with their guardians. . . . Once a girl is betrothed her guardians are expected to be especially vigilant over her chastity, and her future husband should not visit her between the betrothal and the marriage. Should she be discovered to have had relations with another man during this period, he is held to be justified in repudiating the marriage. In the former marriage rites, now obsolete, the husband's female relatives inquired whether the bride had proved to be a virgin and reported the result to her parents, sending a present to her mother if this was the case. Breaches of this rule have never been regarded with great moral reprobation, though an unmarried girl who becomes pregnant passes through a temporary period of disgrace, and her lover is required to make formal amends to her parents. According to native custom a girl who becomes pregnant before marriage must sleep apart from the rest of the household, in a shelter built for the purpose, and cook her own food, which she eats alone. When the time comes for her to give birth her brother should take her to her lover, since the child must be born at the home of its father. After the birth normal relations with her own people are resumed after a formal meal in which the lover and the girl's parents share. If the lover does not marry the girl he is expected to pay compensation to her parents, but in the absence of any ideal of a single life-long sexual partnership, there is not held to be any obligation on him to marry her. Since every child, whether of a married or an unmarried couple, belongs to the clan of its actual father, the child is sent

to them when it is weaned, and the incident is then closed. One such incident would not prejudice a girl's chances of finding a husband; she would not, in short, be presumed to be promiscuous unless she was known to be so. If the lover does marry her he pays only the same amount in bride-price that he would otherwise have paid in compensation, namely, 10s. worth of beer or the cash equivalent.

Chastity for unmarried youths is not insisted upon, although they are warned against indulging in intrigues with married women.

The restrictions on sexual freedom imposed by marriage are of various types. Adultery with a married woman is an infringement of the husband's rights, which he was formerly held to be justified in avenging by assaulting the adulterer; he might, however, be content with compensation awarded by the chief. The Native Law of Fornication and Adultery quoted above is a deliberate attempt to adapt these rules to modern conditions; it represents a compromise between the native belief that the husband is entitled to compensation and the European fear that the right to compensation might lead to abuses, and in practice wronged husbands do seem to derive satisfaction from the punishment of the adulterer although they derive no material gain from it. Adultery by a wife would not, however, normally lead to divorce unless she wished to leave her husband for the adulterer; it would justify him in punishing her, either by beating or by neglect.

Adultery by the husband is not regarded as a breach of his obligation towards his wife. In special circumstances, according to Ganda beliefs, which are probably not now widely held, it was formerly considered to be subject to supernatural sanctions. Adultery by the father of an unweaned child was believed to result in the instant appearance in the child of an illness which rapidly became fatal if not cured by a ritual in which the man's mistress was required to take part. There was, however, no question in this connexion of the anger of any personified supernatural being at a moral offence; the illness was held to result automatically from the action.

This summary of the Ganda code of sexual behaviour shows that a certain specific emotional attitude which is fundamental to Christian teaching on the subject finds no counterpart in the native ideology. This attitude is extremely difficult to define, especially for a writer unversed in the language of psychology, but it can perhaps be described in terms of the doctrine that the body is the temple of the Holy Ghost. The effect of this doctrine is to place indulgence of bodily appetites, beyond the limits prescribed by the Christian code, in a separate category from other moral offences. To the Muganda breaches of the sexual code are wrongful actions from various points of view: they are not sins in the sense that they disturb the relationship of the guilty person with supernatural authorities, and the strength of the feeling which they arouse in disinterested persons is no greater than that attaching to the breach of other accepted rules. Theft would probably in general be more strongly condemned.

Associated with this attitude is the complete absence of the idea of romantic love, either as a necessary condition of marriage or as having marriage as its normal consequence. The fact that a youth is attracted by a girl might be a reason for seeking a liaison with her; it would never by itself be a reason for marrying her. When marriage is under consideration the young man deliberately sets out to look for a wife, and the merits of possible partners are dispassionately weighed.

In the marriage relationship the procreative and the economic aspects are stressed at least as much as the purely sexual. The sterility of a marriage is to-day a strong incentive to make further marriages, and a comment on a man who had taken additional wives after making a Christian marriage was, 'His Christian marriage is finished; his Christian wife no longer bears him children.' In the old days, when the division of labour between the sexes was strict, marriage was an economic necessity to an adult man, since the whole work of cultivation and cooking was done by women.

The wife is expected to take a subordinate position; she should obey her husband and he is entitled to beat her if she does not do so. The household is organized for his convenience; meals should be ready at the times when he likes to eat, and the wife should not cook for herself in his absence. She should ask his permission to go visiting, and if she goes away from home to sleep he fixes the number of days that she may be away. One effect of this relationship is that modern ideas of infant welfare are sometimes introduced by the instructions of the husband. There is, however, a definite conception of the dignity of the household; the husband should not abuse his wife in public; the wife should not tell tales of her husband. Moreover, the husband should listen to his wife's opinions; if he pays no attention to her it is said, 'He does not know she is his wife.' In modern conditions the woman has full control of any money that she may earn by her own efforts; in some households this extends to the receipts from a separate cotton patch; in others, though husband and wife may plant separate patches, the proceeds are pooled.

THE CEREMONIAL OF MARRIAGE

Where formal procedure is concerned the situation is easier to describe. A marriage which is valid by native standards is concluded by a series of formal transactions between the bridegroom and the bride's relatives; and the inauguration of married life is signalized by certain ceremonial actions. . . . The sequence of acts, however, is . . . still essential to the conclusion of a marriage whether or not the Christian ceremony is also performed.

The suitor first approaches the girl directly, and her consent is the necessary preliminary to his formal request for her hand. If she accepts him he announces his desire to marry her in a series of letters, each enclosing a present of money, addressed to herself, her father, mother, and the brother and father's sister designated by the girl, as well as any other relatives whom she may indicate; presents may be sent to a grandfather, and I have one case in which money was sent to a brother of the father. He may also make gifts of food—meat, salt, sugar, tea—to the girl's parents. If her relatives approve of him a day is fixed for his formal introduction to them. On this occasion the girl wears a complete outfit of new clothes which he must present to her. Accompanied by two or three of his own brothers and sisters, he appears at the house of the girl's parents, where her relatives are waiting. The girl's father's sister, speaking in the first person on her behalf while she remains modestly silent, presents him as the man she wishes to marry. The recognition that the girl acts on her own initiative is emphasized by phrases like, 'I have rebelled', 'This is the man who made me rebel' (*okujema,* to throw off authority, also used of a wife who disobeys or leaves her husband), 'I have found my master'.

The girl's brother then announces the amount of the bride-price which he has decided to ask. In addition to the bride-price proper (*omutwalo gwe nyini; omutwalo =* a head-load, the payment of 10,000 cowries made in the period immediately before the introduction of money) various specific presents have to be made. It is common for a lump sum in cash to be asked for, but when this is done these items are enumerated separately in showing how the total is reached. The obligatory presents consist in beer and a live goat for a feast to be made after the girl's departure to her husband, and a garment for the girl's mother. For the beer a tin of paraffin is now frequently substituted; the garment is usually a native bark-cloth—now an expensive item—but cotton clothes may be asked for. In addition the girl's brother may receive a *kanzu* (Arab-style gown) and her father's sister a bark-cloth. If the suitor feels quite unable to pay the amount demanded he may beg that it be reduced. It is recognized that, if this is done, it is done as a favour; there is no question of haggling, still less of the young man refusing to go on with the marriage

because the sum asked is too high. The sum must be paid before the marriage can take place. Sometimes the suitor brings money with him and hands it over on the spot; if not, a date is agreed upon before which it is to be paid. Four months was mentioned to me as the maximum allowable interval, a longer time being held to put too much strain on the girl's patience and her relatives' responsibility for keeping her chaste.

The ceremonial which now accompanies a non-Christian marriage owes more to the specifically European elements of the Christion wedding than to anything in the old Ganda culture. The bride goes to her husband by day, as at a Christian wedding; she may wear the European white dress and veil, and on arrival at her own house will sit at a table with her husband while tea is served and may cut a wedding cake. The characteristically non-Christian procedure is that instead of meeting her husband at a church, or—as in the most modern style—driving to church with him by car, she meets him in the road on the way to his house, and is there formally given to him by her brother; she kneels in token of submission while a drummer plays her husband's clan beat.

After the wedding the bride spends a period of seclusion, during which the work of the household is done by her husband's relatives. In the case of Christian weddings this period is usually a week; the wedding takes place on a Saturday, and bride and bridegroom appear in church on the Sunday a week later. I have no data on the length of the period in non-Christian weddings at the present time; in the past it is said to have been two or three weeks. The formal inauguration of the bride's duties as a wife is made when she serves the food at a feast the materials for which are provided, and the cooking done, by her relatives.

It is clear then that in Ganda culture marriage is an event of serious social importance. It involves careful consideration by both sides of the suitability of the partner, a considerable economic effort on the part of the husband, the conclusion of a contract before a number of witnesses all bound by the ties of kinship to one or other party, and a ceremonial inauguration of the new household.)

GANDA MARRIAGE IN PRACTICE

The effects in practice of the situation described are illustrated by the results of a sociological census taken at Bowa, the head-quarters of the *saza* (largest administrative division under the native government) of Bulemezi.

Of fifty-eight households (including those of unmarried men) within a radius of three miles of the *saza* head-quarters, eight, of which one was that of the Moslem mallam, comprised more than one 'wife'. (For the sake of brevity I follow a prevalent official practice in using the word 'wife' in inverted commas to describe any woman who is living in a man's house, cooking his food, and having sexual relations with him, irrespective of the existence of a contract of marriage between them. If the word is used without inverted commas it implies the existence of such a contract, valid either in European law or native custom.) In two cases there were three 'wives', in the others two. In three cases no formal marriage contract had been concluded. In four the bride-price had been paid, according to the husbands' accounts, for all the women, and in the remaining one the man intended to pay the bride-price of his second wife when he could afford it. In one case the husband had previously made a Christian marriage which had lasted for nine years.

Men living alone numbered nineteen. Of these one was a widower. Nine were married, but for various reasons their wives were not living with them. The number included a Munyoro who had come to Bowa four years previously and vaguely expected his wife to join him 'some time'. Of the remaining eight, four were Baganda, two men of 55 or more, two youths of 20 to 25. The rest were natives of other tribes, two of whom made the oft-heard statement that Baganda women made bad wives. Of seven women who lived alone three were widows,

two had left their husbands to come to Bowa, two had been left there by their husbands.

Of the remainder there were eleven monogamous households in which the original marriage was still in existence. Of these two had lasted over thirty years, two over twenty, three over ten, and the rest only a year or two. Six were Christian marriages, two native marriages, on three I have no data. There is also one case of a second marriage made six years ago by a man whose first wife had died.

There remain thirteen households in which there is only one 'wife', but no contract has been concluded by the couple. In all these except two, one or both of the partners is bound by a previous contract which has not been, and in the existing situation in Buganda, cannot be, dissolved. In four cases the man, and in one the woman, is married by Christian rites.

The salient features of the situation may be summarized by saying that roughly 9 per cent. of the households investigated are based on polygamous contracts of marriages, 19 per cent. on monogamous contracts, in 50 per cent. of the total the parties to a marriage contract are no longer living together, and in about half of these last one or both of the spouses has found a new partner.

From the headman of the neighbouring village of Kawagalo I obtained data on the marital condition of its forty-five households, which I had no opportunity of checking or supplementing by my own observations. Here the number of couples whose first marriage is maintained in being (29) represents a rather higher proportion than at Bowa, and that of persons separated from their original partners (16) a lower. There are three polygamists. Two of these had originally made Christian marriages. In one case both wives left their husband; in the other the Christian wife, who was commended for her good nature, had agreed to her husband's contracting two subsequent marriages, and the three wives lived together in amity.

Married couples may separate for various

reasons. A wife may leave her husband because he beats her, on account of quarrels with a co-wife or as a protest against the introduction of a second wife. The modern husband, who has to house all his wives under one roof, turns out an unfaithful wife, and a man may even send home a woman who has been married to him for some years if he is tired of her sexually and has found a more congenial partner. The separation sometimes occurs when a man moves to another district and leaves his wife behind. He then invariably finds a new 'wife'. Sometimes there is no open breach, but the illness of a parent or relative of that generation obliges a wife to go to visit the sick—the most compelling of kinship duties to the Baganda—and she simply does not return. But as this is the most respectable reason for the absence of a wife, it may frequently be advanced when it is not in fact the whole story. A wife who is ill may leave her husband on the ground that she will be better looked after among her own relatives, to stay with relatives who live nearer to a dispensary, in the hope of finding more effective native medicines, or because she attributes her illness to sorcery. If a child dies the possibility of sorcery is usually canvassed, and its mother, if she seriously suspects it, particularly if she has another child, may leave her husband.

Strictly speaking, she should go to the brother who presided over her marriage. But an alternative open to a woman who can claim any relationship, however remote, to an important chief—it is sufficient if either she or her husband is a member of the same clan as the chief, his wife or his mother—is to put herself under his protection. She can then enjoy the advantages of life at what the Baganda conceive as a pulsating centre of activity—'near the main road you never sleep'—with the possibility of occasional help from the chief or his wife and a plentiful source of casual labour and of temporary 'husbands' in the prison population. Women in these circumstances, however, do not practise prostitution. On the contrary, the 'husband' is often dependent on the woman for

his poll-tax. It seems that a woman rarely leaves her husband to go straight to another man; more often she finds a new partner after she has left him.

NATIVE ATTITUDES

In the daily life of the household and in social contacts outside it the position of the 'wife' is the same whether or not she is legally married. The economics of the Ganda village do not allow the luxury of the kept woman who ministers to her lord in nothing but sexual pleasure. In whatever way the partnership has been formed, the woman must cook, dig, and look after children if there are children in the household. A non-legalized partnership is socially recognized in that the man takes his 'wife' with him to mortuary ceremonies of his relatives—the only remaining Ganda occasion of public ritual. In popular parlance she has the title corresponding to our 'Mrs.' (*muka*, the wife of, used only with the husband's name). She may even take precedence of a legal wife.

Despite the weight of actively propagandist influence against the recognition of marriage by native custom of a contract to be taken seriously, the distinction between a formally contracted marriage and a casual union is perfectly clearly recognized. Just as it is more respectable to be married in church than not, so it is more respectable to have paid the bride-price than not, and the duration of a union also lends it respectability. Couples will often pretend that their association belongs to a more respectable category than is in fact the case. . . . In the case of couples neither of whom is already bound by a Christian marriage, the possibility is mentioned that 'some time' the man will be taken to the woman's relations and a bride-price payment arranged, but I have no data of actual cases. The characteristic to which importance is attached in any marriage which has been legalized by the bride-price payment is that the husband 'knows his relatives-in-law'; that is, the relationship has been formally acknowledged by the persons whose consent to it is legally required.

'Otherwise', said an old woman when lecturing a young man, 'you have no one to complain to if she leaves you. Do you call such a woman a wife?'

Informants will discuss the relative advantages of polygamy and monogamy on their merits independently of the religious sanction for monogamy. A quarrel between co-wives is usually the occasion for somebody to point out this disadvantage of the polygamous household. A series of essays by students at Makerere emphasized the economic burden of polygamy, and it is obvious that the greater the approximation to the European standard of living the greater this burden must be. In the villages, however, it would be difficult to calculate whether the cost of maintaining a wife, in terms of clothing and bought food, outweighed the contribution of her labour to the family income, and the main economic difficulty of the polygamist is that of raising the money for a second bride-price.

The arguments for Christian marriage are not identical with the arguments for monogamy, though there is an obvious point of contact where monogamy is advocated on religious grounds. The ultimate religious ground, that monogamy is ordained by God, is perhaps more often echoed in native comment than the more reasoned arguments used by European Christians; but it is not often echoed with the zeal of those who brought it to Africa. This occurs in abstract references to the subject; but when actual persons are under discussion, it would be unheard of for a man to be unfavourably criticized because he was a polygamist.

The most rational argument that one hears put forward in favour of the Christian contract is that it involves promises by the parties. Women, however, are by no means unanimous in holding that it is to their advantage to be bound by these promises; some regard Christian marriages as something better avoided owing to the heavy penalties for the abduction of a Christian wife, and one man told me that he could not find a woman who would agree to a Christian marriage.

To men, however, the important consideration in any marriage is the bride-price, which must be paid whether the contract is solemnized in church or not; hence to them the crucial question is not the type of contract to make, but whether to enter into a contract at all. One often hears comment on the heavy loss represented by the bride-price if the wife runs away after a few months; and there seems little doubt that this consideration is a strong deterrent to making a marriage contract.

THE COST OF MARRIAGE

I obtained statements of the amount paid in bride-price in eleven Christian and sixteen non-Christian marriages.

In the case of the marriages by native custom the amounts mentioned by informants range from 20s. to 200s. As the 20s. was paid in 1932 and the 200s. at the first marriage of a man who is now elderly, the data do not provide any evidence for an increase in the cash payment. The average payment was 90s.

In the case of the Christian marriages the average (obtained by calculating bride-price and presents separately where informants have given me separate figures) is 130s. Though this figure may be higher than the average payment for the bride-price proper, it is, of course, lower than the average total expenditure on presents to relatives-in-law. Since the two highest payments recorded are 300s. in 1919 and 260s. in 1914, there is here again no evidence of an increase in the amount paid.

But the cases quoted seem rather to support the view that Christian marriage is now an element in the standard of living recognized as suitable to the upper class, the class formed in this generation by the children of the wealthy (large landowners and native government servants) and the more highly educated (native clergy and teachers).

Christian marriage, in fact, as distinct from monogamous marriage, is now an element in that complex whole which may be described as the upper-class standard of living. A man who has had a secondary education and obtained the type of employment to which this is expected to lead, expects to make a Christian marriage as he expects to take his wife home to a house with cement walls and a corrugated iron roof and to provide both her and himself with a complete outfit of European clothes.

The class in which girls would take Christian marriage for granted is probably limited to the families of the really rich. Elsewhere parents and guardians regard it as something to be wished for, and congratulate themselves if it is attained. In practice the weight of pressure from parents and guardians is probably the strongest sanction for the conclusion of a formal marriage.

FACTORS CONTRIBUTING TO THE PRESENT SITUATION

The general picture which emerges from these data is of a society in which two types of marriage contract are recognized as binding, one being the distinguishing feature of an upper class; in which the norms of behaviour which are generally recognized as suitable are still the norms appropriate to the older type of marriage; and in which, in practice, these norms are widely disregarded. For this last state of affairs it is impossible positively to assign causes, or to say which of a number of influences have contributed most to produce it. It is possible, however, to indicate some of the influences which have combined to lead to this result.

The denial of legal recognition to a marriage by native custom, with its corollary, the denial of legal recognition to divorce carried out according to customary forms, has certainly been an important one. It means that no claim can lie for the recovery of bride-price, and thus the economic risks of marriage have greatly increased for the husband at the same time as its actual cost. This policy does not seem to have been a very potent factor in increasing the number of Christian marriages, while it has created a strong deterrent to contracting any marriage at all.

The greater freedom allowed to women is also undoubtedly an important contributory factor to the present state of affairs. This derives from three main sources: the influence of European ideas, modern economic developments, and the introduction of cheap transport.

It still happens that men beat both their wives and their daughters. But it is known that Europeans disapprove of this practice . . . Men do not like to impose the severe discipline of the old days, and women do not meekly accept it. Civilization, as they say, has raised the status of women.

It has also brought them economic independence in the sense that any woman can earn a money income by growing cotton. This can be expended on clothes—the one necessity for which in the old days women depended on their husbands—or it can be used to pay a man to do work such as building which a woman cannot do. Ganda women have never depended on men for heavy agricultural work. Thus women are now no more dependent than men on the marriage partnership for their economic necessities.

Finally, cheap and rapid transport makes it easy for a woman to disappear completely and thus throw off any irksome control. The importance of this factor may be gauged by the phrase that one hears of a girl who has 'gone to the bad', 'she goes to and fro with the buses' or 'she is lost among the bus-drivers'. The bus-driver is the Ganda counterpart of the British sailor with a wife in every port; of the one who had two of his wives at Bowa it was said, 'Who expects a bus-driver to pay bride-price?' The phrase sums up the weakening of sanctions that can only be enforced by personal contact, when circumstances provide a ready means of avoiding embarrassing contacts.

The weakening of the Baganda family, as described in the previous article, has been accompanied by a decline in ceremonies within the family. Before the effects of European contact were felt, the life cycle was elaborately ritualized. The period of embryonic development received especial attention in the taboos and ceremonies observed by the expectant mother. Birth and specific events during childhood were attended by various rituals. The following selection, by John Roscoe, presents a meticulous account of such ceremonies. Roscoe, an Anglican missionary of long experience in Uganda, led the Mackie Ethnological Expedition in 1919. He was a careful observer, excelling in factual description, but his value-judgments reflect his Victorian, ministerial background. For example, when he states that the Baganda child "received no moral training" and that "the mother's affection for it was not unlike that of an animal for its offspring," he is telling us more about himself than about the Baganda.

· 60 · Birth and Childhood
JOHN ROSCOE

Every married woman was anxious to become a mother, and expected to show signs of maternity within a few weeks of her marriage. A woman who had no children was despised, and soon became the slave and drudge of the household.

As soon as a woman knew that she was pregnant she consulted the medicine-man; and he would give her drugs to drink before she took her daily meals. In most instances the husband caused an elderly woman, one of his relations, to come and look after his wife until the child was born. In all cases it was the husband's clan who were specially interested in the pregnancy; they looked after the mother, and made her do whatever they considered to be best for the unborn infant. No woman might allow a man to step over her legs when she was sitting on her mat. Women were never permitted to sit on any raised seat; in fact, the introduction of stools even for men was of later date; both sexes formerly sat on the ground, upon which they spread either skins or mats. Women always sat with their legs placed together, and brought back from the knees, so that the feet were together under the knees to one side; if they wished to change their position, they leant forward on their knees, and moved their feet to the other side and sat back

again. Being taught from childhood to sit in this position, it was not difficult for them to continue thus for hours. For a woman to sit with her legs straight in front of her, or apart, was looked upon as unbecoming; and for any man to step over her legs was equivalent to having intercourse with her; the mere fact of stepping over a wife, or over some of her clothing, was a method frequently followed to end a taboo which necessitated intercourse. A pregnant woman had to be careful not to step over the mat or the feet of a man. Even peasant women were not allowed to sit in the doorway when a man entered the house; they had to move away, otherwise it was thought their condition might be affected, the child might be killed. When a pregnant woman wished to pay a visit anywhere, her husband would send with her a boy belonging to his clan, whose duty it was to beat the grass on either side of the path, if it was a narrow one, in order to take away any evil effects which a man passing beforehand might have left behind. She was not allowed to drink from or to touch any vessel from which a man had drunk, and she had to avoid any contact with the garments which a man had worn. It was looked upon as unfortunate if a pregnant woman came in contact with, or even

[Adapted from *The Baganda: an Account of Their Native Customs and Beliefs*, Macmillan, London, 1911. Pp. 46, 48-50, 54-64, 74-81. Used by permission.]

saw, any child that was not healthy and strong; wild animals also, such as monkeys, were to be avoided, lest they should affect the mother, and the child should be born with large deep-set eyes like the animals' If the woman laughed at a lame person it was thought that her child would be born lame. It was therefore deemed wise to keep wives within an enclosure and to limit the right of access thereto, so that all influences on the unborn child might be for good. During the period of pregnancy a woman had a number of taboos to observe; she was not allowed to eat certain kinds of food; and salt was also forbidden except one kind made from a grass which grows in the swamps, and obtained by burning this grass and washing the ashes and then evaporating the water. She was not allowed to eat any baked plantains, nor might she eat one particular kind of plantain (gonja) which was a favourite food either baked or boiled, certain kinds of beans, yams, the meat from the head of a goat, and an acid fruit (mutungulu) from the swamps. A woman in this condition had to drink a little water before she partook of any food, because it was thought that the child needed it, and that this would save it from being scalded by the food.

For some weeks prior to the birth the woman was daily smeared with butter, and rubbed to make her bones supple. When the time for birth arrived, the old woman called in some one to assist her, and if the birth took place by day, the mother was taken outside into the garden, or into the yard at the back of the house where the people washed. She held on to a plantain or other tree, the second woman stood by her, and supported her, while the other was ready to receive the child. As soon as it was born, it was laid upon a plantain leaf, and the midwife washed out its mouth. . . . In cases of cross birth they would send for a medicine-man, who would assist the woman by gently turning the child; if, however, he found this impossible, he would try to save the woman's life by removing the child. In most clans the first child born to a chief

was awaited with considerable anxiety, because it was thought that the birth of a boy indicated that his father would die; hence, if a male was born, the midwife strangled it, and gave out that it was born dead; in this way the chief's life was ensured, otherwise, it was thought, he would die. If a child was born feet first, it was strangled, for it was thought that it would grow up into a thief and a murderer, and would be a disgrace to its parents, even if it did not kill them. The body of such a child was buried at cross roads, and not in the family ground; it was called *Kija nenge*. If a woman disliked her husband, or if she had any quarrel with him, it might happen that she would try to kill the child during the time of delivery, either by crushing it, or by sitting on it. The midwives at such times threatened the woman, and went so far as to whip her if she did not remain in the best position for the delivery. . . . The afterbirth was called the second child, and was believed to have a spirit, which became at once a ghost. It was on account of this ghost that they guarded the plantain by which the afterbirth was placed, because the person who partook of the beer made from this plantain, or of food cooked from it, took the ghost from its clan, and the living child would then die in order to follow its twin ghost. The grandparent, by eating the food or drinking the beer, saved the clan from this catastrophe and ensured the health of the child. (It was thought that the grandparents, by eating the food or by drinking the beer from the plantains, retained the ghost of the afterbirth in the clan; whereas if a person belonging to another clan ate the food or drank the beer, he thereby carried away with him the ghost of the afterbirth.)

When there was a case of retarded delivery, the relatives attributed it to adultery; they made the woman confess the name of the man with whom she had had intercourse, and if she died, her husband was fined by the members of her clan, for they said: "We did not give our daughter to you for the purpose of adultery, and you should have guarded her." In most cases, however, the medicine-men were able to save the woman's life, and upon recovery she was upbraided, and the man whom she accused was heavily fined. As soon as the child was born, the midwife sent a boy, who had to be a younger brother of the child's father, to fetch a log of wood, which was placed upon the fire and kept burning for the first nine days after the birth. No one was allowed to take any fire or water from the house during the nine days. When they were completed, the log was cast away upon some waste land, and was supposed to remove any evil that might be in the house. No one was allowed to enter the house; the mother had her meals with the midwife, and was said to be lying in *alkali,* and to be unapproachable. When the nine days (or in the case of some clans, seven days) were ended, the woman went out to wash, and her house was swept, and cleansed from all traces of the birth. The woman sent the sponge, with which she washed, to her husband, and he sponged his private parts with it; but in some clans it was customary for the wife to perform this office for her husband. She then cooked a meal, which her husband and the midwife ate with her; after the meal the husband paid the midwife for her services either a goat or a barkcloth, and one hundred cowry-shells, whereupon she returned home. Later on, the husband jumped over his wife and ended the taboo; if he had intercourse with any of his other wives prior to observing these ceremonies, any child born to him would die. A wife lived apart from her husband for three years, while nursing her child; but if she was his only wife, she joined her husband and continued to nurse her baby.

It has been said, and is thought to be a fact, that men who have many wives have only small families by each wife. Certainly the time that was given in these clans to the nursing of each child must have tended to decrease the number of children that a woman could possibly have; still, as they married young, and many of them became mothers at fifteen, and often continued to bear children until they were well over forty,

numbers of them had large families. There are many women who are reported to have had ten and even twelve children where the husband had forty wives. Cases are also recorded of men having had as many as four hundred children. A man with one hundred children was not regarded as having a large family.

Each child had a nurse appointed to take charge of it soon after birth; this girl was expected to be in constant attendance upon the child, and to be ready to amuse it and keep it quiet. Peasant women observed the same rules at birth as chiefs' wives, the only difference being that they had to begin work again at the end of seven days, and lived with their husbands just as they had done before the birth took place. The mother also had to take care of her child, unless the husband could find some one from his clan to come and act as nurse for his wife. It was customary for each mother to take her child out at the first new moon after its birth, and to point out the moon to it; this was supposed to make the child grow healthy and strong. A baby was never put down to amuse itself until the ceremony of placing it on the floor had been performed by the husband's mother; she came at the end of about three months, early in the morning, and after scooping a shallow hole in the floor, placed a piece of barkcloth in it, and seated the child on the barkcloth. The child's mother cooked a feast; her husband and a few friends gathered together to see the ceremony, and afterwards ate the meal. In the evening the husband jumped over his wife to strengthen the child. . . . Until this ceremony of placing the child to sit had been accomplished, the nurse, or the mother, had to carry the child about, or to put it to lie down on its back. A child's early days were never very interesting; it had its bed of thick barkcloth on the floor, near its mother's bed, where a good part of the first three months was spent. It never had any clothing except a string of beads around its waist, and perhaps a string of beads or of wild plantain seeds around its neck; these were worn to give the child strength and to make its neck grow straight. A string was tied round its waist to keep its stomach from becoming too big; this was not tight, but it had medicine on it to protect the child from growing out of true proportions. It underwent its daily washing, which was performed as follows: the child was taken out near the door, a pot of warm water was brought by the nurse, two or three plantain leaves were spread out as a bath-mat, then the mother took the child by one arm, poured warm water over it, and rubbed it down. Sometimes, when the child was refractory and would not allow its face to be washed, she took its feet into her lap, rested its head on her hand, drew the water into her mouth, and squirted it over the child's face, while she rubbed it gently with her hand. No towel was used; the child had to become dry by draining and evaporation; after its bath it was taken into the house again. At the end of a few months children were fed with artificial food, in addition to being nursed; the food consisted chiefly of ripe banana boiled, or steamed, and mixed with milk; the mixture was plastered into the child's mouth as it howled and gasped for breath. From birth until the naming ceremony took place, a child never had its hair cut; the hair was carefully preserved, and often decorated with beads or cowry-shells. If one of the tufts of hair broke off, or was accidentally plucked off, it had to be tied on again, because it was unlucky to allow any hair to be lost until after the ceremony. The child was visited and watched over by the husband's relatives, who took the mother to task if it did not thrive as it should do. Children were never rebuked in early years, and received no moral training. When the time came for an infant to learn to walk, the grandmother came again and tied some small bells on its legs, which answered the double purpose of strengthening its legs, and also of inducing it to make an attempt to walk, in order to hear the bells ring. A child was carried on the nurse's or mother's back in a barkcloth sling, or, in later times, in one of calico; it sat with one leg on either side of the nurse's back, and its arms above the sling. When not in the sling it was put on the nurse's hip with one leg in front of, and one behind its nurse, and her arm around it, thus leaving the other hand of the nurse free for work. As soon as a child showed signs of teething, it was watched anxiously by the mother, for if it cut the upper teeth before the lower, this was regarded as an evil omen that it would ill-treat its mother when it grew up. Women carried their children on their backs in slings, and carried wood or water upon their heads. At home a child was allowed to lie upon the floor, and, when it grew older, it played in the dust; it was not trained in habits of cleanliness, and it grew up more like an animal than a human being; the mother's affection for it was not unlike that of an animal for its offspring. If a man divorced his wife, she was not allowed to take her child with her; it belonged to the husband, it was his duty to look after it as best he could. A mother who was nursing her child would tear it away from her breast, and pass it to her husband, saying, "Take your child." This seems to point to a lack of real love, as also does the fact that children were taken away from their mother after they had been weaned and had little or nothing to do with her afterwards. Still, children, as they grew up, had some regard for their parents; the father was at least feared and respected, while there was something approaching love shown towards the mother. No mother ever thought of kissing her child; there was nothing known among the people like kissing. She might hug it, and pat it, while it was small, when it was cross or had been hurt; and the child would cling to her for protection, when in danger, or turn to her to be comforted when in distress.

Children, when they were old enough to leave their mothers, were taken away to some member of the father's clan. They had, however, a warmer feeling for their mother than for their father. This can be accounted for by the fact that a father had often so many wives and children that the attention which he gave to them could only be of a general character, while the claim on the mother was more direct.

The next event of importance in a child's life was the naming ceremony . . . which gave it its standing in the clan, and it was on this occasion that its legitimacy was established once and for ever. The marriage of the parents was unimportant compared with this ordeal of proving the child's legitimacy. If a woman had intercourse with any man, and became a mother by him, the child, if once it was accepted by the man's clan as his child, took its place among his children, with all the rights of a son whose mother had gone through the marriage ceremony. The gathering for the purpose of naming the child was generally held at the house of the chief of the clan, who took charge of the ceremonies. No child could be brought singly for the ceremonies; there must be at least two, one of either sex; and children of one sex, however numerous they were, could not go through the ceremonies without awaiting at least one child of the other sex. The children were not necessarily all by one mother, or indeed by one father; they might be members of several families; they might also vary in age from a few months to four or five years. The mothers took their children to the appointed place, and each carried with her the piece of umbilical cord which she had preserved carefully from the time of birth; in many clans the mothers wore it tied round their waist, so that it was kept safe. They also had to prepare some salt from the river reeds, and to take it with them to the feast. The head of the clan provided a barkcloth for each mother to sit upon during the ceremonies. When all was ready, the mothers assembled, placed their barkcloths in a row, and each one sat with her child, or children, with her; on the opposite side, also on barkcloths, sat the husbands' mothers, whose office it was to test the cords. A space was left between the two rows, and a large wicker waterproof basket was placed there; into this, beer, milk, and water were poured; each mother then produced the umbilical cord of her child, and handed it to her

mother-in-law, who dropped it into the vessel. In some clans the grandmother touched the cord with oil before she dropped it into the water; as she dropped it in, she said: "This is the child of so and so," and mentioned some of the forefathers of the clan. If the cord floated, the women opposite raised a shrill cry of delight . . . and clapped their hands; if it sank, the child was disowned by the clan, and said to be a child born in adultery. When the test ended, the cords were given back to the care of the mothers, until such time as they were wanted again. A feast was made for all the relatives who attended the ceremonies, while the mothers on that day had only an ordinary meal, because their taboo was not ended. One or two clans, in addition to the ceremony just described, took the cord in the evening, sought out a plantain just about to bear fruit, choosing the kind according to the sex of the child, then cut off the top of the plantain, just below the spot where the leaves branched out, and made an incision in the stem a few inches below, cutting right through to the heart of the tree with a knife used to serve up the cooked plantain food. The cord was inserted so as to rest in the core of the tree, and was left there. Early in the morning they went again to the tree, and if the core of the tree had shot up during the night, so that the piece of cord had come out and was above the place where the tree had been cut, this was regarded as a good sign; the previous decision had been confirmed, and the child was without a doubt a member of the clan. The custom of another clan was to put the cord into a piece of moist cowdung, and throw it against the wall of the house; if it stuck to the wall, this was a good sign, which confirmed the other test; if, however, it fell off twice, this was a sign that the child was not a member of the clan. Other clans preserve the umbilical cord on their bed, or put it with the afterbirth at the root of the plantain tree. When the test of placing the cords in the mixture was ended, the children, sometimes two at a time; were placed upon the back of one of the strongest girls present, and some of the mixture was sprinkled over them, until it was all emptied from the vessel. The head of the clan then presented each boy with a goat skin and each girl with a piece of barkcloth. After the ceremony the people who had already partaken of their meal separated, while the mothers were required to draw water, or to bring firewood, for the head of the clan, before they were allowed to take their evening meal. The meal ended, they sat in the house in a row, with their feet in front of them, and the head of the clan jumped over each one, and, as he did so, the woman would tell her child that he was its father. In many of the clans the husband also jumped over his wife. They all stayed the night at the house of the head of the clan, and early next morning a feast was prepared for the wives who had passed the test for their children. Each mother again sat on her barkcloth in the open, and her mother-in-law sat opposite, holding a piece of cooked fish in her right hand and a piece of cooked plantain in her left. She placed her right hand on the mother's left leg, and her left hand on the mother's right leg, and went slowly through the list of her son's forefathers, and, as she mentioned them, she moved her hands gradually higher, until she reached her daughter-in-law's mouth, into which she put first the boiled plantain and then the fish. The mother ate it, and was thereupon free to rise. The fish was given and eaten as a charm to effect rapid child-bearing, just as the fish swarm by thousands in the shallow waters of the lake. When all the mothers had undergone this ceremony, the children were brought: each grandmother went to her grandchild and mentioned the names of first one, and then another, of her son's forefathers, beginning with the name of the deceased ancestor nearest to her son, but not mentioning any living person. As she rehearsed their names, each time going further back, she watched the child, and when it laughed it was a token to her that the ancestor just named was he whose ghost would be the child's guardian. If the child subsequently fell ill,

or if it did not thrive, they changed its name, and appointed another guardian, because the former was supposed to dislike the child. It was by this name that the child was known in its clan, though not commonly outside; when any matter of importance occurred within the clan concerning the child, the name would at once be mentioned, and be a proof of its membership. After naming her grandchild, the grandmother took it aside and shaved its head, then carefully gathering the hair together, she tied it in a bundle, and placed it at the root of the plantain where the afterbirth was. A feast was made for the mothers, at which they were welcomed and praised by all the members of the husband's clan. Those who failed to pass the test were scolded, forced to confess who was the father of the child, and in some cases were even beaten by the women of the husband's clan. Princes and the King's wives did not wait for several children before the ceremony was performed, though as a rule they too brought both a boy and a girl.

When children were losing their first teeth, it was their guardians' duty to assist them to get rid of the teeth quickly. Yet they seldom, if ever, extracted them for a child, but persuaded it to do this for itself. The [basic] idea was that, if the teeth were not extracted at the right time, the new set would be irregular. They were also anxious that the old teeth should either be preserved, or placed with the afterbirth, and not be thrown away by the child. Some clans preserved the teeth with the hair, while others cast them at the root of the plantain with the afterbirth.

It was the custom for young children to have their heads shaved every two or three months by one of the members of the father's clan; as a rule the hair was placed in the garden, where it would be safe from being tampered with by enemies. No one but a relative, usually a female relative, was allowed to shave either boys' or girls' heads. Both boys and girls were careless about bathing during their minority; custom obliged them to wash their hands before meals, but they seldom did more than that until they were twelve or fourteen. When they approached puberty, they became cleaner, and took more interest in their appearance. It was the custom of grown-up people to bathe daily. Boys were sent to herd goats and sheep, and assist generally in such duties as they were able to perform. They lived in the house, not of their father, but of a relative, and were cared for by his wife, while he himself took care that they were not neglected; their wants were but few, as they wore no clothing until they were about six or seven years old; they were then given a goat skin which was worn slung over the shoulders. When about ten, they were expected to perform light duties such as carrying their relative's beer and mat, or going [sic] messages for him. If the relative saw that the boy was bright and quick he would possibly get him into the household of some chief; there the boy, if he was attentive, might soon make his way and become a trusted servant, and be sent upon important business. He might even become a page to the King, and in this position, if he gained favour by his alertness, promotion would be certain. In other cases a boy remained with his relative, until war broke out, when he accompanied him on the expedition, and perhaps distinguished himself in battle. Much depended upon the boy himself: if he was idle, he might go unnoticed, and never rise to be anything more than a peasant. Once a boy had gained favour with a chief, he could obtain barkcloths or the means to buy them. Other boys, who were less clever, soon found their level as assistants to peasants, taking part in barkcloth making, fence making, and house building, while every time their turn came to supply food for the over-chief, they had to carry it to him to the capital. Boys had a free and happy life while the time of herding lasted; they met together daily, and while the animals browsed, they had ample time for all kinds of games. Their chief game was the throwing of a stick. . . . The stick was fairly stout, and about eighteen inches long; each boy

was armed with two such sticks, and took turns in throwing them. Those who were the most skilled always sent their sticks flying to a safe distance, out of danger from their antagonists.

The national game was wrestling; this was indulged in by men and boys alike; even the King frequently took part in it, though it was never permissible to throw the King; in fact anyone who did so would have been in danger of being put to death. Wrestling was accompanied by beer drinking, and by songs of a doubtful character, while the onlookers clapped their hands in time to the rhythm of the drum which was beaten during the match. A chief whose man had proved successful in the match would frequently give him a wife in appreciation of the skill he had shown. Other outdoor games were a kind of prisoners' base, and a kicking game, in which two youths stood side by side and then kicked sideways, each trying to knock the other over or to drive him off. The chief indoor game was the game of *weso,* which is so common throughout Africa; it is played on a board with holes in it cut in four rows; two persons sit on opposite sides of the board; they have a number of seeds, or smooth stones, which they play into the holes; quickness of sight and rapidity in addition ensure success.

Girls were taught to cook and to cultivate as soon as they could hoe; to be a successful manager of the plantain grove and to be an expert cook were regarded as a woman's best accomplishments. Girls up to about twelve years of age were unclothed, but they had a ring round their waist, made either of lizard skin or from the plantain fibre. When they arrived at puberty, they were given a piece of barkcloth to wear round their loins. Peasant girls were frequently sent to herd the goats, when there was no boy available to do it; even big girls were employed in this work, and often it was a time of danger to them, because they met big boys, and got into trouble with them. It was the woman's duty, in whose charge a girl was placed, to look after her; it was looked upon as a great disgrace to a family, if a girl was with child prior to marriage. Parents would not eat food with a girl who misconducted herself; she was compelled to tell who was the cause of her trouble; and the man was fined a cow and a fowl, and had also to pay the dowry and marry the girl. Even while he was seeking the amount for the fine, the girl had to live with his relations; though she did not intend to marry him, she was obliged to go to his relatives until after the birth had taken place, because the child was their child, and it was they who had to see that the birth customs were observed, and, after the child was weaned, to take charge of it. Such an incident did not prevent a girl from marrying, nor would her husband think less of her, but it prevented her from being taken to wife by a chief, or anyone of importance; consequently every measure was taken to keep girls pure until marriage. They were often, while still young, given in marriage to some chief, when they would be placed in his enclosure under the care of one of his female relations until old enough to become wives. Girls matured at about twelve, though they never remembered their age; they were described as having breasts, and when the breasts began to hang down, they were spoken of as full grown women. Both men and women, when speaking of a girl, indicated her age by the size of her breasts, which they represented by the closed hand. When a girl first menstruated, she was secluded and not allowed to handle any food, nor to enter the house of her brother or uncle; her female relations attended to her wants and fed her. She was described as being "at peace" . . . or being "outside": when she recovered, the relative with whom she was staying had to jump over his wife; or if she was near to them, the girl had to go and tell her parents that she had just recovered, whereupon her father had to jump over her mother. If she was with her brother, she had to go to her mother when she fell ill, and to wait there

until she was well again; she might then return and resume her ordinary duties. The first menstruation was often called a marriage, and the girl spoken of as a bride. When a girl cultivated her first plot of garden alone, and brought the first fruits from it, her relative with whom she lived had to jump over his wife, or her father had to jump over her mother, before they partook of the food. This caused the garden, and all her future work in the garden, to be fruitful. It was for a similar purpose that her father, or the relative with whom she lived, jumped over his wife, at her first menstruation; for if this practice were omitted, the girl would not have children (so it was thought), or they would die in infancy. A girl or woman who did not menstruate was looked upon askance, and if a man married such a woman, then every time that he went to war he wounded her with a spear sufficiently to draw blood; otherwise he would be sure to fall in battle. Such women were also said to have a malign influence on gardens, and to cause them to become barren if they worked in them. Girls seldom played games; they were kept busy for the whole day, and were taught to make mats and baskets to occupy their leisure time; they also drew water and brought in fire-wood.

When a twin had grown up, and went to war for the first time, then if he killed a man, he had on his return to go to his father's house and spend the night there. His father jumped over his mother that night, and the next morning he gave a bark-cloth and a fowl to his son, who then went away to his own residence.

In more ancient times, before princes were killed when their brother began to reign, none of the King's brothers who married were allowed to have sons; any male child born to a prince was put to death by the midwife, and only princesses were allowed to live.

Owing to the clan system, no occasion arose for the adoption of orphans; children belonged to the clan, and when their father or mother died, they were still under the care of some relative who took the place of the father. Women taken captive in war might become the wives of men in high positions, and the children which they had by such men would become full members of the clan, while they themselves were only slaves. On the death of the husband such a woman became the property of his heir; she might be appointed to look after her husband's grave, and in some cases she was respected by the clan. If she had borne children, she would not be so likely to be sold by the heir as would a slave who had never been taken to wife.

The preceding selection included some material about Baganda clans. Restated briefly, the idea was that a child did not acquire clan membership until paternity was established through magical tests. Nowadays such tests have missionary disapproval and at least some children automatically take the clan of their presumed father. Probably tests for paternity are conducted secretly as well. Once clan membership is established in the patrilineal line, it is retained for life. The following selection deals mostly with a particular aspect of Baganda clans, namely totemism. Totems are often associated with clans, but the Navajo, among others, have clans but lack totems.

· 61 · Clans and Totems
LUCY P. MAIR

Totemism—that is to say a ritual connection between animal species and social groups—appears to play a much less important part in the cultures of Africa than in some societies of North America and Australia. At the same time the division into totemic clans is a feature commonly found in the social organization of the Bantu, and since little attention has been paid to it, a note on totemism as it occurs in a culture recently investigated may not be out of place.

The Baganda are divided into some thirty-six exogamous clans, the members of which are linked to one another and distinguished from other groups by respect for a common totem, by the use of a common drum beat on ceremonial occasions, by certain distinguishing personal names, and by special observances connected with pregnancy, childbirth and the testing of the child's legitimacy, as well as by certain mutual obligations. Of these bonds of kinship, it is only the relationship to the totem that concerns us here.

While the totem is not the object of ceremonial, and the rules of behaviour with regard to it appear to be losing their validity, it is interesting that the normal way of asking a man what is his clan is to say, *We dira ki?*—'What is your totem?' It might be objected that if Baganda totemism goes no further than this, it constitutes no more than the use of animal names to distinguish human groups, a practice which, in itself, is hardly sufficient to constitute totemism. But even at the present day totemism means more to the Baganda people than this. A remarkable feature of their system, which does not appear to have been reported elsewhere, is that each clan has two totems, the *muziro* and the *kabiro*. While the *muziro* is the one which gives its name to the clan and the *kabiro* can only be ascertained by specific inquiry, the latter is stated to be

[Adapted from "Totemism among the Baganda," *Man: a Monthly Record of Anthropological Science*, Vol. 35, London, 1935. Pp. 66-67. Used by permission.]

the more important in the sense that breaches of the rules of behaviour towards it have more serious consequences, and are not commonly mentioned, just because of its importance.

The totems are nearly all animals, though they include the mushroom and a fruit called *katinvuma*. They include the cow, sheep and goat, as well as a large number which are hunted for food, and beasts of prey, such as the lion and leopard, which are killed but not eaten. Parts of a dead lion are used for certain medicines, and these are forbidden to the Lion Clan. While the totem animal is commonly spoken of as a 'brother,' there is no myth accounting for totemic divisions by their descent from animal ancestors. The original king of Buganda is said to have allotted the totems along with the clan lands. . . . The major prohibition, as to which all informants agree, is against eating the totem. This is said to produce a rash which sometimes appears on the child of the guilty person. A woman once brought an infant to me with some skin disease and said, 'Perhaps its father ate his *muziro*.' This disease is believed to be curable, but the results of eating the *kabiro* are said to be much more serious, and according to some accounts, death is inevitable.

Accounts differed as regards the killing of the totem animal. Some said that any man might do this, provided he did not eat the flesh, but the more general view was that this latitude was only allowed in the case of a beast of prey against whom the whole village was turned out. In these circumstances, authority had to be obeyed and the killing of the totem was excused because it was done under compulsion—*lwanaku si wakwagala,* 'in sorrow, not of his own free will.' Some informants suggested that a member of the clan concerned should try to avoid being in at the death and might even contrive to let the animal escape as though by accident. It is not believed that the animal would show a similar clemency to a member of its clan during a hunt, but it was stated that a man who met his totem animal by chance would not be attacked if he said, 'I am your brother.'

Modern conditions have introduced two innovations which bear on the relations between an individual and his totem species— the steel trap and the employment of natives on European hunting expeditions. As regards the first, it is agreed that no man should set a trap for his totem animal. The attitude towards the second was rather interesting. Once a man has been engaged to hunt for the Europeans, the latter seems to be made responsible for any offences he may commit against his totem—though here, too, he may make the best of both worlds by intentional stupidity on occasion.

In the native mind the association of the totem with the rules of exogamy seems to be very close. Some school children once asked me how Europeans, if they had no totems, avoided marrying within the prohibited degrees. Here it is, of course, possible that the word 'totem' was used with reference to the whole clan system; as I have mentioned, a person's clan can be known from other distinguishing marks, such as the name. But, on another occasion a man advanced, as a sufficient reason for the prohibition of eating the totem, the apparently inconsequent statement, 'You would not marry your brother.'

The title of the following selection might be misleading to those who think of chieftains as independent leaders. An African chief is generally subordinate to a king, who is sometimes called a paramount chief. Among the Baganda, a chief might better be called a bureaucrat. This selection considers African chieftainship in general, but the discussion centers on the Baganda. It is necessary here to anticipate the discussion of sociocultural change, since chieftainship can best be understood in terms of both the traditions that are giving way and the new practices growing up.

• 62 • Chieftainship

LUCY P. MAIR

One might summarize the sources of the chief's authority by saying that it depended in part only on the supernatural sanctions attached to his heredity and in part on the due performance of his functions. By this I do not mean to suggest that any failure or abuse was instantly met by revolt and deposition, but rather that there was sufficient flexibility in the relations between governor and governed for discontent to make itself felt in ways which it was against the ruler's interest to disregard, while there were in practice often considerable checks on the abuse of an authority which was in theory absolute.

In the area with which I am concerned the functions of the chief might be of three kinds, magical, political, and economic, and his privileges can be closely correlated with the exercise of these functions. Everywhere the paramount chief or king is believed to stand in a special relationship to the land, and in virtue of this relationship he is frequently responsible for the performance of rites upon which the fertility of the land depends and which only he can satisfactorily carry out. It is especially in connection with these magical duties that his hereditary position, linking him as it does with the spirits of his predecessors, is of importance in validating his authority.

The king's hereditary status is certainly an element in maintaining respect for his authority even where, as with the Baganda, he has no magical powers. Here his connexion by descent with the mythological founder of the kingdom at the same time justified his claim to absolute ownership of the country and everything in it and guaranteed his adherence to the tradition which was formally reasserted at his accession—a tradition which, it is worth mentioning, laid down not only the supremacy of the king but his duty to respect certain rights of his subjects.

The maintenance of political authority carried with it advantages to the governed sufficient to make them acquiesce in the burdens which it imposed upon them.

What were these advantages? . . . I can only speak in detail of the tribe which I know at first hand, the Baganda. With them the political functions of the chiefs, who formed a hierarchy appointed by the king and dependent for their position on his pleasure, consisted mainly in the administration of justice and the organization of warfare.

I have myself heard an old peasant say that God showed the Baganda especial favour in giving them chiefs to settle their quarrels. Warfare with them went beyond the mere organization of defence, in itself a service of some importance, to constitute, in the form of raids on neighbouring tribes, a speedier way of increasing their material possessions than any more conventionally economic activity.

In economic matters authority might seem at first sight to have carried with it a position of pure privilege. In the first place, the subject's right to occupy land, and hence his entire livelihood, depended theoretically on the king and practically on the chief to whose village he attached himself. For failure to render the customary services, as for any other action displeasing to the chief, he was liable to eviction. Those who see in African chieftainship nothing but arbitrary tyranny may seem to find here an argument for their point of view, but for an analysis of the working of the institution what is relevant is that the services rendered by the peasant are not given in a one-sided submission to supernatural power or physical force, but in return for rights of fundamen-

[Adapted from "Chieftainship in Modern Africa," *Africa*, Vol. 9, No. 3, London, 1936. Pp. 306-313. Used by permission.]

tal importance. To the Muganda there was no injustice in the fact that these rights were not unconditional. Moreover, he had a ready means of expressing dissatisfaction with his chief by moving to another village.

The rights which a chief could claim from his subjects consisted of a gourd of beer in every brew, a considerable portion of the goods paid over in compensation for any offence tried by him, and services when required in the building of his houses and the fence which surrounded them. He received also his share of the taxes collected through his agency at the command of the king, and on the return from a raiding expedition it rested with him to distribute among his followers that portion of the spoil captured by them which was left when the king had selected his share and, of course, to retain as much of it as he thought fit.

But this system did not mean a constantly increasing accumulation of wealth in the hands of the privileged few, for the simple reason that in the native economy a satiation point was reached early, and when it was reached the rich man turned from the enjoyment of possession to the enjoyment of munificence. Generosity was expected of a chief and was the best way to increase his following; and on the size of his following depended wealth, prestige, and promotion to the control over a wider area.

To the peasant the chief was the ultimate source of his livelihood and a more immediate source of material benefits; he also represented the authority and leadership necessary for orderly relations in peace and the successful organization of war. To the chief his followers brought wealth and prestige provided he dealt fairly with them —a proviso which shows how the institution contained within itself checks on the abuse of a privileged position.

A further check existed in the system of succession. The hereditary principle did not mean that certain individuals were destined by birth alone to succeed to authority. There was always a certain range of choice, which made it worth while for persons who lusted for power to show themselves fit for it.

A feature of the Baganda system which again limited the action both of the king and the chiefs was the existence, side by side with the theoretically supreme authority, of a counsellor whose influence carried very great weight. While the heir could dismiss his father's counsellor, he was not normally expected to do so; so that the new holder of any political position, from the king downwards, usually entered upon his office subject to the advice of an older and more experienced man. This counsellor's advice was asked before any drastic step was taken, such as the deposition of a chief by the king or the eviction of a peasant by the chief; and in the case of the chiefs he was the recognized channel through which peasants who considered that they were unfairly treated could express their grievances.

I have been careful to say, not that the system prevented the abuse of power, but that it set limits to such abuse. Can we say more of the political institutions of the most advanced civilizations? They have their abuses, too, which seem less flagrant perhaps only because they are more familiar.

The entire basis of the chief's position has been altered by the very advent of European government. What was in many areas one of the most important functions of the supreme authority has been completely removed. I mean the organization of war, which in some African societies has justified a system of government much more autocratic than that which I have described among the Baganda. Even where he has retained his judicial authority the modern chief has lost the right to inflict severe punishments for offences against himself. Where new systems of land tenure have been introduced the fundamental economic relationship between chief and people is broken. Christianity and the obsolescence of public ritual have affected this relationship on the religious side. On the other side, authority rests now, not on popularity or on the rendering of specific services to the governed,

but on the power of the European government, which, though it may remove chiefs
from office, seldom does so for the reasons
which would cause native opinion to desire
such a step. It is for this reason—because it
has put the chief out of reach of the sanctions with which he had formerly to reckon
—that a government which maintains his
authority without understanding its real nature may well be condoning abuses of it
which could not in the past have been committed with impunity. Moreover, modern
economic conditions create the possibility of
abuses which could not in the past have been
committed at all. The possibilities of turning one's economic privileges to direct personal advantage are now unlimited; yet the
most superficially literal conception of Indirect Rule involves the maintenance of the
chief's traditional privileges. Because they
have dissociated these privileges from the
corresponding responsibilities, those in authority have sometimes failed to see that
under modern conditions tribute paid to
chiefs is coming to be just that one-sided
burden that it was sometimes thought to
have been before. Yet these same conditions
make any effective protest out of the question.

This is one way in which the nature of
the chief's position as one part of a reciprocal relationship has been misunderstood.
The possibilities of the other party—his subjects as a body, or any one of them—retaliating for his failure to do his due part have
been removed; for it is only those who reject
government through the chief altogether and
propose to replace it by democracy on European lines, who have concerned themselves
with the subjects' point of view, and they
only misinterpret it by forgetting again that
the subject had rights as well as duties.

European governments have assigned to
him many duties which did not form part
of his functions before. Some of these,
such as collection of census figures, enforcement of regulations for the destruction of
old cotton plants, encouragement of such
activities as the killing of rats, might be
described as neutral in their effect on the
relation between chief and subject. But
others, those which involve the use of the
chief's authority in calling upon his subjects
to enter upon distasteful and arduous pursuits which bring them no apparent advantage and throw out of gear the whole
routine of their lives, inevitably produce a
complete distortion of that relationship. I refer, of course, to the use of the chief in obtaining labour for European employers, or recruits in those colonies where conscription is
in force, in collecting taxes imposed by the
government, and sometimes in enforcing
the cultivation by natives of commercial
crops. Where these are among the duties of
the chief, he is simply an instrument of the
superior government and is plainly recognized by the natives as such.

It is true that the prestige of the chief
often leads his subjects to imitate him
in following European ways. Christianity
itself has sometimes been adopted in this
manner, not always without sudden mass
conversion from one sect to another. But for
the chief's example to be effective, the innovation must be in something which is either
a matter of indifference to the people or else
appears to offer them some positive advantage. And further, the apparent advantages
may not always be consistent with the effective working of the complex of native institutions taken as a whole. It is just as easy
for progress to become synonymous with
disruption if an hereditary chief is made its
apostle as it is where the native who claims
to have become civilized is encouraged to
reject the chief's authority—though the process of disruption may be less obvious.

Baganda kingship with its elaborate bureaucracy was well established long before
the first white explorers arrived. Many other Negro kingdoms were also functioning at
this time; the Baganda situation was not unique. It is likely that some ancient Egyptian

ideas about divine kingship filtered through Negro Africa and were adopted in various regions. The Baganda monarchy appears to have been grafted onto the older system of clans and clan chiefs. Perhaps an invading tribe conquered the older inhabitants and set themselves up as the ruling class. The British administrators later helped make the class structure more rigid by creating a group of landed gentry. The following selection describes modern Buganda as a stratified society, one in which there are relatively rigid social classes.

Some confusion about the relationship between the Baganda kingship and British administration can be avoided if certain geographic facts are kept in mind. First of all, Entebbe, the capital of the Uganda Protectorate, is the center of white administration only and does not include any resident African kings. Secondly, each African king in Uganda has his own capital town or city. Buganda has its capital at Mengo, usually considered to be part of greater Kampala. Often, Kampala is called the capital even though this is technically incorrect. Within Mengo, the place with strongest royal associations is Budo Hill.

• 63 • *Social Stratification and the Kingship*

H. A. WIESCHHOFF

Buganda society is a class structure consisting of the aristocrats, who as feudal lords own large tracts of the land and enjoy other privileges, and of large masses of peasants who work the land. The upper class, who keep themselves aloof from the peasants, claims to be of non-Negro origin, although this claim can no longer be supported by physical evidence. Both upper and lower classes are typical Negroes, in spite of the fact that the former came into the country as alien invaders some thousand years ago.

Buganda's political organization may be termed a constitutional monarchy; it has a king whose office is hereditary and who is advised by a council of ministers. Both are controlled by a parliament which, as a legislative and judicial body, is composed exclusively of members of the aristocracy. Many members of the Lukiko, as the parliament is called, are also governors of the several provinces and districts into which the kingdom is divided.

The king and the aristocracy, as the rulers of the country, form a leisure class engaged only in governmental affairs without direct participation in the country's production economy. They own the land which, in true feudal fashion, is worked by the peasants in return for tribute paid to the land owner. Fortunately Buganda has a high fertility, producing good crops, particularly of plantains (a variety of banana) which ... constitute the chief item of Baganda diet. Food is so abundant and so easily grown that the demands of the upper class are met without endangering the welfare or even reducing the living standards of the peasant population, which, as has frequently been stated, is better fed than any other African group. It is perhaps for this reason that the Baganda have been regarded as more intelligent and advanced than other peoples of East Africa. The cleanliness of their houses and clothing, the sanitary conditions, and elaborate personal hygiene, reflect clearly

[Adapted from "Africa," *University Museum Bulletin*, Vol. 11, Nos. 1-2, University of Pennsylvania, Philadelphia, 1945. Pp. 43-46. Used by permission.]

their refined standard of living. Their courtesy among themselves and their decorum to strangers are proverbial.

The fertility of the land has attracted great numbers of people, so that the kingdom with its million inhabitants has one of the densest populations in Africa, living in villages and settlements of considerable size. Density of population combined with the existence of a surplus economy has been peculiarly favorable to the development of domestic arts. The aristocracy depends for its leisurely existence on professional craftsmen who build their houses, produce their furniture, such as beds and stools, and supply utensils of all kinds (oil lamps, cups, and containers). The peasants have become dependent on those professionals who specialize in the making of baskets, earthenware vessels, iron tools, and implements. Not only the production of these objects, but also their marketing in the village square or at roadside workshops, has become an essential feature of Baganda life.

The social stratification is based on property and wealth which finds its most tangible expression in the size of the land holdings and the number of peasants working in them. In addition, it is customary for the well-to-do families to possess large herds of cattle, not for the utilitarian aspects of cattle breeding, but, like horse breeders in our society, for reasons of sport or to exhibit their wealth.

• 64 • Taxes and Revenues

NEGLEY FARSON

The atmosphere of Entebbe is one of altruistic administration. It speaks of unhurried research. You feel, suddenly, that this is the way things *ought* to be in Africa. This is a native country, left as native by the British as possible, yet still held in fief as a British protectorate. If there is any oppression, it is the oppression of one native over another—which is not altogether unknown in Africa. And if the Kabaka of Buganda and the Mugabe of Ankole and the Mukama of Toro are not *absolutely* independent rulers, you will have to admit, when you know the arbitrary despotism of other native chiefs, that such a state of white control is probably the best for the rest of Uganda's black inhabitants; also that the Kabaka is the highest example of an independent native king left in Africa.

Entebbe provokes novel thoughts in your attitude towards Africa.

Subject to the veto of the Governor, the power of the Kabaka is large, if limited, today; it might be compared to the liberty enjoyed by some of the smaller native states in India.

For example, the court of the Lukiko can pronounce the death sentence, although it must be consented to by the Governor, and a final appeal can be made to the Privy Council in England. The *saza* chiefs have criminal powers up to one year's imprisonment and twenty-four strokes. The *gombolola* chiefs can sentence up to three months or ten strokes. Prisoners are confined in native prisons in Buganda, though convicts with over two years' sentence are usually transferred to the Protectorate jails. These native prisons can be inspected by British officers.

The Lukiko (native parliament) has, subject to the veto of the Governor, the right to pass laws for internal legislation in Buganda, such as the right to evict peasants who are on Buganda-owned lands; the right to impose a tax on land, and the right to define native custom in regard to succession anywhere on the 9,003 square miles "left within the gift of the Kabaka" by the 1900 British-Buganda agreement. Of course, the native courts cannot try any white man or any African who is not a Muganda.

Now, although the names of the prime minister, the chief justice, and the minister of finance must be submitted to the British Governor (who has the right to reject them), the Lukiko itself is constituted on oligarchic rather than popular lines. It consists of the three above ministers, the county chiefs, three notables nominated by the Kabaka from each of the counties, and six other notables appointed by the Kabaka from the country at large.

It is not a House of Commons, an elected assembly. There is no form of election. It is a native House of Lords [changed in 1945-46].

And the Baganda—the people, that is—would like to change it. Buganda, with its system of private ownership of land, has a leisured class. These are native landowners, many living on their rents, like English lords. But this leisured class has bred its own destroyers—the Baganda intelligentsia.

And it is between these two factions—the "ruling families" and the intelligentsia, which may come from either the Buhima aristocratic class or the Bantu working class—that the British Government at Entebbe must act as referees, often uncomfortable.

The Kabaka, his ministers, his *saza* and *gombolola* chiefs receive 25 per cent of the poll tax in Buganda; this, in 1938, amounted to £30,880.

Furthermore, there are revenues controlled by the Kabaka's government, such as commutation for obligatory labor for state purposes, land tax, fees and fines from the judicial courts, market dues and licenses, etc., which in 1935 amounted to £128,638.

Apart from the 25 per cent remitted by the British from the total poll tax, the whole of these other revenues may be said to have been imposed by the Lukiko, and the Buganda budget (subject to approval by the British Governor) is made out by the Lukiko itself.

It is felt at Entebbe that too large a part of this native budget is spent on personal emoluments, establishment, and "overhead charges."

The Buganda budget does not *have* to provide items for either education or medical activities, although an annual grant is made of £1,600 to the Protectorate Government for medical stores, and in 1937 there was a non-recurring item in the Buganda budget of £5,000 for the erection and maintenance of dispensaries and maternity centers.

[The Colonial Annual Report for Uganda for 1946 adds a new note to the descriptions of Baganda government when it states:

Constitutionally certain advances have been made, and the awakening of a political consciousness among the people themselves is in evidence. Increased African participation in Protectorate affairs has been brought about by the addition in 1945 of three African members to the Legislative Council. Advance towards democratic forms of local government institutions has been made by the establishment. . . . In Buganda the procedure for the election of popular representatives and for their subsequent nomination through the several grades of Council to the Lukiko, or Parliament of the kingdom of Buganda, has been codified by Native Law. The political consciousness of the people has had among its birth pangs a strike (attended by disturbances) which paralysed public and private services in the area of the Lake shore during a few days in January of 1945, and the dastardly murder of Martin Luther Nsibirwa, at that time Katikiro or Prime Minister of Buganda, on 5th September, 1945. . . .

As regards Provincial affairs, in Buganda the year was quiet after the disturbances of 1945, and the Lukiko, containing for the first time a large number of representatives elected by popular vote, passed several progressive measures, including the important Agricultural Law, 1946.]

• 65 • A King Dies

F. LUKYN WILLIAMS

The death [in 1939] of Sir Daudi Chwa was the first of a ruling Kabaka to occur since the advent of the British Government to Uganda. Not since his grandfather Mutesa died in 1884 had a Kabaka died; Mwanga, his father, after being deposed had died in the Seychelles in 1903, and his body was brought to Buganda and buried with ceremony in 1910. . . . It is clear that most of the old traditional customs connected with death of a Kabaka were carried out then, but modified only slightly by the insistence of the chiefs that Mackay of the C.M.S. should give him a European burial.

Fifty-five years after this event peace and progress had brought about a very different state of affairs. The late Kabaka was a Christian potentate, with at least 52% of his subjects Christian. It was therefore to be expected that the customary ceremonial carried out on the death and burial of a Kabaka would be modified so as not to be repugnant to the religious teaching of the Church and to be in keeping with the progressive ideas of Western civilisation.

The traditional method of dealing with the body of a deceased Kabaka was to embalm it—a process which took about six months—and then bury it. The jaw-bone was removed a few months later and a special temple built to house it.

When the death of Sir Daudi Chwa was reported, the Katikiro, Omulamuzi and Omuwanika, at once proceeded to Lukuli and had the body suitably wrapped in white cloth and carried, as was customary, by hand, to Mengo where it was placed in the council room of Twekobe (Kabaka's house).

On the death of a Kabaka the sacred fire called "Gombolola" which has been constantly burning at the entrance to the Lubiri (Royal enclosure) during his lifetime, is extinguished as a sign that the life of the Kingdom has gone out, and is only lighted again on the accession of the new Kabaka.

In Buganda it was customary to select a successor as soon as possible after the death of the Kabaka, in order that the country might not remain without a head for any length of time. It was usual for the reigning Kabaka to indicate whom of his sons he wished to succeed him and his wishes would be adhered to as far as possible.

The 1900 Agreement allows for the selection of a new Kabaka being made from the descendants of Kabaka Mutesa. He must then be elected by the Lukiko (Council), but his election would not be recognised until it received the approval of His Majesty's Government. On the afternoon of the 22nd. November the son of the late Kabaka, Edward Frederick William David Walugembe Mutebi Luwangula Mutesa, was unanimously elected Kabaka, under the title of Mutesa II.

Towards the close of this eventful day, at 6.00 p.m., Mutesa, who was at school at King's College, Budo, was brought to perform the ceremony of . . . looking on the face of his father and then covering the body with a barkcloth.

The three Ministers, the Katikiro, the Omulamuzi and the Omuwanika, then took the oath of office as Regents, to which they had been appointed, in accordance with the provisions of the 1900 Agreement, during the minority of the Kabaka, who was only fifteen years old.

In the meantime, arrangements had been made to excavate a tomb in the same building in which the remains of Kabakas Mutesa and Mwanga lie at Kisubi.

On the 24th. November, the body was washed and prepared for burial by two women relatives of the [Queen Mother's] clan (bush-buck). A lined coffin had been sup-

[Adapted from "The Kabaka of Buganda," *Uganda Journal*, Vol. 7, No. 4, Kampala, 1940. Pp. 176-185. Used by permission.]

plied by the Public Works Department. This was now closed down and the populace was allowed to pass round it.

A custom in [quite] general use today in Uganda was waived, which is significant of the times in which we live. When a dead man is carried, he is always carried feet first, whereas if a man is carried head first it is a sign that he is alive. It was noticeable that the coffin was on this occasion, as is often the custom of Christian burials, carried head first, and placed in the hearse head first.

The coffin [was conveyed] by hearse and not by hand, thus breaking with all previous custom. It was felt, however, that as time was an important factor in a modern state funeral, the enormous weight of the coffin would have to be carried over three miles, and the excitability of the unprecedented crowds, might . . . delay the cortège.

The pall-bearers were Gombolola Chiefs selected by Kago for the occasion. They carried the coffin from the hearse to the cathedral, where it was met by the Bishop of Uganda and conducted to the chancel steps and placed on a bier, which was draped with a purple pall. The coffin was covered with the Kabaka's flag, on which were placed his orders and decorations and his "engule". ("Engule" is commonly translated "crown".)

The service was attended by His Excellency the Governor, and representatives from every community, race and creed in the country. Representative chiefs had come from all the leading tribes in the country to pay their respects to the late Kabaka. His Highness Mutesa II, attended the service in a private capacity and sat in the choir. After the service the procession formed and the coffin was taken by a direct route to Kisubi.

After the burial the tomb was not filled in or covered for three days, so that the people could file past and pay their last respects to their late Kabaka.

In the afternoon of the 25th. November at 3.0 p.m. the accession ceremonies took place. The chief and most important of these consisted in enthroning the new Kabaka

and showing him to the people. As in the case of his father, who was a minor when coming to the throne, the full ceremonies of accession cannot be completed until he comes of age.

The enthronement took place outside the main gate, Wankaki, of the Lubiri, in the traditional spot on the right as one leaves the Lubiri.

[The Namulondo throne or] stool, made like other African stools, out of one block of wood, has nine legs and was first introduced into the country by the Kabaka Mulondo, who reigned early in the sixteenth century. It is only used in the accession ceremony, and after use is tied up in bark cloth and kept by the members of the Butiko clan.

A new barkcloth was spread on the ground, on which the stool was set. On it were placed the layers of skins which comprise the *ekiwu*: first a cowskin, then a lion skin, then a leopard skin and finally a hyena skin.

A similar carpet was then placed on the right of Namulondo, on which the lady Nanzigu of the Buffalo clan was placed. The original Nanzigu was a wife of Kabaka Kimera, said to be third in the line of Kabakas.

The Katikiro ceremonially carried two new spears and a shield and then stood on the right of the Kabaka. This was a sign that if anyone wished to dispute that Mutesa was not the Kabaka, he was prepared to fight for him. In point of fact, on this peaceful occasion the spears were held point downwards.

The Mugema, the head of the Nkima (Monkey) clan then took the Kabaka by the hand and stood him on Namulondo. He then dressed him in a barkcloth which was given him by the royal barkcloth maker, and tied the knot carefully on the right shoulder.

After placing a mantle of calfskin on top of the barkcloth Mugema addressed the following words to the Kabaka: "Perform your duties well; rule Buganda well; develop into a man and live long."

Kasuju Lubinga then continued the robing of the Kabaka, by placing another bark-cloth on him, but tying the knot on the left shoulder and after placing a leopard skin—the supreme mark of royalty—over the bark-cloth, re-admonished the Kabaka with the words: "Perform all your duties well and rule your people well."

The enrobing was then completed by Mugema who, after receiving a bark-cloth from Kakinda of the Kobe (Yam) clan, adjusted it round the shoulders of the Kabaka and draped it down his back.

It was when the robing was complete that Musoloza relighted the sacred fire, and the rising smoke, proclaiming to all that a Kabaka was reigning, was greeted with acclamation, while the Kabaka stood in full view of his people.

Mukwenda, the Saza Chief of Singo and Sabagabo of Buganda, now brought the shield, called Kamanyi, and two spears and handed them to the Kabaka with the words: "Here are your shield and spears. Fight for your country and conquer nations."

The next event was the placing of a bangle of beads on the left wrist of the Kabaka by Kajubi of the Ensenene (Grasshopper) clan, who then said: "You are Kimera".

To understand the significance of this one must appreciate the early history of Buganda as far as we know it. The tradition of Kimera's birth is thought by some to be in the category of fable rather than of history. Kalemera, his father, the son of the ruling Kabaka, is reputed to have visited Bunyoro, seduced a princess of the royal house, who was the Nsenene clan, and then fled to Buganda, where he died. The mother, though disgraced, managed to save her child by having it brought up by a potter. Later the child was cared for by Mugema. Hence the title, "Kabaka's father", which this chief received and the important part he always played in the accession ceremonies. When the Baganda heard that Kimera was alive, he was asked to come to Buganda and be Kabaka. This tale, whether we believe its historicity or not, or whether it is nearer

the truth to say that Kimera, the Munyoro, invaded and conquered Buganda, undoubtedly helps to explain the connection between Bunyoro and Buganda, between the Hamitic Hima and the Bantu Ganda. There was at some time a movement of infiltration of invasion by a number of clans, said to have come with Kimera. Kimera himself is looked on as the maker of historical Buganda, and many customs and decisions are traced back to the days of Kimera. [Refer to Selection 68.]

The next important ceremony performed was the beating of Mujaguzo. After Mugema had indicated the drums [the chief drummer] brought forward the drum sticks and handed them to Kasuju Lubinga, who in turn handed them to the Kabaka. The Kabaka then beat the Mujaguzo drum called Kawulugumo.

This ranks second in importance among the royal drums, Timba being No. 1 and the most ancient. Kimomera of the Butiko clan, who is assistant royal drummer to Kawula, then handed the drumsticks to the Kabaka, who beat the next Mujaguzo drum, called Namanyonyi.

There was a general cry of acclamation that arose from all throats when the drums were beaten. Mujaguzo was beaten at intervals for the next twenty-four hours. In the old days the drums would not be beaten until the late Kabaka had been duly buried, perhaps six months after his death. The beating of the drums, therefore, also signified that the royal mourning was over.

As no further ceremonies could be performed this day, the Kabaka was carried into the Lubiri in the traditional manner. No Kabaka or his wife walked from place to place, but it was one of the duties and privileges of the Mbogo (buffalo) clan to provide carriers, called Bakongozi, who carried their royal burdens on their shoulders. On this occasion Sekaiba of the Mbogo clan, clad on the shoulders and back with a white goatskin, called the Ekiwu of the Bakongozi, raised the Kabaka on his shoulders and displayed him to the people, so that Buganda could see him. . . . He was then carried through the gateway into the Kabaka's house (Twekobe), while other Bakongozi carried the Lubugas and Prince Juma Katebe, amidst the hand-clapping of the princesses and all people present.

When he was seated the Princes of the Kabaka's clan came and confirmed the accession by paying him allegiance and giving presents of money. The first to come were his grandfathers, or relatives of their generation. These were followed by the aunts and uncles on his father's side, who in their turn were followed by the Kabaka's sisters. Next, Sabalangira, who looks after the Princes, brought Buganda money, i.e. cowrie shells, and after presenting them tied them with raffia on the right wrist of the Kabaka. The Princes of the Mituba then paid allegiance and placed their money on the carpet. All then standing with respect at the corner of the carpet, introduced themselves in turn, saying: "I am your grandfather", or "I am your aunt", or "I am your sister". During the whole of the time that these respects and allegiance were being paid the princes were singing their song *"Kiganda kikira omukwano"*—Relationship surpasses friendship.

At this time the opportunity was taken by . . . dignitaries of Church and State to shake hands and congratulate the Kabaka.

In the meanwhile, the Kabaka's nephews and children of the princesses were collecting outside the Lubiri. Each had a wreath of grass round the head and a reed or a withered banana leaf in the hand, and they sang songs while they slowly approached. They then swept the ground in the Lubiri in front of the Kabaka and were given cents for their work. Sweepers of this nature are called "Bakoza", and it is customary for peasant children to collect in this way and sweep the compounds of chiefs for a small remuneration. In this case the sweeping, being done by royal relatives, signified that the funeral rites were completed.

The new Sabaganzi and his brothers— the uncles of the Kabaka—now came forward to pay their respects and allegiance to the Kabaka. Afterwards they stood and introduced themselves, saying: "I am your uncle".

That night there was much feasting and dancing, accompanied by the almost incessant beating of Mujaguzo drums. The Katikiro and chiefs slept in Twekobe. The Kabaka left in the early hours of the morning, with his tutor, for Budo.

On the 26th. November the Kabaka returned to the Lubiri and gave a feast at midday to his chiefs and notables and to all representatives of foreign tribes who attended the funeral and accession ceremonies.

Before the Europeans came into the country, the religion of the Baganda was complex and specialized. The Christian missionaries who described it did so in tones of horror. Of the missionaries John Roscoe tried hardest to give an objective picture. Even his account exaggerates the brutality and frequency of human sacrifice. Lucy P. Mair, a contemporary British social anthropologist, checked the old accounts and conducted an on-the-spot investigation of her own. Her excellent summary which follows, is not a philosophic discourse on religion but rather an explanation of how it works.

Mair does not include fetishes and amulets in her study. However, Roscoe's careful description of these aspects of the religion is included as the selection which follows Mair's. Amulets and fetishes are alike in that both contain supernatural power, but they are different in that amulets work automatically, whereas fetishes require special attention to retain their power. Frequent offerings must be made to a fetish, or the caretaker must behave in a particular way. A further distinction is that amulets are usually worn on the person, whereas fetishes normally are kept in a shrine.

We discussed Eskimo religion as a separate topic, "The Supernatural World," but for the Navajo and Baganda we have included religion with "'Social Organization and Interaction." This does not mean that religion is of less importance to them; on the contrary, to an increasing extent in more complex societies religion involves special groupings of people rather than individual action. With the Baganda, religious beliefs serve to support the entire social and political structure.

• 66 • *Ancestor-Spirits*

LUCY P. MAIR

Baganda religion, though it was in a sense a cult of ancestors, was something very different from what is usually meant by "ancestor-worship". It was not to the spirits of his immediate ancestors that the Muganda looked for protection or assistance in time of trouble, nor around them that ritual observances centered.

. . . The belief which formed the basis of the whole religious system was that the spirits of the dead remained in close contact with their own descendants, could be placated by means of offerings, and when they wished to communicate with the living could do so by taking possession of a person through whose mouth they spoke.

There is little evidence that the spirits were looked on as a source of blessings. It is occasionally said that a piece of good luck might be attributed to them, but I never came across an actual instance, while cases of their malevolence are constantly quoted. The cult which formerly existed seems to have been mainly directed to placate this malevolence; indeed it is doubtful whether any regular rites were performed until some spirit had demanded them by a visitation. [Furthermore, there seem to have been] no benefits which it was thought to be specifically within their province to confer, nor any recognized formulae of prayer. No accounts of family ceremonies give any indication that the ancestors were believed to be present at them, with the exception of a single statement that the spirits gather to join

in the wailing over a dead man. On the contrary, it was once expressly stated to me that the formal appointment of an heir to take the name and status of the dead person was all the remembrance necessary. This statement illustrates a very significant aspect of the Baganda view of the relation between the living and the dead.

This is not regarded as a prolongation beyond the grave of the ties of mutual obligation by which living relatives are bound, because, on the death of every adult person, his place is filled by someone who is made responsible for the performance of his duties to his relatives. If the heir fails in these duties, the spirit will punish him; but the spirit itself does not remain in continuous contact with those it has left behind. Its active intervention is practically confined to visitations in which it expresses anger at some injury. This is done by "possessing" one of its descendants. The spirit is supposed to enter the stomach by the mouth and cause a type of indigestion . . . whose first symptom is said to be a very cold feeling. This is regarded as the manifestation *par excellence* of spirit possession, but many other illnesses may be ascribed to this cause.

It is in this context of general beliefs that we must examine the ideas of the Baganda concerning the peculiarly powerful and important spirits who formerly, as *lubale,* were the object of a public cult. The *lubale* are the spirits of persons who gave evidence of supernatural powers during their lifetime,

[Adapted from *An African People in the Twentieth Century*, George Routledge and Sons, London, 1934. Pp. 224-226, 229-248, 250, 257-263. Used by permission.]

and who manifested themselves after death not only, like other spirits, for their personal ends but also in order to help the living by foretelling the future and by revealing to them magical means of obtaining wealth, fertility, and success in enterprises of all kinds. This they did through the mouths of prophets who, once possessed, were formally dedicated to their service. Two of them were honoured by human sacrifice—one, Kibuka, the war-god, for the specific reason that he met his death by violence and treachery.

Theoretically, each clan had its own *lubale*, but the cult of each divinity was not confined to the members of the clan. This explains the fact that only a few *lubale* are now universally remembered—Kibuka and Nende, the war-gods, Mukasa, the giver of children and especially of twins, all of whom were particularly honoured by the king, and Kaumpuli, the god of plague. Kings on their death acquired a position analogous to that of *lubale*. That is to say, their spirits could possess the attendant on their tombs and cause him to prophesy. But they did so only for the personal benefit of the reigning king.

The connection between the *lubale* and the members of its own clan was a close but not an exclusive one. Each *lubale* seems to have had a single temple, and this, unless it had been deliberately transferred by the king to a place near the capital, stood in the clan lands and was under the authority of a priest (*Kabona*) appointed by the clan head. A portion of the land was allotted to the god, and the *Kabona* had the same rights over the peasants who lived on it as an ordinary chief. The temple was the scene of the public cult of the *lubale,* and in it were preserved the relics of the god, or some object which was supposed to be his material manifestation (e.g. Kibuka's navel-cord and spear, or the large stone which was sacred to Mukasa). But the cult was open to any one who wished to join in it.

Private prayers, however, were offered only to the *lubale* of the suppliant's clan. He would build a small shrine in his banana-grove and offer beer and cowries there.

The central point in the *lubale* cult was the belief in spirit possession. The *lubale* se-

lected as their mouthpieces certain individuals through whom they spoke, both in answer to inquiries and spontaneously. The connection here between *lubale* and clan was that a prophet was always possessed first by the *lubale* of his own clan, though once his formal initiation as a prophet was completed he might become the vehicle of any divinity.

[There was no] sharp differentiation between the provinces of the various *lubale*. Each individual appealed for the same general benefits to his own clan *lubale,* and, at any rate in the case of the private practitioners, a prophet when consulted did not know which *lubale* would first respond to the invocation. . . . A consultant in search of a cure for illness, of magic to recover stolen goods, of a charm for child-bearing or the acquisition of wealth, would look for a prophet with a reputation for "speaking well", rather than the servant of some particular *lubale*. Any *lubale* could answer such requests. Thus the king when ill would consult Kibuka, the war-god, and I have seen child-bearing charms distributed by a prophet of Kaumpuli, the god of plague, while a chief before he set out for war would consult the local *lubale,* whoever he might be.

At the same time there were certain matters—national safety, national as distinct from personal success in war, dangerous activities such as hunting and fishing, and calamities of various kinds—which were exclusively within the control of individual *lubale*.

I have mentioned already that Kibuka is in fact one of the two gods—or, according to some versions, the only one—to whom human sacrifices were made. The other is the *lubale* of the river Mayanja, whom the king consulted during the accession ceremonies. . . .

Of the *lubale* who presided over calamities, and were appealed to when they occurred, the principal were Kaumpuli, the god of plague, Kawali or Ndawula, of smallpox, Kiwanuka, of lightning, Musisi, of earthquakes, and Nagawonyi, the goddess of drought.

Mukasa was the *lubale* appealed to by fishermen. The hunters' god was Dungu, who, as supernatural owner of all wild animals, would announce to the hunter who approached him before setting out: "I give you such and such a beast; go and kill it!" or might warn him to put off his expedition.

Certain natural objects, such as wells, large rocks, and trees, were also believed to be associated with *lubale,* and treated with respect.

The ceremonial centered always round the "appearance" of the *lubale*—the utterance by his prophet in a hypnotic condition of oracles and answers to inquiries, and, where the temple contained relics of the god, their display before the assembled people. . . . Whether or not there were fixed occasions for consulting the other *lubale,* any individual inquirer had always to arrange in advance the day on which he would approach the god and the gifts he would bring, so that it was generally known when the *lubale* proposed to speak, and those who wished to be present could gather at the temple. The proceedings began with an invocation to the *lubale* uttered either by the *Kabona* or by the prophet himself. The audience then sang the songs especially appropriate to the *lubale* concerned, to the accompaniment not of the usual music but of rattles made of gourds with dry seeds inside or of a double layer of canes with seeds between. The descent of the *lubale* upon the prophet's head was indicated when the latter began to make violent jerky movements and sometimes got up and danced. When these preliminaries were over, he attended to the requests of the persons who had come to consult him, which he was supposed to be able to interpret without their offering any explanation. The ceremony ended with more dancing and singing and the consumption of the beer which the inquirers had brought.

The prestige of the "national" *lubale* rested at least as much upon the elaborate and lavish nature of their cult as upon confidence in the efficacy of their oracles. What struck the popular imagination and is remembered now is the extent of the temple household, the numbers of the gods' servants, his flocks and herds, and, above all, the celebrations which attended a consultation by the king.

The less important temples similarly drew their revenues from the offerings of persons who came to consult the prophet, and acquired their servants in many cases from the children of persons to whom they had given fertility. The private prophet accumulated in the same way his herd of goats and store of barkcloths and cowries from the preliminary gifts which he demanded of consultants and the presents brought him if his advice or medicine was effective. These do not seem to have been stipulated for in advance, but brought as a recognized obligation towards the *lubale,* failure in which would incur his anger.

The prophet was first marked out for his career by the choice of the *lubale,* manifested in his possession by the spirit, but he could not begin to prophesy till he had been ceremonially initiated by an older practitioner. The usual signs of possession by a *lubale* were different from those of possession by a *muzimu* [spirit of a dead person]. The person concerned "went mad", wandered about in a distraught manner, and slept out of doors.

The avowed purpose of the ceremony of initiation . . . is to make the *lubale* speak, but it represents also the formal reception of a new member into the body of practitioners and his public dedication to the service of the god, and it was probably accompanied by some esoteric instruction, particularly as to the efficacy of different herbs and charms. It was presided over by the leading prophet of the neighbourhood—that is the one whose general repute was highest, for there was no fixed order of seniority. The arrangements were made by the father of the person possessed, even if the latter was a grown man, not only because from the nature of his condition he was not responsible for himself but because the ceremony involved the creation of a quasi-filial relationship of the initiate to the initiating prophet.

Usually a number of persons were initiated at the same time.

"The man who initiates him becomes his father; he cannot disobey him."

The prophet was formally handed the insignia of office—a spear and stick, a pair of rattles, a pair of baskets for receiving small offerings, and a cow-hair fly-whisk, which he apparently used to fan himself with when in the frenzy of possession. Prophets of Kaumpuli carry instead a little stick decorated with cowry-shells, with which they beat themselves on the head when possessed.

The new prophet had then to introduce his *lubale* into his own house. . . . He prepared a place in the house to keep his insignia, built a hut for the *lubale* in the banana-grove, and then invited his friends and relatives to a beer-drink provided by his father, at which he spoke for the first time in the name of his *lubale*.

These two types of ceremonial comprise the whole of the organized religious ritual of Buganda. The peculiarities which distinguish it from the religious ceremonies of Bantu Africa are clearly related to the peculiar features of the whole social organization of the people. Just as in economic and political matters, the control of land, and the government of its inhabitants, this organization rested not on kinship ties but on a system of territorial authorities responsible to the tribal head, so in religious observances the unit which acted in co-operation, in so far as it is definable at all, rested on a territorial basis.

Another peculiarity of Baganda religion is that there was no ceremonial in which it was obligatory for any one, outside the servants of the temple, to participate, no occasion for a national gathering such as are recorded almost everywhere among the Bantu, and certainly no gathering of kinsmen at the temple of the clan *lubale*. The cult of the *lubale* by the king himself was certainly regarded as performed on behalf of the nation, but the active participants in it were only the chiefs whom he designated as his messengers. The one tribal gathering took place in connection with the king's accession, and did not include a religious element. The only public manifestation of tribal unity is thus not an affirmation of common dependence upon human head and tribal deity together, but simply of common political allegiance to the king. Religious beliefs do not here serve, as among so many primitive peoples, as a mainstay of the political system.

The prophet's position rested originally on his personal relationship with the *lubale,* made manifest by his possession and recognized as genuine in his initiation. But his subsequent activities were not confined to acting as the *lubale's* mouthpiece, and while the truth of his utterances is mentioned as the criterion of a prophet's success, his prestige rested at least as much upon the use which he made of the magical knowledge which the *lubale* was supposed to reveal to him. This included harmful as well as beneficent magic, and to judge by the stories of present-day magicians, which are a favourite topic of conversation, the real test of greatness was the use which he made of such knowledge to further his personal ends.

Thus the prophet of the established religion appears as one and the same with the sorcerer whose activities are universally dreaded, and among the Baganda, as elsewhere, black and white magic are seen to be linked. It is true that the natives do not clearly recognize this identity. They distinguish between *basamizi* or prophets and *basawo* or doctors, holding that the latter owe their skill to knowledge acquired empirically or learnt from their fathers and not to divine inspiration. But though there probably are persons who deal in native medicines without setting up to be prophets, it is certain that healing by means of herbs and charms was and is an important part of the business of the latter. It is true, too, that sorcerers or *balogo* are invariably referred to as a class apart, who learn their evil secrets heaven knows how—probably from their fathers, as a respectable person learns his craft —and whose identity rarely becomes known, so cunning are they at casting their spells over long distances. But it is quite certain that the activities of prophets to this day include the provision of injurious magic for ends which are regarded as justifiable. . . .

It has already been made clear that the prophets were not looked to for that assistance in economic activities which is so commonly the function of the magician. Though there was a recourse in case of drought, the Baganda had no rain-maker whose magic was regularly called upon, nor any rites associated with the various stages of the agricultural year. In connection with the more hazardous pursuit of fishing from canoes in the lake, magic, and the prophets as its source, seem to have played a wider part.

The one activity in which magic exercised a positive organizing force was warfare. [In] the war itself the prophet played a more influential part than the general. But it was not only over the course of the actual fighting that they predominated. The time and place of the war, the selection of the general, and probably also the districts whose inhabitants were to stay at home "to guard the king", were decided by them in answer to inquiries. One of the prophets went in person with the army, and the general was guided by his daily pronouncements throughout the campaign.

In other departments of life recourse to magic was a purely individual affair, and seldom sought in connection with any particular practical activity. Hunting magic is the main exception to this rule, and of this no one knew much except vaguely that medicine could be obtained to tie into the nets, and when hunting a lion to smear in its footprints and cause it to return. Another case in which magic was used for some specific occasion is litigation; a man would acquire a charm for success before pleading a case.

But the main objects of magic seem to have been of a remedial or, less commonly, of a preventive nature. The *lubale* of plague, of earthquakes, lightning, and drought have been mentioned. The provision of cures for barrenness and for illness of all kinds seems to have represented the greater part of the activity of prophets in general. The war-magic which private individuals could obtain, consisting in medicine to smear on the body in order to turn away the enemy's spears, is of the preventive type, as is the magical precaution taken by a retreating army of stopping the pursuit by placing in the path a cow's hide containing leaves and

—according to one version—the body of an infant.

Then there are various types of purificatory rite which a prophet might recommend to have performed in order to avert a threatened calamity, as often as to put an end to one which had already occurred. The extreme case of such measures is represented by the executions which were ordered by the prophets of Kibuka on behalf of the whole country. To purify a village, a chief might be ordered to kill a man, and would choose a friendless person from among his subjects. A lesser person would make up a bundle of various plants specified by the prophet and have it laid on an ant-hill, or at a crossroad; where the evil would attach itself to the next passer-by. . . . A rite which does not contain this representation in concrete form of a ridding of the evil is the planting of an *mpongo* —a plot of land cleared and sown in one day by joint work of the whole village. In this plot, a quantity of every kind of food-crop was planted, as well as a barkcloth-tree garlanded with banana-leaves. When the millet from this plot ripened, the chief had beer brewed with it and summoned the prophet to drink, and the latter would declare: "The evil has gone to such-and-such a village."

Similarly the magical rites which private individuals performed on their own behalf were all of a precautionary nature.

All the types of sorcery universally believed in operate through the contact or close proximity of the victim himself with the magical object. The belief that parts of the victim's person can be used as the material for sorcery directed against him plays little part in Baganda ideas. There are four main methods of setting the magic to work. One is simple poisoning, which may be done by mixing poison with the victim's food or secretly inserting it in his drinking gourd. The next is the transmission of disease by medicines smeared in the palm of the sorcerer's hand so that the victim touches it when they greet. I was told that the prevalence of cataract which I noticed at Kisimula was due to the unusually large number of sorcerers in the neighbourhood who spread it in this way.

A third method is to bury some object where people will step over it—in the doorway of a house, if a single victim is aimed at; in a public footpath if the intention is to destroy a whole village. The last method is that of sending the magical object to do its work at a distance. This is done most commonly by smoking the medicines in a pipe and blowing the ashes towards the victim.

What is the relation between this system and the new religion which is now, formally at least, accepted by the whole Baganda people? Of course it is officially disowned; the public cult of the *lubale* has vanished, and with it have gone the temples and priesthood which enshrined it—"The temples have fallen down and the *lubale* just wander about," as it was put to me. The wars for which the king depended most upon their guidance are a thing of the past, as are the national dangers against which they warned him, and the royal welfare is now invoked in the liturgy of the Anglican Church. The one fragment that survives is at the tombs of dead kings—of Mutesa at the capital, where his many surviving widows still live, and of Kalema, the short-lived nominee of the Moslems, who drove out Mwanga; here the dead kings' spirits still manifest themselves, though only now for such undignified purposes as the complaint that the spears which adorn their temples are not kept polished. Nor is there any open cult of the ancestors.

But the beliefs as to the existence and behaviour of the *lubale* and *mizimu* remain unshaken, and though some natives say that *lubale,* prophets and all magical practices, and even *mizimu,* are "of Satan", others ascribe the powers of the *mulogo* to Katonda . . . . [Some writers point out that whereas the lubale were superhuman spirits whose prophets could perform magic or tricks to aid a human being in need, there were also supernatural beings, among whom Katonda was the principal. Since he created and ruled the universe, the missionaries used his name for the Christian God.] The latter point of view does not, of course, indicate a metaphysical theory ascribing to God responsibility for the works of the Devil. What it does show is the accommodation, in the native mind, of the new doctrine with the old. Katonda is now taken for granted, though it would be extraordinarily interesting to know how he is conceived—whether, for example, Katonda is thought of as being the same *lubale* whom the Baganda had always known, without realizing his importance or the cult which he desired. He is undoubtedly now the central figure in Baganda theology; he is the protector and giver of blessings *par excellence,* and phrases like "May Katonda protect you!" or "That is Katonda's affair", of any matter of uncertain outcome, are constantly used, and probably with a more literal significance in native language than they have in ours. But Katonda has by no means replaced the other divinities, and, in cases of specific need, it is to them that many natives would first appeal.

I have described the beliefs in magic, good and evil, in the present tense because they are as much alive to-day as they ever were. There may be a few educated natives who really have been reasoned out of such ideas; there are certainly some who have been convinced by the rational explanation of some particular phenomenon, say an epidemic of plague, and have ceased to ascribe it to supernatural causes, but it would be most unsafe to assume that the corollary of such a conviction in one instance must be the rejection of all magical beliefs.

While such beliefs exist the practices to which they give rise cannot die, and the private prophets, though their numbers may be less, still play their part in Baganda life. There are native doctors in every village, who are consulted partly because their medicines are more drastic, and therefore to native ideas more effective, than those dispensed by Government and mission hospitals, but also because of the firm conviction that European medicines are useless against the visitations alike of spirits and sorcers. The secrecy with which the proceedings have nowadays to be carried on has meant a certain alteration in the proportions of their various elements. There can now be no public display of offerings, no festive gathering of suppliants.

The mechanism of control provided by magic over matters that are of intense importance to the individual but uncontrollable by him in any other way—recovery from illness, the fidelity of a wife, a debtor's solvency, success in business—is something for which Christianity does not provide a complete substitute.

There is one class of beliefs that have been directly destroyed by Christianity—those relating to the automatic supernatural punishments, and, in particular, to the punishments for unchastity. Here we are concerned with ideas which, unlike the beliefs in magic, have consequences that run counter to normal human desires, so that the readiness with which they are abandoned is as easily explicable as the capacity with which the magical beliefs are cherished.

Regarded strictly in its religious aspect, as a system of beliefs and practices to which man turns for reassurance in facing the unknown and confirmation of his moral standards, it is very difficult to judge how far Christianity has really been assimilated into Baganda culture. Certainly it means a great deal to them, they know their Bibles thoroughly and unquestioningly accept the literal truth of the mythology, which they harmonize with their own in a manner that is rather amusing.

They accept the formulae, I think, as part of the ritual—the kind of worship that is pleasing to Katonda, just as drumming and dancing pleased the older *lubale*. The differences in Protestant and Catholic ritual they sometimes compare to differences in the ceremonial of the old temples.

Christianity has a very definite importance to the Baganda; but exactly what it signifies to them it is extraordinarily difficult to say. Certainly it does not mean, at this stage, the general acceptance of a new moral code, as a result of which actions formerly permitted meet with the spontaneous disapproval that is aroused by those which age-old tradition condemns. . . . The repudiation of their polygamous wives by many of the chiefs who were first baptized may have had in it an element of conviction that polygamy was displeasing to Katonda, but a great part of its significance must have lain in the performance of an act which publicly differentiated them from their non-Christian neighbours. But the outward and visible signs of Christianity, even if they extend to behaviour in complete conformity with Christian principles, do not necessarily imply the presence of their inward and spiritual counterpart.

As regards the recourse to magic for supernatural aid, my impression is that with the Baganda Christianity has neither discredited nor replaced the traditional methods. What it has done—and this may be the reason why its acceptance has been so widespread—has been to supplement them where they were lacking in the promise of a life beyond the grave, and I believe that in this lies its main significance to the natives in the strictly religious as distinct from the social sense. To look to heaven for the redressing of life's injustices is not, in itself, sufficient to the Muganda, but to be able to look forward to heaven is a matter of great moment.

Christian missions, both by the general education and the specialized training which they give, are doing more than any other single force towards the adaptation of the Muganda to his new life. But their general attitude towards native life, particularly in the sphere of family relations, has been to demand conformity with standards which are not really an inevitable outcome of the Christian doctrine. Because Christianity is the officially recognized religion of the English people, it is assumed that it prescribes the forms in which English life is moulded, and when it is transferred to Africa these forms are too often taken for granted as an essential part of it. The unconscious assumption that a genuine Christian must necessarily behave in all respects like an English gentleman is the product of a culture into which Christianity really has been firmly integrated.

• 67 • Fetishes and Amulets

JOHN ROSCOE

The fetiches . . . were a mixed set of objects of all shapes and patterns. Every home had its supply of them, and no person would have thought himself or his family safe if he had not had a number of them about him. It is impossible to give an adequate idea of the number of these objects, so many and so varied were they; but a few of the most important have been selected....

Fetiches . . . were worn around the neck, arms, and loins for special purposes; for instance, a man, when visiting the King, would wear a fetich as a safeguard against incurring the King's anger; . . . others would wear fetiches to protect them from wild animals, snakes, diseases, and so forth. Women wore them round their waists for fecundity. Those not in use were kept in a particular place in the hut which was reserved for them, and they had frequent offerings of beer made to them. When a man went to war, he carried some with him, to protect him from various dangers, to assist him in battle, and to intimidate the enemy. The fetiches left behind were propitiated daily by his chief wife; offerings of beer were poured out on the floor before them, and prayers to protect the absent husband were addressed to them. If a woman neglected to do this, and her husband fell or was wounded in battle, she was charged with being the cause of his death, and was further accused as an adulteress. The King sent six special fetiches to war with the general.

Only the most skilled medicine-man could make fetiches; herbs had to be carefully selected, and other materials were needed, such as the hearts of lions, leopards, crocodiles, elephants, buffaloes, and other animals, which (it was supposed) would make the owner brave and strong. These materials were pounded together and stuffed into the horns, or they were mixed with clay, made into fetiches, and dedicated by the medicine-man to different gods. They thus became identified with a supernatural being, and in consequence they were possessed by the gods, and were powerful and effective. The secret of making these fetiches was confined to a small number of medicine-men who never divulged it to others, unless they themselves were to reap some benefit by the communication. The people believed that these objects had supernatural powers, they paid large sums of money for them, and treated them with the utmost respect and reverence.

When a King was crowned he sent to his paternal grandmother's clan for a new fetich, *Nantaba.* The grandmother's relatives prepared a gourd . . . and also selected a tree of a special sort . . . for the fetich. . . . [The gourd, with leaves from the tree placed inside, was stitched into a piece of decorated goat skin. A stout stick was cut from the tree trunk. These were taken ceremoniously to the palace.] When they arrived at the palace, a temple was built for the gourd, and one of the King's wives . . . was appointed caretaker of it. . . . Another shrine was built for the stick . . . and it also had a woman-guardian.

Mbajwe was the King's chief fetich, and had its temple, its priest, and a female medium through whom it was supposed to give oracles. This fetich was made of rope in imitation of a serpent, with the head formed of clay and fashioned like a serpent's head. [It had a retinue of attendants: the priest and the medium mentioned above, a chief who was its guardian, a man to carry it, two men to beat the special drums on occasion, another man to procure its food, and a woman to care for the leopard skin rug upon which it reclined. The fetich also

[Adapted from *The Baganda: an Account of Their Native Customs and Beliefs,* Macmillan, London, 1911. Pp. 323-331. Used by permission.]

owned a number of objects—a special bag, an axe, a drum, and a basket. In the temple with it were two smaller fetiches.]

Nambaga was the chief fetich of the common people. It was a horn, usually a buffalo-horn, into which the medicine-men put different ingredients. The open end of the horn, after being filled, was corked with a wooden plug. The plug was frequently decorated with iron, brass, and copper studs driven into it; in the centre of it was a small hole. . . . Into this hole further drugs were poured, if the owner were ordered by the medicine-man to use them either for himself, or for any member of his family. . . .

The fetich *Luboa* was extensively used by hunters and warriors. Hunters believed that the fetich cast a spell over wild animals, and especially over the buffalo, so that they could be approached and speared without the hunter being exposed to attack from them. Warriors, too, believed that in battle the fetich, waved before an enemy, would have the effect of making him powerless to strike, while it nerved the owner, and made his aim sure and effective.

Amulets . . . may be distinguished from fetiches . . . in that the former seldom possessed supernatural powers, but were used chiefly for medicinal purposes. They were carried or worn on the person to be ready for use; some of them were in fact turned into ornaments, and carried about long after they had ceased to be required for their original purpose. The medicine-men were the vendors of amulets; the majority were composed either of wood or of herbs, made into compact shapes. . . . Some of them were for outward application only; others were to be taken internally. . . . They had a wide range of remedies; indeed, almost every ailment known to the medicine-men was treated with some kind of amulet. . . . These amulets were valued so highly by the people that, when the disease was healed, the medicine was not cast aside, but decorated and worn as an ornament, and was thus ready should there be any return of the old symptoms. As charms they were used chiefly for the prevention of disease; their medicinal properties had brought them into notoriety, and they were afterwards regarded as possessing powers to avert the evil which they had originally been meant to cure.

The Baganda had reached a high cultural level before their first contacts with Arab and European explorers. Their farming methods were efficient enough to support a dense population. Arts and crafts were well developed, including that craft basic to advanced technology, the smelting of iron. Their political system was complex, with a kingship based upon a bureaucracy of lower officials and supported by a far-reaching system of taxation.

However, one important invention was lacking in Buganda, the knowledge of writing. Political and legal administration must have been severely handicapped. The maintenance of their armies must have been haphazard. The authority of the king himself was probably difficult to establish.

Taking the place of writing to some extent were symbols of office and an elaborate body of unwritten literature. Myths or folktales give the purported history of the Baganda and back up the traditional authority of the king.

The creation story presented in the next selection, despite being marred by the literary style of its European recorder, gives some idea of Baganda traditions. The reader will perhaps note some incidents similar to other creation stories known by him. Literature develops in large part by the process of placing old incidents or motifs in new combinations. Motifs commonly spread from one group of people to another. Thus, all the African kingdoms near Buganda have creation tales much like the one given here.

The Baganda also have a large number of animal stories. Some of these are moralistic. An animal is arrogant or foolhardy or has some other defect of character. Owing to this trait, the animal is injured or killed.

A favorite series of stories is about the rabbit. Rabbit, the trickster all over Negro Africa, is always able to outwit the larger African animals. The West African Negroes brought rabbit-trickster stories with them when they came as slaves to the New World. The Br'er Rabbit tales made famous by Joel Chandler Harris are based upon African stories.

There are tales about a Baganda boy captured and reared by wild animals. The boy usually spoils things by telling other people of his good fortune. He is then killed or deserted by his animal foster parents. Stories of this type, often called the wolf-boy theme, are worldwide. The cowboy folklore hero, Pecos Bill, for example, was reared by a coyote.

The Baganda, like all people, have many stories about everyday life. Stories about hunts, bewitched persons, wars, and celebrations are common. Early explorers found themselves to be fine material for Baganda folktales. Speke, the first European in Buganda, was believed to be an eater of Baganda babies. Cannibalism of the Basese (people living on the islands of Lake Victoria) was the older theme. Speke was simply cast in the role of a Basese. Incidentally, cannibalism never was common in Africa. Where it does occur it almost always is a religious ritual as it was in the ancient Near East.

Unwritten literature is becoming less important as the percentage of literate Baganda increases. The storyteller, however, still has an eager audience in backwoods Buganda. News and rumors are still spread largely by word of mouth. Each person who passes the news on to another makes it a little more like some familiar tale. Eventually the news may become nothing but a variant form of some widely-known folk tale.

• 68 • *Mythology*
HARRY H. JOHNSTON

History in Uganda goes back with a certain proportion of probability and truth to about the middle of the fourteenth century of our era, when the western coast-lands of the Victoria Nyanza were regarded as loosely held appanages of the two or three Hima kingdoms which stretched over Unyoro, Toro, Ankole, and Karagwe. Possibly for reasons of health the Bahima did little to occupy the richly forested countries of Kiagwe, Uganda, Buddu, Kisiba, etc. They applied the term "Bairo," or "slaves," to the Negro races living in these well-forested countries from which the Bahima aristocrats on the interior plateaux derived coffee berries and bark-cloth. Some 450 years ago (if one

[Adapted from *The Uganda Protectorate,* Hutchinson, London, 1904. Pp. 678-679, 700-705. Used by permission.]

may venture to estimate the lapse of time by native tradition as to the number of kings that have reigned since then) a Muhima hunter from Unyoro, who went by the name of Muganda, or "the brother," came with a pack of dogs, a woman, a spear, and a shield to the Katonga valley. The Katonga marsh-river is a long watercourse, which at the present day separates the Kingdom of Uganda from its dependent Province of Buddu. This hunter, Muganda, was a poor man, but so successful in hunting that large numbers of the aboriginal negroes, the Bairo, flocked to him for flesh. They became so attached to him as to invite him to become their chief, complaining that their distant Muhima sovereign in Unyoro lived too far away for his sovereignty to be of any use to them. Muganda hesitated, fearing to come into conflict with the Bahima aristocracy, who looked upon these lake countries as their hunting ground for slaves. But at last he consented, became the ruler of the country between the Nile and the Katonga River (the modern Uganda), gave his own name to the country, which he called Buganda, and himself took the new name of *Kimera*. The legend runs that the kings of Gala blood in Unyoro and on the Ankole Plateau received the news of a Hima wanderer having become the elected chief of Uganda with equanimity, saying, "What does it matter to us what goes on in those lands from which we draw our slaves?" However, this Norman of Central Africa soon erected his principality into a strong and well-organised power. The people of the coastlands between Busoga on the north and the Kagera River on the west formed a group of Bantu Negroes somewhat distinct from the Unyoro stock to the west of them.

[The ancestry of the king was traced back 30 or more generations to the first man upon the earth. The principal legend about the first man follows.]

THE CREATION

Kintu was the first man, and when he came from the unknown he found nothing in Uganda—no food, no water, no animals, nothing but a blank. He had a cow with him, and when he was hungry he drank her milk.

One day as he roamed about searching for something he saw two girls just dropping down from Mugulu (Heaven, or the Above). He stopped. The girls also stopped a long way off. They were Mugulu's daughters, Nambi and her sister. The girls were much surprised, and Nambi said: "Sister, look at the two things over there. What can they be?" The sister looked, but said nothing. Nambi continued: "We never saw anything like them before. Just go down and see what brings things like these to such a place as the earth."

"How can I?" replied the sister. "Look at those horns!"

"Oh, I don't mean that one; try the other."

The sister then advanced a little way, and when Kintu saw her coming he also advanced to meet her, whereon the sister ran back to Nambi, and they both prepared for flight. Kintu, however, did not continue the pursuit, but returned to the cow.

After some time Nambi and her sister decided to come close to Kintu, and when a hundred paces only separated them Nambi spoke to him.

"Who are you?"

"I am Kintu."

"And what is that?" pointing to the cow.

"That is my cow."

Nambi and her sister withdrew to consider whether this could possibly be true. They returned directly and asked: "We have never seen anything like you before; where did you come from?"

"I do not know."

Kintu at this point milked some milk on to the palm of his left hand and drank it.

"What do you do that for?" asked Nambi.

"That's my food," replied Kintu.

"We see no water here. What do you drink?"

"I drink milk."

The girls then retired for another conference, and Nambi confided to her sister that she believed this was a man; nothing else could do such extraordinary things. They returned to Kintu and submitted their decision, and Kintu said: "Yes, I am a man."

Nambi then told him all about themselves, and suggested that he should accompany them to Mugulu. Kintu agreed on condition that they also took his cow. This they declined to do, and disappeared.

As soon as they arrived they told Mugulu that they had found a man and a cow.

"Where?" asked Mugulu.

"On the earth."

"Not a real man, surely?" and Mugulu smiled as if he did not believe them, but they suspected he knew all the time.

"Oh yes, a real man. We know he is a real man because he wants food, and when he is hungry he drags the udder of his cow, and squeezes out white juice, which he drinks."

"I shall make inquiries."

"He is very nice," said Nambi, "and I wanted to bring him up here. May I go and fetch him?"

"Leave the matter to me," said Mugulu, and the girls withdrew.

Directly they had gone Mugulu called his sons and said: "Go to the earth and test this story about a real man being there. Nambi says she saw a wild man and a cow, and that the man drank the cow's juice. Fetch the cow."

The boys prepared to start at once.

"Soka olinderira" ("Wait a bit"), said Mugulu; "I don't want the man. He will probably die when he sees you; the cow only."

The boys arrived near Kintu's resting-place, and he was asleep. They took the cow and carried her off. When Kintu awoke he did not see the cow, but just then he did not start in search of her, as he supposed she had only wandered a short distance. Presently he got hungry, and tried to find the cow, but in vain. He ultimately decided that the girls must have returned and stolen her, and he was very angry and hungry. He used many words not of peace, and he

sat down and pointed his nails and sharpened his teeth, but there was no one with whom to fight. He then peeled the bark off a tree and sucked it, and thus he fed himself.

Next day Nambi saw Kintu's cow as the boys arrived, and she exclaimed: "You have stolen Kintu's cow! That cow was his food and drink, and now what has he to eat? I like Kintu, if you do not. I shall go down to-morrow, and if he is not dead I shall bring him up here," and she went and found Kintu.

"So they have taken away your cow?"

"Yes."

"And what have you been eating since?"

"I have been sucking the bark of a tree."

"Did you really do that?"

"What else was there to do?"

"Well, come with me to Mugulu and you shall have your cow given back to you."

They went, and Kintu, when he arrived, saw a vast multitude of people and plenty of bananas and fowls and goats and sheep—in fact, everything was there in plenty. And the boys, when they saw Nambi arrive with Kintu, said: "Let us tell our father, Mugulu," and they went and told him, and Mugulu said: "Go and tell my chiefs to build a big house without a door for the stranger Kintu." The house was built and Kintu went into it.

Mugulu then gave the following lavish order: "My people, go and cook 10,000 dishes of food, and roast 10,000 cows, and fill 10,000 vessels with beer, and give it to the stranger. If he is a real man he will eat it, if not, then —the penalty is death."

The food was prepared and taken to Kintu's house. As there was no door, the crowd put their shoulders to one side of the house and raised it up off the ground, and put the food inside, and told Kintu that if he did not finish it all at a meal the result would be death. They dropped down the side of the house again, and waited outside.

Kintu surveyed the mass of food with dismay, and then started to walk around it, muttering his feelings to himself. As he went round the heap his foot slipped into a hole, and on examination he found that it was the opening of a cavern. "Ha! ha!" said he, "this cave has a good appetite; let me feed it," and he took the 10,000 measures of beer and spilled them in, laying the empty vessels on one side; then the 10,000 carcasses of roast cows were pitched into the cavern, and lastly the food from the 10,000 baskets; and then he called to the people outside, after he had closed the hole: "Haven't you got a little more food out there?"

"No," they replied. "Did we not give you enough?"

"Well, I suppose I must do with it, if you have nothing more cooked."

"Have you finished it all?"

"Yes, yes. Come and take away the empty dishes."

The crowd raised the side wall of the house, came inside, and asked Kintu whether he really had disposed of the food. He assured them that he had, and they with one accord cried out: "Then it is a man indeed!" And they went direct to Mugulu and told him that the stranger had finished his meal and asked for more.

Mugulu at first branded this statement as a falsehood, but on consideration he believed it. He pondered for a moment, then taking up a copper axe he said to his chiefs: "Take this to Kintu. Tell him I want material to make a fire. Tell him that Mugulu is old and cold, and that Mugulu does not burn wood for a fire. Tell him I want stones, and tell him that he must cut up rocks with this copper axe and fetch the pieces and light me a fire. If he does so, then he may claim his cow. He may also have Nambi, and he can return to the earth."

The chiefs went to Kintu and told him that Mugulu wanted a fire made of stones, and that he must chop a rock with a copper axe.

Kintu suspected there was something wrong, but he spoke no words to that effect. He put the axe on his shoulder and went out before they allowed the wall to drop to the ground. He walked straight to a big rock, stood in front of it, placed the head of the axe on the rock, and rested his chin on the tip of the handle.

"It does not seem easy to cut," said he to axe.

"It is easy enough to me," replied the axe; "just strike and see."

Kintu struck the rock, and it splintered in all directions. He picked up the pieces of rock, and went straight to Mugulu and said: "Here's your firewood, Mugulu. Do you want any more?"

Mugulu said: "This is marvellous! Go back to your house. It only remains now for you to find your cow," and Kintu went away.

Next morning the chiefs were called before Mugulu, and he said: "Take this bucket to Kintu, and tell him to fetch water. Tell him that Mugulu does not drink anything but dew, and if he is a man he is to fetch it quickly."

Kintu received the bucket and the message, and again he suspected there was something wrong, and he said words within himself, but he spoke nothing to that effect. He took the bucket and went out, and he set it down on the grass, and he said to the bucket: "This does not seem very easy." The bucket replied: "It is easy enough to me," and when Kintu looked down he saw that the bucket was full of dew. He took it to Mugulu and said: "Here's your drinking water, Mugulu. Do you want any more?"

Mugulu said: "This is marvellous. Kintu, you are a prodigy. I am now satisfied that you are a man indeed, and it only remains for you to get your cow. Whoever took Kintu's cow let him restore it."

"Your own sons stole my cow," said Kintu.

"If so," replied Mugulu, "drive all the cows here, and let Kintu pick out his cow if she is amongst them."

Ten thousand cows were brought in a herd. (It will be remembered that Nambi and her sister assumed a fine astonishment at the "horned thing" when they first saw Kintu's cow, and yet this large herd had

belonged to Mugulu all the time. It is however, fatal to cross-examine the story-teller,
as will be seen later on.)

Kintu stood near the herd in great perplexity, lost in thought. A hornet came and
sat on Kintu's shoulder, and as Kintu gave
no heed, the hornet prepared his sting and
drove it home.

Kintu struck at the hornet and missed
him, and the hornet said: "Don't strike, I'm
your friend."

"You have just bit me," replied Kintu.

"It wasn't a bite. Listen. You can never
tell your cow amongst all that herd. Just
you wait until I fly out and sit on the shoulder of a cow. That's yours. Mark her."

The herd of 10,000 cows was driven past,
but the hornet did not move, and Kintu
said aloud: "My cow is not amongst them."

Mugulu then ordered another herd to be
brought, numbering twice as many cows as
the last herd; but the hornet did not move,
and Kintu said aloud: "My cow is not
amongst them."

The herdsmen drove the cows away, and
another herd was brought, and the hornet
flew off and sat on the shoulder of a cow.
Kintu went forward and marked her.
"That's mine," said he to Mugulu. The hornet then flew to another, a young cow, and
Kintu went forward and marked her, and
said: "That also is mine." The hornet flew
to a third, and Kintu went forward and
marked this one also, and said: "That is
mine also."

Mugulu said: "Quite correct; your cow
has had two calves since she arrived in
Heaven. You are a prodigy, Kintu. Take
your cows, and take Nambi also, and go
back to the earth. Wait a bit." Here Mugulu
called his servants and said to them: "Go
to my store and fetch one banana plant, one
potato, one bean, one Indian corn, one
ground-nut, and one hen." The things were
brought, and Mugulu then addressed Kintu
and Nambi: "Take these things with you;
you may want them." Then addressing
Kintu he said: "I must tell you that Nambi
has a brother named Warumbe (Disease or

Death). He is mad and ruthless. At this
moment he is not here, so you had better
start quickly before he returns. If he sees
you he may wish to go with you, and you
are certain to quarrel." Then to Nambi:
"Here is some millet to feed the hen on the
road down. If you forget anything, don't
come back to fetch it. That is all; you may
go."

Kintu and Nambi started, and when they
were some distance on the journey Nambi
suddenly remembered that it was time to
feed the hen. She asked Kintu for the millet,
but it was nowhere to be found, and now it
was clear they had forgotten it in the hurry
of departure.

"I shall return and fetch it," said Kintu.

"No, no, you must not. Warumbe will
have returned, and he will probably wish
to accompany us. I don't want him, and
you had better not return."

"But the hen is hungry, and we must
feed it."

"Yes, it is," assented Nambi.

Nambi remained where she was, and
Kintu returned to Mugulu, and explained
he had forgotten the millet. Mugulu was
very angry at his having returned, and
Warumbe, who just then arrived, asked:
"Where is Nambi?"

"She is gone to the earth with Kintu."

"Then I must come too," said Warumbe
(literally, "Death").

After some hesitation Kintu agreed to
this, and they returned together to Nambi. . . .

They all three proceeded, and reached
the earth at a place called Magongo in
Uganda, and they rested. Then the woman
planted the banana and the Indian corn,
the bean and the ground-nut, and there was
a plentiful crop. In the course of time three
children were born, and Warumbe claimed
one of them.

"Let me have this one," said he to Kintu.
"You have still two remaining."

"Oh, I cannot spare one of these, but
later on, perhaps, I may be able to spare
one."

Years passed by, and many more children were born, and Warumbe again begged Kintu to give him one. Kintu went round to all the children with the object of selecting one for Warumbe, and he finally returned and said: "Warumbe, I cannot spare you one just yet; but later on, perhaps, I may be able to do so."

"When you had three you said the same thing. Now you have many, and still refuse to give me one. Mark you, I shall now kill them all. Not to-day, not to-morrow, not this year, not next year; but one by one I shall claim them all."

Next day one child died, and Kintu charged Warumbe with the deed. Next day again another died, and next day again another; and at last Kintu proposed to return to Mugulu and tell him how Warumbe was killing all his children.

Kintu accordingly went to Mugulu and explained matters. Mugulu replied that he had expected it. His original plan was that Kintu and Warumbe should not have met. He told him that Warumbe was a madman, and that trouble would come of it; yet Kintu returned for the millet against the orders of Mugulu, and this was the consequence.

"However," continued Mugulu, "I shall see what can be done." And with that he called his son Kaikuzi (literally the "Digger"), and said to him: "Go down and try to bring me back Warumbe."

Kintu and Kaikuzi started off together, and when they arrived were greeted by Nambi. She explained that in his absence Warumbe had killed several more of her sons. Kaikuzi called up Warumbe, and said: "Why are you killing all these children?"

"I wanted one child badly to help me cook my food. I begged Kintu to give me one. He refused. Now I shall kill them every one."

"Mugulu is angry, and he sent me down to recall you."

"I decline to leave here."

"You are only a small man in comparison to me. I shall fetch you by force."

With this they grappled, and a severe contest ensued. After a while Warumbe slipped from Kaikuzi's grasp, and ran into a hole in the ground. Kaikuzi started to dig him out with his fingers, and succeeded in reaching him, but Warumbe dived still deeper into the earth. Kaikuzi tried to dig him out again, and had almost caught him when Warumbe sunk still further into the ground.

"I'm tired now," said Kaikuze to Kintu, "I will remain a few days, and have another try to catch him."

Kaikuzi then issued an order that there was to be two days' silence in the earth, and that Warumbe would come out of the ground to see what it meant. The people were ordered to lay in two days' provisions, and firewood and water, and not to go out of doors to feed goats or cattle. This having been done, Kaikuzi went into the ground to catch Warumbe, and pursued him for two days, and he forced Warumbe out at a place called Tanda. At this place there were some children feeding goats, and when they saw Warumbe they cried out, and the spell was broken, and Warumbe returned again into the earth. Directly afterwards Kaikuze appeared at the same place and asked why the children had broken the silence. He was angry and disappointed, and he said to Kintu that the people had broken his order, and that he would concern himself no further with the recalling of Warumbe.

"I am tired now," said Kaikuzi.

"Never mind him," replied Kintu, "let Warumbe remain since you cannot expel him. You may now go back to Mugulu, and 'webale'" ("thank you").

Kaikuzi returned to Mugulu, and explained the whole circumstances.

"Very well," said Mugulu, "Let Warumbe stop there."

And Warumbe remained.

Sociocultural Change and Administrative Policy

>>

Cultural and social change is always going on among all groups of people. The rate of change is variable. In general, the more complex a society, the more rapidly it changes. This correlation is not perfect, owing to other variables, such as conquest by a tribe or country with a different culture. Cultures and societies change as new things are invented, as old traits are lost, and as new things are learned from other people. The last is most important, particularly when combined with the reworking of the borrowed trait into the recipient culture.

We know little about cultural change in Buganda farther back than the last hundred years. One of the biggest changes must have occurred when the foreign plants and animals upon which their economy is based were introduced. Baganda economy was based upon an amalgamation of Far and Near Eastern traits.

Traditional Baganda political institutions seem to have been ultimately derived from ancient Egypt. The cult of dead kings, brother-sister marriage for royalty, and special care for the king's navel cord are specific points of resemblance. Just how Egyptian ideas about royalty came to Buganda is a matter of conjecture. It is probable that the influence was indirect, filtering down through the more northerly Negroes.

European contacts, which came very late, greatly accelerated culture change in Buganda. Most other people of the world felt the effects of Europeans while the latter were still in the feudal age. The Baganda were more fortunate. They were never captured and sold into slavery by Europeans and Americans. They were conquered by arms, it is true, but late enough in the nineteenth century to miss the atrocities practiced earlier.

Furthermore, most Baganda cultural change has come about in a peaceful manner. Sir Harry Johnston, first Special Commissioner of a united Uganda, set a pattern of just

345

and sensible administration that has since been followed. The missionaries have been self-less and devoted to their tasks. Church policies have had their faults, as discussed in Selection 72, but the Baganda owe much to their missionaries.

The remaining selections tell about the changes taking place now and something about Baganda history of the past hundred years. One should realize, however, that the Baganda story is not yet finished. Baganda culture is growing vigorously.

• 69 • History

FRANK J. ESSENE

Little is known about the Baganda prior to 1850[, at which time] the first known visitor from the outside world came to Buganda. He was a deserter from the Sultan of Zanzibar's army, a native of Baluchistan named Isa bin Hussein. This Baluchi was made a court official by King Suna II and given a harem of 300 wives. King Suna died in 1857 and Isa bin Hussein disappeared. But for seven or eight years no soldier "ever had it so good."

Arab traders in search of gold, ivory, and slaves entered Buganda in 1852. Much of their trading was illegal and hence kept secret. Their porters, the Negroes of the east coast, could not be completely silenced, however. Eventually, European traders and explorers heard rumors about a big kingdom on the northern shores of an enormous inland lake. Stories about the Indian deserter were also being circulated. Explorers would soon have penetrated this last big unknown section of Africa in any case. The rumors merely speeded the process.

[An Englishman and a Scotsman,] J. H. Speke and J. W. Grant, managed to get financial backing for an expedition. In 1862, nearly three years after the expedition began, Speke reached Buganda.

Mutesa (Mtésa) had succeeded Suna II as the King of Buganda. Mutesa was a capricious ruler but Speke managed to get along with him. After Grant caught up with Speke, both explorers continued northward. They followed the Victoria Nile part way and finally reached an army outpost in the Anglo-Egyptian Sudan.

Speke's claim of discovering the source of the Nile was disputed by rival explorers. It was not until 1875 when Henry M. Stanley circumnavigated Lake Victoria that Speke was vindicated. Stanley also visited the court of King Mutesa. There, Mutesa allegedly dictated a letter to Stanley asking that missionaries be sent to Buganda. The missionaries were to receive estates, food, and all necessary support from Mutesa. Stanley gave the letter to a British army spy who happened along. The spy was killed but the letter, allegedly stained with the life-blood of the spy, was recovered. *The London Daily Telegraph* published the letter and another scoop was credited to Stanley. (Stanley's story of his "rescue" of Dr. Livingstone had earlier established Stanley's journalistic reputation.)

Stanley's letter brought immediate action. Anglican Church ministers and lay members volunteered for duty in Buganda. Contributions to cover supplies and transportation came in from all over England. In 1877 the first Anglican missionaries were established in Kampala.

The Roman Catholic Church also sent in its missionaries starting in 1879. Even before either Christian church began missionary activity, Mohammedan influences were strong in Buganda. All the Arab traders and many of the East Africa Negro porters were Mohammedans. Some of the Arab traders were part-time missionaries.

Buganda thus received almost simultaneously three fiercely competitive, proselyting religions. Mutesa took advantage of the situation by playing one group off against another. He was fickle in his favors. Usually the last group that had given him valuable presents got preference. Nothing approaching the conditions described in Stanley's letter ever came true. Whether Mutesa reneged on his promises or Stanley had made them up out of whole cloth is impossible to determine.

Mutesa died in 1884. Ten years of civil war followed. In part it was a religious war but economics also was a factor. The Imperial British East African Company tried to get a monopoly of Uganda's export and import trade. The Company had its own private army. However, its profits in trade were less than the expenses of war. By 1890 it was obvious that the Company would never get the country under control. Regular British Army troops began a campaign of conquest in 1893. By 1895 the foundations of the Uganda Protectorate were established.

For five years Buganda was under martial law. The British meanwhile extended their conquests over the rest of Uganda and western Kenya. The British Government earlier made treaties with Germany that set the boundaries of the colonies claimed by each country. Germany's territories at that time included Ruanda-Urundi and Tanganyika which she lost after World War I.

The British decided on a policy of indirect rule in Uganda. Native kings were allowed to keep their thrones though with much limited powers. The British drew up law codes and constitutions. Native laws and customs were allowed to prevail provided they were not contrary to the British-drawn codes.

Buganda was the largest and wealthiest of the native kingdoms. The Uganda Agreement of 1900 gave the Baganda some territory that other kingdoms also claimed. The other claimants have tried to get this territory many times since but always unsuccessfully.

Rail connections changed Uganda from a remote country to one that easily could keep in touch with the rest of the world. Caravan goods became rail freight. Most of the railroad-building crew were laborers from India. An unplanned social change thus resulted. Many of these Indians stayed on in Africa. They and their descendants became traders, artisans, and promoters. Most retail trade in Uganda is now handled by Indians.

British control of Uganda gave a big advantage to the Anglican missionaries. The Catholic missionaries had tried to advance the colonial interests of France and the British Administration did not forget it. The only immediate allies of the Mohammedans were the Arabs. However, the Arabs were too closely identified with the illegal slave trade to add any prestige to the Mohammedan group. The Anglican Church added to its power in various ways. Young Baganda, educated in Anglican schools, got better jobs in government service. Nearly all the Baganda royal house and nobility were Anglican church members.

Modern Uganda is literally a twentieth-century product. Almost all the other selections in this book, particularly the several articles by Mair, describe in whole or part the present-day society. The following selections are detailed studies of some of the social and cultural changes going on today.

• 70 • A Changing Economy

HAROLD B. THOMAS AND ROBERT SCOTT

In Uganda, to-day, the most important question in connexion with the life of the people is whether their development in consonance with British ideas is in their own

[Adapted from *Uganda*, Oxford University Press, London, 1935. Pp. 272-273, 275-277. Used by permission.]

interest. It has been the object of the Administration to superimpose an appropriately coloured version of our own civilization on the structure of native society without causing any serious dislocation of its foundations. Superficially the change in conditions appears so comprehensive as necessarily to have transformed the whole social fabric. A collection of mutually hostile tribes, each adhering to its traditional ways, has been fitted into an organized state which conforms to certain rules of conduct generally related to the framework of British civilization. The transformation has been consolidated, however, not by pressure from without, but by the ability of the natives to adapt alien conditions to their own social organism. The extent to which they have been influenced in certain important directions, notably in agriculture and the care of live stock, will have been realized from previous chapters; it remains to give some account of native society in general which will afford an indication of the effect of British administration on the native mind.

When the 1911 Census was taken in Uganda, the country was only on the threshold of economic development. The total value of the exports of domestic produce from the Protectorate during the financial year 1911-12 was £367,575, of which the sum of £230,850 was in respect of 72,975 cwt. of cotton. In 1931, the year of the latest census, the value of domestic produce exported amounted to £1,978,262, which included the sum of £1,503,307 in respect of 674,714 cwt. of cotton. It would appear reasonable to assume that the change in conditions attendant on this increase in production, particularly in the cultivation of cotton which is almost entirely in native hands, would have been accompanied by corresponding changes in the distribution of population. Economic revolutions, whether gradual or sudden, have usually involved substantial adjustments of the more densely inhabited centres, and it is therefore a matter for comment that a revolution which has, in twenty years, transformed Uganda from a struggling backwoodsman, in enjoyment of a remittance from home, into a substantial and independent producer with a respectable bank balance, has not greatly influenced the distribution of the native population.

It is to be expected that any change in the distribution of the population of Uganda which has been due to the new economic conditions following upon British administration would be particularly noticeable in the Mengo district, the centre of the Buganda Province. In this district are the commercial capital, Kampala, and various areas where European plantations have met with some measure of success. Further, more cotton is cultivated within its boundaries than in any other district of the Protectorate except Busoga. The native population of the Mengo district (as now delimited) represented, in 1911, 42.25 per cent. of the total native population of the Buganda Province; in 1931 the relative percentage was 40.88 per cent. The decrease is entirely in the number of Baganda, and is in part attributable to their low birth-rate, as compared with the death-rate, and in part, probably, to their taking up more fertile lands in other districts of the Province. There is certainly no indication of any general migration outside the Province except in an isolated instance, where 4,000 Baganda are settled in the Kwania county of the Lango district.

Conditions in Uganda . . . are not generally favourable to redistributions of the population, whether in the form of mass movements from one area to another or of large concentrations in the more extensively developed centres. There is no sign that any considerable part of the population is becoming urbanized. The native is fundamentally a peasant whatever his rank or stage of education may be, and neither understands or has any sympathy with a manner of life which is not intimately connected with the land. This attitude is not confined to those who are agriculturists by occupation, but is common to the classes engaged in clerical work and mechanical or other labour, and even to members of the Police Force. The wage-earner is not socially important; he does not consider himself the provider of his family's sustenance, and resents being constrained to accept that position. Money which is earned by whatsoever means is earmarked for the payment of taxes and school-fees and the purchase of luxuries and such necessities as cannot conveniently be manufactured at home. It is regarded as natural and inevitable that each household should have sufficient land to keep it in food, tobacco, and, if possible, alcoholic refreshment, and that each member of the family should take some part in the production of food. This system naturally tends to stabilize each community in its own rural area.

In his own district, if in reach of his own garden, the wage-earner finds himself in the happy position of being obliged to buy no essential article of diet. If he goes elsewhere his bill for food is likely to amount to about five shillings for each adult member of the family each month, and five shillings is between one-half and one-third of a labourer's wages. He cannot even be certain that he will be able to obtain the kinds of food to which he has always been accustomed, and this circumstance restricts, in particular, movement between the plantain areas and the grain areas. The ordinary native will, therefore, endeavour to obtain work near his own home in the first place, or within the area occupied by his tribe. If none is available, he may seek employment for a time in another part of Uganda, but he will return to the family circle when he has accumulated enough money for his immediate needs. The proportion of natives who travel outside their own districts to take up temporary work is not normally large in comparison with the number of those who remain at home. . . . At present the regular cultivation of native land by means of hired labour is not generally favoured, except by the large land-owners in Buganda, since it is too often found that the return on the capital outlay is disappointingly disproportionate to the profits accruing from the unaided efforts of the family. Even when hiring does become part of the economic system, however, it appears improbable that racial prejudice will

allow it to cause any great movement from area to area.

There is generally no shortage of land in the Protectorate for the needs of the natives. The crops which each peasant produces provide in the majority of districts an adequate monetary income, and none of the existing industries is of such a nature as to force the individual to abandon his traditional manner of life. There are no native towns except the *Kibuga,* which adjoins Kampala Township and is the centre of the Native Government of the Buganda Kingdom. The only non-native township which has a distinctively urban character is Kampala, where there is a comparatively small resident native population. Of the natives living in Kampala in 1933, about 1,400 occupied labour lines, servants' quarters or barracks, and less than 500 had their own dwellings. Every day, however, some 4,000 workers of all trades and occupations come into the township from the surrounding countryside and the crowds of morning and evening 'commuters', many of them on bicycles, are a notable feature upon all roads which converge on the township. Conditions in Kampala do not allow of extensive cultivation, nor of the keeping of flocks and herds, and the natives have generally preferred to renounce the amenities of town life and to remain in an environment where they can enjoy what they hold to be the true amenities of life. In the Kibuga and the smaller townships the majority of resident natives continue to live, surrounded by food plots, goats, and fowls, very much in the same manner as obtains outside the township boundaries. In the course of time sanitary restrictions may make it impracticable for them to continue in these ways, and they may change their mode of life. It is more probable, however, that they will seek to change their places of abode to some locality where the sanitary inspector ceases to trouble them.

Uganda is entering the world picture in one respect at least. In 1950, its cotton exports were conservatively valued at forty million dollars. This is about ten times the price that Uganda cotton brought in 1931. Part of the increase is due to price differential, but the tonnage also was much greater. The trend in Uganda is toward ever larger cotton production.

Other phases of Uganda society have not kept pace with the changing economy. Friction was inevitable. The educated Indians, who occupy many responsible positions, were given most of the blame. The following selection describes the situation in plain words. The severe condemnation of Indian traders is doubtless based on actual abuses. But it is also an excellent example of the way in which discontent tends to focus on a minority group, particularly one which can easily be distinguished by its physical characteristics. This role of scapegoat is played by minority groups in every part of the world today. Commonly a group is blamed for situations for which the majority is equally responsible, and in a way that vastly oversimplifies the realities of the situation.

• 71 • Cotton and Discontent in Uganda

The Secretary of State for the Colonies is now on a visit to East Africa where one of his preoccupations will be to inquire into the workings of the Uganda cotton industry. It is time this was done for Uganda cotton is a classic example of how not to do things. Ill-equipped, riddled with dishonest practices, inefficient and a focus of racial animosity, the industry has so far defied official attempts to put its house in order. In 1929 its position was being investigated; in 1938 a Commission reported on its problems. In 1948 yet another Commission had its say; in 1949 there were violent disturbances in Uganda, in which eight people were killed. One of the main grievances was found, by yet another Commission of Inquiry, to be discontent with the conditions in the cotton industry.

What happens in this industry is not merely of local interest. It is the kingpin of the economic life of a country of 5,000,000 souls—in 1949 cotton represented more than £17 million out of Uganda's total export of £23 million. One and a half million acres of land lie under cotton, and the market for it appears limitless.

The growing of cotton is exclusively in African hands, and the output per acre is excessively small. The Director of Agriculture has estimated that the present yield of 230 lb. per acre could quite easily be increased to 500 lb., which means augmenting the value of the crop by well over £10 million. But the agricultural staff which might train the peasants is totally inadequate. The Commission of 1948 found only 22 senior officials, supervising not only cotton, but all agriculture throughout the colony. In the Sudan, with a smaller cotton acreage, 125 scientists and inspectors were employed on cotton alone.

The ginneries are all owned or staffed by Indians. They are small and scattered. Their equipment is antiquated, their buildings old and unhygienic with unsatisfactory conditions for workers. Furthermore, ginning has become a monopoly. Each gin must have a licence, and as there are already too many, no new licences are given. To enter the field one must go through the difficult operation of buying an existing gin. This, until the Government recently came forward with help, has effectively excluded all Africans.

The Africans are naturally resentful, par-

[Adapted from "Cotton and Discontent in Uganda," *The Economist*, Vol. 160, No. 5620, London, 1951. P. 1107. Used by permission.]

ticularly as the Indian ginners are suspected —and have been declared guilty by a Government Commission—of corrupt practices. The 1948 Commission pulled no punches in describing the deliberate cheating of the grower by the ginners and their agents, the buyers. The buyer falsifies the weights, with the result that the grower only receives payment for about 90 per cent of the cotton that he actually hands over. By secret agreement, the buyer and the ginner share the illegitimate profits thus gained. And even if the ginner should be honest, the buyer may not be; he has his own private tricks whereby he gains an extra illicit profit. Numerous devices to defraud and befuddle the illiterate seller are recounted. The race animosity consequently aroused is such that one of the recommendations of this particular Commission was that a local African should always do the weighing.

The ginners are also guilty of neglecting the quality of the cotton they produce. There is an absence of any primary classification of the cotton received, which no subsequent grading of the bales can overcome. In the Sudan there is a strictly controlled system of pre-ginning classification, and only seed of the best quality is reserved for the next season's planting. In Uganda's present layout of small, decentralised ginneries, it seems impossible to achieve anything like this. The storage conditions are also appalling—infested with insects, and rotted by damp.

During the war, with the cessation of private cotton buying in Liverpool and India, arrangements for bulk sales of cotton were introduced by the Uganda Government. More recently a Lint Marketing Board has been created, which fixes the price to the grower for his raw cotton and also the price at which lint is bought from the gins. These arrangements infuriate the Indian ginners, whose profits have been curtailed, and also leave the African growers dissatisfied, as the prices they receive are below those on the world market. The profits made by the Board have been put into a special Cotton Price Assistance Fund, as a buffer against hard times to come. A year ago the balance of this fund—after some money had been used for African welfare—amounted to over £7,000,000. But the Board has made the bad mistake of not explaining itself sufficiently to the Africans, or associating them in its work.

The Government has been far too slow in tackling all these grievances. Proposals made by the Cotton Commission of 1938 were not fully implemented, and in 1948 African organisations were again petitioning for the remedying of malpractices which had been exposed ten years earlier. When these petitions met with little response tempers rose and were played upon by politicians until bloodshed could no longer be avoided. It was obvious what would be the result of such published statements as the following by the Secretary of the Uganda African Farmers Union:—

> Our cotton is our own and we should protect it and rule ourselves and prevent the foreigners who take all the wealth and leave the natives to starvation, while their tummies are growing out, from taking it. Therefore every African of Uganda should avow that it is better to die than give away the wealth of the country of their heredity.

The Government has now announced that it is their policy to provide for the participation of Africans in the ginning industry, and also to train them in the technical and managerial branches of the industry. Co-operative societies have been fostered and two ginneries have already been leased to African co-operatives. But everyone knows that this is insufficient, and that a much more drastic reorganisation is being discussed behind the scenes. It might prove possible to help African co-operatives to take over many more ginneries; an alternative would be the public acquisition of the whole ginning industry. Either course would arouse violent Indian opposition, but the determining factor will be the wishes of the Africans.

Previous selections written by Lucy P. Mair have been largely descriptive. The following article is from the concluding section of her major study of the Baganda. A general picture of how Baganda society functions is given, the areas of greatest friction are discussed, and some suggestions for improvement are made. Although Dr. Mair's book was published in 1934, she anticipated many of the problems discussed in Selections 48, 71, and 73. It is indicative of trends in social science that this book by a leading English anthropologist ends on a thoroughly practical note. The British have set an example that others are now beginning to follow, encouraging anthropologists to aid in administering the affairs of "primitive" peoples. Too often, even in Britain, their recommendations are ignored under pressure of political and economic interests, but increasingly problems resulting from culture contact and change are being studied by the social scientists.

• 72 •   An Analysis of British Policies

LUCY P. MAIR

It is true that many of the old social bonds no longer exist. The ties of kinship outside the individual household—never so strong with the Baganda as among [some other] tribes —have lost most of their importance, while the household itself is a much smaller unit than it used to be. Nor is the village community any longer linked together by the bond of common loyalty to a chief who was not only the sole authority over his subjects but their one source of advancement in life. Success in life is now directly dependent upon individual economic effort; it is no longer the reward of qualities conceived to be socially desirable. For this very reason, there is now much less of the old readiness to share the fruits of success with those kinsmen who used to consider that they had a claim upon them; and even where wealth is the result not of personal effort but of a dispensation from above, as it is in the case of the large landowners, the possibilities of personal satisfaction which it brings are so alluring that they outweigh the attraction of a reputation for generosity. What Baganda society has most to fear is not any economic exploitation from without, but the growth among its own members of a spirit of individualistic acquisitiveness in which every man seeks to exploit his neighbour. One can see the signs of it in the younger landlords, who, free from any responsibility towards their tenants, simply regard them as a source of revenue and constantly devise new ways of interpreting the law to their advantage. At present it is only they who are in a position to exploit, and their efforts are kept in check both by government action and by the ample areas of available land. If, indeed, the goal of a land of peasant proprietors was achieved, it might be merely sentimental to regret the passing of the old obligations of mutual aid, and sufficient to look forward to the substitution for them of social services by the State.

Yet one cannot help wishing that European teaching did not lay quite so much emphasis on the advantages to the individual of commercializing his possessions, and that there was more place in it for the growth of a spirit of corporate loyalty, not, indeed, to church or king—that is sufficiently stressed —but to the smaller group with whom he is in constant contact in the life of the village. Where the old centre of such loyalty in the chief has gone, the village has ceased to be

[Adapted from *An African People in the Twentieth Century*, George Routledge and Sons, London, 1934. Pp. 275-288. Used by permission.]

an entity for any other purpose than that of entry in the land register; and though one could not lay a finger on any definite results, there was a quite tangible difference in the atmosphere of Kisimula, the village that had migrated as a body with old Bugeza, and Matale, the haphazard juxtaposition of a dozen small landlords, who had bought land from Nsubuga, and such tenants as they had collected.

The need has been realized, and the solution sought, in the development of Boy Scout troops in the schools. The Scout movement, in its concentration on practical activities and the training which it gives in intelligent observation, forms a valuable adjunct to classroom studies. But it cannot generate a spirit of co-operation which will be active in circumstances entirely different from those which gave rise to it. Loyalty is not an independent quality which, once created, will remain in existence ready to attach itself to any object which offers; it is part and parcel of the situation in which it is formed, and dies with it. Sentiments cannot be created in one context with a view to their transference to another.

Nor can one hope for great results from the other panacea of European education—football. The enthusiasm with which native schoolboys take to football amply justifies its place in the curriculum; but here, even less than in the Boy Scout movement, can it be assumed that the temporary association which the game creates can alter the players' outlook on social relationships in general.

What is wanted, then, is some positive organization for the joint pursuit of common aims, through which new ties of mutual obligation can be formed. It should be an organization co-extensive with the village community, not a group so large that the active participation of most of its members is reduced to the payment of a subscription. The village co-operative societies, which have already been successfully established in India and Java and are now beginning to be set up in East Africa, probably meet the need in the best possible way. Through such societies, assisted by advice and instruction from agriculture experts, neighbours could be united by their interest in improved methods of cultivation and preparation of the produce for the market; through them such developments might be introduced as the purchase of ploughs, which are at present beyond the means of a single family. Through them, too, it might be possible to cope with what is Buganda's chief problem at the moment—the lack of adaptability of the average cultivator, who, having acquired the habit of growing cotton and nothing but cotton, knowing what cotton requires, and having a general vague feeling that other crops are more difficult, is reluctant to change even to a crop which he is assured will be more profitable. Through them, again, thrift and foresight in planning for the future could be developed. And the principles of loyalty and regard for the interests of others, of the direction of productive effort to ends higher than mere individual gain, which are taught in church and school, could, with this field for their application, become an effective social force.

Given such a focus of village life—and assuming eventual world economic recovery—the future of Buganda should promise well. Yet there are two respects in which the adjustment to modern conditions is sufficiently unsatisfactory to call for comment.

One is in the educational system, which at present is directed almost exclusively to produce young men capable of doing "white-collar" jobs—teachers, native clergy, chiefs, and clerks in Government offices, plantation foremen, and the like. In the eyes of the boys and their parents the first aim of education is to qualify the pupil to earn a good income, and to earn it with the pen or typewriter rather than with the hoe. Yet, if it is assumed as the ideal that every child should receive some organized education, surely this should not consist in the general application of a curriculum devised to meet the needs of what will never be more than a minority.

An incidental disadvantage of the present system lies in the amount of time which has to be devoted to the teaching of English.

Certainly a knowledge of English is an advantage to the Muganda, and there is nothing which they themselves more ardently desire. Certainly, too, if such a knowledge is to be of any value to them, it must consist of more than the memorizing of a mass of words to which their own experience provides no corresponding concept. At Budo School, by the devotion of many hours in the earlier forms to the teaching of English as a language by the most up-to-date methods, this danger is admirably avoided—but at what a cost to the balance of subjects! The requirements of Budo, again, set the pace for the central schools from whom it recruits pupils, and in their case English teaching is often less well-directed. Of the Catholic schools I cannot speak from first-hand observation, but with them the problem is further complicated by the fact that English is often not the native language of the teacher.

One reason for the stress on English is that the only generally recognized standard of attainment is that set by English examinations. Moreover, the Baganda are beginning to demand a university education, and, if they cannot get it on the spot, will go to Ceylon or to England for it. Schools must, therefore, enable them to qualify for entrance.

The second case of serious dislocation lies in the sphere of sexual ethics. The standards laid down by Christian teaching are not taken for granted by the natives as they are by those who still adhere to them in Europe; rather they are regarded as a set of arbitrary rules to be disobeyed when that can be done with impunity. The prohibition of polygamy does not cause serious difficulty, for polygamy is dying out with the passing of the economic system to which it was appropriate and the wars which reduced the number of men. But the prohibition of divorce creates a situation for which no remedy seems possible while it is maintained. Baganda marriage was a contract which could be dissolved, but which was accompanied by guarantees against its frivolous dissolution.

Under Christianity it has become a theoretically indissoluble contract, and what was the pledge of its maintenance—the bride-price—has almost become an inducement to those who should be interested in its stability to encourage its repudiation. In a system which does not admit of divorce the bride-price is an anomaly, and there would be a strong case for its abolition were it not that native feeling would be outraged by the idea of marriages taking place without it. However, the likelihood of such a system becoming firmly established is so remote that this question does not arise. A solution is more likely to be found, as it has been in Europe, in the recognition of civil divorce and in provision of facilities for natives to obtain it; but for this solution to be really satisfactory, it is essential that the refund of the bride-price should be made obligatory.

It remains to estimate the success of the system of government. In one sense, the native authorities are those recognized by tradition, for they are still appointed and promoted by the king. But in another sense they are something very different, for there is no longer any personal tie between them and the people under their control, nor is their acceptability to the populace guaranteed as it used to be by the fact that they depended for their prestige on attracting and retaining a large following. On the other hand, now that the limits of their authority are set so much more narrowly than they used to be, this guarantee is not of great importance; the modern chief is not in a position to oppress his subjects by physical violence or by demands on their services.

Since the Baganda chiefs never derived their position, as so many native authorities do, from any belief in supernatural attributes inherent in certain individuals by virtue of their birth, there has been no violence done to popular sentiment in their conversion to a native civil service, and no reluctance to accept their authority such as is found where there exists alongside the chief appointed by government some other person who, in native eyes, is alone qualified to wield his power.

The only question that has to be asked, therefore, is whether a system of government imposed, as this is, from above, satisfactorily meets the needs of the modern Baganda kingdom. There is a certain demand—not "a great and growing movement", as Dr. Norman Leys describes it, but a demand among the educated Baganda of the capital—for the introduction of popular representation into the Lukiko. I do not think the demand has ever been put forward in the shape of clearly-formulated proposals; if what is asked is the transformation of the Lukiko into a body elected by ballot on a territorial basis, the idea to anyone who has lived in a Baganda village is fantastic. It is hard to imagine the terms in which one would explain to the electorate what they were being invited to do and why. The villagers have views, certainly, which they wish to make known to the Government; they desire, for instance, that it should order the Indians to pay a higher price for cotton. Such views are put forward when a *saza* chief goes the round of the *gombolola* courts.

There is no reason why a council appointed by the votes of the villagers should be any better suited to manage the affairs of the country than the present Lukiko. Presumably some qualifications would be required of a candidate for election; and since the council would require for efficiency at least as high a standard of education as the native civil service, the only persons, other than administrative chiefs, who would be eligible, would be native lawyers and schoolmasters, with some shop assistants. The same difficulty arises with regard to the basis of the suffrage. A property qualification would weigh the scales more heavily than at present on the side of the land-owner; an educational qualification of any real value would reduce the electorate to a body very little larger than that of those eligible for election.

It is unsafe to assume, as the advocates of representative government for African societies do, either that it would in fact secure the interests or desires of the general public, or that it would give them that feeling of responsibility for their own misfortunes which is said to enable European society to bear with fortitude the consequences of its political mistakes. Conferred from above on a populace which is not aware of any desire to manage its own affairs, it can never be anything but a mechanical system, to be manipulated by a few individuals for their own ends, while the majority remain indifferent to its proceedings.

There is probably room—or will be in the future—for the development of channels for the representation of organizations devoted to particular interests. The Native Anglican Church, for instance, puts proposals for legislation before the Lukiko through those chiefs who are represented on its synod. There might be room for its representation in that body in its own right. Again, organizations of native producers may come to feel that their interests deserve more attention than they can get from a council of people with no experience of their special problems. Village co-operative societies, too, might then claim representation. The essence of representative government, after all, is not in some particular mechanism but in the opportunity for the expression of popular opinion—where popular opinion exists.

The serious maladjustments in modern Buganda result from the introduction of European institutions which were not called for by the need for adaptation to new conditions—the creation of a landlord class and the suppression of divorce.

It is not because European institutions are unsuitable to Africans as individuals that their wholesale introduction is deprecated, but because neither African nor any other society can assimilate a complete outfit of alien institutions between to-day and to-morrow. Dr. Leys points out that we believe the early Britons to have been as intelligent as we are and to have differed from us only in "lack of opportunities". Yet he would surely not be prepared to argue that the introduction to prehistoric Britain of mass production and manhood suffrage would have produced a result indistinguishable from the Britain of to-day. Our opportunities have included not only democracy, economic individualism, and higher education, but—up till the last century—time for gradual development.

What will a given change in native institutions produce? The answer to that question is not: Inevitable disintegration, so make no changes. It is to be found in an examination of the institution to be modified, of its place in the society as a whole, its relation to other institutions, and the reasons why it has its peculiar characteristics, and in consideration whether the substitute which is proposed will really take its place, or whether it will leave gaps that other means must be devised to fill. It is by its ability to fulfil the needs of a given society at a given time, and not by its resemblance to the forms to which we are accustomed, that each development must be judged.

African societies have so far produced few, if any, sociologists. Consequently, the demands made by Africans, however intelligent, however highly educated, cannot be taken as decisive in determining the lines along which African development should go. The decision should be made on the results of a scientific study of the actual problems involved.

Nationalistic movements, characteristic of many colonial areas in recent years, are not lacking in Uganda. As might be expected, the Baganda have provided leaders in attempts to break away from real or feared white domination. Baganda Nationalism has received most attention when accompanied by riots. The first part of the following selection is a brief account of the riots of 1949; the second is a summary of a commission's investigation of them.

• 73 • The Uganda Riots

There is much that is familiar in the account of the riots that took place in Uganda last week. They followed the usual pattern of disturbances in the colonial empire, and the Governor's immediate denunciation of the agitators as instigated by Communists was reminiscent, in particular, of the Gold Coast disturbances of early 1948. But whereas in the Gold Coast the main grievance was economic—high prices—in Uganda it seems to have been political. A recent official report had disclosed that African cotton-growers had been cheated on a large scale and for a long time by Indian ginners, which was the excuse for the anti-Indian demonstrations that accompanied the riots. Apart from this, however, the main complaints of the ringleaders, who came from the Bataka Party [explained later in this selection], were directed against the British Government for having agreed to the setting up of the East African High Commission and against the Kabaka of Buganda.

This is not the first time that Balkan politics have been transferred to Buganda. Four years ago there were complaints that the present Kabaka—the king whose rule is recognised by the British under the treaty of 1900—was undemocratic in his choice of Ministers. Since then Mutesa II has made

[From "Trouble in Uganda," *The Economist,* Vol. 156, No. 5515, London, May 7, 1949, p. 835, and "The Uganda Riots," *The Economist,* Vol. 158, No. 5556, London, February 18, 1950, p. 365. Used by permission.]

the Lukiko—the native Parliament—more representative; he is regarded as an enlightened and sensible young man; in fact, government in Buganda has often been held up as an example of indirect rule at its best. But the Bataka party, which has now been proscribed, demanded that the people should be allowed to choose their own chiefs and that the Lukiko should have even more elected members, although its sincerity in this respect can be gauged by its persistent refusal to nominate candidates. In fact, by all reports it is not so much a party as a group of agitators who object to the Kabaka's Ministers because of their advice that the Bataka Party should be abolished. One of its prominent members is now in London; there seems no doubt of its Communist contacts, and it is significant that the trouble began on the day of the first meeting in Uganda of the Central Legislative Assembly of the East African High Commission—the administrative linking-up of the three East African dependencies is as strongly opposed by the Bataka as it is by Russia in the United Nations.

The disturbances are now over. The local troops and police have been reinforced; a Press censorship has been introduced; and a commission of enquiry has been appointed. Doubtless its report and recommendations will follow the usual lines. But it is doubtful whether they will find an easy solution to the main problem—in other colonies no less than Uganda—which is how to direct the Africans' misplaced nationalism into the right channels and prevent what is often not more than a small group of malcontents from becoming a prey to mischief-makers at home and overseas.

* * *

The report of the commission of enquiry into the disturbances which occurred last April in the Buganda province of Uganda was published at the end of last week. It is not altogether a satisfactory document although it will doubtless satisfy any British consciences that may have been troubled when the disturbances broke out. The report commends the police force and the troops for their behaviour in suppressing the riots, places the responsibility for them squarely on the shoulders of an African in this country called Semakula Mulumba, and declares that with one exception none of the grievances alleged by Mulumba and his supporters had any substance. The commissioner, Sir Donald Kingdon, found that the disturbances were a result of a planned rebellion against the Kabaka of Buganda and his Government. Although Mulumba is known to have Communist contacts, there was no evidence of Communist financial or moral aid.

All this is satisfactory as far as it goes, but it does not go far enough. What one would have liked to find in the report is a deeper explanation of what has transformed Uganda from a protectorate which was considered a highly successful example, if not a model, of British colonial rule into one which appears to be becoming increasingly restless and suspicious of British intentions. The disturbances of 1949 were, after all, not the first. There had been serious disturbances in 1945, which culminated in the deportation, without trial, of the ringleaders and had as a sequel the assassination of the Prime Minister of Buganda, Martin Luther Nsibirwa. The intervening years have, moreover, been ones of growing unrest—as witness the enthusiasm with which the Buganda people received the news that Mulumba had presented their grievances to UNO through Mr. Gromyko, the Soviet representative.

Doubtless the commissioner's terms of reference precluded him from investigating last year's riots against a wider historical background—although he mentions the blunder of 1944 when the supervision by the British administrators in Buganda was very greatly relaxed before suitable Africans had been trained to take their place. But the result is that one is left with an uneasy feeling that an opportunity has been missed of examining British policy in a wider setting and that consequently the disturbances may be repeated.

Suggestions for Additional Reading

A first step in gaining a knowledge of Africa in general, or in studying any part of this continent more intensively, is to obtain a systematic bibliography. Such is *Introduction to Africa*, subtitled *A Selective Guide to Background Reading*, prepared by the Library of Congress, European Affairs Division, and published by the University Press of Washington, Washington, D.C., 1952. It includes very few of the older sources but concentrates instead on the more important recent writings. Complete bibliographic references are given, and each source is annotated sufficiently to give some idea of its contents. *Africa: Journal of the International African Institute* (London, Oxford University Press, published quarterly) is also an excellent bibliographic source. Several books on Africa are reviewed in each issue, and the principal contents are five or six anthropological articles. *An African Survey: A Study of Problems Arising in Africa South of the Sahara* by William Malcolm Hailey (London, Oxford University Press, 1938) is a third rich source of references. It also contains many summaries of specific cultural aspects.

The first comprehensive study of Uganda is Sir Harry H. Johnston's *The Uganda Protectorate* (London, Hutchinson and Co., 1902). Many sections of Johnston's large two-volume work were used in preparing this book. Johnston's descriptions of the country and people are quite accurate. His greatest weakness is his theoretical background, particularly in such matters as racial classification.

Harold B. Thomas and Robert Scott, authors of *Uganda* (Oxford University Press, London, 1935), have written the basic reference book on Uganda. Both authors were government administrative officers, as was Johnston, and their book in many ways brings Johnston up to date.

The early missionaries wrote only too voluminously about Uganda. Their writings were for the most part pleas for financial support, the pleading implicit in the horrors they described. Of the missionaries, only John Roscoe wrote generally useful accounts. His *The Baganda* (London, MacMillan and Co., 1911) is only one of several monographs that he wrote on the Baganda and other African kingdoms. *The Baganda* covers Baganda society more thoroughly than any other single source. Roscoe's descriptions are meticulous, but his value-judgments at times seem strange. He was also somewhat handicapped in trying to fit his findings into the doctrine of social evolution. British anthropology at that time had not yet broken away from the theory of set stages in social development. Roscoe himself acknowledged his debt to Sir James Frazer, a leading British anthropologist.

Several of the selections in this text are taken from the *Uganda Journal* (London, Oxford University Press). The *Journal* is the organ of the Uganda Society (originally the Uganda Literary and Scientific Society), whose nonrestricted membership may and do write about anything not concerned with politics. Articles in the *Journal* run from crocodile shooting to a survey of Buganda agriculture.

One of the best sources is Lucy P. Mair's *An African People in the Twentieth Century* (London, G. Routledge, 1934). Dr. Mair is an anthropologist who has specialized in colonial administration. She seems to be a member of Malinowski's functional school of anthropology. Briefly, this school is concerned with how each part of a society interacts with every other part; it is not concerned with historical speculations. As a functionalist, Mair is an excellent antidote for the evolutionist Roscoe. Mair's book considers only Baganda social institutions and perhaps some aspects of culture that have immediate social implications. For a rounded picture of Baganda life, other sources on environment, technology, and history must be added. Dr. Mair has also written several short articles on the Baganda such as the articles on marriage and chieftainship, reprinted in this book.

Certain educated Africans from Uganda have written a few volumes. These include Ham Mukasa, *Uganda's Katikiro in England* (London, 1904); E. M. K. Mulira, *Troubled Uganda* (London, Fabian Publications, 1950); and Akiki K. Nyabongo, *The Story of an African Chief* (New York, Scribner, 1935). Each of these books deals with rather limited aspects of Uganda life but has the obvious advantage of another point of view.

The Uganda Protectorate *Annual Reports,* published periodically by the Government Printer at Entebbe, are valuable sources of information. Various departments and commissions of the Uganda government report on agriculture, education, geology, the cotton industry, land surveys, and mines; they summarize achievements and propose programs. One of the reports on education has been included here.

Among the most recently published material is Edwin S. Munger's *Relational Patterns of Kampala, Uganda* (University of Chicago, Dept. of Geography, Research Paper No. 21, 1951). Dr. Munger concentrates on the problem of how Kampala influences Uganda and, to a lesser degree, other parts of British East Africa. Based upon statistics of rail movements and the like, as well as on personal observations, a lively picture of Kampala as the center of progress is presented. This monograph brings to life the process of sociocultural change. Dr. Munger, in using the human-geographical approach, adds a refreshing and new picture of Baganda life.

Still more recent is the treatment of Uganda in John Gunther's *Inside Africa* (New York, Harper and Brothers, 1955). Gunther is primarily a journalist, preoccupied with providing his readers with the latest information on topics of immediate interest; hence his book does not meet scientific standards of thoroughness. But it takes time to be thorough, and sometimes we cannot wait. The journalist is indispensable, and his work is often interesting.

Some Social-Science Generalizations

PERCY BLACK
AND
HOWARD BECKER

‹‹

EDITORS' NOTE:

The following statement of social-science generalizations forms a fitting conclusion to Part One of our book. You will find that it corresponds in many ways to the Introduction (pp. 2-28), although the two were written independently. The authors of this statement expect you to disagree with or question a number of their assertions, which they would readily admit are in some respects tentative and at many points in need of further illustration and verification. In any event, you will find the ideas offered here challenging.

Percy Black wrote the parts entitled "Looking Back" and "Looking Forward"; Howard Becker is the author of "Looking at Values and Value-Systems." In presenting their ideas, both writers had all six societies in mind, rather than only the three we have already studied.

Looking Back

Crammed with numerous geographic details, racial measurements, and exotic customs, the fact-burdened reader may well ask in desperation, "So what?" "What does it all add up to?" "Is this what social scientists busy themselves with —the amassing of endless facts?"

To answer this query truthfully, we must at once say, "Yes." Social scientists, like all other scientists, do indeed spend much time gathering the basic materials of their science—facts. But that is only part of the answer. Without a blueprint, an accumulation of facts is chaotic. Thus, we may say that what the blueprint is to the architect, principles are to the scientists. The use of principles helps us in making order out of the vast array of facts that each science gathers. Principles are the mortar which holds the facts together; or, seen from another point of view, principles enable us to place groups of facts into a few well-ordered compartments. And so if we are armed with principles, the facts we carry around are no longer disconnected, for the principles make it possible for us to sort like from unlike facts and to arrange them into a system. For, as everyone knows, it is much easier to remember similar things than a mixture of similar and dissimilar ones. With such a device, then, the social-science novice gradually comes to make sense out of what were disordered details.

But in the pages which have gone before, the reader has not been subjected to facts alone; there has been an orderly presentation of the facts as well as a systematic framework which can help us think about any society or ask questions concerning it. We want to know where the people came from, and what are their physical characteristics; what type of physical environment surrounds them and how they adjust to it in meeting their material needs; how they apportion among themselves the various duties involved in living together in groups, and the rules whereby these fixed responsibilities are enforced; how the young are molded to the beliefs, practices, and skills of the older generation; and how these molds are gradually but inexorably changed to meet new conditions from age to age. We also want to know their basic philosophy of life: their manner of thinking regarding their origin and their relation to the universe. And, finally, we shall ask questions regarding their present problems, how they are meeting them, and how, on the basis of their past solutions and basic lifeway, they are likely to evolve into different ways of living.

The careful reader will by this time also have learned a good many principles relating to each aspect of the framework used in this book. Furthermore, he will have developed an ability to compare one society with another and also have gained an outlook which diminishes narrow perspectives and opens a wider social horizon. For only by transcending the narrow confines of our own selves, our own particular group, can we grow in depth, breadth, and wisdom.

The framework and principles, however, of necessity have often been stated in more general and inclusive terms than the facts at hand. We can say with assurance, for example, that all the groups studied have some system of beliefs regarding their relation to the universe and that each group has certain persons who are the main carriers of these beliefs from generation to generation. But we cannot yet say, because facts are lacking, why the Eskimo shaman, for example, is often mentally and emotionally aberrant (at least, from our point of view), whereas the Navajo singer has an altogether different pattern of personality. Again, we can generalize that all groups have some rules regarding who may and may not marry whom, but we cannot say with the same definiteness why one group is matriarchal and another patriarchal or why the levirate is practiced or required in one group whereas it is not practiced, or is perhaps even forbidden, in another. Indeed, to know the answers to many of these questions requires more social scientists throughout the world constantly on the job unearthing the facts.

This brings us back, then, to the point at which we began—namely, facts. Facts alone, we indicated, are not enough, for in and of themselves they do not give us direction. But principles without facts are likewise inadequate; they become directions without a sound basis. Both facts and principles are the bases of science; the one serves as prop to the other. Principles, based on facts, lead us to ask new questions to get more facts, and the new facts often require us, in turn, to modify our principles. The search, thus, is an endless, widening circle—one, however, that inescapably draws the intelligent and curious student on to greater understanding, larger perspective, and deeper insight.

A few more remarks regarding the study of the principles must yet be made. First, these principles in general will answer the following questions: (a) What are the motives of man? (b) What are the bases of society? (c) What are the recurrent relations? No attempt is made here, of course, to state all the possible principles which could cover these questions, or, for that matter, to present them as fully spelled out as possible. This task is left to further courses in social science, although, to be truthful, they are nowhere to be found in any one source at the present time. Secondly, the principles are meant to be useful devices for clarifying many facts and relations. They are like a car: a car is a helpful device in enabling us to extend our range of mobility, but in order to take advantage of this device one has to learn how to operate it. Perhaps the best way to incorporate the principles in our thinking is to keep looking back to the respective societies to see how the principles could best be applied to them. Again, the analogy of the car can be useful here. One must learn not only how to operate it but also how to steer it on different highways through different types of traffic. Likewise, the principles should be learned not merely for their own sake, but rather to enable us to "steer" with them through the different societies. Thus, *looking back* to the societies themselves becomes the means of *looking forward* with the principles.

Some basic principles

HOMO SAPIENS: THE COMMON DENOMINATOR OF HUMAN SOCIETY. Perhaps the most striking conclusion one can draw from a study of different societies is that, although they differ in certain respects, they show even more striking common characteristics. Eskimo and Baganda, Chinese and Southerner, Navajo and Englishman differ in language, customs, economics, and philosophies, but the solid fact remains that they *all do have* language, customs, economies, and philosophies. (References will occasionally be made to the three societies still to be presented in detail—the Chinese Peasant, the Cotton South, and the English Midlands.) This fact seems so obvious that it often escapes our notice—like the air we breathe—but it is, nonetheless, an undeniably important observation. For, guided by this knowledge, we are urged on to find out more about the similarities of men and to search for those factors that bring about the differences.

What are some of these basic commonalities that all men possess? First, we can say that although there are differences in facial characteristics, height, weight, skin coloration, hair distribution, etc., what is more significant is that all men possess bodies with similar nervous systems and internal structures and functions. The same treatment that cures the Eskimo of tuberculosis, for example, also cures the Southerner or the Muganda. Again, the brain structures of any group of men are so similar to those of any other group that even brain specialists cannot tell them apart. Biologically, then, men are more similar to than different from one another. Besides similar nervous systems and internal structures and functions, all men share approximately the same physical potentialities making them unique among animals: great dexterity of the hands, combining strong grasp with delicate manipulation; extremely well-developed stereoscopic and color vision; extremely long infancy and childhood, during which adult care is needed but a great deal is learned. These characteristics give man his unusual opportunities for development beyond the limits reached by other animals, and also set prerequisites that are met by *every* culture.

Second, man possesses a relatively high capacity to learn, which, perhaps more than anything else, sets him apart from the other animals. Since what is learned or developed by one group can be learned or adopted by another—as in the process of diffusion or acculturation, for example—we can say with some assurance that all groups so far studied probably possess about equal learning capacities. In other words, a relatively marked and similar degree of intelligence distinguishes man from the animal world and becomes another common denominator for all men.

Third, man is a symbol-using creature; *i.e.*, he speaks. Language—a system of symbols or words which represent objects and events—enables him to communicate the present, recall the past, and plan the future. Not only does language help man express his ideas but it also influences him to develop *certain kinds* of ideas. That is to say, different groups, because of various experiences, have developed unique systems of symbols, and these in turn, being unique, have influenced men to think and feel and act differently from one another. The Eskimo child, for example, early learns certain words which help him express himself and thereby communicate his ideas; but, since the words were present in the group even before he was born, they have the effect of making him think and feel and act in accordance with the already accepted usage of these words. For example, the Eskimo child very early learns that animal intestines and their contents are a tasty treat, whereas in our society one soon learns that intestines and their contents evoke disgust and are not even to be mentioned. The same can be said for a child or adult in any other society. The conclusion that suggests itself here is that, since words have such a significant influence on men's lives, it is imperative, if we are to understand men, that we know what the words *mean to them* in their everyday lives. This is true, of course, not only among diverse ethnic, cultural, and national groups but also among members of the same family. Misunderstandings arising out of the many shades of meaning that a given word may have for different persons are not uncommon, even among friends. How much more cautious, therefore, we must be in our attempts to understand individuals and groups who have not had the same background and training as ourselves!

We may say, then, in summary, that these three factors underlie the common denominator of human society and culture: (1) man's common biological make-up, (2) his high degree of intelligence, and (3) his great capacity for inventing symbols and transmitting them, thus conveying knowledge from society to society and from one generation to the next. Indeed, these basic characteristics are so highly similar from group to group that the familiar concept of "the brotherhood of man" takes on today increased significance.

MAN, THE TIME-BOUND CREATURE

PAST-BOUND. If it were possible for each generation of men to learn new ideas, new skills, and new ways of living, but not possible to communicate this learning to subsequent generations, then culture would not exist and this book could not be written with the expectation that this and future generations of readers would understand it. Each succeeding generation would start at the same level as the very first generation of men. In actual fact, each generation builds on the accomplishments of all past generations. But we have seen from our study of the various societies that although there is a great deal of continuity from one generation to the next in their style of life, there is, on the other hand, variation as well. Both the continuities and the variations result from man's ability to learn, retain, and use transmissible symbols. A peculiar paradox sometimes arises here because of this twofold ability of man: Although he is capable of change because of his ability to learn new knowledge and adjust to new conditions, he is also resistant to change because of his strong retention of and adherence to the culture transmitted to him from the past. Thus, although each new generation learns new habits of thinking and behaving, often quite incompatible with the thinking and acting transmitted from the past (traditions, customs, folkways, mores), both the old and the new exist side by side. Sometimes the survival of culture traits of the past coexisting with more recently acquired traits has caused great uneasiness on the part of those striving to pass on the older traits to the new generation. That is, being to some extent bound by the past and recognizing at the same time the need for realignment of the past to present conditions, men in all groups have known the pangs of battling within themselves against the old. Men do not live in the past; the past, rather, lives in men.

FUTURE-BOUND. We have seen that man is: (1) a symbol-using creature; (2) capable of transmitting his culture to posterity; (3) able to learn new symbols and transmit these as well, and thus accumulate more supplies in the storehouse of culture; and (4) bound by the symbols of the past, even while he is learning new, and sometimes contradictory, symbols to fit present conditions. All this is true; yet it does not exhaust the uses that man everywhere makes of his symbolizing capacities.

We have dwelt mostly on the past and its influence on the present. How about the future? These relentless drivers, these symbols, give man an incomparable edge over animals by enabling him to reach out into three dimensions at once—the past, the present, and the future. [Reflecting on this, J. L. Myres' definition of culture may seem even more appropriate: "Culture is what remains of man's past, working on his present, to shape his future."]

Animals are primarily embedded in the present, very minutely in the immediate past, and indiscernibly or not at all in the future. Only man invents games and arts and communicates them; only man manipulates his symbols because of the pure esthetic enjoyment he derives from poetry and other creative expressions; only man plays with the skills and customs and symbols he has today in order to reach out and lay hold of what might be tomorrow. Only man asks, "What will tomorrow bring?" and seeks actively to answer this query with all the foresight and planning that he alone has—knowingly rather than instinctively. Only man is capable of foregoing momentary pleasures to plan for possible "rainy days" ahead. So tremendously powerful is this tendency in man that, although it sometimes seems less urgent than the more pressing demands inherited from the past, it is, nevertheless, a crucial counterbalancing characteristic of those societies studied.

THE LIMITS OF HABITAT AND LOCATION

The relations between the lifeway of a people and their physical environment must be appreciated as a basic step toward understanding a society. These relations are viewed in this book in terms of *limits* established by the environment, within which a wide variety of alternative ways of life are possible.

The physical environment, or habitat, has sometimes been regarded as setting patterns that the society *must* follow, but this extreme position has not been adopted here.

The fact that the Eskimo is snowbound much of the year severely limits the kinds of activities that he can perform but does not dictate the specific activities that he will select from the wide range of possibilities open to him. This conclusion is especially evident when we consider that different Eskimo groups living within the same environment do not necessarily have identical cultures. Again, the Navajo, living in an arid region, is forced to adapt himself in certain characteristic ways; but that does not make his culture identical with that of the Arab, who also lives in an arid region. A similar comparison may be made between Britain and Japan. These islands are of comparable size; they have similar raw materials and industries; both, indeed, are seafaring. But who would claim that the lifeways of the one are similar in every respect to those of the other? Indeed, habitat sets limits so wide that many alternatives are usually possible.

Sometimes different societies will solve environmental problems differently because of varying degrees of complexity in their over-all cultural development. Nonliterate societies tend to rely heavily on tradition and may have a limited assortment of technical skills and subsistence patterns. Some literate societies, especially those of modern Europe and America, seek new, nontraditional solutions to certain problems, although tradition may still hold sway in other sectors of their culture and thus prevent the solution of other kinds of problems. Nevertheless, it is important to realize that the particular possibilities and difficulties presented by a habitat will depend greatly on the culture of the people concerned and will not be the same for differing cultures.

An equally important aspect of the physical environment is *location*. Let us imagine that the Navajo reservation were somehow transported to the middle of Africa, so that the Baganda were neighbors of the Navajo. What would the Navajo be like then? And what about the Baganda? Would they both have the same problems of acculturation with which they are faced today? It seems safe to assume that both would have different problems, because their culture contacts would be quite altered from those they now have.

The accessibility of the raw materials of a certain habitat will also not only influence the economy and entire culture of the people living there but will also bring about contacts with other groups and thus introduce influences of quite incalculable complexity. The less accessible a society is to others, the simpler it will remain with respect to the number of culture elements it will develop. For diffusion and culture contacts are possible only if the location of a group is such that channels are open for these processes to occur. When the channels are meager or nonexistent, culture borrowing and culture lending are impossible.

In brief, we may say that although habitat sets the limits of adaptation open to a people, it does not dictate the alternative directions possible. And, although location likewise sets certain limits upon the cultural attainments of a people, it does not dictate the specific culture they will have.

MAN, THE ORGANIZER

Wherever men exist, they are organized. There is no society known that is merely a collection of individuals with no specific relations to one another. Rather, we find that each society is an organization—that is, a relatively stable arrangement of persons and groups with certain accepted responsibilities to one another. Without some unifying arrangement, the group would dissolve and the individuals would drift apart, soon re-forming again or building a new organization elsewhere.

Of course, no social organization is ever in a state of continuous equilibrium. Man reorganizes and disorganizes at the same time. Some societies, especially the more complex ones, have developed means of coping with conflicting interests that develop between and within their subsections and endeavor rationally to make adjustments. In this way a high degree of organization endures indefinitely, even though strains within the organization may arise. On the other hand, there are societies that do not have the inner resources within their patterned arrangements to cope with conflicting interests. These societies may be said to be too stable, too brittle. Thus, when new conditions create unexpected strains, the organization is apt to crack in the wake of widespread internal hostility, unrest, and entire dissolution of large parts of the existing arrangement. We may say, then, that though men organize, they also at times unintentionally disorganize. That organization which foresees the possibility of changes or strain in the future and pre-arranges specific means of coping with them as they arise—*i.e.*, by re-organization—is most likely to avoid or overcome the problems of disorganization.

MINIMUM ESSENTIALS FOR A SOCIETY

Men organize; they form patterned types of enduring social arrangements—but for what purpose? What ends do these patterned arrangements serve and by what means are they achieved?

First, we know that all human beings have certain common biological drives which are termed "needs." These include the need for air, warmth, food, reproduction of the species, water, activity, rest, elimination of bodily wastes, avoidance of bodily harm, etc. Accordingly, every society must be so organized as to enable its members to satisfy these needs at least in some minimum fashion. Unless some form of organization capable of providing for these needs exists, the group cannot long function as a group. Disbanding, internal strife, mass degeneration, mass suicide, or slow death are bound to follow. The first function, then, of any society is the satisfaction of the biological needs of its constituent individuals.

Second, in order for these needs to be satisfied, the social arrangement must be such as to require some degree of order or conformity on the part of the members. Group living, in contrast to a solitary or hermitlike existence, demands responsibilities as well as offering privileges. Thus, in order to ensure that the members will do their part in the socially approved ways, each group has developed channels for meting out reward and punishment through the mores, the law, religion, and other institutions. These agencies serve as systems of checks and balances in rewarding behaviors considered to be in keeping with the group's purposes and punishing those held to be out of step. No society, for example, can long tolerate a state of affairs in which each man is a "law unto himself." Thus, each society has developed some means of preventing bloodshed or avenging it and of adjudicating differences that inevitably arise in the course of social living.

Third, in providing for the biological wants and in the securing of order, a division of labor must necessarily evolve. Different persons will inevitably carry out different tasks. Now, since some labors are more desirable than others, each society has its special forms of differential motivation for the performance of certain tasks essential for group survival. By means of maxims, monetary rewards, group recognition, adulation, special powers and privileges, and so forth, the society achieves some working order among the different persons and groups laboring at their respective tasks. Almost inevitably, too, some degree of pride and self-justification becomes associated with each task. The thinkers and planners, the magicians and priests, the businessmen and tradesmen, the artisans and professional workers, the skilled and the nonskilled—all are differently motivated to perform their tasks; all have a part in keeping the ship afloat.

Fourth, if an organization accomplished all these things for its members yet made no provision for its perpetuation, it would not be a society in the usual sense of the word. It would be rather an association of individuals temporarily grouped for the performance of some mutually desirable goal. Thus, each society encourages reproduction and/or recruitment of its members and ensures that the new members will be socialized in conformity with the group standards and group ends. In this sense, then, a society may be said to be an organization that lives on even though each of its individual members is eventually succeeded by another.

We have now briefly summarized the primary means and ends of social organization. But the picture is much more complex. Every society develops values—i.e., ideas and beliefs and attitudes which are considered of supreme importance to its members. Thus, for example, the Eskimo and Navajo must not displease the spirits, the Baganda chief strives to amass cattle beyond his economic need, the Chinese spares no efforts to please and obey the wishes of the departed, the Southerner espouses the idea of "white supremacy," and the Briton will die for his monarch.

Each society has many values, some, of course, considered more important than others. What especially interests us here is that these values have a profound effect not only on how the members of the society will view the world but also on their social organization. Values among groups sometimes arise out of the experiences of the group under different conditions and activities of the past, sometimes through culture diffusion, and sometimes by forceful imposition of a conquering group—but, however they arise, they always influence the existing social arrangements. To be sure, the same values will affect different organizations in different ways, and the organization in turn will modify the values, but there is always an interaction between them. For example, the introduction of Christianity among the Baganda inevitably brought about changes in their social structure. Marriages were now performed differently and could not easily be dissolved, and polygamy was curbed. In the case of many Eskimo accepting Christianity a crucifix became another type of amulet, and Christ and Mary merely replaced the names of their former gods without greatly changing their previous conceptions of them. Again, China under Communist rule presents a somewhat different picture from that of Russia under the same rule. Thus, values are always assimilated and interpreted in terms of the ongoing social organization and lifeway, and these in turn always react upon and modify the values in some way. In other words, a given type of social organization tends to develop certain value-systems, which, in their turn, influence the functioning and further development of the organization. The resultant interplay of these two characteristics common to all societies is referred to as "socioculture."

The socioculture of a group *must* in some way meet the basic demands necessary for the survival of human groups everywhere. Because these demands are so imperative and so pervasive among all societies, we refer to them here as minimum essentials of a society.

These essentials seem to be so universal that we are strongly urged to the conclusion that the "why" and "how" of sociocultures are variations on a few central themes. The variations do, indeed, differ greatly in degree from the abstract generalizations presented here, and when they do, we are sometimes led—unwisely—to assume that there is variation in kind as well. One thing, however, seems certain: no society can afford to flaunt these essentials for long.

THE PATTERNING OF IDEAL NORMS FOR BEHAVIOR

All societies have differential status and role expectancies according to such categories as age, sex, birth order, precocity, educability, sociability, subgroup membership, occupation, and so on. Standards of behavior are recognized in relation to these statuses and roles, and the individuals tend to act accordingly.

These standards are not necessarily formally taught, but the society nevertheless abides by them and reacts negatively whenever they are transgressed. Traditionally, the child at a dinner table in Britain is "to be seen and not heard." If he is both seen and heard, particularly if he is obtrusive, he may suffer parental displeasure, to put it mildly. The Negro in the deep South has a set status and an associated role. If he seeks to change that status, he may encounter resistance from both the whites and fellow Negroes, both of whom might regard him as "uppity," or "getting out of his place."

In most societies there are also norms of conduct expected of the "ideal" adult personality, toward which parents are expected to rear their children. The daring Eskimo hunter who shares his catch with the community, the flawless craftsman in the English Midlands, and the hard-working, obsequious Chinese peasant are illustrations of the desirable kinds of character fostered in the respective societies. Children, on their part, tend to behave in accordance with both the special statuses they have (either ascribed or achieved) and the ideal adult personality.

The "stamping in" of these norms for behavior is usually brought about by such psychological means as the following: differential reward and punishment, need for and fear of loss of parental or adult affection and attention, identification with parents and other adults, need for and fear of loss of recognition, belongingness and participation in the group, shame and guilt arising from transgression of the norms. Any one or all of these operate in the socialization process, even after the person has effectively internalized the norms and become an accepted member of his group.

THE TRANSFORMATION OF HUMAN NATURE

Human beings, like other animals, are motivated by biological drives but, unlike animals, they learn to become motivated by other needs in accordance with the various demands of their respective sociocultures. Furthermore, these latter acquired needs often are more demanding than the original biological ones (except in situations of extreme stress). For example, persons, like animals, have to satisfy the hunger drive but, unlike animals, they will prefer not to eat (except under duress) unless the food has been prepared according to certain esthetic formulas, and served with appropriate utensils in a more or less dignified manner. Persons, like animals, need sex outlets, but only persons develop codes of ethics, norms of behavior, and mutual expectancies. Persons, like animals, need warmth, but unlike animals will not wear "any old coat" or "any old dress." Persons, like animals, strive to avoid bodily harm, but unlike animals will make the supreme sacrifice for ideas, for flags, for honor, for country, for gods, for race, for class, and so on.

On the basis of these considerations, then, the obvious conclusion that presents itself is that man's biological nature becomes transformed, in the course of sociocultural living, into a new compound. His compound, of course, is by no means devoid of the biological element; rather it is a complex manifold of the biological and the sociocultural. Indeed, it is difficult, if not impossible, to know what man would be like if he were not a product of these two factors continually interacting and influencing the courses of destiny. In other words, we do not know what human nature is "in the raw," except, perhaps, in the characteristics of newborn babies. The latter, however, soon are absorbed by the existing socio-cultures into which they are born, thus depriving us forever of a knowledge of what they would be like if it were possible for them to grow up solitarily. (Only children reared in more or less accidental and partial isolation provide any clues, and these are not of the best, scientifically speaking.) It appears, then, that human nature cannot be understood except as we view its manifestations in relation to the specific sociocultural influences acting upon the common biological base.

Homo sapiens, the biological creature, living together in groups, always produces some form of socioculture; and socioculture, in turn, always invests this creature with something more than the mere biological qualities: it makes him Man—indeed, Man the Reciprocal, *Homo reciprocus.*

MAN, THE PHILOSOPHER

With so much of his life enmeshed in symbol-making, it is hardly any wonder that man should become concerned with himself and his relation to the universe. In most known societies, there is some conception about man's origin and the causes of this origin. Everywhere, spirits and gods, totems and holy objects testify to this serious concern. Magic and animism, mysticism and religion are ever-recurring sociocultural phenomena as man ponders himself and the universe. Questions inevitably arise concerning the "why" of things, and systems of answers built up through experience are passed on from generation to generation as the ultimate truths and the meaning of life.

But these matters are not solely the passing interests of men when they have nothing better to do. They serve, indeed, a much more vital function. They give men a sense of security in the face of a world which they cannot understand —much less control. Disaster and disease, famine and death, interpersonal and intergroup hostilities ever beleaguer and frustrate men. And man's great weapon has been his symbol-making powers. For with them he endeavors to plead with the unseen forces to stave off these natural and social enemies or to ask for redress once they have struck. These philosophies, then, these systems of ideas concerning the "why" of things, appear to be means of overcoming man's weakness in relation to forces he does not comprehend or cannot adequately control.

As man moves from the more simple to the more complex, from knowing less about the world to knowing more, he girds himself with other means of controlling the natural and social orders. Magic gives way to technology, and technology to science. Religion, too, takes on a different meaning. It tends to lose its propitiatory tendencies and becomes more a unifying system of principles that give men breadth and perspective as guides to the "good" life in a complex world. Secularization affects most aspects of life, from the holy to the merely proper, and what is "good" becomes more and more varied. Indeed, the world appears more and more complex as more knowledge accumulates.

In a word, then, we may say that through man's ability to symbolize and in response to ever-recurrent frustrations, man builds up systems of thought that are passed on from generation to generation and that are part of the intricate network of means he has developed for coping with the world.

THE FLEXIBILITY OF HUMAN BEHAVIOR

One of the most remarkable features of *Homo sapiens* which distinguishes him from most, if not all, of the other living creatures is his wide scatter over the face of the earth. Heat and cold, sun and wind, desert and swamp have not stopped this adaptable creature from exploring and inhabiting most areas of the earth's land surface. Biologically, he is so constituted internally as to be able to keep a steady functional equilibrium even under conditions of a relatively wide range of temperature and a great variety of foods, provided that he can make use of accumulated artifacts. The Eskimo, for example, subsists largely on a protein diet of meat and fish products, whereas the Chinese peasant is content for the most part with a carbohydrate diet of rice, wheat, or other plant products.

Man, however, is highly adaptable not only in the biological but also in the behavioral realm. Indeed, his great ability to learn—that is, his ability to acquire new modes of behavior—enhances his biological flexibility. Man can live at the North Pole, for example, but he can do so only because he has learned how to protect himself from the elements. He can live in an unfertile desert because he has learned the art of herding. Human beings, furthermore, are capable of changing their learned behavior if the behavior does not bring satisfactory results—*i.e.*, if it does not satisfy either the biological or the sociocultural essentials, or both. If this were not possible, we should have no notion of culture change: human society and culture would be static, rigid.

Changes of behavior—adjustments—arise out of the necessity to meet new situations. These adjustments occur in relation to two broad dimensions: (1) other personalities, (2) the sociocultural framework.

ADJUSTMENT TO OTHER PERSONS. No one individual faces the prospect of adjusting to *all* of mankind. Throughout his lifetime a person has contact with only a limited number of other people. Each individual, therefore, finds it necessary to adjust to a relatively small circle of other individuals with whom his destinies lie and through whom he derives his status and carries out his several roles. The infinite variety of adjustments which are thus possible influence the formation of different personalities. This, in turn, makes for diversity even in the same socioculture. Indeed, no two persons anywhere are identical in every respect and, as a result, no socioculture anywhere is absolutely uniform. Interpersonality differences make for intracultural differences, and these in turn react upon the former. The spiral is endless.

ADJUSTMENT TO THE SOCIOCULTURAL ENVIRONMENT. The adjustment of the individual occurs not only with respect to other individuals but also in relation to the general frame of his socioculture. All his acts, all his thinking may be said to occur as a result of or in relation to it. The language he uses, the customs he obeys, the philosophy he adheres to, and even the foods he likes are determined by the social and cultural envelope that surrounds him. Even if he is a genius or a madman and, consequently, acts and thinks differently from the rest of his society, his acts and his thinking are nevertheless in relation to *it* and not to some other society. Thus, the deviant personality in one socioculture displays characteristics peculiar to that socioculture and may have little resemblance to the deviant in another socioculture. Briefly, then, the sociocultural environment of a person always represents an exceedingly important factor influencing his behavior in multiform ways.

THE LIMITS OF HUMAN FLEXIBILITY

Though man is capable of learning new ways of doing, thinking, and feeling things as a consequence of changing demands of his environment, or as a result of incomplete satisfaction of a given behavior, he is nevertheless not infinitely flexible. The demands for adjustment must in some way be commensurate with his ability to meet them, and when the demands surpass this ability, tensions result, with consequent unpleasant effects upon the individual and the socioculture. The limits of flexibility are manifested in two broad dimensions: (1) conflicting or inordinate demands of other personalities, (2) conflicting or inordinate demands of the sociocultural framework.

LIMITS OF ADJUSTMENT TO OTHER PERSONS. Each person is a member of several subgroups of his society: His family, his neighborhood, his business or economic group, his status group, his class, etc. Though these groups themselves often reflect the general form of the socioculture and, indeed, give the socioculture its content, it is possible, nevertheless, that they have differing or even conflicting aims and values. But some degree of consistency must be manifest in order to preserve a semblance of order in the socioculture and to avert a state of generalized mutual hostility and aggression among the individuals. When the individual is confronted by diverging and conflicting views, aims, values, meanings, and beliefs of his various subgroups in which he has membership, the tension created is manifested in personality disturbances. That is to say, there are limits to man's ability to adjust to continuous divergent and changing demands of his various subgroups.

LIMITS OF ADJUSTMENT TO THE SOCIOCULTURAL FRAMEWORK. The "form" of a given socioculture is reflected not only in the form of its constituent parts but also in the personality configurations of its constituent individuals. The more nearly harmonious—i.e., integrated—the constituent parts are, the less is the tension experienced by the individuals concerned. Conversely, the more divergent —i.e., unintegrated—the constituent parts are, the more is the tension experienced in achieving personality integration by the individuals concerned.

Thus, we may say that the kind of personalities a given socioculture tends to produce will be more or less reflections of the kind of socioculture it is and the degree of harmony existing among its several different aspects. If the socioculture emphasizes helpfulness and community responsibility, then the individuals will tend to reflect these characteristics. On the other hand, if it is experiencing a great deal of strain, say, between this emphasis and more recent inroads of competitiveness and rivalry, then the personalities, too, will reflect these strains.

THE RELATIVE DEGREES OF INDIVIDUAL FREEDOM

All stable societies impose some degree of restraint upon their constituent individuals. As we have already seen, no enduring organization is possible where each individual is a "law unto himself." However, all societies do allow for individual variations in behavior, even in those situations that are felt to be of importance to the group. These variations rise out of the fact of individual differences in personality and from the fact that different individuals occupy different statuses and consequently are expected to act out different roles. Pressure to conform to group standards is exerted in all societies, but none is so rigidly patterned that variations are impossible. Nevertheless, greater pressure for conformity is exerted in some societies than in others, and consequently smaller degrees of individual variations are possible. However, what is considered to be too restrictive upon individual freedom in one society may not necessarily be so regarded in another. Thus, for example, the American may easily be led to assume that the female in Eskimo society is mistreated into submission by the male, but the Eskimo in their turn may regard the great degree of independence and easy mobility of the American women as a sign of lack of modesty and propriety. The degree of individual freedom thus permitted by various societies is relative to the total matrix of prevailing sociocultural norms.

Where the norms differ, the degree of individual freedom will likewise differ. The latter is dependent on the former.

THE RELATIVITY OF HUMAN BEHAVIOR

Societies may be distinguished by the values that they respect. These represent beliefs and practices that the members consider to be the most important things in life. Any adequate analysis of human social behavior, therefore, cannot be made apart from an understanding of the value-system relative to which the behavior occurs. The same act carried out in two different societies may mean entirely different things because the value-systems are different. Patricide and infanticide in one society may involve the same *actions* as in another, but in the one it may be regarded as a merciful act and thus justified, whereas in the other it may be considered an act of murder and thus condemned. A system of socially sanctioned discrimination and segregation between white and Negro is accepted by some Americans while the same system is hotly disdained by others. In order, then, to gain a scientific understanding of a given behavior among any group of people or of an individual in a given group, it is necessary to gain an understanding of the values prevailing in the respective sociocultural framework. For, after all, most social behavior is *relative* to these values.

Although this relativity can be abundantly documented, many social scientists now recognize the existence of certain behavioral or moral absolutes among societies, although the expression of these absolutes varies. To take a human life, for example, except under special circumstances condoned by a given society, is probably universally considered as a violation of commonly accepted privileges. Everywhere men have rules against murder, but when and how these rules shall apply are relative to the local operating value-systems. One of the great problems of our time is to discover which values are common and which relative. Unless codes are found that are more universally acceptable, mankind is not very likely to awake one day to find misunderstandings miraculously dispelled by sweet reasonableness and brotherly love. Until that day comes we can all benefit by an earnest, unyielding effort to understand others through an understanding of those influences—values, beliefs, social organization, habitat, etc.—that mold them incessantly to a certain fit.

DEFINITION OF THE SITUATION

The principle concerning the relativity of human behavior asserts that the totality of interactions among persons and groups takes place within the broad framework of socially accepted values. But this is only one side of the coin. Men act in given situations not merely in accordance with the expected norms of behavior but also in accordance with how they perceive or interpret these norms. Thus, any given act, in order to be adequately understood, must be studied both in the light of the tangible sociocultural conditions relating to it and also in the light of the interpretation of these conditions *by the actor or actors involved.* A study of both these poles influencing behavior in any given situation is technically referred to as "the definition of the situation." Only a knowledge of the definition of the situation can account adequately for the motivations lying behind an act or a complex of acts either by an individual or a group.

THE STRUGGLE FOR EXISTENCE: COOPERATION AND CONFLICT

We have referred to biological and sociocultural essentials that man must satisfy in some way in order to exist—that is, to exist in groups. Reference has also been made to recurrent problems that arise from both the natural and social orders, forcing man to invent means of coping with these frustrations. These difficulties engender for him a struggle for existence which is characterized by two opposing interactions: cooperation and conflict. Cooperation among men enables them to achieve ends together that they could not achieve alone. At the same time, differences arise with respect to the ends as well as the means to be followed in reaching them. When these differences cannot be solved by "talking things over," hostility or open conflict ensues. In short, dissociation is sometimes as evident in social life as is association. It is also patently evident from a study of the six societies described and analyzed in this book that in each one there are or have been manifestations of men's subjugation of other men. Within societies and among societies, various groups with common interests seek to further their ends even though these may conflict with the ends of other groups. The elders of each group, for example, strive to maintain their positions of authority by fostering the sentiment of respect for and obedience to elders, even though this may create difficulties for the younger generation. Economic classes tend to develop different interests and consequently different orientations, making in turn for rivalries, hostilities, and sometimes even open conflict. As for the subjugation of men of one society by another, every one of the societies studied has experienced or is still experiencing this phenomenon. Indeed, this fact is so blatantly apparent that it needs no emphasis here. The important thing to notice, however, is that although men do, indeed, subjugate one another and often treat one another inhumanely, the balance seems, nevertheless, to be in favor of cooperation. For, if men were not of mutual help to one another towards common goals, it hardly seems possible that men could exist at all.

And, since it is "natural" for men to cooperate, at least as much as to conflict, we can be encouraged to seek out the conditions that give rise to cooperation in order to implement them to the greatest degree for the greatest benefit of all men.

Reciprocal responsibility: the basis of social stability

One of the most striking facts of any society studied is that necessary things somehow get done with some degree of order. The same behaviors relating to the same duties may be observed as occurring again and again till we are led to conclude that there is an ordered patterning involved. People do not trample on one another; they tend to recognize one another as being to some extent like themselves, and they show some degree of consideration for the rights of the other. And, remarkably enough, these mutual behaviors tend to be carried out automatically and spontaneously. One need not tell the Britisher to queue up while waiting for a train to take him to or from work: he does so automatically. Likewise, one hardly need tell the Eskimo hunter to share his catch with the rest of his village—he knows and feels he has a responsibility to them, and they in turn know that they must do the same for him. Signs and propaganda are not needed to urge the Muganda to show his respect for the king, and the king automatically and reciprocally behaves in a manner suiting his station. The list can be multiplied endlessly—man is clearly *Homo reciprocus,* man in reciprocity.

Man's automatically reciprocal behaviors, representing, as they do, a recognition on the part of the society's members that they have responsibilities to one another and to the group as a whole, constitute the elements of ongoing life in any stable society. Without such reciprocal responsibilities, the society breaks down; normlessness (*anomie*) and even revolution take over. These elements of order, then, act as a constraining force in accordance with the value-system of the given socioculture and thereby have the effect of perpetuating the behavior patterns of the past. Yet, without some order, change would likewise be impossible. Reciprocal responsibility acts, thus, at once as a deadweight of the past and a lever of progress to the future. It is the basis of social ethics and morals. It is both cause and effect, description and explanation of social order. Without it societies must decline and perish. It is the elemental lubricant by means of which the more complex systems of social behavior are made possible. In a very important sense, we may say that reciprocal responsibility is the central unit in any social order and that all the other units are dependent upon it for the furtherance of their respective purposes.

When the nations of the world recognize this truism and extend it in their relations with one another, world order and lasting peace will move from the realm of dreams into the reality of everyday life for all men. Man will then be *Homo reciprocus* not merely in families and nations but as that functionally integrated mankind of which sages have long spoken.

Mutual interdependence

We have seen that what a people and its constituent individuals will be like is dependent upon the interplay of a host of factors—habitat, natural resources, maintenance institutions, family system, political system, religious system, etc. Although these facts help determine the character of the ongoing socioculture and of one another, they in their turn are influenced by the totality of their relations. Furthermore, it is impossible to divorce completely, except temporarily for purposes of study, the similarities of various aspects of the respective parts of a common denominator—the "form" or "structure" of the socioculture. Each socioculture has its distinctive form, as well as distinctive content, and it is the form that tends to pervade and influence each part. Thus, we may say that the patterns of and for behavior in different contexts tend to reinforce one another. If this were not so, every activity, every idea, every belief, every value held by a people would be different from every other, and inconsistency, meaninglessness, and chaos would result. And although there is never perfect consistency between the form in one part of the socioculture and another, there tends, nevertheless, to be some "inner necessity" in each socioculture to have as much consistency—as much meaning—as possible.

Looking at Values and Value-Systems

There is no mystery about this "inner necessity," for all sociocultures acquire their distinctive forms in quite natural and understandable ways. One of the most important of these ways is the intertwining, sometimes over a very long growing period, so to speak, of the values that a given people regard as most important. That is to say, values eventually become systematized, so that ramifying through most if not all parts of a socioculture are strands of value, as it were, that careful inspection will show to have a definite pattern or patterns. As Black observed above, such a value-system never has *perfect* consistency; contradictions, omissions, and outright conflicts are often to be found. Nevertheless, even those members of a society who openly defy some aspects of its *ethos* or general value-system—sometimes because they are also members of subgroups representing special interests within the society—are not challenging a vacuum. To rebel against a system means at least that the system exists and that it has enough binding force to be irksome.

In reading about the Eskimo, Navajo, and Baganda, we saw how widely value-systems vary. What appears to the superficial observer to be a single form of conduct is murder in one society but only regrettable necessity in another. The sociofacts are similar, but the mentifacts that lend them meaning are strikingly different. Artifacts also do not speak for themselves; the bangle of beads placed on the left wrist of the Kabaka, signifying his kinship with the early conquerors of Buganda, is not merely a collection of small spheres pierced by a wire that is bent to form a circle three and a half inches in diameter. Here, too, the mentifact must be understood before the artifact can be seen for what, among the Baganda, it effectively is.

We recognize the control exercised by mentifacts in everyday life when, for example, we say of someone, "He's a queer fellow; he's got ideas." What we really mean is not that he has ideas as such, or even new ideas, but that certain ideas are for him values differing from those held by most people. He is a deviant, someone who turns aside or even goes astray on forbidden paths. If we were to question him, he might be able to offer reasons for wandering off the beaten track, and these reasons would be stated in terms of some value-system other than our own.

In fact, we frequently take account of such deviation when we talk about someone who violates a taboo. This term, although a fairly recent one in our language, has become quite widespread; it points to the negative aspects of a value-system. To refer to one of the illustrations in the Introduction, we do not "desecrate or behave disrespectfully toward our flag." As will later be pointed out, such a taboo, although negative, is linked with certain positive or affirmative aspects of our own and similar value-systems which we shall later designate as those focusing on loyalistic sacredness.

So much, then, by way of reiterating what was said in the Introduction and in "Looking Back." It is now desirable, perhaps, to go into more detail about the nature of values, the way they combine into systems, and the relations of such systems with social organization and interaction. The following presentation will necessarily be abstract, and it will be impossible, because of space limits, to provide detailed illustrations for every point. If more extended treatment is desired, the student should make use of Howard Becker's *Man in Reciprocity* (New York, Frederick A. Praeger, Inc., 1956), especially Chapters 10-13.

Any object of any need, at the human level, may be termed a value. For the Eskimo, "slime scraped from a walrus hide together with some of the human urine used in the tanning process" is a food value falling into the realm of "the appropriately sacred"; for the Navajo, sand paintings begun just after sunrise and destroyed before sunset are supernaturalistic values that partake of "holy sacredness"; for the Baganda, totemic exogamy, involving marriage outside the clan, is a kinship value, and as such may be classified as "intimate sacredness."

THE WIDE RANGE AND CULTURAL CHARACTER OF THE SACRED

Let us now try to state more clearly what is meant by sacredness and to see how its main varieties, including those mentioned above, can be located along a sort of scale or continuum that shades over into secular values, which also can be ranged along such a scale.

As our examples have indicated, sacred values are not merely those having to do with the religious, divine, spiritual, and so on. The sacred *includes* the religious, to be sure, but it also takes in a great deal more. In brief, any conduct whatsoever may be viewed as relating to sacred values when it is accompanied by a definite emotionalized reluctance to change those values. Putting it differently, unwillingness or inability, or both—accompanied by distress or other evidence of tension—to alter any aspect of one's "way of life," is sacred evaluation. The person who makes such an evaluation has attitudes so strongly focused on certain values—mentifacts, sociofacts, or artifacts—that he feels and acts in an "upset" way when change in those attitudes or values is even suggested, not to say demanded.

All values, whether sacred or secular, are culturally defined in some manner and degree. If we survive, we must eat something in sufficient quantity and at suitable intervals; but the "something," "sufficient," and "suitable" are dependent on culture, on "what remains of man's past, working on his present, to shape his future." What is sacred to us in eating, clothing, mating, fighting, working, and worshiping is what we have been *taught* in one fashion or another to hold sacred.

The cultural character of the secular

The same is true, in different ways, of secular values. Although the secular is not merely the reverse of the sacred, it can still be said that we *learn* to change and *learn* to like it, and that such acquired ability and/or willingness to change is characteristically secular. When a young Eskimo man no longer seeks the honored status of an independent hunter and learns to be a dependent day laborer instead in order to secure cash for whiskey, he is in search of "the thrillingly secular"; when a Navajo woman wears a soft but expensive Pendleton blanket instead of the scratchier native kind she can cheaply make herself, she is indulging in "the comfortably secular"; when a Baganda landlord no longer feels any quasi-patriarchal responsibility for his tenants, merely exploiting them as sources of revenue, he is acting in accordance with "the consequently secular."

Such instances show that the field of the secular, as here defined, is much broader than that of the avowedly nonreligious, the profane, the skeptical, and the like. The secular *includes* these, of course, but it comprises much beyond them. Concisely, any sort of conduct may be regarded as centering on secular values when a well-marked readiness to seek those values, whatever the changes entailed, is felt or otherwise evidenced. Stated differently, willingness or ability, or both—coupled with desire or similar signs of anticipated gratification—to change one's customary actions in any way whatever is secular evaluation. Those who so evaluate have learned to concentrate on certain tangible or intangible ends in such a way that they may even feel compelled to pursue them by *any* means and regardless of opposition.

Here, too, however, culture plays an important part. No innovation is wholly unprecedented, and in that sense all innovations are cultural; but if they are not to die with their introducers, they must also be imparted to a number of others who must come to appreciate them. That is to say, *changes* in culture must be transmitted, learned, and shared just as definitely as *continuities* in culture. Both sacred and secular value-systems, then, are cultural phenomena.

THE HOLY AS THE EXTREME OF SACREDNESS

We said earlier that values, whether sacred or secular, can be located at various places along a scale or continuum. Such a scale must have end-points if it is to be of any particular use, even though these, in the present state of our knowledge, are somewhat arbitrary. Let us arrange a number of evaluations from estimated maximum reluctance to change sacred values to estimated maximum readiness to seek secular values. We may think of such a continuum algebraically—that is, from maximum plus to maximum minus, with a zero point somewhere near the middle.

Beginning with maximum plus, let us note the fact that, the world over, men have at many if not at all times readily accepted martyrdom for themselves or exacted it of others for the sake of religious values. They have been so compellingly oriented toward what they have viewed as supernatural forces or beings that they have sacrificed themselves or their fellows rather than permit changes in those orientations, or supernatural agencies, or both. Occasionally, it must be granted, it is thought that the supernatural beings or forces themselves punish the impious innovator and that it is not necessary that men intervene in their behalf. Under such circumstances, the violator of the supernaturalistic taboos merely becomes an outcast or may even be permitted to remain a member of the society with prohibited or limited participation in the more important relations such as marriage and leadership. Further, there are cases where holy sacredness is not so rigorously enforced as are certain other varieties—the patriotic or some other kind of the loyalistically sacred, for example. Nevertheless, with few exceptions, the holy in one or another form most frequently appears at the maximum-plus extreme of the sacred-secular scale.

LOYALTY AS HIGHLY SACRED

As we have noted, very close to the holy in power to bring about sacrifice of life is the loyalistic; men have died in droves because of their own or their opponents' loyalties to clans, tribes, castes, factions, parties, or nations. Sometimes, however—and here is the source of one of the exceptions noted with regard to the holy—it is far safer to denounce a god than to become traitor to a group or even to assert independence of it. Here is an illustration:

> Among the Winnebago . . . a man . . . dared to state that he disbelieved in the . . . holiest of the Winnebago deities and . . . expressed his contempt for him. A short time later, the deity in question appeared to the skeptic and pointed his finger at him [which] . . . was supposed to bring

immediate death. The man stood his ground . . . and the deity—Disease-Giver . . .—begged the man to die lest the people make fun of him!

However, the writer to whom we owe this illustration (Paul Radin, *The Method and Theory of Ethnology*, New York, McGraw-Hill Book Co., 1933, pp. 50-51; reprinted by permission) has also written, in the same book (pp. 42-43):

> An individual [among the Winnebago and similar primitive societies] may sin against varying parts of . . . [his social world] without incurring dangerous consequences, but if he sins against any fundamental aspect he must be prepared either to dissociate himself entirely from this world or die.
>
> Possibly we have here one of the reasons for the absence of consistent skeptics or unbelievers and for the nonexistence of revolts against the real structure of society.

Much more evidence along similar lines could readily be furnished; it is clear that the loyalistically sacred, together with several other varieties, may come very close indeed to the holy in life-or-death power, even though, as indicated above, the holy is probably stronger in most instances.

INTIMATE, MORALISTIC, FITTING, AND APPROPRIATE SACREDNESS

Another important kind of sacredness is that connected with what have long been called "primary groups." Ties with playfellows, friends, comrades, premarital companions, mates, family or other kinship-group members, partners, and so on, evoke the phenomena of intimate sacredness. Intimacy, once well and favorably established, is ordinarily viewed as not lightly to be terminated or otherwise altered. The world over we encounter evidence of the supreme devotion that the intimately sacred often calls forth; it, too, may sometimes rival the holy in the zeal it elicits.

Now we may proceed further along the scale. For almost half a century, students of the social sciences have learned that mores are "folkways with built-in morals." Practices that perhaps at first were merely the most convenient and effective ways to get things done eventually become the only right ways, and alterations in them are vigorously resisted. Taking this cue, we may refer to the moralistically sacred as "manners and customs" so entrenched that the violation of them calls up indignation and the suggestion of changing them produces perceptible emotional resistance. The scope of the moralistically sacred is wide; in fact, some social scientists have used the approximate equivalent "folkways and mores" as inclusive of almost everything in the realm of the sacred, with a large part of the secular thrown in for good measure. This seems too sweeping; in the light of the great variety of values and their related attitudes that we must classify, sharper and more numerous distinctions are necessary. "When something's everything, then nothing's anything." Within the limits we have here set up, however, the moralistically sacred is a very useful label.

Obviously, not all breaches of "manners and customs" are viewed with indignation or similar intensely adverse emotion. The overweening violator of the proprieties may encounter only cool contempt, and the awkward newcomer in some group having conventions of a not unduly rigorous sort may meet only with suppressed smiles. To refer to such minimal manifestations of difficulty or dislike of change, terms such as "the fittingly sacred" and "the appropriately sacred" are useful. They represent the sacred on the fringe of fadeout; the shift to the secular is close at hand.

THE PERVASIVENESS OF THE CEREMONIALLY SACRED

Before discussing this shift, however, we must take account of an aspect of sacred conduct that is evident in all its varieties, from the holy to the merely appropriate. This aspect may be designated "the ceremonially sacred." In the realm of the holy—*i.e.*, of the supernaturalistically oriented, of the religious as such—we easily perceive the importance of ceremonial as ritual. Indeed, some investigators of early religion have called attention to the fact that, odd as it may seem, set forms of worship (ritual in the strict sense) may be practiced when the worshipers have only a vague notion of what they are worshiping. That is to say, the holy value—spirit, god, awe-inspiring force—may have no clear designation, but the attitudes of those oriented toward that value may be plainly evident in the repetition of stock ejaculations, phrases, genuflections, and processions. In brief, men may engage in ritual action without having achieved *explicit* religious belief.

The ceremonially sacred, of course, takes in far more than ritual. In the realm of the loyalistic, for example, men may mutually pledge, as did the Founding Fathers, "our lives, our fortunes, and our sacred honor" in an impressive ceremony that, although not repeated, is commemorated every Fourth of July (and commemoration is likewise a ceremony). The intimately sacred, too, has its ceremonies, comprising everything from elaborate vows of blood-brotherhood to mourning to marriage before a justice of the peace. So also has the moralistically sacred, exemplified by ceremonies such as the notarizing of contracts, the awarding of diplomas (with their expressed or implied professional obligations), and a thousand other major and minor routines with moral overtones. Moreover, the fittingly sacred, where at most contempt is expressed toward the deviant, nevertheless has its ceremonials in the intricacies of aristocratic courtesy, "good sportsmanship," diplomatic protocol, and other formalizations of the polite, refined, or respectable. Even the appropriately sacred, in relation to which, in most instances, the social controls are only mildly manifest as good-humored ridicule, has many ceremonial aspects. These, in our society, take the form of "small talk," avoidance of "talking shop," stock formulas for "breaking the ice," greeting, "dating," and leave-taking, suitable ways of adjusting to fellow-workers or classmates—in fact, the whole paraphernalia of what is regarded in the social strata concerned as everyday tactful and considerate conduct. Resistance to change in such conduct is rarely high, but those who are ignorant or impatient of or indifferent to the ceremonials of the appropriately sacred may find themselves the butt of jokes or, at the very least, the cause of poorly concealed amusement. Here again we see what was earlier characterized as "the sacred on the fringe of fadeout." We have again moved from maximum to minimum reluctance to change.

Let us list the more or less arbitrarily designated steps along the scale: holy, loyalistic, intimate, moralistic, fitting, and appropriate, with ceremonial appearing in conjunction with all of them. Commemorative ceremonial, however, which is one important variety, is not manifested with high intensity where the moralistic, fitting, and appropriate are concerned.

THE SYMBOLIZING OF THE SACRED AS PRECEPT

It might be well, in rounding off this part of our discussion of values and value-systems, to call attention to some of the ways in which sacred reluctances are symbolized, implicitly or explicitly, inadequately or adequately. The qualifying adverbs attached to "symbolized" in the preceding sentence point to the fact that many of the forms taken by sacred reluctances can be put into words or other explicit symbols only with difficulty, if at all. The values involved may be only vaguely outlined; the force or spirit, clan, intimate, moral standard, propriety, or routine possessing one degree or another of sacredness may be defined in important respects by shudders of fright, tremors of joy, qualms of nausea, and quivers of ecstasy, as well as by frowns, grimaces, smiles, and rapturous expressions. These and similar phenomena entering into the definitions of sacred values and their correlative attitudes represent only a small proportion, in both number and kind, of the implicit and obscure symbols or potential symbols that not only supplement those that are explicit but in many cases provide crucially important parts of the value-definition.

As long as this is understood, however, little harm will be done here and in our later presentation of folk societies and their characteristically sacred value-systems by referring to the value-defining behavior involved as though it were primarily verbal. We shall use the term "precept," which is ordinarily regarded as designating only compressed bits of folk wisdom such as proverbs. Etymologically, "precept" derives from a verbal construction meaning "to take beforehand" or even "to anticipate." On this basis the term need not refer only to verbal conduct; it can be used to designate any sort of conduct, gesture, or any other form of expression that guides, limits, or defines in advance.

Precepts abound in societies of the kind that we have already studied and in some of the more complex societies still to be described, and have to do with everything from the holy to the appropriate. When they take the form of proverbs, however, or of clusters of ceremonial nods, bows, steps, and postures, they frequently are somewhat vague and hence capable of varying interpretations.

Moreover, this *implicit* character of at least part of the precept, in its concrete aspect, is much more sharply marked where its connections with other values and value-definitions are involved; the systematic links of a given precept with other precepts are almost always implicit. From this it follows that precepts are seldom arranged in such a way as to constitute a creed or code; they are *uncodified*. To be sure, the jumbled masses of precepts encountered in many relatively simple societies are usually intertwined, grown together, or fused; technically speaking, they are *accrete* in the same way as are the outer floral leaves of wintergreen when they finally merge into an inseparable whole. In brief, value-systems composed largely of precepts are likely to be implicit, uncodified, and accrete.

Such preceptive systems possess the characteristics just mentioned largely because these systems are of traditional and nonrational character. The transmitting, learning, and sharing of culture is distinctly informal in the sense that it results from each and every variety of association among intimates rather than from being entrusted to highly specialized instructors functioning in formal organizations. The intimates informally embody, so to speak, what remains of man's past in the given society—*i.e.*, tradition—and this tradition is accepted merely because it *is* tradition. In the Navajo selection telling the story of Old Man Hat, this traditional nonrationality pervading a preceptive or folk society is strikingly in evidence.

PRESCRIPTIVE SYMBOLIZATION OF THE SACRED

Sacred societies, however, often are carriers of value-systems that, although usually developing from precepts, are of what may be called the prescribed type. Sets of prescriptions are represented by the Ten Commandments, the Jewish Torah, the Roman law code of Justinian, the Apostles' Creed, Roman Catholic, Lutheran, and Presbyterian catechisms, British and American common law, and countless other explicitly stated and codified values and their correlative sanctioned attitudes. Not only are the various prescriptions stated with as much precision as is possible at the time in the culture concerned, but in addition this explicitness is buttressed by equally precise systematic arrangement, often deductive in nature. It is true that the deduction is more often than not *ex post facto*. That is, the systematic arrangement of the prescriptions is not initially deductive but rather is the outcome of historical developments and tricks of memorization, for example; and the deductive mortar, as it were, is trowelled between the joints after the structure is already built. Nevertheless, prescriptions are ordinarily *explicit* and *codified*.

At the same time, it is worth noting that prescriptions ordinarily develop out of precepts and that this, together with the *ex post facto* deductive character of the system, renders prescribed value-systems, in practically all cases, markedly *accrete*. Every prescription, even seemingly insignificant ones, is virtually as sacred as every other, and they are all densely intertwined and compacted. In other words, a prescribed value-system may be quite as accrete as one composed only of precepts.

But in spite of such accreteness and the *ex post facto* character of its "deductive mortar," a prescribed value-system must be termed rational in the sense that reasons can usually be given, by those subscribing to it, for every one of its parts and for the system as a whole. The reasoning in question may at times be of no very high quality and may even amount to mere formalism and rationalization, but it is consistently used. This is in strong contrast with the traditional nonrationality of a preceptive value-system, where "That's the way it is and always has been" is the final justification.

To summarize: Preceptive value-systems are implicit, uncodified, accrete, and traditionally nonrational; prescriptive value-systems are explicit, codified, accrete, and at least formally rational.

THROUGH ZERO TO THE FIRST RATIONAL POINT ON THE SECULAR SCALE

Having now surveyed the sacred part of our scale for the evaluation of social change, we must try to get some idea of the transition to the secular part. We shall again follow the practice of trying to arrange the conduct described and analyzed in a sequence from minimum to maximum, but for secularity this practice will prove to be even more difficult and more dependent on estimate or informed guesswork.

Like reluctance to change, readiness to change may verge on zero intensity. The zero point, or better, transitional range, of our sacred-secular scale represents those quite infrequent phenomena evidencing almost complete indifference to change or the lack thereof. Scattered through a given society there may now and again be found a few persons who "don't care much one way or the other" about the conduct of their fellows; however, most members of any society that retains some semblance of coherence do have active concern about even apparently insignificant behavior. Anyone who has ever listened to back-fence or barber-shop gossip will readily agree that evaluational neutrality—in this case, indifference—about trivial matters is not customary.

Be this as it may, when the zero point is passed the secular part of the scale begins. Here readiness to change, for whatever reason, takes the place of reluctance or indifference. Such readiness may, of course, be nearly balanced by an almost equal amount of reluctance—almost equal, but not quite. Change is accepted or even sought; nevertheless, certain limiting reluctances, deriving from the sacred part of the scale, are imposed on its rapidity or scope or both. As we have seen, sacred reluctances may not be clearly symbolized, particularly where precepts are involved. Prescriptions, however, being quite explicit and systematically arranged, are much more definite. Both precepts and prescriptions, concretely considered, lose power as the intensity of sacredness diminishes, but sometimes they transfer a good deal of their remaining efficacy to more abstract formulations that serve as ethical, governmental, professional, and similar principles.

The difference between precepts and prescriptions, on the one hand, and principles, on the other, is to be found in the fact that principles, being always in some degree abstract, admit of many changes in application, whereas precepts and prescriptions, given their concreteness, are virtually impossible to alter without destroying their very nature. Thus it is that when the sacred is salvaged at all, it reappears as the source of principle in the secular realm. Principles are viewed as fundamentally unalterable, and in this sense they incorporate one or another kind of sacredness; at the same time, they are held to be applicable to a wide variety of circumstances, and hence changeable in scope, as time goes on, through implementing amendments and similar adaptations.

The Founding Fathers, for example, built the principle of "unalienable rights" such as those to "life, liberty, and the pursuit of happiness" into the basic documents of our republic. But it has proved necessary to specify those principles by means of a great number of legislative enactments and Supreme Court decisions, to amend the Constitution some twenty-two times, and to repeal one amendment. Most Americans would view our basic governmental principles as by nature inviolable and in fact inviolate, in spite of their strong conviction that the making of necessary changes is praiseworthy. With due regard to difference in circumstances, the same can be said of Britons, as will later be made clear when the general background of the inhabitants of the English Midlands is presented. They, too, adhere to abstract principles—changing their actual use as occasion requires—that in considerable measure derive from a number of sacred attitudes and values.

Pursuant secularity, then, as readiness to change in certain ways, but only in those ways, is inseparably bound up with the sacredness of principles that should never be changed in fundamentals but only in scope and kind of application. Such secularity is rational but is limited by the sacredness of the principles concerned; the means chosen, however new, must still be regarded as "pursuant to the principles." This type of secularity, in most cases, is not strictly deductive in the sense that its innovations are foreseeable because of their logical "that-inevitably-follows-from-this" traits. Rather, certain changes come to be viewed as desirable, and their advocates then say, in effect, "The measures we propose are vitally necessary, and fortunately they are in full harmony with the principles to which we all subscribe." In other words, pursuant rationality may consist in finding justification for changes that were desired long before the possibility of justification was known to exist. It would be a little far-fetched, for example, to assert that all the amendments to our Constitution could have been deduced from fundamental Constitutional principles at the time it was adopted. Nevertheless, careful phrasing of the amendments, plus skillful Supreme

Court interpretation, gives them *ex post facto* deductive connections with our basic principles; these connections and the amendments may then properly be viewed as pursuantly rational.

The way in which principles are applied to specific cases, therefore, is often governed, in part at least, by a desire to limit expedient changes to those that can be brought into accord with the principles. In one quite valid sense, "expediency" means only acting in such ways as to free, release, or extricate— to remove hampering restrictions. In popular usage, however, "expediency" is often disparagingly spoken of as though it were always in direct opposition to "principle." We need grant no such meaning to the term; expedient changes may be consistent with prevailing principles, or they may not be; there is no *necessary* conflict. At the same time, there can be little doubt that changes viewed as expedient, as the easiest ways in the long run to do what must be done anyway, are often difficult to bring into line with pursuant rationality. Moreover, crises of various kinds, as well as changes so rapid that they precipitate crises, may give so little time to those who wish to keep expediency within the limits of principle that their efforts fail.

THE SECOND RATIONAL KIND OF SECULARITY

The consequence is that along with expedient measures that can immediately or ultimately be subjected to pursuant rationality, others are admitted that may eventually defeat all attempts at control and destroy the society they come to dominate. In this book we are able to grant only a trifling amount of space to Fascism, Nazism, and Communism; the most that we can say at this point is that all three are examples of rigid prescription *and* thoroughgoing expediency.

Expediency in such "unlimited" or "consequent" form represents the effort to attain ends by any means whatever so long as these means are not viewed by their users as self-defeating. The "so long as" qualification means that unlimited expediency is unlimited only with regard to the *range* of possible means. Although there are no limitations on the choice of means per se, certain means may be held to be instrumentally worthless or in direct conflict with other and more promising means. Actually, then, *rational* restrictions are imposed in that considerations of immediate utility, long-run effectiveness, or both, of absence of secondary consequences working against such utility and effectiveness, and of economy of effort cancel out or confine the scope of means of some kinds. Only those means chosen because they seem likely to lead successfully to the end are consequent in this sense. Consequent secularity is that type of secularity that is restricted only by rational judgments of instrumental efficiency; it stands in marked contrast with pursuant secularity, which, although likewise rationally limited, is further limited by the demand for consistency with presumably unalterable principle.

Consequently expedient values, as those which are regarded as easiest to attain (at least in the long run), are usually held to be highly desirable by persons not compellingly oriented toward the sacred as proverb or prescription, caring little either way, or holding to the sacred only as an aspect of abstract principle. Many increases in the size and complexity of sociocultures result from consequent expediency: better transportation, agriculture, manufacture, scientific formulation and application are the outcome of such secularity. To put this metaphorically, consequently expedient evaluation produces the profits of progress, but many of what we may call the costs of progress are also the outcome of consequent expediency. Cold-blooded exploitation of employees by employers and vice versa, and exploitation of certain groups of consumers by both, is simply expediency proceeding along rational lines but not effectively limited by precept, prescription, or principle. Total warfare, making use of the services of various experts in ways that are highly consequent, is an even more striking example.

(In this book we give relatively little attention to the dissociative interactions, such as conflict, occurring when value-systems favoring them hold sway; it seems necessary to concentrate on associative interactions and their accompanying organizations. This, however, should not lead the student to think that we regard dissociation as of little importance. On the contrary: if space permitted, our social-scientific objectives would unquestionably be furthered by fuller description and analysis of anarchic murder among the Eskimo, clan feuds among the Navaho, ruling-class conquest among the Baganda long before the day of the British, revolution and civil war among the Chinese, violent racial antipathies and repressions in the Cotton South, and the combative roles played by English Midlanders in strikes, lockouts, and the two World Wars.)

Two Nonrational Points Further Along the Secular Scale

The ends pursued by means selected with rational considerations in mind may of course be quite nonrational or even irrational. To refer to our previous example, we have recently witnessed scientifically conducted total warfare involving fantastic notions of superior and inferior races, of a revival of Caesarism, of an emperor as a descendant of a sun goddess, and of a "proletariat" with the cosmically guaranteed destiny of world domination. Such combinations of rational means and ends of quite opposite character certainly are not the only possibilities in secular conduct. Observe, for example, that *both* may be nonrational—indeed, they may both be so far removed from rational considerations that the distinction between means and end is virtually impossible to make in some cases. Secularity of this kind can be subdivided into at least two varieties, "the comfortable" and "the thrilling."

Comfortable secularity designates readiness to seek any value that yields comfort—as long as the search itself is comfortable! Changes of a comfortable sort are warmly greeted; no restrictions related to the evaluations we have hitherto described remain in force. The ruling maxim, as it were, is: "It's the easiest way; I like it because I like it, and who's to stop me?" Closely related to this is thrilling secularity; the Roman slogan "Bread and the circus" shows the connection. Immediate gratifications are sought from values that when attained provide one or another thrill out of the wide array demonstrably possible. This array may comprise anything from rabid spectatoritis as a Milwaukee Braves fan to sadistic murder committed "just for kicks." The instances chosen are of course extreme; many milder thrills, somewhat resembling the merely comfortable, are everywhere in evidence.

When comfortable and thrilling secularity are in full swing, means and end, as already noted, become difficult if not impossible to distinguish in many cases. Moreover, persons devoted to nonrational search for the new as new tend to follow it avidly at all times and places and to disregard most preceptive, prescriptive, and principled limits. This all-out emotionalized pursuit of the new indicates that relative normlessness prevails, for standards of every kind are changed or abandoned as fancy dictates. The normlessness goes further than the norms themselves in that the connections, whether nonrational or rational, between the norms likewise fluctuate rapidly or disappear. Standard evaluative attitudes and standard values, in other words, occupy at best a very small proportion of the range of needs and objects involved in such extreme secularity. Stating it still differently, the accrete character of preceptive and prescriptive value-systems, or the "rationally regulated" accrete character of principled value-systems, is so drastically altered by the random pursuit of discrete ends as to make the term "system" almost a misnomer.

But note that qualifications have been placed on the scope and degree of normlessness in the foregoing discussion; no society that continues as a society for any length of time is ever wholly normless. That is to say, short of utter societal collapse and dissolution, values and their correlative attitudes are never wholly discrete, never without discernible system, never completely at random. Sometimes societies that have become so addicted to change that normlessness threatens to prevail survive (unless wiped out by conquest or the like) because of a "normative reaction to normlessness" that salvages at least fragments of the associational patterns and other significant parts of the cultures. Around these fragments fresh organizations then crystallize. Omitting further discussion of these qualifications here, however, we can say that the normlessness attending comfortable and thrilling secularity may go a very long way indeed and that the societies in which it is strikingly prevalent are notably unstable.

This now carries us to the end of the secular part of the scale, from the minimum to the maximum of willingness and/or ability to change, from change permissible only in the service of principle to change for the sake of change. We have seen how expedient rationality may veer toward either its pursuant or its consequent subvarieties, and how the emotion-saturated, nonrational search for the new generates both comfortable and thrilling manifestations.

FOLK OR PRECEPTIVELY SACRED SOCIETIES

With the sacred-secular "evaluation continuum of social change" now fully before us, it seems feasible to present several types of societies that embody various aspects and combinations of the value-systems that we have been considering. For our present purposes, these types can be limited to four: folk, prescribed, principled, and normless.

According to the wider definition of "folk" as "a tribe or group of kindred people," the Eskimo and the Navajo are excellent examples of societies having a very high proportion of folk traits, whereas the Baganda possess a number of the prescribed traits along with their predominantly folk make-up. The Chinese peasant combines folk, prescribed, and principled traits in such a way that folk and prescribed traits predominate; and the Cotton South evidences folk, prescribed, and principled traits without a clear predominance of any. The English Midlands are primarily principled, with an easily discernible admixture of other traits.

From these examples, it is perhaps apparent that by a folk society we here mean any society possessing a sacred value-system that is in a high degree traditionally nonrational, implicit, uncodified, and accrete—that is, preceptively sacred. Hence all the "primitive" societies with which anthropologists and similar social scientists chiefly concern themselves are included among the folk societies if they have value-systems that are traditionally nonrational, implicit, uncodified, and accrete. This proviso is necessary because a great many so-called "primitive" societies show features that are not restricted to the folk variety; prescriptive, pursuant, consequent, and even comfortable and thrilling may appear. Indeed, the same proviso is warranted for many of those "backward" or "undeveloped" portions of the larger "advanced" or "civilized" societies with which human geographers, economists, sociologists, and other social scientists are concerned. It is the *proportion* of folk and other characteristics manifested upon which classification depends. Hence, it may be said that for us the Caribou Eskimo represent a folk society, and so also did the American inhabitants of remoter sections of the Cotton South at a date not so very long ago and to a significant extent even now.

But even though "advanced" societies, as we noted, may have "backward" segments of primarily folk type, we must remember that these segments are found in situations strikingly similar to those of the "primitive" societies that can be classified as folk because they are actually pervaded by preceptive sacredness. These situations are varieties of isolation: vicinal, social, and mental.

THE CULTURAL CHARACTER OF ISOLATION AND ACCESSIBILITY

Vicinal isolation (elsewhere called "spatial") refers to the physical absence of other societies in the vicinity with which interaction can go on. Every society has both geographical location and vicinal position. The geographical location has nothing to do with the presence or absence of other societies in the vicinity;

it is specifiable solely in terms of latitude, longitude, altitude, and so on. Vicinal position, on the other hand, at once involves not only relations with other societies but also the level of culture. A people whose only mode of travel is trudging wearily on foot, without even suitable water containers to make desert areas passable, are in a very different vicinal position from that of the inhabitants of the United States, for example, who can fly from the East Coast to the West in a few hours. In the first case, rudimentary culture prevents individuals in the society from overcoming geographical limitations; in the second, vicinal isolation has been replaced by vicinal accessibility by means of the airplane.

It is the culture, in other words, that makes this difference. When it is at a low level, forests are impenetrable, peaks impassable, rivers unswimmable; axes, snowshoes, and rafts change the situation. Although the geographical location of the society remains precisely the same after these cultural developments, its vicinal isolation is diminished because other societies are now vicinally accessible to it. *Nature presents man with his geographical location; culture provides his vicinal position.*

The ability to get in touch with other societies in the vicinity, however, does not automatically guarantee social accessibility. Differences in color and language, for example, may prevent the establishment of associative relations or even lead to extreme dissociation in which one society exterminates another without ever really viewing its members as human beings. In such cases there has been vicinal accessibility but social isolation. Here again culture is operative. Children, for example, *learn* to like or dislike this or that color of skin; they *learn* their own language, and not having learned the language of another society, are as adults ordinarily unable and unwilling to associate with "jabberers," with "creatures that go bar-bar-bar all the time."

The third kind of isolation is mental; although the devising of artifacts may make it possible for people to visit one another and the learning of sociofacts such as trading customs may bridge gaps between societies, mentifacts may still keep isolation intense if not intact. Witness the mental isolation of Gentile from Jew in Nazi Germany. The Jews were not vicinally isolated; they had moved freely among Gentiles for hundreds of years. Some social isolation remained, but it had notably diminished; Jewish lawyers, physicians, and professors had many Gentile clients, patients, and students. Nevertheless, mental isolation still persisted, and an elaborate anti-Semitic "world view" was developed by the Nazis to justify and vastly increase it.

Folk societies evidence all three kinds of isolation in a marked degree. They are not only far away from heavily traveled routes but are also set apart by characteristics such as costume and kinship and in addition cherish the sacred in ways that wall them off from the "infidels," "heretics," "heathen," and "unclean" with whom they do occasionally come in contact. Their culture, although often quite complex in some respects, is in totality relatively simple; and to focus on their value-systems, preceptive sacredness is dominant.

CHARACTERISTICS OF PRESCRIPTIVELY SACRED SOCIETIES

Prescribed societies, our next main type, are usually larger and culturally more developed than preceptive societies. The Baganda, with their elaborate kinship system, their complex and specialized religion, and their absolute monarchy with its intricate bureaucratic administration and legal institutions—all effectively functioning for at least a century before the British came—represent a prescribed society, albeit with a very substantial proportion of preceptive traits. A prescribed society may be defined as any society bearing a value-system marked by sanctioned rationality, explicitness, codification, and accreteness.

This type is inclusive enough to admit most of the larger societies of ancient, medieval, and early modern times. It may be granted, however, that there were periods in the development of ancient Greece, and particularly in Athens, where principle superseded prescription in considerable measure. The same is true of several phases of Roman development and, now and again, of a number of large states in the Near East and elsewhere in the Orient. In Western Christendom, principle emerged out of prescription only slowly and partially until the sixteenth century was well advanced, and even then with great variations from one country to another. In recent modern times, principle was superseded by prescription in Fascist Italy, Nazi Germany, Communist Russia, Franco Spain, and other major or minor totalitarian regimes.

Obviously, prescribed societies are not vicinally isolated in the same degree as most preceptive societies—at any rate, those of recent vintage are not. Nevertheless, political and other barriers may be imposed that counteract cultural facilities for transportation and communication. Refusal to grant exit or entrance permits, for example, may mean that societies are quite as effectively removed from one another's vicinity as they would be if all the devices of modern land, water, and air transportation were suddenly to disintegrate like the wonderful one-hoss shay. Culture, in other words, may counteract culture; mentifacts may give rise to sociofacts that put artifacts out of operation. Ideological conflict may produce an Iron Curtain vicinally isolating a prescribed society. Except for such "cold-war" developments, however, the kinds of isolation most frequently observable in prescribed societies are the varieties of vicinal isolation which result from inadequacy of culture rather than the counteracting of one of its aspects by another, social isolation in many forms, and mental isolation ranging from the Boer conviction of being a chosen people to the class consciousness of the embattled Russian Marxist.

PRESCRIPTION AND SOCIAL ORGANIZATION

Substantial amounts of the social isolation that helps to keep prescribed societies on an even keel are generated or reinforced by state, church, and similar social organizations authoritarian enough to elicit or impose conformity.

Space cannot here be devoted to the various ways in which the state develops and operates, but we can view some of them concretely among the Baganda, the Chinese, the American Southerners, and the English Midlanders. In the English Midlands, prescription plays no very obvious part; but, as recent studies have shown, the reverence of the English for law as law has strong prescriptive as well as principled aspects.

Churches are in many cases prescriptively powerful, especially when they are linked with the state and have ecclesiastical organization, so that the clergyman can call on the soldier for help if need be and, like the soldier, issue prescriptive edicts in a chain of command that reaches down to the simple layman as a sort of religious "buck private." The union of state and church has long prevailed among the Baganda, although since the coming of the British and the advent of widespread Anglicanism together with other kinds of Christianity, the use of force in sanctioning religious decrees has been almost wholly abandoned. The Chinese have never had a state church, and the relatively slight importance of creed in most areas of Chinese religion has made ritual the element of greatest prescriptive importance in religious life, although Chinese religion is usually so intertwined with everyday affairs that the distinction between religious ritual per se and other sacred ceremonial is difficult to make at the empirical level. In the Cotton South, as elsewhere in the United States, there is no state church, nor has there been much *direct* influence of religion on political organization—unless we except the Anti-Saloon League activities of religious leaders such as Bishop Cannon during the Prohibition period. Nevertheless, *indirect* prescriptive pressure, particularly of a Protestant Fundamentalist variety, has played a significant part among whites in many sections of the Cotton South and has had important political effects. Where Negroes are concerned, religious prescription has been quite significant in many ways. In the English Midlands since the Reformation, the Anglican Church, even in the days when its links with the state were still close and effective, did not achieve wide enforcement of its characteristic prescriptions, for the Midlands rapidly became an important center of dissent or nonconformity. Quakers, Methodists, Baptists, and similar sects and denominations promulgated the kinds of religious prescription that were most generally heeded in everyday life.

In prescribed societies, many other institutions besides churches issue prescriptions, some of which may be at variance with others; the school, for example, may inculcate one set, whereas economic institutions promote another. In some parts of contemporary France, for instance, the schoolteacher is often a left-wing Socialist or even Communist, whereas the local factory owner may have the opposite economic orientation. Frequently, however, prescribed societies generate and maintain a fairly uniform set of prescriptions; as we have seen, totalitarian countries provide some of the best examples.

Under totalitarianism, social isolation is often extreme; not only are foreigners distrusted and in many cases excluded, but in addition various groups within the society are viewed with suspicion, at the very least, and are sometimes "liquidated." This points to the fact that under prescription the line between social and mental isolation is often hard to draw. An example is the prohibition of mixed marriage that has so long prevailed among Orthodox Jews, Roman Catholics, and others. Such prohibition socially isolates one group from another and helps to intensify mental isolation; but the social isolation, for all practical purposes, is the outcome of the mental. One reacts on the other, however, and the process is circular; the more mental isolation, the more social, and the more social, the more mental. The upshot is that in concrete instances the two can hardly be disentangled.

PRINCIPLED SECULAR SOCIETIES, PURSUANT RATIONALITY, ACCESSIBILITY

Turning now to isolation and accessibility among principled societies, where the shift from sacred to secular appears, it can be said that except in time of "cold war" or "hot war"—when principles tend to become prescriptions anyway—vicinal accessibility is high. Foreigners and other strangers can readily visit the principled society; the barriers of nature have been levelled, in one way or another, by the advances of culture. Not only can outsiders easily reach the society, but they can also move about in it without suffering social isolation in a marked degree; hence the erstwhile outsider soon becomes an insider. He is admitted to private homes and clubs as well as to hotels and offices, and although a few restrictions usually remain in force, they are not obtrusively evident.

As indicated in the earlier discussion of principled societies, the sanctioned rationality essential to a coherent prescriptive system yields to pursuant rationality. In a principled secular society, therefore, there must always be something to which rationality can be pursuant. Here an illustration from contemporary British life is relevant:

> Given the assumption of the divine right of the ruler, . . . there . . . [developed] a kind of secular absolutism . . . [making] use of derivative legal precepts in administering "the King's Peace." Such legalistic secular absolutism [then underwent] . . . many adaptations called for by changing circumstances, until finally a limited constitutional monarchy in which "the king reigns but does not govern" . . . [was] established. Much of the ceremonial attending the coronation of the [British] monarch . . . [is still] ritual in the strict sense, which is to say that it is oriented toward the deity who presumably grants and guarantees divine right, but many other aspects of the ceremonial . . . [are] merely loyalistically and commemoratively sacred, and some . . . [are] pursuantly secular. In the latter case,

the monarch takes an oath to do nothing that contravenes the supreme law of the realm; "pursuant to the British constitution" he accepts the changes that have led to limitations of his own power, and his subjects also accept them. There may be protests, as when the commoner Stanley Baldwin forced the abdication of Edward VIII, but the protest is often ineffectual; the pursuantly secular wins out over the prescriptively sacred. Yet the sacred core of the monarchy still remains, surviving abdication in the person of a legitimate successor, George VI, and at the latter's death the cry goes up, "The king is dead—long live the queen!" Even though strongly qualified by the sacred aspects of the value-system, . . . [therefore], acceptance of change such as that represented by a limited constitutional monarchy obviously . . . [places British society today] effectively in the domain of . . . [secular principle]. (Howard Becker, *Man in Reciprocity*, pp. 171-172.)

In other words, contemporary Britain has become mentally accessible; what was once a closed sacred system opened at least as early as the sixteenth century to principles deriving from other ideologies and/or countries. Quite recently, therefore, it was possible for the British principled-secular society to follow the pursuant rationality of a monarchical State Socialism once denounced by the Englishman Herbert Spencer as "Bismarckian."

Normless societies

If we bear in mind that normlessness is never complete in any ongoing society, we can perhaps discuss normless societies without perpetually using the word "relatively." Normless societies are unstable, but they have enough continuity to preserve some kind of functional unity over fairly long periods. Only when consequent secularity is virtually unchecked by pursuant secularity and when the comfortable and the thrilling play an overwhelmingly disproportionate part is the society's survival seriously threatened.

It goes almost without saying that the vicinal accessibility of normless societies is very high indeed. Although not all of these societies are or have been predominantly urban—a vitally important qualification based on frontier and similar societies that we lack space to discuss—some of the best examples are those in which cities so strongly affect the rest of the territory that "urbanism as a way of life" is practiced in at least some respects almost everywhere. Strangers are physically present in large numbers and are accepted with little question. The inhabitants of the society themselves either travel freely or, through the mass communications that an advanced socioculture affords, have the results of travel and the cultural contrasts it entails presented to them; as a result there is much actual or vicarious vicinal mobility.

In addition, social accessibility is high; strangers are not only welcomed as sources of novelty but also yield the charm of the exotic. There are relatively few limitations on intermingling of any kind; normless secular societies tend to resemble Singapore, Port Said, Marseilles, London's Limehouse, and New York's Lower East Side. Social accessibility also prevails between classes, castes, and similar groups that tend to remain separate in societies that are not in rapid flux. This is not to say that social stratification is absent in normless societies; however, the various strata shift rapidly and readily interpenetrate: social mobility is marked. This can be seen on ecological city maps; sections once exclusive become quite free-and-easy and heterogeneous. Equalitarian practices are widespread, not so much as the result of principle as of the sheer difficulty of discriminating among essentially anonymous persons.

Mental accessibility in normless societies brings with it "open-mindedness" and a facile tolerance reflecting indifference to principle rather than firm natural-rights convictions. Such tolerance may go so far that criminal conduct is viewed favorably as providing the kind of thrill that imaginary participation in such conduct yields. Surviving sacred formulas survive merely as formulas; they exert little actual control. The society is fully accessible to scientific developments even though these may be destructive of accepted norms. Total warfare, to use our familiar example, abolishing all humane precepts, prescriptions, and principles, is viewed favorably if victory is thereby assured. Over and above this, science is judged praiseworthy, not for its own sake, but because in application it brings improved health, better food, greater ease, and more intense thrills. Mental mobility, in other words, reaches an extreme.

WHAT WE HAVE BEEN DOING, AND THE USES AND ABUSES THEREOF

Having now hastily surveyed the scale of sacred and secular values, and having seen how these combine into systems that are borne by the few main types of societies presented here—societies varying from the isolated to the accessible—we have almost finished our present task. What still remains is largely in the nature of qualification or, better, of warning against certain conclusions that might be drawn too readily from our rough sketch.

Most important, we must remember that the many distinctions we have made are not fully exemplified in real life; we can find *excellent* instances, but not *perfect* ones. Values and value-systems, in everyday affairs, are mixed in many ways, and so are the sociocultures that embody them. We gain insight from such distinctions; and, having such insight, we can more successfully apply scientific methods to the study of "societies around the world"—from our six to as many as are reasonably well-known. But distinctions are only tools. What we really want, and what we may get if we study long and hard enough, is the ability to predict what is likely to happen next in a given society and, with this predictive skill, to be of some assistance in man's exercise of control over his own destiny.

Next, we must not assume that the shift from sacred to secular, as we have presented it here, always proceeds regularly from point to point along the scale without skips, fluctuations, or reversals. Our Eskimo, Navajo, Baganda,

Chinese, and Cotton South societies are all undergoing extremely rapid secularization—so rapid, in fact, that sudden leaps from holy or loyalistic sacredness of the preceptive kind all the way to comfortable and thrilling secularity attended by an advanced degree of normlessness are strikingly manifest.

Further, concentration on secularization should not lead us to ignore its opposite, sacralization. Germany changed from the principled secular society of the Weimar period to the rigidly prescribed sacred society of the Nazis, and if the French Fourth Republic, which now contains a dangerously large Communist minority, were to succumb to totalitarianism, a similar reversal would appear.

Consequently, we must use our distinctions as surgical instruments, laying bare the vital centers in the societies we study, and at the same time bearing in mind the necessity of viewing these societies as ongoing systems—as sociocultures in action—that cannot be fully understood when seen only on the operating table. The merit of our collection of descriptions by many different observers with varying perspectives lies in the fact that the student is thereby enabled not only to use our instruments but also *to see more than dissection can possibly reveal.*

And now let us look forward with Percy Black.

Looking Forward

We have now come to the midpoint of a long journey, but even when we have studied the next three societies and reached the end of this book, our journey will hardly have begun. Students with a yearning to see beyond the dim horizons that we shall eventually have sketched will not rest until they have pushed on further to extend our knowledge of man in society, who is by the same token man in reciprocity. Although there is a great deal that is not yet understood, these eager seekers for the realities of social phenomena must necessarily assume that with increasing evidence and adequate theories, much of human behavior can some day be explained and even predicted. Like the physical and biological sciences, the social sciences recognize the unknown but not, within the confines of mortal experience, the unknowable. With this attitude constantly inspiring them, scientists have been able to push back the boundaries of ignorance about man and the universe of which he is a part. Limitless curiosity, honesty in the report of all observations, searching appraisal of one's own weaknesses as well as strengths, and constructive criticism of *all* methods and theories will ultimately enable scientists to "know" man more adequately than ever before. Until that time, hard, persistent work on the part of the most able students must be both our goal and our recompense.

PART II

THE CHINESE PEASANT

THE COTTON SOUTH

THE ENGLISH MIDLANDS

Introduction

Social Change on a
Worldwide Scale

>>>

We live in a time of spectacular social changes. Each continent has areas where old patterns are yielding to the new, frequently with much discomfiture to many people. Social forces are working at so accelerated a pace that people everywhere wonder what the morrow will bring. A major purpose of this book is to present three case studies of societies that are experiencing varying degrees and kinds of change so that, by comparing them with one another and with our own society, we can gain an understanding of how societies change. Before we turn to a study of the Chinese peasant, the Cotton South, and the English Midlands, we should first examine briefly five of the major social forces at work behind the news items of press and radio throughout the world.

THE STRUGGLE FOR A HIGHER STANDARD OF LIVING

Our present task leads to more concern with dynamics of population growth than with the anthropological classification of people into racial types, to which we devoted some attention in Part One. At the turn of the nineteenth century, Robert Malthus was alarming the people of England with his theory that a population tended to reproduce geometrically (1, 2, 4, 8, 16, 32, 64, and so on) and would greatly outstrip the food supply, which, he thought, increased arithmetically (1, 2, 3, 4, 5, 6, 7, and so on). This would mean that the lowest economic group would forever be on a mere subsistence, or even a starvation, diet. This, of course, does not hold true for most industrialized societies. Does Malthusianism apply, however, to peasant societies? What about migrations of people to less crowded regions in these countries? Do the poorer people reproduce faster than the richer? If so, does this lead to a deterioration in the quality of the population, or is the biological stock unimpaired?

In order to understand the lifeway of a people and their struggle for a higher standard of living, we need to know how they make their living through the utilization of resources at hand or obtainable by trade, and how they distribute the goods that are produced. We also want to know about the kind of property system that determines ownership, inheritance, and the right to dispose of certain possessions. In connection with an economy, we must also consider the occupational specialization and the division of labor.

The Chinese peasant, as we shall see, has traditionally been inclined toward self-subsistence, or producing primarily for his own needs. He trades any surplus crops at the market town and buys the few necessities in return. The study of his economy will also reveal his close association with the soil, the degree to which the land is worked by owners or tenants, and the numerous village organizations created by the peasant to help him face his economic crises.

The Cotton South represents a modified plantation economy, in which the emphasis is on the production of a major crop—cotton—for cash sale. Here the planter has set the social pattern, although the small-scale farmers, or yeomanry, have been an important segment among agricultural producers. After the Civil War, slavery gave way to sharecropping, and many whites as well as Negroes found it hard to make ends meet. The New South, however, has been changing more rapidly economically than most Americans realize. Agriculture is becoming diversified and mechanized, and in some areas commercial farms employing wage workers predominate. Industry is growing at a rapid pace, and in most respects the economy of the South is becoming more like that of the nation as a whole.

The English Midlands has been chosen as the representative of industrial society for the obvious reason that it was the cradle of the Industrial Revolution. A study of its economy reveals a complexity not only in the manifold problems of manufacturing but also in the mechanics of obtaining raw materials and of distributing the finished products to consumers around the world. Banking, storage, insurance, transportation, and wholesaling and retailing establishments, to mention but a few, are essential to an industrial society. The factory system employs large numbers of workers, who organize into unions to deal with management; the government becomes more active in passing and enforcing labor legislation and business and stock-exchange regulations, and in trying to protect the consumer while satisfying the demands of various pressure groups.

Thus, by a careful comparison of the three types of economy described in Part Two, we should be able to trace the multiplication of economic groupings as the consumer demand moves from that of the Chinese peasant to the level of the British middle-class housewife trying to obtain what she considers to be the necessities for her family.

Most of the people of the world go to bed at night still hungry—not through choice but through lack of an adequate food supply. In the past, hunger and famine have been regarded as expected difficulties, to be faced as courageously or resignedly as possible. Even in Britain before the Industrial Revolution, people continued to starve in one part of the country while there was plenty of food in another part, simply because of inadequate transportation facilities. But now, through gossip spreading from market towns, through articles in newspapers and in short-wave broadcasts, rural people everywhere are being told that famine and undernourishment need not forever be considered normal. Although any solution of their problems is far in the future, people are beginning to hope. They hear of the standard of living in America, or of the claims of advancement in the Soviet Union, and they wonder why they also cannot have the things they hear about. This yearning is of itself a potent social force when it leads to action.

This desire for higher standards explains the widespread appeal of agrarian reform in which the land from large estates is distributed among the landless or the small holders. The United States occupation force has recently carried out such a land reform in Japan in the hope of providing a more solid base for the rural society of that country. The Communist-dominated governments also initiate land reforms, but in almost every case to date these have been a prelude to a collectivization of the land which removes it eventually from the ownership of the peasant to whom it was originally distributed.

The Middle East, including the great bloc of Arab states, faces acute agrarian problems because of the ownership of much of the land by a few people, some of them described as feudal in practice and point of view. Land hunger is real and is growing more acute as people increase in numbers and require more food and other items.

Health is said by public-health authorities to be "a purchasable commodity." More and more people around the world want better health for themselves and their children, though a great number still lack an understanding of basic health principles. Unfortunately, where the need is greatest the financial problems are often most serious.

To speak of automobiles, refrigerators, and television sets in connection with the world's standard of living is, to put it mildly, premature. As our study of the Chinese peasant will show, the demands of most peasant people are minimal, from the American point of view. Those who are being caught up in the vortex of change ask simply for food, a new plowshare, common medicines, and a book or two from which their children can learn to read. They want clothing to keep them warm in winter and sufficient income to meet the incidental—though often heavy—expenses of ceremonial occasions. But each generation, largely stimulated by the impact of Western ideas and technology, wants more than the preceding generation. Dreams of plenty and promises of better days ahead are working like leaven among millions of people who hardly dared to dream before. This is a social force not to be taken lightly, especially among people who have recently become conscious of their meager material existence in comparison with the fabulous achievements in other parts of the world.

THE SPREAD OF INDUSTRIALIZATION

A second force of worldwide significance is the spread of industrialization in countries which are trying to catch up with the output of the West. What happens when a peasant countryside becomes part of an industrial society is well described for the English Midlands in pages which follow. In reading this, we may wonder whether China and other countries will undergo the same stages.

From the standpoint of the people involved, the auspices under which industrialization comes and the social philosophy of those responsible for it are also tremendously important. The factory system of our day requires that workers leave their handicrafts in home or small shop and place themselves under the supervision of plant managers; family patterns change with new work schedules and with the receipt of wages, which give independence to the single individual. In other words, industrialization of even a part of a country—whether Mexico, Pakistan, or the Cotton South—means great social change for those involved.

Is industrialization the answer to the acute problem of overpopulation, about which many statesmen feel deep concern? Professor Warren S. Thompson, in his article on the population of China quoted later, points out that the industrialization of Europe and America proceeded as it did because there were new frontiers and unsettled lands to which surplus people could go. This provided new markets and new sources of raw materials, and also eased the pressure of increasing population upon a rising standard of living. But where will the people of India and China go if modern, scientific agricultural practices make their farm labor no longer necessary and if industry does not expand fast enough to give them jobs? Will a higher standard of living ever be obtainable? J. Lossing Buck, Hsiao-t'ung Fei and Chih-i Chang examine in later selections the role that industrialization may play in the development of such countries as China.

The conclusions and decisions of scholars may or may not be put into practice, but many governments the world over are doing all in their power to promote new industries to meet the needs of their people. In imitation of Europe and America, there is a growing tendency to make the machine a fetish and to look to it for progress in terms of material gains.

We of the West started this Industrial Revolution, which is now making its force felt around the world—not only in manufacturing but also in agricultural technology, communications, and transportation. Its power for promoting human happiness is tremendous provided wise heads guide its development.

THE STRUGGLE FOR NATIONAL INDEPENDENCE

In the nineteenth century, in the Balkans, the idea of nationalism was strikingly illustrated where one small country after another imbibed the heady wine of independence and, with Russian help, successfully pushed back the Ottoman Empire, in which the idea of a nation state played almost no part. Before World War I, the Austro-Hungarian Empire was foundering on the stubborn rocks of national aspirations of its minority groups, such as the Czechs, the Croatians, and the Slovenes. In a sense, World War I and Wilson's Fourteen Points won the day for the nation state in Europe. Later on, the concept of statism was developed to so menacing a degree by the Nazi and Fascist regimes that most of the Western World, with other allies, fought World War II to end—among other things—this perversion of the ideal of political freedom.

Is it any wonder, then, that this virus of nationalism, which in its extreme form is recognized as socially disorganizing in a family of nations, should spread to India, Indonesia, the Arab World, and to Africa as it had spread to Latin America almost one hundred years ago? These large areas of the world which have been under the control of, or at least the influence of, Europeans are seeking for themselves the national independence which has already been accepted in the West. This accent on national independence is couched in many slogans and phrases, such as "Asia for the Asiatics," "a drive against imperialism," or "an end to colonialism."

A glance at any day's headlines is apt to show, therefore, some leader in a seemingly faraway country berating those in other lands who have in the past or are in the present supposedly curtailing his nation's independence, whether through economic measures or through a political arrangement of long standing. This drive to be free of outside interference is a social force out of which social changes are being fashioned. To be sure, in many countries people's loyalties are still centered in their family and local village; they have not yet been initiated into the cult of nationalism, but that will happen sooner than most of us realize. It will take considerable time for recently freed countries to realize what other countries are finding out—that patriotism or enlightened love of country is different from the brand of narrow nationalism that makes the nation the supreme value in life.

THE STRUGGLE FOR POLITICAL DEMOCRACY

As we take a worldwide view of social forces at work, we hear many highly articulate leaders demanding for their countries national independence; but far in the background are the almost muted sounds of those who want *individual* independence—or political democracy—too.

In discussing political democracy, we must frankly face the fact that we are apt to take it for granted or credit it with too wide an acceptance. To most of mankind Western democracy is still a rather novel idea, but it is an idea of tremendous power when it is understood by sufficient people in a country. The English Revolution (1688–1689), the American Revolution (1775–1783), and the French Revolution (1789–1799) testify to the power of the ideals of "liberty, equality, and fraternity." Although they did not occur simultaneously, we can, for convenience, combine these three revolutions into what might be called the Western Revolution and describe its political genius as its attitude toward the *importance* and *uniqueness* of the individual. Its heirs became *citizens* rather than *subjects*.

Western political democracy, however, should not be confused with the Marxist brand of economic "democracy," which has always proved unworkable in any extreme form. At times, to be sure, governments must act to safeguard the interests of their citizens in economic as well as other matters, but the democratic test of such action is the rendering of service to the individual and the preservation of his "inalienable rights."

In most of the world, "the dignity of the common man" remains a lofty and unattained ideal. Even though the common man may be given the right to vote, he cannot rise in dignity as long as he is chained to hunger or relegated to a rejected, inferior status because of occupation, religion, or the color of his skin. But the Western Revolution, as long as it is true to its democratic tradition, will continue to champion the dignity of the common man, and those who take it seriously will keep on feeling twinges of conscience as they see violations of this ideal at home or abroad. This is why the Commission on Human Rights of the United Nations has devoted great efforts to drafting a charter of principles toward which all mankind can move, though it be at uneven pace.

A political democracy is not created simply by the drafting of constitutions, the meeting of national assemblies, or the casting of ballots by a large proportion of its people. The satellite countries of Eastern Europe under Soviet influence do all of these things and call themselves the "people's democracies." They lack one indispensable ingredient: respect for the rights of the individual.

It would be wrong indeed to believe that political democracy can assume only the governmental forms fashioned here in America to meet our own needs almost two hundred years ago. Each people will have to use those political forms which, in their own cultural setting, best transform into reality the democratic ideals about which we speak. After all, democracy is more a spiritual force than a political organization. Furthermore, numerous social changes will have to occur before large masses of people become educated enough to understand the role that each must play in the establishment of political democracy as a meaningful force in their lives. There will be many false starts, much misuse of the word "democracy" from an American's standpoint, but broad social changes may eventually result. This is a social force to watch.

THE SECULARIZATION OF DAILY LIFE

Professor Howard Becker, of the University of Wisconsin, makes use of a sacred-secular continuum in viewing the behavior of societies which was presented in some detail at the end of Part One. At one extreme, or pole, it will be recalled, he places those societies in which people behave traditionally, in which custom is sacred, in which the past dictates to the present. In these societies most behavior is nonrational and largely emotional. At the other extreme of the continuum he places the secular societies, those in which the scientific spirit has so permeated the thinking of the people that they subject every phase of life to minute investigation and try to base their conduct on logic, on cold reason. Of course, no actual society exists at either extreme, for each society lies somewhere in between, and the differences are largely those of degree.

Western societies tend toward the secular pole. Accompanying the changes in political ideology of the English, American, and French Revolutions were changes in the attitudes toward time-honored traditions. People who had deposed and beheaded those monarchs who claimed the God-given right to rule could also question other "sacred" traits of their society. This led to various contradictions and controversies in Western society as science and religion began to outargue each other before realizing that there was a place for both, even in a modern age.

Whereas we of the West have had a century for the accommodation of the science-religion controversy, other societies, feeling the impact of Westernization, face the problem almost overnight. For example, in most sacred societies the father's word is law; he is not only respected but usually implicitly obeyed. What happens to the parent-child relationship when a son in a Lebanese village, for example, realizes that he has learned far more about the world than his father can ever learn, that many of his father's commands violate good farming practices and sound health procedures and are at times just outright "superstitious"? Such a son is becoming secularized, as is the society of which he is a part.

Secularization, a truly powerful social force, is coming rapidly to many areas of the world, bringing with it the danger that the old forms of social control may be discredited and discarded before new types of control have been created as a substitute. In such cases, grave social disorganization is apt to result, giving rise to political vacuums to be exploited by aggressive leaders intent on a rise to power through a local revolution.

Thus, we are being reminded that social changes, though considered commonplace in the West, can reach cataclysmic proportions in other societies, where one innovation sets up a chain reaction of effect and countereffect. Is it any wonder, then, that we stress *social change* as the underlying theme of this book and hope that our tracing of change in the three societies to be studied will give us some insight into the revolutionary character of the age in which we live?

The Approach Used in This Book

As was pointed out in the preface, this is a source book of selections chosen so as to provide a sampling of the outstanding authorities on the topics being discussed. We can appreciate the individual flavor of each writer—Martin Yang, an American-trained anthropologist, describing the Chinese village in which he was reared; Hodding Carter, a Mississippi newspaper man, telling of his religious upbringing in the South; or J. B. Priestley, the well-known English novelist, candidly characterizing the Midlands on a trip through that area. Some of the selections are written with objective, scientific detachment; others are more colorful and impressionistic. Some articles may seemingly contradict one another here and there, but this should stimulate us to inquire more deeply into the real state of things.

THE CHINESE PEASANT

Above: China is predominantly a land of farmers, even though it also contains some of the world's greatest cities. Most Chinese peasants rent or own many tiny patches of land, which they farm by primitive methods. The cultivation of rice, which is possible where fields can be flooded, produces an enormous return in food value per acre. *Below:* Farm families are not completely self-sufficient, and for millennia China has had a system of many small village markets, where people in the vicinity may buy and sell.

The enormous population of China has always made manpower abundant and inexpensive, and the high cost of feeding animals has also tended to make man the chief beast of burden. *Above:* The yoke is one of the most common means of carrying heavy loads in China, and when the two baskets are properly balanced, a man can carry a considerable weight. *Below:* To many Chinese the machine-age has meant such small-scale improvements as the sewing machine rather than vast industrial projects, which have been slow in coming.

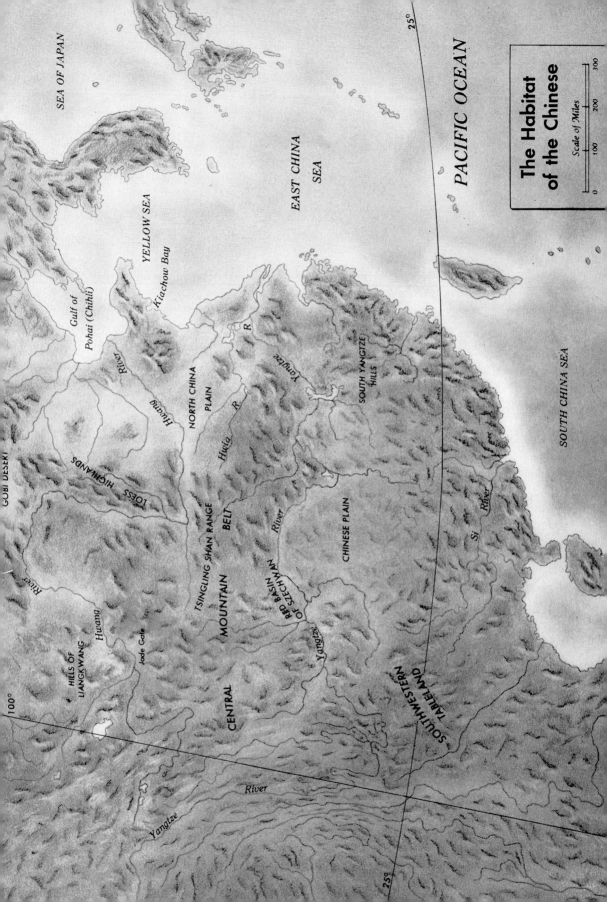

The Habitat
of the Chinese

Scale of Miles

SEA OF JAPAN

PACIFIC OCEAN

YELLOW SEA

Gulf of
Pohai (Chihli)

Kiachow Bay

EAST CHINA
SEA

SOUTH CHINA SEA

GOBI DESERT

LOESS HIGHLANDS

NORTH CHINA
PLAIN

Hwang River

Huia R.

Yangtze R.

SOUTH YANGTZE
HILLS

TSINGLING SHAN RANGE

CENTRAL MOUNTAIN BELT

RED BASIN
OF SZECHWAN

River

CHINESE PLAIN

Si River

HILLS OF
LIANGKWANG

Hwang

Jade Gate

Yangtze

SOUTHWESTERN TABLELAND

River

Yangtze

25°

25°

100°

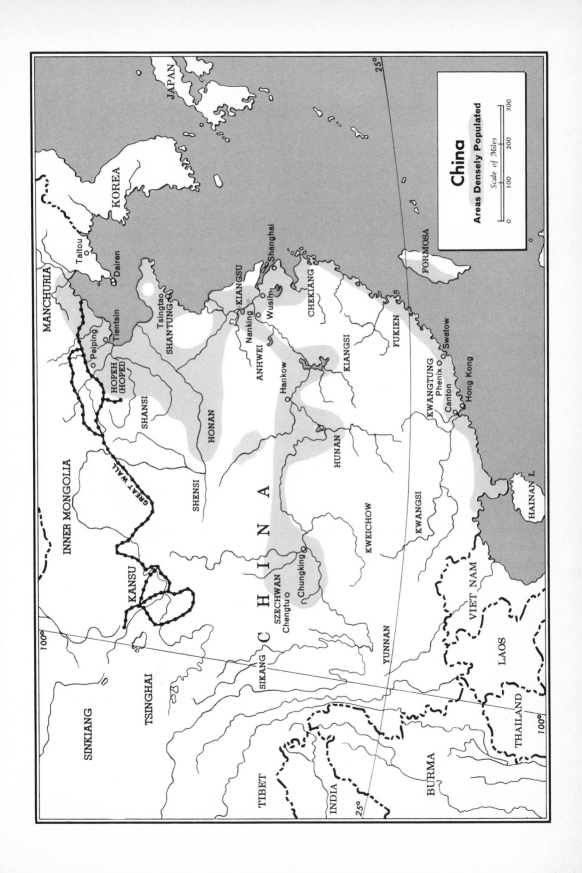

SINKIANG

TSINGHAI

TIBET

INDIA

25°

100°

BURMA

THAILAND

LAOS

VIET NAM

YUNNAN

SIKANG

KANSU

INNER MONGOLIA

MANCHURIA

GREAT WALL

Taitou

Dairen

Peiping

Tientsin

HOPEH (HOPEI)

SHANSI

SHENSI

SZECHWAN

Chengtuo

Chungking

KWEICHOW

KWANGSI

HUNAN

HONAN

SHANTUNG

Tsingtao

KIANGSU

Nanking

Wusih

Shanghai

ANHWEI

Hankow

KIANGSI

CHEKIANG

FUKIEN

KWANGTUNG

Phenix O

Canton

Swatow

Hong Kong

HAINAN I.

KOREA

JAPAN

FORMOSA

25°

100°

C H I N A

China
Areas Densely Populated

Scale of Miles

0   100   200   300

Introduction

>>

The Western world knows vaguely about several Chinas: the almost feudal Manchu kingdom of pigtails and bound feet, which was overthrown in 1911; the homeland of laundrymen, who, incidentally, have all come from a small district around Canton; the China of cultivated leisure, traditional art, and worldly-wise philosophy successfully popularized in the writings of Lin Yutang; one of the "Big Five" in World War II, whose sinews were kept alive by the traffic moving over the tortuous Burma Road; and the Red China of Mao Tse-Tung, the Communist leader who supposedly guides its fortunes in this period of seething social changes.

Yet there is another China, whose face we have learned to know dimly from such works as *The Good Earth* by Pearl S. Buck. This is the Peasant China—not the China of cities and coolies, but the China of villages and farmers. These rural people comprise more than three fourths of the total Chinese population of almost 400 million people. In learning about them, we shall be learning about the basic traits of peasants everywhere.

By no means all nonliterate peoples are considered peasants. For example, the American Indians and most of the tribesmen of Africa lack the specific attributes of a peasant society. A helpful definition is provided by John F. Embree in the preface to his excellent description of Suye Mura, a Japanese village:

> A peasant community possesses many of the characteristics of a preliterate society, e.g., an intimate local group, strong kinship ties, and periodic gatherings in honor of some deified aspect of the environment. On the other hand, it presents many important differences from the simpler societies; each little peasant group is part of a larger nation which controls its economic life, enforces a code of law from above, and, more recently, requires education in national schools. The economic basis of life is not conditioned entirely by the local requirements but by the nation, through agricultural advisers. The farmer's crop is adjusted to the needs of the state. In religion and ritual there are many outside influences to complicate the

simple correlation of rites and social value, festivals and agricultural seasons. While full of local variations, the rituals and festivals are not indigenous to the community nor is the community spiritually self-sufficient.

A longer interpretative discussion of peasant societies is found in Selection 74. This Chinese unit does not attempt to be encyclopedic; rather it serves as an introduction to the ways in which ordinary people live and think, not as statistics but as human beings.

• 74 • Characteristics of Peasant Societies
IRWIN T. SANDERS

The majority of the people in the world today live in folk societies.* These "little people" of the world fill the teeming villages of the Orient, they form the bulk of the population in southern and eastern Europe, and they pass on from one generation to another the colorful costumes and customs of the Latin Americas. In North America evidences of the folk society are numerous: in the French-Canadian villages, among the peons of Mexico, and even in the more isolated areas of the Appalachian mountains.

At first glance it would seem ridiculous to lump together people of so many languages, of so many creeds and colors. However, underneath their apparent divergencies are many ways in which they are much alike.

FOLK SOCIETY A SURVIVAL

One of the most important features of the folk society is that it has stood the test of time. For centuries it has been a way of life to countless millions, carrying with it the au-

* *Folk.* The simpler, uneducated, and less sophisticated members of a population, the masses of a population who by sheer weight of numbers determine the character of the group and preserve and perpetuate its culture traits; also a tribe or group of kindred people. (E. B. Reuter, *Handbook of Sociology*, The Dryden Press, New York, 1941.)

thority of past successes. But now the various folk of the world are finding that they must adjust in part to a twentieth-century mode of living which is as yet virtually untried. It is rather an adventure of man's spirit into the unknown, an adventure which invariably involves a casting away from the moorings that formerly gave the greatest feeling of security. No wonder, then, that peasants look with suspicion and reservation at the new world dawning about them. The folk society represents the tried and true, a survival. The new ways have yet to prove themselves.

Thus one must appreciate the historical continuity of a folk society if one is to understand its nature. It was centuries in the building and it still has a strength that hurried [urbanites] often fail to grasp. Although breaking down in places, like a windmill perhaps rusting and squeaking, it can still prove more than a match for modern Don Quixotes battling with more self-righteous enthusiasm than social wisdom.

ROOTED IN THE SOIL

Members of a folk society are of the earth, earthy. They vary from climate to climate and country to country in the fervor with which they till the soil, but basic to their way of life is the security which agriculture affords. When

[Adapted from "Characteristics of Peasant Societies," *Farmers of the World: the Development of Agricultural Extension*, edited by Edmund de S. Brunner, Irwin T. Sanders, and Douglas Ensminger, Columbia University Press, New York, 1945. Pp. 37-45. Used by permission.]

they choose to work, providing the powers that be are propitious, they know they will reap the fruit of their labors.

Life follows the cycle of the seasons. Because of this, the year has an accentuated variety. The tedium of monotony is periodically broken. The tasks of spring differ from those of fall; the leisure of winter is in striking contrast to the demands of summer.

Thus all of life is strongly colored by the man-land relationship in a folk society. Whether one owns the land oneself, or works for years for those who do, one develops a sense of proprietorship, at times mystical and at times strikingly realistic.

USUALLY FAMILISTIC

Ancestor worship in China may seem to have little in common with a feud in the Kentucky mountains, but in reality both are evidences of the same fundamental belief that the family (with little or no help from the government, from business, from the church) is capable of carrying on the important affairs of life. In a folk society the family tends to occupy two spheres of dominance: over other institutions and over the individual.

The Family·Is the Central Institution. In most folk societies the family is the chief economic unit. It produces not only the food but it also makes the soap, the homespun cloth, and the crude furniture; the family frequently constructs the home. In the person of some elder relative acting as midwife or doctor it brings infants into the world and treats the sick with mysteriously concocted remedies. In other words, the economy of the home is largely self-contained. Provision is usually made, however, for specialization along lines which serve the interests of the group as a whole. A wagonmaker, a tanner, a tinsmith, a master builder, a wood carver—these and many more illustrate the contribution of artisans to the physical welfare of the folk society. As the money economy began its encroachment, specialists in money-lending and merchandising became a part of the picture. Despite their coming, the family group was still considered fundamental.

Nor was formalized government of much importance in years gone by. Elders, representing large family groupings, conducted the affairs of the community in what they considered to be the best interests of all. In familistic societies throughout the world the people still look with resentment upon the imposition of outside officials who try to enforce laws and local regulations alien to the folkway of rule by older family representatives.

Religion, too, has its place in a familistic society but proves a bulwark rather than a competitor of the family system. Quite often the religious leader does little more than officiate when family crises arrive. In areas where Christianity has been accepted by large numbers of people, the Roman Catholic Church has tended to preserve the folk society while Protestant influences have tended to tear it down, moving it in the direction taken by Euro-American society in general. Islam and the other religions of the East are chiefly protectors of the status quo in which loyalty to one's family seldom conflicts with loyalty to one's religious duty.

Educational agencies and organized sources of recreation are little. developed in a folk society. Much training is given in the home, and recreation is supervised by the family or by community opinion in general. Where school systems have been established by outside authorities—governmental or religious—they have tended to neglect the values of a folk society.

The Family Comes First, the Individual Second. Contemporary individualism contrasts strikingly with the familism of the folk society. In the latter, customary controls still govern family relationships, although the conjugal family, made up of parents and children, is displacing the consanguinal family, comprising, in addition, many relatives of the parents. The kinship group traditionally guides the selection of mates by the young, and those earning money outside the home must turn these wages over to the family treasury; in turn, individuals wishing vocational training or education can count upon the support of their relatives, providing their plans follow the family decision. There is also a well-defined division of labor which is based not only on one's sex and age but also upon one's status in the family.

Linked to this subservience to family roles is the fact that one's status in the community largely depends upon the status of one's family. An erring individual reflects upon the family, because in a folk society there has been no attempt to place the burden of moral training upon the school or the religious organization. It remains a family responsibility. Thus, in the community at large, who you are (what family name you bear) is more important than what you are as an individual. Nevertheless, relationships remain personal, in contrast to the impersonality of the [city], where what you have is frequently more important than what you are, or even the family to which you belong.

CONSERVATISM OF FOLK SOCIETY

The conservatism of peasants is rooted in their social values. Because their way of life provides what they consider their most important needs they are satisfied with it. To be sure, social inertia is present too. It is far more comfortable to cling to the old than to embrace the new. Furthermore, in a folk society individuals who seek to adopt a new practice frequently face the ridicule or even the hostility of their fellow peasants, primarily because of what has been called the strain toward consistency, or the tendency to pull all exceptional individuals down to the level of the average. Individual initiative, which is an important element in innovation, is discouraged by the less ambitious. If a person finds such an environment too restrictive he may migrate to the city and become a part of the urban world, with its different set of values and its impatience with the peasant way of doing things.

The folk society still lacks many of the agencies of communication which make modern life so dynamic. Automobiles and good roads, which encourage extreme mobility, are not yet a part of the folk culture; neither are private radio sets, or family subscriptions to daily papers or memberships in monthly book distributing societies. Communication is oral;

the printed page is of little importance even though the literacy rate may be high among certain groups of peasants.

SPATIAL AND MENTAL ISOLATION

Part and parcel of this conservatism is the peasant's isolation, spatially and mentally. Roads, for example, exist primarily for use between village and field or between village and market. Good roads in and of themselves rate low in the scale of values. So does going somewhere just for the sake of going. If a pilgrimage is customary then the person will take a pilgrimage. He does not hanker after the strange sights and experiences of a traveler and, in fact, he usually finds these disconcerting, unenjoyable, and even terrifying. But, upon returning to his native haunts, he does bask in the limelight of being called a Hadji, or by some other title which shows that he has followed a time-honored tradition.

[Very obviously, this] does not mean that some individual who has been to a distant place loses status upon his return. His tales enliven the neighborhood gatherings and, since he usually casts aspersions upon the food, dress, and manners of people abroad, he strengthens the ethnocentric beliefs of his fellows in the superiority of their own way of life. He does lose status, however, if he compares his own folk or society unfavorably with the "outside world," for to that extent he becomes a nonconformist, a disloyal member of the local group.

There is a marked cleavage between the village, the perpetuator of traditional folkways, and the city, the culture-carrier of the scientific age. For one thing, many city dwellers of peasant origin who have accepted the newer social values of the [city] have the zeal of new converts in ridiculing the life from which they have come. Although familiar with what the peasants do and why they behave as they do, these converts develop a bias which makes them highly unreliable as social interpreters. Government bureaus in many capitals are filled with these erstwhile peasants zealously struggling for urban status. Then, again, those whose families have been city dwellers for decades have lost touch with the rural people; they regard them as objects of idle curiosity or as fit subjects for exploitation.

Therefore, where the folk society still maintains a pristine vigor, the peasants build up a [high mental] barrier between themselves and the city dweller which frequency of urban contacts may actually strengthen.

COMPARATIVELY LOW STANDARD OF LIVING

If one should seek an illustration of the changes wrought in Western society by the machine in the past one hundred years let him look first to a folk society. Using this as a starting point modern man can measure his material advancement. Because agrarian societies have an abundance of labor and think seldom in terms of profits, they have little incentive to mechanize their practices in home and field. In many ways they consider the machine a threat and find numerous pretexts for resisting its introduction. They praise what has been made by hand and hunt for flaws in machine-made products.

They produce, where agricultural conditions and size of farms permit, enough for home consumption, with a small surplus to exchange at the market for absolute necessities (such as salt and nails). Living conditions are crude and unsanitary; death rates are high. But this waste of health and life is a part of the fatalistic creed to which most of them subscribe. They have long ago shifted the responsibility to the supernatural and thus are able to adjust to the numerous bereavements that befall them. What the [city man] most frequently associates with a low level of living— unscreened windows, unsanitary handling of meat, improper disposal of sewage, impure and insufficient water, over-crowded houses, raw-boned animals, improper diet—seem relatively unimportant to a peasant. He is more concerned about having sufficient quantities of the kinds of food he likes, having a place to sleep, protection from the weather, and the wherewithal to observe the year's festivities in the recognized fashion. He wants to have enough fuel to see him through the winter, enough provender to keep his animals alive. In some societies, for example in India, many peasants follow an economy of scarcity, calculating how little they will need to grow for the year ahead and concentrating on producing this amount.

AN INTEGRATED SYSTEM

Robert Redfield has effectively stressed the unity found among the various phases of the folk society. In fact, he points out that the ways the group meets its problems "constitute a coherent and self-consistent system." He goes on to point out:

Thus it is not enough to say that in the folk society conventional behavior is strongly patterned; we must also say that those patterns are interrelated in thought and action, so that one tends to evoke others, and to be consistent with others. We may add to this that the more remote ends of living are taken as given. The folk society exists not so much in the exchange of useful functions as in common understandings as to the ends given. In the trite phrase the folk society has a "design for living."

This unity of the folk society has another important implication. Changes which vitally affect one phase of life have their repercussions all along the line. Nowhere today does the folk society described here exist as a pure type. Everywhere it has taken on some of the characteristics of the [larger world]. It operates more and more on a money economy, its members are increasingly being drawn into the orbits of centralized governments, commercial interests are making the peasants trinket and gadget conscious, young people grow restive under the age-old conventions, especially when cities present attractive alternatives. These changes would not necessarily destroy the folk society, which still retains much assimilative power, but their effects deserve careful weighing in terms of each society. Those who seek to change, bear a responsibility that cannot lightly be cast aside, for each innovation launches a train of events which in the long run may produce results not originally desired. This does not mean that the only policy is a "hands off policy," but it does call for careful study of the society one wishes to change. Change there will be. Much will be impersonal and seemingly beyond control. But the consciously planned program of reform, uplift, or regeneration must be thought out and executed against the background of the social fabric, which in a folk society comes all of a piece.

The People and the Habitat

>>>

A peasant society is a survival. China's antiquity is a well-known fact. We speak of Chinese history in millennia instead of in centuries and are impressed by its uninterrupted existence. Modern archaeologists are revising some of the earliest dates in the light of new finds and are moving closer to our own day some of the developments toward "civilization"; but even these revisions do not deny the fact that China is an old, old land, where people have long been struggling for existence in time-honored ways.

The theme of the next selection is this historical development. Such an article has the disadvantage of attempting to telescope topics which deserve much more extended treatment. Fortunately, it can be supplemented by information from any standard history or reference work. It does at least indicate something of the sweep of many periods and without this we are not ready to interpret properly the later sections of this book. Confucius, Mencius, Lao-Tse, and Mo Ti are Chinese sages frequently mentioned in this and later selections. Further information about them can be found in an encyclopedia or other reference work such as Howard Becker and Harry Elmer Barnes, *Social Thought from Lore to Science*, 2nd ed. (Washington, Harren Press, 1952). The systems of thought and the cults to which Confucius and Lao-Tse gave rise are described briefly on page 460.

• 75 • Chinese Continuity
DANIEL H. KULP, II

To a student of things Chinese, their most impressive trait is continuity. One cannot travel in China today, from Shanghai to a small village in the most rural region, without wonder at the age-old devices, at the antiquity of the proverbs, the ceremonies, and the rituals —in short, without feeling that he walks through the ages.

Equally impressive to him are the long horns blown by the priests in the Lama Temple of Peiping, the symmetrical beauty of the altar of the Temple of Heaven, the

[Adapted from "Chinese Continuity," *The Annals of the American Academy of Political and Social Science*, Vol. 152, Philadelphia, 1930. Pp. 18-29. Used by permission.]

Temple or the Tomb of Confucius, the astronomical instruments, the Great Wall, the camel caravans, the two-wheeled carts, the deep-cut roads, the simple plow, the sea-going junk on the Yangtze, the towering waterwheels of Szechwan, the religious processions of Ningpo or Canton, the looms of Nanking or Huchow, the stacks and stacks of volumes of state history, or the proverbs on the lips of a common coolie—quotations from the Odes or from Confucius, Mencius, or Mo Ti.

THE TIME FACTOR

China is a land wherein the fundament of culture was established by transmission from the region northeast of the Caspian Sea, so early that it is identical with that of Europe. In the course of time, war contact with the nomadic Turks on the north and the aboriginals of Asia on the east and the south improved upon this fundament of culture and elaborated it to such a high point that it included not only the technology that could support an ever-increasing population, but also [a highly developed ideology].

THE LAND FACTOR

To appreciate the full importance of the land factor in Chinese continuity, one must remember that topography may work for or against contact. On the one hand, the very location of the geographic area in relation to Europe and the Mediterranean Basin has made for isolation, which accounts in part for the peculiarities of Chinese culture in contrast with the Europeo-American. On the other hand, that same location, being contiguous to the plains on the north and the west, has made for contact with the fighting nomads—to the south, for contact with the uncivilized tribes; while the Pacific Coast afforded opportunity for shipping. These latter conditions operated for a similarity of culture throughout eastern Asia—China, Japan, and Korea.

Not only locus but also size of land mass has made for continuity. [China] contains nearly four and a half million square miles with a climatic range from the subtropical regions of the south to the cold-temperate, almost subarctic, areas of the north. The cold of the high mountains in the west and the south, the heat and the moisture of the Yunnan jungles, the aridity of Turkestan, the constancy of the Han and Yangtze, and the unreliability of the Hwai and Yellow Rivers, all show that any climate of the world may be found somewhere in China.

Then to locus and size must be added fertility, for the wide coastal plains built up by the great rivers flowing into the ocean and revived by frequent floods, or covered with the rich loess deposited by the winds from the Gobi Desert; have been capable of supporting some of the most congested areas of the world.

This same land mass has been the home of the races of China for approximately the last ten millennia.

RACES

China has always been occupied by a variety of races. The picture one gets at the dawn of history is somewhat as follows: on the north the Mongols, the Turks, the Manchus, the Koreans, the Tungus, and minor tribes of Buriats, Goldi, and Dahurs; on the northwest the Sarts and the Hindus; on the west the Tibetans, the Lolos, and the Mantzu; and on the south the Shans, the Miao, the Yao, and the Tung Chia, or cave dwellers. The ancestors of these modern peoples possessed the whole area now known as China. They were the barbarians through whose conquest and by whose tribute the glory that was China was built.

But who were the Chinese? They were invading tribes not racially Chinese at all. They came from Central Asia in successive waves of migration, pushed out by economic competition due to the gradual desiccation of great inland seas, on whose shores once flourished a high civilization. Entering from the northwest, they penetrated the upper reaches of the Yellow River and settled permanently in the lower reaches.

By sending out members of the royal family to rule over the conquered peoples, governmental centers were set up. These later became city-states and centers from which radiated the culture brought in by the invaders. Meanwhile, these rulers and their descendants intermarried with the aboriginals, developed new ruling houses, and merged the weaker city-states into kingdoms, until, by 1122 B.C., the House of Chou emerged supreme in the center of ancient culture and government. During this dynasty, political power was extended to the far south and was organized under a feudal system.

At any rate, the Chou Dynasty represents an era of nearly nine centuries during which the barbarians were gradually assimilated into the "Chinese" culture, although the name China does not attach to land or people generally until Chin Shih Hwang Ti, the first emperor, 221 B.C.

CULTURE

The adaptation of peoples to the various conditions of topography and climate, with a concomitant supply of food resources, through time produces characteristic culture complexes.

In terms of material traits, North and South China represent two great culture areas with differences in their racial bases, the South China complex being fundamentally aboriginal and the North China complex being introduced by invaders.

THE LEGENDARY PERIOD

Even before the establishment of the Chou Dynasty, these northern culture bearers had achieved a [very] high civilization. The people engaged in weaving silk, linen, and hair cloth and practiced dyeing in various colors —red, yellow, blue, and black. They used vessels of bronze and had bows, arrows, spears, battle axes, shields, and armor. Knives, hatchets, and plows were the principal tools. Language was in written form, as is evidenced by the famous bamboo books. Knowledge of music was [quite] high. They used carts drawn by horses for transportation, and chariots in battle. Government was highly organized into a feudal monarchy with five grades of rank—duke, marquis, earl, viscount and baron—even as in Europe. The monarch was

assisted by a premier and a cabinet of six ministers of religion, education, agriculture, works, justice, and communication, with subordinate ones for astronomy, music and forestry.

There is reasonable evidence of the existence of an elementary science and possibly of the establishment of schools. The people had a knowledge of astronomy and used a lunar-solar calendar. Astrology flourished because of their belief in the power of the stars to determine human affairs. There was a definite body of law and a code of punishment. A whole hierarchy of religious beings was worshipped under the leadership of the monarch. Their ethical teachings were high, as for example from the *Shu King:*

> Go not to excess in pleasure. Put away evil without hesitation . . . . Study to have all your purposes in accord with reason. . . . Calamities sent by Heaven may be averted; from those brought upon a man by himself there is no escape. . . . It is not the knowing, but the doing that is difficult.

Any one more or less familiar with China will recognize that with few exceptions these various forms of cultural achievements have continued down to recent times.

CHOU DYNASTY—THE GOLDEN AGE

With the achievements previously attained, it is not surprising that the Chou Dynasty, during its nine hundred years of sway, created what is known as the Golden Age. It was during this period that the main features of Chinese thought and practice were crystallized and stereotyped in such forms that they have continued to the present.

It would be impossible to consider in detail all of the achievements which have continued in one form or another to recent times, but a few will suffice to support the fact of long cultural continuities.

In government, the feudalistic system which was begun during the Hsia and Shang Dynasties continued as the basis of organization and control. The government itself was on a familistic basis with all of the feudal lords at the beginning of the dynasty near relatives to the king. By it, political power was tremendously expanded.

In 684 B.C. the Marquis of Ch'i established a government monopoly in the manufacture of salt and iron in order to increase his wealth. This was the origin of the famous Salt Gabelle, still 'one of the principal sources of revenue. The border tariffs, or what is known now as *Likin,* were established during this period also as a source of revenue. Also one finds the system of tithing, in which the unit of organization was ten households—a system that was retained by the late Manchu Dynasty. Over a tithing were the headmen or village elders, who represented their villages in relation to the government. They were the first census takers and were responsible to the government for the conduct of the villagers and for the upkeep of the physical condition of the villages, such as walls, streets, lighting, police, and village temple and theater. They provided schools, built markets, and adjudged local disputes. They also protected the villagers from the exploitation of the officials, paid the customary taxes, and protested extra impositions. Thus in very early times was established the general scheme of social organization which rendered revenue to the central government and yet provided a high degree of local autonomy—the true basis of the modern democratic movement in China.

By this time also the practice of revolution was firmly rooted. Already, the great cycle of political power had been amply revealed. A powerful lord skilled in fighting enlarged his sway and finally overthrew the last of a decadent dynastic line. He established a new house which waxed in power and glory, only to fall after a period of decadence and corruption to the vigor of some newly emergent leader who listened to the voice of the people, which is "the voice of Heaven."

SOCIAL CLASSES

In a highly paternalistic system, the common people were grouped in nine classes, according to their occupations: (1) farmers, (2) gardeners, (3) woodmen, (4) herdsmen, (5) artisans, (6) merchants, (7) women weavers of silk and linen, (8) servants, (9) unskilled laborers with a superintendent in charge of each group.

Life was highly schematized, at least theoretically, though probably in practice the rigidity of the scheme broke down. That the general stereotype, or theory of organization of life continued is shown by the fact that even today, it is customary to classify people into (1) scholars, (2) landworkers, (3) artisans, (4) merchants, (5) housewives, (6) menials and unskilled workers, and (7) soldiers. Such classes are not to be considered as castes, for any one could become a scholar and a scholar could become an official. Only outcasts, convicts, slaves, actors, ragpickers, barbers, and prostitutes were not eligible to rise in the social scale.

MARRIAGE AND THE FAMILY

The institutions of marriage and the family were established in a form in which they have continued to the present. The marriage broker or go-between, the gifts, the reception of the proposal of marriage in the ancestral temple, and the practice of concubinage were common among the nobility and were imitated by those of lower rank.

Familist ethics of filial piety were stereotyped and put into record and have been influential from that period down to today.

MATERIAL CULTURE

In the buildings of the well-to-do, the characteristic architecture was already developed both in floor plan and decoration. The poor, then as now, lived in mud huts or shacks with walls and roofs made of interwoven reeds. Chairs were not used at that time, though furniture was decorated with mother of pearl, as is common today.

Cookery was highly developed. Food was served in dishes of bamboo, earthenware, and bronze, and eaten with chopsticks.

The dress of the ancient people was quite similar to that common up to the close of the Manchu Dynasty, generally made of silk and linen. The poor people grew fat in winter when they added their many quilted garments, for, then as now, their houses were not heated except with braziers. Jade ornaments were common and combs were instruments of decoration as well as for arranging the hair. The chief amusements were archery, music, drinking, fencing, cockfighting, and hunting.

This period also saw the invention of the compass.

Money was in use, which argues for commercial practices beyond the barter type. It was made of bronze in the form of a conventionalized spade and sword or knife. From the round hole at the end of the latter evolved the [perforated Chinese coin known as the] "cash."

LITERATURE AND PHILOSOPHY

To the Chinese scholar of today, the Chou Dynasty is the Golden Age not because of these various cultural achievements just indicated, but because of the work of the great scholars and philosophers, Confucius, Mencius, Lao Tze, Chuang Tzu, Mo Ti, and Hsün Tzu. Confucius gathered and edited the fragmentary records of early times and thus put into permanent form the accumulations of philosophy, ethics and government. Then it was that the Four Books and the Five Classics took form and through the influence of Confucius' disciples became the basis of Chinese ideology. Of such influence was Confucius that his teachings had become so sacrosanct within two centuries that when Chin Shih Hwang Ti wanted to do away with the feudalism of Chou he was opposed by the conservative scholars because the Master had approved of it. The emperor ordered the classics burned and the scholars put to death, but to no avail.

LATER CULTURAL ACHIEVEMENTS

Among the inventions important in the culture of China today and achieved subsequently to Chou are: modification of ancient script, invention of the brush pen and ink, and beginning of the building of the Great Wall, in the Chin Dynasty; sacrificing at the tomb of Confucius (195 B.C.), rise of alchemy, invention of paper, the great history of Sse-ma Ch'ien—a model for all official histories since —introduction of Buddhism, change of Tao-

ism from philosophy to religion, and civil service examinations, in the Han Dynasty (206 B.C.-220 A.D.); a commercial colony of Arabs and Indians at Canton (300 A.D.) and commissions from Rome by sea, the first Buddhist pagoda built about 250 A.D. and the flourishing of Buddhism and Buddhist art, the use of chairs, and the first record of tea-drinking as a social custom, during the period of the Three Kingdoms and the Sui Dynasty (221-618 A.D.); and during the T'ang Dynasty, Christianity brought by Nestorians and Mohammedanism by the Arabs, rise of the secular theater under the influence of the "Pear Garden," and most important, the invention of printing and the first book, movable type (1041-1049 A.D.), and the issuance of paper money.

THE TECHNIQUES OF CONTINUITY

In any analysis of Chinese society, one can secure a clear understanding of the processes and organizations only by appreciating the basic aspect of familism—a type of society in which all values are referred to family welfare. Furthermore, family welfare in this instance must be defined not only in terms of present generations but more emphatically in terms of family continuity and the welfare of the ancestral spirits. Thus one finds in the functioning of the total familist complex not only the biological continuity of the folk but also the concomitant maintenances, material and spiritual.

The bulk of the Chinese population resides in villages scattered throughout the countryside and these villages generally are occupied by one familist organization or sib. Within the village as a unit of social organization, all the principal institutions may be found—economic, religious, political, judicial, and recreational. The mechanisms of transportation are for the bulk of the population limited to the village and the surrounding fields, which makes the rate of mobility very low.

Thus the land factor, the race factor, and the culture factor through time have combined to produce a milieu especially effective for social continuity. Life is organized on an intimate, personal, blood basis. It is made sacrosanct by the ideals of filial piety and the practices and attitudes of ancestral worship.

ANCESTRAL WORSHIP

Aside from the general condition of isolation of China from the culture currents of the Occident, and aside from the effects of a universal governmental language, the peculiar features that operated for the high degree of continuity in China can be found in ancestral worship. The Chinese youth feels himself constantly surrounded by a world of spirits, who harm or help him according to his attitude and behavior in respect to them. Let him honor them and worship them, and fortune will be his. He holds the same attitude in relation to his immediate progenitors, not only because the principle of filial piety prescribes it, but also because he knows that in time they too will be ancestral spirits. Thus the young are made highly suggestible to values which inhere in the family complex; values which make for the prestige of elders, for obedience, conformity, and social harmony. To depart from the folkways is, therefore, to lose status in the familist group—an event very rare except during the last few decades, when, under the impact of Western cultures, individualization has tremendously increased.

FAMILIST GROUP PRACTICES

There is evidence that from time immemorial, the great majority of the people have been relatively poor, so that the struggle for existence has always been hard. In order to meet these needs, the familist group developed certain mutual aid features which were based partly upon the religious institutions. Usually, each village has a group of voluntary associations through which the members help one another in their economic practices, such as watering fields, harvesting crops, making sugar, repairing dikes, and the like. Connected with the ancestral hall of each village is a certain parcel of land, the income to be used for the upkeep of the hall, the expenses connected with rites and ceremonies of ancestral worship, and the care of the aged and the needy. Normally, therefore, one does not find in Chinese society the need for public charitable aid as in other societies. The beggars and needy folk are usually kin-wrecked, or are small family groups whose economic bases have been destroyed by catastrophic phenomena, such as plagues or floods.

Unless pressed by economic necessity, familist groups continue in one place for long periods of time. The lands are owned by the heads of immediate families, who have inherited them from their immediate fathers and who will in turn parcel them out equally to the male offspring. Thus, through ownership and inheritance, residence is very continuous. This makes for a stable kind of life by reducing contacts and enhancing continuity.

With the exception of some factory production in such cities as Shanghai, Hankow, Tientsin, and Wusih, Chinese industry is domestic handicraft. Masters work in their own home-shops, assisted by apprentices whose families are either relatives or friends of the artisan. Both belong to the same trade guild. The guilds not only have control of standards of work, prices, and apprentices, but also frequently develop their own educational and recreational services. Thus the economic techniques are transmitted under conditions most favorable to continuity, i.e., personal instruction of a practical kind by the masters, and an organization that guarantees the maintenance of sanctioned standards through group pressures.

EDUCATION

The political autonomy of Chinese villages accentuates the foregoing conditions, because it centers responsibility and authority within the village itself.

One responsibility which in time became a matter of pride was the education of the youth in the literature and philosophy characteristic of the country as a whole. This made for the continuity of the national ideology. Each long-established village aimed to produce scholars who could successfully compete in the civil service examinations and thereby become eligible to enter officialdom.

The village scholar conducted his school

with methods of rote memory and strict adherence to the literary language and products
of the past. In forms of composition, thought,
and methods of writing, each generation imitated the great literary products and thus
transmitted the standard patterns from generation to generation.

In addition to the schools, which were the
chief formal agents of transmitting these continuities, well-established villages usually included scholars' halls, dedicated to those who
had successfully passed state examinations—
places where scholars could congregate and
converse on philosophy and religion. The effect of all this was to place the scholar first in
social rank, giving to literary capacity a prestige second only to the worship of ancestors.

As an outgrowth of the literary tradition,
there appeared in China those who corre-
sponded to the minnesingers of Europe; poor,
wandering scholars who traveled from village
to village, or local village scholars, who would
repair to village tearooms and there recount
the tales of ancient folklore, recite poems, or
detail the exploits of the great heroes. Thus,
much of the learning was informally transmitted to the lower classes in the form of
tales and proverbs.

AESTHETICS

Art, too, reenforced the continuities of
Chinese life in the use of the brush and ink,
in the fine forms of calligraphy and also in
the creation of symbolic art highly conventionalized and adapted to achievements with
the brush, under the limitations of the oblong
mural hangings. Even today, one will find
in the scholars' hall or ancestral hall of almost any village, color paintings of the famous ancestors of the family.

But the art of lacquer with the paintings
and decorations flourishes ubiquitously in
connection with ancestral worship. For not
only in the village ancestral hall or the village
temple, but also in the ancestral hall of the
large homestead, one will find beautiful cab-

inets ornately decorated. Within these are
placed the tablets of the ancestors of the
present sib, arranged in a hierarchy, generation after generation, some of them extending back a thousand years or more. The
family lore is replete with the deeds of these
ancestors. They serve as standards of behavior to the young, who are urged to emulate
them.

In the Buddhist and Taoist temples art
has flourished in statuary, architecture, paintings and calligraphy. The pictorial decorations of houses, particularly in the South,
representing heroic deeds or famous people
of tradition, constantly remind the youth of
a glorious past and fill him with pride of
ancestry, race, and culture.

Music is common in every village, for the
truly cultured scholar, the ideal gentleman of
Confucian standard, is skilled in the use of
musical instruments as in poetry and philosophy. Traveling musicians constantly go
about entertaining the patrons of teahouses,
and skilled performers always accompany the
dramatic presentations. Wandering theatrical
troupes go from village to village and present
the ancient historical plays and tales in the
village theater. In all their forms, the aesthetic
arts derive their techniques and standards of
excellence from the past and are effective
means not only of transmitting the ancient
ideologies but also of reenforcing the prestige
of that past.

ANTIQUITY SHAPES THE PRESENT

So in general have the races of China,
locked in a great land mass, through forty
centuries evolved a culture predominantly
organized to secure continuity of practices,
attitudes, and ideals. Innovations and reforms
might occur, rebellions might overturn dynasties, foreign nations might intrigue for
control, yet the general current of life in
the familist agricultural villages swept on,
bearing into the present the vigor of an
ancient heritage.

The continuity of Chinese life, as we have seen above, is based in part on China's
geographical factors of location, size, topographic features, and soil. The next two selec-

tions examine these more closely. The first, by J. R. Schwendeman, looks at China as a whole and provides an over-all view of the Chinese peasant's adjustments to many problems of his habitat. The second, by George B. Cressey, which deals with the regional differences between North and South China, will enable us quickly to locate geographical references made in later selections.

· 76 · Geographic Features of the Habitat of the Chinese Peasant

J. R. SCHWENDEMAN

Nearly one-fourth of all the people in the world live in China Proper. By another comparison, more people live in China Proper than live in the vast lands of North America, South America, Africa, and Australia combined. But these astounding comparative statements only introduce still more incredible facts about the world's most densely occupied habitat.

Most people think of China as a vast empire teeming with people. China is a vast empire, it is true, of 4,516,934 square 'miles, and larger than the United States by more than one million square miles, but only the seaward fringe teems with people. Here on the coastal deltas and flood plains of China's great rivers live at least eighty per cent of the Chinese. This land they occupy so densely would only extend over the approximate area of the Cotton Belt of the United States. It would approach 400,000 square miles and be approximately ten per cent of the Chinese Empire.

A second impressive association, from the geographic point of view, is that the Chinese habitat is among the least desirable of the larger, highly cultured and densely occupied lands of the world. The Chinese are plagued by more problems from the physical environment than most well-occupied lands.

Most of China's land is rough, mountainous, and dry. The fertile plains are almost entirely river-made and largely subject to flood; there are no producing upland plains, such as in the United States and Europe. Loessland, the only exception in China

Proper, is relatively small and is being eaten away by erosion.

China's rainfall is subject to the unpredictable droughts which have been so severe and extensive as to create severe famine conditions. Over North China the rainfall comes almost entirely in the summer months. This feature of the precipitation regime creates serious water supply problems during the winter, and summer floods which destroy growing crops. The year round rainfall of western Europe and eastern United States is vastly more dependable and more evenly distributed.

Moreover, China is poorly supplied with forest products and lacks adequate quantity and quality in many important minerals, especially iron.

Finally, regardless of these many natural difficulties, China's millions strive to live by farming. Three-fourths of the population are peasant farmers. China's cropped lands are little more than half of those of the United States and are not supplemented by the extensive or desirable pasture lands found in the United States and Europe.

The Chinese peasant has taken his well-watered and fertile river valleys and has worked out a system of existence. Perhaps his major failure has been in [not] achieving a balance and diversity in his economy.

POSITION

The people we have referred to as the Chinese peasant, and which we propose to study, live in a large habitat of one and one-half million square miles called China Proper. Politically, China Proper is composed of eighteen provinces located in eastern Asia. While one and one-half million square miles is a huge living space, it is by comparison but a doorstep to the vast interior of Asia, the world's largest continent covering one-third the earth, or 16,494,217 square miles.

Of China's position throughout the ages, already touched upon briefly in the preceding selection, George B. Cressey says,

Southeastern Asia is almost an oasis, largely self-sufficient and isolated from the rest of mankind. Until the era of modern travel, the most perfect barriers surrounded China on all sides. Towering plateaus, arid deserts, tropical forests, and the widest of the oceans all helped to preserve the unity of China. Nowhere near by was there an equal neighbor, except in India which was months away. It is but natural that the Chinese thought of themselves as living in the "Middle Kingdom."

Even today with modern transport facilities, China's isolated position is one of the most secure in the world and her dominantly rough terrain will retard the development of effective communication. Here Cressey says,

Overland travel has been confined to cart roads and flagstone trails, roughly characteristic of the North and the South respectively. Two-wheeled springless carts with narrow iron-studded wheels grind the earth into dusty ruts in the dry season and churn it into deep mud after the rains. Under such conditions one does not travel for pleasure. Sedan chairs are scarcely more comfortable. Where animals are not available long lines of coolies carry salt, tea, cloth and kerosene. . . . Since the means of travel are slow and inefficient, commerce requires an abnormally large number of people. Where man is so numerous and lives so close to the minimum, coolie carriers work for a pittance. It is thus cheaper to wear men down than to keep roads up.

So China remains the most inaccessible of all highly cultured and densely populated areas.

LANDSCAPE

China Proper is mainly a mountainous country. Over much of the area slopes are so steep that normal agriculture is impossible. The most significant mountain range is the Tsingling Shan. This is the mountain range that separates the North from the South, and it is the barrier on which the moist winds from the Pacific lose much of their moisture and against which the cold and dusty northwest winter winds break their force. It separates the moist agricultural lands of Central and South China from the brown and dusty but rich soils of the Northwest so that even the casual visitor to China is struck by these fundamental differences. Soils, crops, natural vegetation, houses and even the habits of the peoples themselves are different. Thus everywhere in China the mountains are a major factor in farming, in erosion control, in floods, and in communication.

Encircling China on the west are such vast mountain walls as the all but impenetrable Tibet, the rugged plateau of Yunnan, and the arid Mongolian Plateau. Access to the interior is only through such occasional passes as the famous Jade Gate near Lanchow.

China Proper has practically no intermediate landscape in the form of low plateaus and upland plains. Opposed to the extreme of rough, hilly and mountainous areas are the low river flood plains and deltas. The largest of these is the combined delta of China's two greatest rivers, the Yangtze and the Yellow. This delta plain is called the Chinese Plain and borders the Yellow Sea in southern extent to the Gulf of Pohai in its northern limits. Its area is about 125,000 square miles. This plain is the heart of classical China and is considered the most occupied land on earth. The present population is approximately 80 million people and 650 persons per square mile.

The alluvial plains of the Yangtze Valley are similar to those of the Chinese Plain but because the Yangtze River is navigable by ocean vessels this plain is commercially more important. This plain is about 75,000 square miles in extent and has a population of nearly 70 million people.

The other plains of China, including the Chengtu Plain of Czechwan, are alluvial in origin and mainly flood plains. They lie mostly along the Chinese coast south of the Yangtze including the large delta and valley plains of the Si Kiang, or are along the inland streams of the great Yangtze-Kiang basin. Together these plains provide the homelands for roughly eighty per cent of China's population, for on these plains productive soil, water supply, water transport, and climate combine to make possible the intensive agrarian economy evolved by the Chinese peasant.

CLIMATE

China Proper extends south-north from the tropics through most of the temperate zone and, therefore, has a wide climatic range. This part of China lies between the twentieth and forty-second parallels north—twenty-two degrees and something over 1500 miles. In North America this would extend from southernmost Cuba to New York.

In addition to this important north-south variation in climate, there are two other major features every student must note. First, there is the continental influence from the world's largest land mass, which is expressed in the monsoonal rhythm greatly intensifying the seasonal distribution of rainfall and temperature. For instance, winter temperatures in China's interior are colder than any other place in the world of equal latitude; and rainfall is largely confined to summer over most of China. Second, the climate is sufficiently temperate to admit of intensive culture but unpredictable and intense extremes in drought and floods occur.

Broadly speaking, China is divided into two climatic provinces, North and South. North China is generally considered the area north of the Tsingling Shan and its extension, the Hwaiyang Shan ranges. In this northern province the winters are cold, windy, dry, and dusty. The average January temperature is 23.5°F. at Peiping in the same latitude as Philadelphia, where the January average is 34.4°F. Philadelphia is subject to extreme continental influences in winter but the continental monsoonal influence of Asia is far more intense. Practically no rain and little snow falls on the average from late September to late May at Peiping, thus creating severe seasonal moisture and water supply problems. The rainy season is mainly restricted to the summer months of June, July, and August. The average July rainfall of nine inches is twice that for any one month of the year in eastern United States. Moreover, the annual fluctuation of summer rainfall is terrific, varying from practically nothing to as much as two feet in a single month. Indeed, a report of twenty-three inches in thirty-three hours is on record. Summer rainfall in the eastern United States is rarely disastrously erratic, either wet or dry.

South of the Tsingling Shan are two distinct types of climate, that of central China of the Yangtze basin and that of the subtropical south. Both show the monsoonal influence in marked seasonal ranges in temperature and rainfall, although both are far from the extremes of North China in this respect. At Shanghai winters are cool to cold, with January averages at 37°F. Summers are hot at 80°F. for July. Rain falls the year round but varies from 1.3 inches for December to 7.4 inches in July. Hence, summer river stages are high and, at times, with excessive rainfall, reach terribly destructive stages.

While subtropical China shows mild winters (60°F.) and hot summers (82°F.) and marked seasonal rainfall distribution (1.1 inches to 15.1 on the average), the erratic tendencies of drought to flood are practically absent. This is true also for the protected inland basin of Szechwan of the upper Yangtze.

The monsoons are the seasonal winds of Asia which are unique among world winds for their seasonal reversal and persistence. In China the prevailing direction is northwest in winter making them cold, dry and dust-laden.

In summer they prevail from the southeast, making them hot and moisture-laden.

Kendrew says, in *Climates of the Continents* (Oxford, 1942),

> In winter atmospheric pressure is very high over Central Asia and the gradient over China steep. Strong winds blow out from the deserts of the interior, which are very cold at this season, and descend as a great cataract over the plateau edge, which is here undefended by mountain ramparts to China. Their descent warms them somewhat but they are still felt as icy blasts, especially in northern China, and they are so strong that they carry clouds of dust and on the China Sea navigation is often interrupted by bad visibility. . . . The winter monsoon is at its strongest in December, January, and February. . . . In May the summer low pressures are already developed over the interior of the continent and they deepen in June and July. The prevailing winds over all China are south and southeast, warm and rainy. . . . The summer monsoon, the season of rain and cloud and damp enervating heat, comes to an end in September. . . .

And many are the ways by which the Chinese peasant adjusts his routine of living to this monsoonal rhythm.

According to *China, Land of Famine,* published by the American Geographical Society:

> Without doubt the worst famines in China have been caused by a lack of sufficient rainfall for a long period. Lack of rain occurs most often in northern and central China. While most other natural disasters result in only a partial destruction of the crops, a drought makes a normally flourishing countryside a barren waste. When it is remembered that in China almost the entire population exists by agriculture, it can be imagined what effect a dry period has, especially if it continues for two or three years, as sometimes happens.

> In time of drought it is only in those districts where irrigation is practiced that any crop at all can be harvested. . . .

It has been estimated by Dwight W. Edwards in his report *The North China Famine 1920-21* that in the great drought of those years, 500,000 people perished and nearly twenty million people were made destitute.

Floods in China are especially destructive since they occur in summer and since the greatest density of population is on the flood plains. Flood disasters occur in both the Yellow and Yangtze basins. The Yellow River is especially a problem since its current has to be contained by dikes for the river bed has been built up by silt until the river flows between its man-made dike banks above the countryside. When a flood occurs and the dikes break, hundreds of square miles—often thousands—are inundated. Sometimes the Yellow River changes its course and disaster results. Such an instance is the flood of 1887-1889 when a break occurred in the southern dike in the province of Honan. According to Chinese official records, more than 2,000,000 people lost their lives either from drowning or from starvation during the resulting famine, and nearly the whole province of Honan south of the river was inundated.

Typhoons and locusts are other calamities which are climatic or arise from climatic conditions. The typhoons are localized to the coastal areas and occur in the fall. Occasionally they are terrifically destructive. Inland they cause torrential rains but the winds lose their violence.

The locusts are listed as one of the three principal natural causes of famine along with flood and drought. This pest, which consumes the growing crops, leaves the countryside as barren as does a protracted drought. They are known to attack and absolutely ruin even trees. In this respect they are more damaging than drought or flood.

NATURAL RESOURCES

From the foregoing accounts it can be readily stated that China's greatest natural assets are her soil, level land, rivers, and other water supply and certain phases of climate. Her greatest handicaps lie in lack of forests and grasses and in the prevalence of mountains and recurring natural calamities.

On the basis of her natural advantages the Chinese provide more food directly from the land than is being accomplished by any other people in the world in a similar area. But it is not quite fair to say that the story of crops tells their sole adjustment to their habitat. In addition, they have a finely adjusted domestic animal economy which provides nonhuman power, a valuable supplement to diet, and moreover these animals subsist as scavengers, feeding upon waste and other inedible products which would otherwise be lost. The story of China's near half-billion fowl— chickens, ducks, geese, and turkeys, 75 million pigs, or 20 million water buffalo and oxen is a fascinating facet of peasant economy. The Chinese also have some cattle, horses, mules, sheep, goats, and burros.

These resources and resource adjustments are major but among such a dense population such mineral resources as salt, clay and stone are vital and such a plant as bamboo is indispensable. Only a brief survey can be given of these many but essential resources.

Because of China's vegetable diet, salt is probably her most vital mineral. Eighty per cent of her supply comes from evaporating sea water and is one of the several important geographic contributions of the sea to China —fish, transportation, especially coastwise, protection, climatic control, and the dilution of continental wastes being other important benefits. Other sources of salt are from the inclosed lakes of Mongolia and the 26 districts of salt wells in Szechwan. Incredible as it may seem, the total number of these wells is estimated at 70,000 and they have been dug by native methods, some to depths of two to three thousand feet!

Sand, clay, and stone for homes, as well as pottery, tile, china, and domestic implements are invaluable in the Chinese Peasant stage of economy. Bamboo, used for every conceivable domestic implement from chop sticks to sedan chairs and musical instruments, would also rank in this category along with wood used for charcoal and weeds and dried stalks of the field used for fuel.

As to economic minerals such as coal, iron, and copper, China ranks as a minor nation. Of these, coal is uppermost. It is widespread over China, but 90 per cent is in the Loess Highlands (Ordos) with the second district in the Red Basin (Szechwan). China uses 40 million tons annually which is small compared to such an industrial nation as the United States which uses nearly 600 million tons. Even so, Chinese industries now use 15 million tons, a good beginning, and Chinese homes use 12 million tons for fuel. Coal in China has additional significance since she has practically no petroleum and must import such products as kerosene, which is widely used.

Iron, the world's most important industrial mineral, is very limited, which is a most serious deficiency. Most important deposits are along the Yangtze Valley with Tayeh in Hupei the leading center. Smaller localities are in Honan and Shantung. (Note these are in China Proper and do not take into account the important deposits in Manchuria.) Iron does not occur near good deposits of coking coal which adds to its use problems. Much as the Chinese peasant uses iron in such simple but universally found implements as the sickle and the hoe, the total annual consumption per capita is only three pounds as compared to 550 pounds per capita in the United States.

Other minerals of significant occurrence are tin, Kochin district in Yunnan; antimony, almost a world monopoly, mainly at Hsikwangshan, Hunan; followed at some distance lower in world rank by manganese and mercury.

While China is not a great producer of silver, she is normally the world's second largest consumer of this metal.

CONCLUSION

Thus it can be discerned that the habitat of the Chinese peasant is complex indeed and cannot be easily evaluated. It is neither a land of extremes such as that of the Eskimo, Navajo, or Baganda, nor yet a land of the many natural advantages enjoyed by the Cotton South or British Midlands.

• 77 • The Geographic Regions of China
GEORGE B. CRESSEY

South China is a land of abundant rainfall. There are many hills but every bit of level land is intensively cultivated. This is the land of canals and paddy fields, of rice and bamboo, of teeming populations crowded into cities with narrow streets. Here the people are somewhat shorter in stature than elsewhere in China and they speak a multitude of dialects. The South tends to be radical and revolutionary, while the North is stolid and conservative.

North China is a land of limited and uncertain rainfall, with large areas of level land but with precarious agriculture and frequent famines. In place of rice and the wet agriculture of the South, the standard crops are millet *kaoliang* [the grain sorghum; literally, "tall grain"], and beans. In place of the greenness of the South, this region is brown and dust-blown for much of the year. In place of canal boats and coolie carriers, there are two-wheeled carts and draft animals. The people are taller and speak a uniform dialect—the Mandarin. Most important of all, the growing season in the North is but four to six months, while in the South it is nine months to a year. Thus, while the North raises one crop or in some places two, the South produces two and three.

These differences are so distinct that they divide China into two great geographic areas, as dissimilar as many countries.

NORTH CHINA PLAIN

The North China Plain is one of the most clearly defined geographic regions in the world. On all sides except the southeast the boundary is well marked by mountains or the sea. Toward the southeast the topographic plain merges with that of the Yangtze, but the limit of the cultural plain is marked by a distinct change in climate, soil, and agriculture.

This great expanse of level land is the gift of the Hwang Ho and the other streams which flow out of the encircling mountains. These rivers have built out a great delta into what was once an arm of the sea. Where they enter the plain from the loess-clad hills of the West, they are so heavily loaded with silt that they are not able to carry all of their burden to the sea, and they deposit some of it along the way. By this process the beds of the rivers have been built higher and higher.

The principal crops are wheat, *kaoliang* or grain sorghum, millet, soy beans, cotton, tobacco, and vegetables. With the exception of the last, none of these crops are commonly irrigated. On acount of the dryness of the winters, one crop per year is the rule in the northern portion of the plain, but south of Shantung, two crops are common. Rice is rarely grown and millions of people eat it only once a year or so, at feasts. Mules, oxen, and donkeys are used on the farms and for hauling two-wheeled carts.

This region has played a leading role in China's history. It has been the seat of most of the great dynasties, and the home of Confucius and the sages.

LOESS HIGHLANDS

The Loess Highlands lie between the North China Plain and the deserts of Central Asia, and thus have climatic characteristics which are intermediate between those of these two regions. Most of the region is semi-

[Adapted from "The Geographic Regions of China," *The Annals of the American Academy of Political and Social Science,* Vol. 152, Philadelphia, 1930. Pp. 1-9. Used by permission.]

arid, with a rainfall of from ten to fifteen inches.

The distinctive feature of the topography is the thick mantle of loess which is spread over hills and valleys alike. This loess is a fine silt dust which has been blown outward from the Gobi and Ordos Deserts and sprinkled over the country as though by a giant flour sifter. In general, it covers all of the country, except the highest mountains, between the Great Wall and the Tsinling Mountains. The thickness of the loess has often been exaggerated, and it probably nowhere averages over three hundred feet.

The steep slopes of the mountains and the dissected loess topography which characterize the Loess Highlands cause human activity to be concentrated in the valley bottoms, which are commonly narrow and capable of but limited cultivation. The loess hills are often terraced, but on account of the scarcity of water they are not irrigated, and crops mature only in the more favorable years. The only areas of green are the thread-like strips along the streams.

In addition to wheat, millet, and *kaoliang*—the principal food crops—there is an extensive cultivation of the opium poppy. On account of the difficulty of transportation, opium is about the only cash crop which can be exported through the mountains, so that opium occupies a position somewhat similar to that of moonshine whisky in the southern Appalachians.

Cart roads connect the principal cities, but most of the region is without wheeled vehicles and depends upon pack animals. In the absence of railroads, which penetrate only the borders of the region, isolation is a dominant factor in the human geography.

It is estimated that the Loess Highlands contain eighty per cent of China's entire coal reserves, with the major portion in the province of Shansi.

MOUNTAINS OF SHANTUNG, LIAOTUNG, AND JEHOL

This region consists of three separate areas grouped around the Gulf of Chihli. These areas form a geologic as well as a geographic unit, for they are made up largely of hard, ancient rocks which have been eroded into bare mountains with steep slopes. Overlying these older formations are, here and there, softer beds, which make islands of more gentle relief.

Although this is one of the smaller of the natural regions of China, its position next to the sea and its proximity to two of the most important agricultural plains give it an increased importance. The cities of Dairen and Tsingtao are among the most important seaports of the country, and, together with Tientsin in the North China Plain, form the principal gateways to North China.

Coal and iron ore are both mined on a large scale, but agriculture is still the dominant occupation, with twenty per cent of the land under cultivation.

MANCHURIAN PLAIN

No other portion of China so closely resembles the United States as does Manchuria. The Mountains of Eastern Manchuria correspond in a way to the Appalachians, the Manchurian Plain may be regarded as a compressed section similar to one across the Mississippi Valley with increasing dryness to the west as in North America, and the Khingan Mountains take the place of the Rockies, although they are much lower and less rugged. Farther west there are deserts in both continents.

The Manchurian Plain is a pioneer land of rapidly expanding agriculture, and in this respect likewise has certain historical similarities to the United States. Although the region south of Mukden has been occupied by the Chinese for many years, a great migration into northern Manchuria has been in progress since 1925. This movement of farmers from old China, south of the Great Wall, reached one million immigrants in 1927, but dropped to two hundred thousand in 1929. This migration from the overcrowded lands of Shantung, Chihli now known as Hopei, and Honan has been due to the attraction of free or cheap land and to the devastation of the North China Plain by wars, bandits, and famine. The extent to which these colonists moved northward because of the pull of the pioneer urge as compared to the push of circumstances in their old homes is an important question, for it has a bearing on the future of this new land.

Kaoliang, millet, and wheat are raised as elsewhere in the North, but it is the soy bean which has been responsible for the marked prosperity of the region. The world-wide sale of beans, bean cake, and bean oil has made this the only region in China where exports exceed imports.

The prosperity and the progressiveness of Manchuria are shown in the fact that it has a greater mileage of railways than all of China south of the Great Wall put together. It is likewise the only area where active railway construction is in progress. Nature has provided a favorable environment; will the Chinese use the opportunity to develop a new and better civilization, or will the land become as overcrowded and famine-threatened as old China?

CENTRAL MOUNTAIN BELT

The Central Mountain Belt is made up of a series of ranges extending from Tibet almost to the Pacific. The topography is rugged in the west, where the elevations rise to three miles, but becomes more gentle toward the east. These mountains cut directly across central China and separate the country into two very diverse parts.

This is a transitional region, which marks the southward limit of loess, cold winters, and dry crops such as millet and *kaoliang,* and the northward extent of water buffalo, rice, tea, and bamboo.

YANGTZE PLAIN

This region is largely made up of the alluvial plain of the Yangtze Kiang below Ichang, although there are some areas of hills which are necessarily included. The lower part of the Hwai Ho and the area around Hangchow Bay are also included. This is a land of canals, with a length of over thirty thousand miles in the delta alone.

The Yangtze is the largest river in Asia and of foremost importance to China. It is navigable for ocean steamers to Hankow, 630 miles from the sea, and by smaller steamers for a thousand miles more. In some sections the banks are diked, but the flood menace is very much less than with the Hwang Ho.

Although this is one of the smallest regions, it has a population second only to that of the North China Plain, with a density of 897 people to the square mile, the highest in all China. This is a region of intensive agriculture, with rice, silk, wheat, beans, cotton, and oil seeds as the principal crops. A large amount of hand labor is used in cultivating the soil. Climatic conditions are favorable and two crops per year are the rule. The rainfall exceeds forty-five inches.

The Yangtze Plain is the social, political, and economic heart of the new China. Modern factories, electric lights, telephones, and imported goods are found in all of the larger cities. The chief industrial cities of the country are found here[, with Shanghai first among them].

RED BASIN OF SZECHWAN

The Red Basin is one of the most enthusiastically praised regions in China. It is said that everything which can be grown anywhere in China may be produced here, for the climate is favorable, the soil productive, and the people energetic.

This basin is surrounded on all sides by high and rugged mountains, so that access is difficult. The only entry of importance is through the gorges of the Yangtze, which lie in the Central Mountain Belt. Fourteen-knot steamers now regularly navigate the rapids, but it was formerly necessary to travel on native junks which were towed up the river by long lines of trackers. Despite its isolation from the outside world, this region has a population of 43,860,118.

Most of the Red Basin is made up of hills of red sandstone, which are more extensively terraced than in any other section of China. There is also a remarkably fertile plain around the city of Chengtu.

Transportation is largely dependent upon man power, to pull junks, push wheelbarrows, carry sedan chairs, or transport loads.

SOUTH YANGTZE HILLS

All of China south of the Yangtze is distinctly hilly or mountainous, and forms a super-region which is known as the South China Highlands. Level land is strictly limited, and there are no broad plains such as those which characterize the North. The South Yangtze Hills include that part of the region which is tributary to the Yangtze Plain.

Cultivation is restricted to the valley floors and the lower slopes of the hills. Rice is the dominant crop, but only limited areas of the hills are terraced. There is normally a surplus for export to the industrial districts along the Yangtze. Tea is an important cash crop and is grown more extensively here than anywhere else in China. Although the capacity of the land to support agriculture is low, the favorable climate causes a dense concentration of people along the rivers.

SOUTHEASTERN COAST

The Southeastern Coast consists of a rocky and irregular shore line backed by picturesque mountains, roughly parallel to the sea, through which swift rivers have cut narrow canyons. Each of these streams has a delta and an important city at its mouth, and these cities and tributary rivers dominate the economic life. Travel is by boat along the rivers or by sea from one city to another, rather than overland.

Fishing is an important industry along the coastal fringe. The building of junks is aided by supplies of timber which are brought down from the mountains. The maritime interests of the region have led the people to migrate to the South Seas in large numbers and the stream of remittances sent back to relatives by these adventurers plays an important part in maintaining the dense population.

This is the typhoon region, with the worst storms from July to September.

HILLS OF LIANGKWANG

This is the tropical region of China, with abundant rainfall and a year-round growing season. The year may be divided into two seasons, a long, hot, humid summer and a short, dry winter. The rainfall exceeds sixty inches. The perpetual greenness is in direct contrast to the brownness of the North during so much of the year.

Agriculture is carried on under intensive conditions and might better be termed gardening than farming, because of the excessive amount of hand labor which is involved. Draft animals are relatively less important than farther north, for the demand for human food is such that there is no land available for forage crops. The water buffalo is the principal farm animal. Two crops of rice per year are the rule, and a third crop of vegetables may also be raised. Other products are sugar cane, tobacco, palm leaves for fans, excellent oranges and other fruits, and mulberry for silk.

On account of the large amount of hilly land unsuited for occupation, the population density of the region as a whole is not particularly high. The real crowding may be seen in the statistical tables, which indicate that the farm land per capita is but 0.18 acre, and that there is the amazing total of 3495 people to each square mile of cultivated land. High standards of living are impossible under such conditions.

Rivers and canals are used for transportation wherever available, while away from the waterways, coolie carriers are employed. There are no cart roads and only three short railways.

Hongkong is the great distributing center for south China, and has one of the finest harbors in the world. Canton is located up the shallow Pearl River and is the political rather than the economic rival of Hongkong.

The people of this region, particularly those from the Canton delta, are among the most progressive in China. Large numbers have gone overseas.

SOUTHWESTERN TABLELAND

This region is a dissected plateau, cut by deep canyons and crossed by high mountains. The average elevation is above a mile, so that although it lies near the tropics it has a delightful, temperate climate. There are several broad plains, and these areas together with the valley bottoms are intensively tilled. Rice is the dominant summer crop, and the opium poppy is conspicuous during the winter.

The Southwestern Tableland is an anthropological museum. Only about half of the people are real Chinese, and the remainder comprise a great variety of primitive peoples. In all cases, the standard of living is low. Difficulties of transportation will doubtless keep this a backward region for some time to come.

One of the world's outstanding population experts is Warren S. Thompson, who for many years has been interested in the study of China's population problems. Like any research worker in this field, he is baffled by the lack of knowledge about the topic, but he is qualified to make good "guesstimates." Whether or not we agree with his opinions as to what should be done to ameliorate the population pressure, we are likely to be impressed with the magnitude of the problem and be critical of those who propose easy solutions.

• 78 • The Population of China: Present and Future
WARREN S. THOMPSON

THE SIZE OF THE POPULATION

Any discussion of the population of China must be prefaced by saying that little is *known* about it. There has never been a census as we ordinarily use that term, nor has any reliable register been maintained either by the local governments or by the central government within the past century. The so-called "censuses" are at most merely the sum of the guesses of local officials, and usually they cover only a part of the country. Any more or less official figure for China's population must therefore be treated as a guess.

I myself am one of those who believe that many, if not most, of the guesses as to China's population in recent years have been too high. . . . On the basis of study and observations made with this definite purpose in mind, I am convinced that we in the West are likely to hold exaggerated notions of both the density and the size of China's population.

I am disposed to *guess* that China's population is somewhere between 325-75 million and that the Empire's population is 375-425 million. These figures seem to me as good as we can hope to arrive at until more reliable data are available. The simple fact is that we do not know what China's population is within very large limits and that any figure used may well be in error by many millions.

But I would like to emphasize the fact that the argument advanced [here] is not affected, whether China has a population of 350 million, or 400 million, or even of 450 million or more. The population is huge in any event, and, in making calculations for illustrative purposes, the round figures of 350 million for China Proper and 400 million for the Empire will be used. Should these figures turn out to be much too small, when China actually comes to count heads, the argument will only be strengthened.

BIRTH AND DEATH RATES

Of more importance to our purposes than the exact size of China's population, or even than precise birth rates and death rates, is a judgment as to the reasonable limits of her potential rate of growth. A variety of evidence is available on this point, and, although none

[Adapted from *Population and Peace in the Pacific,* University of Chicago Press, Chicago, 1946. Pp. 177-183, 188-190, 197-198, 207-210, 215-217. Used by permission.]

of it is satisfactory, it is not altogether useless in trying to get a general view of the population situation in China and in evaluating future growth in broad terms.

It seems reasonably certain that the birth rate in China is not under 40, and my *belief* is that it will average at least as high as that recorded in Formosa (45.6) and possibly even higher. The data on the death rate are even less consistent than those on the birth rate but seem to justify the statement that the death rate probably seldom falls below 35 and then only under conditions quite exceptional in China, such as in a small area where there is some health work or in a "good" year when the harvest is abundant and epidemic disease is mild. Furthermore, the death rate in China is highly variable from year to year and from place to place. . . . This violent fluctuation, much more violent than the fluctuation in birth rates, is probably characteristic of all populations which, like that of China, have practically no health service and live close to the subsistence level even in "good" years.

CONDITIONS DETERMINING CHINA'S POPULATION GROWTH

The conditions that make for a low death rate everywhere have been referred to as "favorable living conditions." Among any people of high birth rate, population growth becomes more rapid as the level of living rises, because this quickly reduces the death rate. . . . With this in mind, I have done my best to find out whether the Chinese level of living had been improving over the last three or four decades. Since definite data are lacking, I was forced to resort to personal inquiry while in the country. I was unable to get anyone to say that living conditions, and in particular sanitary conditions, had improved during the last four or five decades for any but a tiny fraction of the people he knew, although I was frequently told that the well-to-do portion of the Chinese population in the treaty ports (not the more crowded population of the typically native quarters) was better off as regards sanitation.

On the other hand, many older persons believed that living conditions had considerably deteriorated during this period, especially since the fall of the Manchus and the complete breakdown of civil order in many regions. When due allowance was made for the tendency of older people to deplore present evils, it seemed to me that the only reasonable conclusion permitted by these inquiries was that there had been no significant improvement in living conditions, in sanitary practice, or in civil stability among the great mass of the Chinese people in recent decades. If this conclusion is correct, there is no reason to believe that there has been any appreciable decline in the death rate in recent decades which would have resulted in a growth of population comparable to that taking place in many other parts of the East.

POSSIBLE FUTURE GROWTH

Whatever the population is, whatever the birth and death rate, it is of far greater importance from the standpoint of our discussion here to understand the potentialities of population growth in China and the conditions under which these potentialities may become actual. The basic point for our argument is the simple statement which no one will dispute—that China has a huge population, almost certainly not less than 350 million and possibly in excess of 450 million. A second statement which no one at all familiar with living conditions in China will doubt is that the possibility of growth for several decades to come will be measured by the extent of the control achieved over the death rate, since the birth rate will remain high and will [probably] vary within rather narrows limits. A natural increase of only 10 per 1,000 per year in a population of 350 million would mean an increase of over 36.5 million in a decade, while a natural increase of 15 per cent in a decade, such as prevailed in India (excluding Burma) during the decade 1931-41, would raise this to about 56 million. An increase of about 25 per 1,000 per year, such as now prevails among the Chinese in Formosa, would raise the numerical increase to about 98 million.

It must not be forgotten that in China we

are dealing with numbers so much greater than those in the West that we are likely to under-estimate potential future growth. We must face the fact that China will almost certainly grow by 40-60 million in each decade as soon as a few relatively simple economic and political changes are made.

How long can China care for such increases in numbers? How is she to feed, clothe, and shelter such numbers, even at the present subsistence level, twenty or thirty years hence when the first easy economic gains have been achieved?

AGRICULTURAL IMPROVEMENT AND POPULATION GROWTH

The great danger, from the standpoint of a Westerner interested in seeing China achieve a better level of living, is that improvements in Chinese agriculture will take place so slowly that they will only serve to increase the population without raising the level of living. This often does happen among the most poverty-stricken peoples. Any increase in food reduces the death rate and thus raises the rate of natural increase, and very quickly the food available per capita tends to decline to about what it was before the increase in production took place. This happens so imperceptibly, so automatically, that the people themselves generally do not realize it, and thus have no clear choice between better living with little or no increase in numbers and the same low level with larger numbers. The larger numbers come *naturally* with the lower death rate following some easing of the struggle for subsistence because the birth rate remains at its customary level.

This is the usual result when people live as the Chinese are now living.

MIGRATION AND POPULATION GROWTH

Migration might also have a pronounced effect on China's population growth.

If the Chinese had several Manchurias to which they could move freely and cheaply, securing land without cost or at a very low cost as in the settlement of the United States, then we might expect an almost immediate improvement in the level of living for both old and new communities. It seems doubtful [at present] that any such vast migration can be managed in time to prevent the population at home from increasing during the next three or four decades about as fast as improvements in agriculture can be introduced.

In arriving at this conclusion, the probable effects of industrialization on the level of living are not being overlooked. But the speed with which industrialization can effect improvements is often exaggerated by the nationals of industrially backward countries. Furthermore, they seem to attribute all the improvements in level of living in the West to industrialization, to overlook the fact that the West had an abundance of land for settlement at the same time that industrialization was proceeding rapidly. It remains to be seen whether any crowded people having a very low level of living and without a relative abundance of land at its disposal can improve its level of living except very slowly when forced to rely to a large extent on the growth of machine industry.

INADEQUACY OF CHINA'S MINERAL RESOURCES

One must conclude that China's industrial development over a long period will be heavily handicapped by the lack of many important minerals, particularly by her small resources of high-quality iron and copper, and hence that she will be forced to rely heavily on imports from abroad for many types of goods essential to further industrial development and to the improvement of standards of living. It does not follow from such a conclusion that, other conditions being favorable, China cannot go ahead rather rapidly in the immediate future in the development of certain industries, but it does mean that the development of other industries will be handicapped for a long time or even indefinitely.

THE NEED FOR GREATER PER CAPITA PRODUCTIVITY

There is only one sure way to satisfy the larger need of economic goods and services which are essential to better living in China, and that is to make man's labor more productive, although we should not ignore the fact that a more just division of product between landlord and tenant would be very beneficial to a large proportion of the peasants. Likewise the myriad other inequities of the Chinese social system if corrected would help many individuals. But in a country as poverty-stricken as China there cannot be enough of anything to insure decent living to the masses of the people until the productivity of labor is greatly increased.·

If the Chinese are to live better, there must be a larger per capita product to divide, and this can come only if the whole system of agriculture and industry is revolutionized to make the farmer's and industrial worker's labor more productive. Farms must be increased in size (at present there is only about .43 acre of tilled land per person) and consolidated into units large enough to permit the use of improved machinery and to employ the farmer a larger portion of the year; the farmer must also have access to the credit needed to stock and operate an efficient farm unit and on terms which do not make him the virtual slave of the moneylender; research into better crops and farm practices must be established, and a system for the dissemination of its results must be organized.

As long as the Chinese peasant can scarcely produce enough to keep body and soul together, even when he owns his land, there is little hope of better living from the improvement of the distribution of his present product.

JOBS FOR DISPLACED FARMERS

Supposing that the productivity of the agricultural worker can be increased, what, then, is to become of the farmers displaced by the increase in the size of the farm, by the use of more machinery, and by the adoption of more efficient farm practices? Obviously there are only two things they can do; they must go into some kind of industrial or commercial occupation or move onto new land. It seems highly doubtful that a people depending on a rice culture to the extent that the Chinese do can ever reduce their agricultural population to the 20 per cent that is approached in the United States and Australia and still have an abundance of food. But in the light of the studies of Buck and in view of what has actually happened in Japan, it would not appear unlikely that the proportion of the population engaged in agriculture could be reduced from 80-85 per cent to 40-45 per cent, or even somewhat lower, and yet produce enough so that every person could have a more satisfactory diet, better clothes, and a better house than at present, while the community supported a fairly efficient health service.

Such a displacement of population can, of course, take place only if a considerable part of the people no longer needed on the land can be employed in making goods for the farmers and themselves. This means a relatively high degree of industrialization as compared with what now exists. In the course of time China will become increasingly industrialized, but this change cannot come rapidly, and it is not at all certain that it will result in increasing the per capita product available anything like as much as in the West during the past century.

CHINA'S MALTHUSIAN DILEMMA

This race between increasing per capita productivity and population growth is the real Malthusian dilemma, and China is caught on its horns. China is now experiencing the high death rate consequent upon having more children born than can be provided for under the present conditions of production. Probably China can temporarily, and to a limited extent, reduce the hardships of life and hence her death rate by reorganizing her agriculture and by building up her industry; however, we should not expect too much in the near future from industry alone or from agriculture and industry combined in a country already having a dense population and where the birth rate approaches the physiological maximum.

We must think of China as having a strong tendency to increase in numbers for the next several decades and discuss possibilities of improvement with this in mind.

INDUSTRIALIZATION AND THE LEVEL OF LIVING

In order to make consideration of this topic as realistic as possible, certain definite assumptions will be made. They are (a) that political unity and stability will be achieved shortly; (*b*) that the transportation system will be vigorously expanded by this government; (*c*) that industrialization will go forward rapidly, perhaps as rapidly as in Japan after 1905, probably by the government guaranty of foreign loans; (*d*) that agriculture will be extended and improved at a fairly rapid pace through active governmental assistance; and (*e*) that all these advances will continue for the next forty to fifty years. What will then be the living conditions in China? Of course, this question cannot be answered with assurance, but some enlightening considerations can be adduced.

The first measurable effect on population of such a development as assumed here will be an improvement in general health with a marked lowering of the death rate. The basis for this statement is what has happened in most of the West, in Japan, in India, and in other parts of South and East Asia. An increase of population of 10 per cent in each decade would be a very conservative estimate of the increase likely to follow such improvements in living; it is more likely to reach 15 per cent. Just to make easy figuring we will use 400 million as the population of the Chinese Empire, including Manchoukuo.

Assuming a 10 per cent increase in each decade, a population of 400 million in 1940 would become about 585 million in 1980. At a rate of increase of 15 per cent in a decade (which is approximately that of India for the years 1931-41 and less than the rate of the Philippines), China would have approximately 700 million by 1980. Fantastic! Perhaps, but this growth is taking place elsewhere in Asia, and a small measure of the favorable conditions assumed above are just the conditions which are bringing it about.

I have said "favorable conditions assumed," but most Chinese who talk about these matters would say that I have underestimated their resources and have made too much of both the economic and the psychological difficulties in the way of agricultural and industrial development. If this is so, then the prob-able increase in population is also underrated, because if there is faster improvement in the level of living than assumed, there will also be a greater drop in the death rate. Let us not forget that the Japanese figures for the Chinese in Formosa show a rate of increase not of 10 per cent in a decade, nor even of 15 per cent, but of about *25 per cent,* and that as yet there is no sign of any decrease in the birth rate, while the death rate is still falling.

Can the increase in per capita productivity go on fast enough during the next forty to fifty years to care for such an increase in numbers at a substantially higher level of living? The answer must be "No!" Therefore, it will not be any kindness to help China improve her agriculture and develop her industry merely to find that by the end of the century she has twice her present population existing at the level of living now prevailing. From the standpoint both of the welfare of the Chinese people and of our own position in the future when China has a greatly increased population and enough industry to make her a formidable military power, help to China in modernizing her economy *should be made contingent on the willingness of the Chinese leaders to show their people the need for voluntary control of population growth.*

There is not room in the world for the numbers that will naturally come if we teach all the "backward" industrial peoples how to reduce their death rates but do not at the same time show them the necessity of reducing their birth rates and how this can be done. Even with the most earnest efforts to teach these peoples how to control births they will grow rapidly once modern sanitation supported by a more productive industry and agriculture helps them to reduce their death rates. This is inevitable. Consequently, we must consider not only all possible means which can be made available for the care of this inevitable increase—the improvement of agriculture, the expansion of industry and emigration—but also the means of acquainting them with the control of their birth rates.

Making a Living

>>

A peasant society is rooted in the soil. One of the reasons for the survival and continuity of the peasant society is the close affiliation its members have with the land. The man-land relationship is basic. As a first step in understanding the Chinese peasant's economy, we must understand his attitude toward his land. This affords us an insight into the system of property and ownership; into the methods used in tilling the land and raising livestock, and into his need for supplementing agricultural pursuits with related occupations. In this discussion of the peasant economy we also relate the individual farm to the outside world by asking where the surplus crops are sold, where needed supplies are purchased, where farm credit, as well as professional advice about ways of improving production, can be obtained. Since the factors associated with the level of living have been discussed in Selection 3 and will be alluded to in several selections to follow, no attempt will be made here to deal systematically with food, clothing, shelter, and health practices. Throughout the whole unit there are references to cooperatives and other formal organizations which fulfill economic needs for the villagers. These, too, should be regarded as a part of the economy.

A good introduction to the importance of land ownership is the brief discussion included by Hsiao-T'ung Fei in his study of a village on the Yangtze Plain, eighty miles west of Shanghai. Throughout most of China a peasant who owns even a little land can consider himself a landowner and can hold his head high, although his status within the landowning group rises as he obtains more land and shows the other qualities which his fellow villagers admire.

As has been pointed out already, the three societies described in Part Two all serve to exemplify the profound and rapid sociocultural changes going on in the world today. In no aspect of a people's life is such change more easily seen than in the ways in which they make their living—the economic activities basic to all other phases of life. It will be pointed out, particularly in Selection 90, that industrialization and the modernizing of farming methods are affecting China profoundly; but first we shall consider the older but persistent attitudes of the farmers of China.

• 79 • *Land as a Social Value*
HSIAO-T'UNG FEI

. . . The primary function of land is to yield a food supply. But land is not only a means for producing food.

The productivity of land fluctuates according to the amount of attention and labor devoted to it. Furthermore, it is only partially controllable. There are unexpected risks. Thus land acquires its individuality through its variability in reacting to human expectation. Fear, anxiety, expectation, comfort, and love complicate the relation between man and land. People can never be certain what will come from the land. Land provides the means for self assertion, for conquering the unknown and for the pleasures of accomplishment.

Although the productivity of the land can be only partially controlled, this partial control supplies an empirical measurement of workmanship. Honour, ambition, devotion, social approval are all thus linked up with the land. The villagers judge a person as good or bad according to his industry in working on the land. A badly weeded farm, for instance, will give a bad reputation to the owner. The incentive to work is thus deeper than the fear of hunger.

The relative inexhaustibility of the land gives the people a relative security. Although there are bad years, the land never disillusions the people completely, since hope for plenty in the future always remains and is not infrequently realized. If we take the other kinds of productive work, we shall see that the risks involved in them are much greater. The sense of security is expressed in the following statement made to me by one of the villagers:

Land is there. You can see it every day. Robbers cannot take it away. Thieves cannot steal it. Men die but land remains.

The incentive to hold land is directly related to the sense of security. The farmer says, "The best thing to give to one's son is land. It is living property. Money will be used up but land never."

The deeper we analyse the situation, the more it appears, not only that land in general has a particular value to the people, but that the property inherited by a Chia [the extended family] has for it a particular value. Land is transmitted according to fixed rules. People inherit their land from their fathers. The sentiment originating in the kinship relation and reinforced by ancestor worship is manifested also in this personal attachment to the particular plots of land. Religious belief in the importance of the continuity of descendants finds its concrete expression in the continuous holding of land. To sell a piece of land inherited from one's father offends the ethical sense. "No good son will do that. It is against filial piety." This comment sums up the traditional outlook.

Personal familiarity with a particular piece of land as the result of continuous work on it is also a cause of personal attachment to the land. It is very common for people to work on the same piece of land from early adulthood to death. To say that their land is an integral part of their personality is scarcely an exaggeration.

The non-economic value of the land complicates the transactions in land. Although land has its non-economic value, it does not in any sense lose its economic value. The sentimental and ethical reactions to the selling of the land do not rule out completely the possibility of land transactions. People sometimes need money urgently. Economic strain compels them to treat the land as an economic commodity. But I found no case of alienation except under real pressure.

[Adapted from *Peasant Life in China: a Field Study of Country Life in the Yangtze Valley,* by Hsiao-Tung Fei. Reprinted by permission of the Oxford University Press, Inc., New York, 1946. Pp. 181-183.]

If land is of such importance, we can reasonably ask, "Who owns the land?" The next selection indicates that more of the peasants in the wheat area (North China) own their farms than do those in the rice area to the South. This account of farm tenancy has been prepared by a special committee of American and Chinese experts who made a detailed study of the agricultural needs of China, particularly from the standpoint of what the Nationalist government could do to improve the situation. Already in North China at the time of this study, in 1946, the Communist government claimed that it was doing away with tenancy, that landlords were a thing of the past, and that the peasants themselves could own all the land. We shall understand these "agrarian reforms" better once we learn the background facts on land ownership. We shall be interested, later in this book, in comparing the tenancy problem in the Cotton South of our own country with that in China.

• 80 • Farm Tenancy in China

Tenancy is frequently referred to as a major agricultural problem in China. More than a quarter of a century ago, Sun Yat-sen set forth the principle that the man who operates the land should own it. This teaching has given emphasis to the importance of tenancy problems.

Many people, however, hold wrong impressions of tenancy in China, because they are not fully informed of the facts. There are many areas in which practically all the land is owned by farm operators. At the other extreme are many all-tenant communities in which the land is owned by many landlords, and still other areas where a single landlord owns a very large amount of the land. For all China, the best information available indicates that about 30 per cent of the land is rented. Tenancy varies widely in different Provinces and in different type-of-farming areas. In wheat regions, as a whole, probably less than 15 per cent of the land is rented, compared with about 40 to 50 per cent in some of the heaviest rice-producing areas.

Tenancy should be viewed, also, from the standpoint of the proportion of farmers who rent part, or all, of the land they operate.

Many farmers, known as part owners, own some land and rent additional land. They are in a much more secure position than that of tenants. Various sample studies indicate that for all China owner operators constitute approximately half of all farmers, and, of the remainder, part owners probably outnumber tenants.

A larger proportion of farmers in China own some land and rent additional land than in most other countries. One reason for this is that, when small farms are inherited and the land divided between two or more sons, the one who remains on the farm may rent and operate his brother's share. As he accumulates savings, he may buy and gradually pay for the land of other heirs.

Sometimes heirs offer their small tracts for sale, and unrelated tenants, who, through their thrift, have saved some capital, purchase them. In this way, many tenants start on their way to land ownership while still renting part of the land they operate. Many tenants might have become part owners or full owners but for the fact that credit available to them was at such high interest rates they could not afford to use it for land purchase.

[Adapted from *Report of the China-United States Agricultural Mission*, Report No. 2, Office of Foreign Agricultural Relations, U. S. Department of Agriculture, Washington, D.C., May, 1947. Pp. 53-57.]

Many tenants do not desire to own land. They realize that they can advantageously invest their limited capital in operating equipment and farm more land than they would be able to own. Until they are well established financially, the sharing of risks with the landlord in various forms of share renting is a distinct advantage for tenants. Some landlords who are overburdened with debt incurred in buying land have poorer living conditions than many good tenants.

Some landlords have acquired their land through their own thrift as farmers. Many such owners, reaching advanced years, render a service to society by affording wise guidance to young and inexperienced tenants.

Many farmers are tenants on large tracts of land held by landlords or by corporations and rented to many tenants. These tenants have practically no chance to attain ownership. Reclamation areas which require large amounts of development capital become rented land. In some areas large landholdings have been acquired by war lords. When severe famines occur, owners often sell their land to obtain food. The purchasers, usually local people having surplus capital, then rent to the seller or to other farmers.

Landlords frequently acquire land through the foreclosure of mortgages. Oftentimes a borrower must give up his property because of price changes, purchasing land at too high a price, drought, flood, or other misfortunes. The creditor will then rent it either to the debtor or to another farmer.

While some landlords give real aid to their tenants, others may exploit their tenants. The dense population in China and the competition for the privilege of operating the land enable owners to take unfair advantage of their tenants. Also, the large population and its concentration in agriculture have so reduced the size of farms, in many instances, that the division of the crop between the landlord and the tenant does not leave enough for the tenant to maintain a desirable level of living. In addition to requiring his tenants to pay a large portion of their crops as rent, a landlord sometimes requires his tenants to borrow their necessary credit from him at excessive interest rates, to sell their products to him, and to give him labor service, or other benefits. Instances were found of landlords renting their land to the highest bidder. Also, some landlords require their tenants to pay rent before they have produced a crop. This is a real hardship to those who must borrow money at high interest rates to pay their rent in advance.

Many landlords, especially absentee landlords, pay too little attention to their property. Too frequently an owner rents land to one man who sublets it to tenants at excessive rentals. Managers for owners often extort excessive rents, even though the rental is not all paid to the landlord. Not many years ago tenants who were unable to pay their rent were, in some instances, put in prison, or were made virtual serfs of the landlord. Such malpractices and lack of personal supervision on the part of many landlords put tenancy as a system in disrepute.

FORMS OF TENANCY

Methods of renting land in China vary greatly within the same community but more especially between regions. [Nevertheless, more than] one-half the tenancy in China is on a cash basis consisting of: (1) Payments of definite amounts of money, or (2) the market price of a definite amount of crop, or (3) payment of a fixed amount of produce delivered to the landlord.

Share renting, which makes up most of the remaining tenancy, is widespread in China and shows many variations. At Hsinghwa, Kiangsu, for example, several forms of share renting are found which indicate an attempt to adjust land rentals to the productivity of the soil and other factors.

Another form of renting is the "estimated half-and-half," usually associated with absentee ownership, where the yield is estimated before harvest and the rental fixed on this estimate. There is a little "cropper" renting, which is of minor importance, in poorer, or undeveloped, areas, where the landlord furnishes everything except labor and routine management.

MEANS OF SOLVING THE TENANCY PROBLEM

There are two ways of approaching the problems incident to tenancy. First, many of the evils of tenancy may be corrected by introducing better farm-leasing practices; and, second, tenants may be financed in the purchase of land through the development of farm-land credit facilities. Emphasis apparently should be placed on making it possible for tenants to acquire landownership if they are competent and desire to own their own farms. Others will do better as tenants under proper conditions of leasing and supervision. Either approach will succeed only insofar as wise procedures are devised. Likewise, any marked improvement in tenancy must have Government support.

The problem of tenancy in China is similar in principle to that in many other countries. All major countries have faced this problem and out of their experiences has come much valuable information. It is clearly evident that tenancy in itself is not necessarily bad. But, if tenancy is to be considered a good form of land management, arrangements between the landlord and tenant should provide for: (1) A system of farming which will produce large yields and, at the same time, will maintain the productivity of the soil; (2) an equitable division of income between the landlord and tenant based upon their relative contributions; and (3) the removal of the master-servant relationship between the landlord and the tenant. Many instances may be found in China, as in other countries, where these provisions are reasonably met, and others where they are not.

There is probably no more authoritative voice on Chinese agriculture than that of J. Lossing Buck, who, during his long teaching career at the University of Nanking, conducted many studies of actual farm conditions. In order to round out our information on agriculture already obtained from Selections 79 and 80, we turn now to an analysis of Chinese agriculture by Dr. Buck. The village description of Taitou in Selection 88 presents a close-up of the farmer in action, but Dr. Buck provides the broad background for China as a whole, even including such topics as the marketing of crops and livestock, problems of mechanization, and a criticism of the collective farm, which is a part of the program in Red China today.

• 81 • *Some Basic Agricultural Problems of China*
JOHN LOSSING BUCK

I. INCREASING PRODUCTION

Improved Use of Land . . . The best use of land in China is very different from its use in other countries such as the United States of America, chiefly because of a very great difference in population density. Thus, in China greater attention is given to food producing crops for direct human consumption than to pasture and forage for animal con-

sumption. Land which could not be cultivated in the United States is planted for crops in China where farm labor is more plentiful and must eke out an existence. For instance, certain hillsides are terraced at great labor expense, which, if in the United States, would be used only for pasture or forests, or left to the elements. Absence of adequate and cheap transportation in China prevents proper use of land and intensifies her problem of most capable

[Adapted from *Secretariat Paper No. 1*, Tenth Conference of the Institute of Pacific Relations, Stratford-on-Avon, England, September, 1947. Pp. 3, 5-13, 16-18, 20-21, 23-24, 49-53, 58-62. Used by permission.]

use of land. Mountainsides better fitted for forests grow corn on slopes so steep that the tassel of one plant is on the level with the roots of the plant above it.

Tradition may prevent farmers putting some land into better alternative uses. Hill lands in parts of South China may remain in pasture and fuel production because of a prevailing custom that such land is free for all villagers to use for pasture or for gathering of fuel. In other areas land best suited for pasture or forests is often cultivated with resultant large losses from soil erosion. Pressure of population and small farms often force farmers to use land in this way.

In China, the emphasis on food crops has created an unbalanced production between animals and crops. A great source of feed from oil cakes in China is lost by using them directly for fertilizers, rather than for feed. Crop by-products of straw, stalks and chaff, some of which would supply fodder, supply most of the fuel of the country. A substitute fuel would release a portion of these by-products for fodder. The use of oil cakes for feed and crop by-products for fodder should make possible a greater production of animals, which in turn would probably increase the fertility of farms. Moreover, integration of the economy of the range lands in the North and West with agricultural China is still undeveloped. It awaits cheaper and adequate transportation facilities.

A better balance between forest, pasture and crop is also advisable. Some land is being cropped which should be in pasture or forest. Other land is producing grass and bushes cut annually for fuel. Large areas of mountainous land suitable for forests are burned each year for various reasons, the most common being to supply potash to rice paddy fields from water running off the burned slopes. Some of this mountainous land should be in forests to produce lumber and firewood and to insure a water supply for lower agricultural lands; other portions could be used for pasture which together with feed in the form of oil cakes and fodder from crop by-products would provide for the increased animal population already mentioned.

Not only is there an undue attention to crops as compared with animal production, but also to field crops versus horticultural crops. Fruits are considered a luxury and are not a normal part of the diet. Their nutritional value is not recognized.

Multiple cropping is a feature of farming in China. Nearly one-half of the agricultural area of China produces two crops a year. Greater expansion of multiple cropping is possible, especially if more fertilizer is available at reasonable prices. Development of irrigation and drainage will also extend areas of multiple cropping.

The use of water resources for fish and aquatic crops is developed in China to a far greater extent than in most countries. The application of science in production of such crops would increase their output. Moreover, new areas might be utilized for these types of farming.

The amount of uncultivated land in China that might be brought into economic cultivation is often greatly exaggerated. Most of the good lands have been settled.

Increasing Rates of Production . . . One of the most important ways of increasing crop yields in China is through the control of water. Too much or too little water is probably the greatest factor limiting production. Irrigation needs to be extended to lands not now irrigated. Many areas already irrigated require an additional supply of water, either from the main irrigation system or by better equipment to pump water from the available supply. Water needs to be conserved where it falls, or drained off in a way to prevent erosion.

The second most important method by which yields can be increased, is by the use of more fertilizers (both organic and chemical). In general, farmers in China report insufficient fertilizers and insufficient credit to purchase additional fertilizers.

Farm manures could be increased somewhat by greater use of crop by-products for fodder instead of for fuel, providing a fuel substitute could be found. Green manure crops are common in certain parts of China, and can be advantageously extended elsewhere.

Bone meal is another possible source of fertilizer. Before the war Japan used to import large quantities of bones from North China, but China herself needs this source of phosphorus. There are also parts of China where better care of farm manures would increase the available fertility. Night soil [human excreta] is generally used, but its sanitary use from a health standpoint is a major problem.

Perhaps the third most important method of increasing yields of crops and of preventing losses of stored products is the control of insects and diseases. It is estimated that the rice borer alone produces an annual loss of 10 percent of the rice crop.

Improved varieties of crops and nursery stock would definitely increase yields.

Better cultural methods will also increase yields to some extent. Some crops, like cotton and fruit trees, are spaced too closely. Scientific pruning of fruit trees would increase yields. Improved tools would make possible better tillage and timeliness in farm operations, in addition to increasing the output per worker.

Production per animal, as well as quality of product, may be increased profitably by the use of better breeds and strains.

Proper feeding and care is also a prerequisite to greater production. Insufficient feeding is conspicuous in the Northwest range areas where more winter feed, supplemental to the range, is imperative if large losses are to be prevented. Controllable diseases, like rinderpest, cause tremendous losses of stock, including large number of work animals, which in turn affects crop production.

Improving Agricultural Engineering Practices. The Chinese, to a large degree, have adapted their farm implements to suit their conditions, but improvements are both possible and desirable.

Cast and wrought iron and wood are the chief materials used in manufacture. The Chinese used a plow with an iron share and mouldboard some 2000 years before Newbold, about 150 years ago, invented his cast iron plow in the United States.

Although China designed her implements many centuries ago, she has not made many improvements. For instance, it is estimated that a better metal in the hoe to keep the edge sharp and to decrease the amount of sharpening necessary would decrease the labor of hoeing by 15-20 percent.

Present manufacture of agricultural implements is chiefly by artisan families.

Modern techniques should produce better implements at the same cost or, if at higher cost, with enough improvement to enable the farmer to pay for the higher-priced implements because of the decreased labor cost in using them and/or because of increased production.

Modern Machinery. Computations have been made for farm conditions near Nanking to compare (1) cost of plowing with a water buffalo and with a tractor, and (2) the cost of threshing with a flail and with a threshing machine. Based on these data, tractor plowing is over twice as expensive as water buffalo plowing.

The threshing machine has a better chance of success than the tractor even though the machine is used only fifteen days a year. The combine which cuts and threshes in one operation might be more economical than the thresher since it would also save labor needed in cutting with a sickle and in preventing some of the present losses of grain in harvesting.

The combustion engine is an example of a machine successfully and increasingly used in the lower Yangtze valley for irrigation and sometimes for drainage purposes. The water requirements for rice are so great that for many regions where water is not near the field level, human power is not enough and it is too expensive.

The extent to which modern farm machinery can be used depends not only upon its cost but also upon the farm layout. If the fields are too small or too irregular or paths too narrow, machines cannot be used to advantage. With consolidation of holdings, larger fields are possible.

In China, machine methods at present are not as important as in the United States because labor in China is cheaper and more plentiful.

Certain types of small machinery and improved implements should be used but large machinery appears impractical for general use in China at present. If farms were made large enough for large machines, many farmers would be thrown out of work, unless other occupations are created, such as manufacturing, transportation and professions. Another disadvantage of power machinery is that fuel oil must be bought and it is very expensive in China. A cheap source of fuel will hasten mechanization.

The principle to remember is that labor is plentiful in China. The chief need for machinery is (1) to do work that man cannot do, (2) to do work that can be done more cheaply by machinery, (3) to do work more quickly, and (4) to do it sufficiently better to pay for the cost.

Some people think that any great immediate improvement in Chinese Agriculture depends upon use of large machinery. Such an idea is a mistake. China has a large number of farmers in comparison with the amount of land, and often, labor is cheaper than capital for investment in machines. Use of machinery on most farms in China would increase national production only slightly, or not at all. Large-scale farming with machinery would mean a complete change in the size of farms and in their management. Large-scale farming has so many disadvantages that the cost of production is usually greater than on family-sized farms.

Farm structures in China are largely built from local materials. Walls of buildings are constructed from bricks burnt locally, from adobe bricks made by farmers from earth in their fields, or by tamped adobe walls. Roofs are usually of tile or thatch, of wheat or rice straw. Roof sheeting in South China is usually made of rush mats, while in large portions of North China *kaoliang* [grain sorghum] stalks are used for that purpose. Thus the improvement of farm buildings insofar as materials are concerned must be based on an economical source of materials. There is opportunity for improvement in construction of these buildings, especially from the standpoint of sanitation. In many places the interiors of walls could be plastered over to make a smooth wall

and reduce the collection of dust. Perhaps one of the biggest improvements needed is to eliminate earth floors in favor of a floor which provides against dampness and is easily cleaned.

The present method of storing grain is economical from standpoint of materials used, but it appears that losses may be too great. Careful study of the storage problem and of buildings and equipment for storage is essential for preventing losses. Present structures for irrigation, drainage, soil and water conservation and rural roads consist chiefly of stone set in a mixture of earth, sand and lime. Generally, it would appear that the increased use of structures in connection with control of water is essential, but economical materials are necessary.

Transportation and communication in country districts are greatly limited during wet seasons by improperly constructed roads, which often are ditches rather than roads.

Processing of farm products for markets is in a primitive stage and could be greatly improved. Ginning of cotton, baling of cotton, processing and grading tea, and oil pressing, offer opportunities for application of more efficient methods of processing. Also there is need for introducing preservation of food on farms and in rural communities, such as canning, drying and other processes.

II. ORGANIZATION OF MARKETING AND CREDIT MARKETING

Modern methods of marketing in China have advanced slowly. Standardization and grading of export products like tung-oil, raw silk, bristles and tea have been in operation for about a score of years. Also, there are a few good examples of cooperative marketing of cotton, tobacco and oranges developed before and during the war in Central and West China. However, most products are known only by the locality where they are produced. There is no other grading or standardization. Markets are not well organized, and primary markets are chiefly buyer's markets.

False measures or cheating in measuring is common. The standard system of weights and measures is not enforced except in larger cities. Adulteration by small merchants is a common practice. Produce exchange markets in the modern sense do not exist. The miller, or the silk reeler for instance, must send their own buyers to the country, or purchase products through a middleman, who in turn has made his purchase in the country districts.

The adoption of better marketing practices is essential to meet competition of import products. Before World War II, millers in Shanghai imported wheat not because there were no available supplies within China, but because it was easier to send a cable to Australia, Canada or United States for a definite grade of wheat, supply a letter of credit and in due time the wheat of the quality ordered arrived. On the other hand, if the miller purchased wheat within China, it required sending a purchaser to the purchasing areas, buying of small lots of varying qualities, collecting them together, often storing in the open until they could be loaded, and then having the shipment accompanied by the miller's agents to the mill. Such wheat often contained dirt and stones from the threshing floor and required special machinery for cleaning it.

Credit. The credit problem of China is misunderstood in regard to present sources of credit for farmers. The prevailing high interest rates are usually discussed in terms of usury practices by creditors. One of the surprising results of [careful] investigation is that on an average for each locality studied, the landlord supplies not more than one to four percent of the total credit extended to farmers. Friends and relatives of the borrowing farmers extend the larger share of credit from any single source, and this varies from 39 to 83 percent of total credit. More recently credit cooperatives have been organized and for the years 1940-41 a survey of 216 farms and 11 *hsien* of Szechwan show that 48 percent of the credit was obtained from cooperatives. During the war there was considerable extension of cooperative credit by the Chinese Government, but for China as a whole, the percentage of such credit is only a small fraction of total credit obtained by farmers.

A study of 15,000 farms in 22 provinces indicates only 6 percent of the credit was supplied by merchants, or shops operated by merchants. Mortgaging of land is infrequent and amounts to only one percent of the credit received by farmers. Although there may be isolated instances of large proportions of credit granted by landlords or merchants, at supposedly usurious rates, these instances do not portray the true picture for China as a whole.

Organization of Farmers. Organization of farmers [in order] to cooperate for their common welfare is a more difficult task in China, as elsewhere, than is technical agricultural improvement. Farmers can obtain cheaper credit if they organize into groups and apply for one loan for the whole group. Products can be marketed at a lower marketing cost if farmers pool their products and ship them in one lot. Likewise, they can purchase supplies cheaper when buying in larger quantities. Many irrigation projects cannot be successful unless farms are organized into irrigation and drainage districts for administering the problems connected with irrigating or draining their lands. Organization for soil conservation may also be necessary.

If farmers are to receive the benefits of agricultural research, they can do so more easily and more quickly by organizing into groups through which agricultural extension agents of a government extension system can pass on improved practices.

Some organization of farmers has taken place in China. The Bureau of Social Affairs reports the existence of 77,890 cooperatives at the end of June 1945 as partly or solely engaged in agriculture. By the end of 1945 there were 8336 Farmers Associations of which 660 were *hsien* [district] Farmers Associations and 7676 were *hsiang* (township) Farmers Associations.

III. IMPROVING LAND ADMINISTRATION

Land Measurement and Registration. China, like many countries, does not have a complete land survey of privately owned and public lands. The present Land Administration Office, by means of ground surveys in cooperation with *hsien,* have completed surveys of about 600 *hsien*. Samples of these surveys indicate that possibly as much as one-third of the cultivated area of China is not recorded in the Land Office files of the *hsien* land deed offices. Consequently, statistics of cultivated land area in China are far below the actual amount. Moreover, such land is not paying land taxes and thus creates great inequalities in taxation.

Land Taxation. The land tax is the principal source of revenue for *hsien* governments and more recently it is important for provincial governments. Quality of land rather than the farm as a unit is the actual assumed basis for determining rates. However, rates may be determined by landlords with political influence.

Consolidation of Holdings. The problem of consolidation of holdings concerns an existing situation where the number of parcels per farm vary from 1.1 to 5.9 plots and average 5.6 parcels per farm. Each parcel has one or more fields and the average number of fields is 11.6 per farm. This fragmentation of land favored by inheritance customs that provide for division of land among sons, presents a situation requiring careful organization for its amelioration. There are certain advantages and many disadvantages of fragmentation in China.

The advantages of having in one area all the land farmed by one family, therefore, while of utmost importance, need be only briefly mentioned. Boundary lines would thus be reduced in number and extent, saving land and diminishing boundary disputes; larger fields would be possible and time saved in making trips to fields. Further, if land were all in one piece, barriers, such as fences, hedges, or ditches, could be erected to obtain privacy and prevent trespassing, thieving and gleaning. The control of irrigation and drainage water would be more easy; for instance, fields are now so scattered that often it is not economical for a farmer to dig a well for a small plot of ground and it is not always easy for several farmers to cooperate in using the same well. Control of pests, such as rodents, insects, and diseases, would also be less dif-

ficult. The advantages of having land in one piece so outweigh disadvantages that it seems economically advisable to undertake re-arrangement of fields in China.

In any consolidation program it may be necessary to give attention to certain advantages of fragmentation in a country of small farms by consolidating farms to only two or three parcels rather than one parcel.

IV. DEVELOPING TRANSPORTATION, COMMUNICATION AND INDUSTRIES

Transportation and Communication. Agriculture, like other aspects of national economy, is dependent upon well developed systems of transportation and communication. China's waterways and her long coast make it possible to move large quantities of goods by boats, small and large, but shipping facilities need to be increased and modernized. Railroads, although inadequate, have made rail shipments possible on two North and South and two East and West railways, and on other shorter lines.

Modern highways extend 126,000 miles, connecting most of the provincial capitals. Truck transportation is expensive because fuel oil must be imported and transported to the interior.

Transportation costs are high in China both by traditional methods and even by modern transport in comparison with many other countries. Studies . . . show pre-war costs by traditional methods in terms of U.S. dollars per ton mile to be: carrying with a pole, $0.48; motor truck, $0.33; pack horse $0.30; pack donkey $0.24; wheelbarrow $0.20; pack mule $0.17; animal drawn cart $0.13; junk $0.12; rail $0.027; and steamboat $0.024.

The bulk of agricultural products are transported by the high cost traditional methods and one can visualize the effect a complete development of modern transport and communication would have on agriculture as well as the entire economic life of the nation.

The Post Office is remarkably efficient and its service reaches almost every village of the county seat. Likewise all towns, from a county seat upwards, are connected by telegraph.

Most Provincial capitals have their telephone systems but only a few cities have the dial system. Long distance telephone communication is limited and is in early stages of development.

Modernization, additional equipment and extension of services is required for both telephone and telegraph communication. Radio service has developed slowly partly because of the war and partly because of restrictions on receiver sets, restrictions imposed because of the internal political situation.

Large Scale Water Control Projects. No country has greater large-scale water control problems related to agriculture, production of power and navigation than has China. The immensity of the task of water control in the Yellow River watershed almost surpasses one's imagination. It is of course, both an engineering and agricultural problem.

Other important control projects of less magnitude are for the Yangtze River, the Hwia River and others. The occasional severe Yangtze River floods may be [almost] impossible to prevent economically. Two feet of rainfall within two weeks over the whole Yangtze watershed, as occurred in 1931, is a tremendous amount of water to control, especially when such a large portion of the area is already under water for rice culture.

Processing Agricultural Products. Improved processing methods for agricultural products is a crying need in China. Modern methods of milling wheat flour, small power driven rice mills and canning of fruits, vegetables and meats have been successfully introduced. A simple treadle cotton gin, originated by the Japanese, has been increasingly used and is superior to the native hand roller gin. These introductions have proven the advantage of improved processing methods by mechanical power.

Food. [Many] possibilities [exist,] such as (1) extraction and refining of oils of many kinds produced in large quantities in China; (2) grain milling; (3) the processing of grains

for porridges; (4) improvements in grading for standard quality, packaging, storage, warehousing and shipping of foods; (5) meat, poultry, egg and fish processing and packing; (6) fruit and vegetable storage and preservation by canning, freezing and dehydration.

Fibers. Cotton, silk, ramie, jute, wool, hemp, bristles, flax and camel hair are among the fibers produced in China.

Of these fibers, cotton is produced in the largest quantity. China is a land of cotton garments. Cotton is used for cloth, for padded garments and for padding bed quilts. China's climate is favorable for cotton production and she can produce all her requirements. Modern cotton textile mills have been operated successfully in China for years by Chinese owners as well as by foreign firms. China can be self-sufficient in her cotton industry, but erection of a large number of additional mills will be required.

Silk produced by silkworms fed with mulberry leaves is an important industry for domestic and foreign demand of silk. However, to maintain and increase her market for silk, greater attention must be given to rearing silkworms producing high quality cocoons, to baking of cocoons to kill the chrysalis and to improved reeling methods. Hand weavers and a few modern silk fabricating mills produce fine quality silks. Three thousand weavers of silk cloth at Tanyang, Kiangsu, have organized into cooperatives and produce such a fine quality of silk that they are able to compete in the Shanghai markets with machine-made cloth.

Jute grown in North China and hemp in Central China are the chief fibers for string and rope. It is possible that modern methods of processing would be more efficient and would enable a greater production at lower costs.

Flax is grown in the high elevations of the Northwest, but the plant is an inferior variety. Production of fine linens in China appears possible and if embroidered by hand, such linens should supply a lucrative export and reduce import of linen for embroidery and re-export.

Carpet wool is an important export from the Northwest but the Chinese could increase their rug production, supply themselves with more labor and create larger quantities for foreign exchange. Scouring plants for wool should be installed at interior points.

Bristles are exported and a modern processing factory was set up in Chungking during the war. It appears that demand for bristles will continue for certain types of brushes.

Camel hair production can probably be increased to meet foreign demands and improved processing may aid such production.

Hides and Skins. Modern methods of tanning are beginning to be used in small factories in China, but the industry is in its initial stages. Use of leather for western types of shoes and other leather products is increasing. Since China produces large quantities of hides and skins (her density of animal population is as great as that of the United States) the tanning industry will undoubtedly be one of the big developments.

Special Products. Processing of tea for quality grades in large quantities is the only way by which China can increase her tea trade. Modern methods are in use in Formosa and should be adopted on the mainland.

Tung-oil has been one of China's chief exports and its grading in recent years has met foreign market requirements. However, the possibility of improving present methods of extraction requires attention.

Timber production in China is large and transportation of it is chiefly by floating down streams and rivers. There are still a few virgin forests, but they are not easily accessible. Large supplies of timber are also imported for use in coastal and river ports. It is probable that the use of modern sawmill equipment would be economical.

The handicraft industry for export as well as for domestic trade can be developed on a large scale. Most of the raw products would be from the farm or forest and a few are imported.

V. REQUIREMENTS FOR ACHIEVEMENT IN AGRICULTURE

The success of any agricultural program is also dependent upon the type of trained personnel. The amount of trained personnel in China is entirely too small to adequately care for the immense agricultural problems in China. Until there is general education throughout the country, there is no possibility of sufficiently trained agricultural personnel becoming available.

One of the difficulties in China has been that many officials and the general public have not recognized the importance of agriculture in the national economy. In recent thinking, a great deal of emphasis has been placed on industrial development without much reference to agriculture.

The family-farm system of agricultural production is the most practical of all methods for China and will probably continue. Attempts at collective and state farming, modelled after the Russian system, will undoubtedly be made but sudden universal application of collective or state farming is not to be expected. Those who advocate it are in the minority and do not understand the farm management problem involved. The physical factors such as topography, crops and climate are much more varied in China and create production problems quite different from those in Russia.

Under the influence and pressure of reformers, so-called "cooperative farms," collective farms and state farms will be tried in limited areas. It is best that such experiments should be made to avoid a country-wide innovation which would undoubtedly increase costs of production and, hence, costs of food for the consumer. Small experiments will demonstrate success or failure. If they are a failure, the reformers will have to give in. If successful, the method can be applied on a larger scale. The experiments may be costly but it seems to be the only way to resolve present-day contentions.

China is, and must remain, an agricultural country in spite of all possible industrialization. Her resources, according to all present information, are scarcely enough for her own industrialization, although she may have surpluses for export of tin, tungsten, antimony and mercury. At best, she cannot expect to reduce her farm population to less than 50 percent of her total population. This has a different meaning than it would appear to have. At the present time one-fifth of the farmer's income is from sources other than the farm, partly from home industries. With industrialization in China the opportunity for farmers in home industries and local small scale industries will probably increase. The development in China will be one of farmers going into industry for part-time employment, whereas in the United States one sees the industrial worker going into farming as an adjunct to his industrial employment.

Most of the discussion about industrialization in China is misleading and it is probable that not one person in a hundred understands its meaning or import. China's chief concern should be with increasing production per capita. This may be done with her present resources in the fields of both agriculture and industry. There is a tremendous surplus of labor on the farms, which could be used to develop irrigation and drainage projects; to improve land and water transportation; to develop water power, to better land use with proper control of soil and water; to proceed with re-afforestation of mountains; to manufacture farm supplies; to produce improved seeds, nursery stock and improved animals; to process agricultural products for marketing and for consumption; to manufacture improved types of consumer goods; and to develop heavy industry. Utilization of this large resource could be accomplished by a "labor" tax for those who have no money and a money tax for those with wealth. The projects would result in increased production per capita and greater efficiency in production and transportation, and would benefit the taxpayer. In other words, full utilization of labor and capital resources as well as the natural resources within the country would bring about increased production per capita, and therefore a higher standard of living.

Throughout China the peasants support themselves with supplementary occupations. The village on the Yangtze Plain described by Dr. Fei (Selection 79) specializes in the silk industry; in other regions there are other ways of increasing income. The following selection tells of maintenance practices in South China—in Phenix Village, not far from the port city of Swatow. Daniel H. Kulp described this village in 1925, and his study has become something of a classic in the field. There were 650 people in Phenix at the time of the study. Note that peasant villages are never completely self-subsistent; although each family tries to meet its own needs as much as possible, it must still turn to others for required products and services. The market town, where a farmer can sell his surplus produce and then buy needed articles, plays a very important part in the peasant economy (see Selection 81). Many of the simpler needs, however, can be supplied by specialists in his own village or even within his larger kinship group.

• 82 • *Maintenance Practices in a South China Village*
DANIEL H. KULP, II

Farming is the basic industry of the region. It is not the extensive type found north of the Yangtse River, but intensive gardening, with the hoe as the chief implement. Orchards and gardens surround the village; they are particularly large on the north, and east across the

[Adapted from *Country Life in South China: The Sociology of Familism* . . . , Volume I—*Phenix Village, Kwantung, China,* Teachers College, Columbia University, New York, 1925. Pp. 84-101.]

Phenix River. On the south and west there are mainly gardens with a few groves of trees producing fruit and nuts.

The floods always threaten the farmer. Many times the waters will sweep the yams and peanuts from his gardens, but do not harm the trees. For this reason, the people have turned primarily to the development of orchards, thus saving themselves from starvation and ruin. There is not a single farmer in "Gwei Ho" dependent solely upon gardening for his subsistence.

The principal product of the district is oranges. Other products of major importance are, exclusive of rice and grains of other kinds, olives, bananas, persimmons, guava, plums, bamboo. These all grow above ground and are staple products. Cultivated to a less degree are sugar cane, pears, longan, loquat, walnuts, pomelo, lichi, pibaws, yams, peanuts, potatoes, peas, beans of various kinds, and berries of different types.

During the seasons of harvest of the various fruits, especially of plums, pears, pibaws and berries—the perishables—the Chaochow and Swatow markets are glutted and the price drops very low. Cooperative canneries should be opened throughout the region. Then the products could be marketed gradually and the people could secure better incomes from their labors without increased effort.

VILLAGE WEALTH

In general, it can be said that the economic life of the people is one of "deficit." The frequent floods keep them from wealth, as has already been noted. The men depend upon their orchards, which develops in the farmers a tendency to "wait." They get what they can from gardening but count it as extra to their income from fruits. Though they have little to spare, yet they are far from starvation.

There is no doubt that scientific cultivation would raise the income of these people. They do not understand how to improve their crops. Their bananas are small and thin; their plums are bitter; their peanuts are dwarfed. Only the persimmons approach perfection. They should, through farm-demonstration work, learn to select seeds, graft, spray and cleanse

the trees. They have ample time to cultivate in these ways. Only ignorance keeps them from producing fine crops, for the soil is deep and fertile alluvial deposit.

An occasional member of Phenix Village has amassed enough wealth to set up in a business venture but few have been successful. The dream of fortune has led many a young man to seek it in foreign lands. Those who are successful there send home regularly of their incomes. For the region as a whole, according to the consular reports for Swatow, during the year 1911 some three million emigrants in foreign parts remitted to their homes twenty-one million dollars.

Once in a while a fortunate villager returns home with wealth and foreign wife, trailing a flock of queerly-dressed children. It is thus quite natural that a father blesses a departing son. In his emigrant kin he finds an additional source of income. But the sons of luck are few. The majority of the emigrants from Phenix Village come back with empty hands, but richer through sad experience, or else in distant lands complete their journey to "West Heaven."

Some of the Phenix Village men have only migrated as far as Chaochow or Swatow where they are engaged in business. The young men are clerks in stores or banks and the older ones are partners in stores or banks. That one of the heads of the families is contemplating industrial enterprise is shown by his request to the writer for information on the cost of a machine to manufacture shoe nails. From these persons money is sent to their closest kin in Phenix Village.

In addition to their products and their emigrated kin, the third source of income for the families of Phenix Village is the ancestral property. This is established in the following manner: a man of wealth sets aside a part of his property which is not to be divided among his children after his death. This provision guarantees that his descendants, no matter how poor they may become, will have the means of offering sacrifice to his own departed spirit, supplying him with food, money and other things that mean happiness in the other world as they do in this. Such property is considered as belonging to the ancestor even though dead and not as owned by the group. It must be clearly distinguished from other property which may be owned by a familist-group. The income from it is known as the "ancestral fund." Since it is usually more than what is needed to carry on ancestral worship, the living descendants take turns in providing the things required according to custom for the sacrificial ceremonies and the feast that follows for the representative descendants of the ancestor worship. Whatever surplus exists, goes to that person who managed the ancestral property during the year in order to carry on ancestral worship. Inasmuch as some incomes from these ancestral properties are very large, the surpluses are objects of interest. In fact, they may be the only hope for some of the poverty-stricken families. But they further increase the incomes of the wealthy, for the rich are not therefore deprived of their privilege in administering the ancestral estate, providing for ancestral worship, and sharing in the surplus, according to the customary principles of rotation of responsibility.

OCCUPATIONS

The types of occupations by which the people maintain themselves are not numerous. Nevertheless, it is very difficult to determine the exact number of people who follow each type. Most of them pursue several different occupations at different times, according to their needs and opportunities.

Except for agriculture and some handicrafts, there is no special training for the work they do. They try one thing one day and leave it the next without any real loss to anyone. Sometimes they engage in pursuits not at all for commercial purposes, simply out of convenience or for their own needs. Such might be making bamboo-ware,—baskets, etc.,—cutting wood, fishing, raising geese and ducks, gathering fruit. They sell the products of such efforts when they need money or when there is a surplus over the home necessities.

A general division of labor between men and women is to be found in Phenix Village. The men attend to business matters and do most of the field work; the women carry on the home industries. Practically all the village wives, rich or poor, engage in the spinning and weaving of flax into cloth for their own use. The whirr of the spinning wheel . . . and the click of the loom are heard in every part of the village. The servants and slave girls may today sew, sweep, cook, cut wood, or spin, but tomorrow they may be hulling rice or drying it in the courtyard. . . . It is thus impossible to classify the people according to occupations.

Moreover, there are cooperative industrial undertakings, such as sugar-manufacture or boat-sailing of a temporary or irregular nature.

[The occupational distribution of Phenix Village is as follows, the principal occupations being marked with an asterisk:

Agricultural: *farmer, *gardener.
Industrial: *weaver (cotton, flax), woodcutter, carpenter, *fisherman, dyer, varnisher, cook, butcher, broom maker, boatman, silversmith, *bamboo-worker, beancurd maker (now stopped), livestock raiser, herb gatherer, sugar maker, mason, painter of pottery, tailor, hunter.
Professional: *merchant, *fruit dealer, teacher, official, preacher (Christian, now left), doctor, priest, servant, *clerk or salesman, tax collector, fortune teller, gambler, landholder, middleman.

Miscellaneous: emigrant, beggar, nibbler, parasitic idler.]

Some explanation of these occupations may serve to illuminate the manner in which the people carry on their economic activities. Of the two occupations listed under "agricultural," gardening is predominant. By "farmer" is meant all those whose greatest income derives from farming grains and cereals; by "gardener" is meant those who depend upon the cultivation of fruits and vegetables for their income. The farmer is, in most cases, somewhat of a gardener too, but the latter occupation is for him incidental.

Among the industrial and professional occupations butchering, fishing, woodcutting, sugar-making, hunting, landholding, and serving as a middleman are those which are carried on incidentally and intermittently by men. Similarly the women, in addition to their routine duties of the household, cooking, caring for the children, sewing, cleaning and so on, engage in broom-making, the manufacture of hemp twine, basketry, spinning, weaving cloth, raising geese, gathering herbs, and so on.

The prevalence of broom-making rests upon the practical needs of the housewives. They gather the wire grass from the hills, make up thirty to forty brooms in a day, take them to Chaochow where they sell them for an average of one cent apiece and so add to the family income.

Bamboo is very common and is used in a great variety of ways. The shoots of the young trees of certain species are dug up as soon as they break through the ground and are sold for food. One kind, known as the "incense frame" bamboo, is not edible and is allowed to grow to maturity. This is cut down and sold in bulk for the manufacture of incense frames. One hundred *catties,* about one hundred and thirty pounds, sell for thirty to fifty cents, local currency. This type of bamboo is used in the manufacture of baskets, furniture, drying frames, sun shades, beams and pillars in huts, string, rope, fishing tackle, and so on almost *ad infinitum*.

The gathering of medicinal herbs is also an occupation based upon the needs of the home. People regularly scour the nooks and crannies of the hills and mountains in search of the wild plants reputed to possess curative properties.

There are practically as many wholesale fruit dealers as general merchants. The former buy the fruits before the harvest is even ripe; sometimes, when the trees are only in bloom.

The gamblers listed refer to those who keep houses especially for gambling and opium smoking and make a living thereby. Their shops are located just on the northern end of the business section of the village. Being responsible for the good conduct of their patrons, they are men of physical strength, members of strong "branches" of the familist group. They always stand ready, with the assistance of men who have specialized in boxing, to quell disorder or prevent outside interference. Among these the village parasites are found. They pander to everyone in the gambling house and beg gifts from the winners.

THE VILLAGE MARKET

Those who carry on single and clearly distinguishable occupations are the shopkeepers and clerks. Of the twenty-one open shops in the business section only five are run by merchants who are members of the Phenix Village familist-group. The others are rented by people from outside who have come in to do business with Phenix Village.

These shops serve not only the people of Phenix Village but also those of nearby villages who need business service. To meet these needs the shops provide the distributive service. They procure the goods and offer them for sale. It is significant that competition works out here as everywhere. [It is interesting] that thirteen out of twenty-one [shops] deal in food. The others comprise the paper shop, dry-goods shop, coffin shop—the coffins are made and sold in this shop, sometimes to order—and the distinctly service shops, such as barber, opium, and dye shops.

Complete independence of familist economy does not exist either for any part of the village kin-group or for the village as a whole. This market mediates goods between the local producers and the village consumers of ordinary and occasional products and between the city producers and the rural consumers of extraordinary and incidental products.

The meat shops sell pork almost exclusively and some dried fish. The only meat the home produces is from chickens or geese, but the people find it more profitable to sell these and buy bits of pork as they need it.

The food shops sell vegetables, oil, and the like. This provides village families with a wider range of selection of foods for their diets than would be possible were they compelled by the inconvenience of markets to depend solely upon their own products. They grow a limited number of vegetables; other gardeners grow other kinds, and a monotonous diet is thus broken up by buying the different kinds of vegetables put on the market from other gardens.

The work of women is so varied, so important, and so interesting that it is worthy of special and extended treatment. It is possible here only to note its chief phases.

There is no evidence that children are exploited although they are engaged in incidental occupations. Thus they watch the geese, carry water, and assist in the simpler operations about the home. In general the children seem to have too much time for idling.

THE WORK OF WOMEN

The women are engaged primarily in the home work of cooking of food. In the larger homes . . . the kitchens contain the regular large Chinese stoves. These are made of brick, with two pans placed over two fire boxes, quite small and fed with fuel through small openings in the front. The pans are covered with wooden covers; one pan is for cooking rice—which is always steamed—and the other for vegetables and meat.

Frequently, however, the housewives prefer the simple "wind-stove" or *feng-lo* to the large stoves. These are placed in the passageway convenient to the kitchen but outside of it in order to keep the smoke and fumes out of the room in which the people usually eat. These little stoves require less work to handle and are very economical. By burning charcoal in them they are very much cleaner than the large stoves that require ordinary stick-wood and underbrush as fuel. No coal is used for cooking.

Other regular duties are the making of the beds, care of the rooms, sweeping and dusting. When these are attended to, the housewife embroiders or sews for the family. Or she may spin, or weave, make twine, starch it and sun it, make baskets, or prepare rice for cooking. The latter takes much time and falls entirely within the women's sphere of labor and attention.

Quantities of rice are carried on the shoulders in buckets and spread out in the sun to dry. Several times during the day one of the women, probably a servant or slave girl who does the hard work in the wealthier families, will walk through the rice turning it over and over with her bare feet. The winnowing machine is carried into the court, the rice swept together and winnowed. Then it is kept in bags until it is carried out and hulled by pounding. Again it is winnowed, and when needed, is washed in water carried from the well or from the river, and steamed.

There are no conveniences of a modern kind in any of these rural homes even of the best. Women must carry the water; take care of the candles or oil lights—to-day generally of Standard Oil manufacture—and carry them from place to place as needed. The furniture is heavy, especially in the older and wealthier families, and therefore difficult to move about.

And yet life is simple. It does not take long to prepare food for four or five people. A pot of rice, a few vegetables and a bit of meat. Commonly they use in all about sixteen different kinds of vegetables and five kinds of meat, fresh, salt or dried. The latter includes only beef, pork, goose, duck and chicken, and fish.

The intellectual life of the women of all classes is hemmed in by such rural isolation and domestic drudgeries growing out of crude household arrangements. The installation of radio receiving sets could be afforded by at least half the homes of Phenix Village and would greatly relieve the monotony of the wealthier homes and the drudgery of the poorer. A simple village cooperative lighting system could be installed at relatively low cost. These are the only practical improvements that ought to be installed as soon as possible in Phenix Village. Many others could be suggested, but they could not be worked out nor would they be accepted on account of the expense involved.

THE MIDDLEMAN

In addition to the foregoing types of work there should be added three more. Middlemen are very important functionaries in village life. They are necessary because of attitudes of avoidance that prevail among the villagers whenever any situation has possibilities of embarrassment or strain between the people involved. The desire to avoid "losing face" which is the popular phrase for avoiding the feeling of inferiority—or stated positively, the wish for dominance—leads them to deal through intermediaries in land transactions, quarrels, betrothal and marriage, and the determination of prices for products, chickens, pigs, crops and so forth. The women and some farmers use the middleman for their important transactions of the latter sort. The middlemen secure commissions on such work and in the case of land transactions manipulate for "fat" commissions.

This is not a distinct occupation in itself but rather a functional relationship assumed and discharged as occasion offers. In time certain people get the reputation of success through their patience and cleverness. Going back and forth among people in the village and outside, learning confidential matters in connection with the "deals" they put through, they are reservoirs of news and information, which they frequently turn to profit. They are in a sense the village newspaper and feed village conversation with matter for gossip.

BEGGARS

Then there are the nibblers and beggars. The former hang around the streets and food shops and maintain themselves by snatching bits of food whenever the opportunity arises.

The beggars are usually those physically handicapped by heredity or disease, and are thrown upon the mercy of their fellows for maintenance. Their plaintive wail is always most oppressing. Here is a song of the blind:

Oh . . . . !
Teacher, matron and maid,
Do good and help us!
Save us blind children,
Poor blind children!
Parentless children!
Grandfather is sick,
Homeless, poor people, are we!
O . . . . h!
Save us! Oh, save us, rich people!

In the economy of Phenix Village, the beggar in his own way performs a social function as definitely as the farmer, the teacher, the fruit dealer or the gambler. The devout Buddhist hopes to gain "West Heaven," but charity and alms are the fundamental means, enjoined by the priests, of gaining that happiness. The beggar provides the object upon which the faithful may bestow his alms and pity and thus add to his credit in heaven. This is the basis of the kindly feeling that people take in beggars, loathsome as they may be.

In conclusion, the distinctive occupations of the village are agricultural,—farming and gardening, and mercantile. The mercantilists constitute a group larger than the agriculturists: almost one-tenth of the entire village population is engaged in the distribution function.

Exclusive of the types of vocations of the emigrants and the ordinary duties of the housewives, there are in all thirty-nine definite forms of maintenance activities to be found in Phenix Village, comprising productive, service, or parasitic functions.

Social Organization: Familism and Village Life

>>>

A peasant society is likely to be strongly familistic. By now it should be clear that the family is the basic economic unit in peasant China, as it is in most rural societies. Even in the United States, where farm people make up only 15.6 percent of the total population, the ideal seems to be the family-sized farm, which can be taken care of by the members of the family and can provide them with an adequate level of living. But there the comparison with China ends, for our society is not *familistic*.* We tend to stress individualism and to devote segments of our lives to many activities that have little to do with family-centered values. Therefore, as we read about the Chinese family, we must be prepared to notice its all-pervading influence as a pattern of association. The various selections will show the characteristics of the husband-wife, parent-child, in-law, and sibling and cousin relationships, and also follow the processes of socialization and social control through the daily routine.

• 83 • Familism the Foundation of Chinese Social Organization
CHENG CH'ENG-K'UN

Long before the collapse of the Manchu Monarchy in 1911. the social organization in China was founded on a large family system. This system exercised such a powerful influence

[Adapted from "Familism the Foundation of Chinese Social Organization," *Social Forces*, Vol. 23, No. 1, Baltimore, 1944. Pp. 50-59. Used by permission.]

* *Familism.* A social system wherein all behavior, all standards, ideals, attitudes and values arise from, center in, or aim at the welfare of those bound together by the blood nexus fundamentally. The family is therein the basis for reference, the criterion for all judgments. Whatever is good for the family, however that good is conceived, is approved and developed; whatever is inimical to the interests of the family, however they are formulated, is taboo and prohibited (Kulp, *Country Life in South China*, page xxix).

453

that it completely dominated the thoughts and actions of the Chinese people. It taught them the necessity of cooperation, courtesy, patience, and self-control in family relationship. It bred in them a sense of filial obligation toward their parents and respect for their elders. It inculcated in their minds the supreme importance of working for the honor and glorification of the family name. It caused them "to sweep snow in front of their own door, and not to bother about the frost on the roof of their neighbors." It aroused in them family consciousness and not national consciousness, and made them eager to fight for the protection of the graveyards of their ancestors and reluctant to shoulder arms in defense of their country.

How did this large family system come to play such a vital part in the organization of the Chinese nation? It all started more than four thousand years ago when that country was still largely wild and unexplored. There were impenetrable jungles, ravaging floods, and ferocious animals. The people were mostly nomads without fixed habitations and without uniform codes of conduct. [This traditional "history" is somewhat oversimplified.] At that time the advantages of farming had just come to the attention of the government. Emperor Shun recognized that the cooperation demanded in settled agriculture could be achieved only through standardization of human relationships. As a measure of insuring success in this new form of economic enterprise, he, therefore, laid down "Wu Tien" or "the five canons" for the purpose of regulating the relations between sovereign and subject, father and son, elder and younger brothers, husband and wife, and between friends. Of these five canons, three were directly connected with the family, and of the three, filial piety or devotion to and respect for one's parents was the most rigidly and widely applied.

After more than ten centuries of application, filial piety became firmly entrenched in the social order of China. It was upheld by law and sanctioned by philosophers. In Book II of the epoch-making document, *The Constitution of Chow,* supposedly written by the famous Duke of Chow somewhere around the 11th century B.C., it is stipulated that filial piety is the first of the six proper modes of conduct to be taught to the people and that the punishment of the unfilial is the first of the eight laws of punishment. In *Hsiao Ching* or *Classic of Filial Piety,* which is assigned to Confucius and one of his outstanding disciples, Tseng Ts'an, it is also stipulated that there are three thousand offenses against which the five punishments are directed, and none of them is greater than being unfilial.

THREE PRINCIPLES OF FAMILISM

Filial Piety. What was filial piety as applied by the Chinese people? In a country like China where "society" as an idea of human organization did not exist and where nationalism was never greatly developed because of her rarely challenged position, filial piety acquired a great variety of applications. Most of these applications were made and maintained as a result of the approbative evaluations of Confucius, Mencius, and other philosophers of their times. Filial obedience has been recognized the world over as an important virtue of man. But, in China, it was carried to the extreme. Chinese children were not allowed to talk back to their parents, to ignore their commands or thwart their wishes. They were discouraged from criticizing the acts of their father and mother even if these acts were heinous and wicked. Confucius once said: "A man may gently remonstrate with his parents. But if he sees that he has failed to change their opinion, he should maintain an attitude of deference and not oppose them."

Obedience was not the only application of filial piety in China. The Chinese people also served their parents with great devotion and respect. They honored them and supported them and would not do anything which was disgraceful to them. They believed that while parents were alive, a good son should not wander too far afield. They considered a man filial if he followed the footsteps of his parents and did not deviate from their ways. . . . They maintained that the highest achievement of true filial piety was to serve, by means of sacrificial offerings, "those now dead as if they were living."

Furthermore, a filial son in China would take very good care of himself because his body was given to him by his parents. Also he should not show such attachment to his wife and children as to neglect "the nourishment of his parents." Above all, he should have offspring to carry on the name of his family. Once, in his discussion of the last mentioned subject, Mencius enumerated three things which were unfilial, namely: to be without posterity, to encourage parents in unrighteousness, and to desist from giving them succour in their poverty and old age. Of the three, in the opinion of the philosopher, to be without posterity was the most unfilial.

In this great variety of applications, filial piety constituted the first principle of familism in the social organization of China. Many Chinese rulers in history encouraged it by their own examples and, practically all of them, by giving awards of one kind or another to those who had been unusually devoted to their parents. Even alien rulers like the Manchus considered its preservation and promotion of paramount significance to their regime. In 1670 Emperor K'ang Hsi issued an edict of sixteen moral maxims, the first of which enjoins the people to pay great attention to filial piety in order to give due weight to human relationship. After his death, his son and successor, Yung Cheng, caused these maxims to be enlarged and improved, and in 1724 the new emperor decreed that they be read to the people on the first and the fifteenth of each month in every city and town throughout the empire. The decree was in force all the way down to the end of the nineteenth century.

Devotion of Younger Brother to Elder Brother. The second principle of familism was the devotedness of the younger brother to his elder brother. In his oft-quoted "Announcement" to his nephew, the Duke of Chow considered those who were unfilial and unbrotherly more detestable than murderers. The importance attached to love and respect for one's elder brother among the Chinese people may be gathered from the fact that in the past nothing could be a better testimony of virtue than for a man to be spoken of by his relatives and friends as a "dutiful son" and "good brother."

Attitude of Wife toward Husband and Parents-in-Law. The third principle of familism was the proper attitude of a wife to her husband and her parents-in-law. In China when a woman was married she went to live with her husband in the family of his folks. She was expected to serve him, obey his orders, and not to thwart his wishes. It would be in contradiction to the mores for her to leave him under almost any circumstances. The Chinese people conceived of husband as heaven and wife as the earth and, to them, it was against reason for a married woman to change her feeling of duty toward her mate.

More important than the attitude of a woman to her husband was her attitude to her parents-in-law. In China the position of a woman in the family of her husband was extremely difficult. She was supposed to serve her parents-in-law with all human care, courtesy, and respect. According to customary practices handed down from legendary time, at the first crowing of the cock, the daughter-in-law should arise and dress and tidy herself. Then she should go to her parents-in-law and inquire about their health, bring in the basin for them to wash, prepare their breakfast and serve it to them with good cheer. She should maintain the same degree of alertness throughout the day and execute their orders promptly, efficiently, and willingly. Furthermore, she should observe all the rules of decorum in their presence and should neither spit, cough, sneeze, yawn, nor stretch herself, nor lean against anything, nor look askance. These and many other duties used to require as long as three months of instruction before a woman was adequately prepared to enter the house of her husband as wife and daughter-in-law.

UNIQUE FEATURES OF FAMILISM

Complexity. The Chinese family was highly complex when viewed from the standpoint of size. In China it was not uncommon to find thirty or forty relatives living in the same household. [Dr. F. L. K. Hsu reminds us that the large family ideal was achieved mostly among the wealthier families, and that the actual mean or average size of all families is about 5.2 persons, or even less. Just the same, the ideal itself has proven an important social force. These relatives usually included husband and wife and their children, the parents and the grandparents of the husband, his brothers, sisters, cousins, and his brothers' wives. As the children grew up and married, the size of the family increased by the natural process of propagation. To the Chinese people who knew little better than the agricultural mode of life their ancestors had developed, the size of the family meant its economic power. And it was on this basis that they considered it the acme of good fortune to have "five generations under one roof."

The complexity of the Chinese family was greatly intensified by the concubinage system. This system was in existence for more than four thousand years. The legendary sovereigns of China including Huang Ti or The Yellow Emperor and Emperors Yao and Shun all practiced polygyny. In the early part of the Chow Dynasty (1122-255 B.C.) it was a custom for the sovereign to have six grades of spouses representing an aggregate number of one hundred and twenty-six. At the end of the dynasty the custom was changed and the number of spouses of a man depended upon his social status. . . . Among the masses monogamy was the rule. This change in custom continued until the Ch'ing Dynasty (1644-1912) when wealthy farmers and merchants also took concubines. Between 1912 and 1931 many of the ignorant and irresponsible warlords exploited the system to satisfy their lust for sensual pleasure.

The development of concubinage in China was a natural social phenomenon. However evil the system might seem from the modern point of view, its existence was traditionally considered indispensable among the Chinese people. To them, nothing could be more disastrous than for a family to have no male offspring to carry on its name. Therefore, a man was justified to take a concubine or concubines if his wife failed to give birth to a son. This justification was so widely accepted that throughout the ages all government regulations of the system were carefully qualified so that those who did not have male offspring would not be unduly affected. . . . [In the description of Taitou Village (Selection 15) note how uncommon concubinage actually is among the farm people.]

In such a complex family organization, all its members were assigned to their proper positions for the purpose of facilitating the maintenance of domestic harmony. These members included both relatives from a direct line like parents and their children and grandchildren, and those from collateral lines like aunts, uncles, nieces, nephews, cousins, and other more distant relatives. Attached to their respective positions were their respective rights and duties. These rights and duties changed with the change of status of the individual. In the case of a male member, his status was determined by age in conformity with the long-established Chinese social practice. In the case of a female member, her status was determined not only by her age, but also by her ability to help increase the male population of the family. In her relationship with men, a woman's status changed in the following order: Before marriage, she followed and obeyed her father and elder brothers; when she married, she followed and obeyed her husband; and after her husband's death, she followed her sons.

Authority. The second feature was the way by which the family was controlled as one functioning unit. Theoretically, the father was vested with absolute authority consistent with the superior status customarily assigned to men in China. But in actual practice, there was a division of labor between the sexes. While the father occupied himself mainly with the duties of earning a livelihood for the family and upholding its honor, the mother was the center of Chinese domestic life. She generally decided when and where her children should begin their schooling. She arranged the matters concerning their betrothals. She managed the business of the household and directed all the punctilious social relations with kith and kin. She attended to the ceremonies with regard to births, marriages, and deaths, and saw to it that the relationships among the various members of her family were satisfactorily maintained. In reality she held a very exalted position among her children as was amply demonstrated not only by the respect they paid to her when she was living, but also by the mourning rituals they observed after her death. According to Chinese tradition, both father and mother were placed in the same category for first degree mourning except when the father survived the mother.

To strengthen the power of parental control in the Chinese family, a system of mourning was developed. This system was conceived on the basis of kinship and included five degrees. The first degree was observed for father, mother, husband and husband's parents and extended over a period of three years (actually from 25 to 27 months).

From this elaborate system of mourning emerged the cult of ancestor-worship to further strengthen the power of parental control in the Chinese family. This cult conceives the idea that the departed spirits of the ancestors are still hovering somewhere in the neighborhood looking after the welfare of their descendants. In order to keep these departed spirits from losing their sense of justice, the living must continue to demonstrate their respect for the dead. One way of demonstrating such respect was to follow the footsteps of the ancestors and keep to the path of virtue. Evidences of this line of thinking can be found throughout the massive history of China. As early as the fourteenth century B.C. when P'an Keng, the seventeenth ruler of the Shang Dynasty (1766-1154 B.C.) was preparing to move his capital to a better location, his people were unwilling to go with him. Thereupon he made an epochal declaration in which he justified his preparation in these terms: "My present-ent undertaking to move the capital is to give repose and stability to the state. . . . Were I to err in my government . . . my ancestors would send down great punishment for my crime."

Another way of demonstrating respect for one's ancestors was the establishment of places where sacrificial offerings could be made to them after their death. In an ordinary family, the central hall was reserved mainly for this purpose. If the family split up as usually happened in three or four generations, several related families might have a common ancestral temple. In an official family the number of ancestral temples depended upon its status and influence.

In these ancestral halls or temples the Chinese people offered seasonal and anniversary sacrifices to their departed ancestors. During the day of sacrifice the filial son was expected to be deeply engrossed in thinking of his parents. In entering the hall or temple he would seem to see them in the places where their *Ling Wei* or spirit-tablets were set up. On leaving it he would seem to be arrested by hearing the sounds of their movements.

Family Solidarity. The third feature was the solidarity of the family. Centralization of domestic control in the hands of the parents and deification of them after their death were in themselves forces contributing to solidarity. But a more powerful force was the process of conditioning by which the corporate unity of the home was maintained. This process operated for the accomplishment of two chief objectives, namely: collective responsibility in behavior and mutual aid in livelihood. On the one hand children in China were taught that, whatever work they undertook, they must do it with the thought of glorifying the spirits of their ancestors and bringing honor to the family and not to disgrace their good names. In addition, the Chinese government system was such that the administrative authorities found it convenient to hold the family collectively responsible for the conduct of its members. In cases like treason against the State, the crime of one member might cause the death of the whole family irrespective of sex or age. Brought up in these forms of conditioning, the Chinese people naturally learned to think twice before they acted.

On the other hand, children in China were early impressed with the idea that security of the individual in the family lay in mutual aid among its members. They took nourishment of their parents and aged relatives as their first duties in life. They loved their brothers to the same degree as they loved their own "hands and feet." Sometimes a brother would travel thousands of miles across the sea and go through considerable privation to redeem the honor of a bankrupt brother. Oftentimes a successful man would willingly share his wealth with his relatives and use his influence to improve their economic status.

Feeling of Continuity. The fourth feature was the presence of a feeling of continuity in the family. To the Chinese people life was an unending process of succession. One generation died, another came up to take its place and the institutional functions of the family continued.

THE FAMILY AS AN INDEPENDENT SOCIAL UNIT

Circumscribed in this kind of organization, the Chinese large family existed very much as an independent social unit. It was self-contained, self-disciplined, self-perpetuating, and self-sufficient. It fulfilled almost all the functions of an organized society and made the feeling of attachment to it strong and irresistible. Economically, it represented the most radical form of socialistic cooperation. Within its four walls all members worked and lived together. They all did what they could and took what they needed. They were all partners in the same productive enterprise. In their various positions, they were all employers, employees, middlemen, and holders of property. Between them there were no essential differences in social condition. They shared wealth and prestige as well as poverty and degradation.

The operation of this form of socialistic cooperation depended on the subordination of desire for personal profit to the desire for virtue, the significance of which is repeatedly emphasized in Chinese classical literature.

Judicially, the Chinese people believed and practiced the ancient saying that . . . "Disgraceful affairs of the family are not to be made known outside." They kept domestic conflicts very much to themselves. Disrespectfulness to parents, parents-in-law and elders in general, unfaithfulness to husband, disloyalty to elder brothers, and violation of marriage customs were usually hushed up and adjustments made by the parents or, in more serious cases, by the family council which was composed of the elders of the household. When conflicts involved two or more families, the matters were customarily submitted to and settled by the elders of the village which, in reality, was "the family raised to a higher exponent." These village elders, together with the local gentry who were schooled in law and history, formed an unofficial tribunal in which most .of the civil disputes and petty criminal offenses were liquidated. That was why in spite of the fact that China possessed a minutely organized and dynastically revised system of law, her rulers never found it necessary to set up a separate law-enforcing machinery. The Chinese district magistrate was invested with judicial function, but at the same time, he was the warden of local prisons, the overseer of public roads, the registrar of land, the collector of taxes, the superintendent of education, and the commissioner of police.

Socially, members of the Chinese family were all insured against the many misfortunes of life. Whether the person affected was an orphan, a widow, a blind, a crippled, or a decrepit old man, he or she was taken as a charge of the family. Living in such a state of interdependence, the Chinese people never felt the need for organized relief outside the home circle. In fact, until the arrival of missionaries from Europe and America, there was no public philanthropic institution of any permanence within the confines of the Chinese nation.

Education was an important function of the family in China. There, scholars ranked first among the . . . four classes of the people and scholarship was always the basis on which government appointments were made. Nothing would do greater honor to the names of the ancestors than to have scholars and officials in the family. Hence, Chinese parents were generally enthusiastic about giving their intelligent sons every opportunity for education. In well-to-do families, private tutors were hired into the households to prepare the youths for civil examinations which were held periodically by the district, the provincial and the national authorities. In ordinary families, sons were sent to public schools or schools organized and supported by the villagers themselves.

Religious ceremonies constituted another important function of the family in China. Besides worshipping their departed ancestors, the ancient Chinese people worshipped "the spirits of the famous hills, the great streams . . . the land and grain" and made offerings to cats and tigers because they devoured rats and wild boars which destroyed crops in the field. But as a result of the introduction of Buddhism [see the brief explanation of Buddhism which follows this selection] into the country during the first century A.D., the form and content of their worship underwent considerable changes. In their rites of burial and mourning the changes were particularly deep-rooted. As late as the second decade of the present century, the Chinese people were still observing the rites of propitiating the dead which aimed at appeasing the hungry ghost in "Hell" and keeping them from attacking the dead and at invoking the "Compassionate Spirit" so that the dead would be reborn in the "Paradise in the West," the Buddhist concept of "Heaven." Despite the influence of Buddhism religious ceremonies remained essentially a function of the Chinese family.

Like everything else in China, recreation bore the imprint of family influence. The Chinese people arranged and conducted their birthday and wedding ceremonies and annual festivities mainly on the basis of kinship. They dined, wined, drank tea and enjoyed theatrical performances together. Yet they never developed any "community spirit" or feeling of "civic consciousness." They were family-minded and not social-minded. None of the sports which they indulged in called for team-work. Even in card games like mahjong, each person played for himself.

Viewed as a social system, the large family in China worked with considerable effectiveness in a settled agricultural economy. Started from the legendary Emperors Yao and Shun, it stood well the test of forty centuries. It was encouraged in the belief that a nation of cultivated persons and properly regulated families should make a good nation. This belief emphasized the cultivation of the right mental attitude of the individual in human relationship as the most fundamental social function. Confucius regarded it as the key to the establishment of a state of peace and tranquility which he called "the highest excellence." He said: "Trees have their roots and their branches. Affairs have their ends and their beginnings. . . . In ancient time, those who wished to bring about enlightenment to the world, first ordered well their own states. Wishing to order well their states, they first regulated their own families. Wishing to regulate their families, they first cultivated their persons. Wishing to cultivate their persons, they first rectified their hearts. . . ."

Chinese Social Norms. To facilitate the cultivation of the right mental attitude, Confucius developed a system of philosophy which included the three ethical principles of righteousness, benevolence, and propriety. [The latter, in particular,] was a process of social education by which the people were taught to know that to be righteous and benevolent, "the father should be affectionate, the son should be filial, the elder brother should be kindly, the younger brother should be devoted, the husband should be loving, the wife should be submissive, the aged should be gracious, the young should be reverent, the friend should be sincere . . . " This process of social education operated to inculcate into the minds of the people from early childhood a proper understanding of their respective social positions together with their various relationships and duties.

So far, the large family system in China is rapidly being liquidated. The disruptive forces created by industrialization, urbanization, governmental actions in the nature of economic, social, and political reform, civil wars and external conflicts during the last hundred years have all combined to hasten this process of liquidation. But the break-up of the system has not been accompanied by a corresponding rapidity in the reorientation of the mental attitude of the Chinese people. In spite of the introduction of modern education, the influence of four thousand years of familistic tradition is still predominant in practically all phases of their national life. Without a comprehensive knowledge of the development and extent of this influence, it would be difficult to understand the titanic problems which are confronting China in her efforts to adjust herself to the modern world.

Earlier selections have already provided sidelights on the religious life of the Chinese peasant and its connection with the family. To tie together all this miscellaneous information we should first examine standard definitions* of Buddhism, Taoism, and Confucianism and then turn to an article which examines the Chinese religion from the standpoint of daily behavior.

Buddhism. The religion based upon the doctrine originally taught by Gautama Buddha [who lived in India in the sixth to fifth centuries B.C.]. The Great Enlightenment consisted in a perception of the causes of suffering and of the way of salvation from suffering. Buddhism teaches that *Nirvana,* release from liability to suffering, from mortality, is the highest goal attainable, now or hereafter. All beings, gods or men alike, are in need of such salvation. Buddha denied the special virtue of caste, ritualism, and asceticism, and insisted upon the necessity of pity, kindliness, and patience for salvation. Buddhism has developed and still embraces many sects. Buddhism spread through central, eastern, and southeastern Asia, and to Ceylon but is practically extinct in India proper.

Confucianism. The philosophical system of Confucius and his disciples, the basis of much of Chinese ethics, education, statecraft, and religion. Filial piety, benevolence, justice, propriety, intelligence, and fidelity are cardinal virtues. [Confucius lived in China in the sixth to fifth centuries B.C. Mencius was a later Confucian philosopher.]

Taoism. A religion and philosophy of China. Its traditional founder was Lao-Tse, sixth century B.C. Its greatest classic, the *Tao Te Ching,* teaches conformity to the Tao ["The Way"] and simplicity of social and political organization. Taoism is a liberal religion in contrast to the conservative absolutism of Confucianism. Later, the system largely degenerated into magic. Both magical and philosophical Taoism still survive.

• 84 • Chinese Religion and Ancestor Worship
FRANCIS L. K. HSU

The so-called "Three Religions" are: Buddhism, Taoism, and Confucianism. Considerable amounts of ink have been spilled over the question whether Confucianism is a religion or not. Such arguments are irrelevant, for religion in China does not follow the pattern

* Adapted from Webster's *New International Dictionary.* For fuller discussion, see Howard Becker and Harry Elmer Barnes, *Social Thought from Lore to Science,* 2nd ed. (Washington, Harren Press, 1952).

of interreligious exclusiveness of the West; there is no sharp dividing line as between Christians and Mohammedans, or even between Presbyterians and Baptists. Theological formulations may be argued by a few learned monks or priests but the average man has no interest in such things.

CHINESE RELIGION IN ACTION

The first thing that impresses one on entering a Chinese village or market town is the size and number of the temples. The temples are brightly colored, whereas ordinary houses are gray or brown.

The temples are dedicated to a variety of gods, as the Dragon God or the Goddess of Mercy, or they may be dedicated to dignitaries of the community who were deified after death. In market towns, and particularly in district cities there are usually three other kinds of temples: to the God of Wealth, to Confucius, and to the district patron god, who is equivalent in the spiritual hierarchy to the district magistrate in the political one. Several others may also be found, including temples to the Goddess of Measles and to San Kuan (literally three gods—heaven, earth, and man). In some villages there is one to the Sun God, and in the towns and cities there are frequently temples to the God of Agriculture, or the God of War, or to Lu Chu, the most important Taoist god.

Most of the temples, however, house more than one God. Usually they are sacred to a number of gods or goddesses who are from what would be, judged by Western standards, different religions. Consider, for example, a modest temple of the patron of a town in Southwest China. The main altar is dedicated to the patron god, who in this case has the appearance of a warrior. The two side altars are occupied, respectively, by the Goddess of Measles and of Mercy. In front of the main altar are some tablets and images dedicated to the third son of the Dragon God and some lesser spirits.

Identical patterns prevail in ritualistic observance as well as in the concrete arrangements of the temple. To quote from one of my notebooks:

Today saw old Mrs. Y with two grandsons and three granddaughters in the Pan Chu Temple. Offerings are made to every god (that is, every image) in the whole temple, both inside and outside the main hall. Even the dragons winding around the two main pillars of the main entrance received a share of the "food and money."

The old lady first burns paper money in front of the three main shrines. There are four gods occupying these shrines. As the paper burns she kneels down to koutou [kneel and strike the forehead on the ground, whence derives English "kowtow"] fifty times to each of the four gods.

When these gestures of homage are over, she takes some of the food offered at the main shrines and puts it in a tray. She takes this tray and offers it in front of every other image in the temple one by one. In front of each image the procedure is as follows: She offers the tray by lifting it up with both hands to a position over her head. She lays it on the table. She burns some paper money. She kneels to koutou eight or more times. She prays only to the first four gods as she kneels to koutou.

The old lady on this occasion went to express gratitude and to report to the local patron god on the third day after the birth of a grandson; but she wanted to make sure that all gods, whether directly concerned or not, would be pleased, so that the child would grow up well. The yearly cycle of offerings to the gods observed in the same community reflects a similar attitude. Altogether thirty-four days of ritual observances are recorded for the community throughout the year. These include the birthdays of thirty different gods and one occasion on which all gods are worshipped.

[Adapted from *Most of the World: The Peoples of Africa, Latin America, and the East Today*, Ralph Linton, ed., Columbia University Press, New York, 1949. Pp. 775-781. Used by permission.]

During any emergency, such as an epidemic, drought, earthquake, or even after Japanese air raids, prayer meetings take place at which numerous gods and spirits are invoked. At one of these meetings, one scripture contained 608 gods with specific titles, including Jesus Christ and Mohammed, who are called sages and are subordinate to the Jade Emperor, the supreme ruler of heaven. Then the scripture goes on as follows:

In addition to the above the following gods are hereby invoked: Gods of ten directions; all fairies and sages; all fairy warriors and soldiers; ten extreme god kings; gods of sun, moon and nine principal stars; three officers and four sages; the stars of five directions; gods guarding four heavenly gates; thirty-six thunder gods guarding the entire heaven; twenty-eight principal stars of the Zodiac; gods for subjugating evil ghosts; god king of flying heaven; great long life Buddha; gods of Tien Kan and Ti Tze; great sages of Trigrams and Nine Stars; secondary officials of five directions; secondary officials of ten directions; gate gods and kitchen gods; godly generals in charge of year, month, day and hour; gods and spirits in charge of four seas, nine rivers, five mountains, four corners; of hills, woods, all rivers and lakes, wells and springs, ditches and creeks, twelve river sources; every and all gods; Cheng Hwangs and their inferiors; local patron gods; minor local officials; gods of roads and bridges; of trees and lumber; spiritual officers and soldiers under the command of priests; all spirits in charge of protecting the taboos, commands, scriptures and the right way of religion.

THE SPIRIT WORLD

The Chinese believe strongly in an after life; in their conception, the spirits of the dead are closely bound to earth and interested in human affairs. The spirit world is divided into three parts: first, the Upper Heaven, ruled over by an Emperor with an extensive hierarchy of gods beneath him; second, the Western Heaven, where Buddha is the supreme ruler, also with a large group of high gods all of whom are subordinate to the ruler of the Upper Heaven (the exact relationship of the Upper and Western Heavens is never clearly expressed); and third, the Lower Spirit World where the spirits of the dead enter and are processed according to their record on earth. A ruler with ten judges working under him goes over the records. Those who have led good lives are rewarded with titles, leisure, and comfort. Exemplary characters may become gods in the Upper or Western Heavens or may be reincarnated into another existence on earth in which they attain honor and luxury. The wicked are punished by severe tortures, such as being sawed in half or boiled in oil. They may be banished permanently into hell, or reincarnated into another life beset with poverty and degradation, or they may be reincarnated as worms or rats or other lowly animals.

In broad outline this concept is not far different from that held by Western society, but the spirit world and the world of humans is more closely allied in China than in the West. The Emperor of China was known as the Son of Heaven and many heroes of history and legend are considered to be gods reincarnated. New gods are continually being created and many return to earth in reincarnation. The emperor, as son of Heaven, has power over both humans and spirits. Even high bureaucrats, by virtue of the power vested in them by the emperor or because they are gods incarnate, have power over the lesser spirits.

Most important in this link between heaven and earth is the belief that spiritual reward or punishment may come in one's lifetime as well as after death, or may be visited upon one's children. Thus death by lightning, sudden and violent illnesses, as cholera, and serious accidents are generally regarded as punishments originating from the spirit world. For this reason the most important measure against epidemics and accidents is the prayer meeting, in which hired priests invoke the mercy of the superior deities who are presumed to have ordered the disasters as punishment against the community. Conversely, wealth and good fortune are usually held to be rewards originating from the spirit world in payment for good deeds performed by the recipient or his ancestors.

Thus the spirit world and the human world are counterparts of one another. The spirit world is based upon and functional to the existence of the world of humans, and the human world is in turn supervised and guided by the spirit world. They exchange personnel. They endorse the same virtues and condemn similar evils; they express mutual approval or disapproval. In the popular mind the spiritual hierarchy is a part of the social order just as much as the bureaucratic and political hierarchy is. That is why it is irrelevant or even erroneous to speak of different religions in China. To the Chinese there is only a spiritual order which stands as firm as the social order. As there is no question of a community living under two social orders, so it is inconceivable that there should be two spiritual orders. If two religions are both true, they must find their place in the existing hierarchy. A creed for which this adjustment cannot be made is destined to be disregarded or forgotten.

ANCESTOR WORSHIP

The basic religion of China is ancestor worship, but, here again, it is a mistake to regard the cult as a separate religion, for it is part of the larger, all-inclusive structure. The ancestors have gone through the life-death routine of all human beings; that is, they have died and been processed by the Lower Spirit World. They may have been so good that they were received directly into one of the Heavens. Also they may have been reincarnated. If they were evildoers they may have been doomed to eternal punishment; but ancestors, in so far as their descendants are concerned, are different from all other human beings. To their descendants, ancestors are all great men and women with a glorious past and an exalted status. One may believe that someone else's ancestors are in hell, or reincarnated in some base animal form, but no true descendant believes that such a thing could happen to his own ancestors.

To understand this cult one must take cognizance of the family organization and the father-son identification. Between the father and the son there is not only a complete community of interest, but complete social identification. The son not only inherits all his father possesses but he is judged by his father's achievements. Conversely, the father not only has complete rights over his son's wealth but, when the son has reached maturity, the father is evaluated by his son's abilities. When we realize that a particular father and son are but a link in the infinity of many generations in any given family line, we see how the father-son identification becomes the foundation for the religious cult of ancestor worship.

The basic assumptions of the cult are threefold. First, the living owe everything to the departed ancestors, who are, therefore, regarded as persons of great magnitude. Since death only puts the relationship on a somewhat different level, and since the dead have the same needs as the living (namely, food, money, housing, and so on) it is necessary for the descendants to provide for them as if they were alive. Secondly, while the ancestors have already made their imprint on the fate of the descendants, their actions in the spirit world continue to affect the living. Conversely, the actions of the living descendants have bearing on the spirits of the ancestors. Thirdly, the interest of the ancestors is confined to their own descendants, particularly lineal ones. They concern themselves not only with ceremonial occasions—weddings, division of the family, birth of sons—but also take action in emergencies, as when a deserving descendant is about to be flunked by the chief reader in an imperial examination. On ceremonial occasions the presence of the ancestors is recognized by offerings of incense and food. But on occasions of emergency, the ancestors intervene in the form of apparitions.

Thus the ancestral cult shows the same close interrelation between spirit world and human world and the same close correlation between religious structure and social organization. As the family is the foundation of the wider society, so ancestor worship forms the link between the individual and the supernatural.

Familism involves more than common production of economic necessities by family members and more than religion based on reverence for ancestors. It also is closely related to festivals and merrymaking. As we shall see in the following selection, the Chinese peasants have fun as families even more than they do as individuals separately pursuing their own particular recreational tastes.

• 85 • Festivals
T. F. WEI

Fortunately, the monotonous life of the hard-working Chinese is not without a break. Including the Autumn Festival, there are no less than six "Big Festivals" in a year on which people of every walk of life lay aside their work and take their leisure either for ancestor worship, religious ceremony, or feastings and amusements.

The first "Big Festival" of the year, *Ch'ing Ming,* falls on either April 5 or 6 in the Solar Calendar. It is but natural that with the arrival of the true spring of the year an agricultural people like the Chinese invoke the blessing of their ancestors by offering them the first fruits of the harvest newly sown and by refurnishing the mounds and the enclosures in which they may lie. In order to do honour to the spirits of the departed, the usual obeisance, such as the burning of incense-sticks and paper money, is performed before their tumuli.

Excepting those recently bereaved, one sees no sign of grief or mourning in the people wending their way through the country-side, early in the morning of *Ch'ing Ming,* to pay respect to the dead. Although here and there a woman in white "keens" (weeps sorely) over the new grave of her husband or father, the majority who go "to worship at the hill" are clad in clean clothes and assume rather a holiday air as befits those who are on their way to take part in a pleasant picnic.

In fact, besides the solemn duties connected with them, the *Ch'ing Ming* visits to the country-side are looked upon as the first real excursions of the year. School children are especially jubilant when led on an outing on the "Spring Holidays," which always include the *Ch'ing Ming,* although the latter being one of the lunar festivals no longer receives the official recognition of the school authorities.

Next comes the *Tuan Wu* or Dragon Boat Festival which always falls on the fifth day of the fifth moon.

To Western people, the *Tuan Wu* is better known as the Dragon Boat Festival. Dragon boat races are also held in the name of Chu Yuan [a great statesman-poet, fourth century B.C., who drowned himself in protest because an obstinate Prince refused to adopt his reforms], but the honour is supposed to extend to all of those drowned after him. Strikingly resembling dragons, these huge boats are gracefully slim but measure some 90 feet in length. They have high sterns with long steering-paddles rising many feet above the gunwales, while the prows are skillfully carved like a dragon's head with open mouth and cruel fangs and the long body between gaily painted to represent scales. No sooner is the starting signal given than the hundreds of paddles of the racing boats, each kept to time by a coxswain with a bright waving banner, send the slim dragons at top speed through the waters.

According to the Chinese tradition, the fifth moon is regarded as the most poisonous month of the year when the Five Venomous Animals appear: The Snake, the Scorpion, the Lizard, the Toad and the Centipede. Because of all the evil influences being rampant

[Adapted from "Chinese Festivals," *The China Journal,* Vol. 34, No. 3, Shanghai, 1941. Pp. 106-110. Used by permission.]

during the month, the Chinese people have invented a long list of charms and talismans to combat them. On the *Tuan Wu* day, special care is taken to keep off devils and all malevolent creatures, visible or invisible. In addition to hanging out pieces of green, called the calamus, cut in the shape of two-edged swords, and antemisia on their gate-posts, the old folks will insist that every one in the household drink a concoction of sulphur and cinnabar dissolved in wine, as a further guarantee against the undesirables. Mothers never forget to write, by using the wet dissolved sulphur as ink, the character *Wang,* meaning king, on her baby's face, as this ideograph resembles the wrinkle on the forehead of a tiger, the terror of all spirits. Five-coloured threads are tied to the wrists of youngsters to insure them long life and happiness.

The Third "Big Festival," *Chung Yuan,* falls in the middle of the seventh moon or the "Moon of Hungry Ghosts." Being the second *Ying Chieh* of the year, this All Souls' Day is also dedicated to the dead, but it is essentially different from the *Ch'ing Ming* in the fact that the beneficiaries this time are the unhappy spirits who no longer have human descendants to offer them timely sacrifices. It is thought that these hungry ghosts should not be long neglected, otherwise they are likely to meddle maliciously with human affairs. With the introduction of Buddhism into China, the festival, which is traceable to remote antiquity, has become identified with the Buddhist ceremony of the *Yu Lan P'en Hui* commemorating the month during which the souls are released from hell and permitted to wander about to enjoy the worldly hospitality. At the *Yu Lan P'en Hui,* Buddhist priests hold masses everywhere for lonely souls, or such spirits as have suffered injustice or met violent death in their lifetime.

As the service is drawing to a close, preparation is well under way for the start of a grotesque pageantry through the street. The procession is led by the giant figure of *Kwei Wang,* or King of the Devils, with the paper effigies of different ghosts, impersonating the drowned, the hanged and the poisoned, etc.

closely following. Taking part also are the paper imitations of houses, cars, furniture and money. Lastly come the priests continuously chanting the invocation "O mi to Fo"— "Buddha Amida."

The ceremony ends at an open space and always with a bonfire. Everything including the half-consumed incense-sticks must burn so that the ghosts may be able to take them away to the other world.

Exactly one month after the All Souls' Day arrives the Mid-Autumn Festival. This second Festival of the Living may be more appropriately called the Moon Festival as all the myths told of the Festival, carried down to our own days by the flowing stream of tradition, are associated with this luminary. In contrast with the light and heat, symbolic of the Sun, the Moon, typifying softness and cold, early came to be regarded by most peoples of the world as a feminine deity.

Speaking of the celebration of the Festival itself, the moon cakes are the distinctive offerings of the Feast. Just when the moon sails into the high heavens, the service begins. On the altar, plates are set out filled with moon cakes and round fruits like apples, peaches and grapes—all symbolising the full moon.

Now coming to the social pleasures, the feast is usually started in the evening and lasts to midnight—the hour when the moon is at the zenith of her brilliance.

The first of the 10th moon or *Shih Yueh Chao* is the last of the three Festivals of the Dead and decidedly the least celebrated of all the "Big Festivals." Visits are again paid to the ancestors' graves, and the way of offering sacrifices including food, burning incense and candles and paper money, is the same as seen at the *Ch'ing Ming.* Now that the autumn harvest is gathered, opportunity is taken of the comparative leisure of the men to inspect lonely grave-yards and provide coffins and grave-sites for the poor. Among the families recently bereaved, the ceremony known as "burning the clothes" is observed. Paper imitations of warm garments and other household necessities are packed into parcels with paper money and carefully addressed to the ghosts for whom they are intended. In rich families, paper figures of man-servants and maid-servants and imitations of almost all the luxuries of life, e.g., automobiles and houses, etc., are burned together with the other offerings so that the worshippers feel confident that the ghosts receive all the comforts of this world.

By far the greatest, longest, happiest and noisiest of all the Chinese festivals is the New Year. As much preparation is required for the prolonged festivities to come with the New Year, the season normally starts with the 20th of the 12th moon, when a regular housecleaning takes place in every home. On the 23rd (or in South China the 24th) sacrifice to *Tsao Chun,* the "Kitchen God" is offered as he is leaving that night to report on the behavior of each family during the past year to the Jade Emperor of *Yü Wang.* After his feast [has been eaten,] *Tsao Chün's* portrait is carried to the court-yard, either in a miniature sedan chair or on a paper horse. Facing the flames of burning candles and incense-sticks, the image is set alight and sent off skyward to the "Precious-Throne" of the Jade Emperor.

About a week after comes the last day of the year, the greatest paying and settling day among the Chinese. The custom requires that any one who is in debt must by now liquidate the outstanding accounts with his creditors. His failure to do so is considered a matter of great disgrace. However, if he sees no way of paying up, he hides till the New Year morning when he is immune, at least during the New Year holidays, from the bothering of his creditors.

On the New Year Eve the busiest souls on earth are the housewives. They must be responsible for the preparation of scores of dishes and seasonings to satisfy the appetites of both Gods and guests.

When the hour arrives for the offering of sacrifices to the ancestors and Gods, the master of the household, on behalf of his dependents, *ko't'ou* before the altar and ancestral tablets to express his deep gratitude for all the blessings they have so graciously bestowed upon the family during the past year.

After the religious rites are completed, the New Year Eve supper is served to which all members of the family must try their best to attend. Presently, salvos of fire-crackers announce the arrival of New Year and the noise will continue till the dawn of the next morning.

The first day of the year is usually spent at home. The streets are practically deserted and shops tightly shut. It is a day of purely family re-union. After the first day, people begin to make a series of calls on their blood relations and intimate friends.

Feastings, games and amusements complete the picture of the New Year celebrations, which usually last from 4 to 5 days in the cities but much longer in the country districts.

Even after one knows the statuses of family members and the roles each member plays in given situations, the picture is incomplete until one understands the motivational processes of socialization and social control and how these are tied in with differences in status. A good systematic treatment of these matters is afforded by Francis L. K. Hsu, whose book *Under the Ancestors' Shadow* provides one of the subtlest interpretations of Chinese family life.

A peasant society is usually village-centered. The village and the market town tend to make up the peasant's social universe. Wars or famines may uproot him temporarily, or even permanently prevent his return home, but always within him there is the sense of attachment for his own village. As long as he considers himself a peasant, the village is his normal social world. Those who, because of higher education or for other reasons, turn their backs on their peasant origin find it necessary to leave the village and dwell in towns and cities, where there is greater possibility of mobility up the social scale. But individuals such as these frequently have a poignant nostalgia for the village of their youth.

What is there about the village that takes such a hold on its people? Peasant villages are usually muddy in winter, dusty in summer; sanitary conveniences are minimal; work is at times laborious; social control is so strong that an individual can exercise only a limited freedom in his behavior. And yet villages survive as a major locality association for most of mankind. Perhaps it is simply habit; or perhaps Baker Brownell, a philosopher at Northwestern University, has, in his writings, put his finger on an important point. He maintains that in the small community one knows one's neighbors as whole personalities, one is familiar with the totality of the roles that they play, in contrast to the segmental acquaintanceship among people in urbanized areas.

As we have already noted, the family is the first major pillar of peasant life; the community is the second. Many villages in China are family villages in that they are inhabited by members of a single clan, who are interrelated. Many others are made up of people from two, three, or more clans. When the youngsters—or the elders, for that matter—leave the household, self-contained as it tends to be, they find a broader panorama of events in the village square. Commerce is carried on there; the village temple receives frequent visitors; the agents of the local government perform their duties near by; and any local gentry stop in at the tea house. The square also may be the setting for the dramas staged by itinerant actors, although the outskirts of town may be the preferred location.

The village theater, which has a strong hold upon the Chinese people, is being used effectively today by the Chinese Communist government to indoctrinate the people with the new ideology. How and why this is being done will be much clearer after the following account by Arthur H. Smith, whose book on village life in China has been a standard reference since its publication in 1899. Most of his statements still hold true today.

The preceding paragraphs apply to many villages in other parts of the world besides China. An old English village, described in Selection 128, fits the description neatly. In contrast, the villages of the United States vary considerably from their Old World prototypes, as may be seen in Selection 115.

• 86 • The Village Theater
ARTHUR H. SMITH

That the Chinese are extravagantly fond of theatrical representations, is well known to all who live in China. The Chinese trace the origin of the stage to the times of the Emperor Ming Huang, of the T'ang Dynasty (died 762) who, under an alias, is supposed to be worshipped as the god of play-actors. It is a popular saying that if the players neglect to do homage to this patron, they will altogether fail in their representations, whatever these may be.

According to the Chinese themselves, [the Chinese stage] has degenerated from its ancient function of a censor in morals,

[Adapted from *Village Life in China: a Study in Sociology*, Fleming H. Revell, New York, 1899. Pp. 54-69. Used by permission.]

and has become merely a device for the amusement of the people. It is a remarkable circumstance that while the Chinese as a people are extravagantly fond of theatrical exhibitions of all sorts, the profession of play-actor is one of the few which debars from the privileges of the literary examinations. The reason for this anomaly is said to be the degradation of the theatre by pandering to vitiated or licentious tastes. To what extent the plays ordinarily acted are of this sort, it is impossible for a foreigner to decide. The truth seems to be that the general (theoretical) contempt for the stage and its actors in China, is a product of the moral teachings of Confucianism, which uncompromisingly condemn the perversion of the right uses of dramatic representation. But while this (theoretical) view is the one which is constantly met, it is like many other Confucian doctrines, chiefly remarkable for the unanimity with which it is disregarded in practice.

Most Chinese plays are laid out upon so extravagant a scale, as regards time, that they may be spread over many hours, or possibly several days. The dialect in which the actors speak is so different from the spoken language, that it is hard [for the European] to form an idea of what they are saying. The tone adopted is that shrill falsetto, which is not only fatiguing to an Occidental hearer, but almost of necessity unintelligible.

When to these embarrassments are added the excruciating music, the discomfort attending the dense crowds, and the universal confusion which is an invariable concomitant of a Chinese theatre, it is not strange that these representations have for Westerners very few attractions, after the first glance has satisfied curiosity. This indifference on our part is almost unintelligible to the Chinese.

Except in a few large cities, the Chinese have no theatres in our sense of the term, provided with seats and enclosed by walls and roof. The stage is a very simple affair, and is entirely open to inspection. Sometimes it is built like a temple with an open front. But by far the larger part of the rural representations of theatrical companies take place on a temporary scaffolding which is put up for the purpose the night before the plays begin, and is taken down the moment the last play closes. The players resemble their ancient Grecian prototypes in that they are a migratory band, going wherever they are able to find an engagement.

The stage equipments, like the stage itself, are of the simplest order, the spectator being required to supply by his imagination most of those adjuncts in the way of scenery, which in our days, are carried to such perfection in the theatres of the West. There is no division of a play into separate acts or scenes, and what cannot be inferred from the dress, or the pantomime of the actors, they must expressly tell to the audience, as for example who they are, what they have been doing, and the like. The orchestra is an indispensable accompaniment of a theatrical representation, and not only bursts into every interval of the acting, but also clangs with ferocity at such stirring scenes as a battle attack, or to add energy to any ordinary event.

The village theatrical company owes its existence to some rich man, who selects this as a form of investment. As all the available land in the greater portion of China is wholly out of the market, it is not easy for one who has more money than he can conveniently use to decide what to do with it. If he should go into the theatrical business, it is not necessarily with the expectation that the money will yield him a large return, but in order to provide a popular amusement for a great number of people, and at the same time receive a larger or smaller interest on the amount invested.

The value of all [the] various equipments, in a well-furnished theatre, is said to be fully $5,000, and in those of the cheaper sorts, two-thirds or half as much. Each of the three "chests" in which the stage accoutrements are stored, is in charge of three men, who are responsible for the security and the care of the contents of the cases.

The players are divided into classes which are called by different names, the members of each class receiving pay according to the dignity of their position. There are, for example, two individuals, one civil and one military, who represent high-class historical characters .... Another class ... represent personages .... In addition to these are persons of less importance, who represent ladies, officials' wives, young girls, or others. After these come what may be called clowns, who are termed "flowery-faced," ... subdivided into first, second and third. These represent the bad characters ... down to the lowest class who take the most despised and hateful parts of all. In addition to these main characters, there is a considerable force detailed as soldiers, servants, messengers, or to personify boatmen, innkeepers, and the like. The rear is brought up with a large staff of cooks, water-carriers, etc., whose duty it is to provide for the material comfort of the players in their vagrant life.

Aside from the regular theatrical companies one frequently meets with companies of amateurs who have inherited the art of giving performances on a small scale called "a little theatre." They are young farmers who delight in the change and excitement of stage life, and who after the crops are harvested are open to engagements until the spring work begins. There may be only fifteen or twenty in the band, but the terms are low, and the food furnished them much better than they would have had at home, and when the season is over they may be able to divide a snug little sum to each performer.

The manager, or lessee of the theatrical equipment ... engages the players for a term of about ten months, beginning early in the spring, and ending before the close of the year. The whole company may number between fifty and a hundred men, and the best actors may be engaged for sums ranging from the equivalent of a hundred dollars for the most skilled, down to a few tens of dollars for the inferior actors, their food in each case being furnished.

The lessee of the theatre supplies himself with the material for the development of actors, by taking children on contract, or apprenticeship, for a fixed period (often three years) according to a written agreement. At the end of their apprenticeship, these pupils are at liberty to engage in any company which they may elect, for whatever they can get, but during their term of indenture, their time belongs to the man who has leased them of their parents. The motive for such a contract on the part of the parents, is to secure a support for the children. Sometimes children run away from home and make engagements on their own account, attracted by the supposed freedom of the player's life.

The amount which each child receives during the time of his apprenticeship, is the merest pittance, and it is said that in three months at most he can learn all that it is necessary for him to know.

The occasion for the performance of a play is sometimes a vow, which may have been made by an individual in time of sickness, the theatricals to be the expression of gratitude for recovery. In the case of an entire village, it is often the returning of thanks to some divinity for a good harvest, or for a timely rain. A quarrel between individuals is frequently composed by the adjudication of "peace-talkers" that one of the parties shall give a theatrical exhibition by way of a fine, in the benefits of which the whole community may thus partake. In view of the well-known propensities of the Chinese, it is not strange that this method of adjusting disputes is very popular. We have known it to be adopted by a District Magistrate in settling a lawsuit between two villages, and such cases are probably not uncommon.

Sometimes there is no better reason for holding a theatre than that a sum of public money has accumulated, which there is no other way to spend. A foreigner could easily propose fifty purposes to which the funds could be appropriated to much better advantage, but to the Chinese these suggestions always appear untimely, not to say preposterous.

The day previous to a theatre in any village is a busy one. Great quantities of mats are provided, and in a short time some barren spot on the outskirts of the hamlet begins to assume the appearance of an impromptu settlement; for aside from the theatre itself, great numbers of small mat-sheds are put up to be used for cook-shops, tea-shops, gambling-booths, and the like. During the day, even if the village is but a small one, the appearance is that of the scene of a very large fair.

In the larger towns, where fairs are held at more or less regular intervals, it is usual, as already mentioned, to begin them with a theatrical exhibition, on the first day of which hardly any business will be done, the attendants being mainly occupied in gazing at or listening to the play. In such cases the attendants can frequently be safely estimated at more than 10,000 persons. In large fairs there is generally a performance every day as long as the fair holds, an arrangement which is found to be very remunerative from a financial point of view in attracting attendance, and therefore customers.

From a social point of view, the most interesting aspect of Chinese village theatricals is the impression which is produced upon the people as a whole. This impression may be feebly likened to that which is made upon children in Western lands, by the immediate imminence of Christmas, or in the United States by the advent of a Fourth of July. To theatrical holidays in China every other mundane interest must give way.

As soon as it is certain that a particular village is to have a theatre, the whole surrounding country is thrown into a quiver of excitement. Visits by young married women to their mothers' homes, always occasions to both mothers and daughters of special importance, are for a long time beforehand arranged with sole reference to the coming great event. All the schools in all the neighbouring villages expect at such times a holiday during the whole continuance of the theatricals. Should the teacher be so obstinate as to refuse it (which would never be the case, as he himself wishes to see the play) that circumstance would make no difference, for he would find himself wholly deserted by all his pupils.

It is not only brides who take advantage of this occasion to visit their relatives, but in general it may be said that when a village gives a theatrical representation, it must count upon being visited, during the continuance of the same, by every man, woman and child who is related to any inhabitant of the village and who can possibly be present.

It is by no means an uncommon thing to find that in a village which has engaged a theatrical troupe, every family is overrun with such visitors, to such a degree that there is not space enough for them to lie down at night, so that they are forced to spend it in sitting up and talking, which may be easily conceived to be an excellent preparation for the fatiguing duties of the morrow. As a theatre seldom lasts less than three days, and sometimes more than four, it can be imagined what a tax is laid upon the village which is overrun. When it is considered that every married woman who returns to her home, as well as every woman who visits any relative, always brings all of her young children, and that the latter consider it their privilege to scramble for all that they can get of whatever is to be had in the way of food, it is obvious that the poor housekeeper is subjected to a tremendous strain, to which the severest exigencies of Western life afford very few analogies.

The cost of feeding such an army of visitors is a very serious one, and to the thrifty Chinese it seems hard that fuel which would ordinarily last his family for six months, must be burnt up in a week, to "roast" water, and cook food for people whom he never invited, and most of whom he never wished to see. It is a moderate estimate that the expense of entertainment is ten times the cost of the theatre itself, realizing the familiar saying that it is not the horse which costs but the saddle.

The vast horde of persons who are attracted to the village which has a theatre, has among its numbers many disreputable characters, against whom it is necessary for the villagers to be constantly upon their guard. For this reason, as well as on account of the necessity for being on hand to look after the swarms of guests, the people of the village have little or no opportunity to see the play themselves. Guests and thieves occupy all their time! Eternal vigilance is the price at which one's property is to be protected, and the more one has to lose, the less he will be able to enjoy himself, until the danger is over. It is a common observation that, after a theatrical performance, there is not likely to be a single chicken left in a village. To prevent them from being stolen by the expert chicken-thieves, the villagers must dispose of their fowls in advance.

Such being the conditions under which the Chinese village theatre is held, it is surprising that so great a number of theatrical troupes contrive to make a living—such as it is—out of so precarious an occupation, which is likely to fail altogether during years of famine or flood (never few in number), and also during the whole of each period of imperial mourning, when actors are often reduced to extreme misery. One reason for their passionate attachment to the theatre, must be found in the fact that for the Chinese people there are very few available amusements, and for the mass of the country people there is literally nothing to which they can look forward as a public recreation, except a few feast days (often only two or three in the year), the large fairs with accompanying theatricals, or theatricals without fairs.

It is evident that a form of exhibition which is so much valued by the Chinese, may become an important agency in inflaming the minds of the people. This is at times undoubtedly the case. Many instances have come to the knowledge of foreigners, in which theatricals representing the Tientsin massacre or some similar event, have been acted in the interior of China. In some cases this is doubtless done with the connivance of the magistrates, and it is easy to see that the effect upon the minds of the people must be very unfavourable, if it is held to be desirable to maintain among the Chinese respect for foreigners.

In China, as in other lands, it is easy for theatrical representations to deal with current events which have a general interest. In a certain case of warfare involving two different Counties, as to the right to make a bank

to prevent inundation, several lives were lost and a formidable lawsuit resulted. The occurrences were of such a dramatic character that they were woven into a play, which was very popular at a little distance from the scene of the original occurrence.

The representation of historical events, by Chinese theatres, may be said to be one of the greatest obstacles to the acquisition of historical knowledge by the people. Few persons read histories, while every one hears plays, and while the history is forgotten because it is dull, the play is remembered because it is amusing. Theatricals, it is scarcely necessary to remark, do not deal with historical events from the standpoint of accuracy, but from that of adaptation to dramatic effect. The result is the greatest confusion in the minds of the common people, both as to what has really happened in the past, and as to when it took place, and for all practical purposes, fact and fiction are indistinguishable.

Among the most popular Chinese plays, are those which deal with everyday life, in its practical forms. Cheap and badly printed books, in the forms of tracts, containing the substance of these plays, are everywhere sold in great numbers, and aid in familiarizing the people with the plots.

Perhaps the most instructive aspect of Chinese theatricals, is that which takes account of them as *indices* to the theory of life which they best express, a theory in which most Chinese are firm, albeit unconscious, believers. It is a popular saying that "The whole world is only a stage-play; why then should men take life as real?" It is in strict accordance with this view, that the Chinese frequently appear as if psychologically incapable of discriminating between practical realities which are known to be such, and theoretical "realities" which, if matters are pushed to extremities, are admitted to be fictitious.

The spectacular theory of life is never for a moment lost sight of in China, and it demands a tribute which is freely, unconsciously, continually, and universally paid. It is upon this theory that a large proportion of Chinese revelling is based, the real meaning being, "You have wronged me, but I am not afraid of you, and I call upon all men to witness that I defy you." It is this theory upon which are grounded nine-tenths of the acts which the Chinese describe as being done "to save face," that is, to put the actor right with the spectators, and to prove to them that he is able to play his part and that he knows well what that part is. Never, surely, was it more true of any land than of China, that

"All the world's a stage,
And all the men and women merely players."

Chinese villages have formal organizations too. These are purposely created to meet specific needs and must be included in any study of the major patterns of association of Chinese peasant life. Although there are regional differences, Daniel H. Kulp's description of such associations in South China gives a fairly representative picture. You will recall that his study was the basis for Selection 82.

· 87 · Village Associations
DANIEL H. KULP, II

In addition to the familist groupings, Phenix Village contains a number of social groups of an artificial or intentional character. The basis of membership in them is similarity of attitudes with reference to the objectives or values commonly recognized by the members. People are born into familist groupings but they choose to join these associations. The members constantly shift and change so that the composition of the groups is not permanently fixed.

They are all formed to meet a clearly recognized need, which may be present and temporary or in the nature of a future contingency. In the latter case the association develops an organization that provides sufficient continuity to keep it going until its functions have been completed. In one way or another, the groups function for protection, economic gain, and recreation. The means used may be thought of as mutual aid devices. In practically all of them sociability appears quite definitely during their meetings and assemblies.

The six different associations in Phenix Village are the Mutual Aid Club, the Parent Burial Association, the Society for the Manufacture of Sugar, the Irrigation Club, the Boxing Club, and the Music Club. In each case the purpose of the association is clearly suggested by the name.

THE MUTUAL AID CLUB

The Mutual Aid Club is usually of a very temporary nature. It lasts until each member gets his money returned in cash and feasts, when it dissolves automatically without ceremony. It arises out of the needs of the poor people on the one hand and the refusal of the rich families to give loans without sufficient securities, on the other. When a number of poor villagers find themselves in similar circumstances of financial need, they turn to each other for help.

The method of providing this aid has been worked out into a practicable mutual aid device. For example, a certain man needs fifty dollars, presumably for some worthy purpose. He goes to those in the village who are most friendly toward him and who are in similar situations of need and asks them to join his

[Adapted from *Country Life in South China: The Sociology of Familism* . . ., Vol. I, *Phenix Village, Kwantung, China,* Teachers College, Columbia University, New York, 1925. Pp. 189-215. Used by permission.]

"club." He explains his need, the amount of money he wishes to raise, suggests the amount each should pay, which in turn determines the number of people who may be allowed to join.

In this instance, when he has found ten persons who are willing to pay him five dollars each, he has the money he needs. Perhaps a few weeks or a month later, he invites them all to a feast, which costs him about five dollars. This is his first repayment on the instalment plan. The organizer does not pay back in cash but in the feasts which he provides at a cost equal to the amount paid to him by each member. Usually about one month intervenes between each festive occasion. In a club of ten persons in addition to the organizer, it takes ten months until the club ceases to exist. The organizer thus secures with interest, for the first month, fifty dollars, after which he has five dollars less each month until the tenth month when the loan is repaid.

At the first feast each member casts dice once and the one who throws the highest score is paid five dollars by every member of the club except the organizer. . . .

At the following feasts the procedure is repeated until each has been paid his forty-five dollars. Thus each man pays in fifty dollars, gets out forty-five in cash . . . does the organizer a favor . . . enjoys the feast with the food, the companionship and conviviality.

THE PARENT BURIAL ASSOCIATION

The Parent Burial Association partakes of this same characteristic of economic assistance. Its purpose is fundamentally benevolent. In the past it has flourished among the poorer families. In recent times, however, even the rich families have found it worth while to join these associations. It is difficult for them by ordinary procedure, to find help during the period of mourning. At present there are two of these associations in Phenix Village.

What is the need and what is the situation that give rise to this form of voluntary grouping? It has already been mentioned that over half the people of Phenix Village are dependent upon the other half in varying degrees.

Poverty and death are haunting spectres of the poor. They roam through the village and inspire fear that is not physical but social.

It is not that the villager fears death; his belief in Fate relieves him of that worry. But to think of his parent drawing near to the time of departure without adequate funds for proper rites and burial,—this is a real fear. To fail in the provision of rites, feasts, coffin, and funeral would be conduct the most unfilial and condemned by social opinion. The family would be disgraced and the prestige of the village lowered in the estimation of the regional community, so far as gossip would extend on the matter.

Every one, rich or poor, must die; the son knows that the needs arising out of the parent's death are inevitable. Foresight is required of the poor that the material means of the social requirements may not be lacking when the time comes. Such are the attitudes of the poor toward a familist crisis created by the death of a parent.

That it is not death itself that primarily inspires the fear is further attested to by the fact that the rich families also need such associations. They have money and ordinarily are able to employ what help they need. They can finance the material needs of burial ceremonies. With them, as with the poor, the real fear is a fear of inability to meet the required demands of a parent's death as prescribed by community tradition. With them, in contrast to the poor, the need is not for finances but for hands to help in the performance of the humble but necessary duties of laying out the corpse, mourning, and so on. The rich suffer but one need; the poor face two.

The crisis that exists for rich and poor alike arises out of the superstitious attitudes of uneducated people toward touching or handling a dead body. The revulsion against it is deep-seated. The villagers consider a dead body unclean and likely to bring a curse upon those who come into close contact with it. Quite naturally, few seek and all avoid as much as possible the giving of such assistance. So strong is this attitude of avoidance that often not even money can buy for the rich the assistance they need at such times.

That is why, in order not to fail in their traditional duties, they too join the burial associations.

Not only are people needed to handle the corpse and the coffin, but also to assist in the mourning rites. Wailers are needed to exhibit to the countryside the deep grief suffered through the departure of the respected parent. The more wailers, the greater the filial piety and, consequently, the greater the prestige the family achieves. This wailing is not a desirable occupation and villagers avoid it as much as possible. Rich and poor both find it difficult to secure mourners. Here the avoidance attitude is secondary to that regarding the corpse. Sometimes the attitude is even transferred to members of the natural-family which has lost someone by death. People simply prefer to stay away from homes where there are dead bodies.

Some societal device is clearly necessary in order to guarantee the performance of the death duties, the burial rites and ceremonies. The avoidance attitudes must be either neutralized or supplemented; otherwise the social and religious needs of the death-crisis cannot be met. The Parent Burial Association, by creating voluntary bonds of responsibility prior to the appearance of the specific and undesirable duties, represents familist technic of adjustment and resolution of the crisis of death.

THE SUGAR MANUFACTURING ASSOCIATION

Another type of grouping is the Sugar Manufacturing Association. The people form this society to make sugar but even here one finds the religious and social features. When the organization is established they have religious worship in the interests of the success of the undertaking; from time to time they conduct religious worship so that the good spirits may continue to favor them; when they dissolve the organization after the completion of the sugar-making, they conduct worship in gratitude for successful enterprising.

The social nature of this society is even more prominent than the religious. The members work together in a cooperative way; the success of one is the success of all. This interdependence forms a nexus of effort and thought that makes for close group unity. When the day's work is finished, they meet in their common room, built especially for the work of this association, eat, drink, chat and rest.

The general relationship among the members is very democratic, for each member feels himself on an equal footing with every other in responsibility and in participation in the benefits of the association. There is also a desire to deal honestly with one another so that the enterprise may not be wrecked nor the investments of time and money lost. Finally, each is supposed to work zealously so that the financial gains from the undertaking may be as large as possible. Products are thus turned out cheaply and with the maximum elimination of waste and duplicate effort. The incapacity of the individual to conduct such manufacture alone because of the capital needed is compensated for by collectivity.

THE IRRIGATION COOPERATIVE SOCIETY

Another organization of similar type and function is the Irrigation Cooperative Society. This association arises directly out of maintenance practices and needs due to unfavorable climatic conditions. Successful cultivation of rice becomes impossible when droughts set in, for the paddy fields, instead of being flooded, suffer desiccation. The ordinary practice is to dig small holes at the corner of the fields for the collection of water which is then pumped into the fields as they dry up. But when continued lack of precipitation has forced the farmers to use all of the water from these holes, they are compelled to secure water from Phenix River.

Under such unusual and difficult exigencies, the farmer finds himself unable to cope with the crisis. He turns to others for help. Many others in similar situations readily join together and form a cooperative society for the irrigation of their rice fields and so save them from turning yellow before the crop is ripe. Each member pledges himself upon joining the association to cooperate in every way possible with the others, by contributing labor for the enterprise according to the extent of land to be irrigated. Where lands are too extensive to provide this labor through personal effort, the arrangement involves the employment of hands or the payment in kind or cash to other members of the society who may make up a deficiency in labor. Both men and women are found in these organizations. They divide themselves into shifts to work the irrigation pumps and so send a continuous stream of water into the fields.

THE BOXING CLUB

Still another type is the Boxing Club. Some villager who has a slight knowledge of Chinese boxing suggests to a number of young men that a fund be raised to secure the services of an instructor and to rent a place for the "school of self-defense"! An entrance fee is proposed and, when on that basis enough money is collected to launch the school, an itinerant boxing instructor is employed and a suitable place rented. Usually the classes are held in an old school building or temple where the open paved court serves as an open-air gymnasium.

The instruction is given at night when the young men have most leisure. After a few lessons in a series of body movements designed to dispose of an opponent, the pupil is initiated into the mysteries of thrusting, parrying, slashing, and warding with a variety of weapons popular in ancient warfare in China.

At first the movements are learned by mass imitation of the instructor; later they are perfected through practice with a sparring partner to develop experience, confidence and precision. When the sparring begins, and especially when the classes convene while the teacher is instructing in a neighboring village, some of the hardier members "get rough" and troubles arise. Each develops a drive for con-

quest rather than finesse and precision until the organization comes to a more or less sad ending.

THE MUSIC CLUB

Finally, there is the Music Club. It too is an association designed to meet a specific need, and dissolves when the need is met. It rests upon a broad basis of community appreciation of music, for the people commonly find recreation and wholesome enjoyment in it; wherever people gather to spend their leisure time music is provided either by professionals as wandering minstrels or by themselves. The taste for music is a product of the local theatricals which are presented on the stages set up before the temple doors.

Once a year the village turns out for a religious procession, for the success of which there must be attractive music. To provide this music, the young people of the village are canvassed, a group is selected to form a band for the New Year's procession. These people are formed into a school similar to that of the Boxing Club. Money is raised by subscription among the villagers who are rich or interested, in order to supply the instruments and employ a teacher in instrumental music and theatrical singing. This instructor may receive a very high salary, and for the two or three weeks he teaches he is treated as a highly honored guest of the village.

He must teach the children how to handle the musical instruments, such as the gong, the drum, the cymbals, the trumpet, the flute and the violin and banjo, and to chant and sing the songs popularized by the stage.

The pupils are young children of a musical bent, for they can most quickly learn how to handle the instruments and sing the theatrical songs. The high falsetto notes of these songs can best be reached by immature voices. For two or three weeks these children receive instruction day and night. Then the instructor moves on to another village but the band goes on practicing until the religious procession is held. When that great annual event is passed, the club disbands, the members return to their major interests, and the children, to school.

All these associations are really cooperative societies organized to pay the expenses either by cash, by labor, or by kind, of carrying on the activities of the members. The economic nexus runs like a red thread through a string of beads, binding practically all the groups into a fundamental unity of function and purpose.

A fitting addition to the preceding discussion of Chinese rural life is a detailed description of a single village. At this point it is well to review the elementary conceptual scheme around which this book is organized:

1. Society consists of social relations.

2. Each relation is made up of people occupying statuses and playing roles appropriate to those statuses in a given situation.

3. When we classify the statuses we arrive at a number of patterns of association, which we have been describing in considerable detail: the family and kinship system, the locality groupings of neighborhood and community, the economy (as a set of farmers, middlemen, creditors, landlords, tenants, and consumers), the local government, religion, theatricals, and specific purposive organizations.

4. When we classify the roles we get a glimpse into the types of interaction involving competition and conflict, cooperation and accommodation. In some of the selections, also, we paid particular attention to the motivational processes of socialization and social control. The account of Taitou Village, which follows, will add considerably to our information on this score.

5. *Social values,* inherited and thus traditional, carry tremendous weight and help the Chinese peasant rank the various statuses in terms of importance and prestige. We have noted that the scholar and the landowner rate high, the actor and the soldier low. We have seen the relative standing within the family of father and mother, younger brother and older brother, and we shall gain further insight into the status differences among family groups within a village.

6. Another mentifact, or cultural trait of much significance, is the *norm,* which specifies limits of variations allowed in the carrying out of the roles. This gives us a key to the matter of "losing face," so important in the East; it also means that human behavior is predictable to the extent that individuals have been socialized to observe the norms in the performance of their roles.

7. Any society exists only if it possesses a sufficient degree of integration. There must be a correspondence between norms and values, statuses and roles. Patterns of association and processes combine to make up social systems.

Therefore, as we turn to Taitou and its extended treatment, we shall consider it as a small social system—a collection of people interacting with one another in differing ways according to the social relationships existing among them. We shall note the ways in which the integration of daily life is maintained, how the rough edges are worn away; and also the threats to integration in the form of forces coming in from outside. The village studies used thus far include the one by Kulp, in South China (Selections 82 and 87), and the one by Fei, on the Yangtze Plain (Selection 79). Taitou is located on the Shantung Peninsula in North China. Martin C. Yang, the author, is a well-trained social scientist who has brought objectivity and an analytical approach to the study of the village which he once knew well and which he revisited in later years. From our reading thus far we should be able, to some degree, to distinguish features of Taitou life which seem to be local and regional, as well as to identify those characteristics which seem to hold true for peasant China as a whole.

• 88 • A Village of Shantung Province

MARTIN C. YANG

PREFACE

The village of Taitou has been selected as the object of . . . [this] study because the writer was born and reared there, and lived there until he entered high school. Until recent years, he has returned to the village at least once each year, the periods of his visits varying from five days to several months. He has maintained his contacts with his relatives in Taitou and has kept himself informed about the daily life and significant happenings in the village.

THE VILLAGE SITE

The village of Taitou is located on a stretch of level land ringed with mountains on the southwestern shore of Kiachow Bay. Directly across the bay to the east is a small peninsula, on the southern end of which is the city of Tsingtao. This city, which has grown up in recent decades, now provides Shantung and its neighboring provinces with means of access to the outside world. It is a center of commerce, industry, and transportation, and thus plays an important role in the growing trade between rural China and the manufacturing centers in distant parts of the world.

This region is one of the oldest agricultural areas in China. Its people are almost all farmers who cultivate their own land and live in compact villages. There are about twenty villages and a rural town. The town is Hsinanchen—the only marketing center for the region. Taitou is about two thirds of a mile south of Hsinanchen, with which it is connected by a new highway.

The climate of the area is good because of the proximity of the sea and mountains.

The village site can be divided roughly into two parts: the residential area and the immediate outskirts. The former is situated on the north bank of the Taitou River. Here the one main street follows the bowlike curve of the river, with narrower roads branching from it in both directions. A number of small lanes and paths, all running northward, connect with the main street. Most of the residences are located north of the street. The local people call the lanes and paths *hu-tung,* and, if the villagers of a certain *hu-tung* are members of a certain clan, then the name of the clan is added to the *hu-tung's* name. . . .

The central section of the main street is quite spacious. To the south it opens on the river and affords a view of the open country. On the levees built by some of the wealthier families along the riverbank grow rows of willow trees. This part of the main street is something of a social center or public square for the village. In the summer, the villagers

[Adapted from *A Chinese Village: Taitou, Shantung Province,* Columbia University Press, New York, 1945. Pp. ix, 1-2, 4, 6-7, 9, 11-17, 23-28, 30-34, 38, 40-43, 45-48, 50-63, 65-68, 73-76, 79-84, 86-90, 103-117, 119, 123-124, 126-129, 132-135, 137-138, 140-145, 147-158, 160-161, 163, 165-170, 174-181, 183-188, 190-191, 193-194, 198-200, 228, 230, 233-235, 238-242. Used by permission.]

sit on the stones or on the levees under the trees and talk through the hot afternoons. In winter, the old people relax against the walls in the warm sunshine and watch the children at play in the square. Men weaving baskets or knitting straw rain coats or perhaps working on farm tools work out here rather than in their narrow and smoke-filled homes. Some portions of this open space are the private property of different families, who often use their part as an open stable for their animals during the day and also as a place to keep manure and earth before it is removed to the field.

All the better houses are in the central part of the residential area. *Hu-tung* divide the area into four main divisions according to the four clans in the village. The first part, which is almost eight-tenths of the whole area and includes almost all the good houses, is occupied by the P'an clan, the largest in the village. The second is occupied by the Ch'en clan, the third by the Yangs, and the fourth by the Lius . . . The families of each clan cluster together in one section forming a nucleus out from which the clan's territory extends. A few isolated families of each clan have settled among families of other clans or live outside the main residential area . . . Generally, the older and wealthier families occupy the main parts of the residential area, whereas the poorer or smaller families spread in the outlying areas. In the main residential area are the village school, the Christian church, the two oil-pressing shops, and a small foundry. The village school does not have its own building, but occupies one or two rooms of a family house. The Christian church, which was built more than twenty-five years ago, is a good building, the only finer one being the new home of the P'an family.

Immediately beyond the residential area lie the vegetable gardens and the threshing grounds.

Beyond the gardens lie the graveyards of the four clans. There is no general cemetery; each clan buries its dead on land which is believed to be favorable to the future generations of the clan. When the clan becomes large and several branches split off, each branch chooses its own ground for burial.

The southern side of the residential area is quite beautiful in summer. Along both sides of the river there are several stretches of wooded swamps. Not long ago, when the countryside was peaceful and when the P'an families were in their prosperous period, the village was admired by travelers who approached it from the south. Before one reached the edge of the river one could hardly see the village because of a thick green wall of trees. But as the traveler went on, suddenly the village burst into view before him, and in the next instant he was walking before the watching eyes of the villagers and could see the farmers hoeing in the vegetable garden or working on the threshing grounds, women washing their clothes on the river dikes while children played around them, people sitting and working under the tall willow trees, and also the big oxen and mules standing on the river bank. Unfortunately, a great part of that is gone. During the last ten years the P'an family [have] declined rapidly. The woods have been cut, broken river levees have not been repaired, and the tall willow trees are almost gone, as are the oxen and mules.

THE PEOPLE

It is hard to say just how large the population of the village is . . . Each family must post on the top of the front door a card bearing the name, age, sex, kinship status, and occupation of the family members. However, access to this means of counting is impossible, so our estimate must be made on the basis of the size of an average family and the approximate number of families in the villages. . . .

According to the present writer's impression, a family in Taitou . . . [would] average . . . six persons, including parents, children, and grandchildren.

The number of families in the village is also difficult to estimate. More than ten years ago it was generally believed to be about a hundred but there is no doubt that the number has increased in the last decade. Many large families have broken into three or four separate units. None has moved, but a few may have died out. It seems safe to say that there are now about 120 families in the village. If we take these two estimates, then the number of the village's population should be about 720 people.

The death rate among children is high, about two out of every six or seven born. The villagers, for the most part, accept this as a matter of course. If a family loses more children, three out of five for example, the neighbors feel that something must be wrong; either the wife has brought bad luck on the family, or the ancestors have committed actions destructive to God and against human principles. If, on the other hand, all the children in a family live to grow up, the mother and the family are considered very fortunate and unusual. The death rate is highest among children under the age of three; it tapers off decidedly between the ages of five to ten. When a young baby dies, the body is not deeply buried and is easily dug up by wild dogs or wolves. When an old woman asks the name of a neighbor's child and is told that the child is ten years old, she will say, "Good, the child is out of the reach of dogs!" —meaning that the danger of death is past.

The average life span of adults is about sixty to seventy years. Women die earlier than men. This may be because they bear children, work hard, and usually have a diet which is inferior to that of men. When a man of sixty or over is too ill to leave his bed for more than several days at a time, the whole family take it very seriously. When a person under forty dies, the death is regarded as very unusual and great grief is shown by both relatives and neighbors. When a person under sixty dies, the death is still considered unusual, but there is less grief because the deceased has grown-up children to continue the family line and to care for the infirm. If the deceased is over sixty, the death is taken as a matter of course, and only close relatives grieve. In case a person lives longer than seventy or eighty years, his death is a relief to relatives and friends. This is especially true if the family is poor and the young people are not filial. Death may also be a happiness

because the deceased had lived long and had enjoyed a good life; it is good for him to die before he becomes too old to be liked by the younger generations.

The marriage system in this community as in all other Chinese communities is patrilocal—the woman goes to her husband's home. This is the chief form of population displacement; emigration and immigration are rare.

On the whole the population of Taitou is stable. Families rarely leave the village. Individuals move about and many of the young people go to the larger towns to work, but they maintain close ties with their relatives at home and usually come back to the village, eventually to settle down. Any population change in Taitou is more apt to be a result of changing birth or death rates than of shifting population.

AGRICULTURE

In this area, as in all other parts of the country, the cultivated land has for long been elaborately partitioned into very small fragments. A farmer, or a family, does not own one but a number of plots, and these are generally scattered in a number of localities. Homes are not on the cultivated land but are in the village. To get to his farm a farmer has to go to several different places, some of them quite distant. Each field belongs to a different owner and each owner must have some way of reaching his field, so there are numerous roads or paths crossing the land. In the summer, or during the growing seasons, the land resembles many small strips of different colors lying side by side.

Even within the environs of a single village, there is a wide range in the value of the soil. The extreme fragmentation prevents ownership of all the land of a given quality by one or a few families and thereby reduces the possibility of complete crop failure for any one family. Since different land is more or less suited to different crops, a family which has land in several places can grow various kinds of food, will always get some return from its land, and, being, therefore, self-sufficient, has less need to trade. In former times the fields must have been larger. Since a father's holdings are equally divided among all his sons, there is an endless process of division and redivision. Another factor which increases the parceling is the numerous small transactions in buying and selling land. Families buy small bits of land from their neighbors, but seldom whole fields. It is impossible to recombine these fragments, for that would require owners of two or three fields to relinquish them at one time to one person. A family does not sell land unless it absolutely has to, so that the possibility of several families having to sell at once would be extremely rare.

The size of the fields varies greatly. The smallest may be only one-tenth of a *mow* [a *mow* is about one-sixth of an acre], while the largest may be as much as five *mow* or more. Fields in the hills and valleys and in the water [flooded] land are usually small, while those in the level land are large. In the hilly places many tiny fields are terraced on the slopes and bottoms. Sometimes these are just little corners—a plot as large as a *mow* is rare among them. The water land has always been greatly treasured by the villagers, and each small piece is worth a great deal. It has been divided into many plots so that each of the well-to-do families can have one.

About ten years ago there were two or three families each of whom had as much as eighty to ninety *mow* [about 13 to 15 acres] and five or six families who had from fifty to sixty *mow* [about 9 to 10 acres]. In the last decade all these families have either broken into small units, or else been forced to sell their land because of losses inflicted by bandits or because of the extravagance of their children. At present, perhaps no family has a holding greater than forty *mow*.

The main crops are wheat, millet, barley, soybeans, corn, sweet potatoes, and peanuts. A variety of vegetables are grown in the gardens: cabbage, turnip, onions, garlic . . . radishes, cucumbers, spinach, several kinds of string beans, squashes, peas, and melons. There are also many kinds of fruit but none of them in quantity. While there are no orchards, one or two fruit trees may be seen

on the edges of most of the vegetable gardens.

A great part of the land is good for growing sweet potatoes and peanuts, and the yield in these crops is abundant. Because most of the families own only a very limited quantity of land, they have to grow the crops which are most suited to the soil and which offer the best prospects of a good yield. From June to October, sweet potatoes, peanuts, and soybeans occupy almost 50 to 60 percent of the crop land. Next in importance is millet, to which 30 percent is given, leaving only 10 percent for other crops and vegetables. From November to June of the following year, part of the land is devoted to winter wheat and winter barley and part of it is left fallow. Families with larger holdings grow more wheat, millet, and soybeans, while the poorer ones have to raise more sweet potatoes and peanuts. Wheat takes a longer time to grow and requires more fertilizer, and the yield is not high, but wheat flour is regarded as one of the best foods. Wealthy families like it and can afford to grow it. It is also a good cash crop. Sweet potatoes grow well in hilly and sandy soil and do not require much fertilizer, which is an advantage. They are a much more dependable crop, both in quantity and nutritive value, than wheat. Therefore, a family without much land has to grow more *mow* of sweet potatoes than other crops. Since peanuts grow well in soil that is not suitable for wheat, they are the main cash crop of the poorer families. Soybeans are important as a cash crop and also for home consumption; all families grow them in large quantities. Millet is also generally grown and is the most important staple for local consumption.

All but a few families have vegetable gardens. Some vegetables are grown in the open fields. Each family grows from one tenth to one half of a *mow* of turnips. String beans and peas are planted between the rows of the crops or at the edges of the field. A few families also raise water and honey melons. On the water land wet rice is grown. The year's harvest of this crop is not of any significance in the village's whole economy, but it is interesting to note that it gives the village some rice culture which is rare for this area.

Farm implements are generally simple. Those of importance are the plow, two kinds of harrows, a weeding hoe and a digging hoe, wooden and iron rakes, wooden and iron shovels, a harvesting sickle, and different kinds of forks. For threshing, the stone roller and the flail are important. The wheelbarrow is most used, for the mule-cart is not seen in this part of the country. This is perhaps· because the land is hilly and most of the roads are merely narrow paths.

With the exception of a few crude baskets, the villagers do not make their own tools because they can buy all they need at the special country fairs, held twice a year in the market town. Some of the tools are made in neighboring villages where materials are locally available; others are made in distant places and imported by dealers. Before the harvesting or plowing season, itinerant blacksmiths come to the village to repair or reinforce the metal tools or the steel parts.

For fertilizing the fields, both human and animal dung are carefully gathered and preserved. At a corner of the front court or in the backyard a pit and an adjacent pigpen are enclosed by walls or fences which open on the court. The pit is used as a privy and into it are gathered all the manure and other refuse from the barn or from outside; even the ashes from the kitchen are carefully preserved here. When the pit is full, the contents are removed to an open space set aside for the purpose and are covered with a layer of mud. In the pit the mixture has already undergone fermentation and here the process continues. According to the local farmer's experience, raw manure is not good; the fermented mixture is the best fertilizer he knows. When the sowing season arrives, the pile is broken down and the mixture is dried in the sun. It is then made into powder and transported to the fields as needed.

A second important fertilizer is soybean cakes. After the oil has been extracted from the beans, the residue is made into cakes which are used both as animal feed and fertilizer. As fertilizer, the cakes are always mixed with the compost, not only because the farmer cannot afford to use soybean cakes alone, but· because the local people believe that the mixture is more effective.

Green manure is very rarely seen. This is partly due to the lack of mineral fuel. Instead of coal and gas, tree branches and leaves, stalks and wheat and other crops are used as fuel. Although the area is almost surrounded by mountains, wood is still too expensive to be burned as fuel. Consequently, every bit of vegetation that cannot be used for other purposes is carefully gathered and preserved to feed the kitchen stoves. The main sources of animal feed are the stalks of millet, the vines of peanuts and sweet potatoes, and many kinds of grass. In addition, the houses are all thatched with straw, except for a few that have been recently built with tile roofs. The farmer does not consider it economic to use green manure, since there are so many other uses for vegetation. Wheat stalks, for instance, are used for cooking. The ashes are taken out from the stove and mixed with animal manure to fertilize the field. Thus, the stalks serve two purposes: cooking and fertilizing.

Oxen, mules, and donkeys are the customary farm animals. The donkey is the cheapest . . . A family owning less than ten *mow* cannot afford any animal and must either work without one or cooperate with a more fortunate neighbor by exchanging labor for the use of his animal.

Oxen are chiefly used for plowing and sowing, and seldom for pulling wheelbarrows or drawing the millstones. After plowing or sowing an ox remains in the barn, under the shade of the willow trees, or in the sunshine near a wall. Mules are used more frequently— for transporting harvested crops from the field to the threshing ground, pulling the millstones when the donkey is too tired, or for riding to other villages on visits.

Practically every family has a donkey. They are used for every kind of transportation and in many ways in domestic work. Housewives of the village do not often touch the ox, and never try to handle a mule, but they can control donkeys like pets. The absence of a donkey would not only hinder the small farmer in his field, but his wife at home as well.

Although agriculture is the main means of livelihood, many subsidiary occupations supplement income in the slack periods of the farm work. For example, a little foundry was established by two brothers of the P'an family in Taitou. . . . There is also a woodworking shop where one carpenter and an apprentice make furniture parts, plain doors and windows, and a number of simple farm implements. In addition to filling villagers' orders they produce goods to be sold in the market town.

There are three or four cloth weavers. One of them once bought an improved loom and opened a workshop. There he worked for himself and sold his products in the market town or in other villages. Unfortunately, he had to stop because he was short of capital and also because he could not work steadily at it. All the other weavers have only old looms and their rate of production is very low. Recently they have been forced to compete with factory-made cloth which comes in to the country in daily increasing quantities. Young people prefer the fine cloth whenever they can afford it, though the old people still believe that homespun is much better—they say it lasts longer and is better-suited to rough farm work.

A few years ago three families owned oil-pressing shops. In the winter and spring they pressed oil from the locally raised peanuts and soybeans. One of them also opened a shop for making the baskets used as containers for shipping oil to Tsingtao. It was a profitable business and for some time supplied work for ten or more people; but, recently, due to bandit raids and heavy taxes, all the shops have been closed.

There are five or six masons who build houses for the villagers and for people of neighboring villages. Some of them also work periodically in Tsingtao. Their earnings are as good as the carpenters' and several families whose sons are masons have attained a better standing in the community.

It is interesting to note that all these craftsmen are members of poor families. Some have bettered the family status, others have kept their relatives from starvation. Only the oil-pressing shops were owned by members of wealthy families. But we see that nonetheless very few are engaged in industry. What the local people value most is land: big land holdings and a prosperous farm are to them the real signs of prosperity and this is why no rural industry has ever developed into a business of any significance. Necessity is the only incentive, or at least it is the main one, for taking up any means of livelihood other than farming.

There are two kinds of hired farm laborers, the yearly or permanent, and the daily or temporary, laborer. . . . A yearly laborer is not necessarily one who works throughout the entire year. Usually his term of employment runs from the sixteenth day of the first month on the lunar calendar up to the first day of the tenth month. Daily laborers are hired chiefly in the busy seasons, when sowing, hoeing, and harvesting have to be done. Families who have yearly laborers may also hire daily laborers for a few days to get the work done on time. During this period a group of able-bodied men carrying hoes or sickles and wearing straw raincoats and rain hats wait every morning at a corner of the main street in the market town to be hired. This is called locally the "market of laborers." Any farm family who needs help sends someone there to hire a man.

Relations between the family members and the hired laborers are generally congenial. Change in economic status is frequent, so that in the same generation a family who has been hiring laborers may come to the point of hiring their own members out to others. On the other hand, a number of families who were poor may become relatively well-to-do. Since mobility of this kind is great, one family cannot feel superior or inferior to another. Moreover, most of the hired men come from families who own land, though it may be but a small piece, and as long as a family owns even an inch of land they consider themselves on a par with their fellow villagers . . . Workers and owners all follow the same occupation and work together in the fields. All these factors tend to minimize distinctions between wage-earners and employers. But recently the situation has been changing. More disputes rise; laborers demand higher wages and better meals. The employers try voluntarily or involuntarily, to meet these demands, but they complain that it is very difficult to handle hired laborers in these days. . . . The situation as a whole is unfortunate because the rising price of labor is not due to a natural shortage but to social and political chaos. Since the outbreak of civil war, with the attendant increase in banditry and local upheaval, many young people have abandoned the old tradition and have become restless. Some have joined the bandits, others have entered the militia employed by ambitious local chieftains, and others have simply disappeared.

STANDARD OF LIVING

The population of Taitou can be divided roughly into four classes on the basis of food consumption. At the lowest level is the group for whom sweet potatoes are the main item of diet; next are those who have a combination of sweet potatoes and millet; third, those who eat millet and wheat; and at the top, those who eat mainly wheat. All classes eat garden vegetables in large quantity when these are available. The first two groups rarely have animal products of any kind; the last two have them only occasionally.

Among the poor, sweet potatoes are eaten at every meal every day throughout the year. From harvest time until the spring of the following year, they eat fresh sweet potatoes; when these are gone, they eat stored dry slices. These are boiled, or ground into meal which is mixed with other flour to make bread or noodles. Supplementing the potatoes are, first, a kind of gruel made of barley flour and peanut powder; second, a kind of hash made of chopped turnips and soybean juice; and third, one or two kinds of pickles. Occasionally some kind of bread is served.

During the busy season food is more plentiful. Steamed millet or millet bread takes the place of sweet-potato slices, and green vegetables cooked with fat are added to the diet. On a poor family's table, meat, fresh fish, or eggs are seen only on special occasions, when guests are entertained, or for the New Year

celebration. Soybean oil, peanut oil, are used in cooking, and in richer households, pork fat. A poor woman tastes sugar only when she delivers a child.

Food consumption varies with the season.

When sweet potatoes and peanuts are harvested, the busiest time of the year, the diet of a well-to-do family is better than at any time except during the New Year celebration or at special feasts. The food is both plentiful and varied—more pork and beef, more wheat flour, and cabbages are added to the menu. Everybody is well fed, even the beggars look healthy. But as soon as the fields and threshing grounds are cleared up and the hired laborers gone, the diet is again restricted until the coming of the New Year season.

Because wheat flour is the preferred food, a number of social practices center around it. When a marriage is arranged, for example, the most important gift presented by the boy's family is a number of big steamed rolls made of pure wheat flour, each weighing two catties (about three pounds). On top of the roll is pasted the Chinese word "happiness," cut from a piece of red paper. The girl's family distributes some of the rolls to relatives, friends, and neighbors, thus formally announcing the engagement, and returns the rest to the boy's family to be distributed among their relatives and friends.

A group of poor villagers speaking of a Christian preacher, a school-teacher, or a businessman from the market town, will say: "He is a man who eats wheat flour every day, why should he not have a smooth face!" When a person has a run of good luck, his fellow villagers might say: "Just as meat is always served with wheat flour rolls." A successful man is compared by the villagers to winter wheat, which is superior to other cereals because it survives the severest winter weather.

The houses of Taitou can be classified roughly into three types. Those of the wealthiest group are built of stone, burned bricks, lime, and a good grade of wood and roofing material. A stone foundation is laid underground and rises aboveground about six inches. Upon this foundation are built the walls. The lower part of the walls, about four feet high, is built of stone blocks. The blocks used on the front wall are well cut in squares or oblongs; for the back wall irregularly shaped stones are used. Above the lower part is a layer of burned brick. From here on, the wall is constructed of small stones or beaten earth with a layer of lime plastered on the outside. This is topped with an arched wooden roof covered with thatch. The inner side of the wall is set with small, unpolished stones.

The houses of the average income group are constructed in the same way except that the materials used are inferior . . . The houses of the poor are small, made of inferior materials, and not regularly shaped. They are simply huts. . . .

The main house, or the north house, called the *cheng wu,* is usually composed of three to five rooms, while the house on the left or right side of the court generally contains two or three rooms. The width of a main house in the wealthy first group may measure about twelve feet; the length varies greatly. The floors in all kinds of houses are of beaten earth. The walls are papered. The windows are pasted over with thin white paper (sometimes oiled), which usually admits sufficient light and sunshine. The rooms are crowded by the big brick beds and wooden beds, the tables, bureaus, cabinets, and numerous personal belongings. As the kitchen is connected with the bedrooms and the stoves are attached to the tunnels inside the brick beds, the house is kept warm in the winter, but in the summer it sometimes becomes insufferably hot. Temporary kitchens may then be built in the court or in an empty house.

In the house of a well-to-do family one or two rooms are specially furnished and kept for guests. An average family, however, uses the parents' bedroom as a guest room. Guests are almost always relatives so that there is no embarrassment on either side. The parents' bedroom also serves as the dining room for the whole family and their guests in the winter. The large brick bed is covered with a thick layer of straw above which a neat, smooth mat of stripped skins of *kaoliang*

[grain sorghum] stalks is laid. During the winter when the nights are long and it is cold outside, the family usually gathers in the parents' bedroom to work or talk. Neighbors also come and sit on the same bed. Thus, the parents' bedroom is really the center of family life.

A married son and his young wife live in the room across from the kitchen. The door of this room is always kept closed, for the interior should not be seen by the father or by any man who is not of the family. The grown-up daughters always live in the room back of the parents' room so that no one can enter it except by first passing through the parents' room. When male guests or male neighbors are present, the daughters of the house must leave their room beforehand or remain there quietly until the guests or neighbors have gone.

The earth floor of the houses is always dusty, and when it is swept the dust flies about the room. Sometimes water is used to moisten the floor before sweeping, and though this helps, it is not enough. Under the tables, under the wooden beds and bureaus, odds and ends accumulate and heavy layers of dust form. Mothers let their infant children urinate or soil the floor. Because the rooms are crowded, there is not enough fresh air. A pottery bucket is placed in every bedroom for night use. In the winter, when all the windows are carefully pasted over with paper and the doors closed, the air is very foul, especially in the morning. Only when the weather is fine and the doors can be left open is the odor somewhat dissipated.

The farmer's work garments are made mainly of cotton. Silk trousers are worn by quite a few villagers in the summer, but this silk is raised locally and spun at home and is a coarse but very lasting material. In July and August a number of middle-aged wives of the well-to-do families wear linen jackets when working. A number of villagers also possess fur coats or jackets and wear them when they go to the market town or when no manual work has to be done. Wool is used only in winter shoes, winter caps, and winter bed sheets. A few well-to-do families have woolen clothes but do not wear them very often and never for work.

A farmer may have two or three suits of work garments. Cotton-padded jackets and trousers are worn in cold weather. In the spring and autumn the farmer wears a lined jacket and the cotton padding is removed from the trousers. For the summer he has two or three coats and several pairs of trousers. These coats are worn in the winter as underwear, and the same trousers are again padded with cotton.

Everyone has one or two suits of dress clothes. . . . For the New Year celebration, weddings, or formal visiting, the better dress garments are worn. For ordinary occasions, work garments newly washed and pressed are worn. A man's ceremonial dress garment consists of a long gown and a jacket made of fine cloth. A woman's is a skirt and jacket made of fine cloth or silk. Ordinarily a woman wears only a pair of trousers and a jacket, and no skirt. A woman's jacket, whether it is a dress or a work garment must be five inches below her hips and must hang loosely, for if she wears short, tight jackets she will be sharply criticized and suspected of wanting to attract men.

Color is important. Girls, young women, and brides are allowed to wear bright colors— red, pink, purple, or green; the accepted color for grown-up men and middle-aged women is blue. No man under thirty should wear white shirts, and no man under fifty, white trousers. For middle-aged people, cotton-padded trousers may be white, but cotton-padded jackets must not be. Dress garments are usually colored. The long gown is always blue and the jacket black. A woman never wears white unless she is in deep mourning. Men's shoes and caps are always black. Women's shoes are red, pink, or green when they are young, but black when they have passed middle age. Women do not wear hats.

THE COMPONENTS OF A FAMILY

A Chinese family, especially in rural China, is far more than a group of related in-dividuals. In Taitou, as well as in other villages, it is a complex organization of family members, family property, domestic animals, family reputations, family traditions, and family gods. It can be said that the family extends to the as yet unborn generations and to the long-deceased ones. The living traditionally believe that their ancestors' spirits, whether in the ancestral graves or in Heaven, are with them and are keeping watchful eyes upon them at all times. A family's fortune or misfortune is largely controlled by spirits of the ancestors. When the spirits are pleased, the family will receive blessings; but when they have been antagonized, disaster inevitably comes. They must be invited to participate in all special occasions, such as festivals, weddings, and births, and homage must be paid to them at their graves, in the ancestral halls, or before the ceremonial tables of the family. This sense of kinship is strongest at the New Year Festival, a time when the living feel their ancestors to be actually with them.

The importance of the future generations can be seen by the anxiety of the parents to see their sons married, and to accumulate property for their children. With this in mind they work hard and live thriftily so that they can save some capital for the prospective children. They feel guilty when unusually good food is eaten or extra money is spent, not because they cannot afford these things, but because they want to have something to leave to their descendants. A family may have enough houses for all its members to live in, but they keep on buying and building new ones and acquiring land for the future generations. On New Year's Eve, or on other special occasions, family members not only invite their ancestors but also observe rites to symbolize the birth of additional children. Just as the authority of the dead figures in the decisions of the living, the rights of the unborn determine the composition and well-being of the families of which they will become part.

Land is the most important form of property, for it belongs to all the generations. It means much more than a piece of earth on which crops are cultivated; it is the very foundation of the family. Without land a family can never be settled and the family members will never have a sense of security. People and land are the two pillars of the Chinese farm family. When we say a family is broken, we mean that the family's land is gone. In the village a family's status depends very much on the amount of land owned, for this indicates to others how much the family cares for its past and future obligations and how faithfully these are observed.

Domestic animals are an important part of the farm life. In Taitou, these are chiefly oxen, mules, donkeys, dogs, cats, pigs, and chickens. The first four are considered as part of the family and are accorded special treatment. The farmer is most attached to his ox. The feeling is so strong that he may feel worse about the loss of his ox than he would about the death of his infant child, for the loss of the animal endangers the life of the whole family. The slaughter of oxen is condemned by all. There is no law or social custom to forbid the professional butchering of oxen, it is true, but everybody looks down upon anyone who practices it. People believe that no one could become rich in such a business, that the soul of a butcher will be condemned eternally to hell, and that his offspring, if he has any at all, will always be poor and weak. A farmer usually keeps his cow or ox as long as possible. If one day, for some reason, he is forced to sell his animal, there is great sadness in the family. When the farmer turns his animal over to the buyer and sees it being led away, he may shed tears. For one or two days at least the family will maintain silence at the dinner table and the situation will not be relieved until a new cow is purchased.

The intangible components of a family are also important, and the most highly regarded of these is reputation. A family wants to be admired and talked about by people of a neighborhood or of a considerable territory. This is a great source of pride to families of the middle and upper classes who are generally much concerned with what people think of them. There are five ways of achieving reputation, and the first of these is to have members in ranking official positions. If one of the family, for example, is a county magistrate, villagers and others will refer to the family as the *Hsien-chang chia,* or the magistrate's family, and will show great respect to its members. As the official position rises, the family's fame climbs with it.

Scholastic fame comes from having a member in the family who has passed the academic examinations. In the old days, if one of the family passed the first Imperial Examination, the family was known as a *hsiou-ts'ai chia.* Although a *hsiou-ts'ai* was not important, nevertheless on special occasions the family was distinguished by the title from plain farmers.

Since most of the villagers believe that farming is the most dependable and desirable means of livelihood, a family is proud of having plenty of land and many sons who are eagerly cultivating the land. A family which is devoted to agriculture, and has also some scholastic attainment, is the ideal family in the countryside, and usually referred to as a family of farm and study.

Family fame is also built on wealth. [A rich family] will be known over a wide area.

But wealth alone cannot build up family fame. A family may be known as a wealthy one, but not necessarily as one worthy of respect. Two additional factors are needed: first, some distinctive and gracious feature which sets it apart from its neighbors; and, second, a certain degree of socialization which makes it a pleasant topic for discussion.

Conspicuous virtue also enhances a family's reputation. A family may become well known because it has an unusually filial son or an especially good daughter-in-law, or because all its members are so good that the big household has been able to hang together for four or more generations. Filial piety and feminine loyalty are the two most treasured virtues.

A family known as a good neighbor has amicable relations with most of the people in the village. If they are pleasant, mild mannered, and honest, they will be well liked, even if they are not distinguished in other ways. Such people always give way to others. Thus, all the villagers like to do business with them and will speak well of them at social gatherings. There are several families with such a reputation in Taitou.

Family reputation is a basic social value. Not many families have been able to achieve it, nor can it be maintained forever, or even, usually, for as long as a century.

INTRAFAMILIAL RELATIONSHIPS

A young wife must . . . keep from showing that she loves her husband. The general attitude is that a decent wife should love her husband, but must not let her love spoil his career or make him neglect his duty to his family. A good wife stays at her work with her mother-in-law or sisters-in-law during the day, and at night she must wait until all the family members have retired before she can go to her room and be with her husband. . . .

A newly married wife cannot but feel lonesome and strange, because she is really in a strange home with strange people. The sudden separation from her mother, the stern face of her mother-in-law, the . . . dignity of the father-in-law, and above all, her sudden introduction to the continuous housework, all make her feel that she is completely at the mercy of these people. Since she cannot go back to her mother, the only one from whom she can seek protection is her husband. She will generally respond with great warmth and gratitude if she is well received by him.

The partners of an unsuccessful marriage are in an unhappy plight. Divorce is out of the question: they must make the best of it. Outwardly they seem no different from any other couple. They will not quarrel openly; the husband will not beat his wife; she does her work dutifully. However, it is easy to note that the loved wife is active, cheerful, and energetic, while the unhappy wife is listless and slow in her work.

However, if an initially unhappy marriage survives at all, if the hopelessness and sorrow

and burden of work do not break down the unhappy wife, the relationship between the couple improves with time. A woman who survives these hardships without committing suicide or breaking down becomes a heroine in the eyes of her relatives. She has proved that she has patience, far-sightedness, and unusual wisdom and kindness. As the couple grow older and their children reach maturity, their feelings toward each other mellow.

In privacy, romantic love decreases, while the feeling of companionship grows stronger. In their bedroom the wife will tell her husband what has happened in the household during the day and what she thinks about their problems. She will also talk to him about their children. The husband tells her about the crops in the field, the work of his brothers and the hired laborers, and so on. Because of his consciousness of being a man, a filial son, a good brother, and a dignified husband, he is supposed not to listen to, or at least not to believe, his wife's complaints about other household members. In spite of this he frequently accepts her statements, and secretly acts on her suggestions and advice on other matters.

As the husband and wife mature, they come to have their own home and undivided authority over their children. The companionship ripens and is no longer kept secret but becomes the foundation of the newly independent family.

When a couple reaches the age of fifty or sixty, the wife generally becomes the dominant person in the household. She is now the mother-in-law of one, two, or even four daughters-in-law. She is the grandmother of a long line of children and is also the overseer of a large household. The middle-aged sons have almost invariably developed strong attachment to their mother but not to their father. The father's authority in the fields, now that he does not work there, is considerably lessened. He has lost his role in business transactions because he is too old to take the farm products to the market town and deal directly with the dealers. To a certain extent, his importance in relations with the neighbors is diminished, because people find that he is no longer the real authority and that his position as family head is more nominal than real, although he is still respected by all the household.

The relationship between father and child has none of the warmth and freedom existing between mother and child. The father's attitude is dignified, even remote; his authority is unquestioned and he expects submissiveness from his sons. Although in a farm family some informalities are permitted—as, joking in the presence of one's parents, taking a place of equal importance to that occupied by one's father, not rising when the father approaches—yet the father and son relationship is far from free or intimate.

The relationship between mother and son, on the other hand, is comparatively close. Although a boy who reaches the age of ten is dependent entirely upon his father's authority and teaching, this does not interfere entirely with his intimacy with his mother. Because of the lack of female companions and the meager possibilities for recreation, a young man spends much time talking to his mother during his formative years. . . . In her turn, the mother may tell him what she and his father think of him. A son at this time has no one, except his mother, to whom he can tell his thoughts freely, and this provides an unshakable foundation for the long-lasting mother-son relationship.

The affection between mother and son is threatened when the son marries. If the mother is selfish or narrow-minded, as many mothers are, she will become jealous of the young wife. Not a few of the difficulties between mother-in-law and daughter-in-law are unconsciously based on such jealousy. A common saying has it that "A son is lost when he is married."

When a girl is born, she is cared for by her mother in much the same way a boy is. The father maintains his usual attitude of indifference. When the next baby is born, the three- or four-year-old girl has a place of her own or is temporarily taken care of by her grandmother rather than sharing her father's side of the bed as a boy does. When she is six or older, she gradually starts helping her mother to look after the younger sister or brother. By the time she is thirteen, she begins to learn to sew, cook, spin, and many other things. By fifteen, she is indispensable to her mother. Mother and daughter develop an intimate relation, and the father and daughter become more distant. He may have a genuine affection for his daughter, especially if the latter conforms to the prevailing standard of a good girl, but the affection between them must be restrained. His knowledge of his daughter is gleaned indirectly through her mother. Generally, a daughter's marriage is arranged by her mother and only the mother can ask the girl's opinion in the matter. The father is consulted, of course. After the arrangement is made, the mother supervises everything the girl makes for her wedding and also persuades the father to be generous with the dowry. At the wedding both mother and daughter feel sad, which brings them even closer together than they were before. For two or three days before the ceremony, mother and daughter lie awake talking all night. The mother tells her daughter everything she knows about marriage, except the sexual details, and instructs her in the ways in which a bride should behave. Needless to say, the impending separation is difficult for both. When the girl has gone, her mother tries to learn whether or not she has been satisfactorily received by her husband and if she is kindly treated by the senior members of the household. If all goes well, the daughter appears happy when she pays her first visit home and the mother is happy too, but if the situation is not a good one, the daughter will cry at her mother's feet and the mother suffers unspeakably.

Relations between mother-in-law and daughter-in-law are sometimes strained, sometimes harmonious, but always less intimate than those of a daughter and her own mother. A daughter-in-law's obligations to her mother-in-law and to her husband are similar, but there are many points of friction inherent in the situation between the two women.

There are not a few mothers who are softhearted and far-sighted enough to see the importance of cooperation amongst the family members to the well-being of the large household. There are also not a few daughters who have been brought up in homes where broad-mindedness, obedience toward the senior generation, tolerance, filial piety, diligence, frugality, sincerity, and faithfulness have been the objectives in the training of the children. When such a mother and daughter come to live together, they will treat each other with consideration.

During boyhood, brothers are playmates and are on more or less equal terms. Fights between them are not frowned upon. Later, the elder brother is expected to be friendly to his younger brother, but there is some restraint in the situation. The younger one is expected to respect the elder. Before they marry, or when only the eldest has married, they continue to get along well with each other. They work together in the field or at home under their father's direction, and though there may be rivalry or even occasional clashes there is also cooperation, mutual help, and mutual confidence.

In the early years of life, a girl is usually dominated by her brother in play or disagreements. This is due partly to the fact of male priority in a Chinese family. . . . When a boy is twelve or fifteen years old, he begins to feel that it is his duty to protect his sister, even if she is older than he. A Chinese girl over twelve years is not allowed to associate with any boy other than her own brother or her father's brothers' sons. Since her desire for male company grows stronger as she gets older, she eagerly accepts her brother's company and protection. Unmarried brother and sister have a free and intimate relationship. . . . A sister may act as a go-between for her brother and a girl he is interested in. He may confide to her his as yet unrevealed ambitions and he may ask her to speak for him to their mother.

Relations between the wives of brothers may be harmonious but are frequently marred by rivalry. The wives form a team under the direction of their mother-in-law. They help each other by looking after each other's children, by lending each other small articles— a needle, a roll of thread, a piece of cloth, or a little money. They can generally agree as to the order of work, so as to leave time for each to visit her parents. A family with such daughters-in-law will be cited as a model and be praised by all the villagers. Unfortunately, such cases are rather rare. In many large households the rivalry outweighs the harmony, for the wives compete for the favor of the mother-in-law.

The adjustments necessary between the members of a large family are delicate ones and it is only when they can be made with a minimum of friction that a large household can hold together. Jealousies and disagreements between certain members will throw the entire organization out of balance, and, if no immediate remedy is found for the situation, the household may break up. It is the most important duty of the head of a household to keep these relationships functioning smoothly. The task would be impossible, even for a family head of great tact and skill, were it not that so many traditions, rituals, and social sanctions operate as controls in the situation.

There are two basic relationships: that between parents and children (with the emphasis, of course, upon the sons), and that between a son and his wife. Theoretically, these two should be complementary. In practice, however, they are antagonistic to one another. It is true that when parents find a wife for their son they hope that the couple will be compatible and are pleased on the wedding day to receive such congratulations as "Harmony in one hundred years"; "A heavenly sanctioned union"; "Sincerity and love between husband and wife." However, the parents are displeased when the young couple are too devoted to each other, for this menaces the relationship between parents and son, especially that between mother and son. . . . Marriage is not primarily for the happiness of the husband and wife alone, but also for the parents—to help in their work, to wait upon them, to satisfy their desire for grandchildren while they are living, and to continue their "incense and fire" when they die.

Whether a large family can be held together or not depends very much on the congeniality of the married brothers, which, in turn, depends largely. upon their wives.

THE FAMILY AS A PRIMARY ECONOMIC GROUP

Continuing the family line is the main concern of a Chinese farmer, but it is easier to produce progeny than to bring them up. When a man marries, his parents and the spirits of his ancestors are made happy at the thought of the new generation, but the man himself, if he is old enough, feels that a great burden has been put on his shoulders.

The old parents share the responsibility, and though they can no longer work as hard as they did, they save as much as they can of what they have. The parents of many families live more frugally than their children, for they are constantly anxious lest their children face poverty or starvation.

A young wife works harder than anybody else in the family and she lives more thriftily. She does not speak of it, but to her nothing is more important than the security of the family.

All three generations have a common interest in the family's economic security. It is a source of happiness to all: when it is imperiled, all feel the disaster. This is obvious to anyone who sees a family at a time when their important crops are threatened by drought or flood. Not only the older generation manifest great concern, but the young too share the anxiety. If, on the other hand, the harvest of the year is especially abundant and there is a good possibility of having some savings at the year's end, then everybody, old and young, is happy. When a piece of land is bought, even if it be a very small piece, it occasions happiness in the heart of every member of the family. In such a year the family's New Year Festival will be celebrated with great cheer and color.

A farm family is a unit unto itself in production. The family members produce collectively and they produce for the family as a whole, not for any individual member. This holds true for everything.

The work, in the field, on the threshing ground, in the vegetable garden, and at home, is divided among persons according to experience and physical ability. For example, the father is assigned to plant the sweet potato vines, since he is the experienced one. He knows which is the upper end and which the bottom end of the vines and can put them in the right positions. He knows how deep the vines should be planted and also the proper distance between every two plants. Others may also know these things but as yet cannot put them into practice as efficiently. The elder son is asked to carry water from a distant place because he is the strongest in the family. The younger brother and sister are put to pouring water into the small holes because this does not require much experience or strength. Finally, the work of covering the vines and of accumulating earth to support the young plants needs some experience but not much physical strength, and that is why the mother and the elder sister are assigned to these tasks.

We must bear in mind that this organization is not elaborately planned beforehand, but happens very naturally. When the family arrives at the field, the members simply begin their proper tasks; neither the father nor the mother has to give any orders. Needless to say there is flexibility in the arrangement. When there is enough water for a while, the elder son may pick up his father's work for practice. At another time the second son may ask permission to carry water for at least one trip in order to show that he, also, is strong. Or, the elder daughter may insist that she exchange positions with her younger sister on the pretext that the latter should learn a grown-up's work.

In an old-fashioned family, the kind which predominates in Taitou, everyone works or produces for the family as a whole, be he a farmer, a mason, a cloth weaver, a merchant or what not. It goes without saying that those who work on the family's farm work for the whole family. Any earnings made in special trades also belong to the family. If someone keeps a part of his wages, he will be condemned by the family head and suspected by all the other members of the family as being untrustworthy. A merchant who has to do his business outside may spend what he has made for his living expenses and according to his own judgment, but he must turn over all the rest and report what he has spent to the family head. If some of his expenses are found to have been unnecessary, he will be questioned about them in detail. Only when satisfactory reasons are given will his account be closed. If he is already middle-aged and has a prominent position, he may have more freedom in spending his money and the family head may not restrict him too much. But even so, he must know the limits of his freedom and must give the family the lion's share, or the others will complain and the unity of the family will be threatened. When a son goes to work on another family's farm as a hired laborer, his wages are given directly to his father or to his family. He may ask his father to give him a few dollars from his wages, or he may keep or spend the small money given to him by his employer for attending an opera or the local fair, but he is not working for himself but for the family of which he is a member.

The daughters are given a dowry at the time of their marriage, to which they add any money they may have earned and saved while in their parents' home. The young wife can either invest this sum in small home industries or lend it at interest to fellow villagers. When the sum is sufficient, she can buy land with it and this land will belong to the small family unit including herself, her husband and children, and not to the large family of her husband. Her husband's family may cultivate her land and get the harvest. Sometimes the wife may lend her money to the large family, in which case the family would pay it back with interest. . . .

Wives often think of how many *mow* of land and how many *gien* of house each unit will have when the family has separated. They are happy when a piece of land is added to the common property but their happiness is different from the joy of the primary family group. It is not only shallow but each of the wives secretly wishes that the land will become the property of her own group. She may think that the piece of land is largely the result of her own husband's effort and feel it is unfair to make it common property and have it divided equally among the brothers. She may persuade her husband to accumulate personal property by hiding a part of his earnings, if he has any, or by grabbing from the family's income.

The continuity of a family line depends not only on having generation follow generation, but also upon the uninterrupted transmission of the family's common property. Thus, inheritance becomes an important matter in a Chinese family. As we have noted, to the Chinese mind, a family is not merely a group of related people, but also the land, the houses, the livestock, and the family reputation. A prosperous family is one which is increasing in members and in property. In a declining family both are disappearing. This idea is indicated in the common saying "family property depleted and members perished." As long as the property is intact the family exists. When the property is sold, the individual members may still remain, but the family is gone.

. . . Parents who leave nothing to their children will either be blamed for a long time after or be forgotten immediately. Parents who added something to the property, or who restored the original fortune of a family, are inscribed on the family record. They are celebrated by their descendants, and are talked about with pride as long as the family exists.

In this part of the country inheritance is patrilineal, though daughters in some cases have a certain share. Sons have exclusive and definite claims on what the father has left.

The principle of division of land and houses is that an equal share goes to each son. If the division takes place while the parents are still alive, they may prefer to keep a larger share than is given to any of the sons. Whether or not they succeed depends upon their ability to exercise their authority, the opinion of the witnesses, the attitude of the sons, and the size of the total property. Daughters, if unmarried, have a certain amount of money put aside for their dowries. Unmarried sons also have an extra amount for future marriage expenses. Indebtedness is shared equally by the different parties. . . . An important feature is that the youngest son, although not expressly favored, in reality has certain advantages. The mother, or the parents usually choose to live with him, sometimes because he needs further tutelage and protection. In such instances, the parents invariably specify in the contract of division that after their death, their property must be given to the son who has served them. In this way, a further share of the inheritance is given the youngest son. But if the parent or parents live independently after the division of the property, their share will be redivided equally among the sons after their death.

In discussing inheritance we must not neglect the seeming contradiction between the desire of keeping a family's property intact and the desire for more progeny. Once a Western friend told the writer that since the Chinese inheritance system is to divide the family's property equally among the sons he could not understand why Chinese parents want so many sons. Though apparently a reasonable observation, this is not the way Chinese see it. When a son is born even to a poor family, he is not looked upon as someone who will further divide the family's land, but as one who will add to it. When a second son is born, the parents do not worry that their small piece of land will be divided into two parts. Instead, they begin to hope that when their sons are grown up, one will be a hired laborer, another a mason, and they will earn not only their own living but add fifty dollars or so to the family every year. In two or three years, they can buy one more *mow* of land with their savings. Thus, when the parents are old, they will be better off than they now are. This expectation increases with each son born. A son, unlike a daughter, is always looked upon as an economic asset.

THE FAMILY AS A PRIMARY CEREMONIAL GROUP

In the families of Taitou, as in families of other places, there are numerous occasions in the year on which ceremonies are held for dead ancestors, for celebrating good harvests, for worshiping the divinity, or for driving off evil spirits. It is a rule that only family members, or persons of the same family line within a certain number of generations, are allowed to participate. A ceremonial celebration, in fact, is one of the clearest indications of the family's exclusiveness, its conception of itself as a separate entity.

Of the ceremonies observed, those for lamenting and ushering a deceased parent into the long rest and those celebrating the dead ancestors are the most important. The death of a parent, especially of an old one, is taken very seriously.

When a parent dies, all projected affairs are automatically suspended and signs of happiness hidden away. No wedding or rejoicing feast can be conducted during the mourning period; and all things colored red, pink, or purple are put away or covered over with white, blue, or black material. Thus, the most obvious sign of heavy mourning is white; white paper pasted on doors and windows and the wearing of white garments and shoes by the mourners.

Immediately after the body is placed in the coffin, animal sacrifices are made. Offerings, mostly of food, are brought to the family. After the coffin is sealed, it is kept in the house for a period usually of from one to three months, though some wealthy families have been known to keep the coffin at home for nearly a year. This period varies according to the economic and social position of the family. The richer the family, the more elaborate the decoration of the coffin and the length of its retention. While the coffin remains in the house, vegetable dishes are frequently placed before it and incense sticks, candles, paper money, and images are ceremonially offered. Money and foodstuffs are presented to the family to help defray the expenses of the funeral, which otherwise might seriously deplete their resources.

The funeral of a large family always forms a considerable parade. Before the procession starts, the monk of the local Buddhist temple recites a prayer or reads a selection from a classic. When he finishes the chanting, the coffin is immediately moved out of the house. At this moment, all the near kin of the deceased wail loudly and sadly. The coffin is put on a heavy bier which is covered with a red cloth embroidered with dragons. Then the funeral procession begins. Heading it are neighborhood boys or men carrying banners, on which characters are written in praise of the good conduct of the dead. Next comes the brass band playing the mourning music. Then come the paper house, the paper trunks, the paper servants, and many other paper articles which are supposed to be used by the deceased in the other world. Following these is the coffin carrier, and after the carrier is the mourning group with the sons first, then the daughters, then the daughters-in-law, and finally the grandchildren. The [parade] proceeds very slowly and sacrifices may be offered by important friends on the way. Friends or distant relatives who come to lament may also participate in the funeral but they walk in front of the coffin. When the parade is out of the village, the women mourners leave it and return home, but the sons and grandsons follow the coffin to the grave. When the procession reaches the grave, another sacrifice is made before the coffin, which is then put into the grave while each of the mourners drops a handful or a spadeful of earth upon it. After this, they all take off their mourning garments and go home.

After the parents are dead and buried, the descendants try to remember them, to remember their good deeds and words, their glory, and achievements. They are reluctant to believe their parents are gone and rather pretend that they are still living and still with them. Parents' deeds and words still control their children's behavior. It is easy to remember one's parents the first few years after they have died, but it is hard to do so forever. For this reason, the ancient worthies devised and developed an enormous body of ceremonies and a number of feasts by which the forgotten parents remain fresh in their descendants'

minds. These ceremonies and feasts are observed by all families as a matter of course. Whether or not a family really wants to remember its dead ancestors, the ceremonies are practiced and the feasts celebrated. This ceremonial practice is called by Westerners "ancestor worship." In a strict sense, this is a mistake, because the Chinese do not worship their ancestors in the way that gods are worshiped. The Chinese do have the vague idea that their dead parents are with them in an invisible form, but this is a result of consciously trying to keep the memory alive. It should not be interpreted in a religious way; it is a consecration, but in the sense of an unbroken continuity.

MARRIAGE

The Chinese believe that their lives are continued in the lives of their children and that, so long as generation succeeds generation, the predecessors are perpetuated. The maintenance of family continuity is one's greatest responsibility to one's ancestors, for failure to produce offspring means not only the end of the family line but the death of all the ancestors as well. Mencius has said: "There are three things that are unfilial, and to have no children is the greatest of these." The illiterate farmers may not be familiar with the literature, but they are fully aware of their duty in keeping the family tree alive.

The assumption of the responsibilities attendant upon having a wife and anticipating children is the mark of adulthood. An unmarried man of twenty-five is regarded as a boy, whereas a youth of twenty, who is married, is considered a man.

The sons of a wealthy family are married off as a matter of course. In a poor family, however, marriage of sons is an economic problem. Poor parents like to have a number of sons because grown sons are a great asset, but securing wives for them presents difficulties because marriage demands the means to support the additions to the family. But it is also a source of great shame to the parents, especially to the mother, to have a number of grown-up unmarried sons.

Let us assume that the family works hard

and begins to buy land. They accumulate some surplus and pay their debts. The mother will certainly not hesitate to inform her neighbors of the improvement and simultaneously lets her wish for a daughter-in-law be known. At first, the women of the neighborhood may ridicule her, but as the family's economic condition grows better and better, some of the matchmakers will change their attitude and start suggesting girls. Of course, the mother will not risk her chances by making the standard too high, and a match is soon arranged. Great news!

"So, that woman will also have a daughter-in-law."

"Can you imagine, that poor family can also marry their sons."

"Why, it is a decent family. Both old and young work hard and honestly. I cannot see why their sons should not be married."

"Yes, Uncle Sheng is right, if a boy like that cannot marry, I don't see which one of us would deserve a wife."

"Poor family? Who said they were poor? Have not they bought land every year and had their houses repaired? It doesn't matter how much land you have, all that matters is whether a family is rising or declining. I would rather marry my daughter to a plain but growing family than to one which is going down."

After the marriage, the family's social status is raised and, when the daughter-in-law has been seen by all the neighbors, many congratulations are heard from the very women who had made fun of the mother's ambition.

"Well, well, I said you were a lady of great fortune. Just see what a wonderful daughter-in-law you have! Your son really deserves such a beautiful one. By the way, is your second son already engaged? If not, I should like by all means to tell my sister to give you her daughter. As I have said time and again, I don't see where we can find as decent a family as yours."

"Ah, ya-ya, isn't that the Second Aunt? I've just heard that you've married a wonderful daughter-in-law. I have always said that a family like yours should have had a daughter-in-law long ago. But just because your stand-ard is so high that very few girls would suit your sons, so it has been delayed. But any way you got what you wanted. You must be very happy, indeed. Your fate is really a lady's. We are proud of being your neighbors. We should like to come and see your beautiful one. Please do drop in to see us when you are not too busy."

Marriages are arranged by the parents, more specifically by the mother.

Generally, the selection of a daughter-in-law is simpler than that of a son-in-law. The economic condition of the family is more important than the boy's personal qualities, provided he has no particular physical or mental defects, but in the girl's case her family is not subjected to the same scrutiny. The chief requisites for a daughter-in-law are physical health to insure progeny, efficiency in domestic work, a good reputation—which means that the girl is not known for love affairs or disobedience to parents—and, lastly, freedom from physical or mental defects. . . . Frequently the girl's family is of poorer social and economic status than the boy's. The prevailing opinion is that one should not select a daughter-in-law from a family that is much more prosperous than one's own, otherwise the bride may compare the new household unfavorably with the home she has left, complain about the deprivations, and feel superior to the other daughters-in-law.

In choosing a family for one's daughter the situation is reversed. The parents' first consideration is the economic condition of the family—how much land and how many houses the family owns. The girl's mother finds out how many sons the family has and calculates how much each one of the brothers will have when the property is finally divided. It makes a great difference when one compares a family that has twenty *mow* of land but only one son, with one that has thirty *mow* but three sons. If the economic condition is satisfactory, the mother will take the boy's personal qualifications into consideration, but will not make too much fuss about this. . . .

When the two families are satisfied, a formal letter is sent by the boy's family in which the engagement of the girl to the boy is requested. This is accompanied by presents to the girl's parents . . . The girl receives jewelry, dress material, money, and other articles useful to a bride, the amount and quality varying according to the economic condition of the boy's family.

About a half year to three or five years elapses before the wedding. Children of rich families are usually engaged when they are very young and the period may last three years or more, but if a family is poor and it is hard for a son to find a wife, so that he is not young when he is engaged, the wedding takes place immediately after the engagement, with only enough intervening time for the girl to make her wedding dresses.

The wedding outfit includes a number of jackets, shirts, trousers, gowns, underwear, shoes, and bedding. A girl should have at least twelve suits for winter weather and twelve suits for warm weather. All of them should be made of either silk or fine cloth. About ten or twelve pieces of bedding are prepared. All this takes time and the wedding of a well-to-do girl requires a very long period for preparation. In addition, things like trunks, suitcases, boxes, bureaus, cabinets, and toilet articles must be either bought or made. Of course the boy's family supplies some of these things, but the girl's parents must do their best if they do not want themselves and their daughter shamed.

In this period of waiting, the members of the two families are not supposed to see each other often, and even avoid each other except for necessary meetings. In spite of this pattern they remain extremely attentive to each other's affairs. Because the engagement is not as final as marriage, it is not immutable. Although no decent family likes to see the engagement broken, nevertheless, such cases have happened and, if the two families are intimate with each other, a broken engagement will be the occasion of great embarrassment for all. The meeting of the engaged boy and girl before marriage is definitely improper. The boy is not allowed to visit the girl's family and it remains impossible for him to see his fiancee, unless she is seriously ill. Since all but a few of the engagements are

between families of different villages or communities, any meeting of the two parties is difficult at best.

On the morning of the wedding day, the boy's family sends a decorated bridal chair borne by four able-bodied men to the girl's home. . . . When the chair arrives at the girl's home, the bride, who has been waiting for it, is immediately carried into the chair by one of her elder brothers or by an uncle, while the mother weeps and the father stands silent. The bride wears a formal wedding dress or bridal robe of red or deep pink and her face is covered with a piece of red satin. The bridal chair is closed with a curtain so that nobody can see her on the road. Two brothers, close cousins, or perhaps her uncle, accompany her. On the road, the bridal procession proceeds slowly so that the bride will not get seasick, and also so that the enormous and extravagant dowry can be seen and admired by the people in the villages on the way. Meanwhile, the groom, attired in formal wedding gown of blue and jacket of black, waits in the wedding room.

When the bride arrives at the bridegroom's front door, two elderly women come out to meet her, while the men take care of the dowry and welcome the guests who have accompanied the bride. The women's duty is to transport the small boxes in which the bride's toilet articles are contained from the bridal chair to the *hsi-fang* [the room in which the couple will live], and then to take the bride to the place where the wedding ceremony will be performed. This is usually the front court of the home, if the weather is good. In the center of the court is set a table on which are offerings to the gods of Heaven and Earth, a pair of red candles and three sticks of incense. The bride and groom stand side by side in front of the table and pay homage to the gods. Then, facing each other, the bride bows to the bridegroom and he returns the gesture. . . . In the house both the bride and groom make ritual homage to the ancestors, if the family is orthodox enough —otherwise, the ceremony performed in the court is assumed to have been shared by the ancestors. In the *hsi-fang,* the bride is seated on a wooden bed, while the groom takes his place on the brick bed. He is asked to take the red cloth off the bride's head. This is a very important moment to both bride and groom because they are to see each other face to face for the first time. The bride is fed with food which has been brought with her from her home and this is shared by the groom and his parents. After this, the bride is led to pay her respects to her parents-in-law and the groom accompanies her. When they return to their own room both of them will sit on the brick bed and the formal dresses are taken off. The young members of the family and of the neighborhood can now come to see the bride and look at the dowry. The bride is expected to sit on the bed quietly without speaking. The bridegroom also sits there looking very much embarrassed.

The whole family is busy entertaining guests. The two people who have accompanied the bride are the most honored guests and are entertained by senior members of the clan or village leaders, or by the schoolteacher. The feast is the best that the family can afford.

On the evening of the wedding day, the room of the bride and groom is well illuminated with candles and lamps. The room is fully packed with young relatives and intimate friends, who have come to make fun of the bride and groom. Sometimes joking gets out of bounds, but usually it takes the form of jibes at the expense of the groom. . . . After they have all gone, though it may be midnight or still later, the bride and groom perform the last ceremony of the wedding before they retire. This is called toasting each other for the union. A small tray with a bottle of wine and two dishes of vegetables is brought to the room. The door is closed and the couple are alone. They are supposed to drink the wine and eat the food, but in most cases they are unable to do more than pretend to drink and eat after the day's mental and physical strain. Only after this ceremony are the two really united and the titles of husband and wife assumed.

The three things which sanction the marriage are the bridal chair which brings the bride, the parade from the bride's home to that of her husband, and the ritual homage to the gods of Heaven and Earth and to the ancestors of the husband's family. It is well known that in rural China marriage is not recognized through a formal contract signed by the two parties, although the *mei-chi,* marriage-requesting-letter, has been written by the boy's parents and consented to by the girl's. It is not registered in any kind of civil agency.

In other parts of the country, marriages between girls of fifteen and boys of seventeen years old have been reported, but in Taitou the average age is about twenty years. No bride under seventeen, or groom under nineteen, is known. The sons of poor families marry even later.

Marriage is absolutely monogamous, though until recently the possession of two women by one man simultaneously was not illegal. A few years ago, a man of a neighboring village became rich and after he came home to settle down he married a concubine on the ground that his first wife, who was then forty-five, had failed to bear a child. This was frowned upon generally, though it was permitted by the old civil law.

Marriage in Taitou, as well as in most parts of China, is patrilocal and patrilineal. The woman is taken to the husband's family and his clan name is added to hers. Although four different clans are represented in Taitou, marriage between a boy and girl of the same village is discouraged, and no case of intravillage marriage is known to this writer. Some villages are all of one clan and, in such cases, village exogamy is necessary. Another possible reason for the absence of intravillage marriage may be that families related by marriage do not like to live near each other. The engaged couple would be likely to see each other and be tempted into a love affair. Families related by marriage should always be reserved with each other and if they lived in the same village, they would see or visit each other very often. Families in the same village can also very easily become involved in the same village or neighborhood controversies. It would be extremely embarrassing for affinal relatives to find themselves on opposite sides in such a dispute. On the whole, intravillage relations are more intimate than is considered proper for affinal relatives.

In the last thirty or forty years, there has been only one case of divorce. The wife had become pregnant before her marriage. After she was married, she stayed only a few days at her husband's home. When she was paying her formal visit to her mother after marriage, she refused to return to her husband and took refuge with her lover. Neither her family nor her husband's could find her, so her husband could do nothing except to announce a divorce.

This attitude has changed in the last ten or fifteen years, although the change has not as yet been felt in Taitou. Divorces in farm families have been reported in increasing numbers. Most of these recent divorces are results of discrepancy in education. Many young sons and young daughters of well-to-do families now go to the new schools. After graduation, they find jobs in the cities and do not return to farm villages. Away from home, modern boys meet modern girls. They fall in love and want to marry, even though many of them already have wives in their farm homes. In these cases divorce is the only solution. These young men are beyond the ties of the old communities and the family rules cannot reach them; the new government has legalized divorce and the families are financially able to support the wives at home, so that no great difficulty arises. In such cases the young men simply dictate a divorce to their ignorant and old-fashioned wives and then marry and establish new homes in the cities, relinquishing their right to inherit their share of land. . . . Even when the divorce is illegal, as it sometimes is, the family does not take action. The rural people still regard this kind of affair as their own business and would feel it a great shame or embarrassment if the case were brought to public view or dealt with in court. Second, the divorced wives are ignorant of any legal procedure and afraid of strangers. They are heartbroken, to be sure, but they also realize that there is no use in fighting—their husbands are already lost to them.

No social inequality between men and women is so apparent as the discrimination in the matter of remarriage. When a man's wife dies, he is perfectly free to marry again, and he can marry a virgin. The ceremonies, the congratulations, the parade, the happiness of his relatives, occur just as at his first marriage. The dead wife is forgotten altogether, unless she left a child. A widow, however, must not remarry. If she is the wife of a family of status, or if she has a child, especially if the child is a son, she is supposed to remain in widowhood for the rest of her life. Public opinion is that a decent woman should be the wife of only one man.

Sexual relations without formal marriage are morally forbidden. Adultery between persons of the same clan or family is severely condemned. The male suffers permanent loss of social and family position. The woman, if unmarried, will probably commit suicide, for she has lost her chance of being properly married. If a young man has an affair with a girl of a different clan, his punishment may be light—sometimes no more than the laughter of the villagers; but the girl will suffer. There are three or four families in the village whose social standing is so low that the villagers do not think of them in comparison with other families. Sexual immorality in these families is taken for granted and nobody cares unless in some way it shames the community as a whole.

CHILD TRAINING

When a child is about to be born, all the men, unmarried girls, and children are sent away, or, if the house has many rooms, they may merely be banished to some of the empty rooms and told to keep quiet. . . . The necessary articles for the confinement are made ready in the mother's room and the midwife is called. She is usually one of the old women of the neighborhood whose only qualification is the fact that she has delivered other babies; she may also be a witch doctor, and this is considered an added recommendation.

After the child is delivered, its mouth is "opened" with a few drops of water, a ceremonial feeding which is called *kai kou*. . . . The child is wrapped in pieces of cloth and allowed to nurse at the mother's breast.

The third day after the birth is . . . ceremonially celebrated. The child is bathed and clothed in its first garment, a little jacket made of a single piece of red cloth. He is then presented to his grandparents. The family has a feast on this day, but not an elaborate one. . . . Food is also distributed to neighbors and clan members so that they may share the family's joy in the newborn child. Upper-class families take this occasion to thank their ancestors for the birth of the child and to pray for the safety of the new life. Congratulations and gifts from neighbors and clan members are received. Neighboring families usually offer glutinous millet, twenty or thirty eggs, and some brown sugar, since these foods are thought to be the most nourishing for the mother. The gifts come in a fine basket covered with a piece of red cloth and are presented by the mother of the donor's family. She sees the child when presenting her family's gift and praises it and the mother. All gifts must be recorded or at least the givers' names must be remembered, so that similar congratulatory offerings may be made on the birth of a child in the donor's family. These reciprocal presentations go on for many generations.

Also on the third day the baby is given its small name by the head of the family. If there are no grandparents, this duty falls upon the baby's parents. Generally a male child's small name directly or indirectly refers to the family's prosperity or continuity. This is because a boy is expected to be a breadwinner and one who will bring fortune to the family. These expectations create great joy when a boy is born and a high value is placed upon the child. Both the celebration of the birth and an appropriate name reflect the parents' wishes for his health, longevity, and expected talents. Names like *Hsi* (joy) and *Lo* (happiness) indicate the parents' feelings on the occasion. Words like *Pao* (precious), *Kwei* (highness), *Kin* (gold), *Ku* (jade) are often used as names. If the parents feel that the child is a token of the coming of good fortune to the family, they will name him *Fu* (fortune), *Jui-hsiang* (blessing), *Fa* (prosperity), or *P'ing-an* (peace). They may also choose

from among words like *Ch'in* (diligent), *Hsiao* (filial piety), *Shun* (obedience), *Hsueh* (learning), *Ts'ung* (intelligent), *Ch'ang* (strong), *Hu* (tiger), to express their hopes for his being blessed with special gifts.

The birth of a child, especially a boy, is tremendously important to a mother. When the young wife finds that she is pregnant, her thoughts, her interests, her activities, in short her whole personality begins to change. She thinks more and more of the coming of the child and asks her sisters-in-law to tell her what kind of child it will be. She is most interested in ascertaining its sex. She fears the birth pains, but she also looks forward to the honor which will be given to her as the mother of a child.

After the birth of the child, the mother is in constant attendance and generally wants very little assistance. She feeds him at her breast (later he will have liquid and soft foods) day and night. She changes his wet clothes and washes him frequently. She is the only one who attends the child in case of sickness, and it is she who worries most if the illness is serious. The young father shows no interest in his child; on the contrary, he is angry if it disturbs him by crying at night. Occasionally a father hates the very existence of his child. He will not touch it for any reason. He is embarrassed when a relative asks him about it, and to be seen actually holding the baby is a disgrace. He believes that he has helped in "making" the child, and that this in itself was shameful to him. He won't do anything to help because he believes that baby-tending is entirely a woman's job.

When the child is three or four years old, he stays close to his mother most of the time. . . . One always sees a young wife with her child playing beside her as she washes her clothes on the river bank, grinds grain on a street corner, or works in the vegetable garden or on the threshing ground.

At the age of six or seven, a boy will either be sent to the village school, if the family is well-to-do, or be taken to the farm. If he goes to school, his duties at home will be light— sweeping the courtyard or carrying food to the field. During the harvesting seasons, he learns by trying to work within sight of his father.

Boys and girls under ten years may play together but from that time until they are fifteen, they may play together only in groups and remain in places where they can easily be seen by adults. Girls over fifteen are not allowed to talk privately with boys of their own age. Conversation between adolescent boys and girls in the same neighborhood or between cousins is permitted if others are present but bodily contact is strictly forbidden. They may joke with each other, but strictly without reference to sex. Grown-up boys and girls of different neighborhoods do not see each other often and consequently do not talk much. A grown-up girl should not do any favor directly or privately for any young man who is not a member of her family, except with the knowledge and assistance of an adult.

A father should not only keep his hands off a married son but also should refrain from scolding him. When a son is married, he is supposed to be an adult, and the former discipline no longer applies to him. If the son does not behave properly, then his father must talk over any matters that seem to require correction with his family members, including the son's wife, when they are sitting together after supper.

THE RISE AND FALL OF A FAMILY

A farm family's rise is largely accomplished by the buying of land, its fall occasioned by the emergencies that force the sale of land. It is interesting to note that no family in our village has been able to hold the same amount of land for as long as three or four generations. Usually a family works hard and lives frugally until they can begin to buy land. Members of the second generation continue in the same pattern so that more land is added to the family holdings and it becomes well-to-do. Those of the third generation merely enjoy themselves, spending much but earning little. No new land is bought and

gradually it becomes necessary to begin to sell. In the fourth generation more land is sold until ultimately the family sinks into poverty. This cycle takes even less than a hundred years to run its course. The extravagant members die out, and their children begin again to accumulate property. Having suffered, and being fully acquainted with want, they realize the necessity of hard work and self-denial to repair the family fortune. By this time the original big family is gone and in its place there are several small, poor families. Some of these begin to buy land. Thus the same cycle is started again.

Since the rise and fall of the various families is constantly in process, land transactions are also continually going on. Every winter sees the transference of some pieces of land from the jurisdiction of one family to another. The amount of money needed for buying one *mow* of crop land varies according to the quality and location of the land. Each year the price may be different. When a family needs a fairly large amount of money urgently, they usually get it together by mortgaging some of their land. The family which has the money and wants to lend it gives some to the needy family and receives the right of using the land for a certain length of time, with full rights to whatever it produces during that period. A written certificate is issued by the landowner to the money lender, for perhaps three years or longer, and the land cannot be redeemed before the stipulated time has expired. No mortgages are foreclosed. The time may be indefinitely extended, for the money lender can use the land until his money is repaid. The land tax is paid under the name of the owner but it is in fact paid by the person using the land. A family that has to secure money by mortgaging land will feel sad on the New Year and ashamed to walk on the street. The family which has authority to use the land will feel happy, their happiness second only to what it would have been had they actually bought a piece of land.

The direction in which a family is tending can also be seen in its position in the clan, and the general strength, or lack of it, of clan consciousness among its members. When a family has developed into a number of separate households, most of which live in proximity and maintain close relations with each other, it is called a clan. A clan is a group of families connected not only through kinship but also, and more importantly, by means of mutual obligations and privileges. Each family, as well as each individual in it, has duties to perform for the benefit of the others and at the same time has the right to benefit by their efforts. The bond that holds these families together is informal but powerful. Authority is vested not in a particular family or individual but in the group as a whole. The manipulation of this force is the basic function of the clan. When the clan's influence is far-reaching, it indicates that the clan as a whole is strong and has good morale. A clan is the extension of the family and therefore when a clan is prosperous, the families in it are strong; when it is decadent, its families are probably approaching poverty and disruption. A well-functioning clan is really an indication that most of the basic families of that group are developing, not declining.

A clan provides its members with a sense of social orientation and acts as a transitional grouping between the family and the village, uniting them in some ways and bringing them into conflict in others.

In the past the clan had numerous functions. Until very recently there was in China no kind of public social security for the provision of the needy. The clan took care of its members and was supposed to provide for the destitute. Religious organizations or private philanthropy might serve this function in the cities and the market towns, but in the villages the clan was the most important agency. Indeed, one of its chief duties was to see that none of the members should starve or suffer.

Diverse functions of the clan include supporting a school, maintaining a hall for ancestor worship and for disciplining the unfilial or misbehaving members, keeping a clan book and teaching young members the clan's history including the good deeds of their ancestors, and collecting funds to support a brilliant but poor clan member in obtaining advanced education.

So far none of the clans of our village has built an ancestral hall. It seems that the villagers do not have much interest in the elaborate ceremonies of ancestor worship. . . . In other villages, however, one frequently sees the ancestral halls of a large clan. It serves rather as a symbol of a clan's unity than as a functioning institution. Clan consciousness is not active in everyday life, but it can be refreshed when the members see or enter the ancestral hall. On the New Year Festival and other similar occasions the members are summoned to the hall, where they go through some of the ceremonies, listen to the preaching and lectures of the leaders, and discuss clan affairs. This revives the feeling of unity among the kinsmen, and consequently the association of the clan's families becomes stronger than before.

In Taitou no clan has actually given financial support to any of their young members for education, though they have taken interest in similar cases. A member of the Yang clan, for example, had a very good reputation as a student when he was in the market-town school. He was praised by the teachers, the community leaders of the whole market-town area, and also by the senior members of the P'an clan, so that great hope was aroused among all the people of the clan.

. . . The interest is not based solely on an interest in the development of the young man but primarily on the prospective benefits that will accrue to the clan if he turns out to be a success. In the past, the Imperial Examinations were so important that a person who passed even the first one was qualified for some sort of Imperial Honor and was certain to secure a position, albeit a minor one, in the government. The honor and the benefits accruing therefrom were shared by the whole clan. After the establishment of the Republic, the old system was abolished. The number of students in the country has increased greatly and graduation from primary or high schools has become an ordinary event. Even graduation from a university no longer assures one of a government post. These changes have no doubt greatly disappointed the orthodox, both in the country and in the cities, who no longer see the point of expensive training and long years in school. They may continue to send their children to school because the latter insist upon going, but they certainly have lost interest in helping their poor relations go to college.

The new social trend helps to break the clan's control over individual members. In the last fifteen or twenty years most young people have learned to disobey their families and the seniors of their clans. They depend more and more on themselves and show less and less trust in the older generation. The political chaos and the general social disorder have helped to disrupt the old unquestioning reliance upon traditional ways of living. Moreover, under the new system the households of a village are organized into numerous small units. Families and individuals are directly under the authority of the leaders of these units, a fact which has contributed markedly to the decline of the influence of the clan.

VILLAGE ORGANIZATION

From a survey of the surrounding crop land one receives a strong impression of the unity of the village. The fields belonging to village families lie side by side in a circle around the cluster of houses. Although the area overlaps at many points, the boundary line is quite recognizable and there is never any doubt as to which village any piece of land belongs to.

Village solidarity can be seen in many things. Methods of cultivating crops, of threshing, storing, or preparing foodstuffs, of cooking or preparing feasts for the New Year celebration are exactly the same for every family within a single village. In a neighboring village, even though the activities are the same, there will be slight variations in technique. One often hears farm laborers who hire out to different villages tell each other that this village's food is superior (or inferior) to that village's.

Organizations in the village can be roughly divided into three categories: those which cover the whole village, those limited to a single neighborhood, and those based on family associations.

The first village-wide organization is the village defense program, in which every family is required to take part. . . . Wealthy families are expected to equip themselves with rifles, pistols, old-fashioned tube-guns, and the necessary ammunition; other families need to have only a rifle and ammunition. Families that cannot afford to buy rifles are asked to contribute other materials useful in defense. . . . The able-bodied men of all the families are registered and organized into a number of teams. The recruiting system is based on the family unit, each family supplying one grown-up son for duty each night.

Two defense lines were built around the village, the outer one consisting of removable mines—iron tubes filled with powder and scrap iron and connected by wire. The villagers knew where they were and how to pass through the line safely, but a stranger could not enter the village without being trapped by the wires which exploded the mines. The defenses were removed in the daytime for the safety of the villagers. The second line, built within the limits of the village, consisted of a number of fortifications, lane gates, and gun placements on the backyard walls. At night, the young men were assigned, first, to lay the explosive mines and wires for the outer line, and then to patrol the streets, lanes, and strategic points. The village had not been attacked since the organization of the defense. It was rumored that bandits feared to come near it.

The village school, though it had been built by the P'an clan and was mainly supported by them, was attended by boys from the entire village. Until the establishment of the Christian school, this was the only general educational establishment in the village. Girls were not sent to school but trained in the domestic arts at home by their mothers. . . . The school council was made up of the heads of families and this cooperation in managing and supporting the school brought families together.

The villagers regard education as a means

by which a family can raise its position. Children are taught to read names, to understand the content of land deeds, and to recognize the different kinds of paper money orders so that they will not be cheated in business transactions. The sons not needed for farm work are trained for a career, for business or a trade. Calligraphy, account keeping, the use of the abacus, and the learning of the terms for farm products, farm implements, domestic utensils and manufactured commodities also held an important place in the curriculum, and there were some who regarded the school as the place where one learned good manners and absorbed the teachings of the ancient worthies.

In the past, most boys were not in the least interested in their schoolwork. The school itself was a one-room affair with a dirt floor. . . . The tables, benches, and stools were brought by the pupils from their homes. Boys ranging in age from six to twenty years were herded together in one room. The teachers' quarters were partitioned off from the schoolroom and here the teacher sat all day, except when he had calls to make, went to the market town, or was invited out to entertain a guest or to write documents for a village family. At school, his chief function was to maintain order.

Thirty years ago, the first modern school was established in Hsinanchen by the county government. . . . The school in Taitou was also modernized to a certain extent. In these new schools life was interesting to the pupils and, as a result, the attitude toward going to school changed. The textbooks were fascinating; they were written in the contemporary idioms familiar to the pupils and were beautifully illustrated. Above all, they contained interesting stories about children's daily life, which were entirely comprehensible and opened new vistas to the young minds. The arithmetic was new and interesting. Learning the symbols of numbers and new methods of counting was most fascinating. The chalk, the blackboard, the clay stick and the clay plate were all delightful things which had never been seen before. In the old school, singing had been absolutely forbidden, but

now the young teachers cheerfully taught the boys to sing as part of the curriculum. They sang the songs of the coming and going of the swallows, the joy of study, of patriots, and of the flowers and the stars. The boys also learned the symbols of music. Few had any musical talent, but they liked to sing and imitated the teacher with great gusto. Physical education was a regular part of the school day. This was most exciting. In the old days they were punished for making noise or for having fun, now they were taught and led by the teachers in exercises and games. They also had some military instruction.

Another village-wide organization is the collective protection of crops. A crop-watcher is hired by the village every year. His duty is to see that the crops are not damaged by animals nor stolen by thieves. He receives a yearly wage and while he is on duty is supplied with meals by families who have more land than the average.

Punishment of theft is a common concern of the village. Petty theft is dealt with summarily. Sometimes a boy or girl of a poor family may steal some heads of the millet crop, or some string beans, or other crops. If the culprit is caught on the spot by the owner of the field, he may be scolded and forced to give up what he has stolen, or he may get a beating. . . . An adult thief is merely shamed and derided if the theft is a minor one.

Burglary, however, is regarded as a crime. When a home is robbed at night, the owner may use weapons to defend his property, and if the burglar is killed no action will be taken against the man who kills him. If the thief is caught he will either be punished according to village custom or sent to the county government. A man who steals a considerable quantity of the crops, or who breaks open the doors of homes to steal grain, animals, or other useful things at night, is considered a criminal; he is fined or punished by the local leaders according to the local regulations, and though he loses his social position, he may continue to live in the village and eventually redeem his reputation. Those who break into houses to steal money, threatening the family with weapons, are unforgivable criminals and must be taken before the government authorities if they are caught.

Social control is a village-wide affair; its chief instrument is public opinion. For the kind of behavior that is approved by most of the villagers, a person is everywhere honored and praised. Disapproval, therefore, is a powerful check. For instance, though the villagers do not interfere with or harm a promiscuous woman, they sever their relations with her family and ignore the greetings of any of its members. Social isolation is a terrible punishment. Only the three or four families whose social position is so low that they are in a sense immune from public opinion are indifferent to disapproval and fear only physical punishment.

Close neighborhood associations in many cases supersede the village feeling or the clan consciousness. A family of the P'an clan, for example, may have closer relations with some Yang families than with their own clansmen, simply because the Yangs live in the same neighborhood. Frequent contact in daily life brings families together, and consequently the whole village is divided into a number of neighborhoods, or *hu-tung,* which have no reference to the clan. There are nine neighborhoods within the village limits.

People living near by recognize certain social obligations to each other. When there is a marriage, the bridegroom's family distributes steamed rolls made of wheat flour among the neighbors to announce the wedding and extends an invitation to the party. In return, the neighbors offer presents, mostly of food needed for the occasion. . . . In case of a funeral, the neighbors help to build the tomb. They may carry the coffin, or take care of the domestic work while the relatives of the deceased are mourning. This aid is offered voluntarily.

. . . In time of emergency, such as fire, theft, or sudden illness, neighbors are far more helpful than relatives or friends who live at a distance. A common saying runs: "Distant relatives are not as dependable as near-by neighbors."

. . . When a person needs money to pay debts incurred by gambling, opium-smoking, or drinking, he can borrow the sum from his neighbors, but the rate of interest will be exceedingly high and a contract is drawn up. Two men of good credit are required as guarantors and a certain amount of land or a house is demanded as security. These loans extend for short periods and if the payment is postponed twice, the creditor is permitted to cultivate the land of the debtor.

Women of neighboring families gather before their front doors to talk and gossip. Especially in the summertime, when the men are eating at home, the women come out to have a breath of fresh air under the trees. A spontaneous and informal group is formed and the talk ranges from discussion of the daily work to gossip about the marriage of a family at the other end of the village. This continues until the men come out and it is the women's turn to eat. After dinner when the weather is hot and the people don't feel like working, the men and boys go to sleep or play on the main street, on the river bank, or in the groves. The old women go to their bedrooms to take a nap. But the young women and little girls come out again to sit under the trees or in their doorways, bringing with them some piece of work. All of them are members of the same *hu-tung.* They sit about for one or two hours, then return to their homes and resume their important work—sewing, mending, ironing, embroidering, and the like. The men and boys go to the fields.

Because of the need for children's labor in the field and at home and also because there is no surplus money for frivolity, recreation for children is not encouraged and almost no toys are provided for them. Children of the same neighborhood, however, play group games which require little equipment. One of these is *Ta-wa,* a game played with two teams, which requires only some small stones.

Ts'ang-more, a girl's game, is somewhat like blindman's buff.

Another game played by boys is *Ti-Chien-tze.* A group of older boys or young men play with a shuttlecock made by tying some poultry feathers on a coin. This *Chien-tze* is thrown up in the air, and the players try to keep it from touching the ground, kicking or butting it but not touching it with their hands. The game is popular in winter since it is very active and helps the boys to keep warm.

It is easy to draw a checkerboard on the ground and to use stones as checkers. For this reason, checkers is a very popular game in the summer. Younger girls and boys play quietly under the trees on the riverbank with a number of others sitting beside as on-lookers. Sometimes the players get into a serious argument and the spectators take sides with them. While the cows are grazing, the boys sit down and play the game, sometimes letting their animals wander far away over the fields. In the winter a group of young people may gather to learn Chinese boxing or to sing songs in the houses where social gatherings usually take place. During the New Year Festival some active young people may also organize country dramas.

VILLAGE CONFLICTS

In addition to the clan and neighborhood organizations, there are other kinds of intra-village groupings. Families of similar social and economic status, families which support a certain school, and the families which have become Christianized all tend to divide off into special groups.

Families of the same neighborhood may not be as close as families of different neighborhoods, because of status differences. Two or three Liu families, for example, live in the neighborhood where most of the Yang families live. The Lius are very poor and do not have much to do with the Yangs because they feel inferior to them, and the Yangs do not make overtures to them, either. But another Liu family, which has recently become prosperous, has gradually become intimate with the Yangs. Their children were asked to attend the Christian school.

. . . Formerly, the ten or twelve wealthy families of the village had more intimate relations with each other than they had with their neighbors. There was also a group of middle-class families. Their association was not strong but recognizable. The poor families also constituted an informal group. In the past decades, distinctions based upon wealth have broken up because of the decline of the rich families and the general disruption caused by the war. In general, this kind of stratification is rather superficial, for, as we have seen, the status of a family may change in a few generations.

The introduction of Christianity brought about new groupings of families. Ten or twelve families belong to the Protestant church, and five or six families belong to the Catholic church. The Protestant families include the Yangs and Ch'ens and, formerly, also one of the P'an families. The Catholic group is composed of four or five P'an families and two of the Ch'ens. Because Christianity is a new religion and is contradictory in some ways to the traditions and customs of the local society, the two groups of families which identified themselves with this belief are sharply differentiated from other families. This differentiation caused a kind of "we-group" consciousness in each of the two groups. The dozen Yang and Ch'en families have maintained closer relations than would have been likely under other circumstances. The several P'an families which belong to the Catholic church are poor and of very low social status, and are considered by their kinsmen as a group of outcasts. As a result, they have developed a feeling of unity among themselves. Both the Protestant and the Catholic groups regard themselves as "chosen people," thinking that they belong to Heaven while the rest of the villagers are sinners, or people of this world. The preachers of the churches have taught their members to distinguish themselves from the other people. Needless to say, this has tremendously widened the gap between the Christian groups and the rest of the families in the village. But the distinction does not stop here. Protestant-Catholic antagonism has split the two Christian groups. All the non-Christian families practice ancestor worship. They have the Kitchen God in their kitchens, burn incense sticks and kow-tow in the shrine of the God of Earth on the New Year Festival, and patronize the Buddhist temple in the district.

For these reasons, we may consider them as another religious group, though they are by no means organized.

The Christian groups and the other villagers came into difficulty over the question of sharing expenses for practicing opera in the village. The opera was a most important amusement and it was an annual occasion. All the families contributed to it according to their means, except the Christian groups who refused to pay their share. They held that the opera was a kind of thanksgiving to the Dragon God and therefore contradictory to Christianity, and Christians could not give money to it; but that did not prevent the Christian families and their relatives from attending the performance and enjoying the entertainment as much as anyone else. This greatly annoyed the other villagers and the Christian groups were regarded as no longer properly belonging to the village. The villagers' resentment grew when they were told that the Christians were protected by foreign power.

This was not the only friction that occurred between the Christian groups and the other villagers. The Christians were taught that they were God's chosen people, that they no longer belonged to this world but to God's world, and that they must organize themselves into one body against all who were not Christians, and who, therefore, were "sinners." The poor Christians, who felt that they had been oppressed or ill-treated by the wealthy people, wanted to avenge themselves and to express their feeling of injustice. The ambitious members assumed that they were as good as, or even superior to, those who held leadership in the village, the village gentry. They considered it an injustice that they did not have the opportunities to demonstrate their leadership. Besides, the Christians had the attitude that the non-Christians were pitiful because they resisted the "true God" and were, therefore, committing the sin of worshiping false gods. On their side, the non-Christian villagers regarded both the Protestant and the Catholic groups as mean people —people who refused to pay homage to their ancestors, who betrayed their countrymen but made friends with foreigners. Since both sides had prejudices like these, conflicts could hardly be avoided. It was only after people had had time to become more familiar with the religion, and the excitement at the strange things had abated, that the hostile attitude of the non-Christians was lessened. The reconciliation was also attributed to the enlightenment of many of the Christians. In recent years, many well-trained leaders grew up among the Chinese Christians who understand Christianity much better than their predecessors, the first converts, did. These men take a liberal attitude and cooperate in many collective activities with other groups, and refrain from condemning other beliefs.

Clan feuds were a not uncommon source of village conflict. Such a feud existed between some families of the P'an and the Ch'en clans. In the course of it, a Ch'en family was attacked one night by gangsters whose faces were either painted or covered by masks. The family and their relatives all suspected some of the P'ans, but since they could not produce any evidence for their suspicions, the P'ans pronounced the accusation a great insult. Although the case did not develop into a serious clan fight, the bad feeling between the two clans was heightened.

Through many generations the Chinese village gentry have learned an interesting way to end certain kinds of village conflicts. This is to do nothing about it. When two lower-class families get into a dispute, the mothers scold each other on the street, their husbands may have a fist fight, and then it all suddenly stops. The next day their children play together as usual, the adults may not speak to each other for ten days or more, but they conduct their own business as usual and gradually forget the matter. Disturbances of this kind are usually ignored by the village leaders.

Pacification has been for long the measure usually employed to end important village disputes. Usually this is done through the good offices of the village leaders, but when the gentry or the chief clans are involved, the ordinary village leaders do not have sufficient prestige to intervene. In these cases, leaders from other villages are called in. These may be no more capable than the local leaders, but because they are from a different village their presence means more to the conflicting parties, and, therefore, they have a greater "face." Many disputes are thus settled by outside intervention.

The general procedure is as follows: First, the invited or self-appointed village leaders come to the involved parties to find out the real issues at stake, and also to collect opinions from other villagers concerning the background of the matter. Then they evaluate the case according to their past experience and propose a solution. In bringing the two parties to accept the proposal, the peacemakers have to go back and forth until the opponents are willing to meet halfway. Then a formal party is held either in the village or in the market town, to which are invited the mediators, the village leaders, clan heads, and the heads of the two disputing families. The main feature of such a party is a feast. While it is in progress, the talk may concern anything except the conflict. The expenses of the feast will either be equally shared by the disputing parties or borne entirely by one of them. If the controversy is settled in a form of "negotiated peace," that is, if both parties admit their mistakes, the expenses will be equally shared. If the settlement reached shows that only one party was at fault, the expenses are paid by the guilty family.

Very few—perhaps none—of the disputes in this village have been solved by a lawsuit. . . . Villagers forced into a legal case must go to the county seat and hire lawyers, and the ensuing costs are prohibitive for any of the farm families. Nine out of ten families who have sought recourse to the law have had to sacrifice a great part of their small property. Countless stories and proverbs have discouraged farmers from referring their cases to the government. Private mediation has been and is now the most important legal mechanism in rural districts throughout the country. Social justice has been in the past much more important than legal power in protecting the weak against violence of any sort. It is a fact that no matter how small or weak a family may be, if its members behave fairly to the other villagers, both the strong and the lawless will either help it or leave it alone. If it is unreasonably attacked, the attacker would sooner or later be discovered and the whole village would punish him.

Since a number of village conflicts are caused by hurting somebody's "face," it is necessary to discuss the losing or gaining of [the intangible,] "face." When we say in Chinese that one loses face, we mean that he loses prestige, he has been insulted or has been made to feel embarrassment before a group. When we say that a man wants face, we mean that he wants to be given honor, prestige, praise, flattery, or concession, whether or not these are merited. Face is really a personal psychological satisfaction, a social esteem accorded by others.

Perhaps this can be better understood by analyzing the factors involved in losing or gaining face. The first factor is the status of social or other equality between the persons involved. For instance, if a village dignitary asks another to make a social call with him or to grant some other favor and is refused, he will feel that he has lost face. If, on the other hand, a peasant is similarly refused by one of his own rank, he will not have this feeling.

The second factor is the inequality between the social status of the two persons. When a boxer is defeated by an opponent as strong as he is, he will feel sorry but will not lose face. But if the victor is known to be inferior to him, then he will consider his defeat a great loss of face. . . . However, this principle cannot be extended indefinitely. It would not be true to say that the lower the opponent's status, the greater the loss of face. If the insulting person is only a plain peasant or one who has been considered ignorant or mean, a cultured man does not lose face at all, because people will say that the trouble is caused by the peasant's ignorance and is not the other's fault, and if the latter remains impervious to the taunt, he will win great praise from the villagers for being too great to quarrel with a mean person, or so kind that he can forgive another's ignorance.

A third factor is the presence of a witness. In fact, the question of losing or not losing face is based on anticipation of the effect upon a third person or party. If the indignity has not been witnessed or is certain to remain unknown to anyone else, then bitterness may be roused but not the sense of losing face. . . . But the effectiveness of the presence or knowledge of a third party varies with the degree of intimacy between the third party and the persons involved.

Thus, social relationship is a fourth factor. If the third person is intimate with one or both of the opposing parties, the defeated or insulted party does not feel that he has lost face, or at least the feeling will be negligible. But if the third person is not an intimate, the situation is quite different. In the family, for instance, there is no problem of losing or gaining face in relations between husband and wife, parents and children, or between siblings, but there is such a problem between the in-laws. The problem becomes more serious when the social distance extends outside the family to the neighborhood, to the village, and even beyond. Beyond a certain distance, however, this factor becomes ineffective. When a man lives in a completely strange society there is no problem of face, no matter what kind of mistakes he may make, because nobody knows him.

A fifth factor is social value or social sanction. One may commit different and numerous mistakes, but not all of them entail loss of face. In a society where agriculture is the main occupation, one loses face if his farm is not cared for. People pay much attention to filial piety and ancestor reverence, and a family loses face if its members do not hold together as long as their parents are alive or do not conduct a proper funeral for them when they die.

The consciousness of one's own social prestige is a sixth factor. The more conscious one is of his status, the stronger is his fear of losing face. For instance, a liberal or free-minded village gentry would not be particularly disturbed if a junior villager should unwittingly offend him. But if he were highly conventional or orthodox, he would be outraged and

if the offender did not apologize immediately it would become a serious case.

Thus, age becomes a seventh factor in the problem of face. Young people have not as yet acquired much social prestige and therefore do not have much face to lose. On the other hand, old people frequently do not feel loss of face. They can easily be excused (and they always excuse themselves) on the ground that they are old, and besides, experience has made them too mature to be easily embarrassed. Only the middle-aged people, who are very careful to safeguard their social prestige, are serious about losing or gaining face.

Lastly, a person's sensibility is also a factor. A situation that makes one person lose face leaves another unhurt. It is very easy to hurt a sensitive person's feelings and if the slight occurs in the presence of a third person he is certain to feel that he has lost face.

VILLAGE LEADERS

In spite of [recent] changes, the official leaders in Taitou are still essentially of the old category and function in the old manner. A middle-aged man of the P'an clan now serves as the official head of the village. Older people still call him *chwang-chang,* while the young villagers who like to pick up new terms address him as *hsiang-chang.* He takes charge of all public affairs and acts on behalf of the villagers in dealing with the government or with other villages. This man has been in office about ten years. Before him, the *chwang-chang* was his father, and before that, it was a man of the Ch'en clan.

At the beginning of every year a meeting is held to elect a *hsiang-chang,* his chief assistant, and other subordinate officers. Those who attend are the senior members of the families. Every family may be represented by at least one member, though a number of families do not send anyone. . . .

The election is conducted very informally. There is no ballot casting, no hand raising, and no campaign for candidates. The meeting is held in the village school or in some other customary meeting place. When several members of each clan have arrived, the person who presides over the meeting will stand up and say, "Uncles and brothers, now we are all here to discuss the public affairs of our village. As you all know, our *Chwang-chang,* Uncle P'an Chi, has served us very well in the past year. He has worked hard and honestly to pacify disputes, to defend our village, to help families which have been involved in unfortunate controversies, to represent our interests in dealing with the government, and so on. As you also know, to be a public servant in these days is really a headache. Road building, military training for civilians, land surveys, school establishment, village defense, and what not, are all troublesome duties. . . . Uncle P'an Chi has recently said that he feels his age, that he is too tired to bear the heavy burden any longer, and would like to be relieved. I want to know whether we should let Uncle P'an Chi retire and elect another person to be our *Chwang-chang,* or should we ask him to continue. Since this is a matter of importance to our whole village, you are requested to express your ideas and let us know what your opinions are."

This opening address is followed by a moment of silence. Then one of the electors, usually a partially recognized village leader, will say, "Since, as Uncle Heng Li has just said, Uncle P'an Chi has served us well in the past, I cannot see why we should let him retire. I myself, and, I believe, many other fellow villagers, really appreciate Uncle P'an Chi's service, and I do not see any other person among us that is better for the office than he."

"Brother Heng Chun is right," says another representative, who is spinning his home-raised silk on a small spindle and has his long, thin tobacco pipe in his mouth. "We must ask Uncle P'an Chi to continue as our *Chwang-chang.* He has the ability and the experience. Who else can deal with those tricky government servants as he can? I know I couldn't."

. . . When several others have been asked and given an assenting answer, the election is decided, and the village's *chwang-chang* is again in office.

Other officers, such as the *lin-chang, lu-chang* or *chia-chang,* are elected at the same meeting, but in a still less dignified manner. Every villager knows that no upper-class person wants to be elected to any of these offices and knows also that in each neighborhood there are two or three persons who would not refuse to serve. They simply tell one of these persons in each *hu-tung* that he is elected as the *lu-chang* of the neighborhood.

The election is a relatively simple matter since there is no competition for office. On the whole, it may be said that the majority of villagers do not wish to serve in any official capacity and are glad to find among their number an individual who is eager to do so.

The late P'an Chi was considered a successful *chwang-chang* in Taitou, and he may be taken as the type of person who generally became an official leader. He was a man of leisure. He had no farm business to occupy his time, nor was he a craftsman who had to work day and night when business was good. He was the head of a family of three grown sons who were capable of working the family's small holdings of land, so his help in the fields was not needed. He was a man who did not balk at petty deception when the situation warranted it, and he often admitted openly that, for the benefit of the village and for his personal profit, he had to play tricks every so often. He said that not all villagers were honest people and that not all honest villagers would see that some of the means by which the *chwang-chang* received compensation for his services were reasonable. In order to cope with those who were not honest and with those who were honest but unreasonable, subterfuge was necessary.

Once such a person is elected, the probability is that he will remain in office for a long time. Some villagers may not be satisfied with him, but as long as he does not make serious mistakes they will not bother to elect someone else. If he himself really wants to retire, he informs the important villagers of his intention, so that the chairman of the election will make a different kind of opening address and the villagers will not reelect him. If he has done something inexcusable, then either he himself would not have face to hold office any longer or the influential laymen leaders would suggest his dismissal. In this case, the chairman of the meeting would also hint that a new *chwang-chang* should be elected and the villagers would follow the cue. The result of the election is therefore to some extent prearranged and the meeting is a routine matter. The real authority lies in the hands of the laymen leaders. Most villagers understand this and do not attribute too much importance to the office of *chwang-chang*.

The most important duty of the official leaders is dealing with the local or county government on behalf of the villagers. When a government order arrives, the local authority summons the *chwang-chang* of all villages in the district to the market town, where they are informed of their duty. The local *chwang-chang* returns to his village, sees the important laymen first, and discusses with them the way in which the order will be carried out. Then a tentative plan is drawn up. After this has been done, the *chwang-chang* calls a meeting of his assistants and all the other village officers, including representatives of some families of each clan, at which the government order and the tentative plan are presented. After some discussion, the final details for recruiting labor, sharing expenses, and planning the schedule of work are roughly formulated. Then the assistants and other subordinate officers inform all the families of what they are to do. In case some of the villagers complain about the plan or attempt to evade their responsibilities, the *chwang-chang* or his chief assistant will rebuke them on the main street or at a public gathering—provided they are not persons of importance.

Finally, we see that the *chwang-chang* is often the chairman of the few significant village meetings that take place, such as discussions on how to participate in the government's rural reconstruction programs, or the organization of village defense, and so on. We also see that the *chwang-chang* is often asked to be present at the time of the separation of a family. His presence is not actually required in such an instance, but if the brothers have no important relatives or clan head he is the most suitable person to act as a witness to the proceedings.

The *chwang-chang* and his chief assistant receive compensation for their services in money or in entertainment and gifts. Formerly, the *chwang-chang* and other officers were not paid. Expenses were paid out of the public funds and the officers made a commission which took the place of a regular salary. If the actual expenses were ten dollars, for example, they would collect twelve and keep the difference for themselves. No villager ever bothered to make a fuss about this as long as the amounts were small.

In each village there are a number of persons who are in a sense leaders though they hold no official position. Their influence in public affairs or in the community life may be much greater than that of the official leaders, but it may not be evident. They are known essentially as respected laymen. The most notable of these are the village elders, those who have performed special services for the village as a whole, and the schoolteachers.

In a Chinese village a *tsu-chang,* or head of a clan, has some influence over a designated group of families, but his influence is only recognized by the clan and operates within its limits. He is usually an older member but sometimes may be the person who is the wealthiest family head in that particular community, for his wealth allows him to do things others cannot afford. A neighborhood leader is someone who can influence the five or ten families in his *hu-tung,* or small lane, by virtue of his personality or intelligence or general reliability.

There were several other types among the village gentry. One was the gentleman, distinguished by his handsome figure, neat dress, high spirits, good manners, humorous conversation and endless leisure. He was in sharp contrast to the other type of leisured villager who was aggressive, dominating, and inordinately fond of public hearings. Years ago these two types were well exemplified by the heads of two wealthy P'an families. One of them was admired and liked by all the villagers; the other was admired but was not liked because he often showed himself to be stingy in his dealings with hired laborers. These men were not ambitious to be leaders, but they exerted their leadership nonetheless, for it was forced upon them by the position they held in the eyes of the villagers. They were necessarily public figures. This was especially true of the more popular of the two. Because of his mild, impartial, and unassuming manner, he was sought after to mediate disputes that arose between families.

The laymen leaders remain in the background, but their role is so important that without their advice and support the *chwang-chang* and his assistant are unable to accomplish anything. The village gentry are also heads of the chief clans or families. If they object to a program, or even if they merely take a negative attitude, the administration faces an impasse. Laymen leaders do not, as a rule, deal with the government authorities directly. Sometimes the district leader or the county government invites them to a conference to hear their opinions regarding a certain case; not infrequently their advice influences government policy.

. . . The old type of *chwang-chang* does not fit the new requirements, and trained people are replacing him. This has had its effect on the old pattern of subordination to the laymen leaders, who observe this change with a good deal of resentment. The old assurance of their status is gone and in the present insecurity lies the core of much of their antagonism to the new government. They are necessarily the "conservative" element of the population. Their criticism of the government is not specifically directed at policies or the plans for improving the rural areas, but rather at those appointed to carry out these changes.

The teacher of the village school has been traditionally a person who occupied simultaneously several statuses. He was the schoolteacher, head of the P'an clan, a member of the village gentry, and a local scholar. The present teacher is no exception; he is an important layman leader, although he is too young to be his clan's head. The teacher of the Christian school has always been an outsider, so his leadership has not, as a rule, been widely recognized. One of these teachers, however, was a very influential person because he possessed the attributes of a real Chinese gentleman. In addition to his specialized training he was able to paint landscapes, write poems, carve wood and stones, conduct conversations, and appreciate natural beauties. He could also smoke like a gentleman and sip tea like an old scholar. He behaved very conventionally before women and old people, but was humorous when he talked with a group of young farmers. As a result he got acquainted with most of the younger villagers and all the old people spoke well of him. He taught in the school for six or seven years, during which time he exerted a significant influence on the cultural opinions and activities of the village.

INTERVILLAGE RELATIONS

Taitou is closely related to Hsinanchen, the market town and connecting link between the various villages which surround it. The limits of the market-town area are set by the communication and transportation facilities and by the natural physical barriers of the region. There are points at which it may overlap that of another market town, and there are also some "neutral zones" between these areas, but, on the whole, although there is no clear-cut line of demarcation, each market town has a definite and recognizable area, and looks upon the people of certain villages as its primary customers; in turn, it is regarded by the villagers as their town.

Hsinanchen is much larger than any of the villages in its area, and has many good buildings, both commercial and residential. The important streets and avenues all meet at he center of the town to form a public square. The business section has broad streets lined with shops, drugstores, restaurants, and inns. At the northeastern end of the town is the Confucian temple and the new primary school. On the outskirts are the village-type houses of the farming families.

Since Hsinanchen serves more than twenty villages, it has a considerable volume of business. The five or six drugstores sell, in addition to drugs, sugar, oil, spices, and other things. There are also several blacksmith and silversmith shops, three or four bakeries, two hardware shops, one bookstore, two large wine-making establishments, two carpenter shops, three or four small inns and several restaurants. These shops are open all week but are busiest on regular market days. The owners and clerks came originally from the villages where their families still live, and customers patronize those from their own village. Shops are patronized by the same families for generations; farmers go to them because their fathers and their grandfathers went there.

Most of the trade still takes place on the six regular market days, which occur on the first, fifth, tenth, fifteenth, twentieth, twenty-fifth, and thirtieth day of every month. . . . On market days the business life of the town is in full swing. On the evening before the market opens, the professional itinerant traders begin to pour in with their wares; early in the morning come the village butchers with their dressed hogs; the country merchants with their bags of wheat flour, cans of petroleum, bales of spun cotton yarn; and the carpenters with their homemade furniture and farm implements. Later come the traders who deal in dried foodstuffs, fish and seafood, fruits, pottery, chinaware, and scores of other merchandise. Then the farmers begin streaming in from the surrounding villages with their loads of grains, beans, fresh vegetables and fruits, animal feed, and firewood. Some also drive in livestock which they hope to sell or exchange. Later come the people who have nothing to sell but only want to buy. Some member from almost every household in the village is in the town on market day. In the morning every road leading to the town is crowded with people.

All the available space in the town is crowded with booths, counters, and platforms heaped with merchandise. Traders dealing in similar commodities occupy the same section, thus forming more or less specialized markets. The livestock market and the fuel market are located outside the town on the riverbank. People crowd the streets, shout-ing, bargaining, greeting friends, yelling, and swearing. The excitement reaches its peak at noon and then begins to decline. Soon the roads are filled once more with homeward-bound villagers, but the marketing continues until late afternoon.

The market town provides opportunities for farmers from different villages to meet one another, and is in fact one of the few places where they can meet. Chinese farmers always have friends and relatives in other villages and these meetings in the market take the place of visits, which would be more expensive. When the farmers return home they report to the whole family what they have seen and heard and, in this way, people are kept informed about one another.

Most of the leaders in a Chinese rural community have leisure time, which they are apt to spend in the wine shops or the tea-houses in the market town. They talk or argue in the stores on current affairs or historical events and discuss community problems. Many community programs, good and bad, come out of such informal gatherings and many problems have been solved, wisely or not, in these discussions. A score of villages are linked together or separated in conflict whenever their leaders take measures to avoid each other in the market town.

In general, every large market town is crossed by a main road on which persons from the outside world travel. They bring news from distant places. In the town there are telephone and telegraph offices. The post office brings mail into the town to be distributed to the villages. Commercial agents from the county seat or other large cities bring information from their headquarters, which travels to the villages immediately. Teahouses and wine shops generate rumors which are widely spread. There is an old saying that statesmen should listen to the talk in these hidden corners. It is well known that the farmer does not have much to say at home but is a good talker whenever he finds himself in the market town and sits with his fellow villagers in the teahouse.

Since commercialization and industrialization have gradually penetrated the country-

side, the farmer becomes increasingly dependent upon goods not produced by himself. He
produces only the primary foodstuffs on his
farm and in his vegetable garden, and everything else must be bought from the market
town or other cities.

Economic relations with Tsingtao are on
the increase, both in trade and in the employment of villagers. Every year large quantities
of farm products are sold to Tsingtao either
directly by the farmers themselves or through
the grain dealers and vegetable merchants.
The farmer's inclination for growing special
crops and raising certain livestock for the
market in Tsingtao is becoming more obvious
day by day. The increased acreage for growing soybeans, wheat, certain vegetables and
fruits, and the increased amount of poultry
and hogs is all due to the new market. In
return, Tsingtao supplies the farmers with
an ever-increasing amount of manufactured
goods. In every rural market town one can
see huge quantities of factory-made wheat
flour, cotton yarn or cloth, cans of petroleum,
boxes of matches, soybean cakes for animal
feed, and hundreds of other articles. The self-
sufficient economy of the village as well as
of other villages has become [a thing of the
past.]

Sociocultural Change

>>

China today is important not only for what is happening to it as a massive, strategic area of land and a huge population aggregate; it is important because it is a case study in (1) the effect of Western industrialization and other culture traits upon a peasant society, and (2) the more recent effects of a Communist-dominated government upon a property-conscious peasantry. Two matters of such scope cannot be covered adequately in the space available here, but they at least can be touched upon so as to make us aware of the issues involved. The social scientist would consider that these issues are chiefly those having to do with changes in social relations (social change) and modifications in traditional ways of doing things (cultural change).

One of the major changes underway in China before World War II was the rise of an industrial group, small in numbers but great in power. This moneyed, urban-centered group of financiers, manufacturers, and international merchants was threatening the position of the landowning gentry, a class which in the past had provided the scholars, who in turn became bureaucrats and managed governmental affairs. With this shift in power for the nation as a whole, the status of the peasantry required re-examination. The following selection not only provides a keen insight into the social structure of old China, tying in the clan with the gentry, but shows the new forces underway even before the coming of the Communists.

• 89 • Peasantry and Gentry
HSIAO-T'UNG FEI

The gentry differ from the aristocracy in the West in that the former do not form a political party with the responsibility of running a government. Never in the history of China have the Chinese gentry organized their own government. As a class, they never reject any monarch who is able to seize the power and who recognizes the right of land-

[Adapted from "Peasantry and Gentry: An Interpretation of Chinese Social Structure and Its Changes," *American Journal of Sociology*, Vol. 52, No. 1, Chicago, 1946. Pp. 1-16. Used by permission.]

owners. They will enter any government with the purpose of protecting their own kin and local people from the encroachment of the absolute power, but not for the sake of political power itself. They have no sense of political responsibility. They do not even want to remain in their official position for long, and certainly they abhor public duty. Honor and prestige which the official gentry seek at any price have practical values. They mean security to his own clan and to the people of his locality. In fact, even when he is holding an office in the government, he is at the same time working as a representative of his kin and relatives. The latter function is indeed his main job, but, in order to realize it, he has to take the former. Toward his public position he assumes a negative attitude. He is ready to resign whenever his record and influence are well established and can perform his function as protector of his people without a public office. The gentry as a class are outside the government. They take official positions individually. They are moved by social but not by political responsibility. This is why we should not rank them as aristocracy.

It may also be important to point out here that, owing to their pivotal position in the power structure, the gentry have through long history acquired a set of codes of professional ethics. They preach the doctrine of order: every one should behave according to and be satisfied by the position one occupies in the social structure. The task of Confucius was to set down for each social status its canon of correct behavior. The gentry's interest is not in possessing political power but in maintaining order irrespective of who the monarch is. They will serve him as long as he behaves as a benevolent ruler, but if he becomes despotic and suppresses the peasants too hard, the gentry will exert their pressure against him. On the other hand, if the peasants revolt against the ruler, and disturb the social order, they will fight on the side of the monarch. This is their social responsibility. Being a privileged class themselves, they are never revolutionary. Order and security are their sole interests.

. . . A peasant who works on the land is bound to the land as a peasant. Therefore, we may ask how the gentry emerges. Of course, we must admit that, since there is no social barrier preventing a peasant from entering into the gentry if he can afford to lead a leisurely life, there will be those hard-working peasants who strive to rise from the bottom. But it will take them several generations to climb up the social ladder, each generation promoting itself a little. Despite thrift and endurance, this is not only a long but also a haphazard way, because in the rural community misfortunes of all kinds are not uncommon. . . . It will be most rare for a family to keep up its morale for several generations and to have no misfortune strike at them in the meantime.

Another factor which prevents a hardworking and well-to-do peasant family from rising is the high pressure of population. . . . The birth rate is as high as that of the poor peasants and the death rate is comparatively low owing to their better living standard. Such a family grows fast. If it cannot expand its estate at the same rate, its standard of living will sink in the next generation.

It is quite natural that the common tendency among the peasants is not to rise on the social ladder but rather to sink toward the bottom. A petty owner may become a tenant when he sells his land as misfortune befalls him. He may further sink from a tenant to a landless farm laborer. He may in the end die disgracefully or disappear from the village. These outcasts are desperate. They have nothing to lose but their life of drudgery. They leave the village and plunge themselves into banditry or smuggling, or join the army, or seek employment as servants in big gentry houses. These are economically nonproductive jobs, but it is only by taking up such jobs, in addition to good luck, that the outcasts from the rural society can hope to obtain wealth quickly. Only a few reach their aim through various kinds of more or less unlawful ways. But if the ruling class is degenerate and weak, they are the uprising group aiming at power. In Chinese history there are several instances where new dynasties were inaugurated by such desperate outcasts.

In peacetime the few successful upstarts when they have obtained wealth will buy land and insinuate themselves into the leisure class. They are looked down upon and looked at with a prejudiced eye by the gentry. Only gradually and especially by means of affinal alliance, are they admitted into the upper layer of the social structure. Not until one of the family members enters into the scholar group and into officialdom is their position in the gentry consolidated.

The gentry are maintained economically by owning land and politically by occupying a position in officialdom. As a landowning class they have the leisure to learn classical literature which is the professional requirement of an official. For nearly a thousand years the monarch has offered regular examinations to recruit officials from the literati. Only a few low classes are excluded from the right to take part in such examinations. Theoretically men from the peasantry are free to enter into the competition. And there are notable cases in which a son of a poor peasant learned the classics on the back of his buffalo while he was working in the field and attained high honor in the examination. But, after all, these are exceptions, for otherwise such stories would not be circulated like legends. It is true that in China there is no such social class system as the caste system, but it is another question as to whether the Chinese class system possesses high mobility. The mobility between peasantry and gentry has been rather limited. It is needless to add that the existence of the belief among the peasants in the possibility of promotion to the gentry is important because it gives an incentive and eventually stabilizes the structure at large.

Conversely we may ask how frequently the members of the gentry return to peasantry. As far as my own knowledge goes, I cannot find a single case where a good-for-nothing gentleman picks up farming again. It seems impossible that the gentry should return to the farm. Manual labor is highly deplored in the current ideology in China,

even today. The gentry are especially conscious of it. A long gown that signifies leisure is the emblem of honor and prestige and is the last thing a gentleman will cast away. It is worth more than one's life.

Posed on the peak of the social pyramid, the gentry possess prestige and privilege. Prestige and privilege attract the daring and the aggressive individuals from the classes below. The new recruits revitalize the gentry, but, when they are assimilated, they become pacified and neutralized. The energy that may cause upheavals is channeled into the petty mobility in the social structure and is finally eliminated in the pattern of leisurely life. The gentry class is in fact a safety valve in social changes. Conservatism becomes the rule of Chinese society, and China as a culture is singular in the history of human kind in its stability and perpetuation.

Traditional China has not passed. It is present, although in many respects it has been covered by modifications and by novelties. This is why I have consistently used the present tense in the above description. Let no one think that what I have described is only a page of dead history. The essential pattern of the social structure is functioning as ever. That it is changing, I am sure. But the new order will . . . be born from the old through the gradual change of the habitual way of living of the millions.

It seems that traditional China achieved a certain equilibrium from which ensued stability. This equilibrium was upset when China came in contact with the Western powers, with their industrial supremacy.

Modern industry gives the West a power unprecedented in history over agrarian communities. Unlike an age of agriculture when people can live harmlessly alone, the industrial age is an age of expansion, a lure to a world community. Seeking raw material and markets, the industrial nations will not let the Eastern Hemisphere alone. To be sure, trade is for mutual benefit, and industry is the best cure for the poverty of the East. But to the Westerner it is still a mystery why the Chinese of the past generation were so stubborn in refusing to let in Western industrial influences; [yet to] say that the Chinese were prejudiced against new creeds of religion and new ways of production as such is without historical foundation. Buddhism was new to China when it was first introduced, but it was soon incorporated into Chinese religious beliefs and became deeply rooted among the peasants. New crops like the potato and tobacco spread without meeting resistance. To me, the unhappy history of the first period of contact between the East and the West is mainly caused by social factors which can be seen in the perspective I have outlined above.

When the Industrial Revolution started in Europe, it was the middle class who took the lead. Medieval feudalism was receding. But in China at the time of the contact with the West, the middle class was the conservative gentry. The ideal of the gentry is to enjoy leisure under the protection of officialdom. Production is the occupation of the peasants and is considered low. The initiative of the gentry in economic pursuits has long been suppressed. Industrialism is not like Buddhism. When Buddhism made its first appearance, it caught the spirit of the gentleman of leisure. It fitted neatly into the tradition of retirement. Therefore, it was able to recruit from that class a number of talents who spread the creed in China. But modern industrialism, on the contrary, runs counter to the traditional spirit of the gentry. How could industrialism find an easy entrance into China?

The crisis created by the intrusion of Western industrial influences, since the Chinese government failed to resist the powerful intruding force, did not call forth the immediate and effective adjustment of the gentry. They failed because the crisis did not present itself as a direct threat to them. Their interest was in rent-collecting. As long as the peasants were able to pay their rent, the gentry had nothing to worry them. It would have needed foresight to see that Western industrial influences, if not adjusted to the rural conditions in China, would lead eventually to the bankruptcy of the peasants and affect the economic basis of the gentry. But the gentry

lacked foresight. Having no strong sense of political responsibility, they were naturally even less sensitive to the fact that China's political sovereignty was dwindling. The antiforeign policy of the government furthered the aloofness of the gentry, who were submissive in nature.

The rapid intrusion of the Western powers, mainly motivated by commercial interests, on the one hand, and the ineptitude of the Chinese government and the leading class, on the other, resulted in a peculiar adjustment in the first phase of contact between the East and the West. It was characterized by the creation of a special zone of foreign settlement which was later developed into the so-called treaty ports. Order in the ports was maintained by a specially organized government either in the hands of the consuls or in the hands of the representatives of the foreign residents. The Chinese government had no voice in the rule of the special zone. In such zones a type of cosmopolitan community developed.

Cultures come in contact with each other through their agents. In the treaty ports different elements of the Western peoples and the Chinese are gathered. Among the westerners, traders are predominant. Their interest is in making profit. They are not concerned with the wider spheres of social welfare and international good-will which bear no immediate commercial benefit and engender no community security. No efforts have been made on the part of the Western traders to improve the incongruous relation with the people among whom they are living; [instead,] they make deplorable discriminations against the Chinese. These make a respectable Chinese uncomfortable. Humiliation prevents harmonious association. Therefore to such ports a special type of Chinese was attracted. They are known as *compradors*. I possess no sufficient data on the family background of those who form the first line of contact with Western traders, but I strongly suspect that those "secondhand foreigners" were, at least for the early period, recruited from the outcasts of the traditional structure who had lost their positions and sought their fortune through illegal means. Treaty ports are open to them. If they find regular employment in the community, such as servants or interpreters in a foreign concern, they gradually become compradors or first-boys; if they fail, they form gangs. They live in, and take advantage of, the margin of cultural contact. They are half-caste in culture, bilingual in speech, and morally unstable. They are unscrupulous, pecuniary, individualistic, and agnostic, not only in religion but in cultural values. Treaty ports are ultraurban. They are a land where the acquisition of wealth is the sole motive, devoid of tradition and culture.

To the towns in the interior come foreign missionaries. As individuals they are decent people. But they carry, in one hand, the enthusiasm to convert the heathens who are not conscious of their sins themselves and, in the other hand, the privilege of political protection given to the nationals of the Western powers. Religious salvation attracts few because the ordinary Chinese feels no need for a new creed, but the political protection shines in the eyes of those who need extra shelter for their illegal pursuits.

However, as the influences from the West, both political and economical, grow in China, the special group of Chinese, nursed in the treaty ports and in the churches in the interior, gathers importance. Regardless of the type of their character, they occupy a strategic position in China's transition. They are the first few who know foreign languages and the ways to deal with Western people. As their children grow up, they give them modern education and send them abroad to attend Western universities. From this group a new class is formed. They are engaged in professional jobs; at first mainly dependent on foreign sponsors and later on their own feet. But, being reared in a cosmopolitan community, they are fundamentally hybrids. In them are manifest the comprador characteristic of social irresponsibility. It is this class that dominates the first phase of Chinese social and political changes.

Western industrial influence does not stop at the treaty ports. It works its way far into the interior. As I have mentioned above, the bulk of Chinese manufacturing industry is widely scattered in the homesteads of the peasants. The peasants work on their simple looms in their spare time. They have to take up jobs like that because the farm is too small to support them. But handicraft is far less efficient than machine work. Native products cannot compete with the manufactured goods from Western factories. The quality of native products is poor and the cost high. Gradually the native workers lose their jobs. The cheap but good cloth made in factories, for instance, penetrates deep into the remotest villages. This means that thousands of looms in the peasants' homes must stop working. The decline of native industry owing to the invasion of Western industrialism further impoverishes the already poor peasants. Rural depression forces the peasants to sell their land, and more and more peasants sink into tenancy. This is not the end. Tenants have to pay rent to the owners. This means an increase in the peasants' burden. In the area near the modern cities in the coastal provinces, where Western industrial influence is most strong, more than 80 per cent of the peasants are already tenants. The annual drain on rural produce in terms of rent payment is terrific. Many peasants leave their land and become landless laborers. They crowd into the treaty ports to be factory workers or gangsters. Those who remain in the villages linger on, hard pressed under the exacting taxes, rents, and interest. They are desperate.

Rural depression at last threatens the privileges of the gentry. They begin to disintegrate. Those who cling to the traditional privileges have to resort to stronger political backing. They become the spearhead of the oppressors of the peasant movement. They exert pressure on the government to maintain their privilege. However, being an intellectual class, a part of them, the second generation of the old landed gentry, after receiving modern education, take up professional jobs and earn their living independent of land.

Here we find another front of contact between the East and the West. This front is different from that found in the treaty ports. It is mainly cultural. Early in the last period

of the imperial dynasty, a new form of gentry had the opportunity to go abroad, mainly
on government missions or scholarships, and,
unlike the compradors, grew interested in
Western civilization. They were educated in
academic centers, mostly in England. They
translated the works of Adam Smith, Herbert
Spencer, Montesquieu, J. S. Mill, and others
into classical Chinese (which, I believe, are
still the best translations of Western classical
works in Chinese). They tried to dig into
the source of Western civilization and to introduce the best of the West to China. But
it is a slow process, and much slower than
the aping of the irresponsible and superficial
commercial spirit of the foreign traders in
the treaty ports. Slow as it is, it moves on
gradually. The new gentry started the movement of the Chinese renaissance. It was a
movement for vernacular literature, scientific
research, democracy, and modern morality.
This movement was a combined effort of the
returned students and students in Chinese
colleges. Most of them were the children of
the landed gentry.

However, the new gentry share with the
old the same traditional spirit in their lack
of active political responsibility. They frequently voiced their disapproval of the government politics but rarely attempted to assume government responsibilities by taking
up political power themselves. The central
power, since the downfall of the Manchu
Dynasty, has been held by the war lords and
by the treaty-port group. The rising of a
soldier into imperial power is an old story.
In the traditional structure, when a ruler is
degenerate and abuses his unbounded power,
he will encroach on the peaceful life of the
people. The peasant will suffer most. Many
of them will become bandits and begin to
revolt. Inefficient government will not be
able to check the uprising. A new ruler will
appear. In the same way, war lords appeared
in the early years of the Republic. Most of
them were of peasant origin and many started
their career as outlaws. The treaty-port group
rose from the same background and took a
similar way. The difference is that they were
settled in the protection of the cosmopolitan
community and attained their power not
through military strength but through financial strength. They lusted for power, and,
living under foreign traders, they soon realized that the opportunity enjoyed by foreign
traders could be theirs if they could get into
power. With these matured compradors are
the gangsters who form an integral part of
the treaty-port group. They are well organized and disciplined in their gang spirit.
They are daring and unscrupulous. The instability of the Chinese political situation gives
those power-thirsty elements the opportunity
to seize power. Indeed, I am not trying to
minimize the importance of other groups of
the Chinese people in the political struggle.
Successive revolutions were prepared mostly
by the new professional gentry and carried
through by the peasants and workers; but,
owing to the lack of political responsibility
in the gentry and the backwardness of the
peasants, power repeatedly slipped into the
hands of the war lords and the treaty-port
group.

The economic decline of the land interest
on the one hand, and the rising of a new politically conscious treaty-port group, on the
other, undermined the importance of the
gentry in the social structure of China.

By now the reader will be familiar enough with China to appreciate the point of
view of the authors of the next article. Although they recognize the need for "industrialization" in some form, they argue that it must be accomplished in conformity with the
already existing social and economic structure. A mere transferral of European or American industrial patterns would hardly help the millions of Chinese villagers who need to
supplement their inadequate farm incomes. In China, as elsewhere, every aspect of a
people's life is closely interrelated with every other aspect, so that planning any such mo-

mentous change as industrialization must proceed from a firm and comprehensive knowledge of the country and the people. Fei and Chang are Chinese sociologists who have devoted their lives to the systematic development of such knowledge; consequently they write with both insight and authority.

• 90 • Agriculture and Industrialization
HSIAO-T'UNG FEI AND CHIH-I CHANG

INDUSTRY AND COMMERCE IN RURAL ECONOMY

[There are two basic] facts in Chinese rural economy: the first, that traditional Chinese industry is diffused among villages, and the second, that the farmers depend on it for subsistence. The industrial revolution in the West at last threatens the peasants in the Chinese villages in their capacity as industrialists.

The desperation of this situation is felt by every household where income is declining. Any stroke of misfortune will force the peasant owner to sell his land. We have emphasized the fact that Chinese peasants do not sell their land for profit but only when they are in real distress.

DEVELOPMENT OF CO-OPERATIVE RURAL INDUSTRY AS A SOLUTION TO THE LAND PROBLEM

Since a definition of a social situation is a preliminary step toward action, if the agrarian situation is defined in technological terms only, the actions followed will be limited to technological improvements. It is essential, however, for us to recognize that the situation is much more complicated. We do not deny the importance of technological improvement, but we must also understand its limitations. The present study—far from conclusive—at least indicates that the Chinese treatment of rural economic problems merely as problems of agriculture is one-sided. We should like to emphasize our conclusion that the land

problem is aggravated by the problem of rural industry.

An increase in agricultural productivity, [to choose the very obvious] instance, is helpful, indeed; but, by employing all scientific means available, it is estimated that the possible increase can be only about 20 per cent above present productivity. Such an increase is dwarfed in comparison with the rapid decline in price of rural industrial products, such as silk, for example.

Again, take the measure for the equalization of holdings. It is indeed essential, in view of the present unequal distribution of land. But we must remember that, if the government were to pass measures entirely re-allotting all available land to the peasants, the size of a farm would still be under 5 acres, this figure including much which is uncultivable.

There are two ways to enlarge the size of farms: one is the extension of land under cultivation, and the other is reduction in population. Manchuria and northwestern China may offer some relief for land hunger; but how much population can be moved to these parts is still unknown, and the prospect of extension is uncertain. Reduction in population has been the most common solution to the Chinese agrarian situation throughout her history. Periods of prosperity are usually followed by periods of disturbance, in which large numbers of people are wiped out by civil war and famine. Such catastrophes, of course, must not be allowed to occur again. With an improvement in public health, even

[Adapted from *Earthbound China: a Study of Rural Economy in Yunnan*, Routledge and Kegan Paul, London, 1948. Pp. 299-312. Used by permission.]

if measures for decreasing the birth rate are introduced simultaneously, there will not be a quick reduction in population. Therefore, a practical solution cannot be sought along that line either.

The remaining alternative is to move the agricultural population out into other occupations. It seems unreasonable to hope that in the near future the Chinese peasant can live entirely on agriculture. This does not mean that China is born to be poor forever. Her economic potentiality is large, in view of her abundance of manpower and resources. It means only that we must not hope that agriculture alone will save China and give a higher standard of living to the people. If we recognize this fact, the way open to us is one similar to that which has been employed for centuries—the supplementing of agriculture with diffused industry.

It is perhaps important to bear in mind that, given the opportunity, China will inevitably be industrialized; but whether or not this new industrialization will be beneficial to the peasants is the problem. The answer depends upon the form taken by this new industry. If it develops according to the pattern of European and American industry of the last few centuries—that is, if it is concentrated in urban areas and in the hands of a few capitalists—it will only aggravate the distress of the rural population, because it will take away from the village all its homestead industries and thus further decrease the income of the peasants. This process has already been taking place during the last few decades. The further industrialization of China in this way would simply mean that the wealth concentrated in industry will be in the hands not merely of foreign but also of Chinese industrialists—a difference which will not alter the economic condition of the peasants.

It should also be pointed out, at this point, that, if the mass of peasants cannot share in the profits of industry but only suffer from its effects in decreasing their livelihood, the growth of newly developing industry in China will be [severely] checked by a shrinkage of its markets. From this point of view, we can

then lay down the principle that the future form of China's industrial organization must be such that the peasants can share in its profit in order to raise their standard of living, since agriculture alone is unable to do so. In order to achieve this, some part of industry must be decentralized and established in villages or in centers near villages, so that the profits of the industry can be widely distributed among the peasants.

To return to the traditional principle of supplementing the family income of the peasants by industry does not mean to retain the old industrial technology. To argue for retention of traditional industrial practices in the village is impractical. The handicraft technology must be improved by introducing machinery. What we should retain is the fundamental principle underlying the traditional form of this industry—that of a diffused industry suited to the agrarian situation. However, the question which now arises is whether it is possible to have technological improvement under the traditional principle of diffused industry.

Historically, it is true that the industrial revolution was achieved through the concentration of machine equipment and of population. The improvement in technology has been, so far, largely parallel with the development of urban centers. However, this was mainly due to the employment of steam power at the first stage of industrial development. When electric power was introduced, the trend toward concentration of industry changed.

It is [becoming] clear that decentralization of manufacturing plants is not a regression in industrial development but a general tendency in modern industry. Ought China, as a latecomer in the modern industrial world, start with the old pattern and only later move to reorganize? The economic history of the West is a warning against such a policy. The cost involved in such reorganization is great and explains why the decentralized pattern, although it has been proved to be more economical, is slow in being adopted in the West. Large investments in old-style industrial plants prevent a quick adjustment to new technological advances. China thus may have an advantage in starting from the industrial front instead of from the rear. Therefore, it appears that the decentralized industrial pattern is to be recommended, in view both of the traditional background and of modern technology.

[The] success of small-scale rural co-operative factories depends as much upon their external relations with other similar factories and with the markets as upon their internal organization. . . . A large organization, which will co-ordinate the small manufacturing units, is necessary for the new rural industry of China.

Given a co-ordinating organization, manufacturing centers scattered through the villages can work on machine parts or on a specific part in a manufacturing process. They can pool together their products, to be assembled later in a central plant. Thus the advantage of large-scale production is preserved while the concentration of population in urban centers is done away with. For the central co-ordinating management we will look to the government for aid. [Hence] we must point out that such industry must be confined to the manufacturing of consumers' goods. For heavy industry a concentrated plant is necessary. Moreover, if development of transportation lags behind, manufacturing industries will naturally be located near heavy industries. The result will be a rapid concentration in urban centers and the deterioration of the rural areas as pictured above. Thus the sequence in which the various types of industry develop will determine their location.

Let us recognize that we are now at a crossroads. The fate of innocent Chinese peasants is in the hands of those who will decide the pattern of China's industry in the future. No one nation can decide the issue, however; the choice of what sort of a world we are to live in must come with the wide co-operation of the citizens of the world, whose opinion will ultimately decide the case.

Industrialization and the growth of commerce have not been the only sources of social change in China. The new education, stemming largely from a Western orientation, has had a profound effect, as the following selection will show.

· 91 · *Education*
GERALD F. WINFIELD

Perhaps nowhere in the world is learning more revered than in China, yet in no other equally large population is the general level of modern knowledge so low. The entire culture of the country is based firmly on the writings of the sages who lived five hundred years before Christ and who recorded the knowledge of the previous three thousand years and gave to it the prestige and historical influence it still possesses. The greatest and most influential of these sages was Confucius, a teacher on whose work was built the more than 2,000-year-old Chinese educational philosophy and content.

The focus of Chinese education was the system of imperial civil service examinations, first established more than two thousand years ago by the Western Han dynasty.

These examinations, which continued from the year 165 B.C. until they were abolished by imperial edict in 1905, exerted a profound influence not only on education but on the whole social system. Any person who felt himself qualified might take the lowest

[Adapted from *China: The Land and the People*, by Gerald Winfield. Copyright, 1948, 1950, by Gerald Winfield. Pp. 146-167. With the permission of William Sloane Associates, Inc.]

grade of examination given each year in the local hsien magistrate's *yamen*. If successful, the candidate possessing the equivalent of a primary school education was eligible for the provincial examinations and for appointment to one of the lower ranking positions of government. If the candidate then passed the provincial examination, he assumed a more advanced title and was eligible for the national and highest examination as well as for more responsible government positions. Those successful at the highest examinations became full-fledged scholars and, when appointed, sacrosanct officials, who, under the prevailing family system, raised not only themselves but their entire clan to an enviable social position. Because all examinations were literary in content, Chinese education is literary by tradition, and Chinese officialdom down through the centuries has been composed of the literati.

Since official posts carried with them social prestige and opportunities to accumulate wealth, it was not long until education, wealth, and official position became practically synonymous and the perquisites of a relatively small group.

Down the generations families have risen to or lost their foothold in this educated class. They have risen because of the ability of a brilliant son, for it has always been possible for a lad with exceptional ability and with an opportunity to study to obtain official position.

The flaw in this system has always been the problem of the opportunity to study, since the type of learning necessary can be acquired only by many years of effort. Even the most brilliant cannot master the complicated and difficult Chinese language and literature in odd moments. The student must have his entire time free from the demands of other work, and he must have both books and teachers. Consequently a large proportion of educated officialdom came from already scholarly families.

For the successful scholars, education began early in life. It was not uncommon for a child of two or three to begin recognizing characters, and at four or five to study with his father or grandfather, if he was fortunate enough to belong to an educated family. At eight or nine the neophyte began to work with a hired tutor or to attend a small private tutorial school maintained by a retired local scholar or someone who preferred teaching to government service. Almost from the first day of study the child began with the classics, reading the abstruse and profound ideas of Confucius and the other sages, ideas made even more difficult by the highly condensed form of literary writing developed in complicated ideographs. Although the child had little conception of the meaning of the sentences memorized, he was required to hammer away day after day, pounding the classics into his nervous system until he could *pei* them word for word without error. To pei, or "to back," is to turn the back to the teacher and repeat in a high singsong voice the memorized but little understood words of the classic texts.

This classical method of preparation for the imperial examinations produced many thousands of brilliant scholars through the years of China's long history.

On the other hand, the old classical education saddled China with two persistent curses. It has laid the curse of ignorance on the masses, and it has laid the curse of the scholar on the educated.

The curse of ignorance exists because the language structure, the nature, and the teaching methods of classical learning are much too difficult for the average person to grasp in a short time, with the result that the knowledge of the average peasant in China today is severely limited. Most of them spend their entire lives within walking distance of the house in which they were born. Most of them have never seen a map and cannot conceive of anything alien to their immediate experience.

Most Chinese peasants are anything but stupid. Their knowledge of their own folklore and folk history is extensive, although it is frequently far from being historically accurate.

The curse of the scholar, which lies equally heavily on the educated of China, may be summed up in the proverb: "The scholar can neither shoulder a carrying pole nor lift a basket."

All China accepts the fact that an educated man does not work with his hands. Because this tradition is held by [workers] as well as by scholars themselves, many young scientists and engineers returning to China with advanced foreign training, eager to do great things for their country, have their initiative extinguished by community condemnation whenever they engage in shop or laboratory work.

These two great curses of Chinese knowledge, the curse of ignorance and the curse of the scholar, are slowly but surely diminishing. Literacy and the knowledge of things, of people, and of events are slowly spreading.

What of China's education today? If the ability to read a simple book and to write a simple letter is taken as a definition of literacy, what proportion of the Chinese population is literate?

Peiping education authorities estimate that between 30 and 40 per cent of their population can read and write. Buck found that only a little over 15 per cent of the rural population above seven years of age could pass even the lowest test of literacy. In spite of public education efforts carried on since 1905, 75 or 80 per cent of those over seven years of age are illiterate, although more than a hundred million people can read and write. The largest daily newspaper in China has a circulation of over 100,000, but most newspapers are limited to circulations of less than 10,000.

The possibility of a literate population in China did not exist before the literary revolution that began about thirty years ago. Before that time, only the highly telegraphic classical style of writing was employed, using single literary characters to express key ideas in each sentence, a system of writing so condensed that it is almost unintelligible when read aloud. In order to understand literature at all, the reader had to see the characters, and, worse, he had to recognize many rare characters expressing ideas never used in everyday speech.

The literary revolution came when Dr. Hu Shih, began to write with the same word order that is used in speaking. Now, while many scholars still use the literary form, most popular works are written in the spoken language or in what is known as "modern Chinese," in reality a cross between the literary form and the pure spoken language form.

As the literary revolution gained ground, the "Thousand Character" movement was initiated by Dr. Y. C. James Yen. His movement, providing a sort of basic Chinese using only thirteen hundred characters, is the foundation for the mass education movement that has long since spread far beyond the organization he first formed.

Between 1928 and 1943, almost fifty million adults were reported as having made progress toward literacy in two types of schools and in other special adult classes. In addition, courses were broadened to include instruction in citizenship and some technical knowledge.

One of the remarkable achievements of the Chinese during World War II was the steady growth of literacy education for adults in spite of immense handicaps imposed by war. In 1936-1937, the last year of comparative peace, more than three million adults received instruction in reading and writing. In 1942-1943, during the height of the war, over nine million in unoccupied China received such instruction.

It may be inferred from this and other chapters that World War II, which began as the fifth Sino-Japanese War, had an extraordinary effect on education in China and a direct bearing on the rise in the level of literacy. The ultimate effects, when viewed from the safe distance of history, were to unify the Chinese, to give impetus to the development of kuo-yü (Mandarin) as a common spoken language, to create a stronger and more general desire for education, to acquaint large numbers of remote people with modern ideas of health and education, and to create a more general awareness of and interest in the ultimate purpose of government.

Much was gained merely by the shifting of populations, distributing new ideas and materials, breeding modern attitudes and methods.

Literacy in China is extremely low, but there is no doubt that World War II reduced ignorance, even as World War I gave birth to the Mass Education Movement that has made this improvement possible. But what of the general education system?

China's system of modern education may be said to date from the edict of September 1, 1905, which abolished the imperial civil service examinations. Continual loss of wars and territories had suggested to the occupants of the Dragon Throne that something more than classics, humanities, discipline, and contemplation was needed in Chinese education, and that additional educational facilities were necessary. Prior to that time, education was largely private, and girls usually were not considered worth educating. By 1905 there were a number of Chinese who had studied abroad who helped prod the Dragon Throne out of its traditional and antiquated conservatism, and who further influenced the trend of educational organization, curricula, and methods. To assist them there existed a nucleus of foreign mission schools and colleges exemplary of modern education already adapted to Chinese needs.

It may be observed here that in 1932 a group of European-trained educators representing the League of Nations was invited by the Chinese government to inspect the budding Chinese system of education. Among many valuable suggestions, the commission reported that the whole system was much too American.

Although probably the largest number of Chinese to study abroad until World War II were Japanese-educated and many have studied in Europe, Americans have done a great deal directly and indirectly to shape the education of China. The report issued by the League of Nations commission was quite correct in its charge. During the years when the Chinese government was setting the pattern for an education system, American-trained Chinese and American-operated institutions in China provided a ready-made pattern on the spot.

In spite of the amazing educational efforts that brought about unprecedented expansion during the war years, the quality of education declined. The hasty moving of schools resulted in heavy losses of books, materials, and equipment. Living, teaching, and health conditions deteriorated in crowded wartime quarters. [An equally serious] aggravation has been the lack of good textbooks even though efforts were made to produce enough texts with the limited supply of fourth-rate paper available in unoccupied China.

Middle schools in Japanese-occupied territory also had difficulties, although books were more plentiful and better made. English studies were reduced to the number of hours required in Japanese schools; Japanese language was added to the curricula; and textbook contents were modified, especially in regard to civics, history, and social studies generally. Students in occupied China, always aware of and active in national crises, continued to go to school, but developed a resistance to learning. Postwar teachers found that these students had difficulty in learning when they wanted to.

Postwar graduates from all middle schools far outnumbered prewar graduates but are much less well prepared to enter college or even to hold employment.

Higher education in China more than doubled in volume during and in spite of the war, although it too has had to accept lowered standards. When the last imperial dynasty was overthrown in 1911, the college scene was drab indeed, with a few Chinese colleges enrolling only a few thousand students. By 1936-1937, in all China, 108 colleges, universities, and technical schools of college grade were registered with the Ministry of Education. In the academic year of 1936-1937, 41,922 college students were enrolled and 9,154 were graduated. In 1944-1945 there were 145 institutions of higher learning in unoccupied China alone, with 73,669 students enrolled and 10,514 graduating. The rehabilitation of institutions after the war has brought the total number of colleges and universities to 182 and the total number of students enrolled to approximately 110,000. These figures do not include the twenty-seven research institutes and graduate schools above college grade.

With the rate of college graduations exceeding 10,000 a year the total number of college-trained people in China is still probably not more than 250,000, including those who have studied abroad. This total number, which includes a number of people retired from private life or approaching retirement age, is less than half the number graduating from college *each year* in the United States.

The supply of modern trained leadership that China now possesses is totally inadequate to modernize her society [successfully]. From top to bottom, China's education structure is far too small to provide the level of literacy and technical development she urgently needs.

What of the quality of the average Chinese college student? How does he compare with the average American student?

Students in China, like students anywhere, range from the very brilliant to the relatively stupid. On the average their intellectual abilities match those of students in any American college of high academic standing. In terms of application to work and effort to learn, they average considerably better than American students. They are influenced by the long tradition of extreme diligence and discipline imposed by the difficulties of the old classical education and held as the proper qualities of a scholar. In addition they are impelled to great effort by the realization that they are members of a small and highly privileged group with opportunities rare and enviable in China. The paucity of college-trained men in China in relation to a plethora of manpower caused the Chinese government to request that students refrain from active participation in the last Sino-Japanese War. Their potential value as leaders was considered far in excess of their actual value as officers and soldiers.

The change, within forty years, from an educational system that was a veneer of highly refined, almost superficial, philosophical contemplation, possessed of no more than a few institutions of college grade into a network of comparatively modern public schools and colleges numbering at least 510,000 units and bringing some degree of enlightenment to at least 75,000,000 common people, is a stride worthy of historical note. There remains, however, a herculean and expensive task to bring China to the educational level of a modern nation.

Lewis S. C. Smythe, in the personalized article which follows, re-emphasizes the part played by Western education in the changes within China. He also has astute observations to make regarding the coming to power of the Communist regime, which he observed at first hand, and he indicates signs of present dissatisfaction among peasant groups with some of the measures now being carried out.

• 92 • *Recent Social Changes in China*
LEWIS S. C. SMYTHE

CHANGES IN FAMILY LIFE

When I first went to China in the fall of 1928 the students in my class on The Family were debating very hotly two issues: (1) Should sons and daughters have the right to choose their own mates for marriage? Up till about that time the parents had chosen the mates for their sons and daughters. (2) Should girls be treated equally with boys, or

[This adapted article was prepared especially for this book by Dr. Smythe, a trained sociologist, who is now Professor of Christian Community at the College of the Bible, Lexington, Kentucky. Adapted.]

women equally with men, in society? By the time that the Sino-Japanese War ended in 1945 these two questions had been answered in the affirmative among educated groups in the cities. But in country districts, which include over 80 per cent of the population, and among worker groups the old order still prevailed for most members of these groups. The Provisional Code of the Nationalist Republic of China, dated 1931, had granted equality in family matters to women, had granted free choice of mates to sons and daughters on reaching the legal age of 20, and had outlawed the old system of concubinage. But family matters were still handled by families and clans and not according to a Nationalist law book.

When the Chinese Communists took over the government on the mainland of China, many Chinese expected them to "destroy the family" in a manner similar to the Soviet attack on the family in the early years of the Russian Revolution. But contrary to expectations, they were content to legalize the long-standing revolt of the educated groups against the domination of their elders, and especially of the older men. The Marriage Law of the People's Republic of China, promulgated by the Central People's Government on May 1, 1950, was based on the following general principles:

The arbitrary and compulsory feudal marriage system, which is based on the superiority of man over woman and which ignores the children's interests, is abolished.

The New Democratic marriage system which is based on free choice of partners, on monogamy, on equal rights for both sexes, and on protection of the lawful interests of women and children, shall be put into effect.

Polygamy, concubinage, child betrothal, interference with the remarriage of widows and the exaction of money or gifts in connection with marriage shall be prohibited. (From an English translation provided the author by Dr. Theodore H. E. Chen, Division of Asiatic Studies, University of Southern California.)

The only thing in the Chinese Communist marriage law that would be questioned by Americans is its provision for divorce by mutual consent. Since about 90 per cent of American divorce cases are not contested, it looks as though we do in fact what the Chinese Communists legalize but are not able to carry out in fact.

When it comes to the question of what is the cause of these changes in the family life of China, the experts disagree. The latest study, that by Marion J. Levy, attributes it to the effect of industrialization. But as indicated above, I found that the change began in the educated classes and those groups of Chinese that had either studied in Western countries or had had considerable contact with Western ideas. The Communist marriage law was codified by a group of intellectual and professional revolutionaries and not by either the workers or peasants of China. And it is based on Western practice, even while they are criticizing the West.

CHANGES IN ATTITUDES TOWARD "PROGRESS"

In the spring of 1946 a Chinese colleague and I were studying a market town near Chengtu, Szechwan, where most of the land was owned by two large Taoist monasteries. In order to get some historical perspective, we interviewed the leading abbot and asked him what was the most fundamental change that had occurred in the area during the Sino-Japanese War; that is, during the previous 10 years. He startled us by saying: "Before the war these local people were mainly interested in local law suits. Now they are mainly interested in progress." Further inquiry found that it was what we call "material progress," new bus lines, etc., but it also included Western-style education from elementary school up through college and university. The great movements of population during the recent Sino-Japanese War had brought new roads, auto trucks, busses, airplanes (for freight, passengers, and bombs), radio, radio-telephone, more newspapers with more world news; students, intellectuals, missionaries, Christians from East China and more Westerners including G.I.'s; new economic organization in the form of rural credit, consumer, and industrial cooperatives, modern banking; and numerous effects of Western and modern products too numerous to mention. These streams of new and modernizing influences flowed by plane to the larger cities, by trucks and busses to market towns, by wheelbarrow and ricksha from there to the villages. But the total ferment was tremendous.

LAND REFORMS

And yet in the midst of all this ferment, one very fundamental situation in West China remained unchanged; the ownership and control of agricultural land. The only change that occurred was that Nationalist generals got control of more land during inflation than the previous local war lords. But this only strengthened and entrenched the old system.

Sun Yat-sen, "Father of the Chinese Republic," preached a principle of land reform for China: "The cultivator shall own the land he cultivates." The Nationalist Party Congress in 1928 adopted this principle but when the Chinese Communists were threatening the Yangtze Valley in 1948, twenty years later, nothing had been done about it. Meanwhile, the Chinese Communists who had been allied with the Nationalists before 1927, had set up a small area of their own in southern Kiangsi province but were driven out of there by the Nationalist armies in 1934 and made the "Long March" to Shensi province in northwest China. There from 1934 to the end of the Sino-Japanese War in August, 1945, they had experimented with a program that would suit the Chinese peasants. Sun Yat-sen's principle was adopted and put into operation. After the Chinese Communists had conquered all the mainland of China by the end of 1949, they set about carrying out land reform in all parts of their realm. The procedure was to send a group of "experts" into an area smaller than a county and survey the whole situation. Any recalcitrant landlords that did not see the light of the new day were eliminated by various means. Then the land was divided to each family according to the number of mouths. As Hsiao-t'ung Fei pointed out in *Earthbound China,* this did not change the *average* size of land holding, 3.5 acres, but it did level up the land holding of the poorer peasants and gave land to some of the landless proletariat commonly found in many parts of China. Theoretically the landlords received equal treatment. But the Chinese Communists knew the prestige and the social and political power of former landlords in local areas. Consequently, they often put the landlord under a form of house arrest, took all his crops and animals, and then fed his family with a rice dole from month to month. But it was not only the large landlord that was dissatisfied. Anyone that had had more than the average of three and one-half acres of land, felt that he had lost by the deal. Because of the costly military program, the Peiping (Communist) government had to continue high taxes on farmers. The first year in many areas they took a hundred per cent of the rice crop. Consequently, many farmers said, "We received paper deeds for land that we were already cultivating as tenants and lost all our rice crop!" In some instances they turned down improved seed because they said if they used it their land would be given a higher productive rating and their tax rate would be higher.

Life magazine for December 31, 1951, had a very interesting account of how the Chinese Communists had studied an area in northwest China where land reform had been carried out five years before. The complete summary of results of this survey is worth quoting because it shows so many sidelights on Chinese village life today as well as attitudes of the Chinese Communists:

The surveyors reported that the peasants were eating more now, that literacy had increased notably among both children and adults, that the keeping of diaries (which the police like) had become "a mass movement," that village hygiene has improved, that "sexual promiscuity has been reduced 74%," that men beat their wives less frequently and that "drowning of girl babies has stopped." But the old class distinctions have been re-emerging. The investigators were surprised to find that 96 peasant families had sold land to pay for wedding and funeral expenses, an affront to the new social order. About 20% of the peasants had become poor again; an equal percentage "obviously wealthy." This was blamed on the fact that 99 family heads had increased their land holdings, causing prices to rise. They had even begun lending money to less fortunate peasants at the usurious rate of 60% per annum. Peking newspapers discussed the survey tellingly. "Our problem," said the Peking *People's Daily*, "is to find out how to sweep away the decadent dirt from people's consciousness. We must pay close attention to the thought transformation of peasants. We cannot let the peasants' bad self-generated tendencies go unguided."

Actually, the Chinese Communists have not been satisfied with a purely economic sort of Marxism. From the very beginning they have put a great deal of emphasis upon thought transformation, what we call "indoctrination," of the people, from the ignorant peasant to the most educated intellectual, in both city and country. Before I left China "brain washing" was so common that servant women or peasant women walking along the road could be heard to ask each other, "Have you had your mind changed yet?"

CHANGES IN DRESS

A lighter side of wars and revolutions is the "uniform" various groups wear. The first Revolution, in 1911, compelled most Chinese men to have their queues cut off. The Nationalist Revolution in 1926 made most of the educated and urban girls bob their hair. Later the Nationalist officials affected Western-style clothes, well-polished leather shoes, a felt hat, and invariably a cane with a big curved handle. When the Communists came in, they made very simple clothes the order of the day. Later everyone, men and women alike, was supposed to wear a cotton cap, padded trousers and jacket of a dull gray color. But at first only the so-called "progressives," that is, those

who sympathized with the new regime or were opportunists and wanted to get a job, wore the garb of the new order. [In fact, just] before the Communists came, both high school and college students were wearing khaki western-style trousers, shirts with no tie and sleeves rolled up, and leather or tennis shoes. Under the Nationalists the Chinese girls wore permanent waves, but shortly before I left I saw Chinese girls in barber shops having their hair cut Communist-style with long straight bobs, and getting as much enjoyment out of it as they had out of the permanents! The "uniform," including hair-do and cap, provides an easily recognizable symbol of those who want to appear like-minded, just as the bobby-soxers do in America.

CHANGES IN RECREATION AND FESTIVALS

In the old Chinese villages very few of the people could read. So the historical events and novels were repeated over and over in story form by story tellers in the teashops—from which teashops, women of class were excluded, regardless of the type of story. They had to get their stories through gossip. But all could attend the village drama performed on an open air stage with the crowd on the village common. Audio-visual experts in the Nationalist era in China capitalized on this practice by simply putting up a screen and showing movies out of doors to vast crowds. The Chinese Communists brought the new ideas, including caricaturing Nationalist foibles and evils, to the peasants and city workers by all forms of drama and dances.

Festivals have been treated in very much the same way as uniforms. The Nationalists started out to modernize China by making the Chinese coolie wear a shirt in hot weather and abolishing all the old festival practices which they labelled "superstitious." The "foreign New Year" (i. e., January 1st) was given great favor and much celebration while college students were made to attend school all day of the old China New Year (geared to the moon, like our Easter, usually occurring around February 1st). When the Chinese

Communists came in they reversed this and put great emphasis upon the old festivals to appeal to the peasants and workers but modernized the Nationalists' practice of counting years from the first revolution, 1911, and used the system of counting years in a "scientific way," from the birth of Christ!

REGIONALISM

The Nationalists fought any attempt to recognize old regions in China. They feared sectionalism which troubled the United States so much in the Nineteenth Century. But since China, with its inadequate transportation system, is too large to govern easily from one center, the Chinese Communists changed this and installed seven regional governments including several provinces in each region. Manchuria, formerly with three provinces, was one of the first so organized. It gave rise to the idea that Manchuria was going to be separated from the rest of China. The intervention of the Peiping Government in the struggle in Korea probably ended that danger, if there ever was one, because it has brought about another big mass migration of soldiers from what used to be called "China Proper" to Manchuria and campaigns are put on all over the country to buy Russian equipment for Chinese so-called "volunteers" going to Korea by way of Manchuria.

CHANGES STILL IN STORE

We have confined this discussion to indigenous changes in China, although some of them resulted from imported ideas. Even the Japanese invasion of China, 1937-1945, brought only slight changes. In 1946 when we got back to Nanking, we were surprised to find that very few things remained of Japanese culture. [Amazingly, all] that was left in Nanking was the addition of a door to control the draft on the "flower-pot" stove—literally a large earthen flower pot with a grate in it used as a table stove. A few Chinese had inherited Japanese dogs, and the Chinese army had a few Japanese horses. Everything else had "Gone With The Wind." But the Nationalist government in Chungking had copied some of the police control methods of the Japanese! They copied the Japanese in requiring every Chinese, as well as foreigners, to have a "Peaceful Citizen's Pass." When the Communists came in they not only took over the system but used the Nationalist passes more than a year! Since then the Chinese Communist government has done everything in its power to strengthen its control over the Chinese people on China's mainland. How many of their changes will remain after a few years?

Conclusion

In preceding selections, we have seen that the Chinese peasant is still bound to the land, even though often he does not own the land that he tills so laboriously. The population of China is enormous, but relatively few of its people live in cities. The peasants of China most commonly live in villages, which are made up of closely knit family units. For purposes of mutual aid and defense and for the observance of public ceremonies the families of a village work together. But it is expected that an individual will find most of his security against life's misfortunes, will make his living, and will find most of his joys and satisfactions within the confines of his own family group rather than as a member of some larger social unit.

The last selections have shown us the Chinese peasant trying to adjust to new forces which are sweeping the world. He is giving up subsistence farming for the more risky commercial farming in the expectation of greater returns. The local industries on which many villagers have depended for an important part of their livelihood are being destroyed by the penetration of industrial products from the cities. New ideas and ambitions are replacing those that have for centuries been passed from parents to children in a firm and unbroken tradition. China, like the rest of the world, is caught up in violent and sometimes uncontrollable changes.

The Chinese Communists called upon the Chinese peasant to participate both in mass movements and in the army engaged in fighting the United Nations. But still he and his family at home suffer very much the same fate that their ancestors have borne for centuries: they are invited to "participate" in producing food, clothing, and babies; in carrying out the government's mass organization either for public works or for propaganda purposes; and in fighting the Communists' battles for them. But again they find to their sorrow that it is "participation without representation." The directing ideas and the program are all decided in the "emperor's courts" in Peking. A new "mandarinate," which is more powerful than the old one, has penetrated the whole country and night and day watches every villager to see that he does what he has been ordered to do by the same old Peking. But in order to evoke greater effort from more peasants than ever before, these new masters have had to use methods that are slowly but surely arousing the minds of the peasants. Participation in mass movements and in foreign wars is changing their sons so that they will never again be content to settle down in the old village and follow the plow. In time, they too will demand, "No participation and no taxation without representation."

The heavy hand of the centuries bears down on the modern Chinese peasant. China has long seen an oft-repeated cycle which is well described by Olga Lang in *Chinese Family and Society* (p. 7, New Haven, 1946):

> The peasants supported the state and the ruling class with a part of the product of their labor. This was delivered in the form of taxes rather than of rent paid to the landlord. But the system of private landed property which prevailed under the empire led unavoidably to the accumulation of lands in the hands of the landlords who were powerful enough to refuse to pay taxes to the central government. This resulted in the weakening of the state, in agrarian crises, many peasant rebellions, dynastic changes, and foreign invasions and conquests. The long history of China abounds in such dramatic events.
>
> A new dynasty usually began by redistributing the land among the peasants, thus solving the agrarian crisis and strengthening the state machine. But the fundamental social structure with all its weaknesses remained, and soon a new crisis arose.

In other words, as the landlords grew stronger, the government grew weaker. Then, when a strong government was formed and was able to collect its share—or more than its share—of the surplus created by peasant labor, the landlords lost much of their power, if not their lives. But what about the peasant? He was as badly off under one system as the other: he gave the surplus either to the landlord as rent or to the government as taxes. Thus far, the Chinese Communists have simply carried out a strong-government phase of this cycle.

J. H. Boeke (*American Journal of Sociology*, 1952) has compared three attempts to improve the lot of the people of southeast Asia. He points out that both redivision of the land and the Western method of setting up large industries will fail to lift the level of living of the poverty-stricken masses. Boeke urges, instead, helping the Asian peoples to work out democratically their own solutions not only of the land problem but also of agricultural and industrial cooperative programs, educational and cultural development, and governmental reforms. For this a knowledge of the social traits of the people and of the processes of social change will be indispensable.

THE COTTON SOUTH

The old Cotton South depended, in an economic sense, on an enormous production of a single crop which was in great demand in the world market. Means of production were relatively inefficient, especially the use of a vast, unskilled labor force—first Negro slaves and then free Negroes (*top*). Today, not only is cotton growing moving westward, to states where cotton can be grown under irrigation, but the mechanical cotton picker (*bottom*) is working a revolution in the states making up the Cotton South. A tremendous labor force is being released for other occupations—and for migration to other parts of the United States.

The development of industry in the South has been so rapid and so extensive that many Southerners are themselves not completely aware of the change. In the chemical industries, development has been particularly rapid. *Top:* Part of the installations at Decatur, Ala., for the manufacture of Acrilan, one of the new synthetic fibers. Such plants find the South suitable because of the mild climate, the availability of labor, and, in many instances, the accessibility of raw materials. *Below:* The country store, operated by a white storekeeper, serves as one of the few meeting places for the Negroes of the community. As a social center it obviously leaves much to be desired; it represents the wretched conditions under which a large part of the people in the South pass their lives.

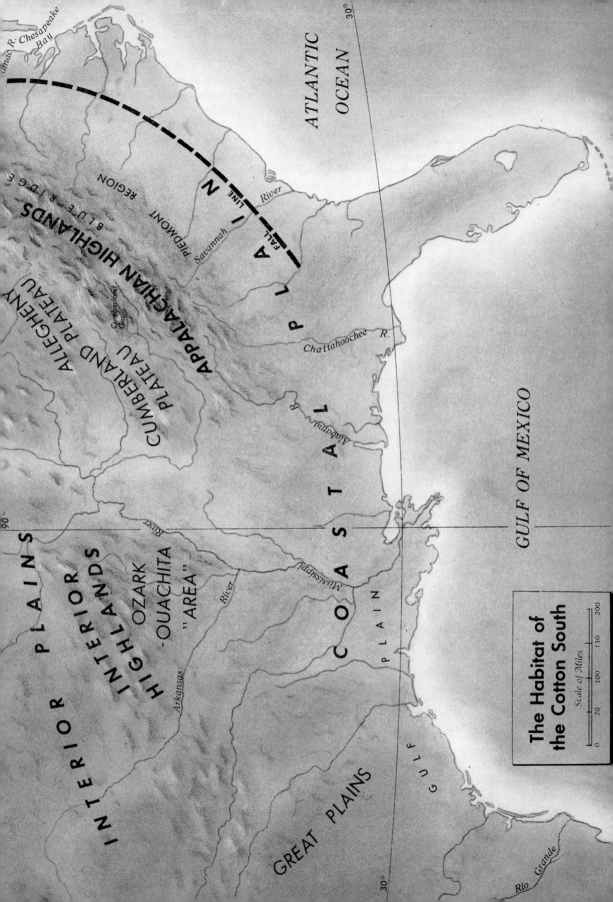

The Habitat of
the Cotton South

Scale of Miles
0   50   100   150   200

ATLANTIC
OCEAN

GULF OF MEXICO

APPALACHIAN HIGHLANDS

ALLEGHENY PLATEAU

CUMBERLAND PLATEAU

Cumberland Gap

BLUE RIDGE

PIEDMONT REGION

FALL LINE

COASTAL PLAIN

Savannah River

Chattahoochee R.

Alabama R.

INTERIOR PLAINS

INTERIOR HIGHLANDS

OZARK
-OUACHITA
"AREA"

Arkansas River

Mississippi River

River

GREAT PLAINS

GULF PLAIN

Rio Grande

Potomac R. Chesapeake Bay

30°

90°

30°

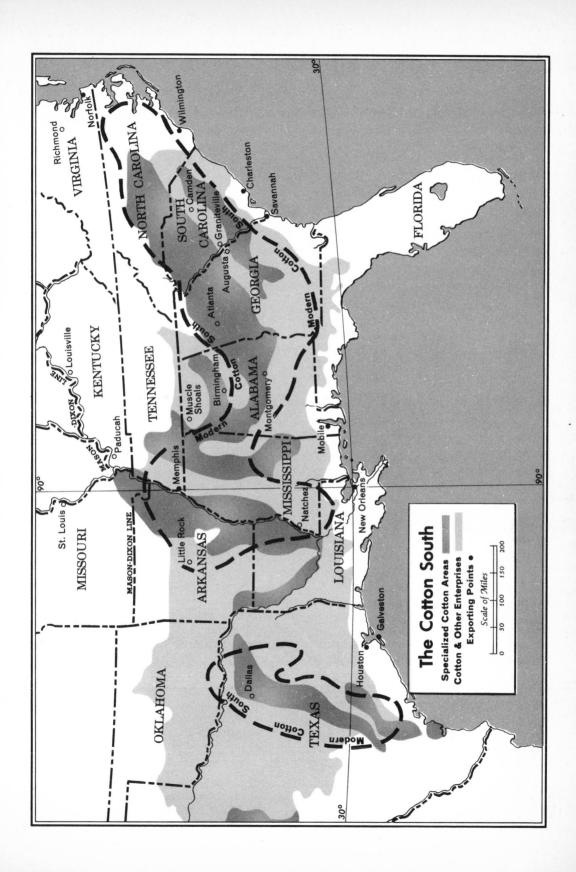

The Cotton South

Specialized Cotton Areas
Cotton & Other Enterprises
Exporting Points ●

Scale of Miles
0   50   100   150   200

Introduction

>>

Life in the Cotton South presents some interesting contrasts to the Chinese peasant way of life. Both regions are agricultural, to be sure, but from its early settlement the Cotton South has stressed cash crops rather than self-subsistent farming. Furthermore, the tradition of the plantation system has strongly influenced Southern life and thought.

Too often we think of the plantation South as an isolated historical development, without realizing that it resembles a type of society still dominant in several areas of the world; furthermore, it is well to remember that the plantation system has in the past been one of the most usual media through which colored races have come into contact with the white races.

· 93 · *The Plantation System*
GEORGE McC. McBRIDE

PLANTATIONS IN THE SOUTHERN STATES

In the British North American colonies the plantations of the south at first depended upon growing tobacco, but precedence was soon yielded to cotton. While these plantations were bound up with the colonial system, they lost their colonial character after the War of Independence and never acquired an imperialist character; but their general economic and labor relations bear striking similarity to those of plantations in colonial and semicolonial countries. Originally the plantations relied for labor upon free or indentured white laborers; but their persistence and expansion were made possible by Negro slavery, without which the plantations could not have developed as they did notwithstanding favorable climatic conditions. The planters, a small group owning millions of slaves, became a sectional ruling class, dominating the economics and politics of the southern states until their power was broken by the Civil War.

[Adapted from "Plantation," *Encyclopaedia of the Social Sciences,* Vol. 12, Macmillan, New York, 1937. Pp. 148-153. Used by permission.]

The abolition of slavery imposed new relations between master and man. Many of the plantations ceased to exist; others, however, adjusted themselves to the changed conditions and operated with Negro tenants, croppers or cash renters; while still others employed their former slaves at a nominal wage or under a system of peonage. In all these cases the laborers were still in a semiservile state. Moreover, while the plantation was usually divided into tracts or parcels of land, instead of being cultivated as a whole by gangs of laborers under direct control of an overseer, it did not lose its distinguishing feature of unified supervision over the choice of crop, the methods of cultivation and the marketing of the yield. In this form the plantation continues to exist in the American south, where it is the characteristic agricultural type.

There are few plantations in the United States north of the Mason and Dixon's line; in climatic rather than in political terms, almost none are found far enough north to have fewer than two hundred days of frostless season. The usual plantation crops, if raised beyond this frost line, are grown on small holdings or with independent laborers. Westward, too, of such a line which passes through northwest Oklahoma and cuts off the western third of Texas the plantation is practically unknown; it is supplanted by the cattle ranch or the irrigation farm, reappearing only, and then in small numbers and in a modified form, upon the delta of the Colorado River and in the mild climate of California. While plantations are thus limited almost entirely to the southern states, none is found in the hill country or in the less fertile areas, where agriculture is carried on in other forms. The plantations are restricted to the regions where soil is best and where land is level or nearly level.

SOCIAL TRAITS OF THE PLANTATION SYSTEM

A plantation society develops a character of its own. The native order is usually disrupted seriously, as families or members of families are uprooted and moved into a new environment, under new superiors who know little of the hereditary customs and institutions of their laborers. In this new setting people of diverse customs must adjust their ways to the habits of their fellows. Such a mingling was strikingly apparent in the slave communities of the southern United States, where Negroes from several parts of Africa were assembled without regard to the differences among them and where the elements of several diverse primitive cultures were further modified by the white civilization into which they had been introduced. The planters' culture too suffered a modification, its language, customs, art, music, literature and even its religion being affected by the slaves. Much the same situation existed in the plantations of Brazil and the West Indies. Something of this social amalgamation is in process in Malaya, where Indian, Javanese and Chinese laborers meet under supervision of Anglo-Saxon, Japanese or Chinese planters, and in Hawaii, where Hawaiian, European and Asiatic cultures mingle.

At the same time the plantation exerts a conspicuous influence in its introduction of new tools, machinery, systems of wages, fashions in clothing, standards of living, notions of sanitation, types of organization, methods of work, sometimes educational institutions and ideas and not infrequently religious beliefs and practices. The effect of these changes is extended beyond the bounds of the plantation and helps to mold the general social order of the district.

A further consequence, and one which seems inherent in the system, is the stratification of society. Upon the plantation and in a plantation society there is a sharp differentiation between the upper class, represented by the owners and the higher (particularly the white) agents of the plantation, and the laboring class. As the line of cleavage between the upper and lower classes is at least partly racial as well as economic, it becomes firmly fixed and individuals seldom pass from one to the other. This division runs through all phases of life, economic, social and political. The laborer may be completely free and still considered of a lower order. The higher foreign employees may be of low social origin in their native land, yet on the plantation they belong distinctly to the upper class. . . . Where such a class division becomes typical of the agricultural population, it inevitably characterizes most if not all of the spheres of life, since the planters generally dominate all circles of society. These differences are emphasized by their introduction into industrial and commercial enterprises, where employees are drawn largely from the rural laboring class and where the lowest foreign employee lords it over the native workers. The aristocracy, mainly agrarian, is sharply separated from the servile class of workers.

In such a social order there is little room for a middle class. The plantation largely markets its own crops; it procures supplies, directly or indirectly, for its entire population; hence the trader class is small and usually dependent upon the estate. Economic groups outside of the plantations are also decidedly limited. The professional class is not numerous. Most of the population bears some relation to the plantation and falls into one or the other of the categories into which its people are divided. Furthermore the plantation tends, precisely as in the old plantation system of the southern United States, to prevent the development of a middle class farming population, in that it crowds out the small agricultural holding. This process was particularly conspicuous in the British West

Indies, where the planters made success for the small farmer virtually impossible. The consequent stratification of society results in political oligarchy. In many regions where the plantation regime is established the laborers are imported from other sections and have no more share in governmental affairs than if they were slaves. Such is the status of the laborers from India, China and the Dutch East Indies employed on the plantations of the Middle East, of many laborers on the banana plantations of Central America and on numerous plantations in Africa. Even where the laborer is a native of the region in which he works, he generally has no legal part in the government or, if accorded such rights by law, he has little opportunity of exercising his privileges. The political situation in the southern United States, in Cuba, Java and Malaya, is characteristic of a society built upon a plantation regime.

The political oligarchy of a plantation country is intimately tied up with foreign interests. Where the country is independent the connection is economic and financial, with an indirect political character. The political connection becomes direct where the plantation country occupies a colonial or semicolonial status, as is usually the case. From the beginning the plantation has been a colonizing force, a means of occupying new lands effectively and of initiating their development.

The author of the preceding selection may be considered unduly critical of the plantation system, but his remarks are based on careful study of the situation in all parts of the world. Some of the less attractive features of the system arise because the plantation is often the scene of rapid social change, resulting from the sudden exposure of a simple society to a highly elaborate commercial or industrial society. In southeast Asia, for example, such exposure for only a few generations has helped precipitate violent movements for political and economic independence

Certain aspects of the plantation system which McBride has mentioned briefly will be the subject of more detailed treatment in the following pages. The people of the Cotton South were colonists, although here the workers as well as the masters came from distant lands. The habitat will be considered, including the semi-tropical features favorable to the plantation system. Besides the economic details of the plantation, we shall note its social effects, which resulted in the extreme social stratification of the Old South. Finally, in order to emphasize the varied aspects and complexities of social change, the Old South will be contrasted with the New South.

The People and the Habitat

»»»

The Cotton South, like every other part of the United States, is inhabited by people of extremely diverse origins. The three major racial groups of mankind are represented: Mongoloid, Negroid, and Caucasian. The Indians are Mongoloids who originally reached the New World from Asia. They have now been greatly reduced in numbers and crowded into a few small sections of their former homeland, where many of them have intermarried with Negroes and whites.

The Negroes make up 29 percent of the population of the deep South and somewhat less in the upper South. Constant migration to the North has made the net increase in numbers of the Negroes less than that of the whites, although both groups have maintained a higher birth rate than the rest of the nation. The ancestors of the South's Negro population were brought as slaves from Africa, most of them from the West Coast or the areas adjacent to it. They were sold into slavery by the Negro rulers of the West African kingdoms or were captured and sold by traders from outside. The Negroes brought to the New World did not have either tribal unity or a common language. People from the same locality and even of the same family were purposely separated to prevent their ganging together against the slave holders. Thus very little of Negro African culture was preserved by this population element. There are few genetically pure Negroes in the United States today, since whites and Negroes have mated ever since the introduction of the Negroes. People with any discernible Negroid characteristics have been classified socially as Negroes, even when they are virtually pure white in physical inheritance. Many people of partly Negro ancestry but of Caucasian appearance pass into the white population every year, usually moving to a new area, where their background is not known.

The white population in the South is predominantly descended from European immigrants of the colonial period—English, Scottish, Irish, and German. Few representatives of later migrations from central, southern, and eastern Europe have settled in the area. For this reason, and also because it has remained chiefly rural in economy, the South has retained many ways of life, attitudes, and even patterns of speech which were once common to the United States as a whole but which have been weakened outside the South by the introduction of new cultural strains and by urbanization.

Since the Civil War there has been a steady flow of whites and Negroes to the northern and western United States. This flow was greatly accelerated during the two World Wars, when people of both races sought jobs in the North. Much of western Oklahoma, New Mexico, and Arizona was populated, when these states were still territories, by white Southerners seeking new land and opportunities. The trend westward has continued, with Negroes joining in the move in the last decade, attracted by new developments in both agriculture and industry. However, the growing industrialization of the South is putting a partial halt to this emigration and is even bringing newcomers into the South from other parts of the nation.

Migration to the North, particularly to the cities, has been more constant on the part of the Negro population of the deep South than the white, and even in depression periods the Negro has kept up his search for better opportunities in jobs, schooling, and social position. Many immigrants to the North have undoubtedly been disappointed by finding many of the same attitudes and restrictions that they had hoped to leave behind.

• 94 • *People as a Southern Resource*
RUPERT B. VANCE, JOHN E. iVEY, JR., AND MARJORIE N. BOND

Anyone who wants to understand the South and the South's place in the nation asks first about the people. Who are the people, and where did they come from? Where do they live? Is there anything about them which is a little different from people in other regions? How well are they using Southern resources?

WHO THE PEOPLE ARE

The South is rich in human wealth. It has a great many people. In 1940 a Census of the United States was taken, and heads were counted all over the country. The nation then had about 132,000,000 people. A few more than 37,000,000 of them were in the South.

Indians are still living in some parts of the South. Oklahoma has more than 60,000. North Carolina has over 20,000. Others are scattered throughout the rest of the region— one or two hundred in some states, one or two thousand in a few others. Altogether the South has about 95,000 Indians. These are all that remain of the people who first lived here.

The South had almost 10,000,000 Negroes in 1940. They live in every Southern state, but most of them—about 8,000,000—are in the Southeast. Negroes make up more than a third of the population in Georgia, Alabama, and Louisiana. Over two-fifths of the population in South Carolina and about half the population in Mississippi are Negroes.

In 1940 the white people in the South numbered close to 28,000,000. Texas has more than five million—a larger number than any of the other Southern states. Kentucky, North Carolina, Tennessee, Georgia, Oklahoma, and Virginia each has over two million white people. The other Southern states each has over a million.

Englishmen were the first to find places for themselves in the new world. Their earliest colony, on the coast of North Carolina, disappeared, but a later settlement in Virginia held its ground. From Virginia the English spread south, where they were joined by Scotsmen. Some of the Scots came straight from their native country. Some lived for a

[Adapted from *Exploring the South,* University of North Carolina Press, Chapel Hill, 1949. Pp. 35-45. Used by permission.]

while in Ireland before they reached America. Because of this they are often called [Scots-Irish or Ulstermen].

Germans moved to the Southern colonies from Pennsylvania, bumping along in wagons over the rough wilderness roads. Irishmen found their way to various settlements along our coast. French families made new homes in the Carolinas and Louisiana. Those who came to Louisiana from France generally settled in the larger communities, especially New Orleans. Other Frenchmen moved south from a part of Canada which was then called Acadia. These Acadian French, who were rural people, chose the Louisiana back-country.

Few newcomers came to the United States for a number of years after the American Revolution. About the year 1820 people started migrating from Europe again. In the beginning this immigration was gradual, like the trickle of a small stream high up in the mountains. After 1880 immigration increased. From 1900 to 1920 it flowed over the states of the north and into the west like a river in flood.

The South was generally left untouched by this flood of new Americans. Few foreigners have come to our region since 1800. From time to time people move here from other parts of our nation. But most Southerners are descendants of the families who first settled along the coast and then spread toward the south and the west.

WHERE THEY LIVE

People in the South have plenty of room. Within the borders marking the Southern region lie more than a million square miles of land. This is more than a third of the nation's area. On this land are less than a third of the nation's people.

The census shows that more than two-thirds of the people in the region live in the country. Most of them are families who depend on farming for a living. Some of them are people who are not farmers. They are in villages which are not classed as towns because they have less than 2500 people. Or they are gathered around the edges outside the limits of towns and cities where they work.

Less than one-third of the Southern people live in towns or cities. Even this urban part of our population is never very far from the country, for the South has no really big cities. The largest in the region are New Orleans, Houston, Louisville, Atlanta, and Dallas, and not one of these is among the ten largest cities in the nation. This means that all Southerners, in town or country or city, live close to the land.

Resources for farming and resources for manufacturing are like magnets drawing the population to them. People live where they can make a living. Those who work in industry settle close to the factories. Those who farm for a living are spread out over the parts of the South where the land and the climate are suitable for agriculture.

The Southern population is largest near our industrial centers. Workers cluster around the coal fields of Virginia and Kentucky, the iron ore deposits near Birmingham, Alabama. They settle down in the Piedmont section of Virginia or the Carolinas and get jobs in the factories making textiles or furniture or cigarettes. They live near Atlanta's processing plants and transportation outlets. They move to oil fields and refineries in Texas or Oklahoma or Louisiana. They go to the great port cities of New Orleans or Houston or Norfolk.

Away from the industrial centers and the main agricultural areas the South has fewer people. Population thins out wherever the chances for work are small.

ARE SOUTHERN PEOPLE DIFFERENT?

[Many of the] specialists studying the South have found a number of ways in which people in our region really differ from those in other parts of the country. . . . In the first place, our families are larger than those in other regions. Southern people, especially people living in the country, have a great many children.

We have a great many children in the South, but only a small proportion of our population is made up of working men and women of middle age. What happens to all the children we rear? Why have they not grown up into a large group of workers? The fact is this: when Southern children grow up, many of them move away. They go to some other part of the country, hoping for a chance to earn a better living than they might if they stayed at home.

White Southerners take part in this moving if the change means work or perhaps better pay. If there is a depression and jobs are scarce, not so many leave. Southerners working in other parts of the country are among those who lose their jobs. When they have no way of making a living, some of them come back home to hunt for work or scratch a living out of the soil.

In good times and in hard times Negroes are leaving the Southern states. They too are looking for better jobs, better pay, greater opportunity. Few of them ever come back, even in a depression. As a result, the Negro population is increasing faster in some other parts of the country than it is in some of the Southern states.

In 1900, for example, South Carolina had 780,000 Negroes, and in 1940 it had 815,000. After forty years the number had increased by only 35,000. In 1900 New York City had 60,000 Negroes. In 1940 it had 478,000—almost eight times the number in 1900. The industrial cities of the Northeast and the Middle States all now have a large Negro population.

Demographers, or students of population, are not only concerned with the numbers and composition of the people they study—that is, with *quantity;* they also investigate the *quality* of the people from the standpoint of health, education, and the possession of basic occupational skills. In the selection that follows, H. C. Brearley, of George Peabody College, who has been aptly termed by Allen Tate as one of the most objective students of Southern life, analyzes the question "Are Southerners really lazy?" In doing so, he suggests that climate and other habitat factors influence Southern behavior *indirectly* rather than *directly,* that health and nutritional levels are low, and that other cultural considerations must be taken into account.

• 95 • Are Southerners Really Lazy?

H. C. BREARLEY

Among friends and enemies, early and late, the Southerner has been condemned for his "laziness." [At] least, the Southerner seems to be a person who, to put it mildly, lacks the initiative and persistence of his Yankee rivals. Is the Southerner's inactivity the result of some inborn deficiency—some taint of the blood? Has a malevolent fate predestined him to a life of sloth and indolence?

Most Southerners vehemently deny the charge of "laziness," but they rarely completely convince themselves or others. One

Southern state has even changed its motto from "Here we rest" to "We dare defend our right." This alters the emphasis from "the lazy South" to "the fighting South," but it does little to explain the far from mysterious bases of these accusations of slothfulness.

The only explanation that is at all acceptable to the Southerner is the placing of the blame squarely upon the immutable providence that gave the region its climate. "The hot weather, you know," is, in fact, one of the South's top defenses against criticism. (As

[Adapted from "Are Southerners Really Lazy?" *The American Scholar,* Vol. 18, No. 1, New York, 1949. Pp. 68-75. Reprinted by permission of the United Chapters of Phi Beta Kappa.]

such, it ranks with poverty, the Civil War and Reconstruction, and the presence of the Negro.) The climatic theory is stated thus by Ellsworth Huntington of Yale University, "In the South we find less energy, less vitality, less education, and fewer men who rise to eminence than in the North, not because Southerners are in any way innately inferior to Northerners but apparently because of the adverse climate."

This comforting doctrine does not, however, bear close examination. In Huntington's own *Civilization and Climate,* from which the quotation is taken, he states that about 63 degrees Fahrenheit is the best temperature for industrial and other manual work. Yet he ignores the fact that much of the South has mean annual temperatures around 63 degrees Fahrenheit, and if averages are deceptive—as they sometimes are—the effects of the South's hot summers cannot be assumed to extend throughout the year. And many visitors from the energetic North give generous praise to the South's briskly cool winters and equable spring and autumn seasons.

Admitting the South's disagreeable summer climate does not necessarily lead to the conclusion that efficiency must thereby be markedly decreased. Careful studies, especially by the New York State Committee on Ventilation, indicate that high temperature and humidity and little movement of air have much less effect upon *true* efficiency than upon *felt* efficiency. However unpleasant may be the effects of hot, damp and stuffy air, they seem to have little measurable influence upon output, provided the worker really concentrates upon his task.

The conclusion seems inescapable that the direct physiological effects of the South's hot summers upon the year's round of activity level of its people must be small indeed. This does not deny the probability that the *indirect* effects of climate may have far-reaching consequences. The climate certainly does affect other parts of the natural environment, such as the incidence of parasites, that in turn may greatly influence the Southerner's energy. Similarly, climatic conditions may combine with cultural factors—for example, in the development of the plantation—to establish attitudes unfavorable to hard work. But the emphasis upon the direct bodily effects of the Southern climate itself is doubtless a satisfying rationalization that leads toward fatalism and the neglect of more reprehensible, but at the same time more remediable, explanations.

Ill health ranks easily among the more significant of these basic reasons for the South's low activity level. A sick man is a tired man, and a half-sick one certainly seems to be "lazy." In 1938 the National Emergency Council reported, "The low-income belt of the South is a belt of sickness, misery and unnecessary death. Its large proportion of low-income citizens are more subject to disease than the people of any similar area" in the United States. The same story is told by the rejections for military service during World War II. Up to June 1, 1944, every Southern state was in the lowest third of percentages of draftees certified as suitable for duty in the armed services. Other data on military rejections give the same tragic report that the South is a region of ill health and physical defect. These conditions do not, of course, arise from any innate weakness, but from ignorance of preventive measures, inadequate medical services, and the inability to purchase proper food and care.

The South also has at least two major parasitic diseases that sap the energy of its people. A decade ago the area was estimated to have 2,000,000 cases of malaria each year. Possibly just as significant as malaria is the presence of intestinal parasites, especially the hookworm that has been aptly called "the germ of laziness."

But ill health may not be as significant as is malnutrition in the making of "laziness."

Semi-starvation in the South is not dramatic, but it is chronic and long continued from generation to generation. For example, Youmans and his associates at Vanderbilt Medical School found that in a comparatively well-to-do middle Tennessee county 14.3 per cent of the whites and 42.1 per cent of the Negroes obtained less than the 1250 calories of food supposed to be the minimum daily requirement for each person. [According to figures published by the Food and Agriculture Organization of the United Nations, the country with the lowest national caloric average is Algeria with 1421 calories (1948-1949). The United States average in 1948-1949 was over 3100.] The primary reason for this deficiency of food, which is probably typical of much of the South, is not ignorance but poverty. In general, the South's per capita annual income is only about 60 per cent of the nation's average. Even in 1947, a relatively prosperous year for agricultural areas, every one of . . . fifteen Southern states had per capita incomes in the lowest third of the entire country. Yet the per capita dollar cost of an adequate diet is approximately the same below the Ohio as it is north of it. The Southerner does not obtain his food at lower prices —he merely goes hungry, or exists upon a cheaper and generally less nutritious diet.

The deficiency of the B vitamins in the diet of Southerners is especially significant. This group of vitamins seem to be necessary for a normal activity level, yet it is often notably lacking upon Southern tables.

If the Southern family is fortunate enough to be above the poverty level, the food may be more wholesome, yet still not adequate. The corn meal of the poor man may be replaced by white flour for hot biscuits, or by boiled polished rice, but both of these cereals reach the table with but a small part of their vitamin-rich natural content. Vegetables, especially the leafy ones, are traditionally cooked by long periods of boiling, perhaps with "a pinch of soda" that effectively neutralizes the vitamin C content. Difficulties of refrigeration, and traditional prejudice against the use of fresh pork during tne summer months, also prevent an adequate intake of foods rich in B vitamins. As a consequence of these factors, middle and upper class Southerners are unfortunately often not as free from malnutrition as are similar groups in other regions of the United States.

In summer the need for the B vitamins, especially for thiamin, is markedly increased, according to studies by Clarence A. Mills and others. By his Panama studies Mills has also found evidence that lean meat and eggs produced in tropical climates are much less rich in thiamin than are similar foods imported from the temperate zones. Other research studies also indicate that food raised on poor or eroded lands, prevalent in the South, is very likely to be short in nutritional value.

The South's lack of an adequate diet is tragically illustrated by the fact that 90 per cent of the nation's deaths from pellagra occur in the thirteen Southern states. Pellagra is a disease resulting primarily from a deficieny of one of the B vitamins, niacin, also known as nicotinic acid. Although only about one thousand Southerners die of pellagra each year, this fact does not begin to indicate the extent of this deficiency disease, since it is estimated that only about one-sixth of the pellagra cases ever consult a physician, and that many thousands of medically unrecognized "near pellagra" victims are to be found among the South's millions of underfed people.

To infer, however, that ill health and hunger are the sole explanations of the low activity level of many Southerners would be a great oversimplification. Other factors may be less dramatic or measurable, but they nevertheless enter into the pattern of life under analysis.

Slavery, for example, resulted in the discrediting of hard manual labor by either whites or blacks, and helped put the Southern gentleman of leisure at the top of the social pyramid. Even today "working like a Negro" is a term of reproach.

Much of Southern farming, especially the cultivation of cotton and of cigarette tobacco, is really only a six- or seven-months task. This has permitted many rural Southerners to cherish the long winter vacation and the midsummer "lay-by time." The relative absence of dairying and poultry and livestock raising has also enabled the Southern rural worker to enjoy much hunting, fishing and plain or fancy loafing, and has made him accustomed to more leisure than even wealthy non-Southerners normally find it possible to attain.

In America, as elsewhere, the rural pattern of life is slower-paced than that of city-dwellers. This slower reaction does not, however, indicate any innate inferiority or inherent laziness. It is merely the result of a less stimulating environment, relatively free from the now-or-never decisions of the man of the city. And the South, it should be remembered, is the most rural region in the United States, and even its larger cities are greatly affected by rural ways and attitudes. A significant part of the South's leisurely manner of living is, accordingly, rural rather than Southern.

The South has suffered much at the hands of the local-color school of writers—native, Northern and European. These writers, with the most honorable of avowed intentions, have so misrepresented the South that Southerners sometimes hardly recognize themselves in literature. The hard-working yeoman farmer is ignored, but the shiftless "poor whites" become the heroes of Tobacco Roads. The self-respecting Negro artisan is crowded out of the pages of books by the more picturesque but atypical migratory singer of "blues." An occasional planter sits upon his veranda and drinks a mint julep, but for every one of these there are thousands of farmers who literally earn their bread in the sweat of their faces.

One favorable aspect of the whole situation is that the principal conditions that have brought about these accusations of wholesale laziness are at least remediable, although not without much expense and cooperative effort.

In the first place, the development of inexpensive air conditioning may soon give many Southerners the equivalent of a more invigorating summer climate.

But the South does not need mechanical refrigeration as much as it needs: (1) larger incomes for its numerous underprivileged groups; (2) more adequate medical care of all types; (3) a varied and nutritious diet for everyone; and (4) a realistic understanding both at home and elsewhere of the conditions and attitudes that have been erroneously interpreted as laziness.

In recent years, moreover, many of the situations that have fostered the South's reputation for laziness have shown significant improvement. The ravages of malaria and hookworm are being markedly decreased. Growing industrial development, more soil conservation, and higher prices for farm products have resulted in some relative increase in income. These larger incomes, the free lunch programs in the schools, and the emphasis upon home gardens and "the seven basic foods," are slowly but surely bettering dietary practices. Hard work more often receives recognition. Possibly the day is not far distant when "these lazy Southerners" will be recognized as an inaccurate stereotype that has gone with the music and the magnolias of the South that almost never was. Man's discovery of the economic possibilities of the Southern environment, as known today, is a matter of several centuries of hard work [by] hundreds of "explorers."

• 96 • Nature's Legacy to the South
ALMON E. PARKINS

Many geographical details of the region which a group occupies have a profound effect on the way in which its people live. In the next two selections the rich natural endowment of the Cotton South will be briefly summarized, as well as some of the serious limitations that nature has placed on man's use of this endowment. Then, the geographic limits of the Cotton South will be more precisely defined and its meaning distinguished from such terms as the South, and the Cotton States.

[Adapted from *The South, its Economic-Geographic Development,* John Wiley, New York, 1938. Pp. 23-29, 35-36, 37-39, 41-54, 56-58. Used by permission.]

They brought back information that stimulated the cupidity of thousands and sent westward wave after wave of land seekers that continued for two centuries or more until the agricultural lands of every section of the South were taken up.

THE LANDS

Two mountain and plateau areas—the Southern Appalachian Highlands and the Ozark-Ouachita area—break the monotony of plains land that spreads from the Potomac to the Rio Grande. Fully three-fourths of the area of the South has elevations less than 1,000 feet above sea level.

The only formidable topographic barrier to the free movement of man and goods is the Cumberland-Allegheny Front, the eastern scarp of the Cumberland-Allegheny plateaus. From the Potomac southward to northeastern Alabama this 800- to 1,000-foot wall (above the Great Valley at its eastern base) has only a few breaks that open westward to the lowlands of the Mississippi basin. The westward-moving pioneers in the South used, for the most part, only one break, the Cumberland Gap, and through this, between 1790 and 1830, streamed more than 100,000 people in search of the rich farming lands of the Transappalachian region.

The Mississippi, though serving in the past as the South's greatest artery of commerce, drawing to the main stream the commerce of the wide-spreading areas, has always restricted the free east-west movement of commerce and people by land. Wide, marshy, pestilential flood plains, a broad strip of water, and valleys filled with unconsolidated mud and sand so deep and soft that finding a substantial footing for heavy bridge piers is difficult have greatly retarded the number of crossing places. In the days of westward movement there were only two important crossing places: one near St. Louis, the other at Natchez. . . . Until the last few years the only bridges across this mighty river between the mouth of the Ohio and the Gulf were at Memphis.

The Coastal Plain. The largest of the physiographic regions is the Coastal Plain, divided into the Atlantic and the Gulf plains. Its area is about 255,000 square miles, larger than France, Belgium, and the Netherlands combined, and nearly a third of the total area of the South. It includes parts of Maryland, Virginia, Kentucky, Arkansas, Oklahoma, and Texas, and the whole of Florida, Mississippi, and Louisiana.

The Coastal Plain is the flattest of the plains lands of the South. It is highest along the inner border, and here rather conspicuous hills are to be found in some states. The outer border is half sea and half land. Shelving sandy barrier beaches topped by sand dunes behind which are lagoons, marshes, and wet flatwoods are the features . . . along most of the coasts of the South from the ocean's edge inland. The width of this low outer tidal border varies greatly. It is widest in eastern North Carolina . . . extending 50 to 70 miles inland from the ocean. Tidewater lagoons and bays along the Atlantic farther south and likewise along the Gulf extend 20 to 30 or more miles inland. Marshes and flatwoods occur still farther to the interior.

Between the low outer marshy, tidal portion of the Coastal Plain and the inner dissected section is the broad flat Middle Coastal Plain, well drained yet flat enough to reduce surface erosion to the minimum. Before the coming of white men this portion of the Coastal Plain bore the best of the longleaf pine forests. It was, and still is, the section most used for agriculture.

The outer belt of the Coastal Plain, except here and there where truck gardens and seaports dominate the landscape, remains much the domain of nature. Several generations of lumbermen in the seventeenth, eighteenth, and nineteenth centuries battled with nature, at times almost obliterating the forest trees with axe, saw, and fire, but each time the trees have come back, though the last generation shows terrible scars of battle. Today much of the cut-over land of the Coastal Plain is in this outer belt. It may become the most active pulpwood-producing area of our country.

Most of the harbors of the South are the drowned mouths of the Coastal Plain rivers, and though they are shallow and subject to silting man finds it is easy to deepen them and excavate new channels. Baltimore and Richmond are at the inner edge of the Plain at its meeting with the Piedmont, but . . . all the other large ports are at or near the outer border of the Plain [such as Savannah, Mobile, New Orleans, Galveston, Houston].

The inner border of the Coastal Plain from central Alabama northeastward is the Fall Line, an "imaginary" line connecting the row of rapids of the rivers that flow across both Piedmont and Coastal Plain. From central Alabama to the Rio Grande a fall line is scarcely discernible. The lower rapids of the Tennessee near Muscle Shoals and the hard rock in the Arkansas River at Little Rock are comparable to the Fall Line rapids, but elsewhere the inner boundary of the Coastal Plain is not sharp.

The Piedmont Plateau. West of the Atlantic Coastal Plain is the Piedmont Plateau, extending from central Alabama northeastward beyond the northern border of the South, on into Pennsylvania. Though called a plateau it is really a plain, a plain of denudation, with only a few hills (monadnocks) rising above the otherwise gently rolling surface. . . . The Piedmont is higher, drier, and healthier than the Coastal Plain. Its flat surface like that of the Coastal Plain in no way erects barriers to man's movements.

The Central Lowlands or Plains, broad and flat and extensive, cover most of Oklahoma and extend southward into Texas. Only a small part of this vast physiographic province is in the South. There are some interruptions in the continuity of the plains—low mountains or rocky ridges.

THE USEFUL MINERALS

The Coastal Plain . . . is young, geologically. The mineral materials forming it are of marine origin derived from animals or are land material that has been deposited in the borders of the sea and worked over on the shores by waves and currents. No metallic minerals occur except bog iron ore that accumulated or was assembled in boggy areas after the Coastal Plain was formed. Sands, gravel, and shell marl are widely distributed.

Clay is less abundant. Fuller's earth [used in filtering] and diatomaceous earth [used as a fine abrasive] are fairly common. Limestone is confined mostly to Florida and near-by portions of Georgia and Alabama.

For some unexplainable cause the petroleum and gas deposits of the Coastal Plain, so far discovered, with one exception, are in the West Gulf Coastal Plain. Salt and sulphur are likewise confined to the West Gulf Plain. The Coastal Plain also has peat and lignite deposits. . . . As long as bituminous coal is available at low prices the lignite deposits will remain mostly unworked.

Gold and silver have been found in the Southern Appalachians but for the most part not in paying quantities sufficient to develop a mining industry. Copper is mined in several localities in North Carolina and southwestern Virginia. . . . Other mineral deposits . . . are mica, feldspar, kaolin (weathered feldspar), soapstone, talc, and magnetite. Granite of excellent quality is taken from many quarries in the mountains and hills of the Piedmont. . . .

THE CLIMATE AND WEATHER

The location of the South, (1) between 25° N and 39° N latitude, (2) in the southern edge of the belt of the Westerlies, and (3) in the southeastern portion of the continent with the sea on the east and the south, and the low relief of the land determine the characteristics of its climate and weather.

The Seasons. Owing to its comparatively low latitude, the South has a high sun during the year as compared to the North. The length of the growing season is longer than in the North, and the length of the day in winter and in summer does not vary so markedly. The median growing season for the Lower South is 240 days and for the Upper South 180 to 210 days, except in the plateau and mountain sections. The growing season for more than half of the South is long enough for two harvests of some crops, and in the Lower South for three. This also means that the hot season is longer. If we assume that a monthly average of 68° and above is *hot* and below 32° is *cold,* the length of the hot season and of the cold season at selected places is as follows:

	Hot	*Cold*
St. Paul, Minnesota	2 months	4 or 5 months
St. Louis	4	1
Montgomery.	5	0
New Orleans.	7	0
Miami	12	0

A high sun is a hot sun. The evaporation of water from the ground and the transpiration from plants are high in most of the South. Much more water is needed for crops in general than in the North, and droughts are more frequent and disastrous. But, surprisingly, the maximum temperature in the summer is, as a rule, little above that of more northerly localities. A comparison of the absolute maximum (the highest temperature ever recorded), up to December 31, 1929, at a few cities is interesting: Atlanta 102°, Montgomery 107°, Louisville 107°, Little Rock 108°, Nashville 106°, Omaha 110°, St. Paul 104° . . ., St. Louis 107°. The summers of the South differ from those in the North in the greater length of the hot spells and their more frequent occurrence. The reverse is of course true of the winter in the two sections. Cold spells are short and infrequent in the South.

The flatness of the Mississippi Basin permits the free movement of the winds whether from the south or from the north. South winds tend to cool off as they move northward, and north winds warm up as they move southward. The Gulf and Atlantic winds tend to give coastal lands for one hundred or more miles inland cooler temperatures than those at localities farther north. The hottest section of the South in the summer is the northern half of the Gulf Coast States.

The Appalachian Highlands are barriers to the movement of winds to only a slight degree, but the ridges do affect the distribution of rainfall. The regions of heaviest rainfall are near the coast and on the east-facing slopes of the ridges of the Southern Appalachian Highlands.

The South is largely in the Hot Summer [av. 68° or higher] and Cool Winter [av. 32°-60°] Region. Only a small part of the Appalachian Highlands has Hot Summer and Cold Winter [av. 32° or lower] temperatures, and only the Gulf Coastal lands and Florida have Hot Summer and Mild Winter [av. 50°-68°] temperatures. This latter temperature region is often known as the Subtropical. The one to the north may be called the Warm Temperate.

Rainfall. . . . About three-fourths of the South has more than 30 inches of rainfall on the average during the year. This we may call the humid portion. Most of the remainder of the South may well be called subhumid, grading into semiarid. The east-facing slope of the Blue Ridge has the heaviest rainfall in the Southern States, one station recording more than 80 inches.

Rain water may be stored in the ground for weeks and months and in the deep porous soils of the High Plains of Texas for a year or two, yet in most parts of the Southern States, with much of the surface in slope and a high summer sun, it is but a matter of a few rainless days before the vegetation with superficial root systems begins to hang out a distress sign. . . . A drought as defined by the Weather Bureau is a 30-day period (consecutive) in which the precipitation during any day is below one-tenth of an inch. . . . Low flat lands suffer less from droughts than hilly lands. A drought of 60 days or more results in a leaf fall in deciduous trees, such as happened in 1925, particularly on slopes. From 15 to 20 per cent (or more) of the forest trees in the drought area were killed. The writer is firmly convinced that *dry spells* (mostly less than 30 days' duration) *are the most widespread and destructive of all weather phenomena to agricultural operators in the South.*

Cold Weather. "Cold spells" or "cold waves" form a second weather phenomenon that affects agricultural operators adversely. The greatest damage is felt in the Lower South where such weather is considered abnormal. In the northern part of the South freezing temperatures are normal experiences from early December to early March, though at any time during this period there may be several days in succession of springlike weather. The severest "cold spells" in the winter come in the rear of well-developed elliptical lows that pass slowly eastward across the Gulf States, provided there is to the northwest of this low a well-developed, slowly moving high. Under such conditions great volumes of cold, clear, dry, biting blasts move southward down the flat Mississippi Basin plains to the Gulf Coast and Florida.

Hurricanes and Tornadoes. A third type of destructive weather phenomenon in the South is the tropical hurricane. Its fury is felt mostly along the Atlantic and Gulf coasts, especially in lower Florida. The newspapers in recent years have so fully described the paths and the destruction wrought that further comments are not necessary here. Some data on the frequency and period of occurrence may be of value. In the 38 years between 1887 and 1925, records show that a total of 240 hurricanes struck or came near our southeastern coasts. . . . Only a few of these 240 were destructive.

Tornadoes, similar in some respect to tropical hurricanes except that they develop on land and cover a much narrower and shorter path, are characteristic of the interior of the Mississippi Basin from the Gulf States to Wisconsin and Michigan. They may be thought of as concentrated hurricanes. The velocity of the wind in the hurricane rarely reaches more than 100 to 125 miles an hour, but in the tornado it may be 300 to 500. Tornadoes are associated with thunderstorms but are distinguished from thunderstorms by their funnel shape. The area of the base of the funnel covers much less than a mile, some not more than a quarter mile. A single tornado may travel a hundred or hundreds of miles before working itself out. Rarely is a path of destruction continuous for this distance, but the tornado may come down to the surface of the earth and leave a record of its presence at only a half dozen places.

Sunshine. Has the expression the "Sunny South" any scientific evidence? The following data for a few selected cities (selected at random) will answer the question:

PERCENTAGE OF POSSIBLE SUNSHINE FOR YEAR

Cities in the South		Cities in the North	
New Orleans..	58	Buffalo	49
Montgomery ..	62	St. Paul	56
Vicksburg	64	St. Louis	59
Miami	67	Des Moines ...	61
Ft. Worth	71	Huron	63

For some non-Southern readers it may not be amiss to be reminded that one does not step into Florida and Gulf climate as soon as one crosses Mason and Dixon's line or the Ohio River. Under normal weather conditions it gets warmer in both summer and winter the farther south one goes, yet every year Nashville, for example, may have colder weather than Illinois in winter and cooler temperatures in the summer, for several days in succession. The summers are not so enjoyable in the middle South as in the middle North; but the winters in the middle North are not as enjoyable as those in the middle South.

There are two major soil groups in the south—one group is sometimes referred to as the lime-accumulating soils, in which moisture rising to the surface and evaporating leaves carbonates, such as lime, in the soil. These lime-accumulating soils are found on the western margin of the Cotton Belt, where the rainfall is so light that the lime accumulation is not washed away. These soils are therefore naturally fertile and are very valuable, since commercial fertilizers are needed far less. In this soil the western part of the Cotton Belt has a considerable advantage over the eastern part.

The other group of soils, prevailing over the eastern part of the Cotton Belt from the

Mississippi Valley eastward, are non-lime-accumulating, because heavier rainfall leaches the lime from the surface. In order to maintain soil fertility an expensive program of fertilizing has to be provided.

The extensive plains, fertile soils, forests, and wild game of the South were largely untouched before 1800. To the Indians this South was a highly desirable habitat. Their simple life found abundant satisfaction in the immediate environment, and nature was not disturbed. Their agriculture, based on corn, beans, and squash, was mainly confined to the rich river bottoms. The vast forested areas were hunted continuously but never to the point of serious depletion of the game. The Indians occupied or used the entire South, but their total number probably never rose above 200,000 for the whole region from the Rio Grande to the Ohio and Potomac.

All of this changed drastically with the intensive exploitation of the area by the white man. The result is a very different type of economic wealth for a vastly larger number of people as well as a different habitat. The creation of a wealthy class from cotton promoted contacts with the entire world in providing for their wants, and nature was often disregarded for the creation and maintenance of this financially exclusive group. But the evils of exploitation pressed hard upon the bulk of the natives. Worn-out lands or lands naturally unfit for cotton production constituted the only space available for many people too poor for any other way of independent life. The bulk of the common people were dependent upon the owners of lands profitably producing cotton. They could not rise above the wages or goods paid for the menial and manual tasks associated with cotton. In this state they were highly vulnerable to habitat handicaps. The mud of winter rendered most of the people immobile and restricted such public functions as education and health; the work required by cotton limited or excluded education and recreation. Disease and insects plagued or ravaged man, beast, and plant with little control.

Paved roads, improved farm equipment and methods, and the control of diseases and insects are throwing into sharp focus such promising aspects of the habitat of the South as its large area, its vast extent of lowland plains above flood level, its accessibility through streams, its extensive coast line and direct overland routes, its temperate climate, its productive soil, and its abundant and varied natural resources. Indeed, many think that no other area in the world exceeds the South in terms of promise.

But some of the greatest problems confronting the South arise in large part from the changes in habitat wrought by man in the era of exploitation. These are described below.

• 97 • Man's Natural Enemies
ALMON E. PARKINS

INSECTS

Space will permit only a brief discussion of a few of the pests known in the South.

The boll weevil is a Mexican pest that first entered southern Texas in 1892. By 1922

[Adapted from *The South, its Economic-Geographic Development,* John Wiley, New York, 1938. Pp. 67-75, 77-79, 81-83, 85-88. Used by permission.]

it had spread over the entire Cotton Belt. In 1921 it was estimated that this one pest reduced the prospective total yield of cotton for the United States 31 to 34 per cent. The loss for Georgia was estimated at 45 per cent, and that for Oklahoma at 41 per cent. The boll weevil, however, has little affected the total crop of cotton. Since it is known that the yield per acre will be less, to maintain the normal cotton crop, the acreage must necessarily be increased and the cost of production is increased.

The cattle tick which carries the germ of the Texas cattle fever has been known in North America since Colonial days, probably having been introduced along with Spanish cattle into Mexico, Texas, and Florida. . . . It is only in recent decades that a thorough study of the disease has been made and a method for the eradication of the tick devised, namely, dipping the animals in a vat of insecticide. In 1906 there were 985 quarantined counties in the South in the infested area. By 1934 the number that had been released was 914 [leaving only 71 quarantined]. . . . Where the tick has been eliminated a surprising improvement and development in the cattle industry have usually resulted. Packing plants have been introduced in many sections, so also have creameries, condenseries, and ice-cream plants.

The Mediterranean fruit fly has been the South's most recent insect scare. Early in 1929 this pest was found well established in central Florida in the citrus-fruit sections. The active measures used won the day for man. This is the first instance in America of an insect pest being entirely destroyed over a large area within a few months.

Owing to the hot moist weather that prevails over a large area, the South is open to ravages by subtropical, tropical, and warm-weather diseases such as yellow fever, cholera, and malaria. But every Southern state has taken active measures against [malaria], and in spite of the poverty and ignorance with which health authorities have had to contend—malaria, ignorance, and poverty are concomitant phenomena—surprising results have been attained.

SOIL EROSION

Studies conducted throughout some twenty years have shown that the Savannah River, which drains the adjacent parts of Georgia and South Carolina, is carrying 135 carloads (50 tons each) of soil (mantle rock) daily to the Atlantic Ocean—more than 2,500,000 tons of suspended material annually. Similar investigations of the Mississippi give the stupendous figure of 340,500,000 tons of suspended rock material being deposited in the Gulf each year. In terms of train loads (of 40 cars, each carrying 50 tons), 466 trains would need to leave the mouth of the Mississippi daily to return this immense amount of rock debris to its original home. According to a report of the United States Bureau of Chemistry and Soils several years ago, Fairfield County, South Carolina, in the Piedmont, had lost 90,000 acres of productive land by gullying. In Stewart County, Georgia, the inner part of the Coastal Plain, 70,000 acres have been made practically useless for agriculture by excessive erosion. In western Tennessee 300,000 acres are reported as having been destroyed. These instances are typical of a process that is going on over a large part of the South.

Erosion, even the sheet wash that is scarcely noticeable, is responsible for much soil depletion, unprofitable farming, tax delinquency, and farm abandonment. The total loss for the country at large, it is estimated by competent Federal Government experts, amounts to $400,000,000 a year. Fully 100,000 acres of productive land are destroyed each year, and in addition a much larger area is being hopelessly impaired. About 50,000,000 acres have been essentially destroyed in the United States, an area equivalent to nearly 625,000 farms of 80 acres each; another 50,000,000 acres are in almost as bad condition. The total loss already is at least $10,000,000,000. More than a third of this—the area of the South is about one-third of the total of the country—should be assigned to the South, for nowhere else in the United States are the conditions quite so favorable for loss by soil erosion. Man, if he intends to build a permanent civilization in the South, must awaken to a realization of the ultimate effects of the slow but relentless destruction of his most valuable of all resources. The vast stores of iron ore, coal, oil, gas, sulphur, and salt, and the power of the thousand streams that roll onward down the slopes to the ocean, can amount to little if the productive power of the soil is impaired. *Soil is a resource that belongs to the public, present and future. Permitting its destruction should be considered a crime!*

Soil erosion—wash and gullying—is active in the South because:

1. During only a few weeks each year, even in the Upper South, is the ground frozen.

2. The staple crops, as cotton and corn, leave the surface of the soil uncovered during the off season, unless the farmer grows winter oats, rye, or wheat, and even these leave much opportunity for erosion.

3. Most of the land is in slope, that is, it has a mature topography and much of the topsoil is of a sort that washes and gullies readily—a light porous upper soil on a denser subsoil.

4. Lastly, because of the cheapness of the land and the prevalence of tenancy (on a large number of farms it is shiftlessness and ignorance), little is done to prevent surface wash and check gullying in its incipient stages.

Soil wash and gullying *can be prevented*. Such waste of land is practically unheard of in Europe. For forty centuries lands have been cultivated in China and Japan and are better today than 4,000 years ago, partly because soil erosion is not permitted. If the South is more susceptible to such processes of land deterioration, *and it is,* the farmers of the South should adjust themselves more than they have hitherto done to the adverse natural conditions and redouble their effort to prevent such losses. [Many] highly productive sections of the Southern States will need millions of dollars spent on levees, drainage ditches, and pumping plants to fit them for agriculture.

WET AND OVERFLOW LANDS

The total area of wet and overflow lands in the South is about 65,000,000 acres. . . .

About 50,000,000 acres of this is potential crop land, but not necessarily economically possible of reclamation at present.

FLOODS AND FLOOD CONTROL OF THE MISSISSIPPI

Floods are perfectly normal phenomena, for most rivers. Southern rivers certainly are no exception. The Southern river that has received the most attention in this country because of its destructive floods is the Mississippi. Nearly every year it has a period or periods of high water, but it is only occasionally that the height of its flood waters becomes excessive. During such times a large area of the flood plain, with its agricultural lands and buildings, cities, and traffic lines, is covered by water, and the usual trend of business affairs is interrupted. Yet these unusual floods are normal, for small floods and large floods must have been the regular order in the life history of the Mississippi for hundreds of thousands of years. . . .

The destructiveness of the flood waters is ever increasing, not necessarily because the floods are higher, although they probably are; but because the number of people that take chances in areas subject to inundation is increasing, and more and more property is being accumulated. No statistical data are available for determining whether the floods of late decades are higher than those of the earlier decades of the historic periods. It seems very clear, however, that though floods are natural happenings man has in various ways . . . in his modification of the natural environment, particularly in the removal of the forests, added a few inches, if not feet, to the "peak" height of the flood waters.

Experiments at Spur, Texas, and at an experimental station on the Piedmont, show that grass cover reduces the run-off materially. Forest cover is equally if not more effective.

The levee system of the Mississippi was devised in the beginning to protect the lowlands from flood; later it was constructed chiefly to improve navigation of the Mississippi. Spillways through which or by which flood waters can reach natural distributaries and be carried away to the Gulf as the water was carried before man interfered, are a second feature worked out for flood control. . . . In portions of the Alluvial Valley the original condition is approached, and yet the work of man is preserved, to some degree at least, by providing a series of overflow basins enclosed by levees.

That the present works will handle *all* future floods no one, of course, can assert, for every now and then nature does the un-expected. The flood of 1937, that brought such appalling disaster to the Ohio Valley, was so easy if the "unprecedented" rains had continued to fall instead of ceasing as they did shortly after the crest of the flood had passed Louisville and Paducah?

handled with ease by the Mississippi works after the flood waters had passed the Tiptonville meander some fifty miles downstream from Cairo. But would the task have been

The preceding discussion has dealt with the habitat problems of the South as a whole, consisting of thirteen states, including on the north Virginia, Kentucky, and Arkansas, and on the west Oklahoma and Texas. Now we shall turn to a more limited area, the *Cotton South.*

Some parts of the South have never raised cotton in significant amounts and are thus excluded from our discussion. Also, some states now raising cotton in quantity, particularly California and Arizona, are not part of the South. The *Cotton South,* as the term is used in this book, refers primarily to the older cotton-producing areas of Georgia, Louisiana, Arkansas, North Carolina, South Carolina, Alabama, and Mississippi. Many of the selections will cover a wider scope, but their focus will be upon these particular states and the way of life which their people developed.

In addition to their many similarities in people and habitat, the states of the Cotton South form a relatively unified section of the country because they share a common historical background. Although some of these states were still wilderness when others were important colonies, they grew to resemble one another in the nineteenth century, particularly in their dependence on slavery and the plantation system. Finally, they were united politically in the Confederacy during one of the most protracted and devastating wars of modern times. After sharing the humiliation of defeat, they continued to be drawn closely together as a consciously "different" social and economic region by their common economic and social problems. Thus, as in other societies we are studying, small diversities are overlaid by a unity of background and traditions from the past and by shared ways of living and meeting the problems of the present.

The Cotton South
J. R. SCHWENDEMAN

Certain portions of the Cotton South of tradition no longer emphasize cotton, and should not be considered as a portion of the modern Cotton South. Among such portions are the following: most of the outer portion of the Atlantic Coastal Plain; the northern portion of the Piedmont Plateau, i.e., north of northern North Carolina; the industrial area about Birmingham, which is a part of the Appalachian Highlands; the Black Belt of Alabama, now agriculturally diversified; the Atlantic-Gulf Coast, with autumnal rains and poor drainage; and the mouth of the Rio Grande, with greater emphasis upon truck-gardening.

Within the modern Cotton South certain

areas specialize on cotton: the Inner Atlantic Coastal Plain; the southern Piedmont; the Northern Alabama area associated with the Tennessee River; the Mississippi Bottom; the Black Waxy (Black Earth) area of Texas; the coastal plain of Southern Texas; and the High Plains (Red Prairies of Texas-Oklahoma). These six areas account for a great part of the cotton land shown in Table 1.

TABLE 1.—PERCENTAGE OF CROP LAND HAR-
VESTED DEVOTED TO COTTON IN COTTON
BELT (1944)

State	Percent
Mississippi	35.4
Arkansas	29.5
South Carolina	24.7
Texas	24.0
Louisiana	23.3
Alabama	22.3
Georgia	16.4
North Carolina	11.7
Tennessee	11.2
Oklahoma	10.5
Missouri	3.1

Florida	1.4
Virginia	0.7
Kentucky	0.2

Outside the South three states in the West are growing cotton by irrigation—New Mexico, Arizona and California. About ½ million acres were used for cotton in 1944 and it is increasing.

Total acreage in 1944 was about 19 million acres of which 18.5 million was grown in the states tabulated above. Of this latter figure only about ½ million acres are grown in the states of Florida, Virginia, Kentucky and Missouri. The Cotton Belt economy falls mainly within the states of North Carolina, South Carolina, Georgia, Tennessee, Alabama, Mississippi, Arkansas, Louisiana, Oklahoma, and Texas, each of which devoted from 10 per cent to roughly 30 per cent of its crop land to cotton. As recently as 1929 the South gave *half* of its crop land to cotton, the total being over 43 million acres. However, the decline in production was not proportional to the decline in acreage—from 14.6 million bales in 1929 to 11.5 million bales in 1944.

• The Natural Limits of the Cotton South
CLARENCE F. JONES AND GORDON D. DARKENWALD

However, these coastal lowlands are well suited to rice culture in southern Louisiana and Texas, to cane growing in the Mississippi Delta, and to fruit and vegetable farming in sandy areas of other sections. The eastern boundary of the cotton belt is in general the border between the outer and inner coastal plains. The outer coastal plain has much swampy land, infertile, sandy soil, and an excessive autumn rainfall of from 10 to 13 inches, all of which tend to restrict cotton culture.

In the old cotton regions of the inner coastal plain and piedmont gently sloping or rolling lands provide good drainage. The yellow sandy loam of the inner coastal plain

The northern boundary follows closely the 210-day frost-free area, which enjoys a mean summer temperature of 77° F. Since the advent of the boll weevil, there has been a tendency to push this line farther north because cold winters kill many hibernating weevils. The western boundary of the cotton belt is about at the 20-inch annual-rainfall line, but 20 inches is sufficient only where soils and the seasonal distribution of the rainfall are favorable. The southern boundary is approximately at the 10-inch autumn-rainfall line. Heavy rains in the fall damage the lint and interfere with picking, while heat and moisture combined in this southern section greatly aid the development of the boll weevil.

[Adapted from *Economic Geography*, Macmillan, New York, 1941. Pp. 206-209. Used by permission.]

is low in fertility, and the brownish red clays and sandy loams of the piedmont are only slightly more fertile. Both are low in humus, but friable and easily worked. The soils of these areas were utilized first because these areas were settled first. The [persistent] application of much fertilizer has maintained cotton farming in these old areas, and, owing to methods of tillage and fertilization, cotton yields are higher here than the average for the entire cotton belt.

Rich alluvial soils of the Tennessee, Mississippi, Arkansas, and Red River valleys, have been responsible for a concentration of cotton production on level bottom lands and adjacent rolling interstream areas, where yields are usually high without the use of fertilizer. The Mississippi Valley region, from southern Illinois to central Louisiana, has the highest yield and produces the longest fiber of the cotton belt. In this region two soil belts, dark silt loams on the flood plains and brown silt loams of adjacent loess plains and hills, are especially fertile. This region, however, has its disadvantages in that the Mississippi goes on frequent rampages, causing great loss of property and life. However, each flood leaves behind a rich layer of silt, some of which, when dry, is picked up by the winds and deposited on near-by lands.

The best cotton soils of Texas are in the grasslands of the central and western parts. Those of the central portion are reddish brown to black, deep, high in humus and calcium carbonate, and easily worked. Both undulating land and flatland respond to machine culture and are not subject to excessive erosion or leaching. The soil of western Texas is dark brown, friable, and high in humus and lime. In these grasslands a smaller rainfall with greater variability and somewhat more extensive methods of farming result in a lower average yield per acre than that in the more humid regions. On the other hand, the drier conditions are hard on the boll weevil.

The Old South, 1850–1860

>>>

The general theme of this book is social change—particularly the kind of change that results when the twin processes of industrialization and urbanization begin to bring about a new social landscape. The South, as much as any area in the country, is now caught in the current of this change; furthermore, it has been studied more intensively than any other large section, with the result that changes can be interpreted against a background of facts. But if we are to study the changing South we must have some idea of what it once was like and recognize the forces that have led to the passing of an old order. How was life in the Old South? What traditional characteristics still leave their impress? Why are Southerners considered different, a point touched upon in Selections 94 and 95?

Obviously, in a book of this sort it is impossible to present a detailed account of the history of the South, interesting though that would be. Instead, the selections that follow present a panorama of what the Old South was like in a single decade, 1850-1860, a period which most historians agree is the basis for most of the traditional concepts about the South which persist to our day. Once the reader is familiar with this period he will have a bench mark against which to look at changes following the Civil War and the other wars of later years.

In the eight selections that follow, notice how the people made their living, their methods of transportation, and their types of dwelling, food, and dress. What was the nature of their family life, their religion, their local government? What were the social distinctions among the whites: the planter, the yeoman, and the "poor white"? Then, too, what was the relationship between the Negroes and whites, institutionalized as it was in slavery? What public issues attracted attention and led to the psychological conditioning of the "Southern mind"?

We can get something of the flavor of life in the Old South if we follow Frederick Law Olmsted on a short part of his rather extended journey during 1853-1854. We join him as he travels through South Carolina, Georgia, and Alabama, describing some of the countryside and chance events, a visit to a plantation, a church service, stopovers in Savannah, Columbus, Montgomery, and Mobile, with intermediate transportation provided by rail, stagecoach, and river steamer. Throughout this account you will note the reaction of a Northerner, who was a trained observer, to a wide range of Southern attitudes. Olmsted was a nationally known landscape architect who helped plan Central Park in New York City and the Capitol grounds in Washington, D. C.

A Journey in the Seaboard Slave States

FREDERICK L. OLMSTED

TRAVEL IN SOUTH CAROLINA

The country was very thinly peopled; lone houses often being several miles apart. The large majority of the dwellings were of logs, and even those of the white people were often without glass windows. The cabin is often elevated on four corner-posts, two or three feet from the ground, so that the air may circulate under it. The fire-place is built at the end of the house, of sticks and clay, and the chimney is carried up outside, and often detached from the log-walls; but the roof is extended at the gable, until in a line with its outer side. The porch has a railing in front, and a wide shelf at the end, on which a bucket of water, a gourd, and hand-basin, are usually placed. There are chairs, or benches, in the porch, and you often see women sitting at work in it, as in Germany.

Cabins, of this class, would almost always be flanked by two or three negro-huts. The cabins of the poorest class of whites were of a meaner sort—being mere square pens of logs, roofed over, provided with a chimney, and usually with a shed of boards, supported by rough posts, before the door.

Occasionally, where the silvery sand was darkened by a considerable intermixture of mould, there would be a large plantation, with negro-quarters, and a cotton-press and gin-house. We passed half a dozen of these, perhaps, during the day. Where the owners resided in them, they would have comfortable-looking residences, not unlike the better class of New England farm-houses. On the largest one, however, there was no residence for the owner, at all, only a small cottage, or whitewashed cabin, for the overseer. It was a very large plantation, and all the buildings were substantial and commodious, except the negro-cabins, which were the smallest I had seen—I thought not more than twelve feet square, interiorly. They stood in two rows, with a wide street between them. They were built of logs, with no windows—no openings at all, except the doorway, with a chimney of sticks and mud; with no trees about them, no porches, or shades, of any kind. Except for the chimney—the purpose of which I should not readily have guessed—if I had seen one of them in New England, I should have conjectured that it had been built for a powder-house, or perhaps an ice-house—never for an animal to sleep in.

We stopped, for some time, on this plantation, near where some thirty men and women were at work, repairing the road. The women were in majority, and were engaged at exactly the same labor as the men; driving the carts, loading them with dirt, and dumping them upon the road; cutting down trees, and drawing wood by hand, to lay across the miry places; hoeing, and shovelling.

The overseer rode about among them, on a horse, carrying in his hands a raw-hide whip, constantly directing and encouraging

[Adapted from *A Journey in the Seaboard Slave States in the Years 1853-54, with Remarks on Their Economy*, Vol. 2, G. P. Putnam's Sons, New York, 1904. Pp. 7-13, 37-69, 82-93, 188-194, 203-205, 207-218, 220-224. Used by permission.]

them; but, as my companion and I, both, several times noticed, as often as he visited one end of the line of operations, the hands at the other end would discontinue their labor, until he turned to ride towards them again.

A VISIT TO A PLANTATION

Nowhere in the world could a man, with a sound body and a quiet conscience live more pleasantly, at least, as a guest, it seems to me, than here where I am. I was awakened this morning by a servant making a fire for me to dress by. Opening the window, I found a clear, brisk air, but without frost—the mercury standing at 35° F. There was not a sign of winter, except that a few cypress trees, hung with seed, attached to pretty pendulous tassels, were leafless. A grove which surrounded the house was all in dark verdure; there were green oranges on trees nearer the window; the buds were swelling on a jessamine-vine, and a number of camelia-japonicas were in full bloom; one of them, at least seven feet high, and a large, compact shrub, must have had several hundred blossoms on it. Sparrows were chirping, doves cooing, and a mocking-bird whistling loudly. I walked to the stable, and saw the clean and neatly-dressed negroes grooming thoroughbred horses. They pawed the ground, and tossed their heads, and drew deep inspirations, and danced as they were led out in exuberance of animal spirits, and I felt as they did. We drove ten miles to church, in the forenoon, with the carriage-top thrown back, and with our overcoats laid aside; nevertheless, when we returned, and came into the house, we found a crackling wood fire, in the old-fashioned fire-place, as comfortable as it was cheerful. Two lads, the sons of my host, had returned the night before from a "marooning party," with a boat-load of venison, wild fowl and fish, and at dinner this evening there were delicacies which are not to be had in perfection, it is said, anywhere else than on a rice-plantation. The woods and waters around us abound, not only with game, but with most interesting subjects of observation to the naturalist and the artist.

Everything encourages cheerfulness, and invites to healthful life.

But I must tell how I got here, and what I saw by the way.

Having some doubt about the road, I asked a direction of a man on horseback, who overtook and was passing me. In reply, he said it was a very straight road, and we should go in company, for a mile or two. He inquired if I was a stranger; and, when he heard that I was from the North, and now first visiting the South, he remarked that there was "no better place for me to go to than that for which I was bound. Mr. X. was a very fine man—rich, got a splendid plantation, lived well, had plenty of company always, and there were a number of other show plantations near his. He reckoned I would visit some of them."

I asked what he called "show plantations." "Plantations belonging to rich people," he said, "where they had everything fixed up nice. There were several places that had that name; their owners always went out and lived on them part of the year, and then they kept a kind of open house, and were always ready to receive company—had a great many Northerners going to see them, those gentlemen had. Almost every Northerner that came here was invited right out, to visit some of them, and, in summer, a good many of them went to the North themselves."

During the forenoon, once or twice, I met a stylish carriage; but much the greatest traffic of the road was done by small one-horse carts, driven by white men, or women.

These carts, all but their wheels, which come from the North, look as if they were made by their owners, in the woods, with no better tools than axes and jack-knives. Very little iron is used in their construction; the different parts being held together by wooden pins, and lashings of hide.

The men with the carts were generally slight, with high cheekbones and sunken eyes, and were of less than the usual stature of the Anglo-Saxon race. They were dressed in long-skirted homespun coats, wore slouched hats, and heavy boots, outside their trowsers. As they met me, they usually bowed, and often offered a remark upon the weather, or the roads, in a bold, but not uncourteous manner.

The household markets of most of the Southern towns seem to be mainly supplied by the poor country people, who, driving in in this style, bring all sorts of produce to exchange for such small stores and articles of apparel as they must needs obtain from the shops.

I shall not soon forget the figure of a little old white woman, wearing a man's hat, smoking a pipe, driving a little black bull with reins; sitting, herself, bolt upright, upon the axle-tree of a little truck, on which she was returning from market. I was riding with a gentleman of the town at the time, and, as she bowed to him with an expression of ineffable self-satisfaction, I asked if he knew her. He had known her for twenty years, he said, and until lately she had always come into town about once a week, on foot, bringing fowls, eggs, potatoes, or herbs, for sale, in a basket. The bull she had probably picked up astray, when a calf, and reared and broken it herself; and the cart and harness she had made herself; but he did not think anybody in the land felt richer than she did now, or prouder of her establishment.

After riding a few miles farther I reached my destination.

Mr. X. has two plantations on the river, besides a large tract of poor pine forest land, extending some miles back upon the upland, and reaching above the malarious region. In the upper part of this pine land is a house, occupied by his overseer during the malarious season, when it is dangerous for any but negroes to remain during the night in the vicinity of the swamps or rice-fields. Even those few who have been born in the region, and have grown up subject to the malaria, are generally weakly and short-lived; but Mr. X. boasts a steady increase of his negro stock of five per cent. per annum, which is better than is averaged on the plantations of the interior.

The plantation which contains Mr. X.'s winter residence, has but a small extent of rice-land, the greater part of it being reclaimed upland swamp soil, suitable for the culture of Sea Island cotton, which, at the present market, might be grown upon it with profit. But, as his force of slaves has ordinarily been more profitably engaged in the rice-fields, all this has been for many years "turned out," and is now overgrown with pines. The other plantation contains over five hundred acres of rice-land, fitted for irrigation; the remainder is unusually fertile, reclaimed upland swamp, and some hundred acres of it are cultivated for maize and Sea Island cotton.

There is a "negro settlement" on each; but both plantations, although a mile or two apart, are worked together as one, under one overseer—the hands being drafted from one to another as their labor is required. Somewhat over seven hundred acres are at the present time under the plough in the two plantations: the whole number of negroes is two hundred, and they are reckoned to be equal about one hundred prime hands—an unusual strength for that number of all classes. The overseer lives, in winter, near the settlement of the larger plantation, Mr. X. near that of the smaller.

It is an old family estate, inherited by Mr. X.'s wife, who, with her children, were born and brought up upon it in close intimacy with the negroes, a large proportion of whom were also included in her inheritance, or have been since born upon the estate. Mr. X. himself is a New England farmer's son, and has been a successful merchant and manufacturer. He is also a religious man, without the dementifying bigotry of self-important humility, so frequently implied by that appellation to a New Englander, but generous, composed and cheerful in disposition, as well as conscientious.

The patriarchal institution could be seen here under its most favorable aspects; not only from the ties of long family association, common traditions, common memories, and, if ever, common interests, between the slaves and their rulers, but, also, from the practical talent for organization and administration, gained among the rugged fields, the complicated looms, and the exact and comprehensive counting-houses of New England, which directs the labor.

The house-servants are more intelligent, understand and perform their duties better, and are more appropriately dressed than any I have seen before. The labor required of them is light, and they are treated with much more consideration for their health and comfort than is usually given to that of free domestics. They live in brick cabins, adjoining the house and stables, and one of these, into which I have looked, is neatly and comfortably furnished. Several of the house-servants, as is usual, are mulattoes, and good-looking. The mulattoes are generally preferred for indoor occupations. Slaves brought up to housework dread to be employed at field-labor; and those accustomed to the comparatively unconstrained life of the negro-settlement detest the close control and careful movements required of the house-servants.

It is a custom with Mr. X., when on the estate, to look each day at all the work going on, inspect the buildings, boats, embankments and sluice-ways, and examine the sick. Yesterday I accompanied him in one of these daily rounds.

After a ride of several miles through the woods, in the rear of the plantations, we came to his largest negro-settlement. There was a street, or common, two hundred feet wide, on which the cabins of the negroes fronted. Each cabin was a frame building, the walls boarded and whitewashed on the outside, lathed and plastered within, the roof shingled; forty-two feet long, twenty-one feet wide, divided into two family tenements, each twenty-one by twenty-one; each tenement divided into three rooms—one, the common household apartment, twenty-one by ten; each of the others (bed-rooms), ten by ten. There was a brick fire-place in the middle of the long side of each living room, the chimneys rising in one, in the middle of the roof. Besides these rooms, each tenement had a cock-loft, entered by steps from the household room. Each tenement is occupied, on an average, by five persons. There were in them closets, with locks and keys, and a varying quantity of rude furniture. Each cabin stood two hun-

dred feet from the next, and the street in front of them being two hundred feet wide, they were just that distance apart each way. The people were nearly all absent at work, and had locked their outer doors, taking the keys with them. Each cabin has a front and back door, and each room a window, closed by a wooden shutter, swinging outward, on hinges. Between each tenement and the next house, is a small piece of ground, inclosed with palings, in which are coops of fowl, with chickens, hovels for nests, and for sows with pig. There were a great many fowls in the street. The negroes' swine are allowed to run in the woods, each owner having his own distinguished by a peculiar mark. In the rear of the yards were gardens—a half-acre to each family. Internally the cabins appeared dirty and disordered, which was rather a pleasant indication that their home-life was not much interfered with, though I found certain police regulations were enforced.

The cabin nearest the overseer's house was used as a nursery. Having driven up to this, Mr. X. inquired first of an old nurse how the children were; whether there had been any births since his last visit; spoke to two convalescent young mothers, that were lounging on the floor of the portico, with the children, and then asked if there were any sick people.

"Nobody, oney dat boy Sam, sar."

"What Sam is that?"

"Dat little Sam, sar; Tom's Sue's Sam, sar."

"What's the matter with him?"

"Don' 'spec dere's noting much de matter wid him now, sar. He came in Sa'dy, complainin' he had de stomach-ache, an' I gin him some ile, sar; 'spec he mus' be well, dis time, but he din go out dis mornin'."

"Well, I'll see to him."

Mr. X. went to Tom's Sue's cabin, looked at the boy, and, concluding that he was well, though he lay abed, and pretended to cry with pain, ordered him to go out to work. Then, meeting the overseer, who was just riding away, on some business off the plantation, he remained some time in conversation with him, while I occupied myself in making a sketch of the nursery and the street of the settlement in my note-book. On the verandah and the steps of the nursery, there were twenty-seven children, most of them infants, that had been left there by their mothers, while they were working their tasks in the fields. They probably make a visit to them once or twice during the day, to nurse them, and receive them to take to their cabins, or where they like, when they have finished their tasks—generally in the middle of the afternoon. The older children were fed with porridge, by the general nurse. A number of girls, eight or ten years old, were occupied in holding and tending the youngest infants. Those a little older—the crawlers—were in the pen, and those big enough to toddle were playing on the steps, or before the house. Some of these, with two or three bigger ones, were singing and dancing about a fire that they had made on the ground. They were not at all disturbed or interrupted in their amusement by the presence of their owner and myself. At twelve years of age, the children are first put to regular field-work; until then no labor is required of them, except, perhaps, occasionally, they are charged with some light kind of duty, such as frightening birds from corn. When first sent to the field, one-quarter of an able-bodied hand's day's work is ordinarily allotted to them, as their task.

But very few of the babies were in arms; such as were not, generally lay on the floor, rolling about, or sat still, sucking their thumbs. The nurse was a kind-looking old negro woman, with, no doubt, philoprogenitiveness well developed; but she paid very little attention to them, only sometimes chiding the older ones for laughing or singing too loud. I watched for half an hour, and in all that time not a baby of them began to cry; nor have I ever heard one, at two or three other plantation-nurseries which I have visited.

From the settlement, we drove to the "mill"—not a flouring mill, though I believe there is a run of stones in it—but a monster barn, with more extensive and better machinery for threshing and storing rice, driven by a steam-engine, than I have ever seen used for grain on any farm in Europe or America before. Adjoining the mill-house were shops and sheds, in which blacksmiths, carpenters, and other mechanics—all slaves, belonging to Mr. X.—were at work. He called my attention to the excellence of their workmanship, and said that they exercised as much ingenuity and skill as the ordinary mechanics that he was used to employ in New England. He pointed out to me some carpenter's work, a part of which had been executed by a New England mechanic, and a part by one of his own hands, which indicated that the latter was much the better workman.

I was gratified by this, for I had been so often told, in Virginia, by gentlemen, anxious to convince me that the negro was incapable of being educated or improved to a condition in which it would be safe to trust him with himself—that no negro-mechanic could ever be taught, or induced to work carefully or nicely—that I had begun to believe it might be so.

We were attended through the mill-house by a respectable-looking, orderly, and gentlemanly-mannered mulatto, who was called, by his master, "the watchman." His duties, however, as they were described to me, were those of a steward, or intendant. He carried, by a strap at his waist, a very large number of keys, and had charge of all the stores of provisions, tools, and materials of the plantations, as well as of all their produce, before it was shipped to market. He weighed and measured out all the rations of the slaves and the cattle; superintended the mechanics, and himself made and repaired, as was necessary, all the machinery, including the steam-engine.

In all these departments, his authority was superior to that of the overseer. The overseer received his private allowance of family provisions from him, as did also the head-servant at the mansion, who was his brother. His responsibility was much greater than that of the overseer; and Mr. X. said, he would trust him with much more than he would any overseer he had ever known.

A CHURCH SERVICE

A majority of the public houses of worship

at the South are small, rude structures of logs, or rough boards, built by the united labor or contributions of the people of a large neighborhood or district of country, and are used as places of assembly for all public purposes. Few of them have any regular clergymen, but preachers of different denominations go from one to another, sometimes in a defined rotation, or "circuit," so that they may be expected at each of their stations at regular intervals. A late report of the Southern Aid Society states that hardly one-fifth of the preachers are regularly educated for their business, and that "you would starve a host of them if you debarred them from seeking additional support for their families by worldly occupation." In one presbytery of the Presbyterian Church, which is, perhaps, the richest, and includes the most educated body of people of all the Southern churches, there are twenty-one ministers whose wages are not over two hundred and fifty dollars each. The proportion of ministers, of all sorts, to people, is estimated at one to thirteen hundred. (In the Free States it is estimated at one to nine hundred.)

The two largest denominations of Christians at the South are the Methodists and Baptists—the last having a numerical superiority. There are some subdivisions of each, and of the Baptists especially, the nature of which I do not understand. Two grand divisions of the Baptists are known as the Hard Shells and the Soft Shells. There is an intense rivalry and jealousy among these various sects and subsects, and the controversy between them is carried on with a bitterness and persistence exceeding anything which I have known at the North, and in a manner which curiously indicates how the terms "Christianity," "piety," etc., are misapplied to partisanship, and conditions of the imagination.

The religious service which I am about to describe, was held in a less than usually rude meeting-house, the boards by which it was inclosed being planed, the windows glazed, and the seats for the white people provided with backs. It stood in a small clearing of the woods, and there was no habitation within

two miles of it. When I reached it with my friends, the services had already commenced. Fastened to trees, in a circle about the house, there were many saddled horses and mules, and a few attached to cars or wagons. There were two smouldering camp-fires, around which sat circles of negroes and white boys, roasting potatoes in the ashes.

In the house were some fifty white people, generally dressed in homespun, and of the class called "crackers," though I was told that some of them owned a good many negroes, and were by no means so poor as their appearance indicated. About one-third of the house, at the end opposite the desk, was covered by a gallery or cock-loft, under and in which, distinctly separated from the whites, was a dense body of negroes; the men on one side, the women on another. The whites were seated promiscuously in the body of the house. The negroes present outnumbered the whites, but the exercises at this time seemed to have no reference to them; there were many more waiting about the doors outside, and they were expecting to enjoy a meeting to themselves, after the whites had left the house. They were generally neatly dressed, more so than the majority of the whites present, but in a distinctly plantation or slave style. A few of them wore somewhat expensive articles, evidently of their own selection and purchase, but I observed, with some surprise, that not one of the women had a bonnet upon her head, all wearing handkerchiefs, generally of gay patterns, and becomingly arranged. I inquired if this was entirely a matter of taste, and was told that it, no doubt, was generally so, though the masters would not probably allow them to wear bonnets, if they should be disposed to, and should purchase them themselves, as it would be thought presuming. In the towns, the colored women often, but not generally, wear bonnets.

During all the exercises, people of both classes were frequently going out and coming in; the women had brought their babies with them, and these made much disturbance. A negro girl would sometimes come forward to take a child out; perhaps the child would prefer not to be taken out and would make loud and angry objections; it would then be fed. Several were allowed to crawl about the floor, carrying handfuls of corn-bread and roast potatoes about with them; one had a fancy to enter the pulpit; which it succeeded in climbing into three times, and was as often taken away, in spite of loud and tearful expostulations, by its father. Dogs were not excluded; and outside, the doors and windows all being open, there was much neighing and braying, unused as were the mules and horses to see so many of their kind assembled.

The preliminary devotional exercises—a Scripture reading, singing, and painfully irreverential and meaningless harangues nominally addressed to the Deity, but really to the audience—being concluded, the sermon was begun with the reading of a text, with which, however, it had, so far as I could discover, no further association. Without often being violent in his manner, the speaker nearly all the time cried aloud at the utmost stretch of his voice, as if calling to some one a long distance off; as his discourse was extemporaneous, however, he sometimes returned with curious effect to his natural conversational tone; and as he was gifted with a strong imagination, and possessed of a good deal of dramatic power, he kept the attention of the people very well. There was no argument upon any point that the congregation were likely to have much difference of opinion upon, nor any special connection between one sentence and another; yet there was a constant, sly, sectarian skirmishing, and a frequently recurring cannonade upon French infidelity and socialism, and several crushing charges upon Fourier, the Pope of Rome, Tom Paine, Voltaire, "Roosu," and Jo Smith.

At the end of the sermon he stepped down from the pulpit, and, crossing the house towards the negroes, said, quietly, as he walked, "I take great interest in the poor blacks; and this evening I am going to hold a meeting specially for you." With this, he turned back, and without re-entering the pulpit, but strolling up and down before it, read a hymn, at the conclusion of which, he laid his book down, and speaking for a moment, with natural emphasis, said:

"I don't want to create a tumultuous scene, now;—that isn't my intention. I don't want to make an excitement—that ain't what I want,—but I feel that there's some here that I may never see again, ah! and, as I may never have another opportunity, I feel it my duty as an Ambassador of Jesus Christ, ah! before I go———." By this time he had returned to the high key and whining yell. Exactly what he felt it his duty to do, I did not understand; but evidently to employ some more powerful agency of awakening, than arguments and appeals to the understanding; and, before I could conjecture, in the least, of what sort this was to be, while he was yet speaking calmly, deprecating excitement, my attention was attracted to several men, who had previously appeared sleepy and indifferent, but who now suddenly began to sigh, raise their heads, and *shed tears*—some standing up, so that they might be observed in doing this by the whole congregation—the tears running down their noses without any interruption. The speaker, presently, was crying aloud, with a mournful, distressed, beseeching shriek, as if he was himself suffering torture. . . . "Oh, any of you wives that has got an unconverted husband, that won't go along with you to eternal glory, but is set upon being separated from you, oh! and taking up his bed in hell—Oh! I call upon you, if you love him, now to come out here and jine us in praying for him. Oh, if there's a husband here, whose wife is still in the bond of iniquity," etc., through a long category.

It was immediately evident that a large part of the audience understood his wish to be the reverse of what he had declared, and considered themselves called upon to assist him; and it was astonishing to see with what readiness the faces of those who, up to the moment he gave the signal, had appeared drowsy and stupid, were made to express agonizing excitement, sighing, groaning, and weeping. Rising in their seats and walking up to the pulpit, they grasped each other's hands agonizingly, and remained, some kneeling, others standing, with their faces towards the remainder of the assembly. There was great confusion and tumult, and the poor children, evidently impressed by the terrified tone of the howling preacher, with the expectation of some immediately impending calamity, shrieked, and ran hither and thither, till negro girls came forward, laughing at the imposition, and carried them out.

At length, when some twenty had gathered around the preacher, and it became evident that no more could be drawn out, he stopped a moment for breath, and then repeated a verse of a hymn, which being sung, he again commenced to cry aloud, calling now upon all the unconverted, who were *willing* to be saved, to kneel. A few did so, and another verse was sung, followed by another more fervent exhortation. So it went on; at each verse his entreaties, warnings, and threats, and the responsive groans, sobs, and ejaculations of his coterie grew louder and stronger. Those who refused to kneel, were addressed as standing on the brink of the infernal pit, into which a diabolical divinity was momentarily on the point of satisfying the necessities of his character by hurling them off.

All this time about a dozen of the audience remained standing, many were kneeling, and the larger part had taken their seats—all having risen at the commencement of the singing. Those who continued standing were mainly wild-looking young fellows, who glanced with smiles at one another, as if they needed encouragement to brazen it out. A few young women were evidently fearfully excited, and perceptibly trembled, but for some reason dared not kneel, or compromise, by sitting.

The last verse of the hymn was sung. A comparatively quiet and sober repetition of Scripture phrases, strung together heterogeneously and without meaning, in the form of prayer, followed, a benediction was pronounced, and in five minutes all the people were out of the door, with no trace of the previous excitement left, but most of the men talking eagerly of the price of cotton, and negroes, and other news.

The negroes kept their place during all of the tumult; there may have been a sympathetic groan or exclamation uttered by one or two of them, but generally they expressed only the interest of curiosity in the proceedings, such as Europeans might at a performance of the dancing dervishes, an Indian powwow, or an exhibition of "psychological" or "spiritual" phenomena, making it very evident that the emotion of the performers was optionally engaged in, as an appropriate part of divine service. There was generally a self-satisfied smile upon their faces; and I have no doubt they felt that they could do it with a good deal more energy and abandon, if they were called upon. I did not wish to detain my companion to witness how they succeeded, when their turn came; and I can only judge from the fact that those I saw the next morning were so hoarse that they could scarcely speak, that the religious exercises they most enjoy are rather hard upon the lungs, whatever their effect may be upon the soul.

FROM SAVANNAH TO MOBILE

I have travelled more than five hundred miles on Georgia [railroads,] and I am glad to say that all of them seemed to be exceedingly well managed. The speed upon them is not generally more than from fifteen to twenty miles an hour; but it is made, as advertised, with considerable punctuality. The roads are admirably engineered and constructed, and their equipment will compare favorably with that of any other roads on the continent. There are now very nearly, if not quite, one thousand miles of railroad in the State, and more building. The Savannah and Macon line—the first built—was commenced in 1834. The increased commerce of the city of Savannah, which followed its completion, stimulated many other railroad enterprises, not only within the State, but elsewhere at the South, particularly in South Carolina. Many of these were rashly pushed forward by men of no experience, and but little commercial judgment; the roads were injudiciously laid out, and have been badly managed, and, of course, have occasioned disastrous losses. The Savannah and Macon road has, however, been very successful. It has always been under the management of

Northern men—was engineered, and is still worked chiefly by Northern men, and a large amount of its stock is owned at the North. I am told that most of the mechanics, and of the successful merchants and tradesmen of Savannah came originally from the North, or are the sons of Northern men.

Partly by rail and partly by rapid stage-coaching (the coaches, horses, and drivers again from the North), I crossed the State in about twenty-four hours. The railroad has since been completed from Savannah to Montgomery, in Alabama, and it is being extended slowly towards the Mississippi; of course, with the expectation that it will eventually reach the Pacific, and thus make Savannah "the gate to the commerce of the world."

At Columbus, I spent several days. It is the largest manufacturing town, south of Richmond, in the Slave States. It is situated at the falls, the head of steamboat navigation of the Chattahooche, the western boundary of Georgia. The water-power is sufficient to drive two hundred thousand spindles, with a proportionate number of looms. There are, at present, probably from fifteen to twenty thousand spindles running. The operatives in the cotton mills are said to be mainly "Cracker girls" (poor whites from the country), who earn, in good times, by piece-work, from $8 to $12 a month. There are, besides the cotton mills, one woollen mill, one paper mill, a foundry, a cotton-gin factory, a machine shop, etc. The laborers in all these are mainly whites, and they are in such a condition that, if temporarily thrown out of employment, great numbers of them are at once reduced to a state of destitution, and are dependent upon credit or charity for their daily food. Public entertainments were being held at the time of my visit, the profits to be applied to the relief of operatives in mills which had been stopped by the effects of a late flood of the river. Yet it is boasted constantly that Slavery is a perfect safeguard against such distress.

I had seen in no place, since I left Washington, so much gambling, intoxication, and cruel treatment of servants in public, as in Columbus. This possibly was accidental; but I must caution persons, travelling for health or pleasure, to avoid stopping in the town.

A day's journey took me from Columbus, through a hilly wilderness, with a few dreary villages, and many isolated cotton farms, with comfortless habitations for black and white upon them, to Montgomery, the capital of Alabama.

Montgomery is a prosperous town, with very pleasant suburbs, and a remarkably enterprising population, among which there is a considerable proportion of Northern and foreign-born business men and mechanics.

I spent a week here very pleasantly, and then left for Mobile, on the steamboat *Fashion,* a clean and well-ordered boat, with polite and obliging officers. We were two days and a half making the passage, the boat stopping at almost every bluff and landing to take on cotton, until she had a freight of nineteen hundred bales, which was built up on the guards, seven or eight tiers in height, until it reached the hurricane deck. The boat was thus brought so deep that her guards were in the water, and the ripple of the river constantly washed over them. There are two hundred landings on the Alabama river, and three hundred on the Bigby (Tombeckbee of the geographers), at which the boats advertise to call, if required, for passengers or freight. This, of course, makes the passage exceedingly tedious.

There was something truly Western in the direct, reckless way in which the boat was loaded. A strong gang-plank being placed at right angles to the slide-way, a bale of cotton was let slide from the top, and, coming down with fearful velocity, on striking the gang-plank, it would rebound up and out on to the boat, against a barricade of bales previously arranged to receive it. The moment it struck this barricade, it would be dashed at by two or three men, and jerked out of the way, and others would roll it to its place for the voyage, on the tiers aft. The mate, standing near the bottom of the slide, as soon as the men had removed one bale to what he thought a safe distance, would shout to those aloft, and down would come another. Not unfrequently, a bale would not strike fairly on its end, and would rebound off, diagonally, overboard; or would be thrown up with such force as to go over the barricade, breaking stanchions and railings, and scattering the passengers on the berth deck. Negro hands were sent to the top of the bank, to roll the bales to the side, and Irishmen were kept below to remove them, and stow them. On asking the mate (with some surmisings) the reason of this arrangement, he said:

"The niggers are worth too much to be risked here; if the Paddies are knocked overboard, or get their backs broke, nobody loses anything!"

[At Claiborne, the] boat being detained, and the bounding bales making too much noise to allow me to sleep, I ascended the bank by a flight of two hundred steps, placed by the side of the slide-way, and took a walk in the village. In the principal street, I came upon a group of seven negroes, talking in lively, pleasant tones: presently, one of them commenced to sing, and in a few moments all the others joined in, taking different parts, singing with great skill and taste— better than I ever heard a group of young men in a Northern village, without previous arrangement, but much as I have heard a strolling party of young soldiers, or a company of students, or apprentices, in the streets of a German town, at night. After concluding the song, which was of a sentimental character, and probably had been learned at a concert or theatre, in the village, they continued in conversation, till one of them began to whistle: in a few moments all joined in, taking several different parts, as before, and making a peculiarly plaintive music. Soon after this, they walked all together, singing, and talking soberly, by turns, slowly away.

There were about one hundred passengers on the *Fashion,* besides a number of poor people and negroes on the lower deck. They were, generally, cotton planters, going to Mobile on business, or emigrants bound to Texas or Arkansas. They were usually well dressed, but were a rough, coarse style of people, drinking a great deal and most of the time under a little alcoholic excitement. Not sociable, except when the topics of cotton, land, and negroes, were started; interested, however, in talk about theatres and the turf; very profane; often showing the handles of concealed weapons about their persons, but not quarrelsome, avoiding disputes and altercations, and respectful to one another in forms of words; very ill-informed, except on plantation business; their language very ungrammatical, idiomatic, and extravagant. Their grand characteristics—simplicity of motive, vague, shallow, and purely objective habits of thought; spontaneity and truthfulness of utterance, and bold, self-reliant movement.

I found that, more than any people I have ever seen, they were unrateable by dress, taste, forms, and expenditures. I was perplexed by finding, apparently united in the same individual, the self-possession and confidence of the well-equipped gentleman, and the coarseness and low tastes of the uncivilized boor—frankness and reserve, recklessness and self-restraint, extravagance and penuriousness.

There was one man, who "lived, when he was to home," he told me, "in the Red River Country," in the northeastern part of Texas, having emigrated thither from Alabama, some years before. He was a tall, thin, awkward person, and wore a suit of clothes (probably bought "ready-made") which would have better suited a short, fat figure. Under his waistcoat he carried a large knife, with the hilt generally protruding at the breast. He had been with his family to his former home, to do a little business, and visit his relatives, and was now returning to his plantation. His wife was a pale and harassed looking woman; and he scarce ever paid her the smallest attention, not even sitting near her at the public table. Of his children, however, he seemed very fond; and they had a negro servant in attendance upon them, whom he was constantly scolding and threatening. Having been from home for six weeks, his impatience to return was very great, and was constantly aggravated by the frequent and long-continued stoppages of the boat. "Time's money, time's money!" he would be constantly saying, while we were taking on cotton, "time's worth more'n money to me now; a hundred per cent. more, 'cause I left my niggers all alone, not a dam white man within four mile on 'em."

I asked how many negroes he had.

"I've got twenty on 'em to home, and thar they ar! and thar they ar! and thar ain't a dam soul of a white fellow within four mile on 'em."

There were three young negroes, carried by another Texan, on the deck, outside the cabin. I don't know why they were not allowed to be with the other emigrant slaves, on the lower deck, unless the owner was afraid of their trying to get away, and had no handcuffs small enough for them. They were boys; the oldest twelve or fourteen years old, the youngest not more than seven. They had evidently been bought lately by their present owner, and probably had just been taken from their parents. They lay on the deck and slept, with no bed but the passengers' luggage, and no cover but a single blanket for each. Early one morning, after a very stormy night, when they must have suffered much from the driving rain and cold, I saw their owner with a glass of spirits, giving each a few swallows from it. The older ones smacked their lips, and said, "Tank 'ou, massa"; but the little one could n't drink it, and cried aloud, when he was forced to. The older ones were very playful and quarrelsome, and continually teasing the younger, who seemed very sad, or homesick and sulky. He would get very angry at their mischievous fun, and sometimes strike them. He would then be driven into a corner, where he would lie on his back, and kick at them in a perfect frenzy of anger and grief. The two boys would continue to laugh at him, and frequently the passengers would stand about, and be amused by it. Once, when they had plagued him in this way for some time, he jumped up on to the cotton bales, and made as if he would have plunged overboard. One of the older boys caught him by the ankle, and held him till his master came and hauled him in, and gave him a severe flogging with a rope's end. A number of passengers collected about them, and I heard several say, "That's what he wants." Red River said to me, "I've

been a watchin' that ar boy, and I see what's the matter with him; he's got the devil in him right bad, and he'll hev to take a right many of them warmin's before it be got out."

The crew of the boat, as I have intimated, was composed partly of Irishmen, and partly of negroes; the latter were slaves, and were hired of their owners at $40 a month—the same wages paid to the Irishmen. A dollar of their wages was given to the negroes themselves, for each Sunday they were on the passage. So far as convenient, they were kept at work separate from the white hands; they were also messed separately. On Sunday I observed them dining in a group, on the cotton bales. The food, which was given to them in tubs, from the kitchen was various and abundant, consisting of bean porridge, bacon, corn bread, ship's biscuit, potatoes, duff (pudding), and gravy. There was only one knife used, among ten of them; the bacon was cut and torn into shares; splinters of the bone and of firewood were used for forks; the porridge was passed from one to another, and drunk out of the tub; but though excessively dirty and beast-like in their appearance and manners, they were good-natured and jocose as usual.

Whenever we landed at night or on Sunday, for wood or cotton, many negroes would come on board from the neighboring plantations, to sell eggs to the steward.

Sunday was observed by the discontinuance of public gambling in the cabin, and in no other way. At midnight gambling was resumed, and during the whole passage was never at any other time discontinued, night or day, so far as I saw. There were three men that seemed to be professional sharpers, and who probably played into each other's hands. One young man lost all the money he had with him—several hundred dollars.

Mobile, in its central, business part, is very compactly built, dirty, and noisy, with little elegance, or evidence of taste or public spirit, in its people. A small, central, open square— the only public ground that I saw—was used as a horse and hog pasture, and clothes drying-yard. Out of the busier quarter, there is a good deal of the appearance of a thriving

New England village—almost all the dwelling houses having plots of ground enclosed around them, planted with trees and shrubs. At a market garden, I found most of the best Northern and Belgian pears fruiting well and apparently healthy, and well suited in climate, on quince-stocks. Figs are abundant and bananas and oranges are said to be grown with some care, and slight winter protection.

The Battle House, kept by Boston men, with Irish servants, I found an excellent hotel; but with higher charges than I had ever paid before. Prices, generally, in Mobile, range very high. There are large numbers of foreign merchants in the population; but a great deficiency of tradesmen and mechanics.

The great abundance of the best timber for the purpose, in the United States, growing in the vicinity of the town, has lately induced some persons to attempt ship building at Mobile. The mechanics employed are mainly from the North.

The great business of the town is the transfer of cotton, from the producer to the manufacturer, from the wagon and the steamboat to the sea-going ship. Like all the other cotton ports, Mobile labors under the disadvantage of a shallow harbor. At the wharves, there were only a few small craft and steamboats. All large sea-going vessels lie some thirty miles below, and their freights are transshipped in lighters.

There appears to be a good deal of wealth and luxury, as well as senseless extravagance, in the town. English merchants affect the character of the society, considerably; some very favorably—some, very much otherwise. Many of them own slaves, and, probably, all employ them; but Slavery seems to be of more value to them in the amusement it affords, than in any other way.

The steamboat by which I made the passage along the north shore of the Mexican Gulf to New Orleans, was New York built and owned by a New Yorker; and the Northern usage of selling passage tickets, to be returned on leaving the boat, was retained upon it. I was sitting near a group of Texans and emigrating planters, when a waiter passed along, crying the usual request, that passengers who had not obtained tickets, would call at the captain's office for that purpose. "What's that? What's that?" they shouted; "What did he mean? What is it?" "Why, it's a dun," said one. "Damned if't ain't," continued one and another; "he is dunnin' on us, sure," and some started from the seats, as if they thought it insulting. "Well, it's the first time I ever was dunned by a nigger, I'll swar," said one. This seemed to place it in a humorous aspect; and, after a hearty laugh, they resumed their discussion of the advantages offered to emigrants in different parts of Texas, and elsewhere.

THE RAPID GROWTH

The territorial Government of Alabama was established in 1816, and in 1818 she was admitted as a State into the Union. In 1820, her population was 128,000; in 1850, it had increased to 772,000; the increase of the previous ten years having been 30 per cent. (that of South Carolina was 5 per cent.; of Georgia, 31; Mississippi, 60; Michigan, 87; Wisconsin, 890). A large part of Alabama has yet a strikingly frontier character. Even from the State-house, in the fine and promising town of Montgomery, the eye falls in every direction upon a dense forest, boundless as the sea, and producing in the mind the same solemn sensation. Towns which are frequently referred to as important points in the stages of your journey, you are surprised to find when you reach them, consist of not more than three or four cabins, a tavern or grocery, a blacksmith's shop, and a stable.

The greater number of planters own from ten to twenty slaves only, though plantations on which from fifty to a hundred are employed are not uncommon, especially on the rich alluvial soils of the southern part of the State. Many of the largest and most productive plantations are extremely unhealthy in summer, and their owners seldom reside upon them, except temporarily. Several of the larger towns, like Montgomery, remarkable in the midst of the wilderness which surrounds them, for the neatness and tasteful character of the houses and gardens which they contain, are, in a considerable degree, made up of the residences of gentlemen who own large plantations in the hotter and less healthful parts of the State. Many of these have been educated in the older States, and with minds enlarged and liberalized by travel, they form, with their families, cultivated and attractive society.

Much the larger proportion of the planters of the State live in log houses, some of them very neat and comfortable, but frequently rude in construction, not *chinked,* with windows unglazed, and wanting in many of the commonest conveniences possessed by the poorest class of Northern farmers and laborers of the older States. Many of those who live in this way, possess considerable numbers of slaves, and are every year buying more. Their early frontier life seems to have destroyed all capacity to enjoy many of the usual luxuries of civilized life.

Notwithstanding the youth of the State, there is a constant and extensive emigration from it, as well as immigration to it. Large planters, as their stock increases, are always anxious to enlarge the area of their land, and will often pay a high price for that of any poor neighbor, who, embarrassed by debt, can be tempted to move on. There is a rapid tendency in Alabama, as in the older Slave States, to the enlargement of plantations. The poorer class are steadily driven to occupy poor land, or move forward on to the frontier.

In an address before the Chunnenuggee Horticultural Society, by Hon. C. C. Clay, Jr., reported by the author in De Bow's *Review,* December, 1855, I find the following passage. I need not add a word to it to show how the political experiment of old Virginia, the Carolinas, and Georgia, is being repeated to the same cursed result in young Alabama. The author, it is fair to say, is devoted to the sustentation of Slavery, and would not, for the world, be suspected of favoring any scheme for arresting this havoc of wealth, further than by chemical science:

I can show you, with sorrow, in the older portions of Alabama, and in my native county of Madison, the sad memorials of the artless and exhausting culture of cotton. Our small planters, after taking the cream off their lands, unable to restore them by rest, manures, or otherwise, are going further west and south, in search of other virgin lands, which they may and will despoil and impoverish in like manner. Our wealthier planters, with greater means and no more skill, are buying out their poorer neighbors, extending their plantations and adding to their slave force. The wealthy few, who are able to live on smaller profits, and to give their blasted fields some rest, are thus pushing off the many, who are merely independent.

Of the twenty millions of dollars annually realized from the sales of the cotton crop of Alabama, nearly all not expended in supporting the producers is reinvested in land and negroes. Thus the white population has decreased, and the slave increased, almost *pari passu* in several counties of our State. In 1825, Madison cast about 3000 votes; now she cannot cast exceeding 2300. In traversing that county one will discover numerous farm-houses, once the abode of industrious and intelligent freemen, now occupied by slaves, or tenantless, deserted, and dilapidated; he will observe fields, once fertile, now unfenced, abandoned, and covered with those evil harbingers—fox-tail and broom-sedge; he will see the moss growing on the mouldering walls of once thrifty villages; and will find 'one only master grasps the whole domain' that once furnished happy homes for a dozen white families.

The selection above necessarily omits Olmsted's references to other Southern states which he visited. His stay in Louisiana, for example, proved a rich experience. His visit to Texas and his inland travels are described in *A Journey Through Texas* and *A Journey in the Back Country,* works which many readers may want to consult.

But Olmsted, like many travelers of his day, has been criticized for thinking of the Southern people as made up of either planters or else "poor whites," or "crackers." The author of the next selection questions how the Confederacy could have fought so costly a war for so long a period if these two classes were the only ones in the South. He found by research that in reality there was a third important group, the yeomanry, who were land-owning, self-respecting, substantial citizens and who gave the South its stability.

• 101 • The Southern Whites
A. N. J. DEN HOLLANDER

The conception of the ante-bellum South current especially among non-southerners presents us with a dual picture of the white society of that romantic region. On the one hand is the southern planter, an aristocratic "colonel" in a soft felt hat with a mint julep in his hand and a darkey hovering deferentially in the background. On the other hand is the "poor-white," a densely ignorant, morally degraded, lawless being, despised alike by planter and slave. He lives in a dilapidated log cabin and ekes out a wretched existence by the half-hearted cultivation of a few corn rows, by hunting squirrels in the pine woods, and by fishing for catfish around the cypress stumps of sluggish streams. There is something wrong with him, something inferior, possibly, in his blood. He eats clay; he goes barefoot and has the "ground itch"; his lips, beard, and chin are yellow with tobacco juice; and he often has a little "blind tiger" on hand to drink or to sell.

Indeed, some such planters and some such "poor-whites" were present in the ante-bellum South, but neither made up the bulk of the population. Any picture of the South in ante-bellum days must portray not the two classes of aristocratic slaveholders and shiftless "poor-whites," but a more complex civilization in which (1) the slaveholders themselves were made up of, first, a small group of wealthy planters owning slaves in large numbers—roughly the gentry—and second, a much larger middle class of smaller planters,

substantial farmers, professional men, and tradesmen; and in which (2) the classes below the slaveholding level were not simply "poor-white," but were first, and in greater numbers, yeomen farmers, artisans, and mechanics, and second, and in much smaller numbers, the true "poor-whites"; indigent, shiftless, and generally inferior.

The number of planters in the ante-bellum South was really small. If a holding of twenty slaves of all ages entitled one to be called a planter, the members of the planter class comprised little more than three per cent of the white population of the slave states, one and one-third per cent in the border states, and four and three-fifths per cent in the cotton states. In 1860 only 2,291 planters held a hundred or more slaves each. More than seventy-three per cent of the slaveholders held fewer than ten slaves. Few farms contained more than five hundred acres. In the whole South such farms comprised not quite three per cent of all the farms containing more than three acres of improved land; not quite two per cent in the border states and not quite three and a half per cent in the cotton states. On the other hand, non-slaveholders constituted more than three-fourths of the southern white population: four-fifths in the border states and more than two-thirds in the cotton states.

[Several] historians of southern antecedents have repeatedly stressed the fact that

[Adapted from "The Tradition of 'Poor Whites,'" in *Culture in the South,* edited by W. T. Couch, University of North Carolina Press, Chapel Hill, 1934. Pp. 403-406, 409-417, 422. Used by permission.]

the old South was not so aristocratic as it is often supposed to have been, that social divisions were not sharp, and that the majority of the people were essentially not unlike those in other parts of the Union and certainly were not hopelessly inferior. Yet little has been done to give an accurate account of the humbler folk, to analyze and evaluate the conditions which surrounded them and influenced their lives. The obstacles to giving such an account cannot be gainsaid. These people were poorly educated, if literate at all, and lived isolated, simple lives; the records they left are few and of small historical value. To the upper classes they were not nearly so important as the slaves, about whom much can be learned from the writings of their masters, who considered their less fortunate neighbors, with the exception only of the overseers, of too little consequence for more than brief mention. Economically, socially, and politically the lower classes were of less importance in the life of the section than in the northern states. To a larger extent than is desirable, therefore, casual remarks and observations of travellers have to be utilized in reconstructing this particular phase of the old South. These sources neither exist in abundance nor can they be used without great caution.

Generally, of those who lived on the farms and did not own slaves—or owned only a few —three types may be discerned.

(1). In the Appalachian mountains, excepting the broader valleys where more prosperous people dwelled, lived the mountaineers, descendants of pioneers who did not complete their westward march. The pioneers had settled in the valleys; their kind and others who came later occupied the areas more difficult of access, spread into the higher valleys, and the narrow coves, there to live in great isolation in the "land of do-without"—a term indicative of destitution indeed. There is no reason to believe that these people were in any sense of low quality or in any way originally different from those who crossed the mountains and settled the Mississippi basin. The mountain *milieu* was principally responsible for the peculiar mode of life which prevailed in the highlands and still prevails with little change in the less accessible parts of the region.

(2). Outside the mountains yeomen farmers made up the majority of the rural white population. Some owned a few slaves and worked alongside them in the fields. Others obtained help from a single Negro. But most of them earned their living exclusively by the toil of their own hands and those of the members of the family. These farmers, though most numerous outside the staple-producing areas, could be found almost anywhere; they were not absent from the black belts. In the upper piedmont, in eastern Tennessee and Mississippi, and along the western and northern borders of the slave states, they were by far the dominant type. In the pine barrens thrifty and sturdy farmers numbered many thousands. They did not make up, of course, a perfectly homogeneous group. Differences in the fertility of the soil, ease of transportation, length of settlement, personal qualities, luck, health, and wealth were reflected in their modes of living. To many a "good liver" the farm gave a comfortable existence and a few luxuries, but at the other end of the scale were a larger number of country dwellers whose well-being was at a lower level than can be called plain. Generally the yeoman farmer and his sons had to work from sun-up to sun-down at a great variety of tasks, and the toils of his wife and daughters are reflected in the homely adage that "woman's work is never done." These people had little to do with money, produced most of what they consumed, usually owned land, stock, and implements, had as a class no debts, were little influenced by fluctuation in staple prices and were socially as well as economically independent. In general they lived on a level that was foreign to luxury and destitution alike. As a group they must be called poor, because their per capita property represented little value, but according to standards existing in the region they were not very badly off. The comparable classes in the free states, however, lived undoubtedly on a superior level.

Crudeness of speech and manners was certainly no indication of meanness of mind any more than it was always an indication of real poverty or even lack of local prestige. The farmers were uneducated; many could not read, more could not write; they took a man's drink whenever there was fit occasion, which was often; they settled their arguments by physical means if they deemed it necessary; they did not work as hard or plan as consistently as their northern colleagues; they were somewhat careless in varying degrees; all were rustic and informal, many were uncouth; urban genteels devised nicknames for them; but as a class they were honest, proud, and independent, had confidence in life, had desires and usually ambition, and in a measure were substantial. In their own eyes and those of others in the South they were respectable citizens. It cannot be assumed that the differences between these farmers and those in the North indicate the lack of any essential qualities by the former. Their physical and moral stamina were such as to stand a severe test in the Civil War. Nor were the attainments of the planters other than those which can be brought about by the inheritance or fortunate winning of property and the consequent advantages of education, refinement, the ownership of property, and the exercise of leadership. Their blood was the same as that of the farmers out of whose ranks all but few had emerged not so long ago.

The complex causes of the general condition of the yeomanry cannot be given more than brief consideration here. The same influences which have held the whole South on a low level of economic development were also hostile to the prosperity of the non-slaveholding whites. The small farmers did not give as much attention as the planters to the production of staple crops for export. But the ideal toward which they strove was that of the planter. There was no other opportunity for profitable investment of capital, and, consequently with the exhaustion of fertility in the east, profits were re-invested in slaves and owners migrated westward in search of more fertile lands. To a certain extent, the presence of the Negro slave undoubtedly had placed a stigma on labor. A self-respecting owner might work in the fields beside his slave, or he might work with a hired slave; but generally, the white man drew the line at hiring himself out to work either in field or factory alongside the Negro. Thus, pre-occupation with the staple crop system, the existence of large areas of fertile lands waiting to be exploited, and the slave system, all combined prevented the development of an integrated agricultural and industrial economy. When capital migrated westward to new and fertile soils, the older regions were left with exhausted soils and without resources for immediate development. These abandoned regions then became stagnant and retained traits of the frontier which have persisted even to the present day.

The plantations developed in the regions suited for them, where soil and topography were favorable, but more especially where transportation was easy. They were in touch with the outside world. Some of the small farmers who, among others, had opened up such districts developed into planters; some of them sold out to engrossing neighbors and left, trekking westward or moving to regions like the upper piedmont, there to join those living already in a region where pressure was not brought to bear upon small holders; others, again, might drift to sterile stretches or to the pine barrens, there to sink to the "poor-white" level; and others, refusing to sell, remained as small farmers. At the end of the ante-bellum period this segregation of groups was fairly well completed. White labor played a minor role in the production of the staples; of the cotton crop it produced not more than fifteen per cent.

Although a number of farmers were in a position to raise crops for the market, as a whole they farmed to feed and clothe themselves with their own produce. When one considers the circumstances under which they found themselves, their small comfort has little that is mysterious. Living on isolated farmsteads, with means of communication rudimentary, public schools scarce and inadequate, in a purely rural environment far from markets, without a surplus to sell, working with a crude technique often on soils which were either not very productive or rapidly eroding and soon exhausted, with little opportunity to rise in the social scale, they necessarily resembled more a poor frontier people than a class of thriving New England farmers. In considering their social position it has to be remembered that the chances for the yeoman and his children in an exclusively rural commonwealth, where large scale agricultural operations prevail, have never and nowhere been very good. For the rest, in making comparisons between the social mobility of the North and the South, sight should not be lost of the fact that in an almost completely rural civilization social capillarity always tends to be less than in an urbanized commercialized area where important steps toward industrialization have already been made. In contemplating the ante-bellum South one must resist the temptation to place slavery persistently in the center and see it as the direct cause of everything. Although Negro slavery and the plantation system were so intimately tied up with each other that it is of little practical value to make an ideological distinction as to the prime importance of either one of them, it may yet clarify thought to remember that the former was only incidental to the latter. It is not improbable that the general condition of the small farmers would have been materially the same had other sources of controllable labor been available for the large scale production of staples. Negro slavery, however, had some concomitants which made it militate still more against people of small means. Chief of these must have been the constant draining away of capital from developing regions by the continual capitalization of labor. Slavery was a clog in the progress of every district where it had established itself and limited in different ways the opportunities for the whites of little or no capital.

(3). The poorest of these farmers gradually merged into the bottom rank of southern rural white people, the listless and squalid dwellers to be found in many widely scattered localities, but chiefly in the sandy ridges of the plantation districts, the pine barrens of the coastal plains, of Florida, and of central and eastern Mississippi, and the sand hills along the fall line. Variously denominated as "sand hillers," "clay eaters," "crackers," and so on, they lived in shiftless poverty on what the half-hearted cultivation of a few acres, hunting and fishing could offer in the way of subsistence, while occasional stealthy bartering with slaves and stealing of cattle and hogs made them a nuisance to planters. Not all of them were squatters or tenants, but the possession of some barren tract made small difference. Travellers described their sickly and slovenly appearance, habitual drinking, tobacco chewing, utter ignorance, strange dialect, inert behavior, and such strange proclivities as clay-sucking, resin-chewing, and snuff-dipping—though the latter custom was not limited to the women of this class.

We have seen that in the ante-bellum South the non-slaveholders were not all of the "poor-white" class. The term "poor-white" has been, however, and still is, responsible for much poorly directed thinking about the South. The limits of the class of people to whom the ante-bellum South applied the term are not clearly laid down. In discriminating southern speech, it was not used to include all white persons who were poor. It was a term of contempt for the indolent hunter-fisher-farmers just described, certain other small farmers, the rude and ignorant cattle rangers of the piney woods, a small number of factory hands, teamsters, and boatmen, and a group of improvident, inefficient and unstable white laborers and poor loafers, but not for all white workmen, artisans, handicraftsmen, and mechanics of small means who, of less importance than in the North, were not absent. The "poor-whites" were those who were both poor and conspicuously lacking in the common social virtues and especially fell short of the standard in certain economic qualities. Laziness, carelessness, unreliability, lack of foresight and ambition, habitual failure and general incompetency characterized them. The term, though used in the South, was not by far so commonly used and certainly not so sweepingly applied as one might suppose on reading comments of northern or European origin.

Various circumstances favored the idea by

outsiders that the non-slaveholding whites of the South stood out in pronounced contrast with the slaveholders. The southern planters formed an aristocratic element in democratic America; their country was accordingly conceived of as a strictly aristocratic, if not feudal, commonwealth. This suggested the three elements of noble planters, servile slaves, and socially dependent "poor-whites."

The itinerary most commonly followed by travellers brought them in contact with the lower piney woods people and "poor-whites" to be found in the neighborhood of plantations. On the other hand, regions like the upper piedmont, eastern Tennessee and eastern Mississippi, where a vigorous yeomanry lived, lay outside the tourist route. Besides the generally crude and poor aspect of the farmsteads, the tumbledown fences, ramshackle outhouses, razorback hogs rooting under the porches, and the coarse "hoecake" or "hog and hominy" of the common people impressed northerners as unfavorably as their ignorance, rough-and-ready easy-going manners, and willingness to be satisfied with little. Frederick Law Olmsted wrote elaborately on this point [see Selection 29]. Visitors from across the Atlantic mostly came South after having glanced over New England and the middle states, and did not fail to notice the existing discrepancies which, indeed, were not flattering to the South. James Sterling, an English tourist, making remarks on the differences between the houses of rich planters and poor

farmers, wrote in 1857: "There is not the same appearance of equally disseminated comfort. There are handsome dwellings here and there, and there are poor, mean-looking homesteads; but one misses the neat farm houses that dot the landscape of New England, and speak of comfort, equality, and intelligence."

The expression "poor-white" has remained part of the stock vocabulary especially of those of non-southern extraction writing on the southern states. This term was originally used particularly by southerners themselves to denote a relatively small class of shiftless human beings, "poor," it is true, and designated "white" to differentiate them from the Negroes whose living standards were not very dissimilar from theirs. The term was early used in its derogatory—and therefore misapplied—sense, of all non-slaveholding white people in the South, by travellers to the South and by propagandists who sought to show the terrible influence of Negro slavery. As the years have passed those so denoted have become a class of much larger size, with more definite limits and special characteristics, and the expression itself has attained greater significance in northern and European nations than it ever possessed in the South. As such it has unfortunately come to embody for many non-southerners an entirely wrong conception of the plain people of the South before the Civil War as well as in later years.

So much, then, for the kinds of white people in the South. What about the Negroes? Not all of them were slaves, nor did all slaves live on large plantations. As a matter of fact, only 46,274 persons owned twenty or more slaves; of these, less than 2,300 persons owned as many as one hundred slaves, according to the census of 1860. Although Selection 100 from Olmsted has already presented some accounts of the smaller plantation, it is of interest to note a vivid picture from *Huckleberry Finn*, in which Mark Twain draws upon his memory of ante-bellum days and describes a small farm belonging to a slaveholding family living near the Mississippi River. We see it as described in the words of Huck himself:

> Phelps's was one of these little one-horse cotton plantations, and they all look alike. A rail fence round a two-acre yard; a stile made out of logs sawed off and up-ended in steps, like barrels of a different length, to climb over the fence

with, and for the women to stand on when they are going to jump onto a horse; some sickly grass-patches in the big yard, but mostly it was bare and smooth, like an old hat with the nap rubbed off; big double log house for the white folks— hewed logs, with the chinks stopped up with mud or mortar, and these mud-stripes been whitewashed some time or another; round-log kitchen, with a big broad, open but roofed passage joining it to the house; log smokehouse back of the kitchen; three little log nigger cabins in a row t'other side the smokehouse; one little hut all by itself away down against the back fence, and some outbuildings down a piece the other side; ash-hopper and big kettle to bile soap in by the little hut; bench by the kitchen door, with bucket of water and a gourd; hound asleep there in the sun; more hounds asleep round about; about three shade trees away off in a corner; some currant bushes and gooseberry bushes in one place by the fence; outside of the fence a garden and a watermelon patch; then the cotton-fields begins, and after the fields the woods.

But for those Negroes who lived on the larger plantations there was a general pattern of life which U. B. Phillips has described in his classic book *Life and Labor in the Old South*. Some contemporary historians think that Phillips' Georgian heritage made him view plantation life too favorably, but the value of his work lies in the minute descriptions of specific plantations, although many of his generalizations are of interest also.

· 102 · Life in Thraldom
ULRICH B. PHILLIPS

The simplicity of the social structure on the plantations facilitated Negro adjustment, the master taking the place of the accustomed chief. And yet these black voyagers experienced a greater change by far than befell white immigrants. In their home lands they had lived naked, observed fetish, been bound by tribal law, and practiced primitive crafts. In America none of these things were of service or sanction. The Africans were thralls, wanted only for their brawn, required to take things as they found them and to do as they were told, coerced into self-obliterating humility, and encouraged to respond only to the teachings and preachings of their masters, and adapt themselves to the white men's ways.

To make adaptation the more certain, it was argued that "no Negro should be bought old; such are always sullen and unteachable, and frequently put an end to their lives." And indeed planters who could afford an unproductive period were advised to select young children from the ships, "for their juvenile minds entertain no regrets for the loss of their connections. They acquire the English language with great ease, and improve daily in size, understanding and capacity for labour." The proportion of children in the cargoes was great enough to permit such a policy by those who might adopt it. But the fact that prices for imported Negroes, even after seasoning, ranged lower than for those to the American manner born is an evidence that the new habituation as a rule never completely superseded the old. Thanks, however, to plantation discipline and to the

[Adapted from *Life and Labor in the Old South*, Little, Brown, Boston, 1929. Pp. 194-217. Used by permission.]

necessity of learning the master's language if merely to converse with fellow slaves of different linguistic stocks, African mental furnishings faded even among adult arrivals.

To the second and later generations folklore was transmitted, but for the sake of comprehension by the children an American Brer Rabbit replaced his jungle prototype. If lullabies were crooned in African phrase their memory soon lapsed, along with nearly all other African terms except a few personal names, Quash, Cuffee, Cudjoe and the like. Eventually it could be said that the Negroes had no memories of Africa as a home.

The plantation force was a conscript army, living in barracks and on constant "fatigue." Husbands and wives were comrades in service under an authority as complete as the commanding personnel could wish. The master was captain and quartermaster combined, issuing orders and distributing rations. The overseer and the foreman, where there were such, were lieutenant and sergeant to see that orders were executed. The field hands were privates with no choice but to obey unless, like other seasoned soldiers, they could dodge the duties assigned.

But the plantation was also a homestead, isolated, permanent and peopled by a social group with a common interest in maintaining social order. In so far as harmony was attained—and in this the plantation mistress was a great if quiet factor—a common tradition was evolved embodying reciprocal patterns of conventional conduct.

The plantation was of course a factory, in which robust laborers were essential to profits. Its mere maintenance as a going concern required the proprietor to sustain the strength and safeguard the health of his operatives and of their children, who were also his, destined in time to take their parents' places. The basic food allowance came to be somewhat standardized at a quart of corn meal and half a pound of salt pork per day for each adult and proportionably for children, commuted or supplemented with sweet potatoes, field peas, sirup, rice, fruit and "garden sass" as locality and season might suggest. The clothing was coarse, and shoes were furnished only for winter. The housing was in huts of one or

two rooms per family, commonly crude but weather-tight. Fuel was abundant. The sanitation of the clustered cabins was usually a matter of systematic attention; and medical service was at least commensurate with the groping science of the time and the sparse population of the country. Many of the larger plantations had central kitchens, day nurseries, infirmaries and physicians on contract for periodic visits. The aged and infirm must be cared for along with the young and able-bodied, to maintain the good will of their kinsmen among the workers, if for no other reason. Morale was no less needed than muscle if performance were to be kept above a barely tolerable minimum.

The plantation was a school. An intelligent master would consult his own interest by affording every talented slave special instruction and by inculcating into the commoner sort as much routine efficiency, regularity and responsibility as they would accept. Not only were many youths given training in the crafts, and many taught to read and write, even though the laws forbade it, but a goodly number of planters devised and applied plans to give their whole corps spontaneous incentive to relieve the need of detailed supervision.

The civilizing of the Negroes was not merely a consequence of definite schooling but a fruit of plantation life itself. The white household taught perhaps less by precept than by example. It had much the effect of a "social settlement" in a modern city slum, furnishing models of speech and conduct, along with advice on occasion, which the vicinage is invited to accept. [However, most] planters did not even attempt an emulation, for not one in a hundred could hope by his own genius and magnetism to break the grip of normal slave-plantation circumstance. The bulk of the black personnel was notoriously primitive, uncouth, improvident and inconstant, merely because they were Negroes of the time; and by their slave status they were relieved from the pressure of want and debarred from any full-force incentive of gain.

Many planters, however, sought to promote contentment, loyalty and zeal by gifts and rewards, and by sanctioning the keeping of poultry and pigs and the cultivation of little fields in off times with the privilege of selling any produce. In the cotton belt the growing of nankeen cotton was particularly encouraged, for its brownish color would betray any surreptitious addition from the master's own fields. Some indeed had definite bonus systems.

But any copious resort to profit-sharing schemes was avoided at large as being likely to cost more than it would yield in increment to the planter's own crop. The generality of planters, it would seem, considered it hopeless to make their field hands into thorough workmen or full-fledged men, and contented themselves with very moderate achievement. Tiring of endless correction and unfruitful exhortation, they relied somewhat supinely upon authority with a tone of kindly patronage and a baffled acquiescence in slack service.

The plantation was a parish, or perhaps a chapel of ease. Some planters assumed the functions of lay readers when ordained ministers were not available, or joined the congregation even when Negro preachers preached. Bishop Leonidas Polk was chief chaplain on his own estate, and is said to have suffered none of his slaves to be other than Episcopalian; but the generality of masters gave full freedom as to church connection.

[As to topics, a] black preacher might meet rebuke and even run a risk of being lynched if he harped too loudly upon the liberation of the Hebrews from Egyptian bondage; but a moderate supervision would prevent such indiscretions. The Sermon on the Mount would be harmless despite its suggestion of an earthly inheritance for the meek; the Decalogue was utterly sound; and "servants obey your masters," "render unto Caesar the things that are Caesar's," and "well done, thou good and faithful servant" were invaluable texts for homilies. The Methodists and Baptists were inclined to invite ecstasy from free and slave alike. Episcopalians and Presbyterians, and the Catholics likewise, deprecating exuberance, dealt rather in quiet precept than in fervid exhortation—with far smaller statistical results.

The plantation was a pageant and a variety show in alternation. The procession of plowmen at evening, slouched crosswise on their mules; the dance in the new sugarhouse, preceded by prayer; the bonfire in the quarter with contests in clogs, cakewalks and Charlestons whose fascinations were as yet undiscovered by the great world; the work songs in solo and refrain, with not too fast a rhythm; the baptizing in the creek, with lively demonstrations from the "sisters" as they came dripping out; the torchlight pursuit of 'possum and 'coon, with full-voiced halloo to baying houn' dawg and yelping cur; the rabbit hunt, the log-rolling, the house-raising, the husking bee, the quilting party, the wedding, the cock fight, the crap game, the children's play, all punctuated plantation life—and most of them were highly vocal. A funeral now and then of some prominent slave would bring festive sorrowing, or the death of a beloved master an outburst of emotion.

The plantation was a matrimonial bureau, something of a harem perhaps, a copious nursery, and a divorce court. John Brickell wrote of colonial North Carolina: "It frequently happens, when these women have no Children by the first Husband, after being a year or two cohabiting together, the Planters oblige them to take a second, third, fourth, fifth, or more Husbands or Bedfellows; a fruitful Woman amongst them being very much valued by the Planters, and a numerous Issue esteemed the greatest Riches in this Country." By running on to five or more husbands for a constantly barren woman Brickell discredits his own statement. Yet it may have had a kernel of truth, and it is quite possible that something of such a policy persisted throughout the generations. These things do not readily get into the records. I have myself heard a stalwart Negro express a humorous regret that he was free, for said he in substance: "If I had lived in slavery times my master would have given me half a dozen wives and taken care of all the children." This may perhaps voice a tradition among slave descendants, and the tradition may in turn derive from an actual sanction of polygamy by some of the masters. A planter doubtless described a practice not unique when he said "that he interfered as little as possible with their domestic habits except in matters of police. 'We don't care what they do when their tasks are over—we lose sight of them till next day. Their morals and manners are in their own keeping. The men may have, for instance, as many wives as they please, so long as they do not quarrel about such matters.' " But another was surely no less representative when he instructed his overseer: "Marriages shall be performed in every instance of a nuptial contract, and the parties settled off to themselves without encumbering other houses to give discontent. No slave shall be allowed to cohabit with two or more wives or husbands at the same time; doing so shall subject them to a strict trial and severe punishment."

Life was without doubt monogamous in general; and some of the matings were by order, though the generality were pretty surely spontaneous. This item, written by an overseer to his employer, is typical of many: "Esaw and Biner has asked permission to Marry. I think it a good Match. What say you to it?" Here and there a man had what was called in slave circles a "broad wife," a wife belonging to another master and dwelling at a distance. Planters of course preferred their slaves to be mated at home.

In the number of their children the Negro woman rivaled the remarkable fecundity of their mistresses. One phenomenal slave mother bore forty-one children, mostly of course as twins; and the records of many others ran well above a dozen each. As a rule, perhaps, babies were even more welcome to slave women than to free; for childbearing brought lightened work during pregnancy and suckling, and a lack of ambition conspired with a freedom from economic anxiety to clear the path of maternal impulse.

Concubinage of Negro women to planters and their sons and overseers is evidenced by the census enumeration of mulattoes and by other data. It was flagrantly prevalent in the Creole section of Louisiana, and was at least sporadic from New England to Texas. The regime of slavery facilitated concubinage not merely by making black women subject to white men's wills but by promoting intimacy and weakening racial antipathy. The children, of whatever shade or paternity, were alike the property of the mother's owner and were nourished on the plantation. Not a few mulattoes, however, were manumitted by their fathers and vested with property.

Slave marriages, not being legal contracts, might be dissolved without recourse to public tribunals. Only the master's consent was required, and this was doubtless not hard to get.

The home of a planter or of a well-to-do townsman was likely to be a "magnificent negro boarding-house," at which and from which an indefinite number of servants and their dependents and friends were fed. In town the tribe might increase to the point of embarrassment. The domestics were likely to consider themselves entitled to luxurious fare. The wife of a Congressman when visiting her home after two years' absence wrote: "I have been mobbed by my own house servants. . . . They agreed to come in a body and beg me to stay at home to keep my own house once more. . . . I asked my cook if she lacked anything on the plantation at the Hermitage. 'Lack anything?' she said, 'I lack everything, what are corn meal, bacon, milk and molasses? Would that be all you wanted? Ain't I been living and eating exactly as you all these years? When I cook for you, didn't I have some of all? Dere now!' Then she doubled herself up laughing. They all shouted, 'Missis, we is crazy for you to stay home.' "

Each plantation had a hierarchy. Not only were the master and his family exalted to a degree beyond the reach of slave aspiration, but among the Negroes themselves there were pronounced gradations of rank, privilege and esteem. [In particular,] the foreman, the miller and the smith were men of position and pride. The butler, the maid and the children's nurse were in continuous contact with the white household, enjoying the best opportunity to acquire its manners along with its discarded clothing. The field hands were at the foot of the scale, with a minimum of white contact and privileged only to plod, so to say, as brethren to the ox.

At all times in the South as a whole perhaps half of the slaves were owned or hired in units of twenty or less, which were too small for the full plantation order, and perhaps half of this half were on mere farms or in town employment, rather as "help" than as a distinct laboring force. Many small planters' sons and virtually all the farmers in person worked alongside any field hands they might possess; and indoor tasks were parceled among the women and girls, white and black. As to severity of treatment, the travelers were likely to disagree.

However the case may have been as to relative severity on farms and plantations, there can be no doubt that the farmers' slaves of all sorts were likely to share somewhat intimately such lives as their masters led and to appropriate a considerable part of such culture as they possessed—to be more or less genteel with their gentility or crude with their crudity, to think similar thoughts and speak much the same language. On the other hand, the one instance of wide divergence in dialect between the whites and the Negroes prevailed in the single district in which the scheme of life was that of large plantations from the time when Africans were copiously imported. On the seaboard of South Carolina and Georgia most of the blacks (and they are very black) still speak Gullah, a dialect so distinct that unfamiliar visitors may barely understand it. And dialect, there as elsewhere, is an index to culture in general.

The life of slaves, whether in large groups or small, was not without grievous episodes. A planter's son wrote to his father upon a discovery of mislaid equipment: "The bridle and martingal which you whipped Amy so much for stealing was by some inattention of Robert's left in Mr. Clark's stable." Again, an overseer, exasperated by the sluggishness of his cook, set her to field work as discipline, only to have her demonstrate by dying that her protestations of illness had been true.

Grievances reinforced ennui to promote slacking, absence without leave, desertion and mutiny. The advertising columns of the newspapers bristled with notices of runaways; and no detailed plantation record which has come to my hand is without mention of them. As an extreme example, here is a summer's account by an overseer, or so much of it as can be deciphered: "August the 20 1844 Randle caught at Mr. Cathram brung home . . . [he had] left on the 12th July 1844 Lem runway on the 25 of July caught on the 2 of August by 1 of Mr Kings negroes Oscar runway on the 27 of August . . . George attempt to git away I coat him and put a ringe and chane on him under the neck Lem runway on the 21 of August September the 3 Beny Bill Elijah Ellie all gawne together and Carline runway on the 3 stayed out 2 days . . . Joe runway on the 11th September."

For steady success, [long] experience taught that the master's authority "should be exercised in a firm but mild manner. He should even to a Negro unite in his deportment the *suaviter in modo* with the *fortiter in re*." This planter continued: "I never saw any degree of courtesy shown to a Negro (that is kept under good subjection) but was returned with usury. Cuffee is hard to outdo in politeness." Another planter accepted the challenge of this task yet more gallantly when urging the value of kindliness and praise: "Give me a high spirited and even a high tempered negro, full of pride, for easy and comfortable management. Your slow sulky negro, although he may have an even temper, is the devil to manage." But as to the female of the species: "The negro women are all harder to manage than the men." A third was almost driven from the planter's career, as he said, "by the great aversion which I have to the manner of cultivating our lands in Virginia by slaves. I feel myself utterly incompetent to the task of managing them properly. I never attempt to punish or to have one punished but I am sensible that I am violating the natural rights of a being who is as much entitled to the enjoyment of liberty as myself." A fourth, less troubled by scruples, was baffled by his problems: "The proper management and discipline of negroes subjects the man of care and feeling to more dilemmas perhaps than any other vocation he could follow. To keep a diary of their conduct, it would be a record nothing short of a series of violations of the laws of God and man. To moralize and induce the slave to assimilate with the master and his interest has been and is the great desideratum aimed at; but I am sorry to say I have long since desponded in the completion of the task." A fifth maintained a strong note of optimism: "The character of the negro is much underrated. It is like the plastic clay which may be moulded into agreeable or disagreeable figures according to the skill of the moulder. The man who storms at and curses his negroes and who tells them they are a parcel of infernal rascals, not to be trusted, will surely make them just what he calls them; and so far from loving such a master, they will hate him. Now if you be not suspicious, and induce them to think by slight trusts that they are not unworthy of some confidence, you will make them honest, useful and affectionate creatures." A sixth, eschewing exalted thought and ignoring profundities, contented himself with being a cheery fellow and relied upon a single prod with a double prong.

By one means or another good will and affection were often evoked. [On certain estates, however,] the whip was as regularly in evidence as the spur on a horseman's heel. That cruelties occurred is never to be denied. Mrs. Stowe exploited them in *Uncle Tom's Cabin* and validated her implications to her own satisfaction in its *Key*. Theodore D. Weld had already assembled a thousand more or less authentic instances of whippings and fetters, of croppings and brandings, of bloodhound pursuits and the break-up of families. Manuscript discoveries continue to swell the record. Here for example is a letter which lies before me in the slave's own writing:

Charlottesville, Oct. 8th, 1852

Dear Husband I write you a letter to let you know my distress my master has sold albert to a trader on Monday court day and myself and other child is for sale also and I want you to let [me] hear from you very soon before next cort if you can I don't know when I don't want you to wait till Christmas I want you to tell dr Hamelton and your master if either will buy me they can attend to it know and then I can go afterwards. I don't want a trader to get me they asked me if I had got any person to buy me and I told them no they took me to the court house too they never put me up a

man buy the name of brady bought albert and is gone I don't know where they say he lives in Scottesville my things is in several places some is in staunton and if I should be sold I don't know what will become of them I don't expect to meet with the luck to get that way till I am quite heartsick nothing more I am and ever will be your kind wife Maria Perkins.

To Richard Perkins

We cannot brush away this woman's tears. But it is fair to show the smile of another when writing in mellow retrospect to her ex-master, years after their severance by emancipation:

Huntington, W. Virginia
Sunday, June 12, 1881.

My old boss i heard that you was still alive and i now take the opportunity to address you a fiew lines i am well and doing well and i hope you are the same i am your servant whom you raised from a child up Catherine Miller who married Henry Miller. i expect you have forgot me but i have not forgot you. i was glad to hear that you was still alive. i have wrote home several times to hear how all the old folks was but i never could find out so i thought i would write you and see if you could tell me. i wish you would send me mine and Mary Janes ages exactly. Mary jane has growed to be such a big girl i don't expect you know her. i would like to see and here you pray once more before I die. i must now come to a close answer right away and tell me every thing that you think will give me any satisfaction about home sweet home. i hope that you will always remember me in your prayers. please excuse short letter and bad writing.

Your old servant Catherine Miller.

Most of the travelers who sought evidence of asperity in the plantation realm found it as a rule not before their eyes but beyond the horizon. [They] concur in their surprise at finding slavery unsevere, though some of them kept seeking evidence to the contrary without avail.

The surprise was justified, for tradition in the outer world ran squarely opposite. And the tradition was reasonable. Slavery had been erected as a crass exploitation, and the laws were as stringent as ever. No prophet in early times could have told that kindliness would grow as a flower from a soil so foul, that slaves would come to be cherished not only as property of high value but as loving if lowly friends. But this unexpected change occurred in so many cases as to make benignity somewhat a matter of course.

The esteem in epitaphs, whether inscribed in diaries or on stone, was without doubt earned by their subjects and genuinely felt by their composers. One reads:

JOHN:
A FAITHFUL SERVANT
AND TRUE FRIEND:
KINDLY, AND CONSIDERATE:
LOYAL, AND AFFECTIONATE:
THE FAMILY HE SERVED
HONOURS HIM IN DEATH:
BUT IN LIFE, THEY GAVE HIM LOVE:
FOR HE WAS ONE OF THEM

For he was one of them indeed, and his name was well-nigh legion. Ancestral halls were fewer far than ancestral servitors, for a planter's migration would vacate the house but carry the personnel.

On the other hand slaves in large numbers were detached from their masters, whether by sale, by lease to employers or by hire to themselves. The personal equation was often a factor in such transactions. Some slaves were sold as punishment, for effect upon the morale of their fellows. On the other hand some whose sales were impelled by financial stress were commissioned by their masters to find buyers of their own choice; some purchases were prompted by a belief that the new management would prove more congenial and fruitful than the old; and still more transfers were made to unite in ownership couples who desired union in marriage.

In the hiring of slaves likewise the personal equation often bulked large, for the owner's desire for a maximum wage was modified by his concern for assured maintenance of physique and morale, and the lessee on his part wanted assurance from the slave of willing service or of acquiescence at least. The hiring of slaves to the slaves themselves was a grant of industrial freedom at a wage. It was an admission that the slave concerned could produce more in self-direction than when under routine control, a virtual admission that for him slavery had no industrial justification. In many cases it was a probationary period, ended by self-purchase with earnings accumulated above the wages he had currently paid his owner.

Slave hiring and self-hire were more characteristic of town than of country. Indeed urban conditions merely tolerated slavery, never promoted it. And urban slaveholders were not complete masters, for slavery in full form required a segregation to make the master in effect a magistrate. A townsman's human chattels could not be his subjects, for he had no domain for them to inhabit. When a slave ran an errand upon the street he came under the eye of public rather than private authority; and if he were embroiled by chance in altercation with another slave the two masters were likely to find themselves champions of opposing causes in court, or partisans even against the constables, with no power in themselves either to make or apply the law.

Town slaves in a sense rubbed elbows with every one, high and low, competed with free labor, white and black, and took tone more or less from all and sundry. The social hierarchy was more elaborate than on the plantations, the scheme of life more complex, and the variety wider in attainment and attitude. The obsequious grandiloquence of a barber contrasted with the caustic fluency of a fishwife. But even the city chain gang was likely to be melodious, for its members were Negroes at one or two removes from the plantation. All in all, the slave regime was a curious blend of force and concession, of arbitrary disposal by the master and self-direction by the slave, of tyranny and benevolence, of antipathy and affection.

The economy of the Old South, as has been indicated in several of the preceding selections, was predominantly agricultural. To understand it one should know how production of cotton, rice, and sugar was carried out both on the larger plantations and the small farms. And what happened to the cotton, the rice, and the sugar when it had been grown and harvested? Since these crops could not be used at home by those who had grown them, they were sold for cash, and this cash was used in the purchase of necessities for the rural people, most of whom were not self-subsistent to the same degree as the Chinese peasant.

The *cotton factor* was the agent who handled the sale of these agricultural commodities and in turn bought for the planters what they needed, ordering many articles from Europe for those with sophisticated tastes.

The following selection, by Alfred H. Stone, although written many years ago, is still one of the best descriptions not only of what the cotton factor did but also of the role he played in the colonial period in helping Europeans start plantations in the New World. This selection and the one which follows on industry give a general outline of the economy of the Old South.

• 103 • *The Cotton Factor*
ALFRED H. STONE

The factor was the home agent of the colonial planter. He was at once his merchant and banker. He bought the goods which the planter had to purchase at home, and sold for him the products returned in exchange. He became an important link in the chain which brought Europe, Africa, and America into commercial association.

Like the plantation slavery system, the West Indian factorage system, with various modifications, was transferred to the Southern colonies of America. It seems to have been the very corner-stone of large-scale, staple, slave-labor agriculture. When the Revolution destroyed the business of English factors, their places were taken by enterprising men in the more important Southern commercial towns. Some of these had been exporting agents and correspondents of English houses. Others were attracted to the business by the promise of large returns, and because it was from the first recognized as an eminently respectable and honorable form of employment for capital and brains; and the social prejudice against trade did not obtain against it.

The importance of the Southern factorage system developed with the growth of the cotton industry. Indigo planting disappeared with the destruction of the English bounty system by the Revolution. Tobacco culture was confined to a more or less restricted area, and did not offer an inviting field for widespread and large-scale capitalistic enterprise. Rice, which took the place of indigo in South Carolina, became an important crop and had its own system of development, in which the factor played a considerable part. In Louisiana the sugar factor became as important a part in the commercial system, as it had been in that of the West Indies. But it was in cotton that the factorage system reached its greatest development, became most powerful, and flourished longest. Cotton was a crop ideally adapted to a capitalistic system of agriculture. It grew through a wide range of geographical

[Adapted from "The Cotton Factorage System of the Southern States," *American Historical Review,* Vol. 20, No. 3, New York, 1915. Pp. 557-565. Used by permission.]

area. Its non-perishable nature lent itself peculiarly to a system which required the concentration of its product at seaboard, at a time when transportation and warehouse facilities were poor, and rough handling, exposure, and long delays would have destroyed the value of any other agricultural commodity. It is therefore the cotton region which offers the student the largest promise of reward for investigation of the system and its effects and ramifications.

The functions of the Southern factor were the same as those of his English progenitor. But the Southern system had one feature not contained in the English. The business here developed relations between factor and client not possible with the West Indian oversea system. The relations between the cotton factor and planter were of the most intimate and confidential character, as close probably as was ever the case between business associates. The ties between them frequently were lifelong and their relations were of a social and personal as well as business nature. How far this close personal association affected plantation policy, it is not possible to say. But it is certain that the counsel and advice of the factor were frequently reflected in the planter's affairs. It was a relationship which often effected a close union of business interests and political, social and economic policies between a large and dominantly influential body throughout the cotton-producing South, and the men who were the leading and dominant figures in the business and financial life of Southern cities. It also raised to the nth power the definite and tangible value of the moral hazard in business. It is not too much to say that the great factorage houses of the South looked quite as much to the character of a customer as to the securities he had to offer. Millions of dollars have been advanced by Southern factors upon the mere personal word of the planter, with no formal security at all, and with only a memorandum to witness the amounts involved. A unique basis of agricultural credit was established, which must be taken into account in interpreting such documentary evidence as plantation and slave mortgages and other securities of record.

Another manifestation of the personal equation was in the opportunities offered by the factorage system to men of little or no capital, usually of the overseer class, to embark in business for themselves. An overseer identified with the successful management of a plantation estate was often as well known to his employer's factor by reputation as the planter himself was personally. Such a one, who possessed the necessary initiative, had little difficulty in establishing a factorage connection on his own account. Many of the largest and most successful planters of the South were men who got their start in this way.

We have seen that the factor furnished the planter with funds; that he acted as a commission merchant in the purchase of plantation supplies, and that he discharged the functions of an agent in selling the plantation product. What were the charges for these services, and what were the characteristic features of the system, which differentiated it from any other relation of principal and agent? And what were its general economic tendencies and effects? The interest rate varied with times, places, and conditions. It probably ranged between eight and twelve per cent. It was usually charged only as funds were actually drawn, though in some instances it was computed on the face of the loan, regardless of the average time of its actual use by the borrower. There was also in some cases a customary brokerage fee of from one half of one per cent to two and one half per cent added to the interest charge. To the price of the goods, wares, and merchandise purchased for the planter was added a commission which varied according to custom from two to ten per cent or more. The customary charge for selling the crop was a commission of two and one half per cent, but sometimes this was as high as four.

These were the only items of open profit to the factor in the transaction. But there were others which helped to make the business attractive, notwithstanding its hazards. In the early days cotton sales were effected through a broker who acted as a middleman between the factor and the resident agent of a foreign mill or merchant. To this broker was paid a commission of one half of one per cent, nominally borne by the mill agent. In practice and custom, however, one-half of this commission was paid by the factor and charged to the planter. This was supposed to be divided between the factor and the broker. The planter was taxed with various other charges, as freight, storage, insurance, drayage, weighing, sampling, mending, and repairing. These were returned on the account of sale to the planter at a uniform rate, fixed by custom or agreement, and were supposed to represent the actual amounts paid by the factor for the service rendered in behalf of the planter. As a matter of fact, custom early developed a system of rebates to the factor on practically all these charges. This seemed to be an inevitable incident of the control by the factor of large quantities of cotton to be warehoused, drayed, insured, compressed, and otherwise handled solely at his direction. Those who were engaged in such business at cotton ports naturally offered the factor the inducements of special rates and drawbacks in consideration of the heavy volume of business which he could divert to their hands.

The exaction of one of these exerted a particularly baneful influence upon the plantation system. This was the penalty commission feature of most advancing contracts between factors and planters, incident to the repayment of all loans in kind, rather than in money. The penalty commission was a [dangerously] simple expedient for stimulating the production of more bales of cotton. It was a proviso coupled to the agreement for paying the customary commission on sales, under which the planter bound himself to pay to the factor a certain sum per bale, sometimes ranging as high as four dollars, for each and every bale by which his actual production fell short of the stipulated number of bales which he agreed to ship. This was in addition to the agreement to plant so many acres in cotton calculated to produce so many bales.

In order to render absolute the factor's control of the entire crop, one of the cardinal features of the system was the requirement that every bale of cotton grown by the planter should be consigned to the factor. If the total crop were one thousand bales, and the first five hundred discharged the planter's debt, an exceedingly improbable supposition, the remaining five hundred bales must nevertheless go forward also. There were few, if any, agricultural lien laws in those days, but this requirement took their place. It also probably made their ultimate enactment less difficult, through common familiarity with the practical operation of their essential principle, which was a certain measure of control, by the financing agent, of the product grown through his assistance.

The broader economic effects of the factorage system would form in themselves alone an interesting and valuable field of inquiry. A primary incident was the concentration of Southern capital, and hence of its real wealth, in the few Southern cities which were its important factorage centres. I am satisfied of the inaccuracy of the commonly accepted idea of ante-bellum Southern wealth as something naturally and essentially rural, as might be expected in a country whose sole business in popular estimation was that of agriculture.

One effect of the system was the retarding of the normal tendency toward the founding and developing of smaller urban communities, common even in an agricultural section. The factorage centres were enormous supply depots, from which were distributed to the interior South, through the factor in bulk, instead of through a local merchant by ordinary processes of retail trade, all the common necessities, comforts, and conveniences of daily life. And it is a mistake to assume that I am here dealing with ancient history. The system outlived by many years the ante-bellum era, and within my memory, in the case of my own family, all the staple articles of domestic and plantation use were bought through my father's factor in New Orleans, and shipped four hundred miles by river, and then hauled by wagons twenty-odd miles further into the interior.

When interior urban development at last took place, it was naturally patterned after that of the seaboard factorage centres. Prosperous and influential factorage houses grew up at what became important interior river points. Here we had a repetition on a smaller scale of the accumulation of cotton and the concentration of capital and wealth which were the rule at seaboard. But this was a step in the direction of the diffusion, not of the break-up, of the system. These interior houses were in the nature of tributaries to the larger streams.

The beginning of the end of the seaboard system did not come until some years after the Civil War. The two most potent instrumentalities in its final dissolution were the railroads and the land-mortgage companies. The development of railroads made it possible for cotton to be shipped direct from the field of its production to that of its foreign or domestic consumption, which in turn made possible a real interior market. The advent of land-mortgage companies made possible a refunding process whereby the whole, or a large part, of a planter's obligations could be financed on a basis of the land alone. His current business could then be transferred on the security of a crop lien and personal property to smaller interior merchants and factors, whose capital, though limited as compared with the old institutions, had become large enough to meet the necessities of the business after the loan companies had assumed a large part of the burden. The country merchant had frequently become a factor through natural gradations, and he was at hand to take care of the smaller business at first, and gradually to extend the field of his operations. Largely from his ranks was developed the country banker, who was an indispensable feature in the slow process of modifying and finally revolutionizing the ancient system. The country factor did business along the same general lines as his city prototype. But where he has taken over the factor's business at all, and this he has largely done, the country banker has practically abandoned the last vestige of the old system. He lends on the same security as the factor, but the business is on the same basis as any other commercial transaction. The railroad and the country merchant and factor, the country compress and the country bank, have been followed by the country buyer, who furnishes the last link in the chain between raw cotton production and consumption. The elimination of the entrepreneur has by no means been accomplished, but the industry has been relieved of a large part of the load which it carried for the greater portion of the first century of its existence. Even in the remote interior a planter can today gin the cotton which yesterday was in the field, and tomorrow receive a check for it from a buyer who will consign it from the planter's platform to its destination at Fall River, Bremen, or Liverpool. Within the span of my personal experience, I have seen the time when a similar transaction would require from two to six months for its consummation, with the intervention of a dozen different agencies of transportation and trade.

One of the chief accents in the South today is industrialization. Not only are Southern communities actively seeking Northern factories but they are also facing up to the profound changes that industry brings to their time-honored way of life. Every Southern state has the equivalent of a planning board or a development commission which is vigorously pushing industrialization within that state. To see such activities in historical perspective we turn to a passage from Dr. Clement Eaton's excellent *A History of the Old South,* which will round out the discussion of the ante-bellum economy. He makes reference to the *factors,* who have been the topic of the previous selection; he also shows how the textile industry, which has had such a phenomenal growth in the South, got its start before the Civil War.

· 104 · The Progress of Southern Manufactures

CLEMENT EATON

Manufacturing in the Southern states did not originate in the post-war "New South," when Henry W. Grady and his fellow editors publicized the expansion of cotton mills. Rather, the South had made an important progress in industry prior to 1860, which was interrupted by the Civil War and resumed in the decade of the 1880's. Southern manufacturing had slowly emerged from the handicraft stage of colonial days. During the eighteenth century and to a lesser extent in the ante-bellum period household industries were carried on by slaves, who were employed on the large plantations to weave cloth, to make bricks, staves, and barrels, to manufacture nails, to boil soap, to do blacksmith work, and even to make artistic furniture. Also in the back country frontier women were engaged in a variety of household industries, particularly the weaving of linsey-woolsey cloth, while their husbands developed into jacks-of-all-trades, making rude furniture, shoes, and agricultural equipment. As late as 1810, according to incomplete census returns, the Southern states were ahead of the rest of the country in the manufacture of homespun cloth and especially in the spinning of flax. In the Piedmont region there were numerous spinning frames in operation, but these rudimentary factories were not equipped with Arkwright machinery, such as had been introduced into New England. The movement of industrialization below the Mason and Dixon line was stimulated to some degree by the War of 1812, but to a much greater extent by the depression of agricultural staples in the period of 1839-1850.

The development of cotton mills in the ante-bellum South was socially more significant than the rise of any other industry, for it pointed the way to utilizing the labor of the poor whites in factories. The Southern states enjoyed at least three advantages in the early development of mills. They had excellent water power along the fall line, they could procure cheap white labor, and they could obtain clean, freshly-picked cotton, undamaged by shipping and exposure. The early Southern mills were small establishments engaged in spinning yarn. South Carolina was prominent in pioneering in the development of cotton mills.

The most influential promoter of the textile industry of the ante-bellum South was William Gregg of Charleston, South Carolina. Trained as a watchmaker and silversmith, Gregg became a successful jeweler in Charleston, thus obtaining the capital which he later invested in the cotton mill industry. His interest in this industry had been attracted when as a boy he had been associated with his uncle in an unsuccessful venture in cotton manufacturing in Georgia. As early as 1836 he acquired an interest in the Vaucluse Cotton Mill. His revolutionary role in the development of Southern cotton mills, however, began in 1844 as a result of a tour of New England which he made to observe the operation of the textile industry in that region.

Gregg determined to build a model cotton factory to demonstrate the value of his ideas. In 1846 he constructed a remarkable cotton mill at Graniteville, South Carolina, not far from Augusta, Georgia. It was built of granite, "airy and commodious," the grounds landscaped and ornamented with shrubbery and flowers. To house the workers he erected eighty-five cottages in the Gothic style, also of granite, each cottage provided with a large garden. His mill people, he boasted, lived "under parental care," for they were not allowed to solace their arduous labor with alcohol, they were required by their leases to their cottages to send their children to school, and no children "of tender age," that is, under twelve years old, were worked in the factory. Thus Gregg started the first compulsory school system in the South.

[Adapted from *A History of the Old South*, Macmillan, New York, 1949. Pp. 423-442. Used by permission.]

Graniteville Factory was operated by water power. The superintendent and overseers were Northern men, but the labor force was composed of three hundred "piney woods" folk. The operatives were chiefly women and children over twelve years of age, for the older people who came from the hill districts and pine barrens did not have the flexibility to make good mill hands. The employees worked twelve hours a day, the men receiving four to five dollars a week, the women three to four dollars per week. The mill cottages rented from sixteen to twenty-five dollars a year. These wages were very low, but they compared favorably with wages paid to mill workers in Massachusetts and to agricultural wages in the South. It was an era when respectable, church-going factory owners exploited human labor without recognizing any injustice in making large profits and giving their employees a pitiful share of the returns of their labor.

Although there were failures, the well-managed textile mills in the South during the decade of the 1850's paid good dividends. The Graniteville Mill in its early years paid a 7 per cent dividend and later as much as 18 per cent. Gregg pointed out that the Southern mills had the advantages over their Northern rivals in securing labor 20 per cent cheaper, cotton at one and one-half cents a pound cheaper, and the superiority of bright, freshly picked cotton over shipped cotton. The Southern mills, almost without exception, manufactured the cheaper grades of cloth, osnaburgs, "nigger cloth," sheeting, and yarn. Moreover, their market remained largely below the Mason and Dixon line.

In North Carolina the Battle family had a pioneer mill at Rocky Mount, but the most important cotton mill leader during the ante-bellum period was Edwin Michael Holt. . . . He gathered the capital for his adventurous enterprise of a cotton mill in his native state from his profits as a farmer, small merchant, distiller, sawmill owner, and miller. In 1837 he erected his mill on Great Alamance Creek in the North Carolina Piedmont, procuring his machinery from the North. With his slaves he made brick for the buildings and cut the timber for his water wheel. His first few years were devoted to spinning yarn, which he transported by wagon to the nearest town, Hillsboro, and to the more distant market of Fayetteville. A considerable amount of his yarn was sold in Philadelphia, Pennsylvania.

In 1853 a French dyer came to Alamance County and was employed by Holt to teach his mill operatives the art of dyeing cloth. Thus the Holt Mill became the pioneer factory south of the Potomac River in introducing colored cotton cloth made by power looms—"the Alamance plaids." By 1861 the Holt Mill had increased from the original start of over five hundred spindles to twelve hundred spindles and ninety-six looms.

The growth of the cotton mill industry in the South was particularly rapid in the last decade of the ante-bellum period. Although the number of factories in 1860, one hundred fifty-nine in eleven Southern states, was exactly the same as reported by the census ten years before, and although there was an actual decrease of 137 in the number of hands reported, the value of the product of Southern mills had risen 43 per cent. On the eve of the Civil War these mills employed 9,906 hands, of whom approximately two-thirds were female, and the average annual wage was $145.41. The South at that time produced one-third of the national output of yarn. Nevertheless, the expansion of the textile industry in the ante-bellum South should not be exaggerated, for the value of cotton goods manufactured by New England in 1860 exceeded the value of the Southern output almost ten times, and the single town of Lowell, Massachusetts, had more spindles running than the whole South.

Another Southern industry was based on the habit of chewing plug tobacco which in the America of the nineteenth century was widespread among all classes. Cigarettes were not manufactured in the South until after the Civil War, while cigars were made principally in the North. But the habit of chewing tobacco was responsible for the growth of an industry which ranked third in importance among the manufactures of the Old South. Only flour and lumber exceeded in value the finished product of tobacco within the Southern states. The tobacco factories, concentrated in Virginia and North Carolina, were chiefly plug tobacco establishments, 98 per cent of them being devoted to this manufacture and only 2 per cent to pipe tobacco.

The manufacture of tobacco below the Mason and Dixon line began as a home industry. The tobacco "twists" thus made were peddled in a horse and wagon through the lower South. In the decades of the 1830's small factories were established in Richmond, Petersburg, Lynchburg, Danville, and in Caswell County, North Carolina. Unlike the cotton industry, the tobacco factories employed slaves as their principal labor force. The larger factories in 1860 employed between fifty and one hundred and fifty slaves, principally men, of whom about half were owned by the factories and the others were hired at rates of from $100 to $200 annually, plus food and maintenance.

The tobacco manufactured in these Southern towns was sold chiefly to factors in New York and Philadelphia. Although some of this chewing tobacco was peddled in the South by wagons, the Southern merchants as a rule ordered their tobacco through New York and Philadelphia, a roundabout method of purchase which enhanced the profits of Northern business men. After the California gold rush, large quantities of Virginia tobacco were sent to the Pacific coast. The Northern factor received a commission of 5 to 7½ per cent of the sale price, and he granted to his customers a credit of eight months. The Panic of 1857 caused the Virginia and Carolina tobacco manufacturers to combine to remedy their grievances against the Northern factors. In December of that year a Tobacco Manufacturers' Convention, consisting of one hundred delegates, met in Richmond and resolved that all factors should limit their credits upon the sale of tobacco to four months and that the commission should not exceed 6½ per cent.

The growth of the tobacco industry in the upper South was phenomenal. By June, 1860, Virginia and North Carolina factories were producing 61 per cent of all plug, smoking, and snuff tobacco manufactured in the United States. Instead of shipping their raw tobacco abroad, as in former times, these states processed two-thirds of the tobacco grown within their boundaries. There had been a steady evolution from small factories to larger units so that in 1860 eighty-five factories, or almost one-fourth in the Virginia-Carolina area, employed fifty or more hands. Richmond, with its fifty-two factories, was by far the largest tobacco manufacturing city in the United States. The eleven Southern states produced a total of $14,612,442 worth of manufactured tobacco and employed 11,321 male and 2,300 female hands.

Prior to the founding of Birmingham, Alabama, in 1871, the iron center of the New South, Richmond was the most important iron-manufacturing city below the Mason and Dixon line. Richmond had the advantage of being located near a coal basin that furnished abundant supplies of cheap bituminous coal. Raw material for the iron-manufacturing industry was obtained from the charcoal-burning furnaces of the Valley of Virginia, which produced a superior grade of iron of great tensile strength.

The greatest iron company of Richmond, and of the South, was the Tredegar Iron Works which was founded in 1837. The masterful personality behind the success of the Tredegar Works was Joseph Reid Anderson, a graduate of West Point Military Academy, who became sales agent of the company in 1841 and seven years later purchased the business for $125,000. The Tredegar Company secured contracts from the United States government to furnish cannon for the navy. By 1860 the company had sold thirteen hundred cannon to the Federal government. The company also manufactured shells, chain cable, rails and spikes for the expanding railroads, and steam machinery for the Louisiana sugar plantations. The market of this Richmond company was largely in the North, for Southerners were prejudiced against buying home-made iron products. The chief contribution of the company to Southern industrial development was the manufacture of over forty locomotives for Southern railroads. During the Civil War the Tredegar Works played a vital role in Confederate armament, one of the reasons for the stubborn defense of Richmond.

The iron industry of Virginia employed slave labor extensively. Half of the labor force of the Tredegar Company, for example, was slaves. Some of the slave hands were owned by the company, but most of them were hired at rates ranging from $100 a year in 1849 to $175 in 1860. These black laborers were taught the skills needed in the iron industry by trained white mechanics imported from the North. In 1847 this situation led to a strike by the white mechanics, who demanded that slaves should not be used in the skilled processes of puddling and rolling. Anderson replied that he would not relinquish his constitutional right to employ or discharge anyone at his pleasure and notified the strikers that they had discharged themselves. After this event he began more extensively to employ slaves, who made satisfactory employees.

In 1860 the milling of flour and cornmeal still ranked at the top of Southern manufactures. A familiar and picturesque sight on the roads of the upper South was a boy like the young Henry Clay riding to the grist mill with a sack of wheat or corn to be ground into flour or cornmeal for the subsistence of the family. In the lower South much of the flour consumed was brought from the Northwest down the Mississippi River. Thousands of small grist mills all over the South served local needs, but the tendency was to concentrate commercial milling in a few urban centers such as Richmond and Baltimore. At Richmond were located the largest grain mills in the world, a single mill having the capacity of producing a thousand barrels of flour a day. Baltimore was also a great flour-milling city. From these two centers vast quantities of flour were exported to the lower South and to Brazil.

The processing of the forest resources of the South was a highly dispersed industry. Numerous small sawmills were scattered throughout the land of Dixie, operated by water power or steam engines, producing over nineteen and a half million dollars of wealth per year. Yellow pine lumber, live oak timber for ships, cypress shingles, staves for barrels, were cut from the illimitable virgin forests. Frequently lumbering was a by-product of clearing the land for the purpose of agriculture. The lumber industry in the South employed approximately sixteen thousand persons, the largest labor force engaged in any Southern manufacturing enterprise. There were also over four thousand persons employed in extracting turpentine from the longleaf pines of the Carolinas and Georgia—a seven and a half million dollar business.

The Southern states also supported a variety of minor industries. In 1860 there were within eleven of the Southern states one female and 3,695 male blacksmiths. Three thousand workers were engaged in the leather industry, producing goods to the value of $4,426,870. The carriage and buggy industry employed over four thousand men constructing vehicles worth nearly four million dollars. The making of steam engines absorbed the energies of 4,328 men, whose annual product was worth $5,624,375. Although the South imported huge supplies of shoes from Massachusetts, nearly four million dollars' worth of shoes were manufactured in the Southern states, representing an increase of approximately 90 per cent during the decade. In the Great Kanawha Valley and at Saltville in the Holston Valley of southwestern Virginia much salt was produced by boiling the brine of the salt springs. Of the 12,717,200 bushels of salt produced in the United States in 1859, Virginia's share was 2,076,513 bushels. The eminent Negro leader, Booker T. Washington, born in slavery, worked in the salt works of western Virginia as a boy. Although some cottonseed oil was produced in the South, there were only two small sugar refineries in the land of Dixie, employing a total labor force of thirty-eight persons.

In one branch of manufacture, the making of cotton gins, the South had a monopoly in 1860. Alabama was the leading state in the Union in the production of cotton gin machinery while Georgia came second. Daniel Pratt, a native of New Hampshire, was the most successful manufacturer of cotton gins below the Mason and Dixon line.

A now forgotten industry which existed in the Old South was the mining of gold. The Federal government derived its entire gold supply for the coining of money between the years 1804-27, from the state of North Carolina. Until the discovery of this precious metal in California in 1848 the Southern states were the chief gold-producing region of the United States.

From an economic point of view the South was never liberated from its colonial status. Although its manufactures were developing in a promising fashion during the last decade of the ante-bellum period, still the South remained largely rural. Two-thirds of all exports from the United States to Europe consisted of Southern agricultural products, rice, tobacco, sugar, and cotton. Nevertheless, much of the profit from the sale of these staples went into the pockets of Northern business men, through the cotton factorage system, the indirect trade with Europe via Northern ports, and the purchase of Northern manufactured goods.

In order to liberate themselves from Northern exploitation, the Southerners considered various proposals: the establishment of direct trade with Europe, the development of Southern manufactures, the boycotting of Northern manufactures, the diversification of Southern agriculture, the building of railroads, and the reopening of the African slave trade. How much the growing sentiment of Southern nationalism contributed to the rise of manufactures below the Mason and Dixon line is impossible to measure.

Southerners felt keenly their dependence on the North for manufactured goods. It was often asserted that Southerners were rocked in a cradle manufactured in the North, dressed in Northern-made clothes, read Northern books and magazines, used Northern plows and agricultural instruments, sent their children to Northern colleges, and were buried in Northern coffins. The agitators for Southern nationalism proposed commercial nonintercourse with the North. Bills were introduced in state legislatures to levy a tax of 10 per cent on all Northern goods imported into the Southern states. Southern Rights Associations were formed to arouse the people not to patronize Northern resorts like Saratoga Springs or Newport, not to subscribe to Northern magazines or newspapers, nor employ Yankee teachers in Southern schools, nor send Southern youth to Northern colleges nor use Northern manufactures. Although the state governments failed to pass drastic laws to carry out such a policy, individuals of extreme Southern feelings did boycott Northern manufactures.

These various efforts to free the South from its colonial status represent an early form of economic planning. Many of the proposals of the ante-bellum "regional planners" and of the Southern Commercial Conventions were sound, but they could not be realized by paper resolutions or the facile dreams of orators. The South was rural, conservative, individualistic, and only by a slow process of education or by drastic economic pressures could Southern ways be radically changed. Furthermore, the South was more prosperous in the decade of 1850-60 than ever before, with cotton selling twice as high as in the preceding decade. If cotton and tobacco had declined disastrously in price at this time, discontent would have aided the reformers and "regional planners." One aspect of the agitation toward economic independence, however, was pernicious—the generation of a bitter anti-Northern feeling in the South. In calling attention to the problems of the South, the Southern Commercial Conventions and the extremists tended to weaken the bonds of the Union.

Although preceding selections have shed some light on the family life of the Old South, further comments seem necessary to point out the close relationship between the home and the economy, between the traditions and the bringing up of children, and between paternalism on the plantation and the acceptance of male supremacy. Arthur W.

Calhoun, in his monumental study of the American family, has collected much information describing the South. The next selection is made up of excerpts from his work.

• 105 • Notes on Family Life in the Old South
ARTHUR W. CALHOUN

Courtship among the southern aristocrats was reminiscent of the age of chivalric gallantry. . . . The girl . . . grew up apart from the great world yet was not provincial. As a child she was self-possessed and able to entertain her mother's callers in proper fashion. She began to have beaux in girlhood and exacted a protracted devotion of her lovers. . . . Girls were kept and cherished in right romantic fashion. Extreme modesty was assiduously cultivated; self-help was not expected. . . . [One] writer says:

No set of girls in Christendom were watched with more vigilant eyes . . . in all ways more surely girdled about, as with a wall of fire, from the sensual temptations of society, at home and elsewhere, than the Southern young women of the more favored sort in these early days.

Page says that the Virginia girl was generally a coquette, often an outrageous flirt, not from heartlessness but as a normal expression of her life. "She played upon every chord of the heart. Perhaps it was because, when she grew up, the surrender was to be absolute. . . ."

There were runaway matches. Greensboro, North Carolina, served as a Gretna Green for Virginians. Excessive restriction upon sex acquaintance furthered such clandestine matches.

But it is particularly in the romanticism of the new southern literature that the woman of the old South shines as queen and saint, a being of rare social gifts and sensibility to exalted sentiments and embodying in her person the quintessence of all that was lovely in the civilization of an effulgent people. Modesty, refinement, and sweet gentility grace the memories of her that linger in the thoughts of her children. Her "highest ambition was to be president of home."

To some extent the status and functions of the middle and upper class women of the old South merited the encomiums that are bestowed. The southern women of the middle class were modest, virtuous, industrious housekeepers, devoted wives and mothers. They were frequently gullible, knowing little of the world, and aloof from public diversions.

In general there could be no complaint of lack of domesticity in southern wives. Marriage prefaced a life-time of self-devotion; sprightly girls became sober, retired wives, bent on making home a man's delight, and devoted to family welfare; their husbands' relatives and connections became their own. After marriage women lived in plantation isolation; only the few that maintained town houses and spent part of the year in Richmond, Charleston, or New Orleans retained their social connections "and for them a staid and modified social life was deemed fitting. For them the dance was over. . . ."

The duties of a plantation mistress were often truly formidable. Many a plantation was a crude industrial plant comparable as to household comfort with a mining camp. On such estates many a lady lived. If slavery released the lady from manual drudgery, it overworked her in other ways; she was typically deficient in vitality, often nervous and sensitive, yet she often had to contend with an aggravated form of the servant problem, for slaveholders did not always manage to get rid of trying and unprofitable servants. Except perhaps a butler and a head housemaid

[Adapted from *A Social History of the American Family from Colonial Times to the Present*, Vol. 2, Barnes and Noble, New York, 1945. Pp. 311-355. Used by permission.]

the help was often idle, incompetent, and in need of constant supervision. . . . A southern lady of an old and wealthy family visiting in New York said: "Your two servants accomplish a great deal more, and do their work a great deal better than our twelve."

Every household operation had to be under scrutiny. Every consumable thing had to be kept locked up, hence the mistress carried a huge bunch of keys and doled out "on incessant requests" whatever was wanted for the household. Continually she was being called upon to attend to some want of one of her many dependents. The plantation nurse brought a list of the sick and the serious cases had to be visited. The wagons came with the carcass of a beef or sheep and the mistress saw to the cutting up. The makers of garments had to receive attention.

Unfortunately there was not much chance for a progressive movement among Southern women. A very interesting *Ladies' Magazine* begun at Savannah in 1819 was forced to suspend at the end of six months for lack of patronage. The lady of the archaic South left little written record. As in the North, woman received no worthy education. An actor remarked in 1842 upon the rarity of daughters of the far South among the vast number of women magazine writers. Gentlemen of the old regime in the South would say, "A woman's name should appear in print but twice— when she marries and when she dies."

Even the chastity of the Southern women (a monopolized excellence) was scarcely a virtue, but rather a matter of course. Men sedulously shielded their female perquisites of white blood. A young lady of South Carolina got a verdict of one thousand dollars against a man (of moderate means) for imputation of unchastity. Education and public opinion were strained to the preservation of the purity of free women, or rather of such as belonged to the master race. Somewhat of the spirit of the regnant male may be glimpsed in the remark of a Natchez gentleman about 1808: "The ladies in general are extremely delicate, which never fails to please, and excite the warmest sensations in the beholder. . . . Tho chaste as the virgin queen before the

Gordian knot is tied, yet indulgent as the Cyprian goddess for ever after."

Death and widowhood in the old South complicated the problem of keeping intact the family name and dignity. . . . In old eastern Virginia it was not expected that a widow would remarry and usually she did not. It was almost a matter of course for a husband to make enjoyment of the estate conditional on non-marriage; the chief gospel was the preservation of family name and these restrictions were not considered cruel.

In so far as city life developed, the simplicity of the family life tended to disappear. At Richmond in 1800 "the higher circle consisted of the families of the neighboring planters, who left their estates to the management of overseers, and spent the larger part of the year in Richmond because of its social advantages." . . . The first tendency of the spirit of Revolutionary days was to do away with artificial social distinctions. Primogeniture was abolished in Virginia and Maryland; so that only by will could estates be maintained intact (as was in fact done in some notable cases for the sake of prestige). In Maryland, following the Revolution there was an open contempt for anything savoring of caste and nobility.

After the Revolution, soil exhaustion in the older states and competition in tobacco reduced old families to poverty and oblivion. . . . By the early [eighteen] thirties at Charleston abolition of primogeniture had undermined old families. "Comparatively few of the old families now remain who are wealthy. . . . Therefore, the sons of the best men of the South are wisely placed in countinghouses in the great trading cities, or . . . bred to some useful calling." (But there were many showy idlers.) The South Carolina planter no longer inherited enough to send his sons to English universities. Division of property was killing patrician notions.

In spite, however, of all contrary tendencies, the family in the South was a much more potent institution than elsewhere in the republic. Old families held the day. In Kentucky, family feuds cost sundry lives. The eldest son of the old Virginia families was regarded as representative of the kin. In old east Virginia, family was a fetish. Estates were entailed to the limit of the law—one generation, and the heir commonly renewed religiously the entail. The tidewater owner of large estates would have been insulted by the idea of selling his home. The ancestral abode was the one spot on earth.

Relationship was traced by Southerners to a remote degree. The bond of fellowship stretched to include all that were worthy, even tho they had removed to distant places. It would be hard to overestimate the power of a great and strongly entrenched southern family connected with a dozen like families all holding a common point of view and action. Marriage and intermarriages and the tangle of consanguinity welded the slave power.

The Old South of the decade before the Civil War was as much as anything else a state of mind, not simply a vague idealization with little meaning but, as our next selection shows, a strong and living force for which the Confederate soldier was ready to die.

Out of what did this romantic legend of the South grow? The following selection, summarizing the changes in the South between 1819 and 1848, does much to answer this question.

• 106 • The Affirmation of Southern Perfection
CHARLES S. SYDNOR

While the relationship of the South to the nation was deteriorating and the power of the South in Congress was declining, changes were taking place within the region itself. Most noticeable, perhaps, was its southwestward expansion, engulfing the Indian lands of the lower South and sweeping across the Mississippi River into eastern Texas. The declining strength of the Southern states in Congress between the 1820's and the 1840's is measured by the loss of three seats by the South while the rest of the nation gained twenty-two seats. Within this same period the southwestward shift of Southern population caused the seaboard states to lose fifteen seats in the lower house of Congress while the rest of the South gained twelve seats.

Beyond the realm of statistical measurement, a more significant political shift had occurred. The strong and nationally respected leadership of Virginia in early years had vanished. By the 1840's, the leading Southern politicians were in the cotton states, and few of them had much influence outside the South. On several counts, [most of] the cotton-kingdom politicians were too aggressive, and their viewpoint was too sectional, for the older and more conservative tobacco South.

Nonpolitical changes were also occurring in the region. These were important, but the sum total of them all was probably less important than the relative changelessness of the South in a nation that was changing fast. The booming cities, the factories, the multiplying railroads, the expanding population, and the changing attitudes and viewpoints above Mason and Dixon's line account for tension between North and South far better than any changes that were taking place in the South.

The South of the 1840's, like the South of the previous century, was a land of farms and

[Adapted from *The Development of Southern Sectionalism, 1819-1848* (Vol. V of *A History of the South,* edited by W. H. Stephenson and E. Merton Coulter), Louisiana State University Press, Baton Rouge, 1948. Pp. 331-339. Used by permission.]

plantations, of few towns and of scattered population, of internal waterway transportation, and of a great export trade to foreign markets. Through all of this period Negro slavery continued. In the formation of the Union and in its early years, the South was accepted as a respectable part of the nation; by the 1840's it was regarded by many Northerners as an obstacle to American social and economic progress and as a moral pariah. The explanation of this change in attitude is to be found in part in the long series of conflicts between the diverging sections, and sectional divergence was due chiefly to those forces that were transforming the North.

As the South declined in political power and as it experienced the growing force of the antislavery movement, the mind of the South was transmuted into something very different from what it had been a generation earlier. This mental change, in its various aspects, was one of the most notable developments in the South between 1819 and 1848.

To speak of the mind of the South implies, perhaps, a unity in the thinking of Southerners when, as a matter of fact, there was much diversity. [However,] within the area of Southern thought and expression, certain traits and qualities had developed which if not universal in the region or even dominant were at least influential and significant.

. . . A great change had come over him [John C. Calhoun] and over many of his generation of Southerners. In the first place, he and they had lost faith in some of the fundamental premises of democracy. Perhaps they had never thoroughly believed that all men were created free and equal and that all had an inalienable right to liberty, but neither had they denied these tenets until the slavery controversy forced them to face the contradiction between slavery and the Declaration of Independence. Compelled to make a choice, they denied the accuracy and validity of the Revolutionary doctrines; and Jefferson, the personification of democratic idealism, they repudiated as a theoretical and dangerous visionary.

Going beyond theories, Calhoun's contemporaries pointed to evils in the actual operation of democratic government. They believed, and with good reason, that grave injuries had been done to the substantial interests of the South during the 1820's within the framework and through the procedures of democratic government. The conclusion was inescapable that a democracy could and often did oppress minorities within itself. Much thought was therefore given to devices for limiting and controlling self-government so as to protect smaller parts against the tyranny of the majority.

Inasmuch as the government to be held in check operated under a written constitution, the discussion turned into constitutional rather than philosophical channels. Champions of the South seldom began with the nature of man or with the good of man and society. Their arguments usually started with the written words of the fundamental document, and thence they proceeded by close reasoning and logical skill that was sometimes amazingly subtle.

The narrow but brilliant operation of the Southern mind on questions of government was accompanied by a restricted and abstract concept of humanity. Although the object of Southern political thought was to afford protection to the individual, far less attention was given to man than to checks and limitations on the machinery of government. It had not been so at an earlier period of Southern history. Jefferson and Madison had tried to build democracy on such goodness and wisdom as could be found in humanity. Calhoun, in contrast, limited himself to the task of devising a system of government that would hold in check the destructive tendencies of man. Yet, the last word must be said for Calhoun. The grim, narrow, pessimistic spirit that had come over him was not altogether and perhaps not mainly of his own creation. The selfish and reckless tendencies in human nature which he was trying to place under legal and constitutional limitations were the forces that had in large measure placed his region on the defensive and made him the champion of a minority.

Along with its concern about problems of government, the mind of the South was becoming preoccupied with the problem of its own social organization. For a long time the South had possessed a distinctive social order, compounded of such elements as ruralism, the plantation system, Negro slavery, and a complex pattern of customs and conventions. To this way of life Southerners had conformed without much thought that they were odd persons living in a curious and different society. But by the 1830's the Southern mind was turned inward to a consideration of its own [social order.] The bitter and extravagant antislavery attack was the major force in making Southerners aware that their region had a way of life that was far different from the rest of the United States.

The first response of Southerners to the vigorous onslaught was frequently one of startled amazement. . . . But defensive forces were soon rallied, and something of a plan of campaign began to emerge. It consisted in small measure of an attack upon the enemy's country, and this was aimed at the Northern characteristic that was most unlike the South, namely industrialism. One of the earliest American critiques of an industrial society, with emphasis on its exploitation of labor, was evolved in the South as a counter-attack against Northern critics of slavery.

But the master plan of the South in this war of words called for a defensive instead of an offensive war. It denied the validity of Northern criticisms, and it evolved into a remarkable apologia of virtually every aspect of the Southern way of life. Inasmuch as the attacking forces charged that Southern life was blighted throughout by slavery, Southern defenders rallied to this point. They claimed that slavery was good, that slavery had a beneficent influence upon Southern life, and that the South like ancient Greece had evolved a noble civilization because the institution of slavery was an integral part of it.

[In the year 1836] Senator James H. Hammond said: "It is no evil. On the contrary, I believe it to be the greatest of all the great blessings which a kind Providence bestowed upon our glorious region. . . . it has rendered our southern country proverbial for its wealth, its genius, and its manners." Some-

what later he claimed that slavery was responsible for the superiority of the moral code, the educational system, the religious beliefs and practices, and other attributes of Southern life. [Further, he said, it] set apart and gave a vigorous individuality to Southern men. Accustomed to commanding, they became leaders wherever they went, demonstrating their prowess in all acquisitions of national territory, and displaying their capacity for political leadership in the predominance of Southerners in the presidency of the United States.

It was also claimed that slavery was the only perfect and permanent foundation for democracy. Because of a servile population, citizens of the Southern states were said to be equal, and "Equality among its citizens is the corner-stone of a republic." Again, it was said that slavery, as it existed in the South, was the only safeguard against anarchy and aggressive skepticism, and that "the destruction of African slavery would be the destruction of republicanism." As proof of this remarkable claim, it was argued that under a system of universal suffrage all political power must eventually fall into the hands of men without education or property, and that property was the great conservative force in government.

In sharp contrast to current pessimism about the economic plight of the South, regional defenders boasted of the indispensable character of Southern staples in the commerce of the world and of the essential importance of the South as a market for the manufactured goods of the North. But their greatest claim to economic excellence was that slavery abolished the usual feud between capital and labor. Thus, the South could escape the discontentment and turbulence of the North because the Southern laborer was freed from the uncertainty and misery of the Northern laborer, especially in depression years.

Having so small a stake in society, the body of Northern labor was "easily, on any occasion of excitement, formed into a mob— so easily swayed by artful and designing demagogues." The impermanent and granular quality of Northern society allowed its members to have much freedom but it gave them little security. In contrast, Southern society was stable because each person, rich and poor, black and white, was firmly rooted in a close-knit, organic social order.

The champions of the Old South claimed that theirs was the ideal social order and the only permanently founded democracy, all because it had, with God's blessing, slavery. Surely, Southerners had come a long way from Jefferson and a long way out of reality.

It would be fruitless to point to fallacies in their reasoning and to the great contrast between the perfections they described and the imperfections [surrounding] them. Although the idealized portrait of the South was false, it was to be a strong and living force in the years ahead. In the long run, the vision of the perfect South was to supply a substantial element in the construction of the romantic legend about the Old South. In the nearer future, it was to give the Confederate soldier something to die for.

Politics in the Old South was an honored calling and a field of great interest. The next selection, although written at times in sweeping generalizations, gives an over-all account of how much power the Southern planters held and what the basis of that power was.

• 107 • The Planter in Politics
WILLIAM E. DODD

The political basis of the plantation system was the county court, and the county court of the South came from the banks of the James and the York rivers. In old Virginia a county court was composed of a group of justices of the peace meeting once a month to try petty cases of law. These justices were the grandees of their respective neighborhoods. They were vestrymen in the established church, owners of plantations, and lords of manors. Their wives were the ladies of the land and their daughters set the hearts of young blades aflame when they appeared in church. They were men of good common sense, familiar with the codes of Virginia and to a less degree acquainted with the precedents of English law courts. Everybody looked up to them; and they made themselves responsible in considerable measure for the good behavior of the countryside. What they thought was right was likely to become law.

Aside from the ordinary business of courts, they sat in administrative sessions to appoint sheriffs and road overseers and to order the building of bridges and schoolhouses. At informal meetings they determined which of their number ought to stand for election to the next assembly, passed upon the conduct of returning members of Congress, and as time went on learned to denounce the conduct of rascally Yankees. The government of Virginia during the first half of the nineteenth century rested securely upon the shoulders of the county justices of the peace.

This was the model upon which South Carolina remade her judicial system when at the end of the Revolution she took into political partnership her great and growing upcountry. The county courts of Georgia, Alabama, and Mississippi were but images of Virginia institutions planted upon a distant soil. Florida and Louisiana readjusted their French and Spanish procedure to fit the

[Adapted from "The Cotton Kingdom: a Chronicle of the Old South," by William E. Dodd, Vol. 27, *The Chronicles of America,* edited by Allen Johnson. Copyright Yale University Press, New Haven, 1920. Pp. 118-121, 146. Used by permission.]

general model, though retaining the Napoleonic code. Texas took her system from Missouri, which in turn had taken hers from Virginia.

The justice of the peace was an institution of the lower South quite as much as of Virginia herself. To know this gentleman of the old school, this humane and good-natured autocrat, mildly proud of himself and keenly resentful of any criticism of his Latin or of his law, is to know the political life of the South as well as of the cotton kingdom, because every justice of the peace, save on the distant frontier, was a slaveholder or likely soon to become such, a conservative in politics and religion, and a member or prospective member of the Legislature.

The political power of the cotton kingdom therefore was firmly lodged in the hands of successful business men. There was never in America a more perfect oligarchy of business men than that which ruled in the time of Jefferson Davis and Alexander Stephens. Laws were made by the owners of plantations; the higher courts were established by their decrees; governors of States were of their choosing; and members of Congress were selected and maintained in office in accordance with their wishes. And, as we have already seen, they were the ruling members of all the churches. Truly nothing of importance could happen in the lower South without their consent. This fact gave to the South its unity of political purpose and that moderation of social change which men of wealth always prefer. Security of property, loyalty to church, and safety in education were the guarantees of the system. . . .

Lincoln was elected. The cotton States prepared to leave the Union. [Despite all odds, there] was then no doubt of final success, and there was little if any serious protest against the ideals that were to be realized.

The New South:

A Changing Economy

>>

The Old, or ante-bellum, South has been portrayed in considerable detail so that we can trace the changes between that era and those which have followed. In this book we do not discuss the Civil War, although it is readily to be recognized that all war—and particularly that war—brought with it great destruction of life and property and also wrought many social and economic changes.

The New South, as the next selection, written in 1921, reminds us, is not necessarily the contemporary South but that which began to take shape after the Civil War. There was no sharp break with the past but rather a turning toward the future by people who had formerly faced only the past.

• 108 • The Background of the New South
HOLLAND THOMPSON

There is a New South, but it is a logical development from the Old South. The civilization of the South today has not been imposed from without but has been an evolution from within, though influenced by the policy of the National Government. The Civil War changed the whole organization of Southern society, it is true, but it did not modify its essential attributes, to quote the ablest of the carpetbaggers, Albion W. Tourgée. Reconstruction strengthened existing prejudices and created new bitterness, but the attempt failed to make of South Carolina another Massachusetts. The people resisted stubbornly, des-

[Adapted from "The New South: a Chronicle of Social and Industrial Evolution," by Holland Thompson, Vol. 42, The Chronicles of America, edited by Allen Johnson. Copyright Yale University Press, New Haven, 1921. Pp. 1-8. Used by permission.]

perately, and in the end successfully, every attempt to impose upon them alien institutions.

The South believed, and believes yet, that it was defeated by the blockade and not by military force. According to this theory, the North won because the South could not manufacture goods for its needs, because it did not possess ships to bring in goods from abroad, and because it could not build a navy to defend its ports. Today it is clear that the South never had a chance to win, so long as the will to conquer was firm in the North. As soon as the War was over, the demand for greater industrial development made itself felt and gained in strength when Reconstruction came; but during that period the people had to devote all their energies to living day by day, hoping for strength to endure. When property was being confiscated under the forms of law, only to be squandered by irresponsible legislators, there was little incentive to remake the industrial system, and the ventures of the Reconstruction government into industrial affairs were not encouraging. Farm property in the South—and little was left except farm property after the War—depreciated in value enormously in the decade following 1860. Grimly, sullenly, the white man of the South fought again to secure domination, this time, however, of his own section only and not of the nation. When this had been achieved, a large portion of the population was overcome by that deadly apathy so often remarked by travelers who ventured to visit the land as they would have visited Africa. The white South wished only to be let alone.

As the years passed, apathy began to disappear in some parts of the South. Wiser men recognized that the old had gone never to return. Men began to face the inevitable. Instead of brooding upon their grievances, they adjusted themselves, more or less successfully, to the new economic and social order, and by acting in harmony with it found that progress was not so impossible as they had supposed. White planters found that the net returns from their farms on which they themselves had labored were greater than when a larger force of negroes had been employed; shrewd men began to put their scanty savings together to take advantage of convenient water power. Securing the bare necessities of life was no longer a difficult problem for every one. Men began to find pleasure in activity rather than in mere passivity or obstruction.

Somehow, somewhere, sometime, a new hopefulness was born and this new spirit—evidence of new life—became embodied in [the phrase] "the New South." The first to use the expression in a way which sent it vibrating through the whole nation was Henry W. Grady, the gifted editor of the *Atlanta Constitution*. In a speech made in 1886 by invitation of the New England Society of New York City, he took for his theme "the New South" and delivered an oration which, judged by its effects, had some of the marks of greatness. "The South," he said, "has nothing for which to apologize. She believes that the late struggle between the States was war and not rebellion, revolution and not conspiracy." He went on, however, to express the feeling that the outcome had been for the best, and painted a picture of the new spirit of the South, a trifle enthusiastic perhaps, but still recognizable.

Today a New South may be said to be everywhere apparent. The Old South still exists in nooks and corners of many States, it is true: there are communities, counties, groups of counties, which cling to the old ideas. In the hearts of thousands of men and women the Old South is enshrined, and there is no room for the new; but the South as a whole is a New South, marked by a spirit of hopefulness, a belief in the future, and a desire to take a fuller part in the life of the nation.

In the rest of our study of the Cotton South, a variety of passages have been chosen to help you compare the Old South with the New. We shall not undertake to trace all of the subtleties of social change for even a single topic over the past six or seven decades;

instead, we shall examine contrasting pictures which in themselves carry suggestions as to why the changes occurred. It is only by comparing the changes in Chinese peasant society with the changes in the Cotton South or in the English Midlands that we can begin to form some clear-cut ideas about the ways in which new ideas are introduced and become a part of any given society.

Social change focuses on changes in social relations. An economy, for example, is made up of the relations among people commonly engaged in what we call economic activities. The industrial system exists as people work together in the roles of capitalist, manager, and worker; the business system is a set of relations between people who have goods or services to sell and those who are willing to buy. The words *banking, transportation,* and *utilities* remind us of money or credit, railroad trains, and power lines, but even these become a part of the economy as *people become associated* together for the purpose of supplying credit, transportation, or electricity.

When, therefore, we look for changes in the economy of the Old South, we try to discover what happened to the relations between the planter and his labor force (or slaves), between the cotton factor and his landlord clients, between the few paternalistic industrialists and their workers.

In the four selections that follow, the emphasis is upon human relations rather than upon commodities or material evidences of an economy, important as these tangible possessions are to any individual or nation. First, what occurred to the plantation system? Secondly, what merchandising arrangement took the place of the factor? Thirdly, what changes paved the way for the increased tempo of industrialization in the South today?

Selection 109, dealing with the social aspects of the plantation system, calls attention to the contrasts between 1860 and 1930. From time to time, reference is made to some intervening year, such as 1910. The author, T. J. Woofter, is a competent social scientist who is not only familiar with sound research methodology but has an intimate acquaintance with the Cotton South. An able corps of co-workers helped him sample in considerable detail the plantation life through the whole cotton region during the early 1930's. This was a time of economic depression, and the federal government was casting about for various rehabilitation programs. This study, *Landlord and Tenant on the Cotton Plantation,* was to provide much valuable information on which later policies were based.

• 109 • Social Aspects of the Plantation System
THOMAS J. WOOFTER, JR.

A plantation is defined for purposes of this study as a tract farmed by one owner or manager with five or more resident families. These may include the landlord, the laborers, share tenants, or renters. Except in the case of renters the landlord exercises close supervision over operators, and except in the case of wage laborers each family cultivates a

[Adapted from *Landlord and Tenant on the Cotton Plantation,* Works Progress Administration, Division of Social Research, Washington, 1936. Pp. xix-xxiv, xxvii-xxix, xxxi, xxxiii, 9-11, 22, 31-33.]

separate piece of land. . . . In those parts of the South where fairly large operative units prevail, the plantation owners, through their control over large acreages of the best land and of large numbers of tenant and laborer families, still dominate the economic, political, and cultural life. Landlord-tenant relationships on the smaller units in such areas are patterned after those on the larger holdings.

In true plantation areas there is a high degree of concentration of land ownership, with a consequent high proportion of tenants among the farm operators. Such areas are further characterized by per capita incomes higher than those in other southern agricultural counties but lower than those in other farming sections of the Nation; small proportions of urban and village dwellers; scarcity of non-agricultural industries; large families; poor school facilities, especially for Negroes; and a highly mobile population, with families frequently on the move in search of better conditions. These areas are utterly subject to King Cotton, booming when the King is prosperous and slumping when the King is sick. Aside from feed for livestock and a limited amount of produce for home consumption, practically no other crop is grown.

As land resources are now used, plantation labor conditions and population trends are largely determined by the pressure of population on these resources. Concentration on one crop—cotton—demands a large labor supply for only part of the year. Landlords prefer large families to meet the labor demands of the peak seasons, thus encouraging a high birth rate. This high rate of population increase in turn perpetuates the plantation system, [for it reduces] the bargaining power of the individual plantation tenant, making it increasingly difficult for him to free himself from the plantation system and become an independent farmer.

Wage labor replaced slave labor on plantations immediately after the Civil War, but share-cropping was soon introduced as a method of labor operations. Most of the plantations are now operated largely by share-croppers—virtually laborers who receive half of the crop in return for working the land. Wage labor continues on a few plantations. Others are operated by various types of tenants, some of whom provide work stock and tools and thus receive a larger share of the crop than the share-cropper and some of whom rent the land outright, paying rent in cash or produce. Often all classes of tenants are found on the same plantations. Of the plantations covered in this study, 71 per cent were operated by families of mixed tenure, while 16 per cent were operated by croppers, 4 per cent by wage hands, 3 per cent by other share tenants, and 6 per cent by renters.

As population pressure increased, whites began to compete with Negroes for places on the land as tenants and laborers. While the vast majority of white agricultural workers were owners in 1860, by 1930 over three-quarters of a million white families in the Southeast had joined the tenant or laborer class. The proportion of white ownership declined steadily with the increase in white tenancy. Whites now make up the majority of tenants in the Old South, as well as in other parts of the country, although nearly all of the plantations in this survey still had Negro tenants, 53 per cent operating exclusively with Negroes, 5 per cent exclusively with whites, and 42 per cent with both. It is evident, therefore, that white tenants are concentrated on the smaller holdings and Negro tenants on the larger.

One of the landlord's major duties, and one upon which the success of his operation depends, is the expenditure of the plantation's working capital, in the purchase of seeds and fertilizer, in plantation upkeep, and in the apportionment of subsistence advances to the tenants for food and clothing. This practice of subsistence advances, to be repaid by the tenants when the crop is marketed, is one of the chief trouble spots for the landlord. The supervision of these advances determines the living standard of the share tenant.

The plantation system is bound up with the cash-crop system. Concentration on cotton increased from the Civil War until the boll weevil invasion soon after 1910. [Drastic] acreage reduction [soon resulted], and as each State reduced its acreage, Texas and Oklahoma added to theirs. When weevil disorganization had passed and the Eastern Cotton Belt began to attain its former production, States west of the Mississippi continued to expand their acreage. As a result, the supply of cotton far exceeded the demand. As a result, the price fell to 6 cents a pound in 1932, causing heavy losses to all producers. Only the semi-self-sustaining farmer, or the planter with resources or good credit, could continue to operate.

. . . The average plantation family in this study was allotted 25 crop acres; croppers had an average of 20 crop acres; share tenants and renters had about 25 crop acres; and wage hands, about 45 crop acres per family.

Although spoken of as a one-crop system, the cropping arrangement of the Cotton South is really a two-crop system: cotton for cash, and corn for food and feed. Most plantations have as much acreage in corn as in cotton. Four per cent of the total expenditure of the plantations studied, however, was for feed which could easily have been grown on the plantations. Up to the inauguration of the cotton reduction program, the plantations of the South tended to be less and less self-supporting, in contrast with the practices of slave plantations which produced a large proportion of their subsistence needs.

Fuel and house rent are part of the tenant's perquisites but the houses furnished are among the poorest in the Nation. Unpainted four-room frame shacks predominate.

The low income for large families provides only a meager subsistence. About one-third of the net income is in the form of products raised for home consumption—a few chickens and eggs, home killed pork, syrup, corn meal, cowpeas, and sweet potatoes. These food items are usually available only in the late summer and fall.

During the months when crops are cultivated, the tenant uses another third of his income, at the rate of about $13 per month, for food—mostly flour, lard, and salt pork—and also for kerosene, medicine, and such clothing purchases as cannot be postponed till fall. Another third is spent for clothing and incidentals, usually soon after the fall "settlement." Thus, by winter, resources are exhausted and "slim rations" begin. Clothing, usually purchased once a year, is of the poorest quality. Often the children do not have sufficient warm clothing to go to school.

Few of the tenants in this study had gardens and only 55 per cent had cows. The effect of poor housing and meager diet was reflected in the health of the families studied.

MOBILITY

Tenants who have not succeeded in locating on good land or with a fair landlord are continually searching for better conditions, many moving from farm to farm each fall. Although they move often, they do not move far. Most of them remain in the county of their birth or locate in adjoining counties.

The rate of farm-to-farm mobility appears to be closely linked with tenure status. The higher the farmer climbs up the "agricultural ladder" the more stable he becomes.

Mobility within the farming occupation is also relatively common as farmers change from one tenure to another.

A third type of mobility is the shift from the open country to town as the tenant periodically tries his luck at the sawmill, the cottonmill, or odd jobs.

The evidence indicates that Negro tenants are a more stable group with respect to residence than white tenants. This is probably accounted for, to a large extent, by the fact that there are relatively fewer opportunities for Negroes outside of agriculture and that Negro tenants are more easily satisfied than are white tenants.

In a study of farmers in South Carolina in 1933, it was found that white tenants move about once every 4 years, and Negro tenants once every 5 or 6 years. White farm owners move about once in 11 years, and Negro owners once in 12 years.

THE AVERAGE COTTON PLANTATION

(Based on rounded averages for the 646 plantations)

The typical cotton plantation operated by 5 or more families in 1934 included a total of 907 acres, of which 385 were in crops, 63 idle, 162 in pasture, 214 in woods and 83 in waste land. Approximately 86 per cent of the 907 acres was owned by the operating landlord and 14 per cent was rented from other owners. Of the crop land harvested, 44 per cent was planted to cotton. On the typical plantation the wage hand cultivated 45 crop acres, the cropper 20, the other share tenant 26, and the renter 24.

The plantation had a total value of about $28,700 of which $21,700 was in land, $3,900 in buildings, $1,900 in animals, and $1,200 in implements. The average long term indebtedness was $11,700.

The typical plantation was occupied by 14 families, exclusive of the landlord's family, of which 3 were headed by wage hands, 8 by croppers, 2 by other share tenants, and 1 by a renter. Of these families, 2 were white and 12 were Negro The average family, the head of which was 41 years of age consisted of about four persons, of whom two to three were employable. The average number of years of residence on the 1934 farm was 8 years for all families, 7 for wage hands, 7 for croppers, 11 for other share tenants, and 13 for renters.

The net plantation income, after deducting expenses, was $6,000. The operator's net income averaged $2,600, leaving $3,400 to be divided among the tenants. If 6 per cent is allowed as the return on the landlord's investment, he received approximately $850 as his labor income, or $2 per crop acre.

Wage hands had a net income of $180, croppers $312, other share tenants $417, and renters $354. The average tenant family received a subsistence advance of $13 per month for 7 months.

TENANT CLASSES

The predominant social characteristic of plantation regions is the class-caste system which is built around the landlord-tenant relationship, for tenancy has become not only a method of making a living but also a way of living. [Review, in this connection, Selection 80, on farm tenancy in China.]

While the plantation proprietorship has continued since pre-Civil War days, merely shrinking somewhat in size, the methods of operation have undergone radical changes. The first of these was, of course, the shift from slave to free labor. The next was the shift from hired labor to half share-cropping, which began very soon after the Civil War. Share-cropping, in which the farm operator contributes only his labor and receives in return a share of the crop, has persisted, but other forms of tenancy have also emerged. The "third and fourth" arrangement is made with tenants who own their work stock. From them the landlord, instead of receiving half, receives a third of the cotton and a fourth of the corn. These tenants, together with other miscellaneous share tenants, are referred to as "other share tenants" throughout this study. Tenants of a still more independent type rent the land outright, receiving the whole proceeds of their crop minus a fixed rental which may be in cash or produce. These tenants are referred to as "renters" throughout this study.

Although share-cropping is predominant, all classes of tenants often mingle on the same plantation. Even though the landlord may prefer half share-cropping, he will often take a tenant on terms of third and fourth share or straight rent if he has a tract vacant, especially when production is expanding. Of the plantations covered in this investigation, 4 per cent were operated entirely by wage hands, 16 per cent were operated entirely by croppers, 3 per cent entirely by other share tenants, 6 per cent by renters, and 71 per cent were mixed in tenure. On the mixed places, however, croppers predominated.

Both white and Negro tenants were often employed on the same plantation. Of the plantations studied 53 per cent were operated entirely by Negro tenants, 5 per cent entirely by white tenants, and 42 per cent by both white and Negro tenants. In general, the percentages of Negroes in the plantation population in each area followed the percentage of Negroes in the rural population.

It must also be remembered that the relations between landlord and tenant are traditionally informal. Detailed agreements are not usually worked out and contracts are practically never written. Such records of advances and repayments as are kept are almost always in the hands of the landlord. This becomes a complicated account when debts from previous years are carried forward and added to current advances. This situation places the absolute control of relationships in the hands of the landlord and the fairness of settlements is largely dependent upon his sense of justice. The tenant's only recourse is to move, which of course does not adjust his past transactions but merely enables him to seek more satisfactory conditions.

Thus the prosperity of landlord and tenant are interwoven and mutually dependent upon three principal factors: (1) the productivity of the land, (2) the efficiency and energy of the landlord, and (3) the ability and energy of the tenant. There is evidence that these factors also interact on each other. In their efforts to farm more efficiently the most able landlords tend to get the most productive land. In their wanderings to better their condition the most able tenants eventually gravitate to the fairest landlords.

It is the absentee landlord who, through ignorance, laxity of supervision, or cupidity, most often allows the "mining" of the land and the loss of the productive top soil through erosion. It is on the absentee-owned plantations that fences and buildings most frequently fall into disrepair. It is these plantations which are least stable in a crisis. [Therefore,] the tenants on these places are the first to find themselves without resources and are often forced either to move to the city or to become laborers or croppers on the more stable farms.

NON-AGRICULTURAL ENTERPRISES

The commissary is one of the most criticized plantation features but may, if fairly administered, be of advantage to the tenant. Usually the commissary is introduced by the operator so that he, rather than the supply merchant, may control the expenditures for subsistence and keep these amounts within the limits of the tenant's ability to produce. The landlord also gets the advantage of wholesale prices with discounts if he is able to finance purchases in cash.

The advantage, or disadvantage, of this practice to the tenant depends entirely upon the extent to which the landlord passes the economies of wholesale buying on to the purchaser and the extent to which the landlord merely substitutes himself for the exploitative merchant.

For performing these varied services, the average landlord makes little more than the cost would be of hiring managers and overseers to do them. Calculated on the basis of salaries paid in 1920 on large plantations, Brannen concluded that the cost of hiring supervision was $1.80 per acre on cotton plantations. According to the present study the landlord profit (after deducting interest on his capital) averaged only $2.01 per crop acre.

SOCIAL CONTRIBUTIONS

Having established and perpetuated a paternalistic relation to tenants and having taken the responsibility for close supervision not only of agricultural operations but also of family expenditures, the landlord is also often called upon for services of a social nature, for the large plantation is a social as well as an economic organism and the matrix of a number of plantations often constitutes or dominates the larger unit of civil government in the locality.

Among efficient landlords, tenant health is one of the major considerations and doctors' bills are paid by the landlord and charged against the tenant crop. Those tenants who have a landlord who will "stand for" their bills are far more likely to get physicians' services than are the general run of tenants. On some plantations socialized medicine is approximated. The landlord pays a flat rate to a doctor who agrees to serve all the tenants for a year, and this charge is distributed on a per visit basis.

Landlords and managers are also expected to "stand for" their tenants in minor legal difficulties such as may grow out of gambling games, altercations, and traffic infractions. This function is, of course, not exercised indiscriminately. A good worker will, in all probability, be "gotten off" and a drone left in the hands of the law. In past decades, the sheriff seldom went on large plantations, minor discipline being one of the manager's undisputed prerogatives. The broad leather strap was the principal instrument of discipline. These practices of plantation discipline have passed, but the landlord assumes responsibility for such tenants as are arrested for minor offenses, especially during the busy season. In the present study 11 per cent of the landlords had, in the year 1934, acted as parole sponsor for tenants and 21 per cent had paid fines.

Use of plantation animals for social or personal purposes is also one of the plantation contributions. Three-fourths of the plantations studied allowed the use of their animals for trips to town and on Sundays, but of these more than one-fourth did not allow such use as often as once a month. Thus, a large proportion of the tenants who did not own work animals either had no means of transportation or had such means available less than once a month.

Landlords are also frequently expected to contribute to plantation social life through aid to churches, schools, and entertainments. The present study revealed that direct contributions to schools were relatively small although the use of land for school buildings was frequently permitted. Planters interviewed reported an average annual contribution to tenants' churches of approximately $13 and to tenants' entertainments of $6. In addition, it goes without saying that plantation

waters are open to tenants' fishing, and plantation rabbits and quail are theirs for the taking. Usually the landlord's contribution of supplies for entertainments such as fish fries, barbecues, and dances is more substantial than his cash contribution.

The contribution of the landlord to plantation efficiency may be summarized as that of the pocketbook and brain. The contribution of the tenant is largely that of supervised brawn. Landlords vary widely in their capability of performing these functions efficiently. Some prefer to stay in town rather than ride over their land. Others work very energetically at their job, thereby contributing materially to their own fortune and to that of their tenants. It is clear that the efficient landlord is not only a capitalist, but also an agronomist, a diplomat, a capable manager, and occasionally a veterinarian and social arbiter.

Tenants have traditionally depended on landlords for services such as those described in this chapter and any plan for replacing the plantation organization with other forms of tenure or small ownership must take into consideration the reality of the managerial function and the practical necessity for supervision of a plantation. It must either provide a similar management until tenants outgrow its need or, through intensive education, train the tenants to perform these duties efficiently.

The selection just concluded shows that many of the features of the 1860 plantations persisted—particularly the paternalism and the provision by the landlord for most of his tenants' needs. Sharecropping was an adjustment to the abolition of slavery; concentration on a single cash crop, with corn as a supplementary crop for food and feed, was the expected rule. But what about those rural people who either worked their own small holdings or worked for landlords who had no commissaries or "staked" the tenant to food from crop year to crop year? The answer was found in the furnishing merchant.

The next selection, by Thomas D. Clark, a well-known historian of the South, explains how the furnishing merchant or country store keeper, with his credit arrangements, took care of the economic needs of poor people as well as of the farmers with the larger land holdings. Dr. Clark traveled throughout the South in 1941-1942 collecting and reading the old ledgers kept by these country merchants, and his findings reflect the careful study he made of the business practices of an earlier day.

· 110 · The Furnishing and Supply System

THOMAS D. CLARK

In the post-Civil War economy of the South the furnishing merchant was a key figure. He became the hub of the new system of agriculture, supplanting in many respects the factor of the earlier years. It was through his stores that goods were made available to customers on their home grounds, and it was he who facilitated the process of economic revival in the badly isolated regions of the South.

Disorganization of the earlier supply system of the South brought about a new condition of trade which wholesale merchants were quick to sense and exploit. Instead of wasting energy on the restitution of the old factorage system of supply, they went to work to develop and expand the crossroads stores. They helped to locate desirable store sites, selected storekeepers, stocked the stores with goods, and supplied money and generous credit when it was needed. Actually they became stationary factors who used the southern merchant as a local intermediary for the distribution of a rapidly increasing quantity of goods. This was to be the merchant's most significant part in the building of the New South. Since there were few local banks, the local merchant was both a source of commodity supply to the people and a channel of capital outlet for extra-regional investors. It was he who served as a direct local contact man for the big wholesale mercantile houses, the fertilizer manufacturers, the meat packers, and the grain, feed, and cotton speculators. A special credit system which was devised by wholesale houses and manufacturers also tied the local merchant up with the nation's banking system.

Goods sold over the counter of the southern general store were nearly all of the cheapest obtainable quality.

Nearly always, customers bought goods with the price uppermost in mind. Getting possession of the article was the primary motive, and eighty per cent of the order notes were written in the form of supplications. Merchants knew this, and they bought stock for their stores accordingly.

Goods were sold customarily at two prices. Cash prices were under those paid for goods charged on the books. Frequently notes came to merchants asking that no book charge be made on an order for goods with the promise to pay in cash within a week or two, and occasionally a landlord would request that his tenant be supplied goods at "high credit prices."

Accounts were closed generally during the months of October, November, and December, and the new books opened in January, February, and March. Accounts were listed just as the purchases were made. At the end of the year the debit entries were added together and an interest charge entered against the total account. The average rate was ten per cent, but a mere statement of the interest rate is only a part of the usury picture. It does not take into consideration either the time element involved or the ultimate interest rate which the customer was forced to pay.

There was an additional interest factor which seldom shows up in store records. When a landlord "stood for" accounts, he often kept either a duplicate record or carried his tenants' charges in his own personal account, and instead of being allowed to settle at the store, the tenant was required to pay the landlord. The tenant was charged both the storekeeper's mark-up and interest costs, and he paid interest to the landlord for taking the risk by "standing for" the account.

The credit system in the South was largely a product of the sore lack of adequate transportation facilities. Perhaps the central theme of all comment on certain of the South's failures was that of diversification of field crops.

Literally hundreds of editorials and special

[Adapted from "The Furnishing and Supply System in Southern Agriculture Since 1865," *The Journal of Southern History*, Vol. 12, No. 1, Gainesville, Fla., 1946. Pp. 24-44. Used by permission.]

feature accounts of poor roads found their way into newspapers. Practically every southern farmer living as much as five miles from a town [confronted] the problem of poor roads every time he hitched his mules to a wagon. What was true of highways was likewise true of railroads and their connections with market centers, and railway freight rates on farm products were so high that often they erased any margin of profit farmers could rightfully expect.

Had transportation and market conditions been different it seems safe to assume, in the light of the facts of business operations and possibilities, that merchants would have welcomed an opportunity to broaden their income basis for their trading areas. There can be little doubt that the fluctuations of cotton production and prices held the same eventual fate for the merchant as for the farmer.

Some merchants made money from their stores. Some of them were able to accumulate a considerable amount of cash savings. Others accumulated little money, but came to own large holdings of land. Most of them were able to build comparatively good homes, but it is doubtful that many of them ever grew rich in the business. When the boll weevil reduced the cotton crop, and when competition of cash stores developed with an expansion of industry, the old line furnishing merchant went into eclipse in the South. His end came only after he had committed countless sins against real southern agricultural progress, and had been properly criticized for it in the newspaper and periodical press, and even in books. But the question remains, what part did the furnishing merchant play? Actually he was never an originator of anything. He was the most direct means by which the lien laws were made to work as a source of credit and banking for his community. His safe bulged with thousands of liens and mortgages. His store was both a source of supply and a market facility. He facilitated the one crop system of agriculture, and as a special agent for the fertilizer companies he sold guano in April to be paid for at high November prices plus an exorbitant profit and interest charge. Also, he helped to channelize enormous amounts of extra-regional capital into the South. [Most] important, he was only a cog in an economic machine which for the South was much larger than the individual influence of merely a simple form of mercantile business.

Even today in the Cotton South some furnishing merchants still do business in ways reminiscent of thirty years ago. But most of them have lost out with the coming of such government agencies as the Farm Security Administration in the 1930's, with the rapid spread of chain stores, which showed what a high mark-up the local merchant had been accustomed to, and with the growing practice on the part of landowners of paying farm laborers in daily wages rather than in a share of the crop.

But there is another important element in the changing rural scene of the Cotton South—namely, farm mechanization. How rapid has this been? What psychological and social factors now favor it? This is the theme of the next selection. To some extent the author of the next selection, Alvin Bertrand, a rural sociologist from Louisiana State University, repeats a little of what Dr. Woofter has discussed in his account of the plantation system of the 1930's, but this repetition gives much-needed emphasis to important points too frequently passed over. We have included two of Dr. Bertrand's footnotes since they explain basic terms for those not versed in some of the social-science vocabulary.

• III • Southern Farm Mechanization in Its Social Setting

ALVIN L. BERTRAND

HISTORICAL BACKGROUND

[The fact is that the] planters of the South generally ignored agricultural machinery many years after mechanization had become common in the North. This lag was related to several factors. Slavery was one of the more important reasons why the early South did not look to technology. The Southern planter of that time was so fully occupied with both slave management and the defense of slavery that he had little time to think of or experiment with new machinery.

W. F. Ogburn's point (in his book *The Social Effects of Aviation*) that an important factor restricting the use of an invention is the existence of a substitute which is available at a lower price or which is simpler or more workable suggests a fourth reason. The presence of an abundant supply of labor undoubtedly retarded the adoption of machinery.

Immigration differentials during the latter part of the 19th century give a clue to another reason why the South lagged behind the North and West in the use of machines. Land-hungry migrants with little cash but new ideas and tools did not find a welcome in the comparatively populated, socially stratified and culturally static South. Consequently, agricultural technology at the production level did not advance far beyond the limited knowledge brought over by the first settlers of this region.

A third reason why the South overlooked mechanization is found in the so-called "factory" system of the plantations. Agricultural endeavors, under this system, are characterized by non-laboring and oft-times non-resident entrepreneurs. It is not difficult to see how a non-laboring farm operator or owner might be slow to experiment with and adopt innovations which did not affect his personal comfort or well-being.

TRADITIONAL INTERACTIONAL PATTERNS

Emerging from the devastation of the Civil War, southern landowners were faced with the problem of getting their lands into production again. At the same time many former slaves were finding their new freedom woefully lacking in the essentials of food and shelter. It was inevitable that the two come to some kind of a working agreement. The system of sharecropping which evolved, following a brief trial of wage labor, has been attributed to both the scarcity of money and a disapproval on the part of the planters to the paying of cash wages. At any rate, the system assured the planter, on the one hand, of a stable supply of labor and the sharecropper, on the other, of a relative security in the furnishing of food, shelter, etc.

Actually the above working agreement represented a truce from the oppositional interaction between planter and laborer developed during the Civil War. The terms of the truce called for a differentiation between groups which reset class lines and again stratified the society as in "antebellum" days. That the system was characterized by wide differentials in standards of living is not surprising. In a stratified society where the masses have no alternative but to gain their livelihood in competition with one another, living standards are bound to vary widely between the upper and lower classes.

With a class system three fields of interaction became possible; between the lower class members, between the upper class members and between the classes. Between lower class members the interaction can be described as a competitive process.

Oppositional interaction between planters, when it was found, can best be described as simple rivalry.

[Adapted from "The Social Processes and Mechanization of Southern Agricultural Systems," *Rural Sociology*, Vol. 13, No. 1, Raleigh, N. C., 1948. Pp. 32-39. Used by permission.]

Inter-class relation, on the other hand, was something entirely different. With land giving them their license, planters, as a rule, felt free to adopt coercive practices in order to control the landless masses.

In summary, it can be said that people connected with the Southern Plantation System, in 1930, were divided into two distinct classes. The ownership of land was concentrated in the upper class and vertical mobility up the agricultural ladder was virtually impossible for the masses. Population pressure and economic dependence made competition a keen process in the lower class, while upper class members were too busy trying to carry on in the face of the depression to worry about labor relations.

THE ROLE OF THE DEPRESSION

The coincidence of our last great depression with the first large scale observance of the machine on the southern fields may lead the casual observer to assign a direct causal relation between the two. No more exercise than a slight review of history proves the error of such an analysis. Though going through many previous periods of hard times the southern scene had retained its familiar one-horse technology intact. It is necessary to hold the fact of the depression as a constant and look for developments which it may have brought about as variables. Two such observations stand out as being characteristic of no previous crisis. They are the unionization, with resulting cooperative action on the part of agricultural workers, and the advent of the AAA with its specific definitions and policies. According to our hypothesis, close scrutiny of these developments should give us the answer to the enigma of why southern planters began mechanization only after 1930.

UNIONIZATION OF SHARECROPPERS RELATED TO MECHANIZATION

The organization, in 1931, of a sharecroppers union in Tallapoosa County, Alabama can be looked upon as the beginning of a series of incidents which changed the relations between "tenant" and landlord and paved the way for mechanization. Never before had

these particular agricultural workers got together in anything like a cooperative organization. Since the first organizers were industrial workers, some reportedly Communist, it seems safe to say that the tenants and laborers themselves respected the existing class interactional patterns (whether because of tradition or fear of upper class retaliation is beside the point) too much to provide the necessary leadership for this kind of organization. At any rate, the speed with which the movement spread pointed out that these lower class members were in a potential state of revolt against the existing order. (Organizers were able, because the prevalent depression brought destitution among the croppers, to stress grievances to good effect. Such things as "tenants" being allowed smaller shares of cotton, less food furnishings, and having to pay exorbitant prices at the plantation store were thoroughly propagandized.) Strangely enough, though the first union's members were all non-white, the later Southern Tenant Farmers Union organized in Poinsett County, Arkansas in 1934 was composed of both races, a precedent seldom set in southern history.

Plantation owners and operators reacted immediately and violently when it became apparent what an organization of their workers could mean. Justifying their action on the grounds that the sharecroppers had violated the sacred precepts of class behavior, some landowners indulged in nearly every type of coercive behavior at their command. Despite all these efforts the unions thrived and managed through their own pressure instruments, strikes, to achieve some of their immediate aims.

This turn-about coercion served notice to all landowners that their labor supply was not assured and furthermore it could and would desert the fields at the most critical times to press any bargain it desired. Only when planters realized that they were unable to rely on traditional interactional patterns to assure them a continuous human labor supply did they begin looking toward the machine as a substitute. And more and more as conflict situations developed between laborer and landowner machinery was substituted for the former. The first part of our hypothesis finds justification in that fact.

THE AAA RELATED TO MECHANIZATION

In answer to the mounting surpluses and stagnant markets which were staring farmers in the face, Congress passed the Agricultural Adjustment Act of 1933. Under this act farmers entered contracts to reduce acreage in specified surplus crops in return for benefit payments, financed chiefly by processing taxes on the commodity concerned. The first cotton contract offer specified that "any producer who is owner, landlord, cash tenant, or managing share tenant and who operates a cotton farm" could be a party to a 1934 and 1935 cotton acreage reduction contract covering his farm. In other words payments were to be made to the farm operator if he could qualify technically as manager.

Since some "tenants" and sharecroppers could qualify as "managing tenants" they were entitled to a pro rata benefit payment for the land taken out of cultivation on their respective plots. Mere laborers, however, had no claim to these payments. Many landlords were quick to realize this difference and to take advantage of it by shifting from sharecropper or "tenant" to cash day labor or mechanized operation. A few, through the "Landlord's Code," were able to abide by the letter of the law with such maneuvers as declaring the tenant "non-managing" if he was "supervised" by a casual riding boss. It is not unfair to say that the "tenant" was left to bear the large share of acreage reduction while the landlord received the major benefits.

Obviously, action of the above sort violated traditional interactional patterns in that planters forsook customary arrangements for the express purpose of profiting at the tenants' expense. When the full significance of his "treatment" dawned on him the tenant was prone to be bitter and uncooperative. This in turn set in motion processes which ended in more displacement of workers by machines. In 1940, only those landowners who had abided by the "meant" conditions of the law

and tenants who had obeyed the traditional class behavior code were operating under a semblance of the old system.

THE WAR AS A CLIMAX

If mechanization was rapidly taking place through the processes just discussed, the coming of the war can be looked upon as the event which capped the climax. A large share of the farm population literally deserted the land. Those who were not being pressed into the armed forces migrated to the industrial centers of the North and West. Thus, the plantations found themselves practically without manpower. As workers became more and more scarce, planters who had mechanized for one reason or another counted themselves very fortunate. On the other hand, landowners who had not turned to technology, in particular those who had lived up to the AAA law and retained their labor supply, found themselves in a predicament. Years of strict compliance with both the letter and the spirit of the law went for naught as the planters who had done most to safeguard the rights of the workers on their lands watched the laborers leave by the thousands at exactly the time they were most needed.

At this point it was impossible to substitute machinery for laborers because the manufacture of agricultural equipment had come to a virtual standstill soon after the National Emergency was declared. Their workers gone, unable to get machinery, and confronted with the relatively favorable situations of their less scrupulous neighbors, such planters resolved never again to be caught in such a dilemma, to free themselves from a dependence upon labor to the highest degree possible.

In this resolve they did and are turning to the relative security of the machine and in so doing are completing the breakdown of old behavior patterns and institutions and creating or adopting new ones. In their turn, sharecroppers, tenants and laborers of the former lower class have had an opportunity to evaluate their previous existence in the light of army travels and industrial "war wages." Neither will be conducive to their return to the areas in the first place, and to the old patterns of interrelationships in the second place.

In conclusion it may be said that the die is cast, the plantation system has or is changing to technology as a result of social processes set in motion by the unionization of agricultural laborers, strengthened by landlord adjustments to the AAA program and brought to a climax by the mass abandonment of the fields by the laborers during World War II.

As mechanization comes to the South, a large pool of potential industrial workers is made available. This, as the following news story will show, is one of the reasons why manufacturing concerns are being attracted to the South. But there are other reasons too. Compare the dramatic account of what is now going on in the Cotton South with Selection 104, which dealt with manufacturing before the Civil War. Such a comparison provides an interesting case study in social change.

· 112 · The Enlightened Revolution

The Old South, the land of cotton, sharecropping and mortgages, is the fastest changing region of the U. S. From the southern Atlantic seaboard west to Arkansas and Louisiana, trim, modern factories have sprung up in the cities, the small towns and the open fields. Since the beginning of World War II, industry has invested billions in the new Southern plants, put 2,000,000 Southerners on new, steady payrolls, and started the dynamics of history's first enlightened industrial revolution.

The big change came with express-train momentum, but it was a long time getting started. The plight of the old Cotton South was well illustrated by Henry Grady, managing editor of the Atlanta *Constitution*. To a Boston audience in 1889, he described the funeral of a "one-gallus" man in Pickens County, Ga. Said Grady:

They cut through solid marble to make his grave, and yet a little tombstone they put above him was from Vermont. They buried him in the heart of a pine forest, and yet the pine coffin was imported from Cincinnati. They buried him within touch of an iron mine, and yet the nails in his coffin and the iron in the shovel that dug his grave were imported from Pittsburgh. They buried him by the side of the best sheep-grazing country on the earth and yet the wool in the coffin bands and the coffin bands themselves were brought from the North. They buried him in a New York coat and a Boston pair of shoes and a pair of breeches from Chicago and a shirt from Cincinnati. The South didn't furnish a thing on earth for that funeral but the corpse and the hole in the ground.

By 1920, the South's industrial revolution had begun—but in the ugly classical pattern that was set a century before in the textile mills of England. Cotton mills moved south to take advantage of hand-to-mouth labor conditions. The "lint-heads," as cotton-mill workers were called, huddled together in drab mill villages, chronically in debt to the company store. They worked a 55- to 60-hour week for around $15 (as compared with a 48- to 54-hour week in New England for about $19).

In the '30s, this classical agony of industrial birth came to a halt. The New Deal put a floor under wages, a ceiling on hours and gave organized labor enough encouragement to worry Southern mill owners. At the same time, U. S. capitalism itself was undergoing

[Adapted from "The South," *Time, the Weekly Newsmagazine*, Vol. 58, No. 24, New York, 1951. Pp. 22, 27. Used by courtesy of *Time*, Copyright Time, Inc., 1951.]

basic changes of attitude and method. More and more industries discovered that well-paid employees did better work and bought a lot more of everybody's products. It is the South's good fortune that the second phase of its industrial expansion comes in a period of enlightened industrial relations unprecedented in history.

What happened in Camden, S. C., is an example of the new kind of industrialization.

By the spring of 1950, a handsome, air-conditioned Du Pont [orlon] plant [began] to operate. Of the 950 employees, about half came from the town, half from the surrounding cotton land. One of the transplanted farmers was Cleatus Threatt, then 25, a World War II veteran whose 65 acres of sandy cotton land were mired in mortgages. One day in May 1950, he was astride his tractor, plowing under a hail-ruined cotton crop, when a friend ran from the neighborhood telephone to tell him that Du Pont had accepted his application for a job. Cleatus had never worked in a factory in his life.

Like most of the South's farmers, he turned out to be good at it. Du Pont put him through a two-month training course, then set him to work as a laboratory technician testing batches of raw materials. In 18 months, he missed only twelve hours of work. His pay climbed from $1 an hour to $1.62 ("I make more now in a week at the plant than I used to make in a month on the farm").

The revolution brought political as well as economic changes to Camden. The town's voters went to the polls and turned out their old-line politicians, voted in an efficient city-manager. Camden's municipal bonds, which had been discounting at 4% and 5%, gained a Class 1 rating: the latest batch discounted at 2%.

Camden's changes have only begun. By mid-1952, Du Pont will complete an additional $25 million expansion of its Orlon plant, and start Camden's spiral whirling again by paying out an additional $7,300,000 a year in wages.

Among the factors in the South's industrial growth are cheap electric power from TVA and private utilities, natural gas piped from Louisiana and Mississippi, and a lowering of Southern freight rates, which used to be much higher than in the Northeast and Midwest.

Industry draws industry. Each new payroll gave the South more money to spend. Northern manufacturers had to decide whether it was cheaper to feed this market by freight or by a new branch plant. An estimated 14% of all U. S. industry now lies in the Southeastern U. S.

Contrary to legend, most of the big corporations which have recently built Southern plants were not primarily searching for cheap labor. Some Southern wages are still lower than Northern, but the gap is sure to narrow. Southern labor offers employers some other, solider advantages. The Southern labor pool is deep. (Mechanical cotton pickers, for instance, and other labor-saving farm machinery are expected to displace 2,000,000 field hands by 1965; many of them will be available for factory work.) The South's labor population is young and quick to learn. Employers who complain that they have to scrape the bottom of the labor barrel in the North find they can pick, choose and train the brightest of young Southerners.

The Southern glad hand has been quick to welcome industrial prospects. In 1936, Mississippi embarked on the "Balance Agriculture with Industry" plan which gave state assistance to local communities so they could build plant facilities. In return, the companies that moved in were supposed to maintain a minimum level of employment for about ten years. Nearly all Southern states borrowed some variation of this technique, or offered special tax reductions to help new factories get going.

Thus far in the revolution, the Negro is still the stepchild, although he is often an indirect beneficiary. Northern corporations, shunning discrimination in their home plants, usually yield to local pressure and restrict Negroes to menial labor. There are notable exceptions. In Memphis, the International Harvester Co. flatly announced that it would hire Negroes without discrimination as to type of job and with equal pay. Out of 2,425 production and maintenance employees, 641 are Negroes.

Industrialization and relative prosperity is stemming the tide of Southerners moving North.

The South's new industry is there to stay.

Part of the revolution described in the preceding selection involves the relationship between management and labor. To what extent is the Southern worker becoming unionized? How successful has been the much-heralded Operation Dixie of the CIO, which set out over three years ago to unionize Southern labor? The author of the next selection points out that today the labor unions are engaged in a "defense of the beachhead." He indicates that "industrial democracy" is an importation to the South and that there are a number of traditional social traits supporting a different type of management-labor relations.

· 113 · The Emergence of Organized Labor

GEORGE C. STONEY

For the past decade the opposing forces of industry and organized labor have spilled dollars, ink, and on occasion even blood in a major campaign for control of the southern worker. At this writing it would seem that labor is fighting a holding operation, its "southern drive" converted to a dogged defense of the beachhead it gained during the early Wagner Act period and the first years of the late war.

This fact—and only a few labor people will question it—is to be regretted, for no one has benefited more from this competition for his loyalties than the southern worker himself.

Mean and unromantic though the struggle be, the economic benefits it has brought to the South are very real.

Those fortunate Yankees who motor to Florida or the Gulf Coast each winter must surely notice the difference—the television aerials on hundreds of small farmhouses north and east of Atlanta; the rows of shiny bicycles outside rickety clapboard schools for Negroes in Mississippi; the remodeled mill villages along the Piedmont range from Danville south through Charlotte and Greenville; the

flashy new store fronts around court house squares in Georgia and Alabama.

In sum, the South in 1951 looks, acts, and feels more like the rest of the United States than at any time in the past century. Most people still cook their beans and collard greens with a slice of salt pork, but now very often that side meat has a good wide streak of lean in it.

Though some mourn lost "charm," the South's new industrial gain is considered good news by most southerners. It should be considered good news by the rest of the country, too. For these thirteen states with roughly a fifth of the nation's population are producing a third of its children, a surplus labor force that—despite remarkable industrialization of the home region—is sending to the North and Middle West millions of new citizens. The annual influx from the South is surpassed in size only by foreign immigration in a few peak years before or just after World War I. What these children have to eat and the way they are educated is obviously of national importance.

McLaughlin and Robock, basing their gen-

[Adapted from "New Opportunity—in a New South," *The Survey*, Vol. 87, No. 4, New York, 1951. Pp. 149-154. Used by permission.]

eralizations on eighty-eight carefully picked case histories, say three main things attract industry to the South: southern markets, southern raw materials, southern labor, in that order of importance.

These findings seem to have surprised almost everyone. For two generations southern leaders had assumed that "cheap, co-operative, native-born labor" was their section's main attraction, and advertised it as such.

McLaughlin and Robock found only a handful of their eighty-eight new plants—those in textiles, garment-making and shoes—were attracted south by the relatively lower wage scales they found. Even the textile and apparel makers seemed resigned to the fact that whatever differential in actual hourly rates of pay they might now enjoy would soon be done away with, leaving them only the differential (one found country-wide) between rates of pay in small towns against those paid in cities.

Why, then, does southern labor still stand as an important attraction to industry and is its unorganized status such a threat to unionized workers in the rest of the country? The most obvious reason is that there is a vast difference between hourly rates of pay and total labor cost per unit of output. In their new southern plants managers seem able to get more production for the dollars they put into pay envelopes. Let's see how this is possible.

The South's high birthrate plus the swift mechanization of agriculture is sending literally millions of new workers into towns who prove more amenable to the new work procedures, increased workloads, the major shifts in what might be called "factory customs" that usually come when a modernized plant is put into operation. This leads to less turnover and lower rates of absenteeism.

It is remarkable, given the widespread popular belief to the contrary, that not one industry studied by the writers of "Why Industry Moves South" had found southern workers less efficient than others and many reported them more efficient, more eager to learn, and—of particular importance—much more willing to work third shifts.

A textile engineer of my acquaintance explained why his chain had decided to open a new plant in South Carolina rather than nearer the main market area:

Land was cheap, he said, allowing them to use the more efficient all-on-one-floor layout. The milder weather made construction a bit cheaper, too. Since most of the workers have cars, the company was able to set their factory down in the middle of the country rather than in or near a town. But the main attraction, he said, was the ease with which they could get people who are willing to work the midnight shift.

Industrial improvements in his line, it would seem, are moving so fast one cannot build a new mill without considering that it may be out-of-date in twelve to fifteen years. So plants are planned for more or less continuous operation. Being able to get labor for a third shift whenever needed without paying a premium would, in itself, make the location of great advantage.

The willingness of young women to spend their nights tending spindles in southern mills has already had a direct effect on work standards in New England, where both managers and union representatives have been forced by southern competition to agree to changes in laws that once protected women from night work in factories.

Until the late 1930's, textiles dominated the Southern industrial picture as completely as cotton and tobacco growing dominated its agriculture. About half the industrial wages earned in the southern states today comes from work in either textile or garment factories. Fortunately, this system of "one crop industry" is changing. In the last decade the expansion of heavy industries paying relatively higher scales of wages has outstripped textile expansion.

Many of these heavy industries have expected that the new employes would be unionized; a few have even encouraged this. Strong and very genuine industrial trade unions exist in the South today in paper-making, rubber, auto assembly, chemicals, and aluminum. They join the strong unions in southern steel and coal that fought their way to recognition in the 1930's.

Few of these new unions could have gained a foothold without extensive financial aid from the North. Most still lean very heavily for direction upon their national organizations.

Ruled by state and local governments who see unionism as a bar to the industrial expansion they desperately need, surrounded by the mass of poor farming people who have the fixed idea that high union wages are responsible for their own low standard of living, plagued by racial difficulties that bring the democratic policies of national unions into dangerous (and easily exploitable) conflict with local customs and beliefs, threatened constantly by the influx of fresh workers from the farms willing to take jobs at almost any price—it is remarkable that these trade unions have made the progress in the South that they have. It is even more remarkable that violence has played such a relatively minor part in their formation.

The situation in textiles is quite different. Here in the South's oldest and still most important industry unions have contracts in fewer than one fifth of the mills, and in many of these their hold is tenuous.

There are good reasons why the CIO unions, in announcing their jointly financed and directed "Operation Dixie," three years ago focused their attention on textiles and have expended most of their effort since that time on this one industry. For in the southern textile situation lies a hard economic lesson for all organized labor.

As long as forty years ago textile manufacturers began moving south out of New England to escape the higher wages and lower work loads being forced upon them there.

With no strong union hold on their main production centers now, textile chains can play non-union plants off against union plants and *vice versa*. Recently, for example, [a certain cotton mill] announced general wage increases in all plants except the one having a union contract. After several months of delay the matter was adjusted, but the union lost its contract the following year. Early in February of this year, when workers threatened to strike the woolen plant of [a firm located]

at Rockville, Connecticut, a notice appeared on the company's bulletin board saying the plant would shut down and move south if work loads equal to those in their southern plants were not accepted.

Until the federal government put a floor under wages with its NRA legislation in the early New Deal days, one found in southern textiles nearly the lowest wages and most appalling living and working conditions in the United States.

The workers the textile plants attracted, again with outstanding exceptions, were people of little education whose childhood on tenant farms or in the back coves of the southern mountains had given them no preparation to fight in an organized way for their own betterment. The custom was to shut them off in mill villages where they continued to live in isolation, a bitter, violent, pitiful group.

Fifteen years of prosperity have made a vast change in this picture. Workers travel in their own cars and live on small farms or in ordinary town neighborhoods.

Given another twenty years of prosperity, the old class distinctions between "mill hands" and other southern wage earners may disappear altogether. Today, however, these class differences remain strong and show themselves clearly in the textile worker's attitude toward himself and his fellows—his lack of self-confidence, his mistrust of his own leaders in dealings with such superior beings as the boss, his preference for leaders that come to him from outside the "mill-hand" group and at the same time his readiness to turn upon that leadership whenever he is cowed.

Sporadic union activity in southern mills has existed for two generations. Every few years long-suffered grievances would erupt into strikes that spread from one mill town to another, often with no reference to immediate causes.

After a period of excitement, a show of solidarity, many bloody brawls and enough shooting to frighten all but the bravest, the orgy would be over. Strikers straggled back through the mill gate, where the foreman waited to blacklist out of employment in his or any other mill in the district the ones he recognized as ring leaders.

Such was the great uprising of the late 1920's, when a handful of Communists were blamed for the months of turmoil around Gastonia and other towns in the Carolina textile strip. Such was the uprising of 1934, with its flying squadrons. Calls would come to a striking group from those still working in the next mill village: "Come pull us out. We want you to shut us down, too." They wanted leadership. They wanted to hit back at the boss. The idea of gaining through unionism a chance to achieve a measure of independence, to gain for themselves as ordinary textile workers a chance to help determine their own destiny and to bear responsibility for their part in it was beyond them.

The strikes of 1937-38 were more solidly based. The CIO had begun the painfully slow process of educating in the fundamentals of trade unionism what textile workers it could reach in this climate notably unhealthy for union organizers. A few contracts were gained.

With the advent of the Wagner Act and the National Labor Relations Board it seemed a new era had come for the textile worker and his union.

Then war-born prosperity, new personnel policies of the larger mills, and those minimum wage laws organized labor itself had fought so hard to get through Congress began to make textile organization even more difficult. The "mill hands" found they were getting better wages and working conditions—as their employers kept informing them pointedly—"without having to pay tribute to any outside union bosses."

Still, grievances did keep popping up and locals were formed. Seemingly realizing the necessity for solid organization rather than emotional outbursts the CIO's textile union leaders set out on a policy of organizing through NLRB elections. Their first few victories brought demands for contracts giving wages and working conditions similar to those won in the northern mills. The industry massed to combat this approach with the same kind of determination

While the textile union was able to win many elections in the mills, the full record shows that this peaceful means of organization brought very few actual contracts into effect. For the election results being legally sanctioned depended ultimately for enforcement not upon strikes but upon the actions of the courts. Court action means delay. While the lawyers squabbled and fenced [pro and con,] the local chapter would have disintegrated, its membership frightened, or disillusioned, or simply fed up. Some hearings were stretched out over a five-year period, and when they eventually reached the U. S. District Court the employers found a remarkably simple solution. They would agree to negotiate, following another election, and the whole round would start over again.

[A recent] report of the Senate's Subcommittee on Labor-Management Relations [clearly] describes textile management's methods of defeating the unions in some detail. It will be sufficient here to say that, despite the still widely scattered ownership prevalent in the industry, methods used by various managements are strikingly similar. Warnings about closing down the mill-if the union wins the election are included in almost uniformly worded letters from the manager to his employes; the same "national religious monthlies" carrying stories about the foreign birth and non-Anglo-Saxon lineage of union leaders appear free of charge in workers' mail boxes; the same pictures of CIO officials dining with Negroes are distributed on handbills; the same law firms are used as consultants in directing both the management's campaign before the elections and in handling whatever Labor Board cases might arise after they are over.

Since the southern textile employers did not give the Senate subcommittee the benefit of testimony, we do not have a similarly documented account of union tactics. It is obvious, however, that the industry group is matching labor's united southern drive with its own.

Industry's view is that the South—and the southern worker—does not want or need unionism and it is going to protect employes from what it considers dues-extortion. The

CIO claims the southern worker is being exploited in the same way that northern workers were before they won union contracts and that they have never been given a chance to make up their own minds about unions, freed from the feudal domination of the boss, the local police, and hostile public opinion.

The unions are not going to cut off their southern drive. Strikes and more strikes can be expected; violence and more violence. The battle will go on between management and labor for America's newest labor market and the South will continue to improve its economic status in the meanwhile.

The New South.

A Changing Social Structure

>>

E conomic forces, as we have already seen, are having great influence in the South today. There are other forces, too, which are altering the older social structure and giving new directions to the dominant social processes. Sociologists use the following three concepts in attempting to understand these forces:

Change. Any alteration of a pre-existing element or complex. Culture change is any alteration of a culture trait or complex; social change refers to an alteration in social relations.

Social forces. The factors involved in a social process; elements that initiate and direct social phenomena. As commonly conceived they include attitudes, appetites, wishes, desires, motives, tendencies, habits, or other items that are assumed to underlie the patterned forms of conduct or to move men to action. Racial prejudices, the love of country, propaganda, scientific research, and so on, are social forces. Five of these were described in the Introduction to this volume.

Social process. The interaction of elements in social change and the transition from one social condition to another.

Probably no one is better qualified to describe the current social changes in the South than Howard W. Odum, of the University of North Carolina, who carried through the pioneering investigations that give much substance to our knowledge of the South today. Odum's *Southern Regions of the United States,* published in 1936, was the outgrowth of years of patient research and represents a landmark in the literature of its kind.

In the article that follows, Odum takes up again the theme of industrial development but then goes on to list other significant social changes. Many of these will be dealt with in greater detail in the remaining selections of this unit.

• 114 • Social Change in the South

HOWARD W. ODUM

For the purposes [before us at present], three main currents of social change in the South will be considered. The first is reflected in the larger area of social and economic changes, including public finance and technological advances. The second has to do with changes that have taken place among the Negroes of the South. The third has to do with changing ideologies and attitudes in the white South.

If we oversimplify our approaches to these three aspects of the South's culture today, we may anticipate our conclusions by noting that, in the first place, the South has changed more rapidly than has the rest of the United States. In the second place there has been an almost complete and revolutionary change in many aspects of Negro life and culture. In the third, except for isolated examples there has been relatively little change in Southern culture with reference to the traditionally Southern bi-racial culture, politics, and inter-regional cooperation, except that temporarily the South appears to have solidified its protest and defense attitudes. These have brought about relatively increased tensions in the structure of the South's total society.

Thus, in our first category, the main changes are comprehended in the following areas: in the increase of wealth and of income; in the rise of the general standard of living with considerable improvement in rural living standards; in urbanization and therefore the bringing about of a better balance between the country and the city; in increased balance between agriculture and industry, and in a balanced agriculture; in increased mechanization of agriculture; in an awakening to the meaning of conserving resources; in great strides in technology, such as research, specialization in manufacturing, transportation, communication, in increase in public works and special public social services; and in increase in public education and public recreation, especially in athletics. Manifestly all these changes reflect an extraordinary transformation in the total Southern economy and culture.

With reference to the Negro, the main changes seem to be in the following areas: a large migration out of the South, and therefore a decreasing ratio of Negro people to the total population; a large migration from the rural South, tending to make the Negro an urban rather than a rural people; a considerable increase in educational opportunities; the rise of a middle and upper class Negro; a rising standard of living; the rise of "the new Negro" and especially a "new" Negro youth; the development of an extraordinarily able Negro leadership; a changing attitude toward segregation; an increase of frustration and aggression; an increase of outside pressures upon the Negro and the South; changes in the Negro worker, especially the woman worker. All these changes, often little known and understood in the South, manifest a significant transformation in race relations and in the ratio of the Negro to the total cultural South.

With reference to the third current of change, namely the ideologies and attitudes of the white South, the story can best be told in terms of reaction and discussion. In general, however, there have been changes somewhat as follows: a freer discussion of all aspects of life and culture with fewer restrictions than formerly; a sharpening of defense and a reinforcing of opposition to changes in segregation practices; an increase in thought and talk about "racism"; revolt against the Supreme Court decisions with reference to voting and higher education and more articulate opposition to federal legislation affecting the South; the still solid South with minor threats of secession from the Democratic party; some progress in southern organization for civil rights; a relatively large number of young college students and returning G. I.'s

[Adapted from "Social Change in the South," *Journal of Politics,* Vol. 10, No. 2, Gainesville, Fla., 1948. Pp. 242-253. Used by permission.]

advocating a more liberal practice with reference to race relations; considerable progress in organized labor advances; strong reaction among the young people who work on farms, in factories, and who operate the trucks and taxis; some recrudescence of the Ku Klux Klan; an ever-increasing pressure from the outside. The net result is reflected in an increasing tension and conflict, affecting all aspects of the South's life and leadership in the nation.

Returning to the assumption that the South is changing more rapidly than the rest of the nation in many of the social-economic aspects of its life and culture, we note that these changes may be measured in several ways. They may be described in terms of absolute gains or losses. They may be measured in terms of relative gains or losses as compared with the rest of the nation. Further comparisons may be made with both the amount of gain or loss and with the rates of change. These may be observed in terms of the South's actual status as compared with the nation, or in terms of the ratio of each measured item's ratio to the South's total, again in comparison with the similar ratio of each item to the Nation's total. Thus, if we look at the situation with reference to urbanization we find that the South started with a low ratio of its population as urban, then increased its urban population more rapidly than the rest of the nation but still has a relatively smaller urban population (in terms of percentages) than the United States as a whole.

Or we may look at certain expenditures for public education. Starting with a low actual expenditure the South's rate of increase is greater than for the nation, as a whole, yet its absolute expenditures still remain far below the nation's average. So, too, the South's expenditure for public education, although constituting a larger ratio of its total public funds than the nation as a whole spends for the same purpose, is still, after its large increase, below the nation's average. Here again, special factors affect the rate of acceleration as in the case of Negro education, in which the South is spending more for Negro education in 1948 than it did for all education a few decades ago.

The nature of the present day trends in the South may be illustrated further by certain specific cases from which it is possible to observe a general pattern of change. Here the South's rate of change is greater than for the rest of the nation, although both its absolute and relative ratio to the total may be smaller. Thus, the estimated population of the three Southern census regions in 1945 was 32.3 per cent of the total for the United States. The total income payments for the same regions were 23.4 per cent, but the percentage increase from 1940 to 1945 was 147 for the South as compared with 116 for the nation. Salaries and wages in the South were 22.3 per cent of the nation's total but the increase for the South was 155 per cent as compared with 125.1 for the nation. The South has 16.9 per cent of total bank deposits representing an increase of 234 per cent, as compared with 142.8 per cent for the nation. In registration of private and commercial automobiles the South has 24.1 per cent, an increase of 2.2 per cent as against a decrease for the nation as a whole of 1.7 per cent. For truck and tractor registrations, the figures were 30.7 and 15 per cent as compared with 9 per cent. In receipts for motor fuel the South's proportion was 38.4 per cent of the total and its increase was 11.1 as compared with a national decrease of 4.5. There were similar large differences in the increase of both private and public telephones, in gross postal receipts and in expenditures for public education. The southern states' ratio for general expenditures for state governments for 1946 was generally greater than for the nation as a whole, including expenditures for education, safety and correction, health, welfare.

These are adequate samplings to indicate trends which are described in more detail in various sources cited. There are other illustrations of changes of a different sort. For instance, there was an increase in the population in four southern states which greatly exceeded the increase for the United States as a whole. This increase manifestly indicated trends due to outside influences which concern the South's relation to the rest of the Nation. In the case of Florida and Virginia there is a clearly measurable flow of population from the Northeast. In Virginia it is an overflow from the District of Columbia and a "pattern of Virginia" appeal. In the case of Florida, it is clearly a case of Florida becoming an "Eastern State" with its winter climate and special urban recreation facilities. In the case of Louisiana, there are Middle America and the Mississippi River, together with the expanded port of New Orleans and the South American hinterlands. In Texas, there was the expansion of war industries and chemical industries and a tendency to become more a part of the West than of the South with an expansion similar to that of the Pacific Northwest's Seattle. These are important trends for the future.

There was thus a trend toward a better balanced culture through the widening range of occupational opportunity, with greater equilibrium between and among agricultural and non-agricultural workers, domestic services and industrial workers, and an increase of social services and scientific workers to approximate a better balance of skilled and trained workers. Alongside these changes, the increase in the population of high school and college students laid the foundation for a continuing increase in the enrollment and growth of higher institutions of learning.

Returning to the second current of social change in the South, there is no doubt that the Negro himself has changed tremendously. It is not only that he has developed important upper and middle classes; it is not only that he has developed a magnificent leadership, and that thousands have taken advantage of higher educational opportunities; it is not only that Negro youth, sensing the epochal spiritual change in racial attitudes and led by Negro leadership of the North and South, is willing to experiment with every type of equal opportunity; it is all this and more.

In *Race and Rumors of Race* we have pointed out how there is a vigorous, lusty enthusiasm and an aggressive attitude and action characteristic of a whole new generation of Negro youth, much of which is as spontaneous and inevitable as would be the growth of the youth of any people.

To those who would face reality, this relatively new and vigorous aggressiveness among young Negroes appears quite natural. In sub-stance, this is what the Negro seems to say:

"We want equal opportunity to live in this the best land in the world. We want a chance to do the best work and to get the best pay. We want to express ourselves fully, and as youth in a youthful race perhaps we are considerably bumptious and noisy. We want the right to travel, to trade, to work without embarrassing segregation laws and customs, and we would like to live anywhere in the community whenever we can make the grade. In more specific instances and cases, we like to go into the drug stores, in the markets, and into other public places as a matter of fact just as other people do; perhaps we want this more because we have not had it, and we are a little immature and naive about it.

"And we like to dream of unreasonable things to be done and ideals to be attained, and we want to do this even as other people do without being considered presumptuous. In the long life line of human beings waiting their turn for service, achievement, privilege, obligation, we want to take our place regularly and not be always slipping back to the end of the line and giving way always to someone else. We are in a transitional stage, boisterous, vocal, unreasonable, and we don't give a damn if we are; we will be heard. We are eager, ambitious, and we got hypnotized with the feeling within ourselves."

There is another major field in which the behavior of Negroes is new as compared with the older southern patterns of work relationships. It is not only that Negroes could earn more money and insist on more pay and larger participation in work of all kinds, with shorter hours and more specialized division of labor. For here the Negro is following a new pattern everywhere. But there is, even among Negroes who have worked long and faithfully in the same fields, a tendency suddenly to change their attitudes and modes of work behavior. Sometimes they don't say much about it. They just change. And sometimes they grumble and just refuse to work in the old way at the old pay. And even though they follow the natural trend, their action results in a critical point of conflict, since it upsets the traditional southern economy of white-Negro work relations.

The greatest over-all change in the Negro South might be described as the development of a high standard of culture and leadership in which achievements in business, literature, art, and education have become commensurate with high standards of culture anywhere. This development is, however, largely unknown and not understood by the white South which continues to discriminate against the Negro by default as well as by intention.

The reflection of the social changes in the South, with reference to traditional southern culture and ideologies, may be measured almost more by reaction within the framework of the other changes than by distinctive changes themselves. In the long run it means that the South in 1948 is a somewhat different South from what it was in the 1920's. The impression, at least superficially, is that there has been an increase in narrow sectionalism as opposed to earlier trends towards interregional arrangements.

During the 1920's and the early 1930's it was commonly assumed that "North" and "South" were no longer valid realities in the new America that was developing, except as they reflected a tragic past which the nation wanted to forget. The First World War had relegated the term "the War," meaning the Civil War, to an outmoded past that took its place alongside other epochs of "only yesterday," or that represented stepping stones on which the nation had already risen to higher things.

Before that, perhaps during the whole of the first third of the twentieth century, there were very substantial trends toward a genuinely realistic reintegration of the South in the nation as, in the regional balance of America, the southern states adopted higher standards of achievement and participated more completely in the total American culture.

There were several reasons for these important trends, perhaps about equally balanced between the regions and the nation as a whole. The leaders of the South had inventoried her resources and her deficiencies and had begun to face the facts in preparation for genuine progress. A new school of historians in the North had rewritten the history of the nation, appraising the South fairly, and had also made realistic diagnosis and criticism of the northern administration after the Civil War. The South had also made extraordinary strides in nearly all phases of its culture and economy. It had developed industry, paved great highways, increased its urban civilization in both the Southeast and the Southwest faster than any other regions. It had pioneered in some aspects of public welfare, public health, and education, and had, with the cooperation and support of the Northeast, strengthened its colleges and universities. It had begun to develop research in both the physical and the social sciences and to apply the results to agriculture and industry, and it was increasing its representation in the national councils of leadership. The South had assumed a new sort of leadership in literature and had become the best documented of all the regions. In all this, the South had liberal cooperation from publishers and educational leaders and philanthropists in the Northeast. And there was pride of achievement not only in the South but in the other regions, particularly in "the Wests," for what the southern regions were doing.

All this was especially marked in the period immediately following the First World War, from 1918 to the early depression years. Then, once again, both the Southeast and the Southwest took larger and more positive part in the affairs of the nation as the Democratic administration developed the New Deal.

Then a strange thing happened, happened twice, once because of the depression New Deal pressure and once because of the pressure of war; namely, a sudden revival of the old sectional conflict and the recrudescence of the terms North and South. It would have been unbelievable if it had not actually happened that this, together with special and intensified revival of the old race conflict, would bring the South to its greatest crisis and the nation again to one of its chief domestic problems since the Civil War.

First, the realistic researches into the resources, deficiencies, and needs of the South, and then the action of the New Deal administration, caused the nation to rediscover the South as a peculiar example of backwardness and later of badness, and to undertake to remake it overnight. The revival of the term "South," in so far as the national administration was concerned and in so far as it began to be used universally by editors and critics, came about in two ways. One was typified in the now famous slogan that the South was the nation's "Economic Problem No. 1." The South was Tobacco Road. It was again missionary territory. But, whatever it was, it was "The South." Secondly, the South came to be synonymous with conservatism or reactionary policies because southern senators and congressmen and state governors and leaders opposed many New Deal policies.

The second intensification of the North-South conflict was brought on by the War, which was expected to unify the nation, and in which the southern states led in enlistment and in all-out support, as a result of the South's racial segregation culture and laws. The nation realized suddenly that the American Dream guaranteed to all its citizens equal rights and opportunities and that while it had gone to war for global democracy, two of its own great regions contained a negation of democracy. It realized further that this negation and this segregation policy applied to the armed forces, because the Army and the Navy and the Air Corps were a part of a white man's world, where the Negro was discriminated against through no fault of his own. And so there was the ever recurring question, "What can be done about the South?" Increasingly, individuals and agencies, private and public, set themselves to the task of "making" the South change. [The] net result was an unbelievable revival of the old bitterness attached to the terms "North" and "South."

It is not possible to estimate how long the present tensions will last or in what direction and at what rates they may continue in the future. At the present time they have a bearing upon all southern achievement and trends, limiting the full extent of economic and industrial development, of educational standards, and of national participation in American life.

Without a doubt, the South is changing, and in some respects changing rapidly. But will the North and the South soon be indistinguishable? Many people of both regions would consider any changes that brought such a result the greatest of misfortunes. However, our regional differences will certainly not disappear entirely, and the increasing similarities in such superficial matters as architecture does not mean that behavior and attitudes are correspondingly similar.

We now move from the area of broad generalizations to the description of a small community, in which the social forces described by Odum can be seen at work.

In the 1940's, social scientists in the Division of Farm Population and Rural Welfare of the U. S. Department of Agriculture decided to study the reasons for stability and instability in American rural communities. They chose six places which were experiencing different degrees of change and observed the daily life in each for a period of several months. Studies were issued for Landaff, N. H., El Cerrito, N. M., Irwin, Iowa, Sublette, Kans., a Pennsylvania Amish community, and Harmony—a Georgia plantation community. It is from the last study that the next selection has been taken. The stress placed upon the social value system affords a key to understanding much about the social structure of any group. Some of these intangibles, or mentifacts, were explained in the preceding selection.

In the heart of the old plantation belt, which stretches across central Georgia from

South Carolina to Alabama, is situated Putnam County. The little community of Harmony, in the northeast part of Putnam County, is composed of approximately 70 families—20 white and 50 Negro. The community extends for about five miles in all directions from its center, at which are located the schools and churches of both the whites and the Negroes. The residences of the white families are scattered, usually about a mile from each other, and near each of them usually live several Negro families.

Harmony is, in truth, two communities with little in common except the understanding that keeps each group to itself and the economic interdependence that requires each to cooperate continuously with the other. Sociologists term a situation of this sort a biracial adjustment, and the community of Harmony provides a good example of its actual functioning. In both communities changes that were set in motion originally by the onslaughts of the boll weevil are being hastened by the pressures of encroaching unbanization and industrialization. As the economy shifts from cotton-growing to dairy farming, the work habits, social relationships, and community structure assume different patterns. Gradually the details of the biracial adjustment will change, but there is little doubt that it will continue to exist for many years to come.

• 115 • The Community Pattern: Harmony, Georgia
WALLER WYNNE

THE COMMUNITY

In the days before the boll weevil, Harmony Community had twice the population it has now, and then its institutions were larger and more numerous. Today, there remains an elementary school and a church for white people; an all-grade school, a church, and a Masonic Lodge for Negroes. Owing to the small number of white children, the community has had difficulty in holding its white school. In fact, the school was closed for several years, and was only recently reopened.

Formerly, the community had some trade services of its own, but now it is entirely dependent upon nearby towns, principally upon Eatonton, the county seat, which is about 8 miles away. To some extent, Madison, the county seat of Morgan County, which adjoins Harmony on the north, serves for trading purposes, and occasionally farmers go about 50 miles to Macon or Athens, the largest cities nearest to the community.

The typical Harmony family is a highly

cooperative unit, and all members of it except the very young contribute to the business of making a living on the farm. The woman's part varies, as between white and Negro families. Generally, white women do only the lighter outdoor tasks such as gardening and caring for poultry but sometimes, usually in emergencies, they help with the milking. Among owner-operators, women almost never do field work; class traditions are against it and the economic status of the family does not require it. Women in white tenant families do not work in the field as a general rule. Negro women, on the other hand, usually work in the field.

Women of the community feel strongly that they should help their husbands earn the family living and they proceed to do it. The wife of one owner said, "I have always thought that a wife should help out all she can, and I have kept some chickens ever since we were married." She contributes to the family income by selling poultry and produce.

Family ties among both white and Negro

[Adapted from *Culture of a Contemporary Rural Community: Harmony, Georgia,* Rural Life Studies, No. 6, Bureau of Agricultural Economics, U. S. Department of Agriculture, Washington, D. C., 1943. Pp. 37-43, 45-51.]

families are strong. Children leave home but their interest in members of their family and their concern for their family's welfare do not perceptibly diminish. Children who live relatively close to their parents visit them rather often; those who live at a distance come less often but usually come at least once a year if circumstances permit.

Children's interest in their parents includes a willingness to help with their support although among white families only a few, if any, are really in need of assistance.

Negro children also are willing to help support their parents. One farmer's children have time and again urged him to give up farming because his health is poor. The earnings of this farmer's children, all but one of whom live in distant cities, are considerably above the average of most Negro sons and daughters in the community. Most Negro children, although willing, cannot contribute to the support of their parents. As a general rule, indigent Negroes are dependent upon public relief.

Among white residents, Harmony Baptist Church is by far the most important institution in the community next to the family, and most families are members of it. A few of the families are Methodists, belonging to a church in an adjoining community, but they sometimes attend the local Baptist church.

People of Harmony are proud of this church, which dates from 1828. The present wooden building was constructed in 1927 after a fire had destroyed the original building. Only a small amount of insurance had been carried, but former residents contributed generously to the rebuilding.

Church services are held one Sunday each month and revival services are held during 1 week each year. For many years the church has been unable to pay for the services of a trained preacher.

Those who had been accustomed to a trained preacher have felt keenly the need for such a person. The present pastor, who lives a considerable distance away, is present in the community only on the day he preaches. One person remarked of the services, "I listen very attentively but I think the while whether I can live through it." Some persons gave the lack of money as the reason the church does not have the type of preacher the members want; the preacher receives $10 each Sunday he preaches. On the other hand, another said that though the people have pride in their church, they are not willing to make the personal sacrifices that would enable them to pay a more highly trained man.

On the Sunday that services are held, the preacher arrives a few minutes before the hour of beginning. He leaves the community shortly after dinner, which he has in the home of one of the church members. The privilege of having the preacher to dinner is not sought after as it was in past years. One woman recalled that formerly a preacher "had to be triplets" to accept his many invitations to dinner. Nowadays the church has to have a committee whose duty it is to find a family that will ask him to dinner. The committee's task is often difficult, for members do not hesitate to say "no" to their request.

Most people are agreed that the church does not have the same hold on the people that it had in years past, and members do not attend church so often as they once did. Several explanations were given for the decline in attendance. One was that people are less religious today, though no one could explain why. The automobile was "blamed" by some: "People go riding instead of going to church." One farmer whose family does not go regularly said that he could not afford to dress as his neighbors do and that he was embarrassed to have people stare at him; another indicated that social differences kept him and his wife at home, though their children attended Sunday School rather regularly; one was critical of the gospel taught at the local church; several said they did not go as often as they should but they could give no reasons.

Among the colored residents the church—Jefferson Baptist Church, the only Negro church in the community—stands first among the formal institutions in the community. Almost all the Negroes join the church at the appropriate age. Some lose their membership through behavior the church does not countenance, because of playing cards for instance, but generally they are readmitted to membership when the Board of Deacons, the governing body of the church, becomes convinced that they have reformed their ways.

Preaching services for the colored people are held one Sunday in every month, prayer meetings are held every Saturday, and Sunday School services every Sunday. Members are required to attend church regularly. If one is absent he must later give a reason, and if he is absent on three consecutive Sundays he is deprived of his membership unless he offers an acceptable reason. Prayer meetings are generally attended only by adults and the older children, but all members of the family go to Sunday School. In addition to its usual services, the church holds, every August, a week of prayer meetings followed by a week of preaching. These events highlight the church year. On the Sunday that closes the 2 weeks of prayer and preaching, people are present from far and wide. These are persons who were born in the community but who have left it to live in other counties, in nearby States, and in distant cities—Chicago, Detroit, New York, and others. Their children who were born outside the community and have never lived there, come too. The old residents have retained membership in the burial society of the church in order to be buried in the churchyard of the community where they were born.

Negroes too are not so interested in their church as they were 50 years ago, according to the Chairman of the Board of Deacons. Then, "folks took a great interest in their church and attended with more regularity than now. They would talk about what the preacher had to say. Nowadays folks can't tell you on Monday what the preacher's text was on the day before." By way of explaining the change he said: "Folks are more sinful than they used to be." He explained this as part of God's plan. "He has a purpose even though we can't understand it." As evidence that folks are more sinful now than in the past, he stated that not so many members take communion now as in the past. According to that church's doctrine, only members without sin may observe the communion rite.

The Harmony Community is served by two schools—one for white children and one for colored. The school for whites is a one-teacher elementary school and has an enrollment of only 11 pupils, 3 of whom live in another community. The teacher does not live here. Harmony children who are of high-school age attend the nearest high school, at Eatonton. They are transported to town by bus at the county's expense, but transportation is not provided for children of grade-school age.

The enrollment at Harmony school has not always been so small. Years ago there were enough pupils to require four teachers, one of them a music teacher. The Harmony school then, older residents declared, was as fine as any in the county.

Opinion was divided on the question of whether schools should be consolidated. Some people hold that "the consolidated school is wrong. It tears down one community to build up another." Such people do not think that the consolidated school offers children a better education or that it is cheaper to operate since the county must provide transportation. Some people, on the other hand, hold that the consolidated school is a fine thing. "I wouldn't send my children to a country school. You have to do justice to children. I took my children out of Harmony school and sent them to Eatonton so they could have a good education. I wouldn't send my children to a teacher that didn't have an A.B. degree." Sampling further: "The consolidated school is progress and it isn't. Children get a better education at the consolidated school but it educates them away from the farm. But if I had children, I would want them to attend." This person recognized what the loss of the school means to the community, declaring: "When you take away the church and school you take the heart out of the community."

The school for colored children combines elementary and high-school subjects. Most of the children are enrolled, and most of them attend regularly. Among the Negro families interviewed, all want their children to have as good schooling as the community affords, but there was not the strong feeling relative to the importance of the school in the community as was found among white residents.

There are no farm organizations in the Harmony Community, and there is only one in the entire county—The Putnam County Farm Board. Only two residents of the community are members of it. Other residents have been invited to become members on several occasions but they have declined because they are unable, for one reason or another, to take a regular part in its activities.

The Putnam County Farm Board is a nonpolitical organization of white farmers and businessmen who have as their goal the improvement of agricultural conditions in the county. Virtually every phase of the farming life of the county is of interest to the Board: Terracing, subsoiling, growing of legumes, planting fruit trees, permanent pastures and pasture improvement, stock improvement, high-producing sires for dairy herds, cow testing, home raising of feed, one-variety cotton planting, etc. Although the Harmony Community has but little representation on the Putnam County Farm Board, residents are highly sympathetic with its objectives.

There is only one cooperative in the county—The Eatonton Cooperative Creamery. It is a mutual, nonprofit, cooperative, processing, purchasing and marketing association, which began operation in 1932. The creamery sells most of its milk—whole milk —on the Atlanta market. Most of the dairymen in the Harmony Community have their milk delivered to the creamery by trucks operated by individuals, as the creamery does not have its own trucks.

When the present cooperative was projected, most dairymen in the community gave it immediate support despite the failure of earlier cooperatives. They think that some organization is necessary if dairying is to be profitable. One dairyman said: "After the last cooperative failed, I said I would never sign again. But I did."

PATTERNS OF INFORMAL ASSOCIATION

Informal cooperation is not now, and never has been, a characteristic of either owners or tenants, whites or Negroes. Exchanging labor, farm tools, and machinery is the exception rather than the rule. This is probably explained by the fact that the plantation system of farming, which existed until fairly recent times, did not require cooperation among farmers, for it was highly self-contained with respect to labor and equipment.

[Although] farmers do not cooperate with one another in carrying on farming activities, they do rally as they have always done, to the aid of one another in times of stress or disaster. Thus, if sickness strikes, neighbors readily lend a willing hand; if a crop is damaged and replanting is necessary, they are ready with equipment and teams and labor if the unfortunate farmer cannot cope with the situation alone.

The pattern of visiting within Harmony Community today contrasts sharply with that of 20 years ago. Then people—both white and colored—visited more often than now. The decrease in the frequency of visiting was attributed partly to a decline in the interest of neighbor in neighbor, but more to "changes of the times."

In the past, white owner families frequently entertained guests, who, without previous invitation, would spend the entire day. Now to visit unannounced is to visit without being welcome although very close friends and relatives are generally welcome at almost any time. The decrease in all-day unplanned visiting was attributed to the fact that families do not have so many servants as they once had and therefore are not prepared to entertain friends on a moment's notice. Only one interviewed family employed more than one servant, and only a few families had even one servant regularly for most families cannot now pay the relatively high wages that servants demand. Spend-the-day guests today are generally persons not from the community but from places rather far away who arrange for the visit in advance.

Commercialized amusement among Negroes is limited to an occasional moving picture in Eatonton. Although children attend more frequently than do their parents they do not go often because of the expense. Only one Negro—an owner—had a radio, but most of the colored people would like to own sets.

LEADERSHIP

There is no well-defined pattern of leadership in the Harmony Community. At the same time, there are evidences of an informal leadership. That is to say, farmers, though they do not recognize an active leadership in the community and apparently think and act independently, are to some extent guided by the opinions and actions of several individuals who are held in high regard by them. In the whole community there is probably not more than one individual who could command the support of the entire community and behind whom the community would unite solidly.

The Negroes of the community are equally without leadership. Until a few years ago, however, there was one man—an owner—who was acknowledged by all as their leader. Since his death, they have not had, and do not now have, a leader, according to the statements of those interviewed.

YOUTH IN THE COMMUNITY

Among the white families there are only a few young people, and there are not more than five single persons between the ages of 16 and 30 years. To appreciate the situation with respect to youth, it is necessary to understand that nearly all children that were born to persons now 50 or more years of age have migrated to the city. Of the few who have remained, only three are farming; the others work in towns or at non-farm occupations.

Most of the children who have migrated had some education beyond high school; many of them had a 4-year college course. Though many of them would probably not have followed farming in any event, all were virtually forced to leave the community because of the lack of opportunities there. The children who left are reported to have been rather successful; one or two have returned to the community, but not for economic reasons.

There are less than 20 white children who are younger than 16 years of age, all of them members of five families.

Among the Negro families there are a good many young people. Many have migrated to urban centers but some of them, particularly the younger ones, have remained in Harmony and have reared children.

Among these youth the most critical problem is the question of economic opportunity. The trend in farm enterprise in Putnam County is away from cotton and toward dairying, but the cultivation of cotton is the one base on which Negro youth can establish themselves as farmers here. The capital requirements for setting up a dairy farm are not within their means, nor, for that matter, within the means of white youth. Several relatively young men who are now establishing, or planning to establish, themselves as dairymen have not acquired capital from their parents nor through farming but have accumulated it over several years by day labor in industrial plants.

Moral standards among Negro youth in the community are apparently higher than they have ever been before. Vice and delinquency and crime are so infrequent as to be minor problems, if even that. There is practically no gambling. The shooting scrapes, very common in the past, are virtually unknown.

VALUE SYSTEM AND ITS SUPPORTING SANCTIONS AND ATTITUDES

Among white farmers two of the most important values that attach to farming as a way of life are: (1) economic security and (2) freedom to manage their own affairs. A farmer may not have any or all of the "luxuries" he would like but "he can always make a living"—enough to eat. Self-sufficiency in that respect is a cardinal principle with every farmer. Each cherishes the freedom to manage his own farm according to his own way. "I am my own boss," is a typical statement.

Security and freedom are not the sole values farmers find in farming. They find enjoyment in it: a good stand of a crop, a fine cow—in those things the farmer finds pleasure and most of the families take pleasure in well-kept yards with flowers and shrubs.

Among Negro farmers, the owner enjoys the same economic security and freedom as the white owners. The renters are their own bosses within obvious limitations, but the croppers have the status of wage hands, despite the fact that they have a share in the crop, and are no more their own masters than are employees of industry. Although neither the renters nor the sharecroppers among the Negroes may be said to have economic security, each does find a certain security in the self-sufficiency he practices.

Although Negro farmers do not value security and freedom of action particularly, they do find satisfaction in farming and attach great value to it. "My glory is turning the earth," one Negro renter said. "I loves to farm, especially when I is encouraged. When my crops come up I got to be in the field day and night seeing 'bout 'em. I likes to see pretty fields all green." Many Negro families take pleasure in having a variety of flowers and potted plants.

The farmers admit certain disadvantages in rural life, but not so many as in the past, and they are not a serious drawback to his enjoyment of farm life. In earlier times the farm families felt keenly their isolation from the outside world. Now they feel this less, or hardly at all. Automobiles, radio sets, daily newspapers, and (just recently when a new system was installed) telephones—all have virtually erased any sense of isolation.

Despite the disadvantages of rural life—which are less for the white farm families than for the colored—few would exchange it for life in the cities. Almost without exception the farmers said that if they had the chance to live their lives again they would select farming as their way of life.

Prominent among the basic "virtues" held in high regard by the farmers is hard work. Most of them have always worked hard. Long hours—from light until dark—were customary. "I used to eat my breakfast at the plow so I could be ready to work when it was light enough. And we worked until you couldn't see. I worked hard." "I was always in the field before it was light and stayed there—except for dinner—until I could hardly see a step ahead of me." These statements are typical.

Not many farmers now work so hard as they did formerly, usually because they are not physically able to work long hours. "People don't work as hard as they used to," one farmer said, and that opinion was expressed by every farmer—white and Negro—without exception.

Farmers expressed a variety of opinions as to why people do not work as hard as they once did. One farmer believed that "the automobile and the fact that there are more things to keep people out late at night" were important reasons, but beyond that he was not [particularly] sure about the explanation. The opinion most generally expressed, however, was that people are not inclined to work hard because they know that the Government will provide for them. But whatever the explanation, all the farmers agreed that the day of hard work from dawn until dark is past. The laborer has breakfast at home and the sun is high before he enters the field; nor can the owner "push" him without running the risk of having him leave. When the sun sets the laborer wants to be not in the field but at the barn.

Farmers are not so thrifty as they were in earlier years, according to general opinion. But even when thrifty, these families were never ones to deny themselves the things that made for as satisfactory and as complete a life as possible, they say. The planter's tradition of a luxurious life was too strong. Not all of the farmers have the planter background, but the philosophy of the planter has conditioned the life of the people to a considerable degree. Thought must be given to the future, but at the same time one must live today. Most farmers have followed and still follow that philosophy. "Money is made round so it will roll," one owner said; one should not squander money, he thought, but one should enjoy life, and therefore he had "never been one to save everything."

According to some people, there has been a marked decline in the habit of saving among these farmers. "Some wear silk that should wear cotton," one owner said. He thought that "various Government programs have encouraged people to spend." This opinion was the one most often given to explain why people are less thrifty now than formerly, but a few thought that "trying to keep up with the other fellow" has been one cause of the changing situation.

These opinions were those of white farmers who were thinking primarily in terms of white people—mostly those living in their own community, but also others within the range of their experience. But the colored people were not entirely excluded from these opinions. Few Negroes, however, have anything to save; most of them are marginal farmers, including renters who own their work stock and equipment. But even among the very few who could save something, however small, there is less inclination to do so now than formerly, according to general opinion. One Negro farmer accumulated more than $1,000 (and later lost it in a bank failure) but he is a rare exception.

Success at farming, informants hold, requires that a farmer not only work hard but that he do his work when it should be done. To neglect plowing a field when the ground is right in order to have some certain pleasure is sure to lead to failure. Farmers have little respect for the man who neglects his work. They do not tolerate tenants who are not steady workers.

White owners in the Harmony neighborhood are highly self-reliant. The success they have achieved has been through their own efforts and by dependence upon themselves. They solve their own problems and they seldom seek advice. Among Negro farmers, the cropper is dependent upon his landlord, and practically every decision with reference to farming is made for him. Renters, on the other hand, have to rely largely upon themselves.

A debt is a matter of honor among these farmers. The ravages of the boll weevil left many in debt, but instead of going into bankruptcy as they might have done, they declined to take that course and eventually paid all their obligations.

"Credit is a good thing, but some abuse it," one farmer said, and his statement is typical of these farmers' attitudes toward going in debt. Indebtedness incurred for a tractor or other farming equipment in order to carry on efficient farm enterprises is considered a perfectly legitimate use of credit, but to buy on credit goods that are not absolutely necessary—household goods, for example—is not considered an appropriate use of credit if the farmer is incurring a debt beyond his capacity to pay. The general practice is to use credit as little as possible.

Negro farmers, in contrast with their white neighbors, have very limited credit facilities and so are unable to incur any considerable debts. Generally speaking, their debts do not extend beyond those incurred for feed and seed loans, for rent, and for "furnish" supplied them. According to their white neighbors, most of them consider indebtedness a solemn obligation and make an honest effort to repay it.

In biracial relationships the patterns of behavior to which Negro and white adhere in the community are essentially those that prevail in other communities of the cotton-growing South. In the realm of customary behavior, the Negroes, for example, address all white adult persons as Mr. or Mrs., or by some title indicative of superior status, as "boss man." Failure to observe this custom would classify a Negro as "uppity," and he would eventually be forced to move from the neighborhood because no farmer would hire him. On the other hand, custom dictates that a white person shall not address a Negro as Mr. or Mrs., and that white and colored people must not shake hands.

Social gatherings of whites and Negroes together are strictly taboo although there are some mixed-group contacts. On special occasions, whites attend functions and funerals at the Negro church. Negroes never attend functions at the white church, but their attendance at funerals of white persons is not uncommon.

In the Old South, society was stratified on lines of class and caste, and this stratification was accepted and firmly fixed. But how have events since the Civil War dealt with this class structure? Has it been revived and maintained on the old lines or has the New South become structured in an entirely different way? In the social scheme of the Old South, the institution of the family was dominant and we have already seen in previous selections how such diverse phases of life as politics, religion, and cotton growing reflected the central position of the Southern family. Has this dominance continued through the years, surviving the upheavals of war and Reconstruction?

For answers to these questions we turn to a book by Francis B. Simkins which traces events in the South from 1820 to the present, emphasizing both the changes that have taken place and the continuity that has persisted from the past.

• 116 • Social Class and the Family in the New South
FRANCIS B. SIMKINS

It is evident that the cream of Southern society was composed of a variety of groups. There was the planter class whose contemporary importance had declined but whose heritage of manners and ideals gave tone to all segments of the upper classes. Added to this section were remnants of the storekeeper group, the lumber barons, the turpentine distillers. Then came the prominent millionaire families, their imitators, and the commercial overseers and their aides. And of course, there were the perennial lawyers and politicians. Supplementing these were doctors, dentists, higher public officials and also army officers whose importance grew as the social functions of government expanded. There were ministers of the Gospel, college professors, and newspaper editors who lent a moral and cultural note to discriminating social groups. A few Negro doctors, ministers, teachers, and business men might be considered in the "ruling" class because of their influence over the Negro masses.

Although the upper classes comprised no more than one-tenth of the Southern people, they formed an aristocracy all their own, and were an integral part of society as a whole. Like the governing classes of England, they adjusted themselves to changes, even receiving talented recruits from the lower orders. Unlike their predecessors of the Old South, these new rulers had no fixed institution to defend. They were either too wise or too practical to make themselves an object of attack by emulating their ancestors who had argued for slavery so strenuously. When they felt obligated to defend their position, they spoke in terms as acceptable to the twentieth century as the pro-slavery argument had been unacceptable to the nineteenth century.

Southerners knew how to make social distinctions—for example, who not to receive in the intimate circle of their homes or clubs. As genuine Americans, however, they did not know how to draw class lines in the cosmopolitan manner. In a society in which so many wore ready-made clothes and owned automobiles, those with exclusive tastes could not dress or ride very differently from others. There were few private schools where children of the upper classes could escape from the social promiscuity of public institutions. The South could not avoid the social confusion so typically American. A friendly critic notes "a feeling of neighborliness, and almost pioneer closeness among the people of all

[Reprinted and adapted from The South Old and New: A History, 1820-1947, by F. B. Simkins, by permission of Alfred A. Knopf, Inc. Copyright 1947 by Alfred A. Knopf, Inc., New York. Pp. 283-295.]

walks of life." The young man or the young woman of anonymous origin could enter the inner circles of society if he or she possessed a requisite amount of charm, good looks, and dancing ability.

Perhaps the most striking characteristic of upper-class Southern society was its almost complete absence of intellectual interests. Leaders of the post-Reconstruction era were Confederate heroes, primitive men whose strength lay in geniality and physical prowess rather than in mental attainments. The next generation of leaders grew up during the cultural famine of war and Reconstruction; some were city-bred with an aristocratic heritage, but the majority sprang from the uncultured yeomanry. Although members of the third generation of leaders were often college-bred, they usually specialized in "campus courses," football, and fraternities. They were induced by editors and professors to support museums and orchestras, but displayed little understanding or enjoyment of these institutions. Theirs was the company of the perpetual Philistines to whom it meant social suicide to discuss intellectual or esthetic subjects. The ladies of the upper classes often attended better colleges than the men and demonstrated little opposition to higher learning. Yet, after graduation, they found more satisfying activities than the pursuit of themes outlined for them in college lecture halls.

Inevitably, such cultural immaturity was reflected in much outright boorishness. Strangers found it difficult to converse with ladies who prattled about their neighbors and were too provincial to discuss topics of general interest. They were disappointed by the soft hands, pink faces, and general corpulence of business men as contrasted to the tanned countenances and lithe figures of the old-time planters. Nor were they prepared to find "hooch" in place of mint julep, the fox trot instead of the Virginia reel, and most of all, perhaps "the grafting of Yankee backslapping upon the normal Southern gentility."

Strangers also discovered that the chivalric code of Southerners meant one set of morals for women, another for men, with much talk about "feminine honor" and "Southern vir-

tue" by those who tolerated a low legal age of consent for illicit relationships. Such shortcomings further indicated the immaturity of the newly rich and the backwardness of the lower classes. The discriminating minority sedulously preserved the aristocratic traditions of good manners and good morals. If money in this society, as elsewhere, was the final arbiter, pride in its possession expressed itself in terms of superior standards inherited from the Old South. Accordingly, impoverished old families could still dictate to the *nouveau riche,* and when a marriage took place between an old and new family, the standards adopted were always those of the old.

To a greater degree than other Americans, Southerners practiced what may be regarded as the essence of good manners: the idea that the outward forms of inherited or imposed ideals should be maintained regardless of what went on behind the scenes. Southern ideals were more extensive and inflexible than those prevailing elsewhere in America. To the rigid code of plantation days was added, in the late nineteenth and early twentieth centuries, the repressions of puritanism imposed by the Protestant clergy, who demanded that the fiddle be silenced and strong drink eschewed "on pain of ruin in this world and damnation in the next." As the land outwardly became more moral, the Southerner expressed his primary love of play and conviviality by "sneaking into the woods with his cards, foregathering with his cronies over a jug behind the barn, slipping away over the river in the nighttime to a cockfight or a breakdown." Although Southerners were among the hardest drinkers in America, one reason they refused to vote for presidential candidate Al Smith in 1928 was because he openly defended drinking. Many critics called this attitude hypocrisy, even deceit; the Southerners, however, insisted upon making a distinction between hedonistic tendencies and long-established ideals. If such evasiveness did not create a perfect code of morals, at least it helped to repress the indecent.

Whether within or without the approved standards of chivalry and puritanism, Southerners have managed to extract the maximum pleasure from the 70 years that have elapsed since Reconstruction. This applied equally to the difficult decades that followed 1865 and the more affluent times of the twentieth century. During the earlier period materials were ingeniously utilized; old jewels, laces, fans and shawls were refurbished; mothers became expert dressmakers and devised refreshments of a simple type. Special stress was placed on the charm and beauty of the Southern girl and an aristocratic self-esteem which blinded the observer to the sound of a creaking floor or the sight of a faded garment. Twentieth-century wealth added material comfort to the social scene, a circumstance that did not necessarily blot out gentility. Some of the social diversions that grew out of these factors survived or developed during the post-bellum period, while others emerged from twentieth-century conditions.

In the decades after the Civil War, the family was the core of Southern society; within its bounds everything worthwhile took place. No one recognized to be a Southerner's social equal dined anywhere other than in his own house or in that of a friend. Good Southern dishes—hot biscuits, fried chicken, custards—could be had only in the home, and the sole type of architecture that appealed was domestic in nature. This absorption in household affairs explains why strangers, unacquainted with Southern home life, found the social scene so dismal. They saw ugly main streets deserted after business hours, and noted an almost complete lack of public entertainment. The hotels were poorly equipped, the restaurants so drab and filthy that they repelled persons of good taste. Southerners who preserved the traditions of comfort and good manners seemed altogether oblivious to these conditions.

After 1910 there were changes in Southern domestic life. Urbanization and industrialization meant an increase in apartment houses, and the abandonment of the family roof by youths seeking the opportunities of a changing economy. The Southerner was frequently lured away from home by the temptation of the automobile and good roads, and became itinerant like other Americans. Hotels became numerous and often achieved the standards of other American public places; restaurants multiplied, and the suburban and rural areas blossomed with community centers given to dancing, dining, and drinking. Public places continued to be almost as backward as in the nineteenth century. In the vast distance between Washington and New Orleans, only with difficulty could the traveler find a restaurant of distinction. The numerous roadhouses were places of bad food, raucous and indiscriminate conviviality, even ruffianism and immorality. They were merely centers of escape for young people tired of the gentility of the home. When these young people married, they joined their elders in losing interest in what happened along the roadside after dark.

There was no significant uprooting of family life. The home in the twentieth century remained the core of a social conservatism fundamentally Southern, still harboring "the tenacious clan loyalty that was so mighty a cohesive force in colonial society." This explains the interminable visits among brothers and sisters, the sheltering of elderly aunts and distant cousins, the care of old family servants, the seeking of favors from relatives in high places, and the tribal conferences whenever a daughter married or a son changed employment. A living symbol of the prevailing domestic stability was the front porch where, in the leisure of the rocking chair, the Southerner endlessly contemplated the past. Here nothing important had happened since the Civil War, except that the screen of trees and banisters had grown more protective.

It was, however, not only the white families of the South who painfully attempted, in the years after the Civil War, to achieve economic security and family unity. And it is not only among the white population that families with roots far back in the antebellum past have occupied places of high social prestige in their communities. Paralleling but quite independent of the new pattern of white social class in the South has been the growth of a pattern of Negro classes. Frequently, as is pointed out below, mulatto families of quite mixed ancestry had already achieved a degree of prominence and economic success before the Civil War, and some of these families have continued to occupy relatively secure and respected positions.

E. Franklin Frazier, the author of the next selection, heads the Department of Sociology at Howard University and has served as president of the American Sociological Society and more recently as chairman of a UNESCO committee studying race relations. Himself a Negro, he has been greatly interested in analyzing the ways in which Negro family life in the United States has changed and developed through the years. He has written authoritatively on the problems of Negro youth and on the Negro family. In the next selection he traces the background of some of the most stable Negro family groups. They form a small minority of Negroes, and in many ways are unlike the less-educated Negro proletariat, but as a group they have played an important part in the difficult passage of their people from slavery to citizenship.

· 117 · The Growth of a Negro Upper Class
E. FRANKLIN FRAZIER

Those elements in the Negro population that have had a foundation of stable family life to build upon have constituted in communities throughout the country an upper social class, more or less isolated from the majority of the population. Up until the first decade of the present century, their numbers were slowly increased by other families that managed to rise, as the favored families in the past, above the condition of the Negro masses. Generally, these families have attempted to maintain standards of conduct and to perpetuate traditions of family life that were alien to the majority of the Negro population. Where they have been few in numbers, they have often shut themselves up within the narrow circle of their own families in order not to be overwhelmed by the flood of immorality and vice surrounding them. In some places they have been numerous enough to create a society of their own in which they could freely pursue their way of life and insure a congenial environment to their children. Often, intensely conscious of their peculiar position with reference to the great mass of the Negro population, they have placed an exaggerated valuation upon moral conduct and cultivated a puritanical restraint in opposition to the free and uncontrolled behavior of the larger Negro world.

In general, homeownership since emancipation offers the best index to the extent and growth of this class of families in the Negro population. By 1890, or a quarter of a century after emancipation, 22 per cent of the families on farms had bought homes; while in the cities and small towns of the country a sixth of the families were living in their own homes. During the next decade homeownership increased slightly in both rural and urban areas; but after 1910 the proportion of farm families owning their homes declined and by 1940 had reached less than 22 per cent. This decline coincided with the rapid urbanization of the Negro and the increase in homeownership in cities. We find in 1940 the highest

[Adapted from *The Negro Family in the United States*, revised and abridged edition, Dryden Press, New York, 1951. Pp. 190-195, 198-205. Used by permission of the University of Chicago Press.]

amount of homeownership among the rural-non-farm families, with one family in three owning its home. Variations in the extent and trend of homeownership during this period can also be observed in the different states.

We shall turn first to . . . two counties in the plantation regions of Alabama and Mississippi, [where] there has been very little farm ownership. In 1910 only 7.5 per cent of the Negro farm families in Issaquena County, Mississippi, owned their homes; while in Macon County, Alabama, where the situation was slightly better, 11.3 per cent were homeowners. However, even in the plantation region where farm ownership is at a minimum, the mulatto families have some advantage over the black families. The family histories of two of the mulatto owners in Macon County will show how they are differentiated culturally in many cases from the majority of landless black tenants.

The head of the first of these families was a mulatto, fifty-eight years old, who was born in an adjoining county. His father, who was born a slave, was the child of a white man. The father managed to accumulate five hundred acres of land which his fifteen children helped him to work. He exchanged this land for land in Macon County a little more than forty years ago in order that his children might be near Tuskegee Institute, though none of them ever atttended that school. The father left his land to his fifteen children, nine girls and six boys. Three of the brothers, including our informant, are still on the land. Our informant, who has been in the present house forty years, is the father of eighteen children. He has kept a careful record of his children's births in a book. Twelve of them were by his first wife, who died in 1919, and the remainder by his second wife, whom he married soon afterward. All the children by his first wife are living, except two who died in infancy. His present wife continues to cook for a white family in which she was employed when she married. Three of the older children are married and live in Montgomery, while the remaining thirteen continue to be a part of the patriarchal household. The family occupies a large well-built four-room house.

The head of this family was the superintendent of the Sunday school connected with the Baptist church in which he has been a deacon "for years." Because of his superior education and position as a landowner in the community, he serves as a clerk-in the church and conducts the prayer meetings.

His farm consists of a hundred and sixty acres, fifty acres of which are in cotton. He owns farm tools, including two sweep stocks, two turn plows, three cotton-planters, and a mowing machine. He also has two mules and four cows which give three gallons of milk a day. His family enjoys a varied diet of beans, peas, peppers, squash, collards, and cabbages from the garden. Though a landowner, he is nevertheless dependent upon the vicissitudes of the agricultural and credit system of the plantation region. Although he "came out even" in 1930, as he remarked, "back debts et us up." The local bank foreclosed on its thousand-dollar mortgage, and he has been making an effort to redeem his land. His two brothers were in the same situation with regard to their holdings.

The history of another family of mixed blood, that owns one hundred and sixty acres and rents four hundred acres of land which is sublet to tenants, will show how the stabilizing of family relations has been bound up with the growth of institutional life among this favored class. The head of this family was born in 1880. According to his story, he was the son of the mulatto daughter of a white man and "a pure Negro excusing him being mixed with Spaniard." Both of his parents were slaves. He was one of ten children and worked for his father until he was twenty-one. He married as soon as he was "emancipated" from the authority of his father. After working six years, he bought the farm in 1907. He attributed his success and desire to have a home to the example set by other colored people, particularly those at Tuskegee.

But we are able to get a further insight into the process by which this family has become stabilized and built up a tradition from other facts in the family history. His grandfather was one of the first deacons in the church which he helped to start right after the Civil War. He explained with considerable pride: "My grandfather was the first one to go there [the church], my father the second, I am the third, my children the fourth and I have some grandchildren who go there which make the fifth generation which practically have been going to that church."

There were seven children in the family, two of whom were boys, twenty-four and eighteen years of age, helping their father on the farm. The oldest daughter was teaching school, while two of her younger sisters were married and living away from home with their husbands. The remaining five children were living at home with their father and a stepmother whom their father had recently married after being a widower for eight years. The house, with its screened windows and rambling rose bushes and vines and potted plants on the porch, stood out in sharp contrast to the hovels inhabited by the multitudes of tenants on the surrounding plantations. Of the six tenant families—three on the rented land and the others on the owned land—five were working "on halves" with an "advance" of ten dollars a month. Although, on the whole, this landowner had been successful, during the previous year he had lost money, while during the current year his tenants for the first time had "come out in the hole."

The well-organized family of a sixty-one-year-old black landowner, who called himself "a pure nigger," shows how, in some cases, those families with a small heritage of stable family traditions and culture create about them communal institutions to maintain and perpetuate their ideals and conceptions of life. When, upon reaching maturity, this man was "emancipated" by his father, he followed the instructions of his father, who had been a slave, and bought his first twenty acres of land. From time to time he added to it, and, with what he received from his father, he owned one hundred and twenty acres in all. He and his wife had been married forty-one years and had an only child, a son, who was born a year after they were married. This son, who was married to a woman with whom he "was raised up," had seven children. Since he was the only child, the mother had

wanted him to remain with his parents; but he had reasoned with her thus: "Mamma, papa went to work and bought him a home and when my children get grown, I want them to see something I have done." So the son acquired a place about a mile away. Nevertheless, he sends his children to the school which, like the community, has been given the name of the family, because his father gave the land for its construction. Although there have been no lodge meetings since the "Mosaics went down," and "community meetings are held mighty seldom," they still get together when they want to "transact any business about just one thing and another for the benefit of the school."

These families are representative of the relatively few families in the plantation area which have managed to forge ahead because of their superior family heritage and thrift. But, like the great mass of Negro tenants, they have been restricted in their development by the plantation system. Their numbers have remained practically stationary in spite of programs encouraging landownership and scientific farming. Individual thrift and a superior social heritage have, in the final analysis, been powerless in the face of the inescapable economic forces inherent in the plantation system. Migration has offered the only escape from the deadening effects of the poverty and the ignorance of the masses of tenants. The decrease, during the decade from 1910 to 1920, in the proportion of mulatto families in Issaquena County, Mississippi, is an indication of this selective migration. On the whole, it is only in those regions outside the plantation area that family life among the rural Negro population has reached a relatively high level of development with the support of an organized community.

The mulattoes in . . . [Hertford County, North Carolina] have shown, until recent years, considerable prejudice toward the blacks with the result that they tended to form separate communities. In two such communities in this county, one taking its name from a mulatto family of free origin and the other from a black family of slave origin, we can see how the rural Negro family has become stabilized under the two very different sets of traditions. Information concerning the origin and history of "Whitetown," (the name of this community, as well as that of the black community, has been changed) the mulatto settlement, was given by the present head of the settlement. Our informant's father, who was born in 1801 and lived within a half-mile of the present settlement, was married twice and had eighteen children in all. The hundred acres of land which he owned were divided among the nine children, who were living at the time of his death. Our informant, who was born in 1853 and has the appearance of a white man, is still active. Although he sold his share for thirty-five dollars, he purchased more land from time to time until he acquired seven hundred acres, the size of the present settlement. The settlement became known by the name of the family around 1860. There was a school in the settlement at the time taught by a member of one of the other mulatto families. Our informant boasted of the fact that, when the "grandfather clause" was passed in order to disfranchise colored voters, he was the only colored man in the near-by town who could vote.

At present there are in the settlement ten children and thirty grandchildren of our informant. His brother, who also lives in the settlement, has six children and one grandchild. Working under the control and direction of the head of the settlement, the children and grandchildren raise cotton, corn, peanuts, peas, and tobacco. In this isolated community with its own school this family has lived for over a century. There has been considerable intermarriage between cousins. They have refused teachers appointed by the county unless they have been very light mulattoes. The family attends a church which was established by a mulatto minister for their benefit. These closely knit families have been kept under the rigorous discipline of the older members and still have scarcely any intercourse with the black people in the county. Seeing these families with their blond and red hair and blue eyes working in the extensive tobacco fields, one would take them for pure Nordic stock.

The other community, composed of black families who boast of pure African ancestry, grew out of a family of five brothers, former slaves, and is known as "Blacktown," after the name of the family. Although the traditions of this community do not go back as far as those of Whitetown, the group has exhibited considerable pride in its heritage and has developed as an exclusive community under the discipline of the oldest male in the family. The founder of the community, the father of our informant, was reared in the house of his master. According to the family tradition the master, "Major Black," was "one of the best white men in the section." Just before he died he called around him all the Blacks, who had taken his name, and said, "I have treated you all right; if I have wronged you, I beg your pardon." The old mansion, which is still standing, is inhabited by the grandson of the major. The paternal relations of slave days are maintained by the grandson and other descendants of the major. When one of the brothers of the original head of the Negro community died, a son of the major came from Norfolk, Virginia, to be present at the funeral.

The boundaries of the present community are practically the same as those of the old plantation, a part of which is rented from the grandson of the major. But most of the land is owned by this Negro family. The oldest of the five brothers was, until his death fifteen years ago, the acknowledged head of the settlement. At present the next oldest brother is recognized as the head of the community. His two sons, one of whom was our informant, have never divided their 138 acres. He and his three brothers, with their children numbering between forty and fifty and their numerous grandchildren, are living in the settlement. Twelve of their children have left the county, and three are living in a near-by town. Our informant left the community thirty-four years ago and worked at hotel work in Boston and as a longshoreman in Philadelphia, but returned after five years away because he was needed by the old folks and longed for the association of his people. One of the sons of the five brothers who founded the settlement is both the teacher of the school and the pastor of the church which serves the needs of the settlement.

These settlements are distinguished from similar clans of blood relatives in the plantation regions of the South by their higher economic status and their deeply rooted patriarchal family traditions. They represent the highest development of a moral order and a sacred society among the rural Negro population. This development has been possible because economic conditions have permitted the germs of culture, which have been picked up by Negro families, to take root and grow. This has been the case with the blacks, as well as with the mulattoes, who, on the whole, have enjoyed superior advantages. Although the mulattoes have less illiteracy, more home-ownership, and comparatively fewer broken families with a woman head, the farm-owners among both classes in this county and the plantation counties as well have a larger number of offspring and more children surviving than the renters and farm laborers in either class. There has been sufficient isolation to shield these families from the disorganizing effects of industrialism and urban life but not enough to produce stagnation. But, as we have observed before, roads and automobiles are gradually destroying the isolation of these regions in the South. Some of the younger generation are venturing into the outside. During 1931 a member of the younger generation in both the black and the mulatto settlements was arrested and punished for transporting illegal liquor.

From these rural communities we turn now to the towns of the South, where amid the shacks and hovels inhabited by the mass of Negro population, a homestead here and there gives evidence of higher aspirations and some heritage of culture. Negroes in the towns and small cities of the South have been constantly drawn from the plantations to work as laborers on road construction, in the mills and the factories, and as domestics in the white families. Usually in these towns and cities there has been a small group of families who have remained segregated from the mass of the Negro population because of their superior economic and cultural status. In some of these communities there has been a single family that has stood out from the mass of the Negro population and endeavored to maintain the standards of family life that were foreign to the masses. A young woman, a teacher, who came from one of these communities tells of the life of her family in a town in Georgia. Her father was the son of a Negro woman and a white man. His white half-sisters became interested in him and helped him to enter one of the Negro colleges established shortly after the Civil War. On her mother's side there had also been some cultural advantages that raised her above the masses of the Negroes. Her maternal grandmother had been a house servant during slavery, and her children were later given instruction by the family that once owned her as a slave. One of these children, her mother, had been encouraged to attend the same school which her father attended. The courtship between her mother and father began while they were in college. Two northern white women, who became interested in her mother and sent her to the Latin High School in Boston, gave her two buildings to start a school in the town of her birth in Georgia. Her father came to teach in the same school and married her mother. The story of her mother's efforts to establish the school and her family's attempts to maintain their own moral standards in the face of the degradation of the masses was related by her as follows:

Our life around M—— was very seclusive. Nowhere to go and nobody to associate with. We were taken away for the summer for vacation to see a little of the world. When my mother first established the school there was quite a bit of opposition. They thought it was at first a Congregational School and they sought to burn it down. She would have to sit up at night with a shawl around her shoulders to watch the buildings going up. Eventually a fire was started but some of the neighbors put it out. After it was erected they kept the children home—they were not going to have any "Congregations" in their families. The people in the community were mostly all Baptists. They said the Congregationalists were not Christians. Although the people there were thrifty and many of them owned their own homes, they had very low moral standards. Our mother and father kept us away from them. It caused hard feelings. We were not allowed to associate with the masses. There was a lot of factories there—canning factories and every child about fourteen years of age had to work. Every year about school time there would be so many illegitimate children born to these girls. My sister and I were the only two girls who didn't work there at the factory.

In the larger cities of the South where these families were more numerous, they were able to create a more congenial environment for their way of life. This was especially true of those cities where there already existed a group of families with several generations of free ancestry and where college communities were located. The development of Negro family life in New Orleans and in Charleston, South Carolina, had its roots among the colored people who were free before the Civil War.

In New Orleans the Civil War and emancipation and consequent industrial and social changes caused the disruption of the free mulatto caste. Many of the free colored people who had themselves been slaveholders were sympathetic toward the confederacy and in some cases participated in the conflict on the side of the South. A review of confederate troops held in New Orleans in 1861 included a regiment of fourteen hundred free colored men. Between the people of this class and the newly emancipated blacks there was little community of interest or sympathy. Some of the members of the free colored caste acquired positions of influence during the Reconstruction Period. One of them was state treasurer from 1868 to 1879. But, when white domination was once more established, the color line was drawn so as to include the former free people of color and their descendants and the former slaves in the same category, and both were subjected on the whole to the same restrictions. Although this brought about some solidarity of interest and feeling between the two classes, many of the descendants of the free colored caste withdrew to themselves, refusing even to send their children to the schools attended by colored people and Negroes of slave ancestry. One of the members of this class wrote concerning the broken morale of his group:

Certain Creoles of our day are reduced to that point of moral impotence that they despise and repulse their kind, even their own parents. Instead of thinking of means of deliverance, they surrender to their weakness, without being able to determine what principles to follow or what resolutions to take, as if they wished to habituate their natures to absolute submission or the obliteration of their individualities. They live in a stage of moral enfeeblement which resembles the last stage of helplessness. In this state of deterioration they not only care little about raising their abased dignity, but they multiply their errors as if to increase their mortification.

The rehabilitation of these families was often effected when they became the leaders of the Negro group or when they intermarried with the ambitious and rising families in the Negro group and mingled their traditions with those of the latter. This was the case with the family of one of the political leaders of the Negroes in the South. Although he was a mulatto, his wife's family, who belonged to the free mulatto caste, objected to their daughter's marrying him because he was a descendant of slaves.

We can get some idea of the outlook of the free mulatto caste from the following excerpt from the family history as related by the daughter:

Upon the death of my grandfather (who was a butcher and had been killed by his slave), my grandmother married an independent tobacco manufacturer. There were twelve children by this second marriage. He and grandma, of whom I have a picture, appear to be white. He looks like an old Confederate soldier. Grandma, when a widow, had refused to marry a man who had fought in the Union Army. She regarded him as responsible for losing her slaves. She consistently refused to salute the American flag. Once when she had to get a passport to go to New Orleans and was ordered to salute the American flag, she spat upon it and put it under her feet. She was not punished for this, either because she was a woman or because she was a beautiful woman. Until her death she regarded Abraham Lincoln as her enemy. Grandma strenuously objected to my father's marrying her daughter because my father was a descendant of slaves. All of her children who are living are now in the white race.

The conflict in traditions and outlook on life was further revealed when the politician wanted their daughter to attend a Negro college and his wife wanted her to enter a convent. As it turned out, the daughter, who married into the colored group and identified herself with them, became a leader of colored women in politics. Her daughter, who was completely identified with Negroes, married a successful businessman who has made a conspicuous success in manufacturing.

In Charleston the cleavage between the mulattoes of free ancestry and the emancipated Negroes, especially those of mixed blood, has never been as wide as in New Orleans. Doubtless . . . there was prejudice against admitting black Negroes into the "charmed circle of aristocracy," as one of the mulattoes referred to her class. But what distinguished these families chiefly from the great mass of the Negro population was not simply their light skins. They took pride in their economic and educational achievements and more especially their culture and purity in family morals.

The emphasis which this class generally placed upon morality in family relations is exemplified in the remark of a member of one of these families that migrated from Charleston to Philadelphia because of an assault during the slavery agitation. In speaking of the attitude of the old Philadelphia families toward the mulatto families from the South, she remarked: "The people there regarded all mulatto women from the South as the illegitimate children of white men, but in the case of our family we could boast of being legitimate."

A brief sketch of the history of one of these old Philadelphia families will throw some light on the origin of the puritanical outlook of this class. The family in question traces its descent from the brother of Absalom Jones, who with Richard Allen organized the Free African Society in 1787. After he broke with Allen, he founded St. Thomas' Protestant Episcopal Church. This pioneer minister's nephew, who was the father of our informant, lived to be ninety-two years of age. As a boy he was bound out, as was customary, to a barber. Later he became the proprietor of three barber shops in the business section of the city and served a select white clientele. Our informant took pride in the fact that his father was one of the founders of the Central Presbyterian Church in 1844 and later wrote its history. He married into one of the old families, one of whose members was appointed to a diplomatic post by the government. There were sixteen children, including our informant. Five of our informant's sisters became schoolteachers, one brother a barber, another a painter, and the remainder went into business. Our informant, who had completed over forty-three years in the Post Office as a clerk, was also the secretary of a building and loan association. He was married to a woman who belonged to one of the old families in New Orleans. They have two daughters who are schoolteachers and a son who is a manufacturing chemist. Our informant still has the eyeglasses which Absalom Jones wore and a chair in his living-room which belonged to his distinguished granduncle.

In other communities of the North where these families have settled they have formed nuclei of family groups that have striven to maintain purity in family morals as well as external forms of respectability. Their numbers have been increased constantly by families that possessed the traditions of the rural families which we have given some account of in this chapter. This small group has been the custodian of the gains which the Negro has made in acquiring culture and civilization. In taking over the manners and morals of the whites, there has been in some instances a disharmony between form and content. But, in most families, insistence upon moral conduct has been supported by genuine sentiment. Where their moral vision has been out of focus and their conscious strivings to attain culture have produced artificiality, this has been the result of their seeing themselves as if in two mirrors. They have seen themselves both in the mirror of their own race, whose ways of life they shunned and disdained, and in the mirror of the white race, in whose image they vainly would have made themselves over. On the whole, these families belong to an age that is past, or before the Negro became a dweller in the modern city.

Religion in the Old South followed the lines of the social classes; thus, the beliefs and practices of the plantation owner and his family were hardly the same as those of his slaves or of the poor whites in the hill counties. On the still-expanding frontier, especially, there was a strong accent on revivalism. Olmsted, in Selection 100, described a revivalistic service he attended in 1853.

For insight into the religion of the New South we make use of a personalized document by Hodding Carter, a newspaperman from Greenville, Miss., who has become a nationally recognized interpreter of Southern attitudes and manners.

• 118 • Faith of Our Fathers
HODDING CARTER

In Tennessee, devout folk still sing praises to the hero of their brush with monkey-minded sons of darkness:

William Jennings Bryan is dead, he died one Sabbath day.
So sweetly was the king asleep, his spirit passed away;
He was at Dayton, Tennessee, defending our dear Lord,
And as soon as his work on earth was done, he went to his reward.
He fought the evolutionists, the infidels and fools
Who are trying to ruin the minds of our children in the schools,
By teaching we came from monkeys and other things absurd

By denying the works of our blessed Lord and God's own holy word.

In Mississippi, Tennessee, and Arkansas, the teaching of evolutionary theories is still technically illegal; and, in the spring of 1948, the University of Arkansas turned down a proposed course which listed the first chapter of Genesis under "Myths of Creation." The camp meeting, brought up to date with loud-speakers and cooling systems, can, in rural Southern localities, outdraw Betty Grable and break even with Jim Folsom, Herman Talmadge, and John Rankin. The political pressures, in certain material directions, of the Baptist and Methodist churches, and to some extent the Presbyterian, are powerful and not uniformly misapplied. New churches con-

[Adapted from *Southern Legacy*, Louisiana State University Press, Baton Rouge, 1950. Pp. 27-37. Used by permission.]

tinue to be built, though it is somewhat more difficult now to fill the pulpits than the pews.

Few Southerners find it easy to look upon these facts with detachment. That thing called the old-time religion is in the blood of most of us, and if it is laughed at, the laughter has as accompaniment an almost inescapable inner, esoteric warning that the ways of God are not to be mocked by man. A little over a century ago, the South of the Scots-Irish farmer and frontiersman was swept by an evangelical flood that submerged the gentlemanly Jeffersonian skepticism and Anglican liberalism, leaving on the Southeastern seaboard alone an isolated high ground of doubt and investigation.

Through the back country rode the indomitable Methodist circuit riders. Rough-tongued men and women were propelled below the surface of rushing rivers and obscure streams by the sanctified hands of self-discovered Baptist preachers, and rose choking, to scream the glory of God and their temporary abnegation of red liquor, eye gouging, and painted Jezebels. This was the Second Awakening, primitive, democratic, and certain, and religious liberalism in the South died before its surge. Victim, too, but of secular and sectional considerations, was the early revivalist concern with the black man's freedom; the Protestant churches of the South became the inspired spokesmen for the institution of slavery, entrenching themselves the more solidly thereby, and Christianity, Northern version, a distorted, satanic misinterpretation of the gospel that doomed the sons of Ham. God had providentially placed the poor, heathen African in the charge of the South. God was on the South's side. It was as simple as that.

"The parties in this conflict are not merely abolitionists and slaveholders," proclaimed the Reverend James Henley Thornwell, Presbyterian divine and president of South Carolina College in 1850. "They are atheists, socialists, communists, red republican jacobins on the one side, and the friends of order and regulated freedom on the other. In one word, the world is the battleground, Christianity and atheism the combatants; and the progress of humanity at stake."

Organized religion in the South became the mighty fortress of the *status quo;* the revival exhorters assumed the dignity and the defense of the ruling classes, uncompromising as ever in their castigation of the sins of the flesh but equally adamant in their justification of man's ownership of man. A Calvinistic God had ordained slavery; those who rebelled against it were in rebellion against God. Narrow fanaticism, strict and literal interpretation of the Bible, defense of the established order and its apostles, orthodoxy discernible even among the anarchical multitude of sects—these were the South's religious answer to the abolitionist, the hell-damned skeptic, the new, restless scientist, and the worldly outsider.

And that, to a lessening and challenged degree, is the religious South's position today.

Yet, it is unfair to so limit the impact of Protestantism upon the South. God was an anthropomorphic Hebraic avenger, with terrible lightning in his eyes, but the Christ child was gentle and forgiving, loving man, loving even the least of these, even the retarded black, God-ordained to be a hewer of wood and drawer of water. A tribal God punished the wrongdoer, but it was the tender Christ who illumined the path of righteousness, who waited beside the still waters, who whispered in the ear of the tempted, who cried out in agony, "Father, forgive them; for they know not what they do."

I know both sides. My family was Presbyterian, not as rigid as the parents of my Baptist and Methodist playmates, for whom dancing and cardplaying were sins only surreptitiously indulged in, but rigid enough and to spare. Sunday school, church, Young People's League, prayer meeting. On Sunday, no funny papers, no movies, no ball games, no profane music. Family prayers every night during a prolific family's summer reunions, with a gay, emancipated aunt at the piano, making ragtime of the gospel hymns, while a horde of cousins, deliciously afraid that God might strike her dead for her rhythmic sacrilege, filled the seashore night with "Shall We Gather at the River," "Beulah Land," and "Stand Up, Stand Up for Jesus." We *knew* God was everywhere. The children's catechism said so. We knew, too, that a still small voice would report to us, and to God, of wrongdoing. And, best of all, we knew that the little Lord Jesus would get us out of trouble if we asked forgiveness. I have never heard a more beautiful phrase than my paternal grandmother's metaphor for the air itself. "God's breath," she said, "it is God's breath." I know, too, that none of us were untouched by the beauty of her faith, by her sureness as to good and evil, in the formative years when consciences grow or wither.

The vengeful tradition persists. Once [I ventured to suggest] editorially that a Holy Roller revival in our town remove itself beyond the city limits because the noise was disturbing to Christians and sinners alike. The participants were handling snakes and white-hot coal-oil-lamp chimneys, getting the shakes and the shouts, and it was not pleasant. So, the next day it was noised around that I was to be denounced in the Unknown Tongue that night. I went to hear it. My Holy Roller friends made certain that their listeners would know who was being denounced. In the middle of the unintelligible jabber-jabber-jabber of the Unknown Tongue, they would occasionally shout my name or that of my newspaper.

Such performances mean religion yet to too many Southerners. Some powerful denominations in Mississippi still conduct state-wide days or hours of prayer whenever the legislature undertakes gingerly to repeal or modify our unavailing liquor laws; but I have not known them to concentrate similarly when forward social legislation is being considered. We have an eighteen-year-old printer's apprentice in my newspaper plant who, in the name of religion, refuses to go to a movie, play cards, dance, or drink even a Coca-Cola. And I know two Protestant ministers to whom inclusion of a rabbi in a ministerial alliance is repugnant because they hold the Jews eternally responsible for the death of Christ.

Tragedy lies in this mean dissipation of the tremendous Southern reservoir of faith.

Fortunately, that tragedy is being increasingly perceived by churchmen and laymen, particularly the younger men and women, and from their awareness comes not only future hope but present action. In seeming contradiction to the constant evidence of misdirected zeal, many churches of the South—Protestant and Catholic alike—are far ahead of their memberships in the areas of social action, which is as it should be and must be. It is not uncommon today for ministers to espouse constitutional rights for Negroes or to bespeak applied Christianity in economic relationships. Some of them pay for their daring. There is much muttering in the South against radical tendencies in the churches, the Federal Council of the Churches of Christ and the YMCA and the YWCA being especial targets, and the spirit of schism is strong. But by the very fact that the minister is still a man apart, ordained by God, his courage and vision can command respect if not emulation. As an example, I can cite the experience of a devoted young clergyman, who less than a year after he came to our town preached a blunt, biting sermon on racial discrimination. He was violently criticized, some members left his congregation, and it was predicted that he would not last a month longer. He is still here and I know that he has won converts.

And where could be found more fertile fields for crusading than the churches of the essentially rural South? There the communal stream runs strong. There, as much as human frailties and human concerns permit, men and women dwell for a short time beyond themselves, seeking refreshment of the spirit, warming themselves in the bright sunlight of the churchyard beneath a brighter if uncomprehended sun. There, fleetingly, they are malleable to good; there the inheritance of ardent faith could pry open the hearts to the words of the preacher who finds his text in Galatians:

"There is neither Jew nor Greek, there is neither bond nor free, there is neither male nor female: for ye are all one in Christ Jesus."

Anyone wishing to understand the South today must know not only about its economy, family life, and religion but also something of its local government. Whereas the
federal agencies spend much time in promoting social change, local government in the
South—and particularly the county government—seems dedicated to resisting change.
The fact that most county officials represent rural constituencies is a partial explanation of
this resistance; another is the continuance of control in the hands of the larger landlords,
who have innumerable political as well as social and economic connections. As we saw in
Selection 107, this was also true of the Old South.

Also an influence, however, was the "populist" movement, which reached into the
South during the 1890's and the years immediately thereafter. The tightly knit control of
the "Bourbons," or privileged aristocratic minority, was shaken to such an extent that
those of less "noble birth" had much more to say about affairs in the Democratic Party.
Then, and periodically since then, "demagogues" arose to voice the discontent of the small
farmers, to play up the race issue with considerable enthusiasm, and to capture control of
various state governments. But such political events, though highly publicized nationally,
have not done much to weaken the hold of "the courthouse clique," in which the voice of
the old-time planter class still has most prestige in the cotton-growing South.

These are important points to bear in mind when reading the following statement
on local government which has been written especially for this volume. John E. Reeves,
a long-time student of this subject, is a member of the Department of Political Science of
the University of Kentucky.

· 119 · Government in a Community of the Cotton South
JOHN E. REEVES

INTRODUCTION

The people of a southern, cotton-growing
community are affected by all levels of government, but it is rural-local government with
which they are most intimately concerned and
for which they are primarily responsible. The
units of government in the rural South consist of county governments, school districts,
and occasionally special districts for drainage
or other specialized purposes. In Louisiana,
the county is called the parish.

The governmental institutions of the
southern cotton-growing community were
brought to this country from Great Britain.
They were adapted to the American scene
and have changed, usually belatedly, to meet
the most insistent demands of a changing
social order, but are still in many respects better suited to a more primitive society. For instance, the system of paying officials by means
of fees (still in effect in most southern jurisdictions for the compensation of such officials
as tax collectors, property assessors, county
clerks, and frequently petty judicial officials)
was well-suited to the time when there was
not enough business to keep officials fully
employed. Again, the area of counties was so
devised as to enable a citizen in the most
remote section of any county to go on horseback or by wagon or carriage to his county
seat, transact his governmental business, and
return to his farm the same day in time to do
his evening milking.

LEGISLATIVE ORGANIZATION

The legislative branch of government is
weak in the county. This results naturally

from the county being primarily an administrative arm of the state, enforcing state law and performing other state functions.

The legislative functions of county government in the Cotton South are performed usually by a county board or fiscal court which is also an administrative board. These governing bodies, by whatever names they may be called, are usually composed of three to nine members and are elected by popular vote, either from the county at large or from districts. In addition to passing a budget, functions of the county board which are legislative in nature are usually confined to (1) providing for certain new functions which the state legislature may make optional at the discretion of the board, and (2) approving land use planning measures which other governmental agencies may wish to put into effect.

OVER-ALL ADMINISTRATIVE ORGANIZATION

The county board, discussed above, is also the chief administrative agency of the county in the Cotton South. It is, however, not an agency which has supervisory authority over all administrative affairs in the county. Many functions may be presided over by independently chosen boards, chief among which are a school board and a health board. Still other functions are performed by popularly elected officials such as a sheriff, tax collector, property assessor, and probably an attorney, coroner, county clerk, and maybe others.

The hydra-headed type of administrative organization in effect in the Southern county is a direct result of the early belief, fostered by Jacksonian democracy, that the more officials elected, the more democratic the government. This belief has persisted despite the fact that practically all of the evidence points to the probability that democratic responsibility and the efficiency of democratic government are reduced by such disjointed organization.

JUDICIAL ORGANIZATION

All civil and criminal cases in the Cotton South are usually tried in the county court

house, the city hall, or in the office of a justice of the peace. Traditionally, the justice of peace court (sometimes referred to as the magistrate's court) was at the base of the judicial system. Although this court still exists in many southern counties, it has been completely abandoned in some of the more enlightened jurisdictions, and functions only to a very slight degree in others.

Next above the justice of the peace court is the county court, sometimes called the probate court. The county court usually has jurisdiction over petty civil and criminal cases, arising anywhere in the county, as well as performing the probate function—i. e., interpreting and enforcing wills, distributing the estates of persons who die intestate (without having drawn a will), and administering estates of deceased persons until the property is allocated to and vests in the heirs or devisees. Generally, too, the judge of this court has charge of all juvenile cases.

Above the county court is the chief trial court of the state. It is generally called the circuit court in the south, but is sometimes known as the superior court or by other title. It has original jurisdiction over all felony cases and over all important civil cases where the sum involved is in excess of a stated amount such as $200 or $300. A district for this court usually includes more than one county with the judge holding court periodically in the court house of each county in his district.

LOCAL POLITICS

Generally those who hold the top official positions in a southern county are beneficiaries of a county political machine affiliated with the Democratic party. The official party organization of the county usually consists of precinct representatives who, on paper, are chosen democratically at "mass" meetings or by secret ballot. However, so few voters participate in these elections that a small group of leaders of the party in the county is nearly always able to determine the choice of precinct representatives, who usually choose a county chairman who is the formal head of the party in the county, but he may be only nominally the head, [because] usually in a rural county ultimate control is lodged in a small group of three to six, some or all of whom hold county offices. By means of patronage and other favors this group can control key figures (rich farmers, country storekeepers and the like) in each precinct, who, by getting out the vote favorable to organization candidates and sometimes by less scrupulous methods, can carry the precinct.

Sometimes county political machines retain power for decades but upheavals are not unknown, particularly if a losing candidate for governor or other high office is backed.

There is often a skeleton Republican organization interested primarily in federal patronage if and when the Republican party wins a presidential election.

The Democratic organization in a rural county is likely to lean to the Dixiecrat point of view. Until recently Negroes have been barred from the ballot both by statutory means and by intimidation. They are still not voting in large numbers.

ADMINISTRATIVE FUNCTIONS

Financial Administration. One of the most important phases of public administration in a southern cotton-growing county is the administration of county finances. The county board is usually responsible for certain functions of financial administration. In addition to passing the budget, which is a legislative function, the board approves all expenditures, establishes salaries, and either directly or through a treasurer makes arrangements for the deposit of funds and the securing of loans.

In any particular southern county, it is almost certain that the county board will not have full authority in relation to finances, since the assessment of property and collection of taxes are usually the responsibility of independently-elected officials. It is in the assessment of property that the worst abuses occur. [As might be expected,] it is usually the rich and politically powerful who are favored. At present there is a concerted effort on the part of state officials in some of the southern states to improve the situation.

Law Enforcement. The enforcement of the criminal law of the state is one of the oldest functions of the county—it is, indeed, as old as the county itself. The southern rural county's law enforcement machinery is still literally the same as in seventeenth century England. The sheriff is the chief police officer of the county, but he has many other duties as well. He is always charged with certain duties in relation to the court and he or one of his deputies must be in attendance at all sessions to wait on the jury, execute and serve writs and other processes, summon witnesses and the like. In most states he is given still other duties—being tax collector in some instances, jailer in others, and county librarian in at least one. The only other local law enforcement official typical of the rural south is the constable and he is rapidly disappearing from the scene.

While the local organization for rural law enforcement has remained the same, the problem has changed drastically. [The] automobile has made it possible for the professional criminal to transfer his operations to the small town, the open country, and the crossroads village, while making the big city his hideout.

The growth of rural law enforcement problems has brought about the establishment of state police forces in some states, and in certain others the highway patrol has general police power in rural areas.

Record Keeping and License Issuing. A county official, frequently the county clerk, is responsible for keeping all records of deeds, mortgages and the like. The same official usually issues various kinds of licenses such as marriage, automobile, hunting, and certain types of business licenses.

Highway Administration. Local roads leading to the county seat, and feeding into through highways, have been the responsibility of county government in the South for many years.

The coming of the automobile brought both the state and the federal government into the through highway field, and required the county to tax its property owners and begin road maintenance and construction in earnest. In recent years the county has received considerable funds from the state to be used on local highways and several of the southern states have inaugurated local or rural highway programs of their own.

Educational Administration. Although in the rural South the modern tendency is to think in terms of the county school system, and more frequently than not there is a county school superintendent with an office in the court house, actually the county government as such is not responsible for school administration. Formerly the superintendent was elected by popular vote and the tax rate and a few other policy matters were determined by a school board. Now, more frequently, the superintendent is chosen by the board which constitutes the governing body of a separate governmental unit—the county school district. Nevertheless, public education is one of the most important, if not the most important, governmental function performed by local officials and employees in the southern county. [The recent Supreme Court decision on school integration has enormously increased its importance.]

Health Administration. Public health work is one of the newer functions of county government, but a rapidly growing one; it is also a field in which both the state and federal governments are particularly active. It is usually optional with the county as to whether it will establish a health program, but if it does it must operate strictly according to state law. In general there are two types of county health organization: (1) a county board of health and a part-time health officer; and (2) a county health board with a full-time health department, under the general supervision of the board. Obviously the first type cannot operate very efficiently. The physician with a private practice who acts as part-time health officer cannot be expected to do more than make routine investigations, enforce sanitation laws, and enforce quarantine if declared by the board or state health authorities. Full-time health departments operate in a majority of the southern counties at present.

Public health work is financed by the local units of government, the state, the federal government, and by grants from such private organizations as the Rockefeller Foundation.

State supervision is exercised over local health work to a greater degree than any other local function. The selection of personnel is subject to state approval and the state department of health usually plans, coordinates and directs the work of the local department to such an extent that it is in effect a branch office of the state department. The recent growth and relative efficiency of health work may give the defenders of "local democracy" reason to ponder.

Welfare Administration. Traditionally the county was the one unit of government in the South which was universally responsible for public welfare administration. Until recently, however, it confined its functions to operating an almshouse for the aged poor, granting niggardly sums to the desperately poor and perhaps granting specified sums at regular intervals to certain classes of indigents such as pauper idiots and to mothers of dependent children. The work has usually been carried on by the county board itself or by a superintendent of the poor, acting also as the keeper of the almshouse.

The county almshouses are generally recognized as unsatisfactory, and Virginia has led the way in establishing district homes for the aged. The federal system of social security may make the almshouse unnecessary in the future. It is almost certain to make one for each county still more undesirable.

Agricultural Extension Work and Soil Conservation. The Federal Smith-Lever Act of 1914 provided for a system of grants-in-aid to the states for the promotion of extension work in agriculture and home economics. Under its provisions, county agricultural agents and home demonstration agents have been established in most cotton-growing counties. The county agent has made a real place for himself among southern farmers. The home demonstration agents have also established a solid reputation with farm housekeepers.

The Agricultural Adjustment Administration has an office in each county which supervises allotment control under the Federal Agricultural Production and Marketing Administration. This office works closely with agricultural agents in assisting the farmer to secure needed fertilizers and in other ways. It is through the Agricultural Production and Marketing Administration that farmers are compensated for staying within the allotted quotas of production.

The Federal Soil Conservation Service has a conservation officer with headquarters in each state and district offices at various places in the state.

Great emphasis has been given to soil conservation in the Tennessee Valley states by the T.V.A., with its manufacture of fertilizer, its reforestation program and its emphasis on prevention of soil erosion and silting.

SUMMARY

In conclusion it may be said that county government performs many important functions for a southern cotton growing community. Among the functions performed by the county are county road construction and maintenance, public health and welfare work, record keeping and license issuing, the administration of petty justice, and agricultural extension and soil conservation work. Education is the function of a separate unit of government. County functions are usually performed by outmoded governmental machinery.

Although all Americans are concerned with the problem of the relationship between Negroes and whites, and many thoughtful and useful studies of the problem have been made, it is impossible to find a common area of agreement on the subject among Americans. We are too easily caught up in a conflict between ideals and realities, between traditions and events, and few of us can be sufficiently detached to consider the question without letting personal feelings enter in. Hoping to get a fair, unbiased survey of the position of the Negro in the present-day life of the United States, the Carnegie Corporation, in 1937, asked the distinguished Swedish social economist Gunnar Myrdal to direct a comprehensive study. Aided by a large group of able researchers, Myrdal left no aspect of the subject untouched. The work was not finished until the end of 1942, and when it appeared in print it was recognized as one of the most controversial books of its time.

Myrdal and his associates have dealt with the United States as a whole, since the Negro's place in a democratic country is a national problem and not a local one. In many ways the situation is more acute in the South, but basically there are few differences except in degree and in detail between one section of the country and another. Therefore, it seems appropriate to depart, in the following selection, from the focus we have maintained on the South and consider the Negro problem for America as a whole.

The conclusion reached by Myrdal can be summed up briefly. He sees the Negro problem as a dilemma between the democratic beliefs held by all Americans and the undemocratic treatment accorded the Negro. He makes no sweeping accusations and provides no simple solutions. Instead, he patiently explores each aspect of American life— jobs, living conditions, law enforcement, schooling, recreation, and so on—determining what Americans do and what they believe should be done, and then examines how the treatment and position of the Negro differ from the treatment and position of other Americans. Most of us are aware of some of the unpleasant aspects of Negro-white relations, and it is often easy to see how specific arrangements and habits have grown and become firmly rooted in American life. What is more difficult is to see the entire dilemma from a distant perspective, undistorted by opinions or prejudices.

In the following selection only a few of the topics covered in nearly 1500 pages can be touched on—and these briefly. Included here are parts of Myrdal's discussion of segregation in housing, of discrimination in economic opportunity and legal treatment, all of them crucial matters in the country as a whole, as well as the South. One of the most complex subjects, caste and class, is dealt with extensively in Myrdal's volume but is omitted here for lack of space. Myrdal found that Negroes in America form a lower caste, which they can never leave, and in which they suffer certain disadvantages regardless of individual ability. This is the nature of a "caste system" in any part of the world. Also, although Americans are often hesitant to realize it, we have a class system, in which every individual is expected to have the opportunity to climb to a higher level. Negroes, however, can climb only within a separate series of Negro classes, since competition for social prestige or status never occurs across the line dividing our castes. Actually, few Negroes are able to rise to the "middle" class level and almost none to the "upper" class, since wealth, education, approved occupations, and the other marks of middle and upper class membership are particularly difficult for them to achieve.

Myrdal concludes his volume with a note of hope that the relations between Negro and white in America will continue to show the lessened friction and increased tolerance that he noted during the beginning of World War II. But he also ends with the sobering warning that the entire world is watching our attempt to resolve this dilemma, for the world is looking to us for leadership in world affairs.

. . . The great reason for hope is that this country has a national experience in uniting racial and cultural diversities and a national theory, if not a consistent practice, of freedom and equality for all. . . . If America in actual practice could show the world a progressive trend by which the Negro became finally integrated into modern democracy, all mankind . . . would have reason to believe that peace, progress and order are feasible. And America would have a spiritual power many times stronger than all her financial and military resources—the power of the trust and support of all good people on earth.

• 120 • *The Dilemma of the American Negro*
GUNNAR MYRDAL

MINORITY PROBLEMS AND THE NEGRO PROBLEM

For some decades there has been a tendency to incorporate the American Negro problem into the broader American minority problem. In the United States, the term "minority people" has a connotation different from that in other parts of the world and especially in Central and Eastern Europe, where minority problems have existed. This difference in problem is due to a difference in situation. The minority peoples of the United States are fighting for status in the larger society; the minorities of Europe are mainly fighting for independence from it. In the United States

[Adapted from *An American Dilemma: The Negro Problem and Modern Democracy*, Harper and Bros., New York, 1944. Pp. 50-58, 380-383, 391-392, 394-396, 523-526, 560-561, 565, 586-588, 599-604, 644-647, 650-662. Used by permission.]

the so-called minority groups as they exist today—except the Indians and Negroes—are mostly the result of a relatively recent immigration, which it was for a long time the established policy to welcome as a nationally advantageous means of populating and cultivating the country. The newcomers themselves were bent upon giving up their language and other cultural heritages and acquiring the ways and attitudes of the new nation. There have been degrees of friction and delay in this assimilation process, and even a partial conscious resistance by certain immigrant groups. But these elements of friction and resistance are really only of a character and magnitude to bring into relief the fundamental difference between the typical American minority problems and those in, say, the old Austrian Empire. Of greatest importance, finally, is the fact that the official political creed of America denounced, in general but vigorous terms, all forms of suppression and discrimination, and affirmed human equality.

From the viewpoint of the struggling immigrant himself, the harsh class structure, which thrust him to the bottom of the social heap, did not seem to be a rigid social determinant. In two or three generations, if not in one, the immigrant and his descendants moved into, and identified themselves with, the dominant American group, and—with luck and ability—took their position in the higher strata. The causal mechanism of this social process has been aptly described as a continuous "push upwards" by a steady stream of new masses of toiling immigrants filling the ranks of the lower social strata. The class structure remained, therefore, fairly stable, while millions of individuals were continuously climbing the social ladder which it constituted. The unceasing process of social mobility and the prospect of its continuation, and also the established Creed of America promising and sanctioning social mobility, together with many other factors of importance, kept the minority groups contented and bent on assimilation.

In trying to reconcile conflicting valuations the ordinary American apparently is inclined to believe that, as generations pass on, the remaining minority groups—with certain distinct exceptions which will presently be discussed—will be assimilated into a homogeneous nation. The American Creed is at least partially responsible for this, as well as for the American's inclination to deem this assimilation desirable. Of course, this view is also based on the memories of previous absorption of minority groups into a dominant "American" population. Even the American Indians are now considered as ultimately assimilable.

In spite of all race prejudice, few Americans seem to doubt that it is the ultimate fate of this nation to incorporate without distinction not only all the Northern European stocks, but also the people from Eastern and Southern Europe, the Near East and Mexico. They see obstacles; they emphasize the religious and "racial" differences; they believe it will take a long time. But they assume that it is going to happen, and do not have, on the whole, strong objections to it—provided it is located in a distant future.

The Negroes, on the other hand, are commonly assumed to be unassimilable and this is the reason why the characterization of the Negro problem as a minority problem does not exhaust its true import. The Negroes are set apart, together with other colored peoples, principally the Chinese and the Japanese. Considerable efforts are directed toward "Americanizing" all groups of alien origin. But in regard to the colored peoples, the American policy is the reverse. They are excluded from assimilation. Even by their best friends in the dominant white group and by the promoters of racial peace and good-will, they are usually advised to keep to themselves and develop a race pride of their own.

To the ordinary white American the caste line between whites and Negroes is based upon, and defended by, the anti-amalgamation doctrine. This doctrine, more than anything else, gives the Negro problem its uniqueness among other problems of lower status groups, not only in terms of intensity of feelings but more fundamentally in the character of the problem. We follow a general methodological principle, presented previously, when we now start out from the ordinary white man's notion of what constitutes the heart of the Negro problem.

When the Negro people, unlike the white minority groups, is commonly characterized as unassimilable, it is not, of course, implied that amalgamation is not biologically possible. But crossbreeding is considered undesirable. Sometimes the view is expressed that the offspring of crossbreeding is inferior to both parental stocks. Usually it is only asserted that it is inferior to the "pure" white stock. The assumption evidently held is that the Negro stock is "inferior" to the white stock. On the inherited inferiority of the Negro people there exists among white Americans a whole folklore, which is remarkably similar throughout the country.

A remarkable and hardly expected peculiarity of this American doctrine, expounded so directly in biological and racial terms, is that it is applied with a vast discretion depending upon the purely social and legal circumstances under which miscegenation takes place. [But] in many regions, especially in the South where the prohibition against intermarriage and the general reprehension against miscegenation have the strongest moorings, illicit relations have been widespread and occasionally allowed to acquire a nearly institutional character. Even if . . . such relations are perhaps now on the decline, they are still not entirely stamped out.

If we now turn to the American Negro people, we can hardly avoid the strong impression that what there is of reluctance in principle toward amalgamation is merely in the nature of a reaction or response to the white doctrine, which thus stands as primary in the causal sense and strategic in a practical sense. It is true that white people, when facing the Negro group, make an ideological application of the general Jim Crow principle —"equal but separate" treatment and accommodations for the two racial groups—and proceed from the assertion that both races are good to the explanation that there is a value in keeping them unmixed. They appeal also to the Negroes' "race pride" and their interest in keeping their own blood "pure." But this is a white, not a Negro, argument. [Moreover, there is still the fact] that the large majority of American Negroes actually are of mixed descent. They already have white and Indian ancestry as well as African Negro blood. And in general they are aware of this fact.

Every widening of the writer's experience of white Americans has only driven home to him more strongly that the opinion that the Negro is unassimilable, or, rather, that his amalgamation into the American nation is undesirable, is held more commonly, absolutely, and intensely than would be assumed from a general knowledge of American thought-ways.

The intensity of the attitude seems to be markedly stronger in the South than in the North. Its strength seems generally to be inversely related to the economic and social status of the informant and his educational level. It is usually strong even in most of the non-colored minority groups, if they are above the lowest plane of indifference. To the poor and socially insecure, but struggling, white individual, a fixed opinion on this point seems an important matter of prestige and distinction.

This attitude of refusing to consider amalgamation—felt and expressed in the entire country—constitutes the center in the complex of attitudes which can be described as the "common denominator" in the problem. It defines the Negro group in contradistinction to all the non-colored minority groups in America and all other lower class groups. The boundary between Negro and white is not simply a class line which can be successfully crossed by education, integration into the national culture, and individual economic advancement. The boundary is fixed. It is not a temporary expediency during an apprenticeship in the national culture. It is a bar erected with the intention of permanency. It is directed against the whole group. Actually, however, "passing" as a white person is possible when a Negro is white enough to conceal his Negro heritage. But the difference between "passing" and ordinary social climbing reveals the distinction between a class line, in the ordinary sense, and a caste line.

This theory of color caste centering around the aversion to amalgamation determines, as we have just observed, the white man's rather definite rank order of the various measures of segregation and discrimination against Negroes. The relative significance attached to each of those measures is dependent upon their degree of expediency or necessity—in the view of white people—as means of upholding the ban on "intermarriage." In this rank order, (1) the ban on intermarriage and other sex relations involving white women and colored men takes precedence before anything else. It is the end for which the other restrictions are arranged as means. Thereafter follow: (2) all sorts of taboos and etiquettes in personal contacts; (3) segregation in schools and churches; (4) segregation in hotels, restaurants, and theaters, and other public places where people meet socially; (5) segregation in public conveyances; (6) discrimination in public services; and finally, inequality in (7) politics, (8) justice and (9) breadwinning and relief.

SOCIAL SEGREGATION AND DISCRIMINATION

Even in the realm of social relations it is of importance that the average Northerner does not think of the Negroes as former slaves. He has not the possessive feeling for them and he does not regard their subservience as a mark of his own social status. He is, therefore, likely to let the Negroes alone unless in his opinion they get to be a nuisance. Upon the ideological plane the ordinary Northerner is, further, apparently conscious that social discrimination is wrong and against the American Creed, while the average Southerner tries to convince himself and the nation that it is right or, in any case, that it is necessary. The white newspapers in the North ordinarily ignore the Negroes and their problems entirely—most of the time more completely than the liberal Southern press. But when they have to come out in the open on the Negro problem, they usually stand for equality. Back of this official attitude, of course, is the fact that most Northerners are

not in direct contact with Negroes. The patterns of social discrimination in the South have originally formed themselves as rural ways of life. In the North the rural sections are, and have always been, practically free of Negroes. Even in the big cities in the North, where there are substantial Negro populations, only a small part of the white population has more contacts with Negroes.

Lacking ideological sanction and developing directly contrary to the openly accepted equalitarian Creed, social segregation and discrimination in the North have to keep *sub rosa*. The observer finds that *in the North there is actually much unawareness on the part of white people of the extent of social discrimination against Negroes*. It denotes the absence of an explicit theory and an intentional policy. In this situation *one of the main difficulties for the Negroes in the North is simply lack of publicity*. It is convenient for the Northerners' good conscience to forget about the Negro.

In so far as the Negroes can get their claims voiced in the press and in legislatures, and are able to put political strength behind them, they are free to press for state action against social discrimination. The chances are that they will meet no *open* opposition.

With the ideological and legal sanctions directed *against* them, social segregation and discrimination have not acquired the *strength, persuasiveness or institutional fixity* found in the South. Actual discrimination varies a good deal in the North: it seems to be mainly a function of the relative number of Negroes in a community and its distance from the South. In several minor cities in New England with a small, stable Negro population, for instance, social discrimination is hardly noticeable.

In the bigger cities, even in New England, the conditions of life for the Negroes have probably never been so idyllic. Since the migration beginning in 1915, the status of Northern Negroes has fallen perceptibly. In the Northern cities nearer the Mason-Dixon line there has always been, and is even today, more social segregation and discrimination than farther North.

One factor which in every Northern city of any size has contributed to form patterns of segregation and discrimination against Negroes has been residential segregation, which acts as a cause as well as an effect of social distance. With residential segregation naturally comes a certain amount of segregation in schools, in hospitals, and in other public places even when it is not intended as part of policy. Personal contacts become, as a matter of course, more or less restricted to Negro neighborhoods. As the Negro sections grew during the northward migration, it became more and more possible for Negroes to have their entire social life in Negro neighborhoods, and white people became conditioned to look upon this as a natural and desirable situation. In this process white Southerners who also moved northward have played a crucial role. To make a manager of a hotel, a restaurant, or a theater interested in trying to keep Negroes out of his establishment, it is not necessary that more than a tiny majority of customers object, particularly if they make a [noticeable] scene. The fact that most Negroes are poor and residentially isolated and, hence, do not patronize white places often, and the further fact that upper class Negroes, who could afford to, abstain voluntarily from visiting places where they are afraid of being embarrassed, solidifies the situation. [The result is that] they abstain from going to places where they actually could go without any trouble. When once this pattern is set by themselves the result might later be discrimination when some Negro tries to break it.

The migrating Negroes have probably been even more influential in spreading Southern patterns in the North than the Southern whites. The low cultural level and poverty of the average Southern Negro stand out even more when he comes North, where general standards are higher. If he comes without any other education, he is at least thoroughly trained in the entire ceremonial system of scraping his foot, tipping his hat, and using self-abasing vocabulary and dialect, and generally being subservient and unobtrusive in the company of whites. [Hence] he will invoke discrimination by his own behavior. The submissive behavior of lower class Southern Negroes is usually not appealing at all to the white Northerner, who has not been brought up to have a patronizing attitude and who does not need it for his own self-elevation.

Even the poor classes of whites in the North come to mistrust and despise the Negroes. The European immigrant groups are the ones thrown into most direct contact and competition with Negroes: they live near each other, often send their children to the same schools, and have to struggle for the same jobs. Obviously attitudes among immigrants vary a good deal. Recent immigrants apparently sometimes feel an interest solidarity with Negroes or, at any rate, lack the intense superiority feeling of the native Americans educated in race prejudice. But the development of prejudice against Negroes is usually one of their first lessons in Americanization. Because they are of low status, they like to have a group like the Negroes to which they can be superior.

I have an impression that the resentment against Negroes in the North is different from that in the South, not only in intensity, but also in its class direction. It does not seem to be directed particularly against the rising Negroes. In the more anonymous Northern cities, the Negro middle and upper classes do not get into the focus of public resentment as in the South. More important is the Yankee outlook on life in which climbing and social success are generally given a higher value than in the more static Southern society, and the ambitious Negro will more often be rewarded by approval and even by admiration, while in the South he is likely to be considered "smart," "uppity" or "out of his place."

Otherwise, the North is not original in its racial ideology. When there is segregation and discrimination to be justified, the rationalization is sometimes a vague and simplified version of the "no social equality" theory of the South.

In this situation, however, not only is intermarriage frowned upon, but in high schools and colleges there will often be attempts to exclude Negroes from dances and social affairs. Social segregation is, in fact, likely to appear in all sorts of social relations. But there is much less social segregation and discrimination than in the South: there is no segregation on streetcars, trains, and so on, and above all, there is no rigid ceremonial governing the Negro-white relations and no laws holding the Negro down. The fact that there are no laws or defined rules of etiquette is sometimes said to cause friction and bitterness because some whites in the North will want Negroes to keep away from them, and Negroes cannot tell which whites these are. But the absence of segregating laws also keeps the system from being so relatively locked as in the South. It allows Negroes to be ambitious.

ECONOMIC DISCRIMINATION

The picture of the economic situation of the Negro people is dark. The prospects for the future—as far as we have analyzed the trends until now—are discouraging. The main practical problem must be how to open up new possibilities for Negroes to earn a living by their labor.

Southern agriculture offers no such new opportunities. It is, on the contrary, likely that Southern rural Negroes will continue to be pushed off the land and thus increase the number of job-seekers in nonagricultural pursuits. In Northern agriculture the main trend will also be a contraction in the demand for labor. The segregated Negro economy will never provide any great number of jobs. It is on the ordinary nonfarm labor market that Negroes have to look for new opportunities. In the nonagricultural pursuits, Negro job limitations, as we have found, are of four different types:

(1) Negroes are kept out of certain industries, North as well as South.

(2) In industries where Negroes are working, they are often confined to certain establishments, whereas other establishments are kept entirely white.

(3) In practically all industries where Negroes are accepted, they are confined to unskilled occupations and to such semi-skilled and skilled occupations as are unattractive to white workers. The main exceptions to this rule are in the building industry where the Negro had acquired a position during slavery but has been losing ground since then.

(4) Finally, there is a geographical segregation. Negroes in the North are concentrated in a few large cities. In the Western centers there is still only a small number of Negro workers. Negroes are even scarcer in the small Northern and Western cities.

Race prejudice on the part of the whites is the usual explanation given for these various types of job limitations. But to relate discrimination to prejudice means little more than to substitute one word for another. Leaving this problem aside for the moment, we may observe that race prejudice and discrimination, in the economic sphere, operate principally in three different ways:

(1) Many white workers, even if they think that Negroes generally should have a fair share in the job opportunities in this country, tend to be opposed to Negro competition in the particular localities, industries, occupations, and establishments where they themselves work.

(2) Some customers object to being served by Negroes unless the Negro has an apparently menial position.

(3) Many employers believe that Negroes are inferior as workers, except for dirty, heavy, hot or otherwise unattractive work. Perhaps even more important is the fact that they pay much attention to the attitudes of both customers and white workers.

All these conditions, in many different ways, are self-perpetuating.

Even in the North the Negro is generally believed to be inferior as a worker. White employees often are strongly against having any Negro co-workers. Yet these attitudes are less general and less well entrenched in the North than they are in the South. Many, perhaps even most, Northerners tend to be rather uncertain and vacillating on such matters. There is nothing in their general ideologies which would support economic discrimination against Negroes. There is no racial etiquette, little emotion about the "social equality" issue, no white solidarity for the purpose of "keeping the Negro in his place." On the contrary, the equalitarian principles of the American Creed dominate people's opinions in the North. [A considerable number of] Northern states and municipalities usually uphold nondiscrimination in public relief as well as in politics, justice, and all other relations between public authorities and the citizens. People in the North are "against" economic discrimination as a general proposition. If the white Northerners had to vote on the issue, a large majority would probably come out for full equality of opportunities on the labor market: they would be in favor of making employment opportunities "independent of race, creed or color." The actual discrimination is, however, as we have seen, the rule and not the exception.

The vicious circle of job restrictions, poverty, and all that follows with it tends to fix the tradition that Negroes should be kept out of good jobs and held down in unskilled, dirty, hot or otherwise undesirable work. Residential segregation and segregation at places of work hinder whites from having personal acquaintance with Negroes and recognizing that Negroes are much like themselves. In the eyes of white workers the Negroes easily come to appear "different," as a "low grade people," and it becomes a matter of social prestige not to work under conditions of equality with them. The fact that Negroes actually work almost only in menial tasks makes it more natural to look upon them in this way. The occupations they work in tend to become déclassé.

When once the white workers' desires for social prestige become mobilized against the Negroes in this way, when they have come to look upon Negroes as different from themselves and consequently do not feel a common labor solidarity with them, "economic interests" also will back up discrimination. By excluding Negroes from the competition for jobs, the white workers can decrease the supply of labor in the market, hold up wages and secure employment for themselves. To give white workers a monopoly on all promotions is, of course, to give them a vested interest in job segregation.

Negroes, on their side, have to try to utilize every opening, even if it means working for lower wages or under inferior working conditions. The abundance of Negro labor, kept idle because of exclusionist policies, must always be feared by white workers. If given the chance, Negroes will accept positions as "sweatshop" competitors—something which cannot fail to increase the resentment of the white wage earners. Sometimes they may even work as "scabs" and so white workers get extra justification for the feeling that Negroes represent a danger of "unfair competition." The Negroes react by being suspicious of the white workers and their unions. For this reason, they are sometimes "poor union material" even if white workers choose to let them in on a basis of equality. White union members then resent the "ingratitude" of the Negroes.

These observations have all referred to the North. The situation in the South is not entirely different, but there are certain significant dissimilarities, some advantageous and some disadvantageous. The factor of ignorance and unconcernedness is important in the South, too. Many white Southerners would undoubtedly give their backing to positive measures to preserve a place for the Negro if they knew more accurately about his plight and about the unfavorable trends. But there is in the South an entrenched and widespread popular theory that the Negro should be held down in his "place."

On the other hand, there are, in the South, many people in the white upper class who feel, as a matter of tradition, that the whites should "look out for" and "take care of" their Negroes. As there are fewer and fewer personal ties between upper class whites and Negroes and the isolation between the two groups is growing, this factor is becoming less and less important as a protection of Negro employment opportunities.

The mere fact that there are many more

Negroes in the South makes them less strange to white people. The white Southerner does not react so much, and for such flimsy reasons, as many Northerners do, to having Negroes around. The employers have more experience with Negro labor and are often not so prejudiced against using it. The workers are more accustomed in many trades to work with Negroes.

The Negroes have also had a sort of protection in the traditional "Negro jobs." These job monopolies, however, have been largely in stagnating occupations and trades. As we have seen, white workers have always been pressing against these job monopolies. Job exclusion in all desirable and most undesirable jobs has, on the whole, been steadily progressing. The Negro's prospects in Southern industry are not promising. The very fact that there are so many more Negroes working there already means that the possibilities for expansion of Negro employment are slighter than they are in the North. The high natural increase of the white population in the South, and the likelihood that many white farmers will be pushed out of Southern agriculture, means that the white pressure to exclude Negroes from jobs will be strong even if there should be considerable industrial expansion.

Particularly in the South the concentration of Negro workers in the unskilled jobs is dangerous for their future employment, as mechanization means a constantly decreased demand for unskilled labor. Unskilled labor itself is changing character. Modern technical development means that formerly unpleasant jobs are becoming "suitable" for white workers. The entrance of women into industry not only means that Negro labor has a new competitor but also intensifies the issue of "social equality." It is difficult to see much hope for the Negro in Southern industry.

LEGAL DISCRIMINATION AND LYNCHING

[The] fact that administration of justice is dependent upon local voters is likely to imply discrimination against an unpopular minority group, particularly when this group is disfranchised as Negroes are in the South. The elected judge knows that sooner or later he must come back to the polls, and that a decision running counter to local opinion may cost him his position.

The dependence of the judge on local prejudices strikes at the very root of orderly government. It results in the danger of breaking down the law in its primary function of protecting the minority against the majority, the individual against society, indeed, of democracy itself against the danger of its nullifying, in practice, the settled principles of law and impartiality of justice. This danger is higher in the problem regions where there is acute race friction and in rural areas where the population is small and provincial, and where personal contacts are direct. Under the same influences as the judges are the public prosecutors, the sheriffs, the chiefs of police and their subordinates. The American jury system, while it has many merits, is likely to strengthen this dependence of justice upon local popular opinion. If, as in the South, Negroes are kept out of jury service, the democratic safeguard of the jury system is easily turned into a means of minority subjugation.

The popular election of the officers of law and the jury system are expressions of the extreme democracy in the American handling of justice. It might, in spite of the dangers suggested, work excellently in a reasonably homogeneous, highly educated and public spirited community. It might also work fairly well anywhere for cases involving only parties belonging to a majority group which controls the court. *The extreme democracy in the American system of justice turns out, thus, to be the greatest menace to legal democracy when it is based on restricted political participation and an ingrained tradition of caste suppression.* Such conditions occur in the South with respect to Negroes.

If there is a deficiency of legal protection for Negroes, white people will be tempted to deal unfairly with them in everyday affairs. They will be tempted to use irregular methods to safeguard what they feel to be their interests against Negroes. They will be inclined to use intimidation and even violence against Negroes if they can count on going unpunished. When such patterns become established, the law itself and its processes are brought into contempt, and a general feeling of uncertainty, arbitrariness and inequality will spread. Not only Negroes but other persons of weak social status will be the object of discrimination. . . . In the South there have been frequent occasions when the legal rights of poor white persons have been disregarded, and even when general lawlessness prevailed. When the frequency of law-breaking thus increases, it becomes necessary to apply stronger penalties than is necessary in an equitable system of justice.

The Negroes, on their side, are hurt in their trust that the law is impartial, that the court and the police are their protection, and, indeed, that they belong to an orderly society which has set up this machinery for common security and welfare. They will not feel confidence in, and loyalty toward, a legal order which is entirely out of their control and which they sense to be inequitable and merely part of the system of caste suppression. Solidarity then develops easily in the Negro group, a solidarity against the law and the police. The arrested Negro often acquires the prestige of a victim, a martyr, or a hero, even when he is simply a criminal. It becomes part of race pride in the protective Negro community not to give up a fellow Negro who is hunted by the police. Negroes who collaborate with the police become looked upon as stool pigeons.

No one visiting Negro communities in the South can avoid observing the prevalence of these views. The situation is dynamic for several reasons. One is the growing urbanization and the increasing segregation of the Negro people. The old-time paternalistic and personal relationship between individuals of the two groups is on the decrease. Another factor is the improvement of Negro education which is continually making Negroes more aware of their anomalous status in the American legal order. A third factor, the importance of which is increasing in pace with the literacy of the Negro people, is the persistent

hammering of the Negro press which, to a large extent, is devoted to giving publicity to the injustices and injuries suffered by Negroes. A fourth factor is unemployment, especially of young Negroes, with resulting insecurity and dissatisfaction.

Lynchings were becoming common in the South in the 'thirties, 'forties and 'fifties of the nineteenth century. Most of the victims in this early period were white men. The pattern of lynching Negroes became set during Reconstruction. No reliable statistics before 1889 are available. Between 1889 and 1940, according to Tuskegee Institute figures, 3,833 people were lynched, about four-fifths of whom were Negroes. The Southern states account for nine-tenths of the lynchings. More than two-thirds of the remaining one-tenth occurred in the six states which immediately border the South: Maryland, West Virginia, Ohio, Indiana, Illinois and Kansas. Since the early 1890's, the trend has been toward fewer and fewer lynchings. The annual average in the 'nineties was near 200; in the 'thirties it dropped to slightly over 10. In 1941 it was down to 4, but there are already more than this in 1942 (July). The decrease has been faster outside the South, and the lynching of whites has dropped much more than that of Negroes. Lynching has become, therefore, more and more a Southern phenomenon and a racial one. Against the decrease in number of victims there has been a marked trend toward greatly aggravated brutality, extending to torture, mutilation and other sadistic excesses.

It is possible to speculate about the causes for the decline in lynching. If our analysis of the background factors is correct, the rising standard of living and the improved education must have been of importance. The fundamentalism and emotionalism of Southern religion have been decreasing. Cultural isolation is being broken by radio, improved highways and cheap motor cars. There is more diversion from the drab and monotonous small town life, and the sex taboos have been somewhat relaxed. The national agitation around lynching, strengthened after the organization of the National Association for the Advancement of Colored People in 1909, has undoubtedly been of tremendous importance in awakening influential people in the South to the urgency of stopping lynching. The sharp decline in lynching since 1922 has undoubtedly something to do with the fact that early in that year the Dyer Anti-Lynching Bill was put through the House of Representatives. It was later killed in the Senate by the filibuster of the Southern senators, and the sellout of Western and Northern senators, but the continuous discussion of the measure from then on has probably been of great importance.

Southern organizations of whites have taken to condemning lynching. Some religious denominations of the South declare against lynching at their annual conventions and sponsor programs on racial matters for white youth. [Moreover,] the great majority of Southern newspapers will come out openly against lynching. State authorities usually try to prevent lynchings, and they have an instrument in the State police systems which can be readily concentrated in any community where people are congregating for a lynching. Behind this movement is the growing strength of Southern liberalism.

RECENT CHANGES AND OUTLOOK FOR THE FUTURE

Against the obstacles of the powerful interlocking system of social, judicial, political, and economic inequalities and disabilities, and in spite of the desire on the part of the majority of Southern whites that the Negroes remain in an inferior social status, and the great indifference and ignorance about it all on the part of most Northern whites, *the Negroes are rising*. They are rising most rapidly in the North, but their rate of rise in the South is not inconsiderable. It is one of the paradoxes of the American situation, ultimately due to the split morality of the nation on the issue of racial democracy, that this rise of the Negroes to a great extent is the result of education and other public efforts, which—solicited by the Negro leaders, pushed by a small minority of Southern liberals, and assisted by Northern philanthropy —is largely provided by the Southern states themselves with the approval of the ordinary Southern whites in political power, acting in partial obedience to the American Creed.

The fundamental character of these efforts and their result have been to diffuse American middle class norms to the uneducated and crude Southern "folk Negroes," emerging out of the backwardness of slavery.

One phase of the rise of the Negroes is the formation of a Negro middle and upper class. A nucleus of such a class was already forming among free Negroes in slavery times. Since then it has been steadily, but slowly, growing, partly as a result of segregation itself, which holds down the Negro masses but opens petty monopolies for a few. These middle and upper class Negroes, who have stepped out of the servant status, live mostly by catering to their own people. [See Selection 117.]

The behavior patterns and attitudes of the small Negro middle and upper class group are of greatest importance for the whole Negro people as they set the standards which are spread from the pulpit and the teacher's desk, by the influential Negro press and through social imitation. As has already been suggested, popular education in America is even more essentially directed on the dissemination of middle class views and ways of life than in most other countries. The cultural rise of the Negro masses means their gradual approach to middle class standards.

Meanwhile the old bonds of intimacy between upper class white families and their Negro servants have been breaking down. This process started immediately after Emancipation but is not yet fully consummated. . . . In so far as Negro professionals increasingly are taking care of the souls and the bodies of Negroes generally, the result is not only the creation of a culturally isolated Negro middle and upper class but also, on the other side of the fence, a new barrier to communication between white people and lower class Negroes. In their daily work also Negroes and whites have been becoming increasingly separated. The only exception in the South to the general trend of increasing separation is the recent coming together of Negro and white workers in the new labor unions.

The isolation we are speaking about—caused by all the barriers to contact involved in etiquette, segregation, and discrimination from the side of the whites and in voluntary withdrawal and resentment from the side of the Negroes—means a decrease of certain types of contacts between the two groups and a distortion of the ones that are left. It is useful here to put the reverse question: What contacts do remain? and what is their significance for interracial relations? To answer these questions there ought to be quantitative studies of the sort we have discussed previously. Since no such studies have been made, our observations have to be general, tentative, and in the nature of somewhat schematic hypotheses for further research.

Negroes constitute about 10 per cent of the American population, and since there has been little attempt to segregate them by region, there is naturally some contact. The patterns of segregation and withdrawal are so effective, however, that even where Negroes are a common sight *there is actual contact with them in practically only three spheres of life: the casual, the economic and the criminal.*

By *casual contacts* we mean all those instances where Negro individuals and white individuals see each other but without the condition of recognizing each other as individuals, or at least for the whites to recognize the Negroes as individuals. [In view of the fact that] the casual contact is one in which the participants have no occasion to regard each other as individuals but only as members of a group, *the main effect of the casual contact would seem to be a strengthening of stereotypes.* Negroes, but not whites, have something of an antidote for the casual contact in their economic contact with whites. The main effect of casual contacts is, therefore, to create and preserve stereotypes of Negroes in the minds of the whites. This is not to say that casual contacts are the only, or even the most important, cause of stereotypes of Negroes. But the impersonality of the comparatively numerous casual contacts al-lows whites to see Negroes as a relatively uniform biological and social type and to ignore the great variations that would become apparent if observation were more attentive. All Negroes come to look alike to the average white person.

Casual contact between Negroes and whites is probably increasing as Negroes—and whites—are becoming more mobile and as the scope of Negro activity is becoming broader. Also it has been taking on a slightly different character as it enters the urban environment. In a city it is sometimes impossible to avoid close physical contact. Negroes and whites jostle each other unconcernedly on crowded streets, and Negroes have been observed to be standing in the white sections of crowded Jim Crow buses. The increase of casual contacts in Southern cities is undoubtedly wearing away somewhat the strictness of racial etiquette.

The increased range of casual contacts in recent years is not unrelated to the growth of a Negro upper class. This is especially important in the North, where there are no laws against Negroes using public facilities. A well-mannered Negro dressed in good taste who appears in a restaurant, a white church, or a railroad station is likely to weaken unfavorable Negro stereotypes rather than to strengthen them. In the South the effect of the appearance of the upper class Negro is somewhat more problematical. In the long run this will probably have a favorable effect, but in many known instances it has led to violence from lower and middle class whites who felt that the Negroes were getting too "uppity." The Negro's physical appurtenances—that is, his home, store, or automobile —will serve as a casual contact in the same manner as his person.

Unlike casual contacts, *economic contacts,* though usually not intimate or protracted, are important enough for the whites and Negroes to see one another as individuals. In the great majority of economic contacts, whites see Negroes as economic inferiors, as when they are servants or other types of menial workers. More rarely they meet as economic equals, as when Negro and white workers work on the same level or when businessman meets businessman or salesman meets customer. Practically never do whites see Negroes as their economic superiors. This is due, of course, to the striking differential in economic and occupational status of whites and Negroes. In contacts arising out of economic relationships, the Negro partner is rarely employer, supervisor, skilled worker, merchant, or professional man. An additional reason for this is the fact that Negroes who occupy these higher economic positions tend to serve and to employ other Negroes. Of course, most whites are vaguely aware that there are Negroes in high economic positions. But it is probable that they everywhere underestimate the number of such Negroes, and it is certain that they rarely have enough contact with them to know them as individuals. From their side, Negroes have economic contacts with whites mainly as superiors and occasionally as equals. They thus tend to have their attitudes of inferiority and dependence—already in existence because of the slavery tradition—reinforced. The same can be said of their attitudes of resentment.

There is one sphere of economic relationship which is extremely important for several reasons. We refer to the Negro as a personal and domestic servant, a position in which he held practically a monopoly in the South until the depression of the 1930's, and in which he is numerically important in the North. The social importance of this relationship derives mainly from the fact that it is very intensive on one side. The Negro maid knows the life of her white employer as few white persons know it; and the Negro janitor and elevator operator knows a great deal of what goes on in his building.

The white employer, on the other hand, does not know the Negro's world just because he has Negro servants. The white employer ordinarily is interested mainly in getting his servant to work, and his attitude toward the servant is, therefore, usually impersonal. We have already commented upon the fact that this relationship has in the main lost in intimacy and personal friendliness. [But in spite of this, what] often happens in the employer-servant relationship is that—depending on the degree of friendliness or appreciation of the white employer and the degree of confidence felt by the Negro servant—the white man or woman makes an exception of his or her servant to the stereotyped conception of the "Negro in general." Similarly, the Negro servant might under happy conditions come to regard his or her employer as an exception to the general run of mean and exploitative white people.

The contacts between white and Negro workers were formerly of the same type. In the trades and handicrafts, the pattern in the South was, and is, that the white worker had a Negro helper. In factories the Negro workers are usually segregated or, in any case, held to certain jobs. As we have pointed out, the mixed trade unions are a new adventure with an uncertain future. It is commonly reported that white workers, if they become accustomed to working with Negro workers, tend to become less prejudiced, and consequently that the Negro workers become less suspicious and resentful. . . . Our general hypothesis is that everything which brings Negro and white workers to experience intimate cooperation and fellowship will, on the balance, break down race prejudice somewhat and raise Negro status. The possibilities for Negroes to rise to the position of skilled workers have, therefore, not only economic significance but also a wider social import as this will tend to weaken the stereotype of the menial Negro.

There are other types of economic contacts between Negroes and whites in which the members of the two groups are of equal or near-equal status. Over a long time span Negro purchasing power has been increasing, and the number of Negro businessmen who can deal as economic equals with whites in a similar position has been rising.

Another sort of economic relationship in which Negroes have a measure of near-equality with whites is that in which the Negro is an entertainer or artist. The Negro as a musician, actor, dancer, or other type of artist is allowed to perform almost freely for a white public in the North—and to some extent in the South—in a way that he can in no other economic sphere outside of the service occupations. His excellence in these fields—cultivated by folk stimulation from earliest childhood and by the realization that other means of earning a living are closed—is recognized. In fact, it is even supported by the stereotypes: the Negro must make up for an intellectual lack by an emotional richness. Nevertheless, a Negro who achieves distinction or popularity in these fields is regarded as an individual, and there can be little doubt that he raises the general prestige level of the Negro population. What has been said of the entertainment and artistic fields is true also of the athletic field, in which Negroes have achieved notable successes.

We mentioned *criminal contacts* as the third most important field of Negro-white relationship. Ordinarily in American societies, as in practically all other societies, criminal relationships are minor. The fact that it is so important in Negro-white relationships has unique causes and unique effects. . . . Whites *believe* the Negro to be innately addicted to crime. The importance of Negro crime as a basis of social relations arises not only out of this fact, but also out of the fact that Negro crime gets great publicity. Even today a large proportion—perhaps a majority—of the news about Negroes that appears in the white newspapers of both South and North is about Negro crimes. When a Catholic or Jew, Swede or Bulgarian, commits a crime that is serious enough to get into the newspapers, it is not usual for his religion or nationality to be mentioned. When a Negro commits a newsworthy crime, on the other hand, only rarely is an indication of his race not prominently displayed. To many white Northerners, this crime news is the most important source of information they get about Negroes.

Crime news is unfair to Negroes, on the one hand, in that it emphasizes individual cases instead of statistical proportions (a characteristic of all news, but in this case unfair to Negroes because of the racial association with especially disliked crimes) and, on the other hand, in that all other aspects of Negro life are neglected in the white press which gives the unfavorable crime news an undue weight.

Crimes against Negroes outside of lynching receive no publicity in the white press. Lynching receives a wide but declining publicity, especially in the North, and such publicity probably serves to raise Negroes—by contrast with Southern whites—in the attitude of Northern whites.

White Southerners are still proud of insisting that they "know the Negro," but the observer easily finds out that the actual ignorance about the other group is often astonishingly great.

Under the old master-servant relationship, the white man's "understanding" of the Negro was not great, but with the disappearance of this relationship even this small amount of sympathetic knowledge declined. What remains is a technique of how to work Negroes and how to keep them "in their place."

The Northerner also is ignorant about the Negro, but his ignorance is less systematic and, therefore, often less deep. As he is ordinarily less inhibited from looking upon the Negro as a normal human being, and as his observation of the Negro is not blinded by the etiquette, he is usually more cognizant of Negro attitudes and capacities and is more willing to lend a sympathetic ear to the Negro's plight. But he is much more ignorant of the conditions which the Negro faces. If the Southerner's whole race philosophy and even his kindliest thoughts are insulting to the new type of Negro emerging out of the cultural assimilation process, the Northerner is likely to insult him out of sheer ignorance.

On his side, the Negro is inclined to be suspicious of the Northerner's good intentions and to retain in the North the cynical attitude and secretive manners that he has developed as a camouflage in the Southern race warfare.

Mutual ignorance and the paucity of common interests is a barrier to, and a modifier of, social contact between even educated and liberal whites and Negroes in the North, even in the extraordinary circles where segregation and discrimination play no role. I have seen Negro and white social scientists together as friends and colleagues. But I know that when their minds meet it usually concerns some aspect of the Negro problem. The Negro is ordinarily not present—and if he is present, he is a stranger—when the whites meet to discuss more general problems. If this is true among liberal social scientists, it is still more true among prejudiced people in all classes. The Negro is an alien in America, and in a sense this becomes the more evident when he steps out of his old role of the servant who lives entirely for the comfort of his white superiors. Ignorance and disparity of interests, arising out of segregation and discrimination on the part of whites, increased by voluntary withdrawal and race pride on the part of Negroes, becomes itself an important element increasing and perpetuating isolation between the groups.

But the system *is* changing, though slowly. Modern knowledge and modern industrial conditions make it cumbersome. The South is becoming "normalized" and integrated into the national culture. Like every other "normal" province, it is beginning to dislike being provincial. The world publicity around the Dayton trial, for instance, did much to censor fundamentalism in Southern religion. A great part of the region's peculiarities in its racial relations is becoming, even to the Southerner, associated with backwardness. The Southerner is beginning to take on an apologetic tone when he speaks of his attitude toward the Negro. To insist upon the full racial etiquette is beginning to be regarded as affectation.

The South has long eagerly seized upon every act of prejudice practiced against the Negro in the North and, indeed, all other social ills of the other region. The visitor finds even the average run of white Southerners intensely aware of the bad slum conditions in Northern metropolises and of the North's labor troubles. Even the Southern liberal has the habit of never mentioning a fault of the South without mentioning a corresponding condition in the North.

Southerners travel and migrate and are visited by Northerners and Europeans. They listen to the radio and read papers, magazines and books directed to the wider national audience. Southern writers—in social science, politics, and *belles-lettres*—aspire to national recognition and not only provincial applause. The thesis that the region is poor and culturally backward, and that this is largely due to the presence of the Negroes and to the Southern Negro policy, has been for a long time developed by Southern authors. The average Southerner is beginning to feel the need for fundamental reforms. Many Southern newspapers have become liberal. Interracial work is beginning to be recognized as socially respectable.

The diffusion of scientific knowledge regarding race cannot be regionalized any more effectively than it can be segregated along a color line. Racial beliefs are becoming undermined, at least for the younger generation in the middle and upper classes. When a person arrives at the point where he says that he knows his views are irrational but that "they are just instinctive" with him, he is beginning to retreat from these views.

The educated, respectable, self-possessed Negro is to the average white Southerner not so often as earlier just the "smart nigger" or the "uppity nigger." As the South becomes urbanized and some Negroes rise in status, it is becoming increasingly impracticable and, in some relations, actually impossible to bracket all Negroes together and treat them alike.

We must not exaggerate these signs of wear and tear on the Southern color bar. *"Social equality" is still a terribly important matter in the region. But it is not as important as it was a generation ago.* One needs only to compare the tremendous upheaval in the South when President Theodore Roosevelt in the first decade of the twentieth century had Booker T. Washington to a luncheon at the White House with the relatively calm irritation the white South manifested in the 'thirties when President Franklin Roosevelt and his gallant lady did much more radical things. It even continued to vote for him. The South is surely changing.

But the changes themselves elicit race prejudice. From one point of view, Robert E. Park is right, of course, in explaining race prejudice as "merely an elementary expression of conservatism," as "the resistance of the social order to change." When the Negro moves around and improves his status, he is bound to stimulate animosity. The white South was—and is—annoyed whenever the Negro showed signs of moving out of his "place." And the white North definitely became more prejudiced when hundreds of thousands of crude Southern Negroes moved in. But conditions for Negroes are improving, Southerners are being jolted out of their racial beliefs, and the group of white people interested in doing something positive for the Negro has grown. The increase in prejudice due to the rise of the Negro is a local and temporary phenomenon in both the North and the South.

The Future of the South

>>

It is difficult to conclude the story of the South with any final summary, because changes are still taking place and the South will not be in the future what it is today or has been in the past. To an even greater extent than some other parts of our country it is beset with problems and is in the midst of difficult readjustments. It has been impossible in this book to cover every aspect of the South, and the careful reader will already have become aware of many omitted topics. But enough has been presented to show the central core of Southern life as a unified and consistent whole, in all its problems and its strengths, its weaknesses and its promises, its clinging to the old with one hand and reaching out to the new with the other. We have seen how social change comes to an agrarian society based on the plantation system, and how the question of racial relationships has changed from a "private" matter for the South to settle in its own way to a burning national issue.

A fitting way to close, we believe, is to turn again to the little volume by Hodding Carter, *Southern Legacy,* and present his summing up. Carter's search for the South's "way out" of its problems is reminiscent of the earnest questioning in Selection 90 by the Chinese sociologists seeking an answer to their country's rural problems.

• 121 • Out of Inquietude
HODDING CARTER

If the South had ever agreed with the rest of the nation that it is primarily a collection of unfavorable statistics, it would have lost long ago the self-esteem which is an essential requisite for cultural survival. But the price of ignoring the statistics is their certain perpetuation.

In the eleven states of the Southeast live some 35 million people, a smaller proportion of the nation's population than they represented fifty years ago. The out-migration quickens. During the war years, the South lost one million more inhabitants than it gained. Of its young men who served in the

[Adapted from *Southern Legacy,* Louisiana State University Press, Baton Rouge, 1950. Pp. 176-186. Used by permission.]

armed forces, one in seven found greener pastures elsewhere after demobilization. Of its young men who remained at home, proportionately more were rejected for physical and mental disabilities than in any other region of the nation.

The states which the one in seven forsook receive only 10 per cent of the nation's industrial wages, although they contain one fifth of the population. The average per capita income of their citizens has more than doubled in twenty years, to $883, but it is only 67 per cent of the national average. It is understandable that the young men are still restless, still intent on the distant field. Their migration has left in the South's labor force far more adolescents and old men than are present in the nation's labor force as a whole. And those who leave and those who remain at home are alike handicapped in their work, for only one third of the South's population has been educated beyond the eighth grade. In this day of the machine, one Southerner in four has less than a fifth-grade education. The principal migration is from the farms of the South. Of the 160 million acres of American farm land which erosion has reduced to inutility, nearly 100 million, more than 60 per cent of the total, lie in the South. On the useful and useless land, two thirds of all Southern farmers try to make their livings by growing cotton and tobacco.

Overproducing its field crops, the South does not yet produce sufficient dairy products, meat, poultry, eggs, vegetables, and feedstuffs to care for its own needs.

Nor is this agricultural instability balanced by industrial productivity. Textiles, wood products, food products, and chemicals account for nearly two thirds of the South's output, textiles making up nearly one third of the total. The South does not yet have industrial capital and management and a trained labor supply. It lacks the great life-insurance companies and investment banks necessary to provide capital investment. It is still primarily an exporter of raw products for processing elsewhere rather than a processor itself.

Against this background of agricultural and industrial lags, other unfavorable statistics are inevitable. The South has the fewest doctors and the fewest hospital beds for each thousand of its population. Its venereal disease, tuberculosis, and infant and maternal mortality rates are the nation's largest. And so on, throughout a somber catalogue.

All of this is well enough known. What is less known is that, except in population loss, the South is moving upward on every gauge by which the progress of a civilization can be measured. Ours is no longer a problem of direction but of acceleration.

More land is being restored in the South through terracing, crop rotation, and pasturing than anywhere else in the nation. Manufacturing income has almost tripled in ten years. In every Southern state, new hospitals are being built, state health departments expanded, disease reduced, school systems extended.

The giant turbines of the Tennessee Valley Authority put water to work for man. The white-faced Herefords graze where once the mined earth cried out for rest. Around the multiplying factories are lined the automobiles of workers from the gutted hills and the once-listless towns. The young saplings rise by plan from the land where the forests were planlessly slain. Everywhere the change is sure.

There is a material and a moral urgency to this Southern metamorphosis.

If the 35 million Southerners were to attain a standard of living equal to that enjoyed by the rest of the nation, their material demands would add 15 billion dollars in needed goods and services to the nation's consumption totals. Could they divest themselves of the searing heritages of mistrust and fear, they would subtract immeasurably from the bill of particulars by which the enemies of democracy seek to negate its meaning throughout the world. These are the South's twin mandates to itself. They cannot be carried out through the force-feeding of new practices and ideals. The realization of their urgency must come from within.

So it is that the South must look behind even as it moves ahead, recognizing the fetters of an agrarian tradition which could have been altogether wholesome, but which was degraded through a one-crop economy, the enslavement of man, and the pitiable make-shift of tenancy on land that men had ruined and were in turn ruined by. The agrarian past must be honestly weighed. Against the manors it reared and the virtues it possessed must be balanced the flight of intellect which it impelled, the prejudices it inspired, the po-litical miasma in which it was shrouded, and the quantitative limitations of the dis-tinctive culture it produced. And we must recognize, too, its peculiar contribution to the American dilemma arising from the pres-ence of the Negro, the abused, retarded, identifiable stranger of 300 years whose sim-ilarity of aspirations and dissimilarity of race have created in the white South a unity of resistance which is the principal cohesive ele-ment in its regional solidarity.

[For myself at least,] the mandatory first step today is to make the availability and the quality of public education in the South at least comparable to prevailing national standards. [And furthermore, the] goal of agricultural-industrial balance must be set beside the goal of education.

Yet even the absolute attainment of eco-nomic objectives would not in itself resolve the racial dilemma that is not restricted to the South but aggravated here because of the numbers involved and attitudes generated by law and folkways for three centuries. Educa-tion, greater economic security, and protec-tive legislation can soften the impact of racial antipathies, but there is no formula for end-ing them except the formula which man dis-covers within himself.

The best that can be expected in the ascer-tainable future from the South's attainment of national levels in income and education is a more rapid amelioration of the discrimina-tory aspects of the white-Negro relationship. The harshest manifestations of prejudice exist where the living standards of the dominant and the submerged groups are alike low, and where the numerical pressures of the sub-merged and dissimilar are interpreted by the dominant as constituting a political, economic, or social threat to the established controls.

Since the living standards are being raised and the numerical pressures reduced throughout the South, greater and rapid amelioration appears certain.

Through migration, the Negro popula-tion in the South is decreasing in relation to the white population, so that in no Southern state and in less than 180 counties is the Negro in a majority. Until now this migration has been principally voluntary and motivated by ambition or resentment or both, but it is being quickened involuntarily as the machine replaces the man and the mule.

The admission that the reduction of the ratio of Negro to white in the South will hasten the South's over-all progress is also an admission of democratic failure; but as tragic as the implication is, the fact remains that if the Negro exodus continues, it will contribute at least as much to the South's economic trans-formation and to white acceptance of the Negro as a citizen as will any other presently foreseeable factor.

But the South cannot wait for this bleak and negative impetus to development. Even if half of the nine million Southern Negroes were to leave, the remainder would consti-tute an unending reproach until they were recognized as citizens entitled to the same political rights and the same economic oppor-tunity and capable of making equal contribu-tions to democratic America.

Such recognition is the paramount neces-sity for the South today, and for all America. The integration of the Negro in our national life has an importance more immediately im-perative than are domestic or even moral con-siderations. [The world is watching us.] The skin colors of three quarters of the world's population are black or brown or yellow. It is to this questioning, undecided majority that the Communist propagandist addresses his calculated disparagement of de-mocracy as bearing a label "For Whites Only —All Others Keep Off."

I would like now to set aside the problems and the statistics and turn again to the legacy of regionalism. The Southerner does not love his country the less because of his self-identifi-cation with the comprehensible part of the whole. America is vast and many-sided, but a man's valley and hillside and state are near and intimate; and if there is any antidote to our mounting reliance upon distant, impersonal, and centralized power it is the regional attachment which, by virtue of long identification with his background, the Southerner possesses to a greater extent than do the rest of America's people.

This may be provincialism, but there is nothing unhealthy in it. The sense of intimate identification with a region fortifies the will to make it more nearly perfect and secure; and as the part is strengthened so is the whole. It is only when loyalty makes the regional patriot blind to imperfection and resentful of inspection that it becomes a de-teriorative force; the obligation to examine, to protest and to propose change must accompany affection, else devotion can destroy. Too many Southerners fail to perceive this corollary; defiant and resentful of the alien critic, they are even more enraged by the native censor, stigmatizing him as a nest-fouler and suggesting that he should go elsewhere if he is not satisfied with what he finds.

I prefer to remain dissatisfied. I hope that there will never come a time when my sons or their sons will look about them and be content; for the soul is nurtured on inquietude: the soul of a man, the soul of a region, the soul of a nation. Out of inquietude the South, so long bemused in the twilight of its self-satisfaction, stirs now before the dawn.

THE ENGLISH MIDLANDS

Left: The term *conurbation* has come into use in England to describe the immense, sprawling industrial cities which have swallowed up outlying towns and adjacent factory districts in their growth. But although they are highly congested, they have a great advantage: they bring together both the means of production, with its highly skilled labor, and a great body of consumers. Coal mining in England (*below*) is of immense importance in providing one of the basic materials for industry. It is hampered by the narrowness of many seams, which makes the use of machinery difficult, thus greatly reducing productivity per man.

Right: Here, as in many parts of England, a factory stands only a few yards from a picturesque old town crossroads. This wide dispersal of industry is as characteristic as is concentration in great urban centers. Among other things, it means that even rural areas are rarely far from factories, mines, or mills. It means, too, that sometimes the English worker lives very close to his place of work, and also very close to the countryside. Even with great industrial growth, farming is important in England, and every effort is still made to produce a substantial part of what the nation eats. *Below:* A harvest group takes a few minutes for the traditional cup of tea.

Orkney Is.

0°

OUTER HEBRIDES

INNER HEBRIDES

HIGHLANDS
SCOTLAND

LOWLANDS

Clyde

NORTH SEA

55°

NORTHERN
IRELAND

Isle of
Man

IRISH SEA

REPUBLIC
OF
IRELAND

Tyne

THE PENNINES

Ouse

Mersey

Trent

WALES

ENGLAND

Malvern
Hills

Wye

Severn

Cotswolds

Thames

ATLANTIC

OCEAN

50°

CHANNEL

50°

ENGLISH

Channel Islands

FRANCE

0°

British Isles

Scale of Miles

0   20   40   60

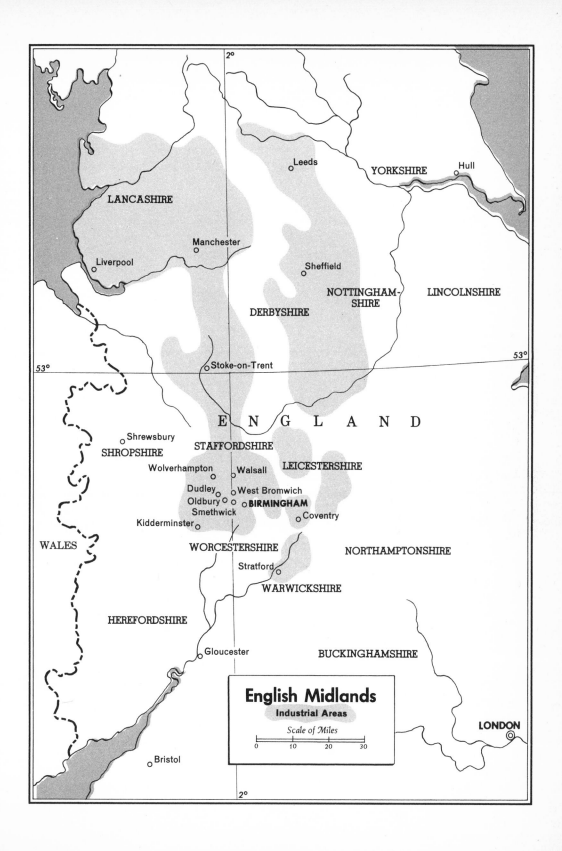

English Midlands

Industrial Areas

Scale of Miles

0   10   20   30

Introduction

>>>

Although it is the most complex of the three societies in Part Two, the English Midlands should not prove the most difficult to understand, because we, too, live in an industrial society. Even our rural areas are closely caught up in the forces and complexities of what is smugly termed "modern civilization." The English Midlands can also be better appreciated when it is realized that industrial society has developed rather rapidly from the background of a society not wholly unlike that of Peasant China. The Cotton South, which has just been dealt with, represents a transitional and rapidly changing society and provides us with perspective for our analysis of the Midlands.

Nevertheless, at the outset of our study of the Midlands, some reorientation in our thinking may be necessary. We shall be dealing with one small part of an island *only slightly larger than Kansas* but with a population about 25 times as great. Furthermore, although the British have absorbed people of many and diverse origins through the centuries, they have not recently experienced such gigantic ethnic assimilation as we have in America. This gives the British people more common characteristics and more homogeneity, although they too have local loyalties and regional differences.

The English Midlands have to be seen in an accurate time perspective, too. When our republic was getting underway, the Industrial Revolution was already working out its transformation of English life. The roots out of which industrial society grew will be described in those selections that tell how the peasantry was transformed into a wage-earning class. But the story of the Industrial Revolution (and that means the story of the English Midlands) is also one of intelligent exploitation of natural resources, of a developing technology in textiles and metal work, and of such occupational specialization that labor unions eventually became an essential feature of the social landscape. A person's labor was transferred from the home to the factory, where centralized power ran many machines at once, where there was effective supervision and mass production. The expense of building a factory and equipping it with machines, of buying raw materials and em-

668

ploying labor meant that new ways of financing had to be worked out. The result was the business corporation, one of the major social inventions of Western society, which made it possible for many individuals to supply capital for an enterprise without acquiring any personal liabilities, in most cases, for the failure and default of the corporation.

Mass production called for increased markets as well as new supplies of raw materials. Profits accumulated to the point that businessmen had to look abroad for ventures in which to invest their idle funds—much of this capital coming to America to finance our transcontinental railroad construction and other enterprises which we now consider essential to our economy.

In the study of England it will be apparent that a democracy can exist within a monarchy, that marked social changes can occur by "evolution rather than revolution," and that the more complex and concentrated the economy, the greater the tendency toward centralized government control. In England, large sections of the economy have been taken over by the government, a process called *nationalization*. It also means *socialization* when viewed in terms of the theory that the people themselves should control the means of production, such as mines, utilities, and the like. This is in sharp contrast to the American emphasis on *private ownership* of utilities and the failure of any Labor Party to emerge in the United States as a politically significant force under the banner of governmental management of our basic industries.

Socialization, however, has another meaning. As we have seen earlier, it is the term used by social scientists to describe the process by which individuals are transformed into socially acceptable persons who know what roles are expected of them in given situations. Some of the selections which follow trace the influences brought to bear upon the growing English boy and girl. In reading of their school experiences, we must remember that in England a "public school" is really what we call a private school. Family life and recreational patterns have some minor differences from ours, but they reflect industrialization in much the same way as they do here. The city becomes an increasingly significant social factor and in its development has attracted the attention of community and regional social planners.

The English value system, though similar in many points to ours, has shades and nuances of its own that influence behavior in subtle ways. Selection 145 presents an excellent description of some of these fine points.

Although the focus is generally on the Midlands, some selections have had to deal with England as a whole, since they deal with the actions of the central government. We shall see, for example, the British plans for nationalization of the economy and of medical care. We cannot, however, overlook the fact that about five years ago a change in the British government began to reverse the program of nationalization, although the fundamental centralization of the British economy has not yet been greatly changed. In many social measures, the United States has followed Britain by a generation or two, and many are wondering whether the centralization there is the course that America will pursue some years hence. It is important to us, in this connection, to understand what the British patterns are, why they appeared, and what similarities and differences in

American and British ways may influence the eventual extension of such patterns to this side of the Atlantic.

It can be seen from the grouping of the selections that we have chosen certain topics for emphasis in connection with this industrial society: (1) the urban concentrations of the people (*conurbations,* in English terminology); (2) the extensive utilization of resources; (3) the historical roots in the Industrial Revolution; (4) the high differentiation of the economy; (5) the strong influence of the economy and the government on other aspects of the social system, such as the family, religion, recreation, social welfare, and education; and, finally, (6) the persistence of many social values even in the face of changes in many other phases of life.

The People

Who are the British? Of what diverse strains is their population made up? For the answer to these questions we turn to *The Face of Britain*, a booklet by the well-known British geographer L. Dudley Stamp. His summary begins with Paleolithic (Old Stone Age) man and his Neolithic successors, long before the coming of the Romans, and tells of successive invasions by tribesmen on the move.

For information about the British people in more recent times, we make use of Eva M. Hubback's *Population of Britain*. This selection will illustrate in detail how demographers (population analysts) go about their task of studying the statistics of birth rates, death rates, and other such data to determine the rates at which groups within the total population are increasing and decreasing. But the most significant fact about the population of Britain today is not the rate at which it is changing but the way in which it is becoming concentrated around a few major urban centers. This process was thoroughly investigated by a Royal Commission, whose report was issued in 1940; two brief passages from this report make up Selection 124.

The last of the selections on the people of Britain considers the urban concentrations of an industrial society, but from a less statistical point of view. Urbanization changes many aspects of a people's life and has had far-reaching effects, which have frequently been completely unforeseen. All towns are not alike, however, either in the reasons for their development or in their problems. It should be borne in mind that even peasant societies have town centers, but the growth of such centers into great metropolises is especially characteristic of industrial society; gradually even the outlying villages are drawn into the orbits of the "conurbations" or are drastically altered by them.

· 122 · The Peopling of the British Isles

L. DUDLEY STAMP

Before the ice-sheets of the Great Ice Age overwhelmed this country Britain was still joined to the continent of Europe. Early man with his implements of crudely chipped flint came into the country by land and settled on river-banks where small clearings could be made, and where his implements are still found buried in gravel-beds. As the cold of the approaching Ice Age became more severe, men took to living in caves, and with the retreat of the ice the climate became milder and thick forests began to clothe the land. The fierce men of the caves with their heavy brow ridges disappeared before a new invader —neolithic man—who brought polished stone implements, and buried his round-headed kinsmen in round graves or barrows. Neolithic man probably arrived in Britain between 3000 and 2000 B.C., and started cultivating the land and domesticating animals. But about the same time—or perhaps earlier —long-headed people who came from the Mediterranean approached Britain from the south-west and settled in Wales and Cornwall. They brought with them the idea of building great stone circles, and these Megalith builders have left as their greatest monuments Stonehenge and Avebury—showing how far they penetrated towards the east. So even at this early age two strains of people inhabited Britain—the one group mainly in Lowland Britain, the other mainly in Highland Britain.

Then came the broad-headed Nordic-Alpine peoples, also from the south-east, with their bronze and, later, iron implements, but even these were but indifferent weapons with which to attack dense forest growth. So these early people laid out their trackways on the ridges where the forest was thinner or absent.

The people of Britain at this time—between 1000 B.C. and A.D. 43—were organised in tribes, and are often referred to in British literature as the "ancient Britons."

In A.D. 43 the Roman conquest of Britain began by an entry in the south-east and a rapid advance north-westwards towards London. A Roman commercial centre was quickly established at the natural crossing-place (still the lowest bridging point) of the Thames, and the Romans imposed a uniform organisation over the whole of Lowland Britain. There they established cities and farms (villae) and made their long straight roads, which still form the basis of the British main road system. [For the most part,] the Romans realised the value of both local and regional site values. [As a consequence,] the great Roman settlements have not only survived but have become [great] foci of modern life. The Romans established their Civil Districts all over Lowland Britain, but never established themselves over Highland Britain or the Celtic fringe. In Wales, the Pennines, and the North they established military camps and military districts, and Hadrian's Wall from Carlisle to the Tyne (at Wallsend) marked for long the limit of Roman influence northwards. Beyond Hadrian's Wall the province of Valencia was but a temporary extension of the Roman domain embracing southern Scotland as far as the wall of Antoninus from the Forth to the Clyde.

The withdrawal of the Romans, owing to the troubles at home, left Britain open to new invaders. The fifth and sixth centuries were the period of invasion, conquest, and settlement by the pagan Angles, Saxons, and Jutes. Lowland Britain became completely Anglo-Saxon, but Highland Britain remained Celtic and Christian, though there were extensive movements amongst the Celts themselves— notably an invasion of Scotland (where the

[Adapted from *The Face of Britain*, British Life and Thought: No. 5, published for the British Council by Longmans, Green and Company, London, 1945. Pp. 11-14. Used by permission.]

Scots from Ireland drove out the native Picts) and Irish invasions of Wales and Cornwall. Whereas the Romans had imposed their control and to some extent their culture, but had eventually departed leaving mainly roads and cities to mark their four-centuries sojourn, the Anglo-Saxons both conquered and absorbed the native inhabitants of Lowland Britain. [Deep into] the forested lowlands of the heart of England the Anglo-Saxons penetrated by river; their settlements were largely riverside settlements, and their chief towns (now the "county towns") nearly always on navigable waterways. [However,] Anglo-Saxons extended the use of the plough and laid the foundations of British agriculture: they gave England her name (Angleland), her language, and many of her institutions.

The Anglo-Saxons were followed by the Danes, who established a Danish Kingdom, but the Norwegian invaders of the eighth, ninth, and tenth centuries were seafaring Vikings who found in the coastlands of Highland Britain an environment more closely resembling that of their Norwegian homeland, and so established themselves as a Scandinavian fringe.

Thus the British Isles at the time of the Norman Conquest (A.D. 1066) comprised an Anglo-Saxon Lowland zone (by this time converted to Christianity), a Celtic Highland zone, and an irregular, Scandinavian fringe. Like the Romans before them, the Normans spread over Lowland Britain, where they constituted a ruling minority crystallising and intensifying the feudal system. They gave to this part of the country many of the finest castles, cathedrals, and churches still extant, for the Anglo-Saxons previously had built mainly in wood. It was not until a century after the conquest of England that the invasion of Ireland began; it was not until 1282 that the Principality of Wales was added to the domain of the Plantagenet Kings. The remaining large portion of Highland Britain resisted both union and conquest until Scotland, in the person of her King James VI, provided a monarch who became James I of [the United Kingdom] in 1603.

At various times since the Norman invasion the cultural and economic life of Britain has been enriched by the arrival of groups of refugee immigrants—notably Flemings and Huguenots.

The visitor to Britain is often at a loss to understand the marked local variations to be found in so small an area in speech, manners, customs, and, to a less extent, in religion, dress, and even physical characteristics. These differences are often accentuated by an intense local patriotism, and their understanding is only possible through an appreciation of the diverse environments and their effect on the evolution of human groups of very different history and background.

In the following selection a few statistical tables have been included; these compress into little space what it might take many paragraphs of text to explain. The birth rate, as you have already learned in the study of the Chinese peasant, shows the number of children born every year per thousand of the population. For example, if 100 children were born within a year in a community of 5000 the birth rate would be 20. The death rate shows the number of people who die every year per thousand of the population. The difference, then, between the birth rate and the death rate is called the natural increase.

We begin to understand what some call "the dynamics of population" when we compare the birth rates and death rates between different social classes, occupations, ethnic groups, or regions. We also find out what effects industrialization has on a people.

• 123 • The Population of Britain
EVA M. HUBBACK

THE GROWTH OF THE POPULATION SINCE 1066

Relatively little is known about the size and growth of the population of England and Wales before 1801, when the first census was taken. Before that time the number of people in this country was largely guesswork. All we can say is that at the time of the Norman Conquest it was probably about 2 millions. It grew slowly, so that in 1600 it was about 5 millions. This slow rate of growth was due mainly to the fact that, although there was a high natural birth-rate and practically no emigration, there was, up to the middle of the fifteenth century, an almost equally high death-rate due to bad social conditions coupled with inadequate medical knowledge. [It] is thought that before the Industrial Revolution about three-quarters of the children born in London died before they were 10 years old.

During the last half of the eighteenth century general prosperity grew rapidly; the introduction of the turnip family into our rotation of crops made it possible to keep cattle alive to produce fresh meat and milk in winter. Scientific discoveries, such as vaccination, and progress in medical knowledge generally greatly reduced mortality—especially infant mortality—and the death-rate began to fall considerably.

During the nineteenth century—although the birth-rate remained as high as it has probably ever been until 1871, when it reached 35 per thousand—the expanding industrial system, with its greatly increased prosperity, led to a much bigger chance of rearing a large family successfully.

This led to such a big increase in the population that it nearly doubled itself between 1801 and 1841, and more than doubled itself during the following sixty years. By 1900,

therefore, it had reached 32 millions in England and Wales. But during the next forty years—up to 1940—the increase only consisted of another 10 millions, since, in spite of the death-rate continuing to fall from 1871, a startling change began to take place about that time in the birth-rate. It fell steadily from 35 in the seventies, until in 1933 it reached a record low level of 14.4 There was a fall in the average number of children per family from over 5 in the 1870's to about 2 in the 1930's—a number obviously too small for replacement purposes.

POPULATION GROWTH AND CHANGES, 1851-1938

As long as the birth-rate is higher than the death-rate there is a natural increase in the population, assuming this effect is not offset by emigration. [The] birth-rate grew steadily from 1851 to 1871, when it began to fall, and by 1938 was less than half what it had been in the earlier period. Suggested causes for this are given later.

The death-rate, which had dwindled, though intermittently, since the middle of the eighteenth century, began also to fall steadily from about 1871, when it was 22.3, to 1938, when it was 11.6. These figures, however, do not fully reflect what had actually happened; for—since the proportion of deaths is highest among young children and old people, and lowest among people between 5 and 50 years of age—the death-rate (like the birth-rate) is affected, not only by changes in social conditions and medical knowledge, but also by changes in the age-distribution of the population. The increase in the proportion of old people, from 9.4 per cent of the population in 1920 to 13 per cent in 1938, meant that the death-rate had not fallen as low as it would have done had the 1920 proportions between old and young been maintained. Had this

[Adapted from *The Population of Britain*, Penguin Books, West Drayton, Middlesex, England, 1947. Pp. 20-35. Used by permission].

happened, the death-rate in 1938 would have been 8.5 instead of 11.6.

The effect of changes in the death-rate at different periods can best be realised in changes in the "expectation of life" at birth in the same periods. (The expectation of life means the average age in years to which a person is likely to live if the death-rate of the year when he was born remained unchanged.) The expectation of life for men increased from 43.7 years in 1881 to 61.8 years in 1938, and for women from 47.2 to 65.8 for the corresponding years. It serves as an admirable indication of changes in social conditions, and is everywhere higher for women than for men. This is partly because baby boys are more difficult to bring up than baby girls, and partly because men are more likely to follow dangerous pursuits than are women.

Owing to the fact that between 1851 and 1938 the birth-rate declined to a greater extent than the death-rate, the natural increase of the population, which is the margin between the two, fell from 13.2 in 1871 to 3.5 in 1938. This indicates the great slowing down in the rate of growth in the population during that period.

Even the rate of natural increase, however, cannot tell us very much about what is happening with regard to the replacement of any given generation by the next, as it does not take into account various other important changes. Neither can the birth-rate, since this relates births to the total population, whereas, of course, it is only women of child-bearing age who can have children. If, therefore, the proportion of women between 15 and 45 years old in the population changes, the birth-rate is bound to alter so long as the number of children produced by each woman remains the same. Since younger women are naturally more fertile than older ones, it will also change if there is a larger proportion of younger to older women within the child-bearing age-group.

We shall have a much better idea of what is happening, then, if births are related, not to the total population, but to every thousand women of child-bearing age. This gives us the *General Fertility Rate,* and shows us that whereas in 1871 1,000 women of these ages were having 154 children a year, in 1938 they were only having 62.1.

NET REPRODUCTION RATE

. . . The net reproduction rate gives the most faithful indication of what is happening with regard to replacement, since it takes into account, not only the birth-rate of the mothers, but also the death-rate of the daughters; and it will be remembered that a net reproduction rate of 1 shows that the present generation of women of child-bearing age are exactly reproducing themselves. The following table shows the course of the net reproduction rate in England and Wales between 1851 and 1938. The turning point came actually in 1922, and the rate became less than 1 from that date. By 1931 it had fallen so low that women of marriageable age were failing to reproduce themselves by a sensible amount. It only reached 1 again in 1946.

TABLE [1.]—NET REPRODUCTION RATE IN ENGLAND AND WALES, 1851-1938

Year	Net Reproduction Rate
1851	1.3
1861	1.4
1871	1.5
1881	1.5
1891	1.4
1901	1.2
1911	1.1
1921	1.1
1931	0.8
1938	0.8

CHANGES IN AGE COMPOSITION

Although the net reproduction rate was less than 1 between 1923 and 1946, there was still some natural increase in our population, as there were so many people, both in and after the reproductive age-groups, who were born at a time when the birth-rate and the number of births per annum were both very much higher. One of the most important effects of any fall in the birth-rate is the change in age distribution of the population. [In] 1938 the number of school-children, 6,860,000, was—even if all lived—too few to replace the young people between 15 and 24, from whom productive workers are selected. These in their turn, being only 7,431,000, were too few to replace the group of potential parents between 25 and 34, who numbered 7,621,000. Of all women over 15, over 40 per cent had already passed the age in which they could have children. One person in four was already over 50 years old.

MARRIAGE RATE AND AGE OF MARRIAGE

So far, in referring to the birth-rate, we have not distinguished between married and unmarried mothers. But since in England and Wales legitimate births in 1938 were 96 per cent of the whole, it is these which constitute the overwhelming majority of births. We must enquire, therefore, into the marriage-rate, i.e. the number of persons married per 1,000 of the population. In this country it has always been high. In 1850, 859 out of every 1,000 women were married; in 1910 the number had fallen to 818, but rose again in 1920-22 to 860, dropping in 1931 to 826, but rising to 900 in 1938. (The marriage-rate in each year is very closely related to the level of economic prosperity.)

Women who marry young may well be expected to have more children than those who marry late in life, partly because they have more years of possible child-bearing ahead, partly because the power to bear children is greatest for women under 25, and becomes greatly reduced near the end of the child-bearing age. Contrary to the popular impression, the average age at which women marry has dropped in recent years. It rose slightly to about 26 years old in 1911, then declined slightly to 25.5 in 1931 and to 24.6 in 1938.

THE BIRTH RATE IN DIFFERENT SOCIAL CLASSES

Neither the birth-rate nor the death-rate is the same in all social classes. Take the birth-rate. As is common knowledge, since 1871 a high birth-rate has in this country generally gone hand-in-hand with poverty; and the birth-rate among unskilled workers was in 1938 probably about 30 per cent higher than among the richer and professional classes, who were, before the war, considerably below replacement level. Thus the poorer half of the nation's parents were producing perhaps two-thirds of the coming generation; and, in general the size of families was inversely correlated with the income level of those in a given occupation.

This difference in the birth-rates of various social classes was most marked when voluntary family restriction first began, since it was the richer classes who first adopted the new ideas and habits. Gradually these spread to the middle classes; later to the higher rank of the working classes and still later to the unskilled workers. This being so, it is not surprising that the difference in the rates between different social classes became less and less, and that recently the biggest fall has been among the lowest-paid workers. Can we in due course expect the present position to be reversed so that there is a direct instead of an inverse ratio between a man's income and the number of his children? . . .

The following table illustrates tendencies up to 1931.

TABLE [2.]—BIRTH RATES IN DIFFERENT CLASSES, ENGLAND AND WALES, 1911, 1921 AND 1931

Class	Births per Thousand Husbands under 55; Wives under 45		
	1911	1921	1931
1. Professional and higher business ranks	119	98	94
2. Lower professional and business ranks	132	104	90
3. Skilled workers	153	141	120
4. Semi-skilled workers	158	162	133
5. Unskilled workers	213	178	153

It will be noticed that by 1921 the difference between Class 1 and the lowest two classes had narrowed, and that by 1931 Class 2 and Class 1 had changed places, Class 1 hardly changing, but all other classes showing a considerable reduction.

POPULATION FIGURES, 1939-46

During the war various startling changes took place in both the marriage- and birth-rates, though the death-rates have remained singularly little affected. It is desirable that these should be considered apart from the pre-war figures, as it is immensely important to try to estimate whether in the future it is the war-time or the pre-war rates which are most likely to hold the field.

Let us start with the marriage-rate. One reason for the startling increase in the number of marriages—especially between 1933 and 1942—has already been suggested. All over the world more people marry when times are good than when times are bad. During the period of worst unemployment in the early thirties, the difficulty of getting a home together was so great that it was not surprising that as employment became better—thanks to the steady increase in building and to rearmament—the rate began to rise.

When the war came, the heightening of the emotional atmosphere and the natural desire of young people to marry when they could still be together, combined with a period of economic prosperity unknown in their lifetime, resulted in a startling increase in the number of marriages. At the beginning of the war an additional reason for the high marriage-rate was that the "marriageable stock" itself had risen since 1931. The bumper crop of babies born in 1920 and 1921, when families were re-united after the 1914-18 war, had reached marriageable age, and a larger proportion of young people were marrying. An extra source of husbands for young spinsters was also to be found in the large numbers of young unmarried men in the American and Canadian Forces.

Since 1939 there has been a marked if intermittent rise in the birth-rate. This was probably partly due to the increased number of marriages, and partly to the desire felt by older married couples for a child before they were separated. The fact that married women could not be directed to employment if they had children under the age of 14 may have contributed to an increased birth-rate. But in spite of the fact that there were nearly a quarter of a million more marriages in the first three years of the war than there would have been if the moderately high marriage-rate of 1936-8 had persisted, nevertheless there were only 190,000 more births than there would have been had the average birth-rate of 1936-8 been maintained. Demobilisation has been followed by the birth-rate rising to 22.7 for the first quarter of 1947.

The most significant figure from the point of view of our future population is the average family size. Further light is required on any possible changes; and an investigation for the purpose is being made by the Royal Commission. Up till the last few years the average family size had remained unchanged since 1930; and—this is the important point—at a size (about 2) lower than replacement level. But the high birth-rate of recent years would suggest that it is extremely probable that it has now increased, though not up to replacement level.

• 124 • Distribution of the Industrial Population in Britain

THE WORLD PHENOMENON OF URBANISATION •

Two outstanding features of population growth have marked the last couple of centuries. The first has been the astonishing expansion of the nations of the Western civilisation. It is stated that at the present time peoples of European origin number approximately 625 millions, constituting about one-

[Adapted from *Report*, Royal Commission on the Distribution of the Industrial Population, London, 1940. Pp. 10-16, 29-30.]

third of the human race. It is not clear how many people of European descent there were in 1800, or what proportion of the world's population they then constituted, but there is authority for the estimate that the increase in their number since 1800 has amounted to about 400 millions, while that of all the rest of the world has probably not been more than 200 or 300 millions. This clearly is a very remarkable expansion.

The death rate in Great Britain in the eighteenth century prior to the Industrial Revolution was undoubtedly high. In London it was probably as high as 50 per 1,000 in 1750, and it was still over 30 per 1,000 in 1800. In the smaller towns and rural districts of England there was a considerably lower death rate than in London and some of the other larger places, but, even so, it was probably not less than 35 per 1,000 in the middle of the eighteenth century for the whole of England. By 1800, it had fallen to between 25 and 30, leaving a considerable margin as compared with the birth rate even if that did not exceed 35 as may well have been the case, and when the second and third censuses had been taken (1811-21) the flood of new life had popularised the phrase, a "redundant population". This decline of the death rate was largely attributable to the Industrial Revolution itself: that Revolution removed two great positive checks which had been operative in greater or less degree until that time, namely, inadequate subsistence and the heavy incidence of disease due to the lack of proper sanitation—sanitation which the growing wealth of the towns was in the succeeding years to provide.

The second remarkable feature of population growth has been the even more rapid proportional rate at which the great urban centres of Western civilisation have spread, overflowing their boundaries and forming sprawling agglomerations of humanity, many of dimensions without precedent in the world's history.

Here again are traceable the effects of the Industrial Revolution. The world in the sixteenth, seventeenth and eighteenth centuries had known teeming cities of traffic and exchange: Venice, the Hansa towns, the City of London, were busy centres of merchandise and population long before steam and the power loom had revolutionised the conditions of industrial production, but the factory and the machine at once gripped, transformed and expanded existing centres of commerce.

Great Britain, the first country to receive the impact of the Revolution through the discoveries of her sons, was also the first to experience the phenomenon of uncontrolled urban growth. Up to the end of the eighteenth century, probably no city in the world had reached a population of a million, but at the census of 1801 Greater London is recorded as having reached a population of well over a million and since then it has retained its place as the most populous conurbation in the world.

The nineteenth century was marked by the persistent and rapid enlargement of the great cities and in Great Britain to-day approximately two-fifths of the total population dwell in the seven million-mark conurbations, while the corresponding proportion in the United States is only about one fifth. Generally speaking, during the last hundred years the million-mark cities have tended to increase their populations at rates at least twice as great as the mean rate of increase for their respective countries; and especially is this characteristic of the capital cities.

DISTINCTIVE FEATURES OF URBANISATION IN GREAT BRITAIN

The world-wide development of intensive urbanisation presents in the case of Great Britain certain distinctive features, two of which are of great importance. First, the acreage of Great Britain in comparison with other Western countries is exceedingly limited in proportion to the size of its population.

[If] England is taken as a unit, the pressure of population shows a figure per square mile of more than 60 in excess of Belgium, which is usually considered the world's most densely peopled national area.

The second distinctive feature referred to above is the vast—and many would add alarming—growth of population in London and South-Eastern England, largely at the expense of the rest of the country.

The concentrations of population in Great Britain may be divided into two groups, namely, the shipping and commercial centres and the centres of mining and manufacturing industry. The two main shipping centres, London and Liverpool, import commodities from all parts of the world, with the result that they have large docks, warehouses and other storage facilities, together with the remaining technical equipment required for unloading and distributing on a large scale. This commercial and distributing function alone provides employment for a considerable population, which in turn gives employment in local industries to a further group. But London, in particular, is more than that. In quite early days it became a centre of handicrafts and cottage industries that have since become factory industries, with the result that it is now an important centre of such industries as leather tanning and dressing; boot and shoe manufacture; the finishing sections of a number of iron and steel trades; tailoring, dress-making, millinery, etc.; the production of paper and of chemicals, dye stuffs and drugs. As a port it was once largely engaged in the building of wooden vessels and it is still an important ship repairing centre; it has also become one of the chief grain milling centres. It is also the largest centre of the timber trade. Having always been the main commercial centre of this country London has grown to be a large factory centre. Its growth as a manufacturing centre has also been fostered by the fact that it is the capital city and the centre of the British commonwealth, the chief centre of the printing and publishing trades, and the Mecca of tourists both from within the country and from other parts of the world, with the result that it maintains public utility services and miscellaneous services on a scale unknown elsewhere in this country. Other large commercial centres, such as Liverpool and Hull, have also built up manufacturing industries, either industries of a local character or "basic" industries using imported materials.

The second group of concentrations of population is based upon mining and manufacture. The main concentrations are the Clyde Valley, the North East Coast, East Lancashire, the West Riding and the West Midlands. Other less pronounced concentrations are to be found in other parts of the country, such as South Wales and the East Midlands. It will be observed that every one of these is situated on a coalfield. In the case of some, more particularly South Wales and the North East Coast, the economy of the community is largely based upon coal production and the sale of coal outside the area. In the case of others, coal is the foundation of manufacturing industries the products of which are the main products that are sold outside the area. Thus, for example, in West Yorkshire the supremacy of coal is challenged by the wool textile industry, which is itself largely based on coal; in South Yorkshire the mining industry has helped to build up a large and still growing steel industry; in the West Midlands the coal industry exists mainly as the handmaid of a large group of miscellaneous metal industries. Thus the coal industry performs a double function by providing a commodity for export to other areas or other countries and by attracting other industries to its own neighborhood. It may be broadly stated that throughout the nineteenth century coal acted as the great magnet to the industrial population other than that which was concentrated in the chief shipping and commercial areas.

The next selection is the result of the efforts of an organization called Political and Economic Planning, which describes itself as,

> . . . an independent non-party group, consisting of more than a hundred working members who are by vocation industrialists, distributors, officers of central and local government, town planners, architects, economists, doctors and so forth, and

who give part of their spare time to the use of their special training in fact-finding and in suggesting principles and possible advances over a wide range of social and economic problems. . . . The group has . . . published full-scale reports on the coal-mining, cotton and iron and steel industries, housing and building, electricity supply, international trade, the Press, the health services, the social services, retirement pensions, continued education from the age of fourteen, and agricultural research.

Four years' work went into the preparation of the report, a small part of which is presented below.

It seeks to provide a comprehensive, balanced and up-to-date summary of the main factors affecting the choice of location of industry, and to supply a basis for a judgement upon the practicability and advisability of attempting conscious stimulation and guidance of industrial development in the national interest. The Report finds in favour of such a policy, but points out its difficulties and limitations, and shows where further examination is needed.

• 125 • Trends in Town Development

Towns are among the oldest social organisms of civilization and have developed a complex life, many aspects of which are only remotely relevant to the problems of location of industry. Nevertheless, the town is, in most cases, the background of industry and is, to a large extent, moulded by the particular nature of its contact with industry, past and present. On the one hand industries, especially those with low location factors, have been established in towns in order to obtain services, labour and markets. On the other hand, towns have grown up round industries, especially those such as coal or cotton with high location factors. It is difficult, therefore, to say to what extent the present distribution of population is the result of, or the reason for, the present pattern of the location of industry. The industrial population and industry have, at any rate, to live side by side, if not intermingled, and it is therefore important to consider their interrelations. These interrelations are both social and economic. There are towns, notably London, in which families from many other areas are eager to live and there are other towns which not only fail to attract outsiders, but fail to hold a number of their own most enterprising inhabitants. The success or otherwise of an industry may depend on the social vitality, the general planning and the efficiency of the services of the town in which it is established. It is easy in considering the location of industry to underrate the importance of this relationship, or even to omit all reference to it. Apart from those costs directly incurred by the individual business there are social consequences arising out of its operations which have to be borne by the community as a whole.

According to the Census, 80 per cent of the 1931 population of England and Wales lived in local government areas classed as urban—that is, in country and municipal boroughs and in urban districts. Up to 1901 there was a rapid rise in the urban percentage, and this was followed by thirty years of relative stability, but, according to the 1936 estimates, the rise has now been resumed.

[Adapted from *Report on the Location of Industry in Great Britain,* Political and Economic Planning, London, 1939. Pp. 148-168. Used by permission.]

... Thus at least four out of every five people in Great Britain are town dwellers. Moreover, areas which are for local government purposes distinct are often in practice parts of one large town. The population is, in fact, much more urbanised and much more concentrated in a relatively few large towns than the figures suggest. The evidence of the Garden Cities and Town Planning Association before the Royal Commission on the Geographical Distribution of the Industrial Population shows that in 1934 more than 20 million persons out of the 45.4 million in Great Britain lived in or very near the fourteen chief urban centres, 15¼ millions living in the six largest towns.

In view of these figures it is rather remarkable that hardly more than 12 per cent of the area of England and Wales is urban (1931), and much of this is not yet built up, although as an offset substantial tracts of land classed as "rural" are more or less built up. Towns from their very nature show a high density of population in relation to their area, but the actual density varies a great deal.

ADVANTAGES AND DISADVANTAGES OF URBANISATION

... Land values in the central areas of the largest towns rise to remarkable levels. It was estimated by the President of the Surveyors' Institution in November, 1935, that properties occupying the best position in the City of London had about doubled in value during the previous fifty years, and Sir Charles Bressey, who quotes this in his "Greater London Highway Development Survey, 1937," states that the cost of comparatively insignificant street widenings sometimes works out at a rate exceeding £2 million per mile. As regards effects on housing, the Garden Cities Association shows that in Manchester the cost of land for the Hulme working-class rehousing scheme is over £7,000 per acre, and the total cost per flat, including site, is over £800; while in central London with land at up to £20,000 an acre, figures in excess of £900 per flat are reached, compared with an average of about £400 for cottage houses with gardens in small towns. The natural result is that

long-needed road facilities are not provided, and housing replacement has been either neglected or provided at a low standard of space per person in order to keep down rents plus subsidies to a not quite intolerable level.

The effects on traffic and health respectively are clearly traceable. An investigation for the Bressey Report showed that the average speed of a well-driven powerful private motor car on main routes through London during working hours in 1936 was not more than 12½ m.p.h., and on considerable stretches in the centre was forced as low as 3½-8 m.p.h., with frequent holdups lasting 1-2 minutes at points of intersection. On the North Circular Road, a suburban highway generally considered very inadequate for traffic needs, the average speed was 23.6 m.p.h., and it seems safe to say that in typical modern street conditions in the British large town, journeys by private car take at least four times as long as they would on unobstructed roads. The growth of towns and of traffic without corresponding improvements in facilities has now, in fact, more than offset in the central areas any speed advantage due to the invention of the internal combustion engine. A powerful car now takes longer to do many journeys than an average cab-horse of forty years ago.

Recent urban growth has meant that large and continually increasing numbers of people are forced by lack of accommodation, high rents, and unsuitable living conditions near their work to live at a distance and travel back and forth twice or in some cases four times every working day. In 1921, the latest year for which such figures are available, at least 800,000 persons were travelling daily to work in central London. The movement, however, includes many opposite currents. Thus Stretford, near Manchester, sent nearly a quarter of its population out to work in other areas, but imported in their place other day-time workers equal to almost half its population. There were already nearly twenty years ago many similar but less extreme cases not only in Greater London, but in most of the chief urban areas. According to the Garden Cities Association "in the year up to June

1937, the people of London made 4,250 million journeys in the London Transport area—436 per head or 2,340 per family. They paid in fares over £41 million or £16 3s. per family. The average journey cost 2.347 pence. In Birmingham in 1936 the journeys were 373 per head and the fares 1½d. per journey, or £8 17s. per family for the year," not counting in either case journeys by taxi or private car. In a small town the corresponding figure is estimated at only £2-£3, and in many cases it is less.

The time taken in such travel for many persons averages 1½-2 hours a day, and on a number of lines a majority of the passengers who travel at peak hours have to stand. The problem of excessive journey time and fares takes different forms in different areas, but is common to the mining valleys of South Wales and the newest industrial belts. A case is known of a large factory outside London, one-quarter of whose workers live an hour or more away from it. On the other hand, there are towns even in the 100,000 size-range, where almost all the workers can still easily walk or cycle to work and go home for their midday meal. According to 'The People's Food,' by Sir W. Crawford and H. Broadley, the proportion of husbands having their midday meal at home is between 50 and 60 per cent in the larger British towns, the proportion being lowest in London (30 to 50 per cent).

The effect of running very heavy traffic in narrow channels between tall buildings, or underground, is greatly to increase exposure to noise, which is very fatiguing and harmful to the nerves. In the carriage of a City tube train travelling at 30 m.p.h. the noise ranges from about 90 to 106 phons—a level at which an adult lion continuously roaring to capacity (105 phons at 18 ft.) would scarcely be audible. Many city streets produce continuous traffic noise reaching 80-90 phons, which is about the level of thunder 1-3 miles away and louder than church bells at 400 yards. The noisiest position by Niagara Falls is stated to yield an average of 105 phons.

Another effect of urban congestion is the very heavy atmospheric pollution already mentioned. An investigation by the Department of Scientific and Industrial Research (summarised in Cmd. 3989, 1931) showed that over a complete year atmospheric pollution from Norwich, a town about two miles in diameter, with relatively very clean air, was significant for a distance of five to six miles down wind from the centre of the city. With a town twenty-four miles in diameter, or a group of neighbouring urban areas twenty-four miles in diameter, pollution would be significant up to about sixty to seventy miles, or more in those cases where the air of the town concerned was dirtier than at Norwich. Smoke is annually responsible for damage measurable in money to the extent of about £40-£50 million—not to speak of an enormous amount of damage on which no money value can be placed. Here is an avoidable national waste equivalent to about 9d. on the income tax. The distorting effect of atmospheric pollution on town development is seen in the emergence of suburbs to windward of the worst affected areas as segregated communities of the richer local inhabitants. Thus smoke plays its part in aggravating class divisions.

A further problem particularly acute in large towns is public cleansing, which is described by the Ministry of Health in its 1936-37 Report as "one of the most costly services provided out of the rates," involving an annual total charge on England and Wales of some £11 million. The towns contribute the overwhelming majority of the 15 million tons per annum of solid waste matter which has to be disposed of in such a way as to avoid nuisance, including about 1 ton of household refuse from every house and about 3 million tons of debris (excluding snow) from 26,500 miles of streets in towns with over 20,000 population.

It is hardly surprising that in spite of modern improvements in sanitation and preventive medicine one of the characteristics of large towns is their unhealthiness. Care must be taken in interpreting statistics on this subject, because there is no standard of measurement for health, and such indirect indices as death-rates present pitfalls. The Registrar-General's Decennial Supplement for England and Wales, issued in 1936, offers something like a reliable yardstick, and shows that taking the national "expected" rate as 100, the actual male death-rate for all county boroughs is 111, and for all rural districts 86. That is, male death-rates in county boroughs are 30 per cent above those in rural districts.

Large towns have usually proved a type of habitat in which the human species can live, but is unable to reproduce itself adequately to maintain its numbers. In the past this has been due mainly to comparatively heavy death-rates: now the same result is brought about largely by the towns' very low birth-rates. In England and Wales, however, there is much less contrast between town and country in this respect than in certain continental nations. In the past the deficiency of the towns has been made good out of the surplus of the country, but this is obviously difficult when the country is producing very little surplus and when its population is reduced to less than one-fourth that of the towns. The period in which it was frequent to find a very large proportion of country-bred people living in large towns has definitely ended, and the towns have increasingly to face replacing their own populations. Yet in many respects recent changes have made urban areas more unsuited than ever to the bearing and rearing of children—as a large number of the drawbacks already described are particularly unfavourable to family life. The large city tends to become a suitable environment only for the able-bodied and unencumbered adult.

Enough has been said to indicate that there are certain disadvantages in concentrating populations in large towns. What are the benefits of the practice and how far do they offset the disadvantages?

The most evident advantage of the town is that it brings large numbers of people, many at a high standard of living, closely enough together for the use of elaborate services and equipment in common. A rich enough family can maintain in an isolated country house its own electric light plant, its own access by metalled roads, its own passenger and goods transport, and its own extensive library, picture gallery, and even zoo, but for the vast majority of families such services have only been brought within reach by devices for their collective provision. The town enables a collection of families grouped together to enjoy a great number of services in common at a low cost.

There is an inherent economy, often of immense importance, in such collective provision, but the nature and extent of this economy is affected by technical changes. In two respects such changes have recently had an important influence. In the first place the old limitations on the size of an efficient town, which were imposed by the limits of walking distance and by difficulties of regular provisioning and water supply have disappeared.

But it must be noted that the same developments which enable the large town to become larger also enable it to be more easily dispensed with. Science increases urban facilities and the size of group which can afford them, and also makes it possible to give the inhabitants of small towns and even of rural areas services formerly restricted to large towns. Electricity, road transport, telephones, wireless, piped water supply, retail delivery and other services are to a large and increasing extent available in rural as well as urban areas, although the cost is sometimes higher and the convenience or range of choice reduced. In a number of cases it is a deliberate policy to even out differences in cost and facilities as between town, suburb and country by making the consumer in the town subsidise the consumer outside it. The result has been not only greatly to enlarge the size of towns, but to blur, sometimes to a surprising extent, the distinction between town and country.

The same trend has led to other consequences. The old-fashioned town offered a relatively meagre range of services, whose effective enjoyment was confined to a small minority of its inhabitants. Lately there has been a progressive expansion, not only of the range of services, but of the proportion of the population which can enjoy them. This has involved in turn a great increase in the number of persons engaged in collective urban services, and has tended at the same time to reduce considerably the size of population needed to sustain a given unit of service. Certain services, such as electricity supply, tend to become available at lower cost the more densely their consumers are concentrated, but others, such as highways, increase in cost per unit of population beyond a certain density. Many of these, however, cannot be supported adequately by thinly scattered communities and they therefore become relatively more costly to provide both above and below certain densities. As the scale of use often varies directly with standards of living, a rise in standards of living may bring a small community up to the appropriate level for supporting a given service, or may push a large town into the zone of higher costs or increasing congestion.

A town which has an appropriate size of population for providing certain services to a privileged minority of its inhabitants may have a much larger population than is necessary or convenient for giving the same services to the whole or even a majority of its inhabitants. If, for example, two-thirds of the inhabitants of many of our large towns suddenly adopted the upper income-group practice of having a bath every morning, it would very seriously increase the difficulties and costs of the existing water supply, based on the assumption that most people have their bath, if any, not oftener than weekly, and on competitive exploitation of remote sources by rival water undertakings. Again, owing to the higher standard of living and the much greater use of road passenger transport, routes which could never have supported a service thirty years ago now do so comfortably, while services which were well used thirty years ago are in many cases hopelessly congested. Our urban street system, already chronically jammed with traffic when one person in twenty owns a car, would in most towns at once become virtually unusable if even three out of twenty started using cars, as in New Zealand.

Much of the confusion in contemporary urban life becomes explicable if it is borne in mind that the town represents, with considerable accretions and with only minor alterations, an organism created to serve a range of technical needs which has long since been outgrown, and a degree of privilege and differentiation in opportunity between sections of the community which no longer exists.

It is important in considering urban advantages to distinguish between those which are now, or shortly will be, shared by non-urban communities, such as telephones and electricity, and those which are likely permanently or for a long time to remain confined wholly or mainly to the town, such as department stores, art galleries, technical schools, and sewage disposal plants. One of the greatest material advantages of the large town is its capacity for low-cost, high-speed delivery of an immense range of goods, and its capacity to make instantly available a great variety of services, from permanent waving to advice on how to start manufacturing ball-bearings. For social purposes, again, towns have advantages which increase probably in direct ratio to their size, as between communities of similar character. There appears to be a tendency in small towns and in country districts for social groups either to cling to an excessively narrow range of interests, or to split up into fragments too small to follow out varying interests without a sense of frustration. In the large town a man can be and often is a member of several different social groups for several different purposes, but in the small town or the country there is an inevitable tendency, where different groups exist, for their memberships to overlap so heavily as to reduce their independent impetus and the sense of freshness gained from belonging to them. The advantage of the large town in this respect is, however, immensely increased by the smallness of the minority at present having the leisure, the education, and the will to take part in many significant activities, and by the overwhelming attraction which it can exert on people with minority interests owing to this and to economic factors.

The Emergence of

an Industrial Society

»»

Sometimes it is best to be technical in order to be clear. This is especially true when references in succeeding selections speak of Britain, Great Britain, the United Kingdom, and the British Isles. Just how do these terms relate to one another?

Great Britain (or Britain) is the large island that consists of Scotland, England, and Wales. Northern Ireland (frequently called Ulster), the Channel Islands, and the Isle of Man, in addition to Great Britain, make up the United Kingdom. The British Isles is the most inclusive term, since it includes the United Kingdom and also southern Ireland or Eire, formerly called the Irish Free State, which zealously asserts its independence from Britain.

In Great Britain itself, our major interest is in the Midlands, but before considering them we shall look at the major geographic features of the island as a whole. Industrialization has not blotted out the attractiveness of many regions or overwhelmed them with the monotonous uniformity that has come to industrial and urban sections. In fact, the habitat of Britain is remarkably varied, and there are many kinds of scenery within a short distance of most cities.

The geography of Britain is complex; many relatively small areas are recognized and their distinctive features are familiar to Britons. Some of the most important of these will be mentioned, and a few of the common English terms used in describing them will appear, such as heath, fell, moor, fen, and weald.

To some extent, the people of an industrial society appear less directly dependent on the physical features and resources of the land on which they live. But, on careful examination, the influence of the land can be seen to be as powerful as for simpler societies.

The selections which follow contain many references to the location of natural resources, such as coal and iron, around which great industrial developments have taken place. Likewise, the development of agricultural areas, main highways, and seaports has been fundamentally affected by aspects of the habitat.

But habitat consists of more than location, surface features, and climate. It also is made up of mineral, plants, and animal resources. The purpose of Selection 127 is to show the close connections among resources, technology, and the growth of industry. Before taking up this selection on the Black Country, which is just north of Birmingham, we ought to get firmly in mind two other of the important regional specializations of England, the Lancashire cotton industry and the Yorkshire woolen industry, since each region boasts different resources and a different historical development.

Most of us, when thinking of the rise of the Industrial Revolution, tend to think first of the developments in spinning and weaving machinery which, together with new sources of power, led to the factory system. As a matter of fact, the textile industry developed outside the Midlands—the focus of our study—but, as the next selection will show, the inventions occurring in the Midlands had considerable effect on the growth of factories elsewhere. Lancashire, to the northeast of the Midlands, was and still is the center of cotton-textile manufacturing. As A. Demangeon, in his book *The British Isles* (London: 1939) has pointed out,

> Owing to its proximity to a great seaport trading with the whole world (Liverpool), to its coalfield, its fast-flowing streams, its damp climate, and its long traditions of industrial skill, Lancashire soon concentrated in its area nearly the whole of the cotton industry of Great Britain. In 1838, it contained three-fifths of the cotton workers in the United Kingdom. . . .

For woolen goods one turned to Yorkshire, which is north of the Midlands. About it Demangeon also writes:

> The West Riding (in Yorkshire) stands in nearly the same relation to the woolen industry as Lancashire does to the cotton. Its lead in the industry dates from the end of the 18th century, when the manufacture of wool migrated to Yorkshire from the eastern and southwestern counties. There it was in touch with Lancashire and its progressive district which had created the great cotton industry. West Riding supplied water power for the mills, clean water for washing the wool, and, above all, coal which was lacking in the eastern and southwestern counties.

If space permitted, it would be of considerable interest to trace the various steps which were taken to give these two areas their worldwide pre-eminence in the manufacture of textiles. For a specific case study of a different industry, however, we have chosen another area—the Black Country, which will be described at greater length in Selection 136. The technological development here is related to the natural resources of coal and iron ore, as well as to the borrowing of numerous scientific ideas from other places. Attention will be given to metallurgy, together with the numerous discoveries and inventions that made the Black Country "black by day and red by night."

The previous references have already introduced the Midlands, the area with which we are concerned in this part of the book. But thus far the question of where the Midlands are has not been answered with precision. By combining many people's ideas, the author of the next selection, which was prepared especially for this book, was able to arrive at a composite which comes as close as possible to defining something about which opinions vary greatly. There is little doubt, however, as to the central area included in the term, and the drawing of sharp boundaries is often deceptive in geography as well as in other spheres.

• 126 • The English Midlands
CATHARINE K. HAYNES

LOCATION OF THE MIDLANDS

The English Midlands—the very use of the term implies the existence of an area which is somehow to be distinguished from the rest of England. We have only to look at the long list of organizations beginning "Midland . . ." in the Birmingham phone directory, to read headlines in a Nottingham paper such as "East Midlands and Festival," to look at such government reports as *North Midlands Coalfield,* or to hear the broadcast of the "Midland News" and the "Midland Quartet" from Droitwich to realize that the Midlands represents something distinctive.

Yet as one goes about trying to discover just what the Midlands is, one finds vagueness on the part of the ordinary person and confusion among the enlightened. As one delves beneath what appears on the surface to be confusion, however, one finds a core of consistency in the definition of the Midland region. During World War I the Ministries of National Service, Labour and Munition in their regional mobilization of the country had a district which was called "West Midlands." Since this time, the "Midlands" has been used to identify the central part of England in an overwhelming proportion of cases where administrative districts were designed. With the nationalization of some of the basic industries of Great Britain,

there has been even more regional administration, with reliance on some form of the term "Midlands" for this central portion. Although these administrative units have not sprung up from the grass roots but have rather been superimposed from the top, there can be little doubt that geographical, economic, and social factors have been taken into account as many of these divisions have been made.

[In the light of this, it] is of primary importance to emphasize that though we may locate a core of the Midlands, it is impossible to draw sharp lines around it. One geographer comments, "From the geographical point of view any attempt to define the exact boundaries of a region is usually a failure." This would appear to be particularly true in a country as small as England, so hemmed in by the sea, so bound together by common tradition, so interwoven by a highly developed network of communication, and so united—in recent decades—"by the overwhelming dominance of urban life."

It becomes clear as one examines these maps of administrative regions that in most cases a division between the East and West Midlands is acknowledged. On occasions, the East Midlands is called North Midlands, but the dichotomy between the two seems to be accepted by administrators. One administrative unit which did not divide the two, the British Broadcasting Corporation, recently witnessed the difference between East and West Midlands. For some time the BBC broadcasted from a station near Birmingham to the whole of the Midlands. So centered in the interests of the West Midlands were its programs that the newspapers of East Midland cities began to complain loudly in their editorial columns. As a result, only recently a station has been set up in Nottingham. This division seems to be reinforced by rather poor communications and transportation between the East and West Midlands, as compared with that between northern and southern points. There is no geographic barrier between the two, though perhaps they fall roughly into two river basins—the Severn and the Trent. One possible explanation is that the heavily populated Birmingham conurbation, lying west of center in the Midlands, has exerted a very heavy pull on the country surrounding it whereas to the East the areas have been more attracted to such cities as Nottingham, Leicester, Derby and have developed their loyalties and economic bonds accordingly.

THE WEST MIDLANDS

First, let us take a closer look at the West Midlands. Perhaps the most commonly accepted definition of the West Midlands today includes the counties of Shropshire, Herefordshire, Worcestershire, Warwickshire, and Staffordshire.

To characterize the West Midlands as a whole, however, would be quite difficult. One writer has said of the Midlands, "Even today many people regard it mainly as a place they cross in order to get somewhere else." Indeed, the picture called to the mind of many an Englishman is that of dingy factory row houses, air grimy with industrial smoke, and vast smouldering heaps of factory and mining waste. This picture is most characteristic of the Black Country, though other industrial areas in the West Midlands have many of these features to a lesser degree. There are contrasts in industrial areas—the Potteries of North Staffordshire are quite different from

the industrial Birmingham, for example. One observer speaks of Kidderminster, the center of the carpet industry, as having "distinct problems which occur nowhere else in the West Midlands." Even the coal mining districts vary. While in the Cannock Chase region the miners are isolated from the rest of society in their grim and straggling mining communities with few amenities and almost no recreation facilities, the miners in the East Warwickshire coal field are drawn from urban areas of mixed communities and enjoy a more varied existence. Turning west, we find the agricultural counties of Hereford and Shropshire, not to mention the more rural parts of Warwickshire and Worcestershire. Some of these areas remain rather untouched by the changes urbanization has wrought on the landscape of other sections. Stratford-on-Avon, for example, lies in as idyllic a country setting as is to be found in England.

Attempt to generalize on the characteristics of the people of the West Midlands [are seldom successful, for as one observer puts it:]

As for the people who live in these counties of central England, what sharp differences they show between one and another, what contrasts in temperament and outlook. Even in speech there is no gradual fading from one variation of a dialect to another as in the North and West, but distinct, abrupt changes in cadence, pronunciation, and words themselves. . . . It has been truly said that in no part of England is the population more heterogeneous.

Another commentator echoes:

No part of England has a character so difficult to assess as this group of loosely united counties. They do not fit into a mould as do, say, East Anglia, the North, or the West Country. They consist of so many dissimilar elements.

Perhaps the very dissimilarity of the people and the rich contrasts within the area serve to distinguish it from other regions in England, more finely drawn.

From all that can be gathered from impressions, the people themselves do not tend to identify themselves with the Midlands. Indeed, county pride seems a rather important factor here, as Mr. George Cadbury indicates:

> County loyalties are very strong, and the county regiments of the Army, county cricket teams, and the like have very considerably fostered this loyalty in recent years. The intrusion of new urban centres, like Birmingham, has blurred the lines a little, but in that case has provided a central regional capital which does not decrease the validity of the county lines at their outer extremities.

There are other indications of localized loyalties, not in the county unit as such, but in a district united around a particular economic pursuit or some other pervasive factor. We see local patriotism quite markedly in the Black Country and the Potteries. Whatever the loyalty, it seems in the light of present information that the West Midlands is an entity of discrete parts, rather than a region strongly bound together by common tradition and marked regional loyalty.

There is one unifying factor which cannot be denied; this is the dominating influence of the Birmingham Conurbation. There can be no doubt that this, the third largest conurbation (and the second largest city) of England, serves and is served by the area around it. Its industry is interlocked with that of the surrounding territory; it draws labor from these districts. It serves as a center of trade and commerce for the area; it draws much of its food from the neighboring farms. Its newspapers are delivered on a wide circle of doorsteps outside the city; people from all around find excellent travel facilities into Birmingham to satisfy their taste for the theatre, music, the pantomime, and the like. The University of Birmingham not only gets strong support from the West Midlands, but also serves it through regional research. As one gets further out on the periphery of the circle of influence, one finds pulls in other directions; such as the pull of Derby on Burton-on-Trent, the attraction of Manchester for the Potteries, the competition with Bristol in the southwestern extremes of the West Midlands. So significant is the dominating influence of Birmingham, however, that some would ap-

pear to use it as the primary criterion for inclusion in the West Midlands.

Let us now turn the spotlight on some of the areas within the West Midlands in order that we may not only see something of the variety of flavor to be found there but also that we may view the relationship of a few of the parts to the whole. It is not within the scope of this summary to give a complete analysis of any or all of these districts; these statements are, rather, to be taken as thumbnail sketches. They represent impressions of astute observers rather than summaries of scientific research—with some exceptions.

BIRMINGHAM

Birmingham, the regional center, is a comparatively young city, as cities go in England. It rose rapidly with the Industrial Revolution; today it enjoys a peculiarly healthy and resilient economy with its great variety of industry—predominantly light engineering. One observer comments that the recent rise of the city has meant relative freedom from the tradition of the landed aristocracy and acute class-consciousness that have been more common in other parts of England. The co-authors of the *West Midland Plan* have this to say:

> During the 19th century Birmingham was preeminently the home of the small man; the skilled artisan and the small manufacturer were the characteristic figures. Movement from one social stratum to another was relatively easy and common; the workman could set up on his own account. The result was a preponderance of the middle classes.

As the city has developed, it has extended outward to accommodate its bulging population; in this process many of the middle class have moved out with industrial and commercial development at the center.

THE BLACK COUNTRY

North and northwest of Birmingham lies the Black Country, an area of some 87,000 acres and with a population of somewhat under a million. It has a density of population of around half that of Birmingham—but this does not mean that there is more room for better living conditions or amenities, for mining, industrial development, and population growth have combined to despoil the land. An observer in 1843 wrote of this area:

> The traveler appears never to get out of an interminable village, composed of cottages and the very ordinary houses. In some directions he may travel for miles, and never be out of sight of numerous two-storied houses; so that the area covered by bricks and mortar must be immense. These houses, for the most part, are not arranged in continuous streets but are interspersed with blazing furnaces, heaps of burning coal in the process of coking, piles of ironstone calcining, forges, pit-banks, and engine chimneys; the country being besides intersected with canals, crossing each other at different levels, and the small remaining patches of the surface soil occupied with irregular fields of grass or corn, intermingled with heaps of the refuse of the mines or of slag from the blast furnaces. Sometimes the road passes between mounds of refuse from the pits, like a deep cutting on a railway; at others it runs like a causeway, raised some feet above the fields on either side, which have subsided by the excavation of the minerals beneath. . . . The whole country might be compared to a vast rabbit warren.

Even today, it is described "from an aesthetic viewpoint . . . (as) hideous in the extreme." The principal trades of the Black Country have been heavy industries—mining and heavy metal works. This industrial organization "either demanded heavy capital as with the iron foundries and heavy metal trades, or next to none, as with the nailers and small independent miners." This structure also called for unskilled and heavy labor; "there was little place in the economy for the middle classes or indeed the skilled artisan," in contrast to Birmingham. Today the Black Country is preponderantly working-class and for the most part, with the exceptions of Wolverhampton, Smethwick and perhaps West Bromwich and Walsall, is extremely poor. As

a consequence, the Black Country towns have almost invariably

> . . . grown up with little provision for middle class or upper class housing and still less for the amenities which these classes require. . . . Recreational facilities reflect this one-sided development. Theatres and large public halls scarcely exist at all; and even the provision of cinemas is poor. The Library service is, with one or two exceptions, conspicuously bad. . . .

It would seem from the above evidence that the Black Country is relatively homogeneous in its landscape, industry, and character of its population. It has, characteristic of working-class areas, a high birth rate and large family size. Perhaps this homogeneity has contributed to the strong sense of identification with the area. Behind this sense of community, moreover, is a body of Black Country fables, customs and the like. It is observed that Black Country men have a distinctive quality about them, reflected not only in their unique dialect but also in such things as a "Black Country humor, with a peculiarly acid character." It cannot be doubted that there is a strong sense of patriotism in this area, but, at the same time, the ties with the Birmingham Conurbation are represented not only by the continuous ribbon of settlement extending from Birmingham but also by marked economic interdependence.

NORTH STAFFORDSHIRE

From the Black Country we continue north to the northern part of the county of Staffordshire. Here we find two industries predominant—pottery and mining. The Potteries have their center in Stoke-on-Trent, which combines the famous Five Towns so vividly pictured by Arnold Bennett. In 1908 he wrote in *The Old Wives' Tale*:

> The Five Towns seem to cling together for safety. Yet the idea of clinging together for safety would make them laugh. They are unique and indispensable. From the north of the country right down to the south they alone stand for civilization, applied science,

organized manufacture, and the century—until you come to Wolverhampton. They are unique and indispensable because you cannot drink tea out of a teacup without the aid of the Five Towns; because you cannot eat a meal in decency without the aid of the Five Towns. For this the architecture of the Five Towns is an architecture of ovens and chimneys; for this it burns and smokes all night, so that Longshaw has been compared to hell; for this it is unlearned in the ways of agriculture, never having seen corn except as packing straw and in quarter'n loaves; for this, on the other hand, it comprehends the mysterious habits of fire and pure, sterile earth; for this it lives crammed together in slippery streets where the housewife must change white window-curtains at least once a fortnight if she wishes to remain respectable; for this it gets up in mass at six A.M., winter and summer, and goes to bed when the public-houses close; for this it exists—that you may drink tea out of a teacup and toy with a chop on a plate.

Perhaps in the nearly fifty years that have passed since this was written, there has not been too much change in the Five Towns. One critic describes Stoke as "a shapeless conglomeration with no real center," marked by "extremely poor living and working conditions." With its lack of diversity of industry, it has had a great problem of unemployment. There is a great amount of part-time work, in which women figure prominently. There is a heavy out-migration from the area because there is so little opportunity for young people and so little selection of occupation. The two industries of the area—pottery and mining—have attracted largely working-class people.

There has been some question about the inclusion of North Staffordshire in the West Midlands for purposes of planning. In contrast to the South Staffordshire coalfields, which is in the heart of the West Midlands, the northern fields belong to the Pennines, "being the western counterpart of the Yorkshire-Derbyshire-Nottinghamshire coalfield

which lies to the east of the Pennine range." "Its unique pottery industry, and the sturdy independence of its people have tended to make it self-contained." It appears to be pulled in two directions—towards Manchester and towards Birmingham—for various purposes. For shopping, services of medical specialists, entertainment, and the like, the people of North Staffordshire usually seek Manchester, while administratively they are definitely tied to Staffordshire. In 1942 one observer commented that North Staffordshire was too small for a subregional planning unit, that "much quiet absorption" into the Midlands was taking place; yet in the process of investigation, preparatory to suggesting the West Midland Plan, Sir Patrick Abercrombie and Herbert Jackson, only a few years later, decided that North Staffordshire should be a separate planning unit in the light of its differences from Birmingham and the Black Country.

As we leave this industrial strip from Birmingham to North Staffordshire, we find the industrial development more dispersed. Shropshire, Herefordshire and the southern part of Worcestershire are predominantly agricultural Though there seem to have been no questions as to the inclusion of Shropshire and southern Worcestershire in the West Midlands, there has been some doubt about Herefordshire. George Cadbury, discussing this doubt, says of Herefordshire:

It is in an entirely separate drainage area down the valley of the Wye, and is cut off from Worcestershire by the barrier of the Malvern Hills. It also has many close affiliations with South Wales and draws many of its supplies from Gloucester. On the other hand, there is no doubt that Hereford folk look to Birmingham, not Bristol, as their metropolis, and the existence of the reasonably good Birmingham-South Wales and Shrewsbury-South Wales railway services, which converge at Hereford, do tend to bind it to the region. Though Hereford traders tend to draw supplies from Gloucester, Hereford farmers tend to send their produce to Birmingham. . . . It is interesting to note that Birmingham University receives grants from all the counties except Herefordshire, and even in this county the Teachers' Training College at Hereford chose to be associated with the Midland Joint Board and is therefore linked with the headquarters at Birmingham University.

To counterbalance Mr. Cadbury's inclination to include Hereford, we find that, a few years later, the counties of Hereford and Shropshire did not join forces with the other West Midland Counties in working out their plan for the Ministry of Town and Country Planning. One commentator stated that these two counties had become wary of cooperating with the more urbanized and industrialized sections, because they felt they had lost ground in past "co-operation."

As we retrace our steps in the direction of the East Midlands, let us return to Staffordshire and enter the East Midlands via Burton-on-Trent, the brewing center. In this city, we have an illustration of the pull between the East and the West Midlands. Administratively, it is a part of the West Midlands, since it is located in Staffordshire. It is, however, only ten miles from Derby and buses run every quarter of an hour from Burton to Derby—a fact which illustrates their close ties. On the other hand, though thirty miles from Birmingham, Burton people seek this larger center for amusement, cultural activities, and more extended shopping. An excellent railway service makes Birmingham with its greater diversity readily accessible to the people of Burton. Here then, we see one instance of the lack of definitiveness in the transition from the West to the East Midlands.

THE EAST MIDLANDS

The East Midlands is even more difficult to define and describe than the West Midlands. Geologically, the East Midlands is linked, via a continuous coalfield with only a minor break, to southern Yorkshire. Northern Derbyshire, part of the Peak area, is really closer to the Pennines than to the East Midlands. Foundries and other heavy metal working industries provide a bond with the Shef-

field area. The emphasis on processing textiles tends to bind the East Midlands to the textile areas of the North. Perhaps less isolated in the past than was the West Midlands, the East Midlands has been more in the flow of English life and has been more under the influence of the traditional social structure.

The East Midlands has equally as much cultural and economic diversity as has the West Midlands, but it lacks the unifying factor of a dominant regional center. In the place of a Birmingham, the East Midlands has several cities with their satellite environs— Nottingham, Leicester, Derby and Lincoln— to mention the most prominent. These cities, unlike the more recent Birmingham, are county towns with a long history and tradition, tending to bind the loyalty of the surrounding areas, but dividing the influence within the region. In this division of power between the various centers, Nottingham has perhaps the edge. A planning official remarked:

Nottingham likes to think of herself as the queen of the Midlands and nothing makes Leicester madder. When Nottingham and Leicester have financial drives for the same cause, all they have to do is put up two barometers—one showing Nottingham results and the other Leicester's. That encourages competition all right.

In 1919 C. B. Fawcett wrote of the Trent Province (East Midlands) and the Severn Province (West Midlands):

In comparison with the Severn Province, the Trent Province may be said to possess much greater physical and historic unity, but distinctly has less economic unity. The last fact is primarily a result of the relative equality of its principal towns. . . . The central position of Nottingham would probably enable it to unify the life of the province; but it is not likely to be able to dominate that life to any great extent.

In 1928, Paul Bryan acclaimed Leicester as the rising power in the East Midlands because it was more favorably located in regard to transport facilities and had been less seriously affected by industrial depression than had

Nottingham. In 1950, however, it appears that Nottingham is rather generally accepted in administrative circles as the headquarters of this region. K. C. Edwards marks in Nottingham the assumption "of many of the functions of a regional capital as envisaged by Fawcett . . . in 1919." It is interesting to note in this connection that some West Midlanders explained the fact that there was no group such as the West Midlanders group in the eastern half of the district because of this lack of a dominant regional center, whereas an East Midlander, keenly interested in planning, said that the reason was the lack of funds to support such a group's activities.

What the East Midlands lacks in unity, it makes up in prosperity. Though there are some areas, such as the declining towns and villages of south-west Northamptonshire and a depressed cotton district and the older part of the coalfield in Derbyshire, which are rather depressed economically, for the most part the area enjoys economic well-being. During the depression, Fogarty writes: "Unemployment in all of the counties except Rutland, and in one or two years Lincolnshire, was well below the national level." One factor in this, we are told, is the excellent balance between industry and agriculture; another factor perhaps lies in the diversity of industry itself. There are rich and fairly recently opened coal resources. The East Midland coalfields have the highest productivity per man as well as the most modern of facilities of any coalfield in the country. The iron resources of the section produce one-third of the nation's foundry iron. The close proximity of these resources to coking coal sources has fostered the growth of foundries. Textiles, boots and shoes, light engineering are but samples of the diversity of industry in this area. There is considerable economic interdependence among various sections of the Midlands and, within reasonable distances, much interchange of labor. One example of this is to be found in the women who come from the mining districts, where there is almost no work for women, into Nottingham to work in the textile industries or cigarette factories.

Informants on the East Midlands would venture few generalizations. One commented that the Non-Conformist Church (such as Baptist, Congregational, Methodist, etc.) is quite strong in the East Midlands as well as in the West Midlands whereas the Anglican church is stronger in the south and particularly in areas where the landed aristocracy hold forth. This section, he ventured, "has a tradition of nineteenth century liberalism, of the small business man's worth, of free trade." For the most part, stress was laid upon the diversity within the area. As in the case of the West Midlands county ties again loom large; in many cases rivalry between counties waxes quite keen.

The Midlands, we must conclude, like the English custard, lacks definitiveness and cohesion. The Midlander does not, as does the Southerner in the United States, feel a strong loyalty to his region. Perhaps he is more like the Mid-Westerner who is less aware of the Mid-West than of his state and his nation.

• 127 • Development of Industrial Technology in the Black Country 1700-1900
W. K. V. GALE

There have been two main phases in the industrial history of the Black Country—the growth and decline of the iron and coal trades over a period of a century and a half, and the development of the area during the last fifty years or so into a centre of light engineering. The iron and coal trades were responsible for the existence of the Black Country as we know it today. Later changes have been incorporated into a structure already existing.

[Adapted from *Birmingham and Its Regional Setting: A Scientific Survey*, Buckler and Webb, Birmingham, 1950. (From a reprint. Pp. 3-20.)]

It is with the first phase of industrial development, and in particular with its technical aspects that we are concerned here.

Definition of the Black Country is not as simple a task as may at first appear. The Black Country has neither physical nor political boundaries, and although it is a concentration of industrial towns, industry alone will not serve as a basis for definition. For if manufacturing industry is taken as the sole consideration, the Black Country could be said to include Birmingham, which it certainly does not. Yet a basis for definition exists in the causes which brought the Black Country into being. In the main there were two causes—the great natural mineral wealth of the area, and the technical developments which made possible the use of that wealth. Economics have played their part in the changes which have affected the area, but the simple fact remains that until it became possible to use the natural resources on a large scale, the Black Country could not develop. Technically, two things were needed to start the growth—a method of smelting and working iron with mineral fuel, and some form of mechanical power to operate the machinery.

The eighteenth century provided both. When they became available, industrial growth began, and proceeded at an ever-increasing rate for many years. The district, which had contained a number of scattered towns and villages, some old, but none of much importance, expanded until it became the conurbation it is today. The earliest date which can be assigned to the beginning of the Black Country is the mid-eighteenth century. Half a century after this the Black Country, "black by day and red by night" with its great concentration of furnaces and smoking chimneys was truly in being.

It is only necessary to mention some of the technical effects of the natural conditions in which the minerals were found. For iron making, it is not only necessary to have ample supplies of ironstone and fuel, because the blast furnace consumes great quantities of limestone as a flux. Refractory clays and sands are also needed to build and repair the furnaces themselves. The Black Country was [notably] fortunate in that it possessed all these requisites. None of the minerals was very difficult to work. The thick coal in some parts cropped out at the surface, and could be won by simply quarrying or adit working.

Charcoal was the only fuel suitable for iron smelting and refining [during medieval times, and even later]. As time went on charcoal became scarce. The use of raw coal was out of the question on account of the sulphurs in it, which produced 'red short' iron—metal which would crumble whenever the smith attempted to forge or weld it at a red heat. Coking the coal was a solution to the problem, and this is in fact how it was solved, but the introduction of such a process was far ahead. It also became possible at a later date to use raw coal in the blast furnace, but this was not until 1828, after the hot blast had been invented. No immediate answer to the fuel problem being found, the charcoal shortage developed into a serious famine. Suitable timber was being used faster than it could be replaced, and the threat of coming to a complete standstill confronted the iron trade.

That process which so many had sought was found at last by Abraham Darby (1676-1717), when he succeeded, from 1709 onwards, in smelting iron with mineral fuel.... Darby first coked the local Shropshire coal, and with the coke obtained, he produced a usable pig-iron. He was primarily an iron-founder—a maker of cast-iron pots—and the iron he made was suitable for his purpose. He did not patent the process, and it was open to anyone to use it.

In the meantime, the iron industry had been growing, if only slowly, in South Staffordshire and Worcestershire. In 1740 four furnaces were in blast in the area, two of them fairly large for the period. By 1788 the number had increased to six, with three building and—significant fact—they all used coke as fuel. The charcoal furnaces were no more. Thus one foundation of the Black Country had been laid, and the development of canals, which was taking place at about the same time, was paving the way for further progress.

THE STEAM ENGINE

The events so far chronicled had set the stage for a new development—the introduction of mechanical power in the form of the steam engine. They had in fact done more—they had rendered its need imperative. The iron trade could expand no more, so long as it was dependent upon water power, and the mines could not be deepened to reach the unworked minerals until they had efficient means of drainage. In these respects the Black Country was, of course, neither better nor worse off than many other areas, and on that score alone not particularly worthy of note; but it was here that the steam engine was developed, and a start was given to that revolution in industry which was to have such a profound effect upon the whole world.

It is worthy of note that somewhere between Wolverhampton and Dudley (the exact spot has not been identified), was the site of the first successful steam engine of what we might call a recognisable type. Thomas Savery (1650-1715) had produced a form of steam pump in 1698, but the engine which Thomas Newcomen (1663-1729) erected near Dudley in 1712, was not only his and the Black Country's first, it was the first workable engine in the world to have a piston and cylinder.

Following the work of Newcomen came the epoch-making inventions of [the Scotsman] James Watt (1736-1819).

At first, Watt's engine, like that of Newcomen, was only capable of effecting reciprocating motion and was thus limited in application to pumping water or working a blowing cylinder. Consequently, its main appeal was on the grounds of increased efficiency over the Newcomen engine and it found particular favour in the districts where coal was expensive.

When the initial difficulties of single-acting engine construction had been more or less overcome, Watt tackled the problem of obtaining rotative motion from his engine. [Earlier, a] Newcomen engine with a crank and flywheel had been set to work in Snow Hill, Birmingham, in 1779, at a mill belonging to James Pickard. The builder of the engine, Matthew Wasborough of Bristol, was granted a patent for the application of the crank to a steam engine in 1780, and Watt was thus prevented from using the simple crank on his own engine.

In place of the crank, Watt devised the well-known sun and planet motion, and in 1782 he took out a patent for a rotative engine. This year is an important one in the history of the steam engine, for Watt also patented the principle of double-acting and expansive working. Two years later Watt introduced and patented an improved method of connecting the piston-rod to the beam—his celebrated parallel motion—and the engine was complete in the form in which it was to remain for about half a century. . . . The effects upon industry of the availability of almost unlimited mechanical power are too well known to need more than a passing reference.

THE EARLY NINETEENTH CENTURY

Tremendous strides were made by the Black Country iron trade in the first quarter of the nineteenth century. Some idea of this expansion can be gained from the fact that while in 1796 the area contained only fourteen blast furnaces, by 1830 there were no less than 123. From a primitive condition the iron trade had progressed to a highly organised industry and its plant and products had developed greatly.

An important development which had begun to spread throughout the Black Country was the introduction of the vertically integrated concern. Though one proprietor had sometimes owned all the mines and works involved in the making of iron, it now became possible for every process to be carried out on the same site. [Some] works carried out the entire process of iron manufacture from mine to finished product, being entirely independent of outside sources for practically all their needs.

The iron and coal trades developed along similar lines so far as the employment of labour was concerned, and well before 1850 both had their firmly established customs. The coal mines were operated by charter masters (locally 'butties') who contracted with the owner to work the mine and provide their own labour. If the mine was a large one several butties would be under contract to the owner, each having his own 'district' or section of the mine.

In the iron trade a similar system prevailed, though owing to its greater complexity there were more divisions in each works. At the blast furnaces, all the owner did was to provide the furnaces and machinery, and employ a manager and two principal assistants. Of these, one, the 'bridge-stocker' took charge of the top of the furnaces, being responsible for handling all raw materials, hoisting them to the charging platform or 'bridge,' and charging them as required. The preparation of the pigbeds and all work at the bottom of the furnaces, including tapping and slag or 'cinder' removal, was the responsibility of the 'stock-taker.' Both these individuals hired whatever labour they required, and in this respect were not answerable to the furnace owner. At the ironworks, the master engaged the puddlers, who themselves employed an 'under-hand' and, usually, a boy to help at the puddling furnace. Each rolling mill (a large works often had several), was operated by a 'roller' working (usually on a tonnage basis) for the master, and, again, employing whatever labour he needed.

Such arrangements, which had grown up slowly, were firmly established by custom, and remained with the trade until recent years. Disadvantages included the ease with which the charter masters could operate the truck system, paying their employees partly in cash and partly in goods. Such a system was open to abuse, and abused it certainly was, though it was no worse in the Black Country than elsewhere.

In 1865 the average output of a blast furnace in the Black Country was 130 to 150 tons per week, although a few made as much as 250 tons, and about twenty furnaces in all were using waste gas to heat the blast or fire the boilers. No less than 2,100 puddling furnaces were then in operation, and although the production of pig iron had fallen somewhat, the trade might have seemed in a wholly healthy condition.

Some of the more far-sighted of the iron- and coal-masters had sounded a note of alarm. William Matthews of Corbyn's Hall, near Dudley, had, in 1860 estimated the duration of the coalfield to be about forty years (in which he was remarkably accurate) and others had referred to the approaching exhaustion of the ironstone mines, and to the increasing difficulty of providing adequate drainage for what mines remained profitable to work.

In the case of ironstone, available local supplies were already insufficient and ores were being obtained from Northamptonshire and other parts of the country. Non-local ores had, in fact, been used as a part of the blast furnace charge for many years.

By far the most important development of the nineteenth century, as far as the Black Country was concerned, was the introduction of a process for making cheap mild steel. In 1856, Bessemer introduced his acid converter process, and cheap steel became a practicable proposition. It came in when the Black Country was enjoying its greatest prosperity. Few people at the time realised its implications, but it had a far reaching effect on the local iron trade. Wrought iron was made in several grades, and by far the greatest output was of the cheaper quality, used for all sorts of purposes where a superior grade was not necessary. As the mild steel process spread, the makers of the lower-grade wrought iron found the new material a formidable competitor.

Just as two principal causes, one the natural mineral wealth, and the other the development of the steam engine had brought the Black Country into being as an iron producer, so two other causes were to bring about decline. The exhaustion of the mineral resources caused the coal trade and the mining of ironstone to become virtually extinct, and the production of pig-iron to follow suit.

The technical developments which made cheap mild steel possible took away a great part of the wrought trade. In the last 30 years of the nineteenth century a great number of ironmasters closed their works.

By 1900, coal production had dropped to about a half of what it had been in 1865, and in the next few years the fall was much more rapid. In 1913 the number of puddling furnaces was estimated at 661 and a further reduction must be recorded since.

ANCILLARY TRADES

The earliest of the ancillary trades was the manufacture of hand-wrought nails, which was probably as old as the iron trade itself. By the eighteen-twenties it employed about 50,000 people, but from then on, the competition of the machine-made nail became increasingly severe. Although it lingered on for many years, the hand-wrought trade is now extinct as far as the Black Country is concerned.

In the case of chains, chain cables and anchors, the Black Country is still the principal centre of production. The making of chains is of considerable antiquity, but the making of anchors was introduced to the district by Noah Hingley, of Netherton, Dudley, in 1848 as an addition to his already existing business of wrought-iron and chain making. There have been changes in technique, but the Black Country today turns out, by modern methods, chains, chain cables and anchors which are without equal.

Engineering is worthy of special note, for the Black Country was the birthplace of many notable engineering achievements. The steam engine underwent most of its early development in our area, and it was in Smethwick that the world's first factory designed and built solely to make engineering products— Soho Foundry—was built. The engineers of the Black Country were equal to all the tasks set them, and steam engines, rolling mill plants, machine tools, and marine engines, all have their place in Black Country history. Locomotives, too, have come from the Black Country, and if the district has not made many, it turned out a very famous early one —the 'Stourbridge Lion.' This locomotive, which was built by Foster and Rastrick at the works of John Bradley and Co. at Stourbridge, was the first to run in the United States. Even shipbuilding was not unknown! In 1822 the Horseley Iron Company of Tipton built and engined one of the first iron steamships, the 'Aaron Manby' which was sent in sections to London and assembled there. It traded across the Channel to France for many years.

Some brief reference to the changes since the area ceased to be a major producer of coal and iron may be made. Many new industries have come to the Black Country, which is now a recognised centre of light engineering. The inherited skill and adaptability of the inhabitants have proved fully equal to all the changes. In working and fabricating iron for a multitude of purposes the Black Country excels, and where once there was a great outward traffic in pig- and finished-iron, there is now a large but opposite, inward traffic of the same materials, which are used in innumerable products. The Black Country still produces pig-iron for foundry and steelworks use, though its output is very small compared with other districts, and its ores and fuel come from outside the area.

Of high grade wrought-iron it is still the premier producer. Though mild steel has superseded wrought-iron for many purposes, the latter is still supreme in some fields, and its use has increased rather than diminished in recent years.

'Made in the Black Country' is still recognised as a hallmark for many products, and by no means the least of these is wrought-iron.

Since an industrial society is inconceivable without industry, it is necessary to trace the growth of what has been termed, for want of a better term, the Industrial Revolution. In England, the Industrial Revolution was preceded by agricultural and commercial revolutions, also of great importance. Furthermore, it was not merely technological but social as well, and it actually represented a cumulative social change rather than merely a sudden inventive achievement. That is, those responsible for the development of various types of machines combined principles and parts which others had already worked out in different connections. Such combinations are possible on a truly revolutionary scale only when there has been a sufficient accumulation of culture traits or individual elements to be successfully put together into new working arrangements.

In order to show the Industrial Revolution in some time perspective, we shall quote, first, a description of the Old Midland Village, a nostalgic and even sentimental picture of what Midland rural life was like before the large-scale growth of industry. It turns back the clock to the early eighteenth century. In reading this account, we must bear in mind that there are still many Midland villages today whose inhabitants live in the old brick and stone houses described, although their outlook differs considerably from that of their forebears who built those houses.

· 128 · The Old Midland Village

WILLIAM G. HOSKINS

A COUNTRY OF VILLAGES

Midland England is more than anything else a country of villages, of compact villages gathered round the church or the green, or strung along a winding street; sometimes perhaps of even more ancient shape—ring-fence villages whose houses, built around the four sides of a hollow square (like the formation of the covered wagons in American frontier days of Indian attacks) reflect the early days of forest and danger on all sides. But whatever the size and shape of the Midland village, we find all the farmhouses and cottages of the parish, the inns and the smithy, are gathered along its streets, and none lie away out in the fields, lonely and remote like those of the wild Devonshire parishes.

In the Midlands the isolated farm and hamlet can hardly anywhere be found: only in the anciently wooded districts that long remained cut-off, like Charnwood Forest in Leicestershire, and in the old wooded parts of Bedfordshire and Buckinghamshire, do we find farms and hamlets away from the parent village, and the characteristic road-pattern of country that has been enclosed direct from the forest. But here, too, the village is still the most prominent type of human grouping.

It is true that even in the counties where the compact nucleated village is most apparent on the Ordnance map, one occasionally comes across red-brick farmhouses in the fields between the villages, but these betray their late appearance by their names—New York Farm, Bunker's Hill Farm, Quebec Farm, Newfoundland Farm. They are the creation of the enclosure awards of George III's day, that revolutionised the old village life all over the Midlands, creating large fields and compact farms, in place of the multitudes of scattered strips in the open fields; but even these isolated farms are few in number, and the enclosure awards, though they transformed the life of the old villages, did not disintegrate them physically. They leeched out all the heart and spirit of the village but left its shell intact.

And so, apart from the industrial districts that mostly lie along a narrow belt of country

[Adapted from *Midland England: a Survey of the Country between the Chilterns and the Trent*, B. T. Batsford, London, 1949. Pp. 61-69, 71-73, 75, 79. Used by permission.]

from the Nene to the Trent where the Victorian prosperity of the hosiery and footwear industries has swamped the old agricultural villages and reduced them to a soggy shapeless mess on the landscape, the Midland village has kept its shape and old likeness. The houses of the village lie all along the streets, mostly facing the street and butting straight on to it without any garden or railings intervening, but sometimes, and usually these are the oldest houses in the place, standing at right angles to it, presenting a blank gable end directly on to the road. The "ancient homesteads", as they are called in the enclosure awards, lay on the village street, or ran back from it; at the back or to one side there was always a small paddock of pasture called "a croft", generally an acre or so in extent (rarely more), and behind the farmhouse was the yard with its buildings (barns, stables, outhouses of all sorts) grouped round it. Somewhere to the side lay the garden and perhaps a small orchard also. All up and down the village streets one finds this constant pattern, with cottages interspersed here and there between the farmhouses, which were well detached from each other; and all over the Midlands, from north to south, this is the familiar pattern—the ancient homesteads clustered within the ring-fence of the village.

BUILDING IN BRICK AND BUILDING IN STONE

In Leicestershire, the farmhouses and cottages will be built mostly of local red brick, especially in the west and south of the county, but here and there in the back lanes the more ancient mud walls can be seen, and less frequently a timbered house of Elizabethan or Stuart times, though these are scarcer in Leicestershire than anywhere else in the Midlands. But the red-brick, which came in generally for village building in the Midlands shortly before 1700 can be, and is, very pleasant in its early styles, with its mellow colouring, slight hand-made irregularities and rough texture, its interesting mouldings and ornament, and the delicate curves of garden walls. There is some excellent building in brick in the Leicestershire villages . . . and a great deal that is seemly and decent, ranging in date

from the 1680's to the 1830's. It is only after 1840 that the real horrors of red-brick as a building material were increasingly explored and, since this coincided with the rapid growth of the two staple Midland industries with their demand for workers, we find in the towns and villages street after street of shiny machine-made brick capped by smooth and shiny Welsh slates, on which no moss or lichen will ever grow: streets and "terraces" proudly dated 1877 or 1884, or some such placid year, rich with lace curtains and large pots of aspidistra blocking the view into the period parlours; streets and roads named after the Jubilee or the Scottish Highlands, or the builder's daughters (Clara Terrace and Laura Villas) or Poplar Avenue which leads briefly to a factory-wall where poplars have long since ceased to blow.

Though the Midlands are mostly overlain with clay, the stone foundations are not far down in most parts. Between the Trent and the upper Welland . . . and again between the Nene and the Ouse . . . the overlying clay is of such thickness as to make the stone inaccessible, and in this district we find villages built of mud and timber (the so-called "wattle and daub" construction) up to the time of James II, and after that of brick. But in the broad belt of country between these claylands the stone—limestone and ironstone mostly—is near the surface, and here we find some of the most beautiful villages in England. There was a time when every village in Northamptonshire, which is the heart of this stone country, had its own quarry, and probably many more than one, for medieval quarries were generally small; and Rutland is even more beautiful in its stone-built farmhouse and cottage architecture, for it has had no manufacturing industry to ravish its old villages. Hardly a single village in Rutland is not worthy of admiration, in whole or in part, and some are outstandingly good.

The Northamptonshire villages and country towns fall into two groups, according to the stone they stand on: those of the north and east of the county are mostly of the grey limestone, extending into Buckinghamshire at Olney, which is largely built of stone; and those of the west and south are built of the even lovelier ironstone or marlstone, as it is variously called. Where the two stones meet, we get some charming mixed colours.

Wherever you go, however, one thing is inescapable from one end of this Stone Belt to the other, and that is that nearly all the best building in every village and country-town falls into the seventeenth and eighteenth centuries, and that within this period there were two generations in particular in which building was at its height, both in quantity and in quality—the two generations between about 1590 and 1650.

THE FIELD SYSTEM AND VILLAGE GOVERNMENT

There were two reasons, perhaps largely peculiar to the Midlands, why this peasant civilisation reached its zenith in this part of England, as well as two other reasons that were common to the whole country. First, that the open-field system, which called for continuous co-operative effort on the part of the village as a whole and so gave a peculiar colour to Midland life, was more character-istic of the great middle zone of England than of any other part. And further, that the Mid-lands, especially north of Watling Street, but to a lesser degree to the south also, were the home of a large class of peasant proprietors, owning from twenty to fifty acres most of them and subservient to no squire or land-lord. So we have a social system from early times founded on the whole village as the unit of work and play and government, and on a considerable class of free men and women who owned at least some of the land they tilled.

Not only were all the lands of the parish—common pasture, meadows, and leys, as well as the great arable fields—used according to the rules prescribed by a completely demo-cratic assembly, but the village governed itself through its own officials, elected by the same assembly, and every man of any standing and responsibility was expected to take his due turn in the rota of officers—constable (most important of them all, for he was the link between his village and the majesty of the general law of the country), churchwarden, overseer of the poor (from 1601 onwards),

field-reeve, pinder (keeper of the village pound), and the lesser offices of village busi-ness: every man took an office according to his capacity to serve it well and there are few, very few, references to men who decline to take their share in the government of the local democracy. This combination of a physically unified village, surrounded by open fields that could not be cultivated except by agreed and common action for which all adult persons had some sense of responsibility, was a good foundation for any civilisation.

Not only that, but the open-field system had another important attribute. Besides call-ing for a truly democratic kind of society, providing opportunities for all men to share in the government and good management of their native villages, it provided opportunities for all, however lowly, to "get on" in a modest way. The man with little or no capital but a pair of strong arms and the will to work was not shut out from economic security and independence as he is today in practically every country in the world (every one at any rate, that has been infected by Western European ideas); but he had his foot on the bottom rung of a ladder which, with his own energy and skill, would take him, not neces-sarily to the top (few nourished that restless ambition) but to a level of modest comfort and self-respect, to some sort of standing in his own little society. [Indeed, even] the more modest among them, not infrequently left to their shepherds or their labourers a few sheep or lambs, or a half-acre or so of crops in the village fields, sometimes apparently not only the crop but the land on which it grew as well.

THE PEASANT ECONOMY

[In addition, there were at least] two other characteristics of this old peasant civili-sation which were more or less common to the whole country in former days, and which were the very essence of the old way of living: I mean its intense "localism", to put it in a word, and (what follows from that) its bal-anced economy.

As to the first of these, I cannot put it better than George Bourne did in one of his best books, *Change in the Village*. "It was of the essence of the old system", he says, "that those living under it subsisted in the main upon what their own industry could produce out of the soil and materials of their own countryside. A few things, certainly, they might get from other neighborhoods . . . but as a general thing the parish where the peasant people lived was the source of the materials they used, and their well-being depended on their knowledge of its resources." All over England, country people had this local knowledge of where everything was to be found and how to make the best use of it; and not only did this give them a minute understanding of the soil and of the whole of their immediate surroundings, and a pride for the skill required in using difficult materials where none others were to be had; but because everything that went into them came out of their native soil, their buildings, which are the only remaining sign of that "home-made civilisation of the rural English", look as though they had grown out of the very earth they stand in, so well matched they are and resting so comfortably on it. They belong to it, just as their builders belonged to it and would in due course mingle their bones with it.

SKILLED CRAFTSMEN

Because the old Midland village aimed at being self-supporting so far as was humanly possible, it found employment for a host of skilled craftsmen within its boundaries, men who lived as much by the land as did their fellows who tilled it and fed their animals on it—the smith, the miller, and the wheelwright (the three most important men of all); the carpenter, the mason, the tailor, the shoemaker, the butcher, the baker, and the saddler and harness-maker. This kind of balanced economy in the old village—and it was an *economy* in all senses of the word to have all these things made or done within the village itself—this kind of economy goes back a very long way, for we find it well developed even in the fourteenth century. The poll-tax returns of 1381 for certain Leicestershire villages, for example, show us a remarkable list of craftsmen. At Hallaton we find carpenters, a brewer, tailors, a barker, a baker, butchers, cobblers, weavers, a cook, a wheelwright, an ironmonger, a shearman, fisherman, in addi-

tion to the purely farming households; and at Medbourne, three miles away, the list includes a miller, a mason, skinners, a carpenter, a butcher, and a "belman". Not all villages were as self-sufficient and as various as this, but most had their smith, wheelwright, miller, mason, and carpenter, and so it was all over the Midlands. If one village had no mason or miller, he could be found in the next surely enough: there was plenty of inter-village traffic, but in general people found all their earthly needs and wants met within a radius of three or four miles at the most, within sight of their own church spire.

Not only was there this balance of activity within the village itself, but the craftsmen themselves kept a similar balance in their own working lives. All, almost without exception so far as I can discover, had a little land near their homes and farmed in their spare time or when, as was inevitable at certain times of the year, trade was slack. There was no enforced idleness for reasons beyond their control: there was always another occupation at hand, always plenty to do, always a pleasant change of occupation and scene there in the background. In the old Midland village, for example, the smith was not only the most important craftsman of the community, but often farmed a small freehold also. . . .

The wheelwright was hardly, perhaps, as exalted a personage as the smith, though he was equally necessary to the life of the village, and he, too, like the carpenter, the tailor, shoemaker, baker, freemason, and weaver had some land and farmed as a side line.

The village baker appears quite early in medieval records in the Midlands, perhaps because in many parts fuel was becoming exceedingly scarce and it was a necessary economy to get bread baked down the street at the bakehouse rather than at home.

THE PEASANT WORLD

Every village was a little organism, with a life of its own and a flavour peculiar to it alone, very nearly self-sufficient and always aiming at being so. Around the village stretched the two or three thousand acres which were the basis of its life, the open fields which were more characteristic of Midland

England than of any other part. This was the peasant's world outside the few streets and lanes that constituted his village, and he knew every inch of it *by heart*. Outside these fields he rarely ventured far nor, for the most part, ever wanted to.

Truly it was at its best a peasant civilisation, a rich many-sided culture. It had its darker side: one could enumerate its many faults soon enough; it was far from perfect. But [men] lived in a place that had meaning and significance for them; their roots went down deep into the cultural humus formed by centuries of ancestors before them on that spot; they "belonged" to that place.

Not only did men live in a place that had meaning for them but they worked in it also, all their lives: home and work were synonymous. And, further, they saw the beginning of their work and the end of it and could therefore take a deep pride in doing it well. But their experience was even wider than this, for they saw their work long before it reached them and long after it had left them. The wheelwright on his evening walk was already marking down in his mind particular trees still growing and planning their use in years yet to come; and when he had finished his cart or wagon he saw it round about the parish for the rest of his life and could still feel the same pride as on the day he turned it out, the best he was capable of. This old qualitative civilisation, disparaged and derided as it is by those who have never troubled to understand it, limited though it was in scope, aimed, not at power, but at perfection and now and then achieved it.

We turn now to a short account of the worldwide changes that lay behind the transformation of the Midlands and, indeed, much of England, from a rural to an industrial region. John L. and Barbara Hammond, who wrote the next selection, are well-known social historians, whose writings reflect a sensitive awareness of the interconnections between social and technological events. In the book quoted here they detail many facets of the fundamental changes that have accompanied the growth of industry in England and the world as a whole. For additional information on the rise of the textile industry, mining, pottery making, and the iron and steel industry their book can be consulted with profit.

• 129 • *The Birth of the Modern World*
JOHN L. HAMMOND AND BARBARA HAMMOND

The Industrial Revolution has created societies in which the plainest lives are ruled by forces that are as wide as the world. In the Middle Ages a man's neighbors were those who lived near him; his outlook was bounded by his village; he could watch the growing of his food, and the spinning and weaving of his clothes. This life, with the charm and the danger of its simplicity, was extinguished by a series of changes, of which the most dramatic were the great mechanical inventions that began in the eighteenth century and have succeeded one another with extraordinary rapidity from that time to this. The new industrial system has been associated throughout the world with the name of England, because the English people played the leading part in making and using the first discoveries. It was from England that the new processes, the new machinery and the new discipline passed to the continent of Europe.

England, unlike Germany and the United States, passed through a revolution of great importance before the introduction of the

[Adapted from *The Rise of Modern Industry*, 5th edition, Harcourt, Brace, New York, 1937. Pp. 1-4, 21-23. Used by permission.]

railway. That revolution was marked by the dissolution of the old village, by the transformation of the textile industries, by changes of a different kind in the Pottery industries, and by a great concentration of capital and power in the industries connected with iron, steel and coal. Its effects were important enough, and decisive enough, to alter the character of English life.

By the middle of the [eighteenth] century it is possible to discern the contributions that England was to make to the solution of the problems created by these new conditions. The immediate confusion has passed; society makes its first efforts to adapt its arrangements to its new life; the distinctive features of a new civilization are emerging from the shadows. Decisions have been taken, institutions have been created, a temper has been formed, beliefs have assumed solid shape that are to influence, for good and for evil, throughout the nineteenth century, first the life of the English people, and later the life of all the most active of the races of mankind.

The Industrial Revolution was in one sense catastrophic, since it had effects that were immediate, and spectacular; in another it was gradual, for it was the climax or the sum of a series of developments, none of them peculiar to England, some of them later in time in England than elsewhere. Any definition of this new society would make it clear that it could not have been called into being by any single set of forces. Its men and women, in Mr. Hardy's phrase, serve smoke and fire rather than frost and sun; they produce for commerce and not merely for subsistence; they use in their daily lives the products of different countries for which they make payment by an elaborate system of exchanges; they live by an economy in which occupations and processes are sharply specialized; they rely for most of their production on the help of machines; the mass of persons taking part in this production have no property in the land, the capital, or the instruments on which it depends. It could not be said of a society so complex as this that it was created by Watt, by Arkwright, by Crompton or by Stephenson. All that can be said is that the inventions by which those names are known throughout the world were decisive events in its history: decisive, because mass production depends on those inventions, and mass production is an integral part of the new system. Those inventions were essential, but among the causes that made the English people what they became, other events were not less significant.

The discovery of the Atlantic routes marked or caused a revolution . . . that took some centuries to produce its full effect. Commerce began to assume not merely a new scale, but a new character; it did not merely employ larger vessels and greater capital, it shipped popular cargoes. When the Dutch and the English first competed in the East, the Spice Islands were counted the chief prize; by the end of the eighteenth century the Spice Islands and India had changed places, and it was doubted whether the cost of keeping those islands was repaid by their profits. For commerce had begun to provide for the many; to depend on popular consumption; to enter into the daily life of the ordinary man. India and America sent new delicacies to England, and in the course of a century, owing to a number of causes—the growth of commercial capital, the development of the arts and machinery of trade, the improvement of transport, changes of habits and manner of life—those delicacies were brought within reach of the poorer classes and passed into general consumption. Tea, sugar and tobacco took the place of pepper, spices and cloves, as the chief articles of commerce.

[Vessels] were now sailing across the Atlantic, or rounding the Cape of Good Hope, bringing cargoes destined, not for palace or cathedral, but for the alley and the cottage. Capitalist commerce was providing for the wants of the peasant and the workman, as well as for the taste of noble or cardinal, rich merchant or prosperous lawyer. Owing to new resources, new products, new materials, new habits, the expansion of wealth and the development of finance, commerce increased rapidly in volume and scale, and this change in degree was accompanied or followed by a change in kind. The day when more profit was to be made by carrying tea for the poor from India, than by carrying pepper for the rich from Java, marked an important stage in the progress of the world to the modern system.

The commercial revolution of the fifteenth and sixteenth centuries was an essential preliminary to the industrial revolution of the eighteenth and nineteenth centuries. For capitalist manufacture on the modern scale was only possible when capital could be applied to the production of goods that were consumed by the mass of the people, and it was the use of capital for this purpose that gave the Industrial Revolution its sweeping character. Commerce and production take the same course. As pepper gives way to tea, so silk gives way to cotton. The relations of Europe and the world outside are reversed: Europe that had drawn on Asia for manufactures takes the lead in production. The conditions arise that make possible so strange a spectacle as that of a Lancashire town using a raw material, not grown on English soil, to produce goods that are exported for popular consumption to India or China. England has learnt how to make greater fortunes from clothing the poor in the simple fabrics of

Manchester, than had ever been made from clothing the rich in the gorgeous fantasies of Babylon or Damascus.

The change from peasant to industrial civilization may be described in another sequence. The wants of the ordinary man were supplied in the early Middle Ages, as in the days of Greece and Rome, either by himself and his family, or by his neighbors; in the next stage these wants were supplied by special persons plying a craft, in a village or small town, organized sometimes in guilds; in the third stage the provision of those needs became the business of individual or group production and large scale merchanting; in the fourth it became the business of large scale production. At that point the world passes to the industrial age: to an age in which commerce and finance are no longer aspects, growing in importance, yet still aspects of its life, but the basis on which a society depends. The English people were the first to develop this system, to enjoy its wealth, to suffer its evils, to struggle with its problems, and to build on this foundation an imposing place and power in the world.

Herbert Heaton, in his article on the Industrial Revolution in the *Encyclopaedia of the Social Sciences*, takes an attitude somewhat different from that of the Hammonds, whom we have just quoted. He shows, for example, that it took 150 years for the Industrial Revolution to get started and another 150 years for the economic transformation to work itself out; and he wonders whether the process can accurately be termed "revolutionary." He does admit, however, that there was a change in tempo about 1750.

Heaton's discussion also reminds us of the contributions that many people and nations made to the preliminary conditions necessary for the Revolution. Heaton indicates, furthermore, that even though the laboring people may have had a hard time of it, the entrepreneurs, or employers who took the risks and managed various business ventures, did not have such an easy time themselves. We include below, as Selection 130, Heaton's summarizing paragraphs. The author was born in England but has taught in American universities for a number of years, at present at the University of Minnesota.

· 130 · *The Industrial Revolution*

HERBERT HEATON

. . . In all lands where it came to displace an established industrial structure the industrial

revolution ran a roughly similar course. The textile industry was usually the first to be affected, then the making of clothes, metal articles and foodstuffs; the large scale manufacture of iron and of steel represented often a distinct step forward but one not easy to take, while the manufacture of machines and producers' goods generally was a hazardous venture. Indeed it is this final step toward complete industrialization which has been most difficult for more recently industrialized countries. In lands coming late to industrialism the easiest success has been won in industries which process the natural or farm products, which produce simple wares such as blankets or plain cotton pieces or which enjoy the natural protection of distance from possible competitors.

Migration of industry from manual domestic or shop conditions to the factory varied in speed from industry to industry. Spinning went quickly; weaving, knitting and some metal trades passed through a transitional workshop period, in which workers were gathered under one roof but continued to use the old equipment. In the clothing industries the sewing machine could be used in the home, and many women clung to the putting out system but had to submit to sweated conditions. The shoemaker and hand loom weaver put up a long fight, and the victory of the laundry and bakery is still far from complete in Europe.

Dependence on coal and water power led to industrial concentration on the coal fields, river valleys and such belts as the fall line in America. Water power had only a limited effect in causing concentration, for it strung the factories all along the banks of rapidly flowing rivers, and for certain textile washing processes an ample supply of water was almost as important as a supply of fuel or power. Where water and coal were found together, as in the Pennine valleys and eastern Belgium, industry was spread over the whole region in villages or towns. For the metal industries location was determined by the coal supply, since it was easier to bring the metal to the coal than vice versa; but this involved the construction of adequate transport facilities, such as the railroad between Lorraine and the Ruhr.

The movement of population to the industrial areas still needs further study. But for England it is now evident that there was no simple mass transfer of people from the south and east to the north and west. The industrial towns grew by drawing workers in from the hinterland, and the void thus made was filled by people from slightly further afield. Journeys were generally short, except in the case of the Irish who swarmed across the Irish Sea to Lancashire, Glasgow and Yorkshire. Only later, when the railroads made longer journeys easier, was there any serious long distance migration. In newer countries, such as the United States, native population was for long streaming away from the eastern industrial centers and a continual inflow of immigrants was necessary to insure an adequate labor supply.

Problems of urban health and housing were probably most acute in those towns which were the homes of the early spinning factories. In looking at them it should be remembered that until 1835 many British manufacturing centers had no adequate municipal government, that knowledge about the essentials of public health was scanty, that cheap production of pipes, bricks and woodwork did not come until about 1840, that house building depended on the willingness of someone to sink capital in dwellings and that the rate of interest current or the profits to be made in industry might be more tempting than the return on house property. [Living] conditions in the early textile towns of New England were very good; only with the coming of wave after wave of foreign laborers did the worst slum conditions appear.

Of labor conditions no easy generalization is possible. Long hours, child labor, employment of women, insanitary conditions, payment in truck, unemployment, low wages, capitalistic tyranny, labor unrest, industrial fatigue, occupational diseases and the "cash nexus" were not inventions of industrial factory capitalism. Night work was a new thing

[Adapted from "Industrial Revolution," *Encyclopaedia of the Social Sciences*, Vol. 8, Macmillan, New York, 1937. Pp. 10-12. Used by permission.]

in the textile industries; but the only novelty about child labor was that children now worked in large groups, were subject to factory rather than parental discipline, discharged more responsible tasks, had to leave the hearth to work and were kept vigorously at their day or night tasks. It should be noted, however, that child labor was universally regarded as natural and that the children's earnings were larger in the factory than they had been at home. When child labor was forbidden, something else—education—had to be developed to fill the waking hours of the young. The hazards to life and limb might perhaps have been prevented before they were attacked by legislation but they had first to be recognized as such, and the apathy toward them was as marked among the operatives as among employers. Such conditions and attitudes repeated themselves in most countries or regions where the factory system was introduced.

As to wages and employment light and shade alternate. In the early stages the new industries, especially cotton and pottery, seem to have paid much higher wages than were prevalent in the older industries, and the demand for hand loom weavers to cope with the flood of machine made yarn raised the rates paid for weaving. In England the long war with France lifted many nominal wages and some real ones, but the slump after Waterloo lowered levels in industry and agriculture alike. The hand loom weaver and some other manual workers suffered when they stuck to their benches in face of the machine; but elsewhere conditions seem to have improved because of rising wages and falling prices after about 1820 or 1830. Some occupations passed from male to female hands, but new occupations were opened up and old ones expanded—metallurgy, mechanical engineering, the construction and operation of railroads, shipbuilding, mining, building— and the opportunities for skilled well paid work multiplied accordingly.

In short, the industrial revolution increased rather than decreased the material welfare of the mass of the population; but some sections suffered from the transition, war and business fluctuations disturbed wages and prices and the dangers latent in the employee's lot became apparent. Unfortunately much of our view of the social aspects of the revolution is drawn from reports of official investigations, which in their very nature are full of complaints and grievances. From them one can paint the industrial revolution as "an orgy of soulless cupidity" (Tawney) and assume that to be the whole picture. But more [thorough and] detailed knowledge of pre-revolutionary conditions tone down the picture and make at least some of the industrial leaders appear more like human beings and less like incarnations of ruthless self-interest. Moreover it is still far from certain how much the revolution was "a triumph of the spirit of enterprise" (Tawney). Enterprise there was but not always triumph, and the industrial field was strewn with the wreckage of men who failed. The trouble with machinery that broke down, with workmen who refused to use it, with customers who demanded long credit yet refused to pay their debts, with booms that burst, with banks that refused any more loans, with wars that closed markets, all made the road stony. Inadequate supplies of working capital wrecked many a venture, and when a successful period came the profits had to be plowed back into the business. The industrial revolution has not yet been studied through the records of bankruptcy, but enough is known to show on what a treacherous sea the entrepreneur of the early machine age launched his boat.

Making a Living

>>>

The complexity of any society depends upon the number of special activities entered into by its members. This specialization, when considered in connection with economic activities, is called the division of labor. In Britain as a whole, and in the Midlands in particular, the division of labor is carried to its greatest extreme. A Midlands factory worker may spend his productive life span operating two or three similar machines. Even the Midlands farmer is a specialist in the sense that he produces almost entirely for a market rather than for his own subsistence and relies upon that market to satisfy many of his needs.

Every specialist has to depend upon others to supply at least some, and often nearly all, of his basic needs. The division of labor operates through the market. Hence, so much trading is needed because of the division of labor that England has been called a "nation of shop-keepers."

A more accurate generalization views Britain as the workshop of the world. In an international division of labor, Britain is the artisan and trader. Britain usually depends, as the individual specialist does, upon others to supply most of its basic needs. During the two World Wars, such supplies were sharply curtailed, and the postwar years have proved little better. A specialist, whether an individual or a nation, is particularly vulnerable to changing conditions.

In the selections that follow, several aspects of the British economy will be dealt with: first, agriculture; then, industry; and, finally, labor. Each is intricately organized and operates in a delicate balance of relationships with other economic activities, both contributing to and depending upon them. One result of this elaborate interdependence has been the recent governmental efforts toward nationalization, aimed at achieving better all-round effectiveness. That nationalization is not felt by all of the British to be the complete or the most satisfactory solution to problems is indicated by current reversals of the program in regard to certain industries. On a smaller scale the daily problems of the housewife also reflect the intricacies of a modern industrial economy, particularly when complicated by the strains of a recent and devastating war.

707

The story of Britain's farming and farmers begins with the most primitive practices and leads to the most modern development. As the next selection points out, Britain's farms today are among the most efficient in the world, being highly mechanized, with good crop yields and with stock breeds that remain at the top of the list.

Wilford Smith, in his *Economic Geography of Great Britain* (Dutton, 1948, p. 173), writes of the agriculture of Britain:

> The agricultural pattern of Britain is exceedingly complex, a mosaic of infinite variety, the country presents as great a variety of landscape as any other land of similar size, farming systems are frequently highly specialized and varied in kind, and present land utilization is strewn with relics of former land use, adapted to past economic conditions, existing side by side with others more closely adapted to the present economy. . . . The physical environment offers possibilities and sets limits, but within these the farmer has an infinite variety of choice open to him and he has not answered the question of what to do with his land always in the same way. There have been striking revolutions in land use.

A brief but authoritative account of some of these changes through the centuries is presented as Selection 131. In reading this and other selections by British authors, we must bear in mind that to the British *corn* means the important small cereal grasses of the country (wheat, especially, and also rye, barley, and oats) and does not refer to *maize*, as it does in American usage. The second of the selections on agriculture shows how farming continues, with certain modifications, in the area closely surrounding a large conurbation, or metropolitan center. These two selections together reveal the part that agriculture plays in the British economy.

• 131 • *The Development of Agriculture in Britain*

About four thousand years ago men in Britain first began to farm. They kept flocks and herds and grazed them on whatever herbage was available. Then they learned to plant crops by pushing a pointed stick into the ground and dropping seed into the hole.

When the Romans came they taught the Britons how to farm the fertile valleys, using the plow and oxen. It remained for the Saxons, however, to establish villages, and from this emerged the Manorial System with its three-field plan, under which the tenants held a number of strips in each of three communal fields. This system remained until the fourteenth century when the need for enclosing land for sheep-raising, due to the expanding wool trade, began the modern field system. These fields were either owned outright by freeholders or farmed by tenants paying a money rent.

The enclosure of the land made possible a further development in arable farming which took place about 1720. The earth was improved by the use of various forms of lime and by the adoption of a four-course rotation of wheat, turnips, barley, clover, a

[Adapted from *Agriculture in Britain,* British Information Services, New York, 1947. Pp. 3-33. Used by permission.]

system of farming encouraged by the great landowners of the time, designed to keep the soil permanently fertile. Britain took its place as the most successful farming country in the world.

British inventions came to the farmer's aid with [the corn drill and the reaper.] There followed chaff-cutters, steam cultivators, steam plows, binders, scarifiers, etc.

At the same time, livestock was improved. Robert Bakewell (1725-95), by the most careful methods, changed the large-boned, coarse, slow-maturing sheep of his era into the well-fleshed animal which he called the New Leicester, whose blood runs in many of the famous sheep breeds of today. The annual sheepshearings were the forerunners of our modern agricultural shows. In 1720 Benjamin Tomkins, a yeoman farmer, was left in his father's will "one cow called Silver and her calf." The descendants of Silver and her calf were selected and improved by the Tomkins family for more than a hundred years, and became the great Hereford breed which thrives equally on the pastures of its native Herefordshire and the ranges of Texas and Australia.

From Yorkshire, at the beginning of the nineteenth century, came Shorthorns, which are found in more places in the world today than any other breed of cattle. A poor Yorkshire weaver named Joseph Tuley, earning less than $5 a week, reared a pig which was to become world famous. Tuley and his wife went short themselves so that their pig might have all it wanted; they washed it and took it for walks on fine days, and in 1851 they entered it at the Royal Show. They were well rewarded. Their pig was the forerunner of the Large White, the most renowned breed of pig in the world.

Of the twenty breeds of cattle, sheep, pigs, and horses of world-wide reputation today, all but three originated in Britain. When the war began in 1939 Britain was the world's leading exporter of livestock.

[Ironically,] the Industrial Revolution—which prompted so many inventions to benefit the farmer—was also responsible in some part for the decline of agriculture towards the end of the nineteenth century. By then food could be brought from abroad more cheaply than it could be grown at home. Between 1867 and 1913 the arable acreage of Britain fell from 17,700,000 to 14,500,000 acres but the demand for more milk and meat for the new urban centers was responsible for increased numbers of livestock. Thus, with the coming of World War I and the ensuing U-Boat campaign Britain faced a serious food shortage. The farmers were appealed to in this crisis and responded by increasing the arable acreage by nearly one and a half million acres in two years, from 1916 to 1918.

The period between the two wars was necessarily one of readjustment. Grain prices fell owing to the large world production and reduced industrial demand, and British farmers had to adapt themselves as best they could to the new situation. Ways and means of helping the farmer during this period were sought. In 1924 subsidies were introduced by the British Government and from that year they were paid on sugar, from 1932 on wheat, from 1934 on milk and cattle, and from 1938 on oats and barley. Successful marketing schemes were also introduced for hops, milk, bacon, pigs, potatoes. These schemes ensured benefits of collective bargaining for members and the raising of standards and quality of products. They also improved collection and supply to distributors, and increased consumption by means of publicity.

Of further help to the farmer was the passing of the Land Drainage Act. By 1942 schemes costing the equivalent of $64 million had been approved under this Act.

During this period Sir George Stapledon's experiments produced improved strains of grasses. It was he who advocated "ley" farming, whereby pastures were renewed every few years by plowing up and reseeding. Farmers began to appreciate more fully the value of good pasture. Even barren hilltops came under the plow for reseeding to grass. With the production of new grasses and careful livestock breeding Britain became, and still is, the "stud" farm of the world.

By 1939 agriculture was still Britain's largest industry, occupying 70 per cent of the land area of England and Wales, and providing employment, directly or indirectly, for over one million people. Yet, despite this fact and all the measures taken during the between-war years, Britain was producing less than one-third of the food she consumed. Moreover, British agriculture was unbalanced. While arable farming had sunk to 12,000,000 acres (the lowest in history), the number of dairy cattle, sheep, pigs, and poultry had never been higher. In order to feed this livestock Britain had to import between seven and eight million tons of feeding stuffs annually: one out of every three tons of food consumed by animals was imported.

Thus, with the outbreak of World War II, British farmers were faced with the greatest task ever set before them. With U-boats again active in the Atlantic and with all available shipping urgently needed for military purposes, Britain was forced to curtail imports of food for the people and feeding stuffs for animals. There were only two ways of doing this. First, a drastic control of food consumption by the people, which was achieved by rationing. Secondly, a maximum increase in home-grown food.

The first step was clearly to increase the acreage of arable land. But this could only be done at the expense of livestock. A question of priorities had to be decided—meat or milk? It was agreed that milk should be priority No. 1, and foodstuffs were accordingly rationed on this basis. Milk prices were subsidized and prices for agricultural produce were fixed in such a way as to encourage the production of foods considered most essential.

One of the worst problems was the gradually increasing labor shortage. Farming was a reserved occupation and the bulk of the men stayed on the farms, but even so about 40,000 went into the armed forces or industry. In order to keep men on farms, a national minimum wage was fixed for the first time in Britain's history, and men were "frozen" as agricultural workers. To ease the situation further a Women's Land Army was recruited, which reached 70,000 at its peak. Workers were transferred, where necessary, from one farm to another. An emergency Land Corps and voluntary Land Clubs grew up and school children were also allowed to help. Men from the armed forces were used when available, as were prisoners of war.

Most startling were the advances made in the use and development of machinery, two-thirds of which was manufactured in Britain. The County Committees set up pools of machinery, and depots were established from which farmers could hire implements at reasonable rates. As a result, British agriculture is now one of the most highly mechanized in the world.

The land itself was improved through drainage schemes (for which the Government undertook to pay half the cost) and by encouraging the use of fertilizers. Already, four months before the outbreak of war, a campaign had been launched and a bonus granted to farmers for plowing up seven-year grass land. Very soon the tillage area was increased by over 60 per cent.

· 132 · Agriculture in the West Midlands

W. B. MERCER

FARMS VS. FACTORIES

Within the Birmingham-Black Country Conurbation 37,000 acres are officially classed as agricultural land. The West Midland Group on Post-War Reconstruction and Planning put the area of undeveloped, "largely-agricultural," land at 68,970 acres.

The type farm consists of the remnants of what was once a holding, together with a few

[Adapted from *Birmingham and its Regional Setting, a Scientific Survey,* Buckler and Webb, Birmingham, 1950. (From a reprint.)]

odd bits of others, with rough grazing on a spoil bank; the buildings a poor little set, the stock a herd of nondescript milking cows. Milk is the mainstay of such farmers as there are.

Most of the agricultural land within the urban area lies, naturally, in the peripheral parishes. Here milk production vies with corn-growing, potatoes and market-gardening.

Market-gardeners cluster around the outskirts. They are a varied band, shading by easy stages from the Saturday afternoon allotmenteer, through the lorry driver whose pal has got a greengrocer's shop, the post-office sorter whose life's ambition is to occupy a smallholding, the petrol-cum-café man who gardens when he is not pumping, the retired policeman, the man who used to be a saddler, and the young fellow but lately in the R. A. F. who has embarked his all in a couple of acres, up to the established nurseryman with a regular pitch in the market and the small firm with shops to feed with home-grown tomatoes.

VEGETABLE GROWING

Three major areas are concerned—Lichfield, Kidderminster and the Avon or Evesham Vale.

[In Lichfield] more than ninety per cent of the vegetables are grown on holdings exceeding five acres; the farmer has become the gardener at least in respect of the major crops. There has indeed been some exchange of function; on the one hand, farmers, with livestock and corn interests tending to reduce their cereals to find room for vegetables, on the other gardeners by origin acquiring land for stock-keeping. . . . Recently, farms have become largely mechanized and there has been much bull-dozing of hedges. Potatoes, roots and green crops occupy anything from a quarter to as much as half of the total area of some farms; potato-growing has indeed been carried to a point which gives cause for alarm, for there have been many evidences in recent years of the build-up of eel-worm populations.

Standard practice in years gone by has included winter-feeding of cattle in yards. The practice still obtains on many farms, despite the relative prices of stores and fat beasts; but two divergent movements are now discernible. Some farms are abandoning feeding in favour of maintenance of store stock only, with sale in-calf or for grass-feeding. Others, borrowing a leaf from neighbours a little farther north, are turning to a policy of arable dairying.

The Kidderminster area differs from Lichfield chiefly in respect of the beet crop. There is a factory in the town, and throughout the district beet is grown on level terms with potatoes. Peas form also a notable crop. The crop is often sold to merchants who pick them.

[The Avon Valley] district figures prominently in monastic accounts of gardening, and doubtless fruit-growing started here at a very early date; but it was primarily a corn-growing area until the construction of the railway in the middle of last century opened up contacts with the fast-growing population of Birmingham and the neighbourhood. Since then development of fruit and vegetable-growing has been rapid, and there has been much deliberate creation, by land-owners and public authorities alike, of small-holdings out of corn-growing farms. Simultaneously, specialised farming by capitalist enterprise has developed. As a result there is now in the valley an enormous aggregation of tiny holdings intermixed with farms of 50 to 500 acres.

The small-holdings are unique. In Evesham itself and two adjoining parishes there are 900 holdings. In another parish, of 1,100 acres, 350 growers occupy 900 acres between them. Practically all the cultivators live in the town or surrounding villages. Fields are small, but, even so, nearly every one is divided like the medieval open field, by paths or ditches, into tiny flats, the total holdings of many growers being made up of parcels in different fields, often in two or three parishes. Nearly every type of vegetable is grown, the most notable being, perhaps, asparagus.

Intensive market-growing originated in Evesham and Pershore. The two centres have long ere this linked up and the industry has spread far afield on both sides of the river, up to Stratford and beyond. Developments in the latter direction have been chiefly amongst capitalist farmers and business men, often with interests in fruit and produce marketing.

THE DAIRYING AREA

The great crescent of Triassic outcrop which enfolds Birmingham has long been noted for its dairy-farming. The output of milk from this region—the so-called "milk belt"—is sufficient to affect materially the nation's supply, and its farmers have rightly enough played a leading role in the development of modern milk marketing.

The area is heavily stocked with dairy cattle. The county of Stafford, for instance, with 550,000 acres of grass and fodder crops, carries a stock of about 116,000 dairy cows and a total of 240,000 stock units—the equivalent, that is to say, of one stock unit to 2.3 acres. That is perhaps an average for the whole belt; the densest stocks occur in the west, and there is a general tendency to ease off towards the east.

MILK AND BEEF IN WARWICKSHIRE

Warwickshire farming before the war was a depressed industry. Eighty-five per cent of its land was in permanent grass, mainly of third-rate quality. On scores of farms, buildings and fixed equipment were steadily becoming derelict. Like other Midland counties it had once been a region of mixed farming, with 80,000 of its 460,000 acres in wheat and 160,000 in tillage; but when the decline in corn prices came in the 1880's, its farmers did not intensify their dairying to the same extent as their western neighbours; they continued sheep and cattle-feeding—enterprises excellent in their way but incapable of yielding high income, prone to lead to economies which take the form of discharging labour, to the merging of fields by the neglect of fences, and thus to ranching, dog and stick farming. Dispensing with labour is the first step in an insidious spiral, which ends with uninhabitable cottages, neglected homesteads, ditches,

drains and fences. No land can be farmed in an husbandlike manner without husbandmen.

There were other deep-seated causes of decline. It had been a county of country seats *par excellence,* affording wonderful hunting. From the turn of the century the days of the country landlord were over and the break-up of estates began. Many farms were "bought" by tenants with insufficient capital to maintain equipment, and agriculture was not then a sufficiently paying proposition to attract Birmingham business interests. In a sense Birmingham did come out into the country, but it came out in search of dormitories only and thereby induced, over a wide area, that curious paralysis of agricultural enterprise which over-spill housing seems fated to cause.

A development of considerable interest in recent years is that of seed growing. There is no doubt that Warwickshire is well suited to the production of most sorts of grass seed and to white clover also, though the latter is a speculative crop. It seems quite possible that grass seed growing can be blended with winter maintenance of cattle, but experience alone can show in what proportion of our winters cattle can graze drills in February, with advantage alike to themselves and the ground.

GRASS LANDS

The Triassic outcrop—mainly of Bunter Sandstone—to the west of Wolverhampton has given rise to a big stretch of predominantly light land extending nearly to the Severn and, in a north-south direction, from Market Drayton to Stourport. The valleys of the streams are usually broad and moist or marshy, well suited to grass. This is the traditional home of arable farming, sheep folding and winter fattening of cattle.

Almost all of it has been heathland enclosed direct in the interests of wool production towards the end of the fifteenth century. A few commons of poor and marshy type remained open until Napoleonic times.

Though it is customary to speak of it as an arable area, it is in truth an area of mixed arable and grass. Farms are in general larger than in most districts in the Midlands; homesteads are conceived on generous lines befitting what may be called a good farming district, though population density is smaller than in the dairying area.

It is good barley land. Though it will grow wheat, this crop competed but poorly with barley until the necessities of the times compelled an extension of the bread grain. Had modern spring wheats been available in pre-war days, possibly bigger areas would have been grown.

The barley, beef and sheep-folding system was at a very low ebb when the sugar beet subsidy was introduced. The new crop "took on" quickly, and its development affords a classic illustration of the forces that come into play when a new industry arises. A new technique had to be devised, methods of cultivation worked out, labour trained to new tasks.

Factories at Wellington and Kidderminster facilitated marketing, and the area under the crop grew steadily—with a brief setback when the sugar subsidy was reduced in 1932—down to the outbreak of war. Beet rather than corn became the keystone of farming. The area under arable cultivation was maintained at a high level.

MIXED FARMING IN THE WORCESTER PLAIN

Worcester is a densely populated county, with a general atmosphere of fruitfulness and modest prosperity. The close-set villages, often developed round what once were small commons and connected by a maze of narrow lanes, are plainly ancient settlements. Early man recognized Worcester as a delectable spot, and the Ridgeway which divides the county from Warwick was a well-worn track when the legions first sighted it. A considerable number of village commons still remain, the most noteworthy on the western side of the Severn.

The chief difficulty in appraising the farming of the Worcestershire Plain, however, lies in its diversity, in the number of enterprises commonly found on one farm. Everyone grows some wheat and some potatoes. . . . There are often a few acres of beet and some fruit is grown on every farm; usually some milk is sold; calves are reared for drafting into the herd, for sale as stores or for fattening, and they may be joined by others purchased for sale later in store or fat condition; there are usually a few pigs and a flock of hens in battery or out on free range, and one field may be let out for the season to a market-gardener who will grow sprouts thereon. All this on 60 acres. If it is a sizable farm there is a small flock of ewes as well, and autumn lambs may be brought in for feeding on the maiden seeds.

In so far as one motif is dominant, it is milk supported by rearing, the emphasis falling on milk where water supplies and buildings are suitable, and on rearing where these facilities are poor.

Vegetables and fruit undoubtedly contribute a big quota to farm income. Fruit is grown everywhere on scales varying from an acre or two of grass orchard, up to the specialist venture of the fruit farmer, pure and simple. It is a long-established enterprise which has evolved slowly.

As has already been mentioned, a complex industrial system must be fed with raw materials from many lands. At first, local resources are usually sufficient but, as they become depleted, they must be supplemented by imports. As industry becomes more highly specialized, there is greater demand for particular kinds of products for which there may be no domestic substitutes; there is also more need to discover new markets for goods produced in almost endless quantities by mass-production methods. Thus, commerce expands and flourishes, illustrating the "dynamic" character of capitalism.

In Selection 133, which follows, mention is made of the goods which pass through London and Liverpool, illustrating the *entrepot* character of these ports. Where goods are moved from one ship to another or from one type of conveyance to another, there is employment for local people and an important source of income.

But commerce and all the technological activities described in previous selections require capital. Thus, financial institutions take deep root in an industrial society, and banking on an international scale provides the mechanism by which worldwide trade can be carried on. Therefore, it is appropriate that the next selection carries the title of Industry (since it presents a bird's-eye picture of manufacturing centers in Britain), Commerce (since it emphasizes shipping and the exchange of commodities), and Finance (since it discusses the balance of trade and Britain's pecuniary resources).

• 133 • *Industry, Commerce, and Finance*

PHILIP CARR

What are the foundations of the industrial, commercial and financial greatness of England, and what are the conditions which are essential to its existence?

The foundations are two—first, maritime transport, and then, coal. The essential conditions are also two—first, the freedom of the seas, and then, the maintenance of purchasing power.

Before the industrial age of the nineteenth century had given coal its enormous importance, London had already become the chief trading center between Europe and the other continents, and afterwards, as a natural consequence, the financial center of the world; and London had attained this position owing mainly to the fact that the goods exchanged between Europe and these other continents were carried almost entirely in British ships. There were geographical and historical reasons for this. The British Isles were favorably placed at the door of Europe and in the temperate flow of the Gulf Stream. The British Navy had successively driven other competitors off the seas—first the Spanish, then the Dutch and then the French.

Thus, by the end of the eighteenth century, England had firmly established herself as a great commercial nation.

In the nineteenth century, she became a great industrial nation as well; and she be-

came so largely because she possessed coal in enormous quantities, in excellent quality and in readily accessible places, so that she had, under her hand and cheap, the power for driving the steam engines, which she had herself invented for her factories, her railways and her ships, which, in turn, provided her with cheap delivery abroad.

The industries were built up in close proximity to, and indeed on the top of, the coal fields; and these coal fields were within easy distance of the seaports—there is no place in England which is not within easy distance of the coast, and the English coast is dotted with good seaports. As sea transport is always much cheaper than land transport, the shortness of the land journey to the factories from the sea for the raw material and from the factories to the sea for the manufactured goods was of great importance in keeping down the selling price of the finished article.

This double advantage was so great that it counterbalanced the fact that all except two of the chief raw materials used for the manufactures, which Great Britain exported overseas, had first to be imported from overseas.

These conditions remain the ones which govern the situation today.

With regard to raw materials used in manufacture, it is still the fact that only two of the important ones, iron and wool, are obtained

[Reprinted and adapted from *The English Are Like That*, by Philip Carr; copyright 1941 by Charles Scribner's Sons, New York, Pp. 184-190, 193-197. Used by permission of the publishers.]

to any considerable extent at home; and even they are not obtained to the full extent that is required.

The great iron industry of Great Britain was built up in the past by using exclusively British ore, and in time of peace Great Britain does still produce two thirds of the iron ore which she needs; but she imports the remaining third.

As for wool, it used to be one of the most famous products and exports of England, and the best qualities are so still. Yet hardly more than a tenth of the woollen yarns and cloths which come from the mills of Bradford, in Yorkshire, or Paisley, in Scotland, and are exported all over the world, is made from the wool of sheep raised in Great Britain.

Several of the metals other than iron have been mined in Great Britain for hundreds of years—the Cornish tin mines, for instance, date back to the Romans—and important industries owe their foundation to these earlier deposits. However, the production has, in all cases, long been insignificant principally because the foreign ore could be obtained more cheaply; and it is upon imported ores that the industries originally created to work the metals of Great Britain have grown to rely.

Finally, all the mineral oil, used to make motor and aviation petrol, as well as for lighting, has to be imported.

When we pass from the minerals below the soil to what is grown above it—animal as well as vegetable—we find that Great Britain is no less dependent upon imports from abroad.

Virtually the whole of the wood used in the country arrives from overseas, as well as the pulp used in paper making, to say nothing of newsprint paper itself.

All the cotton, which is spun and woven in the mills of Lancashire, is imported. Much of the flax which is made into linen in Belfast comes from Russia.

All the tobacco which is smoked in Great Britain is imported.

In the matter of food, the percentage of imports to the whole consumption is no less great—80 per cent of the cereals; 78 per cent of the sugar; 88 per cent of the butter and other fats; 50 per cent of the meat; 33 per cent of the milk; 50 per cent of the fresh fruit.

In addition, Great Britain imports the whole of her enormous consumption of tea, her small consumption of coffee, and her considerable consumption of cocoa.

[It is worthy of note] that, in many cases, the country which is the principal source of supply is itself a member of the British Commonwealth of Nations. This is of considerable importance under war conditions, where finance is concerned, [particularly]. At the same time, these imports have to be carried over the ocean no less than if they were purchased from a foreign country, and the necessity of keeping the seas open and the ships of the merchant service constantly travelling over them remains as vital as ever.

British shipping is therefore at the very foundation of the commercial and financial greatness of the country, and it is also the life line of Great Britain.

I have spoken of shipping to begin with, because that is Great Britain's most essential activity in the sense that if it collapsed, Great Britain could not live. There are, however, other occupations which employ far greater numbers of workers. Look first of all at the productive industries, as they stood before war diverted the activities of so many factories from their normal course. Textiles and clothing, taking cotton and wool together, show the largest figures, the number of the women employed being double the number of the men—the totals in 1931, when the last detailed reports were made, were 1,200,000 women and 600,000 men. The industry in which the greatest number of male workers is occupied is that of metal trades and engineering (1,500,000), followed by agriculture (1,200,000), then by coal mining (1,000,000) and then by the building trades (950,000). Transport of all kinds, including ships, railways and road vehicles, accounts for a larger number of workers (1,750,000) than any of the industries just mentioned; and commerce of all kinds is responsible for almost as many (1,600,000); but these last are rather arbitrary groupings, and are of relatively little interest as an indication of the productive efforts of the country.

The enormous number of people who depend upon the textile industries shows what a great factor these industries are in British prosperity. As far as England is concerned, they are concentrated in South Lancashire for cotton and in West Yorkshire for woollens— that is to say, looking northwards at the map, in that part of the country where the island begins to get definitely narrower. The products of these industries are among the most important of British exports.

The metal-working industries follow the Yorkshire coalfields southwards from Leeds to Sheffield and then to the neighborhood of Nottingham, and are found again, rather to the southwest, on the Midland coal field— Wolverhampton, Birmingham and Coventry.

Around London and Liverpool are other industrial areas, producing various kinds of goods; but they are to be found there, not because there is coal—for there is none—but because, for various reasons, it is more convenient for them to be immediately in touch with a great seaport, where the raw materials arrive and whence the finished goods are despatched, than to be on a coal field.

The shipbuilding industry is established on the estuaries of the Clyde and the Mersey on the West Coast and the Tyne and the Thames on the East.

Among the British industries which manufacture for export, and make the economic greatness of the country, I have spoken of only one or two of the most important; but there are many others. There are ships, locomotives, aircraft and motor cars, the value of whose exports, taken together, was only exceeded, in 1938, by two exports, machinery and cotton, and exceeded that of iron and steel and that of woollens. There are chemicals and dyes whose normal export is worth more than £22,000,000. There are electrical goods, pottery and cutlery, each of which export far more than £9,000,000. There are high-class paper goods, the value of whose export in 1938 was £7,000,000, manufactured oils £5,000,000, and leather goods, £4,000,000.

As for the foreign buyers of these exports, the largest buying country in 1937 was the United States, closely followed by South Africa, Australia and India. France, Germany, Canada and Eire formed a second group. A third group was composed of New Zealand, Argentina, and Russia.

Many communities in the United States today are looking for economic salvation in the coming of more industry to their localities. Chambers of commerce and numerous other organizations are on the alert to persuade expanding business firms to establish plants in their locality. We are learning in this country, as the British learned some time ago, that there are many social factors, such as housing, schools, community spirit, medical services, which influence the decision to move into a specific community. But there are also the economic factors which, in the opinion of industrial management, will promote or hinder the financial success of the enterprise.

It has here and there been mentioned that labor is one of the primary economic factors in the location of industries, and that employer-worker antagonisms have declined. The selection that follows will present a brief picture of the three main sections of the British Labour Movement—industrial, trading, and political. This is followed by a more detailed statement of the industrial side, leaving for later consideration the trading, or cooperative, aspect and the political power of labor.

Anyone familiar with the American labor movement will see many similarities between it and the British trade-union movement. We, too, have the craft unions (forming the American Federation of Labor) and the industrial unions (the Congress of Industrial Organization). But, as in Britain, the distinction between the two types sometimes becomes vague, although the arbitrary boundary is preserved in the formalities of organization. In both countries the collective agreement, or contract, results from collective bargaining between management and labor; when the two cannot agree, the matters in dispute may be left to an impartial arbitration board for decision. In other instances, a mediation board may step in to try to work out a compromise between the two parties.

One striking difference is apparent. In Britain, labor has gone actively into politics with its own political party, but in the United States the leaders of organized labor have preferred to offer support to one or the other major party in return for expected sympathetic treatment. Also, in Britain there is one central body, the Trades Union Congress, which represents all labor, although it has no power to bind the constituent unions. Another important difference lies in the fact that a far greater proportion of English than American workers are unionized. But in both countries labor—and often this means organized labor—must be considered a major factor in the economy and a group of utmost importance in the society.

· 134 · Trade Unionism
G. D. H. COLE

The British Labour Movement has three main sections—industrial, trading and political. For collective bargaining and common action to protect the workers as wage-earners or producers, there exist Trade Unions, covering altogether about 9½ million workers as compared with a total 'occupied' population in civil employment of about 22 millions. For the protection of the workers as consumers, mainly by means of mutual trading and the co-operative organisation of the production of essential goods, there are Co-operative Societies, with a membership of about ten millions, representing a considerably larger total number of consumers. The political organisation, which exists to further workingclass aspirations towards a better social and economic system, is a good deal more complicated, as it is based largely on the Trade Unions and Co-operative Societies. The Labour Party is partly a federation of Trade Unions with certain other bodies, of which the Fabian Society has been one ever since the Party was formed;

and there is also a Co-operative Party which, though separate in organisation, works in close alliance with the Labour Party. We have, moreover, to take separate account, in the political field, of the Communist Party, which has its own organisation and policy, and has steadily been refused admission to the Labour Party as an affiliated body, and also of the Independent Labour Party, formerly affiliated to the Labour Party but now outside it and greatly reduced in numbers, and of a number of other small bodies standing for some form of Socialism, or setting out to organise the workers politically for some special or limited purpose.

The three main sections—Trade Union, Co-operative, and Political—have each their own central co-ordinating bodies. The Trades Union Congress is a federation of national Trade Unions representing the various industries and occupations, and claiming to represent the collective standpoint of organised Labour in industrial matters. The Co-opera-

[Adapted from *The British Working-Class Movement*, Fabian Publications, London, 1949. Pp. 5-11. Used by permission.]

tive Union, which organises the annual Co-operative Congress, links together not only the local distributive Co-operative Societies, or Stores, but also Co-operatives of other types —the Wholesale Societies, the Producers' Societies, and the 'auxiliary' bodies, such as the Co-operative Women's Guilds. The Labour Party includes, in addition to the Trade Unions and other national bodies affiliated to it, the Local Labour Parties organised on a constituency basis, with individual members as well as locally affiliated Trade Union branches and other bodies; and closely associated with it is the Parliamentary Labour Party, consisting of its elected representatives in the House of Commons and the small contingent of Labour peers.

These three main bodies are linked up in turn in the National Council of Labour, which issues from time to time major pronouncements on Labour policy and is designed to promote closer unity between the three sections.

TYPES OF TRADE UNIONS

There were in all, in December 1947, 730 Trade Unions in Great Britain, with over nine million members. The Trades Union Congress had, in the same year, 188 affiliated Trade Unions, with nearly eight million members. . . .

There are three main types of Trade Unions—craft Unions, organising skilled workers belonging to a particular trade or group of trades; industrial Unions, setting out to enroll all the workers in a particular industry, skilled and unskilled together; and general workers' Unions, enrolling mainly less skilled workers from a wide range of industries, but also organising skilled workers for whom no recognised craft Union exists. Typical examples are the London Society of Compositors, the United Pattern-makers' Association, the Amalgamated Association of Operative Cotton Spinners (Craft Unions); the National Union of Railwaymen, the Iron and Steel Trades Confederation, the National Union of Mineworkers (Industrial Unions or close Federations); the Transport and General Workers' Union, the National Union of

General and Municipal Workers (General Workers' Unions). Not all Unions will fit neatly into this classification. For example, the Amalgamated Engineering Union is basically a Union of skilled men in a number of kindred crafts, but has also latterly opened its ranks to include less skilled male workers and, since 1943, women. The National Union of Public Employees resembles a general workers' Union, but is limited to employees of public authorities. The Associated Society of Locomotive Engineers and Firemen is mainly a craft Union of footplate workers, but includes also engine cleaners, most of whom hope to become drivers or firemen later on. There is a good deal of friction between mainly craft, or kindred craft, and industrial Unions over the organisation of both skilled and less skilled workers in some industries— for example, in the railway engineering shops and in the engineering industry generally, and between the National Union of Railwaymen and the Associated Society of Locomotive Engineers and Firemen over the organisation of the footplate grades. This friction, however, is a good deal less acute than it used to be a generation ago; and in many cases rival Unions have reached some sort of working accommodation.

In 1948 there were four Trade Unions with more than half a million members (Transport and General Workers, 1,264,000; General and Municipal Workers, 824,000; Amalgamated Engineering Union, 742,000; National Union of Mineworkers, 572,000). Two others (National Union of Railwaymen, 462,000; Union of Shop, Distributive and Allied Workers, 343,000) had more than a quarter of a million; and there were four more with over 100,000. The six largest Unions included well over half the total membership of the Trades Union Congress; and of these six, the two largest were general workers' Unions, three industrial Unions, and one (the A.E.U.) betwixt an industrial Union and a Union of kindred crafts. Craft Unions tend in most cases to be relatively small, as there are not many very numerous skilled crafts. The largest is the Amalgamated Society of Woodworkers (200,000).

In general *craft* Unions have higher contributions and benefits than others, usually including sick pay and sometimes superannuation as well as dispute benefit. *Industrial* and other Unions catering for a wide variety of workers sometimes have several scales of contributions and benefits, for different classes of members, or provide for voluntary contributions and benefits for sickness. Dispute benefit is provided for in all Unions except some in the public services, which do not use the strike weapon. But in recent years not very much has been spent on this benefit, as authorised strikes have been few ever since 1926. A large part of the expenditure of most Unions has to go on administration costs, including all sorts of services to members in collective bargaining, organization, and defence in legal cases (e.g., workmen's compensation).

TRADE UNION STRUCTURE

The basic Trade Union unit is the local branch (or lodge, among the miners), of which a big Union may have several in a single town. In such cases, the local branches are usually grouped round a District Committee, which is the main local body for handling industrial questions. Many Unions have District or Divisional Councils covering wider areas, usually with a full-time District Organiser; and some of the largest Unions have also full-time local officers. But most local Trade Union work is done voluntarily, or in return for small payments to cover expenses and lost time. Full-time officials are usually employed by the Union nationally, even when they serve a local area, and usually work under the orders of the National Executive.

National Trade Union Executives usually consist of persons working at their trades, and meet only occasionally (quarterly or monthly, with special meetings in case of need). Members are paid small fees ('delegation') to cover expenses and time lost. Most Unions have also Delegate Conferences, annual, biennial, or even triennial, which finally determine policy and make or alter rules. Executive members are sometimes elected by the Conference, and sometimes by ballot vote

of the members. Some Unions use the ballot of members as a frequent means of settling policy issues. This applies especially to the Miners, and to some of the craft Unions. In the general workers' Union the Executive usually has very large powers. The chief full-time officials are often elected by ballot of the membership, but some Unions elect their officials at Conference. Lesser officers are sometimes elected by ballot, but more often chosen by the Executive. Trade Union constitutions differ greatly, in the main according to the organisation of the industry concerned. In some cases—e.g., building, printing, engineering—bargaining is largely local in the first instance, usually with an appeal to a national joint body, and arbitration or strike action in reserve in case of failure to agree. In other industries, from the nature of the case, bargaining is mainly national (e.g., railways, post office); and in many some questions are dealt with nationally and others locally (e.g., coal mining). The central issues of bargaining are standard rates of wages, hours of labour, holidays, overtime pay, and 'recognition' of Trade Unions for purposes of local or factory as well as national bargaining. A good many Unions have *shop stewards* in the factories, to see that membership is kept up, and to take up workshop grievances; but usually such stewards are not given much negotiating power, which is mainly reserved for District Committees and for the national Unions and their officers. One object of this is to prevent works agreements in conflict with national or district agreements; another is the fear that shop stewards may be inclined to throw over Trade Union 'discipline' or to act in violation of agreements not to strike until certain procedures have been followed. During the war, Joint Production Committees were set up in many war factories, for the purpose of improving organisation and output, but these were distinct from Shop Stewards' Committees. After 1945 many of these bodies were discontinued; but there has been a revival since, encouraged both by the Government and by the T.U.C.

Trade Union branches are usually based more on where members live than on where they work, and where there are several branches of a Union in a town the members working in the same factory may be scattered over the branches. Some Unions, however, take the place of work as the unit (e.g., to a large extent Miners, Iron and Steel Workers, Newspaper Printers, Distributive Workers). Those who favour more 'workers' control' in industry usually advocate the extension of shop stewards, shop stewards' committees, Joint Production or Consultative Committees, and branches based on the place of work.

Attendance at Trade Union branch meetings, and also frequency of meetings, differ greatly from Union to Union. In most cases only a small proportion of the members attend, unless there is some special excitement such as a dispute or wage-claim on foot. Many Unions collect subscriptions at branch meetings; but others have collectors who go from house to house, and others collect largely at the place of work, so that members need not attend the branch to pay. Normally, therefore, votes at branch meetings represent directly the views only of the keen minority, though they may, of course, correctly interpret the general opinion.

COLLECTIVE AGREEMENTS

In most big industries there are nowadays national agreements laying down both certain basic conditions of employment and the procedure to be adopted, locally and nationally, in adjusting differences. These agreements usually run for a term of years. In some cases they provide for reference to impartial arbitration in case of failure to agree. A good many Unions use the Government's Industrial Court as a tribunal for this purpose (or the National Arbitration Tribunal—set up during the war, to deal with disputes when strike action was forbidden—and continued since 1945). In a good many cases agreements cover a number of Unions in the same industry; and these Unions are often federated for common action (e.g., National Federation of Building Trades Operatives, National Printing and Kindred Trades Federation).

Strike action was limited up to 1947 (apart from wartime limitations) by the Trade Union Act of 1927, which outlawed the General Strike and any sympathetic strike held to be designed to 'coerce the Government'; but this Act was repealed in 1947, and in general strike action is now limited only by the temporary continuance of the requirement to refer disputes to the National Arbitration Tribunal or to some other court of arbitration. The 1927 Act also prevented Civil Servants from joining with workers in private employment, either in the Trades Union Congress or in the Labour Party, and severely restricted picketing; but the Trade Unions have now recovered the freedom they enjoyed under the Trade Disputes Act of 1906.

THE T.U.C. AND THE TRADES COUNCILS

The central Trade Union body is the Trades Union Congress, with its General Council elected by the delegates as a whole to represent the main industries and groups which act as nominating sections. There are also two seats reserved for women. The General Council acts as the central body to represent industrial Labour, but has no power to bind the affiliated Unions. Neither the General Council nor the T.U.C. itself can call a strike: this has to be done by the separate Unions concerned. The General Strike of 1926 was called by a Special Conference of Trade Union Executives convened by the T.U.C. General Council. There is no general negotiating body to deal with wages and conditions. The General Council has, however, a joint committee with the Employers' National Confederation and the Federation of British Industries for discussion of general industrial questions; and it is represented on a number of general advisory committees of employers and Trade Unionists and on other official bodies set up to advise the Government both on labour matters and on wider questions of production, prices, rationing, etc. Locally, Trade Union branches are federated in Trades Councils, which exist to deal with general questions in their areas, but have no negotiating functions. They are chiefly organising bodies, and agencies of protest against local grievances. The Trades Councils have County

Federations, a National Advisory Committee, and an Annual Consultative Conference; but these federal agencies have little power. The central Trades Councils machinery is in the hands of the T.U.C. General Council.

WOMEN

Of the total of about 9½ million Trade Unionists, about 1¼ millions are women—a rise since 1939 when there were just under a million women in Trade Unions, mostly textile and distributive workers. Women are harder to organise than men, partly because many of them leave employment on marriage, and partly because they are largely employed in less skilled work. Female membership rose greatly during the war, but has fallen since, as many war workers have retired from 'gainful employment'.

By now we should see clearly that an industrial economy has many kinds of occupations and that people demand of it numerous services. Great Britain has moved far toward the socialization of its economy by its nationalization of a number of industries, which is one way of saying that the government undertakes to manage for the people large segments of the economy. The problems that such a program encounters are discussed by Warren Haynes, an American economist who, as a Fulbright Fellow on leave from the University of Kentucky, made a firsthand study of the coal industry in Britain. He has prepared the following summary of his findings especially for this volume.

• 135 • Nationalization in Great Britain
WARREN HAYNES

Nationalization is not a difficult word to define. A nationalized industry is a publicly-owned one; nationalization is the process of converting private assets to public ones. It follows that there is nothing peculiarly British about nationalization; in the United States we have a nationalized post office; the Tennessee Valley Administration was the means by which some assets of private enterprise were nationalized.

In Great Britain the overwhelming victory of the Labor Party in 1945 made it clear that an extensive program of nationalization would be carried out. The Party's platform, "Let Us Face the Future," called for public ownership of a number of industries: coal, gas, electricity, inland transport, iron and steel. It also promised to take over the Bank of England. As soon as it went into office, the Labor Government, headed by Clement Attlee, proceeded to draw up bills to fulfill these promises.

What was the purpose of nationalizing these industries? The Labor Party hoped public ownership of the "basic" industries would assist it in several ways:

1. Through control of investment in these industries, the Party felt it could more readily carry out an economic plan which would eliminate unemployment and assure that resources flowed into socially useful channels.

2. Public ownership of these industries would eliminate private monopoly in their sphere (replacing it, of course, with public monopoly) and would help break down the concentration of economic power in the hands of a few private individuals.

3. Nationalization would be a step in the direction of socialism "which can not come overnight as the product of a week-end revolution." It should assist in the redistribution of personal incomes, an item which

has high priority in most socialist programs.

Nationalization of industry, at least for the immediate future, was to be restricted to "basic industry," which Labor leaders estimated at 20 per cent of all industry. At some future date further measures might be taken. On this, the Party was divided. The extreme Left wished to move rapidly to take over the insurance companies, the shipbuilding concerns, the joint stock banks, the docks, the aircraft industry, the automobile industry, cement, chemicals, and wholesaling. A much larger section of the Party favored a more moderate program; the goal of 20 per cent of industry was quite sufficient for it. There was even a section of the Party (Herbert Morrison was rumored to be its leader) which was opposed to taking over iron and steel, on the grounds that the Government had quite enough on its hands.

Before moving on to specific measures, several points should be made clear. First, nationalization is not a new thing in Great Britain. The Post Office had long been governmentally owned, and the Post Office had owned the telephone systems of Britain since 1892. The British Broadcasting Corporation, a government agency, had a monopoly over broadcasting. The London Passenger Transport Board, the Port of London Authority, and the Central Electricity Board were all examples of government enterprise before 1945. Many of these agencies were established by Conservative governments.

Second, it should be made clear that nationalization of the coal, electricity, gas, and other industries does not in itself constitute "socialism" as defined by the Labor Party, though perhaps it may be considered the core of the Party's platform. Many other measures, springing from the socialist creed, were put into effect between 1945 and 1950. The Health Insurance program, price control, rent control, supervision of monopoly, subsidized housing, town and country planning, and extended social insurance are but a few of these. This report proposes to discuss only a part of the Labor Government's achievement—the progress of the new publicly owned industries.

THE NATIONALIZATION ACTS: 1946-1950

The election of 1945 was followed by a series of complicated nationalization acts, which altogether take up hundreds of pages and have been elaborated by thousands of pages of regulations. The following summary of these acts must of necessity be highly simplified; later sections will go into one of the acts in greater detail—the Coal Nationalization Act of 1946 and will attempt to spell out what nationalization means in practice. For the present, let us summarize all the acts briefly.

1. *The Bank of England Act, 1946* This Act provided for the vesting of the stock of the Bank of England in the Government. This would be comparable to nationalizing the Federal Reserve Bank in the United States; the member banks were left untouched, except that government ownership of the Central Bank perhaps meant closer supervision of their activities. This Act was by no means a revolutionary measure for Britain; the Bank of England had already worked closely with the Treasury. The Conservatives put up little opposition to this measure, recognizing that a small change was involved.

2. *The Coal Industry Nationalization Act, 1946* This Act established a National Coal Board, which was to be responsible to Parliament through the Ministry of Fuel and Power. The Coal Board was to take over the assets of the private coal companies, except some very small unimportant ones. This act will be discussed more fully in later sections.

3. *The Cable and Wireless Act, 1946* This Act provided for public ownership of the stock of Cable and Wireless Ltd. It had the support of all the parties in Parliament and received a unanimous vote. Since the telegraph lines within Great Britain were already publicly owned and had been since 1870, this Act, which took over lines to some foreign countries, was not a radical step. The object of the Act was to unify all the telegraph services into one coordinated system, so that cooperation with Commonwealth and Ameri-

can systems could more readily be attained. The directors of Cable and Wireless were to be appointed by the Government and to come under the Postmaster-General.

4. *The Electricity Act, 1947* A large step toward nationalization of the electricity supply had been taken in 1926, when the Central Electricity Board was set up to coordinate electricity supply. The Central Electricity Board took over control of the generation and long-distance transmission of electricity, but the distribution of electricity was left to the old private companies and municipal systems. The new act provided for public ownership of the whole electricity supply industry: generation, transmission, and distribution. The British Electricity Authority, consisting of ten to twelve members appointed by the Minister of Fuel and Power, was to be the overall coordinating agency. Fourteen Area Boards were also established to distribute the power —thus much authority was delegated to regions. It is interesting that the chairman of the Electricity Authority has been Lord Citrine, formerly a Trade Union leader and General Secretary of the Trades Union Congress for many years.

5. *Gas Act, 1948* Under this Act, the Government took over the gas production and distribution facilities of Great Britain. A Gas Council was established at the center, and twelve Area Boards in the various regions. The organization differed from that in the electricity supply industry in that much more power was delegated to the Areas under the Gas Act. In fact, each Area Board is an almost completely autonomous public corporation, and the Gas Council is primarily a central discussion agency. The Council and Area Boards all come under the Minister of Fuel and Power. The trend towards decentralization, carried even further in the Iron and Steel Act, is one of the most significant developments since 1946.

6. *Transport Act, 1947* This Act established a British Transport Commission consisting of from four to eight members appointed by the Minister of Transport. As in the Electricity Act and the Gas Act, powers were delegated to lower agencies but in this case these agencies were functional rather than regional. The five executives under the Transport Commission are known as the Railway Executive, the Docks and Inland Waterways Executive, the Road Transport Executive, the London Transport Executive, and the Hotels Executive, all of whom are appointed by the Minister of Transport.

The Transport Act is an extremely complicated one. All the railroads were taken over, but only part of the trucks (called lorries).

7. *Iron and Steel Act, 1949* The Iron and Steel Act did not become effective until February 15, 1951. It has been the most controversial of the nationalization measures. The Conservative Party has denounced this Act as unconstitutional, since it feels that the majority of the people do not want it. Accordingly, the Conservatives have promised to reverse the Act when they are restored to power. [Since this was written, early in 1951, the Conservatives have been able to take steps toward accomplishing this reversal.] Furthermore, it is clear that the Labor Party is split on the issue, though Labor Party Members of Parliament voted together for the bill to maintain party unity. This Act differs from the others in that the old firms were left intact as individual units, with their old names, the Government taking over the controlling stock. As far as possible, it was hoped that the same Directors would remain in charge.

An Iron and Steel Corporation was formed to supervise the activities of the individual firms. Small firms, producing under 20,000 tons of iron and steel, were not nationalized. The Iron and Steel Corporation consists of from five to eleven members appointed by the Minister of Supply.

SOME COMMON FEATURES OF THE NATIONALIZATION ACTS

While the above acts have of necessity had to be varied according to the conditions of each industry, there are a few things to be said that apply to all or almost all of them.

1. The Acts demonstrated the belief of

the Labor Party that nationalized undertakings should be run by public corporations; that is, instead of having a government department run the industry, as is done in the case of the post office in both Great Britain and the United States, the authority would be delegated to a special corporation set up for this purpose. In this, these corporations are like the Tennessee Valley Administration or the Reconstruction Finance Corporation in the United States. However, unlike the T. V. A. and the R. F. C., the autonomy of the British public corporations established since 1945 is somewhat limited by the fact that each comes under a Cabinet Minister, such as the Minister of Fuel and Power, the Minister of Transport, or the Minister of Supply. The Minister in each case has substantial powers over general policy, but can not interfere in day-to-day matters.

2. In each act provision was made for parliamentary control. Various control devices are in use: the Minister is always subject to questions from Members of Parliament; occasionally the activities of the boards are subject to open debate; the boards must all present detailed accounts to Parliament which are discussed and debated. In general, Parliament is not supposed to debate day-to-day activities of the boards, but so far it has been found difficult to separate routine affairs from broader policy. For example, there was a considerable discussion in Parliament over the health of Ned, a pit pony (used in mining), who some M.P.'s (Members of Parliament) felt was not receiving proper treatment.

3. In each act there were provisions for compensation to the former owners. The calculation of the amount of compensation has necessarily varied in method from act to act, because each industry involved special considerations. Compensation was paid partly in cash, but mostly in the form of Government securities, which in some cases were to be non-transferable. The amount of compensation has been subject to arbitration and in most cases there is little basis for attacking the fairness of the amounts. The most controversial aspect of compensation has been the nontransferability of some of the Government bonds issued.

4. In most of the Acts, Consumers' Councils have been set up to represent the interests of consumers. These report over the heads of the boards to the Ministers, and each Minister has power to put recommendations of Consumers' Councils into effect. To date, the general feeling, even among Labor Party Members, is that the Consumers' Councils have been ineffective for the most part.

THE COAL INDUSTRY

After [several] years of public ownership, three major issues face the National Coal Board and the other nationalized industries. To date no simple answer to these questions has been found.

1. The first question has to do with decentralization: how far should the Coal Board and other public corporations attempt to delegate powers to local agencies? We have seen that the Electricity Act and especially the Gas Act provided for greater degrees of decentralization than did the Coal Act, but even those acts have been criticized for centralizing too much power in London. The advantages of decentralization are numerous: decisions can be made more readily at the local level; more attention can be given diverse local conditions; there is less chance for red-tape and slow moving bureaucracy to develop; and labor does not feel that its masters are quite so remote. But decentralization is not so simple a question as most critics of the National Coal Board think. There are definite economies in centralizing such things as research; someone has to coordinate coal production plans for the whole industry; if the national Exchequer is to be a source of funds for the industry the national government must have some control; some agency must answer to Parliament for industry; and the workers themselves insist on nation-wide bargaining.

Despite the difficulties, the National Coal Board has been moving toward greater decentralization. Perhaps this development has been too slow; those who have worked in government or army agencies know that it is much harder to break a large unit into small ones than to reverse the process.

2. The second question facing the Coal Board and the other corporations is that of the position of the workers in nationalized industries. On one extreme are those who argue that the workers should have complete control; this might endanger the interests of the general public. Others argue that the workers should have representatives on the Boards, not a few ex-trade-unionists as there are at present, but real representatives voted upon by the workers. The objection to this is not only that such boards might place the workers' interest above the general public interest, but also that such representatives would have a split loyalty between the government on the one hand and the workers on the other. In fact, a large part of the trade unions are opposed to such representation, feeling that the unions must maintain their independence. The alternative that has the greatest support is the proposal that the present separation of management and worker representation through the unions be maintained, but that both management and the workers be educated to work more cooperatively than in the past. The National Coal Board, like the other boards, has set up an elaborate joint consultation machinery through which it is hoped that the workers and managers will be able to communicate their desires and anxieties more effectively. A great deal of experimentation on worker participation in public corporations is likely. So far, no satisfactory formula has been found.

3. The last question has to do with the relation of the public corporations to Parliament. One group argues that the industries should be made departments of the government and that any attempt at autonomy is hopeless. This view recognizes that Parliament is going to snoop anyway so why put up the pretense of independence. The opposite group argues for even greater independence than now exists, to keep the boards as far as possible from politics and so that strictly business, as opposed to civil service, methods be adopted. This issue is still open.

Thus we see that the final form of nationalization has not been achieved; much more experimentation will take place. It will pay us to watch the public corporations in Great Britain, for similar experiments are being carried out in the United States. Each country may learn from the successes and failures of the other.

Social Organization
and Interaction

>>>

An industrial society develops a complex political and social life. In our study of the Chinese peasant we found that the family was the chief pattern of association and thus played a major role in regulating life. In the old Cotton South, also, the family held an important central place, although the relationships among individuals and among groups within the society were considerably complicated by the patterns of stratification resulting from slavery. The New South is today taking over the economic and societal patterns of the rest of the United States and is cooperating in a network of governmental programs of national scope. Thus it has come about that even the traditional speeches on "states' rights" by Southern politicians sometimes have a hollow ring, for the local patterns of control have long since begun to give way to national patterns.

Britain affords us an example of a country in which government, as the agent of the whole (nationwide) social group, has come to the fore and exercised dominant control over many phases of the economy—and, either directly or indirectly, over many of the social patterns and activities. In the United States, on the other hand, we are still heatedly debating the extent to which the "public" federal government should exercise powers formerly or still held by "private" economic groups. But in both Britain and the United States there is no question that the individual's life is dominated by government or business or both, and that the family and the religious group no longer exercise their former degree of authority and control throughout the whole society. Furthermore, in both these societies many activities have come to be oriented toward some aspect of buying and selling or of money-making. Education, for example, is regarded by many people as primarily a matter of teaching people how to make a living, a function it used to perform to only a very slight degree. As another example, the commercialization of recreation is familiar to us all.

As we read the selections that follow, the influences exerted by economic organizations and by the government through those who hold statuses in connection with them will become apparent. We can note, too, how the value system tends increasingly to enlarge such statuses, while legislative bodies and public opinion both seek to limit the ways in which these people in positions of power and trust may behave. The banker as well as the bureaucrat finds himself bound by many more restrictions than formerly, but these are simply a reflection of these individuals' increasing prestige and power. Also, we can try to discover the relative importance of competitive and cooperative activities and the degree to which the compromise or accommodation is accepted in social relations. We shall see, too, the extremely assimilative character of an industrial society. Later selections will also treat of the motivational processes of socialization and social control.

It is well known that social scientists, who try to deal with phenomena systematically, are not the only people who have examined the society in which we live with great care. The travel book and the novel may present much the same information, though in a quite different way. J. B. Priestley, one of the foremost English men of letters, took an extensive trip through England in 1933. What he saw in his visit to the Midlands is presented in the next selection. Priestley's interests ranged widely, touching on not only the physical appearance of places but the work and the recreation of the people there. The nonconformists, whose religious activities interested him, are the Methodists, Baptists, and other Protestants who do not belong to the Established Church of England. Priestley is amused that young people use the Birmingham Corporation Art Gallery as a trysting place, and he tries to decide whether the model town of Bournville is a blessing or a curse to the workers in the chocolate factory there. His observations are revealing, and his ability as a professional writer gives them a vividness that is often lacking in the less personal accounts of the overserious scientist. It should be kept in mind that Priestley made his trip during the depression of the 1930's. Its devastating effect on the people, which is reflected in conditions he observed, was a major factor behind popular demand for the nationalization of certain industries.

• 136 • To Birmingham and the Black Country

J. B. PRIESTLEY

BIRMINGHAM

In the midst of a russet solitude, we came upon a notice board saying, *This is the City of Birmingham*. There was nothing in sight but hedgerows, glittering fields and the mist of the autumn morning. For a moment I entertained a wild hope that this really was the City of Birmingham, that the town had been pulled down and carted away, [for] I had always thought of the place, vaguely, as perhaps the most typical product in civic life of nineteenth-century industrialism, as a city of big profits and narrow views, which sent

[Adapted from *English Journey*, Harper and Brothers, New York, 1934. Pp. 60-90. Used by permission of publisher and author.]

missionaries out of one gate and brass idols and machine guns out of another. It made a great many articles, chiefly in metal, but so far in my life not one of these articles had gained any hold over my affections. Then there were jokes about a foolish Watch Committee there. On the other hand, any guide-book could offer a great many facts on the credit side. In the eighteenth century, Birmingham had a Lunar Society that met every month, and among its members were James Watt, Matthew Boulton, Joseph Priestley, Josiah Wedgwood, Erasmus Darwin, Sir William Herschel, and Samuel Parr: a good all-around team of talents. The number of important inventions, from the steam engine to gas lighting and electro-plating, that either first saw the light or were first brought to perfection in this city, is very impressive. Its commercial success has not been merely a matter of geography and geology, the fact that it has been the centre of a district rich in coal, iron, wood, and sand. History comes into play here. Not being a place of any importance in the Middle Ages, Birmingham was not controlled by the guilds and did not suffer from the various restrictions imposed upon the then larger towns. It was not a chartered borough and therefore Nonconformists were free to settle and work there, and as the industrial revolution was largely nonconformist, Birmingham was able to take full advantage of it. Thus, [through history's cause and effect, it is now] the second city in England. By the time I had considered these matters, the fields had gone and we were passing houses and shops and factories. Did all this look like the entrance into the second city in England? It did. It looked a dirty muddle.

Where the bus finally stopped, a Birmingham citizen asked me if he could carry my two bags to the hotel. He was a young man, this Birmingham citizen: he was dressed in a ragged brown coat and a pair of patched and torn flannel trousers and the wreck of a pair of boots; his face was swollen and it was so long since he had shaved that he was well on his way towards wearing a matted tow-coloured beard. On our way to the hotel, I asked him a good many questions, but many of his replies I cannot give you because he spoke so badly that I could not catch them. But he was twenty-two, had been out of work since he was sixteen, was not receiving the dole, had a father but no mother, and his father was also out of work. It was a fair step to the hotel, and one of my bags, I knew, was heavy; so I told him to put them down and rest the moment he was tired; but there must have been good blood and bone somewhere in that ruin of a young fellow, for he never stopped or even slowed up but moved on at a good pace until he came within a yard or two of the hotel porter, who looked at him in a fashion that most of us would hesitate to adopt in talking to a mongrel that was snapping at our heels. However, I gave him a florin, which was what he usually made, with luck, in a whole day, and he went off delighted. There was a sudden access of civic dignity in the place. Here in Colmore Row you could imagine yourself in the second city of England. There is a really fine view at the end, where the huge Council House turns into Victoria Square. You see Hill Street mistily falling away beneath the bridge that the Post Office has thrown high across the road. If there is any better view in Birmingham than this, I never saw it. For a moment, as you stand there, you believe that at last you have found an English provincial city that has the air and dignity that a great city should have, that at last a few citizens who have eyes to see and minds to plan have set to work to bring comeliness into the stony hotch-potch, that Birmingham has had the sense to design itself as well as its screws, steam cocks, and pressure gauges. This is an illusion, and the only way in which to keep it would be to hurry away from that corner in a closed vehicle and see no more of Birmingham.

I could not do that, but I did the next best thing: I entered the Corporation Art Gallery and Museum, of which I had heard a good deal. The Director of the Gallery assured me that Birmingham had always had its craftsmen too and proved it by showing me case after case of local silver ware, some of it of tasteless design but all of it admirably executed. He also showed me some drawings done by young students—one of them only a boy of fifteen—at the local school of art; and these were surprisingly good. He assured me too that Birmingham could be very generous towards its Gallery and Museum. There were two cases of exquisite Chinese porcelain, and he told me that the necessary sum—I think it was between two and three thousand pounds—to buy these objects of art, which are quite useless and will never declare a dividend, had been raised in a few days. Oddly enough, two other cases of Chinese porcelain, equally exquisite, had been lent to the museum by a famous comedian, whose jests about Birmingham's prudery I still remember.

At the entrance to this art gallery and museum, they put up the daily returns of visitors. The recent average was about eight hundred a day on week-days, with a sudden leap into thousands on Sundays. This is not, I was told, because Birmingham has a passion for art on Sunday afternoon, but because then all the young people promenade up and down the galleries, not looking at pictures but at one another. Apollo has to serve Venus. But what of it? The boys and girls have to begin mating somewhere, and they could obviously begin their acquaintance in much worse places. And you never know. Venus may be a strict task-mistress, but no doubt Apollo is allowed a word now and then. A picture will occasionally catch an eye, then hold it; and so the old leaven of art will start working. There may be new masterpieces presented to this gallery in twenty years' time because a boy and girl were promenading and "clicking" there last Sunday afternoon. The director, a wise man, is of the same opinion.

So long as you keep within a very narrow limit in the centre, Colmore Row, New Street, Corporation Street, Birmingham has quite a metropolitan air, and on the fine afternoon I first explored them, these streets had quite metropolitan crowds in them too, looking at the windows of the big shops and hurrying in and out of cafes and picture theatres.

Tired of walking round, I climbed to the top of a tram. I did not know where it was going, and when the conductor came for his fare, I said I would go as far as the tram went, and took a threepenny ticket. As if it knew what was about to happen, the sun immediately went out. This treachery did not leave us in a kindly dusk—it was too early for that—but only in the middle of quite a different day, lowering and sullen. Then followed one of the most depressing little journeys I ever remember making. The tram helped. But it was Birmingham itself that did most of the mischief. In two minutes, its civic dignity, its metropolitan airs, had vanished; and all it offered me, mile after mile, was a parade of mean dinginess. I do not say that this was a worse tram-ride than one would have had in Manchester, Liverpool, Glasgow, any of our larger cities, or smaller ones either for that matter; I am not making comparisons between cities now.

Possibly what I was seeing was not Birmingham but our urban and industrial civilisation. The fact remains that it was beastly. It was so many miles of ugliness, squalor, and the wrong kind of vulgarity, the decayed anaemic kind. It was not, you understand, a slum. That would not have been so bad; nobody likes slums; and the slum hits you in the eye and you have only to make an effort to get it pulled down. This was, I suppose, the common stuff out of which most of our big industrial towns are made. For [the whole trip] there was nothing [whatever] to light up a man's mind for one single instant. I loathed the whole long array of shops, with their nasty bits of meat, their cough mixtures, their *Racing Specials,* their sticky cheap furniture, their shoddy clothes, their fly-blown pastry, their coupons and sales and lies and dreariness and ugliness. I asked myself if this really represented the level reached by all those people down there on the pavements. I am too near them myself, not being one of the sensitive plants of contemporary authorship, to believe that it does represent this level. They have passed it. They have gone on and it is not catching up. Why were the newest and largest buildings all along this route either picture theatres or pubs? Because both of them offer an escape: they are bolt-holes and safety-valves.

The conductor announced the terminus. I had arrived. I got out, to find that we had climbed to the top of a hill and that a cold wind was blowing over it, bringing dust and grit and filthy bits of paper. On one side was a stretch of high brick wall, which some posters told me was a sports ground. On the other side were some patches of waste ground and some decayed allotments, where the last green rags of gardening were shivering. Further along was a yard filled with rusted parts of motors and scrap-iron. I walked to the end of the brick wall and saw below and afar the vast smoky hollow of the city, with innumerable tall chimneys thrusting out of the murk. The wind dropped, and all along the edge of the pavement the filthy bits of paper settled for a moment before beginning to rustle uneasily again.

BOURNVILLE

I spent the next day, which was fine and warm, at Bournville. There were several good reasons for doing this. To begin with, I was interested in the manufacture of chocolate, having bought and eaten in my time great quantities of the stuff, and having several times, when I was about ten, tried unsuccessfully to make it myself. Then I wanted to see another highly organized giant works, and Cadbury's was one of the biggest in the country. Again, Cadbury Bros. were renowned as employers of the benevolent and paternal kind, and I wanted to see what it was they did. And again, there was Bournville itself, the village. So out I went, through dignified Birmingham, messy Birmingham, to planned Birmingham, which had put on its autumnal colouring and was looking charming.

There are a good many things to be said about Bournville, the village. The first is that it has nothing whatever to do with the firm of Cadbury Bros., Ltd. This came as a surprise to me—as I imagine it will to many people—for I had always thought that the firm built the village for its work-people, on a sort of patriarchal employers' scheme. Nothing of the kind. Here are the facts as they are set out in one of the Bournville publications.

The Bournville Estate was founded by the late George Cadbury in 1895. In 1879, he and his brother Richard, who were partners in business as Cocoa and Chocolate manufacturers, moved their works from the centre of industrial Birmingham to what was then an entirely rural area, four miles from the city. The removal gave George Cadbury an opportunity to put into practice ideas he had long in mind, the result of his contact with working men as a teacher in Early Morning Adult Schools, with which he was connected for over fifty years. He had been led to the conclusion that the root of most social evils lay in the bad housing conditions in which all too many had to live. He was himself fond of country life, and knew its material and spiritual advantages over life in crowded industrial areas, and when the factory was thoroughly established in its new environment he began to see ways and means of giving more and more people the opportunity to enjoy it. He did not, however, contemplate a scheme only for the benefit of his own workpeople; rather, his idea was to make what he called 'a small contribution to the solution of a great problem'—the problem of housing as affecting large industrial towns.

He bought land in the neighbourhood of the factory, and in 1895 began to build Bournville village. Five years later—in 1900 —the estate covered 330 acres, and 300 houses had been built. At that time, in order to secure the perpetuation of his ideas, he handed over the whole property to a body of Trustees—the Bournville Village Trust —on behalf of the nation. He thus gave up entirely his financial interest in it, and secured that all profits—for it was set up on a sound commercial basis—should never accrue to any private individual or body, but be devoted to the development of the Bournville Estate, and to the promotion of housing reform elsewhere.

These then are the facts. It is worth noticing that this Quaker manufacturer, fifty years ago, talked about something that the newspapers and the government are just beginning to talk about now, namely, bad housing. And he not only talked, but he did something. And what he did has proved very successful. His Trust Deed was really a housing plan that could be legally enforced. Thus, he laid down that each house was not to occupy more than a quarter of its own site, that factories were not to take up more than a fifteenth part of any developed area, and that one-tenth of the land, in addition to roads and gardens, should be given up to parks and recreation grounds. Since then, the Trust has really acted like a local authority. It has leased land to Public Utility Housing Societies, which are on a co-partnership basis. These societies—and there are four of them—build houses and then rent or sell them to their members. Some experimental bungalows—each made of different material—have been built, as a test of costs and durability. There are some tiny bungalows, for single persons. There is also a residential club for business women. Some of the owners and tenants work for Cadbury Bros. Others come to Birmingham, and are clerks, artisans, teachers, and so forth. The vital statistics in the booklet I have before me are of some importance. They are taken from an average of the seven years ending 1931. Death-rate per 1,000: England and Wales, 12.1; Birmingham, 11.6; Bournville, 6.5. Infantile mortality per 1,000 live births: England and Wales, 69; Birmingham, 72; Bournville, 56. Some years ago, the heights and weights, age for age, of Bournville children and children from one of the bad areas in Birmingham were compared, and the Bournville children were from two to four inches taller and between four and nine pounds heavier. And the Estate is flourishing.

I saw the whole of the village; if it can still be called a village for now it has the size and population of a small town. Its tree-lined roads, pleasant spaces, villas and gardens are not, of course, the eye-opener they must have been thirty years ago. Nevertheless, they are still infinitely superior to and more sensible than most of the huge new workmen's and artisans' quarters that have recently been built on the edge of many large towns in the Midlands. For example, in many of these estates, no provision whatever has been made for recreation, whereas in Bournville you see everywhere recreation grounds and halls. Model yachting is very popular in this district and it was decided to make another small lake in one of the recently developed areas. The village would look [considerably] prettier [however,] if it did not consist almost entirely of detached and semidetached small villas. I would prefer houses arranged in small courts and squares. I do not understand this passion for being detached or semidetached, for you can have gardens just the same if the houses are built in little rows, but I was assured that [the] tenants greatly prefer to be semidetached. Within these limits, Bournville has done its work very well. If it has rather too many public halls of religion and too few frivolous meeting places for my taste, after all I am not one of its tenants. And its real importance is as an example of what can be done by some careful planning and an absence of the jerry-builder's motives. It is neither a great firm's private dormitory nor a rich man's toy, but a public enterprise that pays its way. It is one of the small outposts of civilisation, still ringed round with barbarism.

As it is human nature and not the manufacture of chocolate that really interests me, I will [not discuss] Messrs. Cadbury as ingenious organizers [but will] consider them as employers. They have of course long been in the top class of the school of benevolent and paternal employers. Their workpeople are provided with magnificent recreation grounds and sports pavilions, with a large concert hall in the factory itself, where midday concerts are given, with dining rooms, recreation rooms, and facilities for singing, acting, and I know not what, with continuation schools, with medical attention, with works councils, with pensions. The factory is almost as busy in the evenings as it is in the daytime. Games, music, drama, lectures, classes, hobbies, conferences, all keep the place in full swing. Once you have joined the staff of this firm, you need never wander out of its shadow. I saw a club-room, fitted up with billiards tables and draughts-boards and the like, where old employees who have been pensioned off come to spend their leisure, playing while their younger comrades are working all round them. The membership of the various clubs and societies is about seven thousand. No form of self-improvement, except those that have their base in some extreme form of economic revolution, is denied a person here. No pastime, except the ancient one of getting drunk, is impossible. Here, in a factory, run for private profit, are nearly all the facilities for leading a full and happy life. What progressive people all over the world are demanding for humanity, these workers have here. Those in charge insist that the firm uses no compulsion whatever and never moves to provide anything until it knows that a real demand exists. It simply offers facilities, they say. And here let me add my conviction that whether all this is right or wrong, the employers themselves have acted in good faith, and genuinely prefer spending a good part of their money on their factory and its employees instead of racing stables and yachts and Monte Carlo.

Is it right or wrong? This is a very pretty problem. It is easy for some academic person, who has never spent an hour in a factory and does not really know how people live, to condemn it on philosophical grounds, but this may possibly be the result of turning off one's imaginative sympathy and not turning it on. We will assume now that our goal is other people's happiness, that what we want is that the mass of people should have a chance of leading the sort of life we lead—or should like to lead—ourselves. Now there is no getting away from the fact that here, owing to this system of paternal employment, are factory workers who have better conditions, more security, and infinitely better chances of leading a decent and happy life, than nearly all such factory workers elsewhere. They have, at least in part, what we should like everybody to have. Thanks to good management and an ever-increasing public passion for chocolate, a goal of some sort has been reached. It is easy, when you are sitting in a pleasant study

and you know that it is unlikely that you will ever have to apply for work in a factory, to say that all this will not do; but could you honestly say as much if you found yourself a factory hand, and a factory hand who worked in bad conditions, who had no security, and whose employers did not care a rap if their people did nothing but drink themselves silly in their leisure? If you strike a balance of ordinary human happiness, in a class that has had all too few chances of it, then here is a definite and enormous gain. The Russians, in their plans for a proletarian millennium, are only taking aim at such a goal as this. What has been promised in Russia—in such matters as hours of work, food, housing, education, amusement—has been actually performed here. No factory workers in Europe have ever been better off than these people. And I doubt if America, even during its very prosperous years, could show us workers of the same kind who had such opportunities for a full, active, healthy life. On any sensible short view, the experiment must be praised.

It is when one takes a longer view that doubts begin to creep in. Is it good for people to see the factory as the centre of their lives, even if that factory offers them so much, and so much that is genuinely significant? Does this system of paternal employment suggest (as Hilaire Belloc pointed out, years ago, in his *Servile State*) the decay of genuine democracy? I believe that this very firm, when it opened a branch factory in Australia, tried to pursue the same policy there but met with a decided rebuff from the Australians, who, whatever their faults, are at least in practice the thoroughgoing democrats they pretend to be. "No," said these Australian employees, in effect, "we don't want your recreation grounds and concert halls, for if you can afford to give us these things, you can afford to pay us higher wages, and we'll take the wages." I do not say that this leaves the paternal employer without a retort, for he can reply: "Very well, if you don't want my welfare schemes, you needn't have them. I will follow the examples of other firms and not give you any recreation grounds or concert halls. But neither will I give you any higher wages. I'll put what I've saved in my pocket." But though he may be worse off in other respects, it is clear that the Australian employee as a political being is occupying the sounder position. He is selling his labour, and nothing else. He is not acknowledging that his employer is a superior creature, whose benevolence may fall upon him like the rays of the life-giving sun. A workman whose whole life is centred in his factory has put all his eggs into one basket. He may enjoy many unusual luxuries, but there is obviously one luxury he cannot enjoy and that is—a spirit of independence. Moreover, he is in danger of believing what his employers are anxious for him to believe and what, in all sincerity, they may believe themselves, namely, that the particular work of that factory is the most urgent and the grandest of human activities, that cocoa is not made for man, but man for cocoa. Pensions and bonuses, works councils, factory publications, entertainments and dinners and garden parties and outings organised by the firm, these are all very well, but they can easily create an atmosphere that is injurious to the growth of men as intellectual and spiritual beings, for they can give what is, when all is said and done, a trading concern for private profit a falsely mystical aura, can drape its secular form with sacramental cloths, and completely wreck the proper scale of values. Very soon, when this atmosphere has been created, you begin to hear talk of "loyalties" that soar high above the common and reasonable fidelity of a decent man trying to do the job for which he is paid. Business cant swells into business mysticism, as it did in the United States before the slump, and there was no end of rubbishy talk about "service" and "loyalty," the kind of talk we get here chiefly from advertising men in their windy conventions. And no institution is fit to dominate men's lives unless it is solemnly dedicated either to God or the commonwealth; and by the commonwealth I do not mean the State, which may be simply a number of selected persons or a dictator and his friends who happen to have collared the army and the police force. If one of these paternal factories were taken over by the State

tomorrow, only one weakness of the system would disappear, the fact that the whole organisation is there for private profit; all the other weaknesses and dangers would remain, for the individual workman would still be compelled to look only in one direction for all the benefits of his life, would run the same risk of losing his independence, could still believe that he was made for his factory and not his factory for him, could confuse and mislay all his values, even though the directors had now to report to a public ministry instead of to a body of shareholders. (Many people easily avoid the pitfalls of business worship or mystical commerce only to fall into the trap of the mystical State, which makes them imagine that a group of institutions and a rough-and-ready organisation for political and economic purposes—let us say a combination of the British Museum, the Metropolitan Water Board, and New Scotland Yard—are somehow more important, of deeper significance to the wide universe, than the sum total of the human beings concerned. And I take this to be the most fashionable and potent illusion of our times; perhaps the father of those warring children, Communism and Fascism.) We must return, however, to the paternal factory system as it is working here and now.

I would say then, in a desperate attempt to conclude the matter and continue my journey, that workers in such places as Bournville have so many solid benefits conferred on them, benefits that must inevitably raise their status, both physical and mental, that in spite of the obvious dangers of the system, they are better placed, as citizens of to-day or to-morrow, than the ordinary factory worker, who is probably not so content either at work or play. On the other hand, I for one would infinitely prefer to see [Bournville] workers combine to provide these benefits or a reasonable proportion of them, for themselves, to see them forming associations far removed from the factory, to see them using their leisure, and demanding its increase, not as favoured employees but as citizens, free men and women.

And now, back in Birmingham in the

dusk, I must offer a score of apologies to Messrs. Cadbury and their busy ten thousand, good hosts all of them and benefactors of the sweet tooth, for using them all as pegs when they had used me as a man and a brother.

BIRMINGHAM

Here are two glimpses of Birmingham life. The first is of the public whist drive I attended on Saturday night. It is worth remembering that card games, like almost everything else in this land of social hierarchies, are not without their class distinctions. Whist was once the favourite card game of the upper classes. Now that those people play bridge, auction or contract, whist has found its devotees in a very different set of people, chiefly the small shopkeeping, artisan and working classes. Why don't these people too play bridge, which is, after all, a much better game? We can only guess. Some of them think bridge much too complicated for them. [But in all probability,] a second and weightier reason is that many of these people do not play bridge because they shrink from imitating the wealthier classes and do not want their friends and neighbours to think they are suddenly "trying to be posh." After all, there is more than one kind of snobbery. We hear a lot about the man who dresses for dinner in Central Africa; but that must not make us forget the existence of a much larger number of men who would die of shame if they were discovered by their acquaintances conveying soup to their mouths above a stiff white shirt. But whatever the reason may be, the fact remains that whist is still the favourite card game of the mass of the English people. The whist drive I attended, one of several advertised in the evening paper, was not a private social function, the equivalent of a bridge party, but a public affair, a combined entertainment and gamble, run by some astute person for profit. The whist drive was held in a certain public hall and began at eight-fifteen. So I raced through my dinner and hurried on to it.

The hall was large, austere in colouring and decoration, and lighted in the most uncompromising fashion by unshaded bulbs of high voltage. It had about as much intimate charm as the average big railway station. I guessed at once that we were in for a formidably business-like evening. Suspended from the ceiling, about a third of the way down the room, was a large indicator, showing the four suits. The remaining two-thirds of the hall, beyond this indicator, was filled with very small chairs ranged round very small tables, most of them not proper card tables but mysterious objects covered with what seemed then, and afterwards, squares of rather dirty blanket material. There were [perhaps] several hundred people there, and most of them seemed to be regular patrons and to know one another. They were mostly middle-aged decent working folk, with only a sprinkling of younger men and women. Nearly all the men smoked, and a fair proportion of the women; but there were no ash-trays. I knocked my pipe out on my heel. What the cigarette smokers did, I do not know. After ten minutes, a man shouted at us through a megaphone and we all went to our tables. The indicator told us what were trumps by lighting up a gigantic ace of clubs. We started. There followed what seemed to me one of the most strenuous hours I have ever spent. To begin with, the games were played at a tremendous speed, aces being banged on kings without a moment's hesitation. Then there was so much to do. You had to fill in your card and to initial the card on each table. If you were the losing man arriving at a new table—and I nearly always was —you had to shuffle the cards before the cut for deal. And three times out of four it seemed to be my fate to deal, and as the packs at each successive table appeared to be older and older and greasier and greasier, so that they were about four inches thick when they were stacked ready to be cut, dealing was an unpleasant business. [Therefore,] what with shuffling, cutting, dealing, playing, gathering tricks up on those bits of blanket, clerkly work with the table card and your own card, changing tables, pushing past enormous fat women, I was kept so busy that after about half an hour of it I was fairly perspiring. And there was never a minute to lose. The whistle blew, as a signal to change tables, the indicator lit up its new suit of trumps, and if you had not finished your game, there were people waiting and looking very cross about it. There was practically no time for conversation, hardly time to smile. What conversation there was about the game, if for once it finished before the whistle blew, I could not understand. [Almost all] my partners were either very big fat women, who bulged over their chairs and the tables, and sweated good-humouredly, or else little witch-like females with sharp noses, tucked-in mouths, and iron spectacles, who held their cards very close to the brooches they wore, hardly ever spoke, and looked very cross, though I do not actually think they were. There were two distinct types among the men: the solid hearty chaps who sat bolt upright, puffing out clouds of smoke and banged each card down as if sheer force might win the trick; and the little thin cunning fellows who sank down and down and half-closed their eyes as they played, like so many Nibelungs. When the whistle blew after the twelfth game, everybody made a rush for the top end of the hall, and reappeared a few minutes afterwards, eating fruits, tarts, and slabs of cake.

This was the interval and by this time I had had quite enough whist-driving, but it seemed to me that if one player disappeared the whole elaborate organisation would be flung into disorder. So I stayed on and played another twelve games, nearly always losing and so going from table to table. There was no excitement at the end, no applause. It was all as brisk and business-like as the whole evening had been. When the last prize had been awarded, everybody cleared off, rather as if they were leaving a factory than making an end of a night's pleasure. I suppose they enjoyed it—which was more than I did—otherwise they would not regularly attend these functions, as they undoubtedly do, but anything superficially less like a night's pleasure I never did see. Considering that many of them must be engaged all day in work that must be at once bustling and boring, it is surprising that they should choose this method of passing the evening. I do not believe that it is card-playing that attracts them there, for nobody could enjoy playing cards at such a speed. The secret is the gamble, the chance of winning two or three pounds for your two shillings. The purely social side of the whist drive was negligible; or at least so it seemed to me, though of course I was a stranger and may have missed some quiet fun. At the end, two impressions remained with me. It is difficult to find words for them here without appearing unpleasantly patronising; but I must take that risk. First, I was struck by the extraordinary ugliness of most of the people there. Nobody has ever called me handsome, and I do not ask for a very high standard of good looks in other people. It is not that these people lacked regular features, fine figures, bright eyes, and so forth. They were, for the most part, downright ugly, really unpleasant to look at closely. The women were either much too fat or far too thin. The men looked like lop-sided oafs, gnomes, hobgoblins. Nearly all looked as if life had knocked them into odd shapes, taken the bloom out of their faces, twisted their features and dulled their eyes. The few native races I have seen could have shown one far better-looking specimens of humanity than these. Possibly the people who go to whist drives are among the least handsome of their kind—this would obviously be true of young women—but even when that allowance has been made, that ugliness remains startling. In twenty years' time, I believe it will have gone. But it does not say much for our way of living that it should be there now. The second impression that remained was of a very different character. These people might be ugly to look at but they were not ugly to be with; in other words, they were surprisingly good-mannered and good-humoured. I never saw one exhibition of bad temper all the evening. Some were obviously much better players than others, and there was money at stake, but nevertheless there was never an embarrassing moment. Even the witch-like, iron-spectacled little women were never actually rude to anybody. They were all patient, decent, good-tempered folk, and they compared extremely favourably, startlingly, with the well-nurtured people I have often seen giving a show of bad manners and egoism at bridge tables, not merely in private but also in functions such as this. The sharp contrast between appearance and manner was very curious. I could make a text of it but will refrain, if only because I want these two impressions to be free from any suspicion of being forced, when actually they were simply what remained to me after an arduous evening.

The second glimpse of Birmingham comes from the following morning, Sunday. I awakened in a strangely quiet hotel, quite unlike the weekday place. The spell of an English Sunday is terrifically potent; even the weather is different. The whole city was blanketed in silence. The streets were wearing their Sunday look: few people in them, hardly any traffic, but a more than week-day allowance of mist hanging about, as if the country had been given permission to send a bit of its autumn weather into town. I ate my customary Sunday morning sausages in an almost empty dining-room, where the waiters were beginning to move like church wardens. You had a feeling, obviously shared by the head waiter, the reception clerk downstairs, the lift attendant, and the two yawning page-boys, that a slab of time like a vast suet pudding had been thrust into your hands, that before Monday dawned there would be time to write an epic poem on the Fall of Jerusalem or to work out successfully every different kind of patience. But I had not this embarrassing wealth of hours because I had decided to do something I had not done for many years, and that was to attend the morning service in a Nonconformist chapel. Birmingham has long been one of the chief strongholds of Nonconformity, and I felt that I could not pass a Sunday in it without visiting one of its places of worship. I found one about ten minutes' walk away. It did not belong to the particular denomination that had claimed me, willy-nilly, when I was a boy, but nevertheless my first discovery was that this service was almost exactly like the ones I remember from thirty

years ago, and that the people taking part in it had not changed a great deal. The chief difference in the congregation was that there were fewer young people in it, and especially young men. I doubt if there were half-a-dozen men under thirty-five in the chapel. If there were any boys present, they escaped my eye. There were a few little girls, a sprinkling of older girls and young women, and all the rest of the congregation and the choir were middle-aged. But I suppose that in my chapel-going days, there would actually have been twice the number of people at this service. And though there was a certain amount of nodding and smiling before, and some hand-shaking after the service, I did not gather the impression that for most of these people this chapel was the centre of their social life; though the notices read out by the minister still suggested that it was.

Nevertheless, when one considers that we are generally supposed to have plunged or blundered into a new world since the war, that vast changes are taking place in every department of our lives, the likeness between this service and the ones I remember was astonishing. The organist looked the same and played the same stuff in the same old way. The choir, with its preponderance of rustling females, its one piercing tenor (I spotted him: eyeglasses and a grey moustache), its uncertain but hopeful basses, its trick of turning everything it sang, no matter how thunderous the music, how wildly oriental the words, into something neat and respectable, the rent garments of prophets converted into a pair of dark striped trousers, was the familiar choir of my boyhood. The deacons who carried round the collection plates were the immortal deacons of my memories: cashiers and shop-keepers, with pointed beards, gold-rimmed spectacles, morning coats, of a terrific respectability, whose very walk, as they returned the collection plates, obliterated the whole doctrine of original sin. Time had not withered them, though in truth they had always been a little withered. As I watched them, I knew that old as I am, a ratepayer and the father of children, I had only to go to the following Saturday's tea and concert and see these mysterious beings suddenly secular and waggish over ham sandwiches and lemon cheese tarts, to be as startled as I was in 1903. We sang as we had always sung. The minister prayed as he had always prayed, not perhaps quite at the same length but still as if he were sternly addressing some powerful but uncertain potentate from the East, who had to be talked to in this fashion before he knew his own mind. There was, as there had been, a children's address, which began by the minister, as ever, suddenly putting on a smile so false and sickly that it was frightening, looking down at three little girls in the second row, and then beginning in an odd voice to talk of some determined whimsicality. When I was a little boy I wriggled in embarrassment at these addresses, and I found myself wriggling all over again that morning in Birmingham. The sermon itself, which was not a bad one, had not changed much; there was the same trick in it of taking a tiny and apparently meaningless text—such as *Then Saul went up* or *These likewise cast lots*—and then finding an astonishing number of deeply significant meanings in it; a method that would soon turn any book, a *History of Rutlandshire* or *Commercial Guide to Sweden,* into a work of the profoundest wisdom. The minister, who had the merit, common among Nonconformist clergymen, of being able to read and sermonise in a sensible manly fashion, had a long dark face and the arched and restless eyebrows of a comedian. Indeed, his whole face was that of a comic actor, probably French; and humor seemed continually to play over it like a breeze ruffling a pond; yet the man behind this face had not a glimmer of this comic spirit and was clearly a very solemn Noncomformist clergyman. Somehow, he had taken to wearing the wrong face, that was all. He fascinated me. Looking as if he were about to speak some terrific drollery out of a comedy by *Labiche,* he would announce the hymn and gravely recite its first four lines.

There was another contrast, however, queerer than that between the minister and his face. And I had not noticed this as a boy

at these services. Then I had taken the general atmosphere of the service and the sect for granted. Now, returning to it after a long absence, I saw how odd it was that these mild Midland folk, spectacled ironmongers, little dressmakers, clerks, young women from stationers' shops, should come every Sunday morning through the quiet grey streets and assemble here to wallow in wild oriental imagery. They stood up in rows, meek-eyed, and pink-cheeked, to sing modestly about the Blood of the Lamb. After a few little coughs, they announced that certain sacred names and symbols induced in them fits of incredible ecstasies. They sat with bent heads listening to accounts of ancient and terribly savage tribal warfare, of the lust and pride of hook-nosed and raven-bearded chieftains, of sacrifice and butchery on the glaring deserts of the Near East. They chanted in unison their hope of an immortality to be spent in cities built of blazing jewels, with fountains of milk and cascades of honey, where kings played harps while maidens clashed the cymbals; and one could not help wondering what these people would do if they really did find themselves billeted for ever in this world of the Eastern religious poets. What, in short, had these sober Northern islanders to do with all this oriental stuff? What did it, what could it really mean to them? Could anything be less aptly shaped and coloured to match their own lives? If this was the time when their thoughts turned to the creator of this universe, when they were asked to **consider the deep truths of life, to face their consciences and search their hearts, why should they be dragged into this far-away fantastic world of goats and vines and deserts and smoking sacrifices and tribal kings? It was almost as if instead of the familiar black-coated minister there had appeared in the pulpit a whirling dervish. Must God, I asked myself, remain forever in Asia? Are these people always to assume that He is still brooding over Babylon? What if He is now brooding over Birmingham?**

THE BLACK COUNTRY

From Birmingham I went to have a look

at the Black Country, which lies to the north and west of the city. This notorious region was strange to me. Now I have seen it, but of course it is still strange to me. You have to live some time in these places to understand their peculiar qualities. All I can do is to offer a few sketches, probably not at all accurate nor free from a certain subjective colouring, for in retrospect it is difficult to disengage the scene from the mood. But perhaps that does not matter: the record of a journey of this kind may be more important if it chronicles a succession of moods than if it captures a succession of scenes. Here, I think, I ought to say a little more about myself. It happens that during the last few years I have been away from industrial districts and have spent most of my time in far pleasanter places. But the first nineteen years of my life were passed in the industrial West Riding, in the shadow of the tall chimneys; and even yet I am not unduly fastidious about my surroundings. So you may take it that throughout this book I am not adopting some absurdly high standard that would make life in half of England impossible. I am not shocked because an iron foundry or a wool-combing mill has little in common with an author's drawing-room or study: I have long known what kind of places men have to labour in. My standard may be rough and ready and somewhat uncertain, but you can assume it is a reasonable one. If I declare that Coketown is a horrible hole, I do not merely mean that it cannot be fitted in to some private fairy-tale Merrie England of my own: I mean that it is a damned horrible hole. And I hope you will take my word for it.

I spent the better part of two days staring at this Black Country. The first day was fine and fairly bright. I went from Birmingham through Smethwick and Oldbury to Dudley, which seemed to me a fantastic place. You climb a hill, past innumerable grim works and unpleasant brick dwellings, and then suddenly a ridiculous terracotta music-hall comes into sight, perched on the steep roadside as if a giant had plucked it out of one of the neighbouring valleys and carelessly left it there; and above this music-hall (its attrac-

tion that week was *Parisian Follies*) were the ruins of Dudley Castle. I climbed a steep little hillside, and then smoked a pipe or two sitting by the remains of the Keep. The view from there is colossal. On the Dudley side, you look down and across at roofs and steeply mounting streets and pointing factory chimneys. It looked as if a great slab of Birmingham had been torn away and then tilted up there at an angle of about forty-five degrees. The view from the other side, roughly, I suppose, to the north-east, was even more impressive. There was the Black Country unrolled before you like a smouldering carpet. You looked into an immense hollow of smoke and blurred buildings and factory chimneys. There seemed to be no end to it. In the vague middle, dominating everything, was an enormous round white tower, which I afterwards learned was a new gasometer. It looked bigger than anything else in sight, and as nothing had dimension that could be measured, it was any size you liked to imagine it. You could think of it, without unduly straining your fancy, as the temple of some horrible new religion. The only sounds that arrived from this misty immensity below came from the tangle of railway lines that gleamed in the foreground of the scene, and these noises were so clear that they might have been picked out and then amplified. There was the scream of a locomotive; there was the clanking of the bumpered wagons; there was the long pu-u-ushing of a train gathering speed. I never remember hearing these railway sounds so clearly. Nothing else came from that enormous hollow. You could easily believe that there were no people down there, that a good locomotive was probably the most playful inhabitant of the region. I was glad that I did not know the names of the towns down there in the smoke; I felt that I was not looking at this place and that, but at the metallic Midlands themselves, at a relief map of a heavy industry, at another and greater exhibition of the 'fifties. No doubt at all that the region had a sombre beauty of its own. I thought so then, and I thought so later, when I had seen far more of its iron face lit with hell fire. But it was a beauty you could appreciate chiefly because you were not condemned to live there. If I could do what I liked with the whole country, I would keep a good tract of this region as it is now, to be stared and wondered at; but I would find it difficult to ask any but a few curators to live in it.

I descended into the vast smoky hollow and watched it turn itself into so many workshops, grimy rows of houses, pubs and picture theatres, yards filled with rusted metal, and great patches of waste ground. There was a cynical abundance of these patches of waste ground, which were as shocking as raw sores and open wounds. In my own West Riding, industry of the grimmest and most uncompromising kind has long been allowed to work its will on the countryside. There, however, the countryside itself is grim and uncompromising. Sometimes the mills, the rows of little houses, the cobbled streets, all seem like natural outcroppings of the Pennine rock. Huddersfield and Rochdale, Keighley and Nelson, may look grim, but the high lands that still separate them look even grimmer. But here in these Midlands, the countryside is mild and friendly. It is on the border of Arden itself. Industry has ravished it; drunken storm troops have passed this way; there are signs of atrocities everywhere; the earth has been left gaping and bleeding; and what were once bright fields have been rummaged and raped into these dreadful patches of waste ground. And nothing I saw there, not even the slums, impressed me more painfully.

The places I saw had names, but these names were merely so much alliteration: Wolverhampton, Wednesbury, Wednesfield, Willenhall, and Walsall. You could call them all wilderness, and have done with it. I never knew where one ended and another began. I remember noticing in Wolverhampton, after half an hour of dingy higgledy-piggledy, the new building of the *Midland Counties Dairy,* white and trim and with immense windows, and thinking how alien it looked there, like the outpost of a new civilisation. I remember arriving at the very end of the earth, where the land appeared to have been uprooted by a giant pig and where there were cottages so small and odd that they must have been built for gnomes, and this end of the earth was called Gornal, and there the women, returning home from the brickworks, wore caps and shawls. The shawls were like those that the weavers used to wear in my own town, but our women had worn their shawls over their heads. Here, however, they wore caps as well, and looked as outlandish as the place they lived in. Afterwards I ran right through the Black Country and came out at the other end, almost within sight of the potteries. On the way back, somewhere between Stafford and Rugeley, I came to a bit of heath country, glowing with autumn, that was as pleasant as you could wish. There the sun went down. It was dark long before I got back to Birmingham; the ravished waste ground, the miserable houses, the muddle of dirty brick, the whole battlefield of industry, sank down and disappeared, and in their places appeared mysterious red gleams of fire and a pretty tracery of lights, so that I was happier staring about me than I had been all day.

My second day there was a Sunday, and in foul weather. Sometimes the raw fog dripped; sometimes the cold rain steamed; but throughout it was thick and wet and chilled. I lunched in one of the smaller towns with a man in the metal trade. There were several Black Country business men there, large hearty fellows, sturdy eaters and drinkers. There had been a sudden flurry of business in the metal trade, and my friend was going back to his office and warehouse in West Bromwich after lunch. I went with him, and on the way was shown, among other things, the last dairy farm in the district. It stood there surrounded for miles by the grim paraphernalia of industrialism; I had only a glimpse of it, a solitary surviving farmhouse in the wet fog, with a few ghostly fields on either side. My friend's warehouse was in— shall we say?—"Rusty Lane," West Bromwich. He keeps sheets of steel there, and no doubt any place is good enough to keep sheets of steel in; but I do not think I could let even a sheet of steel stay long in Rusty Lane. I have never seen such a picture of grimy desolation as that street offered me. If you put it, brick for brick, into a novel, people would not accept it, would condemn you as a caricaturist and talk about Dickens. The whole neighbourhood is mean and squalid, but this particular street seems the worst of all. It would not matter very much—though it would matter—if only metal were kept there; but it happens that people live there, children are born there and grow up there. I saw some of them. I was being shown one of the warehouses, where steel plates were stacked in the chill gloom, and we heard a bang and rattle on the roof. The boys, it seems, were throwing stones again. They were always throwing stones on that roof. We went out to find them, but only found three frightened little girls, who looked at us with round eyes in wet smudgy faces. No, they hadn't done it, the boys had done it, and the boys had just run away. Where they could run to, I cannot imagine. They need not have run away from me, because I could not blame them if they threw stones and stones and smashed every pane of glass for miles. Nobody can blame them if they grow up to

smash everything that can be smashed. There ought to be no more of those lunches and dinners, at which political and financial and industrial gentlemen congratulate one another, until something is done about Rusty Lane and West Bromwich. While they still exist in their present foul shape, it is idle to congratulate ourselves about anything. They make the whole pomp of government here a miserable farce. The Crown, Lords and Commons are the Crown, Lords and Commons of Rusty Lane, West Bromwich. In the heart of the great empire on which the sun never sets, in the land of hope and glory, Mother of the Free, is Rusty Lane, West Bromwich. What do they know of England who only England know? The answer must be Rusty Lane, West Bromwich. And if there is another economic conference, let it meet there, in one of the warehouses, and be fed with bread and margarine and slabs of brawn. The delegates have seen one England, Mayfair in the season. Let them see another England next time, West Bromwich out of the season. Out of all seasons except the winter of our discontent.

Priestley's illuminating comments have proven the point that in centers of industry *the job* is the thing. A growing economy provides more jobs; a shrinking economy leads to unemployment. Recreation frequently becomes an escape from the job rather than a pursuit enjoyed for itself alone. Even family life becomes greatly affected not only by adequacy of income but by the employment of women in industry and commerce. The single woman is given an economic freedom which she never enjoyed when she was dependent on an aging father or a considerate older brother. She can now become her own "breadwinner" and, should she marry later on, she takes into the home something of the independence which she has tasted.

In the selection that follows, Philip Carr describes this changed status of women in England—particularly in the middle-class home. How does this compare with the status of the Chinese woman?

· 137 · *The Status of Women*

PHILIP CARR

... Home life—for the town dweller at least —is gradually becoming flat [apartment] life; and what used to be an important part of

home life, that is to say entertaining friends, takes place elsewhere, in clubs and restaurants, while even the recreation of members of the family chiefly consists of going out. They go out to the cinema, they go out to the theatre, they go out to the country for weekends, they go out to play golf or lawn tennis, or merely for a drive in the car—the car having almost taken the place of the home as the principal interest of many a family.

Home life is still further reduced by the fact that in an English town the head of the family does not return for lunch. He certainly has his breakfast with his wife and his children, if they are old enough not to have theirs in the nursery; and it is a meal taken in the dining room. But breakfast—at least on week days—is not a very conversational meal in England. Father reads his newspaper, which is propped up in front of him on the table. Mother probably does the same; and the children are not encouraged to be chatty. Besides, every one probably has to hurry off to be in time for business.

Home life on ordinary days therefore means dinner in the evening and the hour or two before and after it; and the hour before dinner is probably the only time when a busy man sees his younger children, for they are not allowed to "sit up" for the evening meal, but have their tea in the nursery and are put to bed early.

On Saturday afternoon and on Sunday, the family is—or at least can be—more united; but I have already pointed out that they are not likely to be at home.

When people live in the suburbs or the country, the picture will probably be quite a different one. If they want to receive their friends, they must do so at home; for there are no restaurants to which they can invite them. Besides, the garden is likely to have enabled the home to recover its importance. It may induce the head of the family to spend his leisure there, if his hobby is gardening, which it very likely is. In any case, the house and the garden together will have more personality than can ever be acquired by the town flat.

The position of women in the middle-class English home is in some ways different from what it would be in a Latin country. I have already suggested that perhaps the innate shyness of the English character prevents husbands and wives from easily becoming the familiar associates—almost the business partners—which they so often are elsewhere. Perhaps the reason is partly that English husbands think it is unfair to burden their wives with their office worries. In any case, I fancy that it frequently happens that a wife knows little of her husband's affairs; and the jest about her being able to say no more about his occupation than that "he is something in the City" is not entirely an absurdity. She has been brought up to regard marriage rather as a romantic adventure than as a contract, and her husband is often inclined to encourage the assumption that all the responsibilities are his and none of them hers.

It need hardly be said [here] that although marriages are never arranged in England by parents, nor is there any close bargaining over marriage portions and allowances, and although the great majority of girls who marry in England have no dowry at all, and are not expected by their husbands to bring one, there are young Englishmen who are fortune hunters, and there are plenty of English girls, as well as men, who take a realistic view of the situation, and plenty more who are quite aware that a wife has duties as well as privileges.

This is especially the case since so many young women are now independently earning their living before they marry—since, in fact, the revolution in the social, economic, and political status of women, which began about 1900, but reached its full development only after the other war.

As far as industry and even commerce are concerned, the employment of women has not been brought about solely by the superfluity of the unmarried. It is largely the result of mechanical progress. In factories, human intervention has been reduced to such simple movements that they can be performed after very little training, and, for business offices, young women can soon learn to manipulate a typewriter.

Therefore women are employed in each case, because they do the work as well or even better than men—certainly better and quicker in the case of typewriting and in that of certain deft movements of machine minding—and also because women are nearly always paid less than men for any particular work. They are paid less because they are willing to accept less, and they accept less for two reasons. The first is that at the age at which they begin, they do not depend upon their employment for their living, or at least the whole of their living, as they are generally still at home with their parents. They also accept less, because they regard their employment as merely a provisional affair until they are married—for at that age they assume that they are going to get married. Indeed, they usually do get married, and they usually give up working when they marry. This produces the further result that the great majority of employed women are young. It has been calculated that whereas 80 per cent of the girlhood of England between the ages of eighteen and twenty is earning money in some way, the percentage drops sharply to 65 between the ages of twenty-one and twenty-four and still farther later on. Those who disappear are replaced by another generation of young girls.

I have said that these young girls accept relatively small salaries; but in fact they are not badly paid for the work they do, and probably many boys of their age would be glad to be paid as well. Most boys, however, would hesitate to accept a job which is never likely to lead to anything better; and the field is left open to the young women, of whom there is always a great mass in employment. In the business quarters of the City of London, the whole aspect of the streets has been entirely changed, in hardly more than a generation, by the influx of girl clerks and typists. What was an exclusively male preserve, with hardly a woman to be seen, has become a crowd, in which—at least at the hours when employees arrive and depart—the feminine note predominates.

In the industrial North of England, female labor dates much farther back, back to a period when nobody thought of protecting the girl mill-hand from the competition of the married woman; and in the textile industry, even today, nearly half of the women employed are married.

This invasion of commerce and industry by what may be called the rank and file of the army of women workers has been accompanied by the entrance of women into the higher as well as the lower branches of the Civil Service and also into several of the liberal professions. It is that of medicine which has attracted the greatest number, and it is there that women have attained the highest distinction. Medicine is also the first profession into which women succeeded in gaining admittance. This happened as long ago as 1870, when the London School of Medicine for Women was founded; but for many years, women doctors were few. Even now, when they are accepted as students in most of the London hospitals, there are one or two which still refuse to take them. The great majority allow them to study and to qualify, however, and in 1918 there was a military hospital in France, where the only males were the soldier patients, all the staff—doctors, surgeons and nurses—being women.

Women can now become barristers in England, but only since 1920, while in France they have been able to do so since 1900. They can also be solicitors; but in neither branch of the law has any woman yet risen to any considerable practice. They have been far more successful as architects, as decorators, and also as expert designers of kitchens; and in literature, journalism, painting, sculpture and the theatre they have achieved success and more. They have won fame. Some of them had indeed done so more than a hundred years before any feminist movement was thought of; but it is only in our own time that the number of women successfully practicing any of the arts has been such that the rise to eminence of one of them is no longer a rare phenomenon.

It is also only in our own time that women in England have achieved the full rights of citizenship—that is to say, the right to vote, on an equality with men, at parliamentary and municipal elections, the right to be elected as members of the House of Commons, and the right not to be disqualified, by reason of their sex, from the exercise of any public function. The pressure of demand for these rights became insistent at the same time as the feminine pressure upon the employment market, that is to say, at the beginning of the present century; and it was the result of the same set of circumstances, the excess in numbers of women over men and the consequent mass of unmarried women. The rights were granted immediately after the other war—the parliamentary suffrage in 1918 and the eligibility to the House of Commons a year later—there are now fourteen women members of that Chamber. It was also in 1919 that was passed the Act abolishing the sex disqualification for any Government post. Even now, however, the exercise of these rights in practice cannot be said to be complete. Although a woman can be a member of the House of Commons, it has been decided that she cannot sit in the House of Lords, even when she is a peeress in her own right; and although a woman might in theory be made a Judge or an Ambassador, it is highly unlikely that such an appointment will be made in our time.

The two selections that follow deal primarily with young people and describe the circumstances under which they grow up. If we were to make a detailed study of the socialization process, we would need to know a great deal about early childhood and even infancy, but we nevertheless gain considerable insight into a society by seeing it from the standpoint of the adolescent.

The first selection deals with young girl workers, telling of their housing conditions, their appearance, their jobs, their relationships with their parents, their schooling, and their use of leisure time. It is a revealing, intimate sketch, prepared for this book by Pearl Jephcott, who has written a number of sympathetic studies on the English working girl. There are many references to actual costs of permanents, bicycles, admission to the cinema, and the like. The English monetary terms can be translated fairly easily into dollars and cents. A pound (£) is roughly equivalent to $2.80; it consists of 20 shillings, (each worth 14 cents); a shilling is made up of 12 pence, each worth slightly more than one cent; £2.10 means two pounds, ten shillings, or about $7.00 Shillings and pence are written as 17/6, or $2.46—the cost of a permanent. Pence alone are written 3d. or 6d., about 3 cents or 7 cents, the weekly dues in some of the young people's organizations. This brief explanation does not include all of the intricacies of the English monetary system but it should help us understand the article which follows.

• 138 • Young Girl Workers in English Towns

PEARL JEPHCOTT

There are about one and a half million girls aged 15 to 19 in England and Wales. These notes, however, concern only those girls (though they are the majority) who start work at 15. Most of them are engaged in manual work and are the children of manual workers with the social background that this, broadly, implies. Most of them, too, are town, not country, bred. These two points must be borne in mind and the fact that the picture is a little weighted on the side of the poorer, less intelligent youngster from the less favoured background.

The essential characteristics of adolescent girls are, of course, much the same in Alabama as in Middlesex, in a Chinese village as in a Marseilles tenement. We are familiar enough with these characteristics since all of us have had the experience of being an adolescent, and half of us have our own femininity as a guide to help us interpret younger women. Most of us can recall incidents in our own adolescence when we laboured at good works for three days and were bone idle for the next four. Such reflections help us to sympathize with the adolescent's chameleon-like changes, her emotional heights and depths, her insecurities and her bursts of over-confidence. What we know much less about, and are less sympathetic towards, is the social conditioning that overlays the common framework. We know remarkably little about the differences in the compelling home patterns that each of us has smelled and tasted from the cradle—the differences in family feeding habits and the variations in leisure time customs absorbed through street games and fights and friendships. If it is hard to pin down differences induced by social conditioning in a society with which we have always been familiar, it is a much more hazardous business to try, as these notes are doing, to assess the significant points of the English working class girl for those who know the English scene chiefly at second-hand.

What do English girls look like? That, obviously, is a treacherous question to ask.

Take Maggie Barnes, for example, who lives at 20 Durham Avenue, along with three older sisters. All four girls work in local factories, two as machinists of children's clothes, one at a printer's on a feeding machine. Their father was a Corporation dustman but, through bad health and age, he has now finished with any regular work. Mrs. Barnes is a typical old-fashioned English working woman, country born, a servant until she was married and now the mother of seven grown-up children. The boy whose photo is on the sideboard was drowned in the war and she talks about him often. She is a heavy-bodied, thin faced woman, with wispy grey hair. She wears a black stuff dress, green print apron, wrinkled grey stockings and grey sandals cut away to ease her bunions a bit.

Maggie is the youngest of the family and is 15. She left school four months ago and works at the same firm as two of her older sisters, but she is not yet on a machine. She mostly does odd jobs: giving out work, bundling up the finished vests and knickers, etc. She is round faced and rather heavily built, with medium brown hair. She had a 17/6 perm at Christmas and puts her hair in curlers, but not with much success. Nor does she bother with make up. In the house she wears old white runners, with a hole in one sole, and a red marocain frock with a dipping hem that her Mother bought for 5/- from the bargain shop at the street corner. Over this she wears a royal blue cardigan, a hand-down from her eldest sister who knitted it a couple of years ago. Her spending money, from her £2.10. weekly pay, is 10/- a week. It mostly goes on ice cream, sweets, fares and bits of clothes.

Things are different down the street. The girl there is a year older than Maggie. She is tall, fair and has a fresh complexion on which she spends a good deal of money and time. Her hair is fluffy so she has no perm. She washes it herself, on a Tuesday, at the kitchen sink. She is a capable girl, was in the "A" stream at school, and earns, on piece work, up to £4.10 at the same factory as the Barnes girls work. She hands her pay packet in to her Mother on a Friday night and gets £1 back for her own use. Her Mother takes 30/- for her keep and puts the rest by for the girl's clothes. Her present street costume is a lemon yellow two-piece, bought for £4, with a 12/6 pair of nylons "on a club" at a local shop. She paid for her handbag with her own money, and also her hat, a 24/- riding shape with a draped chiffon bow, in brown. Her name is Pauline Spree.

The artisan home tends to be tightly packed, both inside and outside, but more often than not it is still occupied by only one family. In Maggie's home, for instance, the front of the two ground floor rooms is kept for best. Coats, new bikes, and household goods in general are stored there. The other ground floor room is the hub of the house. It has an open coal fire, on which part of the cooking is done, supplemented by the gas stove in a very small scullery leading off the living room. [Stairs] lead off this room up to two floors and three bedrooms. This means that all of the bedrooms and beds in the house are shared. There is no bathroom so people wash in the scullery. The lavatory is outside the backyard. There is a bit of garden also in this yard but it is not cultivated because Mr. Barnes has an allotment. That, roughly, is a sketch of an old house. Its characteristic feature is compression, and the fact that any personal privacy is almost impossible. At the same time it is snug and if it is in good repair is not too inconvenient to run, from the housewife's point of view.

The working class girls give the impression, by and large, that they have more brothers and sisters than the girl from the professional home. This impression is borne out by population figures which show a fairly close correlation between size of family and social plus economic status. [See Selection 123.] The girls also give the impression that their family life is more closely knit than that of the professional home. The boys, and more so the girls, often show great reluctance to the idea of leaving home to get a better job. Girls, when marrying, will fairly often jib at the idea of having to live even in another part of the same city. The housing shortage has tended to encourage this reluctance. Many couples do not set up house now when they marry but have to live in one or a couple of rooms at an in-law's, a situation which has a good deal of bearing on the younger sister's attitude toward her own future marriage. The attachment to home and neighbourhood is strengthened by another factor, and that is that working class families tend to have more of their relations living nearby than does the professional family.

The great majority of boys and girls, and most of those with whom this article deals,

leave school at the end of the term after their 15th birthday. In a normal 15 to 19 years old population there would probably be about 13% still at school. The 1949 figures for the 82,000 age 14-20 population of the City of Birmingham, for example, showed that 16,700 adolescents were still attending full time schools and colleges while 23,000 were having some form of part time education, possibly chiefly in evening classes.

Schooling in England proceeds in three stages, primary, secondary and further education. These stages were laid down in the Education Act of 1944 which provided more equal opportunities for all children, raised the leaving age to 16 (this to be brought into operation as soon as circumstances permit; and 15 to be the immediate leaving age) and initiated major reforms in buildings, staff and the organisation of schools. Broadly speaking, children go to a primary school from 5 to 11 when, on tests and school records, they pass to the type of secondary school best suited to their abilities—grammar (for the more academic), technical, or secondary modern school. Further education may be taken at evening classes, which many girl clerical workers attend, or at part-time day release schools to which an increasing number of employers now send their juveniles, particularly the boys, for non-vocational education. This generally takes place on one full day a week.

Small boys and girls are generally taught together in mixed schools. At the secondary stage also the same number go to single sex as to mixed schools. Further education which in any case is largely technical, is generally given in separate classes for boys and girls. English schools are relatively small in size as compared with American ones. The secondary modern school attended by many of the girls whose life is described in this article is the largest secondary modern girls' school in the city of 300,000 but has only 440 pupils. It was built 70 years ago and is typical of the older schools in which many town children are still housed.

Most people were glad when the school leaving age was raised. Certainly most girls seem to enjoy their time at school well enough even if some of them feel that the last year did not advance them very much in actual learning. A girl just starting work says that she feels more grown up and better able to tackle her job at 15 than she did a year ago. Many parents, too, are rather concerned because they seem to feel, as is probably true, that the secondary modern school in general has not really decided what the extra year should give these children. They deal largely of course, with the non-academic type, and carry a burden of children with low I.Q.s and of those who are handicapped by unsatisfactory homes. The present syllabus concentrates on widening the child's interests and making her aware of the community in which she lives, by visits to civic institutions, factories, etc. All girls in secondary modern schools get a good deal of domestic training and this is a subject that girls who have left school often say they would like to go on learning.

Although reforms in the 1944 act have helped to democratise education, some correlation between social class and education still persists. The children of working class parents, by and large, still go to the secondary modern or technical rather than the grammar school. There is also still some correlation between the social class of parents and the amount of education beyond the compulsory minimum that parents give their girls as compared with their boys.

The number of advertisements [appearing] regularly reflect the present state of the juvenile labour market when employers are driven to use every possible device to get hold of young workers. This means, of course, that the adolescent can now pick and choose her job and change it in a way that was unheard of before the war. The staff of the Juvenile Employment Bureaux give vocational guidance to all school leavers of secondary modern schools and very many children get their jobs through the Bureaux. On the other hand, some of the more enterprising girls and parents go after jobs directly. A good many girls, especially the shy ones, try to get their first job at a firm where a relative is working, or where the girl's own particular friend is employed.

Roughly speaking, there are three main types of employment that the secondary modern school girls follow. The first is as manual workers in industry; the second as workers in the distributive trades, and the last as clerical assistants in shops, works' offices, etc. To put this in other words—in the year ending June 1948 of all the new girl entrants into insurable employment, about eight went into industry as manual workers, for five who went into shops and seven into all other types of work. It is the children of the larger families who tend to go into industry and to get into the lower grade jobs. There is more job change too in manual than in shop or office work. Though frequent job changes, on the whole, are frowned on by those interested in the welfare of the adolescent (and are equally obnoxious to the employer), there is some case for those adolescents in very routine jobs who almost unconsciously seem to be looking for self education by at least changing the environment in which they have to do the dull and petty job.

For [a great] many girls unskilled factory work is of an extremely routine nature. She does such things as working a button-holing machine, wrapping electric light bulbs in their cardboard cases, picking out the broken edged biscuits from the whole ones as they roll out of the electric oven. This is the kind of job which requires almost nothing more than agile fingers. Unskilled work of this kind, in which even the three R's are not used, does nothing to exercise the wits. There is probably a certain proportion of girls with low I.Q.s whom routine work suits and who would be unhappy in any other environment, but for the majority of the secondary modern school girls, jobs of this kind, even if the girls do not consciously dislike them, have almost certainly a stultifying effect. The repercussions are demonstrated in many ways, particularly in the girl's personal attitudes and in the way in which she spends time after work. She feels frustrated and makes up for this by aggression and cheek. Neither her actual job nor her working environment, often an all feminine one, gives her enough new things to think about. Trivialities assume ridiculous proportions and the girl becomes engrossed in her personal relationships, particularly in those with the opposite sex.

In addition to this, such girls very often have no clear conception of any career before them. They see their job merely as a stop-gap until the day they marry. The idea that a girl should have a career, which she may or may not give up when she marries, has not really taken root in the working class family. This, and the fact that her prospective husband, if he also is in manual work, is probably earning as big a wage at 24 as he ever will, leads the working girl to expect marriage at a relatively earlier age than the girl in the professional home.

Not much material exists on the marriage age pattern of different social levels but the Registrar General's Statistical Review gives the ages at which all women in England and Wales marry, of whom the great proportion will come from working class homes. In the decade before the war 23 was the age at which the largest number of girls married. During the war the peak age dropped, to 20 in the early days of the war, to 21 for 1941, 2, 3. The 1947 figures reflect the immediate post-war conditions of course, but they are not very different from the earlier picture. They show that *more* girls married at 21 in 1947 than at any other age, and that 22 and 20, in that order and in about equal weight, were the next most frequent ages for girls to marry. With this pattern before her the girl is perfectly justified in thinking that she is likely to marry within a few years' time. The expectation influences the whole of her outlook and, in particular, the ways in which she considers it proper to spend her leisure.

Before commenting on the ways in which girls do spend their leisure it is useful to consider how the adults of the girl's family reckon to spend their spare time, and what sort of pattern she observes among her older friends.

The immediate point that such a question calls to mind is that adult working class recreation, on the whole, is an informal affair. Visiting relations bulks largely in the programme. Visiting the local pub, particularly at the weekend, is another regular activity. Older men too, spend a lot of their free time working in their gardens and allotments. The younger ones take part in various sports, either watching or playing, and for men of all ages watching professional football, particularly on Saturday afternoon, is an almost universal activity. Television has not yet become a serious rival to the cinema, and the latter is one of the major recognised ways of spending a free evening. There is a good deal of family cinema going, to the cheaper cinemas, and some families, or perhaps a mother and adolescent daughter, go regularly to the local variety theatre, which exists in most of the larger towns.

The above suggests that many adults among the girl's acquaintances take their pleasures in an informal and unorganised way which does not necessitate joining any society. Of societies that are joined, the churches are of major importance from the point of view of numbers alone. It is a safe bet that more people take part regularly in the social activities provided by the churches than those provided by any other type of body. There is, however, an infinity of these other bodies—clubs and organizations for good works, for games, for hobbies and for cultural activities. But although these are so numerous, social surveys suggest that, on the whole, there are more adults who belong to no leisure time society than those who do belong to one, and that women on the whole belong less than men.

Numerous surveys have been made recently into the way in which adolescents spend their increasing volume of leisure. Most of these enquiries have been directed to the leisure time occupations of working adolescents, implying that those who are still at school at 16 and 17 are presumed to be occupying themselves in ways which adults regard as satisfactory. Three motives seem to have inspired these surveys. In the first place a good many of the seeds of juvenile delinquency seem to sprout during leisure that is aimless. In the second place adults have noted that the girls in very frustrating jobs tend to be the people who fritter away their evenings and week-ends in a very narrow set of activities. And thirdly there has been a growing conviction that it is an adult responsibility to see that all youngsters are given facilities to play the games and practise the hobbies that are recognised as giving so much pleasure and sensible recreation to the boys and girls from more ample homes.

These surveys suggest that on the whole adolescent girls who are at work from 8 A.M. to 5.30 P.M. probably spend the major part of their free time in their own homes. Apart from regular domestic chores, minding the smaller children, etc., they have their personal things to see to and can get enjoyment from hair washing, ironing, etc., in a way that the boys cannot. Not many girls seem to do much actual dressmaking, but knitting is an almost universal occupation. Serious reading of books, as distinct from magazines, is an occupation which seems to run in families and is practised by only a minority of girls who leave school at 15. On the other hand, many still buy the comics regularly and continue to read them, as indeed do the grown ups in their homes. Most of the girls as schoolgirls have read *Girls' Crystal* regularly, and the lower intellectual level of adolescents do not rise much above the level of *Red Star, Miracle* and *Glamour* type of magazine. The only newspapers that seem to be widely read much by this kind of girl are picture papers like the *Daily Mirror* and the *Graphic,* Sunday papers of *The News of the World* type, and the local evening or weekly paper which every home takes.

After about 14 not many girls seem to "play out" or to take part in the street games, "Hot Rice," "Hadrian's Wall," skipping, etc., on which, as children, practically all of them spent a good deal of their leisure. They still go out onto the street, but for slow walks round with a girl friend, for long doorstep talks with a boy, for street corner gossip

with other boys and girls, or for milk bar gang meetings with their particular set.

The girls probably go to the cinema more often than to any other type of paid recreation. About two nights a week seems a typical pattern for a girl with 10/- a week pocket money. Quite often girls will go with their mother or will treat a small brother to a special film, like *Mr. Ichabod and Mr. Toad.* In most artisan districts one cinema makes a point of catering for child and adolescent audiences with serials such as *Jungle Girl* and a generally unsophisticated swashbuckling programme.

Dancing is much less universally practised than cinema going but is generally regarded as a more dashing way of enjoying yourself. An ordinary popular dance hall in a provincial city charges 2/- for 3½ hours of dancing. Young girls often start their dancing under the wing of an older sister, and later on two girl friends will go together. Not very many girls seem to go in a group to dances. Old-time dancing has had a considerable revival recently, and is surprisingly popular even among the Bebop fans.

Cycling is another very regular form of recreation. Most girls manage to get a cycle of their own by the time they leave school probably paying for a £20 cycle by 8/9 weekly installments. There are hundreds of cycling clubs for the real enthusiasts who go in for racing and for 70 mile runs on a Sunday, but for the majority of adolescent girls cycling means not more than going out into the country with a friend for short rides. The popularity of ice and roller skating depends, of course, on what rinks are available. It is regarded as an expensive hobby. A girl who is earning up to £4 a week however will probably afford the 3/6 entrance fee and will save up to buy her own boots. Sports like hockey and tennis are relatively unpopular among working girls. The secondary modern schools are only just beginning to play games of this kind and girls on the whole seem much less able than boys to organise themselves informally into the teams, or even the fours, that such games demand. Swimming probably owes a good deal of its popularity, though it is said to be less universal here than in the States, to the fact that it is a pastime that you can pursue alone.

More than half of the adolescent boy population and a rather smaller proportion of girls, spend some of their evenings at a youth organisation. These are societies for and of young people but sponsored by adults. The latter are concerned to help boys and girls obtain the sort of recreations they enjoy and at the same time try to provide some informal education, particularly for those who have left school at 15. Probably most of the adults connected with youth organisations see the latter as one method of training future citizens of a democratic state and members of a Christian community.

English youth organizations have a long history. Some of the national bodies like the Y.M. and Y.W.C.A., the Boys Brigade and the Girls' Friendly Society date back to the last quarter of the 19th century. These organisations were primarily intended to help the under-privileged young workers of the great cities. The Scout and Guide movement, started before the 1914 war, extended the scope of the youth organisation on, broadly, educational lines. At the beginning of the last war the statutory authorities got into co-operation with the many existing voluntary organisations for young people and, together, a great drive was made under the title of the Service of Youth. This aimed to increase the number of units, to raise their standard and generally to try to get more adolescents linked up with some type of organisation. The liaison between the official education authorities and the voluntary organisations, begun in 1939, still exists and has much strengthened the Youth movement. Funds, premises, and adult leaders are provided from both sources. Organisations, for example, meet in Local Education Authority owned schools and in Church owned Halls. The local boys' clubs arts festival may be run by the National Association of Boys' Clubs while the football and swimming leagues which the same clubs enter for are arranged by the youth organisers of the L.E.A.

All this sounds as if the youth organisations are very much an adult affair. In fact, in the well run units, the young people themselves are asked to take on as much as possible of the responsibility for their own organisation. The relatively small scale of the majority of the units makes this not too difficult. Most organisations have their own, elected Members' Committee. The boys and girls almost invariably pay a subscription, about 3d. or 6d. a week. They decide on programmes, are responsible for the canteen and, under a skilled leader, have a very definite training in democratic methods of control. A fair test of the good unit is how far the boys and girls do really regard the society as their own show.

There are many "boys only" organisations, including the pre-service ones which often have social clubs attached to them. A growing number of societies, especially of the club type, are open to both boys and girls. A decreasing number seem to exist for girls only. The most flourishing of this latter group seem to be for schoolgirls of 12 to 14. The sort of club that some of the girls described in this article belong to has one room with comfortable chairs where people can just gossip; a little canteen serving such things as tea and soft drinks, hot baked potatoes, slices of fried bread, and cheese cobs. It also has one hall big enough for a tap dancing class, for table tennis and for badminton. There is a stage that is a great asset to the drama class, one of the most popular and most valuable activities. One other room is kept for class work under an L.E.A. teacher. Crafts like leather work, embroidery and puppet making and art take place here.

Out of doors the clubs run tennis and cycling sections and camping week-ends, perhaps at a camp house up on the moors owned by all the organisations of the locality. To sum up: the present youth organisations have many weaknesses. They are subject to a good deal of justified criticism and they still fail to attract a large number of those young people who, so far as one can judge, would probably benefit from joining. At the same time, more than half the 14 to 18 population of this country finds it worth while to join voluntarily one or another of the youth organisations which suggests that the latter are meeting a genuine need. Individual youngsters' own enthusiasm and delight in the friendships, the adventures and the activities of their own Brigade or Troop or Club is the most convincing testimonial to the value of the youth movement.

For a somewhat different view of English social organization and processes, we turn to an article by Stephen Spender, the prominent poet, writer, and playwright. Spender presents a picture of the English adolescent as he is influenced through his education by the attitudes and traditions of his society. Particularly important are the development of class consciousness and sex attitudes, and the transmission of spiritual values. It should be kept in mind that in England a "public school" is one that in this country would be referred to as "independent," "private," or "non-tax-supported." Spender's article is based on a lecture he delivered at the Summer Seminar in Education for International Understanding, at Paris in 1947, under the auspices of UNESCO.

• 139 • The Adolescent and the Schools
STEPHEN SPENDER

I am not asked to speak about schools, but about the adolescent. One cannot think of the English adolescent without thinking of a little fragment of human material confronted by a great hierarchy of educational machines through which his young life is going to pass, and from which he will emerge as a member of a community. And the first point to make is that those machines select their material. There are the Elementary Schools, the Secondary Schools, the private Preparatory Schools, the Grammar Schools, the minor Public Schools, the great Public Schools, like Eton and Winchester, Harrow and Charterhouse, and then there are the Universities, Oxford and Cambridge, and what are called, I believe, the provincial Universities. Then, also, a class apart, there are the Girls' Public Schools. There are also the small progressive schools for rich children, which are in revolt against the Public School system.

And Eton and Harrow do not select the boy who goes to the Elementary School. English education is on a class basis. Indeed class feeling is more deeply ingrained in our educational system than anywhere else. I can illustrate this by drawing attention to what I know to be a fact; that many middle class parents who consider that in their own lives they have shed all traces of class feeling, and who may even wish to belong to the working class, yet, when it comes to educating their own children, send them to the public school against whose values they have rebelled themselves. The reason for this is not merely, I think, that such parents consider the Public School the best possible education; they also feel that having a public school education is the sign of belonging to a social class, and they do not feel entitled, just because they have withdrawn from spiritual membership of that class themselves, to impose the choice which they have made for themselves on their children.

Thus, the main social experience of the English child and adolescent is that he belongs to a social class. The child of poor parents is forced continually to think of the job which he will do when he leaves school, the job that will grade him for life. He can only obtain the higher education which will make it possible for him to enter a profession by winning

[Adapted from "The English Adolescent," *The Harvard Educational Review*, Vol. 18, No. 4, Cambridge, 1948. Pp. 229-239. Used by permission.]

scholarship after scholarship, which will take him to the secondary school and finally to the University. If he wins sufficient scholarships to get to a University and then to pass beyond the University into a profession, he will then be absorbed into the broad middle class which is the main stream of English social and cultural life.

The poor are thus in a practical and empirical way made conscious of their place in society during their adolescence by their education. This does not mean that they recognize the superiority of the rich, but it does mean that they realize their own limitations. The social history of the poor man or woman is his or her education. The sons of those who can afford and who do send their children to public schools are conscious of their social position in quite a different way. They know that they belong to a privileged class, and they are conscious of social superiority. In between the public schools and the completely state-supported schools, there is a kind of limbo of minor public schools, day schools and grammar schools, which, unlike the genuine working class schools, have a real consciousness of social inferiority. This attitude is very noticeable amongst those grammar school boys who come up to Oxford and Cambridge: they feel ill-at-ease with the Public school boys. The sense of social superiority of public school boys is only equalled by the energy with which members of the upper-middle class in England sometimes pretend that it does not exist.

[It is only fair to say that] English class feeling is deep rather than narrow. It derives from profound and utmost self-confidence of the ruling classes in themselves, and it has a depth which can absorb newcomers when they have proved that they can also belong to the middle class. This depth and breadth rather than narrowness derives from the fact that we are in a middle-class society with a middle-class culture. The working-class boy who wins scholarships makes his way up until he enters the middle class. Of course, politically, he may remain a revolutionary proletarian, but even such a political attitude does not alter the fact that the revolutionary writer

or the trade-union leader inevitably enters into the middle class of traditional England. The trade unionist and socialist leaders who now appear to be in power in England have worked their way up through the educational system through self-education, into the middle class, which to some extent has broadened itself, by becoming aware of their existence, and absorbing them.

Perhaps I may seem to have strayed from the subject of the adolescent. But I think it is essential to bear in mind that there is a great difference between the experience of the adolescent of working-class parents in England and that of parents who can afford to send their children to the schools where one pays for an expensive education. This difference goes to the very depths of English life. In experiencing this class difference the adolescent experiences a social reality in effective action, which is more or less concealed in adult life. When I say that the poor child who had only a primary education is experiencing the class system, I mean that he is excluded by it from the middle-class tradition which is the main social and cultural stream of English life. And if the poor child gets scholarships and educates himself into one of the professions, into the arts or into politics, he enters culturally into the middle class, and is accepted by it. So we have in England this situation: that class counts very much in so far as the poor and the uneducated are excluded by poverty or ignorance from the middle class, and very little in so far as the middle class has a broad and deep culture which is capable of absorbing into itself every explicit and educated point of view even when it appears to be politically opposed to it. England is an evolutionary rather than a revolutionary country because it has a protean middle class.

Thus, also, we find that the class difference leads to entirely different forms of characteristic adolescent experiences of children of different classes. When we come to physical and physiological development, we find that the difference is very striking, because the public schools take the children away from their homes for nine months in the year and board them. The boarding-school life is undoubtedly healthy, rather spartan-like, and toughening. The poor children do not leave their homes, where, though they may be very poor, they may nevertheless be pampered and spoiled far more than richer children. Sometimes periods of pampering alternate with periods of poverty.

Another great difference between the education of the upper and lower class adolescent is in the development of his attitude towards courtship, marriage, and sexual problems. Here again the child of poor parents takes his or her attitude from the home. The problem for the children who go to boarding schools is that, except in a few schools such as Bedales, where there are both girls and boys, the sexes are artificially separated from each other, at an age when the poor boy is probably walking out with his first girl.

In the English public schools there is no training for courtship and marriage; there is simply a problem called sex, of which everyone is uncomfortably aware. In so far as there is an attempt to deal with this problem, it is pushed on to the science master, who is supposed to explain the biological functioning of sex to the boys, probably by a process of first explaining to them the amours of flowers, then frogs, and so on through the animal kingdom, until the possibility of such a relationship between human beings is indicated. The housemaster, or even the headmaster may be called in, if the sexual problem threatens to break out of this scientific test tube, where the school likes to keep it, and infect the emotional atmosphere of a boy's mind. It is no exaggeration to say that the attitude of most English school masters to sex is simply that it is not a question that should arise in a public school. It should do so after the boy has left school, and then it should solve itself without any previous training through a miracle of love.

A young woman who went to one of the "Girls' Public Schools," and to whom I had shown this paper, commented: "Sex education for girls, as far as I know or have experienced, is pretty well parallel with that of boys. The Botany mistress drops embarrassed hints, or the biology mistress makes a better job of it. Games, hobbies, and all the rest are terrifically encouraged to counteract any nascent interest in boys. At the same time *schwaermerei* on other girls is persecuted by authority—a fact which I am sure does much to stimulate it. . . . In the upper-middle classes I think the education of girls, with its emphases on games, Girl Guides, heartiness and unsentimentality, does tend to produce much too high a percentage of gawky and frigid women who—now that arranged marriages are no longer the fashion—have not the slightest idea how to approach the other sex. 'The English spinster' is, of course, proverbial abroad and is largely the product of bad education in adolescence, which still goes on.

"On the other hand this only applies to the middle class. The working class girl does not seem to have the same difficulties, probably because she imbibes the facts of life and a natural attitude in her more congested home life and while 'helping mother.'"

It seems to me that our trouble in England in these matters is that we do not have an ideal of chastity or even restraint; we insist simply on a complete negation of the instinctional life of children, which often we succeed in killing or perverting. We do not accept the senses and then discipline them: we simply deny them and the consequence of this denial is to drive some English men and women into a pursuit of sensual reality which they have lost.

The English public school is really a kind of small city state, and I think it is only if one sees it in this way that one can really understand its weaknesses and its merits. Like the city state, it is a community small enough and old enough for public opinion to be regarded as impersonal and almost sacred. The floggings, lines and other sensational punishments for which public schools are famous are only really border-line penalties for those who run outside the boundaries of the discipline of the inner city which is created by the extraordinary seriousness with which masters and boys take the school and themselves. A public schoolboy from Winchester who will soon, I am sure, be a cabinet minister, once said to me: "At Winchester, when I was head of my house, I was a greater man than I shall ever be again in my life, even if I live to be a Prime Minister." An appalling remark, from an appalling man, I thought at the time, "but he will certainly be an excellent prime minister!"

Thus the important thing about the public school is that the boys regard all its institutions, all its offices, as sacred; and the masters and parents do also. For a housemaster the choice of prefects and of the boy who will be head of the house is as serious as the choice of a new cabinet for a country, and the boys chosen for these functions take them as seriously as any task they will undertake in the rest of their lives. Of course, there are prefects and head boys who fail, but such failure is parallel to the scandal attaching to a cabinet minister who reveals to his friends the secrets of the Budget.

I think that the explanation of the extraordinary civic sense of responsibility of England is to be found in the English education which teaches boys to take themselves seriously as functions of an institution, before they take themselves seriously as persons or as individuals. This really explains a great deal, both of the merits and defects of the English. It explains why the English are so suspicious of anyone who takes himself as a person seriously, why they mistrust any machinery of thought, such as psychoanalysis, which directs the attentions of the individual too much onto himself and yet why, as responsible members of a community, they show a deadly earnestness about their own positions which leaves no room for cynicism. The [final] effect of the school city-state is to produce a type, what most public schoolmasters would call 'the public school type.' The characteristic of this type is that mixture of good qualities summed up in the minds of schoolmasters by the phrase: *Mens sana in corpore sano.*

The weakness of the system is that it becomes too easy for the masters and the boys themselves to value every activity of the members of the school in so far as it contributes or fails to contribute to the School State and School Type. Games can be regarded in this way. The school team, if it wins matches, contributes to the glory of the school; the discipline of games is a sacred rite within the school tradition; and, moreover, games are supposed to help the boys to lead asexual lives.

Religion, just as much as games, tends to become a part of the school ritual, instead of a window on to a wider, more universal valid order outside it. I am sure that headmasters do not intend this to happen, but nevertheless it does happen. The boy who shows an interest in religion which threatens to take him beyond the spiritual boundaries of the city state is regarded as unhealthy, dangerous, just as much as the boy who takes too great an interest in the arts.

If my analysis is even partly correct it will be seen that our public school education, whilst it instils us with a sense of responsibility to the community, does so at considerable cost to our personal psychology and relationship. In fact, it tends to perpetuate the adolescence of the Englishman, by discouraging the interest in spiritual life for its own sake which leads to spiritual maturity, by teaching us to treat as irrelevant physical instincts which lead men and women to understand each other in a mature and full relationship, and by neglecting the problem of the relationship of the growing child with his parents.

At the same time, if we are a people who never recover from certain adolescent weaknesses, we also acquire in adolescence certain virtues, such as reasonableness, adaptability, generosity, adventurousness, and an astonishingly open mind, combined with a pious attitude toward our institutions. England is supremely the country where the people respond to a national emergency and are capable of that kind of illumination which can see beyond self-interest to the need of the whole country, when it is explained to them, or which can reverse a long-established national policy towards some part of the empire within a few days. Most surprisingly of all, the very class of people who, according to a materialist view, should be most tied up with their own interests, the wealthy public school boys, are the first to sacrifice their lives in a war. Probably, if, in addition to having material interests, they were capable also of developing deep relationships with other people and their families, this capacity for sacrifice would not be so great. The philistines of the undisciplined and undeveloped heart have been among the first to save England in two wars.

In this sketch, nearly everything I have said has tended to emphasize the difference between the adolescent experience of the social classes in England. On the one hand, there are the public school boys, artificially withdrawn from parental affection, and indeed from nearly all affection, during the long years of adolescence; on the other hand there is the poor boy who is a home boy, who is often surrounded by an almost stifling family affection, and who regards 'leaving mum' as the most supremely difficult decision of his life.

Perhaps it would be true to say that if the English adolescent who goes to the boarding public school suffers from lack of affection, the working-class boy (the boy more than the girl) suffers from an excess of it. In the difficult lives of the poor, the home, unless it is a complete failure, as may happen, becomes the centre and supreme compensation for all the disappointments of life. And often there is a touching and perhaps rather oppressive emotional dependence of the parents on the children.

I think that many witnesses who have been in the services during World Wars I and II would agree that, on the whole, the public-school boys are tougher than the working class stay-at-home boys, and that this was very evident between 1914 and 1918, and still evident, though less so, between 1939 and 1945. Perhaps here we have a clue to the unity of English morale: that the upper-class adolescents have retained, to a considerable extent, their toughness and their capacity for leadership. However, toughness is not in itself a sufficient explanation. One has to add to it a few characteristics which really, I think, make the English adolescent exceptional, and which are certainly of value as an experience not to be submerged under the social changes which are taking place all over the world.

The first characteristic, I should call inno-

cence! The English public school-boy is set aside from the experience of the world during his growing years, and plunged into a tradition which has to a great extent remained islanded from the surrounding world. The result is that, with all his faults, he remains to some extent an innocent, and his very defects are based on this innocence. Thus, as I have explained, his snobbishness is based on an almost incredible unawareness of the conditions and existence of the working populations in an industrial civilisation. Now snobbishness is certainly not a virtue, but the fact that this fault is one of innocence instead of one of narrowness and self-opinionatedness means that it can be remedied. So that there exists side by side with the English narrow-mindedness an equally strong open-mindedness, a capacity to see the other person's point of view. [The] other virtues—tolerance, courage, modesty, adaptability, and the rest—are only consequences of this fundamental innocence.

Toughness and an integrity which, with all the faults of the English educational system have not been betrayed, are the contributions of the upper classes to the unity which has enabled English youth to unite for the desperate struggles of two wars. And with all the differences of background and training, the poor recognise and have, themselves, these values. Different as their experiences and environment are, they are given a schooling based on the same idea that education is a training which can create good citizens and strengthen character, and not just a machine for making youths pass examinations. The teacher is responsible, not just for the learning of his pupil, but for his whole development, his physical and moral well-being.

The contribution of the English adolescent experience to the planning of the adolescent education of a world citizen, might well be the idea that a certain isolation of the adolescent from the modern industrial civilisation is necessary. The problem is to isolate him, without at the same time making him unable to deal with the harshest realities of our existence, and of giving him the strength of his virtues. As I have suggested, a weakness of the English

Public School system is that the energies of the boys are too often only directed towards the school itself. [Once again] the school chapel, which, like the school football field, produces a self-worshipping kind of Public School religion corresponding to Public School games, neglects the fundamental educational problem of our time: that is, how, during the period of adolescence, to strengthen in the mind of youth a faith in spiritual values and in human values capable of resisting the materialism and the power policies of the world of enormous conflicting social interests in which we live.

I cannot introduce phrases such as *spiritual values* and *human values* without attempting more precise definitions. By spiritual values I mean the sense that the structure of society exists for the sake of a purpose which is a spiritual purpose, and not just for its own sake. It is simply the sense that all material and social structures exist for the sake of an aim, and that that aim cannot be simply the structure and the material well-being of the society itself, but its vision of a purpose in life. It is the recognition that no civilisation is judged good because its members were of a certain social class or a certain race, but by the values which that civilisation produced; and those values are not just the material conditions within which members of that civilisation lived their lives.

By human values, I mean the realization that human beings, human individuals are each one of them sacred. A business, or a nation, or a political party, or a world organisation, which treats human lives as though they are chattels which can be moved about or cast aside or destroyed without regard for their sacred nature, or as though they were the mud which is dug out of a river bed, when the course of the river is altered, is dehumanising the human spirit, because the whole of humanity, even the humanity of the people who commit crimes against humanity, is involved in acts directed against any section of humanity.

Therefore, I believe that, in the world of to-day, it is necessary that the adolescent have a far greater degree of realisation of himself as a spiritual and also as a physical individual being than exists within the English adolescent experience. At the same time, I think that during this period of transition, the English experience has much from which people in other countries may learn.

This picture of English society would not be complete without a consideration of the role of the church. There is not sufficient space to discuss in detail the numerous organizations through which religious activity finds an expression in Britain, but a look at the membership figures of the major groups will suggest the extent of their importance. The Established Church of England, which is Protestant Episcopal in its form of government, numbers about 2,300,000 full members in England and Wales; the Roman Catholics number more than 2,500,000. Other denominations (Nonconformists) in England and Wales include Methodist, with nearly 1,150,000 members; Congregational Union, 370,000; Baptist, 340,000; Calvinistic Methodist, 230,000; Presbyterian, 80,000; Society of Friends, 20,000; and Churches of Christ, 14,000. In Scotland the Established Church is Presbyterian in form and has 1,250,000 members, the Episcopal Church has 56,000 members, and the Roman Catholic Church 620,000. The Jewish faith in the United Kingdom (which includes Northern Ireland) numbers about 385,000 members. (Statistics from the *American Encyclopedia Yearbook* for 1950.)

Something of the historical background and relationships of these groups will become apparent in the next selection. It was Henry VIII who led the break with the Roman Catholic Church and set up the Anglican, or Established, Church. But even after that break the Catholic Church continued to play a prominent role in English history, its avowed "universality" in contrast to the nationalism that the Church of England encouraged. It was only slowly that opposition developed within England to the doctrine that to be a good Englishman was to be a good member of the Anglican Church. The struggle to divorce religious loyalties from state loyalties led to the Nonconformity movements and eventually spread to the American Colonies, where it contributed significantly to their later Revolution. One of the interesting aspects of the development of Puritanism is the extent to which it may have provided a moral and intellectual atmosphere favorable to the rise of the special economic system we know as capitalism. This and other topics are treated briefly but expertly in the next selection.

• 140 • The Churches and the Rise of Modern England
ERNEST BARKER

THE FIRST REFORMATION:
THE ANGLICAN

There were two Reformations in England —the Reformation which issued in Anglicanism, and that which issued in Nonconformity; and the dualism of the two—reflected, from the end of the seventeenth century, in the opposition of our political parties—has been one of the most peculiar and one of the most potent influences in our national life. It has not only reflected itself in the political organization of parties: it has also appeared in a social division. Anglicanism has been the religion of the gentry, the land, the villages: Nonconformity has been the faith of the middle classes, of commerce and industry, of the towns. The one has fostered the love of tradition, the sense of historical continuity, the passion of national unity; the other has cherished an ideal of the purity of original Christian truth, a belief in the need for basing religious order newly and freshly upon that truth, a doctrine of the indefeasible right of the individual soul to make its own peace with its Maker. To the one the past has been sacred; to the other it has been suspect. The one was naturally drawn to a belief in two parallel and interconnected divine rights— the divine right of the king and the divine

right of the bishop. It stood for authority, and it believed that authority, alike in Church and in State, had two attributes—the attribute of a divine origin and the attribute of a continuous historic tradition. . . . The philosophy of Nonconformity was colder and more rational. The foundation of authority, ecclesiastical or political, was human institution. It was men who had erected presbyters or kings, for ends of edification or protection: it was on a compact between men that their authority rested; and if that authority were not duly used for the ends prescribed, the compact was null and void, and what had been given by men could by men be taken away.

In the Anglican system the king was more than parallel with bishops. He was the bishop of bishops—the supreme head on earth of the Church as well as the State—or at any rate (in Elizabeth's milder phrase) "the only supreme Governor of the realm . . . as well in all spiritual or ecclesiastical things or causes as temporal." Royal supremacy is thus of the essence of the Reformation. The king adds a new province to his existing territory, by acquiring control of things ecclesiastical (hitherto subject to the Pope) in addition to the things temporal which he has always controlled; and he gains at the same time a new consecration for his whole state and position,

[Adapted from National Character and the Factors in its Formation, Harper Brothers, London, 1927. Pp. 195-213. Used by permission.]

and a new appeal to the hearts of his subjects, by becoming, as it were, the chief priest of his people. Loyalty assumes a new fervor: "God bless the King" comes from men's lips with a deeper resonance; "Church and King" is a compelling toast; the principles of the Cavaliers, which became the principles of the Tory party, are launched on their long voyage. The conception and practice of royal headship, which may seem to lower the Church, had for its complement the fact of Establishment, by which the Church was exalted. If the king, who is the symbol of the State, is also the head of the Church, it is inevitable that the Church should be brought into a special relation with the State. On the one hand, the State will guarantee and protect the Church, by acts of legislation or executive process, in its powers and its properties; on the other, the Church will consecrate the State, and, as it were, hold up its hands, in the course of its earthly activities. Establishment means both of these things; but it means particularly the latter.

The conception which underlies establishment is a conception of a single society, which in one aspect we call a State, and in another we call a Church, but which in itself is one and undivided. . . . Before the Reformation there was an English nation, and that nation was organized as a State; but in matter of religion its members belonged to another and wider society, which was the general society of the Latin Church of the West. After the Reformation . . . the nation . . . is now conceived not only as a State, but also as a Church. It receives a new consecration; and the State, as the secular expression of its life, shares with it in that consecration.

This was an ideal; but it never became a fact. Two grave questions occupied the minds of the leaders in Church and State as soon as they attempted to translate the ideal into practice. What was to be the basis of religious unity, and how much was it to include? What was to be done with the dissidents who refused to accept the basis and declined to belong to the single national society in its form of religious expression?

The attempt to make the Church coexten-sive with the nation, and to use external religious observance as a drill to form the habits of Englishmen and to shape national character, encountered an invincible opposition. The ideal of uniformity was answered by the fact of Nonconformity. The Church could not be coextensive with the nation, when a large part of the nation refused to belong to the Church; and there could be no general external drill when thousands insisted upon a free right of internal choice. Nonconformity had always before it the example of Scotland, where, instead of the nation being drilled by external rule into a single religious society, religious society, regarded as something independent and prior, shaped a nation by its inner spirit in the image of its own unity. . . . As the *plebs* established itself in ancient Rome by the side of the *populus* so the Nonconformist congregations established themselves in England by the side of the Established Church. Like the plebeians in early Roman history, they suffered grave disabilities. They could not hold office, municipal or national; and by various statutes they were deprived even of the social right of maintaining schools and giving instruction. . . . It is the Church—the Establishment of the Church, and the Royal Headship of the Church—that is the essence of the Tory party which came into being during the reign of Charles II, just as it is the voluntary religious society, the independence of its congregations, and the general conception of the free Church in the free State, that is the essence of the Whig party which came into existence at the same time. . . . Our party system, almost to the end of the nineteenth century, and until a new third party emerged under the name of Labour, was a legacy of ecclesiastical policies.

THE SECOND REFORMATION: NONCONFORMITY

Nonconformity, like Anglicanism, bequeathed a political party to the nation; and like Anglicanism, but in its own way and with its own quality, it has been a social force in the process of national development. . . . It has spread itself over the world, and made its home in the meeting-houses of Massachusetts no less than in the austere chapels of England; it has steeled our qualities, and accentuated our angularities; it has affected our economic life, and influenced the direction of our foreign policy; it has done much to determine the aspect we have presented to the world, and the judgment which the world has passed upon us.

English Nonconformity has two main streams. The first we may call by the general name of Puritan. Its great period runs from the accession of Queen Elizabeth to the Revolution of 1688. It included (down to 1662) Low Churchmen as well as those who were definite dissidents from the Church; it is represented to-day by Presbyterians, Congregationalists, Baptists, and Quakers. Perhaps its numbers were never very great during the seventeenth century; and when William III attempted a religious census, immediately after the Revolution, he only enumerated 108,000 male Nonconformists to nearly 2,500,-000 Conformists. The volume of Nonconformity was greatly increased in the eighteenth century, when the stream of Wesleyanism was added to its current; and at the present time the Nonconformists of England and Wales (who taken together are almost equal in number to the members of the Church of England) are evenly divided between societies which took their origin from the Puritan movement of the sixteenth and seventeenth century, and those which are derived from the Wesleyan movement of the eighteenth. Remembering this division, and the successive stages in which Nonconformity has played its part and exerted its influence, we must distinguish between the effects of the first and fundamental, and those of the later and secondary period.

Puritanism was rooted and grounded in a positive belief; but there is a sense in which we may say that, in English history, it has been the spirit "which constantly denies." From its beginnings it was engaged in a protestation against the State and a negation of its claims in matter of religion.

There were other ways in which Puritanism fostered political liberty. Its basis was religious individualism; and it fostered a general temper of individualism. Its doctrine of the responsibility of the lonely soul for its own salvation readily allied itself with parallel tenets of secular philosophy, and it helped to encourage their general diffusion. It was the air in which ideas of the Englishman's legal "birthright and inheritance," and even more drastic ideas of the natural rights of all men, flourished in the seventeenth century. All in all, we may say that Nonconformity served as a gathering ground of the various influences (religious, political, and economic) which produced the Liberal or Manchester philosophy of the nineteenth century—a philosophy which not only inspired a party, but determined in no small measure the general life and aspect of Victorian England. "Way for individual enterprise"—this was its teaching; and backed by the manufacturing and commercial classes, which had always been the stronghold of Nonconformity, its teaching triumphed.

If the Puritans were driven, as a tenacious minority, in opposition to the State, to develop the more negative qualities of a minority, there was none the less in their creed a positive quality which was the ground and the rock of their resistance. Puritanism was something more than a challenge to the State. It was the practice of a firm and resolute will ("will . . . is the essence of Puritanism"), set sternly to the kingdom of God and His righteousness; it was a rigour of self-control, and an unrelenting process of self-discipline, by which the will of man was made to fulfil the apprehended purposes of God. It was not for the Puritan to steep his mind in the warm comfort of historic tradition; nor could his spirit float suspended in a cloud of encompassing witnesses, sustained by the communion of an inspired and inspiring Church. His was a new and solitary soul, projected into a bare world for an arduous and lonely struggle; and he must wrestle alone, in the night, with the angel of the Lord. He lived in a spiritual solitude; but he was not a solitary. He could not renounce the world and its works, or embrace the life of the hermit or anchorite; he had been sent into the world to do his Master's business and to fulfil his calling; and it would have seemed to him a surrender of the will and an act of cowardice to flee temptation or to shun struggle.

Loneliness was one of the Puritan virtues, as it was also one of the Puritan defects. They dared to be alone, and they cultivated the high virtues of solitude. Solitude is the preparation and the parent of achievement. . . . But the loneliness of the Puritan was also a defect. He carried a lonely self-reliance to the verge of a lonely selfishness. He rejected any comfort or consolation of society, because he desired to lean on nothing but his own strong will; but he also forgot the just claims of society.

Besides the practice of will, and the cultivation of solitude, the Puritan had a passionate zeal for work which, acting upon an energy natural, as we have seen, to the English stock, and fostered, as we have also seen, by the conditions of the English climate, raised it to a height at which it may sometimes seem almost daemonic. Work was conceived as something sacramental—the outward and visible sign of an inward and visible struggle to do the will of the Lord. The Parable of the Vineyard and the Parable of the Talents were ever before the Puritan's eye. He did not love the Book of Common Prayer, but there was one of its phrases which he took to heart; and he set himself, with all his power, "to learn and labour truly to get his own living in that state of life to which it should please God to call him." The doctrine of Calling . . . was a cardinal doctrine of Puritanism. God had called and "elected" men spiritually to the grace which comes by faith. He had also called and chosen them temporally for some particular employment or business, in which they must labour with diligence, making themselves known by their fruits. . . . Work was thus spiritualized and made an end in itself. . . . It is for this reason that more than one writer has regarded Puritanism as the parent of capitalism. Set together (the argument runs) the Puritan emphasis on work and production, and the Puritan challenge to the State with its consequent claim of a free way for individual initiative—and you have compounded the elements which

constitute the capitalist system. The argument has been challenged by Mr. Tawney [R. H. Tawney, *Religion and the Rise of Capitalism,* 1926] on two main grounds. In the first place, we can trace the origins of capitalism back to an earlier age than that of the Puritan Revolution, and we can find its spirit and its methods already present in the Italian cities of the later Middle Ages. In the second place, Puritanism, in its earlier phase, and down to 1660, opposed itself to the unlimited accumulation of wealth, and its preachers maintained the old mediaeval doctrines of "the just price" and the prohibition (or at any rate the strict limitation) of interest. But if capitalism was earlier than Puritanism, and if Puritanism, in its first beginnings, challenged its methods and its principles, we must also admit (as Mr. Tawney readily admits) that the spirit of later Puritanism was an air congenial to the accumulation of wealth. It was not only that the Puritans were devoted to production in virtue of their doctrine of work and calling. Their discipline of daily life, in itself, and apart from doctrine, was calculated to lay the foundations of success in commerce and industry. They mortified themselves of joys—of luxuries and even of comforts; and a sparing habit of life was productive of saving, which led in turn to banking and the accumulation of capital. The regularity of Puritan life, its stern economy of time, the sense with which it was vested of working in the Great Taskmaster's eye, all tended to produce men of business capacity, ready for the management of affairs and the conduct of large undertakings. In both ways—by supplying the means and by providing the men—Puritanism prepared the way for commercial and industrial greatness, and was a forerunner of the Industrial Revolution.

Down to the end of the seventeenth century Nonconformity was a leaven, small in amount, which yet stirred and moved the whole nation. It grew in volume during the eighteenth century, when Calvinistic Methodism spread through Wales, which in the seventeenth century had been Anglican and Royalist; when Wesleyanism began to count its adherents in hundreds of thousands; and when the Nonconformist bodies generally, by their labours among the new population which was pouring into industry, began to make the volume of their membership more nearly equal to the settled Anglicanism of the countryside. Nonconformity, as we have seen, had always been strong in the towns, among the commercial and industrial classes; and the growth of industrialism and of urban life, which marks the latter half of the eighteenth century, was naturally favourable to the growth of Nonconformity. In that growth it was Wesleyanism which played the greatest and most conspicuous part, affecting not only its own immediate adherents, but also a large section of the Anglican body from which it sprang and which it eventually left. The social influence which it exercised was profound and far-reaching. Wesley and his followers consciously carried their mission among the working-classes, and especially and particularly among the miners. They carried it in the form of a gospel of "enthusiasm" (detestable to the older and more cultivated intelligences of an age of reason) which caught the popular imagination and stirred a popular emotion. But neither their mission nor their influence was confined to a single class. If they went to the poor, they also made converts among the upper classes, and they had their stronghold in the middle class. They gave to that class, which might otherwise have stayed complacent in a fat and dull prosperity, the stimulus of ideals—the aiding of missions; the spread of education; the reform of prisons; the abolition of the slave-trade and of slavery itself. They knitted the middle to the poorer classes in the common bonds of a religious organization: they united them both in the services of the chapel, in which laymen might play their part, and in the common social gatherings of which the chapel was a centre and focus. In this way Wesleyanism stopped the widening of that social gulf which had existed, it is true, before the Industrial Revolution, but which the Revolution, without any counteracting influence, might have made both broader and deeper. By what it did to draw classes to-gether, and by the fact that it supplied a religious channel for the satisfaction of cravings and demands which might otherwise have run into the secular channels of French Revolutionary doctrine, Wesleyanism helped to keep the nation stable in the period of convulsion which marked the passing of the eighteenth into the nineteenth century. But it was not merely a stabilizing force, nor was it content that the comfort of religious enthusiasm should serve to divert men's minds from a sense of social injustice. It supplied, especially from the ranks of its lay preachers, men who led and spread working-class movements for better things—men who could rise above hatred or materialism, and connect ideas of social reform with a keen religious faith. The strength and the hold of the Trade Union and the Labour movement have depended, in no small degree, upon this connection. In other ways it has to be admitted that Wesleyanism inherited and accentuated national defects. It had some of the intolerance of the older Puritanism. It had something of its anxious discipline of life; and it diffused the same cloud of painful observance of the rules of external religion. It did not love the free course of thought, and it was dubious of human science. The tradition of the letter was strong in its teaching; and if the righteousness which it sought to teach was beyond that of the Scribes and the Pharisees, the enlightenment which it attained provoked Matthew Arnold to the adjective "Philistine."

It is possible that the Christian Churches will not exercise in the future the direct influence on national life and character which they have exercised in the past. In particular the influence which Nonconformity in its various forms has exercised during the last three centuries—an influence particularly deep and pervasive—is not likely to be so marked in this century. . . . It is not that Nonconformity has lost ground to the English Church, or, again, that both are losing ground to another Church: it is rather that both have handed to the teacher, and to the school, a torch which was once kept burning by the preacher, and uplifted in church and chapel. When schools and teachers were few, religious bodies had a double duty. They had to mould the characters and to awaken the intelligence of men by their teaching, as well as to touch and move their spirits by their preaching. The spread of a general system of national education may be said to relieve the churches of a part of their ancient duty. It was they who laboured first at the institution of that system; and its foundation stones were laid, over a hundred years ago, by Anglicans and Nonconformists alike, when the different voluntary societies set their hands to the provision of Sunday schools and the founding of day schools.

A system of social relations and institutions that has had, in the past, a far less complex pattern of organization than religion is *recreation*. In industrial societies the amount of time which an individual must devote to his job—making a living—is often drastically reduced, in contrast to peasant and tribal societies. One result is the emergence of "sport" as one of the important forms of recreation available to fill this new-found leisure time. Although an industrial society develops other forms of recreation, we have selected only this one for consideration here.

To those who know Britain well, the following selection may seem one-sided, since there are many leisure-time pursuits besides those described below. Many a Britisher takes pride in his garden; others are extraordinarily fond of excursions into the country by auto, by bicycle, or afoot. The pub, too, is an important center of social life. Nevertheless, we can better understand industrial society when we are aware of its emphasis on mass spectator sports and the role that athletic "games" play in the lives of millions of people. It can well be questioned, however, whether such sports are the ideal "safety valve" for the tensions and monotony of our mechanical age.

• 141 • Organized Sports for Leisure Time
PETER WILSON

A NATION OF SPECTATORS?

The game still traditionally associated with Britain is cricket, whereas in Scotland, Ireland and Wales there is only one first-class cricket county, while in all these countries, as well as in England, soccer is played and certainly watched by ten times as many people. Accurate statistics are difficult to discover, but through the soccer season, of approximately thirty-five weeks, an average of about a million people a week go to watch the forty-four English league matches which take place at least every Saturday.

Various games lay claim to having the greatest popularity amongst actual players. Bowls, for example, with its appeal for both sexes, probably has as many as three million devotees. But I imagine that the sport which has the largest number of active participants is snooker. Estimates vary, but I have been assured by a reliable informant—who is also a snooker enthusiast—that 12,000,000 people annually meander around the green baize table in the clubs and public saloons throughout the country.

It is difficult for the individual totally disinterested in sport to understand the attrac-

[Adapted from "Sport and the Public," *Current Affairs Pamphlet*, No. 59, Bureau of Current Affairs, London, 1948. Pp. 3-10. Used by permission.]

tion which the different forms of it have for their "fans." But in a largely mechanical age where, of necessity, the average individual has to exist in an urban community with few opportunities of self-expression, sport is the ideal safety-valve—and even watching sport provides the ideal opportunity for blowing off the steam accumulated during a week of repetitive and restrictive work.

One of the unhealthy symptoms of the vast attendances which throng with an almost religious fervour to their local football ground each week is the fact that many of them are people who are forced to lead the lives of automata at their work and who, nevertheless or therefore, seem to prefer the mass hypnosis of losing themselves in a giant assembly on what is supposed to be their afternoon of relaxation—when they might be following more individual pursuits.

THE CONSEQUENCES OF WATCHING

For years Britain was supposed to have been the world's schoolmaster in sport, but recently the pupil nations have equalled, and currently surpassed, the originator of most of the more popular international sports. The reason is not hard to discover. The more people who watch, and the fewer people who take part in, the various athletic pursuits obviously affect the general standard of games in any country.

With the possible exception of the U.S.A., British sport probably attracts more spectators, per population, than any other nation. Foxhunting has been described as "the pursuit of the uneatable by the unspeakable," and an equally harsh criticism might be applied to the vast crowds who congregate for their Saturday afternoon soccer-watching, since it could be said that it is the muscular minority being watched by the "miniature" majority.

Yet, with all the criticisms which can justly be levelled against the mass spectator sports, the interest in games like association football is distinctly more healthy than unhealthy. Gambling, through the Pools, has certainly increased the attendance and the interest in soccer. But I have never heard it

suggested, by even the most disgruntled punter, that the honesty of individual teams or players has been affected by the vast sums of money involved.

On the credit side is the fact that supporting games—even in the role of a spectator—means a few hours in the open air; and if only a small percentage feel the urge to emulate their heroes, by going out on common land and kicking a ball about however desultorily, there is at least that advantage over the surrender to the other manufactured entertainments like the cinema or the radio.

An interesting development in sport crowds is the astonishing increase in recent years among women "fans." The more obviously spectacular sports, where little specialized knowledge is required, are clearly the most popular. Outstanding among them is speedway racing, where there must be nearly a fifty-fifty ratio between the sexes. Few women have either the patience or the technical appreciation to attend three-day cricket matches—unless they are very fond of their fiancés or husbands—but at speedway, to a lesser extent at soccer, and in a different way at boxing, the female fan is on the increase and is making her voice heard in more than one sense.

Speedway, although one of the most artificial, is in fact one of the healthiest sports of all from the spectator's point of view. There are few stories of its "crookedness" which have a vestige of truth in them, and although it is an evening sport and many of the arenas are sited inaccessibly, it is the most truly family affair amongst all the major spectacular entertainments.

If the 1940's are to be known as the Atomic Age, the first third of the twentieth century might well be sub-titled the age of sport. Before that time sport was comparatively simple. There was cricket played on the village green and on the private grounds of the great country houses. There was football which was by no means an essentially proletarian game until well into the twentieth century. Prize-fighting was a hole-and-corner business. Track and field athletics were essentially local affairs, and most other sports were largely regional, creating little interest outside the district in which they took place.

The era of speedway racing, ice hockey, cycling, lawn tennis and golf, was still either unknown or far beyond the ken and interest of the man in the street. Horse racing of course there was—but difficulties of transportation and lack of the publicity which nowadays is taken as a matter of course made all but the most famous events relatively unimportant. One sport which attracts its millions nowadays was then completely unknown— dog racing. In the country districts, particularly in the North, fanciers coursed their whippets, but the mechanical hare which was to introduce "roulette on four legs" was not seen until the late nineteen-twenties.

It is difficult, if not impossible, to draw a distinction between sports and pastimes. Fifty years ago you would have been laughed at as a lunatic had you suggested that ping-pong had any function in sporting life other than as a mild *divertissement* for the ladies of the house. Today hard-headed commercial sports impresarios put table tennis on in their ferro-concrete stadia, and attract entrants from more than a score of countries and crowds of over ten thousand.

On the other hand, today croquet is a standing joke to many people; yet Wimbledon, which is one of the most famous names in the world of sport, is still the home of the All England Lawn Tennis and Croquet Club —although I must admit that among all its gracious lawns one does not often notice the one reserved for croquet. Fashions in games, as well as in clothes, alter with rapidity.

If the preceding selections are looked over, it will be apparent that quite a few patterns of association have been discussed, some fairly thoroughly. These include the community, treated in Selections 124 and 125 primarily as a settlement pattern rather than as an area of unified social relations. Other patterns are work and economic groups, particularly the trade union, the family, age and sex groupings, and educational, religious, and recreational organizations.

The next selection turns to quite a different social institution, the British government, and briefly sketches the relations of the Monarchy, the Parliament, and the local government. The enormous importance of the government as an agency of economic control has already been pointed out in the discussion of nationalization, and in Selection 143 its paramount position in the fields of public health and welfare will be shown.

• 142 • The British Government

The British Parliament has two Houses—the House of Lords and the House of Commons. Great Britain has no written Constitution; Government is based on liberties won and Acts passed throughout the generations. Today complete legislative power is invested in the hands of the elected representatives of the people of Britain. The history of Parliament dates back to the thirteenth century when it first became the maker of laws and levier of taxes. The power of Parliament— and with it the liberties of the people—grew throughout the centuries: the law of Habeas Corpus passed in 1678 (by which people could not be held in jail without trial) and the Bill of Rights of 1689, were landmarks.

[Adapted from *A Picture of Britain: Background of a People,* British Information Services, New York, 1946. Pp. 39-46. Used by permission.]

The result of this long history is that the Government of Britain is a blend of modern democracy, traditional customs, survivals and precedents which is sometimes hard to understand. The principle and practice of government is entirely democratic but certain traditional organs and practices have been retained because they are believed to be useful and practical safeguards. An example of this is the function of the House of Lords. By the Parliament Act (1911) most of the real legislative power of the House of Lords was removed. It no longer has an ultimate veto on Bills passed by the Commons. The most it can do is to delay a money Bill for one month, and return an ordinary Bill for reconsideration by the House of Commons three times. The House of Lords provides a valuable debating chamber and a "second thought," while the Commons is the active legislative body.

Great Britain is an hereditary monarchy. The King is the head of the State and fulfills a- very important practical function in providing continuity and helping the smooth working of the Government system. He is also in constant consultation with members of his Government and his experience may contribute much to their deliberations. Most of the King's traditional powers, however, were delegated to the Government or are now unexercised. For instance, the King has a theoretical power to veto Bills but never now exercises it: Ministers are appointed and dismissed in the name of the King, but always on the advice of the Prime Minister. The same applies to the dissolution of Parliament. The King does not enter into party politics but remains above politics as a symbol of the nation as a whole.

The House of Lords has the power to introduce Bills, but confines itself to introducing Bills dealing with uncontroversial and, often, with specialized matters. In addition to the peers who owe their title to birth, a large part of the membership of the House of Lords is made up of peers who have been given titles in recognition of valuable public service in such spheres as law, administration, science, or education. The House has thus a valuable function as a body of experts.

The House of Commons is made up of the directly elected representatives of the people from 640 constituencies. In normal times the maximum duration of a Parliament is five years, at the end of which a General Election must be held. General Elections are also held when the political party in power loses the confidence of the House and wishes to appeal to the country. By-Elections are held in any constituency where the seat becomes vacant through the death of the Member or other cause.

Members of Parliament get a salary of $2,400. Anyone can stand as a candidate for Parliament provided he or she can get eight electors to sign his nomination. He then pays a deposit which he forfeits if he does not get one-eighth of the votes cast. This ruling is to discourage frivolous candidates. A candidate need not live in the area he wishes to represent. A limit is set to the amount which a candidate may spend on his election publicity. Candidates usually stand as the representative of one of the recognized parties, approved both by party headquarters and by the local party committee. They then benefit by the party organization and publicity. In Britain a General Election may come at any moment, so political parties have to consider the wishes of the public in their constituencies all the time; political meetings therefore play a large part in British life. When the voters go to the polls on election day they vote simply for a candidate to represent them in Parliament. Usually they can choose between two or three men representing different parties.

The leader of the political party which has a Parliamentary majority usually becomes Prime Minister and he forms a Cabinet—that is, a group of Parliamentary leaders belonging to his party—most of whom he appoints as heads of Government Departments, responsible for their administration. In addition to its executive function, the Cabinet is responsible for initiating legislation sponsored by the Government.

The Cabinet is responsible to Parliament, and the responsibility is collective: if a measure of major importance for which one Cabinet Minister is responsible is rejected by the Commons, then the Government falls, and a General Election will probably be held. Cabinet Ministers are members of the Lords or Commons and have to face constant questions in Parliament concerning the way the affairs of their Department are being conducted. "Question time" in the House of Commons represents one of the most important of Parliament's functions—the regular checking up on Ministers so that they have always to be ready to explain and defend their activities to the satisfaction of Members.

Local administration is carried out by the Local Authorities who have very extensive powers in the application of laws and in making local bye-laws. They work very closely with such central Government Departments as the Ministry of Health, the Ministry of Education, and the Home Office. Members of Local Councils are elected by direct vote. They receive no salaries.

For the purposes of local government England is broken down into County Boroughs (the largest towns) and Administrative Counties. Under these come County Districts, Urban Districts, and Rural Districts, and under them again, Parishes. Each of these subdivisions has its own council and its own clearly defined responsibilities. Much of the work is done by special Committees of Councillors. Local Authorities derive revenue from local real estate taxes known as "rates," and they also receive considerable grants from the Central Government. They handle Health, Housing, Education, the Police, and often, also, Public Utilities and Transportation in their area.

Trial by jury is a basic principle of English law. All major criminal cases in England are tried by High Court judges in the district in which they were committed. For this purpose circuit judges travel round the country holding courts, which are called "Assizes." There are two courts of appeal from the High Courts, the House of Lords being a final court of appeal. All judges are appointed for life or until retirement. Minor offenses are heard in Quarter and Petty Sessions by honorary Justices of the Peace or paid magistrates who may send the accused to trial, or, for minor offenses, impose a limited penalty.

The Scottish legal system differs in many respects from the English, Scots Law being derived ultimately from Roman Law, while English Law has developed independently.

Before the days of the Industrial Revolution, welfare needs were met chiefly in the family or the neighborhood or else by some charitable, religious organization. But with the rise of the factory system and the insecurities which it brought, increasing attention has been paid to the care of the needy, the ill, the injured, and the aged. The old Poor Law approach was to make poverty a disgrace and regard it as almost entirely the fault of the individual; the newer approach in Western Europe and in the United States is to make use of insurance programs into which wage-earner, employer, and the government participate. Where insurance, governmental or private, is inadequate, some other public funds are distributed.

Britain has gone farther in recent years than any other Western country in its efforts to provide for the emergencies and uncertainties which its citizens face. This new program to provide for the individual's welfare "from the cradle to the grave" has been described as follows in an official information bulletin:

On July 5, 1948, there came into force in Britain five important acts of Parliament dealing respectively with national insurance, industrial injuries, a national health service, the care of children, and a scheme of national assistance for those in acute need. Taken together they constitute what might well be called a new charter of social security, and enable Britain to claim that her system of security for the individual is second to none in the world.

The National Health Service has been the most widely discussed of the Acts because of the debate which has occurred in the United States over "socialized medicine." Both sides to the controversy cite the British experience to prove their points, the medical profession claiming that the quality of medical service in Britain is inferior under state supervision and that government intervention in this area is contrary to the American tradition; proponents of the proposed health bill suggest that many American people are not receiving proper medical attention owing to the concentration of doctors in the cities and the high costs of hospitalization, drugs, and physicians' fees, and that something should be done. And so the arguments run on. The issue can certainly not be settled here, but some light is thrown on the controversy by Rebecca West's calm but penetrating comments on the situation in Britain. She is one of Britain's most distinguished writers and, of course, has a firsthand familiarity with current health problems there, as well as in the United States.

• 143 • The National Health Service

REBECCA WEST

It is . . . [a] fact that the vast mass of the British people, Tory and Labour, doctors and laymen, accept the principle of the National Health Service. They are sometimes disconcerted by the way that that principle works out in practice, grumble noisily—and so they should, or wrongs would never get righted. But I think that few of them would consider it possible to abandon the principle. . . . For it is really true that the National Health Service was called into being because it was what was generally felt to be the only means of fulfilling a useful purpose; or, to be exact, certain useful purposes.

I can best show you what those purposes are by telling you how various people have been affected since July 5, 1948, when the Service was inaugurated by the Minister of Health, in pursuance of a duty laid on him two years earlier by an Act of Parliament.

Ever since then all of us except children and the old have paid certain contributions to the state under an Insurance Act. (When I give figures I will pay no attention to the devaluation of the pound.) On an employed man's insurance card the employer sticks a stamp for which he pays just under $1 and for which the employee pays $1—a total contribution of almost $2. On an employed woman's card the employer sticks a stamp for which the employer pays 65 cents and the employee 75 cents. Boys under eighteen have to have stamps on their cards amounting to rather more than half the value of those on men's cards, and the girls have to account for rather more than half the value of the stamps on a woman's card; and their employers have to pay their share. A self-employed man has to pay $1.25, a self-employed woman has to pay $1. A man who does not follow any employment has to pay just under $1; such a woman has to pay 75 cents.

I sneak in without paying, under the provision that the wife of a self-employed man

[Adapted from "Can a Nation Afford Health for All Its People?", *Ladies' Home Journal*, Vol. 67, No. 9, Philadelphia, 1950. Pp. 139-140, 142, 144, 150, 156. Used by permission.]

can participate in certain benefits, of which the National Health Service is one, on his card.

Of these contributions an average of 10 to 15 cents is allocated to the National Health Service. The rest goes to provide such benefits as old-age pensions and maternity benefits. But the sum of the contributions thus provided for the National Health Service defrayed, at the beginning, only one fifth of its cost. The proportion must be much lower now that the cost has mounted. The deficit, which was originally four fifths and must now be more, is provided from income tax and from indirect taxation, such as the duty on tea, spirits, tobacco, and so on.

The state goes off with this insurance and taxation money in its hand and enters into a contract with the doctors and surgeons and nurses and druggists and hospitals of the land, by which it agrees to pay them certain fees if they give the population free service. So now we all can consult a doctor without paying him, get all medicines prescribed by the doctor without paying the druggist, and go into a hospital without paying for the use of the bed or the operating theater or the radiological or any other department.

Let us first see how it works at the receiving end: on the patients.

You are not being at all realistic if you imagine that the National Health Service is the product of an idealism which will no longer suffer it that people shall be sick and uncared for just because they are poor.

The National Health Service does not make any earth-shaking change in the position of the sick poor. If anybody tells you about little English children in garrets who are now borne away in ambulances to be operated on by world-famous specialists and be nursed back to health by nice starched nurses in hospital wards, and suggests that these children would have been left to die in those garrets until July 5, 1948, put him down as a political propagandist and an unreliable reporter.

The lot of the sick poor has been improved in many secondary ways; but the primary situation of the patient struck down by acute illness when not possessed of means to pay doctors or nurses or hospital authorities has not been dramatically altered.

This is not a criticism of the Service. It simply means that the medical and surgical treatment and hospitalization of people with yearly incomes below $1700 was so well looked after in most parts of England that, though we would all like to make it better still, it would hardly be possible to do so in our present economic circumstances.

The British had no reason to be ashamed of the medical provision they made for their lower-income groups. First of all, they had a useful insurance system. It was introduced by our great statesman, David Lloyd George, in 1911, with the intention of taking care of employed persons who made just enough money to meet their current expenses, but could not be expected to put by the savings which would enable them to cover the cost of sickness. He put the ceiling of this section at $650 annual income. That ceiling has had to be raised twice since; now it is $1700.

This system gave the insured person the right to register with the doctor and go on his panel, as his list of patients was called, and get his medical attention free. The weakness of the system was that it made no provision for the dependents of the insured person; not their wives, not their children, not their old folk. But this was less of a hardship than might appear. Many doctors organized clubs by which insured persons on their panels could get medical attention for their families, by paying something like a quarter a week. Many other doctors never sent in a bill for services rendered to the families of their insured patients, and calculated the extra work as part of the duty they had to fulfill to get their insurance fees.

There was also the district-nursing system . . . which sent out trained nurses to visit people with low incomes in their homes and give them whatever treatment was prescribed by their doctors, even up to midwifery service. This was a remarkable success, attracting a very fine type of nurse. There were also various units for taking care of special classes among the dependents, such as maternity and child welfare, school medical inspection, and school dental services. But there is no doubt that some dependents got left out of any scheme, particularly among women past the childbearing age, and old people. They have benefited enormously from the National Health Service, under which they have the same rights as anyone else.

But where the National Health Service makes a dramatic appearance is in another field: in the middle classes. For them it is as if the sun had come out from behind the clouds, and their relief is a promise as to the state of a happier future.

Take Charles and Joan as an example of the intensity of this relief, and its social purpose. . . . Charles is an officer in the regular army, and therefore they have a house near an army post where Charles is a lecturer, not far out of London.

The other day Charles said, "We have good news for you," and Joan explained. "We're going to have a third baby. On the Health Service, bless it, so I don't mind a bit."

No political philosopher could possibly want a higher testimonial to a piece of social legislation.

Charles's army pay is between $4000 and $5000 a year, out of which they have to pay $1000 in income tax. In order to be near the army post, they have to pay a large rent for the only house which was vacant in the district.

They had their first child a year after the war ended; and it cost them, with doctor and nursing home and a nurse who had to stay two months because Joan was seriously ill after her confinement, over $500. Charles was getting less pay then and this amounted to one-fifth of the spendable income left after he had settled his income tax. Fortunately, he had his war gratuity and that met the bills. Their second child was born in the autumn of 1948, and this time there was no gratuity to fall back upon.

"We don't know what we would have done," says Charles, "if the National Health Service hadn't been set up in the meantime. We can't save off what I get. I suppose we would have had to borrow money and be slaves for the rest of our lives. As it was, we hadn't a headache. We just sat back and were glad the baby was coming."

The main trouble which afflicts the people who use the National Health Service arises, strangely enough, out of its very success. It arises out of the time factor.

If a person's time has more than a certain value it does not pay him or her to use the National Health Service. So many people are resorting to the doctors' offices and to the hospitals that the queues seem endless. Here is one instance in which the poor are actually getting less satisfactory medical attention than they had before the institution of the Service, for in many out-patient departments the time of waiting is doubled or trebled. And it is no joke sitting in a hospital waiting room when you are feeling ill.

This is at present a real defect in the system, and it would be dishonest not to admit its gravity. But time will cure it.

For one thing, these new queues of patients consist partly of people who are seeking medical attention because they do not have to pay for it. Now some of these people really do need medical attention, and could not pay for it; and they may be expected to recur in the queues. But there are others who do not need medical attention, and come simply because they like getting something for (apparently) nothing. Of these some will weary. It is not really very amusing, consulting doctors and going to hospitals. If you object that there have always been paying patients who found it amusing to consult doctors and go to clinics, and never seemed to weary of it, you are forgetting that now that doctors and clinics are no longer paid by these patients, they will probably throw them out.

Certain districts can be named by the Medical Practices Committee, which consists of seven doctors and two laymen, as "closed areas," and the committee may refuse any practitioner permission to set up in such an area if they think that it already contains too many doctors competing for the care of the sick. When this system has been working for some years the existing number of doctors will be fairly distributed all over Great Britain, and there will be no need for any doctor to have more patients on his panel than he can treat without reasonable delay.

But the transitional stage is uncomfortable; and how it could have been avoided I cannot see.

The doctors made a great fuss about coming into the National Health Service, but that was largely because the Minister of Health, Mr. Aneurin Bevan, made a dogfight of the negotiations with the British Medical Association over the terms on which they were to come in; and the secretary of the British Medical Association, Doctor Hill, is a bit of a bulldog himself. But there are working on doctors exactly the same forces which reconciled their middle-class patients to the Service.

I know very well how it used to be in the medical profession, because my sister is a doctor. With the help of the scholarships which Andrew Carnegie, of Pittsburgh, gave to his native Scotland and the self-sacrifice of my mother, she went through Edinburgh University with hardly a penny at the back of her. So, though she was the top of her year in surgery, there was no question of her becoming a surgeon, which is a much more common activity among women in Great Britain than it is in the United States. She had nobody to finance her through the long period of working without reward which was the necessary preliminary to a surgeon's career. She could not even raise the money to buy a practice. Some of the women in her year had parents rich enough to start them as surgeons; nearly all of them, after a few years, had practices bought for them. And notoriously parents have less money to spend on their daughters than on their sons.

Now times are changed. So the National Health Service looks very pleasant to a young doctor who wants to be a general practitioner. He takes his degree, holds some hospital posts, goes into practice in some area that is not "closed," and can have as many National Health Service patients as he can get up to the number of 4000 at an annual capitation fee of $3.50, and a payment for patients in outlying districts based on the mileage he has to cover to get to them, and fees varying from $25 to $35 for obstetric cases. He can also take private patients if he can find the time. He cannot cultivate these better-paying cases at the expense of his National Health Service patients, because he is strictly supervised and his National Health Service patients can file complaints against him before a stern and impartial tribunal. No doctor is engaged by the National Health Service on terms that make him a full-time servant of the state, for that is held to be dangerous. He might become a slave of the state.

On the whole, however, the general practitioner is not displeased by his financial position under the Act. He has security. But how does it affect his work?

Well, this business of overcrowding, of overwork, though it is temporary, is feared by some doctors to be doing permanent harm to medicine. They say that the doctor who finds himself faced with a mob of patients tends to send all of them who have anything but the simplest maladies off to hospital, and so tends to become a diagnostician on a very low level of diagnosis. It is partly, they say, the doctor who yields to this temptation who is responsible for the hospital outpatient queues.

He is also making barren a most fertile field of medicine. For the general practitioner, and only the general practitioner, can get thorough views of illnesses in relation to the whole life of the individual who is suffering from them.

. . . The real charge against the National Health Service [is] that it costs too much.

. . . When the Act was introduced in 1946 it was estimated that it would cost $508,000,000. By the time the Service was inaugurated, two years later, the estimates had risen to $832,500,000. In 1949 the estimates rose still further, and this year we are landed with an estimate for 1951 of $1,600,000,000.

Now it is possible to be too badly frightened by these figures. A great proportion of these sums represents money that would have been spent anyway on medicine, whether the Service had been introduced or not. Individuals would have spent it by direct payments to doctors, nurses and hospitals; now they first pay it to the tax collector, who pays it to the doctors, nurses and hospitals on their behalf. The worry is how much money is wasted on administration costs by this indirect method and whether this wastage is counterbalanced by the quite real saving effected by bulk buying of medical care.

But it is only sane to feel some fright, and indeed considerable fright, at these figures.

They mean that Great Britain is paying out $32 a head for medical care. Now, you cannot pay out what you do not earn. If you consider that out of our population of 50,000,000, 10,355,000 are under nineteen, and that another 5,250,000 are over sixty-five, you will see what a load this bill is on the producing adults between these ages.

You can gather what our plight is by comparing your expenditure with ours. Our national income a year ago was about $42,-480,000,000; yours [U.S.A.] was about $221,-500,000,000. You have more than five times as great a national income as we, which means considerably more margin. But 40 per cent of our income and only 24 per cent of yours goes in taxation. I again beg you, please do not put down that difference just as thriftlessness. We have had two world wars; we really are trying to work out an economy in which all citizens can be guaranteed full employment, which is not a contemptible aim. But it makes life difficult. The mere fact that 16,000,000 of our population—that is, 32 per cent of it—are too old or too young to be in full production explains why it is very difficult for us to have only 60 per cent of our national income at our own disposal as private persons.

The part of the taxation which goes to the National Health Service takes 5½ per cent of our national income.

It is misleading to consider it as an isolated payment. To get its full unpleasantness, consider it in conjunction with another tax—our defense tax. You lay out 3.5 per cent of your national income on that; we lay out 7 per cent of ours. That and the National Health Service account for 12½ per cent of our national income. And that percentage is increasing.

Now, why does the Service cost so much? Partly, of course, because some silly people

are rushing to take advantage of a service which appears to give them something for nothing, and are seeing doctors and buying medicines which they do not really need. But that will wear out in time. . . .

But there is one item which, alone and inevitably, even if every person connected with the giving and receiving end of the National Health Service had behaved like angels, would have made it enormously costly. The Service had to take over the hospitals. They were in such a desperate condition that the National Health Service would have had to be created to get them on their feet, if for no other reason.

Any hospital, in any country, is a frightening economic portent today. Ours were especially frightening because of what happened to them during the war. A hospital is a very delicate and complicated organism and it would have to be a very hardy specimen to survive what was done to nearly all of them between 1939 and 1945.

CONCLUSION

I have left out so many aspects of the Service I wanted to describe, but I hope I have convinced you that the British National Health Service is not just a folly. It is not meaningless. It is a muddle and a monster and a premature baby. It can never work out to everybody's satisfaction, even if it is unmuddled and grows up normal and gets out of the incubator looking fine. Remember this: A National Health Service must be a disappointment, however successful it is. It is bound to be taken as a promise to give the whole population first-class medical and surgical treatment. Well, it can't do that. There are not enough first-class doctors, surgeons, dentists, oculists or nurses to go round, and not enough hospital beds. You are up against a natural insufficiency here; and if you quarrel with it you will have to quarrel with the same insufficiency which makes it impossible to guarantee every citizen a wife as beautiful as Elizabeth Taylor, and a Park Avenue apartment. In any National Health Service a large proportion of the population will have to make do with second-rate attention, and maybe some that is not so good as that. But that would be more grimly true without a National Health Service, and we are better off with one, for it has a purpose, and unless there is another war and unless we all fail in our duties, it should fulfill it.

There are four points which the Service has impressed on me, and I think it may be useful to Americans to hear what they are:

1. The National Health Service of Great Britain is not a piece of Socialist freakishness, but a necessity recognized by intelligent citizens of all parties. The bulk of the population came out of the Second World War unable to pay for medical attention on the scale which was necessary if doctors and nurses were to make a living, and the hospitals were tottering toward insolvency.

If the pressure of history acts on the population and on your hospitals in the same unkind way, you Americans will need, not want —it won't matter whether you want it or not, you will need it—a National Health Service of your own.

2. Start examining the medical landscape early to see if that need is appearing, for the chief thing necessary for the establishment of an efficient health service is time. It has to be based on calculations beyond the power of any community to collect or consider quickly. It is an enterprise comparable to the mobilizing of the Army or Navy or Air Force after the outbreak of a war. Its accountancy alone presents catastrophic possibilities of waste. Ask anybody whose wartime work lay in the finance department of any war-created unit of the Administration if you want confirmation of this statement.

3. It is necessary to frame the conditions of the National Health Service so that it is easy for the persons drawing benefit to understand how much it costs, and who pays for it, and what their own contribution to that payment, direct or indirect, is. Children should be taught the mechanism of the fund in schools, and the figures should be displayed in public places. When people overspent in the old days, they knew it because their purses were empty. Now they can overspend and never know it, because their purses are empty anyway, as they hand over most of their money to the tax collector, and they cannot tell when his purse is empty. This is a new problem arising out of a new and complicated way of living and it has to be met by education.

4. A National Health Service should be lifted out of the political field, because it will be a success or a failure according to the degree to which it is regarded objectively. In America you have a bipartisan foreign policy, and it is just as necessary to have a bipartisan health policy. Nobody should be allowed to cheer or boo anything connected with such a service. The only demonstration allowable is a slight knitting of the brows, such as might be provoked by the working out of a mathematical problem.

In spite of the obvious fact that all these points spring from my sense that our National Health Service is not so good as it might be, I invite you Americans with confidence to come to Great Britain ten years from now and look at it. By then it will be something to be proud of; and you may think we were not so foolish for frankly admitting when times have changed and the old arrangements for meeting the physical crises of life had broken down, and setting about making new ones. There are many different sorts of pioneering.

Throughout this study of the Midlands there has been emphasis on the numerous and profound changes that have taken place in a few generations. The most conspicuous have been in the way the people make their living, in the growth of industrial enterprises, and in the rapid concentration of population in great conurbations. Such changes as the replacement of the wagon and stagecoach by railroads, cars, and trucks have been dramatic in their suddenness and have tended to focus attention on the technological aspects of the recently developed industrial society. But changes have also been marked in the area of social relationships. The changed status of woman from the eighteenth century to the midpoint of the twentieth is a good indication of the way in which the whole of society has had to adjust to the new forces. Community life has become much more complicated, particularly in contrast with the village, which was once prominent in the social scene. Governmental pressures are now observed on every hand, although in Britain—and particularly in the Midlands—there is strong resistance by local governmental authorities to any encroachment from Whitehall (the executive seat of the national government). One-time religious functions, such as support of the needy and promotion of education, have become less important; family life is less centered about the home; and recreational pursuits are much more commercialized.

Paralleling changes in the social organization are modifications in the value system and in the beliefs and ideologies of the people. We have noted in each society described in this book a close correspondence between the status system and the set of social values. In Britain, status is centered in the social classes, whose importance shifts as new ideas and new values prevail.

The last pattern of association to be discussed is social class. The ramifications of British classes are complex and at times contradictory, but C. Arnold Anderson has identified five basic divisions. The top class consists of the royal family. One member of this family, usually a man but sometimes a woman, is the titular head of the British Empire and the symbol of its unity. The second highest class is the nobility, with specific titles which represent social divisions among the nobles. The gentry come next. Sometimes they are called the landed gentry because many own fairly large estates. Some members of the gentry are related to various nobles but do not themselves have titles. The gentry might be called junior-grade nobility. Ranked below the gentry is the middle class or, as an indication of the divisions within it, the middle classes. It consists mostly of city or town people who own small businesses or hold the more responsible positions in business and industry. At the bottom is the lower, or working, class. The most highly skilled workers rate highest within this group and sometimes are counted as lower middle class. Semiskilled workers generally rank below the skilled, and unskilled and casual laborers are at the lowest level of the lower class.

It is generally believed that there is less social mobility in Britain than in the United States, though exact figures for comparison are lacking. Class distinctions are sharper in Britain, and hence it is more difficult for an individual to pass gradually from one class to another. On the other hand, a title of nobility may be inherited by one of the gentry, or a middle-class man may be granted a noble title. Some workers manage to move up into the middle class. Downward movement in the social scale is also possible, usually as the result of economic circumstances.

A study of postwar Britain is a clear case study of how a social structure can be made to harmonize with shifting values, all the while reciprocally influencing the value system so that moderate rather than extreme values are accepted.

The selection that follows has been prepared for this book by Margaret Stacey, who is connected with the first rigorous investigation of social class in Britain. This investigation has taken into account some of the recent research done in the United States. The conclusions set forth here are tentative, for the study has not been finished. They supposedly hold true for a single South Midlands market town which has been increasingly industrialized since the 1930's. What happens to a staid agriculturally oriented community, with some light industry, when an aluminum plant opens up and a flood of managers and workmen come in from outside? This article analyzes the changes chiefly from the standpoint of social class and, in doing so, reveals much about the changes in individual attitudes and social organization.

• 144 • Industrialization and the Class System in Market Town
MARGARET STACEY

Market Town is in the South Midlands of England, but does not form part of that industrial belt known as the "Black Country." It is, in fact, in the English scale, surprisingly isolated. There is no town of comparable size within a radius of 20 miles. It lies in a hollow, protected to the west and north by a line of hills and commands a plain which opens out to the south and east. As a market town it serves an area of approximately ten miles radius, which will be referred to as the Survey Area. For the villages in that area the pull of Market Town is greater than the pull of other neighbouring towns. The frontier of the Survey Area has been defined by those villages which respond equally to these two pulls.

Until the middle of the nineteenth century, the town was strictly a market town, a centre of distribution and exchange. Its industries were ancillary to the agricultural activities of the surrounding country area—flour milling, brewing, and hand-loom weaving for example —and it provided commercial and other services. In 1848 its first industrialisation took place, when a new works for the manufacture of agricultural implements was founded. A canal had been cut earlier (in the 1770's) to link the Midlands to the north with centres of population in the south. In 1850 the first railway was opened. These activities led to the first large-scale influx of "alien" workers, some Irish, but most probably from other parts of this country. The town, therefore, began at

that time to take on a modern industrial complexion, but it should be emphasized that its main new industry was connected with agriculture and, while its products were sold further afield than the Survey Area, nevertheless it stood in a functional relation to the main activity of the area, agriculture. The agricultural implement industry flourished, and the town with it, throughout the last half of the nineteenth century. In the opening years of the twentieth century, however, it failed to maintain its position (largely, as far as one can tell, because the founder had not passed on his business acumen to his son). From about 1911 onwards there is evidence that the town was stagnating. The increase in the population was small and less than the natural increase. It did not share the population expansion of those years that took place in the rest of the country. At the 1931 census, there were some 13,000 souls living in the Borough. In that year an important change began, the results of which form the basis for the present study. A big new aluminium factory began to be built to produce sheet and extruded aluminium. By 1933 it began production and by 1935 large numbers of workers were coming into the town to man the new industry. In a period, therefore, when large areas of the country were suffering from heavy unemployment, Market Town began to prosper and expand again, and to change its nature [so that the] town now has a population of between 18,000 and 19,000 and about 5,000 houses.

In the town itself, about one-third of the working population is now employed in the aluminium factory. The factory is part of a large combine, its ownership is largely Canadian, its raw material is imported, its products have no particular relation to the area and go elsewhere to be finished. The great majority of its senior executives are not natives of the town, and many of its workers are immigrants of 15 years standing at the most. It forms, in fact, a complete contrast to the traditional economic activities of Market Town, based as they were on goods and services produced locally or for local consumption, and run in the main as family concerns or small limited companies. In the inter-war years, other similar changes in the economic structure also took place. Other firms, parts of national or international combines, opened factories in the town, and, a change which has altered the physical appearance of the town, more and more shops were sold to chain stores, some large, some small, but all making the shopping streets of the town centre lose their peculiar Market Town character, and look more like those in any other English town. This process continues.

Figures of employment in the major industrial groups may summarize more concisely the economic structure of the town today:

Industrial Group	Total
Metal processing (chiefly aluminium)	3,300
Distributive trades, hotels, catering and food processing	2,400
Agriculture and horticulture	1,600
Building	1,600
Transport, including railways and storage	1,500
Other manufactures	600
Domestic service (nonresident)	500

The income structure is also interesting. No one in Market Town receives a net personal income of over 2000 pounds per annum, and very few over 1000 pounds. This compares with a national distribution in which, in 1948, 175,000 received net incomes of over 2000 pounds, and 760,000 over 1000 pounds

out of a total of known incomes of 3,210,000 (the numbers of people who earn under 250 pounds per annum are not known nationally and are excluded from this total).

The purpose of this study of Market Town is to analyse the effects of the immigration into the town; more precisely to test whether the town is split into two groups, native and immigrant, and if so, whether this division is deeper and more important than other social divisions. Of other social divisions in the town, social class is one of the most profound. [In general, social class] is a horizontal grouping with no clear boundaries, and upward and downward mobility continually takes place. But how many classes there are and where are the boundaries is not clear. The factors that go to make up the concept, such as occupation, income, education, residence area, manners and, in some cases, family connection, are also fairly clear, but in what proportion these factors combine to determine membership of a social class is unclear. However, it is quite clear that, except at the extremes, income alone is now practically meaningless as a guide to social class in England. Any conclusions must be tentative at this stage. Some points of interest have already become clear, however.

It has generally been considered in England that there are three main social classes: Upper, Middle, and Lower or Working, but that within each of these divisions there is more than one division, particularly in the middle group which is almost always referred to as the Middle Classes. The significant factor which divides the Upper and Upper Middle from the rest would seem to be the possession of a Public School (in the English sense) education. This forms the limit to a man's upward mobility. He may have achieved all the other necessary factors, but he can never quite qualify for the Upper Class without this educational background. If he gives it to his children they will be received into this class so long as they, too, qualify on the other grounds. The significant divide between the middle class and the working class seems to be not so much one of education, but of occupation. Here two factors operate: whether one is employer or employee and whether one's work is manual or non-manual. To be a professional worker, an executive, an owner of industry or shop places one in the middle class; to be a manual worker places one in the working class. On the margin are the low-grade clerical workers.

On this basis in Market Town one finds only two main social classes: the middle and working classes. The upper class in the national sense are absent from the Borough. They are to be found, however, living in the survey area, in the large houses, often but not always, with considerable land attached. At the top level are those with titles who may be wealthy industrial magnates or who may have few possessions apart from house and title. In this group, too, are the "County" families, who, while they may not be titled, qualify for membership. Market Town itself not only has none of these people within its boundaries, but the senior executives of the large-scale industries of the town live outside, too. With the exception of one or two professional workers who qualify for the frontiers of the upper class on grounds of education, the upper class of Market Town itself is part of the national middle class. It is composed of professional men, doctors and solicitors, and the better-off owners of shops and small works in the town. From this group downwards all the shades of the social class pattern are reflected in the town.

Some interesting changes have taken place in the class structure of the town in the last twenty to thirty years. Twenty-five years ago there were one or two "County" families living in the town. Now all are gone. Furthermore, with one or two exceptions, members of the Upper Class living in the surrounding area now play no part at all in the life of the Borough. Managers of chain stores who have come into the town in this period have not been accepted as members of the shop-owning elite. They in some ways form a group on their own and to some extent group with the lower middle class, the responsible clerical worker, and the skilled craftsman. The managers of government departments which have opened new offices in the town again have not fitted into the existing class pattern. Nor have the junior executives of the aluminium industry and of other concerns. Again, and this has occurred throughout the country, there has grown up a new group of clerical workers which has complicated the class pattern.

Any attempt to divide the town rigidly into classes at this stage would be rash. But with all the limitations perhaps the attempt might be worth while. One's impressions and evidence to date would give the following scale. (Occupation, because it seems to be the most important factor, has been used to illustrate the type of people one might expect to find in the groups which comprise the scale. It should not be inferred from this that occupation is thought of as the only, or the finally decisive, determinant of class membership.)

I. (Outside the town)

II. (Outside the town in the main)

III. (In the town and in surrounding villages)

IV. (In the town)

V. (In the town)

VI. (In the town)
VII. (In the town)
VIII. (In the town)

Upper Class: Public School education, possibly title.

Upper Middle Class: Senior executives of large-scale industry not included in I.

Middle Class: Professional men; owners of all except smallest shops and small factories. Bank managers, and senior executives of industry.

Middle Class: Small men working on their own account; junior executives. Managers of chain stores.

Lower Middle Class: Managers of chain stores. Routine clerical workers. Some skilled artisans.

Working Class: Skilled.

Working Class: Semi-skilled.

Working Class: Unskilled.

This scale for what it is worth must be read as a continuum with much overlapping at the boundaries. The tests which give stronger divisions than any others are:

(*a*) Public school education.
(*b*) Employer or employee.
(*c*) Manual or non-manual work.

Not only is the class pattern of the town as a whole changing, but people move from one social class to another. Competition to move upward, to "keep up with the Joneses," to spend visibly, is not so open as one gathers from social studies that it is in the U.S.A., but pressure is nevertheless there. This pressure is not overtly admitted. To state openly one's upward aspirations is not done; indeed, the pattern is rather to deny such aspirations and to deny the existence of social class altogether (a factor which makes it very difficult to study). The pressure to "get on" is often resisted; working class informants have explained how they refused an opportunity to set up in business on their own account, or are worried that their child has obtained a place in the grammar school because it may unsettle him. They prefer a secure place in the working class to the difficulties and insecurities, both real and imagined, of attempting to climb up. Neither is there in Market Town a general conviction that anyone can get to the top if he tries. Those who have "got on" or have "bettered themselves" are admired, if grudgingly; but the general philosophy, particularly in the working class, is to recognize that one is a member of that class and to attempt to improve the lot of the class as a whole, rather than of oneself as an individual, in competition with other members of the class. That mobility is an important factor is, however, clearly observable. In general, it would be true to say that if one stays in Market Town it takes two generations to reach the elite from the lower middle class or the working class.

To assess what effect social class has on the life of the town is difficult, but must be attempted. In the first place, if you are a child in Market Town, your father's social class membership will determine the education you receive, which will in its turn set limits to the amount of upward mobility that is possible for you.

If your father is working class or lower middle class, you will almost certainly go to the State primary school. You will then stand a chance at 11 years of age of winning entrance to the State secondary grammar school. Given equivalent intelligence, your chance of doing this will be greater the higher on the social scale your father is, partly because you will have a better environment for study and more encouragement and partly because of an unconscious bias on the part of the selectors. Despite the aim of the 1944 Education Act to provide "secondary education for all" with its implication of equality and its overt aim to provide education fitted to the "age, ability and aptitude" of the pupil, there is a clearly marked status system. Within the State secondary schools in Market Town, as in the rest of the country, this status grading is in the order grammar, technical and modern, and is related to the status grading of the occupations that pupils from these schools obtain. If you reach the grammar school and do well and your parents are prepared to sacrifice to keep you there beyond the compulsory school-leaving age of 15, you stand a chance of a scholarship or grant to any university in the country, but it is more likely that you will go to a provincial university than to Oxford or Cambridge. Then a great deal of upward mobility would be possible for you short of breaking into the upper class itself.

If, on the other hand, your father is in the middle class, you may be sent to a private school. Here you may get a better or a worse education than you would have at a State school, but you may gain in social prestige. Or the school you go to may be an independent or endowed fee-paying school where you will get an education at least equivalent in merit to a State grammar school and rather more social prestige than if you had gone to the State secondary grammar school.

Again, if your father is a professional man or in the upper middle class, you may well be sent to a Public School, which ranks highest in the social status grading of English schools, although within the Public School system there is a clear status grading again.

In these ways the education most people receive will be determined by their parents' social class and will set some limits to the amount of upward mobility possible for them: not because education is the most significant feature of social class in Market Town, but because of the close connection between education and occupation. This relationship between a parent's social class on the one hand and his child's education and subsequent occupation and, therefore, ultimate social class on the other is becoming to some extent blurred by the increase in opportunities for scholarships, but the pattern remains essentially the same; now more people can go further, but not yet can anybody go all the way.

The second important way in which social class operates in Market Town is in limiting the people one may meet and who, therefore, may become one's friends. This is shown in the membership of formal organizations in the town. By formal organizations we understand any institution which has a formal membership. It therefore includes churches and their ancillary institutions, trade associations and unions, social clubs, cultural organizations and the like. In the main these organizations (excluding the churches) can be divided into two main groups, Middle Class and Working Class. It is only on Government- or Borough-sponsored committees, deliberately balanced, that these two groups meet. Although I have excluded the churches from this description, within them the class pattern is also found. There is a tendency for people higher on the social scale to be in the Church of England and for people lower to be in the smaller non-conformist chapels.

Thirdly, where one lives and in what kind of house is closely connected with one's social class position. This again limits one's possibilities for social contact, although Market Town is still small enough for the residence areas not to be so clearly demarcated as one would find in a city. The ideal to which the town aspires seems to be to own a detached

house in its own ground, screened from prying eyes by walls, hedges or trees, on the higher ground to the south or west or in one of the neighbouring villages. Generally, however, a large semi-detached house is what the elite of the town finally achieve, or an old good class house, sometimes in a terrace. Most of the rest of the middle class and a few of the skilled workers live in semi-detached three-bedroom houses built between or after the wars, and which they buy by instalments. The workers are housed for the most part in Council houses, which they rent, or in nineteenth-century terraced houses.

In sum, therefore, one's social class membership determines the education one's children will receive, the organizations it is possible for one to join, the place one will live and the friends one can make.

Having attempted to assess the extent and importance of social class in the life of Market Town, some attempt must now be made to assess the effect of immigration. One difficulty is immediately encountered in this attempt. It is not enough to say that certain things were before the immigration and certain other things are now, and so the differences are the results of the immigrants coming to Market Town. Along with the arrival of immigrants came an increase in the size of the town. Some of the changes that one observed, therefore, may merely be a response to the increased scale of the town and not to the influence of immigrants as persons. Again, some of the changes may be reflections of changes in the national pattern and not be at all directly connected with the immigration into Market Town.

About half of the inhabitants of Market Town were born and brought up elsewhere. These newcomers came from Yorkshire and Lancashire, from industrial Wales and industrial Scotland, in fact from all those areas that suffered severe depression in the early 1930's. Many came, too, from surrounding villages and small towns and represent part of the "rural drift" of the inter-war years. It is difficult to put one's finger on the tensions that resulted and remain from this influx, partly because it is a technique in Market

Town of dealing with the outcast not to make an open breach but just to leave him alone. Objections to new people, new ideas, or new organizations are rarely, if ever, expressed in public. In general terms it seems that, in the early stages of immigration, it was the immigrants who felt the tension; they complain that they were "left out," did not get service in the shops, and so on. Now it seems to be the old inhabitants who are on the defensive; they give the impression of withdrawing into their own groups and pursuing a policy of noncooperation. Tensions are now revealed over the allocation of Council houses (other things being equal, long residence in the town counts in an applicant's favour); in the fear of Trade Union organizers that in the event of a strike the native inhabitants would not stand solid; in the refusal of owners of shops and small works to follow a lead given by the new large industries.

Apart from changes in the social class pattern which have already been described, there have been changes in the social structure since the recent industrialization of the town. New organizations have been formed, notably a Rotary Club and a Trades and Labour Club. Immigrants play a large role in both of these, which leads one to conclude that they are immigrant organizations, but how far it is simply that the town is now large enough to carry such organizations is difficult to assess. For the rest, the immigrants appear to join organizations rather less than do old inhabitants.

A difference between the immigrant and the old inhabitant is that the latter have many more relations in the town, have family and kin to fall back on and which provide a "ready made" social group. The immigrant has to make his own social group or remain an isolate. For this reason, at one time, we expected that the final analysis would show more immigrants than old inhabitants in formal organizations, but this does not now appear to be the case. A surprisingly large number of immigrants, too, have been shown to have relatives in the town—brothers or sisters, whom they recommended to come, or parents who have retired and taken a house near their children who work here. This may show that the strength of kinship ties is rather greater than one expected in a geographically mobile urban population. But these ties are still clearly stronger for the old inhabitant.

Immigrants show some interesting behaviour differences from the old inhabitants. They go to church or chapel less frequently. It is not simply that they come from places with a less church-going tradition, although this is so in some cases, but that by moving they have broken a habit learned in childhood and connected with one particular church or chapel and have not transferred the habit to a new church in a new town. Some even go so far as to say that they always go to church when they go back home for a visit, but have never been inside one in Market Town. In general, immigrants tend to be rather less traditional in their behaviour than the real Market Town people; they have broken with the traditions of their old town and have not accepted the traditions of Market Town. Again, they are less worried about large-scale organizations. The man brought up in Market Town distrusts a concern which is larger than he can see at one glance.

The aim of this study was to assess to what extent the town was divided into two groups, native and immigrant, and whether this was the most important social division. The tentative conclusion which has been arrived at is that while there is such a division, and that tensions result from it, it is a less profound division than the social class division; less profound because membership in the native or immigrant group does not affect one's total life situation to the extent that social class membership does.

Enduring Social Values

>>>

B efore we read the concluding selection on the English Midlands, it will be worth while to consider for a moment longer the importance of the consciousness of social class. It seems strange to many Americans that the strict adherence to such a status system would not divide English society into conflicting groups and open the way for deep rifts in the national unity. On the contrary, there is relatively little clash or conflict along the lines of the class structure. The reason, to a great extent, is to be found in the almost complete adherence to a set of permanent *values*, a set of attitudes as to what is right and proper and what is expected of an individual in all circumstances. The elements making up the English system of values are numerous, but C. Arnold Anderson has selected the following as among the most significant in making English society stable and unified. (It should be noted that the stress is on *England*; Scotland, North Ireland, Wales, and perhaps Cornwall do not readily fit into Anderson's pattern.)

First, English ideals are epitomized in the phrase "For God, King, and Country."

Secondly, England developed, early in her history, a strong sense of patriotism, a sense of being a nation, and a sense of the people's being subjects of her monarch. This has been constantly reinforced in her literature and is reinforced and complemented by the strong local patriotism toward county and village.

Thirdly, the royal family, and especially the king or queen, are symbols of English ideals.

The Church—that is, the Established Church, to which the upper classes belong— has always exerted a strong influence in English life, even after the extensive development of nonconformist churches.

Propriety, respectability, and diligence are stressed. Ambition and hard work are admired, but they must be tempered with an avoidance of display, with careful conformity to one's "proper" social position, and with morality.

Finally, but by no means of least importance, there is the strong sense of good sportsmanship and fair play, as voiced in the expression, "Let the best man win."

With all this in mind, we can appreciate the final selection by a well-known American historian. It forms a fitting close to our discussion of an industrial society because it is important to remember that, although numerous and rapid changes occur, there must be a considerable degree of stability if a society is to endure. In this selection, by Henry S. Commager, we note the persistence of certain social values and the way in which they give the society a consistency—serving as a social cement. Social change is characteristic of industrialized societies, but it need not result in complete disorganization as long as people perform their roles in terms of widely accepted social values.

• 145 • English Traits
HENRY S. COMMAGER

It is a little over a century ago that Ralph Waldo Emerson landed at Liverpool, spoke famously at Manchester, visited and lectured throughout England, and began writing that wonderful essay on English traits which remains the most astute and penetrating analysis of the English character in our literature. We expect perspicacity from the wisest American of his day: even from Emerson we have no right to expect prophecy, yet what is perhaps most remarkable about "English Traits" is its instinct for the permanent rather than for the transient. For if we review those traits which Emerson distinguished as peculiarly English we find that most of them persist today, flourishing vigorously after a century which has changed profoundly the position of Britain in the world, flourishing defiantly in an England dedicated to austerity and prudence as a century ago she was dedicated to luxury and power.

National character is, to be sure, everywhere wonderfully tenacious, but nowhere is it more tenacious than with the English, who have, after all, something of a patent on tenacity. And this is the first and most obvious of English traits—the stability and permanence of the English character. Come hell or high water, the Englishman remains imperturbably English. He is, it would seem, less affected by the currents and crosscurrents of history than people of any other nation; he is less affected, too, by passing fashions whether of literature or of dress or of food. Nothing will make him false to his word or discourteous to his guest; nothing will keep him from his tea or change his cooking.

Yet what is interesting about all this is that while the underlying character has remained palpably the same, that character itself is no simple thing, but wonderfully complex and even paradoxical. "England is the land of mixture and surprise," wrote Emerson, and the mixture has perplexed most of the interpreters. For the English character is not only stable and uniform, but various and heterogeneous; it is at once obvious and elusive, and almost every generalization must be not so much qualified as confounded.

A materialistic people—who can doubt it? —the English have produced more than their share of mystics and poets, of idealists and transcendentalists, more than their share of the Donnes and Herberts, the Blakes and Shelleys, the Wordsworths and Coleridges, the Foxes and Penns. The greatest colonizing people of modern times, they confess the most passionate attachment to their own country, their own county, their own community: they are at once the most indefatigable globetrotters and the best gardeners. Their wealth and their wanderlust have enabled them to

[Adapted from "English Traits," *The Atlantic Monthly,* Vol. 182, No. 2, Boston, 1948. Pp. 61-65. Used by permission.]

know the best of all other nations, but they remain true to their own: they carry their language with them wherever they go, and though every Englishman delights in French cooking, none permits his chef to imitate it.

A small nation, with a population highly mobile and highly urban, their differences in idiom and dialect and accent are the despair of foreigners; Vermonters and Texans can understand each other better than men from Devon and Lancashire, or from Glasgow and London, and if the observation that the best English is spoken in Dublin is an exaggeration, it is interesting that it should be made: no one ever suggested that the best American was spoken in Toronto. A unified and harmonious people, the English have persisted in class distinctions and divisions far more ostentatious than those to be found in most other countries; while politically they have achieved as great a degree of democracy as any other people, they remain class-conscious, and every Englishman is branded on the tongue with his class mark.

A peaceful people, tender and kind, they are, when aroused, the most belligerent of men, good friends and bad enemies, with the indomitable qualities of the bulldog. Allegedly without a sense of humor, or with a belated one, they have produced, after all, the greatest humorists of our time, and the nation which boasted Herbert Spencer boasted, at the same time, Gilbert and Sullivan. The most law-abiding of people, they write the best of all detective and mystery stories and their literature is stained with violence. Monuments of conformity—no sin is more grievous than to do what is not done—they are at the same time passionate individualists, and the nation where nonconformity is a term of rebuke is that in which eccentricity flourishes unrestrained.

This is all paradox, and it is perhaps an additional paradox that the English character, though sometimes paradoxical, is rarely puzzling and never unreliable. The broad traits are clear enough; they persist through the years, they run through all classes of society. The qualities that tend to unify are far stronger than those which divide. What, then, are the traits which have persisted?

They are a law-abiding people. Probably no other people confess the same profound respect for the law, no other conform so instinctively to the rules and regulations of government or of any organization that has authority. They do not smoke where smoking is forbidden, or walk on grass in defiance of signs, nor do they dabble in the black market or try to evade payments on their income tax, or get out of place in a queue.

That the English pay a price for this trait cannot be doubted. They are, if anything, too law-abiding and too acquiescent. They do not revolt readily enough against bad laws and troublesome regulations, but where law is concerned, they take the attitude that theirs is not to reason why.

The English have a highly developed sense of justice and of right. They want to know where they stand, and they usually do. They believe in fair play, on the playing field and in the law courts and in business. They have little patience with subtlety or cleverness: they do not want rights that can be argued about. They hate all chicanery, all evasiveness and slipperiness. They are upright and downright, foursquare and simple and stanch. They carry their sense of justice over into the political realm—in large matters of national or international policy, in small matters which have their day as questions in the House. Their law is at once just and heartless, and in matters outside the law they are philanthropic but not charitable.

They believe that every man should have his due, neither more nor less, and they have contrived a complex and rigid system to see that each has his due—and no more nor less. The English instinct for observing laws should make most controls superfluous, but much of English life seems organized on the basis of suspicion rather than of trust, and an expensive and pernicious system of checks and controls permeates [everything. The] crossed check is an English invention, and a man could as easily burgle the Bank of England as cash a check where he is not known.

The insistence that every man have his due extends from formal arrangements, like food rationing, to informal relationships, like gratuities: it is the enemy not only of favoritism but of carelessness.

In all this the English are at once the most courteous and the most discourteous of people, and the combination has confused observers for two centuries. It is the courtesy that is instinctive and pervasive, displaying itself formally in the ease of all social relationships and the quiet efficiency of all public ones, and informally in a thousand little acts of thoughtfulness. It is in part the product of training and habit—no children are more courteous than the English; it springs from respect for the individual; it is inspired by natural kindliness. It is to be found alike in individuals, in organizations, and even in crowds.

The discourtesy is a more complicated matter, a mixture of suspicion, indifference, and arrogance, and it is, as often as not, calculated. Its explanation, like that of so many English traits, can be found in the class structure and class-consciousness of English society, and the danger to that structure from anything either incomprehensible or inharmonious. Once an individual is placed, whether as publican or gentleman, as charwoman or lady, all is smooth, but the social sport, whose position and whose claims threaten the structure of the class society, is subject to endless rebuffs.

The English are an intensely practical people, infatuated with common sense. They have produced few great speculative philosophers but many practical ones: Bacon and Locke, Bentham and Mill, Spencer and Huxley, are their typical products, not men like Spinoza or Kant. They like to see a program, and they judge by results. In politics they have a wonderful feeling for the practical and the actual, an instinctive repugnance for the doctrinaire. They distrust all extremes: their Conservatives are liberal and their Liberals conservative, and even their socialism is a bundle of compromises.

For all their open-mindedness and their tolerance, they are an intensely conservative people. They hate innovation, wrote Emerson, and their instinct is to search for a prece-

dent. Even where they are forced to make changes, they change the substance rather than the form, and though English law is certainly as modern as American, the English judge still wears a wig and a King's Counsel takes the silk. They know the advantages of steam heat but distrust anything quite so modern; all the propaganda of the Food Ministry has failed to introduce experiments in cooking, and they still have, as a French wit put it a century ago, but one sauce. Where to an American the fact that something has always been done a certain way is sufficient reason for changing it, to an Englishman it is sufficient reason for retaining it.

For all their conservatism the English are progressive, and it is a peculiarity of the English character to achieve revolution through evolution. Those who speak in the House of Commons are still required to wear a hat, but what they say is rather more radical than anything that can be heard in the American Congress, and if top hats are still required at Eton, education there seems to produce men fit for the responsibilities of the new day. Oxford and Cambridge are still, to all appearances, aristocratic and even feudal institutions, yet they select their students on the basis of talent and each takes a larger percentage of its student body on scholarships than any American university.

For all their conservatism, their phlegm, they are one of the most adventurous of people. What other nation boasts a comparable galaxy of explorers, mountain climbers, navigators; what other could maintain a Hakluyt Society? From the day of Drake and Frobisher to that of Doughty and Burton the English have led the way to the strange places of the earth—always carrying with them their Englishness, even their afternoon tea, for while they are wonderfully adaptable in large matters, they make no concessions in little ones.

Although they are the greatest explorers and colonizers, and have spread the English language and laws throughout the earth, they are the most parochial of people. Even their patriotism is parochial rather than imperial, and Englishmen would find it hard to sing the praises of things they do not know as Americans of the prairie states sing the praises of rocks and rills, of woods and templed hills. The English love their own country rather than their nation, and every acre of England has its historian and its muse. The London *Times* and the Manchester *Guardian* give adequate attention to world news, but few other papers do, and English journalism, generally, is far less cosmopolitan than American.

Though proud of their Empire, the English know little about it, and they know even less of America. More Canadian history is taught at Columbia University than at Oxford, and over a period of a century and a half no English scholar has contributed anything of lasting importance to the study of American history or literature. In matters of language, too, they are parochial. They do not take readily to foreign languages, expecting foreigners rather to learn English, and they are still inclined to think the American language a sort of debased dialect.

English conservatism and parochialism are not unconnected with self-satisfaction. Recent events have, superficially, shaken this Gibraltar-like [sense] of superiority, but it persists in little things, subconsciously as it were. Thus English scholars acknowledge the achievements of Harvard or Columbia or the University of Chicago, but they know in their hearts that Oxford and Cambridge are better, and when they are not on guard their pens slip into the assertion that their higher education is the highest in the world. Most of them are still convinced that the *Times* is the greatest newspaper in the world and that if a book is not in the Bodleian it is not literature.

The English have, needless to say, ground for complacency. It is still true, as Emerson remarked, that they make well those things which are ill made elsewhere in the world. It is not skill alone that accounts for the superiority of their automobiles or their moving pictures over the American, but certain traits of character. They believe in durability, and make things to last—cars and boots and

houses, for example. They take pride in their work, and have infinite patience. They carry into affairs even of business their standards of integrity and propriety: if their books are not always exciting they are almost always well written; if their advertisements rarely lure, they do not outrage decency.

They are a thrifty people—thrifty of property, of speech, of their emotions above all. It is not merely that they prefer understatement to exaggeration; they suspect any public expression of emotion, verbal or by gesture. There is far less public love-making in England than in either America or France, and far less public manifestation of family affection. The English do not shout themselves hoarse at games, but are content to murmur "Well played," and are careful to applaud the play rather than the team.

They are thrifty of the products of their minds, as well. They prefer, on the whole, a performance that is not too brilliant, a conversationalist who is not too clever. Churchill has been suspect, all his public life, for his incomparable oratorical gifts. They distrust the ready speaker, the facile actor, the brilliant player, as they distrust men or women who are too well-dressed. They resist styles, prefer old clothes to new, and have made tweeds and the umbrella national emblems.

They have created a masculine country—a society made for men and run by men; the contrast, here, with either France or America is striking. The English home belongs to the man, not the woman—belongs legally, as far as the ownership is concerned, and psychologically, where furnishings and conveniences are concerned. In the United States, advertisements are directed to women, in England to men, and the advertisers know what they are about. England has few magazines designed primarily for women, and English banks are not fitted with special rooms where women can transact their business. The whole tone of English society is masculine: the importance of clubs, the role of the pub, the concentration of family money on the education of sons.

There are no girls' schools with the standing of Eton or Harrow or Westminster, and only [recently did] Cambridge University concede degrees to women. [All] this, [however,] has nothing to do with politics, or with literature and the arts. There are more women M.P.'s than Congresswomen, and for a generation, now, the best English novelists and critics have been women.

Not the most important, but the most pervasive and the most pernicious of English traits is class consciousness. It is not political, it is only in small part economic; it is social and psychological and philosophical. Its persistence is a tribute to the tenacity of traditional ways of thinking and acting, for it has resisted, stubbornly and successfully, the whole twentieth-century movement of democratization. Originating with the privileged classes, it is retained by the underprivileged, and class sentiment today is stronger with the lower than with the upper classes, and strongest perhaps with the middle.

It reveals itself in a thousand ways, most of them insignificant in themselves, but cumulatively not only important but controlling. In England, alone of English-speaking countries, accent betrays class. There are not only dialects for every section of England, but for each class, and the dividing lines are all but impassable, in less than two generations. The terms "lady" and "gentleman" still have meaning, and have not yielded to the leveling process; other terms, too, confess a special class significance—"top drawer," for example, while the innocuous phrase "not quite" is loaded with dynamite when applied socially. The distinctions between officers and privates in the Army, officers and ratings in the Navy, are more decisive than in the American services, and even in the recent war a public school accent was helpful in obtaining a commission.

Nowhere else have domestics played a comparable role, nowhere was the hierarchy of the domestic staff more implacable, nowhere was Thorstein Veblen's theory of conspicuous waste more fully validated than in pre-war England. The use of the phrase "master and servant" to cover the field of labor relations derives from the Common Law, and there is a social as well as a professional distinction between solicitor and barrister.

Class distinctions extend even into the intellectual realm, where they are least justifiable. The intellectual pre-eminence of Oxford and Cambridge may be challenged, but never the social: it is interesting to note that though both are located in the provinces, it is the other universities—those at Manchester and Birmingham and Liverpool—that are called provincial. Any man can get a good education at the provincial universities, but if he has social ambitions he might as well cut his throat as go to them. A comparable hierarchy prevails in secondary education, and it is little exaggeration to say that half a score public schools, with Dartmouth and Sandhurst, dominate England socially. The class distinctions in newspapers and journals is sharper than elsewhere: the *Times* and the Manchester *Guardian* appeal to a small and select audience, as does the *Spectator* or the *Economist*. Even religious affiliations have a class tincture: the Church of England is the church of the upper, and perhaps the lower, classes, and the term "chapel" still has social connotations. Socially it is almost as fatal to be a Wesleyan as to have gone to a council school or to pay your tailor in pounds. For England alone of all countries has a special coin for social purposes. The guinea is fictitious, to be sure, but no fiction was ever more real, and the distinction between schools, doctors, writers, tailors, who are paid in aristocratic guineas and those who are paid in vulgar pounds is profound.

Logically this pervasive class-consciousness should poison English society, but in fact it does no such thing. English social relationships seem, in defiance of all logic, easy and even happy. Ease, good nature, and happiness characterize English social life.

Crisis tests character. The English character is made for normal times and enables the English to jog along cheerfully from day to day. But it is made for crisis, too. Emerson's memorable speech at Manchester concluded:—

Is it not true that the wise ancients did not praise the ship parting with flying colors from the port, but only that brave sailor which came back with torn sheets and battered sides, stript of her banners, but having ridden out the storm? And so, gentlemen, I feel in regard to this aged England . . . I see her not dispirited, not weak, but well remembering that she has seen dark days before;—indeed, with a kind of instinct that she sees a little better in a cloudy day, and that in storm of battle and calamity, she has a secret vigor and a pulse like a cannon. I see her in her old age, not decrepit, but young, and still daring to believe in her power of endurance and expansion.

Who that knows England today, struggling so gallantly to pay for the grandeur and misery of victory, can doubt that she is at her best in adversity, or refuse to have faith in her power of endurance and expansion?

Conclusions

IRWIN T. SANDERS

There can be no really final conclusions in an introductory book in the social-science field, but it is appropriate to note a few suggestions about further study. First, we can approach new courses and further reading with a high degree of assurance, since we now have an outline of how a society is put together and how its many aspects intermesh. We have considered, at least briefly, the people of which any society is made up, the connections between the habitat and the society that occupies it, the complex of social relations making up an economy, and some of the other patterns that, when added to the economy, make up a society. It has been emphasized that all societies give their own distinctive and individual flavor to the groupings of people and activities that they all contain (for example, family, neighborhood, religion). Each society tends to preserve its distinctiveness as part of its cultural heritage.

Furthermore, some of the basic terms used to describe the nature of society should now be familiar. New "source material" is at hand in every newspaper, book, motion picture, or trip, and analysis of these new situations by means of the appropriate terms and labels can add greatly to an understanding of them. In addition, these basic terms are essential for the effective communication of ideas about the nature of societies or details concerning them.

Again, we have seen how, in all the societies that we have studied, secularization is going on in various ways and degrees, and that here and there traces of its opposite, sacralization, make their appearance. The many authors on whose original works we have drawn have not, to be sure, often used the exact terms found in our section on "Looking at Values and Value-Systems"; nevertheless, they have offered approximate equivalents, frequently quite apt, for the labeling of many of their observations. Of course, these equivalents do not fit together closely, and they often duplicate or overlap each other a good deal. With a little patience, however, we can perform the necessary social-scientific task of translating them into a reasonably consistent vocabulary that will greatly aid us in dealing with values whenever and wherever we encounter them—and that, if we keep our eyes open, is at all times and places. Values and value-systems, to speak metaphorically, are at the very focus of the social-scientific lens; by designating them with some degree of uniformity—perhaps along the lines of the sacred-secular terminology provided in the section mentioned—we make easier not only our own work but also that of others who may wish to utilize it.

Finally, reading about differences in the attitudes and behavior of other people forms a good basis for becoming aware of one's own attitudes and values. What is the "right" way to do things? When is an act proper or improper? Are some norms absolutes, holding true in all circumstances and in all places? What kind of family life or religious belief is "most desirable"? What "should" be the relation of the individual to the government and to the society as an ongoing system? An individual's "social philosophy" is made up of the total of such value-judgments, and, if they are consistent and firmly held, they make for meaningful, harmonious behavior.

Let it be noted, however, that such questions, and the replies to them, go beyond the realm in which the social scientist per se operates. They involve not merely the social-scientific study of values but also the making of value-*judgments* for the guidance of ourselves and others as total personalities and as responsible members of various groups. Such *judgments* we shall and must continually make, but they cannot be made on scientific grounds exclusively. Philosophy and religion play necessary parts, for any value-*judgment* problem, when followed far enough, raises questions about the final ends of life itself, and these questions science should not, and ordinarily does not, attempt to answer.

The Methods of Science and Their Common Focus

These all-too-brief references to value-judgments call for comment on their relation to the methods of science. Even a beginner in the social sciences can recognize a value-judgment and realize that it is an inevitably personal affair in contrast to the detachment of consequently rational kind that is the aim of the scientist. Inclinations toward this or that aspect of the sacred, which we some-times call biases or personal factors, can creep into even as simple a laboratory operation as reading a thermometer, and attempts must be made to replace these inclinations with others of consequently secular kind *when we are acting in our capacities as scientists*. The scientist is searching for prediction and control, broadly considered, and scientific methods are the means that have been found most satisfactory for arriving at *these* ends.

Although scientific methods and their related procedures and techniques are many indeed, they do seem to have a least common denominator. They operate, in general, by assembling facts relevant to a problem, framing a hypothesis about the way in which these facts and others related to them are likely to recur, and then testing the hypothesis by assembling other facts to see if the recurrence does take place within certain limits of accuracy. Such an operation is sometimes called an "interpretation," an "explanation," or "arriving at a valid conclusion," and such designations are entirely proper as long as we realize that we have actually been moving back and forth between evidence and theory related to the evidence until finally we are enabled to say, "If this happens, then this, too, under stated circumstances, will probably happen." There must be some sort of problem that is scientifically relevant before the collecting of evidence or "facts" bearing on it can be suitably carried out; we must then draw preliminary conclusions about "what the facts mean" in terms of possible recurrence, and we must next marshal more facts to see whether our preliminary conclusions can be transformed into finally "true" conclusions. (For further reading on these points, see John Doby, ed., and others, *Introduction to Social Research*, Harrisburg, Pa., Stackpole, 1955, especially the chapter by J. C. McKinney.)

The scientist's "truth," as should be readily seen from the foregoing, is subject to change, always in the direction of a better fit between the "facts" and the "proof." To accept such change as inevitable and indeed desirable, to recognize and welcome the eventual superseding of one's own most cherished work by others who will push it further and improve upon it, the scientist must regard his "truth" as provisional and hence must *as scientist* have secular attitudes and secular values.

It is an entirely proper and normal thing, however, to go beyond what is scientifically provable and to express value-judgments based on precept, prescription, or principle, in the same way in which, in one's roles as citizen, parent, churchgoer, and so on, decisions must be reached for which we have no scientific testing. Still, it is the chief purpose of the social sciences to help us find recurrent regularities (sometimes called "scientific laws") among social phenomena. As these become known, man can act more wisely in the areas of activity to which they pertain. Moreover, we shall have additional knowledge, based securely on social-scientific operations and their valid conclusions—"solid fact" and "sound theory"—from which to determine the range of the value-judgments that will still be necessary.

Seven Social Sciences

Although the social sciences have been mentioned by name from time to time in the foregoing pages, they have not been defined or described in detail. The way in which each approaches the subject of human society will be discussed briefly here, but the only method of thoroughly understanding the content and techniques of a specific science is to read widely in it and if possible undertake research in it. An introductory book such as this cannot, of course, make its reader a social psychologist, an economist, or a political scientist. Only specialized work can do that. But it is also important to realize that society and the culture of which it is a part are interrelated. There is a fundamental unity in man's social world, and if we learn a great deal about a specific aspect of it, we run the risk of overlooking this unity—the interrelatedness of the social universe in which we work.

Since the central theme of this book is social change, we shall try, in discussing the social sciences, to note particularly the way in which each deals with the processes, relationships, and events that make up social change.

1. Cultural anthropology (also called social anthropology)

As would be expected, the chief area of study of the cultural anthropologist is culture, which has been briefly characterized in "Social Change on a Worldwide Scale" and elsewhere. There are at least four cultural processes that apply to social relations, and therefore to social change.

The first of these is *invention,* which can be social as well as material. The originating of a new trait or custom—whether the slit wooden goggles of the Eskimo or the ancestor reverence of the Chinese—is invention. Analysis of any invention will reveal how complex the process is, with each component part of the custom sometimes being a separate invention in its own right.

A second cultural process is called *borrowing* when seen from the point of view of the culture receiving a new trait from another culture but is called *diffusion* when studied simply as the spread of a trait from its point of origin to a second or third place. Most traits within any culture are borrowed; those societies with greatest access to other societies are likely to do more borrowing, thus leading to accelerated social change. A mere listing of all the traits the English have borrowed—even the traditional cup of tea—is convincing evidence for the relation between accessibility to borrowing and receptivity to new traits on the one hand and the growth of complexity in relations on the other.

A third cultural process is *integration,* or the adaptation and incorporation of the new trait into the existing culture pattern. This, too, is a complex process that may involve varying degrees of modification. Somehow or other the rough edges of a new trait have to be rubbed off; it must pass the test of being useful to its new possessors.

Loss of traits, or the discarding of traits no longer needed or suitable, may be listed as a fourth cultural process.

Acculturation is sometimes listed as a fifth cultural process and is used in a dual sense: in the more inclusive sense it means one people's adopting in place of their own culture that of another people, so that only minor vestiges of the replaced culture remain; in the less common sense, it denotes the process whereby an individual acquires the culture traits of the society into which he is born. It can thus be seen that in this second sense socialization, with its emphasis on society, is a part of the broader process of acculturation.

With such processes in mind we can appreciate the role of the archeologist, who reconstructs past cultures and thus learns what they borrowed, invented, and modified. The linguistic expert, by analyzing the structure of a language as well as its vocabulary, can not only find clues to the kind of idea-systems that a given people have now and had in the past but can also trace the history of these systems and point out relations among them. The ethnologist works almost entirely with recent or contemporary societies, examining their artifacts, sociofacts, and mentifacts. The field of anthropology also includes the physical anthropologist, whose work lies outside the social sciences. He considers man as a biological species, and pays particular attention to the inherited physical traits that make up racial variations. By joining the cultural approach, which is the study of man's works, with the physical approach, the anthropologist obtains an over-all view as the basis for developing his science further and more comprehensively. (For a detailed discussion of the mutual contributions among anthropology, social psychology, and sociology, see John Gillin, ed., and others, *For a Science of Social Man,* New York, Macmillan, 1954.)

2. GEOGRAPHY

Like anthropology, geography combines the physical and social sciences, although its whole subject matter is the earth's surface. Physical geography, as its name implies, analyzes and describes the natural environment. Surface features (and their origins), climate, and the distribution of natural resources, to mention but a few topics, can be studied with little reference to man. But geography does not entirely ignore man. Human geography examines the relations between various physical details of the habitat and man's life. With such an approach, and with the inclusion of regional geography and economic geography, it becomes one of the social sciences.

The human geographer's chief concern, therefore, is with mankind's process of adjustment to his physical environment. This is a two-way process: not only is man strongly influenced and limited by the natural environment, but he in turn acts upon and modifies the natural environment. What he does to a forest is reflected in changes in a river's floods and its deposits of sediment. Man's killing off of game animals, such as the buffalo, sets up changes in the vegetation patterns. Some geographers have specialized in the study and classification of the possible resources of livelihood, in terms of "adjustments" such as pastoralism, which is an adjustment to grass (which man cannot eat) by means of sheep (which man can eat, milk, and shear). Social change can then be interpreted as one kind of adjustment giving way to another—agriculture yielding to industry in the case of the English Midlands. Work patterns change and family relations are affected; centralization of economy and government tend to follow, with a loosening of community bonds. This is not due entirely, of course, to man's relation to the habitat, but there is no doubt that the processes of adjustment to natural resources must be considered in any analysis of social change if economic development is to be included. The economy becomes an important contact point between the rest of society and the natural environment.

3. HISTORY

History is the study of man in time. Some historians consider themselves humanists rather than social scientists and conceive of the writing of history as being more akin to the humanities—literature and philosophy—than to the sciences. Their canons of scholarship are strict, and their work is sound, but they leave to those who call themselves social historians the task of introducing scientific method into the study of history. Social historians, too, show a greater interest in changing social relations through time than do many who concern themselves with the philosophy of history. Archeologists, mentioned above, may also contribute to history, deriving information through excavation of sites where man lived and buried his dead. The historian, however, takes as his primary data man's written records and builds his science on them.

The historical process may be likened to the flowing of time. In its simplest aspect the work of the historian means determining the sequence of events so that we can know what happened where and when. This is fundamental for tracing social changes. All social science depends at times upon the analysis of this historical process. Sociologists specializing in the family, for example, are interested in knowing what conditions in the past have been associated with the decline of family life. To the extent that the historian can help them read the record straight, to that extent their conclusions are likely to be valid. But social historians seek to go beyond the chronicling of the order in which things happened; they like to see what kinds of changes are simultaneous or associated. For example, they want to know if an autocratic family system is invariably associated with an autocratic state. Or they may want to know, as Thomas D. Clark demonstrated in Selection 108, just what the relations and functions of some specific occupational group, such as the Southern country storekeeper, really were. With great care they hunt up the contemporary records and come out with the best available answer to such a question. Social historians, therefore, who seek to arrive at some of the uniformities observed through the study of the historical process in several societies, are contributing to the understanding of social change.

4. ECONOMICS

Many economists define economics as the study of how man satisfies his wants—chiefly the material wants (such as the desire for a nourishing meal or a new car) but also "psychological" or nonmaterial wants (such as the desire for greater social prestige, which might be attained by going to an expensive restaurant or owning a car). In this book we have described the sets of social relations within which the economic mechanism operates, but we have not tried to describe how a complex economic system functions.

An introductory economics course would take up the three most important processes connected with satisfaction of man's wants. The first is *production,* or "maximizing the total national dividend"—that is, providing those goods and services which people want in as great quantity as possible. The second process is *distribution,* or the sharing of production. It does not mean distribution in the simple sense of getting products from a factory through a wholesaler to a retail store. Rather, it means who receives what, out of all that is available. What will the investor get for his capital, the manager for his direction, the farmer for his crop? The third process is *consumption,* which is analyzed in terms of customer preference among the many ways in which he may satisfy his wants. Consumption underlies demand, which in turn affects production.

The Cotton South has provided a good case study of the effects throughout the social system when technological changes occur in the production process. Mechanization of agriculture calls for greater capital investment, which the marginal farmer cannot afford; it demands skilled rather than unskilled labor; and it even leads to a change in the distributive relationship between employer and employee. The social changes that result can be seen in migration, in the shifting of landlord-tenant ties, and in new community relations.

5. POLITICAL SCIENCE

As its name suggests, political science is the study of government, or of the distribution of coercive power in society. In Western societies it is customary for us to divide governmental structures into local, state or provincial, and national levels, and to determine within a given society the allocation of power at each level. Power distribution can also be studied, however, in terms of vertical rather than horizontal channels, by a threefold division into the legislative, executive, and judicial functions of the government. The processes by which political power is redistributed vary from the revolution, which results in a sudden and violent shift of power, to such regulated processes as an election, by which certain officials are replaced. Any of these processes not only bring about changes in political structures but have effects upon many other relations. In one sense, even taxation is a process for redistributing economic power, since certain groups may be favored at the expense of others.

In societies different from our own, power can be found distributed in forms that we are not accustomed to think of as "government." Such groups as the family or the clan, or organizations with religious functions, may also "govern," in the sense of exercising control over the individual members of society. Until recently, political scientists had scarcely considered nonliterate societies, but the techniques of analysis can be as profitably applied to them as to our own society.

6. SOCIOLOGY

Sociology focuses on the study of society as a system and tries to describe and understand the interrelations among all the parts of society in terms both of structure and of function. The sociologist is interested in seeing, for example, how the government and the economy are intermeshed, or how the family, the class system, education, and religion fit in with one another, first in specific societies and then in human society in general. He need not become a specialist in political science or in economics in the sense of probing all the inner workings of these institutional arrangements, but he must understand them well enough to be able to see what part they play in a society.

The social processes, or forms of interaction, which the sociologist considers in his analysis of change include cooperation, conflict, competition, accommodation, assimilation, and others. Introductory courses in sociology deal with these in detail, as well as with the concepts of values and norms, which also become altered as social relations change.

For example, a labor dispute between employer and employees which ends in a strike is a conflict situation. The social relations are disturbed, sometimes to such a degree that a state or national government steps in to help work out a settlement. Through what is called conciliation, or a phase of the process of accommodation, each party to the dispute eventually yields on some points and an agreement is reached. This agreement may be written up in a collective-bargaining contract which describes how relations between the employer and employees are to be conducted for a fixed period of time. Thus, social change occurs as people who are dealing with one another—sometimes cooperatively, sometimes competitively, sometimes antagonistically—move from one social situation to another.

Sociologists are trained to view such social phenomena as strikes, race riots, family life, social climbing, or religious organizations as involving people in relations to, with, for, or against one another. Knowing what is happening to these relations helps greatly not only in working out the next step in a given social situation but in seeing the possible effects of any proposed solution upon those participating in it.

Although the subject matter of sociology and anthropology can be seen to overlap to a great extent, sociology is the older of the two disciplines and has concerned itself far more with the study of our own and other highly complex societies. Anthropology has tended to be limited to a consideration of simpler societies, although in recent years it has begun to show as great an interest as does sociology in the literate peoples of the world.

7. SOCIAL PSYCHOLOGY

With social psychology we conclude this brief account of the social sciences. Social psychology is claimed by both psychology and sociology and is sometimes said to belong to neither. This discipline seeks to describe the individual as he behaves in society. Psychology contributes the knowledge about the individual which general psychologists (usually classed as biological scientists) have gained through experimental work. On the other hand, sociology brings to this new hybrid discipline the necessary knowledge of society. The anthropologist also contributes what he has learned about the connection between the culture of a society and the personality of its members. The processes of social psychology, therefore, depend on the point of view from which the individual is studied. One view is in terms of the role-playing process, which leads into a consideration of motivation and socialization. How does a society train its members to play the roles appropriate to their statuses in given situations? How are the social values internalized—made a part of the personality structure of the individual? How are deviants, those who will not conform, made to get into line through the techniques of social control? The connection between such processes and social change is close, whether there is reluctance or readiness to change.

There are many allied fields—such as demography, law, ethics, religion, education, and philosophy—that make important contributions to the social sciences, but they are outside the strict limits of this group of studies and cannot be discussed here.

Summing up, then, we have disciplines dealing with man and his works (anthropology), man's record in time (history), man and his environment (geography), man and his wants (economics), government or power in society (political science), society as a social system (sociology), and the individual and society (social psychology).

It is sufficient for us at this point to learn the central core of each field without attempting to determine its precise boundaries. In the present state of the social sciences every one of them overlaps at many points with several others. Each has numerous unsolved problems, but each gives great promise of future achievements in our search for a better understanding of mankind.

Such categorical descriptions as the ones above can come no closer to expressing fully what the social sciences are like in content, aims, and methods than a verbal description can tell how water tastes. It will depend upon the thirst of the drinker, the source of the water, and the container from which it is drunk. We have tried to provide the opportunity to make a start, but from here on the reader will have to do the sampling.

INDEX